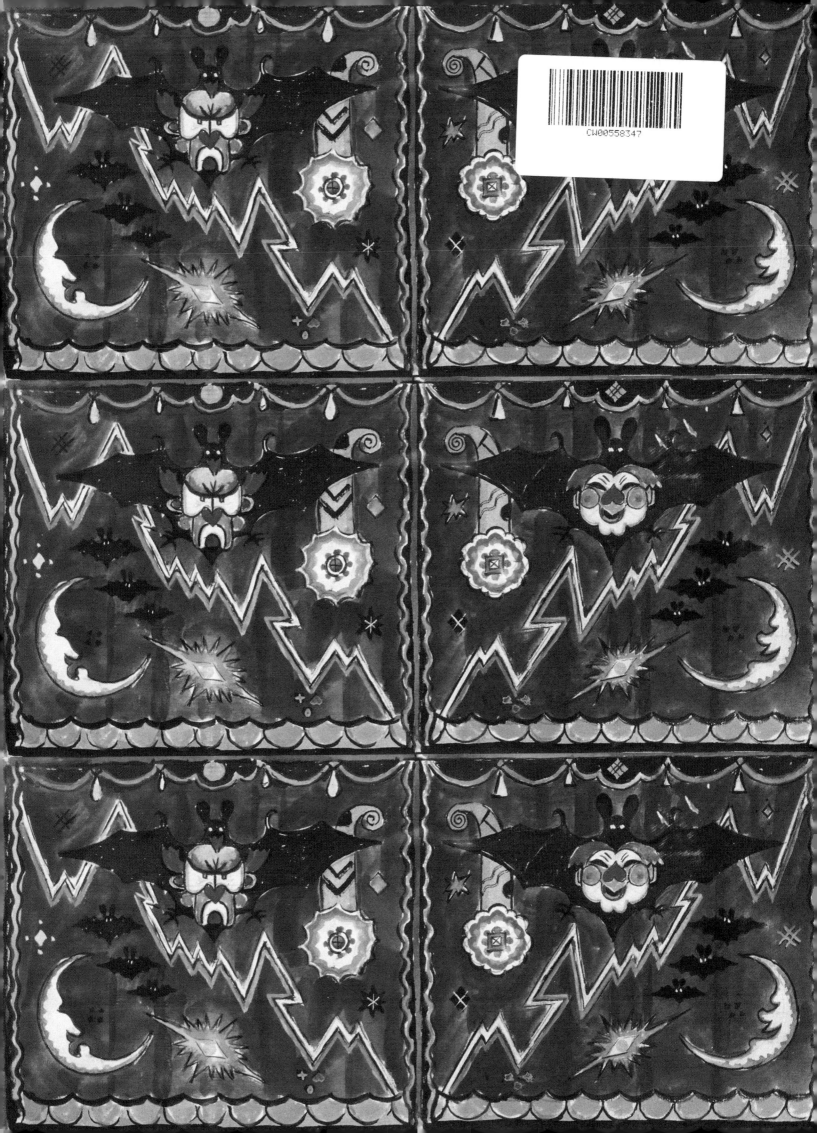

1

VOLUME II

ENCYCLOPEDIA of
RUSSIAN STAGE DESIGN
The Catalogue Raisonné of the Collection of
Nina and Nikita D. Lobanov-Rostovsky

3

John E. Bowlt, Nina and Nikita D. Lobanov-Rostovsky

VOLUME II

ENCYCLOPEDIA of
RUSSIAN STAGE DESIGN
The Catalogue Raisonné of the Collection of
Nina and Nikita D. Lobanov-Rostovsky

ANTIQUE COLLECTORS' CLUB

ISBN: 978 1 85149 719 5

Book design concept: Nikita D. Lobanov-Rostovsky
Photographs: Nikita D. Lobanov-Rostovsky
Colour separations and photocomposition: Antique Collectors' Club Ltd.

British Library Cataloguing-in-Publication Data:
A catalogue record for this book is available from the British Library

Published by Antique Collectors' Club, England
Printed in China for the Antique Collectors' Club Ltd.,
Woodbridge, Suffolk IP12 4SD

Endpapers: Mstislav Dobujinsky: Curtain Design with Quarter-moons for the Chauve-Souris, 1924 (No. 429).

Frontispiece: Léon Bakst: Costume Design for the Blue Sultana, *Schéhérazade*, 1910 (No. 81).

Half Title page: Artist unknown: *Composite Portrait of Sergei Diaghilev and Natalia Goncharova*, ca.1914 (No. 540).

Title page: Natalia Goncharova: Portrait of Sergei Diaghilev, 1916 (No. 562).

CONTENTS

Volume II

Curatorial Information   6

Catalogue Raisonné   10

Note on Transliteration   462

Note on Iconographic References   462

List of Abbreviations   463

Name Index   464

Alexandre Benois: Stage detail: Petrouchka kissing the Ballerina, *Petrouchka*, 1945 (No. 171).

CURATORIAL INFORMATION

The catalogue raisonné of the collection of Nina and Nikita D. Lobanov-Rostovsky could not have been compiled and published without the help of many individuals and institutions. While limitations of space do not permit us to salute each and every one, we offer our special gratitude to our main editor Susannah Hecht. Thanks in no small part to her unfailing attention, ready expertise, and good humor, this book — to use a theatrical analogy — has gestated from a preliminary design to an actual production, one which can now be appreciated globally by a deserving and discerning audience. We also offer thanks to Steve Farrow, whose superb design has helped transform this verbal compendium into a visual delight. We owe a great debt to Olga Shaumyan, whose knowledge and unfailing and meticulous work have proven an invaluable contribution to all aspects of these volumes. Last, but not least, we would like to acknowledge Irina Menshova for her untiring preparation of the comprehensive name index, a major element of the book.

The 1209 entries (1-1196, including late insertions such as 565a) are listed alphabetically according to artist (except for the seven items numbered 1188-1196 and include stage designs, portraits, posters, and other promotional materials. In some cases, the works listed in a particular section may not have been created by the artist in question, but simply relate to his or her undertakings, as in the case of posters advertising an exhibition to which that artist had contributed. A number of ancillary works such as portraits of the artists made by their friends or colleagues are also included in the primary sections.

There are two types of numbers given in square brackets after an entry number. A bare number refers to the full-page color illustration in Volume I, *Masterpieces of Russian Stage Design*. A number prefixed with "R", e.g. "[R1]", indicates that the same work is listed in the Russian catalogue raisonné of the Lobanov-Rostovsky collection, i.e. J. Bowlt and N. Lobanov-Rostovsky: *Sobranie Nikity i Niny Lobanovykh-Rostovskikh. Khudozhniki russkogo teatra. 1880-1930. Katalog-rezone* (Moscow: Iskusstvo, 1994; B179 in the Bibliography, see Volume I). Conversely, "[NIRE]" (not in the Russian edition) indicates that the work was not included in that source. A few of the items are double-sided (e.g. No. 1152 [R383]) and wherever the verso is of particular importance, this has been given a sequential number (e.g. No. 1153 [R383a]). The issue of replicas, versions, and imitations of a given work is a complex one and, while known variants are often mentioned, the listings here are not exhaustive. The Russian version of the catalogue raisonné provides commentary and a black and white photograph for each piece, but since then much new information has come forth and other works have entered the collection. These additions are included here.

The Lobanov-Rostovsky Collection has been represented at exhibitions worldwide and works have been reproduced in numerous books, periodicals, and catalogs. Many such sources are indicated by a bibliographical code within the curatorial data for each item, e.g. B115, plate 1, together with comparative material. General exceptions are lithographs, silkscreens (pochoirs), printed publicity materials reproduced in multiple copies (unless a given item is extremely rare as in the case of No. 1116 [R370]), and also Alexandre Benois's enormous cycle of variants and versions for his several interpretations of *Petrouchka,* which would warrant a separate compilation and analysis. Many of the works have been mentioned in English-language books and catalogs (see, for example, I51), but few have received comparative examination and detailed description in English, and *Russian Stage Design* is intended to rectify that failing.

Léon Bakst: Costume design for a Bayadère carrying a peacock, *Le Dieu Bleu*, 1911 (No. 91).

The iconographic references are not exhaustive and are intended only as a guide to the visual accessibility of the collection within the public domain. In this respect, particular attention is given to early sources of reproduction and to later synthetic repositories, such as the catalogs for the recent commemorative exhibitions devoted to the centenary of the Ballets Russes, e.g. I127. Vexing lacunae still remain in the history of Russian stage design and some artists, e.g. Pavel Dmitriev, still lack essential biographical details. Even so, the more immediate accessibility of archives and the diversification of publishing ventures in the new Russia have generated a flurry of books, articles, and exhibitions concerned with the Russian visual arts, the cultural diaspora, and, specifically, Russian stage design. True, some of these perpetuate traditional mistakes and misapprehensions or merely repeat the standard configuration of names and events. On the other hand, other new publications such as Alla Mikhailova's *Meierkhold i khudozhniki* (G82) and Oleg Leikind, Kirill Makhrov, and Dmitrii Severiukhin's *Khudozhniki russkogo zarubezhia* (H34) correct and expand our knowledge of the subject, often adducing more accurate and comprehensive information. Electronic resources on the internet, while not always accurate, may also provide supplementary bio-bibliographical and visual information. In any case, the appearance of this English-language edition enables us to correct mistakes observed in the Russian edition of the catalog raisonné, add new documentary material, open new sections (e.g. for André Houdiakoff), and update the Bibliography.

A name preceding a reference to an exhibition catalog refers to the compiler, curator or primary author of that catalog. Inasmuch as provenances play an important part in the history of the collection, wherever possible, names of the last proprietors and the dates of transactions are recorded, including full references to relevant auctions.

The date accompanying each entry refers to the date of supposed execution. This has been determined either through the artist's own emendations on the design itself, analogy with similar pieces, reference to the production for which the design was made or in accordance with other documentary evidence. For a variety of reasons, the date of actual execution may not always coincide with the date that appears on the design (e.g. No. 96 [R88]) or it may not correspond to the date of the stage production (e.g. No. 642 [R537]).

Unless stated otherwise, the medium of support is paper and written inscriptions on a given design are assumed to be by the artist. Inscriptions in English, French, German, and Italian are repeated; inscriptions in Russian are indicated as such and translated or transliterated (see Appendices).

Dimensions are in inches and centimeters, height preceding width.

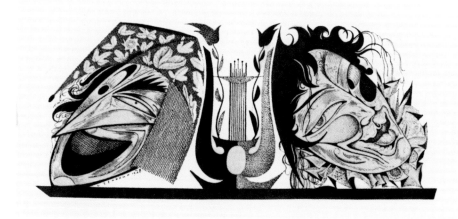

Serge Tchehonine: *Two Theatrical Masks*, 1928 (No. 1047).

Mikhail Larionov: Costume design for an Old Buffoon, *Chout*, 1915 (No. 718).

AIZENBERG, Nina Evseevna

Born 14 (27) June, 1902, Moscow, Russia; died 19 December, 1974, Moscow, Russia.

1918-24 attended Svomas/Vkhutemas, studying under Ilia Mashkov, Alexander Osmerkin, et al.; 1924 began to work as a stage designer for various theaters in Moscow and other cities, contributing to productions of both classical and contemporary works; 1925 onwards contributed to exhibitions; 1926 began to work for the Blue Blouse variety theater, designing, for example, Vladimir Maiakovsky's and Osip Brik's *Radio October* and Mikhail Volpin's *The Queen's Mistake* (1927); 1928 contributed to "Moscow Theaters of the October Decade," Moscow; 1928-30 member of the Moscow Association of Stage Designers; 1929 designed the production of *Le Bourgeois Gentilhomme* for the Maly Theater, Moscow; contributed to the "First Stage Design Exhibition," Moscow; 1930-32 member of the October group and in contact, therefore, with other members such as Gustav Klutsis, Alexander Rodchenko, and Sergei Senkin; 1930-33 helped with agit-decorations in streets and squares for parades; 1935 represented at the "Exhibition of Stage Design Art," Moscow; 1938-41 worked on designs for various gymnastic displays and parades; 1940s-50s worked on many stage productions for various theaters; 1950s painted landscapes; 1964 one-woman exhibition in Moscow.

Bibliography
E. Lutskaia: *Nina Aizenberg. 40 let v teatre.* Catalog of exhibition organized by the Union of Artists of the RSFSR, M, 1964.
A14, Vol. 1, p. 70.
E13, passim.
C144, pp. 40-63.
E15, Vol. 1, passim.
C. Amiard-Chevrel: "La Blouse Bleue" in C57, Vol. 1, pp. 99-110.
S. Sabar: *Nina Aizenberg. Transformations.* Catalog of exhibition at the Hebrew University, Jerusalem, 1991.
A. Sosnovskaia: "'The Blue Blouse'. Nina Aizenberg, Costume Designer" in *Bamakh,* Jerusalem, 1994, No. 137, pp. 77-85 (in Hebrew).
A. Sosnovskaya: "Nina Aizenberg (1902-1974): Russian Designer" in *Slavic and East European Performance,* New York, 2000, Vol. 30, No. 3, pp. 48-73.
Recent exhibitions of stage designs have featured Nina Aizenberg's work. See, for example, I116, pp. 59, 63.

During the decade 1917-27 the concept of theater underwent serious reexamination in the Soviet Union. The rapid establishment and liquidation of many experimental theaters during the early years is sufficient proof of the diversity and energy of the new Russian theater and the fact that the circus, the cabaret, and the open-air mass spectacle now became prominent genres is symptomatic of the abrupt changes that

occurred in the orientation and objectives of the traditional theater. Reasons for this move towards the "lower" forms of spectacle are several: the theater-goer was no longer just a member of a privileged intelligentsia or plutocracy, the circus and variety theater could easily be forged into a political and agitational weapon, and the conventional Russian theater had a limited contemporary repertoire — something that Vsevolod Meierkhold had been complaining about since 1910.[1] As public entertainment, therefore, the dramatic theater was superseded or, at least, supplemented by the circus, the cabaret, the vaudeville, and the so-called "mass action" or "mass spectacle," at least in the early years of the Soviet régime. In the 1920s a number of small variety theaters such as the Blue Blouse opened in Moscow, Leningrad, and other centers.[2] These theaters followed the essential format of the cabaret or vaudeville, although their repertoire differed sharply from that of the pre-Revolutionary cabaret such as Nikita Baliev's Bat (Chauve-Souris).[3] The new variety theaters presented contemporary revues, often of a satirical nature, and they were oriented almost exclusively to the mass audience, the title, of course, eliciting the same kind of association that "blue jeans" elicits in the English-speaking world.

The Blue Blouse, founded in 1923 by the journalist Boris Yuzhanin and his friends, produced works written by progressive writers such as Nikolai Aseev, Osip Brik, Valentin Kataev, and Sergei Tretiakov. Between 1924 and 1926 it issued (irregularly) its own journal with details of engagements, revues, and repertories. True, the Blue Blouse theater denoted a concept or genre of activity rather than a single institution and at one time there were fifteen collectives calling themselves Blue Blouse in Soviet cities. The themes of the Blue Blouse presentations were simple and topical, dealing

with factory life, political events at home and abroad, the inconsistencies of the New Economic Policy, etc., and they were communicated to the audience via declamation, parades, monologues, singing and dancing, even gymnastic displays. Osip Brik described one such popular revue called *Proposing to the USSR:*

> A woman wearing a blue blouse with the inscription "Soviet Russia" came on stage. Then some men also came on stage wearing blue blouses plus top hats and derbies representing England, France, Italy, America. The men sang songs, but they just couldn't get by without proposing to Soviet Russia and kept hanging around her. The woman accepted their collective proposal in a derisive manner and, while making or, rather, singing all kinds of caustic remarks, she agreed to be proposed to.[4]

The Blue Blouse attracted many young artists as designers, including Aizenberg and Boris Erdman, and it was extremely popular, even touring abroad. However, with the imposition of Socialist Realism in Soviet culture in the early 1930s and with the sharp attacks on "bourgeois" forms of art, the Blue Blouse, along with other vaudeville theaters, was disbanded.

Unidentified production, *ca. 1926.*

1a, b, c, d [R1 (a-g)].
Set of Four Variable Shirt or Vest Designs, ca. 1926.
Gouache.
4¾ x 3 in., 12.1 x 7.6 cm.
Provenance: Szymon Bojko, Warsaw, 1977.
1a, 1b, 1c are reproduced in G55, pp. 285-86; I51, p. 48; I77, p. 161.
The fourth item (No. 1d [R1g]) demonstrates how one of these "production costumes"

1a

1b

1c

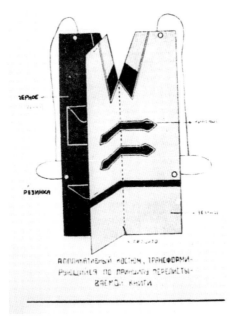

1d

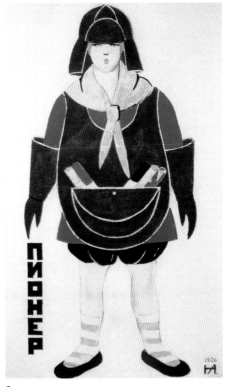

2

can be transformed according to the same principle as turning the page of a book — which Aizenberg explains in the inscription.

Unidentified production, *ca.1926*.

2 [2 in Vol. I; R2].
Costume Design for a Pioneer, 1926.
Pencil, brush, and India ink and gouache.
Signed with the Russian monogram "NA" and dated 1926.
13⅜ x 8⅝ in., 34 x 22 cm.
Other inscription: the lower left carries the Russian word "pioneer" as part of the design.
Provenance: *Ballet, Theatre and Music-Hall Material*, London: Sotheby's, 29 October, 1981, Lot 105 (reproduced).
Reproduced in color in B115, plate 171; and in black and white in E27, p. 124; I77, p. 161.
Similar costumes are reproduced by Vladimir Mrazovsky in his article, "Kostium 'Sinei bluzy'" in *Novyi zritel*, M, 1926, 16 November, p. 6; also see I73, p. 223; and *Nina Aizenberg. Transformations*, p. 16 et seq.

Note: Aizenberg began working for the Blue Blouse in 1926,[5] and one of her first successes was the play called *Radio October*, which Brik and Maiakovsky wrote to commemorate the ninth anniversary of the Revolution. This costume, however, was probably for the Blue Blouse production of Semeon Kirsanov's poem-play called *Kak rebiata-oktiabriata, lishnikh slov ne govoria, poleteli za moria* [How the Octobrist Kids, without Further Ado, Flew across the Seas] in which pioneers (the Soviet counterpart of the boy scouts and girl guides) play a primary role. Alternatively, Aizenberg's costume design here, a "pure use of appliqué,"[6] may have been for the anonymous number called *Pioneers* listed in the repertoire in one of the posters below (No. 8 [R8]). Aizenberg used a simple, but effective innovation so as to

create multi-purpose costumes (demonstrated in No. 1c [R1v] where the same basic pattern is repeated throughout with only minor modifications). The method consisted of:

> painted appliqués which enabled [the actors] to make a "quick change" in front of the audience: Red Army men changed instantly into sailors, sailors into Budennyi soldiers. All parts of the design and decoration could be packed into portable cases which the Blue Blouse actors took with them as they traveled from club to club.[7]

Both the Stenberg brothers and Boris Erdman tried to follow this system in their work for the Blue Blouse, but without particular success, producing costumes better suited for the more conventional theater. Aizenberg, however, was one of

the few Blue Blouse artists who managed to create efficient, quick-change costumes, while retaining the likeness and personality of the given *dramatis persona*. To some extent, Tatiana Bruni was also supporting the Blue Blouse esthetic in her costumes for *Bolt* (see Nos. 393-96 [R360-63]).[8]

The designers of Nos. 3-11 [R3-R10] are unknown. The provenance for Nos. 3-12 [R3-R11] is Viktor Kholodkov, Moscow, 1989.

Aizenberg as contributor:
3 [R3].
Poster Advertising a Presentation by the Shock Group of the Blue Blouse Theater, 1926.

4

6

7

1928 — at the Summer Theaters of the Union of Metalworkers in Golutvin and Kolomna (Moscow Region).
Reproduced in N17.

Aizenberg as contributor:
5 [R5].
Poster Advertising the Blue Blouse Theater, Moscow, ca. 1929.
Lithograph in red and black.
Photomontage.
37 x 28¼ in., 94 x 72 cm.
Inscriptions (as part of the design) provide details on the composition of the so-called Basic Group of the Blue Blouse Theater, its

gigs (e.g. folk dances), and personnel (e.g. designers, including Aizenberg). The date, presumably, is 1929.
Reproduced in B84, p. 17.

Aizenberg as contributor:
6 [R6].
Poster Advertising a Presentation by the Blue Blouse Theater, 1929.
Lithograph in red, blue, and white.
24 x 37 in., 61 x 94 cm.
Inscriptions (as part of the design) provide details on a presentation by the Blue Blouse Theater "before its departure abroad" scheduled for 15 and 16 February, 1929, at

Lithograph in blue and white.
24½ x 36¾ in., 62 x 93 cm.
Inscriptions (as part of the design) refer to presentations at the Club of the Communist University of Workers of the East (Formerly the Chat Noir Theater) on Tverskaia Street, Moscow, 24 January, 1926.

Aizenberg as contributor:
4 [R4].
Poster Advertising Two Presentations by the Blue Blouse Theater, 1928.
Lithograph in black and white.
43¼ x 28¼ in., 109 x 72 cm.
Inscriptions (as part of the design) provide details on the two presentations by the Blue Blouse Theater (the Shock Brigade Group of the Moscow Soviet) "before its departure abroad" — on 25 and 26 August,

8

9

10

11

the Palace of Labor and Art (Tbilisi?).
Reproduced in B179 where the images for
R6 and R7 are interchanged.

Aizenberg as contributor:
7 [R7].
***Poster Advertising a Presentation by the
Blue Blouse Theater, 1929.***
Lithograph in red, blue, and white.
26 x 39¼ in., 66 x 100 cm.
Inscriptions (as part of the design) provide
details on a presentation by the Blue Blouse
Theater "before its departure abroad"
scheduled for 19 March, 1929 (?), at the
City Theater (city not indicated).
Reproduced in N20 and in B179 where the
images for R6 and R7 are interchanged.

Aizenberg as contributor:
8 [R8].
***Poster Advertising the Tour of the USSR by the
Shock Brigade of the Blue Blouse Theater, 1929.***
Lithograph in black and white.
23¼ x 33 in., 59 x 84 cm.
Inscriptions (as part of the design) provide
details on the repertoire and composition of
the company for the USSR tour "before its
departure abroad" scheduled for 8,10,11
January, 1929, at the Lenin Railroad Club in
Alatyr. Printed by the Arzamas Promkombinat
in an edition of 250.

Aizenberg as contributor:
9 [NIRE].
***Template for Poster Advertising the Blue
Blouse Theater's USSR Tour, 1929 (?).***
Lithograph in black and white.
41¾ x 28 in. 106 x 71 cm.
Inscriptions (as part of the design) provide
details on the Blue Blouse personnel.

10 [R9].
***Poster Advertising the Blue Blouse, Moscow,
25, 26, 27 and 29 May, 1926.***
Photomontage on lithograph in black and
white.
35¼ x 24½ in., 90 x 62 cm.
Inscriptions (as part of the design) provide
details on the Blue Blouse personnel,
including its régisseurs (among them, Nikolai
Foregger and Sergei Yutkevich); scriptwriters
(among them, Semeon Kirsanov and Sergei
Tretiakov), and artists (among them,
Aizenberg, Anastasiia Akhtyrko, Boris
Erdman, and the Stenberg brothers).

Aizenberg as contributor:
11 [R10].
***Poster Advertising the Opera-Parody
Carmen by the Blue Blouse Theater,
Moscow, 1930.***
Photomontage on lithograph in black and
white.
28¼ x 21¼ in., 72 x 54 cm.
Inscriptions (as part of the design) provide
details on the Blue Blouse troupe. The left
side illustrates costumes for Carmen, the
Toreador, and José (Brigadier José); the
right — for a Spanish girl and a soldier.
Similar designs for the Spanish girl are
reproduced in I73, p. 223.

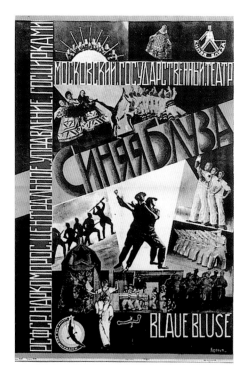

12

Aizenberg as contributor:

12 [R11].
Evgeniia Korbut: *Poster Advertising the Blue Blouse Theater at the State Circus, Moscow*, 1926.
Photomontage on lithograph in blue, yellow, black and white.
Signed lower right in Russian in the plate: "Korbut."
41¼ x 29 in., 105 x 74 cm.
Other inscriptions (as part of the design): "Moscow 3174. Edition of 1500. Published by Ts.U.G.Ts. Printed by Mospoligraf, 1926." Reproduced in color in B115, plate 170.
Information on Evgeniia Korbut has not been forthcoming.

1. See Meierkhold's untitled article in the collection of articles edited by S. Makovsky, et al.: *Kuda my idem*, M: Zaria, 1910, pp. 104-05.
2. The term "blue blouse" is a reference to the blue coveralls worn by industrial workers.
3. For more information on Nikita Baliev and the Bat see entries for Nicola Benois, Lado Gudiashvili, André Houdiakoff, Nicholas Remisoff, Vasilii Shukhaev, and Sergei Sudeikin; also see E1; E21; E52, pp. 19-36, 340-77; and Introduction. For a detailed discussion of Baliev's repertoire see E35.
4. O. Brik: "'Siniaia bluza' i Mosselprom" in *Siniaia bluza*, M, 1928, No. 4, p. 55. Quoted in E15, Vol. 1, p. 330.
5. The date 1923 which accompanies the reproductions of Aizenberg's costumes in G29, plates 61, 62, would seem to be incorrect.
6. V. Mrazovsky: "Kostium 'Sinei bluzy'" in *Novyi zritel*, M, 1926, 16 November, p. 6.
7. E15, Vol. 1, pp. 338. The theater historian, Elizaveta Uvarova, confirmed that item No. 2 was for Kirsanov's poem-play in a conversation with John E. Bowlt in Moscow on 11 May, 1986.
8. For further information on the Blue Blouse theaters see A54, pp. 547-49; A69, pp. 609, 610; C57, Vol. 2, pp. 44 et seq.; E15, Vol. 1, pp. 326-44; E27, pp. 92-132.

AKIMOV,
Nikolai Pavlovich

Born 3 (16) April, 1901, Kharkov, Ukraine; died 6 September, 1968, Moscow, Russia.

1910 the Akimov family moved to Tsarskoe Selo, near St. Petersburg, and then, in 1912, to St. Petersburg; 1914 Akimov attended evening classes at SSEA; 1915 took lessons from Savelii Zeidenberg; 1916-18 attended the New Art Studio under Mstislav Dobujinsky, Alexandre Jacovleff, and Vasilii Shukhaev; 1918 worked in the poster studio of the Petrograd Proletkult; 1920-22 lived in Kharkov, where he taught drawing at the Higher Courses for Workers in Political Enlightenment, and also began his career as a stage designer for productions at the Kharkov Children's Theater; 1922 moved back to Petrograd; 1923 entered the Petrograd Vkhutemas, studying under Dobujinsky and Nikolai Radlov; began to illustrate books, including the collected works of Henri de Regnier; met Nikolai Evreinov; began to design stage productions, at first at small theaters such as Balaganchik [Fairground Booth] and the Free Comedy and later at prestigious theaters such as the Theater of Musical Comedy (Leningrad); the Academic Theater of Drama (Leningrad), the Vakhtangov Theater (Moscow), and the Moscow Art Theater; 1927 contributed to the "Exhibition of Stage Design 1917-X-1927" in Leningrad; 1930 worked for the Leningrad Studio of the Central Directorate for State Circuses; 1932 produced *Hamlet* for the Vakhtangov Theater; 1933 one-man exhibition in Leningrad; 1935 onwards worked predominantly for the Leningrad Theater of Satire (later Theater of Comedy) where, from 1945 to 1949, he was chief designer and producer and then again from 1955 to 1968; continued to design productions until the 1960s.

Bibliography
A. Bartoshevich: *Akimov*, L: Teaklub, 1933.
M. Etkind: *N.P. Akimov – khudozhnik*, L: Khudozhnik RSFSR, 1960.
C28.
A7, Vol. 1, pp. 75-76.
A14, Vol. 1, pp. 108-09.
C61.
G. Levitin: *Nikolai Pavlovich Akimov*. Catalog of exhibition organized by the Union of Artists of the USSR, L, 1979.
M. Etkind: *Nikolai Akimov*, M: Sovetskii khudozhnik, 1980.
I. Lander and P. Makho: *N.P. Akimov*, SP: NP-Print, 2008.
P. Volkova, intro.: *N. Akimov: Teatr – iskusstvo neprochnoe*, M: AST, 2010.
G. Lapkina, ed.: *N.P. Akimov – khudozhnik, rezhisser, teatralnyi deiatel*, SP: State Academy of Theatrical Art, 2011.

Although Akimov received a somewhat fragmentary art education and did not attend a major academy, he was exposed to important artistic influences in Petrograd/Leningrad from an early age. On the one hand, he studied with the Neo-Classical or Neo-Academic

artists Jacovleff and Shukhaev (Nos. 584-88 [R1008-12]; 947-50 [R961-63]) during the "happiest and most useful years of my life",[9] who encouraged his orientation towards the graphic arts as an expressive and forceful medium; on the other hand, he worked closely with Nicholas Remisoff (Re-mi; Nos. 856-57 [R733-38]) and Alexander Yunger, whose satirical spirit appealed to Akimov's keen sense of humor. Akimov was close to Yurii Annenkov and other representatives of the Petrograd bohemia just after the Revolution and worked for some of the cabarets that flourished there, such as Balaganchik and Carousel.[10] Constructivism also played an appreciable role in his evolution — an influence manifest in his designs for Evreinov's *Daesh Gamleta* [Hamlet, Right on] at the Crooked Mirror in 1923-24 and Molière's *Tartuffe* at the Leningrad Academic Theater in 1929, although the "electrification, industrialization and cinematification"[11] of the theater was never Akimov's overriding concern.

As a stage designer, Akimov was versatile and his range encompassed the most diverse productions — from Vsevolod Ivanov's *Armored Train 14-69* in 1927 (Leningrad Academic Theater) to Yurii Olesha's *Conspiracy of Feelings* in 1929 (Vakhtangov Theater), from *Hamlet* in 1932 (Vakhtangov) to Lord Byron's *Don Juan* in 1963 (Leningrad Theater of Comedy). His designs for movies, e.g., for *Cinderella* in 1947, and for theater and movie posters are also worthy of note, and his poster style — a playful distortion often tinged with Surrealist overtones — was especially evident in his Leningrad poster designs of the 1960s and 1970s. In his strict adherence to the dictates of the enclosed space, whether the scenic box or the framed picture, Akimov concentrated on the essential detail that identified and crystallized the ethos of this or that representation. As his early biographer Andrei Bartoshevich remarked in 1933:

> From the very first stages of his independent creative work, Akimov entered the theater, not simply becoming an *artist working in the theater*, a more or less desirable guest artist, but fusing organically with the theater; he became a genuinely *theatrical artist*.[12]

The End of Krivorylsk: *satirical melodrama in fourteen scenes by Boris Romashov. Produced by Nikolai Petrov at the Pushkin Academic Theater of Drama, Leningrad, on 2 December, 1926, with designs by Nikolai Akimov.*

The old values are replaced by the new as the pre-Revolutionary town of Krivorylsk becomes the new Soviet one called Leninsk. The many episodes show the new attributes of Socialist life such as the Party Executive Committee, the movie-house, and the Komsomol, and their inexorable triumph over the legacy of the feudal past.

13 [R12].
Costume Design for Mokronosov, 1926.
Pencil, wash, and black ink.
10¾ x 7⅛ in., 27.3 x 18 cm.
Inscriptions: upper left: "No. 18"; lower right

13

in Russian, in pencil: "Kiselev";[13] below in pencil, in Russian: "The End of Krivorylsk by N. P. Akimov"; on the reverse in pencil, in Russian: "Collection of A. G. Movshenzon."[14] Provenance: Yakov Rubinshtein, Moscow, 1974.

Note: Romashov's topical play about the transformation of a provincial town in the wake of the Revolution premiered at the Theater of the Revolution in Moscow on 20 March, 1926, with designs by Viktor Shestakov. But it was the Leningrad production that made it famous, thanks, in no small degree, to Akimov's designs. Although the sets and costumes still contained Akimov's highly schematic and exaggerated forms, he tempered them with the inclusion of real objects, creating combinations that were "exceptional in their inventiveness."[15] In order to facilitate the scene changes in this multi-episodic play, Akimov mechanized parts of the sets and of the stage itself, so that the resolution was mobile and transformative — but without resorting to "experimentation and tricks."[16] Petrov himself was very pleased with the result and singled out *The End of Krivorylsk* as one of the "productions that any European theater would envy."[17] No wonder, then, that Petrov and Akimov collaborated on many other plays, including Vsevolod Ivanov's *Armored Train 14-69* (1927) also at the Academic Theater, and that Akimov portrayed Petrov in several works.[18]

14 [R13].
Costume Design for a Dance Leader, ca. 1927.
Pencil.
13 x 8½ in., 33 x 21.5 cm.
Inscriptions: cloth annotations in pencil in Russian throughout; lower margin in pencil in Russian: "Dance leader Krumchak; the reverse carries the caricature of a head in profile.
Provenance: Yakov Rubinshtein, Moscow, 1974.
Reproduced in I60, p. 38.

Note: Apart from his stage, poster, and book designs, Akimov was also active as a portraitist, and his interpretations of leading theatrical and artistic personalities form a vital component of his many-sided career. Presumably, item No. 14 [R13] is of a particular individual ("Krumchak" has not been identified) and belongs to the long gallery of Akimov's portraits of celebrities such as Alexei Faiko (1927), Kasian Goleizovsky (1929), Anna Kashina-Evreinova (1922), Nikolai Petrov (1932), Arkadii Raikin (1958), Dmitrii Shostakovich (1931), and Ivan Sollertinsky (1933). Treading a delicate path between academic Realism and caricature, Akimov emphasized the salient characteristics of the model. Akimov seemed to view the world through the magnifying glasses and prismatic lenses that so fascinated him, and the visual result, while often startling, was much more than mere ridicule or estrangement. As Akimov wrote in 1957: "We are convinced — after many sad experiences — that documentary authenticity has nothing in common with the concept of artistic truth."[19]

9.   Etkind, *Nikolai Akimov* (1980), p. 116.
10. For reproductions of Akimov's costumes for the Balaganchik theater see Levitin, *N. P. Akimov,* unnumbered. For a reproduction of a program design for Carousel see Etkind, *Akimov* (1980), p. 19; also see Nos. 47, 48 ([R44, 45]).
11. Etkind, *Nikolai Akimov* (1980), p. 11.
12. Bartoshevich, *Akimov,* p. 24.
13. Presumably, a reference to the Leningrad actor Valentin Georgievich Kiselev (1903-1950). The role of Mokronosov was actually played by Nikolai Simonov, but Kiselev, a friend of both Petrov and Akimov, may have considered taking it.
14. The reference is to the Leningrad collector and theater critic Alexander Grigorievich Movshenson (Movshenzon, 1895-1965).
15. A. Piotrovsky: "Konets Krivorylska" in *Krasnaia gazeta,* L, 1926, 3 December, Evening Issue. Quoted in Etkind, *N. P. Akimov — khudozhnik,* p. 23.
16. K. Tverskoi: "Torzhestvo teatra" in *Rabochii i teatr,* L, 1926, No. 49, 7 December, p. 10. Quoted in C78, p. 186.

14

17. N. Petrov: "Akademicheskii teatr dramy k desiatiletiiu Oktiabria" (1927). Quoted in C31, Vol. 2, p. 323.
18. For reproductions see Bartoshevich, *Akimov* (illustrations unnumbered).
19. C28, p. 133.

ALTMAN, Natan Isaevich

Born 22 December, 1889 (3 January, 1890), Vinnitsa, Ukraine; died 12 December, 1970, Leningrad, Russia.

1901-07 studied painting and sculpture at the Odessa Art Institute; 1910-12 lived in Paris, attending Marie Vassilieff's Académie Russe; influenced by Cubism; 1912 contributed to the satirical journal *Riab* [Ripple] in Vinnitsa; 1912-17 active in the Union of Youth; contributed to many avant-garde exhibitions, including "0.10" and the "Jack of Diamonds"; 1918 professor at Svomas in Petrograd; member of IZO NKP; designed agit-decorations for Uritsky Square, Petrograd, and elsewhere; 1919 leading member of Komfut [Communist Futurism] group; 1910s onwards contributed to many exhibitions at home and abroad, including the "Exhibition of Contemporary Painting and Drawing" (Petrograd, 1918), the "First State Free Exhibition of Works of Art" (Petrograd, 1919), the "Exhibition of Designs for Theatrical Décors of Works from the Studios of the Decorative Institute" (Petersburg, 1922), the "Jubilee Exhibition of the Art of the Peoples of the USSR" (Moscow, 1927), "Artists of the RSFSR over the Last 15 Years" (Leningrad, 1932), "Artists of the Soviet Theater (1917-1935)" (Leningrad, 1935), and the "Exhibition of Soviet Illustrations to Creative Literature over the Last 5 Years" (1931-1936) (Moscow, 1936); 1921 designed the décor for Vladimir Maiakovsky's play *Mystery-Bouffe;* 1923 member of the Petrograd affiliation of the Institute of Artistic Culture (Inkhuk); 1929-35 lived in Paris; 1935 returned to the Soviet Union, settling in Leningrad the following year; 1930s onwards continued to be active as a painter, designer, and illustrator.

Bibliography
B. Arvatov: *Natan Altman,* P: Petropolis, 1924.
G. Kozintsev: *Natan Altman.* Catalog of exhibition at the Leningrad Section of the Union of Artists, 1968.
M. Etkind: *Natan Altman,* M: Sovetskii khudozhnik, 1971.
A. Kamensky: *Natan Altman.* Catalog of exhibition organized by the Union of Artists of the USSR, M, 1978.
M. Etkind: *Nathan Altman,* Dresden: VEB Kunst, 1984.
E. Kuznetsov: *Natan Altman. Teatr, kino.* Catalog of exhibition at MTMA, 1988.
Yu. Molok: "Kak v zerkalo gliadela ya trevozhno…" in *Akhmatovskii sbornik,* Paris: Institut national d'études slaves, 1989, No. 1, pp. 43-52.
J. Bowlt: "Boris Aronson o Natane Altmane" in H32. Vol. 4, pp. 417-420.
A. Shatskikh: "Parizhskie gody Natana Altmana" in H32, Vol. 4, pp. 411-16.

Altman was an artist of many genres and media, although his studio-painting remains of primary interest, especially the portraits. His paintings are distinguished by a fine sense of structure, a quality that he developed from his experience of both French Cubism and particular tendencies within the Russian avant-garde such as Suprematism and agitational art. During the early period, Altman was concerned especially with the intrinsic elements of art and, in the wake of his training in Paris, proceeded to experiment with abstract combinations of textures and colors as in his material selections of 1919-20. He used this knowledge with marked success in his portraits of the 1920s and in his occasional pedagogical endeavors.

That Altman was Jewish by birth, grew up in a strict Jewish family — and yet became a close colleague of Kazimir Malevich, Alexander Rodchenko, and Vladimir Tatlin as he explored the international movements of Cubism and Futurism — is symptomatic of the ethnic diversity of the Russian avant-garde. In turn, exposure to its esthetic and ideological preferences prompted Altman to transfer motifs and subjects from a local vocabulary to a more universal one, as in his Cubist portraits of fellow Jews or his "suprematization" of Jewish letters. His early biographer Max Osborn saw this as one of the radical features in Altman's attitude towards the folkloric legacy: "He wished to study the characteristic elements, to inspect them on the objects that he saw, to remove them from these objects, and, in this manner, to find the paths to creativity which were to have been both private and at the same time objective."[20]

Yurii Annenkov: *Portrait of Natan Altman,* 1921. See No. 46 [R43].

15

15 [R14].
***Portrait of Martiros Sarian,* ca. 1913.**
Pencil.
Signed lower right in Russian "Natan Altman."
5½ x 4¾ in., 14 x 12 cm.
Other inscriptions: on reverse in Russian: "No. 4, portrait of Sarian."
Provenance: Garabed Basmadjian, Paris, 12 March, 1983.

Note: Although Altman was not especially close to the painter Martiros Sarian (No. 896 [R765]), who supported a different artistic system, they occasionally contributed to the same exhibitions and often made caricatures of fellow artists and friends. Judging from the abundant hair and the moustache of Sarian, this portrait could have been made ca. 1913. For a photograph of Sarian at this time see M. Sarian: *Iz moei zhizni,* M: Izobrazitelnoe iskusstvo, 1970, p. 119.

20.   M. Osborn: *Jüdische Graphic / Evreiskaia grafika,* Berlin: Raum, 1923, p. 10.

ANDREENKO
(Andrienko-Nechitailo),
Mikhail Fedorovich

Born 29 December, 1894 (10 January, 1895), Kherson, Ukraine; died 12 November, 1982, Paris, France.

1910-12 painted local landscapes, showing them at the exhibitions of the Society of Lovers of the Fine Arts in Kherson; 1912 graduated from high school in Kherson and moved to St. Petersburg where he enrolled in SSEA; studied there under Ivan Bilibin, Nicholas Roerich, and Arkadii Rylov; also attended Law School at St. Petersburg University; 1914-17 exhibited at Nadezhda Dobychina's Art Bureau, the "Union of Art Workers," and "Contemporary Painting," and also at the "Internationale Ausstellung für Buchgewerbe und Graphik" in Leipzig (1914); worked at Suvorin's Theater, St. Petersburg; during this period met a number of avant-garde artists including Natan Altman, Lev Bruni, and Vladimir Lebedev; active as a painter, stage designer, and magazine illustrator; 1917 finished course work at SSEA and returned to Kherson; 1918-19 lived in Odessa, where he worked as a designer for Konstantin Miklashevsky's Chamber Theater, contributing sets and costumes to the productions of Plautus's *Menaechmi* and the farce *The Four Lady-Killers;* 1920 lived in Bucharest; 1921 moved to Prague; 1923 settled in Paris; by 1928 had moved from Constructivist stage designs and still lifes to Surrealist compositions; later began to paint Parisian scenes in a simple style; continued to design stage projects; began to write short stories and to paint geometric abstractions; 1964 first one-man show at the Galérie Houston-Brown, Paris.

Bibliography
M.V.: "M.F. Nechitailo-Andreenko" in *Teatr-iskusstvo-ekran,* Paris, 1925, February-March, p. 3.
V. Popovich: *Michel Andreenko – Mikhailo Andrienko,* Munich: Suchasnist, 1969.
M2, Vol. 2, pp. 141-42.
G. Dornand: *Mikhail Andreenko, Pionnier et mainteneur du Construcitivisme,* Paris: Chalom, 1972.
V. Popovich: *M. Andrienko.* Paris: Chalom, 1972.
V. and J.-C. Marcadé: "Konstruktivnyi kubizm Andreenko" in *Vozrozhdenie,* Paris, 1973, No. 240, pp. 125-32.
V. and J.-C. Marcadé: "Andreenko's Constructivist Cubism" in *TriQuarterly,* Evanston, Ill., 1973, No. 28, pp. 570-78.
J.-C. and V. Marcadé: *Andreenko,* Lausanne: L'Age d'Homme, 1978.
R. Guerra, intro.: *M. Andreenko: Perekresty. Rasskazy,* Paris: P.I.U.F., 1979.
M. Andreenko: "Zhurnal Sharshuna" in *Russkii almanakh,* Paris, 1981, pp. 387-92.
J.-C. Marcadé: "Pamiati Mikhaila Fedorovicha Andreenko" in *Russkaia mysl,* Paris, 1982, 2 December, p. 13.
M20.
A31, p. 25.
A41, pp. 58-59.
M73, Vol. 26, pp. 67-68.
O. Fedoruk, ed.: *Mikhailo Andrienko i evropeiske mistetstvo XX st.,* K: Abris, 1996.
H34, pp. 84, 85.

Although trained as a studio painter, Andreenko was, from his early days, particularly interested in stage design and he worked at many Russian and European theaters from 1914 onward. Andreenko brought to his theatrical conceptions an appreciation of Cubism and Constructivism, and he was well aware of the scenic experiments of Alexandra Exter. Andreenko's collaboration with the playwright and director Konstantin Miklashevsky at the Chamber Theater in Odessa in 1919 (Exter worked at the Theater of the People's House there the following year) was especially productive — and provocative. Describing the production of the pseudo-classical farce, *The Four Lady-Killers,* staged by Miklashevsky in March, 1919, one reviewer condemned Andreenko's designs as "weak and faceless, with an obvious bias towards the Cubist stereotypes, which were the 'latest rage' in the capitals a few years ago."[21] On the other hand, a second critic praised the production: "As far as the decoration is concerned, the play is a conscientious production. The way in which the perspective of the arches has been resolved is very clever."[22] In his stage designs both for Eastern and Western Europe, Andreenko always elicited conflicting responses, a condition that derived from his very conception of art and reality:

> Newspapers, magazines, posters, neon signs, television, cinema – the result of all this is that the depiction of the real world is deprived of its spirituality... Whether he wants it or not, the artist's thinking has to head in the opposite direction.[23]

16

16 [R15].
Self-Portrait, ca. 1960.
Pencil.
Signed lower right in Russian: "Andreenko."
12½ x 9½ in., 32 x 24 cm.
Provenance: Mikhail Andreenko, Paris, July, 1969.
Reproduced in F107, p. 123; I20, p. 57; I51, No. 2.

Les Millions d'Arlequin: opera-ballet in two acts by Ivan Vsevolozhsky with music by Riccardo Drigo. Projected, but not produced, for the first season of the Opera National at the Royal Opera House, Bucharest, in 1921, with choreography by Boris Romanov and designs by Mikhail Andreenko.

A ballet based on the traditional theme of Pantalone, Harlequin, Columbine, and Pierrot.

17 [R16].
Costume Design for the Smiling Clown, 1921.
Gouache and silver paint.
Signed and dated lower right: "Andreenko 921."
20 x 13 in., 51 x 33 cm.
Identification on the reverse.
Provenance: Mikhail Andreenko, Paris, June, 1968.

17

Reproduced in color in N12; and in black and white in I32, No. 4; I51, No. 3; I77, p. 156; M151, p. 84; P56.

18 [R17].
Costume Design for the Sad Clown, 1921.
Gouache and silver.
Signed and dated lower right: "Andreenko 921."
20 x 13 in., 51 x 33 cm.
Provenance: Mikhail Andreenko, Paris, June, 1968.
Reproduced in color in B115, plate 120; F107, p. 123; and in black and white in I32, No. 3; I51, No. 4; I77, p. 156; M73, p. 89; Q17.

18

Note: Riccardo Drigo (1846-1930), the Italian composer, was conductor of the Imperial Ballet at the Mariinsky Theater, St. Petersburg, from 1886 to 1920. A number of his operas and ballets were produced in St. Petersburg, Moscow, and other Russian cities, including *Harlequinade* (1900), which, when staged outside Russia, became known as *Les Millions d'Arlequin.* Drigo's interpretation of the drama of Columbine, Pierrot, and Harlequin reflected the current fashion for the Commedia dell'Arte in Russia, which also inspired many other literary and artistic works such as Alexander Blok's *Fairground Booth,* Nikolai Evreinov's *Merry Death* (Nos. 924-26 [R941-42]), and Konstantin Somov's painting and designs (No. 953 [R783]). Alexandre Benois was also drawn to the theme and interpreted it in his famous *Petrouchka* (Nos. 159-280 [R133-253]), remembering how Vsevolozhsky had also been inspired:

> When a very old man, [Vsevolozhsky] used to tell me about the profound impression that had been made on him by *The Harlequinades* he had seen in some Paris Theatre. It was with the desire to revive this impression that he created the charming ballet, *Les Millions d'Arlequin* in the theatre he directed, taking the subject from a French *féerie.*[24] In this ballet Harlequin was given exactly the part he played in our old *Balagani.*[25] The pleasant music by Drigo was a welcome addition to this fancy of Vsevolozhsky's and one of the chief items, the famous *Serenade,* became extremely popular and was played by the orchestras of all the world and can often be heard today.[26]

According to one biographer of 1932, Andreenko's sets and costumes for the Bucharest production of *Les Millions d'Arlequin* were so successful that he was invited to become artist-in-residence at the Royal Opera Theater there.[27] The brilliance of Andreenko's designs was paralleled by the bold arrangements of Romanov who retained *Les Millions d'Arlequin* as a major part of his choreographic repertoire. His Berlin version, staged at the Russisches Romantisches Theater in 1922 with designs by Vladimir Boberman, Fedor Hosiason, and Léon Zack (see Nos.1178-81 [R488-91]), also won Romanov wide acclaim.

Tsar Fedor Ioannovich: *tragedy in five acts by Alexei K. Tolstoi. Produced at the Ruské komorní divadlo (Russian Chamber Theater), Prague, 1922, with music by Alexander Grechaninov and designs by Mikhail Andreenko.*

Son of Ivan the Terrible, Tsar Fedor Ioannovich (Ivanovich) who reigned from 1584-98, is presented as an indecisive leader. In spite of his plans for imperial expansionism and economic prosperity, he is the victim of court intrigues and is no match for the clever Boris Godunov and the boyars, especially the wily Shuisky brothers.

19

20

21

19 [3; R18].
Costume Design for a Boyar's Daughter,
1922.
Watercolor.
Signed and dated lower right: "Andreenko
1922."
15½ x 7 in., 39.5 x 18 cm.
Provenance: Mikhail Andreenko, Paris,
June, 1968.
Reproduced in color in C7, plate 298; and in
black and white in I40, No. 3; I51, No. 5;
I77, p. 157.

20 [4; R19].
Costume Design for a Young Man, **1922.**
Watercolor.
Signed and dated lower center: "Andreenko
1922."
15½ x 7 in., 39.5 x 18 cm.
The reverse carries the inscription: "Michel
Andreenko, 125 Bd. Sébastopol, Paris 2, N
10 Maquette du costume Russe"
Provenance: Mikhail Andreenko, Paris,
June, 1968.
Reproduced in color in C7, plate 298; M151,
p. 84; and in black and white in I40, No. 4;
I51, No. 6; I77, p. 157.

21 [R20].
Costume Design for Tsar Fedor, **1922.**
Watercolor and gold paint.
Signed and dated lower right: "Andreenko
922."
16¾ x 7¼ in., 42.5 x 18.5 cm.
Provenance: Mikhail Andreenko, Paris, July,
1969.
Reproduced in black and white in I40, No.
1; I77, p. 157.

22 [R21].
Costume Design for Tsarina Irina, **1922.**
Watercolor and gold paint.
Signed and dated lower left: "Andreenko 922."
16¼ x 7¼ in., 41.3 x 18.5 cm.
Provenance: Mikhail Andreenko, Paris, July,
1969.
Reproduced in black and white in I40, No.
2; I77, p. 157.

Note: The poet and playwright Alexei
Konstantinovich Tolstoi (1817-75) portrays Tsar
Fedor as a tragic figure, a "good and weak
sovereign, with an unerring sense of values
and a complete inability to impose his good will
on his crafty councilor."[28] Because of this
equivocal interpretation, Tolstoi's play, written
in 1868, was long banned from the Russian
stage. It premiered at the Moscow Art Theater

only in 1898 when it scored an immediate
success thanks to the acting of Ivan Moskvin
and Olga Knipper. As a matter of fact, the
Moscow Art Theater took its production of *Tsar
Fedor Ioannovich* to Prague in 1906, thus
creating a precedent for the 1922 presentation.
Andreenko designed several historical plays in
Prague, including Dmitrii Merezhkovsky's *Paul
I* (also for the Russian Chamber Theater in
1922) and Denis Fonvizin's *The Minor* (for the
Czech Folk Theater).

Unidentified production, *Paris, 1924.*

23 [R22].
Set Design with Two Bridges, **1924.**
Collage.
Signed and dated lower left: "Andreenko
1924."
11 x 11¾ in., 28 x 30 cm.
Also signed on the reverse.
Provenance: Mikhail Andreenko, Paris,
June, 1968.
Reproduced in I32, No. 1.

24 [R23].
Set Design with a Vase, **1925.**
Collage.
Signed and dated lower right: "Andreenko
1925."
18½ x 16 in., 47 x 40.5 cm.

22

23

Other inscriptions: the reverse carries Andreenko's home address.
Provenance: Mikhail Andreenko, Paris, June, 1968.
Reproduced in I32, No. 2; I51, No. 7; I77, pp. 111 and 157; P26.

Note: These sets may have been created for a scenic experiment rather than a fully fledged production. Comparable pieces are illustrated in color in C7, plates 296, 297, the Nationalbibliothek, Vienna, has a similar

24

design in its collection, and another similar design is illustrated in *Teatr-iskusstvo-ekran* (Paris, 1925, February-March, p. 3). Andreenko did work on a number of productions in Paris in the mid-1920s, including Catulle Mendés' *Maris Contents,* staged by Fedor Komissarzhevsky at the Théâtre de l'Arc-en-Ciel, and Tristan Tzara's *Mouchoir de Nuages* at the Théâtre de la Cigale during the 1926-27 season. Whether these sets were for a specific spectacle or were a reminiscence of designs for the Chamber Theater in Odessa and Prague, they extend Andreenko's primary concern with the notion of scenic construction and dynamic volume. Describing Andreenko's designs for the première of Paul Hindemith's *Nusch-Nuschi* in Prague in 1922, two critics have emphasized this distinctive feature:

> In his sets, Andreenko would break the stage up into separate sections by means of arc-like ladders, which enabled him to suggest in a colorful manner several portions of a city or a port, side streets, gardens, and so forth. This was a Mediaeval tradition transposed into contemporary terms.[29]

Alexandra Exter was investigating a similar approach to the stage at this time (see Nos. 474-97 [R982-1003]).

21. A. Koiransky: untitled review in *Nashe slovo*, Odessa, 1919, 21 March, p. 3.
22. Anon.: "Kamernyi teatr" in *Yuzhnaia Rus*, Odessa, 1919, 15 March.
23. M. Andrienko: "Notaki pro suchasne mistetstvo" in *Suchasnist*, Munich, 1966, No. 4. Quoted in V. and J.-C. Marcadé, *Andreenko*, p. 574.
24. Ivan Aleksandrovich Vsevolozhsky (1835-1909) was Director of the Imperial Theaters in Moscow from 1881 until 1886 and then in St. Petersburg until 1899.
25. See entries on Alexandre Benois' *Petrouchka* below.
26. F7, p. 33. Also see the Russian version of these memoirs in F54, p. 380 (second edition).
27. V. Sichinsky writing in 1932. Quoted in Popovich: *M. Andrienko,* p. 14. Andreenko confirmed this in a conversation with John E. Bowlt in Paris on 17 December, 1981.
28. D. Mirsky: *A History of Russian Literature*, New York: Knopf, 1960, p. 243.
29. V. and J.-C. Marcadé, *Andreenko,* p. 573.

ANISFELD, Boris (Ber) Izrailevich

Born 2 (14) October, 1879, Beltsy, Bessarabia (Moldova); died 4 December, 1973, Waterford, Connecticut, USA.

1895-1901 studied at the Odessa Drawing School; 1901-09 studied at IAA under Dmitrii Kardovsky, Ilia Repin, and other professors; 1905-07 contributed caricatures to journals of political satire; 1906 contributed to the exhibitions of the "World of Art," the "Union of Russian Artists," Moscow, and the "Salon d'Automne," Paris; thereafter exhibited frequently in Russia and abroad; 1907 designed the production of Hugo von Hofmannsthal's *Die Hochzeit der Sobeide* at Vera Komissarzhevskaia's Theater, St. Petersburg; thereafter very active as a stage designer; 1908 with Alexandre Benois and Alexander Golovin worked on the designs for Sergei Diaghilev's production of *Boris Godunov* in Paris; 1909 with Golovin and Nicholas Roerich worked on the designs for Diaghilev's production of the *Maid of Pskov;* 1911 created the décor and costumes for Diaghilev's production of *Sadko;* 1912-14 designed many ballet and drama productions such as Milii Balakirev's *Islamey,* Leonid Andreev's *Ocean,* and Michel Fokine's *Une Nuit d'Egypte;* 1913 collaborated with Anna Pavlova on a production of *Les Préludes* for the Manhattan Opera House, New York; 1914 designed Vaslav Nijinsky's production of *Les Sylphides* in London; 1918 via Siberia and Japan emigrated to the US; 1918-20 one-man exhibition at the Brooklyn Museum, New York, and other institutions; 1919 designed Xavier Leroux's *La Reine Fiammette* and Maurice Maeterlinck's *L'Oiseau Bleu* for the Metropolitan Opera, New York, the first of several major productions for New York, Chicago, and other US cities; 1921 designed Sergei Prokofiev's *Love for Three Oranges* for the Chicago Opera company; 1922 designed Nikolai Rimsky-Korsakov's *Snow Maiden* for the Metropolitan Opera; 1926, after working on designs for Puccini's *Turandot* (not produced), gave more attention to painting and to teaching; 1928 became a professor at The School of the Art Institute of Chicago, where he taught for more than thirty years.

Bibliography
V. Voinov: "B.I. Anisfeld" in *Novaia studiia,* M, 1912, No. 3, pp. 17-18.
C. Brinton: *Boris Anisfeld.* Catalog of exhibition at the Brooklyn Museum, New York, and other institutions, 1918-20.
M2, Vol. 2, pp. 140,141.
J. Flint: *Boris Anisfeld. Twenty Years of Designs for the Theater.* Catalog of exhibition at the National Collection of Fine Arts, Washington, D.C., 1971.
V. Zavalishin: "Pamiati Borisa Anisfelda" in *Novoe Russkoe Slovo,* New York, 1974, 13 January, p. 4.
S. Terenzio: *Boris Anisfeld.* Catalog of exhibition

at The William Benton Museum of Art, University of Connecticut, Storrs, 1979.

N. Weber and M. Chatfield-Taylor: *Paintings by Boris Anisfeld.* Catalog of exhibition at Adler Fine Arts, New York, 1979-80.

J. Taylor et al.: *Boris Anisfeld 1879-1973.* Catalog of exhibition at Gilman Galleries, Chicago, 1981-82.

R. and E. Kashey, et al.: *Boris Anisfeld in St. Petersburg 1901-1917.* Catalog of exhibition at the Shepherd Gallery, New York, 1984.

R. Mesley: *Boris Anisfeld, "Fantast-Mystic."* Catalog of exhibition at the Art Gallery of Ontario, Toronto, 1989.

N. Metelitsa et al.: *Boris Anisfeld.* Catalog of exhibition at Ohio State University, Lima, 1994. M73, Vol. 26, pp. 68-69.

R. Salykhova and M. Ignatieva: *Boris Anisfeld v Rossii.* Catalog of exhibition at the GMTMA, 1994.

S. Bekkerman: *Boris Anisfeld,* New York: A.B.A Gallery, 2001.

C. Chatfield-Taylor: *Works on Paper from the Estate of Boris Anisfeld 1879-1973.* Catalog of exhibition at the Shepherd and Derom Galleries, New York, 2007.

Boris Anisfeld. Catalog of auction at MacDougall's, London, September-October, 2008.

E. Lingenauber and O. Sugrobova-Roth: *Boris Anisfeld. Catalogue Raisonné,* Dusseldorf: Libertas, 2011.

Anisfeld came to the discipline of stage design via studio painting and book illustration. His early illustrative work for the satirical journals *Zhupel* [Bugbear] and *Adskaia pochta* [Hellish Post], for example, reveal a rich fantasy of demons, serpents and *femmes fatales,* and his stage designs (1907 onward) and frescoes for St. Petersburg mansions (1910 onward) elaborate these images. No doubt, Diaghilev chose Anisfeld for the Paris production of *Sadko* in 1911 precisely for this reason, and Anisfeld's exotic imagination was no less suited to Fokine's productions of *Islamey* and *Une Nuit d'Egypte* in 1912-13. Anisfeld retained his love of the fantastic and the mysterious during his émigré period sometimes to the chagrin of established artists and critics. In a polemical exchange of letters with Christian Brinton, Leila Mechlin, Secretary of the American Federation of Arts, remarked in 1918 that Anisfeld's paintings "are without the element of beauty; in some instances even unsightly and incomprehensible. They are ill-drawn, showing the human form distorted, and one, *The Crucifixion,* is little short of blasphemous — horrifying to one who reveres Christ."[30] The public success of the Brooklyn Museum show was ample proof of the rashness of Mechlin's statement.

Anisfeld was one of several St. Petersburg artists who brought a strong appreciation of the *fin de siècle* and the *style moderne* to stage design. Although overshadowed by Léon Bakst (one of Anisfeld's early influences), artists such as Boris Grigoriev, Nikolai Kalmakov, Sergei Sudeikin, and Anisfeld constituted a second generation of Symbolists in Russia, contrasting sharply with the abstract trends of the Suprematists and Constructivists during the 1910s and 1920s. A convinced figurative painter and sculptor, Anisfeld was always guided by his maxim "I paint what I feel, not what I see... my scenery comes from the feelings aroused."[31]

25

25 [R24].
Self-Portrait, ca. 1928.
Pencil.
Signed lower right in red ink: "B. Anisfeld."
11 x 8 in., 28 x 20.5 cm.
Provenance: the artist's daughter, Mara Otis Chatfield-Taylor, Washington, DC, October, 1965.
Reproduced in D41, p. 268; F107, p. 123; I14, p. 61; I51, No. 8.

Sadko: opera-ballet by Nikolai Rimsky-Korsakov with book by Adolph Bolm. Produced by Sergei Diaghilev at the Théâtre du Châtelet, Paris, on 6 June, 1911, with choreography by Michel Fokine and designs by Boris Anisfeld.

The production was only of Scene 6 from Sadko.

See No. 308 [R275] for complete plot synopsis.

26 [R25].
Costume Design for One of the Two Trumpeters, ca. 1911.
Watercolor, pencil, and India ink.
17⅞ x 13 in., 45.5 x 33.1 cm.
Inscriptions: upper left in Russian: "No. 15, 2 trumpeters"; upper right in Russian: "male ballet."
Provenance: *Dance, Theater, Opera, Music-Hall,* New York: Sotheby, Parke Bernet, 12 June, 1981, Lot 20 (reproduced).
Reproduced in I51, No. 10; and Lingenauber and Sugrobova-Roth, *Boris Anisfeld,* p. 188.

26

27 [5; R26].
Costume Design for a Member of the Peasant Chorus, ca. 1911.
Watercolor.
17½ x 13 in., 44.5 x 33.1 cm.
Inscriptions: upper left in Russian: "No. 21, 10 costumes"; upper right in Russian: "Male Peasants' chorus."
Provenance: Cyril Beaumont, London, February, 1965.
Reproduced in I14, No. 3; and Lingenauber and Sugrobova-Roth, *Boris Anisfeld,* p. 219. For reproductions of analogous costume designs see L142, Lot 95.

Note: The Paris production of *Sadko* was a success not only because of the superior cast (Princess Volkhova was danced by

27

Lubov Tchernicheva, whose lightness and grace engendered associations with Mikhail Vrubel's portrait of his wife in the same role in 1898),[32] but also because of the sets and costumes. One Paris critic spoke of Anisfeld as the "real magician behind these animated visions" and praised the artist for his "tumbling tresses of aquatic vegetation, his horizons of blue, luminous and fairy-like waves."[33] However, Diaghilev was not altogether pleased with Anisfeld's designs, regarding them as too serene. According to Fokine, Diaghilev, in a rare lapse of good taste, brought from the Lido an "entire trunk of live crabs and all kinds of garbage for the underwater kingdom... He did not sense how unsuitable these really were to Anisfeld's decorations and costumes, even if he had bought them in Venice."[34] Anisfeld repeated some of his Underwater Kingdom costumes for the 1914 production of *Sadko* at the People's House, St. Petersburg. Diaghilev revived the opera-ballet for the American season in 1916, but he replaced the Anisfeld designs with new ones by Natalia Goncharova, and Adolph Bolm revised the choreography.

28

Islamey: *ballet in one act by Michel Fokine based on music by Milii Balakirev orchestrated by Sergei Liapunov. Produced by Michel Fokine at the Mariinsky Theater, St. Petersburg, on 10 March, 1912, with choreography by Michel Fokine and designs by Boris Anisfeld.*

The wife of the King of the Black Islands gives her husband a cup of wine that she has drugged. Forewarned of her ruse, he pretends to drink the wine and fall asleep. Hiding the King behind a curtain, the wife entertains her black lover, but at the climax of their embraces, the King enters, killing the man. Terrified by her husband's intrusion, the wife flings herself over a precipice.

28 [6; R27].
Costume Design for an Arab Female Dancer, ca. 1912.
Gouache, pencil, silver and gold paint.
Signed lower right in Russian in pencil: "B. Anisfeld."
17⅜ x 12 in., 44.2 x 30.6 cm.
Provenance: the artist's daughter, Mara Otis Chatfield-Taylor, Washington, DC, October, 1965
Reproduced in color in B88, p. 31; B115, plate 25; L88, Lot 200; and M151, p. 108; and Lingenauber and Sugrobova-Roth, *Boris Anisfeld*, p. 199; and in black in white in A34, p. 45; H32, p. 396; M73, p. 89; N115. This item is one of the group of dancers in Anisfeld's décor reproduced in color in F19 between pp. 352 and 353. A similar costume is reproduced in color in I. Barsheva: *Muzei-kvartira I.I. Brodskogo*, M: Izobrazitelnoe isskustvo, 1985, plate 80.

Note: A gesture to the fashion for heady mixtures of Eastern sex and violence, the production of *Islamey,* with its theme from *A Thousand and One Nights,* was much in keeping with Fokine's own esthetic

preferences at this time (cf. *An Egyptian Night* at No. 30 [R29]). The dances during the love scene were especially rousing and Anisfeld's vivid colors, reminiscent of those of Bakst's, extended the dynamism of the plot — even though the ballet lasted only seven minutes. According to one source, Fokine also designed a few costumes for the Mariinsky production.[35]

Les Préludes: *ballet in one act by Michel Fokine based on music by Franz Liszt inspired by Alphonse de Lamartine's Méditations Poétiques. Produced by Michel Fokine for Anna Pavlova in Berlin in December, 1912, and then at the Mariinsky Theater, St. Petersburg, on 13 March, 1913, with choreography by Michel Fokine and designs by Boris Anisfeld.*

The ballet has no established plot. Evoking Botticelli's paintings, the action treats the eternal struggle between life and death, good and evil.

29 [R28].
Costume Design for a Young Girl, ca. 1913.
Pencil and watercolor.
Signed lower right in pencil in Russian: "Boris Anisfeld."
19 x 11¾ in., 48.3 x 30 cm.
Other inscriptions: upper left in black ink: "No. 10,1"; on the right in pencil in Russian: "green wig."
Provenance: the artist's daughter, Mara Otis Chatfield-Taylor, Washington, DC, October, 1965.
Reproduced in I14, No. 4; I51, No. 9.

Note: Les Préludes was one of two ballets that Fokine produced for Pavlova at the theater that she rented in Berlin at the beginning of 1913, the other being *The Seven Daughters of the Mountain King* (based on Mikhail Lermontov's poem called *The Three Palms*). For *Les Préludes* in

29

Berlin, Pavlova and Lavrentii Novikov danced the principal roles (Tamara Karsavina and Fokine in St. Petersburg) and, according to Cyril Beaumont, both Artur Nikisch and Richard Strauss attended the premiere.[36] The scenery was "rather cubist in treatment"[37] and Fokine's choreography was "in the spirit of Duncan."[38] It was long thought that this particular costume was for *Sadko* (cf. Nos. 26, 27 [R25, 26]), but comparison with a similar design in the GMTMA and with a photograph of Anisfeld's setting for *Les Préludes* (which seems to include this item) indicates that this earlier assumption was incorrect.[39] Alternatively, the design might be for the Good Fairy in her magic green cap in *The Blue Bird* (see No. 31 [R30]), although the absence of wings undermines the probability. The green flecks on the dress also bring to mind the costume for *Aziade* (see No. 38 [R37]).

An Egyptian Night (Une Nuit d'Egypte); *also known as Egyptian Nights: one-act ballet based on a novella by Théophile Gautier with music by Antonii Arensky and choreography by Michel Fokine. Produced at the Royal Theater, Stockholm, on 14 March, 1913, by the Fokine Ballet Company with designs by Boris Anisfeld.*

In Fokine's variation on the theme of Cleopatra, Amoun and Bérénice are lovers, but Amoun's attention is diverted by the appearance of Cleopatra. In exchange for Cleopatra's favors, Amoun agrees to die and drinks a cup of poison after a night of love. Meanwhile, however, the High Priest has replaced the poison with a sleeping draft. As Cleopatra sails away with Antony, the High Priest consoles the distraught Bérénice, telling her to awaken her love.

30

30 [7; R29].
Costume Design for Cleopatra's Slave Worn by Michel Fokine, 1913.
Gouache and pencil.
Initialed lower right in pencil in Russian: "B.A."
12¼ x 19 in., 31 x 48.3 cm.
Other inscriptions: lower center in pencil in Russian: "Cleopatra's slave."
Provenance: the artist's daughter, Mara Otis Chatfield-Taylor, Washington, DC, October 1965.
Reproduced in color in B115, plate 24; F107, p. 123; H32, p. 396; I14, No. 5; I51, No. 11; and Lingenauber and Sugrobova-Roth, *Boris Anisfeld*, p. 212.

Note: Fokine created his choreography for *An Egyptian Night* after examining Arensky's score in the library of the Mariinsky Theater, St. Petersburg, and he presented the ballet there on 8 March, 1908 (with Fokine as Amoun, Pavlova as Bérénice, and Vaslav Nijinsky as Cleopatra's Slave). Fokine recalled his initial preparatory work:

> When I staged *Egyptian Nights* I was thinking only of ancient Egypt. I would pay hurried calls to the Hermitage Museum's Egyptian department... and study the material there. I surrounded myself with books on ancient Egypt. In short, I saturated myself with this different Egyptian world...
>
> I staged the dances in Egyptian style then entirely new... the positions were in profile. The lines of the groups were angular. The palms of the hands were flattened out. In short, a style which twenty or thirty years later became the indispensable trademark of the modernists (Indeed, in the last few years I have had occasion to watch many ballets of a most stereotyped kind, but as long as the palms of the

hands were flattened out, they were invariably labeled "modern").

> These profile positions, angular lines, and flat palms were sustained all through the ballet. This was also new, this was also a reform. But I certainly do not wish to claim that these techniques must be applied to all dances, everywhere.[40]

The artistic result of Fokine's choreographic experiments and Anisfeld's bold designs caused the critic Valerian Svetlov to regard *An Egyptian Night* as the "destruction of all the traditions of the good old days. It is a 'transvaluation of values'... of classical technique, the destruction of the 'canon',"[41] and the Emperor Wilhelm, who attended one of the *Cléopâtre* performances, even declared that archaeologists could learn much from the reconstruction.[42]

Even though *An Egyptian Night* marked the beginning of a new epoch in ballet (Diaghilev presented the modified version called *Cléopâtre* for his 1909 Paris season [see Nos. 75-79 [R71-75]), Fokine was paying homage to a current fashion for Egypt. As early as 1901 a ballet called *Nights in Egypt* had been staged at the Hermitage Theater, St. Petersburg, and during the 1900s and early 1910s a number of movies dealing with Ancient Egypt were shown in St. Petersburg and Moscow. The fashion gained momentum in the 1920s, inspiring more ballets and divertissements such as *An Egyptian Ballet* (danced by Anna Pavlova in 1923) and *The Romance of a Mummy* (also danced by Pavlova in 1925). One critic observed in 1910 that:

> While Diaghilev took *Egyptian Nights* off to Paris, the Petersburg Coliseum was showing movie scenes under the title *Cleopâtra*. A group of ballet people went to see it and imagine their universal surprise when they saw everything that Fokine had presented in *Egyptian Nights*. The entire theme, the entire action right down to the last detail has been borrowed from the movies.[43]

Whatever the sources for Fokine's conception, he used *An Egyptian Night* as a vehicle for integrating dance, decoration, costume, and mime, and in the 1913 Stockholm and Berlin versions he even danced the part of Cleopatra's Slave. An enthusiast of artistic synthesism, Diaghilev could not help but be attracted by Fokine's fanciful restoration and interpretative skills, including *Cléopâtre* in his first Paris season. Anisfeld himself was fascinated by the Middle and Far East and worked on many productions that required "Oriental" motifs, including *Le Roi de Lahore* (1924), *Aziade* (1926), and *Turandot* (1926) (see Nos. 37-39 [R36-38]).

The Blue Bird (L'Oiseau Bleu): *opera of lyric comedy in four acts with libretto by Maurice Maeterlinck and music by Albert Wolff. Produced at the Metropolitan Opera, New York, on 27 December, 1919, by the Metropolitan Opera Company with designs by Boris Anisfeld.*

Mytyl and Tyltyl, children of a woodcutter, seek the Blue Bird of Happiness. Helped by the Good Fairy and by her magic green cap, the children visit the Land of Memory, the Palace of the Night, the Garden of Happiness, the Cemetery, and the Kingdom of the Future. Suddenly they wake up — to find themselves at home on a Christmas morning.

31 [R30].
Costume Design for the Joy of Understanding, 1919.
Watercolor.
Signed lower right in pencil in Russian: "Boris Anisfeld."
15 x 10¼ in., 38 x 26 cm.
Other inscriptions: on left side in French and Russian: "Sk 29, 3 joies inconnus; 3 chorus angel with"; on right side: "Axman" (a reference to the soprano Gladys Axman [1895-1968], who sang the part); mid-right: "le levs."
Provenance: the artist's daughter, Mara Otis Chatfield-Taylor, Washington, DC, October, 1965.
Reproduced in color in Lingenauber and Sugrobova-Roth, *Boris Anisfeld*, p. 221; and in black and white in I14, No. 12; similar designs are reproduced in J7, Lot 56; J32, Lot 54; I51, No. 12; and Lingenauber and Sugrobova-Roth, *Boris Anisfeld*, p. 221.

Note: This production of the opera *The Blue Bird* was the world premiere and Maeterlinck himself was present. The event was transformed into a spectacular gala in aid of various charities, and Mrs. William K. Vanderbilt, Jr., patroness of the Bluebird Campaign for Happiness, even

31

declared that New York should be painted blue — to which end she had a blue mailer printed. It was a latterday Symbolist gesture that might have been more appropriate to the ambiance of Moscow and St. Petersburg in the early 1900s, when Maeterlinck's play had enjoyed a particular success, especially in its interpretation at the Moscow Art Theater from 1908 onwards.[44] Anisfeld's decorations and costumes for the New York presentation received unqualified praise and ensured him several subsequent engagements with the Metropolitan. As one critic wrote: "It was the artist rather than the composer who was the star of the evening. Boris Anisfeld is the alchemist in color who provided these magnificent settings."[45]

The Love for Three Oranges: *a farcical opera in four acts by Sergei Prokofiev based on the comedy by Carlo Gozzi. Produced at the Civic Opera Company, Chicago, on 30 December, 1921, with designs by Boris Anisfeld.*

The son of the King of Clubs suffers from a hypochondria that defies all curative attempts to make him laugh. The Prime Minister, Leondro, and the King's niece, Princess Clarissa, wish to thwart the cure in the hope that they will rule instead of the Prince. The latter is protected by Tchelio, the Magician, whereas Leondro is protected by Fata Morgana, the Witch. One day Fata Morgana, by chance, makes the Prince laugh, and then puts a curse on him according to which he falls in love with three oranges that he pursues through many lands and adventures. Finally, the Prince comes home to rule with Ninetta, one of the Princesses imprisoned in the oranges. The evildoers are revealed, but Fata Morgana helps them escape by ushering them through a trapdoor.

32 [R31].
Costume Design for a Devil, 1921.
Gouache, pencil, and green ink.
Signed in the center in green ink: "Boris Anisfeld."
11½ x 9½ in., 29 x 24 cm.
Other inscriptions: top left corner in pencil: "No. 8"; top right in green ink: "Farfarello" with the caption underneath "The Love of Three Oranges."
Provenance: the artist's daughter, Mara Otis Chatfield-Taylor, Washington, DC, October, 1965.
Reproduced in color in Lingenauber and Sugrobova-Roth, *Boris Anisfeld*, p. 232; and in black and white in I14, No. 6.

Note: The idea for an opera called *The Love for Three Oranges* was suggested to Prokofiev by Vsevolod Meierkhold who, in 1914-16, was editing a journal of the same name in Petrograd, i.e. *Liubov k trem apelsinam.* Prokofiev received the commission in January, 1919, and he set to work immediately so as to ensure its readiness for the fall season in Chicago. Prokofiev did, indeed, finish the piece over the summer, but the conductor Cleofonte Campanini, who had proposed the project, died, and the premiere was delayed. Because of Prokofiev's demand

32

for compensation to cover the period of postponement (the entire production cost in Chicago was $250,000), the opera continued to be delayed — until Prokofiev withdrew his requirement and a new contract was drawn up.[46] The enterprise was fraught with difficulties and the opera became a box office draw only in later years. Anisfeld's daughter, Mara Otis Chatfield-Taylor, recalled:

> Prokofiev came here and lived very near us in New York. He wrote part of the score of *Love of Three Oranges* in my father's studio. From what my father said, he wrote it all in three weeks. They would collaborate about the sets and costumes and how to arrange it all. My father loved the music the minute he heard it — so did I — but when it opened in Chicago, every critic was in a panic because they all hated the music.

At the opening everyone yelled only for the artist, because my father's scenery and costumes were absolutely glorious. When people would ask him about the music, he said, "Wait twenty years and you'll like it."[47]

A number of important Soviet artists also produced designs for *The Love for Three Oranges,* including Isaak Rabinovich (No. 855 [R732]).

Snegurochka (The Snow Maiden): *opera in a prologue and four acts by Nikolai Rimsky-Korsakov after the play by Alexander Ostrovsky. Produced as the American premiere at the Metropolitan Opera, New York, on 23 January, 1922, with designs by Boris Anisfeld.*

Spring and Winter have a fair daughter, Snegurochka. They know that if Yarilo, the Sun-God sees her, she will die, so before they depart for the north, they entrust their child to the Spirit of the Wood. There then begins a complicated love intrigue: Snegurochka falls in love with Lel, a young shepherd, while a wealthy youth falls in love with Snegurochka, and the fair Kupava falls in love with him. Tsar Berendei calls a court of justice to pronounce upon these doings. Unhappy in her predicament, Snegurochka, through the intercession of Spring, falls in love with Misgir. But Yarilo has warmed her heart and she melts away while Misgir throws himself into the lake. Even so, the opera ends with a rousing invocation to the Sun-God, led by Lel.

33 [R32].
Costume Designs for the Four Shepherdesses, 1921.
Pencil, colored crayon, and gouache.
Signed and dated lower left: "Boris Anisfeld 1921."
10½ x 14¼ in., 26.5 x 36 cm.

33

34

35

34 [R33].
Costume Designs for Three Gusli Players, 1921.
Watercolor and red pencil.
Signed and dated lower right in red pencil: "Boris Anisfeld 1921."
11¾ x 13¾ in., 30 x 35 cm.
Other inscriptions: upper margin in red pencil in French: "Joueurs de Guzli, 5 costumes."
Provenance: the artist's daughter, Mara Otis Chatfield-Taylor, Washington, DC, October, 1965.
Reproduced in I14, No. 11; and Lingenauber and Sugrobova-Roth, *Boris Anisfeld*, p. 237.

35 [R34].
Costume Designs for the Nobleman Bermiata and His Wife Elena the Beautiful, 1921.
Watercolor.
11 x 12½ in., 28 x 38 cm.
Inscriptions: upper center in red pencil: "Bermiata et sa femme"; upper left, in pencil, illegible.
Provenance: the artist's daughter, Mara Otis Chatfield-Taylor, Washington, DC, October, 1965.
Reproduced in color in N188, p. 2; and in black and white in and Lingenauber and Sugrobova-Roth, *Boris Anisfeld*, p. 237.

36 [R35].
Stage Details, 1921.
Watercolor, ink, and pencil.
Initialed lower right: "B.A."
11 x 15 in., 28 x 38 cm.
Annotations throughout in orange ink and pencil regarding size and number of objects.
Provenance: the artist's daughter, Mara Otis Chatfield-Taylor, Washington, DC, October, 1965.
Reproduced in I14, No. 9; and Lingenauber and Sugrobova-Roth, *Boris Anisfeld*, p. 238.

Note: Snegurouchka enjoyed an immediate success at the Metropolitan Opera as much for the "Slavic" costumes as for the singing. Anisfeld's daughter recalled:

> [Anisfeld] closely supervised the making of all the costumes he designed — sometimes he painted on them directly — but occasionally the prima donnas insisted on their own ideas. Lucretia Bori was Snegourotchka… and her idea of a Russian snow maiden was a Sonja Henie costume with maribou feathers and white boots. It was awful, but Bori had a beautiful voice and she was a darling woman— but this costume drove him absolutely bananas.[48]

For obvious reasons, *Snegurouchka* attracted many other Russian designers, not least Viktor Vasnetsov (No. 1115 [NIRE]), Konstantin Korovin (Nos. 651-59 [R546-54]), and Nicholas Roerich (Nos. 887-90 [R745-48]).

Provenance: the artist's daughter, Mara Otis Chatfield-Taylor, New York, 1971.
Reproduced in color I20, No. 4; J7, Lot 65; and Lingenauber and Sugrobova-Roth, *Boris Anisfeld*, p. 237. The Wadsworth Atheneum possesses a similar set of costume designs for "Berendeevki Maidens." See G86, p. 58.

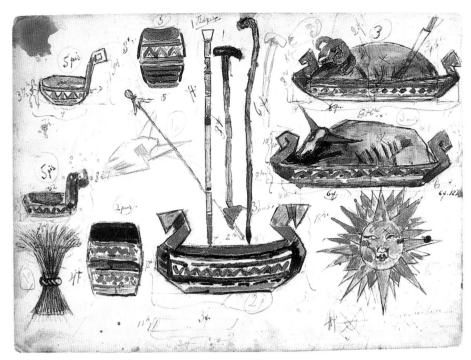

36

38

Le Roi de Lahore: *opera in four acts and eight tableaux by Jules Massenet. Directed by Wilhelm von Wymetal at the Metropolitan Opera House, New York, on 29 February, 1924, with choreography by Rosina Galli and designs by Boris Anisfeld.*

Alim, the King of Lahore, wishes to marry Sita, the niece of the High Priest Timur, but Scindia, Alim's perfidious minister and rival, spreads the false rumor that Sita has a lover. For this she is condemned to death. There then ensues a battle with Sultan Mahmud during which Scindia murders Alim, but the God Indra sends him back to earth disguised as a beggar. Sita — now betrothed to Scindia, the new King of Lahore — recognizes Alim and, refusing to part with him, she kills herself. Thus the union of Sita and Alim is brought about, albeit in death.

37 [R36].
Costume Design for Scindia in Act II, 1924.
Gouache, gold paint, and pencil.
10 x 7⅜ in., 25.5 x 18.7 cm.
Inscribed top right in pencil: "Scindia Act II"; lower right: "Silver"
Provenance: the artist's daughter, Mara Otis Chatfield-Taylor, Washington, DC, October, 1965.
Reproduced in I14, No. 7; and Lingenauber and Sugrobova-Roth, *Boris Anisfeld,* p. 240; similar designs are reproduced in J7, Lot 69; J11, Lot 40. The piece was used as a color frontispiece for *Paintings by Boris Anisfeld.*

Note: Massenet's reenactment of the Hindu epic *Mahabharata* was yet another reflection of the vogue for Orientalism on

37

the European and American stage in the 1910s and 1920s — manifest in *Schéhérazade, Le Dieu Bleu, Aziade, Turandot,* etc. *Le Roi de Lahore* was much to Anisfeld's liking and he illustrated some of his most exotic fantasies in this production — enhanced by Giacomo Lauri-Volpi in the title role.

Aziade: *one-act ballet by Mikhail Mordkin with music by Joseph Giutel. American premiere produced by Mikhail Mordkin for the Mikhail Mordkin Russian Ballet Company, Philadelphia, on 28 October, 1926, with choreography by Mikhail Mordkin and designs by Boris Anisfeld.*

Aziade, an oriental beauty, is a free daughter of the desert. Sheik Hussein forces her to become his mistress, but she takes her revenge by poisoning him.

38 [R37].
Costume Design for Aziade, 1926.
Gouache.
Signed and dated lower right: "Boris Anisfeld 1926."
14 x 10 in., 35.5 x 25.5 cm.
Other inscriptions: upper right in red ink: "Aziada Ballet" followed by other remarks, including the name "Shabelska", a reference to the Polish dancer Maria Shabelska (1898-1980).
Provenance: the artist's daughter, Mara Otis Chatfield-Taylor, Washington, DC, October, 1965.
Reproduced in I14, No. 13; and Lingenauber and Sugrobova-Roth, *Boris Anisfeld,* p. 246.

Note: One of two ballets that Mordkin brought to the USA on his 1926 American tour (the other was *Carnival*), *Aziade* was but a pale reflection of Fokine's *Schéhérazade* (also from *A Thousand and One Nights*). Mordkin had first produced his version of *Aziade* in Moscow, in 1918, with dancers from the Bolshoi Theater and with an ambitious visual scheme that included stairs, colored lights, and projectors. However, even with Anisfeld's spicy costumes, the Philadelphia production had only limited appeal.

Turandot: opera in three acts by Giacomo Puccini (completed by Franco Alfano) based on a drama by Carlo Gozzi. Projected, but not produced, by the Metropolitan Opera, New York, in 1926, with designs by Boris Anisfeld.

A cruel Chinese Princess, Turandot, announces she will marry only that suitor who can solve three riddles. Inability to do so brings death. Calaf solves the riddles and then announces that he will choose death if Turandot can guess his name (Calaf=Love). Her cruelty dissipates in the presence of his love and she agrees to marry him.

39

39 [R38].
Costume Design for Adelma, a Tatar Princess, 1926.
Watercolor, ink, and pencil.
13⅛ x 10 in., 33.5 x 25.5 cm.
Inscriptions: upper right: "Adelma" with illegible annotations in pencil.
Provenance: the artist's daughter, Mara Otis Chatfield-Taylor, Washington, DC, October, 1965.
Reproduced in I14, No. 8; and Lingenauber and Sugrobova-Roth, *Boris Anisfeld,* p. 258; similar designs are reproduced in J7, Lots 77, 79; see also *Boris Anisfeld. Twenty Years of Designs for the Theater,* p. 31.

Note: Anisfeld designed sets and costumes for a production of *Turandot* scheduled for the Metropolitan Opera, New York in 1926, and the opera was, in fact, staged there on 16 November, 1926 (first American performance), but with designs by Joseph Urban. Some of Anisfeld's costumes for *Turandot,* especially for Adelma, demonstrate his interest in a more stylized, linear style, sharing strong affinities with Constructivism.

30. Letter from Leila Mechin to Christian Brinton dated 25 September, 1918. Published in the *New York Times,* New York, 1918, 19 October.
31. William B. Murray: "Boris Anisfeld Brings His Art to America" in *Vogue,* New York, 1918, 1 December, p. 56.
32. Vrubel's portrait of his wife, Nadezhda Zabela-Vrubel, is in the RM.
33. Review in *Le Gaulois,* Paris, 1911, 7 June. Quoted in D26, p. 109.
34. F19, p. 470.
35. G2, see caption to Nos. 873-77 there.
36. D5, p. 102.
37. Ibid.
38. D19, Vol. 1, p. 454.
39. Reproduced in D5, between pp. 102 and 103.
40. F17, p. 127.
41. V. Svetlov: "Balet" in *Peterburgskaia gazeta,* SP, 1909, No. 56, 27 February, p. 4.
42. Notice in *Den,* SP, 1913, No. 66, 10 March, p. 6.
43. Vidi (=Boris Shidlovsky): "Teatralnyi kurier" in *Peterburgskii listok,* SP, 1910, No. 13, 14, January, p. 5. For Fokine's own remarks on this production see the newspaper *Den,* SP, 1913, 10 March.
44. For information on the Moscow Art Theater production see C66, pp. 965-75, 1093-105. Also see Wladimir Egoroff, Maurice Maeterlinck, *L'Oiseau Bleu. Féerie en 6 actes et 12 tableaux,* Paris: Charpentier and Fasquelle, 1911. It is of interest to compare Vladimir Egorov's designs for the Moscow production of the play with Anisfeld's resolution of the opera.
45. (unsigned): "'The Blue Bird' in Music and Picture" in *Art and Decoration,* New York, 1920, January, p. 187.
46. Information taken from S. Krebbs: *Soviet Composers and the Development of Soviet Music,* London: Allen and Unwin, 1970, pp. 145-46.
47. *Paintings by Boris Anisfeld,* unpaginated.
48. Ibid.

ANNENKOV, Yurii Pavlovich (pseudonym: Boris Temiriazev)

Born 11 (23) July, 1889, Petropavlovsk-on-Kamchatka, Russia; died 18 July, 1974, Paris, France.

1892 the Annenkov family relocated to St. Petersburg; 1908 Yurii Annenkov entered St. Petersburg University and also began to take art lessons at Savelii Zeidenberg's private studio; 1909-10 attended the studio of Yan Tsionglinsky (Jan Ciągliński); 1911-12 worked in Paris, studying under Maurice Denis and Félix Valloton; 1913 back in St. Petersburg began to work for the Crooked Mirror satirical theater where he designed the sets and costumes for Nikolai Evreinov's *Homo Sapiens* and other plays; 1913-14 close to the Union of Youth group of artists and writers, including Nikolai Kulbin and Jean Pougny; worked as an illustrator for various magazines including *Satirikon* and *Teatr i iskusstvo* [Theater and Art]; during these years Annenkov often visited the *dacha* region of Kuokkala, where bohemians such as Evreinov, Mikhail Matiushin, and the Pougnys resided in the summer; this

proximity led to a number of joint ventures, e.g., Annenkov's illustrations (and Kulbin's) to Evreinov's three-volume *Teatr dlia sebia* [Theater for Itself] (Petrograd, 1915-16), and to his cover for the separate edition of Evreinov's *Predstavlenie liubvi* [Presentation of Love] (Petrograd, 1916); 1917 onward designed a number of experimental productons, including George Kaiser's *Gas* (1922) and Alexei Tolstoi's *Mutiny of the Machines* (1924); 1918 contributed decorations to the May Day celebrations on the Field of Mars, Petrograd; 1920 with Mstislav Dobujinsky and Vladimir Shchuko decorated the mass drama *Hymn to Liberated Labor* in front of the old St. Petersburg Stock-Exchange; 1921 designed the mass action *The Storming of the Winter Palace;* 1922 member of the World of Art association; contributed to the "Erste Russische Kunstausstellung," Berlin; 1924 emigrated to Paris; during emigration Annenkov was active as a studio painter, stage and movie designer, and book illustrator, e.g., for Pierre Bost's *Le Cirque et le Music-Hall,* Paris: Au sans pareil, 1931.

Yurii Annenkov: Portrait of Vsevolod Meierkhold, 1922. Lithograph.

Bibliography
M. Babenchikov: "Annenkov — grafik i risovalshchik" in *Pechat i revoliutsiia,* M, 1925, June, Book 4, pp. 101-29.
P. Courthion: *Georges Annenkov,* Paris: Chroniques du Jour, 1930.
M2, Vol. 2, pp. 141-42.
G. Andreev: "Na razgromlennom Parnase" in *Novoe Russkoe Slovo,* New York, 1974, 15 September, p. 3.
A. de Saint-Rat: "The Revolutionary Era through the Eyes of Russian Graphic Artists" in *Sbornik. Study Group on the Russian Revolution,* Leeds, 1979, No. 2, pp. 34-43.
B. Berman: "Zametki o Yurii Annenkove" in *Iskusstvo,* M, 1985, No. 2, pp. 34-39.
A. Struzhinskaia: "Khudozhnik teatra Yurii Annenkov" in *Voprosy teatra,* M, 1993, No. 13, pp. 223-47.

H34, pp. 89-93.

A. Tolstoi: "Stilizatsiia avangarda (Yurii Annenkov: vstrecha simvolista s avangardistom) in B288, pp. 322-34.

A. Tolstoi: "Parizhskii kontekst kollazhei Yuriia Annenkova" in B296, pp. 160-81.

A. Tolstoi: "Boris Grigoriev i Yurii Annenkov. K voprosu o russkom ekspressionizme" in *Grigorievskie chteniia,* M: 2009, No. 4, pp. 196-216.

A. Tolstoi:"Annenkov-Blok. Dialog vokrug illiustratsii" in V. Vanslov et al.: *Russkoe iskusstvo*, M: Nauka, 2009, Vol. 3, pp. 169-207. K283, pp. 90-95.

I. Obukhova-Zelinskaia: "Yurii Annenkov v Italii" in *Archivio Russo-Italiano*, Salerno, 2011, No. 8, pp. 279-95.

Annenkov's memoirs (F25, F73) and articles (e.g., N2) also provide a valuable insight into his artistic worldview and cultural milieu.

Before the Revolution Annenkov was close to theatrical personalities in St. Petersburg, especially Evreinov, becoming a regular designer for Evreinov's Crooked Mirror cabaret and Vera Komissarzhevskaia's theater — where he designed Charles Dickens's *A Christmas Carol* (1914) and Fedor Sologub's *Night Dancers* (1915). Annenkov also did many portraits of playwrights, actors, and critics, some of which are reproduced in his memoirs (F25).

While not a central supporter of the Cubo-Futurist and Constructivist movements, Annenkov was much concerned with the intrinsic qualities of art, especially with the expressive quality of line. Shortly after designing Evreinov's *The Chief Thing* for the Theater of Free Comedy, Petrograd, in 1921 (see No. 1008 [R832]), Annenkov asserted that "art will attain the high-point of its flowering only after the artist's imperfect hand has been replaced by the precise machine."[49] Indeed, some of Annenkov's compositions of this time were, in fact, geometric and even non-objective, indicating his strong orientation toward industrial art in the early 1920s. In spite of this brief interest in machine art, Annenkov achieved his greatest results in portraits and book illustrations, especially in his masterly drawings for Alexander Blok's poem *The Twelve* (1918). Annenkov had many imitators, not least Alexander Arnshtam, and his influence as a decorator and graphic artist can be traced in the work of several important stage designers of the 1920s such as Nikolai Akimov (see Nos. 13,14 [R12,13]) and Valentina Khodasevich (see Nos. 601-04 [R862-65]).

40

40 [R39].
Self-Portrait, 1920.
Pencil.
Signed and dated lower left in Russian: "Yu. Annenkov 1920."
15½ x 10¼ in., 39.4 x 26 cm.
Provenance: the artist, Paris, March, 1967.
Reproduced in F107, p. 124; I14, p. 61; I51, No. 14; M22 (a).

Unidentified production, Petrograd, ca. 1915.

41 [R40].
Costume Design for a German Soldier.
Watercolor, pencil and black ink.
Initialed lower left in Russian: "Yu. A."
8¾ x 7 in., 22.2 x 17.8 cm.
Other inscriptions: upper right in Russian: instructions to the dressmaker: "German

41

soldier; second German soldier dressed in the same way, but all yellow to be substituted with red. White gloves."
Provenance: Igor Dychenko, Kiev, 1975.
Reproduced in I40, No. 5; I51, No. 15.

Note: It is reasonable to suppose that this design was for one of the numerous revues staged by Evreinov at the Crooked Mirror during World War I. Annenkov was especially active as a designer there between 1913 and 1915 and, presumably, this costume was for one of the several anti-German sketches produced at the Crooked Mirror during the First World War. However, another possibility might be the play *Knight of Malta* designed by Annenkov for the Troitsky Theater, Petrograd in 1915 (the GMTMA has a costume for a fat man for this production not dissimilar to item No. 41 [R40]). The simple forms, bright colors, and allusions to the Turks (the half-moon on the soldier's buckle and the use of the Turkish word *asker* [soldier]) bring to mind the patriotic *lubki* (broadsides) that Aristarkh Lentulov, Vladimir Maiakovsky, Kazimir Malevich, and other artists were producing in Moscow and Petrograd during the first years of the War.

The GMTMA also contains a number of Annenkov costume and set designs for a "model operetta" called *Black and White* composed by Semeon Timoshenko and Vladimir Shmidtgof for Nikolai Petrov's production at the Free Theater, Petrograd, in 1920. This propaganda play, with an introduction by Anatolii Lunacharsky, contained satirical references to American Capitalists, German militarists, English colonials, etc., and the GMTMA designs for this are also close to No. 41 [R40]. However, the inscriptions on the design in question are written in the old orthography and, therefore, in principle, would predate the Revolution, although, certainly, its use did not disappear immediately. On the other hand, Annenkov seems to have adjusted to the new orthography at once, judging by his other handwritten inscriptions of ca. 1920.

The Crooked Mirror, one of several intimate theaters active in St. Petersburg and Moscow just before and after the Revolution, was founded in 1908 by the critic Alexander Kugel and his wife Zinaida Kholmskaia. In 1910 Evreinov became director of the Crooked Mirror and, until its closure in Petrograd in 1917 (see No. 814 [R696]), he commissioned and/or produced approximately 100 plays. Evreinov, Kugel, and Annenkov attempted to provide a theatrical experience very different from that offered by the Imperial theater system. As Evreinov wrote, they wished "to create a very special kind of theater, mobile, simple, 'sharp', one that can provide space for individuality and that is quite free of routine."[50]

42

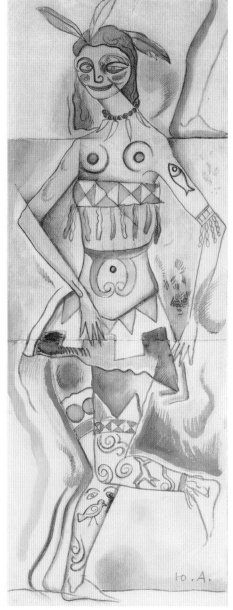

43

The First Distiller: *comedy in six acts by Lev Tolstoi. Produced by Yurii Annenkov and Vsevolod Meierkhold on 13 September, 1919, in the Coats of Arms Hall of the Hermitage, Petrograd, with designs by Yurii Annenkov.*

An imp, one of the Devil's agents, plays tricks on a peasant hoping that he will call on the Devil's name. The imp is summoned by his chief for failing to deliver any peasants to hell by swaying them from their belief in God. Disguised as a laborer, the imp proceeds to initiate the peasant into the joys of drink made from corn, and soon the entire village has taken to alcohol. The peasants fight and slander one another, thus moving away from the straight and narrow path. The imp delivers his converts to hell and his chief is very pleased.

42 [R41].
Stage Design for the Scene in Hell, 1919.
Gouache and pencil.
Initialed and dated lower left in Russian: "Yu. A. 1919."
10¼ x 12½ in., 26 x 31.7 cm.
Other inscriptions: on reverse in Russian: "*The First Distiller* by L. Tolstoi, Hermitage Theater, Petersburg, 1919."
Provenance: the artist, Paris, March, 1967.
Reproduced in color in B115, plate 104; and in black and white in G49, p. 101; I32, No. 5; I51, No. 16; I77, p. 139.

43 [8; NIRE].
Costume Design for the Baba-Yaga (Witch), 1919.
Watercolor and pencil on paper on board.
Initialed lower right in Russian: "Yu. A."
18½ x 6½ in., 47 x 16.5 cm.
Provenance: Gleb Ivakin, Kiev, November, 1999. In a letter to Nikita D. Lobanov-Rostovsky dated 23 November, 1999, Ivakin writes: "This sketch by Yu. P. Annenkov was acquired by my father from the artist's wife, the actress Elena Borisovna, in 1968. In fact, the sketch was made for her — she danced the 'Baba Yaga'."
Reproduced in color in F107, p. 126.

Note: Annenkov did, indeed, make the design for his wife, Elena Borisovna Galpern (1895-1980), who danced the part. Annenkov used circus acrobats for the hell scene in Act II so as to create a flying ballet. Rumor has it that this "mixture of farce and *moralité*"[51] inspired the foundation of the Eccentric Group of actors and artists (FEKs) in 1921 with Grigorii Kozintsev, Georgii Kryzhitsky, and Leonid Trauberg; and, according to Trauberg, Annenkov's production was the "first truly Futurist play."[52] Annenkov's brilliant conception prompted one critic to describe the spectacle as a "modernized *lubok* with its elements of the music-hall and the circus."[53] Alexandra Exter used a similar resolution in her designs for revues in the mid-1920s, although, in all probability, she was unaware of the Annenkov designs (cf. Nos. 476, 487, 493 [R984, 993, 999]). Forty-five years later, the American musical *Jesus Christ, Superstar* incorporated the same methods into a totality that critics identified as unprecedented and avant-garde.

The Storming of the Winter Palace: *mass spectacle by Nikolai Evreinov, Alexander Kugel, Konstantin Derzhavin, Dimitrii Temkin, and Nikolai Petrov. Produced in the Winter Palace Square, Petersburg, on 6 November, 1920, with designs by Yurii Annenkov and music by Guigo Varlikh.*

A dramatization of the storming of the Winter Palace during the Revolution, involving 6000 actors, 500 musicians — and 100,000 spectators who viewed the action from Uritsky (now Winter Palace) Square.

44 [9; R42].
Panoramic Festive Decoration for Uritsky Square, 1920.
Watercolor and pencil.
Signed and dated lower left in Russian: "Yu. Annenkov, 1920."
8 x 23½ in., 20.3 x 59.7 cm.
Provenance: the artist, Paris, March, 1967.
Reproduced in color in B115, plate 103; and in B. Gascoigne, *World Theatre,* Boston: Little, Brown, 1968, p. 290; B6, pp. 312-13;

Ю·Аннєнковъ, 1920.

44

132, No. 6; I51, No. 17; I77, p. 143; a similar design in the BTM is reproduced in color in B26, plate 134; photographs of the actual spectacle have been reproduced several times, e.g., in C7, Nos. 390-93, and C55, pp. 50-51. For a plan of the action on Uritsky Square see *Nicolas Evreinoff 1873-1953,* Catalog of exhibition at the Bibliothèque Nationale, Paris, 1981, p. 8.

Note: The Storming of the Winter Palace was one of several mass actions planned for the major cities just after the Revolution, although few were realized.[54] While the genre of the mass action was international and of long standing (cf. the elaborate, organized mass festivals at the time of the French Revolution), its apologists in Soviet Russia felt that it could and should be adjusted directly to their own ideological needs. Alexei Gan, an enthusiastic supporter of the agit-movement, explained:

> The mass action is not an invention or a fantasy, but is an absolute and organic necessity deriving from the very essence of Communism... The mass action under Communism is not the action of a civic society, but of a human one — wherein material production will fuse with intellectual production. This intellectual/material culture is mobilizing all its strength and means so as to subordinate unto itself not only nature, but also the whole, universal cosmos.[55]

The *Storming of the Winter Palace* was an ambitious, but ill-conceived enterprise, since, in relying on the "masses" as an integral part, it required enormous manpower that could not be controlled in any adequate manner. Annenkov recorded the details of the White, or Right, Tribune in the production:

> 125 ballet dancers
> 100 circus people
> 1750 supernumeraries and students
> 200 women, preferably students
> 260 secondary actors and
> 150 assistants.[56]

As one of the producers wrote:

The spectacle begins... We have flags, telephones, electric bells in our hands. Actors come out on to the steps of the Stock Exchange... It was obvious that they were not moved or excited by the idea of the scenario or by the project itself.[57]

45

45 [R579, where attributed to Nikolai Kulbin].
***Book Cover Design Incorporating a Portrait of Nikolai Evreinov,* Petrograd, ca. 1921.**
Watercolor, black ink, and pencil.
12⅝ x 10⅞ in., 32.2 x 27.5 cm.
Provenance: auction, London: Sotheby's, September, 1978.
Reproduced in color in B115, plate 147; F107, p. 221; and in black and white in G55, p. 284; I77, p. 164; M140; and R15.

Note: One of the most remarkable fields of endeavor in Annenkov's artistic career was his portraiture. From the very beginning, Annenkov liked to depict his social and cultural contemporaries either directly from life or from photographs. Anna Akhmatova, Natan Altman, Abram Efros, Nikolai Evreinov, Georgii Ivanov, Lenin, Viktor Shklovsky, Fedor

Sologub, as well as self-portraits, were among Annenkov's subjects, and he included many of these likenesses in his book *Portrety* [Portraits], which carried appreciations by Evgenii Zamiatin, Mikhail Kuzmin, and Mikhail Babenchikov.[58] Annenkov arrived at his peculiarly "prismatic" style of drawing faces through various routes — his training in French Cubism, his interest in photography, and his perception of objects and specific details as "externalizations" of character — an approach that earned him the title of "Neo-Realist" (along with Boris Grigoriev, Alexandre Jacovleff, Vasilii Shukhaev, et al.).[59] Kuzmin wrote of Annenkov:

> Apart from transmitting the outer movements... Annenkov is most inclined to convey the mobile elements, the wavering atmosphere, the vital current issuing forth from his immobile model (animate or inanimate). In this lies the main secret of his portraits. Without being naturalistic, they are extremely realistic.[60]

This design is assumed to be a project for a cover or frontispiece of one of Nikolai Evreinov's books (the name Evreinov, written in the new orthography, is part of the design), even though none of the Evreinov editions carries this particular composition.[61] The playwright Nikolai Nikolaevich Evreinov (1879-1953) was a favorite model for artists of the 1910s-20s, especially for Yurii Annenkov and Kulbin, and Evreinov even wrote a book about his experiences as a sitter.[62] Artists were attracted to Evreinov because of his dynamic and often eccentric personality:

> How young Evreinov was then, how passionate and inexhaustibly witty! A pupil of Rimsky-Korsakov, how marvelously he improvised at the piano! How incredibly he used to tap his forehead, the crown of his head, the back of his neck, his cheekbones — with teaspoons, making folk melodies and opera arias![63]

Evreinov also considered himself to be a Futurist painter.[64]

46

46 [R43].
Portrait of Natan Altman, 1921.
Woodcut.
Initialed and dated in Russian "Yu. A. 1921."
5 x 4¼ in., 12.7 x 11 cm.
Provenance: Yurii Annenkov, Paris, March, 1967.
Reproduced in M81, p. 90; H32, Vol. 4, p. 417. This portrait is based on the original drawing in India ink (formerly in the collection of Irina Zhivotovskaia-Dega) in Yu. Annenkov, *Portrety,* P: Petropolis, 1922, p. 55; B212, p. 13; F25, Vol. 2, p. 160; B215, p. 13. Yet another version, in pencil and crayon, is reproduced in L88, Lot 242.

Annenkov as contributor: *Posters for the Free Comedy Theater, Petrograd, 1922-23.*

47

47 [R44].
Designer unknown: *Poster Advertising Four One-Act Plays for the Period 5-10 December, 1922.*
Lithograph.
31⅞ x 25⅜ in., 81 x 64.5 cm.

Provenance: Solomon Shuster, Leningrad, March, 1984.
Reproduced in color in M151, p. 62.
The poster provides information on the various numbers to be presented on 5–10 December, 1922, i.e. *The Descent of Hans into Hell, Passion, Revue of the Fairground Booth,* and *Nue.*

48

48 [R45].
Designer unknown: *Poster Advertising Four One-Act Plays, for the Period 9-14 October, 1923.*
Lithograph.
31⅞ x 25¼ in., 81 x 64 cm.
Provenance: Solomon Shuster, Leningrad, March, 1984.
Reproduced in M151, p. 62.
The poster provides information on the various numbers to be presented during 9-14 October, 1923, i.e. *A Strong Feeling, Five Dollars, Destinée*, and *The Little House in Batavia;* reference is also made to a fashion show from the Atelier of Fashions (the Moscow fashion house with which Annenkov, Alexandra Exter, Kuzmin, Vera Mukhina, et al. were associated).

Note: Assisted by the theater director Nikolai Petrov, the poet Lev Nikulin, and Mariia Andreeva (Maxim Gorky's wife), Annenkov founded the Free Comedy Theater in Petrograd in November, 1920, on the premises of the pre-Revolutionary theater known as the Pavillon de Paris. The Free Comedy, located in a cellar on Sadovaia Street, was decorated by Annenkov, and its aim was to put on short, topical plays that had not been produced elsewhere. Among the successes of the Free Comedy was the production of Evreinov's *The Chief Thing* on 20 February, 1921, with designs by Annenkov (see No. 1008 [R832]). However, the Free Comedy, where, incidentally, Annenkov's

brother Boris was an actor, also attracted broader audiences, especially the new Soviet bourgeoisie, who had emerged as a result of the New Economic Policy (NEP), through its production of titillating numbers such as *Passion* and *Nue* (advertised on No. 47 [R44]) and *A Strong Feeling* and *Destinée* (advertised on No. 48 [R45]).

Both posters make reference to the title *Balaganchik* [Fairground Booth], which was the name of the little theater or nightspot that operated in the same building as the Free Comedy (at first in the basement and then on the second floor).[65] According to one of the actresses who played there, Fairground Booth was actually a "straight" theater in the sense that it did not rely on spontaneous numbers as the cabarets did, and was small, intimate, "like a large close-knit family."[66] Compered by Petrov (known more familiarly as Kolia Peter), who had also acted as the host for the Stray Dog cabaret in St. Petersburg, the Fairground Booth catered to a varied audience, although, as these two posters demonstrate, it employed distinguished actors and actresses, e.g., Vera Leonidovna Yureneva (1876-1962) and Rina Vasilievna Zelenaia (1902-91), both mentioned in No. 47, who were popular stars in the early 1920s. The Fairground Booth closed in 1926 (?)[67] and the Free Comedy in the early 1930s.

49

49 [R46].
Portrait of Mikhail Larionov, 1950.
Black ink.
Initialed and dated lower right in Russian: "Yu. A. 1950."
10¼ x 7¾ in., 26 x 19.7 cm.
Provenance: the artist, Paris, August, 1966. Now in a private collection.
Reproduced in F22, Vol. 2, p. 212; F107, p. 145; I14, p. 62; I51, No. 137; M151, p. 35.

Note: Although Annenkov and Larionov had been acquainted in Russia before the Revolution and contributed to exhibitions together, they did not become close friends until the 1920s in emigration. Annenkov had fond memories of their meeting in Paris:

> Larionov ('Larionych', Misha) was a true and cordial friend. Tall, with a rather peasant-like appearance (even in a tuxedo) and always full of turbulent ideas, he was an inexhaustible collocutor, and a philosopher with a hint of wiliness in his half-closed eyes — but which were without malice or ill-will.[68]

Larionov gave his portrait of Sergei Diaghilev (No. 733 [R621]) to Annenkov in 1949.

49. Yu. Annenkov: "Estestvennoe otpravlenie" in Arena. *Teatralnyi almanakh*, P, 1924, p. 114.
50. C21, p. 400. For information on the Crooked Mirror, see C. Moody: "The Crooked Mirror" in *Melbourne Slavonic Studies*, Melbourne, 1972, No. 7, pp. 25-37; E52, pp. 205-92; and C123. For repertoire listing and extended commentary see C84, passim.
51. V. Shklovsky: "Dopolnennyi Tolstoi" in *Zhizn iskusstva*, P, 1919, No. 259-60, 4-5 October, p. 2.
52. Conversation between Leonid Trauberg and John E. Bowlt, M, 20 March, 1986. Also see E47.
53. N. N-v: "Pervyi vinokur" in *Zhizn iskusstva*, 1919, No. 250, 24 September, p. 1. Shklovsky, however, felt that Annenkov had actually produced a travesty of the folk theater, observing that the "folk theater is not only a theater of movement as such, but also a theater of verbal dynamics" (V. Shklovsky: "Narodnaia komediia i 'Pervyi vinokur'" in *Zhizn iskusstva*, 1920, Nos. 425-6-7, p. 1). According to Shklovsky, Annenkov had ignored the word — "Yurii Annenkov's sin before the word is unforgivable" (ibid.).
54. Apart from *Storming of the Winter Palace,* the following mass actions should be mentioned: *Action for the III International* (1 May, 1919), *Death of the Commune* (18 March, 1920), *Mysterium of Liberated Labor* (1 May, 1920), the *Blockade of Russia* (20 June, 1920), *Towards the World Commune* (19 July, 1920) — all in Petrograd; *Pantomime of the Great Revolution* (7 November, 1918) — in Moscow. For useful commentary on the international mass action see J. Gregor: *Theaterarchitektur, Massentheater und Kleintheater*. Rome: Bardi, 1934.
55. A. Gan: "Borba za massovoe deistvo" in C3, p. 73.
56. F25, Vol. 2, p. 126.
57. Quoted in C5, pp. 428-29; where the original source is not indicated. For further information on the mass action, including the *Storming of the Winter Palace,* see Yu. Annenkov: "Revoliutsiia i teatr" in *Parizhskii vestnik*, Paris: Embassy of the USSR, 1925, Nos. 66 and 67 for 22 and 23 July, pp. 2-3 both; C31, Vol. 1, pp. 272-76; C. Amiard- Chevrel: "Les Actions de masse" in *Les Voies de la Création Théâtrale*, Paris, 1979, No. 7, 1979, pp. 243-76; N. Evreinov: "Vziatie Zimnego dvortsa" in *Krasnyi militsioner*, M, 1920, No. 14, 15 November, pp. 4-5; B72, Vol. 2, pp. 194-200; C84, pp. 191-208.
58. Yu. Annenkov: *Portrety*, P: Petropolis, 1922. Reprinted by Strathcona Publishing Co., Royal Oak, N.D. (1978?).
59. E. Zamiatin: "O sintetizme," ibid., p. 24.
60. M. Kuzmin: "Kolebaniia zhiznennykh tokov," ibid., p. 48.
61. Annenkov included a sketch of Evreinov in the second volume of the latter's *Teatr dlia sebia* [The Theater for Itself] (P: Sovremennoe iskusstvo, 1915-17). For another Annenkov portrait of Evreinov see F25, Vol. 2, p. 110.
62. N. Evreinov: *Original o portretistakh*, M: Gosizdat, 1922.
63. F25, Vol. 2, p. 117.
64. See, for example, the reproduction of Evreinov's painting *Dancing Spanish Lady* in *Stolitsa i usadba*, P, 1914, No. 11, between pp. 14 and 15. Evreinov refers to this here as the "first Futurist picture in the world."
65. For information on the Fairground Booth see E15, Vol. 1, p. 314; E27, p. 74; N. Kramova: "Balaganchik" in *Novoe Russkoe Slovo*, New York, 1986, 17 October, pp. 8, 14.
66. Kramova, p. 8.
67. Kramova says 1926 (p. 14); Elizaveta Uvarova says 1924 (E27, p. 74).
68. F25, Vol. 2, pp. 222-24.

ARNSHTAM (ARNSTAM), Alexander Martynovich

Born 28 March (9 April), 1880, Moscow, Russia; died 6 October, 1969, Paris, France.

1901 studied philosophy at the Kaiser-Wilhelm Universität, Berlin; ca. 1906 graduated from Law School at Moscow University; attended Konstantin Yuon's and Ivan Dudin's Art School in Moscow; then studied at the Académie de la Grande Chaumière and La Palette in Paris; 1908 onward in St. Petersburg; contributed vignettes and illustrations to many journals of the time such as *Zolotoe runo* [Golden Fleece] and *Solntse Rossii* [Sun of Russia]; 1913 contributed to the "Graphic Art" exhibition in St. Petersburg; 1914 worked for Konstantin Nezlobin's theater in Petrograd; 1915-17 contributed to the "World of Art" exhibitions; 1917 edited and designed *Khudozhestvennyi zhurnal* [Art Journal]; 1920 moved to Moscow where he continued to work as a designer and illustrator; 1922 emigrated to Berlin; 1920s made portraits of actors and artists; worked for Russian cabarets, including the Chauve-Souris, and designed several ballets for Berlin theaters; designed and illustrated books for émigré publishers such as Academia, Gelikon, and Ladyzhnikov; also designed the sets for movies such as *Heimkehr* (1928), *Die letzte Kompagnie* (1930), and *Rasputin, der Dämon der Frauen* (1932); 1933 via Spain moved to Paris; 1933-42 lived in Paris, where he continued to work as a stage and movie designer; 1938 designed the sets and costumes for Maurice Tourneur's production of the movie *Katia* (Boris Bilinsky designed the female costumes); 1943 left Paris for the Zone Libre; 1945 returned to Paris; 1950s-60s continued to work as a designer.

Bibliography
A. Levinson: "Khudozhnik A. Arnshtam" in *Vershiny*, P, 1915, No. 31-32, p. 17 (whole issue designed by Arnshtam).
A14, vol. 1, pp. 195-96.
H25, pp. 22-23.
M2, Vol. 2, p. 143.
M. Magidovich: "Aleksandr Arnshtam" in *Novyi Mir iskusstva*, SP, 1998, No. 4, pp. 18-20.
K. Arnshtam: "Zhizn s illiustratsiei" in *Evropeiskii vestnik*, London, 1999, No. 32, pp. 8-11.
V. Gusev et al.: *Aleksandr Arnshtam / Alexandre Arnstam*. Catalog of exhibition at the RM, 2000.
K. Arnshtam, ed.: *Aleksandr Arnshtam. Vospominaniia*, SP: Novikov, 2010.

Arnshtam's social trials and tribulations were characteristic of his tragic generation of Russian artists displaced and disoriented by the October Revolution and the post-Revolutionary diaspora. His emigration from Petrograd to Berlin and to Paris paralleled the similar itineraries of many other Russian artists and writers of the time such as Yurii Annenkov, Boris Bilinsky, Ivan Bilibin, and Georges Pogedaieff, who opted to test their fortunes in the West rather than face the uncertainties of the Bolshevik régime. Like

Annenkov and Bilibin, too, Arnshtam was already a mature and established artist when he left Russia, a professional who was now forced to adjust to the harsh realities of a new language, a new culture, and a new clientèle — a brutal confrontation that later on prompted other émigrés, including Bilibin, Sergei Konenkov, and Vasilii Shukhaev, to return to the Socialist motherland.

Trained in St. Petersbrug, Berlin, Moscow, and Paris, Arnshtam was an accomplished draftsman whose illustrations, vignettes, and tailpieces graced the major art and society magazines of Russian Modernism. He was an enthusiast of the graphic arts and was quick to encourage the artistic talents of others, including children, inspiring the idea of a children's journal dedicated entirely to their art and edited entirely by them.[69] Indebted to the conventions of *Jugendstil* and the World of Art, Arnshtam imbued his drawings with a clarity and calculation reminiscent of the elegant filigrees of other stylists such as Annenkov, Miss (pseudonym of Alexandra Remizova, sister of Re-mi), and Vladimir Levitsky. He emphasized these qualities in his celebrity portraits of the 1920s, evoking — in their abrasive linearity and stiletto sharpness — the febrile nightlife of a decadent Berlin. Yet he also used these qualities to good effect in his movie designs of the late 1920s onwards, as in *Tod über Shanghai, Katia,* and *l'Amour autour de la maison.* Along with Bilinsky and Re-mi, Arnshtam became one of the leading movie designers of the Russian emigration, his *Katia,* according to some observers, causing a "real revolution in French cinematography."[70]

50

50 [NIRE].
Self-Portrait, **1926.**
Pen and ink
Signed with the initials and dated lower right: "AA 926."
23¾ x 18⅛ in., 60 x 46 cm.
Provenance: the artist's son, Cyril Arnstam, Chaville (Paris), 2004.

51

51 [R47].
Portrait of Nikita Baliev, Director of the Chauve-Souris, 1926.
Pen and ink.
Signed and dated lower right in German and Russian: "Alexander Arnshtam, 17 December 1926."
15 x 15 in., 38 x 38 cm.
Other inscriptions: lower left in Russian: "Nikita Baliev"; on the reverse "Arnshtam-Nikita Balieff. Schauspieler B.Z. a M. V. 17.XII.1926."
Provenance: the artist, Paris, March, 1966. Now in a private collection.
Reproduced in I14, p. 60; I51, No. 18; Arnshtam, *Vospominaniia,* between pp. 128 and 129 (Cf. Nos. 859 [R736], 948 [R962]).

Note: Nikita Fedorovich Baliev (the Russianized version of the Armenian name Mkrtich Balian, 1877-1936) was the founder and director of the cabaret The Bat / Chauve-Souris active in Moscow (1908-19) and then in Europe and the US (1920-36). With his hearty laugh and inimitable accent, Baliev scored a remarkable success as an impresario and a variety artist with the European and American publics during the 1920s. Baliev was portrayed by many artists, including Yurii Annenkov, Nicholas Remisoff, Vasilii Shukhaev, Sergei Sudeikin, and the sculptor Viacheslav Andreev. Arnshtam contributed designs to a number of Berlin productions of the Chauve-Souris.

52 [R48].
Design for the cover of Nikolai Evreinov's book Teatr kak takovoi [Theater as Such], 1923.
Pen and ink.
Initialed and dated lower right "A.A. 1920" above the word "Berlin."
8⅞ x 6½ in., 22.5 x 16.5 cm.
Provenance: the artist, Paris, March, 1966. Reproduced in I14, No. 16, where it is described wrongly as a cover for Evreinov's play *The Chief Thing;* Q17.

Note: Teatr kak takovoi [Theater as Such], which saw several editions, was one of Evreinov's most important tracts on the so-called conditional theater, or theater of convention. This cover was for the Berlin

52

Academy (Akademiia) edition of 1923, which also carried illustrations by Arnshtam. The early 1920s was one of the most fruitful periods in Evreinov's life: he published no fewer than ten books between 1921 and 1925, some while he was living in Berlin from the late fall of 1922 through January, 1923. Arnshtam was also busy in Berlin, designing and illustrating books such as Evgenii Zamiatin's *Ogni sviatogo Dominika* [The Lights of Saint Dominic] (1922), Samuil Vermel's *Alkhimiia teatra* [The Alchemy of Theater] (1923), and Teffi's (Nadezhda Buchinskaia's) *Shamram* (1922). This particular cover, which incorporates a portrait of Evreinov (cf. 45 [R579]), has been reproduced several times, e.g., H13, between pp. 32-33. For another of Arnshtam's designs for *Teatr kak takovoi* (published in Berlin in 1923) see *Aleksandr Arnshtam / Alexandre Arnstam,* p. 59.

53

53 [R49].
Portrait of the Actor Ivan Moskvin, 1927.
Pencil.
Signed and dated in Russian: "Moskvin 1927 Alexander Arnshtam"; and in German in the center "I. Moskvine, A. Arnshtam 927"
12½ x 14¾ in., 32 x 37.5 cm.
Provenance: the artist, Paris, March, 1966. Reproduced in I40, No. 6.

Note: Ivan Mikhailovich Moskvin (1874-1946) was one of Russia's greatest actors and was a permanent force at the Moscow Art Theater from its very inception. Moskvin played many roles in plays by Anton Chekhov, Nikolai Gogol, Maurice Maeterlinck, Alexander Ostrovsky, and Ivan Turgenev, to mention only a few. The exact circumstances under which Arnshtam made this portrait are not known, although Moskvin was also in Berlin in 1922-23 as an actor with the Blue Bird cabaret and as part of the Moscow Art Theater on tour.[71] Presumably, he was in Berlin again in 1927 when Arnshtam drew this portrait.

69. For information on this episode see M. Magidovich: "Deti Mira iskusstva" in *Novyi mir iskusstva,* SP, 1998, No. 5, p. 2-5.
70. Magidovich, "Aleksandr Arnshtam", p. 20.
71. See H31, pp. 114, 175.

ARONSON, Boris Solomonovich

Born 15 (28) October, 1900, Nezhin, Chernigov Region, Ukraine; died 16 November, 1980, New York, USA.

1910s studied under Ivan Seleznev at the Kiev Art Institute and took private lessons from Alexander Murashko and then Ilia Mashkov in Moscow; 1917 helped to found a museum of modern art in Kiev; studied in Alexandra Exter's studio; 1920 organized the "First Jewish Art Exhibition" for the Culture-League in Kiev to which Iosif Chaikov, El Lissitzky, Nisson Shifrin, Alexander Tyshler, et al., also contributed; 1921 moved to Moscow where he studied under Ilia Mashkov at Vkhutemas; attended performances of the Habima Theater; 1922 designed plays for the Yiddish Chamber Theater in Moscow; left for Berlin where he studied etching and the graphic arts; designed the cover for Nikolai Nikitin's *Nochnoi pozhar* [Night Fire] (1924); 1923 published a monograph on Marc Chagall; emigrated to the USA, where he soon made his name as a stage designer; 1926 contributed to the "International Theater Exhibition" in New York; 1927 one-man show at the Anderson Galleries, New York; 1928 subject of monograph published by Waldemar George; 1929 illustrated Nikolai Evreinov's *Theater in Life;* 1930s onwards worked on many stage productions such as *The Gentle People* (1939), *The Great American Goof* (1940), *Cabin in the Sky* (1940), *Snow Maiden* (1942), *Pictures at an*

Exhibition (1944), View from the Bridge (1955), JB (1958), Fiddler on the Roof (1964), Company (1970), Pacific Overtures (1976), and The Nutcracker (1977).

Bibliography

W. George: Boris Aronson et l'art du théâtre, Paris: Chroniques du jour, 1928.
H6, p. 46.
T. Wood: Boris Aronson. Catalog of exhibition at the Vincent Astor Gallery at Lincoln Center, New York, 1981.
F. Rich and L. Aronson: The Theatre Art of Boris Aronson, New York: Knopf, 1987.
A. Comins-Richmond: "Nikolai Evreinov: A Letter to Boris Aronson" in B183, pp. 323-34.
F. Rich: Boris Aronson. Stage Design as Visual Metaphor. Catalog of exhibition at the Katonah Gallery, Katonah, New York; and the Harvard Theatre Collections, Cambridge, Mass., 1989-90.
J. Bowlt: "Boris Aronson o Natane Altmane" in H32, Vol. 4, pp. 417-20.

Much influenced by Alexandra Exter and then by Marc Chagall in the early days, Aronson applied the principles of Constructivism (as, for example, in the 1925 Bronx production of Final Balance) before turning to a more lyrical style. One of Aronson's greatest qualities as a designer was his constant aspiration to express the ethos of the spectacle rather than simply decorate the narrative. As Elia Kazan commented:

> Boris insisted that you talk about what the play meant until he was sure you'd said everything you had to say. Contradictions did not bewilder him; he embraced them. His goal, in the end, was the same as your own, to make the play have its meaning.[72]

Perhaps the most valid description of Aronson the designer is to be found in his own response to Chagall's panneaux for the Jewish State Chamber Theater in Moscow of 1920-21:

> [Chagall] has synthesized the Harlequinade of the Jewish theater and the grotesquerie of the Jewish ghetto, he has created a plastic pantomime in which his somersaults of fantasy attain an extraordinary acuity.[73]

Such characteristics enabled Aronson to achieve fame as a primary stage designer in the US, contributing to productions in the Group Theater, the Metropolitan Opera, Radio City Music Hall, and many other New York theaters.

The Snow Maiden (Snegurochka): ballet in one act and four scenes by Serge Denham with music by Alexander Glazunov. Produced for the Ballet Russe de Monte Carlo by Bronislava Nijinska at the Metropolitan Opera House, New York, on 15 October, 1942, with designs by Boris Aronson.

See No. 33 [R32] for plot summary.

54

54 [R50].
Costume Design for the Raven, 1942.
Gouache and colored crayons.
Signed lower right: "Boris Aronson."
18⅛ x 11⅞ in. 46 x 30.1 cm.
Provenance: Dance, Theatre, Opera, Music-Hall and Film. Décor and Costume Designs, Books, Posters and Photographs, Sotheby, Parke Bernet, New York, 1981, 16 December, Lot 75 (reproduced).
Reproduced in color in the commemorative program Ballet Russe de Monte Carlo, American Tour, 1942-1943, New York, 1942, unpaginated center page (and also in the 1943-44 tour program) together with an illustration of the scenery containing the Raven on stage; a similar design is reproduced in Boris Aronson (1981), p. 13. For a reproduction of the set incorporating the Raven, see G21, plate 17.

Note: During the 1940s, Aronson, as stage designer, divided his loyalties between an illustrative and accessible interpretation and a more abstract, formal one. As a visual narrator, therefore, he could provide the engaging sets and costumes for The Snow Maiden and a "documentary Realism" for the production of The Detective Story (1949) at the Hudson Theater in New York. Certainly, during the dark moment of WWII, the bright colors, scenic asymmetry, and humanized birds and trees for The Snow Maiden afforded a light relief and were a far cry from the more radical and startling sets

for The Great American Goof (1940), which the Museum of Modern Art exhibited forthwith as a prime example of avant-garde design. In any case, with Nijinska as choreographer and Alexandra Danilova, Nathalie Krassovska, Igor Youskevitch, and Frederic Franklin as principal dancers, The Snow Maiden was well received by American audiences, proving that for Aronson, as Waldemar George observed in 1928, "le décor n'est pas une fin en soi ou une démonstration, mais un élément de l'action dramatique."[74]

72. E. Kazan: untitled appreciation in Boris Aronson (1981), p. 19.
73. B. Aronson: Shagal, Berlin: Petropolis, 1923, p. 25.
74. W. George, Boris Aronson et l'art du théâtre, p. VIII.

BAKST, Léon (Rozenberg, Lev Samoilovich; Rozenberg, Leib-Haim Izrailevich)

Born 27 April (9 May), 1866, Grodno, Belarus; died 27 December, 1924, Paris, France.

1883-86 audited courses at IAA; from 1890 onward active in book design and illustration, contributing graphic ornaments to diverse publications such as the Symbolist journals Mir iskusstva [World of Art], Zolotoe runo [The Golden Fleece], and the satirical pamphlet Zhupel [Bugbear]; 1890-93 illustrated magazines such as Khudozhnik [Artist] and Peterburgskaia zhizn [St. Petersburg Life]; 1891 visited Europe, the first of many trips abroad; 1898 co-founded the World of Art society; assumed technical responsibility for its journal; 1901 with Alexandre Benois, Evgenii Lancéray, and others worked on the decorations for a production of Sylvia scheduled for the Mariinsky Theater, St. Petersburg; 1902 made his debut as a stage designer for productions of Le Coeur de la Marquise and Hippolytus in St. Petersburg; collaborated with Sergei Shcherbatov and Vladimir fon Mekk (von Meck) on the Contemporary Art business enterprise in St. Petersburg; 1903 designed the production of La Fée des Poupées (Die Puppenfee) choreographed by Nikolai and Sergei Legat; thereafter active in numerous drama, opera, and ballet productions; 1907 traveled in Greece with Valentin Serov; 1909 designed Sergei Diaghilev's production of Cléopâtre in Paris; 1909-10 published a long article on modern art in Apollon [Apollo] in St. Petersburg, one of many essays on culture; 1910 designed Diaghilev's production of Schéhérazade in Paris; thereafter collaborated with Diaghilev, Ida Rubinstein, and other impresarios on productions in Europe and the USA; 1910s active as a fashion designer; 1923 and 1924 visited the US. Bakst's sensuous art attracted many young Russian artists including Boris Bilinsky, Erté, and Simon Lissim.

Bibliography:
Much has been written and published on Bakst and a number of substantial bibliographies have already been compiled. In this respect, special mention should be made of the Select Bibliography that Alexander Schouvaloff included in his monograph in 1991, i.e. *Léon Bakst: The Theatre Art,* London: Sotheby's, 1991, pp. 255-65.
Among other important publications are:
C. Spencer: *Leon Bakst,* London: Academy Editions, 1973; second edition 1995.
C. Spencer: *Bakst.* Catalog of exhibition at The Fine Art Society, London, December, 1973-January 1974.
I. Pruzhan: *Bakst,* L: Iskusstvo, 1975.
C. Mayer: *Bakst.* Catalog of exhibition at The Fine Art Society, London, 1976.
N. Borisovskaia: *Lev Bakst,* M: Iskusstvo, 1979.
I. Pruzhan: *Bakst,* L: Aurora, 1987.
E. Sznajderman: *On Stage: The Art of Léon Bakst.* Catalog of exhibition at the Israel Museum, Jerusalem, 1992.
H. Carmeli and D. Lurie: *Léon Bakst. The Sleeping Beauty.* Catalog of exhibition at the Tel-Aviv Museum of Art, 1992.
S. Golynets: *Lev Bakst,* M: Izobrazitelnoe iskusstvo, 1992.
D. Souhami: *Bakst. The Rothschild Panels of the Sleeping Beauty,* London: Wilson, 1992.
E. Naslund: *Léon Bakst. Sensualismens Triumf.* Catalog of exhibition at the Dansmuseet, Stockholm, 1993.
C. Spencer: *Bakst and the Ballets Russes.* Catalog of exhibition at The Fine Art Society, London, 1995
E. Bespalova: "Bakst v Amerike" in *Nashe nasledie,* M, 1997, No. 39-40, pp. 132-37.
E. Bespalova: "Leon Bakst's Textile and Interior Design in America" in *Studies in the Decorative Arts,* New York, 1997-98, Fall-Winter, Volume V, N 1, pp. 2-28.
J. Bowlt, ed.: *Theater of Reason, Theater of Desire: The Art of Alexandre Benois and Léon Bakst.* Catalog of exhibition at the Thyssen-Bornemisza Foundation, Lugano, 1998; and the Museum für Kunsthandwerk, Frankfurt, 1999.
E. Ingles: *Bakst and the Art of Theatre and Dance,* London: Parkstone, 2000.
E. Bespalova: "Bakst v Chikago" in *Russkoe iskusstvo,* M, 2004, No. 1, pp. 38-45.
E. Bespalova: "Nastennaia zhivopis Baksta dlia doma Rotshildov v muzee 'Uodesdon'" in *Russkoe iskusstvo,* M, 2004, No. 3, pp. 36-47.
E. Bespalova: "Khudozhnik i pevitsa. Tvorcheskii soiuz Lva Baksta i Marii Kuznetsovoi" in *Russkoe iskusstvo,* M, 2006, No. 4, pp. 54-67.
E. Bespalova: "Tretiakovskii period v tvorchestve Baksta" in *Russkoe iskusstvo,* M, 2008, No. 1, pp. 106-17.
E. Bespalova: "Parizhskii teatr Baksta i Kuznetsovoi" in *Russkoe iskusstvo.* M, 2009, No. 4, pp. 104-15.
C. Spencer: *Bakst in Greece,* Athens: Gema, 2009.
E. Baiguzina: *L.S. Bakst v poiskakh antichnosti,* SP: Nestor-Istoriia, 2009.
E. Terkel: "Lev Bakst: 'Odevaites' kak tsvetok!' / Lev Bakst: 'Dress Like a Flower!'" in *Tretiakovskaia galereia / Tretiakov Gallery,* M, 2009, No. 4, pp. 28-43.
D. Boult (J. Bowlt): "Neobkhodimo ukrasit povsednevnuiu odezhdu" in *Teoriia mody,* M, 2010, No. 15, pp. 243-54.
Yu. Demidenko:"Lev Bakst – khudozhnik mody" in *Teoriia mody,* M, 2010, No. 15, pp. 217-42.
E. Terkel: "Bakst kak dizainer" in L. Iovleva, ed.: *Tretiakovskie chteniia 2009,* M: Ekspress 24, 2010, pp. 172-86.
J. Abbot: "Russian Art & Design in the Evergreen Museum and Library" in *Slavic and Eastern European Information Resources,* London, 2010, No. 11, pp. 246-64.
E. Terkel: "'Uspekh redkostno ogromnyi'. Amerika v zhizni Baksta / America in Léon Bakst's Life and Art" in *Tretiakovskaia galereia / Tretiakov Gallery,* M, 2011, No. 2, pp. 59-75.
E. Terkel and J. Boult (Bowlt), eds.: *L.S. Bakst. "Moia dusha otkryta." Literaturnoe i epistoliarnoe nasledie,* M: Iskusstvo XXI vek, 2012.
V. Parisi, trans.: *Léon Bakst: In Grecia con Serov,* Milan: Excelsior, 2012.
E. Terkel: "Lev Bakst i Zinaida Gippius" in L. Iovleva, ed.: *Tretiakovskie chteniia 2010-2011,* M: INIKO, 2012, pp. 204-19.

Of all the members of the World of Art group, Bakst deserves the highest acclaim for his contribution to both studio painting and the decorative arts. In broad terms, Bakst evolved from line to color: "From a graphist I've turned into a pure painter," he wrote to the critic Pavel Ettinger in 1910.[75] "It's easier to sense and to synthesize form through paint — it turns out more authentically, more tangibly," he wrote to the artist Anna Ostroumova-Lebedeva the same year.[76] In his Paris stage productions (between 1909 and 1914 he designed twelve for Diaghilev), Bakst astounded audiences by his munificence of color and tactile forms. His exposure of the dynamic force of the human body was a simple and radical development, and contrasted sharply with the traditional notion of the theatrical costume as a means of disguise and ornament. If his costumes and sets could be criticized at all, it was that they were too visual —"the spectacle dominates the music too much."[77] Yet, although Bakst himself was aware of the incongruity, as he asserted in his article "In the Theater No One Wants to Listen Any More, People Just Want to Look" of 1914,[78] perhaps he never really wished to resolve it. Certainly, Bakst was quite aware of the swiftness with which fashion and style changed, as he implied in his article on Futurism and Classicism of 1922.[79] Occasionally, he would adjust his designs to the dictates of mode and money, an attitude that compromised some of his later creations such as *The Sleeping Princess* of 1921 (Nos. 96-101 [R88-93]), which relies for its effect more on extravagance and exaggeration rather than on subtle harmony.

Among Russian stage designers, Bakst enjoyed the widest recognition. As early as 1904 some of his costume designs were reproduced in postcard form (Nos. 59-71 [R55-67]), his success was meteoric, and his talent burnt itself out quickly. There was something overripe, something fateful about Bakst's art, as if it mirrored his own morbid hypochondria. In 1913, at the height of his fame, Bakst remarked: "And it's strange [for me] to be feeling horribly indifferent and almost despondent."[80] The paradox of Bakst's career lies in the fact that the surfeit of his colors and the lushness of his forms seem to draw their

55

strength from an epoch fast declining, doomed to imminent destruction. One of his obituarists, Alexander Pleshcheev, seemed to understand this in entitling his farewell "Enough."[81]

55 [R51].
Artist unknown: *Portrait of Léon Bakst, ca. 1920.*
Pencil.
17¼ x 11⅜ in., 44 x 30 cm.
Presumably, the portrait was made by one of Bakst's many students.
Provenance: *Ballet and Theatre Material,* London: Sotheby's, 13 March, 1980, Lot 80 (reproduced). Now in a private collection.
Reproduced in F107, p. 126; I51, No. 19.

56 [R52].
Portrait of the Artist Konstantin Somov Seated in a Chair, 1899.
Pencil
Signed in pencil in Russian lower right: "L. Bakst"
12¼ x 9⅝ in., 31 x 24.5 cm.
Other inscription: in Russian lower right: "To my friend K. Somov 1899."
Provenance: Yakov Rubinshtein, Moscow, 1974. Now in a private collection.
Reproduced in F107, p. 151; S. Yamshchikov: "Esli kollektsioner istinnyi" in *Sovetskaia kultura,* M, 1982, 12 February, No. 13, p. 5.

56

57

58

Hippolytus: *tragedy by Euripides, translated and edited by Dmitrii Merezhkovsky. Produced by Yurii Ozarovsky at the Alexandrinsky Theater, St. Petersburg, on 14 October, 1902, with designs by Léon Bakst.*

Hippolytus is the son of Theseus, King of Athens. Phaedra, Theseus's Queen, is in love with Hippolytus — which is the doing of Aphrodite, whom Hippolytus has slighted, preferring a life honoring the chaste and athletic Artemis. When Phaedra's passion is revealed to Hippolytus, he reacts so violently that Phaedra fears his anger and kills herself. Due to an oath not to admit the real course of events, Hippolytus cannot tell the truth to Theseus. Theseus, therefore, banishes him. As Hippolytus is riding away, a bull of unnatural size appears from the sea and frightens his horses who stampede, and Hippolytus is dragged to his death. Artemis then appears to tell the truth to Theseus, but not in time to save Hippolytus, who dies in the arms of his father.

57 [R53].
Costume Design for a Wise and Prominent Man from the Suite of Theseus, 1902.
Gouache and black ink.
Signed lower right in Russian: "L. Bakst."
11½ x 8½ ins.; 29.2 x 21.6 cm.
Other inscriptions: upper center in Russian: "Hippolytus; wise and prominent man from the suite of Theseus, 2 costumes"; lower right "details for first costume"; upper left "upper tunic, second costume."
Provenance: the artist's niece, Mila Barsacq, Paris, November, 1966.
Reproduced in I14, No. 26; I51, No. 20; and in Spencer, *Leon Bakst*, fig. 26; a similar design is reproduced in J7, Lot 2; also see J4, Lot 16; and J8, Lot 9, where similar costumes are reproduced as designs for *Phèdre*. Bakst made analogous designs for the production of Sophocles's *Oedipus at Colona* in 1904, some of which are reproduced in G20, fig. 41a; J21, Lot 64; Pruzhan, *Bakst* (1975), p. 66; also see B20, p. 144.

58 [R54].
Costume Design for One of Phaedra's Slaves, 1902.
Watercolor and pencil.
Signed lower right in Russian: "L. Bakst."
11 x 8¾ in., 28 x 22.2 cm.
Other inscriptions: upper right in pencil in Russian: "Maid and slave of Phaedra. 5 costumes"; lower right: instructions to the dressmaker.
Provenance: Issar Gourvitch, Paris, June, 1966.

Note: Bakst had a difficult task explaining his conception of Ancient Greece to Merezhkovsky and Ozarovsky, for, as he wrote to Vladimir Teliakovsky in April, 1902, he feared that a "mutual misunderstanding between the writer [translator] and the artist will ensue, the former demands from the latter things that contradict the style and conditions of the scene."[82] Indeed, Bakst's designs did not win universal support and after the dress rehearsal, Konstantin Korovin was asked to "improve" the clouds in Bakst's décor. Still, the production did receive positive reviews, for, as the critic Yurii Beliaev wrote, "These were not the usual Greeks on stage in a *style empire* or, worse, Greeks from an operetta; these were Greeks from Etruscan vases, from sepulchral bas reliefs… The costumes were beautiful, new."[83] Andrei Bely, the Symbolist poet and philosopher who knew Bakst from his sittings for several portraits,[84] also emphasized the authenticity of Bakst's reincarnation of Hellas in his essay of 1906:

> [Bakst's] drawings from the life of antiquity are almost a scientific tract. The truthfulness, almost the archaelogicality of his costumes and his poses point to the seriousness of his creative work. But at the same time you can sense another, more profound truthfulness — a truthfulness to nature.[85]

Hippolytus marked the first of Bakst's professional designs for spectacles dealing with antiquity and it expressed his profound interest in the ancient civilizations. As Ida Rubinstein remarked of Bakst: "From the depths of time he summoned the artistic coarseness, the nakedness of that era when Oedipus cried out and Antigone wept."[86] Evidently, Bakst was much taken by the particular position and profile of the "wise and prominent man" since he adjusted the costume to several other productions. It is of interest to compare this resolution of the sets and costumes for the 1902 version of Euripides's tragedy with the designs by Alexander Vesnin, Konstantin Medunetsky, and the Stenberg brothers for Alexander Tairov's productions of Racine's *Phèdre* in 1922 and 1923 (cf. Nos. 789 [R665], 969-71 [R795-97], 1137-42 [R377-82]).

Léon Bakst: Old Man in Blue Cape, *Le Martyre de Saint Sébastian*, Hand-colored lithograph, 1911.

Léon Bakst: Hand-colored lithographs: Old Man in Brown Cape, *Le Martyre de Saint Sébastian*, 1911; Old Priest, *Le Dieu Bleu*, 1912; Black Guard, *Sleeping Beauty*, 1921; A Page, *Aladin*, 1919

„ФЕЯ КУКОЛЪ"

Балетъ въ одномъ дѣйствіи и 2-хъ картинахъ.

музыка I. Байера.

Представленъ въ первый разъ на сценѣ Эрмитажнаго театра въ С.-Петербургѣ 7-го февраля 1903 г.

Постановка Льва Бакста.

Костюмы:

1. Фея куколъ.
2. Англичанка.
3. Ея дочь.
4. Кукла Испанка.
5. Кукла Китаянка.
6. Кукла Японка.
7. Кукла Француженка.
8. Одна изъ фарфоровыхъ куколъ.
9. Горничная.
10. Костюмъ кордебалета.
11. Почтальонъ.
12. Денщикъ.

59

„LA FÉE DES POUPÉES"

Ballet en un acte et deux tableaux

Musique de J. Bayer.

Mis en scène d'après les dessins de M-r Léon Bakst
au théâtre Impérial de l'Ermitage

Février 1903.

Costumes:

1. La fée des poupées.
2. Une dame anglaise.
3. Sa fillette.
4. Une poupée espagnole.
5. Une poupée chinoise.
6. Une poupée japonaise.
7. Une poupée française.
8. Une poupée en porcelaine.
9. Une femme de chambre.
10. Costume du corps de ballet.
11. Un facteur.
12. Une ordonnance.

Т-во ГОЛИКЕ И ВИЛЬБОРГЪ.

La Fée des Poupées (Die Puppenfee): ballet divertissement in one act by Josef Bayer. Produced by Nikolai and Sergei Legat at the Hermitage Theater, St. Petersburg, on 7 February, 1903, and then at the Mariinsky Theater, St. Petersburg, on 16 February, 1903, with choreography by Nikolai and Sergei Legat, musical additions by Petr Tchaikovsky, Riccardo Drigo, Anatolii Liadov, Anton Rubinstein, and Louis Moreau Gottschalk, and designs by Léon Bakst.

A toy shop on Nevsky Prospect in St. Petersburg boasts an enormous selection of toys and dolls that impersonate the owner, the mailman, and the many passersby such as a Spanish lady, a French lady, etc. The most important of the dolls is the Fairy Queen who animates her charges, so that the entire toy shop comes to life as the dolls march, dance negro dances, waltz, etc.

59 [R55].
Wrapper for set of postcard reproductions of costumes for *La Fée des Poupées*, 1904.
Lithograph.
6⅛ x 7½ in., 15.5 x 19 cm

60-71 [R56-67].
Postcard reproductions of costumes for *La Fée des Poupées (Die Puppenfee),* 1904.
Each reproduction is chromolithography on card, measuring 5½ x 3⅝ in., 14 x 9.3 cm.
Provenance: the artist's niece, Marie Constantinowicz, Paris, June, 1966. Now in a private collection.

Note: La Fée des Poupées marked Bakst's debut as a ballet designer. His set and costume designs expressed playfulness, ingenuity, and "geographical accuracy," but not the dazzling sensuality for which Bakst is now remembered. His décors appealed because they were a "faithful copy"[87] of the Gostinyi dvor (shopping arcade) on Nevsky Prospect in St. Petersburg in the 1850s. To some extent, Bakst — and the Legats — were appealing to a fashion for the naive and unassuming artifact, especially for the art of the toy, which interested the World of Art artists in particular. In fact, Benois maintained that his own collection of toys, reproductions of which also appeared as postcards in 1904, had actually inspired some of Bakst's

renderings for *La Fée des Poupées.*[88]

The set of twelve postcards was published in St. Petersburg in 1904 (not, as is often stated, 1903) by the Society of St. Eugenia, an impressive organization that published numerous artistic postcards. For further discussion of the St. Eugenia Society see No. 74 [R68], for a complete listing of its postcards see Yu. Vulfson: *Illiustrirovannyi katalog otkrytykh pisem v polzu Obshchiny Sv. Evgenii* (M: Bonfi, Vol. 1, 2005; Vols. 2, 3,4, 2006; see Vol. 1, pp. 204-06, for reproductions of the set of the twelve Bakst postcards) and for a one-page reproduction of another set see Spencer, *Bakst,* p. 41. For some commentary see A28, unpaginated. Color reproductions of some of Bakst's original watercolors for the 1903 production upon which the postcards were based are reproduced in Golynets, *Lev Bakst,* plates 132-37. The set was not Bakst's first collaboration with the Society of St. Eugenia, which in 1902 had published a reproduction postcard of his picture *A Favorite Poet* (see Vulfson, Vol. 1, No. 171).

60

61

62

63

64

65

60 [R56].
The Fairy of the Dolls, the Fairy Queen.

61 [R57].
An English Lady.

62 [R58].
The Daughter of the English Lady.

63 [R59].
A Spanish Lady Doll.

64 [R60].
A Chinese Lady Doll.

65 [R61].
A Japanese Lady Doll.

66

68

70

67

69

71

66 [R62].
A French Lady Doll.

67 [R63].
One of the China Dolls.

68 [R64].
The Maid.

69 [R65].
A Costume Design for the Corps de Ballet.

70 [R66].
The Mailman.

71 [R67].
The Batman.

Two caricatures: *The following two caricatures of the brothers Nikolai Gustavovich Legat (1869-1937) and Sergei Gustavovich Legat (1875-1905) by Alexei Vladimirovich Taskin (1871-1942) were created around the time of their joint production of* La Feé des Poupées.

72

72 [R69].
Caricature of Nikolai Legat, ca. 1903.
Pencil.
Signed lower left in pencil in Russian: "Drawn by A.V. Taskin"; and lower left in pencil in Russian: "Nikolai Legat."
9½ x 6¾ in., 24 x 17 cm.
Other inscription: upper right : "II."
Provenance: Solomon Shuster, Leningrad, March, 1984.

73 [R70].
Caricature of Sergei Legat, ca. 1903.
Pencil.
Signed lower center in pencil in Russian: "Drawn by A.V. Taskin"; and lower right in pencil in Russian: "Sergei Legat."
9½ x 6¾ in., 24 x 17 cm.
Other inscriptions: upper right: "III."
Provenance: Solomon Shuster, Leningrad, March, 1984.

Note: Alexei Taskin was a professional pianist who accompanied ballet and opera companies, specifically at the Mariinsky and Alexandrinsky Theaters in St. Petersburg. In this way, he played for many celebrities, including Medea Figner, Michel Fokine, the Legats, and Anna Pavlova. An affable and sociable man who "scatters gentilities,"[89] Taskin was a talented caricaturist as well as an able musician.

Taskin has copied, in somewhat modified form, the famous self-caricatures by the Legats, which were reproduced in color in their album *Russkii balet v karikaturakh* [The Russian Ballet in Caricatures] (SP: Progress, 1903). This book contains ninety-four caricatures of dancers and dance supporters signed by the two brothers, including their sister Evgeniia Legat, Fokine, Tamara Karsavina, Georgii Kiaksht, and Marius Petipa. Nikolai Legat recalled how the brothers arrived at the idea of caricaturing the Russian ballet:

> Our room was covered with all sorts of sketches. Our tastes lay in the direction of the grotesque, and one day we suddenly thought of trying our hand at caricatures. First Serge had a go at me, and hit off the comic traits of my head very successfully. I followed suit and made a very funny drawing of him. Next we went at our colleagues in the theatre, and from that day became recognized cartoonists.
>
> One day we showed a few cartoons at the opera, and Stravinsky (father of Igor) urged us to publish an album, to which he would be the first subscriber. We followed his advice and published a collection done in water colours.[90]

Nikolai Legat continued to caricature ballet and artistic personalities in later years, e.g., Anton Dolin and Kira Nijinsky, and some of his drawings are illustrated in his memoirs.[91] The original watercolor caricatures of the Legat brothers that Taskin copied, now in the BTM, are also reproduced there (opposite p. 46 and opposite p. 26, respectively).

74 [R68].
Poster Advertising the Postcards of the Red Cross Society, 1904.
Lithograph in red, brown, black, and white.
Signed in the plate center right in Russian: "Bakst."
18¼ x 24¾ in., 46.5 x 63 cm.
Other inscriptions: lower left corner in Russian: "Printed by the Kadushin lithographic workshop, St. Petersburg"; lower right corner in large type: "On sale everywhere"; in small

73

type: "Permit for printing by the St. Petersburg censor, 22 March, 1904."
Provenance: *Russian Pictures, Icons and Russian Works of Art*, London: Sotheby's, 15 February, 1984, 15 February, Lot 57 (reproduced).
Reproduced in L19, Lot 10; M73, p. 89; another copy is in the collection of the Karelia Museum of Visual Arts; the original gouache for the poster is reproduced in L13, Lot 57.

Note: Bakst is not usually remembered for his commercial advertisements, even though he was active in this area, designing, for example, a number of programs, bookplates, and posters in the late 1890s and early 1900s such as the poster for the Philanthropic Bazaar of Dolls (1899; illustrated in Pruzhan, *Bakst*, p. 47), the Russian section at the Viennese Secession of 1908 (illustrated in B114, p. 77; and B159, p. 38), for the

74

Caryathis recital (No. 93 [NIRE]), and this piece. The Red Cross (also-called the Society of St. Eugenia) was founded in St. Petersburg in 1882 and, in order to attract funds, undertook a series of publishing ventures, including postcards (1892 onwards). Among the sets of postcards that it issued were reproductions of works by modern Russian artists including Alexandre Benois, Ilia Repin, Mstislav Dobujinsky (Nos. 425-27 [R460-62]), and Nicholas Roerich as well as Bakst. In 1904 Bakst produced twelve postcards based on his costumes for *La Fée des Poupées* (see Nos. 59-71 [R55-67]) and his poster was intended to increase the sale of this set.

The poster also has a sentimental content inasmuch as the woman depicted is Liubov Pavlovna Gritsenko (1870-1928), the third daughter of the collector Pavel Tretiakov. Bakst had recently met her and, in 1903, painted her portrait (reproduced in Pruzhan, p. 73). The couple married the following year after Bakst converted to Lutheranism, his fiancée's religion.[92] It is not known who the little girl is, although it is fair to assume that she is Gritsenko's daughter by her first marriage (to the painter Nikolai Gritsenko). Liubov Gritsenko and the little girl are, presumably, looking at the postcards for *La Fée des Poupées*. In composition and theme this poster brings to mind one of Bakst's first sallies into the world of promotional materials, i.e. his poster for the Philanthropic Doll Bazaar organized in St. Petersburg in 1899 to benefit the city's maternity homes (for a reproduction see B297, p. 26).

Cléopâtre: *a choreographic drama in one act based on Antonii Arensky's* An Egyptian Night *(see No. 30 [R29]) with musical additions by Nikolai Cherepnin, Alexander Glazunov, Mikhail Glinka, Nikolai Rimsky-Korsakov, and Sergei Taneev. Produced by Sergei Diaghilev at the Théâtre du Châtelet, Paris, on 2 June, 1909, with choreography by Michel Fokine and designs by Léon Bakst.*

The plot of Cléopâtre, *while similar to that of* An Egyptian Night, *is at once more salacious and more tragic. Amoun, an Egyptian youth, has seen the Queen of the Sapphire Nile, Cleopatra, and has defied her courtiers, renounced his humble mistress Ta-Hor, and offered his life for a sign of Cleopatra's favor. The Queen is amazed at his devotion and, while her slave girls dance bacchanales with the black servants, she succumbs to his passion. Yet, his triumph is short; swift death by poison follows. The vast hall supported by massive columns is deserted, and as the Royal galley carries Cleopatra down the sacred river, the faithful Ta-Hor falls lifeless on the body of her faithless lover.*

75 [10; R71].
Costume Design for Cleopatra, Worn by Ida Rubinstein, 1909.
Pencil and watercolor.
Signed lower right in Russian: "Bakst."
11 x 8¼ in., 28 x 21 cm.
Provenance: Mrs. Havemeyer, New York, February, 1968.
Reproduced in color in the Souvenir Program,

75

76

Ballets Russes, for a benefit in aid of the British Red Cross at the Théâtre National de l'Opéra, Paris, 29 December 1915; as the cover for I20; and in B115, No. 1; D41, p. 55; F107, p. 126; G61; G99, p. 62; I68, p. 6; as the cover for I115 and on p. 129; I127, p, 121; as the cover for N188 and on p. 4; in black and white in H32, p. 398; I20, No. 5; I51, No. 21; M75; M86; M131; M161; N107; N114; N122; N157; O3; R2; R17; in Spencer, *Leon Bakst,* fig. 41; G39, Fig. 40, and in many other sources. The design was also issued as a postcard by the Fondation Ryback, Paris (André Barry, no date). For a photograph of Rubinstein in this costume, see Spencer, *Leon Bakst,* p. 57. A curious version, dated 1911 and described as a costume for Anna Pavlova, is in the BTM and is reproduced in K61, No. 232. Bakst also designed similar costumes for Salomé in Oscar Wilde's tragedy (1910, TG; reproduced in color in K67, No. 1) and in Richard Strauss's *La Tragédie de Salomé* (1914, TG; reproduced in G31, fig. 149).

76 [R72].
Costume Design for Jewish Dancer in Blue and Gold, 1910.
Pencil, watercolor, and gold paint.
Signed and dated lower left in pencil: "Bakst, 1910."
11 x 8¼ in., 28 x 21 cm.
Other inscriptions: upper right in pencil: "Cléopâtre" and "Juive."
Provenance: Evgenii Gunst, Moscow, May, 1967.
Reproduced in color as the cover to I41; in B115, No. 3; and M23; and in black and white in N118; a similar design dated 1909 is reproduced in J27, Lot 127; and L88, Lot 162, where it is labeled as a costume for a Syrian dancer. Another similar design, also dated 1909, and, presumably, the original inspiration for many allied costumes of 1909-11, is reproduced in Spencer, *Leon Bakst,* plate 7 under the title *Danse Syrienne*. A later design labeled *Costume Design for a Syrian Dancer* is reproduced in the catalog of the exhibition

"Léon Bakst" held at the Galleria del Levante, Milan, 1967 (fig. 4), and another version also dated 1910 and described as a costume for *Schéhérazade* is reproduced in D15, p. 22. The design in question would appear to be one of Bakst's many retrospective copies of original sketches.

77 [11; R73].
Costume Design for a Male Dancer Holding a Tambourine in the "Danse Juive," 1910.
Gouache heightened with gold paint, and pencil.
Glued to the reverse is a thin piece of paper with costume annotations in French and initialed "L.B." These data indicate that the piece is a Bakst authorized studio copy made to be sent to the costume maker.
13⅜ x 9½ in., 34 x 24 cm.

77

Other inscriptions: top right in pencil: "Danse Juive, Fig. 29."
Provenance: *Arts Décoratifs du XXème Siecle,* Monaco: Christie's, 1 February, 1987, Lot 43. Now in a private collection. Reproduced in color as the cover to B88; and in A34, p. 15; B115, No. 2; F107, p. 105; I68, p. 7; I77, pp. 66 and 169; G79, p. 129; and in black and white in O1; P16; R15. A similar design is reproduced in color in Spencer, *Leon Bakst,* plate VIII; Golynets, *Lev Bakst,* plate 141; and in black and white in Pruzhan, *Bakst* (1975), p. 131.

78

78 [R74].
Costume Design for the Syrian Harpist, 1910 (?).
Watercolor.
Glued to the reverse is a thin piece of paper with costume annotations in French and initialed "L.B." These data indicate that the piece is a Bakst authorized studio copy made to be sent to the costume maker.
13 x 9½ in., 33.2 x 24 cm.
Other inscriptions: fabric annotations on right side.
Provenance: *Arts Décoratifs du XXème Siècle,* Monaco: Christie's, 1 February, 1987, Lot 33. Now in a private collection. Reproduced in color in B115, plate 4; F107, p. 425; and in black and white in M86.

79 [R75].
Costume Design for a Bacchante, 1910 (?).
Watercolor.
13 x 9½ in., 33.2 x 24 cm.
Inscriptions: notes and pencil markings throughout followed by the initials "L.B." Glued to the reverse is a thin piece of paper with costume annotations in French and initialed "L.B." These data indicate that the piece is a Bakst authorized studio copy

79

made to be sent to the costume maker.
Provenance: *Arts Décoratifs du XXème Siècle,* Monaco: Christie's, 1 February, 1987, Lot 40 (reproduced). Now in a private collection.
A similar design, dated 1909, is reproduced in color in J18, Lot No. 49; another similar design dated 1910 is reproduced in black and white in Pruzhan, *Bakst,* p. 131.

Note: Cléopâtre was one of the most successful ballets of the Diaghilev Saisons Russes. Bakst's costume design for Rubinstein as Cleopatra, while sensuous and provocative, was also carefully organized. As he wrote to Diaghilev in April, 1911: "My mises-en-scène are the result of a very calculated distribution of paint spots against the background of the décor... The costumes of the primary characters are like dominants, like flowers amidst the bouquet of the other costumes."[93] Bakst's con-

ception of Cleopatra, whom Alexandre Benois once defined as the "most beautiful woman in antiquity,"[94] brought forth impassioned praise at the Paris premiere, causing Jean Cocteau to speak of her as "penetratingly beautiful like the pungent perfume of some exotic essence."[95] Certainly, these costumes epitomize the elements that made Bakst world-famous — the lushness of forms focusing on erogenous zones, the marvelous combination of bright and clear colors, and the finely detailed draftsmanship.

Bakst arrived at his resolution of the designs for *Cléopâtre* after a brief, but valuable experience as a stage designer in Russia, and these costumes were reminiscent of his designs for the presentation of *Salomé* projected by Michel Fokine and Vsevolod Meierkhold for the Mikhailovsky Theater, St. Petersburg, in November, 1908 (part of this spectacle was produced privately in St. Petersburg in December, 1908 with Rubinstein in the title role). *Cléopâtre* was perhaps the most harmonious of the several collaborations between Bakst and Rubinstein, the exotic dancer and whimsical impresario who, for all her caprices, never doubted the "incomparable originality" of her designer.[96]

Thaïs: opera in three acts based on a novel by Anatole France adapted by Louis Gallet with music by Jules Massenet. Produced by Marie Kousnezoff in the Great Hall of the St. Petersburg Conservatoire on 16 January, 1910, with designs by Léon Bakst.

Athanael, a Cenobite, decides to convert the courtesan Thaïs from her life of debauchery to a life of religious quest. Thaïs accepts his plea and enters a convent. However, Athanael then realizes that he has fallen in love with her. Rushing to her convent, he is in time only to see her die. Stricken with grief he falls beside her.

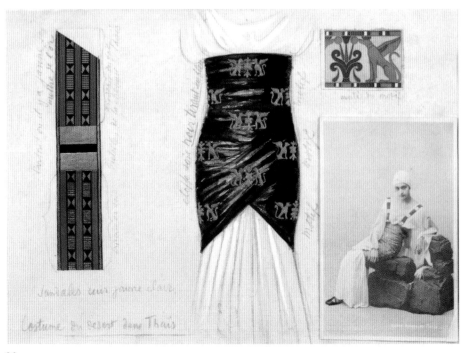

80

80 [R76].
Costume Design for Flore Revalles in the Role of Thaïs, 1910.
Watercolor, pencil, and gold, with a photograph of Flore Revalles wearing the costume.
Inscribed and annotated in pencil by Bakst with instructions to the dressmaker.
8¼ x 11½ in., 21 x 29.2 cm.
Provenance: the artist's niece, Bertha Tsipkevitch, Paris, February, 1969.
Reproduced in I40, No. 12; J5, Lot 33.

Note: Flore Revalles (1889-1966; also known as Flora Revales), a celebrated beauty and one-time companion of the conductor Ernest Ansermet, was both a dancer and an opera singer. In 1915 Diaghilev invited her to join the Ballets Russes and she took part in the 1915-16 season at the Metropolitan Opera, New York, dancing in Schéhérazade in January, 1916. She appeared with Nijinsky's troupe in 1916 in New York and again with Diaghilev's company in 1917, but thereafter concentrated on her career as a singer. Marie Kousnezoff (Mariia Nikolaevna Kuznetsova, 1880-1966), a singer with the Mariinsky Opera in St. Petersburg, who in emigration directed the Opéra Privé de Paris, achieved acclaim for her interpretation of Thaïs at the Paris Opéra. It is interesting to note that Bakst also designed a costume for Kousnezoff in a 1910 production of Thaïs (see G30, plate 3). On Kousnezoff, see also Nos. 367-68 [R337-38].

Schéhérazade: choreographic drama in one act with music by Nikolai Rimsky-Korsakov, book by Léon Bakst and Alexandre Benois, and choreography by Michel Fokine. Produced by Sergei Diaghilev at the Théâtre National de l'Opéra, Paris on 4 June, 1910, with designs by Léon Bakst.

The Shah Shahriar, suspecting his favorite wife, Zobeida, of being unfaithful, pretends to go out hunting. As soon as he leaves, the ladies of the harem persuade the Great Eunuch to let in the black slaves. An orgy ensues led by Zobeida and her favorite negro. The Shah suddenly returns and orders the transgressors to be executed. Seeing that he hesitates to punish her, Zobeida stabs herself and dies at the feet of her Shah.

81 [12; R77].
Costume Design for the Blue Sultana, 1910.
Watercolor and pencil.
Signed on reverse upper left in pencil: "Bakst."
11⅝ x 9 in., 29.5 x 23 cm.
Other inscriptions: on reverse instructions to the printer of the reproduction of this design in the Christmas issue of l'Illustration (Paris,1927): "Hauteur totale de la femme = 18.5 cm. Ne pas detourer et laisser toute marge;" the reverse carries a stamp in green ink: "G. Rasamatt, Dépositaire exclusif des oeuvres de Léon Bakst, 11, rue Louis Francais, Paris XIII, 22 avr., 1927"; also label of the previous owner, "Mr. Hopkinson, Londres" (=Cecil Hopkinson).
Provenance: by private treaty at Sotheby's, London, 1 August, 1981. Now in a private collection.

81

Reproduced in color in l'Illustration (Paris, 1927, December [Christmas issue]); as the cover to M14; and in B115, plate 6; F107, p. 425; G99, p. 166; I117, p. 281; I130, p. 105; O13, p. 115; I115, p. 134; reproduced in black and white in D10, p. 51; I51, No. 23; I77, p. 169; N17; N128 (b); M147; M148; M161; Q3; R1; R18; the gouache and gold version of this design, formerly in the collection of James A. de Rothschild, now in a private collection, has been reproduced many times, e.g., in the Souvenir Program Serge de Diaghileff's Ballet Russe (New York: Metropolitan Ballet Co., 1916, unpaginated) and in Spencer, Leon Bakst, plate 19. In some sources the gouache and gold design is referred to as the Red Sultana, e.g., A. Levinson, Bakst (London:

Bayard, 1923), plate 33; Zhar-ptitsa (Berlin, 1922, No. 9) opposite p. 8; Pruzhan, Bakst (1975), p. 140. However, the title Blue Sultana is more correct inasmuch as the primary identifying characteristic is the predominant blue of the Sultana's turban.

Note: Ida Rubinstein, with whom Bakst had collaborated since 1904, was the model for the Blue Sultana, and, with her oriental features and lithesome silhouette, she epitomized Bakst's ideal of feminine beauty. Bakst applied the basic conception of this costume to all the female participants in Schéhérazade and, to some extent, he repeated methods that he had already explored in Cléopâtre. As a dramatic exercise in sex and violence, Schéhérazade appealed to a Parisian public nurtured on the poetical and artistic fantasies of the European Symbolists. The dominant conception of woman as a fateful enchantress shared by writers and artists such as Charles Baudelaire, Aubrey Beardsley, Gabriele d'Annunzio, and Alexander Blok found a direct expression in the Blue Sultana's "long, viscid, and terrifying sharovary [trousers] symbolizing her voluptuousness, cruel as the sting of a wasp."[97]

82 [14; R78].
Artist unknown: Set Design for the Last Scene: the Return of the Sultan Shariar, ca. 1910.
Oil on canvas.
43¾ x 51¼ in., 110 x 130 cm.
Provenance: Bedel Storage House, Paris, June, 1966. Now in a private collection.
Reproduced in color in B115, plate 5; M86, p. 76; M161, p. 44; Yu. Gogolitsyn: "'Provoditel velikikh idei...'" in Antik.info, M, 2005, No. 26, p. 85; and in black and white in B44, p. 291; N114.

82

Note: This depiction of the orgy from *Schéhérazade*, painted probably by one of Bakst's disciples, or perhaps by Lucien Lelong, rather than by the master himself, is clearly inspired by Bakst's actual décors for the ballet and repeats many of the details — the hanging lamps, looped drapes, brash greens and reds (cf. the famous set in watercolor, gouache and gold in the Musée des Arts Décoratifs, Paris, reproduced, for example, in Pruzhan, *Bakst* [1975], pp. 132-333; also see the documentary photograph in the GMTMA reproduced, for example, in I89, pp. 96-97). While reminiscent of Bakst's preferred themes and compositions in his studio paintings (cf. the oil *Siamese Sacred Dance,* 1901, TG, reproduced in Pruzhan, *Bakst* [1975], p. 76), the canvas contains awkward perspectival and anatomical resolutions that are surely not Bakst's. It is of interest to compare No. 82 [R78] with the actual setting of the last scene — see the documentary photographs in G63, pp. 116, 117.

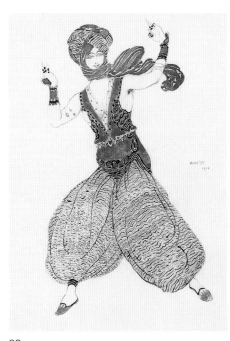

83

83 [R79].
Costume Design for Almée, 1910.
Watercolor, gold paint, and pencil.
Signed and dated: "Bakst 1910."
13 x 9 in., 33 x 23 cm.
Provenance: the artist's niece, Bertha Tsipkevich, Paris, February, 1969. Now in a private collection.
Reproduced in color in *Comoedia Illustré,* Paris, special number for 15 June, 1910, centerfold (unpaginated); as the cover to the exhibition catalog *Léon Bakst,* Paris: Hotel de Jean Charpentier, 1928; G61; in black and white in I40, No. 10; N114.

84 [13; R80].
Costume Design for a Slave, 1910.
Watercolor.
Signed upper right: "Bakst."
10¼ x 6½ in., 26 x 16.5 cm.
Inscriptions: references to colors to be used in five costumes are along right side.

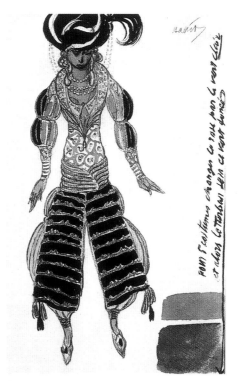

84

Provenance: the artist's niece, Marie Constantinowicz, Paris, June 1966. Now in a private collection.
Reproduced in I14, No. 24.

Narcisse: *mythological ballet-poem in one act by Léon Bakst with music by Nikolai Cherepnin and choreography by Michel Fokine. Premiered by Sergei Diaghilev in Monte Carlo on 26 April, 1911, and in Paris at the Théâtre du Châtelet on 6 June, 1911, with designs by Léon Bakst.*
Narcisse declares his love to Echo. But the jealous Nymphs explain that his love will not be requited. Narcisse leaves Echo to go with the Nymphs and, in retribution, is condemned to love himself hopelessly. Narcisse kneels before a pool, sees his reflection, falls enamored, but is unable to gain a mutual affection. Fatigued, he bows to the ground and changes into a flower. Echo, in turn, changes into a stone.

85 [15; R81].
Costume Design for a Bacchante, 1911.
Gouache and pencil.
Stamped signature lower right: "Bakst."
19¼ x 13 in., 49 x 33 cm.
Provenance: the artist's niece, Bertha Tsipkevitch, Paris, November, 1966.
Reproduced in color in M157, p. 13; and in black and white in I14, No. 27; a similar design is reproduced in Borisovskaia, *Bakst,* p. 87.

86 [16; R82].
Costume Design for a Boeotian, 1911.
Silkscreen heightened with gold paint.
Signed and dated in the plate: "Bakst 1911."
19⅞ x 15¾ in., 50.5 x 40 cm.
Reproduced in color in B115, plate 7; and in black and white in J49, Lot 828; M114 and

R18. The silkscreen is from an unauthorized edition of ca. 1924 made in the US. The size of the edition is unknown, but it is assumed to have been less than fifty. The original watercolor and pencil design for this Boeotian is in the collection of the GMTMA.

Note: The miniature ballet that Bakst based on one of Ovid's *Metamorphoses* resembled a "tragic idyll" according to Andrei Levinson,[98] and with its fauns and satyrs, looked forward to *L'Après-midi d'un faune* of the following year. Although the main roles were filled by Tamara Karsavina (Echo), Vaslav Nijinsky (Narcisse), Bronislava Nijinska (a Bacchante — the present design may have been for her), and Vera Fokina (a young Boeotian), the emphasis was not on virtuoso dancing, but rather on "free plasticity." As Vera Krasovskaia

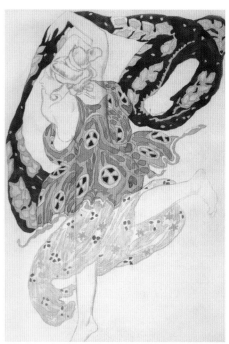

85

86

87

remarked, the influence of Isadora Duncan could be observed in the collective endeavor to unite drama, music, and song as well as in the "hellenistic" design of the chore-ography.[99] Perhaps because of its intimate mood, *Narcisse* did not score a particular success and, as Serge Grigoriev recorded, the Paris public found it rather tedious.[100] Bakst's costume designs for Narcisse, especially his costumes for the Boeotians (Nos. 85, 86 [R81, R82]), are among his most striking, and his typical concentric motif was to leave a strong imprint on fabric design and decoration in the 1920s.

Le Martyre de Saint Sébastien: *a mystery play in five acts by Gabriele d'Annunzio with musical interludes by Claude Debussy and choreography by Michel Fokine. Produced on 22 May, 1911, by Ida Rubinstein at the Théâtre du Châtelet, Paris, with designs by Léon Bakst.*

According to pious legend, Sebastien joined the Roman army under false pretenses in order to plead with the Christian prisoners to be firm in their faith under persecution. His efforts won him many converts, including the Prefect of Rome. However, when Diocletian, who had made Sebastien captain of his guard, discovered that Sebastien was a Christian, he ordered him shot to death by archers.

87 [NIRE].
Poster for Le Martyre de Saint Sebastien, 1911.
Colored lithographic reproduction printed by Eugene Verneau and Henri Chachoin, Paris.
15½ x 49¼ in., 39.3 x 123.5 cm.
Provenance: *Poster Auctions International*, New York, 1998, 8 November, Vol. 27, Lot 202. Now in a private collection.
The poster, consisting of two sheets with costume designs for minor characters, decorated the streets of Paris before the premiere. It has been reproduced numerous times, e.g. in Schouvaloff, *Léon Bakst. The Theatre Art*, p. 118 (also see the documentary photograph of the performers' line-up on p. 122). As is evident from his designs for *Oedipus at Colona* (1904) or *L'Après-midi d'un faune* (1912), Bakst often favored a strong horizontal sequence of figures.

88

88 [R83].
Costume Design for one of the Archers of Emère, 1911.
Gouache, silver, and gold paint, and pencil.
Stamped signature lower right.
11⅜ x 9 in., 29 x 23 cm.
Provenance: the artist's niece, Bertha Tsipkevich, Paris, June, 1967.
Reproduced in I20, No. 6; I51, No. 24; a variant, dated 1922, is reproduced in C7, plate 91. A preliminary sketch for this Archer is in the collection of the Metropolitan Museum of Art, New York.

Note: Le Martyre de Saint Sébastien, one of the several collaborations between Rubinstein and Bakst, enabled the former to make her first independent appearance on the Paris stage in the role of St. Sebastien. In any case, d'Annunzio, one of Rubinstein's ardent admirers, wrote the play especially for her. Although recent critics speak of the success of Bakst's designs for this pro-duction,[101] not all reviewers of the time were enthusiastic. Anatolii Lunacharsky, for ex-ample, dismissed the designs simply as an "anachronistic mixing of styles."[102]

La Péri: *one-act ballet based on a Persian fairy-tale with music by Paul Dukas and costumes by Léon Bakst. Rehearsed by Diaghilev's Ballets Russes in Monte Carlo in 1911, but not produced.*

Iskender searches for the flower of Immortality and finds it — as an emerald talisman in the form of a lotus — in the hands of Péri, a Persian fairy. Iskender steals it, but falls in love with Péri. She awakens and sees the flower, now purple with desire, in Iskender's right hand. In order to regain her property, she proceeds to dance. The flower turns white and gold and Iskender is forever fused with it.

89 [front cover; R84].
Costume Design for the Péri, 1911.
Gouache, pencil, and gold paint.
Stamped signature lower right: "Bakst."
26¾ x 19⅛ in., 68 x 48.5 cm.
Provenance: the artist's niece, Bertha Tsipkevitch, Paris, June, 1967. Now in a private collection.
Reproduced in color in A34, p. 58; B115, plate 8; G61; G70; G99, p. 162; I115, p. 143;

89

N13, plate 30; O23; and Golynets, *Lev Bakst,* plate 162; in black and white in I20, No. 7; I40, No. 11; I51, No. 25; I77, p. 169; M140; N111; N114; M107; N24; N43; this design is a larger version of the more familiar design, formerly in the Serge Lifar collection (see J14, Lot 22); the latter has been reproduced in color many times, e.g., in Pruzhan, *Bakst* (1975), p. 162; B11, plate 40; and R15. Cf. the lithographic version of the same costume in No. 90 [R85].

90

90 [19; R85].
Costume Design for the Péri, 1911.
Hand-colored lithograph.
Signed and dated in the plate: "Bakst 1911."
12¼ x 9 in., 31 x 23 cm.
Other inscriptions: stamped signature of the atelier lower right; inscribed upper right by Bakst in the plate: "Péri, N. Trukhanova." This is No. 35 out of 50 copies published in 1911, based on the original sketch (see No. 89 [R84]). Evidently, a second printing of this lithograph was also made later, probably after Bakst's death. This would explain why some sheets of the lithograph, in slightly paler colors, carry an embossed signature and the indication that the edition was in one hundred copies. For a color reproduction of Bakst's original costume for Nijinsky, who was to have danced the part of Iskender (a later design is in the collection of the Metropolitan Museum, New York), see Spencer, *Leon Bakst,* plate 16; and D41, ill. 73.
Provenance: the artist's niece, Bertha Tsipkevich, Paris, February, 1969. Now in a private collection.

Note: It is generally assumed that Diaghilev cancelled the ballet, because of an argument between Diaghilev and Dukas concerning the dancer Natalia Vladimirovna Trukhanova (Nathalie Trouhanova, 1885-1956; see No. 767d [R646g]), who, according to Dukas, should have danced the title role, and

because of Bakst's alleged procrastinations. However, Trukhanova's own account of the events is rather different. According to her memoirs, Trukhanova directed a small company of French dancers who used to put on annual Concerts de Danse de N. Trouhanova in Paris. In 1911, her then companion Dukas played her the score for his new opus, *Péri,* which he wanted Trukhanova to dance. However, Trukhanova was not impressed by the music: "This is a *danse des vaches* from the mountains," she exclaimed, "but Péri is not a mountain cow, she is a flower!"[103] After conferring with Trukhanova, Dukas changed the music and she agreed to dance it, but, as she recalled, *Péri* was not an easy ballet because it relied on only two characters and, unless danced well, it could become tedious. In order to make her character representation as authentic as possible, Trukhanova spent several months studying oriental art in London.

One day, Diaghilev and Nijinsky dropped by Trukhanova's Paris studio and invited her to stage and dance *Péri* for the Ballets Russes — with choreography by Michel Fokine and designs by Bakst. Flattered by Diaghilev's attentions, Trukhanova agreed, but she soon discovered that Diaghilev's company had taken an instant dislike to her — Fokine never showed up and Nijinsky expressed no interest in being her partner. When, a few days before the scheduled premiere, Adolf Bolm replaced Nijinsky as Iskender, Trukhanova threw a fit, walked out, and left the Diaghilev company. However, she continued to work on her version of *Péri* and, with choreography by Ivan Clustine and designs by René Piot, it was produced by her own company in June, 1912. The production was well received and, not immodestly, Trukhanova contended that "it proved to be the very best French choreographical and musical work of the entire early 20th century."[104]

Nina Lobanov-Rostovsky describes the costume design for the *Péri* as follows:

> Léon Bakst's reputation as the greatest, and certainly the most influential artist of twentieth-century ballet design, has been based for the most part on his sensual orientalist costumes for *Schéhérazade, Cléopâtre, Thamar, Le Dieu Bleu,* and *Les Orientales,* and two costumes for *La Péri,* all designed for the *Ballets Russes.* Swirling scarf, peacock-hue ornaments, colourful costume, head-dress feathers, and pert, exposed breast make *La Péri* one of the most enchanting and desirable of all Bakst's beautiful female costumes. It is quintessential Bakst. As a collector of *Ballets Russes* costume designs, if asked to choose one Bakst, I would choose *La Péri.*
>
> When we bought our beautiful *La Péri* costume design in 1967, from Madame Tsipkevich, one of Bakst's nieces in Paris, she told us that ours was a larger repeat of Bakst's beautiful 1911 original, which was "in an old French collection." We were of course curious to know which collection but didn't

manage to find out. It was, therefore, a wonderful surprise to be asked by Sotheby's to view and then write about the *La Péri* prototype, which had been consigned to them for auction by a member of the original collector's family.

La Péri is a Persian tale about a peri (a Persian fairy) who, expelled from heaven, seeks to return there after various earthly adventures, by using a magic talisman. Diaghilev commissioned Bakst to create a ballet scenario on this topic with music by the French composer Paul Dukas. Bakst was also to design the set and costumes. It was scheduled for the 1911 *Ballets Russes* season in Paris, but not produced, the chief reason being that Dukas had insisted that the lead role be given to his mistress – the plump, amateurish dancer Natalia Trouhanova, who did not belong to the *Ballets Russes* company. Endless arguments ensued between Diaghilev, Dukas, the choreographer Fokine, and Bakst. Trouhanova didn't come to Monte Carlo for rehearsals, and the ballet was cancelled. Nijinsky was to have been her partner in the role of the warrior Iskender. Fortunately, both Bakst designs for Trouhanova's and Nijinsky's gorgeous costumes had already been photographed for publicity purposes, and had been printed in souvenir programs announcing the forthcoming *Ballets Russes* season. This brought the designs to the attention of balletomanes and art lovers in Paris. (In April 1912, Trouhanova performed in a concert version of *La Péri* but not in Bakst's costume).

The art dealer and collector Jules Chavasse purchased the original costume design directly from Bakst. After Chavasse's death in early 1919, his collection was sold at auction in Paris, on 6th June 1919, and the costume design for *La Péri* was acquired by a nephew for 900 francs. It remained in the family until now. It is rare to come upon a prototype Bakst costume design with such an impeccable provenance.

So beautiful and desirable was the costume, that a hand-coloured print based on the original design was issued in 1911 in an edition of 50 copies. Later, after Bakst's death in 1924, another larger hand-coloured print was created in an edition of 100.

No one is certain about the whereabouts of the prototype for Iskender, but a beautiful, large later version is in the collection of the Metropolitan Museum in NYC. The larger versions of both La Péri and Iskender were borrowed and hung together at the fine Diaghilev exhibition and first ever Diaghilev Festival at Groeningen, the Netherlands, in December 2004 – March 2005. It was a treat to be able to admire them on the same wall. Viewers of both sexes remained rooted in front of the alluring, dancing figure of *La Péri.*[105]

Le Dieu Bleu: *one act ballet by Jean Cocteau and Frédéric de Madrazo with music by Reynaldo Hahn based on a Hindu legend. Produced by Sergei Diaghilev at the Théâtre du Châtelet on 13 May, 1912, with choreography by Michael Fokine and designs by Léon Bakst.*

At a Hindu ceremony, a young man is about to enter the priesthood, but the maiden who loves him tries to stop this. The High Priest condemns her action and gives her over to the monsters of the temple. However, the maiden invokes the Goddess and the Blue God, who deliver her from this fate. The divinities retire gracefully as the two lovers are reunited.

91

91 [18; R86].
Costume Design for One of the Bayadères Carrying a Peacock, 1911.
Watercolor, pencil, and silver paint.
Signed and dated lower right: "Bakst 1911."
12¼ x 9 in., 31 x 23 cm.
Other inscription: upper right: "3 Bayadères avec paons Dieu Bleu."
Provenance: John Carr-Doughty, Leicester, 3 November, 1981.
The design has been reproduced many times, e.g., in color in Spencer, *Leon Bakst,* p. 157; B115, plate 9; F107, p. 126; G99, p. 175; I115, p. 144; I117, p. 306; in black and white in I15, fig. 34; I51, No. 26.

Note: Before the production of *Le Dieu Bleu*, Fokine had been impressed by the Ballet Troupe of the Royal Siamese Court that had danced in St. Petersburg in 1900 and he suggested that Diaghilev undertake a ballet related to the culture of Southeast Asia. Diaghilev liked the idea and commissioned Bakst to design the sets and costumes for the ballet, which Diaghilev scheduled for 1911 and then postponed until the following year. Bakst's set for *Le Dieu Bleu* representing the Hindu temple surrounded by

gigantic cliffs and lush tropical foliage is among his most exotic (for a reproduction of the version in the Centre Georges Pompidou, Paris, see I89, p. 91. The costumes also extended Bakst's fertile imagination: he made a generous application of the pearls, pendants, and scarves that he loved so much and even had Nijinsky (the Blue God) painted blue. Still, despite such splendor and the dancing by Karsavina (the maiden), Lidia Nelidova (the Goddess), and Nijinsky, *Le Dieu Bleu* was not an overall success, at least from the choreographic standpoint, and many observers found the result both tedious and pretentious. On the other hand, Cyril Beaumont was rather impressed with the spectacle, at least at its premiere in London in February, 1913:

> The best thing about *Le Dieu Bleu* was its setting, in which Bakst proved that while he could evoke all the cruelty and voluptuousness of the East, as in his setting for *Schéhérazade*, he could also, by a different combination of color and design, conjure up the mystery and sense of awe produced by the East in a mood of religious exaltation.[106]

La Pisanella, ou la Mort Parfumée: *comedy in a prologue and three acts by Léon Bakst and Gabriele d'Annunzio, with music by Ildebrando da Parma Pizzetti. Staged by Vsevolod Meierkhold for Ida Rubinstein at the Théâtre du Châtelet, Paris, on 2 June, 1913, with choreography by Michel Fokine and designs by Léon Bakst.*

The Latin West, feudal and mystic, clashes with the rigid and solemn Byzantium, while the imperishable perfume of Hellas rises from the land of Cyprus, whence Aphrodite sprang forth.

92 [NIRE].
Costume Design for the Arbaletier, 1913.
Watercolor and pencil.
Signed lower right: "Bakst."
12⅛ x 8⅛ in., 30.7 x 20.5 cm.

92

Provenance: the artist's niece, Bertha Tsipkevich, Paris, June, 1967.
Reproduced in I20, p. 16, No. 11.

Note: In plot and mood close to *Le Martyre de Saint-Sébastien* (see No. 87 [NIRE]), *La Pisanella, ou la Mort Parfumée* was one of Bakst's most luxurious presentations. The sweeping sets evoking the antiquities of Cyprus and the fabulous Crusader costumes, in particular, impressed audiences and critics alike, the more so since some of the main costumes were executed by the Maison Worth. Eduoard de Max as the Prince of Tyre, Rubinstein alternating as a nun and a beggar, and her searing Dance of Death choreographed by Fokine drew loud applause. In a letter to D'Annunzio Bakst even referred to Rubinstein as "La divine."[107]

Dance recital by Elise Jouhandeau, *Paris, ca. 1916. The exact details of Jouhandeau's recital have not been forthcoming.*

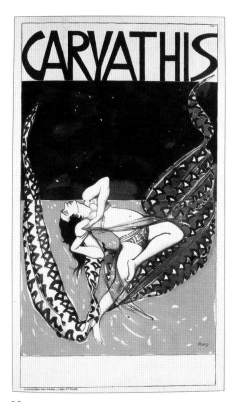

93

93 [17; NIRE].
Poster Advertising a Dance Recital by Caryathis (Elise Jouhandeau), ca. 1916.
Hand-colored lithograph.
Signed in plate lower right: "Bakst."
77¼ x 48⅞ in., 196 x 124 cm.
Other inscriptions: on lower right margin, details of the printer: H. Chachoin Imp[rimerie], Paris, Visa No. 15310; on lower right margin, printer's logo.
Provenance: *Poster Ecstasy. Poster Auctions International,* New York, 1998, 8 November, Vol. 27, Lot 201 (reproduced).
Reproduced in color as the cover for F107 and p. 126. Copies of the poster have been reproduced on numberous occasions, this one, for example, in I117, p. 317. The copy in the collection of the Metropolitan Museum of

Art, New York, is reproduced in Jean Crespelle: *La Folle Epoque*, Paris: Hachette, 1968, plate 9; and in *Bakst*. Catalog of exhibition at The Fine Art Society, London, 1976, p. 36; another, in a private collection, is reproduced in color in K223, plate 33, and in black and white p. 84; also see J21, Lot 49; yet another is in the collection of the Israel Museum, Jerusalem, and is reproduced in E. Sznajderman: *On Stage: The Art of Léon Bakst. Theatre Design and Other Works.* Catalog of exhibition at the Israel Museum, Jerusalem, 1992, p. 17. The same museum possesses preliminary sketches for the poster, two of which are reproduced, ibid., p. 16.

Note: In this indulgence of the senses Bakst has pictured Elise Jouhandeau (1888 [sometimes given as 1891] -1971), wife of the writer Marcel Jouhandeau and a Parisian occasional dancer who bore the stage name Caryathis — a reference to the maidens who danced sacrificial rituals in the Temple of Artemis Caryathis in Ancient Greece. Jouhandeau also took part in the *Fête Nègre,* which Paul Guillaume and Blaise Cendrars organized at the Théâtre de Champs-Elysées in Paris in 1919 and for the Ballets Suédois. Erik Satie composed the music for *La Belle Eccentrique* for her, which was performed in 1921. Drawing on his ample slavegirls and Boeotians of *Schéhérazade, Narcisse,* and similar exotic ballets, Bakst intensifies their serpentine lines, heady colors, and erogenous zones to produce a poster that treads a fine line between breathtaking brilliance and vulgar satiety, perhaps reminding us more of cloying Hollywood spectacle than of free artistic dance. Unfortunately, the exact occasion for this commission is not known, although the rampant energy and electric passion with which Bakst has imbued the image might indicate an obsession with Jouhandeau's physical charms rather than with her balletic talents. Some idea of her artistic aspirations and emotional encounters can be gained from her autobiography, bearing the histrionic title, *Les spleens empanachés. Joies et douleurs d'une belle excentrique* (Paris: Flammarion, 1960).

According to the explanation accompanying Lot 201 in the catalog for *Poster Ecstasy. Posters International,* it is reasonable to assume that the date of this poster is "ca. 1916" rather than the traditional "ca. 1919." This is because the French publisher, "Imp. H. Chachoin, Paris", had used a visa number — indicating that the poster was published under government authority after passing censorship during the First World War.

The Sleeping Beauty: *ballet in a prologue and three acts and apotheosis based on a fairy-tale by Charles Perrault; original music by Peter Tchaikovsky and original choreography by Marius Petipa and Ivan Vsevolozhsky. Produced by Anna Pavlova in abbreviated form at the Hippodrome Theater, New York, on 1 September, 1916, with modified choreography by Ivan Clustine and designs by Léon Bakst.*

The Princess Aurora receives gifts from the Fairy of the Lilacs, the Fairy of the Crystal Fountain, and the other fairies in celebration of her christening. However, the parents of the Princess forget the wicked fairy, Carabosse, who, in revenge, casts an evil spell, plunging the princess, her attendants, and all within the Castle into an everlasting slumber. However, one hundred years later Prince Charming happens upon the scene, awakens Princess Aurora with a kiss, thereby arousing everyone else from the deep slumber. Amidst general jubilation, the happy couple marry.

94

94 [R87].
Costume Design for One of the Counts Hunting, 1916.
Gouache, gold paint, and pencil.
Signed lower right and dated: "Bakst 16."
11½ x 5¼ in., 29.2 x 13.3 cm.
Provenance: Issar Gourvitch, Paris, June, 1966. Now in a private collection.
Reproduced in I14, No. 19; a similar design is reproduced in J4, Lot 44.

Note: Tchaikovsky's *Sleeping Beauty* had its premiere at the Mariinsky Theater, St. Petersburg, in 1890 with lavish designs by Mikhail Bocharov, Matvei Shishkov, and others. As Tchaikovsky's most popular ballet, it saw many revivals in Russia, not least in 1914 at the Mariinsky with designs by Konstantin Korovin. Bakst had worked on the theme of *The Sleeping Beauty* since at least 1909, when he designed the *pas de deux* for the Blue Bird presented within *Le Festin* (as *Firebird*) in Paris that season. In 1914 Bakst was commissioned by James A. de Rothschild to paint seven panels on the subject, and reluctantly, he continued to work on these until 1922. In 1916 Anna Pavlova and her company took part in the *Big Show* at the New York Hippodrome with a 48-minute version of *Sleeping Beauty,* shortened eventually to 18. Although Bakst did not go to the USA to supervise the implementation of his designs at the Hippodrome, the visual aspect of the production enjoyed a particular success: "Harmony of color constantly delights the eye, for with all the bizarre effects characteristic of Bakst there was never a jarring note"[108] — effects, of course, which returned with amplitude in Bakst's work for *The Sleeping Princess* five years later.

95 [NIRE].
Portrait of Ivan Bunin, 1921.
Pencil.
Signed and dated lower right: "Bakst 1921"
13½ x 8¼ in., 34.3 x 21 cm.
Provenance: the artist's niece, Bertha Tsipkevitch, Paris, 1964; acquired from Nikita D. Lobanov-Rostovsky by Ilia Zilbershtein, who, in turn, presented it to the Museum of Private Collections, Moscow.
Reproduced in F100, p. 182; F107, p. 254; I51, p. 79; J4, Lot 44.

95

The Sleeping Princess: *ballet in a prologue and three acts based on a fairy-tale by Charles Perrault,* The Sleeping Beauty; *original music by Peter Tchaikovsky and original choreography by Marius Petipa and Ivan Vsevolozhsky. Produced by Sergei Diaghilev at the Alhambra Theatre, London, on 2 November, 1921, with choreography by Nicholas Sergeyev and additional choreography by Bronislava Nijinska, partial reorchestration by Igor Stravinsky, and designs by Léon Bakst.*

See No. 94 [R87] for plot summary.

96

96 [R88].
Costume Design for Galisson, Tutor to Prince Charming, 1922.
Watercolor and silver and gold paint.
Signed and dated lower right: "Bakst 1922."
17⅞ x 10⅜ in., 44 x 26.5 cm.
Provenance: Issar Gourvitch, Paris, June, 1966.
Reproduced in color in André Levinson: *L'Oeuvre de Léon Bakst pour la Belle au Bois Dormant* (Paris: Brunoff, 1922), plate 4; and B115, plate 10; in black and white in I20, No. 10; I51, No. 27 (where back to front); a very similar design is reproduced in C7, plate 93, where, in spite of its inscription in the upper right, the piece is described as a costume for Louis XIV; Borisovskaia, *Lev Bakst,* plate 56, describes the piece as a costume for the Court Minister; Levinson in *Bakst, Catalogue,* opposite p. 179, identifies the costume as Galisson; also see K50 (b), unnumbered; and J34, Lot 17.

97 [R89].
Costume Design for La Fée de Sagesse (The Good Fairy), ca. 1921.
Gouache, pencil, silver paint, and ink.
Signed lower right in ink: "Bakst."
10¼ x 11⅜ in., 26 x 29 cm.

97

Cloth annotations throughout.
Provenance: the artist's niece, Bertha Tsipkevitch, Paris, September, 1966.
Reproduced in color in I130, p. 160; M157, p. 13; and in black and white in I14, No. 18; there exist several versions, e.g., J15, Lot 63.

98 [R90].
Costume Design for a Young Girl in Act I, ca. 1921.
Pencil and watercolor.
Cloth annotations throughout.
11⅜ x 6¼ in., 29 x 16 cm.
Provenance: the artist's niece, Bertha Tsipkevitch, Paris, September, 1966.
Reproduced in I14, No. 20.

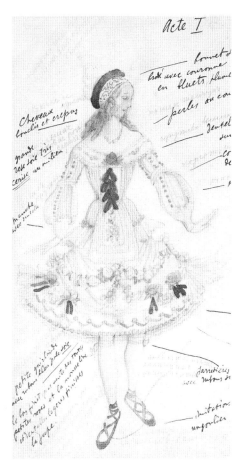

98

99

99 [20; R91].
Hunting Costume Design for the Duchess, ca. 1921.
Gouache, pencil, and gold paint.
Stamped signature lower right: "Bakst."
24⅞ x 18⅞ in., 63 x 48 cm.
Provenance: the artist's niece, Bertha Tsipkevitch, Paris, September, 1966.
Reproduced in I14, No. 22; I117, p. 373.

100 [21; R92].
Costume Design for Prince Charming at Court, ca. 1921.
Gouache, pencil, and gold and silver paint.
Stamped signature lower right: "Bakst."
24⅞ x 18⅞ in., 63 x 48 cm.
Provenance: the artist's niece, Bertha Tsipkevitch, Paris, September, 1966.
Reproduced in I14, No. 23; I117, p. 373.

100

101

103

102

101 [R93].
Costume Design for One of the Queen's Guards, ca. 1921.
Gouache, pencil, and gold and silver paint.
Stamped signature lower right: "Bakst."
19⅝ x 13 in., 50 x 33 cm.
Provenance: the artist's niece, Bertha Tsipkevitch, Paris, September, 1966.
Reproduced in I14, No. 21.

Note: For the 1921 production Diaghilev had hoped to use Alexandre Benois's talents for historical evocation, but Benois was in Russia so, instead, Diaghilev invited Bakst to design the ballet. True to his nature, Bakst invented a rhetorical and ambitious scheme of décors and costumes, spending two and half months in London to create three décors and 300 costumes, drawing on his experiences of *La Légende de Joseph* (1914), *Sleeping Beauty* (1916), and the *Dames de Bonne Humeur* (1917), in particular, and fusing the most varied styles. His stage directions even specified that all the people and animals in the Castle should remain still until the Prince awakened the Princess, but the dogs, cats, and birds refused to cooperate. The sumptuous décors and costumes drained Diaghilev's financial resources and, as a result, Sir Oswald Stoll, who managed the Alhambra production, confiscated them and this led to a final rupture between Diaghilev and Bakst. However, Diaghilev did stage part of *The Sleeping Princess* in Paris on 18 May, 1922 (*Le Mariage d'Aurore*), but with sets and costumes by Alexandre Benois and Natalia Goncharova (see No. 567 [R435]).

Of course, none of this explains the date of "1922" on a number of Bakst's costumes for *The Sleeping Beauty*. Larissa Salmina-Haskell (G30, p. 14) argues that Bakst may have dated some pieces this way in order to avoid sequestration; other critics presume

that Bakst repeated some of the designs in 1922 for reproduction in André Levinson's book, *The Designs of Léon Bakst for "The Sleeping Beauty"* (London: Benn, 1923; Paris: Brunoff, 1922). It is also not improbable that Bakst simply duplicated certain designs out of financial considerations, the more so since the 1921 pieces, when taken out of the storeroom in 1922, were "found to be so perished that it was impossible to use them."[109] (For a discussion of the entire episode see D7, pp. 191-214; and J. Bowlt: "Il teatro dell'eccesso" in I117, pp. 85-93. Many of the original costumes were auctioned in 1968 (see J2, Lots 118-74) and 1995 (see J53, Lots 53-90).

Artémis Troublée: ballet by Léon Bakst with music by Paul Paray and choreography by Nicola Guerra. Produced on 28 April, 1922, by Ida Rubinstein at the Théâtre National de l'Opéra, Paris, with designs by Léon Bakst.

The ballet is based on the story of Phaedra. See No. 57 [R53] for plot summary.

102 [22; R94].
Costume Design for a Female Dancer Holding the Train of Her Dress, 1922.
Watercolor, pencil, and silver paint.
Signed and dated upper right: "Bakst 1922."
17⅜ x 9½ in., 44 x 24 cm.
Provenance: Simon Lissim, Dobbs Ferry, New York, June, 1969.
Reproduced in color in G61; B115, plate 11; in black and white in I20, No. 8; I51, No. 28; M161; N43; P6; Spencer, *Leon Bakst*, p. 150; N37.

103 [R95].
Costume with an Egyptian Motif for a Female Dancer, 1922.
Watercolor, pencil, and silver and gold paint.
Signed and dated lower right: "Bakst 1922."
17⅜ x 9¼ in., 44 x 24 cm.
Provenance: Simon Lissim, Dobbs Ferry, New York, June, 1969.
Reproduced in B115, plate 12; I20, No. 9; I51, No. 29; M161, p. 44; Spencer, *Leon Bakst*, p. 151.

Note: According to contemporary reviews, *Artémis Troublée* was one of the less auspicious collaborations between Rubinstein and Bakst. Rubinstein, who filled the title role, was even censured for her "clear imprint of dilettantism."[110]

Phaedre: tragedy in verse in three acts by Gabriele d'Annunzio with music by Ildebrando da Parma Pizzetti. Directed by Armand Bour and produced by Ida Rubinstein at the Théâtre de l'Opéra, Paris, on 7 June, 1923, with designs by Léon Bakst
See No. 57 [R53] for plot summary.

104 [NIRE].
Preliminary Study for the Décor in Act I (outside the palace), 1923.
Pencil.
Signed lower right: "Bakst."
9⅞ x 11 in., 25 x 28 cm.
Provenance: the artist's niece, Bertha Tsipkevitch, Paris, September, 1966.
Reproduced in I40, p. 43.

105 [NIRE].
Preliminary Study for the Décor in Act I
(inside the palace), 1923.
Pencil.
Signed lower right: "Bakst."
8¾ x 11 in., 22.5 x 28 cm.
Provenance: the artist's niece, Bertha
Tsipkevitch, Paris, September, 1966.
Reproduced in I40, p. 44.

Note: Ida Rubinstein danced the title role.
This was a revival of the work first
produced on 9 April, 1909, at the Teatro
Lirico, Milan. For Rubinstein's Italian tour in
1926, Pizzetti's music was replaced by a
new score by Arthur Honegger.

La Nuit Ensorcelée: *ballet in two tableaux*
with book by Léon Bakst set to the music of
Frédéric Chopin adapted by Emile Vuillermoz
and orchestrated by Louis Aubert. Produced
at the Théâtre de l'Opéra, Paris, on 19 July,
1923, with choreography by Leo Staats and
designs by Léon Bakst.
The scene is set in Paris in the 1850s
where, in a dream, two little girls find a
magnificent doll — the Fairy Queen.

106 [NIRE].
Preliminary Stage Design, 1923.
Pencil on paper squared out for enlargement
Signed lower right: "Bakst."
6 x 10¾ in., 15.5 x 27 cm.
Provenance: the artist's niece, Bertha
Tsipkevitch, Paris, September, 1966.
Reproduced in I40, p. 44.

107 [R96].
Portrait of Prince Vladimir Argutinsky-
Dolgorukov, 1923.
Pen and ink.
Signed and dated lower right in Russian:
"Bakst 1923."
6 x 6 in., 15.5 x 15.5 cm.
Provenance: the artist's niece, Bertha
Tsipkevitch, Paris, February, 1969.
Reproduced in I20, p. 59.

Note: Prince Vladimir Ivanovich Argutinsky-
Dolgorukov (1874-1941), an esthete,

104

105

107

106

collector, and balletomane, a "true *grand seigneur* with charming manners,"[111] was close to the World of Art associates, especially Bakst, Benois, Diaghilev, and Somov. Morally and materially, he contributed to the establishment of the Ballets Russes in Paris and, in 1910, helped save the season by countersigning a bill for 10,000 French francs.[112] Argutinsky-Dolgorukov was a favorite subject for the World of Art artists, who liked to satirize this easy-going, affable aristocrat — (cf. Benois's 1909 sketch of him in the RM; also see No. 304 [R273]).

75. Letter from Léon Bakst to Pavel Ettinger dated 15 September 1910. Quoted in Pruzhan, *Bakst* (1975), p. 135.
76. Letter from Bakst to Anna Ostroumova-Lebedeva dated 12 November 1910. *Ibid*, p. 135.
77. Henri Ghéon writing on *Schéhérazade* in 1910. Quoted in F16, p. 88.
78. L. Bakst: "L.S. Bakst o sovremennom teatre. Nikto v teatre bolshe ne khochet slushat, a khochet videt" in *Peterburgskaia gazeta* , SP, 1915, 21 January.
79. L. Bakst: "Futurizm i klassitsizm" in H1, 1922, No. 7, p. 10.
80. Letter from Léon Bakst to Liubov Gritsenko (Liubov Bakst) dated 17 June 1913. Quoted in Pruzhan, *Bakst* (1975), p. 185.
81. A. Pleshcheev: "Dovolno (Pamiati Baksta)" in *Teatr-iskusstvo-ekran* , Paris, 1925, January, p. 11.
82. Letter from Léon Bakst to Vladimir Teliakovsky dated 11 April, 1902. Quoted in Pruzhan, *Bakst* (1975), p. 60.
83. Yu. Beliaev: "'Ippolit" in *Novoe vremia* , SP, 1902, 16 October.
84. Two of these, of 1905 and 1906, in the State Literary Museum, Moscow, are reproduced in I. Andronnikov, et al. (eds.): *Pamiatniki kultury. Novye otkrytiia. Ezhegodnik 1978*, L: Nauka, 1979, pp. 95, 96. A third, in the collection of the Ashmolean Museum, Oxford, is reproduced as plate 1 in G30.
85. A. Bely: "Bakst," Andronnikov et al., *Pamiatniki kultury*, op. cit., p. 97.
86. "Ida Rubinshtein o sebe" in *Solntse Rossii* , SP, 1913, No. 25, p. 12.
87. Newspaper report of the time. Quoted in D19, Vol. 1, p. 69, where neither author, nor source are given.
88. F7, p. 230. Also see Benois' article on toys, i.e., "Igrushki" in *Apollon*, SP, 1912, No. 2, pp. 49-54.
89. P. Buchkin: *O tom, chto v pamiati*, L: Khudozhnik RSFSR, 1963, p. 93.
90. F6, pp. 43-44.
91. F6. For contextual commentary see D35.
92. Bakst converted to Lutheranism, and not, as is often assumed, to Orthodoxy. See letter from Alexandre Benois to Walter Nouvel dated 31 May, 1903 in RGALi, f. 938, op. 1, ed. khr. 46, l. 130.
93. Letter from Léon Bakst to Sergei Diaghilev dated 28 April 1911. Quoted in Pruzhan, *Bakst* (1975), p. 130.
94. F54, Vol. 2, p. 510.
95. Quoted in Spencer, *Leon Bakst*, p. 59.
96. "Ida Rubinshtein o sebe," op. cit.
97. Ya. Tugendkhold: "Russkii balet v Parizhe" in *Apollon* , 1910, No. 8, p. 70.
98. A. Levinson: *Staryi i novyi balet*, P: Svobodnoe iskusstvo, N.D. p. 40.
99. D19, Vol. 1, p. 365.
100. D11, pp. 52-53.
101. For example, Philippe Jullian, a leading historian of Symbolism, felt that the alleged success of *Le Martyre de Saint-Sébastien* "went to the designer, then at the height of his career" (quoted in Spencer, *Leon Bakst*, p. 141).
102. A. Lunacharsky: "Parizhskie pisma. Misteriia o muchenichestve sv. Sebastiana" in *Teatr i iskusstvo*, SP, 1911, 10 July.
103. D88, p. 167. For more information on Trukhanova and *La Péri*, see L. Garafola: "Soloists Abroad: The Pre-War Careers of Natalia Trouhanova and Ida Rubinstein" in B183, No. 2, pp. 7-39.
104. Ibid., l. 199.
105. Commentary (edited) by Nina Lobanov-Rostovsky to the auction catalog for Sotheby's: *Russian Art*, London, 12th June, 2007, p. 126.
106. D7, p. 58.
107. Letter from Bakst to D'Annunzio dated 7 April, 1913. Quoted from A. Maver Lo Gatto), ed.: "Otto lettere inedite di Léon Bakst a D'Annunzio" in *Quaderni del Vittoriale*, Milan, 1978, No. 7, January-February, p. 59. Bakst also referred to her as "un être fabuleux" (letter dated 29 July, 1911; ibid., p. 56).
108. *New York Evening World*, New York, 2 September, 1916. Quoted in D. Vaughan, "Further Annals of the Sleeping Beauty: Anna Pavlova 1916" in *Ballet Review*, New York, 1969, Vol. 3, No. 2.
109. D7, p. 229.
110. N. Zborovsky: "Teatr M.N. Kuznetsovoi" in *Teatr i zhizn*, Berlin, 1922, May, No. 10, p. 15.
111. D11, p. 6.
112. Baron Dmitrii Gunzburg and Diaghilev also cosigned the bill. See D12, p. 216.

BARANOFF-ROSSINÉ, Vladimir Davidovich (Shulim-Volf Leib Baranov)

Born 1 (13) January, 1888, Bolshaia Lepetikha, near Kherson, Ukraine; died 25 January, 1944, Auschwitz, Germany.

1908 graduated from the Odessa Art Institute; moved to St. Petersburg, enrolling in IAA; 1907-08 under the name L.D. Baranov contributed to the "Wreath-Stephanos" exhibition in Moscow, and in 1908 to the "Link" in Kiev; 1910 moved to Paris; adopted an alias Daniel Rossiné, coined from Don Quixote's horse Rocinante; 1910-14 lived in the artists' colony La Ruche, moving closely with Natan Altman, Alexander Archipenko, Marc Chagall, Jacques Lipshitz, and other radical artists; also in touch with Hans Arp, Robert and Sonia Delaunay, Fernand Léger, and Amedeo Modigliani; 1911 onwards contributed regularly to Paris exhibitions, including the "Salon des Indépendants"; 1913 created the sculpture *Symphony No. 1*; 1914, interested in the color-sound theories of Alexander Skriabin; 1910s elaborated and then built his so-called Optophone; a synesthetic machine in which each key corresponded to a particular color, producing sounds, colored lights, and patterns simultaneously; 1915-17 lived in Scandinavia; 1917 returned to Russia; taught at the Petrograd Svomas; 1918 helped decorate Petrograd for the first anniversary of the October Revolution; contributed to the "World of Art" exhibition; close to the Jewish Society for the Promotion of the Arts in Moscow; 1919 contributed to the "First State Free Art Exhibition" in Petrograd; 1922 taught at the Moscow Vkhutemas; associated with Inkhuk and GAKhN; 1923-34 played chromatic music on the Optophone at Vsevolod Meierkhold's Theater of Revolution and at the Bolshoi Theater; also played music by Grieg, Rachmaninoff, and Wagner, projecting corresponding colors onto a screen; 1925 emigrated to Paris; 1930s invented instruments for determining the quality of precious stones; invented the pattern of the military camouflage uniform, predating its "official inventor" Georges Braque.

Bibliography
J.-C. and V. Marcadé: *Vladimir Baranoff-Rossiné.* Catalog of exhibition at the Galerie Jean Chauvelin, Paris, 1970.
V. Wilson: *Vladimir Baranoff-Rossiné.* Catalog of exhibition at the Rutland Gallery, London, 1970.
J. Leymarie et al.: *Baranoff-Rossiné.* Catalog of exhibition at the Musée National d'Art Moderne, Paris, 1972-73.
J.-C. Marcadé and A. Weber: *Wladimir Baranoff-Rossiné.* Catalog of exhibition at the Galerie Brusberg, Berlin, 1983.
H34, pp. 118, 119.
H51, passim.
J.-C. Marcadé and V. Kruglov: *Baranov-Rossiné*, M: Trilistnik, 2002.
A. Sarabianov: *Vladimir Baranov-Rossine*, M: Trilistnik, 2002.
A. Shatskikh and N. Avtonomova: *Vladimir Baranov-Rossine*. Catalog of exhibition at the GMII, 2007.

Along with Altman and Archipenko, Baranoff-Rossiné was one of the many Russian and East European expatriates who lived and worked in France before and after the First World War. Some of them were Jewish, hailing from the Ukraine and Belorussia, who found an ethnic haven in the cosmopolitan Paris after the racial and social discriminations which Russian institutions (not least, the Academy of Fine Arts in St. Petersburg) often imposed upon their aspirants. Residing abroad, therefore, Baranoff-Rossiné acquainted himself with the latest artistic trends, especially "Cézannism", Cubism, Futurism, and Orphism, which, naturally, informed his esthetic vocabulary. However, from the earliest days, a distinguishing feature of Baranoff-Rossiné's compositions was the emphasis on rhythm and on a sinuous, "melodic" line which is often more reminiscent of the Symbolist concern with rhythm as the essential, synthetic, and cohesive foundation of life. In turn, Baranoff-Rossiné often referred to music in his pictures and sculptures, both in the harmonious organization of the painted surface (as in *Samovar,* 1916) and in the titles of works (e.g. *Symphony No. 1,* 1913, or *Song of Songs,* 1920). After all, one of Baranoff-Rossiné's more celebrated achievements was his construction of the Optophone, which, following the observations of Vasilii Kandinsky and Scriabin on the potential correlations of certain colors with certain sounds, "played" a double discipline of color-sound, prefiguring the bolder experiments of Boris Bilinsky with his "musique en couleurs" and Leopold Stokowski and Walt Disney with their *Fantasia.* In transcending the traditional perimeters of the arts, Baranoff-Rossiné seemed to take a particular delight in "combining the uncombinable."[113]

108

108 [23; NIRE].
Stage Design on the Theme of The Birth of Venus, 1917.
Gouache, watercolor, black ink, and pencil.
Signed with initials lower right.
19¾ x 25⅝in., 50 x 65cm.
Other inscriptions: verso carries stamp of authentication signed by the artist's wife and with the artist's archival reference number: "233."
Provenance: *The Russian Sale,* London: Bonhams, 24 November, 2008, Lot 67 (reproduced).
Reproduced in: Marcadé and Kruglov, *Baranov-Rossine,* p. 117; Sarabianov, *Vladimir Baranov-Rossine,* p.149.

Note: A studio painter and occasional sculptor, Baranoff-Rossiné rarely ventured into the theater, although he was involved in the open-air agit-decorations for Petrograd and gave public performances of his Optophone at the Theater of the Revolution, the Bolshoi Theater, and the Russian Academy of Artistic Sciences in Moscow. *Stage Design on the Theme of The Birth of Venus*, therefore, is an unusual piece in the artist's repertoire, and its theatrical destination and function are unclear. True, Baranoff-Rossiné did produce a similar *Jugendstil* exercise, also dated 1917, for what seems to be a drop curtain[114] (reminiscent of Alexander Golovin's sumptuous decorations for Mikhail Lermontov's *Masquerade* at the Alexandrinsky Theater, Petrograd, of the same year) , but such theatrical sallies were rare and Baranoff-Rossiné seems never to have designed the sets and costumes for an actual production. On the one hand, with its swirling, effervescent mix of peacocks, swans, feathers and arbors, *Stage Design on the Theme of The Birth of Venus*, pays homage to the *fin de siècle* vocabulary of artists such as Thorn Prikker and Jan Toorop; on the other,

the reference to Botticelli's *Venus* reminds us of Baranoff-Rossiné's own fascination with the amorous principle, reflected in his rich interpretations of Adam and Eve in the Garden of Eden. As he declared in 1931: "Il faut faire sur le papier ou la toile les choses qu'il est impossible de construire dans la nature. C'est là l'art authentique."[115]

113. Sarabianov, *Vladimir Baranov-Rossine*, p. 62.
114. For a color reproduction see Sarabianov: *Vladimir Baranov-Rossine*, p. 147.
115. Statement by Baranoff-Rossiné dated 5 April, 1931. Quoted in J.-C. Marcadé: "Baranov-Rossiné: L'Inventeur" in *Wladimir Baranov-Rossiné. Sonderdruck aus Brusberg Berichte*, Berlin, 1983, August, No. 29, p. 1.

BEKHTEEV, Vladimir Georgievich

Born 3 (15) April, 1878, Moscow, Russia; died 21 June, 1971, Moscow, Russia.

1894-95 attended the Nicholas Cavalry Academy, St. Petersburg, graduating as a lieutenant; 1901 took private art lessons with Yan Tsionglinsky (Jan Ciągliński); 1902-05 attended Heinrich Knirr's studio in Munich; 1905 contributed to the "New Society of Artists" in St. Petersburg; 1906 lived in Paris; 1906-08 travelled in France, Italy, Tunis; 1909 joined the Neue Künstlervereinigung in Munich; 1910 contributed to the "Jack of Diamonds" exhibition, Moscow; 1911 joined the Blaue Reiter group; with Alexej Jawlensky joint exhibition at the Barmer Ruhmeshalle, Barmer; 1912-13 exhibited with Der Sturm, Berlin; until 1914 lived in Europe, before returning to Russia for mobilization; 1917 enlisted in the Red Army; member of the Department for the Pre-

servation of Monuments and Antiquities in Moscow; 1921 became artistic director of the First State Circus, Moscow, designing many spectacles for it; early 1920s turned increasing attention to book design; 1925 contributed to the "Exposition Internationale des Arts Décoratifs" in Paris; late 1920s-40s concentrated on book design and illustration, working on a cycle of illustrations for Mikhail Lermontov's *Hero of Our Time* and for translations of Western classics for the Academia publishing-house; 1939-45 evacuated to Shymkent in Kazakhstan; 1945 returned to Moscow; 1950s returned to studio painting; 1961-64 one-man exhibitions in Moscow.

Bibliography
E. Tager: "V.G. Bekhteev" in *Iskusstvo knigi*, M, 1967, No. 4, pp. 98-106.
D. Kogan: *Vladimir Bekhteev*, M: Sovetskii khudozhnik, 1977.
D. Kogan: *Vladimir Georgievich Bekhteev*. Catalog of exhibition, M: Union of Artists of the USSR, 1970.
I. Galeev: *Vladimir Bekhteev*. Catalog of exhibition at Art-Divage, M, 2005.
Publications dealing with the Blaue Reiter group in Munich often carry references to Bekhteev and his work. See, for example, H. von Tavel et al.: *Der Blaue Reiter*. Catalog of exhibition at the Kunstmuseum, Bern, 1987, passim.

Many artists of the Russian avant-garde were attracted to the circus as an "alternative space", which, even if governed by its own canons and conventions, encompassed conditions that were distant from the cultures of the traditional theater and the studio painting. In the circus the "stage" was an arena open to a democratic public at 360⁰, the customary difference between performer and public was overcome by dialogue and repartee. The pyrotechnical display of juggling, the unpredictability of jungle beasts, the risk of falling from a trapeze, the outlandish antics and costumes of the clowns, and, in general, the glitz and gaudiness of the circus inspired Fedor Bogorodsky, Vasilii Kamensky, Mikhail Larionov, Kazimir Malevich, Vladimir Maiakovsky, Kirill Zdanevich, and many other artists to visit the circus and sometimes even to moonlight as extras. After all, the Cubo-Futurists were the first to welcome Anatolii Durov to their fold, — with his laughing act, his pigs, and top hats, the greatest Russian clown of the 1910s.

The post-Revolutionary theater "legalized" this enthusiasm. Established artists, writers, directors, and administrators such as Bekhteev, Vasilii Kandinsky, Alexander Kuprin, Vsevolod Meierkhold, and Anatolii Lunacharsky led an intense campaign to incorporate the circus into the hierarchy of the dramatic arts or, rather, to accept the circus as a discipline equal in sophistication to the ballet and the opera. Bekhteev, Boris Erdman (No. 457 [R1004], Nikolai Foregger (No. 511 [NIRE]), Karl Hoerschelmann (No. 579 [R861]), and Georgii Yakulov, in particular, also accepted the circus as a serious and exacting laboratory for visual

109

111

109 [R326].
Self-Portrait with Guitar (also-called Harlequin), ca. 1915.
Gouache, watercolor, black ink, and pencil.
7½ x 6 in., 19.2 x 15.3 cm.
Reproduced in M25, p. 18.
The oil painting of 1915, for which this is a preliminary design, is reproduced in Kogan, p. 37.
Provenance: Dora Kogan, Moscow, 1974.
Now in a private collection.

Unidentified production for the Moscow State Circus, 1921.

110

110 [R327].
Costume Design for a Circus Horse-Rider, ca. 1921.
Watercolor and pencil.
14¼ x 10¾ in., 39 x 27 cm.

Inscriptions: at top in pencil in Russian "Costume Design for a female horse-rider"; upper left margin in ink in Russian: "A. Gorsky at work"; the reverse carries another sketch for a costume crossed out. The reference is to the balletmaster, Alexander Alexeevich Gorsky (1871-1924).
Provenance: Dora Kogan, Moscow, 1981.
Reproduced in I51, No. 31; a similar design is reproduced in Kogan, *Vladimir Bekhteev*, p. 39.

111 [R328].
Costume Design for a Devil, ca. 1921.
Pencil.
13¼ x 11 in., 34 x 27 cm.
Provenance: Dora Kogan, Moscow, 1974.
Reproduced in I32, No. 7; I77, p. 149.

experiment, especially in the realm of the costume and accessories, and they made a vital contribution to what the Contructivists might have called the *prozodezhda* of the circus. As Bekhteev wrote in his tract, *The Circus:* "We artists love the human body, its strength and agility developed to perfection. Consequently, we love acrobats and jugglers, riders and toreadors, we love circus people in all their manifestations."[116] In this respect, Bekhteev was paying homage to an artistic vogue inasmuch as Nikolai Evreinov, Foregger, Meierkhold, and other directors and choreographers of the time were trying to transfer elements of clowning, farce, and acrobatics from the circus to the professional stage. At the same time, Bekhteev opposed the Victorian traditions of the circus costume by referring to Cubism and Constructivism in his designs, although, as Dora Kogan, his first biographer wrote, they "lacked the inner energy, tension and dynamic charge absolutely necessary to the spectacle of the circus."[117]

Bekhteev designed most of his circus pieces between 1921 and 1924, when he was also active as a costume designer for Lev Lukin's Moscow Free Ballet. What drew Bekhteev to the circus and modern dance was their spontaneous movement rather than mechanical reflex and mere gymnastic exercise (which, for example, attracted the Italian Futurists, Fortunato Depero and Prampolini). As Bekhteev's close friend, the theater critic Alexander Fevralsky, commented: "The essential material in the theater is the living, human body. Our main attention should be given to its correct and intensive development. More sharp and bold movements, more acrobats, more tricks. Take everything we can from the circus. Discount literature and 'psychology'."[118] Direct extensions of this sentiment were to be found in Bekhteev's own designs, in Meierkhold's productions of *The Magnanimous Cuckold* and *The Death of Tarelkin* (see Nos. 974-80 [R800-06]), and in Yakulov's conceptions for *Signor Formica* (see Nos. 1159-60, [R1014-15]) and *Giroflé-Girofla* — all of 1922.

112

113

114

112 [R329].
Costume Design for Two Clowns, ca. 1921.
Pencil and watercolor.
5 x 7½ in., 13 x 18 cm.
Provenance: Dora Kogan, Moscow, 1974.
Reproduced in I32, No. 8.

113 [R330].
Costume Design for a Clown Numbered 52,
ca. 1921.
Pencil and watercolor.
12½ x 8¾ in., 32 x 22.5 cm.
Reproduced in color in I77, p. 92; and in
black and white in I32, No. 9; I77, p. 149;
P12; T17; T23; T31.
Provenance: Dora Kogan, Moscow, 1974.

114 [R331].
Costume Design for a Clown Numbered 13,
ca. 1921.
Pencil and watercolor.
8½ x 5½ in., 22 x 14 cm.
Reproduced in I32, No. 10; I77, p. 149. A
version in a private collection is reproduced
in I74, No. 4, where it is identified as a
costume design for a clown called Beliaev
(identity not established).
Provenance: Dora Kogan, Moscow, 1974.

115

115 [R332].
Five Costume Sketches, ca. 1921.
Central costume in watercolor, remaining
four in pencil.
17½ x 12¼ in., 45 x 31 cm.
Provenance: Dora Kogan, Moscow, 1974.
Reproduced in I32, No. 11; J23, Lot 95.

116 [R333].
Costume Design for a Gymnast, ca. 1921.
Watercolor.
17½ x 12¼ in., 45 x 31 cm.
Reproduced in I32, No. 11; J23, Lot 95.
Provenance: Dora Kogan, Moscow, 1974.

116

117

117. [NIRE].
Costume Design for a Clown, ca. 1921.
Pencil and watercolor.
12½ x 8¾ in., 32 x 22.5 cm.
Provenance: Dora Kogan, Moscow, 1974.

116. Quoted in Kogan,*Vladimir Bekhteev,* p. 36.
117. Ibid., p. 43.
118. A. Fevralsky: "Dialektika teatra" in *Zrelishcha,* M,
    1922, No. 7, p. 9.

BELOBORODOFF,
Andrea (Beloborodov,
Andrei Yakovlevich)

Born 16 (28) December, 1886, Tula, Russia;
died 24 February, 1965, Rome, Italy.

1905-15 attended IAA; 1910s made interior
designs for the Yusupov Mansion on the
Moika, St. Petersburg; 1920 moved to
London, where Prince Felix Yusupov entrusted him with the decorations for the
Blue Ball (in which Anna Pavlova danced);
designed an open air theater for Pavlova's
Hampstead residence, Ivy House; late
1920s-34 lived in France; in Paris he was in
close touch with the Benois family,
Mstislav Dobujinsky, Konstantin Somov,
and other World of Art artists; 1924 one-
man exhibition at the Galerie Charpentier;
began to work as a *vedutista* and book
illustrator; made interior designs for the
Hotel Van Heukelom in Paris; 1930
contributed to the exhibition "Art Russe" in
Bruxelles; illustrated Maurice Paleologue's
de luxe edition *Rome;* 1934 moved
permanently to Rome; soon known for his
interpretations of antiquity; 1930s-40s
contributed to many exhibitions in Italy and
other countries; 1939 met the industrialist

118

Maurice Sandoz; 1948-53 designed the interior of Sandoz's Roman villa; 1942 designer and technical advisor for the movie *Noi vivi*; 1954 made costumes and sets for Tchaikovsky's *Mazeppa* at the Maggio Musicale Fiorentino, Florence.

Bibliography
T. Varsher: "Triumf khudozhnika A.Ya. Beloborodova v Rime" in *Segodnia*, Riga, 1937, No. 31.
Mostra personale di Andrea Beloborodov. Catalog of exhibition at Al blu di Prussia, Naples, 1955.
A. Shishkin: "Andrea Beloborodov and Italy" in *Europa Orientalis. Archivio Russo-Italiano*, Salerno, 2005, No. IV, pp. 369-84.
D. Dzhuliano (G. Giuliano): "Perepiska M.V. Dobuzhinskogo i A.Ya. Beloborodova" in *Europa Orientalis. Archivio Russo-Italiano*, Salerno, 2011, No. VII, pp. 126-87.

Andrei Beloborodoff is remembered primarily for his pictorial renderings of Rome and fantastic Italian cities, disturbing and lugubrious. Devoid of human beings, transfixed by their august geometry, and yet pervious to the elements, Beloborodoff's monuments and ruins are at once reminders of past glory and apocalyptic symbols of the ultimate transience of all civilizations. Beloborodoff was not a leading stage designer, although in the 1940s and 1950s he tried his hand at sets and costumes for movies and operas. As his biographer, Dmitri Ivanov has pointed out,[119] Beloborodoff, a fine musician, was fond of the theater, and, as a student in St. Petersburg, was a regular visitor to concerts, the opera, the ballet, and the classical drama. He also maintained a strong interest in architectural and interior design, as is demonstrated by his resolutions for the Sandoz villa in Rome, "one of his most remarkable architectural works."[120]

Les Sylphides: *romantic reverie in one act by Michel Fokine based on music by Frédéric Chopin orchestrated by Igor Stravinsky, with additional music by Alexandre Glazunov, Anatolii Liadov, Nikolai Sokolov, and Sergei Taneev. Produced by Sergei Diaghilev at the Théâtre du Châtelet,*

Paris, on 2 June, 1909, with choreography by Michel Fokine and designs by Alexandre Benois.

Based on Fokine's pas de deux from Chopiniana, *this ballet carries no concrete plot, but is intended as a balletic reproduction of Romantic engravings from the 1840s.*

118 [R97].
Anna Pavlova Dancing in "Les Sylphides," 1921.
Lithograph (61/100) after the 1909 composition and poster by Valentin Serov. Signed and dated lower left in the plate "AB[eloborodoff] 921."
11¼ x 9½ in., 28.6 x 24.1 cm.
Other inscriptions: signed with the initials in Russian: "VS" and dated "909" lower right.
Provenance: Anna Tcherkessoff, daughter of Alexandre Benois, Paris, 1980. Now in a private collection.

Note: Much has been written about the ballet *Les Sylphides*, the title that Benois gave to this ensemble of Romantic movements,[121] and both Benois and Fokine spoke of it fondly in their memoirs.[122] As far as Beloborodoff's lithograph of the famous Serov design and poster is concerned (see No. 909 [R777]), this is an unenhanced repetition of the original tempera of 1909 (200 x 175 cms.), now in the RM.[123] The poster that incorporated Serov's interpretation of Anna Pavlovna Pavlova (1881-1931), produced to coincide with the premiere of *Les Sylphides* and displayed in Paris in May-June, 1909, also carried the words "Théâtre du Châtelet Saison Russe Mai Juin 1909 Opéra et Ballet." Most balletomanes of the time agreed that Serov had "caught Pavlova's lines,"[124] and one observer even went so far as to maintain that the poster "attracted more responses in the press than Pavlova herself."[125]

Serov played an active role in the enterprise of the Ballets Russes and, in general, in the world of ballet, theater, and opera. He did at least one other sketch of Pavlova, and, of course, participated in the design of sets and costumes for the Diaghilev productions (see Nos. 910-11 [R778-79]). Beloborodoff was also in contact with the Diaghilev circle, especially in emigration, and he shared the passion of Léon Bakst, Serov, and Somov for bygone cultures — one reason for his strong friendship with the Symbolist philosopher and poet Viacheslav Ivanov in Rome. Anna Ostroumova-Lebedeva, a member of the World of Art group, recalled that Beloborodoff's architectural landscapes were "stylish, the tones were combined with measure and taste, but the pulse of life was not in them."[126] It is not known why Beloborodoff was chosen to lithograph the Serov poster in 1921, although, presumably, it was a commercial rather than an esthetic transaction, given the initial popularity of the original.

119 D. Ivanov: "Andrei Yakovlevich Beloborodov." Unpublished manuscript, pp 3-4. In a private collection.

120 Ibid., p. 15. We would like to take this opportunity to thank the late Dmitri Ivanov for providing John Bowlt with biographical materials on Beloborodoff. For Beloborodoff's interpretations of Rome, see his folio, i.e. J. Neuvecelle and H. de Regnier, introd.: *Andrea Beloborodoff. Ventriquatro vedute di Roma*, Roma: Bestetti, 1961.
121 See, for example, D18, p. 66 et seq.; D26, p. 122 et seq.; I42, pp. 23-25.
122 F7, p. 275 et seq.; F19, p. 179 et seq. Also see Karsavina's memoirs, i.e., F40. Pavlova, Karsavina, and Nijinsky were the lead dancers in *Les Sylphides.*
123 For a color reproduction of the tempera see D. Sarabianov: *Valentin Serov*, L: Aurora, 1982, No. 188.
124 A. Pleshcheev: "Vidennoe i slyshannoe" in *Vozrozhdenie*, Paris, 1935, 13 October. Quoted in F34, Vol. 2, p. 473.
125 L. Novikov: "Ya delil s nei slavu" in *Anna Pavlova*. M, 1956. Quoted in F34, Vol. 2, p. 473.
126 A. Ostroumova-Lebedeva: *Avtobiograficheskie zapiski*, M: Iskusstvo, 1974, Vol. 3, p. 122.

BENOIS,
Alexandre Nikolaevich
(Benua, Alexander Nikolaevich)

Born 21 April (3 May), 1870, St. Petersburg, Russia; died 9 February, 1960, Paris, France.

Son of Nikolai Leontievich Benois, academician and architect, and of Kamilla Albertovna (née Kavos), a musician; uncle of Nadia Benois, Evgenii Lanceray, and Zinaida Serebriakova; 1885-90 attended Mai's Gymnasium, St. Petersburg, where he met some of the future members of the World of Art group; 1887-88 audited classes at IAA; 1890 visited Germany; 1890-94 attended Law School at St. Petersburg University; 1895-99 curator of Princess Mariia Tenisheva's collection of modern European paintings and drawings; 1896 organized a Russian section for the Munich Secession; first trip to Paris; began to paint scenes of Versailles, a favorite

Mstislav Dobujinsky: *Portrait of Alexandre Benois*, 1914. See No. 424 [R459].

Georgii Vereisky: *Portrait of Alexandre Benois*, 1921. See No. 1131 [R373].

Georgii Vereisky: *Portrait of Alexandre Benois*, 1922. See No. 1121 [NIRE].

Georgii Vereisky: *Portrait of Alexandre Benois*, 1922. See No. 1122 [NIRE].

theme for the rest of his life; 1898 co-founded the World of Art, becoming a regular contributor to its magazine and exhibitions; established himself as an authority on seventeenth- and eighteenth-century French culture; 1899 onward illustrated many books including Pushkin's *The Bronze Horseman* (1905) and his own book *Toys* (1905); 1900 made his debut as a stage designer for the one-act opera *Cupid's Revenge*; 1901-02 published his *History of Russian Painting in the XIX Century*, one of several important studies in art; 1902 onward created designs for numerous stage productions both in Russia and abroad; 1907-16 edited the journal *Starye gody* [Bygone Years]; 1907 designed *Le Pavillon d'Armide*, which Diaghilev then included in his Paris season for 1909; 1911 designed Diaghilev's Paris production of *Petrouchka*, for which he also wrote the libretto; 1912-15 artist-in-residence at the Moscow Art Theater; 1918-26 curator at the Hermitage, Petrograd; 1926 emigrated to Paris, where he continued to paint, design and publish.

Bibliography

M. Etkind: *Aleksandr Nikolaevich Benua*, L-M: Iskusstvo, 1965.

G. Bernardt: *Aleksandr Benua i muzyka*, M: Sovetskii khudozhnik, 1969.

A. Gusarova: *Aleksandr Benua*. Catalog of exhibition at the TG, 1972.

E. Klimoff: "Alexandre Benois and His Role in Russian Art" in *Apollo*, London, 1973, December, pp. 460-69.

R. Buckle: *Alexandre Benois*. Catalog of exhibition at Hazlitt, Gooden and Fox, London, May, 1980.

Collection Alexandre Benois. Collection J. de Vichet et à divers amateurs. Dessins Anciens. Aquarelles par A. Benois. Catalog of auction at Hôtel Drouot, Paris, 16 November, 1984.

G. Dorfles: *I Benois del Teatro alla Scala*. Catalog of exhibition at La Scala, Milan, 1988.

M. Etkind: *A.N. Benois i russkaia khudozhestvennaia kultura*, L: Khudozhnik RSFSR, 1989.

V. Frolov, ed.: *Dvesti let semie Benua v Rossii*, SP: Dom Benua, 1994

Z. Lerman: *Aleksandr Nikolaevich Benua i Ermitazh*. Catalog of exhibition at the Hermitage, SP, 1994.

V. Gusarov: *Petergof v akvareliakh Aleksandra Benua*, SP: Iskusstvo Rossii, 1996.

I. Khabarov, comp.: *Aleksandr Benua. Khudozhestvennye pisma. Parizh 1930-1936*, M: Galart, 1997.

T. Vergun: *Semia Benois*. Catalog of exhibition at the Elizium Gallery, Moscow, 1998.

J. Bowlt: *Theater of Reason, Theater of Desire: The Art of Alexandre Benois and Léon Bakst*. Catalog of exhibition at the Thyssen-Bornemisza Foundation, Lugano, 1998; and the Museum für Kunsthandwerk, Frankfurt, 1999.

K. Azadovsky, ed.: *Rainer Mariia Rilke i Aleksandr Benua*, SP: Egida, 2001.

V. Kruglov: *Benua*, SP: Khodozhnik Rossii, 2001.

E. Näslund: *Alexandre Benois och Konstens värld*. Catalog of exhibition at the Dansmuseet, Stockholm, 2002-03.

N. Aleksandrova and T. Esina, eds.: *A.N. Benua. Moi dnevnik 1916-1917-1918*, M: Russkii put, 2003.

I. Vydrin, ed.: *Aleksandr Nikolaevich Benua i Sergei Pavlovch Diagilev. Perepiska (1893-1928)*, SP: Sad iskusstv, 2003.

I. Vydrin, ed.: *Aleksandr Nikolaevich Benua i Mstislav Valerianovich Dobuzhinsky. Perepiska (1903-1957)*, SP: Sad iskusstv, 2003.

A. Winestein, ed.: *Dreamer and Showman: the Magical Reality of Alexander Benois*. Catalog of exhibition organized by Boston Public Library, Boston, Mass., 2005-06.

G. Sternin and Yu. Podkopaeva: *Aleksandr Nikolaevich Benua: Khudozhestvennye pisma 1908-1917*, SP: Sad iskusstv, 2006 (first of three volumes).

I. Zakharov, ed.: *Aleksandr Benua. Dnevnik 1916-1918*, M: Zakharov, 2006.

M. Etkind: *Aleksandr Benua kak khudozhestvennyi kritik*, SP: Zvezda, 2008.

Yu. Solonovich et al.: *Versalskie grezy Aleksandra Benua*, SP: Palace Editions, 2010.

I. Zakharov, ed.: *Aleksandr Benua. Dnevnik 1918-1924*, M: Zakharov, 2010.

An Important Private Collection of Works by Alexandre Benois. Catalog of the auction organized by Sotheby's, London, on 29 November, 2011.

Distinguished in many métiers — writing, painting, art history, criticism — Alexandre Benois is remembered primarily as a painter of architectural ensembles and theatrical designer.[127] The numerous sets and costumes of Benois demonstrate a

Zinaida Serebriakova: *Portrait of Alexandre Benois*, 1955.[128] See No. 908 [R773].

remarkable ability to adjust the eye to many epochs, nations, and moods, a talent that he manifested early in life. Benois inherited from his mother a veritable cult of the theater and his boyhood dream was to become a stage designer. Nurtured on a St. Petersburg culture of the 1870s and 1880s, Benois was deeply affected by its passion for the drama, the opera, and the ballet, and, before his departure for Germany in 1890, he had already seen *Sleeping Beauty, Queen of Spades,* and many other productions. No doubt, these early experiences prepared Benois for his work on the one-act ballet *Sylvia* by Léo Delibes in 1901, when Prince Sergei Volkonsky, Director of the Imperial Theaters, prompted by Sergei Diaghilev, decided to prepare a special production. Benois was appointed chief designer and worked on the spectacle with Konstantin Korovin, Bakst, Lanceray and Serov, but because of an argument between Diaghilev and Volkonsky, the ballet was not produced.

Benois's real debut as a stage designer came in 1902 when he was commissioned to design the Mariinsky production of *Götterdämmerung* (presented in 1903). Although some critics, including Diaghilev, felt that the result was unimaginative, others praised Benois: "His décors ... produced the impression of true life and were very convincing. At times the spectator quite forgot that this was a theatrical 'action'."[129] Indeed, Benois's attention to accuracy of historical detail was the hallmark of his stage sets and costumes, exemplified by *Le Pavillon d'Armide,* in which he produced a splendid, encyclopedically precise evocation of the age of Versailles. Benois's success in the 1907 *Le Pavillon d'Armide* confirmed his artistic vocation and thereafter he was involved in numerous theatrical projects. Also in 1907 Benois helped establish the Antique Theater in St. Petersburg (for which he designed the drop curtain); the following year one of his designs was used for the Paris production of *Boris Godunov;* in 1909 he designed *Les Sylphides* (with choreography by Michel Fokine) for Diaghilev's first Paris season of the Ballets Russes; he also entered into negotiations with the Moscow Art Theater that led, in 1912, to his appointment as artist-in-residence (through 1915) and to his close association with Konstantin Stanislavsky. 1910 saw the Paris production of *Giselle* with sets and costumes by Benois, and the following year *Petrouchka,* perhaps the climax to Benois's career as a stage designer. But *Petrouchka* was an exceptional celebration of design, for all too often Benois tended to work as a diligent archivist, following traditional concepts of stage design, and he did not always reach the flights of fancy maintained by his colleague and rival Bakst.

119 [242; R98].
Portrait of Mstislav Dobujinsky, 1908.
Watercolor.
Signed lower right in Russian: "Aleksandr Benua."
8⅝ x 10⅞ in., 22 x 27.5 cm.
Other inscriptions: upper left in pencil: "Villa du Midi 28.VI.1908"; beneath the signature in

119

Russian: "Draw[ing] of Dobujinsky. VI.1908." Provenance: the artist's daughter, Anna Tcherkessoff, Paris, June, 1968. Now in a private collection.
Reproduced in color in F107, p. 143; M157, p. 33; M161, p. 46; and in black and white in I20, p. 58; I51, No. 71; N114; N115; *Deutsche-Russische Zeitung,* Berlin,1997, June, No. 6, p. 13.

Note: Benois made this portrait while he, Dobujinsky, and their families were residing at the Villa du Midi, a *pensione* on the shore of Lake Lugano. The portrait shows Dobujinsky seated on the terrace. Lake Lugano was a favorite vacation spot for the Benois family and Alexandre Benois wrote of it fondly.[130] Benois created several similar portraits of his friend — cf. the pencil portrait of 1911 in the collection of the Hermitage, St. Petersburg.

120 [R99].
Portrait of Prince Alexandre Shervashidze, 1906.
Pencil.
Signed and dated in Russian: "Aleksandr Benua VII 1906."
7⅞ x 10 in., 20 x 25.5 cm.
Inscriptions: lower left: "Prince Alex. C. Chervashidze à Primel"; lower right in Russian: "Prince Shervashidze painting my portrait."
Provenance: the artist's daughter, Anna Tcherkessoff, Paris, June, 1968. Now in a private collection.
Reproduced in I20, p. 60; I51, No. 213; I130, p. 121.

Note: Benois drew this portrait of Shervashidze in July, 1906, when the Benois and Shervashidze families were

vacationing in Primel in Brittany. Although Benois did not have a very high opinion of the artistic merits of his colleague, he later recalled the encounters in Primel with some sympathy, finding Shervashidze to be tolerable, if not especially stimulating:

> Later on as well, Shervashidze remained the same person of misty charm, the same 'collapsible soul' who, willingly, would submit to the opinion and will of others and would not wrestle with his almost irresistible tendency towards *dolce far niente.* This did not stop him from always being neatly dressed, from being distinguished by a great restraint in matters of food and drink.[131]

Still, Benois's and Shervashidze were very different individuals, both psychologically and esthetically, and their polemic on the pages of the journal *Zolotoe runo* [The Golden Fleece] in 1906 demonstrated the incompatibilities of their respective artistic worldviews.[132]

120

Many of Benois's designs carry detailed inscriptions regarding the resolution of this or that costume or set. Since these inscriptions are often long and of a highly technical nature, only the more significant commentaries have been included in the entries below. Benois made many copies, variants, and versions of his initial designs, especially for *Le Pavillon d'Armide, Giselle,* and *Petrouchka,* and often he omitted the actual (often later) date of execution on such pieces. Consequently, while a particular set or costume may seem to be for an early production, it may, in fact, be a later rendering — a state of affairs that creates major problems in dating and chronology. If concrete evidence for the real date of execution is lacking, the designs below have been left undated.

Le Pavillon d'Armide: *ballet-pantomime in three scenes based on Théophile Gautier's story* Omphale. *Produced at the Mariinsky Theater, St. Petersburg, on 25 November 1907 with scenario by Alexandre Benois, music by Nikolai Cherepnin, choreography by Michel Fokine and designs by Alexandre Benois. The ballet was then performed by Sergei Diaghilev's Ballets Russes at the Théâtre du Châtelet, Paris, on 19 May, 1909, becoming a primary part of the Ballets Russes repertoire.*

The young Vicomte de Beaugency, caught unawares in a storm, finds himself in the castle of the Marquis de Fierbois, a magician. He is lodged in an enchanted pavilion decorated with an exquisite tapestry depicting the beautiful, but now deceased Marquise Madeleine as Armide surrounded by her Court. At the stroke of midnight the tapestry comes to life and Love drives away Time. The Vicomte becomes infatuated with the embroidered Armide, and his happiness is crowned as Armide recognizes him as her long departed lover René and gives him her scarf as a mark of her love. King Hydrao enters, whom the Vicomte recognizes as none other than his host. When the Vicomte awakens, the Marquis shows him Armide's scarf resting

A set of 7 postcards of Benois's sketches for *Le Pavillon d'Armide,* S. Petersburg, 1914.

Odalisque

Pasha

Armide

Reynaldo

Courtier

Lady at Court

Gentleman at Court

on the clock. Observing that Armide in the tapestry no longer wears her scarf and that he is the victim of an enchantment, the Vicomte falls unconscious.

121

121 [1; R100].
Design for a Program Cover, 1952.
Watercolor and pencil.
9⅞ x 6¼ in., 25 x 16 cm.
Inscription: at the foot of the design: "13.VII. à 8.30 du soir."
Provenance: the artist's daughter, Anna. Tcherkessoff, Paris, April, 1979. Now in a private collection.
Reproduced in G55, p. 282; I51, p. 70; N91, p. 136. The design shows Diaghilev holding the curtain as Petrouchka peeps out. On stage *Le Pavillon d'Armide* is being performed. The design was a project for the cover of the catalog of "The Diaghilev Exhibition" in Edinburgh and London in 1954 (see I7) on which Benois worked at least eighteen months in advance. A similar design, incorporating No. 121 [R100], was actually used inside the catalog (on p. 12). Cf. No. 159 [R133].

122 [R101].
Portrait of Nikolai Cherepnin Playing the Piano and the Violinist Viktor Valter, 1928.
Pencil.
9½ x 5¾ in., 24 x 14.5 cm.
Inscription: lower left: "N. Tcherepnine joue avec délectation les oeuvres de son fils Alexandre, le violiniste Walter lui tourne les pages. Rue Ferou, 9 (Paris 6). Eté 1928;" lower left in Russian: "Today, April 27, 1945, I learned on the telephone about his [Tcherepnine's] death."
Provenance: the artist's daughter, Anna Tcherkessoff, Paris, June, 1968.
Reproduced in I20, p. 59.

122

Note: Benois had known Nikolai Nikolaevich Cherepnin (Tcherepnine) (1873-1945), the composer of the music for *Le Pavillon d'Armide,* since before 1907, the year of its St. Petersburg production with Benois's designs, and he maintained this friendship throughout the Russian and

French years (Cherepnin married one of Benois's nieces). As Benois remembers, Cherepnin was the first to report to him in Paris in 1907 that *Le Pavillon d'Armide* had been accepted for production at the Mariinsky Theater in St. Petersburg and that discussions of staging and choreography were already going ahead with Alexander Krupensky and Michel Fokine. Benois felt happy that "in spite of my absence, I was not forgotten — either as the author of the subject or as the creator of the entire visual aspect — I was obliged to Cherepnin for this."[133] One result of this collaboration was that Benois drew a number of portraits of Cherepnin, including one dated 1907.[134] Viktor Grigorievich Valter (Walter) (1865-1935), the distinguished violinist, was leader of the Mariinsky Theater orchestra.

123 [R102].
Design for the Tapestry, 1907.
Gouache, ink, and pencil.
6¼ x 6¾ in., 16 x 17.2 cm.
Inscriptions: on lower margin in ink: "première esquisse pour un gobelin, 1907. Le Pavillon d'Armide, ballet d'Alexandre Benois."
Provenance: the artist's daughter, Anna Tcherkessoff, Paris, September, 1978.
Reproduced in I41, No. 43; and I51, No. 35. There exist several versions of the design for the tapestry (here depicting Armide and René). One is in the BTM and is reproduced in color in G33, plate 52; a sketch for the 1909 version in the TG, is reproduced in color in B20, p. 227.

123

124

125

Other inscriptions: upper left in pencil:"Le Pavillon d'Armide, création à St. Petersburg 1907;" upper right: "L'Épouse favorite du Pasha (Madame Anne G. Vassilieva)."
Provenance: the artist's daughter, Anna Tcherkessoff, Paris, September, 1978.
Reproduced in G55, p. 50; I41, No. 35.
Anna Grigorievna Vasilieva (1874-1913) danced the Pasha's Favorite Wife in the 1907 production and appeared as one of the Harp Players in the 1909 one.

127

124 [R103].
Costume Design for Vaslav Nijinsky as Armide's Favorite Slave, 1907.
Watercolor, pencil, ink, and gold paint.
Signed lower left in French: "Alexandre Benois."
11¾ x 9 in., 30 x 23 cm.
Other inscriptions: signed a second time on the reverse and dated 1907, and a third time at front bottom in ink; upper left in pencil: "Le Pavillon d'Armide; version à St. Petersbourg, 1907. Premier rôle confié à Vaslav Nijinsky. Premier costume porté par lui"; upper right in pencil: "L'Esclave favori d'Armide, W. Nijinsky"; bottom margin in ink: "A mon cher petit fils bienaimé Alexandre Tcherkessoff pour son jour d'anniversaire, le 19 VIII 1958. Alexandre Benois"; on reverse in pencil: "Alexandre Benois, 1907 Le Pavillon d'Armide (W. Nijinsky) no. 8"; also Italian Customs' stamp in blue ink.
Provenance: the artist's daughter, Anna Tcherkessoff, Paris, February, 1979.
Reproduced in I41, No. 26; I51, No. 40; N91, p. 137; N107, p. 79; another version is in the collection of the Victoria and Albert Museum, London, and is reproduced and described in G36, No. 14; a third version is in a private collection and is reproduced in G51, plate 8; also see G22, p. 59; the Dance Collection of the New York Public Library at Lincoln Center also possesses a version. Benois gave the 1907 version a deep pink and silver costume in order to approximate a mid-eighteenth century ballet dress, but for the Paris 1909 production he changed the colors to white, silver and orange. For the reproduction of a 1909 version see J12, Lot 5.
   Alexandre Yurievich Tcherkessoff (1926-84), an artist, was the son of Anna Tcherkessoff, i.e. Benois (see No. 140 [R114]), and Georges Tcherkessoff (see Nos. 1099-100 [R891-92]).

125 [R104].
Costume Design for Susanne de S., 1907.
Watercolor, gold paint, pencil, and black ink.
Signed lower right in ink and dated: "Alexandre Benois 1907."
10 x 6⅛ in., 25.5 x 15.5 cm.
Other inscriptions: upper left, partly erased: "Le Pavillon d'Armide 1907;" upper right: "Armide, version à la création 1907 St. Petersbourg."
Provenance: the artist's daughter, Anna Tcherkessoff, Paris, September, 1978.
Reproduced in G55, p. 52; I41, No. 41.

126 [R105].
Costume Design for the Favorite Wife of the Pasha, 1907.
Watercolor, gold paint, black ink, and pencil.
Signed lower left in pencil "Alexandre Benois."
9½ x 8 in., 24.5 x 20 cm.

126

127 [R106].
Costume Design for one of the Ladies at Armide's Court, 1907.
Watercolor, silver and gold paint, black ink, and pencil.
Signed lower right in ink: "Alexandre Benois."
9⅛ x 6⅝ in., 23.2 x 16.8 cm.
Other inscriptions: upper left in pencil, in French: "Le Pavillon d'Armide, 1907"; upper right: "Les Dames de la Cour d'Armide."
Provenance: the artist's daughter, Anna Tcherkessoff, Paris, September, 1978.
Reproduced in G55, p. 47; I41, No. 32.

128

128 [R107].
Costume Design for One of the Chevaliers at the Court of Armide, 1907.
Watercolor.
Signed and dated lower left in ink: "Alexandre Benois 1907."
9⅛ x 6⅛ in., 23.2 x 15.6 cm.
Other inscriptions: upper left in pencil: "Le Pavillon d'Armide;" upper right: "les seigneurs à la cour d'Armide les costumes ont servit pour les noces d'Aurore."
Provenance: the artist's daughter, Anna Tcherkessoff, Paris, September, 1978.
Reproduced in G55, p. 47; I41, No. 33; a version is reproduced in J4, Lot 126.

129 [25; NIRE].
Costume Design for One of the Ladies and Gentlemen in Waiting at the Court of Armide, 1907.
Watercolor.
Signed in ink across the bottom of the

130

131

drawing: "Alexandre Benois."
9⅛ x 6⅛ in., 23.2 x 15.6 cm.
Other inscriptions: upper left in pencil, identifying characters.
Provenance: artist's daughter, Anna Tcherkessoff, Paris, September, 1978.

130 [R108].
Costume Design for One of the Guards, 1907.
Watercolor, gold paint, black ink, and pencil.
Signed lower left in pencil: "Alexandre Benois."
10¼ x 6½ in., 26 x 16.7 cm.
Other inscriptions: upper left in pencil in French:"Le Pavillon d'Armide, 1907"; upper right: "Les Gardes."
Provenance: the artist's daughter, Anna Tcherkessoff, Paris, September, 1978.
Reproduced in G55, p. 48; I41, No. 34.

131 [R109].
Costume Design for One of the Buffoons, 1907.
Watercolor, gold and silver paint, black ink, and pencil.
Signed and dated lower left in pencil: "Alexandre Benois 1907."
9¼ x 5½ in., 23.5 x 14.2 cm.
Other inscriptions: upper left in pencil:"Le Pavillon d'Armide"; upper right: "Les Bouffons (Messr. Rozai, B. Romanov, etc.)."
Provenance: the artist's daughter, Anna Tcherkessoff, Paris, September, 1978.
Reproduced in G55, p. 49; I41, No. 37.
The references are to the dancers Georgii Alfredovich Rozai (1887-1917) and Boris Georgievich Romanov.(1891-1957).

132 [NIRE].
Costume Design for One of the Buffoons, 1909.
Pencil, ink and gouache, heightened with white and gold,

13½ x 9½ in., 34 x 24 cm.
Inscribed in Russian with copious costume notes.
Provenance: sold by the artist's daughter, Anna Tcherkessoff, at *Diaghilev Ballet Material*, London: Sotheby's, 13 June, 1967, Lot 68 (reproduced).
Also reproduced in K86, p. 9. Now in a private collection.

Note: Writing about the first night of *Pavillon d'Armide,* Serge Grigoriev recalled that the "the only item which caused much excitement was the exceptionally spirited dance of the Buffoons, led by Rozay."[135]

129

132

133

134

135

Richard Buckle, who helped with the program notes for the 1967 Sotheby's catalog wrote: "This dance, led by Rosai [Rozai] in 1909, was the first terrific manifestation of Russian character dancing (as opposed to classical) in the West and brought down the house."[136]

133 [NIRE].
Costume Design for the Lord Chamberlain, 1908.
Watercolor, gold and silver paint and ink
Signed and dated lower left: "Alexandre Benois 1908."
14¾ x 10¼ in. 37.5 x 26 cm.
Annotations to dressmaker in pencil in French. Upper left: "12 (10?, 8?). Chancellier, Seigneur de la cour d'Armide. Cordon de l'argent en moiré azure. Maillot blanc." Right side: 84. 178. Chapeau en satin blanc de dentelles or. Col en guipure blanche. Costume en satin blanc avec application en lamé or. L'echarpe-ceinture en satin rose aux bout de lamé, ajoute or. Boutons fermés en choux de lamé or."
On reverse, in the center, signed in pencil and numbered: "Alexandre Benois No. 34."
Provenance: *Impressionism and Modern Art*, London: Christie's, 5 April, 2006, Lot 146 (reproduced).

134 [NIRE].
Costume Design for One of the Ladies of Armide's Court (No. 83), 1908.
Watercolor, ink, gold and silver paint
Signed and dated lower left: "Alexandre Benois 1908."
14¾ x 10¼ in.; 37.5 x 26.2 cm.
Other inscriptions: top left, in pencil: "12 (10? 8?). Dames de la Cour d'Armide."
Annotations in pencil to the dressmaker, mostly in Russian, stipulating colors and fabrics to be used. Top right: "179. 83." In French: "Cheveux poudrés blancs. Col en dentelles d'argent. Dentelles d'argent tuyautée posées le long du devant de

corsage qui lui est en satin rose a bordures de diamants. Robe en vierics. Jupe en soie applications en lamé or de rosets. Jupe du dessous en drap d'argent (en lamé). Souliers à haut talons en satin blanc."
On reverse, inscribed top right by Benois:"Paysans No. 24, 25" and signed on left side "Alexander Benois, No. 35."
Provenance: *Impressionism and Modern Art*, London: Christie's, 5 April, 2006, Lot 147 (reproduced).

135 [R110].
Costume Design for one the Shadows, 1909.
Watercolor, black ink, and pencil.
Initialed and dated: "AB 1907."
12½ x 8¼ in., 31.7 x 21 cm.

Provenance: the artist's daughter, Anna Tcherkessoff, Paris, February, 1979.
Reproduced in G55, p. 51.

136 [NIRE].
Stage Design for Scene 1: The Arrival of Viscount René, 1909.
Watercolor, gouache, and pencil
Signed and dated.
19½ x 25 in., 49.5 x 63.5 cm.
Inscription: on the reverse: "Alexandre Benois 1907 Le Pavillon d'Armide 1èr tableau. l'arrivée de René."
Provenance: *Diaghilev Ballet Material*, London: Sotheby's, 13 June, 1967, Lot 65 (reproduced).
A close copy is reproduced in J57, Lot 196.

136

137

138

139

137 [R111].
Stage Design for Scene III, 1909.
Watercolor, pencil, pen and ink.
Signed on the reverse in pencil and dated.
8⅞ x 11⅞ in., 22.5 x 30 cm.
Inscriptions: on the reverse: "Alexandre Benois, Le Pavillon d'Armide, IIIe tableau (même décor qu'au Ier) IIème version pour Diaghilev Paris, 1909: collection du Prince de Lieven" (Prince Petr [Petrik] Alexandrovich Lieven [1887-1943], author of D6, was a childhood friend of Benois).
Provenance: the artist's daughter, Anna Tcherkessoff, Paris, September, 1978.
Reproduced in color in I40, No. 45; and I51, No. 34; also see N107; the original sketch for the 1907 production is in the RM and is reproduced in B20, p. 224; another version of this is reproduced in C31, fig. 108; also see Etkind, *Aleksandr Nikolaevich Benua,* fib. 34 and F7, p. 101 (auctioned as Lot 2 in J15); a similar design is in J1, Lot 65, and J46, Lot 56. Benois was especially fond of this décor and applied it to many productions such as *Casse-Noisette* (Ballets Russes de Monte Carlo, New York, 1940) and *Andrea Chénier* (La Scala, 1951). Benois had even used an analogous design for the production of Alexander Taneev's *Cupid's Revenge* at the Hermitage Theater, St. Petersburg in 1900.[137]

138 [R112].
Stage Design for Armide's Garden, Scene II.
Watercolor, India ink, pencil, and gouache.
Signed lower left in ink: "Alexandre Benois."
18¾ x 24⅞ in., 47.5 x 63.2 cm.
Other inscriptions: the title "Le Pavillon d'Armide" follows the signature.
Provenance: *Dance, Theatre, Opera, Cabaret,* New York: Sotheby's, 6 December, 1979, Lot 15 (reproduced). Now in a private collection.
Reproduced in color in B115, plate 20; D16, p. 18; I117, p. 266; I130, p. 57; M157, p. 12; and in black and white I51, No. 36; N114; N165; R18; a variant of this for the 1907 production is reproduced in G31, fig. 109; sketches of the building in the background are reproduced in *Alexandre Benois,* Catalog, fig. 103; for similar designs also F7, p. 292; J1, Lot 66. The 1907 original of the set for Scene II differed markedly from the 1909 version (Cf. No. 121 [R113]).

139 [26; R113].
Stage Design for Armide's Garden, Scene II, 1909.
Watercolor and collage.
Signed lower right: "Alexandre Benois."
17¾ x 24¾ in., 45 x 63 cm.
Other inscriptions: inscribed on the reverse:"Le Pavillon d'Armide, IIe tableau.

Les jardins d'Armide. Pas de trois dansé par M. Nijinsky et Mesdames Tamara Karsavina et Alexandra Fedorova, Paris, 1909"; the same inscription appears in ink in the front left corner.
Provenance: the artist's nephew, Mikhail Benois, Madrid, May, 1968.
Reproduced in color in G61; in black and white in G20, p. 104; G22, p. 58; I30, No. 12; I51, No. 37; and N114. A version of this, minus the waterfall in the center, is in the Wadsworth Atheneum and is reproduced in color in G58, plate 35, and in black and white in I11, p. 20; another is in the collection of the Fine Arts Museums of San Francisco and is reproduced in I44, fig. 16; an undated version is also in the collection of the Republic Museum of Visual Arts, Grozny (Chechen Republic) and is reproduced in B20, p. 225. Also see J46, Lot 55. According to I22, fig. 27, this design for Armide's Garden resembles Matvei Shishkov's design for Scene II of the original production of Tchaikovsky's *Sleeping Beauty* at the Mariinsky Theater, St. Petersburg, in 1890. The 1909 version of the set for Scene II of *Le Pavillon d'Armide* differed markedly from the 1907 original (cf. No. 138 [R112]).
Tamara Platonovna Karsavina (1885-1978) and Alexandra Alexandrovna Fedorova (1884-1972) danced the pas de trois with Nijinsky.

140

141

140 [R114].
Costume Design for Armide and Her Pages, 1909.
Watercolor, ink, pencil, and gold paint.
Signed lower left in pencil: "Alexandre Benois."
8¾ x 13⅛ in., 22.3 x 33.2 cm.
Other inscriptions: upper right in pencil: "Le Pavillon d'Armide. Madame Karsavina (Paris, 1909)"; lower margin inscribed: "A ma chère fille Atichka, pour son anniversaire de 1954."
Provenance: the artist's daughter, Anna Tcherkessoff, Paris, September, 1978.
Reproduced in G99, p. 174; I41, No. 40; I51, No. 39; a variant is reproduced in G22, p. 59; another in J1, Lot 70; another variant dated 1907 is reproduced in D20, p. 90. The design is reminiscent of some of Benois's studio paintings of the early 1900s such as *The King's Walk* (1906, TG).
"Atichka" here refers to Benois's daughter, Anna (1895-1984), who married the artist Georges Tcherkessoff (see note to 124 [R103]).

141 [R115].
Costume Design for the Vicomte, 1909.
Watercolor, gold paint, black ink, and pencil.
9¼ x 6⅜ in., 23.5 x 16.2 cm.
Signed lower left in pencil.
Inscriptions: upper left in pencil: "Le Pavillon d'Armide"; upper right in pencil: "René de Beaugency en Renaud version de Paris, 1909, Mr. Mordkine (création 1907 à St. Petersbourg Mr. P. Gerdt)."
Provenance: the artist's daughter, Anna Tcherkessoff, Paris, September, 1978.
Reproduced in G55, p. 52; I41, No. 39.
Mikhail Mikhailovich Mordkin (1880-1944) danced the 1909 Vicomte, Pavel Andreevich Gerdt (1844-1917) the 1907 one.

142

142 [27; R116].
Costume Design for the Marquis de Fierbois Dressed as King Hydrao in the Land of Dreams, 1909.
Watercolor, ink, and silver paint.
Signed lower left: "Alexandre Benois."
14¾ x 10⅞ in., 37.5 x 27.5 cm.
Other inscriptions: upper left: identification by Benois in pencil.
Provenance: the artist's nephew, Mikhail Benois, Madrid, May, 1968.
Reproduced in I20, No. 12; I51, No. 38; I117, p. 269; M29, p. 80; Q24.
A version is in the Wadsworth Atheneum and is reproduced in I11, No. 19.

143 [R117].
Costume Design for the Marquis de S. in Real Life in the First Scene, 1909.
Watercolor, black ink, and pencil.
Signed lower right in ink: "Alexandre Benois."
8⅞ x 6 in., 22.5 x 15 cm.
Other inscriptions: upper left: "Le Pavillon d'Armide"; upper right: "le Marquis de S.: 1er tableau; version de Paris 1909 (M. Boulgakov) création à St. Petersbourg 1907, M. Solianikov."
Provenance: the artist's daughter, Anna Tcherkessoff, Paris, September, 1978.
Reproduced in G22, p. 59; G55, p. 48; I41, No. 42. There are several versions of this costume. See, for example, I11, No. 18; I44, No. 17; J4, Lot 25.
Alexei Dmitrievich Bulgakov (1872-1954) danced the 1909 Marquis, Nikolai Alexandrovich Solianikov (1873-1958) the 1907.

143

144

145

146

147

144 [R118].
Travelling Costume Design for the Vicomte René de Beaugency.
Watercolor, black ink, and pencil.
Signed lower right in pencil.
9¼ x 6 in., 23.5 x 15.2 cm.
Other inscriptions: upper left in pencil: "Le Pavillon d'Armide"; upper right: "René de Beaugency."
Provenance: the artist's daughter, Anna Tcherkessoff, Paris, September, 1978.
Reproduced in I41, No. 44.

145 [R119].
Costume Design for Nijinsky as the Favorite Slave, 1909.
Watercolor, pencil, and black ink.
Signed lower left in pencil "Alexandre Benois," and on reverse.
11⅞ x 9 in., 30 x 23 cm.
Other inscriptions: upper left in pencil:"Pavillon d'Armide, version de Paris, 1909"; upper right in pencil: "L'Esclave favori d'Armide pour W. Nijinsky (pas de trois avec Mlles. Karsavina et Alexandra Fedorova)"; on reverse in pencil: "Alexandre Benois, L'Esclave préféré d'Armide (W. Nijinsky) version de Paris 1909. No. 9," and Italian Customs stamp.
Provenance: the artist's daughter, Anna Tcherkessoff, Paris, February, 1979. Now in a private collection.
Reproduced in G55, p. 46; I41, No. 27.

146 [R120].
Costumes for the Favorite Wife of the Pasha and the Pasha, 1909.
Pencil.
12¼ x 9¼ in., 31 x 23.5 cm.
Inscription: the reverse carries a certificate of authenticity from Anna Tcherkessoff,

Benois's daughter (see No. 140 [R114]).
Provenance: the artist's daughter, Anna Tcherkessoff, Paris, February, 1979.
Reproduced in G55, p. 50; I41, No. 28.

147 [R121].
Costume Design for One of the Two Confidantes of Armide, 1909.
Watercolor, gold paint, pencil, and red pencil.
Signed lower left in pencil: "Pavillon d'Armide version de Paris, 1909."
12½ x 9½ in., 31.5 x 24.2 cm.
Other inscription: upper right in pencil: "les deux servantes d'Armide (pas de trois avec W. Nijinsky), Mlles. T. Karsavina et A. Fedorova."
Provenance: the artist's daughter, Anna Tcherkessoff, Paris, February, 1979.
Reproduced in I41, No. 38.
Karsavina and Fedorova danced the two Confidantes in 1909.

148 [R122].
Costume Design for One of the Ladies at Armide's Court, 1909.
Watercolor, gold paint, black ink and pencil.
Signed lower left in pencil: "Alexandre Benois."
11⅝ x 9 in., 29.5 x 22.8 cm.
Other inscriptions: upper left, in pencil: "Le Pavillon d'Armide ballet d'Alexandre Benois, version 1909 à Paris"; upper right: "Dames a la Cour d'Armide"; on reverse in pencil: "Alexandre Benois 1907 Le Pavillon d'Armide Dames de la Cour d'Armide;'" and Italian Customs stamp.
Provenance: the artist's daughter, Anna Tcherkessoff, Paris, February, 1979.
Reproduced in G55, p. 46; I41, No. 31.

148

149

150

151

149 [R123].
Costume Design for a Black Boy (Armide's Page).
Watercolor, gold paint, black ink, pencil.
Initialed lower right in pencil: "A.B." and signed on reverse: "Alexandre Benois."
9½ x 6⅛ in., 24.2 x 15.7 cm.
Other inscriptions: pencil annotations to dressmaker throughout
Provenance: the artist's daughter, Anna Tcherkessoff, Paris, September, 1978.
Reproduced in I41, No. 36.

150 [R124].
Costume Design for the Postilion.
Watercolor, black ink, and pencil.
Initialed lower left: "AB."
8¼ x 6½ in., 21 x 16.5 cm.
Other inscriptions: upper right in pencil: "Le Pavillon d'Armide Le Postillon qui arrive au dernier moment."
Provenance: the artist's daughter, Anna Tcherkessoff, Paris, September, 1978.
Reproduced in I41, No. 29.

151 [R125].
Costume Design for 12 O'Clock, One of the Twelve Characters in "The March of the Hours", 1909.
Watercolor, silver paint, black ink, and pencil.
Signed lower right in pencil: "Alexandre Benois."
9 x 5¾ in., 23 x 14.5 cm.
Other inscriptions: upper left in pencil: "La Marche des Heures"; the number "XII" is also inscribed in the hat.
Provenance: the artist's daughter, Anna Tcherkessoff, Paris, September, 1978.
Reproduced in G55, p. 49; I41, No. 30.

Note: Le Pavillon d'Armide of 1907 was Benois's first professional theatrical

engagement after the production of *Götterdämmerung* in 1903, and it was one of his most successful. *Le Pavillon* provided Benois with a theme requiring both a childish simplicity and a precise historical sense. As Fokine affirmed, each detail received Benois's scrutiny:

> The color of a braid, of a galloon on the dress of an extra which you couldn't even make out on stage through your binoculars — Benois gave much thought to these things and selected them after careful consideration. He wished the galloon to shine — but not too much. He didn't want "cheap" flashiness.[138]

The St. Petersburg production was an unqualified success especially since Anna Pavlova danced Armide and the aging but still elegant Gerdt danced the Vicomte, while Nijinsky danced Armide's Slave and Karsavina, Lidiia Kiaksht, Lubov Tchernicheva, and Fedorova danced variations in the Divertissement. Diaghilev's response — "This must be shown in Europe"[139] — prepared the way for the no less auspicious production in Paris in 1909.
Paris audiences saw a rather modified and shortened version of *Le Pavillon* with certain musical rearrangements and with a new cast of primary roles — Mordkin danced the Vicomte, Vera Karalli — Armide, and Alexei Bulgakov — the Marquis, while Karsavina, Fedorova, and Nijinsky were retained (this was Nijinsky's first ballet appearance in the West). Benois also re-examined his contribution and

succeeded in greatly improving the décor and costumes, which had been made especially for the Paris stage. In

the St. Petersburg version I had been worried by the neighbourhood of lilac, pink and yellow, and by the somewhat motley details of the décor for the second scene. These defects I now corrected.[140]

Benois did not entirely remove these "motley details" and some critics still accused him of too much emphasis on historical bric-à-brac. Writing in 1916 Andrei Levinson observed that Benois's *Le Pavillon:*

> is not the luxurious and capricious dream of the colorist, igniting the canvases of the décors with an incandescent play of colors; it is, first and foremost, the recreation of the past. The searching curiosity of the artist-researcher who delights in every typical or unusual detail… was able to create a very interesting and diverse picture, but, inevitably, from a purely painterly standpoint, it lacked unity.[141]

Giselle: *ballet-pantomime in two acts by Vernoy de Saint-Georges, Théophile Gautier and Jean Coralli with music by Adolphe Adam. Produced by Sergei Diaghilev at the Théâtre de l'Opéra, Paris, on 18 June, 1910, conducted by Paul Vidal, with choreography by Michel Fokine (after Jean Coralli and Jules Perrot) and designs by Alexandre Benois.*

Albrecht, a Duke, in love with a village maiden Giselle, has disguised himself as a peasant in order to woo her, but the game-keeper Hilarion, also in love with Giselle, is jealous and shows her Albrecht's princely sword, proving Albrecht's duplicity — for the latter is engaged to Bathilde, the Prince of Courland's daughter. Her heart broken, Giselle loses her reason and kills herself

with Albrecht's sword. The Wilis come to
Giselle's grave and she rises from the dead.
Albrecht comes and dances with her until
she disappears. Hilarion also comes — is
captured by the Wilis and is drowned by
them. The Wilis then approach Albrecht,
but he succeeds in defending himself with
the cross on Giselle's grave until Giselle
and Albrecht leave its protection
whereupon they are forced to dance
interminably until he drops exhausted. As
dawn comes, the Wilis retire, Giselle
returns to her grave and Albrecht
prostrates himself thereon.

152 [R126].
***Stage Detail for the Dance in Act II:
Albrecht is at the Grave of Giselle While She
Appears behind Him as a Wilis.***
Gouache, ink, and pencil.
Signed on reverse in pencil.
12½ x 19¼ in., 32 x 49 cm.
Other inscriptions: in the left margin in ink:
"Le dessin définitif qui devait servir de
vignette pour la carte d'invitation à la
répétition générale (laquelle n'a pas eu
lieu). Eté abandonné dans le cabinet de M.
Voirolle [name crossed out] M. Thomas;"
there then follows another inscription also
crossed out, i.e., "Je crois même qu'on en
avait tiré des preuves mais pris de dégout
pour toute la bôite de l'opéra — n'y suis
plus retourné."
Provenance: the artist's daughter, Anna
Tcherkessoff, Paris, April, 1979.
A close version is reproduced in *Alexandre
Benois,* No. 55.

152

153

153 [R127].
Costume Design for a Hunter with a Spear.
Watercolor and pencil.
Signed lower right in red pencil.
12½ x 9½ in., 32 x 24.2 cm.
Inscribed by Benois in red pencil upper
right: "Giselle, un chasseur"; lower right:
"No. 10."

154

Provenance: the artist's daughter, Anna
Tcherkessoff, Paris, April, 1979.

154 [R128].
Costume Design for Giselle.
Watercolor and pencil.
Initialed in pencil lower right.
9¼ x 6 in., 23.5 x 15 cm.
Inscribed by Benois upper left in pencil:
"Giselle."
Provenance: the artist's daughter, Anna
Tcherkessoff, Paris, April, 1979.
A version of this is reproduced in G22, p.
67; I11, p. 27. For a photograph of Tamara
Karsavina wearing the costume for the
1910 production (in the GMTMA) see D17,
p. 49. From this we can see that the

costume is a peasant dress in pale blue silk
trimmed with white silk and blue velvet.
The low neck is bordered with cream crepe
with clusters of blue and cream velvet and
silk ribbons. The short crepe sleeves are
bordered with blue velvet ribbons. A white
silk apron is attached to the knee-length
skirt.

155 [R129].
Costume Design for a Page.
Watercolor, black ink and pencil.
Signed lower right in pencil: "Alexandre
Benois."
14¾ x 9⅝ in., 37.5 x 24.5 cm.
Inscribed upper right in pencil: "Giselle";
lower left in pencil: illegible.
Provenance: the artist's daughter, Anna
Tcherkessoff, Paris, April, 1979.

155

156

156 [R130].
Costume Design for the Prince of Courland.
Watercolor and pencil.
Initialed in pencil lower left.
9⅞ x 6⅜ in., 25 x 16.2 cm.
Inscribed upper left: "Giselle Le Prince de Courland."
Provenance: the artist's daughter, Anna Tcherkessoff, Paris, April, 1979.

157 [R131].
Costume Design for the Princess Bathilde, Cousin of Albrecht, Duke of Silesia.
Watercolor and pencil.
Initialed in pencil lower left.
11¾ x 9 in., 30 x 22.7 cm.
Inscribed upper left in pencil: "Giselle, Bathilde."
Provenance: the artist's daughter, Anna Tcherkessoff, April, 1979.

157

158

158 [R132].
Costume Design for a Page Carrying a Hawk.
Watercolor and pencil.
Signed lower right in pencil.
12¼ x 9½ in., 31.2 x 24 cm.
Inscribed upper left: "Giselle"; upper right: "Les pages du Prince."
Provenance: the artist's daughter, Anna Tcherkessoff, Paris, April, 1979.
A similar work is reproduced in I44, No. 37.

Note: One of the most popular ballets in the international repertoire, *Giselle* followed closely in the wake of *Le Pavillon d'Armide*, Diaghilev's other non-Russian ballet in the early sequence of the Ballets Russes in Paris. Benois commented:

> What is the secret charm of this ballet? It is mainly due, one must confess, to its simplicity and clearness of plot, to the amazingly impetuous spontaneity with which the drama is developed. There is barely time to collect one's thoughts before the heroine, who but a moment ago charmed everybody with her vitality, is lying stiff and cold and dead at the feet of the lover who has deceived her.[142]

But in spite of Benois's designs and the cast headed by Karsavina (Giselle) and Nijinsky (Albrecht), the Paris audience of June, 1910, was not prepared for this traditional ballet — when their taste for the exotic and the barbaric had already been aroused by *Cléopâtre* and *Schéhérazade*. In any case, as Karsavina mentioned on several occasions, Nijinsky did not seem to be suited emotionally to this particular plot. Pavlova (whom Diaghilev had wanted to dance Giselle) and Mordkin starred in the New York production of *Giselle* the same year, which, on the contrary, enjoyed a marked success. The critic Carl van Vechten described his impressions at the Metropolitan Opera:

> It is doubtful if such dancing has ever been seen on the Metropolitan stage save when these two Russians were here last season, and it is certain that

there never has been more enthusiasm let loose in the theatre on a Saturday afternoon than there was yesterday.[143]

Benois returned to *Giselle* several times, not least for the Paris Opéra in 1924 when he decided to try and restore the original 1841 production. As a result, Benois made many versions of costumes and set details (as he did for all his major ballet and opera projects) and these are exhibited and offered for sale regularly (see, for example, J43, Lots 25-29). It is not known for which particular production, if any, Nos. 152-58 [R126-32] were intended.

Petrouchka: *burlesque ballet in four acts by Alexandre Benois and Igor Stravinsky. Produced by Sergei Diaghilev's Ballets Russes at the Théâtre du Châtelet, Paris on 13 June, 1911, with music by Igor Stravinsky, choreography by Michel Fokine, and designs by Alexandre Benois.*

The scene is St. Petersburg ca. 1830 on Admiralty Square at Carnival time. In the midst of the merry-making there appears an Old Showman in oriental costume who displays his puppets — Petrouchka, the Ballerina, and the Moor — who proceed to perform a brisk dance. The Old Showman has endowed his puppets with human sentiments. The next scene shows a dark room where Petrouchka languishes after being cast there by the Showman. The Ballerina visits him, but departs, frightened by his amorous overtures. She then proceeds to flirt with the Moor in his luxurious chambers. Petrouchka appears on the scene, but is chased away by the Moor. Back outside the fairground booth, Petrouchka suddenly runs through the crowd, pursued by the Moor who cuts him down with his scimitar. A policeman explains that Petrouchka is only a puppet, and as the Showman drags the toy back to his booth he suddenly sees the ghost of Petrouchka on the roof. Alarmed, the Showman takes to his heels.

With the exception of No. 184 [NIRE], items 159-280 [R133-R253] are now in a private collection.

159 [24; R133].
Cover Design for the Catalog of "The Diaghilev Exhibition," 1954.
Watercolor, wash, and black ink.
Signed and dated lower left: "Alexandre Benois 1954."
11¼ x 8⅝ in., 28.5 x 22 cm.
Other inscriptions: on reverse in pencil: "Alexandre Benois" and "Frontispice pour le Catalogue de l'Expos. Diaghilev organisée par Richard Buckle à Edinburgh et à Londres 1954."
Provenance: the Alexandre Benois family estate via the artist's son-in-law, Rémi Clement, Paris, September, 1984.
Reproduced in color full page on p. 9 of the Edinburgh and p. 12 of the London catalogs of "The Diaghilev Exhibition," 1954 (see I7).
Also reproduced in color in B115, plate 200; D13 (frontispiece); F29, opposite p. 385; F107, p. 128; G. Ashton, *Petrushka,* London:

159

Aurum, 1985 pp. 11; M157, p. 12; I127, p. 96; and in N110, p. 57. See No. 108 [R100]. The design shows a portrait of Diaghilev in the oval at the top supported by a reclining Columbine and Pierrot. The curtain is being held by the Magician while Petrouchka peeps out. On stage the Vicomte and Suzanne de S. are performing in *Le Pavillon d'Armide*.

160 [R134].
Portrait of Igor Stravinsky Playing the Piano Score of "Petrouchka" in the Hall of the Teatro Costanza, Rome, 1911.
Pencil.
Signed lower right in pencil and dated: "Alexandre Benois, 1911, Rome."
8⅝ x 5⅜ in., 22 x 13.7 cm.
Other inscriptions: upper margin: "Igor Stravinsky jouant la partition de Petrouchka à une des répétitions du ballet qui se faisaient dans la buvette du 'Théâtre Costanza' à Rome, mai 1911"; upper left: "Fokine avoue qu'il ne comprend rien dans les rythmes de la danse des cochers!"; lower left: "Il fait une chaleur d'étuve!"
Provenance: the artist's daughter, Anna Tcherkessoff, Paris, June, 1968.
Reproduced in D13, p. 51; Etkind, *A.N. Benua i russkaia khudozhestvennaia kultura*, p. 262; I130, p. 175; another version is reproduced in I20, No. 59 and I51, No. 42; yet another is reproduced in L19, No. 154. The drawing shows Stravinsky playing the piano at a rehearsal of *Petrouchka* at the Teatro Costanza, Rome, in May, 1911. This was a time when, in stifling heat, everything seemed to be going wrong, when:

> Fokine found the rhythms for the ensembles unjustifiably complicated. Benois resented the threatened interference of Leon Bakst. Diaghilev wanted the score to end on a major chord. Stravinsky insisted that it close on an unfinished phrase.[144]

161 [R135].
Receipt from Igor Stravinsky to Sergei Diaghilev, 1915.
The Russian text reads: "From S.P. Diaghilev I have received one thousand three hundred and fifty francs for Petrouchka [done] for the Russian Musical Publishing-House. I have also received two hundred and thirty francs in addition to the money I received in Switzerland from checks (for account of the three-year *Oiseau de Feu* contract). Paris. 31 December, 1915. Igor Stravinsky."
The reverse (on Hotel Edward VII stationery) reads "1350 fr. pour Petrouchka pour l'Edition Musicale Russe, + 250 fr. pour l'Oiseau de Feu à compte contract de 3 années."
Provenance: Issar Gourvitch, Paris, April, 1979.

Petrouchka was one of Benois's favorite spectacles and he returned to it as a designer and studio painter many times. The sets, stage details and costumes below are for various productions (1911, 1930, 1947, 1956, etc.) and, throughout his life, Benois continued to repeat, modify and elaborate the basic images that he had invented for the Paris premiere in 1911. Because most of the set and costume designs exist in many versions, are reproduced often (e.g., G22, pp. 63-65, I11, Nos. 22-32; I28, Nos. 16-25; I44, Nos. 19-25,), and appear regularly in the sale room (e.g., J30, Lots 60-69; J37, Lots 36-40; L212, Lots 74-83), variants and reproduction sources for the following pieces are not listed. For a comprehensive discussion of the theme of Petrushka, including the ballet *Petrouchka*, see C95.

160

161

162

163

162 [28; R136].
Stage Design for the Backdrop for the Fair,
Scenes 1 and 4, 1947.
Watercolor, gouache, and pencil.
Signed in ink lower left: "Alexandre Benois."
12¾ x 18¾ in., 32.5 x 47.5 cm.
Other inscription: lower right: "Petrouchka.
For the 1947 production at La Scala, Milan."
Provenance: the artist's daughter, Anna
Tcherkessoff, Paris, 1968.

Reproduced in M161, p. 47.
One of the visual sources for this repre-
sentation was Konstantin Makovsky's
painting called *Popular Promenade during
Shrovetide on Admiralty Square, St.
Petersburg* (1869, RM; reproduced, for
example, in A. Gubarev et al.:
*Gosudarstvennyi Russkii muzei. Zhivopis
XVIII – nachalo XX veka. Katalog,* L: Aurora,
1980, p. 192), which "delighted" Benois

(F54, Vol. 1, p. 247). It is also possible that
Benois knew Andrei Popov's *Balagans in
Tula* (1868, TG).

163 [29; R137].
Design for the Backdrop for Petrouchka's
Room, Scene 2, 1948.
Watercolor, gouache, and pen.
Signed in ink lower left: "Alexandre Benois."
9¼ x 14 in., 23.5 x 35.5 cm.

164

165

Other inscriptions: lower right: "Petrouchka, II Tableau 1948"; the reverse carries a pencil portrait of the Magician.
Provenance: the artist's son, Nicola Benois, Milan, January, 1970.
Probably for the 1949 production at the Paris Opéra.

164 [R138].
Design for Backdrop for the Moor's Room, Scene III, 1946.
Watercolor, gold paint, and gouache.
Signed in ink lower left: "Alexandre Benois 1946."
8½ x 12⅜ in., 21.5 x 31.5 cm.
Provenance: the artist's daughter, Anna Tcherkessoff, Paris, June 1967.
This design may have been for the 1947 production at La Scala.

165 [30; R139].
Design for the Backdrop for the Moor's Room, 1956.
Watercolor and gouache.
Signed in ink lower left: "Alexandre Benois."
10¼ x 11¾ in., 26 x 30 cm.
Provenance: Vladimir Hessen. New York, 1964.
For the 1956 production at the Staatsoper, Vienna.
See Nos. 169 [R143], 170 [R144].

166

167

166 [31; R140].
Curtain Design with Night Scene with Fantastic Creatures in the Sky, ca. 1957.
Watercolor and gouache.
Signed in ink lower left: "Alexandre Benois."
9¾ x 12¾ in., 32.5 x 25 cm.
Provenance: the artist's nephew, Mikhail Benois, Madrid, May, 1968.

167 [R141].
Curtain Design with Night Scene with Fantastic Creatures in the Sky and with the Admiralty Tower in the Background, 1957.
Watercolor and ink.
Signed lower left in ink: "Alexandre Benois."
12⅝ x 19¼ in., 32 x 49 cm.
Provenance: the artist's son, Nicola Benois,

Milan, January, 1970.
Reproduced in M161, p. 42.
For the 1957 production at the Copenhagen Opera House.

168

169

168 [R142].
Curtain Design with Night Scene of a St.
Petersburg Square with a Stage Set in the
Foreground, 1956 (Cf. No. 169 [R143]).
Watercolor, gouache, and ink.
Signed and dated lower left: "Alexandre
Benois 1956."
12 x 17 in., 30.5 x 43 cm.
Inscription on the back in French: "1er

tableau. Covent Garden."
Provenance: the artist's son, Nicola Benois,
Milan, January, 1970.
For the 1956 production at Covent Garden,
London.

169 [R143].
Set Design for Scene 4: Nightfall is
Imminent, 1956 (Cf. No. 168 [R142]).

Watercolor and ink.
Signed and dated lower left: "Alexandre
Benois. 1956."
9 x 11¼ in., 23 x 28.5 cm.
Other inscription: lower right in black ink:
"Petrouchka, rideau d'avant-scène."
Provenance: Vladimir Hessen, New York, 1964.
For the 1956 production at the Staatsoper,
Vienna. (See Nos. 165 [R139], 170 [R144]).

170

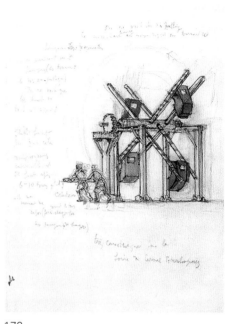

172

170 [R144].
***Detail for the Last Scene: The Showman
Carries Away the Puppet of Petrouchka
While the Ghost of Petrouchka Appears on
the Roof of the Fairground Booth, 1955.***
Watercolor, ink, and pencil.
Signed lower left in pencil: "Alexandre Benois."
12 x 8½ in., 30.5 x 21.7 cm.
Other inscriptions: lower right: "pour
Kochno, IV.1955."
A similar design at the Musée de l'Opéra,
Paris, is reproduced in color in D17, p. 67;
I45, p. 33; also see Ashton, p. 9. This
design, a gift from Benois to Boris
Evgenievich Kochno (1904-91), Diaghilev's
secretary, was used as a detail for the

production of *Petrouchka* at the Staatsoper,
Vienna, in 1956. Vienna had seen
Petrouchka with Benois's designs in 1913
and Erika Hanka had produced a version
there in 1947 with designs by Robert Kautsky
(also see Nos. 165 [R139], 169 [R143]).
Provenance: Alexandre Djanchieff, Paris,
February, 1978.

171 [32; R145].
***Stage Detail: Petrouchka Kissing the
Ballerina, 1945.***
Watercolor, pencil, and black ink.
5 x 7¼ in., 13 x 18 cm.
Inscription: "22.XII.45. pour Madame Wilson."
For contextual commentary and color
reproduction see Ashton, pp. 18-19.
Provenance: the Alexandre Benois family
estate via the artist's son-in-law, Rémi
Clement, Paris, September, 1984.

172 [R146].
Stage Detail: Ferris Wheel.
Watercolor, pencil, and ink.
10⅝ x 7½ in., 27 x 19 cm.
Inscriptions carry technical details.
Provenance: the artist's daughter, Anna
Tcherkessoff, Paris, November, 1979.

173 [R147].
Stage Detail: Samovar and Tea Vendor.
Watercolor, pencil, and ink.
Initialed lower left.
4¾ x 4¼ in., 12 x 10.7 cm.
Provenance: the artist's daughter, Anna
Tcherkessoff, Paris, April, 1979.

174 [R148].
Stage Detail: Merry-Go-Round, 1956.
Watercolor, pencil, and ink.
Signed lower left and dated: "Alexandre
Benois, 1956."
6¾ x 9¼ in., 17 x 23.5 cm.
Provenance: the artist's daughter, Anna
Tcherkessoff, Paris, April, 1979.

173

171

175 [R149].
***Stage Detail: Two Devils in Hell: Part of
Petrouchka's Room, 1930.***
Watercolor and pencil.
Initialed in pencil and dated: "AB 1930."
6¼ x 7½ in., 16 x 19 cm.
Provenance: the artist's daughter, Anna
Tcherkessoff, Paris, November, 1979.

176 [R150].
***Stage Detail: Left Side of the Stage in Act I,
1936.***
Watercolor, black ink, and pencil.
Signed in ink and dated: "Alexandre Benois
1936."
12¾ x 9⅝ in., 32.3 x 24.5 cm.
Provenance: the artist's daughter, Anna
Tcherkessoff, Paris, November, 1979.

174

175

176

178

177

177 [R151].
Stage Detail: Decorations for the Top Part of the Booth on Left side of the Stage, ca. 1957.
Watercolor, pencil, and ink.
8¼ x 10⅝ in., 21 x 27 cm.
Instructions in upper parts in French: "Tableaux ornant le hall de la baraque à gauche du décor."
Provenance: the artist's daughter, Anna Tcherkessoff, Paris, April, 1979.

178 [R152].
Stage Detail: Sweetmeat Vendor at His Stand, 1957.
Watercolor, pencil, and ink.
Signed lower left in pencil and dated: "Alexandre Benois 1957."
4¾ x 4¾ in., 12 x 12 cm.
Other inscription: lower margin: "offenes Laden mit Süssigkeiten."
Provenance: the artist's daughter, Anna A. Tcherkessoff, Paris, April, 1979.

179

181

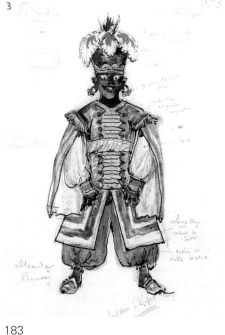

183

179 [R153].
Stage Detail: The Magician's Little Theater, ca. 1957.
Watercolor, gold paint, and black ink.
Signed in pencil lower center in French "Alexandre Benois."
9½ x 6 in., 24 x 15.3 cm.
Provenance: the artist's son, Nicola Benois, Milan, January, 1972.

Unless stated otherwise, most of the following costume designs are signed and dated "Alexandre Benois 1911-1956" and would seem to relate, therefore, to the 1956 productions of Petrouchka *at the Staatsoper, Vienna, and Covent Garden, London. Full reference to the signatures is suspended in this section.*

180 [33; R154].
Costume Design for Petrouchka.
Watercolor, ink, and pencil.
Signed lower left.
10⅞ x 7½ in., 27.5 x 19 cm.
Identifications in upper margins; cloth annotations throughout.
Provenance: the artist's son, Nicola Benois, Milan, September, 1969.

181 [34; R155].
Costume Design for the Ballerina, 1947.
Watercolor, gold paint, pen, and pencil.
Signed lower left and dated 1947 in pencil.
10⅞ x 7½ in., 27.5 x 19 cm.

Identifications in upper margins; cloth annotations throughout.
Provenance: the artist's son, Nicola Benois, Milan, September, 1969.

182 [R156].
Costume Design for the Blackamoor with a Club.
Watercolor and pencil.
12⅝ x 9½ in., 32 x 24 cm.
Identification in upper right.
Provenance: exchanged for two *Petrouchka* costume designs (an Officer of the Guards and a Peasant Woman) with Princess Maria Niscemi (wife of Prince Alexander Romanoff), New York, June, 1969.
Possibly for the 1920 production at the Bolshoi Theater, Moscow.

180

182

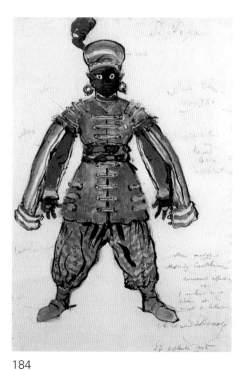

184

185

186

187

183 [R157].
Costume Design for the Blackamoor.
Watercolor, silver paint, ink, and pencil.
Signed lower left in pencil.
10⅞ x 7½ in., 27.5 x 19 cm.
Identifications in upper margins; cloth
annotations throughout
Provenance: the artist's son, Nicola Benois,
Milan, January, 1970.

184 [35; NIRE].
Costume Design for the Blackamoor.
Watercolor.
Signed and dated lower right in pencil:
"Alexandre Benois, 27 Septembre 1945."
10⅞ x 7½ in., 27.5 x 19 cm.
Identification in the upper margin; some
cloth annotations and a dedication.
Provenance: artist's daughter, Anna A.
Tcherkessoff, Paris, November, 1979.

185 [R158].
***Costume Design for the Half-Naked
Blackamoor, 1947.***
Watercolor, black ink, pencil, and gold paint.
Signed and dated in pencil lower right.
9 x 6¼ in., 23 x 16 cm.
Inscribed in upper margin: "Petrouchka,
Nouvelle version pour le Nègre"; on left
side: notes referring to the headdress
"Variante couronné en coquillages posées
sur cheveux crépus; collier en coquillages
en partie dorés."
Provenance: the artist's son, Nicola Benois,
Milan, September, 1969.

186 [R159].
***Costume Design for the Charlatan (The
Magician).***
Watercolor, ink, and pencil.
Signed in pencil lower left.
10⅞ x 7½ in., 27.5 x 19 cm.
Identifications in upper margins; cloth
annotations throughout.

Provenance: the artist's son, Nicola Benois,
Milan, September, 1969.

187 [R160].
***Costume Design for the Magician's Two
Drummers.***
Watercolor and ink.
Signed in pencil lower left.
11¼ x 7½ in., 29.2 x 19 cm.
Character and costume annotations.
Provenance: the artist's son, Nicola Benois,
Milan, September, 1969.

188 [R161].
***Costume Design for the Sad Barrel Organ
Grinder.***
Watercolor, ink, and pencil.

188

Signed in pencil and dated lower left.
10⅞ x 7½ in., 27.5 x 19 cm.
Identifications in upper margins; cloth
annotations throughout.
Provenance: the artist's son, Nicola Benois,
Milan, September, 1969.

189 [36; R162].
***Costume Design for the Second Barrel
Organ Grinder.***
Watercolor and black ink.
Signed lower right.
12¼ x 9 in., 31 x 23 cm.
Provenance: the Alexandre Benois family
estate via the artist's son-in-law, Rémi
Clement, Paris, September, 1984.

189

190

192

194

190 [R163].
Costume Design for the Merry Barrel Organ Grinder.
Watercolor and pencil.
Signed in pencil lower left.
9½ x 6½ in., 24 x 16.5 cm.
Identifications in upper margins; cloth annotations throughout.
Provenance: the artist's son, Nicola Benois, Milan, September, 1969.

191 [R164].
Costume Design for the Ballerina Who Accompanies the Sad Barrel Organ Grinder.
Watercolor, ink, and pencil.
Signed in pencil lower left.
10⅞ x 7½ in., 27.5 x 19 cm.
Character and cloth annotations throughout.
Provenance: the artist's son, Nicola Benois,

Milan, September, 1969.

192 [R165].
Costume Design for the Ballerina Who Accompanies the Merry Barrel Organ Grinder.
Watercolor, ink, and pencil.
Signed in pencil lower left.
10⅞ x 7½ in., 27.5 x 19 cm.
Character and cloth annotations throughout.
Provenance: the artist's son, Nicola Benois, Milan, September, 1969.

193 [R166].
Costume Design for the Rejoicing Merchant with Harmonica, 1952.
Watercolor, ink, and pencil.
Signed lower right in pen and dated 1952.
9½ x 6½ in., 24 x 16.5 cm.
Character and cloth annotations throughout.

Provenance: the artist's son, Nicola Benois, Milan, September, 1969.

194 [R167].
Costume Design for the First Gypsy Who Accompanies the Rejoicing Merchant.
Watercolor and pencil.
Signed in pencil lower left.
9½ x 6½ in., 24 x 16.5 cm.
Identifications and date in upper margin; cloth annotations.
Provenance: the artist's son, Nicola Benois, Milan, September, 1969.

195 [R168].
Costume Design for the Second Gypsy, 1951.
Watercolor, ink, and pencil.
Signed and dated lower left: "Novembre 6, 1951, Milan, San Camillo."

191

193

195

196

198

200

11⅝ x 8⅛ in., 29.5 x 20.5 cm.
Character, staging, and cloth annotations
throughout.
Provenance: the artist's son, Nicola Benois,
Milan, September, 1969.

196 [R169].
**Costume Design for the Second Gypsy: Back
View**
Watercolor, ink, and pencil.
9⅞ x 7½ in., 25 x 19 cm.
Character and cloth annotations throughout.
Provenance: the artist's son, Nicola Benois,
Milan, September, 1969.

197 [R170].
**Costume Design for the Old Man
(Showman).**
Watercolor, pencil, and ink.
Signed lower left.
10⅞ x 7½ in., 27.5 x 19 cm.

Character, cloth, and staging annotations
throughout.
Provenance: the artist's daughter, Anna
Tcherkessoff, Paris, February, 1979.

198 [R171].
**Costume Design for the Old Man
(Showman) Seated.**
Watercolor and pencil.
Signed with initials and dated lower left.
12⅝ x 9¼ in., 32 x 23.5 cm.
Inscription upper center in pencil: "Le Died."
Provenance: the artist's son, Nicola Benois,
Milan, September, 1969.

199 [R172].
Costume Design for the Bear Tamer.
Watercolor, ink, and pencil.
Signed in pencil lower left.
10⅞ x 7½ in., 27.5 x 19 cm.
Character and cloth annotations through-
out.

Provenance: the artist's son, Nicola Benois,
Milan, September, 1969.

200 [R173].
Costume Design for the Police Officer.
Watercolor, ink, and pencil.
Signed with the initials lower left in pencil.
10⅞ x 7½ in., 27.5 x 19 cm.
Character and costume annotations
throughout.
Provenance: the artist's daughter, Anna.
Tcherkessoff, Paris, February, 1968.

201 [R174].
Costume Design for a Policeman.
Watercolor and pencil.
12¼ x 9½ in., 31 x 24 cm.
Provenance: Semeon Balan, Long Island,
New York, 1964.

197

199

201

202

204

206

202 [R175].
Costume Design for a Watchman.
Watercolor, ink, and pencil.
Signed in pencil midleft.
10⅝ x 7½ in., 27 x 19 cm.
Costume and cloth annotations throughout.
Provenance: the artist's son, Nicola Benois, Milan, September, 1969.

203 [R176].
Costume Design for the Chief Wet Nurse.
Watercolor, ink, and pencil.
Signed in pencil lower left.
10⅞ x 7½ in., 27.5 x 19 cm.
Cloth and character annotations throughout.
Provenance: the artist's son, Nicola Benois, Milan, September, 1969.

204 [R177].
Costume Design for One of the Six Wet Nurses in Pink.
Watercolor, gold paint, ink, and pencil.
Signed in pencil lower left, and in center.
10⅝ x 7½ in., 27 x 19 cm.
Character, cloth, and costume annotations throughout.
Provenance: the artist's son, Nicola Benois, Milan, September, 1969.

205 [R178].
Costume Design for One of the Six Wet Nurses in Blue.
Watercolor, ink, and pencil.
Signed in pencil left center.
10⅝ x 7½ in., 27 x 19 cm.
Character, cloth, and costume annotations throughout.
Provenance: the artist's son, Nicola Benois, Milan, February, 1968.

206 [R179].
Costume Design for One of the Six Wet Nurses in Blue (Back View).
Watercolor and pencil.
Signed in pencil lower right.
9½ x 6½ in., 24 x 16.5 cm.
Identifications in upper margin; character, costume, and cloth annotations throughout.
Provenance: the artist's son, Nicola Benois, Milan, December, 1969.

207 [R180].
Costume Design for One of the Four Coachmen in Red.
Watercolor, ink, and pencil.
Signed in pencil left center.
10¾ x 7½ in., 27.5 x 19 cm.
Character, cloth, and costume annotations throughout.
Provenance: the artist's son, Nicola Benois, Milan, September, 1969.

203

205

207

208

210

212

208 [R181].
Costume Design for One of the Four Coachmen in Blue.
Watercolor and ink.
Signed in pencil left center.
10⅞ x 7½ in., 27.5 x 19 cm.
Cloth and costume annotations throughout.
Provenance: the artist's son, Nicola Benois, Milan, February, 1968.

209 [R182].
Costume Design for a Groom, 1947.
Watercolor and ink.
Initialed in pencil and dated lower right.
10⅞ x 7½ in., 27.5 x 19 cm.
Character and cloth annotations throughout.
Provenance: the artist's son, Nicola Benois, Milan, September, 1969.

210 [R183].
Costume Design for an Aristocratic Old Lady.
Watercolor, ink, and pencil.
Signed left center.
10⅞ x 7½ in., 27.5 x 19 cm.
Character and cloth annotations throughout.
Provenance: the artist's son, Nicola Benois, Milan, September, 1969.

211 [R184].
Costume Design for Footman to the Aristocratic Old Lady.
Watercolor, ink, and pencil.
Signed in pencil left center.
10⅞ x 7½ in., 27.5 x 19 cm.
Character and cloth annotations throughout.
Provenance: the artist's son, Nicola Benois, Milan, September, 1969.

212 [R185].
Costume Design for an Aristocratic Lady Walking.
Watercolor and ink.
Signed in pencil right center.
9½ x 6⅛ in., 24 x 15.5 cm.
Character and cloth annotations throughout.
Provenance: the artist's son, Nicola Benois, Milan, September, 1969.

213 [R186].
Costume Design for the Son of the Aristocratic Young Lady.
Watercolor, ink, and pencil.
Signed in pencil center left.
9¼ x 6½ in., 23.5 x 16.5 cm.
Identifications and date in upper margin together with character and cloth annotations.
Provenance: the artist's daughter, Anna Tcherkessoff, Paris, February, 1968.

209

211

213

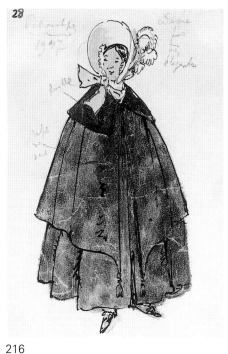

214

216

217

215

218

214 [R187].
Costume Design for the Aristocratic Lady with Her Son.
Watercolor, ink and pencil.
10¼ x 7⅛ in., 26 x 18 cm.
Character and cloth annotations throughout.
Provenance: the artist's son, Nicola Benois, Milan, September, 1969.

215 [R188].
Costume Design for the Young Count, 1936.
Watercolor and ink.
Signed in pencil lower left and dated 1936.
12⅝ x 9½ in., 32 x 24 cm.
Character and cloth annotations throughout.
Provenance: the artist's son, Nicola Benois, Milan, September, 1969.

216 [R189].
Costume Design for the Not Very Elegant Lady.
Watercolor, ink, and pencil.
9½ x 6¼ in., 24 x 16 cm.
Character and cloth annotations throughout.
Provenance: the artist's son, Nicola Benois, Milan, September, 1969.

217 [R190].
Costume Design for the Very Elegant Man Walking.
Watercolor and ink.
Signed in pencil lower left.
9 x 6½ in., 23 x 16.3 cm.
Character and cloth annotations throughout.
Provenance: the artist's son, Nicola Benois, Milan, September, 1969.

218 [R191].
Costume Design for the Old French Emigré.
Watercolor and ink.
Signed lower left in pencil.
9½ x 6¼ in., 24 x 16 cm.
Character and cloth annotations throughout.
Provenance: the artist's son, Nicola Benois, Milan, September, 1969.

219 [R192].
Costume Design for the Aristocratic Gentleman Walking, Wearing a Fur Hat.
Watercolor and ink.
Signed in pencil lower left.
9 x 6½ in., 23 x 16.5 cm.
Character and cloth annotations throughout.
Provenance: the artist's son, Nicola Benois, Milan, September, 1969.

220 [R193].
Costume Design for the Aristocratic Gentleman Walking, Wearing a Top Hat.
Watercolor and ink.
Initialed in pencil lower left.
10¼ x 6¼ in., 26 x 16.5 cm.
Character and cloth annotations throughout.
Provenance: the artist's son, Nicola Benois, Milan, September, 1969.

219

221

223

221 [R194].
Costume Design for the Country Squire Walking.
Watercolor and ink.
Initialed in pencil lower left.
10¼ x 6¼ in., 26 x 16.5 cm.
Character and cloth annotations throughout.
Provenance: the artist's son, Nicola Benois, Milan, September, 1969.

222 [R195].
Costume Design for the Man with the Peep-Show.
Watercolor and ink.
Signed in pencil lower left.
10⅜ x 7¼ in., 26.3 x 18.5 cm.
Character, costume, cloth, and accessory annotations throughout.
Provenance: the artist's son, Nicola Benois, Milan, September, 1969.

223 [R196].
Costume Design for the Blini Vendor.
Watercolor and ink.
9⅝ x 6 in., 24.5 x 15.4 cm.
Character, costume, cloth, and accessory annotations throughout.
Provenance: the artist's son, Nicola Benois, Milan, September, 1969.

224 [R197].
Costume Design for the Young Pastry Vendor.
Watercolor and ink.
Signed lower left.
9½ x 6¼ in., 24 x 16 cm.
Character, costume, cloth, and accessory annotations throughout.
Provenance: the artist's son, Nicola Benois, Milan, September, 1969.

220

222

224

225

227

229

225 [R198].
Costume Design for the Hot Drinks Vendor, 1947.
Watercolor, ink, and pencil.
Signed in pencil lower right and dated 1947.
9½ x 6¼ in., 24 x 16 cm.
Character and accessory annotations.
Provenance: the artist's son, Nicola Benois, Milan, September, 1969.

226 [R199].
Costume Design for the First Merchant Walking.
Watercolor and ink.
Signed in pencil lower right.
9½ x 6¼ in., 24 x 16 cm.
Character and cloth annotations throughout.
Provenance: the artist's daughter, Anna Tcherkessoff, Paris, February, 1968

227 [R200].
Costume Design for the Old Merchant Woman (Back View).
Watercolor and ink.
Signed in pencil mid-left.
9½ x 6¼ in., 24 x 16 cm.
Costume and cloth annotations throughout.
Provenance: the artist's son, Nicola Benois, Milan, September, 1969.

228 [R201].
Costume Design for the Second Merchant Walking.
Watercolor and ink.
Signed in pencil lower right.
9½ x 6¼ in., 24 x 16 cm.
Character and cloth annotations.
Provenance: the artist's son, Nicola Benois, Milan, September, 1969.

229 [R202].
Costume Design for the Young Merchant with Pretensions to Elegance.
Watercolor and ink.
Signed in pencil lower left.
9½ x 6¼ in., 24 x 16 cm.
Character and cloth annotations.
Provenance: the artist's son, Nicola Benois, Milan, September, 1969.

230 [R203].
Costume Design for a Salesman in a Foodstore.
Watercolor and ink.
9½ x 6¼ in., 24 x 16 cm.
Character and cloth annotations.
Provenance: the artist's son, Nicola Benois, Milan, September, 1969.

226

228

230

231

233

235

231 [R204].
Costume Design for an Officer in the Ulan Guards Regiment.
Watercolor, ink, and pencil.
10½ x 7¼ in., 26.8 x 18.5 cm.
Character and cloth annotations.
Provenance: the artist's son, Nicola Benois, Milan, September, 1969.

232 [R205].
Costume Design for an Officer in the Guards Regiment.
Watercolor, ink, and pencil.
Signed in pencil lower left.
10½ x 7⅛ in., 26.8 x 18 cm.
Character, costume, and cloth annotations.
Provenance: the artist's son, Nicola Benois, Milan, September, 1969.

233 [R206].
Costume Design for a Student in the Cadet Corps.
Watercolor, ink, and pencil.
Signed in pencil lower left.
10½ x 7⅛ in., 26.8 x 18 cm.
Character, staging, costume, and cloth annotations.
Provenance: the artist's son, Nicola Benois, Milan, September, 1969.

234 [R207].
Costume Designs for Two Soldiers Walking.
Watercolor and ink.
10⅞ x 7½ in., 27.7 x 19 cm.
Character, costume, and cloth annotations.
Provenance: the artist's son, Nicola Benois, Milan, September, 1969.

235 [R208].
Costume Designs for the Drum Major in the Pavlovskii Guards Regiment and a Young Boy.
Watercolor, ink, and pencil.
Signed in pencil lower right.
10⅞ x 7¼ in., 27.5 x 18.5 cm.
Costume and cloth annotations.
Provenance: the artist's son, Nicola Benois, Milan, September, 1969.

236 [R209].
Costume Design for a Cossack Guards Officer, 1936.
Watercolor, ink, and pencil.
Signed in pencil and dated mid-right margin "1936."
12¼ x 9½ in., 31 x 24 cm.
Provenance: the artist's son, Nicola Benois, Milan, September, 1969.

232

234

236

237

239

240

237 [R210].
Costume Design for a Cossack Officer.
Watercolor, pencil, and ink.
Signed in pencil lower left.
9½ x 6¼ in., 24 x 16 cm.
Identification and date in upper margins together with cloth and costume annotations. Provenance: the artist's daughter, Anna Tcherkessoff, Paris, February, 1979.

238 [R211].
Costume Design for a Retired Soldier Playing a Balalaika.
Watercolor, ink, and pencil.
9¾ x 6½ in., 24.7 x 16.6 cm.
Character, costume, and cloth annotations. Provenance: the artist's son, Nicola Benois, Milan, September, 1969.

239 [R212].
Costume Design for an Artisan Playing the Harmonica.
Watercolor and ink.
Signed lower left.
9⅞ x 6⅜ in., 25 x 16.3 cm.
Character and cloth annotations.
Provenance: the artist's son, Nicola Benois, Milan, September, 1969.

240 [R213].
Costume Design for a Workman, One of the Three Drunkards.
Watercolor and ink.
9⅞ x 6⅜ in., 25 x 16.3 cm.
Character and cloth annotations.
Provenance: the artist's son, Nicola Benois, Milan, September, 1969.

241 [R214].
Costume Design for a Peasant, One of the Three Drunkards.
Watercolor and ink.
9⅞ x 6⅜ in., 25 x 16.3 cm.
Character and cloth annotations.
Provenance: the artist's son, Nicola Benois, Milan, September, 1969.

242 [R215].
Costume Design for the Masks – the Devil, 1947.
Watercolor and ink.
Signed in pencil lower center and dated 1947.
10¼ x 7½ in., 26.2 x 19 cm.
Character, costume, and cloth annotations. Provenance: the artist's son, Nicola Benois, Milan, September, 1969.

243 [R216].
Costume Design for the Masks – a Coachman Dressed as a Wet Nurse.
Watercolor and ink.
Signed in pencil lower right.
10 x 6½ in., 25.5 x 16.4 cm.
Character, costume, and cloth annotations. Provenance: the artist's son, Nicola Benois, September, 1969.

238

241

242

244

246

244 [R217].
Costume Design for the Masks – a Hungarian, 1946.
Watercolor, ink, and pencil.
Signed in pencil lower left and dated "1946."
9½ x 6⅛ in., 24.2 x 15.5 cm.
Character and cloth annotations.
Provenance: the artist's son, Nicola Benois, Milan, September, 1969.

245 [R218].
Costume Design for the Masks – a Female Hussar.
Watercolor, ink and pencil.
Signed in pencil lower right.
9⅞ x 6¼ in., 25 x 16 cm.
Character, costume, and cloth annotations.
Provenance: the artist's daughter, Anna Tcherkessoff, Paris, September, 1984.

246 [R219].
Costume Design for the Masks – a Young Girl Disguised as a Hussar, 1957.
Watercolor, ink, and pencil.
Signed lower left and dated.
9½ x 6½ in., 24 x 16.5 cm.
Character and cloth annotations throughout.
Provenance: the artist's son, Nicola Benois, Milan, September, 1969.

247 [R220].
Costume Design for a Peasant.
Watercolor and ink.
Signed in pencil center left.
9¾ x 6¼ in., 24.6 x 16 cm.
Character and costume annotations.
Provenance: the artist's son, Nicola Benois, Milan, September, 1969.

243

245

247

249

248

248 [R221].
Costume Designs for Two Masks – the She-Goat and the Stork.
Watercolor and ink.
Signed in pencil lower right.
9⅝ x 12⅜ in., 24.5 x 31.5 cm.
Character and cloth annotations.
Provenance: the artist's son, Nicola Benois, Milan, September, 1969.

249 [R222].
Costume Design for the Goat, 1936.
Watercolor, black ink, and pencil.
12¼ x 9⅝ in., 31 x 24.5 cm.
Signed and dated center right in pencil.
Inscribed lower right in pencil: "Mr. Fokine [illegible]."
Provenance: the artist's daughter, Anna Tcherkessoff, Paris, February, 1979.

250 [R223].
Costume Design for the Goat (Devil).
Watercolor.
12¼ x 9½ in., 31 x 24 cm.
Character annotation in Russian in upper right.
Provenance: Semeon Balan, Long Island, New York, 1964.

251 [R224].
Costume Designs for Two Masks – the Two Demonic Monsters.
Watercolor, ink, and pencil.
Signed in pencil lower right.
9⅞ x 7⅝ in., 25 x 19.3 cm.
Character and construction annotations.
Provenance: the artist's son, Nicola Benois, Milan, September, 1969.

250

251

252

254

252 [R225].
Costume Design for the Masks – Cupid.
Watercolor and ink.
Initialed in pencil lower right.
9⅝ x 6⅛ in., 24.5 x 15.7 cm.
Character, costume and cloth annotations.
Provenance: the artist's son, Nicola Benois, Milan, September, 1969.

253 [R226].
Costume Design for a Mask – Carefree.
Watercolor, ink, and pencil.
9½ x 6⅛ in., 24.3 x 15.5 cm.
Character and cloth annotations.
Provenance: the artist's son, Nicola Benois, Milan, September, 1969.

254 [R227].
Costume Design for Three Masks – a Calf, a Fox, and a Pig.
Watercolor and ink.
Signed in pencil lower left.
9½ x 12½ in., 24.3 x 31.7 cm.
Character and costume annotations.
Provenance: the artist's son, Nicola Benois, Milan, September, 1969.

255 [R228].
Costume Design for a Boy Disguised as a Pig.
Watercolor, black ink, and pencil.
Signed lower left in pencil.
12¾ x 9⅞ in., 32.5 x 25 cm.
Other inscription: upper left corner in red pencil: "No. 105."
Provenance: the artist's daughter, Anna Tcherkessoff, Paris, February, 1979.

256 [R229].
Costume Design for the Second Blacksmith.
Watercolor, ink, and pencil.
9⅝ x 9 in., 24.5 x 23 cm.
Costume and cloth annotations throughout; inscribed "d'après Steladovsky."
Provenance: the artist's daughter, Anna Tcherkessoff, Paris, February, 1968.
The identity of Steladovsky has not been established.

253

255

256

66

257

68

259

260

258

261

260 [R233].
Costume Design for a Woman of the People,
1936.
Watercolor and ink.
Signed in pencil center left and dated.
9 x 11¾ in., 23 x 30 cm.
Character, costume, and cloth annotations.
Provenance: Yurii Annenkov, Paris, August,
1966.

261 [R234].
Costume Design for a Peasant Woman.
Watercolor, ink, and pencil.
Signed in pencil lower right.
12½ x 9 in., 32 x 23 cm.
Character and cloth annotations.
Provenance: the artist's daughter, Anna.
Tcherkessoff, Paris, February, 1968.

257 [R230].
Costume Design for the Masks – a
Troubadour, **1947.**
Watercolor, ink, and pencil.
Signed in pencil and dated lower right "A.
Benois. 1947."
9½ x 6⅛ in., 24.3 x 15.7 cm.
Provenance: the artist's son, Nicola Benois,
Milan, July, 1969.

258 [R231].
Costume Designs for Five Children of the
People, **1947.**
Watercolor and ink.

9½ x 12¾ in., 24 x 32.5 cm.
Character and costume annotations.
Provenance: the artist's son, Nicola Benois,
Milan, September, 1969.

259 [R232].
Costume Design for a Merchant Woman.
Watercolor, ink, and pencil.
Signed in pencil lower right and qualified
"d'après T…" (illegible).
9¼ x 6½ in., 23.5 x 16.5 cm.
Identifications and date in upper margin.
Provenance: the artist's son, Nicola Benois,
Milan, September, 1969.

262

265

262 [R235].
Costume Designs for Three Women of the People.
Watercolor, ink, and pencil.
9¼ x 12⅞ in., 23.5 x 32.7 cm.
Character and costume annotations.
Provenance: the artist's son, Nicola Benois,
Milan, September, 1969.

263 [R236].
Costume Design for a Peasant Walking.
Watercolor, ink, and pencil.
Signed in pencil lower left.
9¼ x 6¼ in., 23.5 x 16 cm.
Identifications and date in upper margin
together with two cloth annotations.
Provenance: the artist's son, Nicola Benois,
Milan, September, 1969.

264 [R237].
Costume Design for a Young Peasant Walking.
Watercolor, ink, and pencil.
Signed in pencil lower left.
9½ x 6¼ in., 24 x 16 cm.
Identifications and date in upper margin
together with cloth annotations throughout.
Provenance: the artist's son, Nicola Benois,
Milan, December, 1969.

265 [R238].
*Costume Design for the Old Servant
Accompanying the Elegant Lady, 1952.*
Watercolor, ink, and pencil.
Signed in pencil lower left.
11⅝ x 8⅛ in., 29.5 x 20.5 cm.

Other inscription: lower left: "Novembre 1,
1952, San Camillo, Milan."
Provenance: the artist's son, Nicola Benois,
Milan, December, 1969.

266 [R239].
Costume Design for a Cherkess Officer Walking.
Watercolor, ink, and pencil.
Signed in pencil lower left.
9¼ x 6¼ in., 23.5 x 16 cm.
Identifications and date in upper margins
together with cloth annotations.
Provenance: the artist's son, Nicola Benois,
Milan, December, 1969.

263   264   266

267

267 [R240].
Costume Design for an Athlete: Hercules Shown in Action, 1952.
Watercolor, ink, and pencil.
Signed lower right in pencil and dated lower left.
11⅝ x 8⅛ in., 29.5 x 20.5 cm.
Other inscription: lower left in ink: "1.XI.1952, Milan, Clinique San Camillo."
Provenance: the artist's son, Nicola Benois, Milan, December, 1969.

268 [R241].
Costume Design for a Tea Vendor.
Watercolor, ink, and pencil.
Signed in pencil lower left.
9½ x 6¼ in., 24 x 16 cm.
Identifications and date in upper margin.
Provenance: the artist's son, Nicola Benois, Milan, December, 1969.

268

269

269 [R242].
Costume Design for an Acrobat Show Woman, 1952.
Watercolor, ink, and pencil.
Signed lower left in pencil.
8¾ x 7½ in., 22.2 x 19 cm.
Other inscription: "Arrive avec l'athléte aux poids lourds et le jongleur. Avant et après son numero elle revêt ce manteau."
Provenance: the artist's son, Nicola Benois, Milan, December, 1969.

270 [R243].
Costume Design for Young Boy Juggler, 1952.
Watercolor, ink, and pencil.
Signed lower left.
8¾ x 7½ in., 22.2 x 19 cm.
Other inscription: lower left: "1.XI.1952, Milano, San Camillo."
Provenance: the artist's son, Nicola Benois, Milan, December, 1969.

271 [R244].
Costume Design for a Merchant Woman Walking.
Watercolor, pencil, and ink.
9¼ x 6½ in., 23.5 x 16.5 cm.
Identifications upper margin together with cloth annotations.
Provenance: the artist's son, Nicola Benois, Milan, December, 1969.

270

271

272 [R245].
Costume Design for a Chamber Maid Walking.
Watercolor, ink, and pencil.
9¼ x 6½ in., 23.5 x 16.5 cm.
Cloth annotations.
Provenance: the artist's son, Nicola Benois, Milan, December, 1969.

273 [R246].
Costume Design for the Granddaughter of the Old Countess.
Watercolor, ink, and pencil.
Signed in pencil lower right and dated: "Milano, 14.X.52"
9½ x 6½ in., 24 x 16.5 cm.
Identification and date in upper margin together with cloth annotations.
Provenance: the artist's son, Nicola Benois, Milan, December, 1969.

272

273

275

277

274 [R247].
Costume Design for the Frivolous Young Lady.
Watercolor, ink, and pencil.
Signed in pencil lower left.
9¼ x 6¼ in., 23.5 x 16 cm.
Identification and date inscribed upper margin in pencil.
Provenance: the artist's son, Nicola Benois, Milan, December, 1969.

275 [R248].
Costume Design for the Old "Battlefield" Officer.
Watercolor, ink, and pencil.
Initialed in pencil lower left.
9¼ x 6¼ in., 23.5 x 16 cm.

Character and cloth annotations.
Provenance: the artist's son, Nicola Benois, Milan, December, 1969.

276 [R249].
Costume Design for the Young Girl Dressed as a Polish Maid, 1956.
Watercolor, black ink, and pencil.
Signed and dated lower right in pencil.
12¼ x 9½ in., 31 x 24 cm.
Inscribed throughout in English, French, and Russian.
Provenance: the estate of Alexandre Benois via the artist's son-in-law, Rémi Clement, Paris, September, 1984.

277 [R250].
Costume Design for the Young Count Holding his Coat, 1956.
Watercolor and ink.

Signed and dated lower left in pencil.
12½ x 9 in., 32 x 23 cm.
Inscribed throughout in English, French, and Russian.
Provenance: the Alexandre Benois family estate via the artist's son-in-law, Rémi Clement, Paris, September, 1984.

278 [R251].
Costume Design for the Young Girl Dressed as a Kitchen Boy, 1956.
Watercolor, black ink, and pencil.
Signed and dated lower left in pencil.
12¼ x 9½ in., 31 x 24 cm.
Inscribed throughout in English, French, and Russian.
Provenance: the Alexandre Benois family estate via the artist's son-in-law, Rémi Clement, Paris, September, 1984.

274

276

278

279

280

279 [R252].
A Costume Design for the Balloon Seller and a Little Boy of the People, 1956.
Watercolor and black ink.
Signed and dated lower left in pencil.
12¼ x 9¼ in., 31 x 23.5 cm.
Inscribed throughout in English, French, and Russian.
Provenance: the Alexandre Benois family estate via the artist's son-in-law, Rémi Clement, Paris, September, 1984.

280 [R253].
Costume Design for a Dancing Fox (Fancy Dress), 1956.
Watercolor and black ink.
Signed and dated lower left in pencil.
12¼ x 9½ in., 31 x 24 cm.
Inscribed throughout in English, French, and Russian.
Provenance: the Alexandre Benois family estate via the artist's son-in-law, Rémi Clement, Paris, September, 1984

Le Rossignol: opera in three acts with incidental dances by Igor Stravinsky and Stepan Mitusov based on a tale by Hans Christian Andersen. Produced by Sergei Diaghilev's Ballets Russes at the Théâtre National de l'Opéra, Paris, on 26 May, 1914, with choreography by Boris Romanov and designs by Alexandre Benois.
The tale of the Emperor and the nightingale who enchants him with a song, but who is then banished in favor of a mechanical bird. Finally, however, the nightingale is brought back as the Emperor is dying, and she effects his cure by her song.

281 [37; R254].
Costume Design for One of the Blue Mandarins, 1914.
Watercolor, silver paint, black ink, and pencil.
Signed lower right in ink and dated: "Alexandre Benois, 1914."
18⅝ x 9 in., 47.3 x 23 cm.
Other inscriptions: upper left in pencil: "Le Rossignol, un Mandarin"; upper left blue stamp of French Customs; upper right in pencil "Les Mandarins Bleus"; another design is on the reverse (see No. 282 [R254a]).
Provenance: the artist's daughter, Anna Tcherkessoff, Paris, February, 1979.
Reproduced in Souvenir Program *Russian Opera and Ballet* (London: Royal Theatre, Drury Lane, London, 1914), unpaginated; in color in N188, p. 6; I127, p. 218; and in black and white in I41, No. 51; I51, No. 44; I117, p. 354; a design for another Mandarin, along with several other costumes for *Le Rossignol,* is in the collection of the Ashmolean Museum, Oxford, and is reproduced in G30, No. 14; the RM also possesses comparable designs, some of which are reproduced in G21, figs. 115-17.

282 [R254a].
Costume Design for a Mandarin, 1914.
Colored pencil.
18⅝ x 9 in., 47.3 x 23 cm.
This sketch is on the reverse of No. 281 [R254]. It bears the inscription upper right in ink: "No. 64, Alexandre Benois, Le Rossignol, un Mandarin."
Reproduced in I41, No. 51; I51, No. 45.

283 [38; R255].
Costume Design for the Third Japanese Envoy with a Golden Box on the Lid of Which Stands a Mechanical Nightingale, 1914.
Watercolor and black ink.
18⅞ x 13 in., 48 x 33 cm.
Inscriptions: upper left in pencil: "Madame Miamzine, No. 26"; right margin in Russian: "hairdo from velvet, black velvet"; lower right in French: "copie d'après une estampe japonaise (de Toyokuni)."
Provenance: the artist's daughter, Anna Tcherkessoff, Paris, November, 1979.
Reproduced in G55, p. 283; I51, No. 46; I117, p. 352.

284 [R256].
Costume Design for a Japanese Envoy with Sword, ca. 1914.
Watercolor, black ink, and pencil.
18⅞ x 13 in., 48 x 33 cm.

281

282

283

284

Inscriptions: upper left in pencil: "M. Charonoff"; right margin in Russian: "hairdo from velvet, black velvet"; lower right: "copie d'après Kuniyoshi."
Provenance: the artist's daughter, Anna Tcherkessoff, Paris, November, 1979.
Reproduced in G55, p. 283; I51, No. 47.
The bass baritone Basile Charonoff (Vasilii Semeonovich Sharonov, 1867-1929), sang the part of a Japanese envoy.

Note: Stravinsky and Mitusov began working on the opera *Le Rossignol* in 1910, if not before,[145] and Benois was captivated immediately by the music. Benois was drawn to designing the piece since he had long wanted to express his interpretation of the art of the Far East:

> At first I thought of keeping to the style of the *chinoiseries,* which were so popular during the eighteenth century. But as I worked on, I became rather irritated by their obvious absurdity, and my own enthusiasm for what was authentically Chinese began to reflect itself in my conception. As for the costumes, colored Chinese broadsheets served as invaluable material... Ultimately, I achieved something distant from pedantic precision, something of a crossbreed, but something that fitted Stravinsky's music perfectly.[146]

The decorative effect of the Paris production was impressive. Anatolii Lunacharsky referred to Benois's "fantastic *chinoiserie,*"[147] and the critic Alexander Maslovsky praised the artist for his "knowledge of style and psychological penetration."[148] Even so, Diaghilev staged *Le Rossignol* with Benois's designs only twice in Paris and four times in London, before changing the opera into a one-act ballet and entrusting the designs for this to Matisse (produced in Paris in 1920).

285 [R257].
Portrait of Maurice Ravel, 1914.
Pencil.
Signed lower right in pencil and dated "Alexandre Benois, 5 juin, 1914, St. Jean de Luz."
8⅝ x 5¼ in., 21.8 x 13.4 cm.
Inscription: lower left in pencil: "Maurice Ravel ayant pris son bain en train de croquer un 'plaisir'."
Provenance: the Alexandre Benois family estate via the artist's son-in-law, Rémi Clement, Paris, September, 1984.
Reproduced in A4, p. 285. A very similar version, in the collection of the Bibliothèque

Nationale, Paris, and dated July, 1914, is reproduced in C. Samuel: *Prokofiev,* Paris: Editions du Seuil, 1960, p. 95, and in Bernardt, *Aleksandr Benua i muzyka,* between pp. 192 and 193.

Note: The Benois family often used to vacation at the seaside resort of St. Jean de Luz, near Biarritz, and Benois painted and drew a number of pictures on that subject (cf. the drawing in the GMTMA, reproduced in Etkind, *Aleksandr Benua,* No. 61; and the watercolor in the collection of the late Nicola Benois, Milan). Nicola Benois recalled those summer days:

> 1914 was the last year when we could go abroad. We made a long journey to Italy and then moved to France – to Saint-Jean-de-Luz, near Biarritz, as guests of Maurice Ravel, with whom my father had to do some work. They had been friends for some time and would later create the famous *Bolero* for Ida Rubinstein. Ravel was a minute man, but affable. He lived with his mother, an old and kind lady who was very nice to me.
> Ravel liked to go bathing with me. He was not a great swimmer, but he had fun playing in the water. I still have a watercolor that my father did where you can see Ravel in a white dressing-gown between his wife and my mother while I'm taking the sun lying on the sand and my two sisters are walking towards the sea followed by Ravel's little dog.[149]

286 [NIRE].
Portrait of the Poet Sergei Esenin, Petrograd, November, 1915.
Pencil.
Dated "11 November 1915."
6¾ x 4⅜ in., 17 x 11 cm.
Benois's inscriptions in French and Russian affirm that Esenin was sporting a "style russe" and exaggerating his "Russianness."
Provenance: the artist's daughter, Anna

285

286

Tcherkessoff, Paris, June, 1964; given by Nikita D. Lobanov-Rostovsky to Ilia Zilbershtein, who, in turn, presented it to the Museum of Private Collections, Moscow. Reproduced in I. Zilbershtein: "Neizvestnyi risunok" in *Ogonek,* M, 1985, No. 40, p. 22; F100, p. 184; F107, p. 254; I20, p. 58. According to Zilbershtein, Benois drew the portrait during a poetry reading at the home of Iosif Gessen in Petrograd early in November.

The Stone Guest: *play in five acts by Alexander Pushkin. Produced by Vladimir Nemirovich-Danchenko and Alexandre Benois at the Moscow Art Theater on 26 March, 1915, with designs by Alexandre Benois.*

Returning in secret to Madrid from exile for murdering the Commander Don Alvaro, Don Juan and his man Leporello come upon the Commander's beautiful widow, Donna Anna, in prayer before her husband's stone statue, and Don Juan determines to seduce her. That evening at the house of his former love, the actress Laura, Don Juan kills the Commander's brother Don Carlos in a duel. Then, after gaining access to Donna Anna's presence disguised as a hermit, he proclaims his love for her using an assumed name, and wins a rendezvous for the following evening. In jest he invites the Commander's stone statue to stand guard outside the door of his widow, and the statue nods assent. Next evening Don Juan reveals his true identity, and, overcoming her scruples, wins a kiss from Donna Anna. At this the Stone Guest enters and grasps Don Juan's hand in a stony grip. Together they sink into the ground.

287 [39; R258].
Set Design: Don Juan Addressing the Statue.
Watercolor.
Initialed lower right: "AB."
12⅝ x 15¾ in., 32 x 40 cm.
Provenance: Peter Tretiakov Gallery, New York, 1967.
Reproduced in I14, No. 38.

Note: In 1909 Benois began to collaborate with the Moscow Art Theater and worked on a number of productions there, including Molière's *Le Malade Imaginaire* and Goldoni's *La Locandiera* (both 1913), but his designs for the cycle of Pushkin's "Little Tragedies" in 1915 (*Mozart and Salieri, The Stone Guest* and *Feast during the Plague*) marked the high point of his involvement in Stanislavsky's theater. Actually, Benois continued to spend most of his time in St. Petersburg and abroad and was rarely at the Moscow Art Theater, something that led to several misunderstandings between him and the producer Vladimir Nemirovich-Danchenko.

For this production of *The Stone Guest,* Don Juan was performed by Vasilii Kachalov, Donna Anna by Mariia Germanova, Laura by Vera Baranovskaia, and Don Carlos by Alexei Stakhovich. Mark Etkind has reported that Benois conceived the décor as:

severe and majestic: a small cemetery by the ancient walls of Madrid, the

287

stones of the tombs, the silhouettes of the cypresses rising in the blood-stained yellow sunset and, in the distance, the towers of a monastery disappearing into the setting sun… The gloomy walls of the cathedral, the enormous, marble sarcophagus and the huge statue of the Commander. [150]

Perhaps because of this heavy resolution, the audience was not especially pleased and reviewers complained that the designs had "consumed the action"[151] and rendered Pushkin's text "inaudible."[152] Benois was very unhappy about the reception of his *Stone Guest* and, as a result, proffered his resignation to the Moscow Art Theater.

Le Bourgeois Gentilhomme: *play in five acts by Jean-Baptiste Poquelin Molière. Staged by Alexandre Benois for the Petrograd Academic Theater of Drama, Petrograd, on 14 April, 1923, with designs by Alexandre Benois.*

The bourgeois Jourdain wishes to rise to an aristocratic station, ordering splendid new clothes and learning the fine arts of fencing, dancing, and philosophy The cash-strapped nobleman, Dorante, tells Jourdain that he has mentioned his name to the King at Versailles. Although already married, Jourdain dreams of marrying a Marchioness, Dorimene, and having his daughter Lucille marry a nobleman. But Lucille is in love with the middle-class Cléonte, who in disguise, presents himself to Jourdain as the son of the Sultan of Turkey. Jourdain is taken in and consents to have his daughter marry foreign royalty. The play closes with a false and ridiculous ceremony at theTurkish court.

288 [NIRE].
Costume Design for the Master of Philosophy, 1922.
Watercolor and black ink.
Signed and dated lower right: "Alexandre

Benois 1922."
11⅞ x 7⅛ in., 30 x 19 cm.
Other inscriptions: Identification in upper right in Russian: "Teacher of philosophy. A.A. Usachev." The reference is to the actor Alexander Usachev (1863-1937), who played the role of the Master of Philosophy. The celebrated Kondrat Yakovlev played the role of Jourdain.
Instructions throughout to the dressmaker.
Provenance: present from Ildar Galeev, Moscow, 2009.
For Benois's own commentary on this production see F29, pp. 104-07; and Zakharov, *Aleksandr Benua. Dnevnik 1918-1924*, pp. 391-94.

288

La Dame aux Camélias: play in five acts by Alexandre Dumas fils. Staged by Armand Bour and produced by Ida Rubinstein at the Théâtre de Sarah Bernhardt, Paris, on 27 November, 1923, with designs by Alexandre Benois, Oreste Allegri, and Georges Mouveau.

Marguerite Gautier, a consumptive beauty with a dubious past, is about to submit to the Comte de Varville's demands and become his mistress, when Armand Duval (Alfredo Germont) falls in love with her and carries her off to the country. However, Armand's father (Georgio Germont), alarmed at the disgrace the association will bring on his family, prevails on Marguerite to leave Armand. She returns to her former life of dissipation with the Count. When Armand next meets her, he challenges the Count to a duel and wounds him, only to learn the real reason for Marguerite's defection and to be convinced of her love. The lovers are reconciled at Marguerite's deathbed, and she dies in Armand's arms.

289

289 [40; R259].
Set Design for Act II, 1923.
Gouache.
Signed on reverse and inscribed: "La Dame aux Camélias, Acte II, Le Boudoir de Marguerite, Version Définitive."
16⅛ x 22½ in., 41 x 57 cm.
Provenance: the artist's daughter, Anna Tcherkessoff, Paris, June, 1968.
Reproduced in color in B115, plate 21; and in black and white in I20, No. 14. A version in the collection of the Nationalbibliothek, Vienna, is reproduced in C7, Figure 70.

Note: Rubinstein (as Marguerite Gautier) also performed Act V of *La Dame aux Camélias* at a charity matinée for Russian refugees at the Théâtre Edouard VII, Paris, on 21 April, 1923. Another "preview," also in aid of Russian refugees, was given at the Théâtre des Champs-Elysées on 14 June, 1923.

Le Médecin malgré lui: comic opera in three acts by Jules Barbier and Michel Carré after Molière, with music by Charles Gounod and recitatives by Erik Satie. Produced by Sergei Diaghilev at the Théâtre de Monte Carlo on 5 January, 1924, with choreography by Bronislava Nijinska and designs by Alexandre Benois.

Martine, wife of Sganarelle, wishes to take revenge on her husband for beating her. She meets the domestics of a gentleman Géronte, who is seeking a doctor to cure his daughter Lucinde, who is dumb. Martine says that her husband is a wonderful doctor, but that he works only if beaten. After much beating, Sganarelle confesses to being a doctor and cures Lucinde. The play ends happily ever after with the marriage of Lucinde and Léandre.

290 [R260].
Stage Design for Act II, 1924.
Gouache.
Signed lower left: "Alexandre Benois."
11⅜ x 15½ in., 29 x 39.5 cm.
Other inscriptions: lower right: "Le Médecin Malgré Lui, Act III."
Provenance: Vladimir Hessen, New York,

December 1975.
Reproduced in color in B115, plate 23; and in black and white in I40, No. 21; I51, No. 48; and R11. A version is reproduced in *La Revue de "l'Oeuvre"* (Paris, 1924, No. 1); another version is in F7, opp. p. 379; yet another, formerly in the possession of Anna Tcherkessoff, Paris, is reproduced in I42, No. 334.

290

291

291 [R261].
Costume Design for a Peasant, 1923.
Gouache and ink.
Signed and dated lower left: "Alexandre Benois. 1923."
14½ x 10⅜ in., 37 x 26.5 cm.
Annotations throughout.
Provenance: the artist's daughter, Anna Tcherkessoff, Paris, June, 1967.
Reproduced in I40, No. 22.

292 [R262].
Costume Design for the Doctor, 1923.
Gouache and ink.
Signed and dated lower right: "Alexandre Benois. 1923."
11⅞ x 9½ in., 30 x 24 cm.
Provenance: the artist's daughter, Anna Tcherkessoff, Paris, June, 1967.
Reproduced in I40, No. 28.

292

293

293 [41; R263].
Costume Design for the Ethiopian, 1923.
Gouache, ink, and silver paint.
10⅜ x 7⅝ in., 26.5 x 19 cm.
Annotations throughout.
Provenance: the artist's daughter, Anna Tcherkessoff, Paris, June, 1967.
Reproduced in I40, No. 24.

294 [R264].
Costume Design for M. Fouqué, 1923.
Gouache and pencil.
Signed and dated lower left: "Alexandre Benois. 1923."
18¾ x 12½ in., 47.5 x 31.6 cm.
Annotations throughout.
Provenance: the artist's daughter, Anna Tcherkessoff, Paris, December, 1979.

294

Note: To honor the centenary of Charles Gounod, Diaghilev staged three of his operas at Monte Carlo – *La Colombe, Philémon et Baucis,* and the famous *Médecin malgré lui* based on Molière's play. Diaghilev and Benois had not collaborated since *Le Rossignol* in 1914 mainly because Benois had been living in Russia, and this seemed an ideal opportunity to heal old wounds and reestablish artistic contact. But, as Benois himself soon realized, he and Diaghilev were now distant to each other. True, both were fond of Molière and Benois had designed a cycle of his plays for the Moscow Art Theater in 1912 and 1913, but from Diaghilev's point of view, Benois as a designer was already passé. Sergei Grigoriev described the production as follows:

> This opera went well, much assisted by a delicious décor by Benois... it was a whole ten years since we had seen him; and during that long time Diaghilev's taste had completely changed and he did not admire Benois anymore. I remember how Benois stood with me in the wings and said with a shrug, "Diaghilev no longer likes my décors. I can't understand it." But I could understand it, well enough. Diaghilev during the years had moved to the left; and work such as Benois's now seemed to him academic.[153]

295 [R265].
Cover Design for the 1924-25 Season Program of the Chauve-Souris (The Bat), 1924.
Watercolor, ink, and pencil.
Signed lower left in ink and dated: "Alexandre Benois 1924."
15 x 12⅝ in., 38 x 32 cm.
Other inscriptions: on reverse in pencil: "Alexandre Benois. 1-ère idée du Programme pour Balieff automne 1924."
Provenance: the artist's daughter, Anna Tcherkessoff, Paris, February, 1979.
Reproduced in color in F107, p. 107; M73, p. 90; a close version in the collection of René Guerra is reproduced in K189, p. 62. The design served, with some minor changes, as

295

the cover for the 1924-25 Paris season program, i.e., *Théâtre de la Chauve-Souris de Nikita Balieff* (see Nos. 345-48 [R310-13]). For information on Nikita Baliev and The Bat see entries for Nicola Benois, Lado Gudiashvili, Nicholas Remisoff, and Vasilii Shukhaev. This was one of Baliev's most successful seasons (also see No. 578 [R443]).

Unknown production, *Paris, 1925.*

296

296 [NIRE].
Costume Design for Voltaire, 1925.
Watercolor and black ink.
Signed bottom left: "Alexandre Benois."
18½ x 12¾ in.; 47 x 32.5 cm.
Other inscriptions: instructions to the dressmaker.
Provenance: the artist's daughter, Anna Tcherkessoff, Paris, 1964. Now in a private collection.
Reproduced in I14, p. 23.

Le Roi Fait Battre les Tambours: *short sketch in the repertoire of the Chauve-Souris theater and part of the 1924-25 Paris season. Based on an old French song known in English and American productions as* The King Orders the Drums to Be Beaten. *Designers varied, but Alexandre Benois designed the 1924-25 Paris season production.*

297 [R266].
Costume Design for a Court Jester.
Gouache and black ink.
Signed in ink lower left: "Alexandre Benois."
18⅛ x 12 in., 46 x 30.5 cm.
Provenance: the artist's daughter, Anna Tcherkessoff, Paris, June, 1967.
Reproduced in I40, No. 15; G61.

298 [R267].
Portrait of Vasilii Shukhaev, 1926.
Pencil and ink.
9½ x 8¼ in., 24 x 21 cm.
Inscription: left margin in Russian: "V.I. Shukhaev

297

at a meeting of the World of Art at Bilibin's on 31 May, 1926. This meeting [illegible] the inglorious end of a glorious, famous society."
Provenance: the artist's daughter, Anna Tcherkessoff, Paris, June, 1968. Now in a private collection.
Reproduced in I20, p. 60; I51, No. 216.

Note: As an active member of the revived World of Art society in the 1910s, Shukhaev and his close friend Alexandre Jacovleff were in constant contact with Benois. In Paris, too, Shukhaev was a frequent visitor to the Benois family and was a member of Le Monde Artiste. Actually, in spite of the pessimistic inscription on this piece, the World of Art did not die immediately. According to a note in the archive of Boris Grigoriev, dated 1 April, 1927, the World of Art meetings continued, with "Benois, Bilibin, Dobujinsky, Larionov, Milioti, Serebriakova, Stelletsky, Shchekatikhina, Jacovleff" discussing further exhibitions.[154]

298

Le Coq d'Or: *opera-ballet in three acts with music by Nikolai Rimsky-Korsakov and libretto by Vladimir Belsky based on a fairy-tale by Alexander Pushkin and adapted by Alexandre Benois. Produced by the Grand Opéra, Paris, on 12 May, 1927, with choreography by Michel Fokine and designs by Alexandre Benois.*

Tsar Dodon wishes to defend his kingdom against his enemies and, to this end, he accepts the gift of a Golden Cockerel from an Astrologer: the Cockerel will warn of danger. In return, the Tsar promises the Astrologer anything he desires. Suddenly, the Cockerel cries: "Danger!" The Tsar's sons go off to war, and the Tsar follows them only to find his army vanquished and his sons dead. Just then, a huge tent arises from the battlefield and the languorous Tsaritsa Shemakhan emerges therefrom. Fascinated, the Tsar joins her in a dance, makes a fool of himself, but still receives her consent to marry. The wedding procession makes its way to the Tsar's Palace when suddenly the Astrologer appears, demanding the Tsaritsa as his reward. The Tsar smites the Astrologer – and the Cockerel smites the Tsar. The Tsar and the Tsaritsa then disappear as the Astrologer explains to the audience that everything – apart from the Tsaritsa and himself – has been a dream.

299 [R268].
Costume Design for the Tsar's Chamberlain with the Head of a Ram, 1927.
Watercolor, black ink, and pencil.
Signed lower left in pencil: "Alexandre Benois."
15 x 10⅜ in., 38 x 26.5 cm.
Other inscriptions: in pencil upper left: "Le Coq d'Or, 1927"; upper right: "No. 66, Chambellans du Tsar; Hommes aux Cornes; un Gentilhomme de la Cour Gigantesque"; along right side in pencil is the outline of a man used for scale comparison; the reverse carries a pencil design for a devil.
Provenance: the artist's daughter, Anna Tcherkessoff, Paris, November, 1979.

299

300

301

302

303

303 [R272].
Costume Designs for the Cyclops in the Procession together with Scale Figure, 1927.
Watercolor and pencil.
Signed in pencil mid-right: "Alexandre Benois."
15 x 11 in., 38 x 28 cm.
Other inscriptions: upper left in pencil: "Le Coq d'Or 1927." "Le Cortège; les Monstres Cyclopes"; on reverse: "Alexandre Benois, 1927. Le Coq d'Or; Les Monstres du Cortège, Les Cyclopes. No. 65 (Italian customs stamp). Coll. A. Tcherkessoff."
The piece also carries a figure drawing to the left of the two Cyclops.
Provenance: the artist's daughter, Anna Tcherkessoff, Paris, December, 1979.

304 [R273].
Portrait of Prince Vladimir Argutinsky-Dolgorukov and Jean Giraudoux, 1928.
Pencil.
6¾ x 4¾ in., 17 x 12 cm.
Inscription: lower margin: "Argutinsky, Giraudoux X [=October] 1928."
Provenance: the artist's daughter, Anna Tcherkessoff, Paris, June, 1968.
Reproduced in I20, p. 58.

Note: Both Bakst and Benois sketched the kindly Prince Vladimir Argutinsky-Dolgorukov on several occasions (cf. No. 107 [R96]). For Benois, Argutinsky-Dolgorukov had a special appeal inasmuch as he helped to promote the first production of *Le Pavillon d'Armide* in St. Petersburg in 1907. Benois remembered him as a "very attractive, very sympathetic man" and claimed to have discovered and developed the aristocrat's artistic flair.[155] Jean Giraudoux (1882-1944), the author and esthete, who is sitting in the armchair here, was also supportive of the Russian ballet and in the 1930s did much to promote the talents of Serge Lifar.[156]

304

300 [R269].
Costume Designs for Two Midgets and a Court Chamberlain with a Pig's Head, 1927.
Watercolor, black ink, and pencil.
Signed lower right in pencil: "Alexandre Benois."
15 x 11¼ in., 38 x 28.5 cm.
Other inscriptions: also signed and dated mid-right; upper left in pencil: "Le Coq d'Or, 1927"; mid-left: "Nains Marchant dans la Procession"; "Enfants de 14 ans"; upper right: "Chambellan du Tsar"; on reverse in pencil is another signature and a customs stamp "No. 66."
Provenance: the artist's daughter, Anna Tcherkessoff, Paris, November, 1979.

301 [R270].
Costume Design for a Boyar, ca. 1927.
Gouache and pencil.
15 x 11⅝ in., 38 x 29.5 cm.
Provenance: the artist's daughter, Anna Tcherkessoff, Paris, June, 1968.
Reproduced in I40, No. 14.

302 [R271].
Costume Designs for the Cyclops in the Procession, 1927.
Watercolor.
Signed lower right in pencil: "Alexandre Benois. 1927."
14½ x 10⅜ in., 37 x 26.5 cm.
Provenance: Yurii Annenkov, Paris, August, 1966.

305

306

307

La Valse: ballet in two parts by Maurice Ravel. Produced by the Ida Rubinstein Ballet at the Théâtre de Monte-Carlo on 15 January, 1929, with scenario and choreography by Bronislava Nijinska and designs by Alexandre Benois.

The first part of the ballet, lacking a definite plot, opens with a series of waltzes danced by various couples and during this lighthearted, romantic pastime three girls chase a boy. In the second part, with its mysterious music, the boy looks for one of the ballerinas. Suddenly, Death appears as a figure in black, forcing one of the girls to dance. Now also vested in black, she dies.

305 [R274].
Costume Design for One of Two Young Girls, 1928.
Watercolor.
Signed and dated lower right in pencil: "Alexandre Benois. 1928."
9 x 12¼ in., 23 x 31 cm.
Other inscriptions: upper left in pencil: "La Valse n 14"; upper right in pencil: "2 Demoiselles"; center right in pencil: "en blanc bleu rose."
Provenance: Olga Poliakova, Paris, 1966.

306 [NIRE].
Costume Design for an Officer, 1928.
Gouache and pencil.
12¼ x 9⅜ in., 31.25 x 23.75 cm.
Other inscriptions: numerous inscriptions top left side.
Provenance: the artist's daughter, Anna Tcherkessoff, Paris, September 1974.
Reproduced in I40, p. 50.

307 [NIRE].
Costume Design for a Hussar, 1928.
Gouache and pencil.
12⅝ x 9⅜ in., 32 x 23.75 cm.
Other inscriptions: numerous inscriptions top left side.
Provenance: the artist's daughter, Anna Tcherkessoff, Paris, September 1974.
Reproduced in I40, p. 50.

Sadko: opera in four acts and seven scenes by Nikolai Rimsky-Korsakov with libretto by the composer Vladimir Belsky. Produced by Marie Kousnezoff's Opéra Russe à Paris in the Théâtre des Champs-Elysées, Paris, on 7 June, 1930, with designs by Alexandre Benois and choreography for the sixth scene by Bronislava Nijinska.

As the merchants of Novgorod rejoice, Sadko, a singer from Novgorod arrives and entertains them with his song. The scene then changes to the shores of Lake Ilmen where Sadko's singing attracts a group of swans who turn into beautiful maidens, including Volkhova, the Sea Princess. Volkhova confesses her love for Sadko, but then returns to her father, the King of the Ocean, announcing that Sadko will presently catch three golden fish and travel in foreign lands. Sadko does, indeed, catch the fish, embarks on a voyage in the merchants' ships, and finds treasure. But Sadko becomes marooned on a plank of wood at sea and

plunges to the ocean floor and the Underwater Kingdom. Sadko then wakes up to find himself at the edge of Lake Ilmen and to witness the arrival of his ships laden with treasure.

Nos. 308-38 [R275-304] are now in the collection of Gennadii Rozhdestvensky, Stockholm.

308 [R275].
Set Design for Scene II (Sadko Sings on the Shore of Lake Ilmen), 1930.
Pencil and gouache.
Signed and dated lower left: "Alexandre Benois, 1930."
12 x 17⅞ in., 30.5 x 45.5 cm.
Inscribed: "Sadko Act II. Opéra Russe à Paris" with a dedication in Russian to Nikolai Yanchevsky, who sang one of the Corals.
Provenance: Theatre, Ballet and Music-Hall Material, London: Sotheby's, 23 October, 1980, Lot 237 (reproduced).
Reproduced in J27, Lot 247; a similar design

308

309

311

312

311 [NIRE].
Costume Design for St. Nicholas, 1930.
Watercolor and pencil.
12⅝ x 9½ in., 32 x 24 cm.
Inscribed: upper left in pencil: "77, Sadko, Paris 1930"; upper right in Russian: "Saint Nicholas the Miracle-Worker."
Provenance: the artist's daughter, Anna Tcherkessoff, Paris, June, 1967.

312 [R279].
Costume Design for an Indian Boy (One of the Indian's Two Attendants), 1930.
Watercolor, pencil, and ink.
Initialed and dated lower left "AB 1930."
11¾ x 8¼ in., 30 x 21 cm.
Inscribed upper left in pencil: "No. 36, Sadko, Paris"; upper right in Russian: "Indian suite, 2 boys."
Provenance: the artist's daughter, Anna Tcherkessoff, Paris, November, 1979.

is reproduced in the souvenir program *Opéra Russe à Paris. Théâtre des Champs-Elysées*, 1930, spring, unpaginated.

309 [R276].
Set Design for Act IV (the Port of Novgorod), 1930.
Watercolor and gouache heightened with white.
Signed lower left in Russian: "Alexandre Benois."
16⅛ x 25¼ in., 41 x 64 cm.
Provenance: the artist's daughter, Anna Tcherkessoff, Paris, April, 1983.
Reproduced in color in G79, p. 130. A similar design is reproduced in color in the souvenir program *Opéra Russe à Paris. Théâtre des Champs-Elysées*, 1930, spring, undated; and in Etkind, *Aleksandr Nikolaevich Benua*, op. cit., plate 84.

310 [R277].
Set Design for Scene 6 (the Palace of the King of the Sea), 1930.
Watercolor.
Signed and dated lower left: "Alexandre Benois 1930."
15⅜ x 23 in., 39 x 58.5 cm.
Inscribed lower right "Sadko, VIe scène."
Provenance: the artist's daughter, Anna Tcherkessoff, Paris, June, 1967.
Reproduced in color in the souvenir program *Opéra Russe à Paris. Théâtre des Champs-Elysées*, 1930, spring, unpaginated; in black and white in G19, p. 55.

313

315

317

313 [R280].
Costume Design for a Pancake Seller, 1930.
Watercolor and pencil.
Initialed lower right "AB."
12¼ x 9½ in., 31 x 24 cm.
Inscribed upper left in pencil: "No. 66, Sadko, 1930. Paris"; upper right in pencil in Russian: "Blinshchik [pancake seller]."
Provenance: the artist's daughter, Anna Tcherkessoff, Paris, June, 1967.

314 [R281].
Costume Design for a Varangian, 1930.
Watercolor and pencil.
12⅝ x 9½ in., 32 x 24 cm.
Inscribed upper left: "33a, Sadko, pour Paris, 1930."
Provenance the artist's daughter, Anna Tcherkessoff, Paris, June, 1967.

315 [R282].
Costume Design for Ocean (Neptune), King of the Sea, Holding a Club and Trident, 1930.
Watercolor and pencil.

12⅝ x 8¼ in., 32 x 21 cm.
Inscribed upper left: "Sadko, Paris, 1930."
(Cf. No. 335 [R301]).
Provenance: the artist's daughter, Anna Tcherkessoff, Paris, June, 1967.

316 [R283].
Costume Design for a Fish with Open mouth, 1930.
Watercolor and pencil.
Signed and dated lower left: "Alexandre Benois, 1930."
12⅝ x 8 in., 32 x 20.3 cm.
Inscribed upper left: "Sadko"; upper right "Habitants du Monde sous Marin."
Provenance: the artist's daughter, Anna Tcherkessoff, Paris, June, 1967.
Reproduced in Q3.

317 [R284].
Costume Design for a Bream, 1930.
Watercolor and pencil.
Initialed and dated lower left: "AB, 1930."
12¼ x 9½ in., 31 x 24 cm.
Inscribed upper left: "No. 89"; upper right in Russian: "2 Bream, ballet." The sheet also carries a pencil outline of the Bream *en face*.
Provenance: the artist's daughter, Anna Tcherkessoff, Paris, November, 1979.

318 [R285].
Costume Design for a Coral, ca. 1930.
Watercolor and pencil.
12⅝ x 9½ in., 32 x 24 cm.
Inscribed upper left in pencil: "88, Sadko, version de Paris"; upper right in Russian: "4 corals, ballet" (The Paris program, however, mentions only three Corals).
Provenance: the artist's daughter, Anna Tcherkessoff, Paris, June, 1967.

314

316

318

319

321

323

319 [R286].
Costume Design for One of Eight Dwellers of the Sea, 1930.
Watercolor.
12¾ x 9 in., 32.5 x 23 cm.
Inscribed upper left: "Sadko, version de Paris 1930"; upper right: "Habitants du fond de la mer."
Provenance: the artist's daughter, Anna Tcherkessoff, Paris, June, 1967.
A version is reproduced in J4, Lot 145.

320 [R287].
Costume Design for a Dweller of the Sea, ca. 1930.
Watercolor, pencil, and silver paint.
Signed lower right in pencil: "Alexandre Benois."
11⅜ x 7⅞ in., 29 x 20 cm.
Other inscription: upper left: "Sadko";

upper right: "8 Habitants de la mer."
Provenance: *Ballet and Theatre Material*, London: Sotheby's, 6 June, 1979, Lot 29 (reproduced).

321 [R288].
Costume Design for a Sea Monster Holding a conch in Left Hand, 1930.
Watercolor.
Signed and dated lower right in pencil: "Alexandre Benois, 1930."
12 x 8¼ in., 30 .5 x 21 cm.
Other inscription: upper left: "Sadko, 1930"; upper right: "Monstres marins portant des coquillages, Ballet."
Provenance: the artist's daughter, Anna Tcherkessoff, Paris, November, 1979.

322 [R289].
Costume Design for a Sea Monster Holding a Conch in Right Hand, ca. 1930.
Gouache and silver paint.
11¾ x 8¼ in., 30 x 21.5 cm.
Inscribed upper left in pencil: "No. 81, Sadko,

version Paris"; upper right: "4 Monstres."
Provenance: the artist's daughter, Anna Tcherkessoff, Paris, November, 1979.
A version is reproduced in J4, Lot 145.

323 [R290].
Costume Design for a Dweller of the Sea Wearing a Three String Necklace of Pearls, ca. 1930.
Watercolor, pencil, India ink, and silver paint.
Signed lower right in pencil: "Alexandre Benois."
11⅜ x 7⅞ in., 29 x 20 cm.
Inscribed upper left in pencil: "Sadko"; upper right: "8 habitants de la mer."
Provenance: *Ballet and Theatre Material*, London: Sotheby's, 6 June, 1979, Lot 29 (reproduced).

324 [R291].
Costume Design for a Seahorse, 1931.
Watercolor and pencil.
Initialed and dated lower left in pencil: "AB 1931."
11 x 9¼ in., 28 x 23.5 cm.

320

322

324

325

327

329

Other inscriptions: upper right: "2"; upper left: "No. 90, Sadko (version de Paris)." Cf. No. 337 [R303].
Provenance: the artist's daughter, Anna Tcherkessoff, Paris, November, 1979.

325 [R292].
Costume Design for a Crayfish (back and front), 1930.
Watercolor and ink.
Signed and dated lower right in pencil: "Alexandre Benois, 1930."
12¼ x 9 in., 31 x 23 cm.
Other inscriptions: upper left: "No. 90"; upper right "8 Ecrevisses."
Provenance: the artist's daughter, Anna Tcherkessoff, Paris, 1979.

326 [R293].
Costume Design for a Crab, 1930.
Watercolor.
Signed and dated lower right in pencil:

"Alexandre Benois, 1930."
11⅜ x 8¼ in., 29 x 21 cm.
Other inscription: upper left: "Sadko, version de Paris, 1930"; upper right: "Monstres Marins."
Provenance: the artist's daughter, Anna Tcherkessoff, Paris, 1979.

327 [R294].
Costume Design for a Jellyfish, 1930.
Watercolor and ink.
Signed and dated lower right in pencil: "Alexandre Benois, 1930."
10¾ x 6¼ in., 27.3 x 16 cm.
Other inscriptions: upper left: "No. 82"; upper right :"2 Méduses, choeur."
Provenance: the artist's daughter, Anna Tcherkessoff, Paris, 1979.

328 [R295].
Costume Design for a Pike in a Skirt, ca. 1930.
Watercolor.
11¾ x 8¼ in., 30 x 21 cm.

Inscribed upper left: "No. 56F"; upper right in Russian: "1 pike, choir (1 out of 2 pikes)." The design is almost the same as No. 329 [R295a] except for the overlay skirt, since this item is attached to the lower part of the design.
Provenance: the artist's daughter, Anna Tcherkessoff, Paris, 1979.

329 [R295a].
Costume Design for a Pike, ca. 1930.
Watercolor.
Other data are the same as in No. 328 [R295] and the design is also the same, except for the overlay skirt.

330 [R296].
Costume Design for a Fish with a Striped Head, 1930.
Watercolor.
Signed and dated lower right: "Alexandre Benois, 1930."
11 x 8¼ in., 28 x 21 cm.

326

328

330

331

Other inscription: upper left: "Sadko, version de Paris, 1930."
Provenance: the artist's daughter, Anna Tcherkessoff, Paris, 1979.

331 [R297].
Costume Design for a Fish with Spikes, 1930.
Watercolor.
12⅝ x 9½ in., 32 x 24 cm.
Inscribed in pencil upper left: "Sadko, version de Paris, 1930."
Provenance: the artist's daughter, Anna Tcherkessoff, Paris, June, 1967.

332 [R298].
Costume Design for a Trumpet Player, 1930.
Watercolor and pencil.
Initialed and dated lower right: "Alexandre Benois, 1930."

332

333

11 x 9¼ in., 28 x 23.5 cm.
Other inscriptions: upper left: "no. 78"; upper right in Russian: "3 trumpet players."
Provenance: the artist's daughter, Anna Tcherkessoff, Paris, 1979.

333 [R299].
Costume Design for a Starfish, 1930.
Watercolor and pencil.
Initialed lower right: "AB."
11¾ x 8⅛ in., 29.7 x 20.7 cm.
Other inscriptions: upper left: "No. 89, Sadko, 1930"; upper right: "5 étoiles de la mer."
A version is reproduced in the souvenir program *Opéra Russe à Paris. Théâtre des Champs-Elysées,* 1930, spring, unpaginated.
Provenance: the artist's daughter, Anna Tcherkessoff, Paris, June, 1980.

334 [R300].
Costume Design for a Silverfish Holding a Scarf in Left Hand, 1930.
Watercolor and pencil.
Initialed and dated lower right: "AB 1930."
12⅜ x 9½ in., 31.5 x 24 cm.

334

335

Other inscriptions: in pencil upper left: "No. 87, Sadko (Version de Paris)"; upper right in Russian: "8 silver fish. (Ballet)."
Provenance: the artist's daughter, Anna Tcherkessoff, Paris, April, 1983.

335 [R301].
Costume Design for Ocean (Neptune), King of the Sea, Holding a Trident, 1930.
Watercolor.
Signed and dated in pencil lower right: "Alexandre Benois, 1930."
12⅝ x 8⅝ in., 32 x 22 cm.
Other inscription: upper left: "No. 32, le Roi de la mer, Sadko, Rome"; numerous annotations on reverse.
Cf. No. 315 [R282].
Provenance: the artist's daughter, Anna Tcherkessoff, Paris, April, 1983.

336 [R302].
Costume Design for a Peasant Girl, 1931.
Watercolor and pencil.
Signed lower right in pencil: "Alexandre Benois."
12⅝ x 9 in., 32 x 23 cm.
Other inscriptions: upper left: "Sadko, Rome"; upper right: "Fille Paysanne"; mid-right: "pour Rome, 1931."
Provenance: the artist's nephew, Mikhail Benois, Madrid, May, 1968.

337 [R303].
Costume Design for a Seahorse, 1931.
Watercolor.
Signed lower left in pencil: "Alexandre Benois."
12¼ x 8⅝ in., 31 x 22 cm.
Other inscriptions: in pencil upper left: "Sadko, pour Rome, 1931, Ballet sous-marin"; upper right: "2 hippocampes."
Cf. No. 324 [R291].
Provenance: the artist's nephew, Mikhail Benois, Madrid, May, 1968.

337

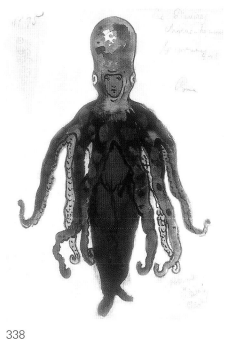

336   338

338 [R304].
Costume Design for an Octopus, 1930.
Watercolor and ink.
Signed and dated lower right in pencil:
"Alexandre Benois, 1930."
11¾ x 7⅞ in., 30 x 20 cm.
Other inscriptions: upper left: "No. 95";
upper right: "Les pieuvres, choeur-
hommes, 4 costumes, Rome."
Provenance: the artist's daughter, Anna
Tcherkessoff, Paris, 1979.

Note: Between June, 1930, and February,
1931, the Opéra Russe à Paris, directed by
Prince Alexei Tsereteli (Zereteli) and Colonel
Wassily de Basil (pseudonym of Vasilii
Grigorievich Voskresensky), staged *Sadko* no
less than four times with the Nijinska
choreography and the Benois designs, i.e., at
the Théâtre des Champs-Elysées, Paris
(premiere on 7 June, 1930); at the Gran
Kursal, San Sebastian, Spain (12 September,
1930); at the Théâtre des Champs-Elysées
again (25 December, 1930 — selections
only); and then during the second Opéra
Russe season in Paris in January and
February, 1931. Perhaps the most impressive presentation was the first when Nijinska
had just become maître de ballet in the
Opéra Russe and made her debut as such
with *Sadko*. Directed by Alexandre Sanin,
conducted by Albert Coates, and with the
coloratura soprano Lidiia Lipkovskaia, the
basso Kapiton Zaporozhets, and other
important singers and dancers, the June
1930 *Sadko* scored a resounding success.
After Nijinska left to form her own company
in January, 1931, her position was taken over
by Boris Romanov the following April. Later
in 1931 Benois designed another production
of *Sadko* at the Teatro Reale dell'Opera in
Rome and Nos. 335-38 [R301-04] are for this.

Boris Godunov: *opera in a prologue and four
acts by Modest Mussorgsky with libretto
based on a play of the same name by
Alexander Pushkin. Prepared, but not
produced, by the Staatsopera, Munich, in
1943 with designs by Alexandre Benois.*

*The faithful at Novodevichii Monastery are
informed that Boris has not yet decided to
take the crown. He does so and there is
much rejoicing. Five years later, during a time
of famine and plague, Boris no longer enjoys
the same sympathy. Grigorii, an apprentice
of the monk Pimen, has dreamed that he
was the murdered Dmitrii, the rightful heir to
the throne. Grigorii, pursued by the police,
escapes from the monastery. Boris is warned
of the Pretender by the cunning Prince
Shuisky and he continues to be haunted by*

*the dead Tsarevich. Meanwhile, Marina,
Dmitrii's sweetheart, incites him to march on
Moscow. In anguish and remorse Boris dies,
and the opera ends with an empty stage,
except for the village idiot.*

339 [R305].
Set Design for Act I (Pimen's Cell), ca. 1943.
Gouache.
16½ x 23¼ in., 42 x 59 cm.
Inscribed on the reverse: "Décor pour la
scène de Pimen, Boris Godounov."
Provenance: the artist's daughter, Anna
Tcherkessoff, Paris, February, 1968.
Reproduced in I40, No. 13.
That this design was intended for a 1943
Munich production was confirmed by
Nicola Benois.

339

340

The Sleeping Beauty: *ballet in a prologue, three acts, and an apotheosis based on a fairy-tale by Charles Perrault; original music by Peter Tchaikovsky and original choreography by Marius Petipa and Ivan Vsevolozhsky. Prepared, but not produced for La Scala, Milan, in 1953 with designs by Alexandre Benois.*

See No. 94 [R87] for plot summary and see Note after No. 101 [R93].

340 [R306].
Set design, 1953
Gouache.
Signed and dated: "Alexandre Benois 1953."
12 x 16½ in., 30.5 x 42 cm.
Provenance: Vladimir Hessen, New York, June, 1967.
Reproduced in I40, No. 16.

341 [R307].
Costume Design for a Lady with Falcon, ca. 1927.
Watercolor and black ink.
Signed lower right in pencil: "Alexandre Benois."
12 x 9½ in., 30.5 x 24 cm.
Other inscriptions: upper left in pencil: "La Belle au Bois Dormant"; upper right: "Dame à la chasse."
Provenance: Vladimir Hessen, New York, 1967. Now in a private collection.
Reproduced in I40, No. 17.

342 [R308].
Costume Design for the Big Black, 1927.
Gouache.
Signed and dated lower right: "Alexandre Benois 1927."
12⅜ x 9½ in., 31.5 x 24 cm.
Annotations throughout.
Provenance: the artist's daughter, Anna Tcherkessoff, Paris, June, 1967.
Reproduced in I40, No. 18.

Note: Benois designed several versions of *The Sleeping Beauty* and the excerpt from it, *Aurora's Wedding*. The fact that No. 342 [R308] is dated 1927 (No. 341 [R307] is undated, but comes from the same pro-

venance, is on the same paper, and of the same format, and, therefore, probably from 1927 also) indicates that it was used for one of the productions of *Aurora's Wedding* that year, e.g., for Diaghilev's presentation in Milan in January or in London in July.[157]

127 See, for example, "La décoration Théâtrale. Une conversation avec M. Alexandre Benois" in *Le Figaro*, Paris, 1929, 11 June.
128 Serebriakova was the niece of Benois.
129 F5, Vol. 2, p. 37.
130 See F54, Vol. 2, pp. 491-98.
131 F54, Vol. 2, p. 432. On p. 433 of the same source Benois also refers to a pencil portrait that Shervashidze made of Benois at this time (1905-06), but he does not mention the watercolor portrait that, apparently, Shervashidze is painting in the work under discussion. For Benois's description of Primel see ibid., p. 428.

132 See the two articles: A. Benua: "Khudozhestvennye eresi in *Zolotoe runo*, M, 1906, No. 2, pp. 80-88; and A. Shervashidze: "Individualizm i traditsiia," ibid., 1906, No. 6, pp. 64-72. Benois criticized contemporary artists for trying to be individualists at all costs and, thereby, for contributing to what he regarded as the artistic confusion of his time. Shervashidze, on the contrary, argued that individualism was a beneficial and productive condition.
133 F54, Vol. 2, pp. 458-59.
134 The 1907 portrait is in the RM. It is reproduced in F54, Vol. 2, between pp. 512 and 513.
135 D11, p. 56
136 J1, p. 52.
137 The composer of *Cupid's Revenge*, Alexander Sergeevich Taneev, was a "very nice, but little talented dilettante" (F54, Vol. 2, p. 303) and should not be confused with the celebrated composer of the same name.
138 F19, p. 188.
139 F7, p. 266.
140 Ibid., pp. 291-92.
141 A. Levinson: "Russkie khudozhniki-dekoratory" in *Stolitsa i usadba*, P, 1916, 1 May, No. 57, p. 12. For a detailed discussion of Benois's designs for *Le Pavillon d'Armide*, including many relevant illustrations, see Alden Murray: "A Problematical Pavilion: Alexandre Benois's First Ballet," in G55, pp. 23-52.
142 Quoted in G. Balanchine: *Balanchine's Complete Stories of the Great Ballets*, New York: Doubleday, 1954, p. 185.
143 Quoted in ibid., p. 186.
144 I9, p. 40
145 According to Stravinsky (F32, p. 379), he began to think about *Le Rossignol* as early as 1908.
146 F54, Vol. 2, p. 535.
147 A. Lunacharsky: "Russkie spektakli v Parizhe" in *Sovremennik*, 1914, Book 14-15. Quoted in Etkind, p. 99.
148 A. Maslovsky: "Balety S. Diagileva i russkie khudozhniki" in *Teatr*, Berlin, 1922, April, No. 9, p. 6.
149 R. Allegri: "Nicola Benois, il più grande scenografo del nostro tempo racconta la sua vita" in *Gente*, Milan, 1981, No. 44, p.75.
150 Etkind, *Aleksandr Benua*, pp. 109-110.
151 Quoted in ibid., where original source is not given.
152 Ibid.
153 D11, p. 192.
154 Formerly in the collection of the late Cyrille Grigorieff, Cagnes-sur-mer, France.
155 F54, Vol. 2, pp. 36-37.
156 F31, pp. 154, 238.
157 For some information on the 1927 productions see D26, pp. 481, 492, 511.

341

342

BENOIS, Nadia (Benua, Nadezhda Leontievna)

Born 17 (29) May, 1895, St. Peterburg; died 8 February, 1975, Gloucestershire, England.

Daughter of the architect Leontii Nikolaevich Benois, niece of Alexandre Benois, and cousin of Nicola Benois, Evgenii Lanceray, and Zinaida Serebriakova.
1914-15 attended the New Art Studio under Alexandre Jacovleff and Vasilii Shukhaev in Petrograd; 1916 married Johann (Jona) Platonovich Ustinov; 1917-19 studied at the Pegoskhuma; 1920 emigrated to England; 1921 birth of son, Peter Ustinov, later to achieve fame as an actor, director, and writer; 1920s-30s recognized for her Impressionist landscapes and still-lives; had several one-woman exhibitions in London, including the Adelphi Gallery (1924) and Arthur Tooth (1929, 1932, 1936); 1939 designed the Sadler's Wells production of *Sleeping Princess;* 1930s-50s designed ballets and films, collaborating, for example, with Marie Rambert at the Rambert Dance Company; among her stage commissions are *Dark Elegies* and *Nutcracker;* among her film commissions are *Vice Versa* and *Private Angelo,* both produced by Peter Ustinov.

Bibliography
J. Manson: "Nadia Benois" in *Apollo,* London, 1929, Vol. 9, pp. 137-38
S. Vincent: "In the Studio of Nadia Benois" in *The Studio,* London, 1936, Vol. 112, pp. 260-65. H34, pp. 139, 140.
T. Vergun: *Semia Benua.* Catalog of exhibition at the Elizium Gallery, Moscow, 1998.

Nadia Benois grew up in a family whose primary passion was for the visual arts and her early exposure to the architectural drawings of her father, to the stage designs of her uncle Alexandre, and to the land-

scapes of her uncle Albert left a strong imprint on her creative psychology. While never attaining the universal recognition of Alexandre or of his son, Nicola, Nadia Benois worked for distinguished companies, including the Ballet Rambert and Sadler's Wells, and her works entered the collections of prestigious museums, including the Tate Gallery and the Victoria and Albert. Nadia Benois maintained her family ties with the Benois and the Serebriakovs in France and was in touch with art critics such as Mary Chamot and Herbert Read in England. Both her studio painting and her applied art are characterized by a spontaneity and lightness that led observers to remark on the absence of the "fatal weariness" that, allegedly, beset most Russian artists and writers.[158]

The Sleeping Princess: *ballet in a prologue and three acts based on a fairy-tale by Charles Perrault,* The Sleeping Beauty*; original music by Peter Tchaikovsky and original choreography by Marius Petipa and Ivan Vsevolozhsky. Produced by the Sadler's Wells Ballet Company at Sadler's Wells Theatre, Islington, London, on 2 February, 1939, with designs by Nadia Benois.*
        See No. 94 [R87] for plot summary and see Note after No. 101 [R93].

343 [NIRE].
Costume Design for the Guest, 1939.
Watercolor and pencil.
Signed lower right in pencil: "N. Benois."
4½ x 3½ in.; 11.5 x 9 cm.
Other inscriptions: in black ink: "A Guest Prologue + Act I Sleeping Princess Sadlers Wells. Merry Christmas and Happy New Year from Klop, Nadia, and Peter."[159]

Note: Although Nadia Benois's sets and costumes were considered to be rather modest, especially after Bakst's sumptuous precedent of 1921 (see Nos. 96-101 [R88-R93), the Covent Garden production scored a resounding success, not least because of the dancing by the nineteen year-old Margot Fonteyn as the Princess and Robert Helpmann as her Prince. At that moment the Sadler's Wells Ballet Company was only eight years old, but it demonstrated a high degree of professionality, showcasing over seventy dancers for this premiere — in the presence of Queen Mary.

158 Vincent, "In the Studio of Nadia Benois", p. 265.
159 "Klop" (literally, "bedbug") was the nickname of Nadia Benois's husband, i.e., Johann Ustinov; "Peter" here refers to their son. See N. Benois: *Klop and the Ustinov Family,* London: Sidgwick and Jackson, 1973.

BENOIS, Nicola (Benua, Nikolai Alexandrovich)

Born 19 April (2 May), 1901, St. Petersburg, Russia; died 29 March, 1988, Milan, Italy.

Son of Alexandre Benois and cousin of Nadia Benois, Evgenii Lanceray, and Zinaida Serebriakova. Studied painting with his father and Orest Allegri in St. Petersburg; also attended IAA / Svomas in Petrograd, taking lessons from Dmitrii Kardovsky, Mikhail Matiushin, and Vladimir Tatlin; helped his father with a number of stage productions before creating his own designs for productions in Petrograd theaters such as *Julius Caesar* and Alexander Glazunov's *The Seasons;* in these early years he also painted sets after designs by Alexander Golovin, Vladimir Shchuko, et al.; 1923 with Boris Kustodiev's son, Kirill, painted ceiling decorations for the cabaret Little Berry; 1924 emigrated, thereafter working for many theaters in Paris, London, and elsewhere, including the Chauve-Souris in Paris where he designed revues, such as *I Miss My Swiss* and *Amour et Hiérarchie;* 1926 worked for Ida Rubinstein's ballet company in Paris; visited Maxim Gorky on Capri; 1927-32 chief designer for the Teatro Reale dell'Opera in Rome; 1936 onwards worked as artist-in-residence at La Scala, Milan, creating the sets and costumes for ca. 150 spectacles there; at various times in the 1920s-40s also worked at the Teatro Colón in Buenos-Aires.

Bibliography
M2, Vol. 2, pp. 148-55.
A14, Vol. 1, p. 367.
G.Tintori: *Nicola Benois. Scenografo e pittore.* Catalog of exhibition at the Museo Teatrale alla Scala, Milan, and the Sala Ex Cavallerizza, Brescia, 1980-81 (this is one of several exhibitions in Italy).
I. Kadina: "Master stsenografii Nikolai Benua," in *Iskusstvo,* Moscow, 1981, No. 12, pp. 42-47 (Italian translation:"Un maestro della scenografia. Nikolaj Benois" in *Rassegna Sovietica,* Rome, 1984, July-August pp. 163-76).
Nicola Benois's memoirs are of particular interest. See R. Allegri: "Nicola Benois, il più grande scenografo del nostro tempo racconta la sua vita" in *Gente,* Milan, 1981, No. 44, pp. 72-73, 75-76; No. 45, pp. 58-62, 64, 69; No. 46, pp. 132-34, 137-38, 141; No. 47, pp. 82-87, 91; No. 48, pp. 132-35, 138, 140, 145; No. 49, pp. 98-99, 101-06; No. 50, pp. 177-78, 180.
I Benois del Teatro alla Scala. Catalog of exhibition at La Scala, Milan, 1988.
T. Vergun: *Semia Benua.* Catalog of exhibition at the Elizium Gallery, Moscow, 1998.
H34, pp. 140, 141.
M175.
P. Deotto: "Nikolai Benua. Teatralnyi khudozhnik mezhdu Rossiei i Italiei" in M. Talalai, ed.: *Russkie v Italii: Kulturnoe nasledie emigratsii,* M, 2008, pp. 505-43.

a Guest
Prologue + act I
Sleeping Princess
Sadlers Wells.

Merry Christmas and Happy New Year from Klop Nadia + Peter

Nicola Benois inherited his father's love of the theater and, during his long career as a stage designer, worked on more than 300 opera and ballet productions. Nicola Benois began his profession as an international designer for Nikita Baliev's cabaret, the Chauve-Souris (The Bat), in 1924, and Nos. 345, 346 [R310, R311] are among his earliest attempts at costume design. Nicola Benois was one of many young émigrés who worked for the Chauve-Souris in the 1920s in Paris, London, New York, and other cities — a colorful variety show that attracted European and American audiences by what Viktor Shklovsky would have called its "counterfeit Russian provincialism."[160]

Along with Lado Gudiashvili, Vasilii Shukhaev, his father, and, above all, Sergei Sudeikin and Nicholas Remisoff, Nicola Benois contributed much to the color and movement of the Chauve-Souris in Paris, London, and New York. His designs for the revues *I Miss My Swiss* and *Amour et Hiérarchie* provided him with valuable artistic experience for his more ambitious designs for grand opera and ballet in later years such as Mussorgsky's *Boris Godunov* and Tchaikovsky's *Queen of Spades*. During the 1930s-50s Nicola Benois achieved a solid reputation for his refined combinations of historical ethos and personal fantasy, creating scenic illusions while always heeding the music. He wrote:

> la couleur est une évolution musicale; la lumière aussi; et musicales sont la ligne des figures dans leurs diverses attitudes, et la ligne du paysage, et même celle des choses dans leur divers aspects.[161]

344

344 [R309].
Self-Portrait, 1969.
Pencil.
Signed lower right and dated: "Nicolai Benois 1969."
15 x 11¾ in., 38 x 30 cm.
Provenance: the artist, Milan, February, 1969.
Reproduced in F107, p. 128; I20, p. 57; I51, No. 49; M91; M151, p. 96.

Amour et Hiérarchie. Une Bouffonerie du Temps Passé: *revue with libretto by Petr Potemkin and music by Alexei Arkhangelsky. Produced by Nikita Baliev's Chauve-Souris at the Théâtre Fémina, Paris, 1924, with designs by Nicola Benois.*

A young and charming lady receives her admirers — a soldier, a lieutenant, a lieutenant colonel. Military discipline compels each suitor to leave as his successor arrives. The final visitor is a general and he claims the lady's heart.

345

345 [42; R310].
Costume Design for the General, ca. 1924.
Watercolor.
Signed lower left: "Nicolai Benois."
18⅞ x 12⅝ in., 48 x 32 cm.
Other inscriptions: lower left in ink in Russian: "To dear Semeon Mikhailovich from N.A. Benois" (a reference to Simon Lissim; see Nos. 745-50 [R626-30]). This costume design, worn by the actor Mikhail Dalmatoff, was given by Nicola Benois to Simon Lissim.
Provenance: Simon Lissim, New York, June, 1967.
Reproduced in color in the Souvenir Program for the Théâtre Femina, 1924, p. 5; and other souvenir programs; and in black and white in A34, p. 76; I20, No. 17; and I51, No. 50; a photograph of a scene from *Amour et Hiérarchie* showing the lady and her four suitors is reproduced in the Souvenir Program *Balieff's Chauve-Souris* (New York, 1924-25; cover design by Alexandre Benois — see No. 295 [R265]), p. 10. Another version of this design is reproduced in J32, Lot 113 (i); also see G68, p. 161.

346

346 [R311].
Costume Design for the Soldier, 1924.
Watercolor.
Signed and dated lower right: "Nicolai Benois 1924."
18⅞ x 12⅝ in., 48 x 32 cm.
Other inscriptions: lower left: "Costume du soldat pour l'Amour et Hiérarchie"; lower right: "M. Ermoloff." The reference is to the actor Mikhail Ermolov, who wore this costume.
Provenance: the artist, Milan, February, 1969.
Reproduced in I20, No. 16; I51, No. 51.

Note: Introduced into the repertoire of the Chauve-Souris in 1924, *Amour et Hiérarchie* was an immediate hit and reappeared regularly in subsequent seasons. When it was performed in England and the USA, its title was changed to *Love in the Ranks*. N. Benois remembers:

> I was introduced to Baliev and immediately he put me to the test by entrusting me with the designs for a sketch called *Love in the Ranks*. I tried to execute it with humor, and it had such a success that Baliev engaged me to design all the other sketches. That was my first victory in a foreign land.[162]

Gostiny Dvor (Une Bouffonerie de l'Ancien Petersbourg): *revue with music by Alexei Arkhangelsky. Produced by Nikita Baliev's Chauve-Souris at the Théâtre Femina, Paris, 1925, with designs by Nicola Benois.*

Two shop assistants, working in a fine clothes and dry goods store located in an old Russian shopping-mall (Gostiny Dvor), are flirting with two lady customers. Indignant, the owner (the merchant) tries to send his assistants away, but, beseeched by the ladies, he is obliged to forgive them.

348

347

Note: Gostiny Dvor was the last in the series of fifteen sketches or revues that Baliev produced in the 1924-25 Paris season of the Chauve-Souris. The souvenir program for the season, i.e. Théâtre de la Chauve-Souris de Nikita Balieff (Paris: Brunoff, 1924), carries a color reproduction of the set designed by N. Benois in which the Shop Assistant and the Merchant can be seen (p. 16). This was one of the most successful seasons for Baliev (Nos. 295 [R265], 297 [R266], 428-29 [NIRE], 578 [R443], 949 [R963]).

347 [R312].
Costume Design for One of the Shop Assistants, 1925.
Watercolor, pencil, and ink.
Signed, dated, and identified lower right in brown ink in Russian: "Nikolai Benois, Paris, 1925, The Bat."
18⅞ x 12⅜ in., 48 x 31.5 cm.
Other inscriptions: upper left in brown paint in Russian: "Gostinyi Dvor," plus the name of the actor and singer "Ermoloff"; upper right in brown paint in Russian: "1st Shop Assistant. The reference is to Mikhail Ermolov (see 346 [R311])
Provenance: the artist, Milan, January, 1980.

348 [R313].
Cotume for the Merchant, 1925.
Watercolor and ink.
Signed, dated, and identified lower right, in brown paint, in Russian: "Nikolai Benois, 1925, The Bat."
19¼ x 13½ in., 49 x 34.3 cm.
Other inscriptions: upper left, in brown paint, in Russian: "Gostinyi Dvor"; upper right in brown paint in Russian: "Merchant (Come into the shop)."
Provenance: the artist, Milan, January, 1980.

The Tale of Tsar Saltan: *opera in three acts by Nikolai Rimsky-Korsakov with a libretto by Vladimir Belsky after a poem by Alexander Pushkin. Produced by Alexandre Sanin at the Teatro Colón, Buenos Aires, fall, 1926, with choreography by Bronislava Nijinska and designs by Nicola Benois.*

Of three sisters, Povarikha, Tkachikha and Militrisa, the Tsar has chosen the youngest, Militrisa to be his bride. The jealousy of the two elder sisters drives the Tsaritsa and her son, the Tsarevich Gvidon, from the kingdom. But they find refuge on the magical island Buyan where they are befriended by a beautiful swan who turns into a Tsarevna and marries Gvidon. Gvidon is sent back to his father's court in the guise of a bumble-bee and the truth is revealed with a happy ending, including the Cinderella-like forgiveness of the elder sisters.

Note: According to the Nijinska Archives (see I65, p. 82), Nijinska choreographed operas at the Teatro Colón only between February and August, 1926. Nicola Benois, however, maintained that this particular collaboration occurred in the fall of 1926.

349 [43; R314].
Stage Design for the Prologue, 1925.
Watercolor, gold paint, and pencil.
Signed and dated lower right: "Nicolai Benois 1925."
16½ x 25 in., 42 x 63.5 cm.
Provenance: the artist, Milan, July, 1969.
Reproduced in color in B115, plate 196; F107, p. 516; M151, p. 96; and in black and white in I20, No. 15; I51, No. 52. There exist several versions of this design, e.g., J27, Lot 234; J44, Lot 133 (cf. No. 350 [R315]).

349

350

The Tale of Tsar Saltan: *opera in three acts by Nikolai Rimsky-Korsakov with a libretto by Vladimir Belsky after a poem by Alexander Pushkin. Produced by Alexandre Sanin at La Scala, Milan, on 19 March, 1929, with designs by Nicola Benois.*
See No. 349 [R314] for plot summary.

350 [R315].
Stage Design for the Prologue, 1928.
Watercolor, gold and silver paint, and pencil.
Signed lower right in ink: "Nicola Benois."
19¼ x 27½ in., 48.8 x 69.7 cm.
Provenance: the artist, Milan, January, 1980. Now in a private collection.
Reproduced in I51, No. 53; M43 (b). A similar design, dated 1930, is reproduced in

J27, Lot 234; and L88, Lot 204. Another version is reproduced in color in a set of 16 postcards, *Nikolai Benua* (M: Izobrazitelnoe iskusstvo, 1978); in 1929 La Scala also published individual black and white postcards and one of them carries a version; see also *Iskusstvo,* M, 1981, No. 12, p. 43 (cf. No. 349 [R314]).

351 [R316].
Costume Design for One of the Four Servants, 1928.
Gouache and pencil.
Signed lower right in blue pencil and dated: "N. Benois, 1928."
14 x 10¼ in., 35.5 x 26 cm.
Other inscriptions: Initialed upper left in red

pencil "NB"; upper right in blue pencil in Italian: "Zar Saltan, I & III Atti, 4 inservienti; 2 di ballerini."
Provenance: the artist, Milan, June, 1980.

352 [R317].
Costume Design for the Messenger, 1929.
Watercolor and colored pencil.
Signed lower right in red pencil and dated: "N. Benois, 29."
12¼ x 9½ in., 31 x 24 cm.
Initialed upper left in red pencil "NB."
Other inscriptions: annotated throughout in French in red and black pencil.
Provenance: the artist, Milan, June, 1980.

Boris Godunov: *opera in a prologue and four acts by Modest Mussorgsky with libretto based on a play of the same name by Alexander Pushkin and Nikolai Karamzin's History of the Russian State. Produced by Alexandre Sanin at La Scala, Milan, in May, 1927, with designs by Nicola Benois.*
See No. 339 [R305] for plot summary.

353 [R318].
Costume Design for Andrei Shchelkalov, Clerk of the Duma, 1927.
Gouache and pencil.
Signed lower right and dated: "Nikolai Benois, 1927."
18⅛ x 11¼ in., 46 x 28.5 cm.
Other inscriptions: lower left in Russian: "Boris Godunov in La Scala Theater"; upper right character identification: "Scelkaloff"; middle right: "15 (?) V 1927"; cloth annotations along right side.
Provenance: the artist, Milan, June, 1980.

354a

354a-f [a in R319].
Six portraits of Fedor Chaliapin, **1929-30.**
Charcoal.
Signed and dated in charcoal in Russian, lower right: "Nikolai Benois. Rome. 1929-30 season"(a); "N. Benois '29" (b-e); "Nikolai Benois. '29" (f).
18⅛ x 12⅝ in., 46.2 x 32 cm.
Other inscriptions: across lower margin in black pencil in Russian: "F.I. Chaliapin attaches the beard for Boris [Godunov]."
Provenance: the artist, Milan, January, 1980. Reproduced in C52, Vol. 2, between pp. 384 and 385 (where variants are also reproduced); G55, p. 286; a version is in J27, Lot 231.

Note: This portrait of the great basso, Fedor (Theodore) Chaliapin (Fedor Ivanovich Shaliapin, 1873-1938), in the role of Boris relates to the Rome premiere of *Boris Godunov* on 19 April, 1929, at the Teatro Reale dell'Opera (in the 1927 Milan production, Carlo Galeffi sang the title role). Both Chaliapin and Nicola Benois received immediate critical acclaim, one reviewer asserting that "Chaliapin was truly great... Benois's sets are very beautiful and the lighting is perfect."[163] Alberto Gasco, correspondent for *La Tribuna* was more explicit:

> With a flicker of the eyelash, a sigh, an imperious or feverish gesture of the hand he [Chaliapin] manages to reveal complex and profound feelings. He imparts an extraordinary firmness of line, an almost frightening clarity to the figure of "Boris." ... The scenarios are of a rare chromatic beauty and of an impeccable style. To the painter Nicola Benois let us give a really heartfelt "Bravo!"[164]

354b

354c

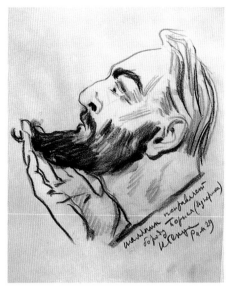

354d

354e

354f

Mefistofele: *opera in a prologue, four acts, and an epilogue by Arrigo Boito. Produced by Gianandrea Gavazzeni under the direction of Margarita Wallmann at La Scala, Milan, on 4 March, 1964, with designs by Nicola Benois.*

Mefistofele appears to Faust as a friar and then reveals himself as the spirit that denies all things. Faust agrees to accompany Mefistofele in return for one hour of peace. Rejuvenated, Faust travels through many adventures with Mefistofele and elicits the love of Margaret. Margaret loses her mind, and, outside her cell, Faust pleads to Mefistofele for her life. In a moment of clarity Margaret tells Faust that she has drowned her baby, and then dies as Mefistofele appears. After other experiences, including an encounter with Helen of Troy, Faust returns to his laboratory and, despite the machinations of Mefistofele, resists him. Faust dies in prayer.

356

357

355 [R320].
Costume Design for One of the Monsters at the Witches' and Devils' Gathering, 1963.
Watercolor, pencil and ink.
Signed and dated lower right: "N. Benois, 63."
12¼ x 9½ in., 31 x 24 cm.
Provenance: the artist, Milan, September, 1969.

A Midsummer Night's Dream: opera in three acts by Benjamin Britten based on the play by William Shakespeare. Produced at the Bolshoi Theater, Moscow on 28 October, 1965, with designs by Nicola Benois.

The complicated plot concerns a group of lovers — Theseus and Hippolyta, Hermia in love with Lysander but who is loved by Demetrius, and Helena, the friend of Hermia, once betrothed to Demetrius. They gather on Midsummer Eve when, unknown to them, the fairies, ruled by Oberon and his Queen Titania, also assemble. Through various mischiefs involving a "juice of love," administered by Oberon's page Puck, the affections of the lovers are transferred; and Bottom, the stupid weaver, is also made to wear an ass's head. But all ends well: the proper lovers are reunited and Bottom reaches Athens in time to perform in Pyramus and Thisbe.

356 [R321].
Costume Design for a Tree Trunk, 1965.
Watercolor and pencil.
Signed and dated: "Nicola Benois, 65."
19⅞ x 14 in., 50.5 x 35.5 cm.
Provenance: the artist, Milan, July, 1969.

357 [R322].
Costume Design for Dandelion, 1965.
Watercolor and pencil.
Signed and dated in Russian: "N. Benois, 65."
19⅞ x 14 in., 50.5 x 35.5 cm.
Other inscription: top right in pencil in Russian: "Onion. Pepper."
Provenance: the artist, Milan, July, 1969.

355

358

359

360

360 [R324].
Portrait of Nikita D. Lobanov-Rostovsky, 1981.
Charcoal and white paint.
Signed and dated lower right in Russian:
"Nikolai Benois '81."
19½ x 27½ in., 49.5 x 70 cm.
Other inscription: signed in pencil lower
center: "Nicola Benois."
Provenance: the artist, Paris, November,
1981. Now in a private collection.
Reproduced in F107, p. 135; I51, p. 2; M20;
M43 (a); M175; M211.

Note: In this portrait Nicola Benois has
conceived the collector as a slightly
mysterious, but joyous, individual who is
helping to preserve a part of European
culture (hence Valentin Serov's *Rape of
Europa* [see No. 914 [R781] in the center of
the picture) and who, at the same time,
possesses a slightly demonic attitude towards the world – hence Nikolai Kalmakov's
Costume Design for a Devil (see No. 599
[R503]) in Lobanov's left hand.[165]

358 [R323].
Portrait of Nikita D. Lobanov-Rostovsky, 1980.
Charcoal.
Signed upper left in a stage design in
Russian: "Nikolai Benois."
17⅞ x 27⅜ in., 45.5 x 69.5 cm.
Other inscriptions: on the book cover in
Russian: "To Dear Nikita Dm. Lobanov-
Rostovsky, collector and preserver of
theatrical art." Benois drew the portrait on
21 June, 1980, in Milan.
Provenance: the artist, Milan, 21 June,
1980.
Reproduced in M10, p. 275.

359 [NIRE].
Portrait of Nikita D. Lobanov-Rostovsky, 1980.
Charcoal and whitewash.
Signed and dated lower center right:
"Nicola Benois 1980."
14½ x 9½ in., 37 x 24 cm.
Provenance: the artist, Milan, 21 June,
1980.
Reproduced in color in F107, p. 130.

160 V. Shklovsky: *Zoo Or Letters Not About Love.*
Trans. Richard Sheldon. Ithaca: Cornell University
Press, 1971, p. 89.

161 N. Benois: "Le Metteur en Scène Théâtrale" in G.
Frette: *Décors de Théâtre.* Milan: Görlich, 1956, p.
XIV. For information on N. Benois's activities at La
Scala after World War II, see G. Gavazzeni (intro.):
La forma dinamica dell'opera lirica, Milan: Lelli and
Masotti, 1984.

162 Allegri: *Gente,* 1981, No. 46, p. 138.

163 Anon.: "Boris Godounow al Teatro Reale" in
Corriere d'Italia, Rome, 1929, 20 April, p. 3.

164 A. Gasco: "'Boris Godunoff' al Teatro Reale
dell'Opera" in *La Tribuna,* Rome, 1929, 20 April, p. 3.

165 From a conversation between Nicola Benois,
Nikita D. Lobanov-Rostovsky, and John E. Bowlt
in Paris, 15 November, 1981 (published in *Novyi
zhurnal,* New York, 2000, December, No. 221, pp.
151-74).

BERMAN, Eugene
(Evgenii Gustavovich)

Born 4 (16) November, 1899, St. Petersburg, Russia; died 14 December, 1972, Rome, Italy.

Until 1908 lived in St. Petersburg; 1908-14 traveled in Germany, Switzerland, and France with his family; 1914 returned to Russia; took art lessons from Pavel Naumov and the architect Sergei Gruzenberg; 1918 emigrated to Paris, where he lived until 1939; 1919 enrolled at the Académie Ranson, attending courses under Edouard Vuillard and Maurice Denis; 1922 traveled in Italy; 1924 first major exhibition at the Galérie Druet, Paris, with his brother Léonide, Pavel Tchelitchew, and others; late 1920s became interested in Italian Renaissance art and architecture; 1930 first American one-man exhibition at the Julien Levy Gallery, New York; 1930s interested in, and influenced by, Salvador Dalí; designed for the Ballet Russe de Monte Carlo; 1936 made his debut as a stage designer with scenery for the second Hartford Music Festival in Connecticut; 1937 became an American citizen; 1941 one-man exhibition in Boston; 1950 one-man exhibition in Buenos Aires.

Bibliography
J. Levy: *Eugene Berman,* Freeport, NY: Books for Libraries Press, 1947.
G. Arnberg: *The Theatre of Eugene Berman.* Catalog of exhibition at the Museum of Modern Art, New York, 1947.
M2, Vol. 2, pp. 155-156.
R. Lynes, introd.: *The Graphic Work of Eugene Berman,* New York: Potter 1971.
"Eugene Berman." Obituary in the *New York Times,* New York, 15 December 1972, p. 52.
M. Duncan: *Eugene Berman in Perspective.* An exhibition of selected works from the Robert L. B. Tobin Collection at the University of Texas, Austin, 1975.
R. Tobin: *Eugene Berman and the Theatre of Melancholia.* Catalog of exhibition at the Marion Koogler McNay Art Museum, San Antonio, Texas, 1984.
M. Duncan et al.: *High Drama. Eugene Berman and the Legacy of the Melancholic Sublime.* Catalog of exhibition at the Marion Koogler McNay Art Museum, San Antonio, Texas, 2005.

Like Nicola Benois, Dmitri Bouchène, Simon Lissim, and Léon Zack, Berman was one of the last representatives of Russia's Silver Age — of the Alexandrine culture that informed the World of Art group and molded Sergei Diaghilev's Ballets Russes. Active in France, Italy, and the USA, Berman maintained close connections with Russian artists and dancers, collaborating, for example, with Serge Lifar on the 1938 production of *Icare* in Monte Carlo. It is of interest to note that for the original 1935 production, Lifar asked Dalí to make the decorations, but the fruits of Dalí's "superabundant imagination"[166] could not be utilized. Evidently, Berman provided a

still visionary, but practical, alternative, and Lifar was pleased with the 1938 sets and costumes. Berman's designs for *The Devil's Holiday* in 1938 and 1939 enabled him also to put his playful fantasy to good purpose, even if — as one enthusiast has observed — the result was reminiscent of the artist's concurrent fashion projects for *Vogue* magazine.[167]

Devil's Holiday (Le Diable s'Amuse): *comic ballet in three scenes and a prologue with music and libretto by Vincenzo Tommasini drawn on themes from Paganini. Produced by the Ballet Russe de Monte Carlo at the Metropolitan Opera House, New York, on 26 October, 1939, with choreography by Frederick Ashton and designs by Eugene Berman.*

The Devil, disguised as a wealthy foreigner, plays tricks on people; a Venetian nobleman, his daughter, her fiancé, a beggar, etc. A ball, a carnival, and a masquerade provide the circumstances for the Devil's high jinks. But midnight strikes and, his holiday over, the Devil disappears.

361

361 [R325].
Hair Design, 1939.
Watercolor.
Initialed and dated: "E.B. 1939."
10⅜ x 8⅝ in., 26.5 x 22 cm.
Other inscriptions: lower margin in French: "Coiffure pour le Diable s'Amuse."
Provenance: K. Sergeyeva, New York, 1967.
Reproduced in I14, No. 39; I51, No. 54; I77, pp. 102 and 130. The Museum of Modern Art, New York, possesses a set of designs for the 1939 production — see G. Goode, *The Book of Ballets, Classic and Modern,* New York: Crown, 1939, pp. 90-91; G21, plates 89, 90.

Note: Although Ashton choreographed this production of *The Devil's Holiday,* with sets and costumes by Berman, and Alexandra

Danilova and Simon Semenoff in the leading roles, it did not enjoy a particular success. Sol Hurok commented:

> Done at the opening of our 1939-40 season, at the Metropolitan Opera House, under the stress and strain of a hectic departure, and a hurried one, from Europe after the outbreak of the war, it suffered as a consequence... Ashton had been able only partially to rehearse the piece in Paris before the company made its getaway, eventually to reach New York on the day of the Metropolitan opening, after a difficult and circuitous crossing to avoid submarines. On arrival, a number of the company were taken off to Ellis Island until we could straighten out faulty visas and clarify papers. I am certain *Devil's Holiday* was one of Ashton's most interesting creations; it suffered because the creator was unable to complete it, and as a consequence, America was never able to see it as its creator intended, or at anything like its best.[168]

166   F23, p. 134.
167   Letter from Robert L. Tobin to John E. Bowlt dated 14 September, 1981.
168   F11, p. 130.

BILIBIN, Alexander Ivanovich

Born 4 (17) February, 1903, St. Petersburg, Russia; died 10 October, 1972, Harting, England.

Eldest son of Ivan Bilibin and Mary Chambers-Bilibina.
1914, being congenitally deaf, sent to a school for the deaf in Switzerland, learning to lipread English and Russian; late 1910s onwards lived with his mother in England; 1924-28 studied at the Central School of Arts and at the Royal Academy, London, under Charles Sims, Ernest Jackson, Walter Sickert, Ambrose McEvoy, and others; also studied drawing under his father, helping him with decorations for the Russian Orthodox Church in Prague; 1930s designed for various English and Russian troupes, in particular, the Mikhail Mordkin Ballet; 1935 and 1937 one-man exhibitions at the Royal Academy; exhibited with the London Group and Artistes Silencieux in Brussels; 1936 stayed abroad when his father returned to the USSR; 1941 designed *Mask of the Red Death* (after Edgar Allan Poe) with choreography by Michel Fokine (not produced); member of the Royal Society of Watercolour Artists, life member of the Chelsea Art Club, and regular contributor of decorations to the New Year parties at the Albert Hall.

Bibliography
Nothing substantial has been published on Alexander Bilibin. Some references will be found in F30, including his reminiscences of his father (pp. 142-46).
M2, Vol. 2, p. 157.

362

363

Reproduced in Joel Carmichael: *Cultural History of Russia,* New York: Weybright and Talley, 1968, opposite p. 217; B75, p. 426; I14, No. 51; I51, No. 58.
No production of *Boris Godunov* with designs by Alexander Bilibin seems to have been staged in 1941.

BILIBIN, Ivan Yakovlevich

Born 4 (16) August, 1876, Tarkhovka, near St. Petersburg, Russia; died 7 February, 1942, Leningrad, Russia.

1890-96 attended gymnasium in St. Petersburg; 1895-98 attended SSEA; 1896 attended Law School at St. Petersburg University; 1898 visited Munich, then Switzerland and Italy; 1898-1900 attended Princess Mariia Tenisheva's art school in St. Petersburg, taking courses under Ilia Repin; 1899 onward close to the World of Art artists, contributing to the journal and exhibitions; contributed illustrations to editions of Russian fairy tales; 1900-04 attended the Higher Art Institute of IAA; 1904 made designs for Nikolai Rimsky-Korsakov's *Snegurochka* produced in 1905 at the Prague National Theater; published an article on the popular art of Northern Russia in the *World of Art* magazine; 1905 contributed to satirical journals such as *Zhupel* [Bugbear]; 1907-11 worked on designs for Sergei Diaghilev's production of *Boris Godunov* in Paris; traveled to England; began to teach at SSEA; began work on designs for Rimsky-Korsakov's *Sadko* at the People's House, St. Petersburg; 1909 designed Sergei Zimin's production of *The Golden Cockerel* in Moscow; 1915 decorated ceilings for the Kazan Station, Moscow; 1917-19 lived in the Crimea; 1920-25 lived in Egypt and then moved to Paris; 1920-30s continued to work as a stage and book designer; made decorations for the Russian Orthodox Church in Prague; 1936 returned to Leningrad; where he taught at the Academy of Arts.

Bibliography
N. Misheev: "I. Bilibin" in H5, 1928, No. 40, pp. 1253-59.
M2, Vol. 2, pp. 157-158.
F30.
G. and S. Golynets: *Ivan Yakovlevich Bilibin,* M: Izobrazitelnoe iskusstvo, 1972.
S. Golynets: "Tvorchestvo I. Ya. Bilibina v gody pervoi russkoi revoliutsii" in *Voprosy otechestvennogo i zarubezhnogo iskusstva,* L, 1975, pp. 109-23.
S. Golynets: *Ivan Bilibin,* L: Aurora, 1981.
O. Semenov: *Ivan Bilibin,* L: Detskaia literatura, 1986.
F. Gray et al.: *Russian Stories. Ivan Bilibin.* Catalog of the exhibition at the University of Brighton Gallery, Brighton, England, 1993.
A. Bode: *Ivan Jakovlevič Bilibin. Der russische Märchenillustrator,* Wielenbach: Erasmus Grasser, 1997.
Anon.: "Vladimir Chuguev, zhizn vne zhurnalizma" in *European Herald,* London, 1999, May, pp. 7-8.

Unknown production, 1935.

362 [NIRE].
Costume Designs for Two Heraldic Creatures, 1935.
Watercolor.
Signed lower right in Russian and dated: "A. Bilibin '35."
19⅛ x 24 in., 48.5 x 61 cm.
Provenance: the artist, London, February, 1966.
Reproduced in I14, p. 25, No. 40.

Boris Godunov: *opera in four acts by Modest Mussorgsky.*
        See No. 339 [R305] for plot summary.

363 [44; R334].
Design for the Proscenium Curtain for Act I, 1941.
Sepia, brown and black chalk.
Signed and dated lower right in Russian: "A. Bilibin 1941."
18½ x 23 in., 47 x 58.5 cm.
Provenance: the artist, London, February, 1966.

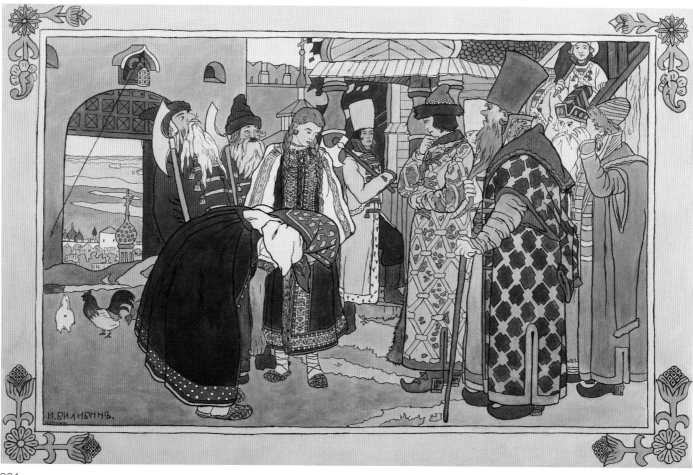

364

G. Klimov: *Ivan Bilibin. Po materialam sobraniia E.P. Klimova,* M: Terra, 1999.
T. Verizhnikova: *Ivan Bilibin,* SP: Aurora, 2001.
V. Beliakov, comp.: *I.Ya. Bilibin v Egipte 1920-1925,* M: Russkii put, 2009.
H64, especially Chapter 3.
T. Verizhnikova, comp.: *I. Bilibin: Zhizn i tvorchestvo. Suzhdeniia ob iskusstve. Sovremenniki o khudozhnike,* SP: Aurora, 2011.

Although Bilibin was not an intimate friend of Sergei Diaghilev or Alexandre Benois, they considered him — in the early years — to be a brilliant designer, and when Diaghilev decided to produce *Boris Godunov* in Paris in 1908, he chose Bilibin to be the costume designer. Bilibin was a fanciful painter, a careful historian, and also an avid collector of antique Russian art. For example, embroideries from his private collection were included in the prestigious "Exhibition of Icon-painting and Artistic Antiquities" in St. Petersburg in 1911-12 and he published a pioneering article on the popular art of Northern Russia in the *World of Art* journal.[169]

Bilibin brought to *Boris Godunov* a valuable experience of the stage and, familiar with the fashions and styles of 16th- and 17th century Russia, he achieved a precise and vivid reincarnation of that epoch. That Bilibin paid every attention to the smallest detail of cut and pattern is evident, for example, in his exotic gown for Boris — immortalized in Alexander

Golovin's portrait of Chaliapin in that role.[170] Bilibin also produced splendid historical costumes for Anna Pavlova and Mikhail Mordkin, which they wore for various divertissements in the 1910s.

Bilibin never betrayed his allegiance to the national art of Russia even in emigration and perhaps that is why he felt a close kinship with Nikolai Rimsky-Korsakov and, like Mikhail Vrubel, found in his operas a deep source of artistic inspiration. Consequently, Bilibin was involved in a number of important productions of works by Rimsky-Korsakov: he designed sets and costumes for *The Golden Cockerel* (Moscow, 1909), for *Sadko* (St. Petersburg, 1914), and for *The Tale of the Invisible City of Kitezh and the Maid Fevronia* (Brno, 1934). Bilibin's work for Sergei Zimin's production of *The Golden Cockerel* attracted particular attention and was praised for the vivid colors of the sets and scintillating patterns of the costumes. Bilibin was very familiar with this theme and with other subjects of Medieval Russian culture from his research into, and illustrations of, Russian fairy stories (for which he is now remembered above all). Through his intense stylization and bright colors, Bilibin tried to express the ethos of ancient Slavdom, even though, as one artist said in reference to Bilibin's interpretations of Pushkin's Russian tales, "he had neither Pushkin's nanny, nor, of course, his genius."[171]

Vasilisa the Beautiful: children's play based on the Russian fairy tale. Possibly a project for a children's theater in St. Petersburg in 1908.

Vasilisa the Beautiful is hated by her step-mother and stepsisters, but she overcomes their evil intentions with the help of a doll willed to her by her late mother. One of the penalties that they impose upon Vasilisa is to obtain fire from Baba-Yaga, the witch who eats people. The doll protects Vasilisa through this adventure and she brings back a skull containing light to her stepmother and stepsisters — a light so bright that it burns them to cinders. Vasilisa then moves in with an old lady who is so struck by Vasilisa's needlework that she shows the Tsar a specimen of her cloth. He is so captivated by Vasilisa's work and then by her beauty that he falls in love with her and they marry.

364 [R335].
Artist unknown: Stage Design for the Scene at the Palace Gate (the Old Lady Brings Vasilisa to the Tsar's Palace), 1908.
Watercolor, gold paint, and black ink.
Signed lower left in Russian: "I. Bilibin" with the word "copy" in Russian and the date "08" underneath.
19⅛ x 29⅛ in., 48.5 x 74 cm.
Provenance: Gregory Frumkin, London, June, 1970.
Reproduced in color in F107, p. 283; I77, p. 10; and in black and white in I77, p. 125; M86; M161; N112, p. 57, where the work is attributed to Bilibin.

Ivan Bilibin: Postcards of costume designs for the opera *Boris Godunov*, 1909,
published by The Society of St. Eugenia Charitable, St. Petersburg.

Note: The original painting, dated 1900 and showing the old lady who has brought Vasilisa to the gates of the Tsar's palace, belonged to the Ministry of Finance in St. Petersburg before the Revolution (present whereabouts unknown). A version of this picture was used as an illustration to the fairy tale of the same name *(Vasilisa Prekrasnaia)* published by the Department for the Preparation of State Papers in St. Petersburg in 1902. According to the former owner of this work, Bilibin made the copy for the son of the then British Ambassador to Russia, who, in 1908, was Sir Arthur Nicolson. However, this watercolor lacks the

vigor and precision of Bilibin's style and the question of another artist's hand (perhaps a copy by one of Bilibin's students) is a pressing one. The former owner also maintained that this was for a production at a children's theater, but there is no record of such a spectacle designed by Bilibin in the mid-1900s. Bilibin did work on designs for a Prague production of *Snegurochka* in 1904 (realized in 1905) that, in style, is reminiscent of this particular set. Bilibin also worked on stage designs for the famous *Golden Cockerel* production in Moscow in 1909 and for *Sadko* at the People's House, St. Petersburg, in 1914, and both cycles of

designs have affinities with the piece under discussion.[172] The image of Vasilisa was modeled after Anna Pogosskaia, daughter of the Populist writer Alexander Fomich Pogossky (1816-74).[173]

Boris Godunov: *opera in four acts by Modest Mussorgsky. Produced by Sergei Diaghilev for the first Saison Russe at the Théâtre National de l'Opéra, Paris on 19 May, 1908, with set designs by Alexandre Benois, sets and costumes by Alexander Golovin, and additional costumes by Ivan Bilibin assisted by Dmitrii Stelletsky.*

See No. 339 [R305] for plot summary.

365

366

367

365 [NIRE].
Costume Design for a Married Woman from Olonets Region, 1908.
Watercolor and black ink.
Signed and dated lower right in Russian: "I. Bilibin 1908."
15 x 10⅝ in., 38 x 27 cm.
Provenance: Issar Gourvitch, Paris, November, 1966.
Reproduced in I20, p. 19, No. 20. A very similar design, dated 1905, is reproduced in L170, Lot 113.

366 [R336].
Costume Design for a Boyar, 1908.
Watercolor.
Signed and dated lower right in Russian: "I. Bilibin 1908."
13⅜ x 9⅞ in., 34 x 25 cm.
Other inscription: center right side in Russian: "Boyar."
Provenance: Issar Gourvitch, Paris, November, 1966. Now in a private collection.
Reproduced in color in B115, plate 19; and in black and white in I14, No. 43; I51, No. 55; M148; N157; R1; R11. There exist several variants of boyars' costumes made by Bilibin for this and later productions. See, for example, the Souvenir Program
for the *Opéra Privé de Paris. Première Saison,* Paris, 1929, unpaginated.
Both *Costume Design for a Married Woman from Olonets Region* and *Costume Design for a Boyar* were reproduced as color postcards in 1909 by the Society of St. Eugenia of the Red Cross, St. Petersburg, as part of a set of eight costume designs by Bilibin for *Boris Godunov.*

Note: Bilibin contributed a great deal to the success of the first major Russian season in Paris in 1908 since he researched and collected historical costumes specifically

for this production of *Boris Godunov.* Diaghilev recalled:

> Wanting to have the costumes for *Boris* as splendid and authentic as possible, I had sent out a sort of expedition under the painter Bilibine, the well-known expert on old Russia, to search the northern provinces, particularly those of Arkhangelsk and Vologda. Bilibine went from village to village buying up from the peasants a mass of beautiful hand-woven sarafans, head-dresses and embroidery, which had been hoarded in chests for centuries.[174]

Bilibin returned to *Boris Godunov* in 1931 for Alexander Ulukhanov's production for the Opéra Russe de Paris, but although he used similar costumes, the result did not repeat the phenomenal success of the 1908 production — when Fedor Chaliapin sang Boris in Bilibin's dazzling costume under the baton of Felix Blumenfeld.

The Tale of Tsar Saltan: *opera in three acts by Nikolai Rimsky-Korsakov with a libretto by Vladimir Belsky after a poem by Alexander Pushkin. Produced by Nikolai Evreinov for Marie Kousnezoff's Opéra Privé de Paris at the Théâtre des Champs-Elysées, Paris, in late January, 1929, with designs by Ivan Bilibin and some costume designs by Alexandra Shchekatikhina-Pototskaia, executed by Alexandre Shervashidze.*
See No. 349 [R314] for plot summary.

367 [R337].
Costume Design for the Tsarevich Gvidon Disguised as a Bumble-bee, 1929.
Watercolor and pencil.
Initialed lower right in Russian and French

and dated: "1 January, 1929."
12¼ x 9¼ in., 31 x 23.5 cm.
Other inscriptions: lower right in Russian: "Bumble-bee."
Provenance: the nephew of Alexandre Benois, Mikhail Benois, Madrid, May, 1968.
Reproduced in color in N188, p. 8; in black and white in I20, No. 21; I51, No. 56.

368 [46; R338].
Costume Design for the Guard, 1929.
Watercolor.
Signed lower left, initialed in Russian, and dated: "1929"; also signed in French: "J. Bilibine."
16½ x 11¾ in., 42 x 30 cm.
Other inscriptions: lower left in Russian: "Tsar Saltan; the Guard."

368

Le Gardien, de "Tzar Saltan"
Décors et Costumes de J. Bilibine

GRANDE SAISON DES OPÉRAS RUSSES

Le Navigateur, de "Tzar Saltan"
Décors et Costumes de J. Bilibine

OPÉRA PRIVÉ DE PARIS
Direction :
Maria KOUSNEZOFF-MASSENET

Théâtre des Champs-Élysées
13 et 15, av. Montaigne, - Élys. 72-42. 72-43

10	Mai	Kitège
11	Mai	Tzar Saltan
12	Mai	Prince Igor
15	Mai	Kitège
16	Mai	Tzar Saltan (matinée)
19	Mai	Prince Igor
20	Mai	Tzar Saltan
22	Mai	Prince Igor
23	Mai	Snegourotchka (matinée)
24	Mai	Kitège
26	Mai	Prince Igor

Les gravures sont extraites du programme de l'Opéra Privé de Paris édité par la Publicité Commerciale & Théâtrale 46, Rue de Provence - Paris

"Succès"

Orchestre des Concerts Symphoniques
Walter STRARAM
65 exécutants

Directeur de Musique et Ier Chef d'Orchestre
EMIL COOPER
ancien Ier Chef d'Orchestre des Théâtres Impériaux de Russie

Chef d'Orchestre :
Alexandre LABINSKY

Chœurs Mixtes
de l'Opéra Privé de Paris
70 personnes

Danses Polovtsiennes du "Prince Igor" réglées par
Michel FOKINE
Maître de Ballets des Théâtres Impériaux de Pétrograd

LES DÉCORS ET LES COSTUMES
d'après les esquisses des artistes peintres
C. KOROVINE et J. BILIBINE
Les costumes sont exécutés dans les
ATELIERS DE L'OPÉRA PRIVÉ DE PARIS

L'atelier de l'Opéra Privé reçoit les commandes

Program for Opéra Privé de Paris repertoire, May 1929 with two costume designs by Ivan Bilibin.

Provenance: Alexandre Djanchieff, Paris, February, 1978.
Reproduced in color in the Souvenir Program for the *Opéra Privé de Paris. Première Saison*, Paris, 1929, unpaginated; and in B115, plate 188; and in black and white in F30, between pp. 240 and 241.

Note: Bilibin had a long-standing attachment to this fairy tale, the full title of which is *The Tale of Tsar Saltan, of His Son the Glorious and Mighty Bogatyr Gvidon Saltanovich, and of the Beautiful Tsarevna Swan*. Bilibin's illustrations to the 1905 edition of the tale are among his most

successful, and he used a similar style and imagery for his cover of the program for this production (which was also used for subsequent programs at the Opéra Privé). In 1928 Bilibin created a set of illustrations for a proposed new edition of *Tsar Saltan* and he returned to the opera itself in 1937 with a lavish production at the Kirov Theater, Leningrad. Bilibin's designs for the 1929 version were well received, as Gustav Bret of *l'Intransigeant*, affirmed: "Musique, décors, costumes, cette représentation du *Tsar Saltan* est une joyeuse et magnifique fête de la couleur."[175] Bilibin's wife, Alexandra Shchekatikhina-Pototskaia, also

helped with the costumes (cf. Nos. 919-23 [R966-69]). Marie Kousnezoff (see No. 80 [R76]) founded her Opéra Privé de Paris in 1928. Although she attracted talented artists, producers, and dancers such as Bakst, Benois, Bilibin, Konstantin Korovin, Nikolai Evreinov, Boris Romanov, Bronislava Nijinska, and Alexandra Balashova, she ran into financial difficulties, especially after a disastrous American tour. In 1930 her company was taken over by Prince Alexei Tsereteli and Colonel Wassily de Basil and was renamed the Opéra Russe de Paris, but the new enterprise soon folded.[176]

369

Provenance: *Ballet and Theatre Material*, London: Sotheby's, London, 9 June, 1983, Lot 31 (reproduced).
Reproduced in color in B115, plate 189; I77, p. 65; I117, p.284; J22, Lot 7; in black and

370

The Tale of the Invisible City of Kitezh and the Maid Fevronia: *opera in four acts by Nikolai Rimsky-Korsakov with a libretto by Vladimir Belsky. Produced by Marie Kousnezoff's Opéra Privé de Paris, Paris, on 27 February, 1929, with designs by Alexei Korovin.*

Prince Vsevolod, in disguise, comes upon Fevronia in her humble hut. Taken by her songs of nature, he falls in love with her and the couple agree to marry. The people of the city of Little Kitezh await the bride and groom, but the dignitaries are dissatisfied that the Prince will marry a peasant girl, and they ask the drunkard Grishka Kuterma to insult her. As the people drive Grishka away, sounds of battle are heard, and the Tatars suddenly appear, looking for the road to the city of Kitezh. They capture Fevronia and persuade Grishka to lead them to their destination. The Tatars fight over their maidenly prize, but suddenly the mirage of the fairy city of Kitezh appears, and, fearful, the Tatars run away. Fevronia, believing her Prince to be killed, wishes for death, but he appears and bears her off to Kitezh.

369 [R339].
Stage Design for Paradise in Act 4, Scene 2 (the City of Kitezh), 1929.
Watercolor.
Initialed and dated lower right in Russian: "I.B. 1929"; signed below in French: "J. Bilibine."
21½ x 28⅜ in., 54.5 x 72 cm.
Provenance: the nephew of Alexandre Benois. Mikhail Benois, Madrid, May, 1968. Now in a private collection.
Reproduced in color in B115, plate 190; and in black and white I20, No. 19; I51, No. 57; M175. A very similar design, in the the RM, is reproduced in color in G. and S. Golynets, *Bilibin,* p. 170; and in S. Golynets, *Bilibin* (1981), No. 147. Also see G30, No. 29.

Note: Bilibin created this set for the 1929 production of *The Tale of the Invisible City*

of Kitezh organized by Marie Kousnezoff for her Opéra Privé. But, for reasons unknown, she gave the actual commission to Alexei Korovin (see Nos. 630-41 [R525-36]). However, Bilibin, who used the basic principle of this set in several designs (e.g., for *The Golden Cockerel* in 1909 and *L'Oiseau de Feu* at the Teatro Colón, Buenos Aires, in 1931), reworked it for a production at the City Theater, Brno, on 8 November, 1934.

L'Oiseau de Feu: *ballet in two scenes with music by Igor Stravinsky based on the Russian fairy tale. Produced at the Teatro Colón, Buenos Aires, on 5 (?) September, 1931, with choreography by Michel Fokine and designs by Ivan Bilibin.*

The young prince Ivan Tsarevich finds the Firebird in a forest glade at night. In exchange for her freedom, the Firebird gives the Tsarevich one of her golden feathers. Twelve princesses come upon the scene and one takes the fancy of the Tsarevich. Enamoured of him, she begs him to flee because of the wizard Kashchei. The Tsarevich waves the feather and the Firebird forces the demons of Kashchei to dance until they drop. The Firebird then shows the Tsarevich a huge egg in a tree, the soul of Kashchei, and Tsarevich proceeds to throw it to the ground — destroying the wicked Kashchei and his court. The Tsarevich and his maiden then celebrate their wedding.

370 [R340].
Costume Design for a Goat in the Suite of Kashchei, 1910/1931.
Watercolor and gouache over pencil.
Initialed in Russian and dated 1910; signed lower right in French: "J. Bilibine."
15 x 10⅝ in., 38 x 27 cm.
Other inscriptions: on reverse in heavy black ink: "J. Bilibine, Ballets Russes de S. Diaghileff, 1910"; also two French customs stamps for export.

white in A34, p. 79; I77, p. 125; M68; P16; P38; and in J37, Lot 31, where it is described as an item for *Le Festin* of 1909.

Note: Bilibin based his image of the goat on a popular 18th-century Russian *lubok* (cheap hand-colored print) called *The Bear and the Nanny-Goat Idle Away Their Time.*[177] The date at the right of the design plus the inscription on the reverse may indicate that Bilibin submitted this design to Diaghilev for the 1910 production of *L'Oiseau de Feu* in Paris. The 1931 attribution, however, is based on a documentary photograph of 1931, in which the head of the goat can be seen.[178]

371

371 [R341].
Cover design for a program for Colonel de Basil's Ballets Russes de Monte Carlo, 1931.
Watercolor, black ink, and pencil.
3⅝ x 2⅞ in., 9.1 x 7.2 cm.

169 I. Bilibin: "Narodnoe tvorchestvo russkogo Severa" in *Mir iskusstva*, SP, 1904, No. 11, pp. 303-18.

170 Golovin's portrait of Fedor Chaliapin in the role of Boris Godunov wearing Bilibin's costume (1912) is in the RM.

171 V. Levitsky: "Molodye gody I.Ya. Bilibina i russkoi grafiki" n F30, p. 136.

172 For reproductions and commentary see G. and S. Golynets, *Bilibin*, pp. 88-90, 133.

173 According to Cyril Katkow in a letter from him to Wendy Salmond dated 28 October, 1984. Katkow was an assistant of Bilibin in Paris.

174 D26, p. 105.

175 Gustav Bret in *l'Intransigeant*, 1929. Quoted in the Souvenir Program of the *Opéra Privé de Paris. Première Saison*, Paris, 1929, unpaginated.

176 For information on Kousnezoff-Massenet (Kuznetsova) see *Teatr*, Berlin, 1922, No. 9, p. 15; and 1929, No. 1, p. 15; D31, p. 5; E. Bespalova: "Khudozhnik i pevitsa. Tvorcheskii soiuz Lva Baksta i Marii Kuznetsovoi" in *Russkoe iskusstvo*, M, 2006, No. 4, pp. 54-67; and E. Bespalova: "Korovin v parizhskoi chastnoi opere Marii Kuznetsovoi," ibid., 2011, No. 4, pp. 105-13. Also see Konstantin Korovin section.

177 For a reproduction of this *lubok* see, for example, Yu. Ovsiannikov: *Lubok*, M: Sovetskii khudozhnik, 1968, plate 42.

178 See Golynets: *Bilibin* (1981), p. 205. Vera Popova, who executed the masks for the 1931 production in her Paris workshops, has described her activities in Golynets, *Bilibin* (1970), p. 233.

BILINSKY, Boris Konstantinovich

Born 21 September (4 October), 1900, Benderi, Bessarabia, Moldova; died 3 February, 1948, Catania, Sicily, Italy.

1910s attended Military Academy and University in Odessa; 1920 left the Ukraine for Berlin, where he studied stage design under Max Reinhardt; early 1920s worked for the Blaue Vogel and other cabarets; 1923 settled in Paris, where he started to work for a number of theaters, including l'Arc en Ciel; established contact with Léon Bakst, Simon Lissim, Léon Zack, and other Russian artists; 1925 received a Gold Medal at the "Exposition Internationale des Arts Décoratifs" in Paris for a poster design; 1928 established his own advertising corporation, Alboris; 1920s-30s involved in many opera, ballet, and movie productions, working with Nikolai Evreinov, Serge Lifar, Bronislava Nijinska, Boris Romanov, and other directors and choreographers for various Russian ballet and opera companies, such as the Opéra Russe à Paris and the Ballet Russe de Monte Carlo; among his celebrated set and/or poster designs for movies were those for *Le Lion des Mogols* (1924), *Metropolis* (1926), *Casanova* (1927), and *Monte Cristo* (1929); created an illustrative cycle for the theme of St. John's visions of the Apocalypse; among his ballet and drama designs were those for *Symphonie Fantastique* (1933) and *Pelléas et Mélisande* (1933 and 1937); 1938 designed the female costumes for Maurice Tourneur's production of the movie *Katia* (Alexander

Arnstham designed the other costumes and the sets); 1939-47 lived in Rome; worked for Titanus Films and also for La Scala in Milan, designing, for example, Aurelio Milloss' *Follie viennesi* for the 1946-47 season; also designed jewelry and leather goods; with Walt Disney discussed the idea of transposing part of his "musique en couleurs" to cinema.

Bibliography:

A. P-V: "B.K. Bilinsky" in *Teatr i iskusstvo*, Paris, 1924, No. 2 , p. 10.

E. Znosko-Borovsky: "A propos de quatre artistes (Larionov, Léon Zak, Modzalevsky, Bilinsky)" in *La Revue de "l'Oeuvre"*, Paris, 1927, November, No. 1, pp. 24-26.

S. Lissim: "Boris Bilinsky" in *Mobilier et décoration théâtrales*, Paris, 1931, Année 11, pp. 425-28.

S. Lissim: "Boris Bilinsky; décorations théâtrales et cinématographiques" in *Art et les artistes*, Paris, 1937, December, pp. 101-04.

Anon.: *Boris Bilinsky. Cinema, Teatro, Musica.* Catalog of exhibition at the Casa d'Arte Bragaglia, Rome, 1940.

S. Shcherbatov: "Nezavershennyi 'Apokalipsis'" in *Russkaia mysl*, Paris, 1948, 12 March, p. 5.

Anon.: *Scenografia e balletto. Acquarelli e tempere di Bilinsky.* Catalog of exhibition at the Capannina di Porfiri, Rome, 1955.

M3, Vol. 3, pp. 207-209.

Anon. (S. Lissim?): *Boris Bilinsky.* Catalog of exhibition at the Leonard Hutton Galleries, New York, May-June, 1975.

V. Bilinsky-Clémenti: *Boris Bilinsky (1900-1948).* Catalog of auction at Hôtel des Ventes, Bayeux, France, 1993, 25 April.

O. Medvedkova: "Borisu Belinskomu [sic] s voskhishcheniem" in *Russkaia mysl*, Paris, 1993, 18-24 June, p. 14.

I88, passim.

V. Bilinsky-Clémenti: "Colored Music: The Pictorial Transcriptions of Boris Bilinsky" in B183, No. 2, pp. 508-15.

H38, passim.

R. Clémenti-Bilinsky: *Boris Bilinsky, Dessins pour l'Opéra, le Théâtre et le Ballet, 1927-1947.* Catalog of exhibition at the Mairie du 7e Arrondissement, Paris, 1999.

A. Karetnikov: "Meriia 7-go raiona Parizha ustroila vystavku Borisa Konstantinovicha Bilinskogo" in *Evropeiskii vestnik*, London, 1999, No. 32, p. 15.

R. Clémenti-Bilinsky: "Un fonds oublié: les archives de Boris Bilinsky" in *Cinémaction*, Paris, 2000, No. 97, pp. 74-80.

V. Crespi Morbio: *Bilinsky a La Scala*, Turin: Allemandi, 2011.

Bilinsky is remembered for his artistic contribution to the European cinema in the 1920s and 1930s, when he worked as a set and/or poster designer for important productions such as *Casanova* (1927), *Metropolis* (1927), *Schéhérazade* (1928), and *Le Diable Blanc* (1929). As a commercial artist, Bilinsky was much sought after, especially by the Russian émigré producers working in the French film business at Montreuil, such as Nicolai Malikoff, Victor Tourjansky, and Alexandre Volkoff, and his vivid style suited their effervescent scenarios.

However, in spite of this close association with the entertainment industry, Bilinsky was a serious and introspective artist who

treated his scenographic commissions as "rubbish [but] sometimes it all amuses and diverts."[179] Symptomatic of Bilinsky's philosophical inclination was his profound interest in the Apocalypse and Book of Revelations, which inspired his sequence of illustrations — stirring visions of the end of the world that could almost constitute the frames of a motion picture. Bilinsky hoped that these Apocalyptic scenes could in some way be connected with a musical score, making for a synthesis of music and image. After all, for Bilinsky, music was the noblest form of art, because it was an abstract and universal signpost to the spiritual — or to the "Mysterium" that fascinated Alexander Skriabin (one of Bilinsky's favorite composers). Like Skriabin and Vladimir Baranoff-Rossiné (see No. 108 [NIRE]), Bilinsky believed that music could be translated into colors and vice versa, and that a system of transcription could be elaborated, as he tried to explain in his notes:

> Once I have selected the musical piece that I want to translate pictorially, my spirit then endeavors to saturate itself in the atmosphere of the music so as to penetrate its style, its character, its predominant colors, and its rhythm. [In this way my spirit] will apprehend the vibrations and attune me to the musician.[180]

Unfortunately, Bilinsky's untimely death cut short his researches on color-sound translation, although perhaps his ideas did come to fruition in the Walt Disney production of Leopold Stokowski's *Fantasia* of 1940.

372 [R342].
Self-Portrait, ca. 1925.
Pencil, heightened with watercolor.
Signed lower right in white with the monogram :"BB."
9⅞ x 7⅞ in., 25 x 20 cm.
Other inscription: on the reverse: "Paris, 2/vii."
Provenance: Federico Bartoli, Rome, 1984.

372

Le Lion des Mogols: film by Jean Epstein after a narrative by Ivan Mozzhukhin (Mosjoukine). Produced by Jean Epstein for the Société des Films Albatros, Montreuil-sous-Bois, near Paris, with décors by Alexandre Lochakoff and costumes by Boris Bilinsky. Released on 12 December, 1924.

The young Mogol officer Roundghito saves the captive princess Zemgali from the lust of the Great Khan, but is obliged to leave his native country. Anna, an actress, falls in love with him, but she proves to be an exiled Mogol princess and the sister of Roundghito. When the Khan dies, they return to their country and Roundghito, now the crown prince, marries Zemgali.

374

373

373 [R348].
Costume Design for a Mountebank, 1924.
Watercolor.
Signed lower left: "Boris Bilinsky."
20⅞ x 14 in., 53 x 35.5 cm.
Other inscription: lower right in French: "Bateleur."
Provenance: the artist's daughter, Valeria Bilinsky-Clémenti, Paris, July, 1969.
Reproduced in I20, p. 20.

374 [R354].
Costume Design for Anna, 1924.
Watercolor, silver paint, and pencil.
Signed lower right with the monogram: "BB."
19¼ x 12⅝ in., 49 x 32 cm.
Other inscription: lower left in French: "Madame Lissenko" (a reference to Natalia Lisenko, 1886-1969, who played the part of Anna).
Provenance: the artist's daughter, Valeria Bilinsky-Clémenti, Paris, July, 1969.
Reproduced in I40, No. 36, where it is described as a costume for the opera *Polovtsian Dances.*

375

375 [R355].
Costume Design for the Prince, 1924.
Watercolor and gold paint.
Signed with monogram lower right: "BB."
20⅛ x 14 in., 51 x 35.5 cm.
Other inscription: lower left in French: "Prince" (played by Ivan Mozzhukhin).
Provenance: the artist's daughter, Valeria Bilinsky-Clémenti, Paris, July, 1969.
Reproduced in I40, No. 37, where it is described as a costume for the opera *Polovtsian Dances.*

Note: Epstein's *Le Lion des Mogols* was Bilinsky's first involvement in movie design

and his costumes attracted immediate attention, eliciting comparison with Léon Bakst's ballet costumes of the same period. Bilinsky also designed the poster for the motion picture which was awarded a Gold Medal at the Paris "Exposition Internationale des Arts Décoratifs" in 1925.[181]

Geheimnisse des Orients (Schéhérazade): film directed by Alexandre Volkoff based on the Arabian Nights. Produced for the Universum Film Aktiengesellschaft (UFA-Film), Berlin, 1928, with costumes by Boris Bilinsky and sets by Alexandre Lochakoff.

In a magical Middle East of lovely maidens and dashing princes, a poor Egyptian cobbler — through comic twists of fate — wins and loses the friendship of a Sultan.

376

376 [R343].
Costume Design for Prince Hussein, ca. 1928.
Watercolor and silver paint.
Signed lower left: "Boris Bilinsky."
15¾ x 12⅝ in., 40 x 32 cm.
Provenance: the artist's daughter, Valeria Bilinsky-Clémenti, Paris, July, 1969.
Reproduced in I40, No. 38; I77, p. 130; I117, p. 277; a costume for Shah Shahriar in the same motion picture is reproduced in J31, Lot 101.
The costume was worn by the comic actor Gaston Modot.

Note: The UFA version of *Schéhérazade* was the German answer to Robert Leonard's audacious *Restless Sex* released from Hollywood in 1920 with designs by Erté. Bilinsky was an obvious choice for the costume designs here since he had already collaborated with Volkoff on the latter's

Casanova released in Paris in 1927. Of the same generation as Erté and Umberto Brunelleschi, Bilinsky brought a highly spiced and honeyed Orient to Western audiences, maintaining the fashion that Bakst had created. Bilinsky used similar designs for a booklet called *Schéhérazade* (title in Arabic, Paris: Langlois, ca. 1930) that promoted the Schéhérazade cabaret that opened in Paris in 1927 (in 1934 Bilinsky was invited to design the interior decoration). In all these contexts Bilinsky stressed the rich, but taut organization of the Persian miniature, something that made the Volkoff *Schéhérazade* "one of the great productions of the current season... Mr. Bilinsky has brought much artistic fancy and taste to the picture by his costumes."[182] It should be added that, for Bilinsky, the principal attraction of the cinema was because it gratified his desire to attain a true synthesis of sound and movement — the "sound assumes a spatial, visual form while the image resounds and moves in time."[183]

377

Ruslan and Liudmila: *opera in five acts by Mikhail Glinka after a poem by Alexander Pushkin. Produced by Nikolai Evreinov for Prince Alexei Tsereteli and Colonel Wassily de Basil's Opéra Russe à Paris on 24 May, 1930, with choreographic numbers by Bronislava Nijinska, choreography for the dream sequence by Boris Romanov, and designs by Boris Bilinsky. On 4 June, 1931, the production opened at the Lyceum Theater, London, before going on to Madrid.*

Ruslan, a knight, and Liudmila, daughter of Prince Svetozar, celebrate their wedding despite a prophecy of fatal danger. Thunder and gloom suddenly come upon the merrymakers, and Liudmila is abducted. Svetozar promises his daughter's hand and half his kingdom to the one who finds her. Ruslan finds out that Chernomor has taken Liudmila, and, after finding her in the Gardens of Chernomor, cuts off Chernomor's beard, thus depriving him of his magic power. Ruslan awakens Liudmila from her slumber and the two are reunited.

377 [47; R344].
Stage Design for Prince Svetozar's Feast for Liudmila's Wedding, 1930.
Watercolor, silver and gold paper collage.
Signed and dated lower left: "Boris Bilinsky 30."
19¼ x 25 in., 49 x 63.5 cm.
Provenance: the artist's daughter, Valeria Bilinsky-Clémenti, Paris, July, 1969.
Reproduced in color in the Souvenir Program for the *Opéra Russe de Paris* (Paris, 1930), unpaginated; and in I51, p. 16; and in black and white in I20, No. 22; I77, p. 130; T9. Costumes for the same production are reproduced in J31, Lot 29; a similar set design is reproduced in color on the cover of H8, 1 June, 1930. This piece is rather similar to Ivan Bilibin's and Alexei Korovin's designs for the 1929 Paris production of *The Tale of the Invisible City of Kitezh and the Maid Fevronia* (Cf. Nos. 369 [R339], 630 [R525]).

378 [R346].
Costume Design for a Waiter, 1930.
Watercolor and pencil.
Initialed lower left. "BB."
19⅝ x 13 in., 50 x 33 cm.
Provenance: the artist's daughter, Valeria Bilinsky-Clémenti, Paris, July, 1969.
Reproduced in I40, No. 34.

379

378

379 [R347].
Costumes for Two Russian Noblemen, 1930.
Watercolor and pencil.
Signed with monogram and dated left: "BB. 30."
20⅛ x 14 in., 51 x 35.5 cm.
Provenance: Nicolas Wyruboff, Paris, July, 1969.
Reproduced in I40, No. 31.

The Polovtsian Dances: *excerpt from Alexander Borodin's opera* Prince Igor. *Produced by Prince Alexei Tsereteli and Colonel Wassily de Basil's Opéra Russe à Paris and the Compagnie des Ballets Russes de Bronislava Nijinska for the Théâtre de la Danse Nijinska at the Théâtre National de l'Opéra Comique, Paris on 23 May, 1932, with designs by Boris Bilinsky.*

The scene is laid in an encampment of the Polovtsians where Prince Igor and his son, Prince Vladimir, are prisoners. Although a prisoner of Khan Konchak, Prince Igor is still treated with respect and fiery dances are staged in order to distract him. Thus Khan Konchak hopes that Prince Igor will consent not only to a lasting peace with the Polovtsians, who are ruled by the Great Khan, but also to the union of Prince Vladimir and Konchakovna, the Khan's beautiful daughter. However, Prince Igor manages to escape, while Prince Vladimir is unsuccessful in his bid for freedom. However, all ends happily, since Prince Igor joins his wife Yaroslavna, while Prince Vladimir is allowed to remain with the Polovtsians as husband to Konchakovna.

La Princesse Cygne: *ballet based on an excerpt from Rimsky-Korsakov's opera* The Tale of Tsar Saltan, *starting from Act II, Prince Guidon's arrival at the deserted island of Buyan. Originally produced by Ida Rubinstein in Paris in 1928, with choreography by Bronislava Nijinska. Then produced by Prince Alexei Tsereteli and Colonel Wassily de Basil's Opéra Russe à Paris and the Compagnie des Ballets Russes de Bronislava Nijinska for the Théâtre de la Danse Nijinska at the Théâtre National de l'Opéra Comique, Paris, on 2 June, 1932, with choreography by Bronislava Nijinska and costume and set designs by Boris Bilinsky.*

See No. 349 [R314] for plot summary.

382

381

380

380 [R353].
Costume Design for a Persian Slave Dancer with Flying Braids, 1932.
Watercolor.
Signed lower right: "Boris Bilinsky."
19 x 12⅝ in. 48.3 x 32 cm.
Provenance: the artist's daughter, Valeria Bilinsky-Clémenti, Paris, July, 1969. Now in a private collection.
Reproduced in I40, No. 35.

381 [48; R345].
Costume Design for a Boyar, ca. 1932.
Watercolor and pencil.
19⅝ x 13 in., 50 x 33 cm.
Inscriptions: color and cloth annotations in Russian and French in the margins for the dressmaker; on reverse: identification and certification by Bilinsky's daughter, Valeria Bilinsky-Clémenti: "La princesse Cygne fait par mon père Bilinsky."
Provenance: the artist's daughter, Valeria Bilinsky-Clémenti, Paris, July, 1969. Now in a private collection.
Reproduced in I40, No. 29; I51, No. 61; a similar design is reproduced in the Souvenir Program, *La Nijinska Ballets Russes. Théâtre de la Danse,* Paris, 1934, unpaginated; another similar design is reproduced in black and white in J31, Lot 94.

382 [R349].
Costume Design for a Warrior, ca. 1932.
Watercolor and pencil.
Signed lower left: "Boris Bilinsky."
19⅞ x 12¾ in., 50.5 x 32.5 cm.
Annotations in pencil throughout.

Provenance: the artist's daughter, Valeria Bilinsky-Clémenti, Paris, July, 1969.
Reproduced in I20, No. 23.

383 [R350].
Costume Design for a Russian Peasant Woman, 1932.
Watercolor.
Signed and dated lower left: "Boris Bilinsky 32."
17⅜ x 12⅝ in., 44 x 32 cm.
Provenance: the artist's daughter, Valeria Bilinsky-Clémenti, Paris, July, 1969.
Reproduced in I40, No. 28; a replica, but unsigned and undated, in the collection of The Fine Arts Museums of San Francisco, is reproduced in I44, p. 37.

383

384

384 [R351].
Costume Design for a Russian Peasant Man,
ca. 1932.
Watercolor and pencil.
Signed lower right: "Boris Bilinsky."
19 x 12⅝ in., 48.3 x 32 cm.
Provenance: the artist's daughter, Valeria
Bilinsky-Clémenti, Paris, July, 1969.
Reproduced in I40, No. 27.

Note: Traditionally, it has been assumed
that this item was a costume design for the
1932 *La Princesse Cygne.* However,
according to Bilinsky's grandson, René

385

Clémenti-Bilinsky, "A partir de 1937, tous
les dessins signés portent le paraphe B.
Bilinsky en lettres capitales."[184] Consequently, the piece may be for a later
production.

385 [R352].
Costume Design for the Prince, ca. 1932.
Watercolor and pencil.
Signed lower left: "Boris Bilinsky."
19 x 12¼ in., 48.3 x 31 cm.
Provenance: the artist's daughter, Valeria
Bilinsky-Clémenti, Paris, July, 1969.
Reproduced in I40, No. 30.

386

387

386 [NIRE].
Costume Design for the Jail Watchman, 1932.
Watercolor.
Signed lower right: "B. Bilinsky."
19½ x 12⅝ in., 49.5 x 32 cm.
Provenance: the artist's daughter, Valeria
Bilinsky-Clémenti, Paris, July, 1969. Now in
a private collection.
Reproduced in I40, p. 53.

387 [NIRE].
Costume Design for a Russian Priest, 1932.
Watercolor and ink.
Signed lower right: "B. Bilinsky."
19⅝ x 12⅝ in., 50 x 32 cm.
Provenance: the artist's daughter, Valeria
Bilinsky-Clémenti, Paris, July, 1969. Now in
a private collection.
Reproduced in I40, p. 53.

179 Shcherbatov, "Nezavershennyi 'Apokalipsis'", p. 5.
180 S. Lo Presti: "Vedere la musica" in *La Sicilia,*
     Catania, December, 1946 / January, 1947.
181 We would like to thank René Bilinsky-Clémenti,
     grandson of the artist, for providing this infor-
     mation to John Bowlt.
182 Anon: "Po studiiam" in *Illiustrirovannaia Rossiia,*
     Paris, 1929, 16 February, p. 15.
183 Statement in *Boris Bilinsky* (1940), unpaginated.
184 Clémenti-Bilinsky, "Un fonds oublié", p. 77.

BOGOMAZOV, Alexander Konstantinovich

Born 14 (20) March, 1880, Yampol, near
Kharkov, Ukraine; died 3 June, 1930, Kiev,
Ukraine.

1896-1902 attended the Kherson Agricultural
Institute; 1902 enrolled at the Kiev Art
Institute; met Alexandra Exter; 1905 took part
in political demonstrations and strikes for
which he was expelled; moved to Moscow;
attended Fedor Rerberg's private studio and
Konstantin Yuon and Ivan Dudin's Art School;
1907 returned to Kiev; from then onwards
contributed regularly to exhibitions, including
the Union of Russian Artists and the Moscow
Society of Independent Artists; 1908 contributed to the "Link"; 1911 traveled in Finland;
1912-15 taught at a school for the deaf and
dumb in Kiev; 1913-14 associated with the
Moscow Cubo-Futurists; 1914 with Alexandra
Exter organized the "Ring" exhibition in Kiev;
began to elaborate his artistic theories,
culminating in the completion of his book
Iskusstvo zhivopisi [The Art of Painting]; 1915
took up residence in Geriusy in the Northern
Caucasus, where he painted and taught; 1919
taught at the First State Painting and
Decorative Studio in Kiev; 1919-20 designed
agit-transport, including trains; became head
of the Art Education Section in the All-
Ukrainian Visual Arts Committee; 1922-30
professor at the Kiev Art Institute; 1927
founder-member of ARMU (Association of
Revolutionary Art of the Ukraine).

Bibliography
A14, Vol. 1, p. 435.
I. Dichenko: "Pravda krilatikh obraziv" in *Moloda*
gvardiia, K, 1974, 23 August, p. 4.

I. Dichenko: "Teoretik i praktik revoliutsionogo mistetstva" in *Moloda gvardiia,* 1979, 5 December, p. 6.
D. Gorbachov: "Na soniachnikh vantakh" in *Ukraina,* K, 1980, No. 20.
I. Dychenko: "Aleksandr Bogomazov" in *A-Ya,* Paris, 1986, No. 7, pp. 46-51.
B77, passim.
D. Gorbachov: "Prorochili rukopis" in *Ukraina,* Kiev: Akademiia nauk Ukrainskoi RSR, 1989, No. 23, pp. 456-66.
A. B. Nakov: *Bogomazov.* Catalog of exhibition at Musée d'Art Moderne, Toulouse, 1991.
A. B. Nakov "Ot futuristicheskoi ekspressii k konstruktivnomu formalizmu" in *Iskusstvo,* M, 1993, No. 1, pp. 69-73.
E. Dimshits, ed.: "Spogadi dochki O. Bogomazova" in *Ukrainske mistetstvoznavstvo,* K, 1993, No. 1, pp. 141-54.
A31, p. 77.
A41, pp. 218-19.
D. Gorbachov, intro.: *O. Bogomazov: Zhivopis ta elementi / A. Bogomazov: Painting and Elements,* K: Popova, 1996.
B237.
H. Makarenko: *Khudozhni obrii Oleksandra Bohomazova,* Sumy: Oblasna naukova biblioteka, 2000.
A. Liubimova: *Aleksandr Bogomazov,* SP: Palace Editions, 2008.

While David Burliuk, the "father of Russian Futurism," was known for his extravagance and sociability, Bogomazov, the Cubo-Futurist, was very different in character, spirit, and artistic intention. Both men were leaders of the Ukrainian avant-garde, recognized their debt to domestic and foreign conventions, and had much to say about the new art. Indeed, Bogomazov's treatise on the art of painting of 1914, indebted to both Symbolist ideas and innovative Cubo-Futurist theory, was an immediate product of this Ukrainian versatility and tolerance. Even before Ivan Kliun and Kazimir Malevich, Bogomazov, in his treatise, reduced the process of painting to its intrinsic elements – line, color, mass, volume, rhythm – while appealing to the esoteric dimensions peculiar to the philosophical worldviews of Pavel Filonov, Vasilii Kandinsky, and Mikhail Matiushin. On the one hand, Bogomazov offered a black square (one year before Malevich did) as the departure point for the new art; on the other he drew upon the Symbolist legacy of synesthesia and the musical analogy: "There are sounds which are clear, rich, powerful… and there are colors which are sad, strident, happy."[185]
Bogomazov's paintings and drawings of the mid-1910s, with their rapid force lines and repeated articulations, demonstrate (just as Olga Rozanova's do) a clear understanding of Italian Futurism, and even if he never saw a picture by Severini or a sculpture by Boccioni, he would have known about the Futurist theories from the Russian translations and from the eager discussions conducted in Kiev by the Burliuks, Benedikt Livshits, and, above all, Exter.

388

388 [R356].
Self-Portrait, 1914.
Charcoal.
Initialed and dated lower right in Russian: "AB 1914."
15⅞ x 11⅞ in., 40.3 x 30.2 cm.
Other inscription: under the initials in Russian: "Self-Portrait."
Provenance: the artist's widow, Vanda Monastyrskaia, Kiev, 1971.
Reproduced in F107, p. 476; N106. A similar self-portrait is reproduced in L3, Lot 82.

389 [R357].
Costume Design for a Female Dancer, ca. 1915.
Watercolor.
14½ x 9 in., 37 x 23 cm.
Inscription: identification on the reverse by the artist's widow, Vanda Monastyrskaia.

389

Provenance: the artist's widow, Vanda Monastyrskaia, Kiev, 1971.
Reproduced in color in B115, plate 78; I77, p. 71; and in black and white in I32, No. 13; I51, No. 62; I77, p. 127; N107, p. 79; Dychenko, p. 49.

390

390 [R358].
Costume Design for a Georgian Dancer, ca. 1915.
Pencil.
8¾ x 7⅛ in., 22.3 x 18 cm.
Provenance: the artist's widow, Vanda Monastyrskaia, Kiev, 1971.
Reproduced in I32, No. 14; I51, No. 63; I77, p., 127; Dychenko, p. 49.

Note: Even a cursory survey of Bogomazov's paintings and drawings, especially the charcoal drawings of 1913-16, reveals an almost excessive preoccupation with rhythmic systems. The images jump, spin, collide, and coalesce, while the perspectives advance literally by leaps and bounds, as though the artist were trying to imitate the vision of the frog's eye with which he once filled an entire canvas.[186] Both in his theoretical statements and in his artworks, Bogomazov often described a cyclical movement, whether in girls playing with a yo-yo or men sawing wood, in vibrations and reverberations or in music and dance.[187] Yet Bogomazov was concerned not with the mere outward manifestations of rhythm (as the Italian Futurists tended to be), but rather with its deeper, intrinsic motivation, with questions such as: What is rhythm and whence does it come? As he wrote in his essay for the "Link" exhibition of 1914: "Rhythm is a Mysterious Director managing everything: color, line, word, sound, etc."[188] Although Bogomazov does not seem to have designed any stage productions, he regarded the performing arts as a carrier of this rhythm and in true

Symbolist tradition perceived the theater as the highest form of artistic synthesis.[189]

The two designs for female dancers (Nos. 389-90 [R357-358]) executed by Bogomazov while he was head of the Graphic Arts Division of the Geriusy Studio for Higher Education in 1915-16, illustrate his conception of rhythm as a pervasive force that connects all phenomena. Certainly, such compositions bring to mind the dancing themes of the Italian Futurists, such as Gino Severini's *Dancer in Blue* (1912, Mattioli Collection, Milan), even though, once again, Bogomazov was aspiring to evoke the "cosmic" or total rhythm and not simply mechanical repetition. As he wrote in his 1914 essay:

> the artist's relationship to a given piece of nature, to an object, is his relationship to the sensation of the rhythmical values contained within its elements.[190]

185　A. Bogomazov: "Izkusstvo zhivopisi" (1914), typescript, private collection, p. 107. The full text of Bogomazov's treatise was published by Dmitrii Gorbachev in 1996 (see *O. Bogomazov: Zhivopis ta elementi / A. Bogomazov: Painting and Elements*) and in French translation by André B. Nakov (see *Bogomazov*, 1991, pp. 1-77).

186　See Gorbachov, *O. Bogomazov: Zhivopis ta elementi.*

187　For reproductions of works incorporating these motifs see, for example, L4, Lots 37-60; and Dychenko, "Aleksandr Bogomazov."

188　A. Bogomazov: untitled essay in exhibition catalog, *Koltso*, Kiev: Art and Artisan Students' Workshop for Printing, [1914], p. 1. An English translation of the text is in B75, pp. 105-06.

189　Dychenko has also pointed to certain parallels between Bogomazov and the Symbolists. See Dychenko, op. cit., p. 48.

190　Bogomazov, "Elementy zhivopisi", p. 67.

BOUCHÈNE, Dimitri (Bushen, Dmitrii Dmitrievich)

Born 26 April (8 May), 1893, St. Tropez, France; died 6 February, 1993, Paris, France.

Spent childhood and adolescence in St. Petersburg; 1912 graduated from the Second St. Petersburg Gymnasium; attended SSEA; 1913 visited Paris; 1915-17 curatorial assistant at the Museum of the Society for the Encouragement of the Arts, Petrograd; 1918, 1922, and 1924 contributed to the "World of Art" exhibitions; close to Alexandre Benois, Konstantin Somov, and the critic Sergei Rostislavovich Ernst (1894-1980), his life-long companion; 1918-25 Assistant Curator of Ceramics and Jewelry at the Hermitage; 1922 illustrated the Russian edition of Henri de Regnier's stories, the first of several illustrative cycles for books and journals; 1925 settled in France; attended the Académie Ranson; 1926 onward active as a stage designer in Paris, Monte Carlo, Milan, Amsterdam, and other cities; among his designs were those for productions of Jean Giraudoux's *Tessa* (1934) and *Electra* (1937), and Maurice Yvain's *Blanche Neige* (1951, with choreography by Serge Lifar); late 1920s onwards designed textiles and clothes for Paris fashion houses; 1977 illustrated Anna Akhmatova's *Le Poème sans Héros* (Paris: Librairie des Cinq Continents); 1991 one-man exhibition at the Hermitage, Leningrad.

Bibliography

L. Lvov: "Sredi khudozhnikov. Tvorchestvo Dmitriia Bushena" in *Mir i iskusstvo*, Paris, 1930, No. 9, pp. 5-6.

A4, p. 72.

S. Ivensky: *Mastera russkogo ekslibrisa*, L: Khudozhnik RSFSR, 1973, pp. 102-05.

V. Veidle: *Posledniaia kniga serebrianogo veka"* in *Russkaia mysl*, Paris, 1977, 8 December, p. 9.

Dimitri Bouchène. Catalog of auction at Nouveau Drouot, Paris, 1981, 30 March.

Dimitri Bouchène. Catalog of auction at Nouveau Drouot, Paris, 1982, 22 February.

N. Lobanov: "Dmitri Dmitrievich Bouchène" in B44, pp. 303-05.

Dmitri Bouchène. Catalog of auction at Nouveau Drouot, Paris, 1983, 7 March.

Dmitrii Bushen. Catalog of exhibition at the Hermitage, L, 1991.

B. Lossky: "Poslednii iz 'Mira iskusstva'" in *Russkaia mysl*, Paris, 1993, 5 March, p. 15.

A. Vasiliev: "Pamiati khudozhnika" in *Russkaia mysl*, Paris, 1993, 5 March, p. 15.

H34, pp. 185, 186.

K252, pp. 123-35.

One of the last members of the World of Art group, Dimitri Bouchène maintained the refined, decorative traditions of his elder colleagues such as Léon Bakst, Alexandre Benois, and Mstislav Dobujinsky. As a studio painter, stage designer, fashion designer, and book illustrator, Bouchène entered into fruitful collaboration with many figures of the Paris *beau monde* in the late 1920s onward. Although he never worked for Sergei Diaghilev, Bouchène joined forces with primary dancers and choreographers, such as Michel Fokine, Serge Lifar, and Kurt Jooss. Writing of the world premiere of Fokine's *Les Eléments* with designs by Bouchène at the London Coliseum in 1937, Arnold Haskell remarked that the "costumes, by D. Bouchenne [sic], are partly beautiful in spite of a great license in period, partly verging on revue."[191] Haskell's equivocal description points to the essential characteristic of Bouchène's personality — his willingness to curb his fertile imagination only when absolutely necessary and to take great risks in search of an exciting visual result, whether in illustrating a children's story [192] or designing a sophisticated ballet. No doubt Diaghilev would have appreciated this.

L'Oiseau de Feu: *ballet in two scenes with music by Igor Stravinsky based on the Russian fairy tale. Produced for the 13th Gulbenkian Ballet Festival at the Tivoli Theater, Lisbon, on 24 May, 1969, with choreography by Serge Lifar and designs by Dmitrii Bouchène.*

See No. 370 [R340] for plot summary.

391 [R369].
Curtain Design, **ca. 1969.**
Gouache.
Signed lower right in pencil: "Bouchène."
15¾ x 23⅜ in., 40 x 59.5 cm.
Other inscriptions: lower left in pencil: "L'Oiseau de Feu."
Provenance: the artist, Paris, October, 1980.
Reproduced in I51, No. 64; a similar watercolor is reproduced in *Dimitri Bouchène* (1982), Lot 81.

Note: Serge Lifar first choreographed *L'Oiseau de Feu* for the Théâtre National de l'Opéra in 1954 with designs by Georges Wàkhevitch. He repeated the choreography for this 1969 version, but his innovative system did not appeal to the critics who were used to the 1914 Diaghilev version by

391

Michel Fokine. One reviewer even referred to the Lisbon production as a "travesty of the original."[193] However, Bouchène's costumes and sets were impressive and critics agreed that he had resolved "les problèmes soulevés par les couleurs en mouvement, le rhythme de la danse et l'interprétation des acteurs."[194]

191 A. Haskell: "Fokine World Premiere" in *The Daily Telegraph*, London, 1937, 25 June.
192 A good example of Bouchène's playful illustrations for a children's book is *Vanka-pioner v Gostsirke* [Vanka the Pioneer in the State Circus], L: Committee for the Popularization of Art Editions, 1925.
193 F. Hall and J. Cobb: "Thirteenth Gulbenkian Festival, Lisbon" in *Ballet Today,* London, 1969, July-August, p. 19.
194 *Hommage à Dimitri Bouchène.* Catalog of auction at Nouveau Drouot, Paris, 30 March 1981, p. 12

BRAILOVSKY, Leonid Mikhailovich

Born 23 May (4 June), 1867, Kharkov, Ukraine; died 7 July, 1937, Rome, Italy.

392

1886 enrolled in IAA and received several prizes during his coursework, e.g., a Small Gold Medal in 1894; 1891 onwards exhibited regularly in St. Petersburg and Moscow, e.g., at the "Society of Water-colorists"; 1895-98 studied in Paris and Rome; 1898 professor at the MIPSA;1890s onwards celebrated for his watercolor renderings of antiquities and medieval Russian architecture; 1900s taught at CSIAI; 1900s-10s supported the Neo-Russian style in his designs for buildings and books; 1909-10 contributed to Vladimir Izdebsky's "International Exhibition of Paintings, Sculpture, Engraving, and Drawings"; 1910-11 contributed to Izdebsky's "Salon 2" in Odessa; 1910s designed productions for major theaters such as *The Merchant of Venice* and Molière's *Le Médecin malgré lui* for the Maly Theater, Moscow, and Mozart's *Don Juan* for the Bolshoi Theater, Moscow; 1912 designed the tombstone for Anton Chekhov's grave at the Novodevichii Cemetery in Moscow; 1916-17 contributed to the exhibitions of the "Moscow Association of Artists" and "Contemporary Painting" in Moscow; 1917 left Moscow for the Crimea; contributed to the "First Exhibition of Paintings and Sculpture by the Association of United Artists" in Yalta; 1918 contributed to the "Art in the Crimea" exhibition in Yalta; 1921 member of the Union of Russian Art Workers in Belgrade; contributed to the exhibition "L'Art Russe" in Paris; 1924 took up residence in Rome; 1920s-30s with his wife Rimma, contributed to many exhibitions, including the "Salon d'Automne" in Paris in 1927.

Bibliography
A. Novitsky: "L.M. Brailovsky i ego proizvedeniia" in *Stroitel*, SP, 1905, No. 5, pp. 321-25.
Anon.: "Beseda s Brailovskim" in *Teatr,* M,

1912, No. 1146, pp. 4-5.
A14, Vol. 2, p. 60.
I. Menshova, ed.: *Muza.* Special issue of *Experiment,* Los Angeles, 2007, No. 13, passim.
H34, pp. 171-73.
Some of Brailovsky's designs for Crimean architectural projects are reproduced in S. Barkov et al., eds.: *Ezhegodnik Obshchestva arkhitektorov-khudozhnikov.* SP, 1908, pp. 22-23.

Brailovsky was a painter, an architect, and a stage designer, and, before his final emigration, achieved a certain recognition for his Art Nouveau houses and dachas as well as for his sets and costumes. While fleeing the Bolshevik north in 1917-18, Brailovsky and his wife Rimma Brailovskaia (1877-1959), an embroidery designer and book illustrator, became close friends of Vera and Sergei Sudeikin then taking refuge in the Crimea. Consequently, they often saw each other in Miskhor, Gaspra, and Yalta, entertained mutual acquaintances, such as Ivan Bilibin and the musician Miron Yakobson, and contributed to the same kind of cultural life that they had promoted in St. Petersburg and Moscow, such as the "First Exhibition of Paintings and Sculpture by the Association of United Artists" in Yalta in December, 1917, and Sergei Makovsky's "Art in the Crimea" exhibition in Yalta in October-November, 1918.

Simon Boccanegra: *opera in three acts and a prologue by Giuseppe Verdi with text by Francesco Maria Piave after a play by Gutiérrez. Possibly for a production in Belgrade in the 1920s.*

Boccanegra agrees to accept the plebeians' nomination to the position of Doge in Genoa and thereby confronts Fiesco, the patrician. Fiesco laments the

death of his daughter, who has just borne Boccanegra's child. Much later Fiesco's granddaughter (Boccanegra's daughter) reappears as Amelia in the Palace of Grimaldi with her lover Gabriele, although she is also loved by Paolo, a plebeian. The antagonism between Boccanegra (now the Doge) and the patricians Adorno (alias Gabriele) and Fiesco (disguised as Andrea) continues, as Amelia finds herself at the center of rival desires. Finally, she marries Gabriele, but, through a dastardly plot, Boccanegra is poisoned by Paolo.

392 [R359].
Stage Design, ca. 1922.
Black pencil on parchment.
Signed lower right in pencil: "L. Brailovsky."
13⅛ x 17⅞ in., 33.5 x 45.5 cm.
Provenance: Marianna Jedrinsky (who lived in Jugoslavia when Brailovsky was also there), Paris, March, 1981.

BRUNI, Tatiana Georgievna

Born 24 October (6 November), 1902, St. Petersburg, Russia; died 16 September, 2001, St. Petersburg, Russia.

Born into a musical and artistic family, her father, Georgii, being a professor of music and one of Sergei Prokofiev's early teachers; 1918-20 attended SSEA; 1920-26 attended Pegoskhuma-Svomas under Osip Braz, Alfred Eberling, Nikolai Radlov, and others; 1923 worked as a stage designer for the Institute of Rhythm and the Theater of the Proletarian Actor, designed Prokofiev's *Moments Fugitives*; also worked on productions for George Balanchine's Young Ballet; during the 1920s emerged rapidly as a leading member of the new Leningrad school of stage designers that included Nikolai Akimov and Valentina Khodasevich; worked for the Theater of Drama and Comedy, Leningrad Ensemble of Stage Workers, and other companies; 1931 created the costumes for Dmitrii Shostakovich's *Bolt*; 1937 designed a production of *La fille mal gardée* for the Maly Opera Theater, Leningrad, thereafter becoming artist-in-residence (designing 24 productions there); 1930s onwards also worked as a designer for other companies, including the Kirov and Leonid Yakobson's Choreographic Miniatures, contributing to the success of numerous productions of classical and modern ballets; 1941-42 remained in Leningrad during the siege; 1942 evacuated to Perm, where she also designed ballets and operas such as *Swan Lake, Don Quixote, Giselle,* and *Sleeping Beauty*; 1950s onwards taught at Nikolai Akimov's Leningrad Ostrovsky State Theater Institute.

Bibliography
A14, Vol. 2, pp. 82-83.
L. Elizarova: "Tatiana Georgievna Bruni" in E. Davydova, comp.: *Leningradskie khudozhniki teatra*, L: Khudozhnik RSFSR, 1971, pp. 95-121.
T. Drozd: "Roman ee zhizni" in *Sovetskii balet*, M, 1984, No. 4, pp. 29-32.
E. Binevich: "Tatiana Bruni" in G50, No. 6, 1984, pp. 78-90.
G. Levitin: *Tatiana Bruni*, L: Khudozhnik RSFSR, 1986.
T. Bruni: "O balete s neprekhodiashchei liuboviu" in *Sovetskii balet,* M, 1991, No. 5, pp. 33-37.
I99, pp. 166-67.
Tatiana Bruni: The Magic of Russian Ballet and Opera Stage Designs. Booklet for exhibition at the Kirov Academy of Ballet, Washington, D.C., 1999.
Tatiana Bruni, Legend of the Kirov – and a Rare Collection of Russian Avant-Garde Artists from the 1920s and 1930s. Booklet for exhibition at the Russian Cultural Center, Washington, D.C., 2011.
Recent exhibitions of stage designs have featured Tatiana Bruni's work. See, for example, I116, p. 78.

Tatiana Bruni belongs to a vigorous generation of Soviet stage designers active in Leningrad in the 1920 and 1930s, a generation that includes Moisei Levin, Ekaterina Petrova, Elizaveta Yakunina, and, above all, Akimov. Like Alexandre Benois, Tatiana Bruni hailed from a family of gifted artists and architects (her grandfather was the painter Fedor Bruni, rival of Karl Briullov and curator of paintings at the Hermitage in 1849-64) and her natural disposition was towards the fine arts. As an impressionable teenager of thirteen, she visited the exhibition of set and costume designs and posters by Konstantin Korovin, Kazimir Malevich, Nicholas Roerich, Sergei Sudeikin, Vladimir Tatlin, etc., from the collection of Levkii Zheverzheev (sponsor of the 1913 production of *Victory over the Sun*) in Petrograd in 1915, a confrontation that resolved her to become a professional stage designer. Bruni's subsequent training, especially under Eberling at Pegoskhuma,

helped develop her innate sense of color and precision of form, a combined skill that served her well in the many subsequent commissions, especially for the ballet — a "love that passes not."[195] Among the more than eighty spectacles that she designed are *Giselle, The Nutracker, Eugene Onegin, Sleeping Beauty,* and *Swan Lake*. The Kirov Academy of Ballet in Washington D.C., honored Bruni with an exhibition of her ballet and opera designs in January, 1999.

Bolt: *ballet in three acts and seven scenes with music by Dmitrii Shostakovich and book by Viktor Smirnov. Dress-rehearsed, but not produced at the Academic Theater of Opera and Ballet, Leningrad, on 6 April, 1931, by Viktor Smirnov with choreography by Fedor Lopukhov, costumes by Tatiana Bruni, and sets by Georgii Korshikov.*
Under the supervision of Kozelkov, a Soviet factory, running at full steam, symbolizes the dynamic tempo of the new life. But certain negative individuals, including a hooligan Lenka Gulba, and his cronies, wish to hinder industrial progress, and their co-workers dismiss them from the factory shop. Wishing to have his revenge, Gulba tries to persuade the young worker Gosha to break a lathe by inserting a bolt in it. Boris overhears the conversation and goes to the shop to anticipate their action. But Lenka locks him in, thereby compromising him and Boris is arrested. In the end, however, Gosha tells the truth and Lenka is arrested.

393 [49; R360].
Costume Design for Kozelkov's Girlfriend in Act II.
Watercolor and black paint.
12⅝ x 9¼ in., 32 x 23.5 cm.
Inscriptions in pencil in Russian: upper right: "2nd Act. Kozelkov's girlfriend. Kostrovitskaia. 1 costume"; lower right:

393

"No. 33/3."
Vera Sergeevna Kostrovitskaia (1906-79) danced the part of Kozelkov's girlfriend.
Provenance: Rosa Esman Gallery, New York, 1979.
Reproduced in I77, p. 161; T4; T14; T15. The GMTMA also possesses a costume for the same subject; for a color reproduction see K210, p. 51.

394

394 [50; R361].
Costume Design for Lenka Gulba's Girlfriend.
Watercolor over pencil.
12 x 9 in., 30.5 x 23 cm.
Inscriptions in pencil in Russian: along right side: "Lenka's girlfriend"; in upper right: "Kostandi, 1 costume." The reference to Kostandi is, presumably, to the actor, clown, and acrobat Yurii Konstantinovich Kostandi (1876-1933).
Provenance: *Russian Pictures, Icons and Russian Works of Art*, London: Sotheby's, 15 February, 1984, Lot 109.
Reproduced in I77, p. 161.

395 [51; R362].
Costume Design for a Komsomol Girl on a Rope Ladder (Act III, Scene 2).
Watercolor over pencil.
15½ x 14 in., 39.4 x 35.5 cm.
Provenance: *Russian Pictures, Icons and Russian Works of Art*, London: Sotheby's, 15 February, 1984, Lot 109.
Reproduced in I77, p. 161. A similar design for the Komsomol Girl by Bruni is reproduced in C79, p. 109; and a comparable costume, for a textile-worker, is also reproduced in K50 (a), p. 389 (where it is misattributed to Lev Bruni) and in K50 (b), unpaginated. For color reproductions of other costume designs by Bruni and Korshikov in public and private collections see I74, pp. 33-36, and I79, Nos. 869-74.

Note: Bolt was one of the several experimental ballets and operas that

395

Shostakovich wrote just before and after 1930, others being *The Golden Age* and *The Limpid Stream*. In all cases, the critical reception was, to say the least, divided. The Soviet establishment considered such works "formalist" and their depiction of socio-political reality as "distorted." Although *Bolt* was an industrial ballet with real hammers and machines (reminiscent, therefore, of Sergei Diaghilev's production of Sergei Prokofiev's *Le Pas d'Acier* in 1927; see Nos. 1165-67 [R1020-22]) and relied for its effect on "political intermezzi, choreographic posters and radio loud-speakers,"[196] it was regarded as an inaccurate, if not pernicious, portrayal of Soviet industry, and the dress rehearsal was a fiasco. As a result, *Bolt* was withdrawn immediately even though its premiere was scheduled for 8 April (two days after the dress rehearsal), when, in fact, another spectacle was given in its place.[197] The choreographer and the composer were severely reprimanded, a dark presage of the brutal censure of Shostakovich's opera *Lady Macbeth of Mtsensk* in 1936 with its "leftist confusion instead of natural, human music."[198] Shostakovich himself was "in terrible shape. Everything was collapsing and crumbling. I was eaten up inside,"[199] and

under the pressure of events he published his recantation.[200]

As far as the designs for *Bolt* are concerned, Bruni and her husband Georgii Nikolaevich Korshikov (1899-1944) relied substantially on the 1920s conventions of the agit-theater (see Nos. 1-12 [R1-11]), the ROSTA Windows (advertisement windows of the Russian Telegraph Agency, for which Vladimir Lebedev, Vladimir Kozlinsky, Vladimir Maiakovsky, et al. worked) and the TRAM theaters (Theaters of Working Youth) — that wished to "create a theater capable of reflecting the most acute, most urgent, and topical questions and problems worrying young Soviet people."[201] In this way, Bruni tried to present social types rather than individuals, the "general recognizable features of this or that hero."[202] The Leningrad historian Tatiana Drozd described the Bruni costumes as follows:

> Their imagery is fulsome, their con-struction is original. The positive heroes — the Sportsman and Sportswoman, the Textile-Worker, the Working Woman, and others — were dressed in lightweight, simple costumes which exposed the actor's body to a maximum and revealed its plasticity. The costume-masks for the negative characters — the Drunkard, the Loafer, the Bureaucrat — were more complex, heavier. They concealed the body of the actor, deprived him of individuality, made him look like a moving mannequin.[203]

In spite of the negative response, Bruni maintained that the ballet was "obviously ahead of its time... In fact, *Bolt*, cruelly destroyed at its birth, subsequently, became an inexhaustible source from which ballet masters still derive specific elements, even today."[204]

Unidentified production for the Leningrad Circus, ca. 1950,

396 [R363].
Set Design for the Procession, ca. 1950.
Watercolor, pencil with black ink, and gold paint.
8¼ x 23¼ in., 21 x 59 cm.

Provenance: Garabed Basmadjan Gallery, Paris, September, 1974.
Reproduced in I37 (1982), pp. 12 and 13.

Note: According to Valentina Korshikova, daughter of Tatiana Bruni and Georgii Korshikov, this design was made in the late 1940s or 1950s for a so-called Parade Avenue of the Leningrad Circus.

195 Translation of the title of Bruni's article on ballet "O balete s neprekhodiashchei liuboviu", op. cit.
196 I. Sollertinsky: Untitled essay in the program *Bolt. Balet v 3-kh deistviiakh.* M: Nauka, 1976, p. 40.
197 Information supplied by Tatiana Drozd in letters to John E. Bowlt dated 30 November, 1984, and 15 February, 1985.
198 Article in *Pravda,* M, 28 January, 1936. Quoted in B. Schwarz: *Music and Musical Life in Soviet Russia 1917-1970,* New York: Norton, 1972, p. 123.
199 S. Volkov, ed.: *Testimony. The Memoirs of Dmitri Shostakovich,* New York: Harper and Row, 1979, p. 85.
200 See Schwarz, op. cit., p. 75.
201 Z. Stepanov: *Kulturnaia zhizn Leningrada 20-ykh—nachala 30-ykh godov,* L: Nauka, 1976, p. 40.
202 Binevich: "Tatiana Bruni," p. 82.
203 T. Drozd: "Roman ee zhizni," p. 31.
204 Quoted in Elizarova: "Tatiana Georgievna Bruni," p. 99. For other information on Bruni's designs for *Bolt* see Levitin, *Tatiana Bruni,* pp., pp. 24-38.

BURLIUK, David Davidovich

Born 9 (21) July, 1882, Semirotovshchina, near Kharkov, Ukraine; died 15 January, 1967, Southampton, New York.

Born into a talented family: his mother was a painter as were his brother, Vladimir, and two sisters, Liudmila and Nadia, while his brother Nikolai was a poet; 1894-98 attended various high schools in Sumi, Tambov, and Tver; 1898-99 and 1901 took art courses in at the Kazan Art Institute; 1899-1900 and 1901 attended the Odessa Art Institute; 1902-03 studied under Anton Ažbè in Munich; 1904 attended the Académie Cormon in Paris, mid-1900s coorganized and/or contributed to various exhibitions, including "Wreath-Stephanos" (Moscow, 1907-08), the "Link" (Kiev, 1908), and the "Jack of Diamonds" (Moscow, 1910); 1907-13 the estate of Chernianka, near Kherson, which Burliuk's father

managed, became a meeting-place of young artists and poets; in 1912 the ancient name of the locality, Hylaea, became the title of the group, which included Velimir Khlebnikov, Alexei Kruchenykh, Benedikt Livshits, and Vladimir Maiakovsky; 1908-17 lived in St. Petersburg, Moscow, and Iglino (near Ufa); 1909-11 contributed to Vladimir Izdebsky's "Salons"; 1910 coedited the miscellany *Sadok sudei* [A Trap for Judges]; thereafter published and/or edited many Futurist books such as *Trebnik troikh* [Prayerbook of Three] and *Tango s korovami* [Tango with Cows]; 1910 returned to Odessa; 1910-14 studied at MIPSA where he met Maiakovsky (both expelled in 1914); 1911 contributed to the *Blaue Reiter* exhibition; 1912 contributed to the *Blaue Reiter* almanac in Munich; married Mariia (Marusia) Elenevskaia; compiled and published *Poshchechina obshchestvennomu vkusu* [A Slap in the Face of Public Taste]; 1913-14 with Vasilii Kamensky and Maiakovsky made a Futurist tour of Russia; 1915 family moved to the Urals; 1917 Burliuk back in Moscow; 1918 with Maiakovsky worked on the movie *Not Born for Money;* 1918-19 lived in Siberia; 1920-22 lived in Japan; 1922 settled in New York; 1925 welcomed Maiakovsky on his visit to New York; 1930-66 with Marusia published a journal called *Color and Rhyme.*

Bibliography
K. Droior: *Burliuk*. New York: Wittenborn, 1944
H. Ladurner: "David D. Burljuks Leben und Schaffen 1908-1920" in *Wiener Slawistischer Almanach,* Vienna, 1978, vol. 1, pp. 27-55.
K. Kuzminsky: *Titka rodiny*, Orange, Conn.: Goloveiko, 1982.
J. Bowlt, ed.: *A Slap in the Face of Public Taste. A Jubilee for David Burliuk and the Cause of Russian Futurism.* Special issue of *Canadian-American Slavic Studies,* Irvine, 1986, Vol. 20, Parts 1-2.
H25, pp. 160-64.
A28, Vol. 1, pp. 367-70.
David Burliuk. Catalog of exhibition at the Nesterov State Art Museum, Ufa, 1992 (exhibition did not open).
David Burliuk. Faktura i tsvet. Catalog of exhibition at the Nesterov State Art Museum, Ufa, 1994.
B. Kalaushin: *Burliuk, otets russkogo futurizma,* SP: Apollon, 1995.
David Burliuk 1882-1967. Catalog of exhibition at the RM, 1995.
B184, pp. 39-52.
Z povernenniam v Ukrainu, pane Burliuk. Catalog of exhibition at the National Art Museum, K, 1998. B280.
Anon.: *David Burliuk,* New York: A.B.A. Gallery, 2001.
N. Evdaev: *David Burliuk v Amerike,* M: Nauka, 2002.
A. Panov et al.: *Modernism in the Russian Far East and Japan, 1918-1928.* Catalog of exhibition at the Machida City Museum of Graphic Arts, Machida, Japan, and other venues, 2002, passim.
M. Shkandrij: "Steppe Son: David Burliuk's Identity" in *Canadian-American Slavic Studies,* Idyllwild, 2006, Vol. 40, No. 1, pp. 65-79.
E. de' Pazzi: *David Burliuk. His Long Island and*

397

His World, Long Island: Writers Ink Press, 2007.
A. Kapitonenko: *Nash David Burliuk,* Sumi: D. Burliuk Foundation, 2007.
E. Lucie-Smith: *David Burliuk: Russian Modernist.* Catalog of exhibition at LewAllen Modern, Santa Fe, 2008.
M. Shkandrij: *Futurism and After: David Burliuk 1882-1967.* Catalog of exhibition at the Winnipeg Art Gallery, Winnipeg, 2008.
D. Karpov, comp.: *David Burliuk.* Catalog of exhibition at the Maiakovsky Museum, M, 2009.
N. Voiskounski: "Futurism and After: David Burliuk (1882-1967)" in *Tretiakovskaia galereia,* M, 2010, pp. 78-85 (special issue devoted to America and Russia).
H34, pp. 180-84.
H51, passim.
A. Chernov, ed.: *D.D. Burliuk. Pisma iz kollektsii S. Denisova,* Tambov: Denisov, 2011.
Burliuk's memoirs are of interest. See, for example, F78; L. Seleznev, ed.: *David Burliuk. Interesnye vstrechi,* M: Ruskaia derevnia, 2005.

No history of 20th-century Russian culture can be written without substantial reference to the life and work of David Burliuk, and there can be no question that the Russian avant-garde would not have developed quite as dramatically if Burliuk had not undertaken his many creative and organizational activities. As his fellow Futurist, Vasilii Kamensky, once said: "The name of David Burliuk was, and always is, an international name, like the sun in the heavens."[205] Put more succinctly, he was, as Vasilii Kandinsky called him, the "Father of Russian Futurism."[206] Burliuk was in close personal and artistic contact with the major poets and painters of his time such as Natalia Goncharova, Khlebnikov, Mikhail Larionov, Kazimir Malevich, and Maiakovsky. Many of them, such as Goncharova and Larionov, fell out with this boisterous individual, but others, not least Maiakovsky, retained a life-

long fondness for him. Burliuk organized many of the Futurist happenings — art exhibitions, polemical debates, poetry recitations, publishing enterprises — and he himself was a man of inexhaustible energy, assuming the role of poet, painter, theorist, rhetorician, and impresario.

397 [R364].
Vladimir Burliuk: Portrait of David Burliuk, 1913.
Lithograph in black and white.
8 x 5⅞ in., 20.3 x 15 cm.
Provenance: Viktor Kholodkov, Moscow, 1989.
First reproduced in V. Khlebnikov, V. Maiakovsky, D. and N. Burliuk, *Trebnik troikh,* M: Kuzmin and Dolinsky, 1913. Reproduced many times thereafter, e.g., in M151, p. 55.

Note: Vladimir Davidovich Burliuk (1886-1917), David Burliuk's younger brother, was a painter of originality and sensibility — evident especially in his so-called *vitrages* and *cloisonnés.*

398

398 [R365].
Portrait of Nikolai Burliuk, 1913.
Lithograph in black and white.
7⅝ x 6⅛ in., 19.5 x 15.5 cm.
Provenance: Viktor Kholodkov, Moscow, 1989.

Note: Nikolai Davidovich Burliuk (1890-1920) was the youngest of the three Burliuk brothers. He was a poet of some merit and also a theorist, but published comparatively little.

399

400

399 [R366].
Portrait of Vladimir Maiakovsky, 1913.
Lithograph in black and white.
7⅞ x 6½ in., 20 x 16.4 cm.
Provenance: Viktor Kholodkov, Moscow, 1989.
First reproduced in V. Khlebnikov, V. Maiakovsky, D. and N. Burliuk, *Trebnik troikh,* M: Kuzmin and Dolinsky, 1913. Reproduced many times thereafter, e.g., in M151, p. 55. The poet Benedikt Livshits also reproduced it as a Maiakovsky self-portrait. See his memoirs, *Polutoraglazyi strelets,* L: Izdatelstvo pisatelei, 1933, p. 169.
In the 1910s Burliuk and the poet Vladimir Vladimirovich Maiakovsky (1893-1930) were close friends.

400 [R367].
Portrait of Nicholas Roerich, 1929.
Pencil.
Signed and dated lower right: "Burliuk 1929."
15 x 12 in., 38 x 30.5 cm.
Provenance: Vladimir Hessen, New York, 13 June, 1981. Now in a private collection.
Reproduced in D. Burliuk, *Rerikh,* New York: Burliuk, 1929; I51, No. 199; O3.

Note: Artistically and emotionally, Burliuk was very distant from Nicholas Roerich. However, during the 1920s, both men played active roles in the colony of Russian artists in New York and they enjoyed an affable relationship in spite of their different worldviews. Indeed, as a leader of the Cubo-Futurists in Russia before the Revolution, the ebullient Burliuk and his colleagues had regarded Roerich, along with Alexandre Benois, Konstantin Somov, and other members of the World of Art, as pillars of conventional taste and had criticized them many times. Even so, Burliuk commenced his 1928 survey of Russian art in America with an appreciation of Roerich[207] and Roerich allowed Burliuk to organize the "Exhibition of Paintings by David Davidovich Burliuk" at the Roerich Museum, New York, in January 1930. The exact occasion for this

portrait is not known, although it seems to be a sketch for the oil portrait of Roerich that Burliuk painted also in 1929 (present whereabouts unknown; reproduced in D. Burliuk, *Art Bulletin,* New York: Burliuk, 1932, unpaginated). Burliuk painted and drew many portraits of Russian émigrés during his American residence, including those of Nikolai Feshin and Boris Grigoriev.

David Burliuk as contributor (previously attributed to Kirill Zdanevich):
401 [R493].
Designer unknown: Poster Advertising the Tiflis State Theater: "Famous Moscow Futurists Who Will Deliver a Scholarly Lecture on Art and Literature", 1914.
Lithograph in black and white.
7½ x 10¼ in., 19 x 26 cm.
Inscriptions advertize the proceedings of the

meeting scheduled for 27 March [1914] at the Tiflis State Theater, e.g., "Vasilii Kamensky, pilot and aviator of the Imperial All-Russian Air Club, will lecture on 'Airplanes and the Poetry of the Futurists'...; David Burliuk on 'Cubism and Futurism (in Painting)'...; Vladimir Maiakovsky on 'The Achievements of Futurism'...; V. Maiakovsky, V. Kamensky and D. Burliuk will read their poetry."
Provenance: Viktor Kholodkov, Moscow, 1989.
The poster has been reproduced several times, e.g., in B104, p. 202; M. Poliakov, comp., *Vasilii Kamensky,* M: Kniga, 1990, ill. 10; and Yu. Molok, ed., *Vasilii Kamensky: "Tango s korovami,"* M: Kniga, 1991, p. 4. In B179, p. 145, it is reproduced on the wrong page, i.e., it should head the description of R493 on the preceding page and not of R494.

402 [R368].
Designer unknown: Poster Advertising a Program of Poetry Declamations and Lectures under the General Title of "The Futurists and the Life Force" at the Poets' Cafe, Moscow, 26 February, 1918.
Lithograph in black and white.
10¼ x 8⅜ in.; 26 x 21.2 cm.
Provenance: Viktor Kholodkov, Moscow, 1989.

Note: The Poets' Café, located in a former laundry at 1, Nastasinskii Lane, just off Tverskaia Street in Moscow, was organized by Kamensky in the fall of 1917. Like its rival the Café Pittoresque (see No. 738 [R624]), the Poets' Café was a regular meeting-place for the "dreadnoughts of contemporary art,"[208] for the Moscow bohemia — and also for "sailors, Red Army soldiers, and workers."[209] Until its closure in the spring of 1918, many of the avant-garde writers and artists visited the Café and through their high jinks and constant

401

402

audience-baiting, the Café achieved the reputation of a radical "anti-bourgeois" institution.[210]

According to the inscriptions, contributors to the program included the Futurists David Burliuk, Yakov Cherniak, Anna and Vladimir Goltsshmidt, Kamensky, and Maiakovsky; and the Imaginists Alexander Klimov, Alexander Kusikov, and Sergei Spassky. The principal events scheduled included a Futurist masquerade "with two valuable prizes for the best costumes" (18 February), a lecture by Vladimir Goltsshmidt (photographed in the poster) on the "Sunlit Joys of the Body" (21 February), a lecture by Kamensky on "Art Today. This Is What Futurism Is" (23 February), an evening of Russian *bylina* sung and recited by Anna Goltsshmidt (26 February), and Cherniak's spring debut with an evening of "études and fairy-tales" (1 March).

205 Letter from Vasilii Kamensky to David Burliuk dated 23 January, 1927. Published in D. Burliuk: *Entelekhizm*, New York: M. Burliuk, 1930, p. 3.
206 This statement is ascribed to Kandinsky in the exhibition catalog *Oils, Watercolors by David Burliuk*, New York: 8th Street Gallery, 1934, p. 3.
207 See H6, pp. 7-10.
208 *Teatralnaia gazeta*, M, 1917, 17 December. Quoted from V. Katanian, ed.: *Maiakovsky. Literaturnaia khronika*, M: Gosudarstvennoe izdatelstvo khudozhestvennoi literatury, 1961, p. 91.
209 *Tvorchestvo*, Vladivostok, 1920, No. 5. Quoted from ibid., p, 92.
210 For further information on the Poets' Café see V. Lapshin: "'Kafe poetov' v Nastasinskom pereulke" in G44, Vol. 2, pp. 178-88; Italian version: "Il Caffè dei poeti' nel Vicolo Nastas'inskij" in *Rassegna sovietica*, Rome, 1985, No. 1, pp. 122-35. Also see E41 for 13 November, 1992.

CHAGALL, Marc (Shagal, Mark Zakharovich)

Born 7 (19) July, 1887, Vitebsk, Belarus; died 28 March, 1985, St. Paul-de-Vence, France.

1907 enrolled in SSEA; 1908 switched to Savelii Zeidenberg's private art school and then to Elizaveta Zvantseva's school, where he studied with Léon Bakst and Mstislav Dobujinsky; 1910 moved to Paris; 1912 contributed to the "Salon des Indépendants" and the "Salon d'Automne"; also contributed to the "Donkey's Tail"; 1913 contributed to the "Target"; 1914 contributed over forty works to the "Jack of Diamonds" exhibition in Moscow; one-man exhibition in Berlin; early 1910s meets radical artists and writers such as Guillaume Apollinaire, Blaise Cendrars, the Delaunays, and Fernand Léger, 1914 one-man exhibition at Galerie Der Sturm, Berlin; 1915 married Bella Rozenberg (Rosenberg); 1917 moved back to Vitebsk; 1918 became head of the Vitebsk Popular Art Institute, although he was soon ousted by Kazimir Malevich; 1920-21 worked as a stage designer for Alexei Granovsky's State Jewish Theater in Moscow; 1922 via Kaunas emigrated to Berlin; paid particular attention to lithographs and woodcuts; contributed to the "Erste Russische Kunstausstellung"; 1923 settled in Paris; 1924 first comprehensive retrospective at the Galerie Barbazanges-Iodebert, mid-1920s painted gouaches for the La Fontaine *Fables;* represented at many exhibitions in Paris, particularly at the Galerie Katia Granoff; frequented Côte d'Azur; 1931 visited Palestine in preparation for his work on the Bible etchings; 1935 visited Poland; 1941-46 lived in the US; 1942 designed *Aleko* for Mexico City and New York; 1946 one-man exhibition at the Museum of Modern Art, New York; 1952 his daughter, Ida, married art historian Franz Meyer; 1966 finished his Bible illustrations; 1963 painted new ceiling for the Paris Opéra; 1968 exhibition of his works from private collections organized by the Academy of Sciences in Novosibirsk; 1973 traveled to Moscow in connection with a small retrospective of his work there.

Bibliography

Chagall is the subject of a very large number of monographs, catalogs, and articles. The titles below are a representative selection only.
F. Meyer: *Marc Chagall*, New York: Abrams, 1964.
S. Alexander: *Marc Chagall*, New York: Putnam, 1978.
S. Compton: *Chagall*. Catalog of exhibition at the Royal Academy of Art, London, and the Philadelphia Museum of Art, 1984-85.
A. Kamensky: *Chagall: Periode Russe et Soviétique 1907-1922*, Paris: Editions du Regard,1988 (also English and German editions).
S. Compton: *Marc Chagall. My Life—My Dream. Berlin and Paris, 1922-1940*, Munich: Prestel, 1990.
C. Vitali et al.: *Marc Chagall. Die russischen Jahre 1906-1922*. Catalog of exhibition at the Schirn Kunsthalle, Frankfurt, 1991.
S. Goodman et al.: *Marc Chagall and the Jewish Theater*. Catalog of exhibition at the Solomon R. Guggenheim Museum, New York, 1993.
S. Pagé et al.: *Marc Chagall. Les années russes, 1907-1922*. Catalog of exhibition at the Musée d'Art moderne de la Ville de Paris, 1994.
S. Forestier and F. Paquet: *Marc Chagall. Le Ballet, l'Opéra*. Catalog of exhibition at the Musée National Message Biblique Marc Chagall, Nice, 1995.
B. Reifenscheid: *Chagall und die Bühne*, Bielefeld: Kerber, 1995.
M. Bohm Duchen: *Chagall*, London: Phaidon, 1998.
S. Compton: *Chagall. Love and the Stage 1914-1922*. Catalog of exhibition at the Royal Academy, London, 1998
B. Harshav: *Marc Chagall. A Documentary Narrative*, Stanford: Stanford University Press, 2004
E. Selezneva: *Mark Shagal. Zdravstvui, Rodina!* Catalog of exhibition at the the TG, 2005.
C. Zevi and M. Meyer: *Chagall delle meraviglie*. Catalog of exhibition at the Complesso del Vittoriano, Rome, 2007.
V. Rakitin: *Shagal*, M: Iskusstvo XXI vek, 2010.
A. Seban, et al.: *Chagall et l'avant-garde russe*. Catalog of exhibition at the Centre Pompidou, Paris, 2011-12.

Although Léon Bakst once told the young Chagall that he would never make a successful stage designer, Chagall, throughout his long career, retained a love of the theater and of the histrionic. From his early years, Chagall cherished the hope that he would become a stage designer — "to work for the theater had long been my dream."[211] Chagall made his real debut as a stage designer during 1920-21 when he worked on various productions at Granovsky's Jewish State Chamber Theater in Moscow, designing, for example, plays by Shalom Aleichem:

> The fabulous nature of Shalom Aleichem's dramas suited Chagall's temperament. The intuitive understanding for the folk that Chagall exhibited in his paintings complemented the carnival nature of Aleichem's works.[212]

Still, Chagall was not content with a merely folkloristic interpretation and he proceeded to apply Cubist, geometric principles to his sets. This did not appeal to the more moderate critics, as Abram Efros asserted:

> Chagall showed that he did not have a theatrical streak... He did not want to know the third dimension, or the depth of the stage and arranged all his sets parallel with the footlights, in the same way as he arranged his paintings on the walls or on an easel... he does not adapt to stage perspective...[213]

Chagall had little professional experience of the classical Russian theater and his involvement in the important production of *Aleko* in 1942 is unexpected. No doubt, Chagall identified some of the social and psychological problems of his own people with those of the gypsies. Alexander Pushkin's romantic treatment of the nomadic people and his intense descriptions of nature must also have appealed to Chagall's imagination. Never a Realist, Chagall's fantasy annoyed more sober observers of reality such as commissars and bureaucrats in post-Revolutionary Vitebsk newly painted by Chagall and his colleagues: "Why is the cow green and why is the horse flying through the sky, why? What's the connection with Marx and Lenin?"[214] Perhaps Chagall the painter with his improbable and fanciful pictures belongs, ultimately, more to the discipline of theater than to that of painting.

Aleko: *ballet in four scenes based on Alexander Pushkin's poem* The Gypsies *with music by Peter Tchaikovsky arranged by Erno Rapée. Produced by the Ballet Theatre (now American Ballet Theater) at the Palacio de Bellas Artes, Mexico City, on 8 September, 1942, with choreography by Leonide Massine and designs by Marc Chagall. The production was then given on 6 October, 1942, at the Metropolitan Opera House, New York.*

Aleko, a Russian gentleman, is bored with life. He joins the gypsies and falls in love with Zemfira, daughter of the King of the Gypsies. However, she is unfaithful to him, and, mad with jealousy, Aleko slays the girl and her gypsy lover.

403

403 [R939].
Costume Design for an Old Man (Zemfira's Father), ca. 1942.
Watercolor and pencil.
Signed lower right in ink: "Marc Chagall."
12¾ x 9¾ in., 32.3 x 24.7 cm.
Other inscriptions in Russian in pencil: lower left: "Old man"; lower right: "Aleko."
Provenance: *Dance, Theatre, Opera,* New York: Sotheby, Parke Bernet, 15 December, 1977, Lot 103 (reproduced).
Reproduced in F107, p. 133; I51, No. 66; I77, pp. 119, 157; I117, p. 574; J19, Lot 103; M73, p. 95; M161, p. 46. A number of designs are also reproduced in J29, Lots 124-30; for a complete list of designs see G28, p. 270.

Another costume design for Zemfira's Father is in the collection of the Museum of Modern Art, New York. For other costumes for *Aleko* see *Marc Chagall. Le Ballet, l'Opéra,* pp. 42-87, and Reifenscheid, *Chagall und die Bühne,* pp. 102-16.

404

404 [52; R940].
Costume Designs for Aleko and Zemfira, ca. 1942.
Watercolor and pencil.
Signed lower left in pencil: "Marc Chagall."
15⅛ x 10¼ in., 38.5 x 26.2 cm.
Other inscriptions: lower right in pencil in Russian: "Aleko's trousers"; in English: "sketch for Aleko."
Provenance: Leonard Hutton Gallery, New York, 7 December, 1979.
Reproduced in color in B115, plate 119; F107, p. 132; G70; I61, p. 449; I68, p. 17; I77, p. 96; I117, p. 574; M151, p. 53; N188, p. 58; and in black and white in G55, p. 287; H32, p. 417; I51, No. 65; I77, p. 157; M88; M112; N112, p. 55, M36; P47. It was also reproduced in color in the souvenir poster for I77. For reproductions of related costume designs see *Marc Chagall* (Centre Pompidou) pp. 156-59, and *Chagall* (Royal Academy), pp. 250-53.

Note: Because of union problems, Chagall was forced to take his ballet from New York, where it was scheduled to premiere, to Mexico City. The effect of this move was beneficial for, as Franz Meyer writes, the "tropics brought out a new color sensibility."[215] After an intense collaboration with Massine and with the unfailing assistance of Bella, his wife, Chagall created a masterpiece that drew nineteen curtain calls and overshadowed all the other numbers in the program. When the ballet opened at the Metropolitan later in 1942, the success was no less immediate, the more so since George Skibine and Alicia Markova, in the lead roles,

were already known to American audiences. John Martin, dance critic for the *New York Times,* wrote:

> [Chagall] has designed and painted with his own hand four superb backdrops which are not actually good stage settings at all, but are wonderful works of art... So exciting are they in their own right that, more than once, one wishes all those people would quit getting in front of them.[216]

211 F24, p. 165.
212 See Jean-Claude Marcadé: "Le contexte russe de l'oeuvre de Chagall" in *Marc Chagall. Oeuvres sur papier,* pp. 18-23.
213 A. Efros: "Khudozhniki teatra Granovskogo" in *Iskusstvo. Zhurnal Gosudarstvennoi Akademii khudozhestvennykh nauk.* M, 1928, No. 4, pp. 62-63.
214 F24, p. 137.
215 Meyer: *Marc Chagall,* p. 440.
216 John Martin: Review of *Aleko* in the *New York Times,* October, 1942. Quoted in Alexander, *Marc Chagall,* p. 359. Chagall was much appreciative of Martin's opinion, as he indicated in a speech that he gave at a dinner in Martin's honor in New York in January, 1943. See M. Shagal: "Rech na bankete v chest Zh. Martena" in *Zaria,* New York, 1943, 15 January, No. 2, p. 6. For more information on Chagall and *Aleko* see E. Surits: "'Aleko': sotrudnichestvo Miasina i Shagala" in *Balet,* M, 1999, May-June, pp. 14-16.

CHERVINKA (Chervinko), Ivan Ivanovich

Born 1891; died 1957 (some sources state 1950).

1900s took private lessons; 1918 entered the Popular Art Institute / Art-Practical Institute in Vitbesk; 1919 member of the Creative Committee of Unovis; 1919-23 student of Kazimir Malevich; member of Unovis; close to Ilia Chashnik, Vera Ermolaeva, Lazar Khidekel, Nikolai Suetin, and other Suprematists; designed Unovis poster for the Central Cooperative Alliance called *All for One and One for All;* 1920-21 played a major role in the preparation of the two issues of the magazine *Unovis;* 1922 stayed behind in Vitebsk after many other Unovis students left for Petrograd to work with Malevich; 1923 contributed to "Exhibition of Paintings by Petrograd Artists of All Directions" in Petrograd; 1920s taught drawing at a high school near Vitebsk;1928 one-man show near Vitebsk. Part of his archive was destroyed during World War II.

Bibliography
Nothing substantial has been published on Chervinka. For contextual information see:
E. Basner et al. *Krug Malevicha,* SP: Palace Editions, 2000, p. 147.
I. Vakar and T. Mikhienko, eds.: *Malevich o sebe. Sovremenniki o Maleviche,* M: RA, 1004 (two volumes).
A. Shatskikh: *Vitebsk. Zhizn iskusstva 1917-1922,* M: Yazyki russkoi kultury, 2001.
A. Shatskikh: *Vitebsk. The Life of Art,* New Haven: Yale, 2007.
Also see Bibliographies for Malevich and Suetin.

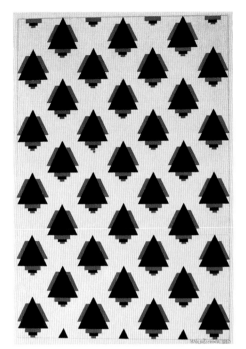

405

405 [NIRE].
Suprematist Textile Design with Black Triangles, 1920.
Gouache and black ink.
Signed and dated lower right in Russian: "I. Chervinka. 1920."
8⅝ x 6¼ in., 22 x 16 cm.
Provenance: *Modern and Contemporary Art,* London: Bonham's, 2005, 20 June, Lot 25 (reproduced).
Reproduced in color in F107, p. 357.

406 [NIRE].
Suprematist Design with Red Circles, 1920.
Gouache and black ink.
Signed and dated lower right in Russian: "I. Chervinka. 1920."
8⅝ x 6¼ in., 22 x 16 cm.

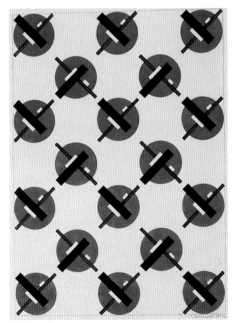

406

Provenance: *Modern and Contemporary Art,* London: Bonham's, 20 June, 2005, Lot 25 (reproduced).
Reproduced in color in F107, p. 357.

Note: It is hard to determine the function and purpose of these textile designs, although it is assumed that the surviving printed cloth sample (1920) which he produced for Malevich, based on a Malevich Suprematist design, was intended simply as an esthetic and material experiment, rather than as the prototype of a dress or upholstery design.[217]

217 For a reproduction see Shatskikh, *Vitebsk. The Life of Art,* p. 139

DELAUNAY, Sonia (Terk, Sonia Ilinichna)

Born 14 (26) November, 1885, Gradizhsk, Ukraine; died 6 December, 1979, Paris, France.

1890 moved to St. Petersburg from the Ukraine; 1903 visited Karlsruhe; 1905 made her first trip to Paris; enrolled at the Académie de la Palette; established contact with Amédée Ozenfant and André Dunoyer de Segonzac; 1907 began to paint in a Fauvist manner under the influence of Van Gogh and Gauguin; 1910 married Robert Delaunay; they established their studio on the Rue des Grands-Augustins where they worked until 1935; 1911 produced first examples of professional applied art; 1912 met Georgii Yakulov in Paris; 1913 close to Guillaume Apollinaire and Blaise Cendrars; contributed to the "Herbstsalon" at the Galerie Der Sturm, Berlin; 1914 exhibited *Prismes Electriques* at the "Salon des Indépendants"; moved to Madrid at the outbreak of World War I; 1915-16 traveled in Portugal; 1918 designed the costumes for Diaghilev's production of *Cleopatra* in London; 1920 back in Paris made contact with Dada writers and artists; 1923 created Simultanist textile designs for a Lyon corporation; 1924 with Jacques Heim opened a fashion atelier; 1925 contributed to the "Exposition Internationale des Arts Décoratifs," Paris; 1929-30 produced two albums, *Tissus et tapis par Sonia Delaunay* and *Compositions. Couleurs, Idées;* 1935-37 with Robert worked on a vast mural for the "Exposition Internationale" (Paris, 1937) for which she received a Gold Medal; 1939 with Robert, van Doesburg, Rambosson, and others organized the first exhibition of Réalités Nouvelles at the Galerie Charpentier; thereafter continued to paint and design in Simultanist style.

Bibliography
J. Lassaigne: *Sonia Delaunay.* Catalog of exhibition at the Galerie Gmurzynska, Cologne, 1975.
A. Cohen: *Sonia Delaunay,* New York: Abrams, 1975.
G. Le Rider and others: *Sonia et Robert Delaunay,* Paris: Bibliothèque Nationale, 1977.
R. Buck et al.: *Sonia Delaunay. A Retrospective.* Catalog of exhibition at the Albright-Knox Art Gallery, Buffalo, and other institutions, 1980.
A. Malochet: *Atelier Simultané de Sonia Delaunay 1923-1934,* Milan: Fabbri, 1984.
B. Contenson: *Delaunay (Sonia et Robert).* Catalog of exhibition at the Musée d'Art Moderne de la Ville de Paris, Paris, 1985.
H. Serger and W. Werner: *Sonia Delaunay.* Catalog of exhibition at La Boetie, New York, and Kunsthandel Wolfgang Werner, Bremen, 1986-87.
A. Madsen: *Sonia Delaunay,* New York: McGraw-Hill, 1989.
M73, Vol. 26, pp. 75-76.
S. Baron and J. Damase: *Sonia Delaunay. The Life of an Artist,* London: Thames and Hudson, 1995.
M. Schneider-Maunoury: *Sonia and Robert Delaunay: Paintings and Works on Paper.* Catalog of exhibition at the Galerie Gmurzynska, Cologne, and Danese, New York, 1997.
J.-L. Delaunay: *Robert and Sonia Delaunay. Paris Weltausstellung 1937.* Catalog of exhibition at the Galerie Gmurzynska, Cologne, 1997.
Sonia Delaunay. Ritmo e colore, 1923-1934. Catalog of exhibition at the Galleria di piazza San Marco, Milan, 2002.
Brigitte Leal: *Robert et Sonia Delaunay. Donation Sonia et Charles Delaunay.* Catalog of exhibition at the Centre Pompidou, Paris, 2003.
Dzh. Malmstad and Zh.-K. Markade (J. Malmstad and J.-C. Marcadé): *A.A. Smirnov. Pisma k Sone Delone 1904-1928,* M: NLO, 2011.
Sonia Delaunay's memoirs are also of interest; see F56.

Although Delaunay left Russia as a very young woman and never returned there, she — and her husband Robert — always maintained a close communication with Russian artists, choreographers, impresarios, and designers, especially during the 1910s and 1920s. Indeed, a number of Delaunay's experimental undertakings done in Paris found immediate parallels among the avant-garde communities in Moscow and St. Petersburg. As early as 1904-05 she was exchanging ideas on sound and color with the literary historian and musicologist Alexander Smirnov;[218] and her Simultanist color illustrations to Blaise Cendrar's *La Prose du Transsibérien et de la petite Jehanne de France* (Paris, 1913) were held in high regard by the Russian Cubo-Futurists, while her bold fabric designs of the 1920s are curiously similar to those of Liubov Popova and Varvara Stepanova done in Moscow — something that was especially clear at the "Exposition Internationale des Arts Décoratifs" in 1925. The connections between the Delaunays with their theory of Simultanism and the color theories of Aristarkh Lentulov and Georgii Yakulov should also be noted, although Yakulov maintained that Simultanism, was his invention, "making himself hoarse shouting that [Robert] Delaunay had robbed him."[219]

Primarily, Sonia Delaunay was a designer of clothes and textiles rather than a stage decorator, although she was active in this capacity just before and after 1920. In 1918 she worked on Diaghilev's production of *Cleopatra* in London; in 1919 she designed the inaugural revue for the Petit Casino in

407

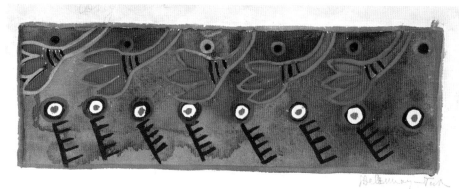

408

409

Madrid; and in 1923 she designed the *Soirée du Coeur à Barbe* directed by Ilia Zdanevich (Iliazd) and Serge Romoff for the Cherez group in Paris. In this way, Delaunay established a fruitful relationship with the Paris Dada circle, leading, for example, to her fanciful costumes for Tristan Tzara's *Le Coeur à Gaz* in 1924. In these spectacles, Delaunay applied her notion of Simultanism, which, according to one critic, is "based on colour relations that can be observed in their action on one another… contrasts are completed by harmonies based on dissonances."[220]

Cleopatra (Cléopâtre): *a choreographic drama in one act based on Antonii Arensky's* An Egyptian Night *(see No. 30 [R29]) with musical additions by Nikolai Cherepnin, Alexander Glazunov, Mikhail Glinka, Nikolai Rimsky-Korsakov, and Sergei Taneev. First produced by Sergei Diaghilev at the Théâtre du Châtelet, Paris on 2 June, 1909 (see No. 75 [R71]). Produced by Diaghilev again at the Coliseum Theatre, London on 5 September*

1918 with sets by Robert Delaunay and costumes by Sonia Delaunay.
See No. 75 [R71] for plot summary.

407 [R444].
Fabric Design No. 1, ca. 1918.
Watercolor and black ink.
Signed lower right in pencil: "S. Delaunay-Terk."
4¾ x 13⅝ in., 12 x 34.5 cm.
Other inscriptions: upper right in ink: "1"; on reverse upper left in ink "No. 19/5"; lower right French Customs stamp.
Provenance: the estate of Leonide Massine, New York, December, 1979.
Reproduced in *Sonia Delaunay. A Retrospective,* p. 156; I51, No. 67; I77, p. 131.

408 [R445].
Fabric Design No. 2, ca. 1918.
Gouache and black ink.
Signed lower right in pencil: "S. Delaunay-Terk."
5 x 12¼ in., 12.7 x 31 cm.
Other inscriptions: upper margin in pencil: "pièce longue"; on reverse upper left in ink:

"No. 10/1" and French Customs stamp.
Provenance: the estate of Leonide Massine, New York, December, 1979.
Reproduced in *Sonia Delaunay. A Retrospective,* p. 156; F107, p. 515; I51, No. 68; I77, p. 131.

409 [R446].
Fabric Design No. 3, ca. 1918.
Gouache and black ink.
Signed lower right in pencil: "S. Delaunay-Terk."
4¾ x 12¼ in., 12 x 31 cm.
Other inscriptions: upper right in ink: "3"; on reverse upper left in ink: "No. 19/1" and French Customs stamp.
Provenance: the estate of Leonide Massine, New York, December, 1979.
Reproduced in *Sonia Delaunay. A Retrospective,* p. 156; I51, No. 69; I77, p. 131.

410 [NIRE].
Fabric Design, 1918.
Gouache.
Signed lower left: "Sonia Delaunay."
12⅜ x 9½ in., 31.4 x 24 cm.
Provenance: Celia Ascher, New York, May, 1972.

Note: These fabric designs are a vivid illustration of Sonia Delaunay's radical position vis-à-vis the conventional patterns in cloth design of her time. She substituted traditional ornamentation with geometric motifs and exotic imagery, and her bright, contrasting color combinations, coupled with graduated tints and harmonies, anticipated a central direction of future fashion. Indeed, these *Cleopatra* fabrics are very similar to Delaunay's own fashion textile designs of the mid-1920s. Even though it has been reported that Delaunay was re-elaborating her *Cleopatra* designs for her *Livre Noir No. V* in 1924 (Malochet, *Atelier Simultané,* p. 26), it is assumed that Nos. 407-10 [R444-46] are indeed from 1918; cf. the items reproduced in *Delaunay (Sonia et Robert),* p. 227.

410

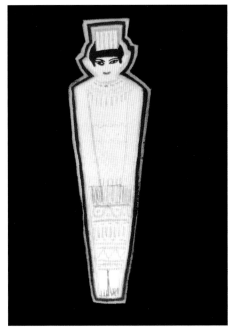

411

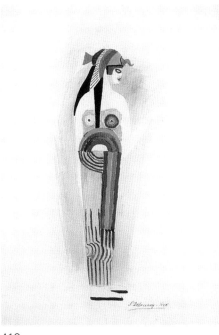

413

412

411 [R447].
Cleopatra as a Mummy, ca. 1918.
Gouache.
15⅛ x 11 in., 38.5 x 28 cm.
Provenance: the estate of Leonide Massine,
New York, December, 1979.

412 [R448].
Mummy Design for Cleopatra's Screen, ca. 1918.
Watercolor and ink.
12⅝ x 9⅝ in., 32 x 24.4 cm.
Provenance: the estate of Leonide Massine,
New York, December, 1979.
A variant is reproduced in *Delaunay (Sonia et Robert)*, p. 225, fig. 209.

413 [53; R449].
Costume Design for Cleopatra, ca. 1918.
Watercolor.
18⅞ x 13⅝ in., 48 x 34.5 cm.
Provenance: the estate of Leonide Massine
via Leonard Hutton Gallery, New York, June
1982.
Reproduced in color in B115, plate 118; F107,
pp. 141, 221; I117, p. 324; M151, p. 70; N156,
p. 75; and in black and white in I77, p. 131;
M36; M107, p. 91; M140; N88; R15. Cf. No.
414 [R450]. A variant is reproduced in
Delaunay (Sonia et Robert), p. 224, fig. 225.

Note: Sergei Diaghilev revived *Cléopâtre* for
London audiences with the original choreography by Fokine and with Lubov Tchernicheva, Leonide Massine, and Lydia Sokolova
dancing the title roles (Cleopatra, Amoun, and
Ta-hor). Of course, it was difficult to even
approach the famous designs by Léon Bakst
for the 1909 version, but Robert and Sonia
Delaunay provided an exciting resolution. Cyril
Beaumont, who attended the production at
the Coliseum, recalled:

> [There] was a new setting by Robert
> Delaunay, conceived in the violently
> contrasted colours and cubist shapes
> then regarded as the most advanced
> artistic expression. The setting was
> certainly striking and theatrically effec-
> tive, but the colouring was strident and
> irritating... There was also a new
> costume for Cleopatra, designed by
> Sophie [sic] Delaunay; it was another
> vivid conception in yellow, red, and gold
> not improved by a segment of mirror-
> glass affixed to the girdle, which winked
> like a heliograph every time it caught the
> light... Tchernicheva made a regal
> Cleopatra, whom she portrayed as a cold,
> enigmatic, sadistic being... Massine was
> interesting as Amoun... at his best in the
> death scene. Sokolova was a good Ta-

Hor, and the episodes of her love for
Amoun and despair at his death were
well mimed, but not distinguished by any
original touches.[221]

Cf. Nos. 30 [R29], 75-79 [R71-75]. Note that
Delaunay's costume for Cleopatra was
auctioned in London in 1968 (see J2, Lot
75). For color reproductions of other
relevant designs see K50(b), unnumbered;
and *Delaunay (Sonia et Robert)*, pp. 224-25.
For a black and white photograph of
Tchernicheva wearing a Cleopatra costume
and for other costume designs see *Sonia
Delaunay* (unpaginated).

Aida: *opera in four acts by Giuseppe Verdi.
Produced at the Teatro Liceo, Barcelona,
1920, with designs by Sonia Delaunay.*

*Radames, chief guard at the Pharoah's
court in Memphis, dreams of conquering the
enemy, the Ethiopians, as a reward for which
he demands the release of his beloved, Aida,
daughter of the Ethiopian leader, Amonasro.
Amneris, the Pharoah's daughter, is in love
with Radames and is jealous of Aida. In order
to gain advantage, Amneris lies to Aida that
Radames has been killed, even as Radames
returns victorious with the Egyptian forces.
Among the prisoners is Amonasro. Inadvertently, Radames commits treason and is put
in prison for this, while Aida and Amonasro
escape. Amneris then tells Radames that she
will free him if he renounces his love for Aida,
but he refuses. The High Priest then
commands that Radames be buried alive
and, as the sentence is carried out, Aida
appears next to him — never to be parted
again.*

414 [54; R450].
Costume Design in Simultanist Style for Amneris, 1920.
Watercolor, gouache, and pencil.
Signed and dated: "Sonia Delaunay-Terk;
XI.1920."
19⅝ x 15 in, 50 x 38 cm.

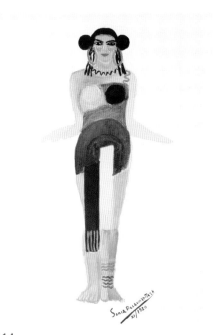

414

Provenance: *Important Impressionist and Modern Drawings and Watercolours,* London: Sotheby's, 5 July, 1979, Lot 436 (reproduced).

Reproduced in color in B115, plate 117; I77, p. 74; I117, p. 324; and in black and white in H32, p. 405; I77, p. 132; N188, p. 18; in the catalog of *Important Impressionist and Modern Drawings and Watercolor,* London: Sotheby's, 1979, 5 July, Lot 436; in *Sonia Delaunay,* p. 143; and in Cohen, *Sonia Delaunay,* p. 79. This costume is very similar to the one that Delaunay designed for *Cleopatra* in the 1918 London production; for a reproduction see J2, Lot 75; also see *Delaunay (Sonia et Robert),* p 226.

Note: Aga Lahowska, who sang the part of Amneris, wrote to Delaunay in December, 1918, regarding the forthcoming production of *Aida:* "L'opéra est tellement vieux et si connu que pour pouvoir l'entendre avec intérêt, il faut le vêtir de neuf."[222] Delaunay, who designed the costumes for Aida and Amneris, followed this advice and produced designs that were no less vivid than her costumes for *Cleopatra* of 1918.

Designs not intended for particular productions

415

415 [R451].
Costume Design for a Female in Simultanist Style, 1917.
Watercolor.
Initialed and dated lower right: "SD 1917."
10⅝ x 8¼ in., 27 x 20.9 cm.
Other inscription: lower right: "409."
Provenance: Gimpel Gallery, New York, November, 1971. The piece is missing from the collection and is presumed to have been stolen.
Reproduced in I20, No. 25; I77, p. 130.

416

416 [55; R452].
Three Costume Studies (Left to Right: Costume Design for a Lady, 1923; Simultanist Dress. Rhythm without End, 1919; Costume, 1919), 1925.
Silkscreen.
15 x 22 in., 38 x 56 cm.
Provenance: Marina Henderson, London, June 22, 1983.
The three costumes on one page are from the folio *Sonia Delaunay, ses peintures, ses objets, ses tissus simultanés, ses modes,* Paris: Librairie des Arts Décoratifs, 1925 (edited and prefaced by André Lhote, with poems and short texts by Blaise Cendrars, Joseph Delteil, Tristan Tzara, Philippe Soupault, et al.).

Note: Just as Léon Bakst and Alexandra Exter transferred some of their lessons from stage to fashion design, so Delaunay extended the ideas that she used in *Cleopatra* and *Aida* to her dress designs of the 1920s. In this discipline, Delaunay worked on several levels: providing total ensembles (from purse to gown to automobile) for the wealthy Parisienne, as well as simple *tissu-patrons,* or cut-out patterns, that the working woman could use. While applying Simultanist devices to her dress creations, as evidenced by her concentration on color rhythm and rotational pattern, Delaunay concerned herself with "liberating" the female body and was a primary supporter of the sack. In the words of André Lhote, she covered the "sweet undulations of the human body with geometric architectures."[223] Delaunay was well represented at the "Exposition Internationale des Arts Décoratifs" in Paris in 1925 and Lhote's luxury edition carrying twenty color silkscreens served as useful propaganda for her fashion ideas and for her fashion boutique on the Pont Alexandre III. To some extent, however, the color plates in this book might also be regarded as illustrations to the accompanying poems by Cendrars et al., especially when we

recall her illustrative work for the *Prose du Transsibérien* (see above).

218 See J.-C. Marcadé, ed.: "La Correspondance d'A.A. Smirnov avec S.I. Terk (Sonia Delaunay). 16 Sept., 1904 — 8 Avril, 1905" in *Cahiers du monde russe et soviétique,* Paris, 1983, July-September, pp. 289-327.
219 F48, p. 176.
220 J. Lassaigne: "Sonia Delaunay or the Sovereignty of Colour" in K52, p. 79.
221 D7, pp. 109-10.
222 F56, p. 79.
223 A. Lhote: "Document X" in *Sonia Delaunay, ses peintures,* op. cit.

DENISOVSKY, Nikolai Fedorovich

Born 12 (25) February, 1901, Moscow, Russia; died 25 May, 1981, Moscow, Russia.

Son of the engraver Fedor Denisovsky. 1911-17 attended CSIAI; 1917-19 attended Svomas; close contact with Alexander Deineka, Konstantin Vialov, and other members of the future OST; during this period studied under Georgii Yakulov; 1918 designed agit-decorations for the first anniversary of the Revolution; 1919 founder-member of Obmokhu, contributing to all its exhibitions through 1923; worked predominantly on posters, e.g., for the Red Army; also designed decorations for a traveling village theater and an educational theater in Moscow; member of Glavprofobr (Chief Committee of NKP); 1922 contributed to the "Erste Russische Kunstausstellung" in Berlin, and, as secretary to the exhibition, traveled with it to Berlin and Amsterdam; 1924-27 worked extensively as a caricaturist in journals such as *Krokodil* [Crocodile], *Bich* [Lash], and *Buzoter* [Rowdy]; painted a portrait of Lenin in his coffin (1924); 1925-32 member of OST, contributing to its exhibitions; 1929 traveled to the Donbas coal basin to paint industrial themes; 1930 traveled to the Kerch Metal Plant and to the gold mines of Siberia, painting and collecting material for his book illustrations; 1931 onwards painted portraits of Party dignitaries such as Stalin, Semeon Budennyi, and Kliment Voroshilov; 1935 visited Magnitogorsk; 1941-45 designed posters for the Okna TASS (propaganda windows of the Soviet Telegraph Agency).

Bibliography
V. Kostin: *OST*, L: Khudozhnik RSFSR, 1976. A14, vol. 3, pp. 337-38.
N. Denisovsky: [Autobiography] in V. Lobanov, ed.: *Sovetskie khudozhniki*, M: Izogiz, 1937, vol. 1, pp. 71-72.
V. Lobanov: *Vystavka rabot khudozhnika N.F. Denisovskogo. 35 let tvorcheskoi deiatelnosti.* Catalog of exhibition at the Union of Soviet Artists of the USSR, M, 1956.
L. Kolesnikova: *Khudozhnik Nikolai Denisovsky 1901-1961*. Catalog of exhibition at the State Maiakovsky Museum, M, 2004.
K281, pp. 162-71.

417

417 [R453].
Caricature of Vladimir Maiakovsky Holding a Lion on a Leash, 1924.
Collage with photographs of Maiakovsky's head and of the lion, with pencil and black ink.
Signed and dated in ink lower right: "Denisovsky 1924."
13¼ x 9¼ in., 33.7 x 23.5 cm.
Inscribed on the reverse in pencil in Russian by Denisovsky: "N. Denisovsky. Caricature of Maiakovsky for the journal *Krokodil.*"
Provenance: Viktor Kholodkov, Moscow, 1982. Now in a private collection.
Reproduced in O1.

Note: Denisovsky began to work as a caricaturist for the Moscow journal *Krokodil* [Crocodile] in 1924, rendering satirical likenesses of celebrities of the time such as

the poet Vladimir Vladimirovich Maiakovsky (1893-1930). The reader of *Krokodil* could recognize Maiakovsky instantly through not only the inclusion of a real photograph of his face, but also the literary allusion found in the lion being led by Maiakovsky: in 1923 Maiakovsky had co-founded the avant-garde journal *Lef* [=Left Front of the Arts] to which a number of radical writers and critics such as Boris Arvatov, Osip Brik, and Nikolai Chuzhak contributed. Since the Russian word for "lion," i.e., *"lev"*, sounds like the acronym of the journal's title *(Lef)*, the reference is clear.

Denisovsky first met Maiakovsky when the latter paid a visit to Svomas in 1919 just before Denisovsky graduated. "The image of Maiakovsky," Denisovsky recalled, "engraved itself on my memory forever."[224] For his part, Maiakovsky also admired Denisovsky and, for example, was very pleased with the artist's designs for the 1925 publication of his poem "Chto takoe khorosho i chto takoe plokho" [What's Okay and What's Not].[225] For Denisovsky and for most of his colleagues, Maiakovsky was the first poet of the socio-political and cultural revolution, the "true leader of young art people."[226] The man to the left of the collage, looking up to Maiakovsky's powerful figure, is the writer, Osip Maksimovich Brik (1888-1946), co-founder of *Lef*.

224 N. Denisovsky: "Vospominaniia N. Denisovskogo" in *Literaturnaia gazeta*, M, 1937, No. 19, p. 3.
225 V. Maiakovsky: *Chto takoe khorosho i chto takoe plokho*, M: Priboi, 1925. In a letter to Lilia Brik of 26 July, 1925, Maiakovsky refers to the Denisovsky illustrations. See B. Jangfeldt, ed.: *V.V. Maiakovsky i L.Yu. Brik. Perepiska 1915-1930*, Stockholm: Almqvist and Wiksell, 1982, p. 139. Denisovsky also designed the layout for the book *Vladimir Maiakovsky* edited by Vasilii Katanian in 1930.
226 Denisovsky's autobiography, op. cit., p. 71.

DMITRIEV, Pavel Sergeevich

Born 1841, St. Petersburg (?), Russia; died ca. 1900, St. Petersburg (?), Russia.

1861-71 studied architecture at IAA; 1871 received the title of Artist without Rank for his design for the St. Petersburg Stock-Exchange; 1880s designed covers for the satirical journal *Shut* [Buffoon].

Bibliography
Although little is known of Dmitriev's life and career, the two following titles provide information on the kind of subjects and styles that he favored in his design work.
E. Kuznetsov: *Russkie narodnye gulianiia po rasskazam A.Ya. Alekseeva-Yakovleva*, L-M: Iskusstvo, 1948.
A. Nekrylova: *Russkie narodnye gorodskie prazdniki, uveseleniia i zrelishcha*, L: Iskusstvo, 1984.

418

418 [R455].
Design for a Diorama Illustrating an Event from Russian History, ca. 1872.
Watercolor.
Signed lower right in Russian: "Architect P. Dmitriev."
16⅝ x 10¾ in., 42.2 x 27.3 cm.
Provenance: Iosif Lempert, Paris, April, 1977.
Reproduced in B44, p. 293.

419 [R456].
Design for a Diorama Illustrating an Event from Russian History, 1872.
Watercolor.
Signed lower right in Russian: "Architect P. Dmitriev."
16½ x 10⅝ in., 42 x 27 cm.
Provenance: Iosif Lempert, Paris, April, 1977.
Reproduced in B44, p. 293.
The building in the right background is the spire of the Admiralty.

419

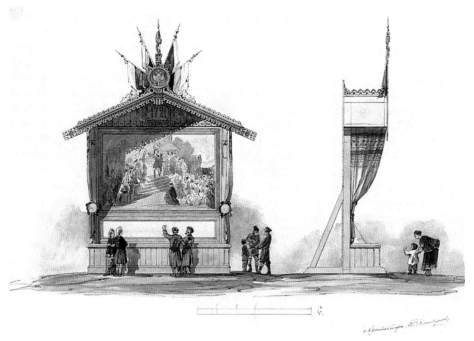

420

420 [R457].
Design for a Diorama Illustrating an Event from Russian History (Front and Side Views), ca. 1872.
Watercolor.
Signed lower right in Russian: "Architect P. Dmitriev."
12¼ x 16½ in., 31 x 42 cm.
Other inscription: the date "1721" is incorporated into the stage.
Provenance: Iosif Lempert, Paris, April, 1977.
Reproduced in B44, p. 292; B88, p; 35.

Note: The date 1721 is, presumably, a reference to the peace treaty signed between Sweden and Russia on 30 August, 1721, after the long war between those two nations. Peter I emerged as the unquestioned victor and, thenceforth, was called Peter the Great and granted the title of Emperor.

421 [R458].
Set Design for a People's Theater or "Balagan", 1872.
Watercolor.
Signed and dated in Russian: "Architect P. Dmitriev, 1872."
15½ x 13 in., 39.5 x 33 cm.
Other inscription: above the stage in Russian: "People's Theater."
Provenance: Iosif Lempert, Paris, April, 1977.
Reproduced in B44, p. 292.

Note: The *balagan* (plural: *balagany* (from the Persian word *balakhane* meaning "upper room") was a temporary structure used for theatrical events and erected usually in market-places and at bazaars. The Field of Mars in St. Petersburg became the site of one of the most famous *balagan* complexes active on holidays and feast-days such as Shrovetide. The *balagan* assumed particular importance as a genre of folk theater in the mid-18th century and it survived into the early 20th.

The repertoire of the *balagan* consisted of farces and folk dramas such as the *Emperor Maximilian and His Disobedient Son Adolf* (see No. 1014 [R837]) and it relied substantially on the Russian interpretations of the Italian comedy or Punch and Judy show (cf. the ballet *Petrouchka*). Oriented towards the common masses, the *balagan* attracted audiences through circus tricks, juggling acts, and fantastic transformations. Acrobats, clowns, gymnasts, and jugglers were among the primary artistes, while the *zazyvala*, or touter (compère), also played an important role in haranguing the audience, parodying the actors, and making snide remarks about current events and celebrities.

A professional architect, Dmitriev designed a number of attractions for the Field of Mars in the early 1870s, including *balagany* and dioramas, which he produced

421

in a Neo-Russian, or Neo-Nationalist, style (cf. Alexandre Benois's designs for *Petrouchka* at Nos. 159-280 [R133-253]; Andrei Riabushkin at No. 865 [R761]; and Viktor Vasnetsov at No. 1115 [NIRE]).

DMITRIEV, Vladimir Vladimirovich

Born 31 July (13 August), 1900, Moscow, Russia; died 6 May, 1948, Moscow, Russia.

1916-17 attended Elizaveta Zvantseva's Art School in Petrograd; visited Vsevolod Meierkhold's Studio on Borodino Street; 1917 under Meierkhold's guidance, prepared designs for a production of Velimir Khlebnikov's *Death's Mistake* (not realized); 1917-18 attended Meierkhold's Kurmastsep (Courses in the Art of Stage Productions); 1918-22 attended Pegoskhuma-Svomas, studying under Kuzma Petrov-Vodkin; 1918 designed a production of Henrik Ibsen's *Nora* for the Luna-Park Theater; 1920 designed Emile Verhaeren's *Les Aubes* for Meierkhold's production at the Theater of the RSFSR No. 1 in Moscow; 1921 designed Vasilii Kamensky's *Stenka Razin* for the Theater of the Baltic Fleet in Petrograd; 1920-22 taught at the Art School for Sailors in Petrograd; organized the group called Young Ballet, which included George Balanchine and Leonid Lavrovsky; 1923 contributed to the "Exhibition of Paintings by Petrograd Artists of all Directions, 1919-1923" in Petrograd; 1926 designed Fedor Lopukhov's production of *Pulcinella* for the Leningrad Theater of Opera and Ballet (Kirov), and in 1927 *Le Renard;* 1928 onwards worked frequently for the Moscow Art Theater, designing Lev Tolstoi's *Resurrection* there in 1930 and *Anna Karenina* in 1937; 1930-48 worked frequently for the Bolshoi Theater, Moscow, designing, for example, Tchaikovsky's *Queen of Spades* in 1931; 1939 moved to Moscow.

Bibliography
N. Tretiakov: *V. Dmitriev,* M: Sovetskii khudozhnik, 1953.
N. Chushkin and M. Pozharskaia: *Vladimir Vladimirovich Dmitriev.* Catalog of exhibition at the All-Union Theatrical Society, M, 1954.
E. Kostina: *Dmitriev,* M: Sovetskii khudozhnik, 1957.
A14, Vol. 3, pp. 395-96.
G38, pp. 99-143.
N. Chushkin: *Vladimir Vladimirovich Dmitriev.* Catalog of exhibition at BTM, 1976.
V. Berezkin: *V.V. Dmitriev,* L: Khudozhnik RSFSR, 1981.
A. Mikhailova, intr.: Dokumenty i fakty iz istorii otechestvennogo teatra XX veka, M, 2004, No. 3, pp. 346-92; 594-602.

Vladimir Dmitriev belongs to the second generation of Russia's avant-garde and, like many of his colleagues in Leningrad, such as Nikolai Akimov, Valentina Khodasevich, Moisei Levin, and Elizaveta Yakunina, he chose to develop his artistic talent in the theater. To a large extent, Dmitriev's orientation was determined by his early exposure to the theater — his mother was an actress at the Alexandrinsky Theater and as a teenager he met leading theater people of the time, such as Alexander Golovin, Meierkhold, and Sergei Sudeikin. Dmitriev worked for the major theaters of Leningrad and Moscow and, as one of his biographers has remarked, he "lived by his interests in the theater; he gave it all his powers, all his distinctive artistic talent."[227] Dmitriev designed over 150 theater productions and also published theoretical essays on stage design.

Nowadays we tend to remember Dmitriev for his early experimental projects — such as the designs for Meierkhold's production of *Les Aubes* in 1920 (when Dmitriev was only 20 years old) — which, in their emphasis on real materials in three dimensions, anticipated the Constructivist sets by the Stenberg brothers and Alexander Vesnin for the Chamber Theater. However, in spite of the "excesses" of *Les Aubes*, Dmitriev tried always to illustrate the plot and action of a given play through his sets and costumes, adapting his artistic talent accordingly, rather than to use them simply as the extension of an esthetic credo. Consequently, he did not hesitate to create a "straight" decor for a production of *Eugene Onegin* at the Kirov in 1925, or the following year to visualize Sergei Prokofiev's *Love for Three Oranges* as a *balagan*. Because of his artistic flexibility, Dmitriev was also able to adjust to the ideological pressures of the 1930s-50s when the "wise policies of the Party which sharply condemned formalism in art helped artists, including stage designers, to step onto the road of Realist creativity."[228]

The Love for Three Oranges: *a farcical opera in four acts by Sergei Prokofiev based on the comedy by Carlo Gozzi. Produced by Sergei Radlov at the State Academic Theater of Opera and Ballet, Leningrad (now the Mariinsky Theater) on 18 February, 1926, with designs by Vladimir Dmitriev (USSR premiere).*

See No. 33 [R31] for plot summary.

422

422 [R454].
Design for the Stage Curtain in Act I, Scene 2, ca. 1926.
Watercolor and pencil.
12¾ x 10¼ in., 32.5 x 26 cm.
Reproduced in color (upside down) in I60, p. 40. Another design with similar elements is reproduced in color in C79, p. 100. For reproductions of other relevant designs see V. Berezkin, *V.V. Dmitriev*, pp. 56-66.
The reverse carries a stage design for Act III, Scene 3 (see No. 423 [R454a]).
Provenance: Viktor Kholodkov, Moscow, 1986.

423

423 [R454a].
Stage Design for Act III, Scene 3, The Desert, ca. 1926.
Watercolor and pencil.
Signed lower right in Russian: "Dmitriev."
12¾ x 10¼ in., 32.5 x 26 cm.
Other inscription: lower margin in Russian: "V.V. Dmitriev. Love for 3 Oranges."
The reverse carries a design for a stage curtain for Act I, Scene 2 (see No. 422 [R454]).
Provenance: Viktor Kholodkov, Moscow, 1986.

Note: Interested in the Italian Comedy, in the *balagan* tradition, and in the circus, not least thanks to his association with Vsevolod Meierkhold, Dmitriev was happy to accept Sergei Radlov's invitation to design *The Love for Three Oranges*. Although the bold colors of Léon Bakst and, more immediately, the expressive geometries of Alexandra Exter come to mind here, Dmitriev's stage designs for *The Love of Three Oranges* were original and effective. They functioned as follows:

In the spectacle Dmitriev used a painterly-volumetrical system of decorations... Two exquisite spiralling white ladders disappearing into the depths on either side of the stage, a

platform in the background and painted backdrops "inserted" into the general blue ground of the spectacle were what defined the artist's general spatial composition. Painterly effect was achieved not only via the painted landscapes, but also via the combination of the red carpet on the panel with the yellow (on the blue ground) of the long, narrow panels coming down from the gridirons and confining the scenic parameter.[229]

Against this audacious decoration, Radlov and Dmitriev used all manner of circus and comic acts, leading Prokofiev to observe that:

In comparison to what I've seen hitherto, this is the best production. The brilliance and lightness of the Prologue, the running tables, flying Truffaldino, the trapezes, the headspinning tempos — all these things were accomplished... thanks to the talent of those who created the spectacle — Dranishnikov, Radlov, and Dmitriev.[230]

Given twenty-six times, the production was the most attended opera in Leningrad in 1926, not only because of the music and the scenery, but also because the cast included the distinguished singers Mariia Maksakova and Ivan Ershov. Not everyone, however, was pleased with this "light, merry, and jocular" result.[231] The critic Alexei Gvozdev, for example, complained that Dmitriev was the wrong choice for designer, because he was too close to the "luxurious decorativeness of the old operatic theater... which Prokofiev is ridiculing."[232] Perhaps Gvozdev would have been happier with Isaak Rabinovich's more grotesque designs for the 1927 production of the same opera at the Bolshoi Theater in Moscow (No. 855 [R732]) or with Alexander Khvostenko-Khvostov's project (No. 607 [R860]).

227 Tretiakov, *V. Dmitriev*, p. 5.
228 Ibid., p. 9.
229 G53, p. 154.
230 S. Prokofiev: "Ob 'Apelsinakh'" in *Rabochii teatr*, L, 1927, No. 7, p. 9. Quoted in V. Berezkin, *V.V. Dmitriev*, p. 63. The reference is to Vladimir Dranishnikov, who conducted the orchestra.
231 F68, p. 80.
232 A. Gvozdev: "Liubov k trem apelsinam" in *Zhizn iskusstva*, L, 1926, No. 7, p. 15. Quoted in Berezkin, *V.V. Dmitriev*, p. 76.

DOBUJINSKY (Doboujinsky/Dobuzhinsky), Mstislav Valerianovich

Born 2 (14) August, 1875, Novgorod, Russia; died 20 November, 1957, New York, USA.

1885-87 attended SSEA; took lessons from Lev Dmitriev-Kavkazsky; 1898 graduated from Law School, St. Petersburg University; 1899 attended the studios of Anton Ažbe and Simon Hollósy in Munich; 1901 back in St. Petersburg; close to the World of Art group, contributing to its journal and exhibitions; thereafter worked as a designer for many journals such as *Zhupel* [Bugbear], *Apollon* [Apollo], and *Zhar-ptitsa* [Firebird]; 1906 illustrated Alexander Pushkin's *The Station Master* (published 1934); 1907 co-founder of the Antique Theater, St. Petersburg; 1909 designed Konstantin Stanislavsky's production of Ivan Turgenev's *A Month in the Country*; thereafter designed many productions for the Moscow Art Theater, including Dostoevsky's *Devils* (1913) and Dmitrii Merezhkovsky's *Let There Be Joy* (1916); during World War I served as a medical orderly; 1918-19 taught at Pegoskhuma-Svomas, Petrograd, and the Vitebsk Popular Art Institute; active member of the House of Arts, Petrograd; designed a production of Schiller's *Die Räuber* for the Bolshoi Dramatic Theater, Petrograd; 1924 emigrated to Kaunas; taught in the State Art School and established his own teaching studio; 1935-39 lived in England; 1939 emigrated to the US; in the 1930s and 1940s contributed to many stage productions in Europe and the USA.

Bibliography

M2, Vol. 2, pp. 158-173.
Anon.: *Mstislav V. Dobujinsky*, New York: The Group of Friends of Mstislav V. Dobujinsky, 1973.
A. Gusarova: *Mstislav V. Dobujinsky 1875-1957*. Catalog of exhibition at the TG, 1975.
J. Bowlt: "The Early Graphic Work of Mstislav Dobujinsky" in *Transactions of the Association of Russian-American Scholars in USA*, New York, 1975, Vol. 9, pp. 249-86.
F45.
T. Wood: *Mstislav V. Dobujinsky. Half a Century of Theatrical Art*. Catalog of exhibition at the Center for the Arts, the New York Public Library at Lincoln Center, New York, 1979.
A. Gusarova: *Mstislav Dobuzhinsky*, M: Izobrazitelnoe iskusstvo, 1982.
F72.
G. Chugunov: *M.V. Dobuzhinsky*, L: Khudozhnik RSFSR, 1988.
M73, Vol. 26, p. 76.
L. Byckling, ed.: *Pisma Mikhaila Chekhova Mstislavu Dobuzhinskomu*, P: Vsemirnoe slovo, 1994.
G. Chugunov, comp.: *Vospominaniia o Dobuzhinskom,* SP: Akademicheskii proekt, 1997.
F96.
A. Riumin: *M.V. Dobuzhinsky. Azbuka "Mira iskusstva"*, M: Nashe nasledie, 1998.
G. Chugunov, comp.: *M.V. Dobuzhinsky. Pisma,*
SP: Bulanin, 2001 .
A. Gusarova*: Dobuzhinsky,* M: Belyi gorod, 2001.
O. Lapo and L. Petrova, comps.: *Dobuzhinskie chteniia,* Velikii Novgorod: Commission on Culture, Cinema, and Tourism, 2001.
I. Vydrin, ed.: *A.N. Benua i M.V. Dobuzhinsky. Perepiska,* SP: Sad iskusstv, 2003.
V. Belikov: *"Ya" i "drugie" Mstislava Dobuzhinskogo.* Catalog of exhibition at the Marc Chagall Museum, Vitebsk, 2004.
Mstislav Dobuzhinsky. Catalog (two volumes) of the auction organized by Y.M. Le Roux-C. Morel, J.J. Mathias, and Baron Ribeyre et Associés at the Drouot Montaigne, Paris, on 24 June and 22-23 November, 2005.
Yu. Girba: *Mstislav Dobuzhinsky. Ot Litvy do Ameriki.* Catalog of exhibition at Our Artists Gallery, M, 2008.
For a list of Dobujinsky's stage designs see M2, Vol. 2, pp. 159-73.
D. Dzhuliano (G. Giuliano): "Perepiska M.V. Dobuzhinskogo i A.Ya. Beloborodova" in *Europa Orientalis. Archivio Russo-Italiano,* Salerno, 2011, No. VII, pp. 126-87.

Dobujinsky once wrote to Nina Berberova: "I'm drowning up to my ears in the theater."[233] Although he was referring to a specific production in his letter, Dobujinsky's reputation rests in general on the many sets and costumes that he designed for the ballet, the opera, and the dramatic stage. He started his career as a stage designer in 1907 with his contribution to Meierkhold's production of Alexei Remizov's *Besovskoe deistvo* [A Devilish Act] at Vera Komissarzhevskaia's Theater, St. Petersburg, and in 1908, for Nikolai Evreinov's production of Adam de la Halle's *Jeu de Robin et Marion* at the Antique Theater, St. Petersburg. Perhaps Dobujinsky's most celebrated stage ensemble was for Stanislavsky's production of Ivan Turgenev's *A Month in the Country*, although, seen in retrospect, the sets seem to lack the inventiveness and brilliance that we associate with Dobujinsky's collaboration with the Saisons Russes, such as *Papillons* and *Midas* (Nos. 425-27 [R460-62]).

Even so, *A Month in the Country* enabled Dobujinsky to explore the culture of one of his favorite epochs — the Russian Biedermeier style — and, in turn, to think about allied subjects, such as the Russian *style empire* and Russian chinoiserie, as well as the artistic parallels between Nikolai Gogol and E.T.A. Hoffmann.

Dobujinsky's most intense involvement with the theater was in the 1910s, when he worked both for ambitious enterprises such as Vladimir Nemirovich-Danchenko's production of Alexander Blok's *The Rose and the Cross* at the Moscow Art Theater in 1917, and for more intimate concerns such as the cabaret and night-club the Comedians' Halt in Petrograd. Apart from his decorative work, which he extended to murals for the Kazan Railroad Station, Moscow, in 1916 and even to Revolutionary agit-designs for the Admiralty in Petrograd in 1918,[234] Dobujinsky continued to illustrate books, travel widely, maintain a voluminous correspondence, and create his splendid graphic views of London, Amsterdam, St. Petersburg, and Vilnius.[235] It

was Dobujinsky's universality, his constant transcension of temporal and spatial locales that prompted the critic Erik Gollerbakh to assert that "more than anyone, Dobujinsky has reflected the soul of our epoch in his works."[236]

Alexandre Benois: *Portrait of Mstislav Dobujinsky, 1908.* (See No. 119 [R98])

Georgii Vereisky: *Portrait of Mstislav Dobujinsky, 1922.* (See No. 1124 [NIRE])

424 [R459].
Portrait of Alexandre Benois, 1914.
Pencil.
Signed lower margin in ink in Russian:"Drawn by M.V. Dobujinsky" and dated "28.XI.1914." 8½ x 5⅛ in., 21.5 x 13 cm.
Other inscriptions: lower margin in pencil in Russian: "At the house of Princess N.P. Gorchakova."
Provenance: Anna Tcherkessoff, daughter of Alexandre Benois, Paris, October, 1968. Now in a private collection.
Reproduced in F107, p. 127; I20, No. 5; I51, No. 32; M151, p. 14; N128; and in M. Pozharskaia: *Aleksandr Golovin,* M: Sovetskii khudozhnik, 1990, p. 192.

Note: Princess Natalia Pavlovna Gorchakova (née Kharitonenko, 1880-1964) and her husband Prince Mikhail Konstantinovich Gorchakov (1880-1961) were ardent collectors of painting, and their St. Petersburg

424

house contained superb examples of Canaletto, Borovikovsky, Rokotov, etc.; in fact, Nicola Benois remembers it as one of the most important private collections of Old Master paintings that he had ever seen.[237] Alexandre Benois, Dobujinsky, and other World of Art artists often visited the Gorchakovs to discuss matters of art. The late Anna Tcherkessoff, daughter of Alexandre Benois, wrote of this portrait: "Evidently, it was done after a private dinner, after which ensued various interesting conversations between the close friends."[238]

Midas: *a mythological comedy in one act adapted from Ovid's* Metamorphoses *by Léon Bakst with music by Maximilian Steinberg. Produced by Sergei Diaghilev at the Grand Opéra, Paris, on 2 June, 1914, with choreography by Michel Fokine and designs by Mstislav Dobujinsky.*

The god Dionysius grants Midas, King of Phrygia, a dispensation of dubious merit: everything he touches turns to gold — including food. As a result, Midas almost starves to death, but Dionysius allows him to divest himself of this gift by bathing in the Pactolus torrent.

425 [R460].
Costume Design for a God, 1914.
Postcard.
Initialed and dated lower right in Russian: "M.D. 914."
5¾ x 3⅝ in., 14.5 x 9.2 cm.
Other inscription: along left border in Russian after the code number 64-25: "M. Dobujinsky. Costume Design for the ballet 'Midas' (Russian Ballet Season in Paris 1914)."
Provenance: Nicola Benois, Milan, 1964.

426 [R461].
Costume Design for Gamadriada, 1914.
Postcard.
Initialed in Russian and dated lower left: "M.D. 914."
5¾ x 3⅝ in., 14.5 x 9.2 cm.
Other inscription: along left border in Russian after the code number 64-26: "M. Dobujinsky. Gamadriada. Costume Design for the ballet 'Midas' (Russian Ballet Season in Paris 1914)."
Provenance: Nicola Benois, Milan, 1964.

427 [R462].
Costume Design for the Dancer Tamara Karsavina, 1914.
Postcard.
Signed in the plate in Russian: "M. Dobujinsky."
5¾ x 3⅝ in., 14.5 x 9.2 cm.
Other inscriptions: along the lower end in Russian: "M. Dobuzhinsky. Costume Design for the Ballet *Midas* for T.L. Karsavina"; lower right corner: "Code no. 64-22."
Provenance: Nicola Benois, Milan, 1964.

Note: Diaghilev accepted Bakst's idea for a balletic interpretation of Ovid's *Metamorphoses* with music by Steinberg as early as 1912.[239] In *Midas* and other renderings Bakst wanted to present a "Greece not of the classical tradition, but an everyday Greece with a touch of the comic."[240] However, in spite of Bakst's efforts and the dancing of Adolph Bolm, Margarita Froman, and Tamara Karsavina, the result was rather tedious. Serge Grigoriev recalled:

> Fokine by this time was exhausted. Not only had he composed three ballets; he had also danced at nearly every performance. It was not surprising, therefore, that in the composition of the last ballet on our list — *Midas* — his inspiration failed him, particularly since neither the subject itself, nor Steinberg's music, attracted him. Doboujinsky's designs for the décor — after Mantegna — were also somewhat uninspired; in short, *Midas* was still-born.[241]

All three postcards were issued by the Society of St. Eugenia (the Red Cross organization in St. Petersburg). For details on this society see Nos. 59-71 and 74 [R55-68].

425

426

427

428

430

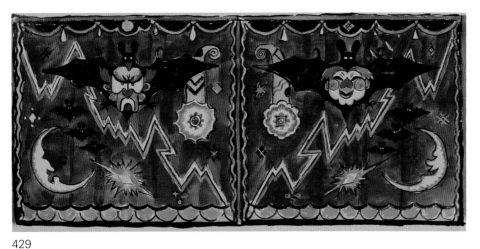

429

Reproduced in color in black and white in A34, p. 124; M73, p. 91; R15. For reproductions of similar costume designs see L147, Lot 71; L159, Lots 400-02; L164, Lots 195-97; and L182, Lots 551 and 552.

431 [R464].
Costume Design for a Cossack with Hands on Hips, 1926.
Watercolor, pencil, and ink.
Signed lower left with the monogram and dated in ink: "2.VII.1926."
12½ x 9⅝ in., 31.8 x 24.3 cm.
Provenance: *Alexandre Sementchenkoff Collection*, London: Christie's, 22 October, 1987, Lot 620 (reproduced). Now in a private collection.

Curtain designs for Nikita Baliev and his Théâtre de la Chauve-Souris at the Théâtre de la Madeleine, Paris, 1924.

428 [NIRE].
Curtain Design for the Chauve-Souris, 1924.
Gouache, gold and silver paint.
4½ x 7 in.,11.5 x 17.7 cm.
Left side of the image bears the Cyrillic initials "LM" for *Letuchaia mysh* (the Russian for "bat"), right side, correspondingly, bears the letters "CS" for *Chauve-Souris*.
Provenance: Anastasie Kopřivová, Prague, June, 1986.

429 [NIRE].
Curtain Design with Quarter-moons for the Chauve-Souris, 1924.
Watercolor.
9⅜ x 19¼ in., 23.7 x 49 cm.
Provenance: Anastasie Kopřivová, Prague, June, 1986.
Reproduced in F107, p. 486.

Note: It is assumed that these two designs were intended as designs for the

intermediary curtain for one of Baliev's productions at the Théâtre de la Madeleine rather than for a permanent drop curtain.

Platov's Cossacks in Paris (Les Cosaques de Platov à Paris): *revue by Petr Potemkin with music by Alexei Arkhangelsky and designs by Mstislav Dobujinsky. Produced by Nikita Baliev and his Théâtre de la Chauve-Souris at the Théâtre de la Madeleine, Paris, in the fall of 1926.*

The famous General Platov, who had lost one ear at battle, was the head of a regiment of cossacks that were part of the Russian occupation forces in Paris in 1814.

430 [56; R463].
Costume Designs for Two Cossacks Flirting with Two Girls, 1926.
Watercolor, pencil, and ink.
Signed lower left with the monogram in ink.
12½ x 9⅝ in., 31.8 x 24.3 cm.
Provenance: *Alexandre Sementchenkoff Collection,* London: Christie's, 22 October, 1987, Lot 619 (reproduced). Now in a private collection.

431

Raymonda: *ballet by Lidiia Pashkova and Marius Petipa with music by Alexander Glazunov. Produced by Nicholas Zverev for the Lithuanian National Opera and Ballet at the Kaunas State Theater, Kaunas, on 28 February, 1933, with designs by Mstislav Dobujinsky.*

Raymonda is betrothed to the knight Jean de Brienne, but he must leave for a crusade. During his absence, Abderakhman, the Saracen knight, tries to seduce her, but Brienne returns, overcomes his rival and wins back his lady. The marriage festivities are inaugurated by a rousing Hungarian divertissement.

432

432 [R466].
Portrait of Nicholas Zverev, 1932.
Pencil.
Signed with the monogram and dated lower right: "1932."
13⅜ x 10 in., 34 x 25.5 cm.
Provenance: Michael Glinski, Paris, January, 1969.
Reproduced in I20, p. 57.

Note: Nicholas (Nikolai) Matveevich Zverev (1888-1965), who produced the Kaunas version of *Raymonda*, worked for Sergei Diaghilev's Ballets Russes between 1912 and 1926. He then toured with various companies with Vera Nemtchinova (his first wife; see No. 433 [R467]), Anton Dolin, and Leonid Massine. From 1936 until 1945 he was associated with the Ballet Russe de Monte Carlo. Dobujinsky made this portrait when they were both living in Kaunas.

433 [R467].
Portrait of Vera Nemtchinova, 1933.
Pencil, watercolor and gouache.
Signed and dated lower right in Russian: "Mstislav Dobujinsky 1933."
Other inscription in Russian preceding the signature: "To dear Raymondochka from your true and dedicated MVD."
Reproduced in I40, No. 40; M88.

433

Provenance: Michael Glinski, Paris, January, 1969.

Note: Vera Nikolaevna Nemtchinova (1899-1984), one of Diaghilev's greatest dancers in the early 1920s, scored her first major success in *Les Biches* (1924) and then *Les Matelots* (1925). Leaving Diaghilev's Ballets Russes the following year with her then husband, Nicholas Zverev (see No. 432 [R466]), she founded her own ballet company (see Nos. 1057-59 [R930-32]) and became a leading dancer with the Lithuanian State Ballet in Kaunas from 1930-35, taking the title role in *Raymonda*. After that she joined the Ballet Russe de Monte Carlo.

434 [R468].
Costume Design for a Spanish Dancer of the Panaderos, 1932.
Gouache and pencil.

434

Signed and dated lower left: "M. Dobujinsky, 1932."
13⅜ x 8⅝ in., 34 x 22 cm.
Other inscriptions: the margins carry instructions to the dressmaker.
Provenance: the artist's son, Vsevolod Dobujinsky, New York, 1966.
Reproduced in color in N188, p. 20; and in black and white in I14, No. 45.

The Sleeping Beauty: *ballet in a prologue and three acts based on a fairy tale by Charles Perrault with music by Peter Tchaikovsky and original choreography by Marius Petipa. Produced by the Lithuanian National Opera and Ballet at the Kaunas State Theater, Kaunas, on 18 April, 1934, with choreography by Nicholas Zverev after Petipa, and designs by Mstislav Dobujinsky.*

See No. 94 [R87] for plot summary.

435

435 [R469].
Costume Design for One of the Three Ivans or Buffoons in Act III, 1934.
Watercolor and pencil.
Signed lower right with the monogram and dated 1934.
14 x 10 in., 35.5 x 25.5 cm.
Other inscription: upper left: "Les Foux."
Provenance: the artist's son, Vsevolod Dobujinsky, New York, November, 1967.
Reproduced in B115, p. 193; I20, No. 26; I51, No. 72.

436

437

436 [NIRE].
Set Design for the Prologue, 1936.
Pencil, India ink, and watercolor.
Signed lower right with the monogram,
inscribed and dated 1936.
6⅛ x 8⅞ in., 15.6 x 22.5 cm.
Provenance: the artist's son, Vsevolod
Dobujinsky, New York, November, 1967.
Reproduced in I14, No. 41.

437 [NIRE].
Set Design for Acts I and III, 1936.
India ink, watercolor, and gouache.
Signed lower right with the monogram,
inscribed and dated 1936.
6⅛ x 7⅜ in., 15.6 x 18.75 cm.
Provenance: the artist's son, Vsevolod
Dobujinsky, New York, November 1967.
Reproduced in I14, No. 42.

***Le Mariage d'Aurore* (also known as *Les
Noces d'Aurore* and *Le Mariage de la Belle
au Bois Dormant*):** *extract from the ballet*
La Belle au Bois Dormant *(Sleeping Beauty)
produced at the Théâtre de la Monnaie,
Brussels, in 1938 with choreography by
Nicholas Zverev and designs by Mstislav
Dobujinsky.*

*This ballet, which shows the dances at
the marriage feast of* Sleeping Beauty *(see
No. 94 [R87]) has no developed plot.
Among the guests are the various fairies
and nobles, the Blue Bird, Little Red Riding
Hood, the Shah Shahriar from* Schéhérazade,
and other fabulous personages.

438 [R470].
Costume Design for the Wolf, 1937.
Watercolor, silver and gold paint, black ink,
and pencil.
Signed and dated lower right: "MD 1937."
13¾ x 9⅞ in., 35 x 25 cm.
Provenance: the artist's son, Vsevolod
Dobujinsky, New York, June, 1968. Now in
a private collection.
Reproduced in I20, No. 33.

438

Swan Lake: *ballet in four acts by Peter
Tchaikovsky with libretto by Vladimir
Begichev and Vasilii Geltser and original
choreography by Vaclav Reisinger. Produced by Nicholas Zverev for Les Ballets
de Monte Carlo, Monaco, in April, 1936,
with choreography by Nicholas Zverev and
designs by Mstislav Dobujinsky. Only Act II
was performed.*

*Princess Odette is turned into a swan
by the magician Rothbart. At midnight,
however, she and her companions regain*
*their human form, and at one such trans-
formation, Prince Siegfried falls in love with
her, swearing to rescue her. Expected to
choose his bride one night at a castle ball,
Siegfried is bewitched by Odile, daughter
of Rothbart, who — as a black swan —
looks like Odette. When the latter appears,
Siegfried realizes that he has broken his
oath, but he is forgiven by Odette. Rothbart
then conjures up a storm and the two
lovers are drowned.*

Scenic Mimes: *choreographed by Bella Reine, New York, 1943.*

439

439 [NIRE].
Costume Design for a Beggar, 1942.
Charcoal and gouache.
Signed lower right with the monogram, dated 14 December, 1942; and dedicated to Bella Reine.
17¼ x 12¼ in., 43.7 x 31.2 cm.
Provenance: the artist's son, Vsevolod Dobujinsky, New York, November, 1967. Now in a private collection.
Reproduced in I14, No. 43.

440

440 [NIRE].
Costume Design for an Old Woman with Spikes, 1942.
Charcoal and gouache.
Signed lower right with the monogram, dated 1942, and dedicated to Bella Reine.
19⅞ x 15 in., 50.6 x 38.1 cm.
Provenance: the artist's son, Vsevolod Dobujinsky, New York, November, 1967. Reproduced in I14, No. 44. Now in a private collection.

Note: Of Russian-Jewish origin, Bella Reine (1897-1983) was born in Lithuania, but studied classical and free dance in Petrograd before emigrating to France in 1923. Married to the Symbolist painter Ivan Bozherianov, Reine was especially interested in the visual arts, including the work of Marc Chagall and Pablo Picasso, and also cultivated friendships with celebrated performers, such as Maurice Chevalier and Serge Lifar. Living in the USA during World War II, Reine made her living by dancing pantomime numbers and giving private lessons. Presumably, the production in question was a pantomime.

Mam'zelle Angot: *ballet in three scenes by Charles Lecocq with music arranged by Efrem Kurtz and orchestrated by Richard Mohaupt, choreography by Leonid Massine and designs by Mstislav Dobujinsky. Produced by the Ballet Theatre (now American Ballet Theater) at the Metropolitan Opera House, New York, on 10 October 1943.*
    Mlle. Angot, who is betrothed to a barber, is in love with a political caricaturist. The latter, while drawing a cartoon of a government official, falls in love with his mistress, a noble lady. The official does not like the cartoon and sends the caricaturist to jail where Mlle. Angot joins him. The caricaturist then flees from jail and arrives at a reception where he declares his love for the noble lady, but it transpires that Mlle. Angot and the noble lady are old school friends. Mlle Angot then exposes the affair between the official and the noble lady and finds that she really does love the barber.

441 [R471].
Costume Design for l'Homme Orchestre, 1943.
Gouache.
Signed lower right: "Dobujinsky."
15 x 10 in., 38 x 25.5 cm.
Other inscriptions: upper right: "l'Homme Orchestre"; upper left: "Mam'zelle Angot"; left margin carries instructions to the dressmaker in French.
Provenance: Nicola Benois, Milan, February, 1968.
Reproduced in I20, No. 30; I51, No. 73.

441

442

442 [R472].
Costume Design for the Raffles Vendor, 1943.
Gouache.
Signed lower left in pencil and dated: "M. Dobujinsky, 1943, NY."
14½ x 9⅞ in., 37 x 25 cm.
Other inscriptions: upper left in pencil: "Mam'zelle Angot"; upper right: "Le vendeur des prix."
Provenance: Nicola Benois, Milan, February, 1969.
Reproduced in color in B115, plate 195; F107, p. 143; and in black and white in I14, No. 46.

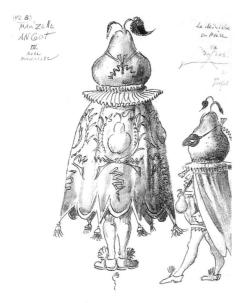

443

443 [R473].
Costume Design for the Minister Dressed as a Pear, ca. 1943.
Pencil and black ink.
Signed lower center with monogram.
12⅝ x 10 in., 32 x 25.5 cm.
Other inscriptions: upper left: "Mam'zelle Angot. III Acte. Masquerade"; upper right: "Le ministre au poire."
Provenance: the artist's son, Vsevolod Dobujinsky, New York, June, 1968. Now in a private collection.
Reproduced in I20, No. 31.

444 [R474].
Costume Design for the Cocoa Vendor, 1943.
Watercolor and ink.

444

Signed lower right margin with the monogram and dated "43."
15 x 10 in., 38 x 25.5 cm.
Other inscription: top left in French: "Mlle Angot"; upper right: "Marchand de Coco. Extra."
Provenance: the artist's son, Vsevolod Dobujinsky, New York, June, 1968.
Reproduced in I20, No. 32.

Note: For commentary, see "Ballet Theatre Opens Season with Novelty" in *Musical America,* New York, 1943, October, p. 15.

Khovanshchina: *opera in five acts by Modest Mussorgsky, completed by Nikolai Rimsky-Korsakov, with libretto by Mussorgsky and Vladimir Stasov. Staged by Edward Johnson at the Metropolitan Opera, New York, on 16 February, 1950, with choreography by Laurent Novikoff and designs by Mstislav Dobujinsky.*
The leader of Ivan Khovansky's streltsy (military corps) tries to organize a palace coup and to put his son Andrei on the throne instead of the young Tsars, Ioann and Peter. His endeavor, however, fails. These black deeds, set in the colorful ambiance of Old Russia, are countered by the touching love affair between Andrei and the maiden Marfa.

445

445 [NIRE].
Costume Design for an Old Believer, 1950.
Pencil, India ink, and watercolor.
Signed lower right with the monogram and dated 1948; inscribed top left.
13 x 8⅞ in., 33.1 x 22.5 cm.
Provenance: the artist's son, Vsevolod Dobujinsky, New York, November, 1967. Now in a private collection.
Reproduced in I14, No. 46.

446

446 [NIRE].
Costume Design for Martha, 1948.
Pencil, charcoal and gouache.
Signed lower right with the monogram and dated 1948; inscribed top right.
12¼ x 9⅝ in., 31.2 x 24.3 cm.
Provenance: the artist's son, Vsevolod Dobujinsky, New York, November, 1967.
Now in a private collection.
Reproduced in I14, No. 47.

Note: This 1950 production (in English) was the premiere of *Khovanshchina* at the Metropolitan Opera and scored an immediate success, not least because of the strong cast of singers — Rise Stevens, Polyna Stoska, Charles Kuhlmann, Jerome Hines, and Lawrence Tibbett — conducted by Emil Cooper

The Love for Three Oranges: *a farcical opera in two acts by Sergei Prokofiev based on the comedy by Carlo Gozzi. Directed by Vladimir Rosing and produced by Theodore Komissarjevsky for the New York City Opera at the City Center, New York, on 1 November, 1949, with ballet choreography by Charles Weldman and designs by Mstislav Dobujinsky.*
See No. 32 [R31] for plot summary.

447 [R475].
Design for the Proscenium Curtain, ca. 1949.
Watercolor.
8⅝ x 13 in., 22 x 33 cm.
Provenance: Jill Weldon, step-daughter of the violinist Nathan Milstein, New York, 1966.
Reproduced in I14, No. 44.

447

Wozzeck: *Opera in three acts with music by Alban Berg. Staged by Theodore Komissarjevsky at the New York City Center Opera, New York, on 3 April, 1952, with designs by Mstislav Dobujinsky.*

The soldier Wozzeck shaves his Captain, who says that Wozzeck lacks morality, citing his bastard child from Marie. Wozzeck answers that virtue is not for the poor. Marie succumbs to the advances of the Drum Major and Wozzeck confronts Marie with his suspicions. Reminiscing about their life together, he kills her with a knife, which he throws into a pond. Covered in blood, he wades into the pond to recover the knife and drowns. Marie's child is told that his mother is dead, but he fails to comprehend.

448 [NIRE].
Costume Design for Marie, 1952.
Charcoal and gouache.
Signed lower right with the monogram and dated 24 March, 1952.
12½ x 9⅞ in., 31.9 x 25 cm.
Provenance: the artist's son, Vsevolod Dobujinsky, New York, November, 1967.
Reproduced in I14, No. 45.

Coppélia: *ballet-pantomime in two acts by Charles Nuitter and Arthur Saint-Léon based on E.T.A. Hoffmann's tale* The Sand Merchant *with music by Léo Delibes. Produced by the Ballet Rambert at the Cambridge Arts Theatre, Cambridge, England, on 7 May, 1956, with choreography by Marie Rambert and designs by Mstislav Dobujinsky.*

The scientist, Dr. Coppelius, has constructed a beautiful automaton, Coppélia,

and Franz, Swanhilde's beloved, falls in love with her. One night Swanhilde and her friends enter the workshop of Dr. Coppelius and discover the secret. When the Doctor arrives, all flee, except for Swanhilde, who hides. Franz climbs through the window, is seized by the doctor and forced to take a potion, for the Doctor wishes to transfer the life forces of Franz to his automaton. Unknown to the Doctor, Swanhilde takes Coppélia's place and "comes to life." Franz also wakes up and Swanhilde tells the Doctor of the trick. Swanhilde and Franz are then reconciled.

449 [57; R476].
Costume Design for the Chinese Doll, 1956.
Gouache, ink, gold and silver paint, and pencil.
Signed lower right with the monogram and dated: "16.VII.1956."
14½ x 9½ in., 37 x 24 cm.
Other inscriptions: upper left: "The Chinese Doll."
Provenance: the artist's son, Vsevolod Dobujinsky, New York, November, 1967. Now in a private collection.
Reproduced in color in B115, plate 195; and in black and white in I20, No. 27; I51, No. 74; and L88, Lot 199. Many costumes by Dobujinsky for *Coppélia* of ca. 1956-57 are in the collection of the Center for the Performing Arts, the New York Public Library at Lincoln Center.

450 [R477].
Costume Design for the King Doll, 1956.
Gouache, ink, pencil, silver and gold paint.
Signed and dated lower right "1956."
14½ x 12 in., 37 x 30.5 cm.
Other inscriptions: upper left: "King Doll"; upper right: "Coppélia."
Provenance: the artist's son, Vsevolod Dobujinsky, New York, November, 1967. Now in a private collection.
Reproduced in G61; I20, No. 29; M45; and L88, Lot 196.

448

449

450

451 [58; R478].
Costume Design for the Astrologer Doll,
1956.
Gouache, pencil, and gold.
Signed with monogram and dated lower
right "1956."
14¾ x 12 in., 37.5 x 30.5 cm.
Provenance: the artist's son, Vsevolod
Dobujinsky, New York, November, 1967.
Now in a private collection.
Reproduced in I20, No. 28; L88, Lot 193; Q13.

Note: Dobujinsky designed several productions of *Coppélia,* including one staged
by the Lithuanian State Ballet in Kaunas in
1933, and another staged by the Ballet
Russe de Monte Carlo at the Alhambra
Theater, London, in 1956. For some commentary on the 1956 version, see C.
Barnes: "Ballet Rambert" in *Dance and*
Dancers, London, 1956, July, pp. 28-29.

The Bronze Horseman: *ballet in three acts and*
thirteen scenes by Reingold Glière based on
the poem by Alexander Pushkin. Produced at
the Kirov Theater, Leningrad on 27 June,
1949. with choreography by Rostislav
Zakharov and designs by Mikhail Bobyshev.

451

After one of the occasional inundations
of St. Petersburg, Evgenii finds that his lady
love has been drowned. Demented with

grief, he blames Peter the Great, founder
of this inauspicious city — monumentalized
in the famous bronze statue — for his
misfortune. In Evgenii's diseased imagi-
nation the statue comes alive and pursues
him until he drops.

452 [R479].
The Bronze Horseman, ca. 1949.
Charcoal, black ink, and white gouache.
Signed lower right: "M. Dobujinsky."
12¼ x 15¾ in., 31 x 40 cm.
Provenance: Alexandre Djanchieff, Paris,
September, 1978. Now in a private collection.
Reproduced in color in F107, p. 143; M151,
p. 33; a similar version is reproduced as No.
81 in K9.

Note: Dobujinsky's rendering of Etienne
Falconet's famous statue of Peter the Great
on Senate Square (known in Soviet times
as Decembrists' Square) in St. Petersburg
(Leningrad) has no direct connection with
Glière's ballet. However, inasmuch as
Glière, like many Russian musicians,
writers and artists, was fascinated and
inspired by the monument, it is relevant to
include Dobujinsky's image here.

452

453

A La Vieille Russie's store at 785 Fifth Avenue, where it was located from 1941-1961, prior to moving to its present location down the block at 781 Fifth Avenue and 59th St.

453 [R465].
Interior of the Russian Antique Store, A La Vieille Russie, **ca. 1950.**
Gouache.
Signed lower left with the Russian monogram.
9½ x 15⅛ in., 24 x 38.5 cm.

Provenance: the artist's son, Vsevolod Dobujinsky, New York, December, 1971. Reproduced in I40, No. 39; M28.

Note: This item was formerly described as a stage design for the production of Ivan Turgenev's comedy, *A Month in the*

Country, at the Theater Guild, New York, on 17 March, 1930. However, new evidence, including this documentary photograph, indicates that Dobujinsky's gouache was of the interior of the antique store A La Vieille Russie, which between 1941 and 1961, was situated on the corner of Fifth Avenue and 60th Street in New York. The scene was commissioned by the then owners of the store, Alexander and Ray Schaffer, shortly before the store relocated one block south to 781 Fifth Avenue. The glass display case visible in the arch on the right of the gouache is still at A La Vieille Russie.[242]

233 Letter from Mstislav Dobujinsky to Nina Berberova dated 11 November, 1949, in N. Berberova: "Pisma M.V. Dobuzhinskogo k N.N. Berberovoi" in *Slavica Hierusalymitana,* Jerusalem, 1980, No. 4, Letter No. 15.

234 For details on Dobujinsky's agit-designs see A. Strigalev: "M.V. Dobuzhinsky v revoliutsionnye gody" in Yu. Korolev: *Sovetskoe monumentalnoe iskusstvo '75/77,* M: Sovetskii khudozhnik, 1979, pp. 244-56; Dobujinsky's own statements in the same issue (pp. 257-70) are also of relevance.

235 For commentary on Dobujinsky's scenes of Lithuania, Latvia, and Estonia see I. Korsakaite et al.: *Iskusstvo Pribaltiki,* Tallin: Kunst, 1981, pp. 167-78.

236 E. Gollerbakh: *Risunki M.V. Dobuzhinskogo,* M-P: State Publishing-House, 1923, p. 34.

237 R. Allegri: "Nicola Benois, il più grande scenografo del nostro tempo, racconta la sua vita" in *Gente,* Milan, 1981, No. 47, p. 87.

238 Letter from Anna Tcherkessoff to John E. Bowlt dated 29 September, 1981.

239 F63, vol. 2, p. 198.

240 F63, vol. 1, p. 462.

241 F63, vol. 1, p. 462.

242 We are grateful to Nina Lobanov-Rostovsky and to Mark, Paul, and Peter Schaffer of A La Vieille Russie, New York, for this information.

DUNKEL, Eugene (Dunkel, Evgenii Borisovich)

Born 30 April (12 May), 1890, Vernyi (Alma-Ata), Russian Turkestan (Kazakhstan); died 10 April, 1972, Pelham, New York, USA.

1893 onwards lived in Riga; ca. 1900 studied under Ivan Trutnev at the Vilnius Sketching School; 1904 enrolled in MIPSA; studied under Konstantin Yuon; 1907-16 attended SCITD, studying under Petr Lambin; 1913 entered IAA, studying under Dmitrii Kardovsky; contributed to the "5th Exhibition of the Association of Independents," Petrograd; worked at the Troitsky and Mariinsky Theaters and the Theater of Musical Drama, Petrograd; 1916 worked for the journal *Solntse Rossii*; 1917 mobilized and sent to the Rumanian front; 1919 via Ekaterinoslav and the Crimea went to Bulgaria; 1920 worked in Greece as a portrait painter, then moved to Paris; 1923 arrived in New York, where subsequently he designed ballets, operas, and dramas staged by the Metropolitan Opera Company, the Ballet Theater (after 1940), and other companies; 1928 contributed to the exhibition "Paintings, Sculpture and Drawings by American and European Artists" at the Brooklyn Museum; 1929 one-man exhibition at the Galerie J. Allard, Paris; 1920s-50s worked on many Broadway musicals, ballets, and operettas; 1938-40 made sets for the Ballet Russe de Monte Carlo; 1930s worked for CBS Radio, designing settings for studio audiences; painted murals for the Latin Quarter Restaurant and other restaurants in New York; also worked for Mikhail Mordkin's ballet company in New York; 1943 with his brother Andrei designed sets for part of the exhibition "Fun and Folly" at the Museum of the City of New York; 1953 executed the scenery after Jean Corot for *Les Sylphides* at the Royal Opera House, Covent Garden, London, danced by American Ballet Theater; 1957 contributed to the exhibition "Artists of the Theater," New York.

Bibliography
H6, p. 47.
Eugene B. Dunkel. Catalog of exhibition at the Dunkel Scenic Studios, New York, 1959.
M2, Vol. 2, pp. 173-75.
"Eugene B. Dunkel, 81, a Scenic Designer." Obituary in the *New York Times,* 12 April, 1972, p. 48.
H34, p. 270.

The Enchanted Kingdom: *film (?) projected, but not produced, for the Paramount Picture Corporation, New York, 1925. Plot not known.*

454

454 [R480].
Stage Design, 1925.
Watercolor, pencil, and gold paint.
Signed and dated lower left in pencil: "E. Dunkel, 1925."
18 x 30 in., 45.7 x 76.2 cm.
Other inscriptions: on reverse in ink in a mixture of Russian and English: "Sketch for a decoration for the Paramount theater, *The Enchanted Kingdom,*" and signed in pencil "Dunkel."
Provenance: the artist's daughter, Elizabeth Dunkel, New York, June, 1971.
Reproduced in I51, No. 75. A similar design, for a 1924 production of *The Tale of the Invisible City of Kitezh and the Maid Fevronia,* is reproduced in I14, No. 49.

Note: According to George Dunkel, son of Eugene Dunkel, his father was closely associated with the Famous Players Company, also known as the Famous Players-Lasky Corporation, directed by Adolph Zukor in New York.[243] This corporation became the Paramount Picture Corporation in the mid-1920s. The Famous Players-Lasky Corporation produced vaudeville presentations as well as movies. Since the movie copyright catalogs for 1925 list no movie called *The Enchanted Kingdom*, a reasonable assumption is that this design might have been for one of the many revues staged by the Famous Players. The leaping deer on either side of the arch in this set bear a striking resemblance to the beasts that recur in Gudiashvili's drawings and paintings of the early 1920s (cf. No. 577 [R442]).

243 Letter from George Dunkel to John E. Bowlt dated 8 October, 1981.

EISENSTEIN (Eizenshtein), Sergei Mikhailovich

Born 10 (22) January, 1898, Riga, Latvia; died 11 February, 1948, Moscow, Russia.

1915-18 attended the Institute of Civil Engineering, Petograd; 1918 joined the Red Army; while enlisted, worked in amateur theater and helped in decorations for the so-called agit-trains; 1920 moved to Moscow where he joined the First Working Theater of the Proletkult as a designer and instructor; 1921-22 attended the State Higher Directors' Studios under Vsevolod Meierkhold, where he helped design a number of productions, including Jack London's *The Mexican*; collaborated with Nikolai Foregger, Meierkhold, and other producers; 1923 director of the Proletkult theater laboratories; studied the circus and music-hall, working with the FEKS group (Factory of the Eccentric Actor); close to the Lef group; 1924 began to direct movies and to work for the First State Movie Factory, producing *Strike*; 1925 produced *The Battleship Potemkin;* 1927 *October;* 1929 *The General Line;* 1929-32 traveled in Europe and America; 1930-32 on location in Mexico for his film-epic *¡Que Viva Mexico!;* 1932 onwards taught at the State Institute of Cinema in Moscow; 1938 produced *Alexander Nevsky;* 1944 produced first part of *Ivan the Terrible* (second part finished in 1946 and released in 1958).

Bibliography:
S. Yutkevich, ed: *Sergei Eizenshtein. Izbrannye proizvedeniia v shesti tomakh,* M: Iskusstvo, 1964-71.
S. Yutkevich: *Eizenshtein, Teatralnye risunki,* M: Soiuz kinematografistov SSSR, 1970.
V. Shklovsky: *Eizenshtein,* M: Iskusstvo, 1973. F41.
M. Rocher-Jauneau: *Eisenstein 1898-1948. Suite de dessins.* Catalog of exhibition at the Musée des Beaux-Arts, Lyon, 1978.
Y. Barna: *Eisenstein,* Bloomington: Indiana University, 1983.

P.-M. De Santi: *L'Officina di Eisenstein: dai Disegni ai Film,* Turin: Mole Antonelliana, 1981 (Catalog of exhibition February-April, 1981).
J. Leyda and Z. Voynow: *Eisenstein at Work,* New York: Pantheon, 1982.
R. Yurenev: *Sergei Eizenshtein. Zamysly. Filmy. Metod,* M: Iskusstvo, 1985.
L. Kleberg and H. Lövgren, eds.: *Eisenstein Revisited,* Stockholm: Almqvist and Wiksell, 1987.
D. Elliot: *Eisenstein at Ninety.* Catalog of exhibition at the Museum of Modern Art, Oxford, 1988.
I72.
D. Bordwell; *The Cinema of Eisenstein,* Cambridge, Mass.: Harvard University Press, 1993.
A. Nikitin: *Moskovskii debiut Sergeia Eizenshteina,* M: Intergraf, 1996.
I. Axjonow: *Sergej Eisenstein, Ein Porträt,* Berlin: Henschel, 1997.
N. Kleiman, ed.: *Sergei Mikhailovich Eizenshtein. Memuary,* M: Trud, 1997 (two vols.).
N. Kleiman et al.: *Sergei Mikhailovich Eizenshtein. Montazh,* M: Muzei kino, 2000.
L. Hanson and N. Kressel: *Eisenstein at 100: A Reconsideration,* New Burnswick: Rutgers University Press, 2001.
O. Bulgakova: *Sergei Eisenstein. A Biography,* San Francisco: Potemkin Press, 2002.
O. Calvaresi and V. Ivanov, eds.: *Sergej Michailovič Ejzenštejn. Quaderni teatrali e piani di regia (1919-1925),* Savveria Monnelli: Rubbetino, 2004.
M. Klejman and M. Sesti: *Ejzenštejn: La Musica del Corpo.* Catalog of exhibition at the Parco della Musica, Rome, 2004-05.
I. Eskevich: *Opticheskie manevry v okrestnostiakh Eizenshteina i Pikasso,* M, 2005.
V. Zabrodin: *Eizenshtein: Kino, vlast, zhenshchiny,* M: NLO, 2011

Eisenstein is now remembered for his avant-garde movies such as *Strike* and *Battleship Potemkin* and for his bold exploration and application of devices such as montage, frame, cut, and closeup. However, Eisenstein came to his experimental films after a brief, but intense apprenticeship as a stage designer and actor with brash new companies in Petrograd and Moscow, such as FEKS and Mastfor (Nikolai Foregger's workshop), collaborating closely with young artists and scenarists, such as Georgii Kozintsev, Grigorii Kryzhitsky, Leonid Trauberg, and Sergei Yutkevich. The plays that Eisenstein designed then, such as *Good Treatment of Horses* (1922) and *The Mexican* (1923), made clear reference to the circus and the music-hall and he applied their bright colors and stick figures to his sets and costumes. As he said of his films:

> The center of gravity of their effect lies not so much *in the explosion as in the supercharging process of the explosion.* The explosion can happen. Sometimes it happens at the intense climax of the preceding suspense and sometimes not, sometimes it's almost absent.[244]

Efficacy, shock, economy, mechanical precision are qualities that Eisenstein continued to emphasize in his films of the 1920s and early 1930s, until political imposition forced him to entertain more by dramatic narrative and ideologial message as in *Alexander Nevsky* and *Ivan the Terrible.*

Ivan the Terrible (Part I): *film produced by the Central Cinema Studio, Alma-Ata, USSR in 1944. Scenario and direction by Sergei Eisenstein; artistic direction by Iosif Shpinel; settings and costumes executed from Eisenstein's sketches by Lidiia Naumova.*

Ivan IV (the Terrible) is being crowned Tsar in the Uspensky Cathedral in the Moscow Kremlin. He declares that the boyars' power will thenceforth be limited, and that his aim is to unite all the Russian lands. After marrying Anastasiia Romanova, Ivan leads his armies to Kazan and storms its fortress. On his return to Moscow, he falls sick. The boyars now rise up, and their spokeswoman, Efrosiniia Staritskaia, poisons Anastasiia. His faculties returned, Ivan swears to end the boyar power once and for all, and to this end sets off to find new courtiers. The film ends with the people beseeching Ivan to return to Moscow.

455

455 [R971].
Costume Design for a Fat Oprichnik in Monk's Clothing, 1942.
Pencil.
Signed with monogram and dated: "22.IX.1942."
8⅛ x 5⅛ in., 20.5 x 13 cm.
Other inscriptions: upper right in Russian: "Fat Oprichnik (in monk's clothing)."
Provenance: Lidiia Naumova, Moscow, May, 1983.

Reproduced in I40, No. 48. A similar design for a 1942 Maeterlinck production is reproduced in Yutkevich, *Eizenshtein,* No. 28.

456

456 [R972].
Drawing of Prince Andrei Kurbsky on His Knees in front of Anastasiia, 1942.
Pencil.
Signed with monogram and dated: "14.IV.1942."
12¼ x 8⅝ in., 31 x 22 cm.
Other inscriptions: lower left, in pencil in Russian: "Kurbsky on his knees in front of Anastasiia."
Provenance: Lidiia Naumova, Moscow, May, 1983
Reproduced in A34, p. 132; I40, No. 49.

Note: Eisenstein's *Ivan the Terrible* followed his other lavish historical reconstruction, *Alexander Nevsky,* that was awarded the Order of Lenin in 1939. Their success compensated Eisenstein for the bleakness of the preceding decade marked by his difficult sojourn in the USA and Mexico in 1929-32 when he was filming *¡Que Viva Mexico!* and his personal dissatisfaction with *Bezhin Meadow.* During the 1930s Eisenstein was criticized for distorting reality thanks to his experimental techniques, but *Ivan the Terrible,* narrative and patriotic, was appropriate to Russia's wartime mood and to Stalin's own autocratic psychology — and it marked Eisenstein's momentary rehabilitation. Alexander Birkos, the film historian, has described the episode:

> The film was originally planned as a trilogy, but only Parts I and II were completed... The showing and release of Part I was a great triumph for Eisenstein, who received the then

coveted Stalin prize in February 1946. Then following a heart attack, Eisenstein suffered disgrace after the official previewing of Part II. This part was less flattering to the Russian tsar and critics attacked the director for erroneous interpretations of Ivan's character.[245]

Although Eisenstein did receive Stalin's permission to continue working on Part III, after editing Part II he suffered a second, fatal heart attack and, consequently, the trilogy was never completed.

Eisenstein was also prolific as a stage designer, manifesting an appreciation of many styles and historical epochs, especially in the 1920s when he was close to Foregger, Meierkhold, Yutkevich, and other avant-garde theater people. At that time he investigated various methods, although, obviously, he was especially drawn to Constructivism (cf. No. 1139 [R378]). Although Nos. 455 [R971] and 456 [R972] have little of Eisenstein's radical spirit of the 1920s, they still demonstrate his creative energy and unusual resolutions for key points in the movie.[246]

244 Yutkevich, *Sergei Eizenshtein. Izbrannye proizvedeniia v shesti tomakh,* Vol. 1 (1964), p. 95.
245 E11, p. 50.
246 Eisenstein's sketches for the sets and costumes for *Ivan the Terrible* have been reproduced in many sources, e.g., in Leyda and Voynow: *Eisenstein at Work,* pp. 125-45. For Eisenstein's own ideas and scenario for the movie see Yutkevich, ed., *Sergei Eisenshtein,* Vol. 1 (1964), pp. 189-200; Vol. 6 (1971), pp. 197-420.

ERDMAN (also known as Drutskoi and Drutsky), Boris Robertovich

Born 4 (16) February, 1899, Moscow; died 28 February, 1960, Moscow.

Brother of the playwright and producer Nikolai Erdman (1902-70). ca. 1917 took lessons from Ilia Mashkov; 1917-18 actor at the Chamber Theater, Moscow; 1918 made his debut as a stage designer in Smolensk; 1919 joined the Circus Section of TEO NKP; 1920 designed a production of *The Stone Guest* for the Safonov Theater, Moscow; ca. 1920 close to the Imaginist group of writers headed by Vadim Shershenevich; designed and illustrated some of their literary works; 1920s worked in GITIS (State Institute of Theatrical Art) in Moscow, collaborating with Vsevolod Meierkhold and other celebrities; 1923 worked with Nikolai Foregger and Kasian Goleizovsky on experimental dance; designed productions for the Blue Blouse variety theater; 1925 contributed to the "Exposition Internationale des Arts Décoratifs" in Paris; designed Sergei Vasilenko's ballet *Joseph the Beautiful* staged by Goleizovsky at the Experimental Theater, Moscow; 1925-30 designed choreographic productions by Natalia Glan, Goleizovsky, and Lev Lukin for Vera

Drutskaia and Alexander Rumnev's Evenings of New Dance in Moscow; ca. 1927 lived in Odessa; worked with Isaak Rabinovich; 1930 designed Yurii Olesha's *Three Fat Men* for the Moscow Art Theater; 1941-45 headed the Art Section of the State Circus, Moscow; 1950-60 headed the Art Section of the Stanislavsky Dramatic Theater, Moscow.

Bibliography
Sherpets: "B. Erdman. Imazhinizm v zhivopisi" in *Sirena,* Voronezh, 1919, No. 4, pp. 63-68.
A. Sidorov: "Boris Erdman, khudozhnik kostiuma" in *Zrelishcha,* M, 1923, No. 43, June, pp. 4-5.
I. Merzliakov: "Khudozhnik-eksperimentator teatra" in *Rabochii i teatr,* M, 1935, No. 12, pp. 5-7.
E. Lutskaia: "Khudozhnik satiricheskogo spektaklia" in *Teatr,* M, 1955, pp. 117-26.
Also consult M. Alfieri: "La vita e l'opera di Nikolaj Erdman" in *Rassegna sovietica,* Rome, 1981, November-December, pp. 85-100; A. Svobodina, ed.: *Nikolai Erdman. Piesy. Intermedii. Pisma. Dokumenty. Vosmpominaniia sovremennikov.* M: Iskusstvo, 1990, passim; and V. Vulf, ed.: *Nikolai Erdman. Angelina Stepanova: Pisma,* M: AST/Astrel, 2011.
Recent exhibitions of stage designs have featured Boris Erdman's work. See, for example, I116, pp. 60, 61, 80.
For a list of Erdman's stage designs of the 1920s and early 1930s, see I5, pp. 106-07.

A vital force in the crucible of early Soviet culture, Boris Erdman was in close touch with the leading reformers of that era, including Meierkhold, Valentin Parnakh, Vsevolod Pudovkin, and Viktor Shklovsky, and some of his magazine illustrations, caricatures, and set and costume designs are connected directly with them. Erdman made drawings for the main theatrical magazines of the early 1920s such as *Ermitazh* [Hermitage] and *Zrelishcha* [Spectacles], he collaborated with important troupes such as the Chamber Theater, the Experimental-Heroic Theater, Goleizovsky's Chamber Ballet, Nikolai Foregger's Mastfor (Foregger's workshop), and the Blue Blouse agit-theater, and he paid particular attention to the less orthodox media of theatrical expression, especially the cabaret and the circus.

Erdman belonged to the first Soviet generation of stage designers that also included Boris Ferdinandov, Petr Galadzhev, Valentina Khodasevich, Vasilii Komardenkov, Nikolai Musatov, Ilia Shlepianov, and Sergei Yutkevich. Drawing upon the geometric traditions of Alexandra Exter, in particular, their art was distinguished by a refractive, almost metallic finish, by geometric precision, and by a "miniaturization" that presented the human body as a robot or automaton, and their designs, often inspired by the cinema, might best be described in the cinematic terms of montage, cut, framing, closeup, and dissolve. Naturally, their art reflected the main features of the "Roaring Twenties" — commercial advertising, mass communi-

cation, and the circus and the cabaret, and Erdman's designs were also laboratorial in the way that Goleizovsky's Chamber Ballet, Alexander Tairov's Chamber Theater, and Boris Nevolin's Intimate Theater were, i.e., confined spaces for the cultivation of rare species observed by an élite. Erdman drew upon the acrobatics of Vladimir Fogel, the clowning of Vitalii Lazarenko, Parnakh's jazz, and Foregger's "machine dances."

The critic and historian Alexei Sidorov, one of Erdman's earliest advocates, said of his costumes that "in their play with right angles, asymmetry, and contrast, [Erdman's] costumes resolve the tasks of the inner character."[247] In collaboration with Sergei Eisenstein, Galadzhev, and Yutkevich, Erdman designed the installations that Foregger used for his so-called parades at Mastfor. Extracting "maximal comic effect from the absurd incongruity of form and content,"[248] Foregger and Erdman drew upon the staccato technique of the cabaret in which short numbers or skits pass before the audience in rapid succession like the frames of a movie. Together with Galadzhev, Nikolai Musatov, and Goleizvosky, Erdman also designed some of Goleizovsky's eccentric dances and Spanish dances for the Chamber Ballet in 1922-23, rendering the almost nude dancers as streamlined components of a machine. These exercises were one more manifestation of the "eccentric culture" that Parnakh identified with "unexpected combinations of movements, peripatetics, and unprecedented harmonies (syncopation, dissonances, new tempos)."[249]

457 [59; R1004].
Costume Design for a Circus Horse-Rider, ca. 1921.
Pencil, watercolor and silver.
10 x 7½ in., 25.4 x 19 cm.
Provenance: Dora Kogan, Moscow, June, 1973.
Reproduced in I32, No. 15; I51, No. 76

Note: In February, 1919, TEO NKP under Anatolii Lunacharsky established a special Circus Section. Ilya Ehrenburg, Erdman, Goleizovsky, Vasilii Kamensky, Sergei Konenkov, Pavel Kuznetsov, Pavel Markov, and other artists, writers, and producers worked for the Section, the purpose of which was to "care for the artistry of the circus, to help the laborers of the circus... to cleanse their art of impurity... to determine [its] strength, agility, and courage, to incite laughter, and to delight in a brilliant, vivid, and exaggerated spectacle."[250] Like Foregger (No. 511 [NIRE]) and Goleizovsky, Vladimir Bekhteev (Nos. 109-17 [R326-33]) and Georgii Yakulov, Erdman wished to bring the discipline of the circus into closer contact with the "high" art forms of the ballet and the drama, to which end he published a number of statements on the subject.[251] His approach to the circus costume was serious and innovative and he tried to adopt the lessons of Cubism and the geometric style to his own resolutions.[252] Erdman's designs were

457

especially successful for the equestrian numbers popular in the State Circus in 1921-22 such as *The Struggle for a Horse, Mrs. Denny's Riding Lesson,* and *Mr. Brown's Riding Lesson.* The design in question may have been for one of these numbers.

247   Sidorov, "Boris Erdman, khudozhnik kostiuma," p. 4.
248   C89, p. 97.
249   V. Parnakh: "Novoe ekstsentricheskoe iskusstvo" in *Zrelishcha,* M, 1922, No. 1, p. 5.
250   A. Lunacharsky: "Zadacha obnovlennogo teatra" in *Vestnik teatra,* M, 1919, No. 3. Quoted in F3, p. 26.
251   See, for example, his article "Nepovtorimoe vremia" in *Tsirk i estrada,* M, 1928, No. 3-4, pp. 6-7.
252   See his article "V poiskakh 'trekhmernoi' dekoratsii" in *Vestnik teatra,* 1920, No. 50, pp. 7-8.

Vera Ermolaeva, 1923.

ERMOLAEVA, Vera Mikhailovna

Born 2 (14) November, 1893, Kliuchi, Saratov Region, Russia; died 26 September, 1937, Dolinka Prison Camp, Karaganda, Kazakhstan.

1902-03 family lived in London, Innsbruck, and Lausanne; 1905 family moved to St. Petersburg; 1906-11 studied at the Obolenskaia Gymanasium in St. Petersburg; 1911-13 enrolled in the studio of Mikhail Bernshtein; contact with members of the Union of Youth, including Pavel Filonov, Kazimir Malevich, and Mikhail Matiushin; 1914 studied in Paris; 1915-17 enrolled at the Archaelogical Institute, Petrograd; 1918 member of IZO NKP; 1918-19 worked at the City Museum, Petrograd; member of the Today Workshop of artists; met Vladimir Maiakovsky; 1919 published an article on store signboards in *Iskusstvo kommuny* [Art of the Commune]; began to work on illustrations for children's books, establishing contact with Yurii Annenkov, Vladimir Lebedev, and others; moved to Vitebsk, becoming rector of the Popular Art Institute / Art-Practical Institute there until 1922; invited Malevich to teach there; 1920 worked on a studio production of the Cubo-Futurist opera *Victory over the Sun;* early 1920s influenced by Malevich's Suprematism; joined Unovis and contributed to its several exhibitions; published article on Cubism in the Unovis almanac; 1921 designed production of Maiakovsky's *War and Peace* in Vitebsk; 1922 contributed to the "Erste Russische Kunstausstellung" in Berlin; followed Malevich to Petrograd where, until 1926, she headed the color laboratory within Ginkhuk; mid-1920s onward illustrated children's books by Nikolai Aseev, Daniil Kharms, Alexander Vvedensky, Nikolai Zabolotsky, and other writers, and editions of Ivan Krylov's fables; 1928 made poster for the Oberiu evening at the Press House; 1928-31 worked as illustrator for the children's journal *Ezh* [Hedgehog]; 1934 arrested; 1935 received three-year sentence for anti-Soviet activities; 1937 accused of collaboration with counter-revolutionary groups.

Bibliography

E. Kovtun: "Khudozhnitsa knigi Vera Mikhailovna Ermolaeva," in *Iskusstvo knigi 68/69.,* M., 1975, No. 8, pp. 68-81.
K52, pp. 100-10.
K55, pp. 146-47.
I12, vol. 4, pp. 45-46.
E. Kovtun: "Vera Ermolaeva" in *Tvorchestvo,* M, 1989, No. 6, pp. 24-26.
K216.
E. Petrova et al.: *V kruge Malevicha,* SP: Palace Editions, 2000.
A. Shatskikh: *Vitebsk. Zhizn iskusstva 1917-1922,* M: Yazyki russkoi kultury, 2001.
A. Shatskikh: *Vitebsk. The Life of Art,* New Haven: Yale, 2007.
A. Zainchkovskaia et al.: *Vera Ermolaeva,* SP: Palace Editions, 2008.

I. Galeev: *Vera Ermolaeva (1893-1937).* Catalog of exhibition at the Galeev Gallery, M, 2009.

Ermolaeva, the "Gioconda of Vitebsk,"[253] began to play an active role in the Russian avant-garde after her teaching appointment to the Vitebsk Popular Art Institute in 1919 (in 1921 the Institute changed its name to the Vitebsk Art-Practical Institute). The faculty included artists who were to become members of the Suprematist group known as Unovis: Nina Kogan directed the preparatory classes, Ermolaeva drawing and painting, and El Lissitzky graphics and architecture. In the fall of 1919, Ermolaeva, who by then was rector, honored Lissitzky's request to invite Malevich to join the faculty, and the story of how Malevich ousted Marc Chagall from the position has been recounted in the many biographies of the two artists. Apart from Ermolaeva, Kogan, and Lissitzky, Ilia Chashnik, Ivan Chervinka, Lazar Khidekel, and Lev Yudin were also resident in Vitebsk in 1919, and during 1919-21 a number of other important artists also passed through, including Mstislav Dobujinsky, Robert Falk, and Jean Pougny.

By the end of 1919, Malevich had established a strong group of Suprematist supporters, including Ermolaeva, and this served as the basis of Posnovis (= Followers of the New Art) founded in January, 1920, which then changed its name to Unovis. As a member of Unovis, Ermolaeva participated in a number of joint projects, not least the studio production of *Victory over the Sun,* for which she designed the sets and costumes.[254] Ermolaeva had already collaborated, at least indirectly, with Malevich in the theater when she designed a book cover (?)[255] for Vladimir Maiakovsky's *Mystery-Bouffe* (produced by Vsevolod Meierkhold with costumes by Malevich in 1918), but *Victory over the Sun* marked the high point of her commitment to Suprematism. Although she joined Malevich in Petrograd in 1923, she soon moved away from Suprematism to concentrate on book illustration.

Victory over the Sun: *opera in two actions with prologue by Velimir Khlebnikov, libretto by Alexei Kruchenykh and music by Mikhail Matiushin. First produced at the Luna Park Theater, St. Petersburg, on 5 December, 1913, with designs by Kazimir Malevich. Produced by Unovis (Affirmers of the New Art) in Vitebsk on 6 February, 1920, with designs by Vera Ermolaeva and some costumes by Kazimir Malevich.*

The first action of this Cubo-Futurist opera is concerned with the capture of the sun, which occurs offstage; the second with a Futurist evocation of the tenth century which takes place in a curious house-like setting after the conquest of the sun. Various characters bemoan the loss of the old world or praise the new, contributing to a plot line that often seems illogical. Characters include two Futurist strongmen, a traveler through time, a representative of the past, and a combination of Nero and Caligula.

458

458 [R481].
Stage Design for Action II, 1920.
Woodcut.
10⅞ x 13¾ in., 27.5 x 35 cm.
Provenance: André B. Nakov, Paris, June, 1977.
Reproduced in many sources, e.g., Q12. The first reproduction was in the almanac *Unovis,* Vitebsk, 1920, No. 1; see also K3, unpaginated (where it is described as a linocut); K42, p. 189, etc. The size of the edition of this woodcut, which sometimes carries watercolor additions, is unknown (cf. Nos. 752-64 [R632-43]; 770-84 [R648-62]).

253 The description is Marc Chagall's. Quoted in F. Meyer: *Marc Chagall,* New York; Abrams, 1964, p. 272.
254 For a detailed discussion of the 1913 production of *Victory over the Sun* with some references to the 1920 one, see C. Douglas: *"Victory over the Sun,"* in G55, pp. 69-89; and . N. Firtich et al.: *Ot Gogolia k "Pobede nad solntsem": Traektoriia russkogo avangarda.* Special issue of *Zapiski russkoi akademicheskoi gruppy v SShA,* New York, 2009, Vol. 35. In connection with the exhibition "The Avant-Garde in Russia 1910-1930: New Perspectives" at the Los Angeles County Museum and the Hirshhorn Museum and Sculpture Garden, Washington, D.C. (1980-81), the California Institute of the Arts, Los Angeles, produced *Victory over the Sun* in English translation, with costumes made according to the original designs, and with supplementary music. The performances on 5, 6 and 7 September 1980 in the Los Angeles County Museum were very successful in spite of the difficulties surrounding the recreation of such a complex spectacle. Performances were also given later at the Hirshhorn Museum. Other versions of *Victory over the Sun* were given at the Seibu Museum, Tokyo, in connection with K61 (fall, 1982), at the Brooklyn Academy of Music, New York (November, 1983), at the Atelier de Création Populaire for the festival "1905 Russie — 1917 — URSS 1935" in Toulouse (March, 1984), and at the Alabama-Halle, Munich (April-May, 1984). Supervised by G.I. Kubanova, the Leningrad Studio also put on productions in Leningrad and Moscow in 1989.
255 For a reproduction of the piece see *Knizhnye oblozhki russkikh khudozhnikov nachala XX veka.* Catalog of exhibition at the RM, 1977, p. 33.

ERTÉ (pseudonym of Romain de Tirtoff, Roman Petrovich Tyrtov)

Born 23 November (5 December), 1892, St. Petersburg; died 21 April, 1990, Paris.

Born into an upper class family, his father being an admiral in the Imperial Naval School and an elder brother Nicholas, being military governor of St. Petersburg; late 1890s already designing clothes for his mother, aided by the family's resident dressmaker; early 1900s frequented St. Petersburg theaters; 1910s attended Ballets Russes performances, including *L'Après-Midi* and *Sacre du Printemps;* 1912 arrived in Paris, France becoming his home thereafter; 1913 secured a contract with Paul Poiret – who coined the name "Erté" (the pronunciation of the initials of "Romain de Tirtoff"); 1914 designed costumes for the scene "Le Musée Cubiste" in the Paris music-hall revue *Plus Ça Change;*.1914-23 lived in Monte Carlo; 1915-36 contributed 240 covers and 2,500 pen-and-ink drawings and *gouache* designs to *Harper's Bazaar;* 1910s-30s also designed for the stage, including costumes for the exotic Dutch dancer Mata Hari and Madame Rasimi, 1919-36 designed costumes for the Folies-Bergère, the Ziegfeld Follies, and shows such as Irving Berlin's *Music Box Revue;* also worked for Hollywood films; 1925 participated in the Paris journal *Art et Industrie;* designing utility household objects and domestic interiors; 1940s involved in the theater in Paris, London, and elsewhere; 1960s onwards close to Eric and Salome Estorick of the Grosvenor Galleries, London and New York; 1960s

made sheet metal sculpture with oil pigments called *Formes Pictorales.*

Bibliography
S. Estorick: *Erté's Theatrical Costumes in Full Color,* New York: Dover, 1979.
C. Spencer: *Erté,* New York; Potter, 1970.
R. Barthes: *Erté,* Milan: Rieti, 1972.
F42.
S. Blum: *Designs by Erté,* New York; Dover, 1976.
T. Walter: *Erté,* New York; Rizzoli, 1978.
Erté (Romain de Tirtoff): *Erté's Costumes and Sets for "Der Rosenkavalier",* New York: Dover, 1980.
M. Lee, ed.: *Erté. Das druckgraphische Werk,* Berlin: Propyläen, 1983.
M. Lee, ed.: *Erté. Skulpturen,* Berlin: Propyläen, 1986.
M. Lee, ed.: *Erté. Neue Druckgraphik,* Berlin: Propyläen, 1987.
Erté (Romain de Tirtoff): *Kunst ist mein Leben,* Berlin: Propyläen, 1989.
Anon.: "Obituary: Erté (Romain de Tirtoff)" in *The Times,* London, 1990, 23 April.
A. Rudzitsky: "Velikii ukrainskii khudozhnik Erté (1892-1990)" in *Antikvar,* M, 2010, No. 9, pp. 65-70.

Erté's theatrical innovations were countless, including "living curtains" (showgirls with plumes and pearls, festooned by embroidered trains, *costumes collectifs* (immense, single costumes shared by a group of performers, with a single theme, e.g., *Silk* (now in the Victoria and Albert Museum, London); and *tableaux vivants* (e.g., *L'Or*). Thanks to William Randolph Hearst, Erté worked in Hollywood, although his style was considered to be inappropriate to the movie capital. Even so, he designed *The Restless Sex* (1919) for Hearst's Cosmopolitan Films, a sequence called *Bal des Arts* (a ballroom setting with a "Babylonian hanging-garden"), offering a blend of Art Nouveau and emergent Art Deco of the 1920s, and Louis B. Mayer's film *Paris* (not produced). But when, later on, he was again called on by Hollywood to work on films about Paris, he declined the offer, arguing that Hollywood had no understanding of the real Paris. In any case, Erté made that city his home, designing for the lyric stage, including the genres of music-hall and revue, and for individual celebrities such as Mary Garden and Victoria de Los Angeles. He also designed for the ballet companies of Colonel de Basil and the Marquis de Cuevas and in 1980, already advanced in age, designed an especially exuberant production of *Der Rosenkavalier* for Glyndebourne. Whether Erté's judgement of Hollywood was correct or not, he also trod a thin line between elegance and vulgarity, his style being highly formulaic and contrived, but always precise and controlled. Indeed, Erté was a master not only of esthetic composition, of color and graphic line, but also of stage machinery and acting techniques. On the other hand, Eré's creative energy was astounding and, far from waning with the years, his fascination with costume design and the female form continued to provide ammunition for scintillating exhibitions such as "Erté at Ninety" and "Erté at Ninety-Five," which the Eric Estorick Gallery in London, one of his most loyal supporters, organized with pomp and circumstance. As Robert Pincus-Witten observed in 1970: "If the authentic germ is that of Beardsley, the question must be asked, who in the period developed this taste more than Erté, elaborated it with more racy instinct, conceit and savoir faire?" [256]

Aladin, ou la Lampe Merveilleuse. *Variety show produced by the Folies-Bergère, Paris, in 1929, with designs by Erté.*

A poor youth in China, Aladdin (Aladin), is recruited by a sorcerer to the Maghreb. The sorcerer persuades Aladdin to retrieve a wonderful oil-lamp from a magic cave. Trapped in the cage, Aladdin retains a magic ring lent to him by the sorcerer, which, inadvertently, he rubs and a genie appears, who takes him home. When his mother tries to clean the lamp, a second, more powerful genie appears, thanks to whom Aladdin becomes rich and marries Princess Badroulbadour, the Emperor's daughter. The sorcerer returns, tricking Aladdin's wife into giving him the magic lamp and orders the genie to take the palace to his home in the Maghreb. But Aladdin retains the magic ring and summons the lesser genie, who, if unable to undo the magic of the genie, transports Aladdin to the Maghreb. The sorcerer's more powerful and evil brother tries to destroy Aladdin by disguising himself as an old woman. Badroulbadour falls for the disguise, commanding the "woman" to stay in her palace. Aladdin is warned of this danger by the genie of the lamp and slays the imposter.

459 [60; NIRE].
Costume Design with Chinese Dragons, 1929
Gold paint and gouache
15¼ x 11⅛ in., 38.8 x 28.2 cm.
Signed lower right quartile. Verso bears studio stamp reading: "ERTÉ, Romain de Tirtoff, 124, Rue de Brancas, Sèvres (S.-&-O. [=Seine et Oise]);" further rubber-stamped with "Composition originale", numbered in ink "No. 1484", and inscribed with "Aladin."
Provenance: *The Russian Sale,* London: Bonham's, 24 November, 2008, Lot 46 (reproduced).
Reproduced in F107, p. 163.

Note: With more than 150 costume and décor designs, including sumptuous renderings for the Sultan and his entourage, *Aladin* was one of Erté's most ambitious theatrical enterprises. From the *Book of One Thousand and One Nights* (the *Arabian Tales*) and with its loose references to spirits of fire and beautiful princesses, *Aladin,* of course, projected Erté's exotic temperament and Oriental bias. For his costumes he incorporated these and other elements, producing a rich mélange of Chinese, Siamese, and Persian references,

459

offered through the tinsel of Hollywood and Paris fashion houses. Indeed, Erté's emphasis on the slender and sensuous female silhouette with the towering headgear, the symmetrical sleeves, and the scintillating colors here brings to mind his concurrent designs not only for other theatrical productions such as *Louis XIV* and *Casanova,* but also for his sumptuous illustrations in *Ladies' Home Journal, Cosmopolitan, Vogue,* and *Harper's Bazaar.* The sheer luminosity of such designs demonstrates that, far from "disappearing beneath the tidal wave of industry." [257] Erté possessed the unfailing capacity to come back and surprise.

256 R. Pincus-Witten: untitled essay in *Erté.* Catalog of exhibition at Sonnabend, New York, 1970, unpaginated.
257 A. Hicks: "Master of Remote Beauty" in *The Times,* London, 1990, 23 April.

Alexandra Exter, 1919.

EXTER (née Grigorovich), Alexandra Alexandrovna.

Born 6 (18) January, 1882, Belostok, Ukraine (now Białystok, Poland); died 17 March, 1949, Fontenay-aux-Roses, near Paris, France.

1892-99 attended St. Olga Women's Gymnasium in Kiev; 1901-03 attended the Kiev Art Institute; 1904 married her cousin, the lawyer Nikolai Ekster (Exter), who died in 1918; 1906-08 re-enrolled in the Kiev Art Institute; 1908 onward was a regular visitor to Paris and other European cities; contributed to several Kiev exhibitions, including David Burliuk's "Link," the first of many involvements with the avant-garde; first book illustrations; 1909-14 lived abroad frequently; acquaintance with Apollinaire, Braque, Picasso, Soffici, and other members of the international avant-garde; 1910 contributed to the "Triangle" and "Union of Youth" exhibitions in St. Petersburg; 1910-11 contributed to the "Jack of Diamonds" exhibition Moscow; 1912 moved to St. Petersburg; associated with the Union of Youth; 1913-14 lived mainly in France; 1914 organized the "Ring" exhibition in Kiev; 1915 prompted by Kazimir Malevich and Vladimir Tatlin began to investigate non-objective painting; 1915-16 contributed to "Tramway V" and the "Store"; began her professional theater work with designs for *Thamira Khytharedes* produced by Alexander Tairov at the Chamber Theater, Moscow; 1917 designed *Salomé* for the Chamber Theater; 1918-19 ran her own studio in Kiev, where many artists of later fame studied such as Isaak Rabinovich, Alexander Tyshler, and Pavel Tchelitchew; 1918-20 worked intermittently in Odessa as teacher and stage designer; 1920 moved to Moscow; married the actor Georgii Nekrasov; worked at the Theater of the People's House, 1921 contributed to the exhibition "5 x 5 = 25," Moscow; designed Tairov's book *Zapiski rezhissera* [Notes of a Director]; 1921-22 taught at Vkhutemas; 1923 turned to textile and fashion design for the Atelier of Fashions, Moscow; member of design team for the *Izvestiia* Pavilion at the "All-Russian Agricultural Exhibition", Moscow; began work on the costumes for the movie *Aelita* (released 1924); 1924 emigrated to Paris; contributed to the Venice Biennale; with Léon Zack and Pavel Tchelitchew worked for the Ballets Romantiques Russes; taught at Léger's Académie Moderne; 1925 contributed to the "Exposition Internationale des Arts Décoratifs" in Paris; during the 1920s and 1930s continued to work on stage and interior design; 1925 designed costumes for seven ballets performed by Bronislava Nijinska's Théâtre Choréographique; 1926, with Nechama Szmuszkowicz, created a set of marionettes; 1927 exhibition at Der Sturm, Berlin; 1929 exhibition at Quatre Chemins, Paris; 1937 exhibition at the Musée des Arts et Métiers, Paris; 1937-46 illustrated a number of elegant editions for children such as Marie Collin-Delavaud's *Panorama de la Montagne* (Paris: Flammarion, 1938) and *Panorama de la Côte* (Paris: Flammarion, 1938) and her own *Mon Jardin* (Paris: Flammarion, 1936).

Bibliography:
Ya. Tugendkhold: *Aleksandra Ekster,* Berlin: Zaria, 1922.
M2, Vol. 2, pp. 175-76.
M6.
M8.
Ausstellung Aleksandra Ekster. Catalog of exhibition at Der Sturm, Berlin, 1927.
Alexandra Exter. Théâtre (Maquettes, Décors, Costumes). Catalog of exhibition at the Galérie Quatre Chemins, Paris, 1929.
A. Tairov: *Alexandra Exter. Décors de Théâtre,* Paris: Quatre Chemins, 1930.
Alexandra Exter. Théâtre. Catalog of exhibition at the Musée des Arts et Métiers, Paris, 1937.
P. Faucher: *Alexandra Exter: divadlo: skizy, dekorace, kostymy.* Catalog of exhibition at the Uměleckoprůmyslové Muzeum, Prague, 1937.
A. B. Nakov: *Alexandra Exter,* Paris: Galerie Chauvelin, 1972.
J. Bowlt: "A Veritable Amazon of the Russian Avant-Garde" in *Art News,* New York, 1974, September, pp. 41-43.
A. Koval: *Ausstellung Russische Avantgarde. Alexandra Exter. Michel Andreenko.* Catalog of exhibition at the Galerie Werner Kunze, Berlin, 1974.
S. Lissim et al.: *Artist of the Theatre, Alexandra Exter.* Catalog of the exhibition at the Center for the Performing Arts, the New York Public Library at Lincoln Center, New York, 1974.
J. Bowlt: *Alexandra Exter. Marionettes.* Catalog of exhibition at the Leonard Hutton Galleries, New York, 1975.
K52, pp. 112-30.
M. McClintic: *Alexandra Exter, Marionettes and Theatrical Designs.* Catalog of exhibition at the Hirshhorn Museum and Sculpture Garden, Washington, D.C., 1980.
R. Cohen: "Alexandra Exter's Designs for the Theater" in *Artforum,* New York, 1981. Summer, pp. 46-49.
E. Tomilovskaia et al.: *Aleksandra Ekster. Eskizy dekoratsii i kostiumov.* Catalog of exhibition at the Bakhrushin Museum, M, 1986.
M. Kolesnikov: "Aleksandra Ekster. Ot impressionizma k konstruktivizmu" in *Sovetskii balet,* M, 1987, No. 6, pp. 61-65.
M20.
G. Kovalenko: "Teatr i zhivopis Oleksandri Ekster" in *Ukrainskii teatr,* K, 1988. No. 4, pp. 25-27 (in Ukrainian).
M32.
M. Kolesnikov: *Aleksandra Ekster.* Catalog of exhibition at the BTM, 1988.
Aleksandra Ekster (1884-1949). Catalog of exhibition at the Odessa Art Museum, Odessa, 1989.
M. Kolesnikov: "Aleksandra Ekster i Vera Mukhina" in *Panorama iskusstv,* M, 1989, No. 12, pp. 89-110.
G. Kovalenko: "Ekster v Parizhe" in *Teatralnaia zhizn,* M, 1990, No. 17, pp. 20-23.
B109, pp. 117-40
F. Ciofi degli Atti and M. Kolesnikov: *Alexandra Exter e il Teatro da Camera.* Catalog of exhibition at the Archivio del '900, Rovereto, 1991.

G. Kovalenko: "Aleksandra Ekster v Parizhe" in *Teatr,* M, 1992, No. 2, pp. 103-22.
G. Kovalenko: *Alexandra Ekster.* M: Galart, 1993.
D. Gorbachev: "Exter in Kiev — Kiev in Exter" in *Experiment,* Los Angeles, 1995, No. 1, pp. 299-322.
M73, Vol. 26, pp. 77-78.
G. Kovalenko: "'Tsvetovaia dinamika' Aleksandry Ekster (iz byvshego sobraniia Kurta Benedikta)" in G. Vagner, et al., eds.: *Pamiatniki kultury. Novye otkrytiia,* M: Nauka, 1996, pp. 356-65.
G. Kovalenko: "La peinture cubo-futuriste d'Alexandra Exter" in *Ligeia,* Paris, 1998, No. 21-24, pp. 104-19.
K224, passim.
K236.
J. Chauvelin: *Alexandra Exter 1882-1949.* Catalog of exhibition at the Musée Château de Tours, Château de Tours, 2009
G. Kovalenko: *Aleksandra Ekster,* M: Moscow Museum of Contemporary Art, 2010 (two volumes)
P. Railing: *Alexandra Exter Paints,* Forest Road, East Sussex: Artists' Bookworks, 2011.

Alexandra Exter was one of the few artists of the avant-garde capable of maintaining the theatrical principle that Léon Bakst applied with such aplomb, i.e., the ability to transcend the confines of the pictorial surface and to organize forms in their interaction with space. Exter's awareness of this interaction was evident in her first collaborations with Tairov (when she also worked closely with Vera Mukhina), i.e., the productions of *Thamira Khytharedes* (1916), *Salomé* (1917), and then her later endeavors such as *Romeo and Juliet* (1921) and the *Death of Tarelkin* (1921, projected but not produced by the First Studio of the Moscow Art Theater). When the critic Tugendkhold observed of *Thamira Khytharedes* that Tairov and Exter had managed to "make an organic connection between the moving actors and the objects at rest,"[258] he was already indicating the direction that Exter would follow. It was precisely in this production that the conventions of the *Stilbühne* were dropped and replaced by a kinetic resolution in which the actors and scenery played equal roles. Exter's concentration on the "rhythmically organized space"[259] pointed forward to her Constructivist designs for the movie *Aelita*, to her costume designs for Bronislava Nijinska's Choreographic Studio in Kiev and then Théâtre Choréographique in England and Paris,[260] and to her set of marionettes of 1926.

In the dynamic medium of film, where focus and sequence change constantly, formal contrast is transmitted by a rapid variability of light, and light itself plays a constructive role, Exter perhaps attained the high point of her scenic career. Her concern with the formative value of light was, however, already evident in her stage designs of 1916-17 in which she relied on saturated lighting as well as on the painted surface for effect: "From top to bottom the box of the stage is full up with bridges, platforms; mirrors flash."[261] During the 1920s, as in *Aelita*, Exter incorporated the

properties of transparency and reflectivity into her system, anticipating Sergei Diaghilev's production of *La Chatte* in 1927 with designs by Naum Gabo and Antoine Pevsner. Exter never ceased to experiment with stage design, applying her ideas to drama, the ballet, revues, and modern dance. In 1925 she even invented "epidermic costumes" for a ballet project in which the dancers were painted, not dressed. As her one-time student, Alexander Tyshler, said: "In her hands, a simple paper lampshade turned into a work of art."[262]

Ignatii Nivinsky: *Portrait of Alexandra Exter, 1928.* (See No. 802 [R684])

Thamira Khytharedes (Thamyris Kitharodos): *a Bacchic drama in twenty scenes by Innokentii Annensky produced by Alexander Tairov at the Chamber Theater, Moscow, on 2 November, 1916, with music by Henri Fortier and designs by Alexandra Exter.*

Thamira, son of the Thracian King and the nymph Argione, has won great fame for his playing of the kithara, or cithern (a kind of lute). His pride has reached such proportions that he even challenges the Muses. But Thamira is beaten by them in the musical competition and as a punishment his eyes are gouged out and his musical talent revoked.

460 [61; R973].
Costume Design for a Bacchante with Hands Outstretched, 1916.
Gouache and gold paint.
20 x 13⅛ in., 50.8 x 33.3 cm.
Inscription: the reverse carries the stamp and signed authentification of Simon Lissim indicating the design to be from the Exter estate and is dated "February, 1952, Dobbs Ferry, New York, USA."
Provenance: Merrill C. Berman, Rye, New York, 1979.
Reproduced in color in B115, plate 136; I68, p. 13; I77, p. 85; I117, p. 540; M151, p. 119; N156, p. 75; as the cover for I60; B151, p.

460

62; and Chauvelin, *Alexandra Exter,* fig. 75; and in black and white in Tugendkhold, *Aleksandra Ekster,* plate XIII; I77, p. 137; M68; M93; P8; P13; P55; U3. For reproductions of other costumes see G17, plates 21-24; G31, no. 289.

461

461 [62; R974].
Costume Design for a Female Dancer with Part of the Tunic Held out in Front, 1916.
Gouache and gold paint.
17¾ x 18½ in., 45.2 x 47 cm.
Provenance: Simon Lissim, Dobbs Ferry, New York, March, 1971.
Reproduced in color in B115, plate 135; F107, p. 158; I68, p. 25; I77, p. 84. N188, p. 60; and J. Chauvelin ed.: *Alexandra Exter,* Paris: Max Milo Editions, 2003, fig. 75; and in black and white in H32, p. 390; I77, p. 137; N13; N130; P5; P16; P29; S2; S17; S26; S30. For reproductions of other relevant costumes see G17, plates 21-24; G31, no. 289; and Chauvelin, *Alexandra Exter,* fig. 76.

462

462 [63; NIRE].
Costume Design for a Dancing Bacchante with Bare Bosom, 1916.
Gouache on blue paper.
Signed lower right in Russian: "A. Exter."
18¼ x 15½ in., 46.5 x 39.5 cm
On reverse described, annotated, and numbered upper left in Russian:" Exter Alexandra / 'Thamira Kythared' / Bacchante / N 59."
Provenance: *Vente François de Ricqlès,* Paris: Salle Drouot, 30 May, 2001, Lot 49.
Reproduced in F107, p. 427; K288, p. 8.

Note: Innokentii Fedorovich Annensky (1856-1909) completed his tragedy *Thamira Khytharedes* in the summer of 1906. His interpretation of the Greek myth, which Sophocles had also used as the basis for a dramatic text (now lost), connected immediately with the St. Petersburg and Moscow fashion for Ancient Greece and Rome during the Modernist period. This retrospective cult was especially prevalent among the Symbolist poets and philosophers such as Valerii Briusov, Viacheslav Ivanov, Dmitrii Merezhkovsky, and Faddei Zelinsky, and Léon Bakst, especially, paid homage to the interest in his paintings and stage designs. Like his colleagues, Annensky, no doubt, discerned a certain parallel between the tragic sense of Greek mythology and the twilight years of Imperial Russia, although it was the notion of artistic genius and esthetic form, of the *"Grenzfragen* of the field of musical psychology and esthetics"[263] that really inspired Annensky's investigation into this ancient legend.

Exter worked on three major productions for Tairov's Chamber Theater in Moscow — *Thamira Khytharedes* (1916), *Salomé* (1917), and *Romeo and Juliet* (1921). *Thamira Khytharedes* was Tairov's "first genuine scenic manifestation,"[264] even though, as a literary work, the drama itself was not especially radical. Tairov was

attracted to Annensky's text by its juxtapositions of high and low vocabulary, by its interweaving of tragedy and satire, and by the dispensations with Classical Greek dramatic rules (e.g., the chorus is not always present and the characters do not always speak in verse). Much under the influence of Edward Gordon Craig, Adolphe Appia, and Sergei Volkonsky (Appia's apologist in Russia), Tairov and Exter conceived the stage as a volumetrical, constructive space, wherein the "cubes and pyramids and the system of inclined platforms, along which the actors moved, created an image of Ancient Greece."[265] As Tairov himself recalled, the guiding force of the sets and costumes was rhythm: "in transferring the necessary rhythmical constructions into the maquette, we gave up the entire central part of the backdrops to platforms which revealed the Apollonian rhythm inherent in the figure of Thamira."[266]

To many observers, *Thamira Khytharedes* was the "most significant phenomenon of the Moscow theater season,"[267] thanks both to the sets and costumes and also to the high professionalism of the actors (Nikolai Tsereteli played the role of Thamira), and it marked a turning-point in the history of the Chamber Theater. If indebted to the principles of Appia, in particular, Exter's monumental solutions also used Cubism as the common stylistic denominator:

> Cubes and cones in large blocks painted in restrained black and blue arose and slid over the steps of the stage. The two currents of volumes corresponded to the two levels of Annensky's tragedy and the two rhythms of Tairov's production. The "Apollonian statics" were centered on the majestic staircase that enclosed the cypress-like cones; the "Dionysian dynamics" were defined by the inclines and cubes at the wings...

The costumes for *Thamira* — the bearers of the dynamic principle — were often beyond the limits that Tairov had established. The vividity, abrasiveness, and whirlwind-like movement of their cut and coloration were almost too much for the eye. In this sense, the actual costume designs are instructive:

> The stage tended to extinguish and deaden them. But on paper... they are possessed by agitation, almost a commotion.[268]

As the critic Konstantin Derzhavin observed, Exter's "three-dimensional, extra-painterly resolution of the scenic space"[269] marked the real break with traditional, Naturalist theater. Her "pure antiquity... in a Cubist stratification"[270] pointed towards the Constructivist settings at the Chamber Theater by Alexander Vesnin (e.g., *Phèdre* of 1922) and the Stenberg brothers, all of whom held Exter in high regard (cf. Nos. 969-71 [R795-97], 1137 [R377]).

463

repeated her 1916 curtain here when Tairov decided to revive *Thamira Khytharedes* in 1920. This second production was, however, "but a pale reflection of its [first] brilliance."[278]

La Cueva de Salamanca: *play in eight comedies by Miguel Cervantes. Rehearsed, but not produced, by Konstantin Stanislavsky at the Moscow Art Theater as part of a dramatic production of five short, comic plays called* Cervantes's Intermezzos *in 1921 with designs by Alexandra Exter.*

Leonarda and her maid Cristina plan to unite with their lovers while Leonarda's husband is out of town. A young student seeks shelter in their house and agrees to keep the ladies' affairs secret. When, unexpectedly, Leonarda's husband returns, the student saves the day with his tale of magic from the Cave of Salamanca.

464

463 [64; R975].
Curtain Design for the Chamber Theater, Moscow, 1920.
Gouache.
Signed and dated upper right in Russian: "Alexandra Exter, 1920/II 17, Moscow."
20⅞ x 28½ in., 53 x 72.5 cm.
Provenance: Yakov Rubinshtein, Moscow, 1974.
Reproduced in color in B115, plate 134; F107, p. 158; I117, p. 539; and Kovalenko, *Aleksandra Ekster* (1993), p. 50; and in black and white in I37 (Yaroslavl), p. 7; I61, p. 317; I77, p. 137; M73, p. 92. The original design of 1916 is reproduced in C2, between pp. 146 and 147; G17, p. XV; as the cover to *Aleksandra Ekster* (Bakhrushin Museum, 1986); G66, plate 20; I81, p. 88; and elsewhere.

Note: Exter came to the world of the theater through her interest in the applied arts, specifically, dresses, scarves, cushions, etc., exhibited in Moscow as early as 1913.[271] Her interest in the stage curtain as a medium of experiment derives from this innate concern with fabric, material, pattern, color application, sewing, and weaving — an aspect of Exter's career that tends to be overshadowed by her more celebrated studio paintings and sets and costumes.

The original and later versions of the curtain in question were not for the permanent drop curtain of the Chamber Theater — as is usually supposed, since Exter began her theatrical career only in 1916.[272] Alexander Tairov opened his Theater in December, 1914, with a production of *Sakuntala* with designs by Pavel Kuznetsov (cf. No. 690 [R577]), and for almost two years he searched for an artist who would manifest a "sense of the

active element of the theater."[273] Exter filled this need, and Tairov invited her to design the curtain for the 1916-17 season of the Chamber Theater — which opened on 22 September with a production of *The Merry Wives of Windsor* (designs by Aristarkh Lentulov) and continued with *Veil of Pierette* (designs by Anatolii Arapov), *Thamira Khytharedes* (designs by Exter), *La Cena delle Beffe* (a project designed by Vera Mukhina, see Nos. 798b-99 [R671-72]), and *The Straw Hat* (designs by Ivan Fedotov). Exter's curtain, with its heraldic imagery and mythological animals, seems to relate to all these dramas simultaneously. The curtain was, however, only one component of Exter's total design, for the vestibule, stairs, and proscenium arch were also decorated in the same way. Abram Efros recalled:

> The displacements and "dislocations" of her wall-paintings created with ardent, I would say, passionate conviction, arrested us by their pathos — right at the entrance, and then led us upstairs into the foyer and came full circle in the auditorium with the magnificent curtain. It fell majestically between the sculpted portal done in Cubo-Baroque style — with its black and white sabers, heraldic beasts and dark colored stripes.[274]

The result was, as Efros mentioned, that Lentulov's designs for the first play of 1916-17 paled beside Exter's painted environment.[275] The young artist Vladimir Dmitriev, an admirer of Exter's work, remembered "Exter's wall-painting on the stairs... her super theater curtain."[276] Exter also designed a special curtain for *Salomé* (9 October, 1917),[277] and, evidently, she

464 [65; NIRE].
Costume Design for a Barber with Hand on Hip, 1924.
Gouache
20⅞ x 13¾ in., 53 x 35 cm.
Signed, dated and inscribed: "Moscou, 1921."
Provenance: *Russian Pictures, Works of Art and Icons,* London: Sotheby's, 30 November, 2006, Lot 107 (reproduced).
Reproduced in color in Chauvelin, *Alexandra Exter,* fig. 177.
For referemces to the project see *Zhizn iskusstva,* P, 1921, Nos. 685-87 and 700-01.

Aelita: 100-minute film by Fedor Otsep and Alexei Faiko after the novel by Alexei N. Tolstoi. Directed by Yakov Protazanov for Mezhrabpom-Rus, Moscow, 1924; with sets by Isaak Rabinovich assisted by Sergei Kozlovsky and Viktor Simov, costumes by Alexandra Exter assisted by Vera Mukhina; and camera work by Yurii Zheliabuzhsky and Emil Schünemann. Released 25 September, 1924.

During the harsh time of Military Communism, the engineer Los, whose wife is attracted to Erlikh, a "bourgeois remnant," constructs a spaceship to Mars to discover a better life. Although he falls in love with the Queen of the Martians, he sees that Martian society is a feudal one in need of revolution. After acquainting himself with the values of the Martians' decadent society and organizing a revolution, Los wakes up on earth. He realizes that it has all been a dream.

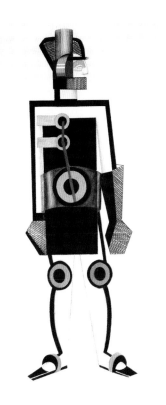

466

467

465

465 [66; R976].
Costume Design for Aelita, Queen of the Martians, 1924.
Gouache and ink.
27 x 18⅜ in., 68.6 x 46.7 cm.
Inscribed mid-left margin in Russian: "Aelita."
Provenance: Simon Lissim, Dobbs Ferry, New York, March, 1971.
Reproduced in color in B115, plate 140; Kovalenko, *Aleksandra Ekster* (1993), p. 130, and Chauvelin, *Alexandra Exter*, fig. 204; and in black and white in *Krasnaia niva*, M, 1924, No. 15, p. 361; Faucher, *Alexandra Exter: divadlo: skizy, dekorace, kostymy*, No. 18; B88, p. 43; H32, p. 419; I20, No. 34; I32, No. 16; I51, No. 79; I67, p. 57; I77, p. 148; I117, p. 543; N91, p. 138; N180. For other illustrations, including stills from the movie, see *Teatr, iskusstvo, ekran*, Paris, 1925, January, p. 28; V. Rakitin, "Marsiane A. Ekster" in *Dekorativnoe iskusstvo*, M, 1977, No. 4, p. 29; Michel Louis: "Aelita ou le rêve de l'homme ridicule" in *Archives d'Architecture Moderne*, Brussels, 1977, July, pp. 33-49.

466 [R977].
Costume Design for a Martian, 1924.
Gouache.
Signed and dated lower right in Russian: "A. Exter, 1924."
20⅞ x 13⅞ in., 53 x 35 cm.
Provenance: Simon Lissim, Dobbs Ferry, New York, 1965.
Reproduced in Faucher, *Alexandra Exter: divadlo: skizy, dekorace, kostymy*, No. 19; I14, No. 56; I32, No. 17; I48; I51, No. 80; I62, p. 117; I77, pp. 116, I117, p. 543; M91; P6; P22; P38; P41; P50; Lissim et al., *Artist of the Theatre*, p. 28; Kovalenko, *Aleksandra Ekster* (1993), p. 133, and Chauvelin, *Alexandra Exter*, fig. 196.

467 [R978].
Costume Design for Gor, Guardian of Energy, 1924.
Gouache.
Signed and dated lower right in Russian: "A. Exter, 1924."
20⅞ x 13⅜ in., 53 x 34 cm.
Other inscription: lower right: "Costumes Aelita, 1924."
Provenance: Simon Lissim, Dobbs Ferry, New York, 1965.
Reproduced in Faucher, *Alexandra Exter: divadlo: skizy, dekorace, kostymy*, No. 21; I14, No. 57; I32, No. 18; I51, No. 81; I77, p. 148; I117, p. 543; Lissim et al., *Artist of the Theatre*, p. 28; Kovalenko, *Aleksandra Ekster* (1993), p. 133; and Chauvelin, *Alexandra Exter*, fig. 197

468 [67; NIRE].
Costume Design for a Female, 1924.
Watercolor and gouache
22 x 16 in., 56 x 40.5 cm.
Inscription in French: "Projet pour un costume féminin"

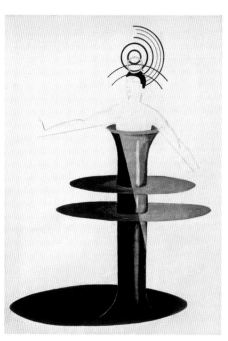

468

Provenance: *Tableaux Modernes*, auction organized by François de Ricqlès at the Salle Drouot, Paris, 2001, 30 August, Lot 28 (reproduced)
Reproduced: in color in Chauvelin, *Alexandra Exter*, fig. 206; I117, p. 543; and in black and white in Faucher, *Alexandra Exter: divadlo: skizy, dekorace, kostymy*, No. 23.

469

La Dama Duende (The Phantom Lady):
comedy in three acts by Pedro Calderón de la
Barca. Produced by Mikhail Chekhov at the
Second Studio of the Moscow Art Theater on
9 April, 1924, with designs by Ignatii Nivinsky.

This comedy of confused identities
treats of the elaborate love affair between
one Don Manuel and Doña Angela, the sister
of Don Juan. By installing a glass partition
between her chambers and the room of her
brother's guest, Don Manuel, Doña Angela
enamored of Don Manuel, is able to move
back and forth quickly and silently. After a
skirmish between Don Luis (the brother of
Don Juan) and Don Manuel, after the passing
of anonymous love letters, after a scolding by
Don Juan, solicitous of his sister's welfare
(she being a recent widow), Doña Angela, the
phantom lady, accepts the hand of Don
Manuel, while her maid Isabel accepts the
hand of Cosme, Don Manuel's servant.

471

469 [68; NIRE].
Costume Design for a Martian, 1924.
Watercolour and gouache
20⅞ x 14⅛ in., 53 x 36 cm.
Inscription: "Projet de costume féminin"
Provenance: *Tableaux Modernes*, auction
organized by François de Ricqlès at the
Salle Drouot, Paris, 2001, 30 August, Lot 29
(reproduced).
Reproduced in color in Chauvelin,
Alexandra Exter, fig. 202; I117. p. 543; and
in black and white in Faucher, *Alexandra*
Exter: divadlo: skizy, dekorace, kostymy,
No. 22.

Note: Aelita was Exter's only major
commitment to the art of film, although
sources mention her involvement in other
movies such as *Daughter of the Sun*,[279] and
she also constructed her marionettes in
1926 for a movie projected, but not
produced, by Peter Gad in Paris. Based on
Alexei Tolstoi's novel *Aelita* of 1923, the
movie was part of the current fashion for
sci-fi culture just before and after the
Revolution and it paralleled the serious and
less serious examples of "sky art"
contemplated by Alexander Labas, Vladimir
Liushin, Kazimir Malevich, Vladimir Tatlin,
and other artists during the 1920s. In her
pioneering designs, Exter set an example
that anticipated our more contemporary
resolutions of space fantasies such as *Star*
Wars. With its easy plot, box office stars
(Yuliia Solntseva as Aelita and Yurii
Zavadsky as Gor), and audacious costumes
by Exter, *Aelita* could not fail to attract both
Russian and Western audiences, even
though film critics have genuine
reservations about this "cosmic
Odyssey."[280]

470

470 [69; R979].
Costume Design for a Woman with a Fan, ca. 1924.
Watercolor, ink, and pencil.
21⅝ x 15½ in., 55 x 39.5 cm.
Provenance: Simon Lissim, Dobbs Ferry,
New York, 1965.
Reproduced in color in B115, plate 138;
F107, p. 584; and in black and white in C7,
fig. 199; G42, p. 205; I20, No. 35; I32, No.
19; I51, No. 82; I77, p. 143; I117, p. 542. A
variant in the collection of the late Donald
Oenslager is reproduced in Lissim et al.,
Artist of the Theatre, p. 28.

471 [70; R980].
Costume Design for a Man with a Ruff, 1924.
Gouache and collage.
Signed and dated lower right in Russian:
"A. Exter 1924."
16⅞ x 21⅝ in., 43 x 55 cm.
Provenance: Simon Lissim, Dobbs Ferry,
New York, 1965.

Reproduced in color in B115, plate 139;
F107, p. 584; and in black and white in C7,
fig. 200; I14, No. 55; I32, No. 21; I51, No. 83;
I68, p. 12; I77, p. 143; I117, p. 542; N128 (b);
O31; and Lissim et al., *Artist of the Theatre*,
p. 28. A variant was auctioned in J19, Lot 88.

472 [71; R981].
Costume Design for a Woman with a Farthingale, 1924.
Gouache and collage.
Signed and dated lower right in Russian:
"A. Exter 1924."
16⅞ x 21⅝ in., 43 x 55 cm.
Provenance: Simon Lissim, Dobbs Ferry,
New York, 1965.
Reproduced in color in B115, plate 137;
F107, p. 584; G79, p. 134; and in black and
white in G55, p. 227; I14, No. 54; I32, No.
20; I51, No. 84; I68, p. 12; I77, p. 143; I117,
p. 532; M73 (a); P15; Q3; Lissim et al.,
Artist of the Theatre, p. 28; and on the
cover of C. Kelly, ed., *An Anthology of*
Russian Women's Writing, 1777-1992,
Oxford: Oxford University Press, 1994; also
see J36, Lots 191, 192.

472

473 [NIRE].
Costume Design for Doña Angela, 1926.
Gouache.
24⅝ x 16⅛ in. 62.5 x 41 cm
Signed and dated lower right in French: "A. Exter 1926."
Provenance: *Peintures Russes,* Salle 1, Drouot-Richelieu, Paris, 19 May, 2004, Lot 87 (reproduced).
Reproduced in F107, p. 584.
The attribution to Exter has been questioned.

Note: There is some question as to the attribution of No. 473 [NIRE] to Exter and, in any case, as to the exact date and application of her stage designs for *La Dama Duende,* although it is known that she worked on an unrealized production at the Moscow Art Theater as early as 1919. Moreover, according to Lissim et al., *Artist of the Theater* (p. 38), Exter also designed costumes for a 1921 production at the Second Studio of the Moscow Art Theater, but other sources (e.g. C182) omit any reference to such a production. However, Mikhail Chekhov did produce *La Dama Duende* there on 9 April, 1924, with designs by Ignatii Nivinsky, a former student of Exter, although, in his book (G42, pp. 203-04),

473

Donald Oenslager refers to this production as a collaboration between Chekhov and Exter. It is possible that Chekhov first gave the design commission to Exter, but since

she emigrated to Paris early in 1924, she or Chekhov may have passed on the project to Nivinsky (see No. 801 [R682]). There is no evidence to assume — as has been done traditionally — that Exter worked on a separate Paris production also in 1924.[281]

Various projects.
Exter made the following designs (Nos. 474-80 [R982-88]) between ca. 1925 and ca. 1927. In greater or lesser degree they all relate to the set of fifteen *gouaches au pochoir,* or silkscreens, that she compiled for the album *Alexandra Exter. Décors de Théâtre* (see Nos. 483-97 [R989-1003]). Nos. 476 [R984], 479 [R987], and 480 [R988] are the original gouaches for the silkscreen duplicates. None of the designs seems to have been used for an actual production, although the intensity with which Exter worked on them indicates that she was expecting commissions.

474 [72; R982].
Stage Design for a Revue, ca. 1925.
Gouache.
Signed lower right: "A Exter."
20 x 26⅜ in., 51 x 67 cm.
Provenance: Simon Lissim, Dobbs Ferry,

474

New York, May, 1969.
Reproduced in color in B115, plate 141; I117, p. 543; N66; and in black and white in

Faucher, *Alexandra Exter: divadlo: skizy, dekorace, kostymy*, No. 84; I20, No. 36; I32, No. 23; I51, No. 85; I77, p. 158; P42; P44.

475 [R983].
Stage Design for "King Lear", ca. 1925.
Gouache.
Signed lower right: "A Exter."
18¾ x 25 in., 47.5 x 63.5 cm.
Provenance: Simon Lissim, Dobbs Ferry, New York, 1965.
Reproduced in I14, No. 53; I32, No. 22; I51, No. 86; I77, p. 158; I117, p. 545; P36; P56; and in Lissim et al., *Artist of the Theatre*, p. 30.

476 [73; R984].
Stage Design for a Spanish Pantomime, ca. 1926.
Gouache and black ink.
Signed upper right: "A. Exter."
19½ x 20½ in., 49.5 x 52 cm.
Other inscription: on reverse a label from the 1937 Prague exhibition carrying the words "Span pantomima."
Provenance: Alina Izdebsky-Pritchard, New York, June, 1977.
Reproduced in color in B115, plate 142; C8, frontispiece; F107, p. 427; Kovalenko, *Alexandra Exter* (1993), p. 153; I117, p. 547; and M151, p. 119; and in black and white in *Teatr, iskusstvo, ekran,* Paris, 1925, January, p. 19; Faucher, *Alexandra Exter: divadlo: skizy, dekorace, kostymy*, No. 68; C7, No. 193 (where it is dated 1926); I51, No. 87; I77, p. 158; N105. Exter repeated the design as a silkscreen for her *Décors de Théâtre* in 1930 (cf. 493 [R999]. An identical design, in the collection of the Theatermuseum, Cologne, is reproduced in I62, p. 106.

475

Note: According to one source, this piece is:

> designed to serve the significant rhythmic emotion contained by a play, and is demanded by dynamic representation and interpretation. It suggests the transition from neo-realism to concrete realism and shows the use of color.[282]

Huntly Carter, author of the above, then goes on to repeat what he identifies as Exter's "construction formula":

> Given that the intensity of the emotion of the play (tragedy, comedy, etc.) is strictly subordinated to the essential intensity of the "construction," it is necessary that this construction be conceived for the emotional movement.[283]

477 [74; R985].
Stage Design and Lighting Study for Scene 3 of the Play **Don Juan,** ca. 1926.
Gouache.
Signed lower right: "A. Exter."
20 x 27 in., 50.5 x 69.5 cm.
Provenance: Simon Lissim, Dobbs Ferry, New York, March, 1971.
Reproduced in color in B115, plate 143; I117, p. 545; and in black and white in Faucher, *Alexandra Exter: divadlo: skizy, dekorace, kostymy*, No. 99; I77, p. 158.

476

Note: The design is for a play by Solomon Poliakov-Litovtsev and Petr Potemkin projected in Paris in 1926, but not produced. In 1929 Exter returned to the subject in her designs for the ballet *Don Juan ou Le Festin de Pierre* (cf. Nos.481-82 [NIRE]).

478 [R986].
Stage Design for the Duel in "Othello," ca. 1927.
Gouache.
Signed lower right: "Alex. Exter."
18¼ x 23⅝ in., 46.5 x 60 cm.
Other inscriptions: on reverse a French customs' stamp and label from the 1937 Prague exhibition carrying the words: "A. Exterova, No. 1 Shakespeare Othello Dekorace."
Provenance: Galina Izdebsky, New York, October, 1977.
Reproduced in color in B115, plate 144; F107, p. 278; Chauvelin, *Alexandra Exter*, fig. 316; and in black and white in Faucher, *Alexandra Exter: divadlo: skizy, dekorace, kostymy*, No. 1; I51, No. 88; I77, p. 158; T5; T6. A similar design is reproduced in C7, No. 195.

477

478

479

480

479 [R987].
Lighting Design for a Tragedy, ca. 1927.
Gouache.
Signed lower right: "A Exter."
20¼ x 20 in., 51.5 x 51 cm.

Provenance: Sonya Ryback, Paris, September, 1971.
Reproduced in color in B115, plate 145; and Kovalenko, *Alexandra Exter* (1993), p. 146; and in black and white in Faucher,

Alexandra Exter: divadlo: skizy, dekorace, kostymy, No. 65; I32, No. 38; I51, No. 89; I77, p. 158; M183, p. 7; P5; P7; P10; P19; P31; P35; P37; P43; and Lissim et al., *Artist of the Theatre*, p. 30.
This design is reminiscent of one of Exter's sets for the 1921 production of *Romeo and Juliet* at the Chamber Theater, Moscow (cf. G10, Vol. 2, fig. 153.). Exter repeated the design as a silkscreen for her *Décors de Théâtre* in 1930 (cf. 494 [R1000].

480 [R988].
Stage Design with Two Dancers Holding a Hoop, ca. 1927.
Watercolor.
Signed lower right: "A Exter."
18⅞ x 25¼ in., 48 x 64 cm.
Provenance: André Boll, Paris, 1965.
Reproduced in color in B115, plate 146; Kovalenko, *Alexandra Exter* (1993), p. 220; and I117, p. 548; and in black and white in I32, No. 39; I51, No. 90; I77, p. 158; and Lissim et al., *Artist of the Theatre*, p. 30. Exter repeated the design (minus the hoop) as a silkscreen for her *Décors de Théâtre* in 1930 (cf. 497 [R1003]).

Don Juan, ou Le Festin de Pierre: *ballet in three acts with libretto by Ranieri de' Calzabigi, and music by Christoph Willibald Ritter von Gluck. Projected, but not produced, for Elsa Kruger (Elza Kriuger) at the Opera House, Cologne, in 1929.*

Don Juan serenades Donna Elvira, but her father, the Commander, enters with sword drawn to protect his daughter and, in the ensuing duel, Don Juan kills the Commander. Don Juan is banqueting with friends, when a terrible knocking is heard at the door. Opening the door, Don Juan discovers the marble statue of the dead Commander, which invites Don Juan to dine at his tomb. The Commander steps from his tomb, and although Don Juan confronts the Commander with frivolity, irrevocable judg-

481

482

483 [R989].
Stage Design for Othello, Act I, with Three Performers on Stage.
Signed in pencil lower right in Russian: "Aleks. Exter."

484 [R990].
Stage Design for Othello, Act II.
Signed in pencil lower right in Russian: "Aleks. Exter."

483

ment is passed upon him: to the strains of a passacaglia, graves fly open, flames rise, and Juan descends into Hell.

481 [NIRE].
Costume Design for Don Juan, ca. 1929.
Watercolor and pencil.
Signed lower right: "A. Exter."
27¾ x 16⅞ in., 60.5 x 43 cm.
Provenance: Simon Lissim, Dobbs Ferry, New York, March, 1965. Now in a private collection.
Reproduced in I20, No. 37.

482 [NIRE].
Costume Design for a Female Dancer, ca. 1929.
Gouache and ink.
Signed lower right: "A. Exter."
24⅜ x 16½ in., 62 x 42 cm.
Provenance: Simon Lissim, Dobbs Ferry, New York, March, 1965. Now in a private collection.
Reproduced in I20, No. 38.

Décors de Théâtre (Set of silkscreens).
Nos. 483-97 [R989-1003] are stage designs, all 13 x 20 in. (33 x 50.5 cm.), from the album of fifteen silkscreens (pochoirs) *Alexandra Exter. Décors de Théâtre,* Paris: Editions des Quatre Chemins, 1930. The set of silkscreens, all by Exter, was published in an edition of about 150 copies, and each piece was identified by its own title. The album was prepared and prefaced by Exter's old friend, Alexander Tairov, director of the Chamber Theater. For color reproductions of all fifteen pieces see, for example, J27, Lot 232. Nos. 485 [R991], 486 [R992], and 492 [R998] carry dedications by Exter to the sculptor and patron Vladimir Alexeevich Izdebsky (1882-1965). Provenance: all fifteen were acquired from Galina Izdebsky, New York, October, 1969.

484

485

485 [R991].
Stage Design for Faust with Flags on Stage.
Inscribed lower right in pencil in Russian:
"To dear Vladimir Alexeevich [Izdebsky]
from Alexandra Exter, January, 1948."

486 [R992].
Design for Cirque with Male and Female Performers.
Inscribed in ink lower right: "Souvenir d'A.
Exter à l'ami Izdebsky, Janvier, 1948, Paris.
Act 2 de Cirque."
The ballet *Circus* was composed by the
dancer Elsa Kruger (Elza Kriuger).

486

487 [R993].
Design for Cirque with Six Performers in Capes.
Signed lower right in Russian: "Aleks. Exter."
Reproduced in color in N159.
The ballet *Circus* was composed by the dancer Elsa Kruger (Elza Kriuger).

488 [75; R994].
Stage Design for an Operetta with Action on Five Platforms.
Signed in pencil lower right in Russian: "Aleks. Exter."
Reproduced in color in N159; and in Kovalenko, *Alexandra Exter* (1993), p. 152.

487

488

489

489 [R995].
Stage Design for an Operetta with Four Figures Climbing.
Signed in pencil lower right in Russian: "Alex Exter."

490 [R996].
Stage Design for Don Juan and Death: Actor Center Stage.
Signed in pencil lower right in Russian: "Alex Exter."
Reproduced in black and white in Faucher, *Alexandra Exter: divadlo: skizy, dekorace, kostymy*, No. 100.

490

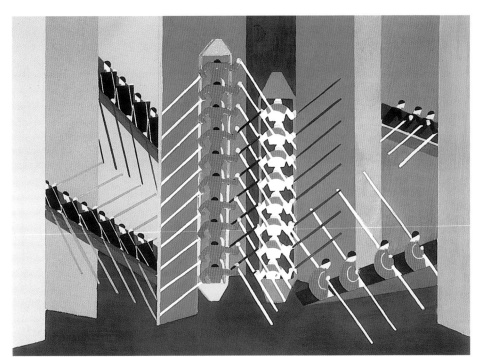

491

491 [R997].
Design for a Revue with Six Rowboats.
Signed in pencil lower right in Russian: "Alex. Exter."
Reproduced in color in N159; and in black and white in Faucher, *Alexandra Exter: divadlo: skizy, dekorace, kostymy*, No. 86.

492 [76; R998].
Stage Design for a Revue with Action in Center and on Both Sides of Stage.
Inscribed in ink lower right in Russian: "To dear Vl. Al. Izdebsky from Al. Exter, January, 1948."
Reproduced in color in Kovalenko, *Alexandra Exter* (1993), p. 152; and in black and white in M86.

492

493

Alexandra Exter: Poster of Scenic Construction – Preliminary Version, 1926.

493 [R999].
Stage Design for a Spanish Pantomime with Four Guitar Players.
Signed lower right in Russian: "Alex. Exter."
Cf. the original gouache and ink composition for this at No. 476 [R984].

494 [R1000].
Lighting Design with Two Intersecting Beams.
Cf. No. 478 [R986] and the original gouache and ink composition for this at No. 479 [R987].

Alexandra Exter: Poster of Scenic Construction, 1926.

494

495

495 [R1001].
***Stage Design for Don Juan in Hell, the Stage
Composed of Stairs.***
Signed in pencil lower right in Russian: "A.
Exter."

496 [R1002].
***Stage Design for The Merchant of Venice
with Three Circular Lights.***
Signed lower right in Russian: "A. Exter."
Reproduced in color in Kovalenko,
Alexandra Exter (1993), p. 149.

496

497

498

497 [R1003].
Stage Design with Two Dancers Holding a Hoop.
Signed lower right in Russian: "A. Exter." Cf. the original gouache at No. 480 [R988].

Note: In her Constructivist stage sets Exter manipulates staircases and platforms with their emphatic verticals and diagonals to produce a remarkable play of movement, light, and color. The design for a *Revue* (No. 474 [R982]) is an impressive example of this principle, animated with dancers in dynamic interplay. The set for *King Lear* (?) (No. 475 [R983]) uses a combination of arches and steps in a "Baroque-Futurist" style that maximizes the scenic space. In the *Spanish Pantomime* (Nos. 476 [R984], 493 [R999]) the geometry of planes is challenged by the colored gradations of the surfaces. In the duel scene from *Othello* (No. 478 [R986]) the beams of light construct space elements wherein the actors perform, while the lighting design for a tragedy (No. 479 [R987]) seems to dematerialize the scenic space itself. In all these set designs, Exter was attempting to illustrate the "dynamic use of immobile form"[284] that she had applied in her first works for the Chamber Theater, Moscow. Following the examples of the designers Appia and Thomas Gray (cf. G10, Vol. 2, figs. 37-41, 65-68), Exter became particularly interested in the architectural possibilities of the stage and often used arches and steps to enhance and "expand" the space on stage (as, for example, in the sets for *Don Juan* in No. 477 [R985] and for Elza Kriuger's production of the ballet of the same name scheduled for the Cologne Opera House in 1929). Exter's student and colleague Isaak Rabinovich also supported this system, as evidenced by his sets for the productions of *Don Carlos* at the Theater of Comedy, St.

Petersburg, and *The Sorcerer* at the Jewish State Chamber Theater, Moscow, in 1922, as well as for *The Love for Three Oranges* of 1927 (see No. 855 [R732]).

Seven against Thebes: play in eleven sections by Aeschylus. Projected, but not produced in Paris ca. 1937 with designs by Alexandra Exter.

When Oedipus, King of Thebes, realizes that he had married his own mother and had four children with her, he blinds himself and curses his sons to divide their inheritance (the kingdom) by the sword. The two sons, Eteocles and Polynices, agree to rule Thebes in alternate years, but after the first year, Eteocles refuses to step down so Polynices raises an army to take Thebes by force. Each of the seven captains that lead the army against the seven gates of the city of Thebes is described. The commander of the troops before the seventh gate is revealed to be Polynices, the brother of the King. Eteocles resolves to meet and fight his brother before the seventh gate and exits. Following a choral ode, a messenger enters, announcing that Eteocles and Polynices have killed each other in battle.

498 [NIRE].
Costume Design for the Messenger, 1937.
Gouache
Signed lower right: "Alex Exter."
20¼ x 12⅝ in., 51.5 x 32 cm.
Provenance: Simon Lissim, Dobbs Ferry, New York, 1965. Now in a private collection.
Reproduced in I14, p. 31, fig. 52.

258 Ya. Tugendkhold: "Pismo iz Moskvy" in *Apollon,* P, 1917, No. 1, p. 72. Exter also contributed five tipped-in tone plates to a special, limited edition of *Thamira Khytharedes* in 1919 (I. Annensky: *Famira Kifared,* SP: Grzhebin, 1919).

259 C11, p. 70.
260 See I65, passim.
261 I1, p. 29.
262 Quoted in O. Voronova: *V.I. Mukhina.* M: Iskusstvo, 1976, p. 43. For a photograph of dancers wearing Exter's "epidermic costumes" see K13, p. 31.
263 Letter from Innokentii Annensky to Alexandra Borodina dated 2 August, 1906. Quoted in A. Fedorov, ed.: *Innokentii Annensky. Stikhotvoreniia i tragedii,* L: Sovetskii pisatel, 1959, p. 630.
264 P. Markov: "O Tairove" in C35, p. 17.
265 Ibid.
266 A. Tairov: *Zapiski rezhissera,* in C35, p. 163.
267 Ya. Tugendkhold: "Pismo iz Moskvy", op. cit., p. 72. Nikolai Efros was also enthusiastic. See N. Efros: "Famira Kifared" in *Rech,* P, 1916, 12 November, No. 312, p.3.
268 G17, p. XXIV.
269 C11, p. 70.
270 G17, p. XXII.
271 Tugendkhold, *Exter,* p. 17.
272 Ibid., p. 16.
273 Tairov, *Zapiski rezhissera,* in C35, p. 163. In 1916 Mukhina seemed also to have made designs for a drop curtain for the Chamber Theater. See, for example, the illustration that is described as "Study for a stage design" in R. Klimov, ed.: *Mukhina,* M: Iskusstvo, 1960, Vol. 3, ill. 147.
274 G17, p. XXI.
275 Ibid.
276 Memoir by V. Dmitriev dated 1945. Quoted in V. Berezkin: *V.V. Dmitriev.* L: Khudozhnik RSFSR, 1981, p. 13.
277 The *Salomé* curtain is reproduced in Tugendkhold, op. cit., plate XIX.
278 Tairov, op. cit., p. 172.
279 C7, plate 197.
280 V. Rakitin: "Marsiane A. Ekster" in *Dekorativnoe iskusstvo,* M, 1977, No. 4, p. 29. For a detailed discussion of *Aelita* see Louis, "Aelita."
281 This argument finds further support in the fact that a number of Exter's so-called "Spanish dance" costumes were reproduced in Moscow in 1924. See A. Sidorov: "Iskusstvo tantsa v SSSR" in *Sovetskaia kultura. Itogi i perspektivy.* M: Izvestiia TsIK SSSR i VTsIK, 1924, p. 325.
282 C8, frontispiece caption.
283 Ibid., p. 330.
284 Tugendkhold, "Pismo iz Moskvy.", op. cit., p. 17.

FALK, Robert Rafailovich

Born 16 (28) October, 1886, Moscow, Russia; died 1 October, 1958, Moscow, Russia.

Studied music and painting from early age; 1902-05 studied under Konstantin Yuon and then with Ilia Mashkov; 1905 entered MIPSA, studying under Abram Arkhipov, Leonid Pasternak, and Apollinarii Vasnetsov, and later with Valentin Serov and Konstantin Korovin; 1909 converted from Judaism to Christianity; 1910 traveled in Italy; member of the Jack of Diamonds group, taking part in its exhibitions; 1910s influenced by Cézanne and Cubism; 1919 member of IZO NKP; 1921 member of the Moscow chapter of Kultur-Lige; 1918 helped with the organization of Svomas; 1918-28 taught at Svomas-Vkhutemas-Vkhutein; 1924 co-founded the group called Moscow Painters; 1925 onwards involved in theater productions such as *The Night in the Old Market, The Travels of Benjamin III, Uriel Akosta,* and *Enchanted Tailor;* 1928-38 lived in France; 1938 returned to Moscow; 1939 two one-man shows; 1941 evacuated to Bashkiria and then to Central Asia; 1940s-50s considered to be formalist and alien to the Soviet régime; 1950s-60s popular with the dissident generation; 1962 contributed to exhibition commemorating the "30th Anniversary of the Moscow Artists' Union"; 1964 one-man exhibition in Erevan; 1966 one-man exhibition in Moscow.

Bibliography
D. Sarabianov: *Robert Falk.* Catalog of exhibition at the Moscow Section of the Union of Artists of the USSR, M, 1958.
D. Sarabianov: *R.R. Falk.* Catalog of exhibition at the State Picture Gallery of Armenia, Erevan, 1965.
M. Sarian: *R. Falk.* Catalog of exhibition at the Moscow Section of the Union of Artists of the USSR, M, 1966.
D. Sarabjanow: *Robert Falk,* Dresden: VEB Verlag der Kunst, 1972.
D. Sarabianov: *Robert Falk. Risunki, akvareli, guashi.* Catalog of exhibition at GMII, 1979.
A. Shchekin-Krotova, comp.: *R.R. Falk. Besedy ob iskusstve. Pisma. Vospominaniia o khudozhnike,* M: Sovetskii khudozhnik, 1981.
T. Levina: *Robert Falk,* M: Slovo, 1996.
A. Emdin, comp.: *Robert Falk. Khudozhestvennyi dnevnik,* M: NGS, 2002.
V. Chaikovskaia: *Tri lika russkogo iskusstva XX veka. Robert Falk, Kuzma Petrov-Vodkin, Aleksandr Samokhvalov,* M: Iskusstvo XXI veka, 2006.
D. Sarabianov and Yu. Didenko: *Zhivopis Roberta Falka. Polnyi katalog proizvedenii,* M: Elizium, 2006.
I. Zolotukhina: *Risunki R.R. Falka.* Catalog of exhibition at the Sakhalin Regional Art Museum, Yuzhno-Sakhalinsk, 2006.
I. Galeev: *Robert Falk.* Catalog of exhibition at the Galeev Gallery, M, 2012.

Falk is remembered not as a designer or illustrator, but, above all, as a studio painter who in the 1920s and 1930s paid particular attention to the work of Cézanne. Much appreciative of French art in general, Falk

499

was not supportive of Russia's extreme tendencies, observing an academic distance from the more vociferous artists such as David Burliuk and Kazimir Malevich. However, Falk was a leading member of the Jack of Diamonds group and, along with Petr Konchalovsky, Alexander Kuprin, Ilia Mashkov, and Vasilii Rozhdestvensky, tried to steer an even course between the more xenophobic sympathies of the avant-garde and the sense of measured form ensured by Cézanne, Matisse, and Picasso in particular. Partly because of this "French connection", Falk was much admired by the emerging unofficial artists of the 1950s onwards — while being criticized, sometimes harshly, by the status quo. Falk's still-lives and portraits, in particular, highly suggestive, emotionally suspended, and carefully constructed, left an appreciable influence on more contemporary artists such as Dmitrii Krasnopevtsev and Vladimir Veisberg.

The Travels of Benjamin III: *epos in three acts adapted by Iekhezkel Dobrushin from the novel by Mendele Mocher Seforim. Produced at the State Jewish Theater (GOSET), Moscow, on 20 April, 1927, with music by Lev Pulver and designs by Robert Falk.*

Benjamin is a fool in a town of poor Jews. One day Benjamin is struck suddenly by a desire to travel, and joined by Sendrel, he sets out to find the Jewish kingdom mentioned in legends of the Ten Lost Tribes. But barely escaping from their own wives, the two travel only as far as nearby towns and kidnappers, taking advantage of their naiveté, sell them into the Tsarist army. They try to escape, but the army's inane response forces the audience to question the division between absurdity and dream.

499 [77; NIRE].
Set design, 1927.
Gouache on paper laid down on cardboard.
17¾ x 23¼ in., 45 x 59 cm.
Signed lower right: "R. Falk."
Provenance: *Russian Art,* Sotheby's, London, 1 December, 2009, Lot 402 (reproduced).
Reproduced in F107, p. 467. For reproduction of a parallel design see L198, Lot 403; for other designs see I122, pp. 159-63. For reproductions of costume designs see C168, between pp. 154 and 155.

Note: Given the virtual renaissance of national Jewish culture in Russia during the 1910s, demonstrated by the establishment of the Jewish National Museum, the Jewish Society for the Encouragement of the Arts, and the many Jewish ethnographic and folklore centers which sprang up in St. Petersburg, Moscow, and Kiev, it is surprising to learn that young Jewish artists such as Natan Altman, Falk, and El Lissitzky did not give their exclusive attention to Jewish history. Indeed, it would be a mistake to identify their ethnic commitment only with their recognizable ethnic subjects.

Rather, the Jewishness of such artists may lie in other more subtle, more abstract qualities characteristic of Jewish culture as a whole — an emphasis on the literary or didactic purpose of art, a reductive or "Talmudic" treatment of images as in Falk's still-lives or Lissitzky's Prouns, and in what Maxim Syrkin regarded as a "spontaneity", an "intimacy", and a "cosiness" of visual expression.[285] In any event, the 1910s witnessed an attempt to identify Jewish art not through the veracity of depictions of everyday scenes, but, on the contrary, through an artist's ability to assimilate and reprocess themes and styles which, ostensibly, had nothing to do with the traditions of the shtetl and the Pale of Settlement.

Perhaps it was because of this duality that Falk, the cosmopolitan Muscovite who saw Cezanne as his first inspiration, experienced a momentary gravitation towards Jewish life and culture — not as a documentary resource but as an instrument of theatrical stylization. Granovsky's theater, after all, was concerned more with the "spirit" of Jewish life than with any anthropological representation and, like Falk, used irony and hyperbole to transmit this condition — which harmonized well with the absurd story of *The Travels of Benjamin III.* Still, Falk did not feel at home in GOSET and, a studio painter at heart, he preferred the serious oil on canvas to the provisional costume and set design. An applied and, therefore, ancillary art, stage design — for Falk — could not express the "authentic, inner visual and psychological processes" of the artist.[286]   After *The Travels of Benjamin III*, Falk concentrated on studio painting, although he did fulfil occasional commissions for other theater productions during the 1930s-50s.

285   M. Syrkin: "Evrei i iskusstvo" in *Evreiskaia nedelia,* M, 1916, No. 25, p. 40
286   R. Falk: "Besedy ob iskusstve" in Shchekin-Krotova, *R.R. Falk,* 1981, p. 27.

FEDOROVSKY, Fedor Fedorovich

Born 14 (26) July, 1883, Chernigov, Ukraine; died 7 September, 1955, Moscow, Russia.

1907 graduated with a Gold Medal from CSIAI where he studied under Konstantin Korovin and Mikhail Vrubel; 1907-18 taught there; 1906 contributed to the exhibition of the Moscow Association of Artists; 1907 took part in a stage design competition organized by Sergei Zimin's Opera Company in Moscow, shortly thereafter joining the Company as artist-in-residence; 1910 designed *Snegurochka* for the Zimin Opera Theater, Moscow; 1913 designed *Khovanshchina* for Sergei Diaghilev's production in Paris; 1914 designed *May Night* for Diaghilev's production in London; 1915 contributed to the "World of Art" exhibition, Moscow; 1918-23 taught at the restructured CSIAI, i.e., Svomas–Vkhutemas; 1922 designed a production of Bizet's *Carmen* at the Bolshoi Theater, Moscow; 1925 represented at the "Exposition Internationale des Arts Décoratifs" in Paris; 1930s-40s involved in many operatic productions such as *Boris Godunov* (1927 and 1946) and *Prince Igor* (1934).

Bibliography
N. Giliarovskaia: *Fedor Fedorovich Fedorovsky,* M-L: Iskusstvo 1946.

Yu. Platonov: *F.F. Fedorovsky,* M-L: Sovetskii khudozhnik, 1948.
E. Kostina: *Fedor Fedorovich Fedorovsky,* M: Sovetskii khudozhnik, 1960. G38, pp. 277-306. M2, Vol. 2, pp. 176, 177.
E. Kostina: "Khudozhnik muzykalnogo teatra" in *Iskusstvo,* M, 1983, No. 12, pp. 34-40.
S. Pokrovskaia: *F.F. Fedorovsky.* Catalog of exhibition at the Starye gody Gallery, M, 1997.
Recent exhibitions of stage designs have featured Fedor Fedorovsky's work. See, for example, I116, pp. 26,73.

Fedorovsky was, first and foremost, an artist of the stage, and, unlike most of Russia's theatrical designers, regarded studio art as a secondary occupation. Fedorovsky made his real debut as a stage designer in 1910 with his sets and costumes for Zimin's production of *Snegurochka* in Moscow, although he was certainly active with a number of stage projects before that (including *Carmen* as early as 1907). Like his principal mentor, Konstantin Korovin, Fedorovsky is remembered for the color and movement that he brought to the Russian theater, especially to the pageants of Russian history such as *Khovanshchina* and *Boris Godunov,* and to this day the former is still given with his sets and costumes at the Bolshoi. Although an artist of uneven talent, Fedorovsky questioned the refined elegance of the World of Art artists such as Alexandre Benois and Mstislav Dobujinsky, preferring the primitive vitality of Medieval Russia to the sophistication of Versailles — something that he expressed in the broad, assured brush strokes and ample proportions of his designs. As one critic has written:

Fedorovsky... loves the theater and theater decoration, "scenic architecture" as a creative recreation of what was not, of what could not have been... He needs the world of the fairytale or the world of the historical legend, the world of great passions and heroic exploits.[287]

Khovanshchina: *opera in five acts by Modest Mussorgsky, completed by Nikolai Rimsky-Korsakov, with libretto by Mussorgsky and Vladimir Stasov. Produced by Sergei Diaghilev for the Ballets Russes at the Théâtre des Champs-Elysées, Paris, on 5 June, 1913, with musical emendations by Maurice Ravel and Igor Stravinsky, choreography by Adolph Bolm and designs by Fedor Fedorovsky.*
See No. 445 [NIRE] for plot summary.

500 [78; R848].
Two Costume Designs for Prince Khovansky, 1912.
Gouache.
Signed and dated lower right in Russian: "Fedorovsky 1912."
34 x 40 in., 86.5 x 101.5 cm.
Provenance: private art gallery, Paris, June, 1966.
Reproduced in color as the centerfold in *Comoedia Illustré,* Paris, 1913, 5 June, unpaginated; in B115, plate 27; D1, unnumbered plate; D41; G99, pp. 180, 181; and F107, p. 99; and in black and white in A34, p. 147; I20, No. 39; I51, No. 91; N88. A watercolor version for the left-hand figure appeared as the cover illustration for the Souvenir Program of the *Ballets Russes. Théâtre des Champs-Elysées* (Paris, 1913);

500

501

a design similar to the left-hand figure is reproduced in Giliarovskaia, *Fedorovsky*, p. 57.

501 [79; R849].
Costume Designs for Persian Slave Dancers in Act 2, 1912.
Gouache.
Signed and dated in right margin in Russian: "Fedorovsky 1912."
29⅜ x 42 in., 76 x 106.7 cm.
Provenance: private art gallery, Paris, June, 1966.
Reproduced in color in *Comoedia Illustré*, Paris, 1913, 5 June, unpaginated; in B115, plate 26; D1, unnumbered plate; I128, p. 107; N188, p. 52; I117, p. 529; and in black and white in I40, No. 40. A close version is reproduced in Platonov, *F.F. Fedorovsky*, unpaginated; and Pokrovskaia, *F.F. Fedorovsky*, p. 13.

502 [80; R850].
Costume Designs for the Boyar Shaklovityi and the Scribe, 1913.
Watercolor and gouache.
Signed and dated lower right in Russian: "Fedorovsky 1913."
32 x 32 in., 81.4 x 81.4 cm.
Other inscriptions: left margin in Russian: instructions for the dressmaker.
Provenance: private art gallery, Paris, June, 1966.
Reproduced in color in the Souvenir Program of the *Ballets Russes. Théâtre des Champs-Elysées*, Paris, 1913; B115, plate 28; and in black and white in I40, No. 41. A close version is reproduced in Platonov, *F.F. Fedorovsky*, unpaginated; and I128, p. 105.

Note: With Fedor Chaliapin in the principal role, with half-naked dancing girls in exotic costumes, and with Tamara Karsavina, Lubov Tchernicheva, and Vaslav Nijinsky in the choreographic numbers, *Khovan-*

shchina provided a splendid context for Fedorovsky to indulge his love of spectacle. One observer wrote:

> In Mussorgsky's *Khovanshchina* everything is tragic, on a grand scale, powerful. And this was embodied in the décors, sets and make-up by Fedorovsky. He resolved everything in exaggerated forms. Everything told of strength and power: mighty boyars appeared on stage, looking like gigantic oaks in their huge fur hats and brocaded, unbending caftans with straight, lapidary folds.[288]

Although cognoscenti criticized Diaghilev for tailoring the opera to the tastes of the Paris public, they were unanimous in their praise of Fedorovsky's designs. Anatolii Lunacharsky even spoke of the "cyclopic" effect of Fedorovsky's evocation of Old Russia.[289] Fedorovsky himself, who felt that the color harmonies

502

in *Khovanshchina* were of the utmost importance, returned to the opera in 1918 (for the Theater of the Soviets of Workers' Deputies) and in 1949 (for the Bolshoi Theater), although these versions enjoyed only a fraction of the Paris success.

287 G35, p. 97.
288 A. Lunacharsky in his review of the 1913 Russian season in Paris. Quoted in Giliarovskaia, *Fedorovsky*, p. 48.
289 G38, P. 296.

FEDOTOV, Ivan Sergeevich

Born 7 (19) May, 1881, Moscow, Russia; died 2 February, 1951, Moscow, Russia.

1901 graduated from CSIAI; 1902 began to work as a stage designer for the Moscow Private Opera; 1905 designed Maxim Gorky's *Children of the Sun* for Vera Komissarzhevskaia's Theater in St. Petersburg; 1908-17 worked for Sergei Zimin's Opera Company in Moscow; 1913 and 1914 contributed to the "Jack of Diamonds", Moscow; 1917 onwards worked as a stage designer for many productions in Moscow, Leningrad, and Kiev; 1918 worked for the Theater of the Soviets of Worker's Deputies in Moscow, where he designed many productions: Giacomo Puccini's *La Bohème*, Gioacchino Rossini's *Barbiere di Siviglia*, and Otto Nicolai's *Die Lustigen Weiber von Windsor*; 1920 worked at the Terevsat (Theater of Revolutionary Satire) in Moscow with Mak (Pavel Ivanov), Vasilii Komardenkov, Ivan Maliutin, et al.; 1920-21 worked at the Theater of the RSFSR No. 1 under Vsevolod Meierkhold and Valerii Bebutov; designed Fedor Komissarzhevsky's production of *The Marriage of Figaro* for the Art Education Union of Workers' Organizations, Moscow, and the agit-play *The Sleeping Soldier* at the Theater of Revolutionary Satire, Moscow; 1921 worked for the Children's Theater, Moscow; 1924 contributed to the exhibition "Stage Design of the Last 5 Years" in Kazan; 1934-51 artist-in-residence at the Central Theater of the Soviet Army, Moscow; 1930s-40s continued to design many plays; 1935 contributed to the exhibition "Artists of the Soviet Theater; 1917-1935" in Moscow and Leningrad; 1946 became Merited Art Worker of the RSFSR.

Bibliography
A7, Vol. 5, p. 435.
F. Syrkina and A. Shifrina: *Vystavka proizvedenii zasluzhennogo deiatelia iskusstva RSFSR, laureata Stalinskoi premii Ivana Sergeevicha Fedotova (1881-1951)*. Catalog of exhibition at the All-Union Theater Society, M, 1960.
L. Vedekhov: "Khudozhnik Fedotov" in *Teatr*, M, 1982, No. 2, pp. 109-14.

Fedotov was a professional stage designer in the sense that, unlike most of his colleagues — whether Léon Bakst or

Liubov Popova — he took courses in the discipline of stage design at a major design school (i.e., the Stroganov Institute), graduated with a diploma in stage design, and then applied his expertise immediately by working for major theaters in Moscow and St. Petersburg. Like Mak (Nos 765-67h [R644-46z]) and Ivan Maliutin, Fedotov worked simultaneously as a caricaturist and stage designer, combining these two talents with particular success in his projects for sets and costumes at Terevsat in the early 1920s.[290]

Terevsat was one of the many ephemeral theaters born of the Revolution that used satire and parody to expose the defects of the *ancien régime,* and instruments of agit-prop to stir the spirits of the proletarian audience. Fedotov, Maliutin, and Vasilii Komardenkov were typical of a generation of stage designers that, if not as radical in their visual resolutions as Vladimir Dmitriev or Alexander Rodchenko, still impressed their audiences by humor and satire, clarity of illustration, and historical recognizability. This might explain why Fedotov felt equally at home with Komissarzhevskaia and Meierkhold, Komissarzhevsky and Zimin, and could move easily between a traditional Italian opera and a rousing celebration of the Soviet armed forces. As Flora Syrkina has commented:

> Fedotov appears to us as a very fine master, an inexhaustible worker, an artist of delicate taste. His sketches — and they retain independent artistic value — preserve the fragrance of a production [that may already belong] to the past.[291]

Die Lustigen Weiber von Windsor: *comic opera in three acts by Otto Nicolai with libretto by Herman von Mosenthal based on William Shakespeare's five-act comedy* The Merry Wives of Windsor. *Produced in April, 1918, at the Theater of the Soviet of Workers' Deputies from the Rogozhsko-Simonovsky Region, Moscow, by Fedor Komissarzhevsky with designs by Ivan Fedotov.*

Mrs. Ford and Mrs. Page discuss the love letters they have received from Sir John Falstaff. Falstaff arrives to pay attendance on Mrs. Ford, but their dalliance is interrupted by the entrance of Mr. Ford, although Falstaff manages to hide in time. Falstaff later returns to the household dressed as an old woman, and Mr. Ford searches for the culprit in vain. The last act occurs in Windsor Forest, where Falstaff makes love to both Mrs. Ford and Mrs. Page, while Anne, Mrs. Page's daughter, and her suitor Fenton, also while away the time. All is resolved and the opera ends with a trio and chorus.

503

503 [R851].
Costume Design for Mrs. Ford, Moscow, 1918.
Watercolor.
Signed and dated lower right in Russian: "I. Fedotov 1918."
10⅝ x 8⅝ in., 27 x 22 cm.
Provenance: Alexander Rabinovich, New York, June 13, 1981.
Reproduced in I51, No. 92.

Note: Fedotov designed seven productions for the Theater of the Soviet of Workers' Deputies in Moscow, including *La Bohème* (1917), the *Barber of Seville* (1919), and *Fidelio* (1919), although *Die Lustigen Weiber von Windsor* seems to have been his most successful.[292] Fedotov was not especially experimental as a designer, but, for that reason, his art appealed to the average theater-goer. He was, for example, against Cubism and Constructivism in the theater, as he emphasized in a statement of 1936:

> A design devoid of abstract lines and forms that say nothing will increase the significance of the spectacle and will be more organic for its entire resonance.[293]

290 For information on Terevsat see C144, pp. 26-39.
291 F. Syrkina: Untitled essay in *Vystavka proizvedenii,* op. cit., p. 7.
292 For a review see V. Bebutov: "'Vindzorskie prokaznitsy' Shekspira–Nikolai–Komissarzhevskogo v teatre S.R.D." in *Izvestiia khudprosotdela Moskovskogo Soveta rabochikh, soldatskikh i krestianskikh deputatov,* M, 1918, No. 3-4, May, pp. 12-16.
293 Untitled statement by Fedotov. Quoted in Flora Syrkina in her preface to the catalog *Vystavka proizvedenii,* p. 5.

FÉRAT, Serge (Serge Jastrebzoff; also Sergei Nikolaevich Rudnev, and Sergei Nikolaevich Yastrebtsov)

Born 28 March (9 April), 1881 (sometimes given as 28 May, 1878), Moscow, Russia; died 13 October, 1958, Paris, France.

As a child, visited England, France, Italy, and Germany with his family; lived and studied in Kiev; late 1890s studied law; 1901 went to Paris along with Baroness Hélène d'Oettingen, purportedly his father's mistress; settled permanently in Paris; enrolled at the Académie Julian, studying under Marcel Baschet and William Bouguereau; 1906 onwards contributed to exhibitions, including annually (1914-1928) to the "Salon des Indépendants"; early 1900s frequented the Lapin Agile cabaret and became friends with Henri le Douanier Rousseau; 1910s in touch with Guillaume Apollinaire, Georges Braque, Pablo Picasso, and other modern artists and writers; started to form a collection of Cubist paintings; painted in a Cubist style, often on glass; 1911 onwards known as Serge Férat; 1914 volunteered for military service and worked at the Hôpital du Gouvernement Italien; 1917 onwards designed for theaters, including Apollinaire's *Les Mamelles de Tirésias* (costumes by Irene Lagut) at the Renée Maubel Conservatoire in Paris; interested in the circus, for which he designed sets and costumes; 1918, with d'Oettingen, took over the journal *Les Soirées de Paris* edited by Apollinaire; 1925 contributed to the "Section d'Or"; 1935 one-man exhibition at the Galerie Bonjean, Paris; 1937 designed sets for Pierre-Albert Birot's puppet play *Matoum en Matoumoisie* staged at the "Exposition Universelle"; 1938 one-man exhibition at the Galerie de Beaune, Paris; 1949 contributed designs to Ilia Zdanevich's anthology of *Poésie de mots inconnus;* 1930s-50s continued to paint landscapes and interiors; designed tapestries for the Beauvais manufactory.

Bibliography
J. Cocteau: *Serge Ferat,* Rome: Volori Plastici, 1924.
V. de la Brosse-Ferrand et al.: *Hommage à Serge Férat.* Catalog of auction organized by Art Curial at Hotel Dassault, Paris, 2007, 22 October.
J. Warnod : *Serge Férat, un cubiste russe à Paris,* Paris: de Conti, 2010.
A. Berès: *Serge Férat 1881-1958.* Catalog of exhibition at the Galerie Berès, Paris, 2010.
H34, pp. 581, 582.

504

Ferat was a prominent member of the Paris avant-garde, moving closely with Apollinaire, Braque, Juan Gris, and Picasso, in particular, and supporting the Cubist esthetic in his paintings and designs. One of his most important pictures was *Lacerba*, which, under the name Edouard Férat, he contributed to the 1914 "Salon des Indépendants." Apollinaire noticed Ferat's compositions there, praising them for their "fine colouring that promise major works to come."[294] The reference to the Florentine Futurist magazine *Lacerba* demonstrates another of Ferat's interests, i.e. Italian Futurism; in fact, his picture *Lacerba* was reproduced in the magazine *Lacerba* for 15 July, 1915, and Valori Plastici of Rome published Jean Cocteau's monograph on him in 1924.

Unknown production, *1920*

504 [NIRE].
Design for a Circus Performance, Paris, 1920.
Gouache and ink
Signed lower right: "S. Férat."
6¼ x 8½ in., 16 x 21.5 cm.
Provenance: *Russian Art,* London: Sotheby's, 27 November, 2007, Lot 296 (reproduced).
Reproduced in color in F107, p. 420. Ferat repeated the motifs of *Circus Performance* in a number of concurrent compositions. See, for example, *L'Ecuyère* (1920-21) reproduced in Berès, *Serge Férat 1881-1958,* p. 224.

294 G. Apollinaire in *L'Intransigeant,* Paris, 1914, 2
     March.

FILONOV, Pavel Nikolaevich

Born 27 December, 1882 (8 January, 1883), Moscow, Russia; died 3 December, 1941, Leningrad, Russia.

1897, an orphan, Filonov moved to his married sister's apartment in St. Petersburg; 1897-1901 attended SSEA; 1903-08 attended the private studio of the Academician Lev Dmitriev-Kavkazsky; 1908-10 attended IAA; 1910 expelled from the Academy; 1910-14 close to the Union of Youth, contributing to three of its exhibitions; 1912 traveled for six months in Italy and France; 1913 with Iosif Shkolnik designed Maiakovsky's tragedy *Vladimir Maiakovsky;* 1914 published his first manifesto *Sdelannye kartiny* [Made Paintings]; 1914-15 illustrated Futurist booklets; 1915 published his own poem with illustrations, *Propeven o prorosli mirovoi* [Chant of Universal Flowering]; continued to elaborate his Ideology of Analytical Art and Theory of Madeness; 1916-18 served on the Rumanian front; 1919 contributed to the "1st State Free Exhibition of Works of Art" in Petrograd; 1923 contributed to the "Exhibition of Paintings by Petrograd Artists of All Directions, 1919-1923"; briefly associated with Ginkhuk; published his "Declaration of Universal Flowering" in *Zhizn iskusstva* [Life of Art]; 1925 established the Collective of Masters of Analytical Art (the Filonov School); 1927 supervised the designs for Igor Terentiev's production of Nikolai Gogol's *Inspector General* at the Press House, Leningrad; 1929 supervised the designs for a production of the agit-play *King Gaikin I* at the Vasilievsky Island Metalworkers' Club; 1929-31 one-man exhibition planned at the Russian Museum,

Leningrad, but not opened; 1931-33 supervised the illustrations for the Academia edition of the *Kalevala;* 1932 contributed to the exhibition "Artists of the RSFSR of the Last 15 Years" in Leningrad and then Moscow (1933); 1936 delivered a lecture at the House of the Artist, Leningrad; 1967 first one-man exhibition in Novosibirsk.

Bibliography
V. Anikieva and S. Isakov: *Pavel Filonov.* Catalog of exhibition at the RM, 1930.
J. Křiž: *Pavel Nikolajevič Filonov,* Prague: Nakladatelství československých výtvarných umělců, 1966.
M. Makarenko: *Pervaia personalnaia vystavka. Pavel Filonov 1883-1941.* Catalog of exhibition, at the Picture Gallery of the Siberian Section of the USSR Academy of Sciences, Novosibrisk, 1967.
N. Misler and J. Bowlt: *Pavel Filonov: A Hero and His Fate,* Austin: Silvergirl, 1983.
E. Kovtun: *Pavel Filonov.* Catalog of exhibition at the RM, 1988.
J.-H. Martin et al.: *Pavel Filonov.* Catalog of exhibition at the Centre Georges Pompidou, Paris, 1990.
J. Harten and E. Petrowa: *Pawel Filonow.* Catalog of exhibition at the Kunsthalle, Düsseldorf, 1990.
N. Misler and Dzh. Boult [J. Bowlt]: *Pavel Filonov.* Moscow: Sovetskii khudozhnik, 1990.
N. Misler and J. Bowlt: *Die Physiologie der Malerei. Pawel Filonow in der 20er Jahren / The Physiology of Painting. Pavel Filonov in the 1920s.* Catalog of exhibition at the Galerie Gmurzynska, Cologne, 1992.
N. Misler and J. Bowlt: *Malévitch – Filonov.* Catalog of exhibition at the Galerie Piltzer, Paris, 1992.
B170.
A. Parnis: "Smutian kholsta" in *Tvorchestvo,* M, 1994 (special issue), pp. 4-5.
J. Bowlt: "Pavel Filonov kak khudozhnik barokko" in *Voprosy iskusstvoznaniia,* M, 1995, No. 1-2, pp. 496-504.
B184, pp. 70-74 (English edition).
Yu. Markin: *Pavel Filonov,* M: Izobrazitelnoe iskusstvo, 1995.
B192, pp. 510-16.
E. Kovtun: "Filonov v 1930-e gody" in B207 pp. 392-99.
F94.
L. Tkachenko: *Filonov,* SP: Znak, 2000.
G. Ershov: *Pavel Filonov,* M: Belyi gorod, 2001.
E. Kovtun, intro.: *Pavel Filonov. Dnevniki,* SP: Azbuka, 2000.
E. Petrova: *Pavel Filonov,* SP: Palace Editions, 2001.
N. Misler, I. Menshova, and J. Bowlt: *Pavel Nikolaevich Filonov.* Special issue of *Experiment,* Los Angeles, 2005, No. 11.
Dzh. Boult (J. Bowlt). N. Misler, and A. Sarabianov: *Filonov. Khudozhnik. Issledovatel. Uchitel,* M: Agei Tomesh, 2006 (two volumes).
E. Petrova et al.: *Pavel Filonov: Ochevidets nezrimogo / Pavel Filonov: Seer of the Unknown.* Catalog of exhibition at the RM, 2006.
I. Galeev et al.: *Filonovtsy. From the Masters of Analytical Art to the Post-avant-garde.* Catalog at Art-Divazh, Moscow, 2007.
A. Laks, ed.: *Pavel Filonov. Sbornik statei,* SP: RM, 2007.

L. Pravoverova, comp.: *Pavel Filonov. Realnost i mif,* M: Agraf, 2008.

J. Bowlt and N. Misler: "The Seeing Eye, the Knowing Eye" in M. de Peverelli, M. Grassi, and H.-C. von Imhoff, eds.: *Emil Bosshard, Paintings Conservator (1945-2006). Essays by Friends and Colleagues,* Florence: Centro Di, 2009, pp. 11-28 (Russian translation in Laks, *Pavel Filonov,* pp. 145-53).

M. Sokolov: *Pavel Filonov,* M: Art-Rodnik, 2008.

L. Vostretsova: *Pavel Filonov, Pobeda nad vechnostiu.* Catalog of exhibition at the Museum of Visual Arts, Ekaterinburg, 2009.

I. Pronina: "Puteshestvie avangardista Pavla Filonova v Lione" in L. Iovleva, ed.: *Tretiakovskie chteniia 2010-2011,* M: INIKO, 2012, pp. 167-80.

Filonov was a central member of the Russian avant-garde, although in theory and practice he differed profoundly from the more familiar representatives of the movement. By 1912 he was already a "Cubo-Futurist" and was fully aware of the potential of the new Russian art. He declared: "Make paintings and drawings that are equal to the stone churches of the South-East, the West, and Russia in their superhuman exertion of will."[295]

Like his colleagues, Natalia Goncharova, Mikhail Larionov, and Kazimir Malevich, Filonov was fascinated by primitive art and proceeded to develop an individual, inimitable style that took account of the methods of the Russian icon, the *lubok* (broadsheet), woodcarving, etc. Still, Filonov was careful to emphasize the need to master the craftedness, or "madeness," of the artistic discipline and, for this reason, also supported certain 19th century Russian artists (Ivan Aivazovsky, Vasilii Vereshchagin, etc.) who, according to him, possessed remarkable technical skill. Filonov bade his students make "any work you want with any material, so that the artist and the spectator are affected by its maximum professional and ideological value."[296] Filonov reached this artistic worldview through many avenues — strict academic training, strong interest in Symbolism especially as reflected in the painting and drawing of Mikhail Vrubel, Neo-Primitivism, and, perhaps unexpectedly, clear recognition of the Northern European Renaissance. The parallels between the graphic emphasis of Cranach, Dürer, and Filonov, or between the allegorical concerns of Bosch and Filonov are particularly worthy of comment.

Filonov did not romanticize or idealize, but, instead, depicted the cold and bitter world of the northern hemisphere in accordance with a tradition that tended to focus on the cruelty and ugliness of everyday life rather than to titillate and entertain. No doubt, Filonov saw Cranach's studies of wild boars before painting his own *Wild Boar* of 1912-13 (RM) and there is a striking compositional parallel between Grünewald's *Three Heads: Anti-Trinity* (1523-24, Kupferstichkabinett, Berlin) and Filonov's portrait of his sister (1923-24, RM). As far as Bosch and Breugel are concerned, Filonov's was attracted to them by their fantasy and allegory, their preoccupation with eschatological symbols, their common sense of imminent, universal transformation, and their vivid evocations of heaven and hell.

As his major oils demonstrate, Filonov drew on a private, hermetic conglomeration of symbols, whereas Bosch at least was operating with a more accessible lexicon of alchemical, astrological, and folkloristic terms. But in both cases, the organization or, rather, disorganization of discrete images creates a gigantic acrostic whose ganglia have almost disguised the organic core of the painting. For Filonov's students such imagery held a diabolical attraction.

Vladimir Maiakovsky. A Tragedy: *play in verse in two acts with prologue and epilogue by Vladimir Maiakovsky. Directed by Vladimir Maiakovsky and produced by the Union of Youth at the Luna Park Theater, St. Petersburg on 2 December, 1913, with designs by Pavel FIlonov and Iosif Shkolnik.*

Various strange characters, fragments of Maiakovsky's persona, recount the tragedy of the poet's anguish in the City-Hell which cripples and dismembers its inhabitants. The poet is surrounded by grotesque individuals such as a man without an ear, a man without a head, and a man with black cats, who misunderstand him, mimic him, and reject him.

Filonov as contributor:
505 [NIRE].
Program, 1913.
Printed paper.
Inscriptions provide information on the production (see below)
8¾ x 6 in., 22 x 15.7 cm.
Cf. 891 [R758].

> Full text of the program:
> ASSOCIATION OF PAINTERS "UNION OF YOUTH"
> WORLD PREMIERS OF FUTURISTS OF THE THEATER
> LUNA-PARK THEATER
> (former Kommissarzhevskaia Theater, 39 Ofitserskaia Street)
> PROGRAM
> Monday, 2 and Wednesday, 4 December
>
> ───────────
>
> VLADIMIR MAIAKOVSKY
> Tragedy in 2 acts with a prologue and epilogue by Vladimir Maiakovsky
> Cast of characters
>
> Vladimir Vladimirovich Maiakovsky, a poet, aged 20 to 25
> His woman friend, standing 4 to 6 meters tall, doesn't speak
> An old man with black dry cats, a couple of thousand years old
> A man missing an ear
> A man with a stretched forehead
> A man missing a head
> A man missing an eye and a leg
> A man with two kisses
> Women with tear drops, tear pearls and tear pools
> An ordinary young man
> A girl, a boy, newspaper vendors et al.
>
> Prolog:
> Act I: In major key. City.
> Act II: In minor key. City.
>
> Directed by Vladimir Maiakovsky.
> Stage sets for the prologue and epilogue: P.N. Filonov
> Stage sets for Acts I and II: I. Shkolnik
> Costume designed by P.N. Filonov
> Starts at 9 pm. Ends no later than 11 pm.
> Safekeeping of coats at 10 kopeks per person.
>
> ───────────
>
> Permit for printing issued on 28 November 1913, No. 6922, by the Deputy Mayor of St. Petersburg, Chamberlain Mr. Lysogorsky. At the Imperial Theaters Printers.

Note: *Vladimir Maiakovsky* was the first of two spectacles presented by the Union of Youth as part of the repertoire of the newly established Theater of the Futurists, at first known as the Budetlianin Theater, the other spectacle being *Victory over the Sun* designed by Kazimir Malevich (see Nos. 770-84 [R648-62]). The sets for the prologue and epilogue were painted by Filonov and for Acts I and II by Shkolnik, a fellow member of the Union of Youth. Unfortunately, Filonov's designs were destroyed during a flood in Leningrad in 1924, but it is known that he also created most of the costumes. Mark Etkind described the visual arrangement of *Vladimir Maiakovsky* as follows:

> The scenographic composition of the spectacle bore a circular character: the action was framed by a square panneau which served as a pictorial headpiece for the prologue and as a tailpiece for the epilogue: a lubok-like, cheerful pile of painted toys and in the middle a "big, beautiful rooster."[297]

The most comprehensive description of *Vladimir Maiakovsky* belongs to the actor Alexander Mgebrov, who attended the premiere and, as a matter of fact, sat next to the poet Velimir Khlebnikov.

> The lights went down and up went the curtain… A half-mystical light palely illuminates the stage enclosed in cloth or calico and the tall backdrop made of black cardboard — which, essentially constitutes the entire decoration. What this cardboard was meant to represent, I don't know… but the strange thing is that it was impressive: there was a lot of blood and movement in it.[298]

Collective of Masters of Analytical Art *(also known as the School of Filonov)*

In June, 1925, Filonov was given space in the Academy of Arts, Leningrad, in order to conduct courses with a group of students, which as he recorded, gave rise to the

Collective of Masters of Analytical Art. It was among these *filonovtsy,* or *filonidy,* who included Tatiana Glebova, Boris Gurvich, Pavel Kondratiev, Alisa Poret, Andrei Sashin, and Mikhail Tsibasov that Filonov disseminated the principles of his theory of Analytical Art. Although by 1927 the Collective, or School, numbered over forty, it was never a really cohesive group and, in 1930, divided into two factions. The smaller faction remained loyal to Filonov; the other quickly disbanded and some of its members, e.g., Evgenii Kibrik, assumed a private and public position hostile to Filonov.

Although the Collective of Masters of Analytical Art is often referred to as a school, it would be misleading to regard it as a system or program of regular classes, coursework, and homework. As one pupil recalled later, the sessions with Filonov "bore the character of consultations. Pavel Nikolaevich would make brief remarks, sometimes they would be abrupt. No one ever objected."[299] Filonov addressed his

students as comrades and, while quite aware of his own artistic supremacy, maintained that anyone could learn to be an artist if the principles of Analytical Art (madeness) were followed and applied.

The Collective embarked upon several joint ventures, including exhibitions, stage productions (such as the 1927 *Inspector General*), and the 1933 illustrated edition of the *Kalevala* (L: Academia). The Collective was ousted from the Academy in 1927 and five years later ceased to exist officially with the passing of the Party Decree *On the Reconstruction of Literary and Artistic Organizations.*[300]

The Inspector General: *satire in five acts by Nikolai Gogol. Produced by Igor Terentiev at the Press House, Leningrad, on 9 April, 1927, with music by Vladimir Kashnitsky and designs by the Collective of Masters of Analytical Art supervised by Pavel Filonov.*

The elders of a provincial town, led by the governor, hear that an inspector general

from St Petersburg is coming to examine their various institutions. In a case of mistaken identity, they assume that the young fop Khlestakov, a visitor to their town, is the inspector general, and they proceed to deceive, flatter, and bribe him in order to conceal the state of civic affairs. Khlestakov is delighted at this unexpected attention and goes on his way greatly contented with their bounty. But, to the horror of the elders, the real inspector general suddenly arrives, culminating in the famous "mute" scene as the curtain descends.

506

506 [R853].
School of Filonov: Poster for **The Inspector General, 1927.**
Lithograph in red, black, and white.
29⅜ x 22 in., 74.5 x 56 cm.
The center tabloid contains the details of the production in Russian: "Theater of the Press House. Inspector General by Gogol. Artists: Masters of Analytical Art from the School of Filonov. Composer: Vladimir Kashnitsky. Producer: Igor Terentiev. Leningrad, April, 1927." The lower margin carries the publication details: "Published by the Press House. Leningrad Literary District No. 3460. Leningrad. Edition of 5000 copies. Order No. 877 at the Evgenii Sokolov Workers' Press, 29 Red Commanders' Prospect."
The poster has been reproduced several times, e.g., in V. Liakhov: *Sovetskii reklamnyi plakat 1917-1932,* M: Sovetskii khudozhnik, 1972, No. 100; Misler and Bowlt, op. cit., p. 71; E38, No. 22; I60, p. 39.

Note: The poster shows costumes used in the Prologue to the Terentiev production of *The Inspector General,* i.e., these costumes were not used in the comedy itself (cf. Nos. 507-09 [R854-56] for versions of the original watercolors). Although the poster was a collective endeavor and the individual designers did not sign their names, it is possible to identify the following sections (Nos. 506a-506d [R853a-R853g]):

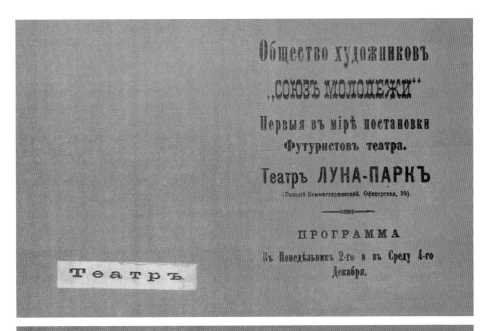

505

506a

506c

507

Nos. 507-09 [R854-56] are preparatory designs for the final versions of the costumes. All the items bear various rubber stamps, including one with the stamp of the Ministry of the Interior. This is because shortly after the production of *The Inspector General,* the designs by Filonov's pupils were confiscated by the police. All three of the designs below may be by Andrei Sashin, although they may have been composed later, if not by Sashin, then by another hand. In fact, these three items replicate, in smaller format, the designs for the same costumes in the State Russian Museum in St. Petersburg (reproduced, for example, in K145, Nos. 319-320). One discrepancy is that the imprints of various official stamps from the period of the Civil War shown on top of the paint layer must predate 1927.

506a [R853a].
***Costume Design for Stepan Ukhovertov, a Warden* by Andrei Timofeevich Sashin (1896-1965).**
The original watercolor of this design, now in the RM, is reproduced in color in K62, No. 50; B89, plate 320; and B90, p. 107. See No. 507 [R854] for a version of the watercolor.

506b [R853b].
***Costume Design for a Priest* by Rebekka Mikhailovna Leviton (1906-87).**
This was a supplementary character since Gogol's original cast does not contain such a figure. See I73, pp. 214-15 for other designs by Leviton.

506b

506d

506c [R853v].
***Costume Design for a Merchant* by Artur Mechislavovich Liandsberg (1905-1963).**
See I73, pp. 215-16 for other designs by Liandsberg.

506d [R853g].
***Costume Design for a Policeman* by Nikolai Ivanovich Evgrafov (1904-1941).**
The original watercolor is reproduced in K90, fig. 67. See I73, pp. 216 for another design by Evgrafov.

507 [R854].
***Costume Design for Stepan Ukhovertov, a Warden,* 1927.**
Watercolor, pencil, and black ink.
9 x 8 in., 23 x 20 cm.
Rubber-stamped upper right in Russian: "Ministry of Supplies, Northeastern Province of Russia." The reverse carries another sketch (see No. 508 [R855]).
The final version (see 506a [R853a]) incorporates the pencil head on the right of this figure into the figure itself, while the head here depicted on the police-officer's coat is raised towards the padlock. Also see 508 [R855].
Reproduced in color in B115, plate 149; M81; and in black and white in A34, p. 374; I77, p. 127.

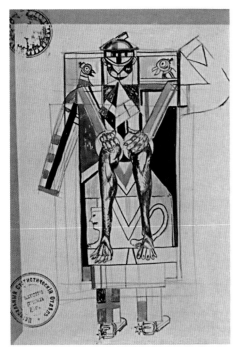

508

508 [241; R855].
Reverse of the Costume of Stepan Ukhovertov, a Warden, 1927.
Watercolor, black, and pencil.
8¾ x 5¾ in., 22.5 x 15 cm.
This sketch is on the reverse of No. 507 [R854].
Rubber-stamped left side with two imprints from the Central Statistical Department of the Ministry of the Interior.
Reproduced in color in B115, plate 150; and in black and white in I77, pp. 108, 127. The final design of this preparatory work is reproduced to the right of the main figure in C89, p. 253, upper left hand corner.

509 [R856].
Costume Design for a Tavern Waiter, 1927.
Watercolor, black ink, and pencil.
8½ x 7 in., 22 x 17.5 cm.
Rubber-stamped lower right in Russian: "Commander [illegible]."
Reproduced in color in B115, plate 151; I77, p. 73; and in black and white in I77, p. 127; M93. The final version is reproduced in color in B89, plate 319; also see C89, p. 253, lower right.

Note: Early in 1927 the Futurist poet, theorist, and painter Igor Terentiev was commissioned by Nikolai Baskakov, director of the Press House, Leningrad, to stage a production of *The Inspector General.* Terentiev accepted the offer and invited Filonov to supervise the sets and costumes, the implementation of which was entrusted to the Collective of Masters of Analytical Art. Terentiev himself had already worked as a producer in Leningrad and Tiflis (Tbilisi) and had just founded a new theater laboratory at the Press House.[301] Terentiev and Filonov immediately found a common language evident not only from their respective approaches to Gogol's play, but also in the ways they both dismissed conservative art. But although this commission was a prestigious one, the interpretation so provoked the resentment of both

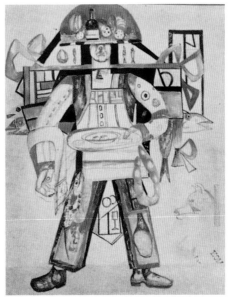

509

the public and the press that both men and their coworkers became the targets of exceptionally strong censure and abuse.

After several delays, the premiere of *The Inspector General* took place in the remodeled Press House Theater on 9 April, 1927. The august premises (the Press House occupied what had been the Shuvalov mansion) were also decorated by a "sculpture-cum-bas-relief"[302] and "nightmarish paintings of a madman's hallucinations"[303] by Filonov's pupils — what is traditionally called the "Exhibition of Masters of Analytical Art." The actual sets and costumes for the production designed by Filonov's disciples (including Nikolai Evgrafov, Glebova, Artur Liandsberg, Poret, and Sashin)[304] were sharply criticized for their "irreverence" to Gogol:

> The red, green and blue costumes for the performance, done by the "masters of the Filonov school", above all, confuse the viewer. Apparently, Filonov's scenic exercises, these multicolored costumes are meant to take *The Inspector General* out of its historical framework… but these costumes are simply a caprice, altogether dilettantish, spurious, provincial and absurd.[305]

Furthermore, the designs, which, incidentally, were contributed collectively and without individual signatures, were linked to what were considered salacious antics in Terentiev's interpretation:

> In these multi-colored, painted, Chinese-cum-Parisian costumes which reduce decadent esthetism in the theater to self-sufficient snobbism, the actor performs a series of very indecent numbers… [The producer] makes the governor sit in a WC, the governor's wife go around in her pantaloons and another guy go about with a night potty… To the strains of Beethoven's *Moonlight Sonata* Khlestakov takes his candle and goes

into the toilet depicted in the form of a tall, black box looking like a telephone booth. And that's where Khlestakov perches himself with Mariia Antonovna.[306]

In spite of the negative reception of Terentiev's production of *The Inspector General* and the Filonov contribution, Filonov and his Collective were commissioned to decorate a second stage production in April, 1929. This was the play *King Gaikin I* (also-called *Activist Gaikin*), an agit-presentation where, as Filonov implied in a lecture at one of the performances, "essentially, the decoration of the spectacle was nothing less than an agitational, traveling exhibition for the *filonovtsy.*"[307] It was staged for the Vasilievsky Island Metalworkers' Club in Leningrad and, evidently, was not as experimental as *The Inspector General.*[308] In his autobiography, Filonov mentions a fourth theatrical involvement in the 1920s, for a play called *Lenka's Canary,* but information on this piece is not available.

510

510 [R857].
Alisa Poret: *Poor People. Panel Section for The Press House, 1927.*
Pencil.
8¾ x 4⅞ in., 22.3 x 12.5 cm.
Inscribed on the reverse in Russian by Poret: "First sketch for the decoration in the Press House, Leningrad, Lumpen proletariat, 1926 [=1927]. On the advice of P.N. Filonov I transferred the large head to the top."
Reproduced in I60, p. 41. See final version, an oil on canvas, illustrated as Lot 83 in L3. A similar panel, attributed to Pavel Kondratiev, is illustrated in L48.

Note: Poor People by Alisa Ivanovna Poret (1902-84), one of Filonov's primary students,[309] was part of a large oil panel that she and her colleague, Tatiana Nikolaevna Glebova (1900-85),[310] designed for the Press House in 1927. Glebova recalled that they "used the same canvas divided into two (Poret on the subject of *Poor People*, Glebova on the subject of *Prison*)."[311] The occasion for this undertaking was the production of *Inspector General* at the Press House, during which time Filonov and his Collective also organized their "Exhibition of Masters of Analytical Art." Filonov did not participate in the show, although he gave a public lecture there and used the events to promote his views on what he perceived to be the impasse that modern art had entered and how art could escape. In his lecture Filonov did not mention the actual pieces on show (ca. 20 paintings, some stage designs, and one sculpture) or the artists (ca. 31), but divided his report into fifteen theses that he had already advanced on several previous occasions. In his typically brusque manner, he concluded that "along the entire front art is dying" — except for his own system, of course.[312]

Among the other artists represented at the Press House (apart from Poret and Glebova), were Alevtina Mordvinova on the subject of *The Hanged Man*, Yurii Khrzhanovsky on the subject of *Soldiers of the Red Army*, Vsevolod Sulimo-Samuillo on the subject of heads, Saul Rabinovich and Innokentii Suvorov with their sculpture of a worker throwing a member of the bourgeoisie over his shoulder, etc. The general response to these works was not especially positive, as contemporary reviews demonstrate:

> The splendid hall in the style of Louis XVI [the Press House] gained nothing from the spaces between columns being completely covered in canvases by the Filonov followers.[313]

It is tempting to interpret *Poor People* as a commentary on the predicament of Filonov and his pupils, i.e., their uneasy position vis-à-vis the cultural establishment in Leningrad at this time. However, while they were certainly criticized, they were not yet ostracized — until the arrests of individual members began in the early 1930s.

295 P. Filonov, D. Kakabadze, A. Kirillova, E. Lasson-Spirova: *Sdelannye kartiny*, SP, 1914. English translation in Misler and Bowlt, *Pavel Filonov*, p. 135.

296 Letter from Pavel Filonov to Vera Sholpo, 1929. Quoted in Misler and Bowlt, *Pavel Filonov*, p. 26.

297 M. Etkind: "'Soiuz molodezhi' i ego stsenograficheskie eksperimenty" in *Sovetskie khudozhniki teatra i kino ' 78*, M, 1981, No. 3, p. 157.

298 A. Mgebrov: *Vospominaniia* (1932). Quoted in V. Katanian: *Maiakovsky. Literaturnaia khronika*, M: Gosudarstvennoe izdatelstvo khudozhestvennoi literatury, 1961, p. 53, 54.

299 O. Pokrovsky:"Trevogoi i plamenem", undated manuscript, private collection, p. 14.

300 For more information on the Collective of Masters of Analytical Art see Misler and Bowlt, *Pavel Filonov*, passim.

301 For information on Terentiev see T. Nikolskaia: "Igor Terentiev v Tiflise" in L. Magarotto, M. Marzaduri, G. Pagani Cesa, eds.: *L'Avanguardia a Tiflis*. Venice: Università degli studi di Venezia, 1982, pp. 189-209; also S. Kudriavtsev, ed.: *Terentievskii sbornik*, M: Gileia, 1996 (No. 1) and 1998 (No. 2).

302 Untitled note in the newspaper *Smena*, L, 1927, 6 April, p. 3.

303 "Shkola Filonova" in *Krasnaia gazeta* (Evening Issue), L, 1927, 5 May, p. 5.

304 Filonov compiled a list of his students who worked at the Press House. See Misler and Bowlt, *Pavel Filonov*, p. 34.

305 Piotrovsky: "'Revizor' v teatre Doma pechati" in *Krasnaia gazeta* (evening issue), 1927, 11 April, p. 4.

306 M. Zagorsky and A. Gvozdev: "'Revizor' na Udelnoi" in *Zhizn iskusstva*, L, 1927, 19 April, p. 5.

307 V. Gross: "Filonov v teatre" in *Krasnaya gazeta* (evening issue), 1929, 29 April, p. 13.

308 For further information on *King Gaikin I* see Misler and Bowlt, *Pavel Filonov*, p. 38; and "Filonov v teatre" in *Krasnaia gazeta* (evening issue), 1929, 29 April, p. 13.

309 Nothing substantial has been published on Poret. Her own memoirs are of interest. See A. Poret: "Vospominaniia o Daniile Kharmse" in *Panorama iskusstv*, M, 1980, No. 3, pp. 345-59.

310 For information on Glebova see the catalogs of her exhibitions, *Tatiana Glebova*, L: Union of Artists of the RSFSR, 1981 (with essays by Glebova and Evgenii Kovtun), and *V.V. Sterligov, T.N. Glebova*, L: RM, 1995 (two volumes, with introduction by Evgenii Kovtun). Also see *Experiment*, Los Angeles, 2010, No. 16 (devoted to Tatiana Glebova and Vladimir Sterligov). For a color reproduction and discussion of Glebova's contribution, i.e., *Prison* (now in the Museo Thyssen-Bornemisza, Madrid), see B154, p. 117.

311 T. Glebova: "Souvenirs sur Filonov" in *Cahiers du Musée national d'art moderne*, Paris, 1985, No. 1, p. 119. For contextual discussion and relevant illustrations see Bowlt and Misler, "The Seeing Eye, the Knowing Eye."

312 P. Filonov: "*Vystuplenie Fil*onova na dispute v Dome pechati," undated manuscript, private collection, p. 9.

313 "Shkola Filonova", op. cit. According to eye witnesses (the sculptor Saul Rabinovich and the movie director Leonid Trauberg), the decorated hall blended with the dramatic production itself, the more so since the actors, wearing their dazzling costumes, sometimes walked out into the auditorium (conversations between John E. Bowlt, Nicoletta Misler, and Saul Rabinovich, M, March and June, 1986; and between John E. Bowlt, Nicoletta Misler, and Lev Trauberg, M, March, 1986). This must have functioned especially well in the case of the costume for Stepan Ukhovertov which Sashin designed as a sandwich board (see No. 507 and 508 [R854, 855]).

FOREGGER (von Greifenturn), Nikolai Mikhailovich

Born 6 (18) May, 1892, Moscow, Russia; died 8 June, 1939, Kuibyshev, Russia.

1914 contributed to the Kiev journal *Muzy* [Muses]; 1918 organized own private theater in Moscow called the Theater of the Four Masks concentratinbg on Medieval French farces; 1919 onwards cultivated a particular interest in the circus; gave a lecture on the subject at the International Union of Circus Artists in Moscow; 1919-20 with Sergei Eisenstein, Mikhail Chekhov, et al. taught at the First Working Theater of Proletkult; with Alexander Tairov, Georgii Yakulov, et al. coorganized the First State School of Theatrical Art and the First State Theater for Children in Moscow; 1920-24

directed his studio called Mastfor (Foregger's workshop) in Moscow where he organized Constructivist and Eccentrist spectacles and acrobatic dances, including *Good Treatment of Horses* and *Dances of the Machines* (1923); close to, and influenced by, Vsevolod Meierkhold; 1924-26 produced a number of ballets, including *Constructive Gopak* and *Dance of the Budennyi Cavalry;* 1929-34 worked at the Kharkov Theater of Opera and Ballet, producing *Polovtsian Dances, Footballers*, etc.; 1934-36 worked at the Shevchenko Theater, Kiev; 1938-39 director and artist-in-residence at the Kuibyshev Theater of Opera and Ballet.

Bibliography

N. Sheremetievskaia: "Nikolai Foregger — postanovshchik tantsev" in *Teatr*, M, 1972, No. 5, pp. 134-42.

M. Gordon: "Foregger and the Dance of Machines" in *Drama Review*, New York, 1975, March pp. 68-73.

N. Foregger: "Experiments in the Art of the Dance", ibid., pp. 74-77.

D28, passim.

A20, p. 550.

A. Chepalov: "Nikolai Foregger and the Dance of Revolution" in B183, Vol. 2, pp. 359-70.

I104.

I107.

A. Chepalov: *Sudba peresmeshnika, ili novye stranstviia Frakassa*, Kharkov: AVEK, 2001.

E. Faccioli: *Nikolaj Michajlovič Foregger (1892-1939). Dal simbolismo al realismo socialista*, Rome: Bulzoni, 2007.

D116.

Foregger's vocabulary and iconography owed much to the time and motion studies conducted by Alexei Gastev at the Central Institute of Labor in Moscow (TsIT) in 1921 onwards, especially to the notion of the mechanical or machine dance. Gastev's call for a reaction against "frozen contemporary intellectual culture" and his emphasis on the need to "move your own body" could well have been voiced by Foregger.[314] However, it would be misleading to assume that Foregger was merely extending and "estheticizing" the TsIT program or using his repertoire as a didactic illustration of Gastev's ideas. Political propagation was alien to Foregger (one reason why Mastfor was shortlived) and, ultimately, his real desire was to restore "fun" to the theatrical performance and reinvest it with the condition of the circus. As he asserted in his article on avant-garde theater and the music-hall, it was often the lighter genres such as the circus that popularized the salient ingredients of avant-garde performance:

> The circus has shown the actor the significance of the body as a flexible, obedient, and expressive instrument and has taught him how to deal with material; the music-hall will teach him how to create, how to grapple with the work on hand and the properties of the images of contemporary theater.[315]

Inasmuch as parody and satire constituted a major part of the Mastfor curriculum, it was logical that the clown and slapstick comedy would have attracted Foregger and his immediate colleagues, Eisenstein, Vladimir Mass, and Sergei Yutkevich. Of course, they were not alone in their enthusiasm for the circus and for the restoration of its respective skills of the clown, the acrobat, the juggler, etc. After all, Meierkhold looked to the circus for theatrical inspiration, while David Burliuk, Vasilii Kamensky, Vasilii Kandinsky, Vladimir Maiakovsky, Alexander Osmerkin, and many other poets and painters of the avant-garde emulated clowns, counted Anatolii Durov and Vitalii Lazarenko among their closest friends, and also worked in circuses (see Nos. 110-17 [R327-33]; 457 [R1004]). Even Foregger's antagonists, Kasian Goleizovsky and Lev Lukin, found a model for their eccentric dances in the "eccentrism" of the circus. True, the most aggressive of the Constructivist theorists, Alexei Gan, did not share this enthusiasm for the modern circus, arguing that the individual acts of the clowns, jugglers, and horse-riders demonstrated dexterity, but they were disparate and lacked a synthesizing ideology or organizing principle[316] — a "formlessness" (besformennost) which, however, Foregger regarded as a positive quality.[317]

Although it is now difficult to understand, let alone reconstruct, the actual role and distribution of machine dances within such spectacles, we can assume that Foregger used his repertoire to "despise the logic of the word and sweep away the psychologism of content"; in their place Foregger — this "heir to the Medieval charlatans" — introduced the "subjectless theater, born of the tempo and rhythm of the action."[318] That is why Foregger took the machine as a departure point, i.e., he identified a perfect expediency, efficacy, and economy in the movement of a piston or a gear-wheel, qualities that he also identified potentially with the human body; that is also why Foregger used music simply as a metronomic, not a mellifluous, accompaniment to his machine dances.[319]

Unknown production, *1920s.*

511 [NIRE].
Costume Design for a Clown Wearing Spectacles, ca. 1925.
Watercolor and colored pencil.
14 x 9⅞ in., 35.5 x 25 cm.
Provenance: Issar Gourvitch, Paris, June, 1974.

Note. Painter, art critic, designer, and balletmaster, Foregger, like Goleizovsky, was one of the most dynamic practitioners of Constructivism in ballet in the early 1920s.[320] He was, as Meierkhold once said, among the few "healthy individuals"[321] in the performing arts of that time and used many theatrical media — the music-hall, the circus, the mystery play, and the balagan —

511

to energize the drama and the dance as with this costume for a clown. As the critic and historian Pavel Markov mentioned in 1924:

> [Foregger] builds the play of the actors as combinations of... unexpected devices. He brings the text of what is being played close to contemporaneity. He regards movement and dance from the standpoint of the modern street. He uses a noise orchestra in his production, he creates dances that communicate the work of the machine, his actors perform comic roles with devices taken from clowning and the circus.[322]

314 A. Gastev: *Kak nado rabotat,* M: VTsSPS, 1924, pp. 13 and 72.
315 N. Foregger: "Avangardnoe iskusstvo i miuzik-kholl" in *Ermitazh,* M, 1922, No. 6, pp. 5-6.
316 A. Gan: "Ravnenie na tsirk," ibid., No. 9, p. 8.
317 P. Aleksandrov: "Foregger i Mass," ibid., No. 5, p. 6.
318 Ibid.
319 Frank (=Vladimir Liutse-Fedorov): "Mekhani-cheskie tantsy Mastfora" in *Zrelishcha,* M, 1923, No. 26, pp. 16-17.
320 For some of the ideas on dance and drama that Foregger expressed and practised while directing Mastfor see C31 (1975), pp. 358-59; also Foregger, "Experiments in the Art of the Dance", op. cit.
321 C32, p. 50.
322 Quoted in C31 (1968), p. 159.

Naum Gabo, ca.1950.

GABO, Naum (pseudonym of Pevzner, Naum [Neemia] Berkovich)[323]

Born 5 (17) August, 1890, Briansk, Russia; died 23 August, 1977, Waterbury, Connecticut, USA.

1910 graduated from Kursk High School; entered medical school at Munich University; attended Heinrich Wölfflin's lectures; transferred to the Polytechnic Engineering School in Munich; 1913 visited Italy, studying the collections of the Old Masters in Venice, Milan, Bologna, and other cities; 1913-14 visited Paris, where his brother Antoine Pevsner was studying; contact with the Cubists; 1914 visited Scandinavia; 1915 made his first wood and metal constructions in Norway; 1917 returned to Russia; 1920 compiled and published the *Realist Manifesto* (cosigned by Antoine Pevsner) in conjuction with the Moscow exhibition of works by Gabo, Pevsner, and Gustav Klutsis; 1919-22 designed a number of esthetic and utilitarian objects, some kinetic, such as a project for a radio station and a monument for a physics laboratory; 1922 emigrated to Berlin; took part in the "Erste Russische Kunstausstellung"; contact with the Novembergruppe; 1920s contact with Mies van der Rohe, Vasilii Kandinsky, Paul Klee, Walter Gropius, and other leading modern artists and architects; 1924 with Pevsner exhibited at the Galerie Percier, Paris; 1926 contributed to the De Stijl group show at the Little Review Gallery, New York; 1927 with Pevsner designed sets and costumes for Sergei Diaghilev's production of *La Chatte* in Monte Carlo, Paris, and London; 1932 settled in Paris; took a leading part in the Abstraction-Création group; 1936 moved to England; 1946 moved to the US; 1962 visited Soviet Russia; 1971 knighted for his services to art by Queen Elizabeth II.

Bibliography
R. Olson and A. Chanin: *Gabo – Pevsner.* Catalog of exhibition at the Museum of Modern Art, New York, 1948.
H. Read and L. Martin: *Gabo,* London: Lund Humphries, 1957.
N. Gabo: *Of Divers Arts,* New York: Pantheon, 1962.
A. Pevsner: *Naum Gabo and Antoine Pevsner,* Amsterdam: Augustin and Schoonman, 1964.
Gabo. Catalog of exhibition at the Tate Gallery, London, 1977.
S. Nash and J. Merkert: *Gabo.* Catalog of exhibition at the Dallas Museum of Fine Arts, the Tate Gallery, London, and other institutions, 1985-86.
J. Merkert: *Naum Gabo. Ein russische Konstruktivist in Berlin 1922-1932.* Catalog of exhibition at the Berlinische Galerie and elsewhere, 1989.
J. Merkert et al.: *Naum Gabo und der Wettbewerb zum Palast der Sowjets, Moskau 1931-1933.* Catalog of exhibition at the Berlinishche Galerie, Berlin, and the IVAM, Valencia, 1993.
M. Belodubrovsky, comp.: *Russkii avangard i Brianshchina,* Briansk: BGPU, 1998.

Naum Gabo. Catalog of exhibition at Annely Juda Fine Art, London, 1999.

C. Lodder and M. Hammer: *Gabo on Gabo,* Forest Row, East Sussex, UK: Artists' Bookworks, 2000.

C. Lodder and M. Hammer: *Constructing Modernity. The Art and Career of Naum Gabo,* New Haven: Yale University Press, 2000.

Alexander Rodchenko – Naum Gabo: Spatial Constructions. Catalog of exhibition at the Galerie Gmurzynska, Cologne, 2001.

M. Harrison: *Gabo and Colour.* Catalog of exhibition at Annely Juda Fine Art, London, 2004.

N. Sidlina: *N. Gabo,* M: Gordeev, 2011.

While often regarded as a primary contributor to the establishment of Russian Contructivism, Gabo was an artist indebted more to Western European than to Russian influences and, contrary to common opinion, was not closely associated with the Russian avant-garde. The *Realist Manifesto* that he cosigned and published with his brother in Moscow in 1920, with its affirmation of "depth as the only pictorial and plastic form of space,"[324] may have coincided with the radical rejection of painting in favor of construction that Rodchenko and Tatlin were advocating, but, as Nikolai Khardzhiev emphasizes, at that time Gabo was an "unknown debutant."[325]

This is not to detract from Gabo's status as a major contributor to 20th century sculpture in the West. Like Kandinsky and El Lissitzky, Gabo was an artist of international experience who assimilated the most disparate infuences (medicine, engineering, Cubism, the Symbolism of Mikhail Vrubel, the theories of Wölfflin) and tailored them to suit the precise contours of his artistic vision, whether a kinetic sculpture, a costume design for *La Chatte* or a monument in Rotterdam. Moreover, Gabo remained loyal to his conviction that the new art should be formal and abstract, unsullied by local ethnic, ideological or anecdotal bias. As he once told Herbert Read: "Artists cannot go on forever painting the view from their window and pretending that this is all there is in the world, because it is not."[326]

La Chatte: *ballet in one act by Sobeka (a composite pseudonym where S=Sauguet, B=Balanchine, K=Kochno) based on a fable by Aesop reworked by Boris Kochno with music by Henri Sauguet. Produced by Sergei Diaghilev's Ballets Russes at Monte Carlo on 30 April, 1927, with choreography by George Balanchine and designs by Naum Gabo and Antoine Pevsner. The production was then given in Paris on 27 May, 1927, at the Théâtre Sarah-Bernhardt.*

A young man, in love with a cat, beseeches Venus to change her into a woman. Although granting his wish, Venus also causes a mouse to enter the scene. The woman chases the mouse and is transformed back into the cat. As a result, the young man dies of a broken heart.

512

512 [R394].
Costume Design for the Woman (Cat), ca. 1927.
Pencil on graph paper.
Signed lower right in Russian: "Gabo."
10¾ x 8¾ in., 27.3 x 22.2 cm.
Other inscription: stamped upper left with the identifying mark of the Serge Lifar collection.
Provenance: *Ballet Material and Manuscripts from the Serge Lifar Collection,* New York: Sotheby's, 9 May, 1984, Lot 54 (reproduced).
Reproduced in color in J43, Lot 54; and in black and white in I77, p. 132. Two other costume designs, formerly in the Lifar collection and now in the Wadsworth Atheneum, are reproduced in I11, pp. 46, 47; duplicates of these minus the Gabo annotations, in the Library of the Grand Opéra, Paris, are reproduced in K50 (b), unnumbered; another costume, also from the Lifar collection, is reproduced in J43, Lot 53; also see G52, p. 41; I61, p. 249; other relevant designs are reproduced in Nash and Merkert, *Gabo,* pp. 173-74. Photographs of the actual sets and costumes have often been reproduced — e.g., in G43, No. 15. For Eileen Mayo's rendering of the set see I31, p. 70.

Note: The preparation for, and production of, *La Chatte* was one of the rare occasions when the two artist brothers Gabo and Pevsner (No. 823 [R689]) applied their abstract principles of Constructivism to a utilitarian context, and the result was astonishing. Somewhat in the manner of the designs by Alexandra Exter, Sergei Kozlovsky, Vera Mukhina, Isaak Rabinovich, and Viktor Simov for *Aelita* of 1924 (see Nos. 465-69 [R976-78]) and of Lissitzky's designs for his exhibition rooms of 1926 and 1927-28, Gabo and Pevsner used light, not color, as a main artistic force. By constructing transparent and refractive surfaces from mica, celluloid, black oilcloth, etc., they created a mobile and variable décor that reflected and magnified the movements of the dancers.

In turn, the bizarre plot of the ballet was expressed by the eccentric décor, consisting of abstract geometric shapes distributed throughout the scenic space and looking like "radio or gymnastic apparatus."[327] In other words, just as the plot was based on the physical displacement of one creature by another, so the objects that related to this transubstantiation were just as displaced and, with the exception of Pevsner's statue of Venus, resembling his concurrent celluloid torsos (e.g., *The Dancer* of 1927-29 at the Yale University Art Gallery), were deprived of figurative value. Moreover, the circular stage itself revolved, therefore changing its appearance, while the statue acted as a gravitational center of the entire kinetic structure:

> Omnipotent as the symbol of a classical goddess, the vacuum mannequin towered over the real bodies of her dancer subjects, who complemented her rigidity with violent gymnastic dance.[328]

Alicia Nikitina, who danced the Cat-Woman in the Paris production, replacing Olga Spessivtseva, the Monte Carlo Cat-Woman, recalled:

> After only a couple of hours' rehearsal, I danced *La Chatte* with Serge Lifar. Our schematic movements were matched perfectly by the reflective constructions and costumes of Gabo.[329]

La Chatte was one of several "industrial" spectacles inside and outside Russia that relied for their scenic effect on modern hi-tech materials and streamlined actions.[330] Meierkhold's first Constructivist presentations such as *The Magnanimous Cuckold* of 1922 and *The Death of Tarelkin* of 1923 (Nos. 974-80 [R800-06]); Bronislava Nijinska's *Le Train Bleu* (1924), and Leonid Massine's *Le Pas d'Acier* of 1927 (Nos. 1165-67 [R1020-22] which was in the same Paris season as *La Chatte),* were other expressions of this esthetic. It is also worth recalling Diaghilev's first "urban" ballet, *Jeux,* of 1913, produced at the "noonday of Futurism"[331] — such a vivid reflection of "contemporary life"[332] that Diaghilev thought of dating it as 1930 in the program.[333] As Nikitina mentioned:

> Once again [*La Chatte*] was a really new ballet, a true creation that did not resemble anything that had been shown before. Balanchine's choreography was the finest he had ever done, Sauguet's music, so melodious, so expressive, inspired me remarkably and was in such harmony with the fairylike background of transparent and colourless constructions. It was another feather in Diaghilev's cap.[334]

True, Lifar liked to claim the success for himself, as he wrote in his commentary on *La Chatte:*

> that very day [26 May, 1927] Spessiva [Spessivtseva], by some accident, hurt her foot. It was impossible to cancel the première of *La Chatte* announced for the next evening, for that would certainly have compromised the whole of our Paris season. Meanwhile Balanchine was insisting that Danilova (who knew the part) should take her place while Diaghilev held that Nikitina was the only adequate substitute. As I had always been, and still was, on very good terms with her, I offered to get her to agree to stay with us through the season. Then, with no more than a single day in which to rehearse, I took her right through her part in *La Chatte.* At the performance she acquitted herself to perfection, and scored a deserved success though, it is true, I helped her greatly by carrying her, most of the time, on my arms.[335]

But whether Lifar really "helped Nikitina greatly" or whether Nikitina herself was responsible for her success in spite of Lifar "humming an incredibly false tune"[336] is immaterial. The result, as one observer wrote, was: "the height of perfection in architecture and sculpture by Gabo and Pevsner, and in sculpturesque choreography by Balanchine."[337]

323 Gabo's full name appears in several Russian variations, including Naum Berkovich, Naum Abramovich, and Naum Borisovich. See Notes to Antoine Pevsner.
324 N. Gabo and A. Pevsner: "The Realistic Manifesto" in B12, p. 213.
325 N. Khardzhiev: "Stati ob avangarde" in B217, p. 136.
326 Gabo in conversation with Herbert Read in Read and Martin, *Gabo*, p.176.
327 Such, apparently, was the response of many of the spectators. See I15, p. 227. For a detailed description of the visual aspect of *La Chatte* see D26, pp. 483-86; and M. Hammer and C. Lodder: "A Constructivist *pas de deux:* Naum Gabo and Sergei Diaghilev" in B183, pp. 80-99. For documentary photographs see D51, pp. 164-68.
328 R. Olson and A. Chanin: "Antoine Pevsner" in *Gabo – Pevsner*, p. 56.
329 Alicia Nikitina in conversation with John E. Bowlt, August, 1976, Monte Carlo.
330 Elizaveta Surits has discussed the impact of such ballets in B31, pp. 112-37, and D28. Also see B183, Vol. 2.
331 F4 (second edition, 1948), p. 236.
332 A. Levinson: *Staryi i novyi balet,* P: Svobodnoe iskusstvo, 1918 (?), p. 84
333 F4, op.cit. For a discussion of *Jeux* see Lord Chernian: "Lev Bakst and Vaslav Nijinsky: The 1913 Production of *Jeux*" in G55, pp. 53-68.
334 A. Nikitina: *Nikitina,* London: Allan Wingate, 1959, p. 78.
335 D8, p. 449.
336 Nikitina, op. cit., p. 76.
337 V. Kameneff: *Russian Ballet through Russian Eyes,* London: Russian Books and Library, 1936, p. 31. Naturally, not all responses to the designs for *La Chatte* were so positive. Raymond Cogniat, for example, in his *Décors de Théâtre* (1930) saw them as "seductive — but arbitrary" (G12, p. 13).

GALADZHEV, Petr Stepanovich

Born 28 December, 1900 (10 January, 1901), Stary Krym, Crimea, Ukraine; died 5 October, 1971, Moscow, Russia.

1909-17 studied at CSIAI; 1910s worked as a set director's assistant at Sergei Zimin's Opera Theater, Moscow; 1917-20 studied at Svomas/Vkhutemas under Vladimir Favorsky and Dmitrii Shcherbinovsky; then attended a studio at the Workers' Art Education Union under Fedor Komissarzhevsky; 1919 first commercial collages and reliefs; started acting career; 1920-25 student at the State Cinematography Polytechnic under Lev Kuleshov; 1921 onwards created designs for The Lukin Ballet Studio, Moscow; started to publish caricatures and vignettes in journals such as *Ekho* [Echo], *Ermitazh* [Hermitage], and *Zrelishcha* [Spectacles]; 1922 created designs for *Fantasy,* choreographed by Kasian Goleizovsky to music by Alexander Scriabin for the Chamber Ballet, Moscow; 1920s worked for prestigious companies such as the Crooked Jimmy Cabaret and the Blue Blouse agit-theater; moved closely with experimental actors, directors, moviemakers, and choreographers such as Sergei Eisenstein, Nikolai Foregger, Zinaida Tarkhovskaia, and Yurii Zavadsky; 1920s onwards involved in numerous movies, either acting (as in Lev Kuleshov's *The Extraordinary Adventures of Mr. West in the Land of the Soviets* of 1924) or designing the sets and costumes; 1925 created cover design for sheet music of Matvei Blanter's *Solara,* Moscow; contributed to the "First Exhibition of Graphics" at the Press House, Moscow; 1940 onwards designer for the Soiuzdetfilm All-Union Children's Film Studios and later for the Gorky Film Studios; acted in thirty-six films; made sets for over fifty films, including *Kashchei the Immortal, Donetsk Miners,* and *When the Trees Were Tall,* and directed three movies; 1965 designated Meritorious Art Worker of the RSFSR; 1971 received a USSR State Prize for his work in the film *By the Lake.*

Bibliography
M. Fedorov: *Petr Stepanovich Galadzhev.* Catalog of exhibition at the Union of Artists of the USSR, M, 1961.
A14, Vol. 2, p. 391.
K. Isaeva: *Petr Stepanovich Galadzhev.* Catalog of exhibition at the Moscow Kino Center, 1990.
J. Bowlt: *Pjotr Galadschew.* Catalog of exhibition at the Galerie Alex Lachmann, Cologne, 1995. I81.
N. Galadzheva: "Petr Galadzhev — pervostepennyi sluzhitel kino" in *Kino-glaz,* Moscow, 1992, No. 1, pp. 28-32.
V. Winokan: *Pyotr Stepanovitch Galadshev.* Catalog of exhibition at Galerie Natan Fedorowskij, Berlin, 1994.
A. Borovsky: *Petr Stepanovich Galadzhev.* Catalog of exhibition at the House of Photography, Moscow, 2003.

N. Galadzheva, ed.: *Khudozhnik kino Petr Galadzhev,* M (publishing-house not indicated), 2010.

Galadzhev's many renderings of drama, ballet, cabaret, and film productions in the 1920s, often reproduced as covers or accompaniments of texts in magazines such as *Zrelishcha,* if collected and collated, would constitute a vivid panorama of the Constructivist performing arts. Although these are often artist's impressions rather than actual projects, they are also stark exercises in black and white kinetic miniatures which present the human body as an energic automaton whose steps and gestures move to the calculated rhythm of wheels and levers. Indeed, the refractive, almost metallic finish of Galadzhev's renderings of Goleizovsky's *Tombeau de Columbine* or Faiko's *Lake Liul,* might best be described in the cinematic terms of montage, cut, framing, closeup, and dissolve. But Galadzhev's images also depend for their effect on a microsopic play of force lines contained within the frame of the text, printed page, stage or screen, and we remember the artist's advice to students: "Examine an insect under a magnifying-glass and you'll see something unprecedented, something that you could never have imagined!"[338] Galadzhev's drawings are laboratorial in the same sense that Alexander Tairov's Chamber Theater, Goleizovsky's Chamber Ballet, and Boris Nevolin's Intimate Theater were, i.e. strictly delineated spaces for the cultivation of uncommon species observed by a chosen few.

Lake Liul: *detective melodrama by Alexei Faiko. Produced by Vsevolod Meierkhold assisted by Abram Room and Vladimir Uspensky at the Theater of Revolution, Moscow, on 8 November, 1923, with designs by Viktor Shestakov.*

Set in the Far West or Near East. Against a background of luxurious hotels, posh shops, high-clsss restaurants, and dancing halls, the Capitalist world is being obliterated by revolution, The revolutionary Anton Prim crosses over to the service of bourgeois society, but is shot by the workers whom he betrayed.

513 [NIRE].
Stage Design, 1923.
Black ink.
Initialed lower left in Russian as part of the design: "PSG."
9⅞ x 13½ in., 25.2 x 34.4 cm.
Inscriptions in Russian read: "[The Store] Excelsior Lake Liul"' in French: "Reclame."
Provenance: private transaction, Moscow, 2000. Now in a private collection.
A version of this design, identifed as a "theatrical production of 1921" and made for the journal *Zrelishcha,* is reproduced in Fedorov, *Petr Stepanovich Galadzhev,* unpaginated.

513

Cine-Eye: *78-minute, black-and-white silent documentary film by Dziga Vertov with script by Dziga Vertov, camera work by Mikhail Kaufman (Dziga Vertov's brother), and promotional materials by Petr Galazdzhev. Released by Kultkino-Goskino, Moscow, in 1924.*

The new state, the USSR, is described through the realia of everyday Soviet life such as the Young Pioneers, war against tuberculosis, a lunatic asylum, cooperatives, and a physics lessons for workers.

514 [NIRE].
Poster Design for *Cine-Eye*, 1924.
Black ink.
Initialed lower left in Russian as part of the design: "PSG."
13¼ x 9⅝ in., 33.5 x 24.6 cm.
Inscriptions left and right as part of the design in Russian: "KINO"; middle: "EYE."
Provenance: private transaction, Moscow, 2000. Now in a private collection.
There exist a number of variants of this design. See, for example, Galadzheva, *Khudozhnik kino Petr Galadzhev*, p. 478.

515 [NIRE].
Cover Design for the Journal "Sovetskii ekran," No. 33, 1925.
Black ink.
Initialed lower left in Russian as part of the design: "PSG."
12¾ x 9⅞ in., 32.5 x 25 cm.
Inscriptions as part of the design: lower margin and upper right in Russian: "KINO."
Provenance: private transaction, Moscow, 2000. Now in a private collection.
Reproduced in *Punkt, Linie, Kreis, Fläche*, Catalog of exhibition at the Galerie Orlando Zurich, 2012, p.39.

Death Ray: *feature film by Lev Kuleshov, based on a script by Vsevolod Pudovkin, starring: Vladimir Fogel, Petr Galadzhev, Alexandra Khokhlova, Andrei Fait, Vsevolod Pudovkin, et al. Released by Goskino in 1925.*

The Soviet self-taught engineer Podobed has invented a terrible weapon of destruction — the death ray — to fight the Imperialists. Proletarians abroad receive this weapon from the USSR and with its help dethrone the reign of Capitalism.

516 [81; NIRE].
Poster Design for a Street Cinema on Wheels for the Fim "Death Ray", 1925.
Gouache and blue ink on gridded thick white paper.
Initialed lower left in Russian: "PSG."
23⅝ x 31½ in., 60 x 80 cm.
Inscriptions in Russian throughout, including the instruction that the contraption is to be made of plywood and cellulose.
Provenance: private transaction, Moscow, 2000. Now in a private collection
Reproduced in color in Bowlt, *Pjotr Galadschew*, p. 54.

Circle (a.k.a. Duty and Love): *feature film by Alexander Gavronsky and Yulii Raizman; with script by Sergeii Yermolinsky and Vadim Shershenevich, camera work by Leonid Kosmatov, and artistic direction by Vasilii Komardenkov, starring Bella Chernova, Petr Galadzhev, Anatolii Ktorov, Vera Popova, et al. Released by Gosvoenkino (State Military Cinema) in 1927.*

A prosecutor's aide Boris Bersenev neglects his wife Vera, who is attracted to the playboy Vladimir Poliansky. But he turns out to be an embezzler of government money and soon appears in court before Bersenev. Having recognized Poliansky as the lawyer who had offered him shelter during his persecution by the Tsarist police, Communist Bersenev decides to let the case proceed along legal channels.

517 [82; NIRE].
Poster Design for Yurii Raizman's Film "Circle", 1927.
Gouache and blue ink.
Initialed lower left in Russian "PSG."
31½ x 23⅝ in., 80 x 60 cm.
Provenance: private transaction, Moscow, 2000. Now in a private collection.
Reproduced in color in Bowlt, *Pjotr Galadschew*, p. 47; and in *Punkt, Linie, Kreis, Fläche*, Catalog of exhibition at the Galerie Orlando Zurich, 2012, p.40. The face is of the actress Bella Chernova.

514

515

516

517

518

519

Reproduced in color in Bowlt, *Pjotr Galadschew*, p. 45.

The Knot: *melodramatic film directed by Vladimir Shirokov, with camera work by Valerii Alexeev, script by Alexander Balagin, set design by Dmitrii Kolupaev, and starring Valentina Kuindzhi, Nikolai Kutuzov, Andrei Gromov, Leonid Yurenev, et al. Released by Sovkino, Moscow, in 1927.*

The sharks and shady dealers nurtured by the partial return to the Capitalist system during the New Economic Policy are overcome by the true Communists.

519 [83; NIRE].
Poster Design for the film "The Knot", 1927.
Gouache and blue ink on gridded paper.
Initialed bottom center-right in Russian: "PSG."
23½ x 33⅞ in., 59.5 x 86 cm.
Inscriptions (as part of the design) throughout in Russian, with names of actors and production company.
Provenance: private transaction, Moscow, 2000. Now in a private collection.
A similar, unsigned poster is reproduced in color in Bowlt, *Pjotr Galadschew*, p. 55.

338 P. Galadzhev: "K tebe – khudozhnik kino." Quoted in Isaeva: *Petr Stepanovich Galadzhev,* unpaginated.

S.W.D. *("S.W.D." is the acronym of* Soiuz velikogo dela = *Union of the Great Cause): feature film by Grigorii Kozintsev and Leonid Trauberg; with camera work by Andrei Moskvin, and art direction by Evgenii Enei; starring Sergei Gerasimov, Konstantin Khokhlov, Andrei Kostrichkin, Sofia Magarill, Petr Sobolevsky, et al. Released by Sovkino, Leningrad, in 1927.*

518 [NIRE].
Poster Design for the Film "S.W.D.", 1927.
Gouache and blue ink.

Initialed lower left in Russian "PSG."
33⅝ x 23⅝ in., 85.5 x 60 cm.
Inscriptions in upper margin: pencil figures from 1 to 16 corresponding to a grid. Other inscriptions (as part of the design) in Russian: across the top, in black: "cinema drama in 6 parts"; along left margin: "Union of the Great Cause"; along right margin: "Dir. Kozintsev – Trauberg"; across the bottom: "Production of Leningrad Sovkino Factory."
Provenance: private transaction, Moscow, 2000. Now in a private collection.

GAMREKELI, Iraklii Ilich

Born 5 (17) May, 1894 Gori, Georgia; died 10 May, 1943 Tbilisi, Georgia.

1920s attended the Tiflis School of Painting and Sculpture; 1921 onwards active as the stage designer of plays, ballets, operas, movies; close to the producer and playwright Kote Mardzhanishvili (Konstantin Mardzhanov); 1922-43 chief designer for the Shota Rustaveli Dramatic Theater in Tiflis/Tbilisi where he designed many important productions such as *Hamlet* (1925), *Othello* (1937), and Schiller's *Die Räuber* (1933); 1923 contributed to the "First Exhibition of the Group of Young Artists" in Tiflis; 1924 contributed to the "Exhibition of the Society of Georgian Artists" in Tiflis; member of the group of experimental artists and writers called H2S04; 1927 contributed to the "Jubilee Exhibition of Art of the Peoples of the USSR" in Leningrad; began to work on movie designs with his debut in *My Grandmother* of 1929; 1930s-40s worked extensively for the Griboedov Russian Dramatic Theater in Tbilisi; 1932 designed Reingold Glière's ballet *Red Poppy* for the Paliashvili Theater of Opera and Ballet in Tbilisi; contributed to the exhibition "Construction and Art of the National Republics" in Moscow; 1939 became a member of the Communist Party of the Soviet Union.

Bibliography
N. Gudiashvili: *Iraklii Gamrekeli*, M: Sovetskii khudozhnik, 1958.
A7, Vol. 1, p. 1098.
Sh. Amiranashvili and L. Lomtatidze: *Vystavka proizvedenii zasluzhennogo deiatelia iskusstv GruzSSR khudozhnika I.I. Gamrekeli (1894-1943)*. Catalog of exhibition of stage sets and costumes organized by the Union of Artists of the USSR, M, 1962.
A14, Vol. 1, p. 406.
L. Lomtatidze: *Iraklii Gamrekeli*, Tbilisi: Teatralnoe obshchestvo Gruzii, 1982.
Ts. Kukhianidze: *Iraklii Gamrekeli*, Tbilisi: Khelovneba, 1988.
Recent exhibitions of stage designs have featured Iraklii Gamrekeli's work. See, for example, I116, p. 79.

Gamrekeli was introduced to the world of stage design through Mardzhanov, Sandro Akhmeteli, and other distinguished Georgian producers. Indeed, it was Mardzhanov who "discovered" Gamrekeli after seeing the artist's illustrations to Oscar Wilde's *Salomé* at an exhibition in Tiflis in 1921. Mardzhanov was impressed and, as a result, invited Gamrekeli to design his production of *Salomé* at the New Theater the following year. This was so successful that Mardzhanov again invited Gamrekeli to work on a production of Lope de Vega's *Fuente Ovejuna* the following year at the Rustaveli Dramatic Theater — which marked the real beginning of Gamrekeli's "Constructivist" phase. "In this work [*Fuente Ovejuna*] you could already see the style that would be characteristic of my subsequent works," wrote Gamrekeli later,[339] thinking, no doubt, of the painted

volumetrical shapes and special light effects that he had applied and would continue to apply. Under these auspicious conditions, Gamrekeli began his professional career as a stage designer, becoming Georgia's foremost designer of plays, operas, ballets, and movies in the 1920s-30s.

Gamrekeli's theatrical experiments are distinguished by their subtle, unexpected resolutions, e.g., multi-level constructions or multi-purpose objects — something identifiable with the designs for *Mystery-Bouffe* (Nos. 520-24 [R395-99]) or for the movie *My Grandmother* (1929) in which

> The action in one of the episodes unfolded at a round table on short legs which served simultaneously as a stage. Doors were attached to the outside of this peculiar table-stage — which created the sensation of an endless corridor in some kind of institution, but, from the inside, looked like closets standing behind the backs of the people sitting at the table.[340]

This description brings to mind Alexander Rodchenko's moving, circular construction for *One Sixth of the World* of 1931 (No. 875 [R756]), although there is no reason to assume that Rodchenko was paraphrasing Gamrekeli. Rather, both men were working in the Constructivist idiom and both, therefore, were interested in the kinetic and transformative use of construction on stage. In the 1930s, Gamrekeli, like his compatriot Lado Gudiashvili, adapted to the demands of Socialist Realism and turned to a more traditional decorative interpretation. Even so, his designs, e.g., for the Georgian plays *Georgii Saakadze* (1940) and *Vasilii Kikvidze* (1941) (both produced at the Rustaveli Theater), continued to appeal to the histrionic sense of his exuberant audience.

Mystery-Bouffe: "A Heroic, Epic, and Satirical Depiction of Our Epoch" in prologue and six acts by Vladimir Maiakovsky. Projected but not produced for the Shota Rustaveli Dramatic Theater, Tiflis, in September, 1924, by Kote Mardzhanishvili (Konstantin Mardzhanov) with designs by Iraklii Gamrekeli.

The entire Earth, except for the North Pole, has been liquidated by a flood. Taking refuge in an ark at the North Pole are "seven pairs of clean" (including an Indian Rajah, a Russian speculator, a German, a Priest, an Australian, Lloyd George and an American) and "one pair of each unclean" (including a Red Army soldier, a lamplighter, a driver, a miner, a servant, a smith, a washerwoman, an engineer and an Eskimo fisherman). The unclean deceive the clean and throw them overboard. Conquering many barriers, the unclean then visit hell and, after depositing the clean there, go on to heaven, which they leave in disgust. They return to a new Earth — to the Promised Land of the Communist paradise. The two rival groups are supplemented by many other personages such as devils and saints, an intellectual, a lady with boxes (an emigrée), a conciliator, etc.

520

520 [84; R395].
Stage Design for Act I (Version), 1924.
Watercolor, gouache, and black ink.
Signed lower right in black ink in Russian: "1924 Ir. Gamrekeli."
14 x 10⅜ in., 35.5 x 26.5 cm.
Other inscriptions: the reverse carries the following in blue pencil in Russian: "Mystery-Bouffe. Meant to be staged in the open air [illegible] Mardzhanov."
Provenance: Viktor Kholodkov, Moscow, 1989.
Reproduced in color in B115, plate 165; as the front cover to I77; and in black and white in I77, p. 141; N176; O26; P55; A. Favorsky, comp.: *Maiakovsky — Piesy*, M: Detskaia literatura, 1976, after p. 64.

521 [R396].
Stage Design for Act I (Another Version), 1924.
Grey wash and black ink.
Signed lower right in black ink in Georgian: "I.I. Gamrekeli."

521

8½ x 6⅞ in., 21.5 x 17.5 cm.
Other inscription: the reverse carries the following in pencil in Russian: "Sketch for the décor of Mystery-Bouffe by V. Maiakovsky. Staged by Mardzhanov. Painter-constructor Iraklii Gamrekeli. The play is meant to be staged in the open air."
Provenance: Viktor Kholodkov, Moscow, 1989.
Reproduced in color as the cover for I97; and in black and white in I96, p.134; I97, p. 92.

522 [R397].
Stage Design for Act I (Variant with Three Fish Heads), 1924.
Watercolor and black ink.
10 x 6⅞ in., 25.3 x 17.5 cm.
Provenance: Viktor Kholodkov, Moscow, 1989.

523 [85; R398].
Stage Design for Act II, 1924.
Watercolor.
10¼ x 8⅞ in., 26 x 22.5 cm.
The design carries the following Russian inscriptions as part of the composition: on left curtain: "Act II"; on right curtain: "V. Maiakovsky"; on top curtain: "A2 near No. P1 32"; on the boot: "BLIA/KhA R H2SO4 G [illegible]."
Provenance: Viktor Kholodkov, Moscow, 1989.
Reproduced in color in B115, plate 167; and in black and white in I77, p. 141; I96, p.134; I97, p. 92.

524 [86; R399].
Stage Design for Act III, 1924.
Watercolor.
Signed lower left in Russian: "I. Gamrekeli."
10⅝ x 8⅝ in., 27 x 22 in.
The design carries the following Russian inscriptions as part of the composition: on left curtains: "Act III. Miracles"; on right curtains: "V. Maiakovsky"; on upper right curtain: AAA UUUU"; on the potty: "Purgatory"; on the stove: "Hell"; on the base: "'Gretts' Kitchen."
Provenance: Viktor Kholodkov, Moscow, 1989.
Reproduced in color in B115, plate 166; I96, p. 63; and in black and white in I77, p. 141; I96, p.134; I97, p. 92; O26.

Note: If they had been implemented, Gamrekeli's designs for Mardzhanov's pro-

posed production of *Mystery-Bouffe* would surely have surpassed those of Viktor Kiselev (Nos. 608-18 [R504-14]) in eccentricity and fantasy. In Nos. 520-22 [R395-97], for example, a highly schematic planet Earth sits upon a block of ice and in the third of these designs is supported by three sea monsters against the Northern Lights. Certainly, Gamrekeli seems to have been well informed of the latest audacious experiments in Constructivist theater that Vsevolod Meierkhold was encouraging in Moscow and Leningrad. His set designs here are immediately reminiscent of Liubov Popova's for *The Magnanimous Cuckold* (1922), of Varvara Stepanova's for *The Death of Tarelkin* (1922; Nos. 974-80 [R800-06]), and — above all — of Vasilii Fedorov's for Alexander Ostrovsky's *Forest* produced by Meierkhold in January, 1924.[341] Moreover, Nos. 520 [R395] and 521 [R396] seem to have been inspired directly by Sergei Eisenstein's set for the production of George Bernard Shaw's *Heartbreak House* projected (but not realized) by Meierkhold in 1922.[342] No doubt, Maiakovsky, who visited Tiflis in September, 1924, and discussed the proposed presentation of his play with Mardzhanov, described the Moscow experiments carefully to both producer and designer.

Judging by the designs here, Mardzhanov and Gamrekeli conceived of *Mystery-Bouffe* as an instrument for the approbation and propagation of the avantgarde in general and not just as a particular play with its defined plot and characters — rather in the way that Meierkhold treated Fernand Crommelynck's *Magnanimous Cuckold*. In other words, their interpretation was liberal, not literal, and they added many digressions and extraneous interpolations. First of all, the play was scheduled to take place outside, on Mount David in Tiflis, and not inside a theater hall. Secondly, Gamrekeli, at least, added a number of private references especially in Acts II and III, which are not a part of Maiakovsky's original text. For example, Maiakovsky's stage directions for Act II call for "The deck of an ark" and there is no mention of a lady's boot (although a cobbler is among the "unclean," and a boot is one of the live objects that inhabits the Promised Land in Act VI).

524

Furthermore, Gamrekeli refers to his own group allegiance through his inclusion of the formula H_2SO_4 (sulphuric acid), for this was the name of a Tiflis Dada faction to which Gamrekeli belonged — propagating the decomposition of conventional cultural values (cf. No. 1184 [R494]).[343] In true Maiakovsky spirit, Gamrekeli is also using words and fragments of words in a creative, if sometimes scandalous manner. For example, the boot in his design for Act II carries the letters "BLIA/KhAR" (cf. *bliakha* meaning "buckle") which might be read as *bliakhar* (minus the terminal soft sign) meaning "metal-plate worker" (perhaps a reference to the smith who is one of the "unclean" in the play) or a concertied form of the words *bliad* (whore) and *ebar* (fucker). Such erotic and salacious effects (also note the night potty in No. 524 [R399] as the representation of Purgatory) would have appealed to Maiakovsky. But there are also more neutral plays of words, e.g., the "'Gretts' Kitchen" also in No. 524 [R399], which has direct associations with the words *grekh* (sin), *greshnik* (sinner), and *gret* (to warm, heat), and which therefore, illustrates the actions of the devils in Hell in Act III as they sing "I like a ragout made of juicy sinners." It is reasonable to assume that the production did not take place precisely because of this "shocking" and "irrelevant" complex of connotations.[344]

339 I. Gamrekeli: [Memoirs], undated. Quoted in Gudiashvili, *Gamrekeli*, p. 8. For information on Mardzhanov see D. Kantadze: *Riadom s Mardzhanishvili*, M: VTO, 1975; L. Pizzini: "Creatività e fantasia di un regista russo K.A. Mardzanov" in *Il Cristallo*, Bolzano, 1996, Vol. 38, No. 1, pp. 101-12.
340 E. Tsitsishvili: *Dizainovoe proektirovanie v Gruzii*, Tbilisi: Khelovneba, 1985, pp. 27-28.
341 For a reproduction of Fedorov's set for *The Forest* see I26, p. 86.
342 For a reproduction of Eisenstein's set for *Heartbreak House* see G49, plate 184.
343 For information on H2SO4 see J. Bowlt: "H2SO4: Dada in Russia" in S. Foster, ed.: *Dada Dimensions*. Ann Arbor: UMI, 1985, pp. 221-48.
344 For commentary on Gamrekeli and Mardzhanov during the 1924 theater season in Tiflis see D. Kantadze: *Riadom s Mardzhanishvili*. M: VTO, 1975, pp. 109-31

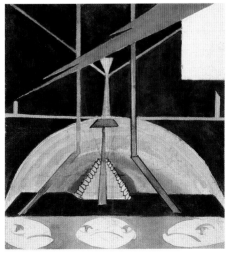

522

523

GAN, Alexei Mikhailovich

Born 1893 (some sources give 1888), Moscow (?), Russia; died 1942, Novosibirsk, Russia.

1918-20 attached to TEO NKP in Moscow as head of the Section of Mass Presentations and Spectacles; end of 1920 dismissed from NKP by Anatolii Lunacharsky because of his extreme ideological position; close association with Inkhuk; co-founded the First Working Group of Constructivists; 1922 published his book *Konstruktivizm* [Constructivism]; turned to designing architectural and typographical projects, movie posters, bookplates, etc.; 1922-23 editor of the journal *Kino-foto* [Cine-Photo]; 1924 contributed to the "First Discussional Exhibition of Associations of Active Revolutionary Art" in Moscow; 1926 contributed to the "First Exhibition of Graphics" in Moscow; 1926-30 member of OSA [Association of Contemporary Architects] and artistic director of its journal *SA* [Contemporary Architecture]; 1928 member of the October group; 1934-35 lived in Khabarovsk; died in a prison camp.

Bibliography
B12, pp. 214-25.
B59, passim.
A. Lavrentiev: *Aleksei Gan,* M: Gordeev, 2010.

Alexei Gan is remembered above all for his support of the Constructivist movement and for the booklet, *Konstruktivizm,* his volatile manifesto of 1922 (its cover was designed by Alexander Rodchenko). Naturally, the publication was prompted by the many debates on construction and production which took place at Inkhuk during 1921 and in which Boris Arvatov, Osip Brik, El Lissitzky, Liubov Popova, Rodchenko, Varvara Stepanova, and Nikolai Tarabukin played a formative role. Indeed, some of the ideas in *Konstruktivizm* were reflected in another primary Constructivist declaration of 1922, i.e. *Iskusstvo v proizvodstve* [Art in Production], which also drew upon the Inkhuk program. Moreover, the First Working Group of Constructivists, of which Gan was a member, was already active in 1921. At loggerheads with studio artists, Gan was an indefatigable apologist of industrial art, the cinema, and architecture, although his terminology and literary style did not always make for clarity:

> Tectonics is synonymous with the organicness of thrust from the instrinsic substance... Texture is the organic state of the processed material... Construction should be understood as the collective function of construction...[345]

525 [R400].
Poster for the "Exhibition of Works by Vladimir Maiakovsky", 1931 (Proof).
Lithograph in black and white.
25⅝ x 17¾ in., 65 x 45 cm.
(See Nos. 526-28 [R401-03]).

525

526

526 [R401].
Poster for the "Exhibition of Works by Vladimir Maiakovsky", 1931 (Variant).
Lithograph in red and black on white paper. Signed lower right margin in the plate in Russian: "Alexei Gan."
Text lower right crossed out in ink by Gan.
25⅝ x 17¾ in., 65 x 45 cm.
(See Nos. 525, 527 and 528 [R400, 402, 403]).

527

527 [R402].
Poster for the "Exhibition of Works by Vladimir Maiakovsky", 1931 (Variant).
Lithograph in red and black on white paper. Signed lower right margin in the plate in Russian: "Alexei Gan."
25⅝ x 17¾ in., 65 x 45 cm.
Other inscription: the title in Russian: "Exhibition of Works by Vladimir Maiakovsky" as part of the design; this is followed in small print by the details of location, schedule and publication, i.e., "Literary Museum of the Lenin Public Library and the Society for Assisting the Literary Museum at 18, Marx-Engels Street," etc. The publication details provide the date, i.e., 30 October, 1931, at Mosoblpoligraf on Glavlit Street, Moscow, in an edition of 2000. (See Nos. 525, 526, and 528 [R400, R401, R403]).
Reproduced in D. Ades: *Posters.* New York: Abbeville, undated, p. 52; E38, No. 36.

528 [R403].
Poster for the "Exhibition: Life and Works by Vladimir Maiakovsky", 1931 (Final).
Lithograph in red and black on white paper.
31½ x 21¼ in., 80 x 54 cm.
Inscriptions: "Published by the State Literary Museum. Chief Editor Vladimir Bonch-Bruevich. Edition of 2000. Printed at Izvestiia of the Deputies of Soviet Workers of the USSR, Pushkin Square, Moscow." Reproduced in color in M157, p. 54.
(See Nos. 525-27 [R400-02]).

Note: On 1 February, 1930, the exhibition "20 Years of Work" opened at the Writers' Club on Vorovsky Street in Moscow (which later became the main office of the Union of Writers of the USSR). Under the auspices of the Federation of Soviet Writers and Ref (Revolutionary Front of the Arts), Maiakovsky organized this overview of his literary and artistic achievements

528

(over a hundred of his books together with posters, notebooks, magazines, etc. were on display), as if sensing perhaps that his days were numbered (he committed suicide on 14 April, 1930). A catalog and poster were issued in connection with "20 Years of Work."

The exhibition in the Writers' Club was open until 15 February, 1930, when it went to Leningrad for a week. It then returned to Moscow where it was opened in the Krasnaia Presnia Komsomol House. From the very beginning, Maiakovsky had indicated that, after the exhibition closed, he would donate all the materials to the Literary Museum of the Lenin Library. The materials were, indeed, transferred there and another exhibition was organized in October (?), 1931, in order to mark this

valuable accession. The event was accompanied by lectures and excerpts from the movies in which Maiakovsky starred (according to the small print on Nos. 526-27 [R401-02]).[346] This poster was designed by Gan for the Literary Museum exhibition, i.e., not for "20 Years of Work." Gan was a friend of Maiakovsky and they had been especially close during their mutual support of Constructivism and industrial design in the early 1920s. Gan incorporates a photo-portrait of Maiakovsky taken by Abram Shterenberg at "20 Years of Work."[347]

Gan as contributor:
529 [NIRE].
Designer unknown: Poster Advertising the Exhibition "Vladimir Maiakovsky, 1893-1930", 1936.
Lithograph in red, blue, and white
Photomontage with seventeen photographs of which ten are designs by Maiakovsky
27½ x 41¾ in., 70 x 106 cm.
Inscriptions in lower margins: Literary Editor: N.A. Vinogradova; Artistic Editor: Erik Gollerbakh; Editor-in-Chief: E.S. Dobin. Edition of 4000. Published by Izobrazitelnoe iskusstvo, Leningrad, 1936.

345 B12, pp. 218-25.
346 For information on the 1930 exhibition "20 Years of Work" see Maiakovsky's own catalog, i.e., 20 let raboty Maiakovskogo, M: Federation of Soviet Writers, 1930. In 1973 the exhibition was reconstructed in the premises of the Union of Writers of the USSR, where the Writers' Club had been, and a brochure (unsigned) was published called Posetiteliam vystavki "20 let raboty Maiakovskogo," vozobnovlennoi k vosmidesiatiletiiu so dnia rozhdeniia poeta, M: Literaturnaia gazeta; a booklet compiled by Konstantin Simonov was also published, i.e., Maiakovsky delaet vystavku, M: Kniga. Also see K38.
347 In the poster Gan has blacked out the background of Shterenberg's photograph which contains some of the Maiakovsky posters for Okna ROSTA which were at "20 Years of Work." For a reproduction of the undoctored photograph see Simonov, Maiakovsky, p. 50.

GOLOVIN, Alexander Yakovlevich

Born 17 February (1 March), 1863, Moscow, Russia; died 17 April, 1930, Detskoe Selo, near Leningrad, Russia.

1881-89 attended MIPSA; at first studied architecture and then switched to painting when he took courses from Vasilii Polenov, Vladimir Makovsky, and Ivan Prianishnikov; 1889 visited Paris, the first of several trips to Europe; 1890s supported Art Nouveau and Jugendstil; close to the Neo-Nationalist artists such as Elena Polenova, Mariia Yakunchikova, and Viktor Vasnetsov at Abramtsevo; contact with the founding members of the World of Art group; 1898 debut as a stage designer at the Bolshoi Theater, Moscow; 1898-99 with Konstantin Korovin designed the interior of the Handicraft Section for the Russian Pavilion at the "Exposition Universelle," Paris (1900); 1899 contributed to the first "World of Art" exhibition; thereafter exhibited regularly with various professional societies; 1900 with Mikhail Vrubel et al. decorated the frieze on the Metropole Hotel, Moscow; 1901 designed The Maid of Pskov for the Bolshoi Theater; 1902 became artist-in-residence at the Imperial Theaters, St. Petersburg; 1900s contributed to many stage productions at home and abroad; 1908 designed the sets for Sergei Diaghilev's presentation of Boris Godunov in Paris; 1909 with Nicholas Roerich and Dmitrii Stelletsky designed Diaghilev's production of The Maid of Pskov in Paris; 1908-19 worked closely with Vsevolod Meierkhold; 1910 worked on Diaghilev's production of L'Oiseau de Feu in Paris; 1910s painted portraits of theatrical celebrities; 1917 designed the production of Mikhail Lermontov's Masquerade at the Alexandrinsky Theater, Petrograd; 1917 until his death continued to work mainly as a stage designer, contributing to productions of Le Chant du Rossignol (Mariinsky Theater, Petrograd, 1919), Orpheus (Ida Rubinstein, Paris, 1926), Shakespeare's Othello (Moscow Art Theater, 1930), etc.

Bibliography
E. Gollerbakh, *A. Ya. Golovin. Zhizn i tvorchestvo*, L: Akademiia khudozhestv, 1928.
F16.
B. Almedingen: *Alexander Yakovlevich Golovin.* Catalog of exhibition at the Academy of Arts of the USSR and the All-Union Theatrical Society, M, 1956.
M2, Vol. 2, pp. 177-178 (for a listing of his theatrical productions).
A. Bassekhes: *Teatr i zhivopis Golovina*, M: Izobrazitelnoe iskusstvo, 1970.
B. Almedingen: *Golovin i Shaliapin*, L: Iskusstvo, 1977.
I. Gofman: *Alexander Golovin*, M: Izobrazitelnoe iskusstvo, 1981.
S. Onufrieva: "Golovin — khudozhnik Aleksandrinskogo teatra" in G50, Vol. 7, pp. 287-310.

529

I. Gofman: *Golovin-portretist,* L: Khudozhnik RSFSR, 1981.

M. Pozharskaia: *Aleksandr Golovin,* M: Sovetskii khudozhnik, 1990.

Mejerchol'd e Golovin. Don Giovanni in Russia. Catalog of exhibition at La Manna d'Oro, Spoleto, 1992.

Golovin, along with his friend and rival Konstantin Korovin, is one of the most celebrated of Russia's stage designers, and in the 1920s was still remembered internationally as the artist of the costumes for Diaghilev's 1908 production of *Boris Godunov* in Paris.[348] Diaghilev commissioned Golovin to design all the sets and costumes for the *L'Oiseau de Feu* production of 1910, although neither Diaghilev, nor Michel Fokine were pleased with everything: "Golovin's costumes were beautiful... [he] provided wonderful costumes for all the participants; only two [of the three] didn't come off."[349] Consequently, Diaghilev asked Léon Bakst to redesign three costumes, including the one for Tamara Karsavina as the Firebird, and these harmonized with Golovin's exotic, highly ornate sets and curtain.

From 1901 onwards, Golovin was artist-in-residence at the Imperial Theaters, St. Petersburg, and brought to the Saisons Russes a rich experience of scenic design. A member of the World of Art, Golovin knew Diaghilev from the early days, even though his artistic approach was closer to that of the Moscow stylists such as Vladimir Egorov than to that of his St. Petersburg contemporaries. Like other artists of his generation, especially K. Korovin, Golovin took Western artistic ideas and exaggerated them vividly, rhetorically. Golovin's concentrated application of the Jugendstil esthetic evident in his designs for *L'Oiseau de Feu* and, above all, for Vsevolod Meierkhold's production of Lermontov's *Masquerade* in 1917, brought forth much criticism and what Mstislav Dobujinsky said in the latter context might be extended to many of Golovin's decors:

> Where is the common artistic idea, where is the center... and where is composition, if there is any? It's precisely this, the really essential, that is missing... And what's all this fabulous splendor for, and, anyway, what is it in front of us?[350]

In response to such remarks, the phlegmatic Golovin commented:

> I feel that, in my decorative work, I have managed to express a particular style germane to my painting. I am often asked: "How did you *find* your style? How did you arrive at this style?" In my opinion, it's impossible to answer this question. Everyone knows and understands *what* style is but the artist who possesses stylistic distinctiveness is unlikely to be able to explain how he came to possess it. "I was born like that," that is the only possible answer.[351]

Georgii Vereisky: *Portrait of Alexander Golovin,* 1925. See No. 1130 [R372].

Swan Lake: *ballet in four acts by Peter Tchaikovsky with libretto by Vladimir Begichev and Vasilii Geltser and choreography by Vaclav Reisinger. Produced at the Chinese Theater at Tsarskoe Selo (Tsar's residence outside St. Petersburg) on 2 February, 1902, with designs by Alexander Golovin.*

See No. 436 [NIRE] for plot summary.

530 [R404].
Set Design for Act III. A Hall in the Castle, ca. 1902.
Gouache.
Signed lower right in Russian: "A. Golovin."
17¾ x 21⅝ in., 45 x 55 cm.
Provenance: private transaction, Moscow, 1984.

Reproduced in I60, p. 13; and M65. A similar piece, made for the 1901 Bolshoi Theater production of *Swan Lake,* is reproduced in Bassekhes, p. 27. This may be the design referred to as lost in F16, p. 352.

At the Gate of the Kingdom (Ved Rigets Port): *verse drama in eight acts by Knut Hamsun. Produced by Vsevolod Meierkhold at the Alexandrinsky Theater, St. Petersburg, on 30 Septermber, 1905, with designs by Alexander Golovin.*

The first in a set of three plays (followed by The Game of Life *and* Sunset Glow*),* At the Gate of the Kingdom *is set in Christiania. The constant hero is Ivar Kareno, a student and progressive thinker, who is presented to us at the age of 29. As Kareno moves through the trilogy accompanied by his wife and other characters, his actions demonstrate that a young man below 30 may be a rebel, but at age 50 and beyond he will become conservative and exchange his radical views for the comfortable haven of complacent seniority — only to be replaced by another young rebel of 29.*

531 [NIRE].
Set Design for Act I, 1905.
Watercolor.
Inscribed and dated on reverse.
8⅞ x 15 in., 22.5 x 38.2 cm.
Provenance: Issar Gourvitch, Paris, November, 1966.
Reproduced in I20, p. 24; No. 42.

Carmen: *opera in four acts by Georges Bizet with libretto by Henri Meilhac and Ludovic Halévy based on a novel by Prosper Merimée. Produced by Vasilii Shkafer at the Mariinsky Theater, St. Petersburg on 10 March, 1908, with designs by Alexander Golovin.*

Don José, a corporal, tells of his love for Micaela, a peasant girl. But Carmen, a

531

533

gypsy girl, appears and tries to seduce him. She throws a flower to him and he picks it up. After a contretemps in the cigarette factory, Carmen is arrested by José, but, bewitching him, escapes. José joins her at a tavern and, after drawing his sword against Captain Zuniga, is forced to flee with her to the mountains and to join the smugglers. Micaela comes looking for him. Escamillo the Toreador and Don José duel over Carmen. Later, driven by jealousy, Don José kills Carmen, only to prostrate himself in remorse over her body.

532 [R405].
Sketch for Carmen's Hairstyle, ca. 1908.
Watercolor.
16½ x 13⅛ in., 42 x 33.5 cm.
Inscribed lower right in pencil in Russian: "silver combs."
Provenance: Issar Gourvitch, Paris, November, 1966, who had acquired it from Vera Komissarzhevskaia before 1910.
Reproduced in I14, No. 69. A full length design by Golovin for Carmen wearing the same hairstyle, in the BTM, is reproduced in F16, p. 82; Gofman, *Golovin*, p. 59. A similar face and hairstyle appear in two costume designs reproduced in G83, pp. 57, 58, 61.

Note: The singer of Carmen for this production was Marie Kousnezoff (see No. 80 [R76]), and this sketch is, therefore, also her portrait. Judging by contemporary accounts, she was successful in her role — "a vivid Carmen, exhaling the sun and fire of the south... she has much distinctive, ferocious grace."[352]

L'Oiseau de Feu: *ballet in two scenes with music by Igor Stravinsky based on the Russian fairy-tale. Produced by Sergei Diaghilev for the Ballets Russes at the Théâtre National de l'Opéra, Paris, on 25 June, 1910, choreography by Michel Fokine, sets by Alexander Golovin, costumes by Alexander Golovin, and Léon Bakst.*
    See No. 370 [R340] for plot summary.

533 [R406].
Costume Design for Tamara Karsavina as the Firebird, ca. 1910.
Watercolor and pencil.
Signed lower right in Russian: "A. Golovin."
13¾ x 10½ in., 35 x 26.7 cm.
Other inscription: upper left in Russian: "The Firebird."
Provenance: Ilia Zilbershtein, Moscow, March, 1972.
Reproduced in A34, p. 167; F107, p. 257; G99, p. 176; I40, No. 51; I51, No. 93. A photograph of Karsavina wearing the costume is reproduced in D24, p. 68. A version of this design, in the GMTMA, is reproduced in I89, p. 108.

Note: This was one of the three costumes by Golovin (for the Firebird, the Tsarevna, and Ivan the Tsarevich) that did not appeal to Diaghilev, and he asked Bakst to make substitutes. Bakst produced three variants for his Firebird costume (reproduced, for example, as the cover to I. Pruzhan: *Bakst,* L: Iskusstvo, 1975; B123, No. 34; D10, p. 51; D41, plates 42, 44, 45; J24, Lot 31; also see G59, pp. 41-42), including the version which

Karsavina actually wore[353] and which was made into the famous porcelain figurine (see J4, Lot 260). Bakst's three costumes, deemed by some critics as fit for a Persian fairy-tale,[354] blended easily with Golovin's other designs, especially with the splendid set for Kashchei's Kingdom (see Onufrieva, *Golovin,* plate 31; D41, plate 43). In his reminiscences, Stravinsky even forgot Bakst, so impressed was he by Golovin's designs: "I am, of course, far from attributing this success solely to the score; it was equally due to the spectacle on the stage in the painter Golovin's magnificent setting and the brilliant interpretation by Diaghileff's artists."[355] Golovin returned to the *Firebird* in 1921 for a lavish production at the Mariinsky Theater in Petrograd: for reproductions of costumes see L112, Lots 154-63.

348 For example, Walter Propert lavished praise on Golovin. See D1, pp. 13-14.
349 F19, p. 263. Fokine refers to two rejected costumes (presumably, out of three), but other sources contradict this, and, in fact, it is not entirely clear whether Diaghilev rejected one, two, or all three of Golovin's costumes. Most reports indicate that the main design, i.e., for Karsavina as the Firebird, was never worn and that the Bakst substitute was used from the very start. However, in her book (D24, p. 68) Nesta Macdonald writes that "of Golovine's beautiful designs for L'Oiseau de Feu, only that for the Firebird herself was unsuccessful. It was worn by Karsavina for the first few performances, in Paris in 1910, when, in the same bill, she and Nijinsky danced their *pas de deux* from Le Festin — re-named L'Oiseau d'Or. Just as the title, Oiseau de Feu, had confusingly been transferred to Stravinsky's new ballet, so, too, was Karsavina's costume — Bakst's glorious fantasy of flame-coloured plumes."
350 Amadeo (pseudonym of Mstislav Dobujinsky): "Naprasnaia krasota" in *Rech,* P, 1917, 9 March, No. 67.
351 F16, p. 52.
352 Zigfrid: "Mariinskii teatr. Novaia postanovka opery, Karmen" in *Obozrenie teatrov,* SP, 1908, No. 358, 13 March, p. 4.
353 For a photograph of Karsavina wearing the Bakst costume see *Studiia,* M, 1912, No. 42-43, p. 9.
354 Jean Louis Vaudoyer on *L'Oiseau de Feu,* 1910. Mentioned in Gollerbakh, *A. Ya. Golovin. Zhizn i tvorchestvo,* 1928, p. 38.
355 F20, pp. 29-30. According to Evgenii Gunst, Golovin's sets were painted (i.e., realized after Golovin's designs) by Nikolai Sapunov. See E. Gunst: untitled essay in *Sapunov,* catalog of exhibition at the Central House of Writers, M, 1963, p. 12.

GONCHAROVA (Gontcharova), Natalia Sergeevna

Born 21 June (3 July), 1881, Nagaevo, Tula Region, Russia; died 17 October, 1962, Paris, France.

1892 onward lived in Moscow; 1901 enrolled at MIPSA to study sculpture; met Mikhail Larionov who encouraged her to paint; she became his life-long companion (they were married in 1955); 1906 contributed to the Russian Section at the "Salon d'Automne," Paris; 1908-10 contributed to the three exhibitions organized by Nikolai Riabushinsky, editor of the journal *Zolotoe runo* [The Golden Fleece] in Moscow; 1910 with Larionov and others founded the Jack of Diamonds group and participated in the first exhibition; 1911-14 contributed to the subsequent exhibitions organized by Larionov: the "Donkey's Tail" (1912), the "Target "(1913), and "No. 4" (1914); ca. 1910 worked in Primitivist, Cubist, and, in 1912-13, Futurist and Rayonist styles; 1910 one-day exhibition at the Society for Free Esthetics, Moscow; 1913 (Moscow) and 1914 (St. Petersburg) major retrospective exhibitions; 1914 (29 April) with Larionov left for Paris to design Sergei Diaghilev's production of *Le Coq d'Or;* Galerie Paul Guillaume, Paris, and Galerie Der Sturm, Berlin, held an exhibition of both artists' work; 1915 returned briefly to Moscow, where designed Alexander Tairov's production of Carlo Goldoni's *Il Ventaglio* at the Chamber Theater, Moscow; 1916-17 after traveling with Diaghilev's company to Spain and Italy, settled in Paris with Larionov; 1919 with Larionov exhibited at the Galerie Barbazanges, Paris; 1920-21 contributed to the "Exposition internationale d'art moderne" in Geneva; 1922 showed at the Kingore Gallery, New York (both exhibitions also included work by Larionov); 1924 designed puppets for Yuliia Sazonova's Puppet Theater, Paris; 1920s onwards continued to paint, teach, illustrate books, and design productions, including Boris Romanov's *A Romantic Adventure of an Italian Ballerina and a Marquis* for the Chauve-Souris, New York (1931); after 1930, except for occasional contributions to exhibitions, Larionov and Goncharova lived unrecognized and impoverished; 1954 their names were resurrected at Richard Buckle's "The Diaghilev Exhibition" in Edinburgh and London; 1961 Art Council of Great Britain organized a major retrospective of Goncharova's and Larionov's works.

Bibliography
E. Eganbiuri (pseudonym of Ilia Zdanevich): *Mikhail Larionov Natalia Goncharova,* M: Miunster, 1913.
Exposition des Oeuvres de Gontcharova et Larionow. L'Art Décoratif Théâtral Moderne. Catalog of exhibition at the Galerie Sauvage, Paris, 1918.
A. Liberman: *The Artist in His Studio,* New York: Viking, 1960.
M. Chamot and C. Gray: *A Retrospective Exhibition of Paintings and Designs for the*

Mikhail Larionov: *Portrait of Natalia Goncharova,* ca. 1910. See No. 697 [R590].

Theatre. Larionov and Goncharova. Catalog of the exhibition at the City Art Gallery, Leeds; the City Art Gallery, Bristol; and the Arts Council Gallery, London, 1961.
M2, Vol. 2, pp. 178-180.
T. Loguine: *Gontcharova et Larionov,* Paris: Klincksieck, 1971.
M. Chamot: *Gontcharova,* Paris: La Bibliothèque des Arts, 1972.
Rétrospective Gontcharova. Catalog of exhibition at the Maison de la Culture de Bourges, 1973.
G. Orenstein: "Natalia Goncharova. Profile of the Artist-Futurist Style" in *The Feminist Art Journal,* New York, 1974, Summer, pp. 1-6.
Nathalie Gontcharova 1881-1962. Catalog of exhibition at the Galerie Wolfgang Ketterer, Munich, 1978 (?).
M. Chamot: *Goncharova. Stage Designs and Paintings,* London: Oresko, 1979.

Mikhail Larionov: *Portrait of Natalia Goncharova,* ca. 1930. See No. 698 [R591].

K. Bakos: *Goncsarova,* Budapest: Corvina, 1981.
Michel Larionov. Nathalie Goncharova. Catalog of exhibition at Galleria Martini & Ronchetti, 1983.
Natalia Goncharova. Catalog of exhibition at the Marion Koogler McNay Art Museum, San Antonio, Texas, 1987.
Goncharova. Catalog of exhibition at the National Art Gallery, Wellington, New Zealand, 1987.
N. Gurianova: "Voennye graficheskie tsikly N. Goncharovoi i O. Rozanovoi" in *Panorama iskusstv,* M, 1989, No. 12, pp. 63-88.
J. Bowlt: "Natalia Goncharova and Futurist Theater" in *Art Journal,* New York, 1990, spring, pp. 44-51.
M. Tsvetaeva: *Nathalie Gontcharova,* Paris: Clémence Hiver, 1990.
M73, Vol. 26, pp. 78-79.
B109, pp. 52-79.
T. Durfee: "Natalia Goncharova: Two Letters" in *Experiment,* Los Angeles, 1995, No. 1, pp. 159-68.
G. Kovalenko: *Natalia Goncharova. Mikhail Larionov. Vospominaniia sovremennikov,* M: Galart, 1995.
Le Paris des Années Vingt. R. Kawashiva, N. Gontcharova et M. Larionov. Catalog of exhibition at the Shiseido Gallery, Tokyo, 1995.
J. Boissel et al.: *Nathalie Gontcharova, Michel Larionov.* Catalog of exhibition at the Centre Georges Pompidou, Paris, 1995. Opened as *Natalia Goncarova Michel Larionov* at the Fondazione A. Mazzotta, Milan, 1996.
R. Gayraud, ed.: *Nathalie Gontcharova Michel Larionov par Elie Eganebury.* Paris: Clémence Hiver, 1996.
Natalia Gontcharova and the Russian Ballet. Catalog of exhibition at Julian Barran, Ltd., London, 1996.
N. Misler: "Apocalypse and the Russian Peasantry: The Great War in Natalia Goncharova's Primitivist Paintings" in *Experiment,* Los Angeles, 1998, No. 4, pp. 62-76.
K224, passim.
E. Iliukhina: *M. Larionov. N. Goncharova. Parizhskoe nasledie v Tretiakovskoi galeree. Grafika, teatr, kniga, vospominaniia.* Catalog of exhibition at the TG, 1999.
K236, pp. 155-83.
A. Lukanova, comp.: *Larionov. Goncharova. Shedevry iz parizhskogo naslediia. Zhivopis,* Catalog of exhibition at the TG, 1999.
D. Yifat: *Natalia Goncharova. A Pioneer of the Russian Avant-Garde.* Catalog of exhibition at the Tel-Aviv Museum of Art, Tel-Aviv, 2000.
G. Kovalenko, ed.: *N. Goncharova, M. Larionov,* M: Nauka, 2001.
E. Basner et al., eds.: *Natalia Goncharova. Gody v Rossii,* St. Petersburg: Palace Editions, 2002.
N. Gromova, intro.: *Tsvety i goncharnia. Pisma Mariny Tsvetaevoi k Natalie Goncharovoi 1928-1932,* M: Dom-Muzei Mariny Tsvetaevoi, 2006.
J. Sharp: *Russian Modernism between East and West: Natalia Goncharova and the Moscow Avant-Garde,* New York: Cambridge University Press, 2006.
B. Kemfert and A. Chilova: *Natalja Gontscharowa. Zwischen russischer Tradition und europäischer Moderne.* Catalog of exhibition at the Opelvillen, Rüsselsheim, the Kunsthalle, St. Annen, Lübeck, and the Angermuseum, Erfurt, 2009-10.
A. Parton: *Goncharova. The Art and Design of Natalia Goncharova,* Woodbridge, England: Antique Collectors' Club, 2010.
D. Bazetoux: *Natalia Gontcharova: son oeuvre*

entre tradition et modernité, Brussels: Arte-Print, 2011.
Also see Bibliography for Mikhail Larionov.

A remarkable poise, common sense, and pragmatism characterized Natalia Goncharova, and she demonstrated her qualities not only in sophisticated paintings, but also in talented designs for books, fashion, and the stage. Chronologically the primary woman artist of twentieth-century Russia, Goncharova both cultivated an intellectual interest in the traditional handicrafts and primitive rituals of Old Russia and used these as subjects for her pictures and designs. Her study of Russian peasant costume and ornament, for example, prepared the way for her folkloristic evocations in Diaghilev's *Le Coq d'Or* (1914) and *L'Oiseau de Feu* (1926) as well as for her illustrations to Alexei Kruchenykh's *Pustynniki* [Hermits] (1913) and to the Paris edition of the *Conte du Tsar Saltan* (1922). Goncharova's recognition of the vitality and potential of national Russian art forms inspired her and Larionov to organize an exhibition of "Icons and Broadsheets" in Moscow in 1913.

Naturally, Goncharova's attitude influenced the formal arrangements of her painting, contributing to her intense stylization, her forceful color combinations, and her "naive" perspectives and proportions, all of which prompted critics to identify her as "Asian" rather than "European." She declared in 1913: "I have turned away from the West... For me the East means the creation of new forms, an extending and deepening of the problems of color..."[356] Goncharova's *joie de vivre,* her sympathy for the simple and immediate pleasures of life perhaps dictated her preference for a figurative painting of dancing peasants, ethnic costumes, beasts, and birds. The apparently non-objective works of Goncharova's Rayonist period (1912-13) and "cosmic" period (1950s) might be regarded as momentary digressions from her fundamental, primitive esthetic. As a matter of fact, Goncharova's Rayonist works often rely on a figurative and primitive point of departure (e.g., her painting *Artistic Possibilities of a Cockerel*), and her depictions of peasants at work and play leave the

534

impression of greater spontaneity and sincerity than the sometimes labored abstract works. Perhaps this explains the unqualified success of Goncharova's designs for *Le Coq d'Or.*

Le Coq d'Or: *opera ballet in three acts with music by Nikolai Rimsky-Korsakov and libretto by Vladimir Belsky based on a fairy-tale by Alexander Pushkin and adapted by Alexandre Benois. Produced by Sergei Diaghilev for the Ballets Russes at the Théâtre National de l'Opéra on 24 May, 1914, with choreography by Michel Fokine and designs by Natalia Goncharova assisted by Mikhail Larionov.*
See No. 299 [R268] for plot summary.

534 [87; R407].
Stage Design for Act I, ca. 1914.
Watercolor.
Signed lower right: "N. Gontcharova."
28½ x 41½ in., 72.5 x 105.5 cm.
Provenance: Irina Bashkiroff (a student of Goncharova's), New York, May, 1974. Now

in a private collection.
Reproduced in color in B88, p. 37; B115, plate 29; B122, p. 263; I67, p. 55; I115, p. 178; I117, p. 349; I130, p. 107; M23; M157, p. 34; Parton, *Goncharova,* p. 254; Yu. Gogolitsyn: "'Provoditel velikikh idei...'" in *Antiq.info,* M, 2005, No. 26, p. 85; and in black and white in G12, plate 9; I51, No. 95; I77, p. 132; N112; N114, No. 37; N167; R18. There exist several versions of the set for Act I (which is also similar to the set for Act III). For reproductions of versions, see I1, p. 15 (same as D23, color plate 2); D41, plate 125; Souvenir Program of the New York 1946-47 season of the *Original Ballet Russe. Col. W. de Basil,* unpaginated color plate; J21, Lot 29 (also reproduced in color on the cover); J2, Lot 25; also see J7, Lot 137. For reproduction of designs for Act III, see N. Gontcharova and M. Larionov: *L'Art Décoratif Théâtral Moderne,* Paris: La Cible, 1919, unpaginated color reproduction (also in G23, fig. I50); J26, Lot 111; J2, Lots 47-49 (the actual backdrop and arch); also see D41, plate 131. Another backdrop, sometimes referred to as a curtain, is reproduced in three versions in G36, fig. 51; I7, p. 37; J23, Lot 29. Also see D1, unpaginated; and I50, p. 40. Goncharova repeated motifs from her sets for *Le Coq d'Or* in other contexts, e.g., for her unrealized *Foire Espagnole* of 1916; see G10, Vol. 2, fig. 258. See also No. 559 [R430]. For other reproductions and commentary see J. Homann: *"Le Coq d'or." Natalia Goncharova's Designs for the Ballets Russes.* Catalog of exhibition at the Busch-Reisinger Museum, Cambridge, Mass., 2003.

535 [R408].
Stage Design (Project), ca. 1914.
Black ink.
7½ x 11¾ in., 19 x 30 cm.
Provenance: Alexandra Tomilina, widow of Mikhail Larionov, Paris, 1965.
The figure of Prince Gvidon (Guidon) on the left appears in many versions. See, for

535

536

537

example, D1, unpaginated; D13, p. 61; G12, No. 7; I44, p. 48; J12, Lot 6. Goncharova later used the image of Prince Gvidon for one of her panels for Serge Koussevitsky's Paris home in 1922. See J7, Lot 40.

536 [R409].
Costume Design for the Tsaritsa Shemakhan, ca. 1914.
Watercolor.
15 x 6½ in., 38 x 16.5 cm.
Inscriptions: upper left: instructions in Russian to the dressmaker; on reverse in Alexandra Tomilina's hand: "Fait par N.

Gontcharova" and stamp of Larionov's studio.
Provenance: Alexandra Tomilina, widow of Mikhail Larionov, Paris, 1965.
Reproduced in I14, No. 70; I51, No. 96; N98; similar designs are reproduced in G10, Vol. 2, figs. 145, 148; G19, p. 18.

537 [R410].
Costume Design for One of the Princes, ca. 1914.
Black ink.
16½ x 11 in., 42 x 28 cm.
Inscriptions: numerous annotations in Russian giving indications for materials and colors; on reverse in French in Alexandra Tomilina's hand: "Fait par N. Gontcharova" and stamp of Larionov's studio.
Provenance: Alexandra Tomilina, widow of Mikhail Larionov, Paris, 1965.
Reproduced in I14, No. 72.

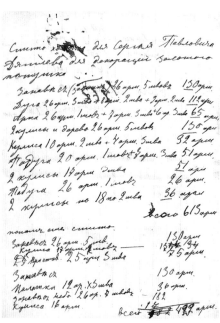

538

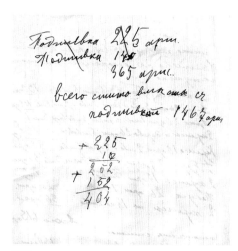

539

538 [R411].
Recto. *Listing of Cloth Used for Various Elements of the Production (Curtains, Side-Scenes, etc.)*, ca. 1914.
Ink on lined white paper.
8⅞ x 6⅞ in., 22.5 x 17.5 cm.
Inscriptions: details in Russian (recto): "Listing of cloth for the décors for the Golden Cockerel for Sergei Pavlovich Diaghilev." There then follow the designations and lengths.
Provenance: Alexandra Tomilina, widow of Mikhail Larionov, Paris, 1965.
See 539 [R411a].

539 [R411a].
Verso. *Listing of Cloth Used for Various Elements of the Production.*
Black ink on white paper.
8⅞ x 6⅞ in., 22.5 x 17.5 cm.
See 538 [R411].

540

540 [R412].
Unidentified artist: *Composite Portrait of Sergei Diaghilev and Natalia Goncharova*, ca. 1914.
Black ink.
12 x 7⅞ in., 30.5 x 20 cm.
Provenance: Konstantin Stramentov, London, February, 1979.
Reproduced in G99, p. 177; I41, No. 63; I51, No. 97; I91, p. 22.

Note: The rendering of Diaghilev on the left is taken from a caricature by Pavel Egorovich Shcherbov (1866-1938) entitled *Salzburg* (1898; reproduced in A. Savinov: *P.E. Shcherbov*, L: Khudozhnik RSFSR, 1969, p. 19; see ibid., pp. 58, 61 for commentary). In Shcherbov's caricature Diaghilev, who is presented as a rag and bone man (hence his pick-axe and unshaven appearance), is pointing to Princess Mariia Tenisheva, who had purchased Mikhail Vrubel's picture *Morning at Diaghilev's* exhibition "Russian and Finnish Artists." This exhibition was held in St. Petersburg in 1898 in the section of town known as Solianoi gorodok [lit. Salt Town] — hence the title *Salzburg*. The rendering of Goncharova on the right is taken from her Cubo-Futurist painting called *Lady in a Hat* (1913, now in the Musée d'Art Moderne, Centre Georges Pompidou, Paris; reproduced in both catalogs of Goncharova's one-woman shows in Moscow and then St. Petersburg in 1913 and 1914). The text in this double portrait reads in translation: "The famous Diaghilev, as drawn *jokingly* by P.E. Shcherbov, our famous caricaturist. This same Diaghilev invited Mrs. Goncharova to paint the decorations for Rimsky-Korsakov's opera *The Golden Cockerel*. Her self-portrait, drawn *not jokingly*, is placed above this text. Dotted lines indicate what has been added by artists from the *Igralishche*. The figure 5 is taken from Goncharova's masterpiece *Lady*."[357]

Note: Goncharova's designs for *Le Coq d'Or* were probably her most successful, and the fact that she repeated and modified her sets and costumes, and that the spectacle itself was revived many times indicate her own fascination with this opera-ballet. Critics who saw the premiere agreed that Goncharova's "setting inaugurated a new phase of stage decorations,"[358] for she implemented successfully Benois's proposal that the opera *Coq d'Or* actually be staged as a ballet-opera (action mimed by dancers with singers in choral formation on steep ramps on either side of the stage — shown clearly in No. 534 [R407]):

> Le problème... consistait à trouver un emplacement où loger une masse de 90 solistes et choristes que la fosse d'orchestre ne pouvait contenir... Gontcharova proposa d'installer les chanteurs sur la scène, assis les uns au dessus des autres, sur des gradins, à la façon dont la *Douma des Boyards* est représentée sur les images populaires russes...[359]

Fokine, who choreographed *Le Coq d'Or* in 1914 and who, because of Goncharova's notoriety as a Cubo-Futurist, had grave misgivings about Diaghilev's selection of her as the designer, quickly changed his mind. He wrote in his reminiscences:

> Gontcharova not only provided beautiful décors and costume designs, but she also manifested an extraordinary, fantastic love for her work on *The Golden Cockerel*. It was touching to see how, with their own hands, she and Larionov painted all the props. Each piece on stage was a work of art. What great work! Seeing the enthusiasm of the two artists, I was amused to recall the fears and rumors.[360]

Even the generally reserved Prince Sergei Volkonsky exclaimed:

> What imagination! Mrs. Gontcharova, our famous 'Futuristic' painter has gone beyond all confines of what a child's fantasy can construct. [361]

Liturgie: *ballet in seven movements by Natalia Goncharova and Mikhail Larionov with choreography by Leonide Massine and designs by Natalia Goncharova. Rehearsed under Sergei Diaghilev for the Ballets Russes in Lausanne, spring, 1915, but not produced.*

The ballet, based on the Passion of Jesus Christ, proceeds through a series of choreographic tableaux treating the Annunciation, the Ascension, the Resurrection, etc. The ballet was to have been performed with interludes of Russian church music.

Note: The eighteen designs numbered 541-58 [R413-29]) relate to the portfolio of sixteen silkscreens (pochoirs) that Goncharova compiled in 1915, i.e., N. Gontcharova and L. Miassine: *Liturgie. 1915. 16 Maquettes Reproduites au pochoir d'après les Aquarelles originales et signées par l'auteur*, Paris: M.P., 1915. Since the edition of this album was very small (probably thirty-five copies), the full set is a rarity, although individual sheets sometimes appear.[362] Curiously enough, comparison of what should be duplicate silkscreens sometimes reveals discrepancies from piece to piece. This might be explained by Goncharova's own emendations on certain copies and also by the alleged existence of a second edition of the portfolio. G10, Vol. 1; p. 170, H14, p. 30; and I15, p. 130, carry a reference to the following title: Nathalie Gontcharova: *Liturgie. Album de 18 Costumes au Pochoir*, Paris: Povolotzky, 1927. Although it has not proved possible to locate a copy of this second edition, it is tempting to assume that such a publication did exist. This would explain, for example, the existence of certain designs which, while destined obviously for *Liturgie,* were not printed in the 1915 edition (e.g., the design for a backdrop entitled *Liturgie* and dated 1915 in the collection of the Metropolitan Museum of Art, New York, and reproduced in D1, unnumbered; and G22, plate 4; also cf. the analogous drawings for various personages connected with *Liturgie* reproduced in J7, Lots 143-48; J9; J20, Lots 7-8ii; J23, Lot 24; J24, Lots 87-90ii; also see the set designs described as projects for *Liturgie* in the collection of the Museum of Modern Art, New York, i.e., *Nativity* and *Flight into Egypt,* which are reproduced in I61, pp. 222 and 224). Many of the original gouaches for *Liturgie* are in the collection of the TG.

For reproduction of the full run of this set see Parton, *Goncharova*, pp. 264-68; for the reproduction of the set in the TG, see Boissel, *Nathalie Gontcharova, Michel Larionov*, pp. 99-102; for reproductions

from yet another set of *Liturgie* see L164, Lot 209.

The paper used for the silkscreens bears the watermark "J. Perrigot Arches (France)."

Unless otherwise indicated, provenance for items 541-58 [R413-29] is Alexandra Tomilina, widow of Mikhail Larionov, Paris, 1967.

N. GONTCHAROVA

"Liturgie"

1915 - Lausanne

16 Maquettes

Reproduites au pochoir d'après les Aquarelles originales et signées par l'Auteur.

541

541 [R413].
Label for "Liturgie", 1915.
Printed label.
5⅛ x 4⅛ in., 13 x 10.5 cm.
This label, designed, presumably, by Goncharova, appears on the front side of the portfolio *Liturgie*.

The following sequence of silkscreen costumes for *Liturgie* follows the numbered order in the portfolio (indicated in parentheses after each catalog number). The eleventh silkscreen, the Six Winged Seraph, is represented by the original watercolor for this 552 (11) [R423a]. The copy of *Liturgie* presented to the BTM by Goncharova in 1927 and still preserved there was used as the primary source for consultation and comparison. The silkscreens were sold through the bookshop Les Quatre Chemins: Editions Artistiques, Paris, owned by Anna and Elena Gabrilovitch, friends of both Larionov and Goncharova, who also published their previous works starting in 1919. This set is reproduced in full in Parton, *Goncharova*, pp. 264-68.

542

543

544

542 (1) [R414].
Costume Design for a Man from the People, 1915.
Gouache/silkscreen.
Signed lower right: "N. Gontcharova."
25 x 17½ in., 63.5 x 44.5 cm.
Other inscriptions: lower left: "Homme du Peuple, Liturgie."
The original watercolor and gouache design, now in a private collection, is reproduced in Parton, *Goncharova*, p. 338. A sketch for the costume is reproduced in K290, p. 31.

543 (2) [R415].
Costume Design for St. Anne, 1915.
Gouache/silkscreen.
Signed lower left: "N. Gontcharova."
24 x 16 in., 61 x 40.5 cm.

Provenance: Alexandra Tomilina, widow of Mikhail Larionov, Paris, 1967.

544 (3) [88; R416].
Costume Design for a Cherub, 1915.
Gouache/silkscreen.
Signed and dated lower right corner: "N. Gontcharova 1915."
24 x 14¾ in., 61 x 37.5 cm.
The original collage for this design is reproduced in C7, plate 138. It was auctioned in June, 1967 (see J1, Lot 50); also see J40, Lot 57. The Cherub is depicted from the back, although in a similar design, formerly in the collection of Alexandr Tomilina and now in the TG, the central person faces the viewer (for a reproduction see Iliukhina, *M. Larionov. N. Goncharova. Parizhskoe nasledie v Tretiakovskoi galeree*, p. 59).

545 (4) [89; R417].
Costume Design for St. Andrew, 1915.
Gouache/silkscreen.
Signed lower left: "N. Gontcharova."
25 x 17¾ in., 63.5 x 45 cm.
A drawing for this design is reproduced in J7, Lot 144.

545

546

547

548

546 (5) [90; R418].
Costume Design for St. Mark, 1915.
Gouache/silkscreen.
Signed lower right: "N. Gontcharova."
29⅞ x 22 in., 76 x 56 cm.
Other inscriptions lower left: "St. Marc,
Liturgie."
A variant (the original watercolor?) is
reproduced in G10, Vol. 2, fig. 305. The
original gouache with collage, formerly in

550

the collection of Alexandra Tomilina and
now in the TG, is reproduced in Iliukhina,
*M. Larionov. N. Goncharova. Parizhskoe
nasledie v Tretiakovskoi galeree*, p. 57.

547 (6) [R419].
Costume Design for Judas, 1915.
Gouache/silkscreen.
24 x 15 in., 61 x 38 cm.
The original watercolor for this design is in
the Victoria and Albert Museum, London,
while a related drawing is in the collection
of the Virginia Museum of Fine Arts
(reproduced in Chamot, *Goncharova*, p. 66).

548 (7) [91; R420].
*Costume Design for One of the Magi (the
Abyssinian King?), 1915.*
Gouache/silkscreen.
Signed lower right in pencil: "N.
Gontcharova."
25 x 17½ in., 63.5 x 44.5 cm.
A sketch for a second magus is reproduced
in K290, p. 30.

549 (8) [92; R421].
Costume Design for St. John, 1915.
Gouache/silkscreen.
Signed lower right: "N. Gontcharova."
24¾ x 16¾ in., 63 x 42.4 cm.
Other inscriptions lower left: "Liturgie;
Apôtre Jean."
A variant (the original watercolor?) is
reproduced in G10, Vol. 2, fig. 305.

550 (9) [R422].
Costume Design for a Shepherd, 1915.
Gouache/silkscreen.
Signed lower left: "N. Gontcharova."
24 x 12 in., 61 x 30.5 cm.
Other inscriptions: lower left: "Berger,
Liturgie."
Cf. No. 558 [R429].
Now in a private collection.

551

549

551 (10) [93; R423].
Costume Design for St. Peter, 1915.
Gouache/silkscreen.
Signed lower right: "N. Gontcharova."
24 x 16½ in., 61 x 42 cm.
Other inscriptions: lower left: "St. Pierre,
Liturgie."

552 (11) [94; R423a].
*Costume Design for the Six-Winged Seraph,
1915.*
Watercolor, pencil, and ink
Signed and dated in lower right: "N.
Gontcharova, 1915."
28¾ x 21½ in., 73 x 54.7 cm.

552

Other inscription lower left: "A Monsieur Ram Gopal, ce magnifique danseur que j'espère revoir bientôt à Paris. N Gontcharova. Paris 1940." (The reference is to Ram Gopal [1912-2003], the "Indian Nijinsky", who moved to Europe in 1938). Provenance: *The Russian Sale,* London: Sotheby's, 7 October, 1998, Lot 136 (reproduced).
Reproduced in color in F107, p. 441; G99, p. 171; I94, p. 67; N188, p. 15.

554

555

553

553 (12) [R424].
Costume Design for Christ, **1915.**
Gouache/silkscreen.
25 x 15 in., 63.5 x 38 cm.

554 (13) [R425].
Costume Design for a Roman Soldier, **1915.**
Gouache/silkscreen
22½ x 15 in., 57 x 38 cm.
Inscribed lower left: "Soldat."

555 (14) [95; R426].
Costume Design for an Apostle, **1915.**
Gouache/silkscreen.
30 x 22 in., 76.2 x 56 cm.

556 (15) [96; R427].
Costume Design for St. Matthew, **1915.**
Gouache/silkscreen.
Signed lower right: "N. Gontcharova."
29¼ x 21½ in., 74.3 x 54.7 cm.
Other inscriptions: lower left in pencil: "Apôtre."
Provenance: *Ballet Designs,* London: Sotheby's, 4 June, 1981, Lot 114 (reproduced), where it is described as a costume design for St. Mark.
A variant (the original watercolor?) is

reproduced in I19, p. 21. A drawing for the design is in the collection of Victoria and Albert Museum, London (see G36, No. 62). A watercolor version is reproduced in J36, Lot 182.

557 (16) [97; R428].
Costume Design for One of the Magi, **1915.**
Gouache/silkscreen.
Signed lower right: "N. Gontcharova."
24 x 16½ in., 61 x 42 cm.
Other inscriptions: lower left: "Roi Mages."
A similar design for One of the Magi, with the figure facing right to left, formerly in the

556

collection of Alexandra Tomilina and now in the TG, is reproduced in Chamot, *Goncharova,* p. 66; and in in Iliukhina, *M. Larionov. N. Goncharova. Parizhskoe nasledie v Tretiakovskoi galeree,* p. 58.

558 [R429].
Costume Design for the Shepherd, ca. **1915.**
Gouache and pencil.
Stamped with the monogram lower right and signed upper right in Russian: "N. Goncharova."
18½ x 11⅞ in., 47 x 30 cm.
Other inscription in Russian: "To the young man [illegible]."
Reproduced in I40, No. 53. A watercolor version, dated 1914, is reproduced in Chamot: *Gontcharova,* p. 144. This gouache is the model for the

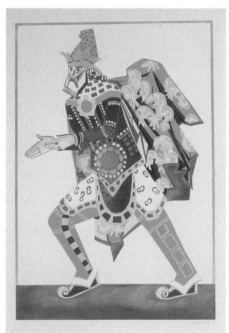

557

gouache/silkscreen that appeared in the album *Liturgie* (see No. 550 [R422]).

Note: The visual theme of *Liturgie* was not new to Goncharova. She had just published her portfolio of fourteen lithographs entitled *Misiticheskie obrazy voiny* [Mystical Images of the War] (M: Kashin, 1914), and when she had been a very young girl, she had prepared eighteen sketches of religious figures for a church. Goncharova often made pictures with Biblical subjects, including the cover to the collection of reproductions published by the Jack of Diamonds group in Moscow in connection with the opening of their first exhibition in December 1910, and a set of nine oil panels which she painted in 1911 and displayed at the "Donkey's Tail" the following year. This set included a painting called *The Four Evangelists* (now in the RM), which the Moscow censor took down from the show "on the grounds that the name Donkey's Tail was incompatible with the treatment of religious themes."[363] Actually, if the censor had looked more closely, his wrath might have been mitigated by the fact that, the irreverent "Donkey's Tail" notwithstanding, Goncharova was simply borrowing methods from the old icon painters in a pious and unpretentious manner — as a visual comparison demonstrates (cf. C7, figs. 132-38).

Goncharova worked on the ballet *Liturgie* with Diaghilev and Massine in Lausanne in 1915. This was a productive time for Goncharova since, between arriving in Lausanne in the late summer of 1915 and the end of 1916 (in July, 1916, she accompanied Diaghilev to San Sebastien) she created designs for a total of four ballets, not one of which, unfortunately, was produced (*Liturgie*, *España* [see No. 559 (R430)], *Triana*, and *Foire Espagnole*). This intense activity produced not only numerous designs for sets and costumes, but also three portfolios of silkscreens — *Liturgie, Album de 14 Portraits Théâtraux* (Paris: La Cible, 1916) and *L'Art Décoratif Théâtral Moderne* (Paris: La Cible, 1919), the last two of which were joint undertakings by Goncharova and Larionov.

As far as the ballet *Liturgie* was concerned, Goncharova's labors were in vain. Diaghilev hoped that Stravinsky would write the score for the ballet, but the composer refused to be party to a theatrical presentation of the holy story (which was to have included a Mass). Diaghilev hoped that there would be four interludes with Stravinsky's music, but when the composer rejected the idea, he entertained the notion of mere sounds as an accompaniment. Diaghilev wrote to Stravinsky from Rome on 8 March 1915:

> After twenty-two rehearsals of *Liturgie*, we have come to the conclusion that absolute silence is death… Therefore, the dance action will have to be supported not by music but by sounds — that is to say, by filling the ear with harmonies.[364]

558

But even though Diaghilev discussed such a sound accompaniment with the Italian Futurist Filippo Marinetti, hoping that a Futurist orchestra might help, nothing came of the project. Leonide Massine recalls that Diaghilev also tried to obtain copies of some ancient chants from Kiev, but because of the upheavals of the War, he never received them, much to the chagrin of the young choreographer:

> For me *Liturgie* had been not only a technical challenge, but even more the first artistic realization of a theme which had taken root deep in my subconscious when I was a child. I found it profoundly satisfying to interpret the scenes of the life of Christ in ballet form.[365]

Goncharova was not Diaghilev's first choice of designer for *Liturgie*. According to the writer Ivan Bunin, Dmitrii Stelletsky had been asked to make the costumes, but he had refused because — like Stravinsky — he did not approve of the presentation of such a deeply religious subject on stage. (In fact, Walter Propert still echoed reservations about the potential censorship hazard in 1921.)[366] In turn, Stelletsky recommended Goncharova, and she even made a design for an iconostasis, except that she confused the places of the Virgin and the Saviour. They were supposed to dance without music, on a double floor so that the sounds of their feet would echo. Stravinsky was supposed to compose chorales for the entr'actes.[367]

Even if Goncharova did position the Virgin and the Saviour wrongly in this iconostasis (which is hard to imagine), she regarded her *Liturgie* costumes as a cycle, each one organically connected to the next. The set of silkscreens illustrates this conception — which lay at the basis of Goncharova's principle of costume design:

> Les costumes peuvent se nuire mutuellement ou se faire ressortir l'un l'autre. Un costume peut passer presque inaperçu à côté d'un autre… Cela peut se comparer à un jeu de cartes aux règles rigides et compliquées, mais aux combinations innombrables.[368]

España: *ballet based on Maurice Ravel's music for* Rhapsodie Espagnole *with choreography by Leonide Massine and designs by Natalia Goncharova. Rehearsed under Sergei Diaghilev for the Ballets Russes in Rome, fall, 1916, but not produced.*

559 [98; R430].
Costume Design for a Spanish Dancer, ca. 1916.
Gouache/silkscreen.
Initialled lower right and dated 1914.[369]
19½ x 12¾ in., 49.5 x 32.5 cm.
Provenance: Robert Brown, New York, December, 1969.

Note: This gouache/silkscreen was reproduced for the first time under the title *Costume Espagnol* in the portfolio by Goncharova and Mikhail Larionov, *L'Art Décoratif Théâtral Moderne* (Paris: La Cible, 1919) in an edition of 515 copies.

This collection contained five silkscreens, folio (folded) by Goncharova and Larionov, three lithographs printed in color

559

(two by Goncharova and one by Larionov), two line blocks by Larionov and one colored lithograph. The text by Valentin Parnakh was illustrated with eleven tipped-in photographic reproductions of stage designs by the two artists. Goncharova's contribution was based on her scenic work for Diaghilev, especially on the projects that he undertook in Lausanne and then in San Sebastien in 1915-16; Larionov's images were also from largely unrealized productions (see Nos. 705-09 [R597-600]). The portfolio was published in the wake of the exhibition "Art Décoratif Théâtral Moderne" that Larionov organized at the Galerie Sauvage, Paris in 1918.[370]

Goncharova joined Diaghilev in San Sebastien in July, 1916, where, together with Leonide Massine, they worked on several ballet projects (see note to *Liturgie* above). *España* was going to consist of a series of Spanish dances based on Ravel's music and, according to one source, the wearer of this particular costume was to have been Catherine Devilliers.[371] Goncharova repeated the basic composition in a number of parallel works (the TG, for example, possesses a preliminary drawing for the gouache/silkscreen), and her various pictures called *Spanish Ladies* have been widely reproduced (e.g., in C7, figs. 140, 141). A painting called *Spanish Woman,* in a private collection, Paris (reproduced in K24, p. 31), and a painting with a collage in the collection of Robert L. B. Tobin, San Antonio, are very similar to *Costume Design for a Spanish Dancer.* In addition, Goncharova's portrait of Tamara Karsavina included in the portfolio *Album de 14 Portraits Théâtraux* (for a reproduction of the original watercolor see K141, p. 61) and the later portrait of her now in the collection of the Nationalbibliothek, Vienna (reproduced in C7, fig. 114; Chamot, *Goncharova,* p. 73), also bear a close resemblance to the work under discussion. Goncharova made many sketches on the theme of Spanish ladies (see Chamot, *Goncharova,* p. 74; J24, Lot 65).

Unfortunately, because of the privations of the War, Diaghilev was unable to produce *España,* although he continued to be fascinated by Ravel's music and, according to his notebooks for 1923-24, he intended to use *Rhapsodie Espagnole* as well as Isaac Albeniz's *Triana* (on which Goncharova also worked) as part of a music festival in Austria.[372] Although Goncharova did not see the realization of her designs, they provided her with a rich source of artistic ideas during the late 1910s and 1920s, and they left a strong impression on all who saw them:

> En regardant les espagnoles que Mme. Gontcharova a composées pour la musique de Ravel, quelqu'un qui se refuse à comprendre le cubisme me disait dernièrement sur un ton ironique: "Mais ce sont des cathédrales, mon cher!…" Elles ne peuvent, en effet, de la scène nous donner aucune autre impression que de cathédrales à

travers lesquelles on voit toute l'Espagne agenouillée dans sa foi mystique, tout un peuple enivré par le soleil et la couleur.[373]

14 Portraits de Théâtre 1915-1916; Lausanne, St. Sebastian; reproduits aux pochoirs d'après les aquarelles originales et signés par l'auteur, Paris: La Cible, 1916. A portfolio set of fourteen theatrical portraits by Goncharova designed in Lausanne and St. Sebastian and published as silkscreens in a limited edition of 35 copies. Goncharova painted the original gouache versions of these highly stylized portraits in Lausanne and St. Sebastian when she and Larionov accompanied Serge Diaghilev's dance troupe to Spain for a Ballets Russes season. A complete set is in the collection of tne GMII. Another set was sold at Sotheby's, London, on 27 November, 2007.

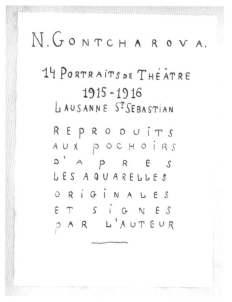

560

561

560 [NIRE].
Cover for 14 Portraits de Théâtre, 1916.
Gouache au pochoir/silkscreen.
6¼ x 4⅝ in., 16 x 11.8 cm.
Provenance: *The Russian Sale,* London: Bonham's, 26 November 2007, Lot 109 (reproduced).
For reproductions of the entire set of portraits see L164, Lot 224.

561 [NIRE].
Portrait of Leonide Massine, 1916.
Gouache au pochoir/silkscreen.
6¼ x 4⅝ in., 16 x 11.8 cm.
Signed in pencil, lower right: "N. Gontcharova."
Provenance: *The Russian Sale*, London: Bonham's, 26 November, 2007, Lot 109 (reproduced).
For the reproduction of another copy see Parton, *Goncharova,* p. 271. For reproductions of the entire set of portraits see L164, Lot 224.

562

562 [R431].
Portrait of Sergei Diaghilev, 1916.
Gouache au pochoir/silkscreen.
Signed lower right with the initials: "N G."
19⅝ x 12¼ in., 50 x 31 cm.
Provenance: Robert Brown, New York, December, 1969.
Reproduced in Goncharova and Larionov, *L'Art Décoratif Théâtral Moderne.* The original gouache for this so-called *Mechanical Costume,* formerly in the collection of Alexandra Tomilina, Paris, is reproduced in G49, p. 159; I51, p. 144; J34, Lot 35; M9. The portrait is captioned in French "grime" (i.e., "make-up").

563

564

565a

Zlodeichik: *ballet projected at the Opera House, Sofia, in 1922, with choreography by Boris Kniaseff and designs by Natalia Gonchraova.*

563 [NIRE].
Costume Design for a Wicked Woman, 1922.
Watercolor.
Signed lower right: "N. Gontcharova."
13 x 7⅞ in., 33 x 20 cm.
Provenance: Boris Kniaseff, Athens, July, 1966.
Reproduced in I14, No. 74.

Note: Information regarding a ballet called *Zlodeichik* and choreographed by Kniaseff has not been forthcoming. The current attribution and identification were supplied by Kniaseff to Nikita Lobanov-Rostovsky at the time of acquisition.

Grand Bal des Artistes; also known as Grand Bal Travesti Transmental and Grand Bal de Nuit: *charity ball organized by Natalia Goncharova, Mikhail Larionov, et al. for the Union of Russian Artists at the Salle Bullier, Paris, on 23 February, 1923, with publicity designs by Natalia Goncharova and Mikhail Larionov.*

564 [R432].
Poster Advertising The Grand Bal de Nuit, 1923.
Colored lithograph.
Signed in the stone: "N. Goncharova."
46⅞ x 31⅛ in., 119 x 79 cm.
Other inscriptions: "Grand Bal de Nuit / le 23 Février" forming part of the design; lower margin contains details of the event plus the name of the printer, i.e., Joseph-Charles, Paris.
Provenance: Nicholas Lynn, London, 1979.
Reproduced in Loguine, *Gontcharova et Larionov*, p. 138; J37, Lot 164 (damaged

version); D72, plate 27; L19, Lot 153; M73, p. 92; Parton, *Goncharova*, p. 303.

565 [R433].
Ticket No. 1075 for The Bal Banal on 14 March, 1924, 1923. Price 10 Francs.
Brown and grey print on cream paper.
8 x 5½ in., 20.4 x 14 cm.
Signed in the plate lower left and dated: "N. Gontcharova, 923."

565

Other inscriptions: the following words form part of the design: "Salle Bullier, 31 Ave. de l'Observatoire, vendredi le 14 mars 1924. Bal Banal organisé par l'Union des Artistes Russes. Billet No. 1075 Prix = 10 Fr." The seal of the Union des Artistes Russes is rubber stamped on the top and bottom of the ticket above the perforated margins.
Provenance: Alexandra Tomilina, widow of Mikhail Larionov, Paris, 1967.
Reproduced in B17, No. 272c; and B34, p. 109.

565a [NIRE].
Ticket for a Box for The Bal Banal on 14 March, 1924, 1923.
Black print on blue-grey paper.
11⅝ x 6¼ in., 30 x 16 cm.
Signed in the plate lower left and dated: "N. Gontcharova, 923."
Provenance: *Vintage Posters,* London: Bloomsbury, 14 November 2012, Lot 167.
This is a variant of No. 565 [R433], but for the box.

565b

565b [NIRE].
Ticket for a Box for **The Bal Banal** *on 14 March, 1924,* **1923. Price 15 Francs.**
Black print on beige paper.
13 x 6½ in., 33 x 16.5 cm.
Signed in the plate lower left and dated: "N. Gontcharova, 923."
Provenance: *Vintage Posters,* London: Bloomsbury, 14 November 2012, Lot 167. This is a variant of No. 565 [R433], but priced at 15 francs.

566, 566a [R434].
Two-sided Program for The Bal Olympique, **1924.**
Black print on yellow paper and black print on blue paper.
Signed in the plate lower right under the costume design: "N. Gontcharova."
25⅝ x 10 in., 65 x 25.5 cm.
Other inscriptions: beneath the costume design: "Gontcharova. Projet pour le Bal Olympique pouvant servir aux deux sexes; recommandé aux personnes pressées. Matière: Papier ou calicot coloriés." Below

this follow the events of the Program. On the reverse: "Bal Olympique. Vrai Bal Sportif costumé organisé par l'Union des Artistes Russes à Paris le vendredi 11 Juillet 1924 de minuit à 6 h. du matin à la Taverne de l'Olympia 28 Bd des Capucines (2me entrée 8 rue Caumartin)." From this it is clear that Goncharova's costume design was meant to be simple and unisex.
Provenance: Drouot-Richelieu, Aguttes Auction House, Paris, 2005, 19 December, Lot 182 (reproduced).

566

Goncharova as contributor:

566b [NIRE].

Jean Metzinger: *Poster for* **the Bal de la Grande Ourse** *on 8 May, 1925.*

Green and yellow on off-white paper.
Central image signed in the plate: J. Metzinger.
19⅝ x 12⅝ in., 50 x 32 cm.
Other inscriptions by Goncharova in ink: underneath the central image: "A Madame Muller" and "N. Gontcharova," who perhaps contributed to the design of the poster; on top, over the image in Goncharova's hand: "Invitation." Small yellow script on the bottom advertises the ball to be held from 10 pm till 6 am.
Provenance: Vintage Posters, London: Bloomsbury, 14 November 2012, Lot 167 (reproduced).

Mme. Müller is Nüta (Anna) Müller-Groholski, great niece of the Russian painter Nikolai Sverchkov.

Note: Goncharova and Larionov were involved in the organization of at least four charity balls in Paris during the 1920s, i.e., the *Grand Bal des Artistes,* or *Grand Bal Travesti Transmental* (23 February, 1923, at the Salle Bullier), the *Bal Banal* (14 March, 1924, at the Salle Bullier), the *Bal Olympique, Vrai Bal Sportif* (11 July, 1924, at the Taverne de l'Olympia), and the *Bal* (also *Balle) de la Grande Ourse* (8 May, 1925). All were sponsored by the Union of Russian Artists.

The *Grand Bal des Artistes,* held at the Salle Bullier on the Ave. de l'Observatoire near the Closerie des Lilas restaurant, was the most ambitious of the four and, as

566b

Larionov's flyer proclaims (No. 725 [R616]), it was a "Foire de Nuit" rather than a "Bal de Nuit."[374] The program included four dance bands and two bars serving "pommes frites anglaises et cocktails"[375] and the dancing was supplemented by all kinds of happenings:

> Gontcharova et sa boutique de masques, Delaunay et sa Compagnie Transatlantique de pickpockets, Larionov et son Rayonnisme, Léger et son orchestre-décor, Cliazde [=Iliazd] et ses accès de fièvre au 41e degré.[376]

Supervised by a committee that included Goncharova and Larionov, the *Grand Bal* was a philanthropic venture for the Union of Russian Artists — a society that brought together many of the Russian émigré painters and critics such as Viktor Bart, Sonia Delaunay, Serge Romoff, Léopold Survage, and Ilia Zdanevich (cf. No. 1185 [R495]). Goncharova and Larionov designed much of the publicity material for this *Bal,* including the program (by Larionov, see No. 725 [R616]), the flyer (Larionov), and the ticket (Larionov, see No. 726 [R617]) as well as the large poster (Goncharova). Larionov also invited Russian and French colleagues, the "plus grands génies du monde,"[377] including Bart, Albert Gleizes, Juan Gris, Fernand Léger, Pablo Picasso, and Survage to sponsor and design forty *loges,* or boxes, which were then sold in aid of the Union.

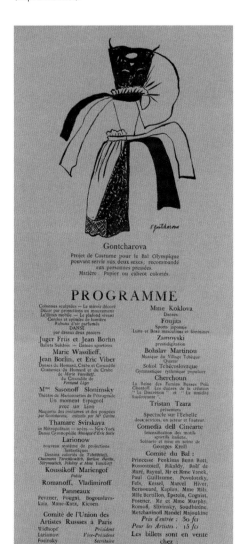

566a

Marie Vassilieff also designed a poster for one of the Bullier balls (see No. 1116 [R370]).

As with her other publicity materials for the *Bal Banal* (flyer and ticket) and the *Bal Olympique* (poster, program, and ticket), Goncharova incorporated motifs from her contemporary paintings and ballet designs, and in style and composition this poster brings to mind a number of canvases such as *Bathers* (1917-23, Grosvenor Gallery, London) and the several renderings of Spanish women.

Le Mariage d'Aurore or Le Mariage de la Belle au Bois Dormant: *extract from the ballet* La Belle au Bois Dormant (Sleeping Beauty). *Produced by Sergei Diaghilev for the Ballets Russes on 18 May, 1922, at the Théâtre National de l'Opéra, Paris; choreography by Marius Petipa with modifications by Bronislava Nijinska; designs by Alexandre Benois and Natalia Goncharova.*

See No. 94 [R87] for plot summary.

567 [99; R435].
Costume Design for the Shah Shahriar, ca. 1922.
Gouache, gold, silver and pencil.
Signed lower right: "N. Goncharova."
16¼ x 10⅞ in., 41.3 x 27.5 cm.
Provenance: Alexander Malitsky, Bay Shore, New York, May, 1974. Now in a private collection.
Reproduced in color on the cover of the Souvenir Program for the *Ballets Russes à l'Opéra*, Paris, 1922, May-June; in the Souvenir Program for *Colonel W. de Basil's Ballets Russes*, New York, 1935, unpaginated; and in A34, p. 164; F107, p. 140; I117, p. 372; I130, p. 109; Parton, *Goncharova,* p. 351; and in black and white in I40, No. 54; I51, No. 112.

567

Note: Le Mariage d'Aurore (also-called *Les Noces d'Aurore*) became a good box office draw and it was revived several times by Diaghilev and then de Basil. Benois was responsible for the designs except for the costumes for the episode known as the "Contes des Fées," which Goncharova created. In the 1922 season the part of Shah Shahriar was danced by Nikolai Semenov.

Les Noces: *choral ballet in four scenes by Igor Stravinsky. Produced by Sergei Diaghilev for the Ballet Russes on 13 June, 1923, at the Théâtre de la Gaité-Lyrique, Paris, with choreography by Bronislava Nijinska, and designs by Natalia Goncharova.*

Les Noces *treats a traditional Russian, peasant wedding — the consecration of the bride, the consecration of the bride-groom, the leave-taking of the bride, and the wedding celebration.*

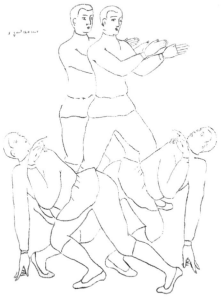

568

568 [R436].
A Group of Four Dancers, ca. 1923.
Pencil.
Signed upper left: "N. Gontcharova."
19⅞ x 15 in., 50.5 x 38 cm.
Provenance: John Carr-Doughty, Leicester, England, 3 November, 1981.
Reproduced in I13, plate 6; I9, p. 27; I51, No. 113; I117, p. 381; Parton, *Goncharova,* p. 362; and in many other sources. There exist numerous variants and tracings of this drawing, a composite costume design and choreographic study. There is a replica in the collection of the Victoria and Albert Museum, London (see G36, No. 69); a version with gouache added was formerly in the collection of Boris Kochno (see D16, p. 187 for color reproduction, and pp. 189, 191 for photographs); another version is in the collection of the Wadsworth Atheneum (see I11, p. 99); also see J31, Lot 37.

Note: Stravinsky worked for several years on the score of *Les Noces* (originally called

Les Noces Villageoises); in fact, in his correspondence with Stravinsky, Diaghilev refers to *Les Noces* as early as November, 1914. According to Kochno, Goncharova designed three different versions for *Les Noces,* one in vivid, folkloristic style and another in half-tones with gold and silver embroidery; but Diaghilev rejected these, suggesting that she design the costumes like everyday work clothes with trousers and shirts for the men and tunics for the women.[378] Goncharova took this kind of clothing as her model, modified it, and produced "costumes très sobres ... de deux couleurs: marron et blanc."[379] This simple resolution integrated fully with her austere background:

> a plain backcloth and wings, together with one or two central 'flats,' in which windows of varying colours were inserted to indicate changes of place.[380]

Bronislava Nijinska, the choreographer for this production was also audacious in her resolution:

> *Les Noces* opened up a new path in choreography for me: promoting the corps de ballet to a primary artistic level. I did not want there to be a dominant performer (soloist) in this spectacle. I wanted all the dancers to fuse in one movement and to create a whole. In my choreography the mass of the ensemble was meant to "speak" — able to create just as many choreographic nuances as the orchestra mass does musical ones.[381]

With Felia Doubrovska as the principal dancer, *Les Noces* scored a great success in Paris, although its showing in London in 1926 brought forth much negative comment.[382]

The Firebird (L'Oiseau de Feu): *ballet in two scenes with music by Igor Stravinsky based on the Russian fairy-tale. Produced by Sergei Diaghilev for the Ballets Russes at the Lyceum Theater, London, on 25 November, 1926, with choreography by Michel Fokine and designs by Natalia Goncharova.*

See No. 370 [R340] for plot summary.

569 [100; NIRE].
Costume Design for One of the Monsters, ca. 1926.
Watercolor.
Signed upper right: N. Gontcharova."
17¾ x 6¾ in., 45 x 17 cm.
Other inscriptions: cloth annotations throughout.
Provenance: *Russian XIX and XX Century Art Auction,* London: MacDougall's, 15 June, 2007, Lot 69 (reproduced).
Reproduced in Parton, *Goncharova,* p. 366.

570 [101; R437].
Backcloth Design for the Finale, ca. 1926.
Watercolor.
Signed lower left: "N. Gontcharova."
28 x 40 in., 71 x 101.5 cm.

569

Provenance: Irina Bashkiroff (a student of Goncharova), New York, May, 1974. Now in a private collection.

Reproduced in color in B115, plate 44; F107, p. 140; G70; I77, p. 133; I115, p. 196; I117, p. 283; and as the cover to I40; I130, p. 97; Parton, *Goncharova,* p. 357; and in black and white in D10, p. 93; I51, No. 114; partial reproduction in C7, plate 144; G28, plate 54A; Goncharova used part of this design for her cover for the Souvenir Program for *Colonel W. de Basil's Ballets Russes,* New York, 1935-36 season. There is a variation of this design in the collection of the Victoria and Albert Museum, London (reproduced in color as the cover of G59 and on p. 43; for other reproduction and commentary see G36, No. 87; Chamot, *Gontcharova,* p. 81). Another version is reproduced in D13, opp. p. 97. A photograph of the 1935 de Basil revival of *L'Oiseau de Feu* in Monte Carlo showing No. 570 [R437] is in G14, p. 35; and of the 1954 Covent Garden revival in I54, p. 16.

Note: The designs for the 1910 production of *L'Oiseau de Feu* had been ruined by rain during storage in a railroad car in 1922. Consequently, Diaghilev commissioned Goncharova to replace the Golovin's original

pieces, his castle, for example, now becoming a fabulous Christian City — a scene that had been left out of the 1910 production. This rendering, reminiscent to Serge Grigoriev of "ancient Russian icons,"[383] was used for the several revivals of *The Firebird,* including the 1961 Royal Ballet production in Moscow. Mary Chamot has described the result as a "perfect instance of how the décor of an imaginative artist can enhance the dramatic and emotional effect of music and dancing."[384]

Chota Roustaveli: *ballet in four acts with music by Arthur Honegger, Alexandre Tcherepnine, and Tibor Harsányi, based on Shota Rustaveli's epic tale* The Knight in the Panther's Skin. *Produced by Serge Lifar on 5 May, 1946, at the Théâtre de Monte Carlo with choreography by Serge Lifar and designs by Alexandre Shervashidze.*

Under Queen Tamara, Avtandil is sent by his beloved Tinatin, ruler of Arabia, to find a mysterious knight clad in a panther's skin, who turns out to be Prince Tariel. Avtandil helps Tariel find his beloved, Nestan-Darejan, the daughter of the King of India, who is held captive by evil spirits. Avtandil and Tariel free her and a double wedding ensues.

570

571 [NIRE].
Costume Design for Tariel Clad as a Panther,
1943.
Watercolor.
Signed top left corner: "N. Gontcharova."
15 x 8⅞ in., 38 x 22.5 cm.
Other inscriptions: on the right: faint pencil drawing of a torso and illegible inscriptions; on the bottom in brown pencil, in another's hand: "Tariel, Algaroff", and underneath in blue pencil: "et Trailine"; and Lifar collection stamp in the right corner.
Provenance: gift from Serge Lifar, Paris, 1965. Now in a private collection.
Reproduced in I14, No. 73; Parton, *Goncharova,* p. 382.
Reference is to Youli Algaroff-Metzl (Yulii Vladimirovich Algarov, 1918-1995), who danced Tariel, and to Boris Trailine (1921-2012), a Greek-born Russian dancer, who also performed in the same ballet in 1946.

Note: Goncharova held great store by Lifar's wartime project of the Georgian epic, for which she produced numerous sketches for costumes and sets. However, at the last moment Goncharova withdrew her designs, Shervashidze was asked to substitute, and, in fact, the premiere took place only after the War and in Monte Carlo, not in Paris. Not immodestly, Lifar recalled of his production that

> From far and wide there came a discerning public to witness the performance. I felt at once that contact with life had again been made… I had proved that the Dance was not dead in Europe.[385]

571

356 Goncharova. From Preface to the catalog of her one-woman exhibition, M, 1913. Translation in B12, pp. 56, 58.
357 The word *igralishche,* an uncommon derivation from the word *igra* (play, game), does not have a clear meaning here. It could refer to a group of artists in 1914 who called themselves by the term, but there is no record of such an association; more probably, it refers to the group of scene decorators who worked for Diaghilev's company. As for the painting *Lady in a Hat,* this was already a celebrated, if not, notorious picture by the fall of 1913, having been reproduced, for example, in connection with Goncharova's and Mikhail Larionov's endeavor to open a Futurist theater in Moscow — in the journal *Teatr v karikaturakh,* M, 1913, No. 1, p. 14.
358 G20, p. 127.
359 G24, p. 32.
360 F19, p. 316.
361 S. Volkonsky: *Otkliki teatra,* P: Sirius, undated, p. 57. For other Russian commentary on the *Coq d'Or* in Paris see A. Rimsky-Korsakov: "'Zolotoi petushok' na parizhskoi i londonskoi stsenakh" in *Apollon,* SP, 1914, No. 6-7, pp. 46-54.
362 Individual sheets appear regularly at auction. See, for example, J30, Lots 112-15.
363 F48, p. 89.
364 Letter from Sergei Diaghilev to Igor Stravinsky dated 8 March, 1915. Quoted in D17, p. 101.
365 F28, p. 74.
366 See D1, p. 41
367 Diary entry by Ivan Bunin for 16 August 1929, in M. Grin, ed.: *Ustami Buninykh,* Munich: Posev, 1981, pp. 230-31.
368 N. Gontcharova: "Le Costume Théâtral" in M. Georges-Michel and W. George: *Les Ballets Russes,* Paris: Vorms, 1930, p. 22. For a detailed discussion of the entire episode of *Liturgie,* see V. Antonov: "Neudavshiisia zamysel Diagileva" in *Russkie novosti*, Paris, 1953, No. 427, p. 6. Also see D26, p. 296. For further commentary see A. de Stael: "Apostoly Goncharovoi" in *Teatr,* Berlin, 1922, No. 14, pp. 8-9.
369 It is highly unlikely that Goncharova designed this costume in 1914. Presumably, the date 1914 was added later and perhaps not by Goncharova.
370 There is some confusion regarding the number and type of editions of *L'Art Décoratif Théâtral Moderne.* The 1919 edition is the most familiar one, although this was divided into three kinds, i.e., 1) of 15 copies, *édition de tête,* numbered A to O; 2) of 100 copies of lesser quality; and 3) of 400 copies with an inferior color mix. According to J31, Lot 165, there was then a 1921 edition, and according to I15, p. 324, there was even a 1930 edition. John Bowlt is indebted to Andrei de Saint-Rat for these bibliographical details.
371 Another gouache/silkscreen of this costume, auctioned in London in June, 1981, was described as a "design for Catherine Devilliers in *España"* (see J30, Lot 141, and cf. No. 710 [R601]). Catherine Devilliers (Ekaterina Devilier), a ballet dancer, had been one of the leading attractions at the Blue Bird cabaret in Berlin in 1922 before her further emigration to Paris.
372 See D8, pp. 322-23.
373 S. Romoff: "Le Cubisme dans l'Art théâtral" in *L'Art,* Paris, 1919, May, p. 11.
374 The flyer is reproduced in Loguine, *Gontcharova et Larionov,* p. 132.
375 Ibid.
376 Ibid. The reference is to Ilia Zdanevich and his 410 group (see No. 1184 [R494]).
377 Loguine, op. cit., p. 132.
378 D17, p. 189.
379 S. Grigoriev: "Gontcharova et Larionov. Peintres-Décorateurs des Ballets de Diaghilev" in Loguine, *Gontcharova et Larionov,* p. 113. For more information on Bronislava and the production of *Les Noces,* see N. Van Norman Baer: "The Choreographic Career of Bronislava Nijinska" in B183, pp. 60-78.
380 D11, p. 186.
381 B. Nizhinskaia: "'Svadebka' Stravinskogo" in *Novoe russkoe slovo,* New York, 1983, 9 November, p. 5. For further information see I66, pp. 32-36.
382 See the statement by H.G. Wells condemning the "deliberate dullness of the London critics" in D17, p. 190.
383 Grigoriev: "Gontcharova et Larionov," p. 113.
384 Chamot: *Gontcharova,* p. 81.
385 F23, p. 307.

GRIGORIEV (Grigorieff), Boris Dmitrievich

Born 11 (23) July, 1886, Moscow, Russia; died 8 February, 1939, Cagnes-sur-Mer, France.

1899 graduated from high school in Rybinsk; 1901 the Grigoriev family moved to Moscow; 1903-07 studied at CSIAI under Dmitrii Shcherbinovsky (1905-07); 1907-13 attended the Higher Art Institute of IAA, taking courses under Dmitrii Kardovsky and Alexander Kiselev; 1908 onward contributed to many exhibitions including the "Triangle," the "Impressionists," the "World of Art" and the Munich "Secession"; 1912-13 contributed caricatures to the journal *Satirikon* and then, in 1914, to *Novyi satirikon* [New Satyricon]; 1912-14 lived in Paris; studied at the Académie de la Grande Chaumière; made drawings and paintings of Paris life, some of which were published in 1918 in the collection *Intimité;* traveled in Italy, Greece, Hungary, and Switzerland; 1916 with Sergei Sudeikin and Alexandre Jacovleff decorated the interior of the Petrograd cabaret The Comedians' Halt; during these years was patronized by Alexander Burtsev, a collector and editor of the journal *Moi zhurnal dlia nemnogikh* [My Journal for the Few] in which Grigoriev's works were reproduced; 1917-18 worked on a cycle of pictures which became the basis of the *Raseia* [Russia] published in Russia in 1918 (and Germany in 1922); 1918 taught at CSIAI; 1919 designed *Snegurochka* for the Bolshoi Theater (not produced); emigrated to Berlin; 1921 arrived in Paris, where he had a one-man show at the Galerie Povolozky (December, 1921-January, 1922); in the early 1920s was close to Jacovleff and Vasilii Shukhaev; 1923-38 visited the US many times; 1923 took part in the "Exhibition of Russian Painting and Sculpture" at the Brooklyn Museum, New York; 1927 built a house at Cagnes-sur-mer, the Villa "Borisella"; 1928 professor at the Academy of Fine Art, Santiago, Chile; one-man show at the Museo de Bellas Artes there; 1930 returned to France; 1935 appointed Dean of the New York Academy of Applied Arts; 1936 visited Chile; 1938 returned to Cagnes-sur-mer.

Bibliography
N. Punin: "Tri khudozhnika" in *Apollon*, P, 1915, No. 8-9, pp. 1-14.
V. Dmitriev and V. Voinov: *Boris Grigoriev. Intimité*, P-Berlin: Yasnyi, 1918.
A. Tolstoi et al.: *Boris Grigoriev. Raseia*, Potsdam: Müller, and Berlin: Efron, undated; Russian edition: *Boris Grigoriev. Raseia*, Potsdam: Müller, and P-Berlin: Efron, 1922.
N. Radlov: "Boris Grigoriev" in his *Ot Repina do Grigorieva*, P: Brokgauz and Efron, 1923, pp. 49-58.
C. Brinton : *Boris Grigoriev*. Catalog of exhibition at the Worcester Art Museum, Worcester, Mass., 1924.
L. Réau et al.: *Boris Grigoriev. Faces of Russia,* Berlin and London: Sinaburg, 1924. Editions also in French and German.
C. Farrère et al.: *Boris Grigoriev. Boui Bouis,* Berlin: Razum, 1924.
A14, Vol. 3, pp. 174-75.
C. Grigorieff: *Boris Grigorieff*. Catalog of exhibition at the Château-Musée de Cagnes-sur-mer, 1978-79.
T. Galeeva: "Risunki Borisa Grigorieva" in *Sovetskaia grafika*, M, 1986, No. 10, pp. 251-62.
R. Antipova: *Boris Grigoriev*. Catalog of exhibition at the Pskov State Combined Historical, Architectural, and Art Museum, Pskov, 1989.
R. Antipova, comp.: "Pisma" in *Nashe nasledie*, M, 1990, No. 4, pp. 44-60.
V. Dudakov: "Boris Grigoriev" in *Russkaia mysl*, Paris, 1990, 25 May, p. 11.
A. Kamensky: "Boris Grigoryev's 'Russia'" in *Moscow News Weekly*, Moscow, 1990, No. 8-9, p. 23.
S.-A. Stommels: *Boris Dmitrievich Grigoriev*, Nijmegen: Quick Print, 1993.
T. Galeeva: *Boris Grigoriev*, M: Galart, 1995.
A42, pp. 197-99.
H34, pp. 239-43.
G. Pospelov: *"Liki Rossii" Borisa Grigorieva*, M: Iskusstvo, 1999.
R. Antipova, ed.: *Boris Grigoriev i khudozhestvennaia kultura XX veka. Materialy III Grigorievskikh chtenii*, Pskov: Pskov State Combined Historical, Architectural, and Art Museum, 2004.
V. Terekhina: *Boris Grigoriev. Liniia. Literaturnoe i khudozhestvennoe nasledie*, M: Fortuna EL, 2006.
T. Galeeva: *Boris Dmitrievich Grigoriev*, SP: Zolotoi vek, 2007.
R. Antipova: "Perepiska Borisa Grigorieva s baronessoi Mariei Vrangel" in *Novyi zhurnal*, New York, 2010, No. 261, pp. 85-126.
V. Kruglov et al.: *Boris Grigoriev*, SP: Palace Editions, 2011.

Like his friends Jacovleff and Shukhaev, Grigoriev was a member of the second generation of World of Art, supporting the traditions of Alexandre Benois, Léon Bakst, Mstislav Dobujinsky, and Konstantin Somov. Like them, Grigoriev regarded line as a visual element of great importance and even in his paintings treated it as his dominant method of expression. In its emotional intensity, Grigoriev's line sometimes brings to mind the later German Expressionists such as Otto Dix and George Grosz. As Grigoriev once said: "Line encloses all the weight of form within its angles and dispenses with all the immaterial... Line is the creator's swiftest and most intimate medium of expression."[386] In his piquant *intimités* of bordello scenes, Grigoriev also maintained the strong erotic tradition of the World of Art, although for him titillation was to be found in heterosexuality rather than in homosexuality.

The incisive contours of Grigoriev's drawings seem to evoke the very lifeforce of Russia:

> Portraits of souls, cosmic stylizations. Beneath the impression of a chance characteristic feature of a face, he sees the eternal, permanent physiognomy of the chance model; it is not an episodic visage but, so to say, its astral essence.[387]

So impressive was Grigoriev's artistic skill that the critic Nikolai Punin, one of the first champions of Grigoriev's art, compared the artist to a coachman who knows every quirk of his horses, their strengths and weaknesses.[388] But not everyone liked Grigoriev's often harsh Realism, as the writer Georgii Grebenshchikov indicated in a letter to Grigoriev of 1935:

> your art does not delight in the sense of mastery, IT DOESN'T MAKE ME JOYFUL. Imagine — I like you, but I'm afraid of your art. It emphasizes the negative features of life, the body, and even nature too much.[389]

572 [102; R438].
Four Dancers on a Stage, 1913.
Gouache.
Signed and dated lower left in Russian: "B. Grigoriev 13."
16⅞ x 33¼ in., 43 x 84.5 cm.
Other inscriptions: on reverse in pencil in Russian: "B. Grigoriev 13."
Provenance: *Russian Paintings, Drawings,*

Watercolours and Sculpture, London: Sotheby's, 5 March, 1981, Lot 132 (reproduced).

Reproduced in color in B115, plate 75; F107, p. 141; I77, p. 147; I117, p. 528; M157, p. 52; and in black and white in *Moi zhurnal dlia nemnogikh,* SP, 1913, Vol. 8-10, unpaginated; I51, No. 115. For reproductions of similar designs see L211, pp. 38-41; and Kruglov et al., *Boris Grigoriev,* pp. 72, 73. Two similar designs were in the collection of the late David Sigalov, Kiev. A similar scene dated 1913 in the collection of Evgeniia Chudnovskaia, St. Petersburg, entitled *Low Season in Paris (Fashionable Dance),* is reproduced in color in Galeeva, *Boris Grigoriev,* No. 7; an analogous scene is reproduced in color in L113, Lot 80.

Note: This sketch seems to depict a scene from a Paris cabaret such as Le Chat Noir (cf. L1, Lot 59) and in both subject and style recalls the sardonic exaggerations of Sudeikin — in the early years a major influence on Grigoriev. That to some critics Grigoriev's drawings were merely "coarse imitations of Sudeikin" [390] is not surprising, given the personal and professional proximity of the two artists, for example, their joint collaboration (with Jacovleff) on the interior designs for the Comedians' Halt, the Petrograd cabaret established in 1916.[391] Some of Grigoriev's scenes of cafés, bars, and more dubious establishments are reproduced in his album *Intimité* of 1918.

Note: The theme of this work relates closely to Grigoriev's favorite motifs of the masquerade, the café-chantant, and the *femme fatale,* which he drew and painted in St. Petersburg, Berlin, and Paris. Analogous drawings are reproduced in the de luxe album by Vsevolod Dmitriev and Vsevolod Voinov, *Boris Grigoriev. Intimité,* and in Grigoriev's *Boui Bouis* (also see Galeeva, *Boris Dmitrievich Grigoriev,* pp. 31-91). Grigoriev played an active, although brief role in émigré publishing-houses in Berlin, including Slovo, of which the publicist and historian Boris Isaakovich Elkin (1887-1972) was director.

386 B. Grigoriev: "Liniia," in Tolstoi, *Boris Grigoriev. Raseia,* unpaginated.
387 A. Shaikevich: "Mir Borisa Grigorieva," ibid.
388 Punin, "Tri khudozhnika," p. 1.
389 Letter from Georgii Grebenshchikov to Boris Grigoriev dated 7 June, 1935, formerly in the collection of the late Cyrille Grigorieff, Cagnes-sur-mer, France.
390 Essem: "Tovarishchestvo nezavisimykh" in *Russkaia khudozhestvennaia letopis,* SP, 1913, No. 3, March.
391 For information on Grigoriev's involvement in the Comedians' Halt see V. Perts and Yu. Piriutko: "Klub khudozhnikov, artistov i poetov" in *Dekorativnoe iskusstvo,* M, 1983, No. 11, pp. 29-34; and E37.

GRIGORIEV, Mikhail Alexandrovich

Born 13 (25) May, 1899, St. Petersburg, Russia; died 25 September, 1960, Leningrad, Russia.

1918-20 attended the Petrograd Svomas under Dmitrii Kardovsky, Kuzma Petrov-Vodkin, and Vasilii Shukhaev; 1920s worked as an artist for newspapers and magazines such as *Krasnaia gazeta* [Red Newspaper] and *Ogonek* [Little Flame]; 1927 worked on agit-designs for the celebration of the tenth anniversary of the Revolution; 1927 onwards worked predominantly as a theater designer for a wide variety of plays and operas for the Theater of Comedy, the Bolshoi, the Theater of the Young Spectator, etc.; 1940s painted and drew anti-Nazi pictures and cartoons; 1948-58 artist-in-residence for the Komissarzhevskaia Dramatic Theater in Leningrad; 1950s several one-man exhibitions in Leningrad.

Bibliography
M. Grigoriev: *Kogda khudozhniku shestdesiat,* L-M: Iskusstvo, 1964.
A14, Vol. 3, pp. 178-79 (contains a list of publications).

While distant from the more celebrated masters of Leningrad stage design such as Nikolai Akimov, Tatiana Bruni, and Leonid Chupiatov, Grigoriev achieved a solid reputation for his capable, if eclectic, decorations in Leningrad theaters. His repertoire was vast, including drama, opera, and the ballet, ancient and modern, and he could move easily between Gozzi and Schiller, Mark Twain and Dumas, Ostrovsky and Tchaikovsky, Molière and O'Henry. As chief designer for the Komissarzhevskaia Dramatic Theater, Grigoriev supported a plain style alleviated by an occasional "orientalism" or reference to the late Romantic splendours of Mikhail Bocharov and Matvei Shishkov. Grigoriev was also the author of essays on questions of scenography and on individual stage designers such as Sofia Yunovich, while he himself became the focus of much critical acclaim in the 1950s-60s.

Unknown production, 1930s.

574 [NIRE].
Design for a Curtain, 1930s.
Watercolor
3¼ x 4⅛ in., 8.3 x 10.5 cm.
Provenance: private transaction.

573

573 [103; R439].
Four Masked Actors, 1920.
Pencil, watercolor, and gouache.
Signed, inscribed, and dated on the reverse in Russian: "To dear B.I. Elkin, Boris Grigoriev, Berlin, 920."
14⅛ x 12 in., 36 x 30.5 cm.
Provenance: Marina Henderson, London, March 1981.
Reproduced in color in B115, plate 76; I77, p. 147; M157, p. 52; N188, p. 16; and in black and white in I51, No. 116; J22, Lot 107; M73, p. 91.

574

GRIGORIEV, Pavel Alexeevich

Born 15 (27) January, 1846, St. Petersburg (?), Russia; died after 1884, St. Petersburg (?), Russia.

1865 studied architecture at IAA; 1868 switched from student to auditor; 1872 awarded Silver Medal; 1880s designed a number of productions, including *Boris Godunov* and *Tsar Ivan the Terrible* for St. Petersburg theaters; also contributed caricatures to the St. Petersburg journal *Shut* (Buffoon).

Bibliography
Nothing substantial has been published on Pavel Grigoriev. For some information see S. Isakov et al., eds.: *Imperatorskaia Sankt-Peterburgskaia Akademiia khodozhestv*, P: Golike and Vilborg, 1915, Vol. 2, p. 320.

Aldona (I Lituani): *lyrical drama in three acts and a prologue by Amilcare Ponchielli based on a libretto by Antonio Ghislanzoni. Produced in St. Petersburg on 8 November, 1884, with dances arranged by Marius Petipa and designs by Pavel Grigoriev.*
In 14th-century Lithuania, Corrado Wallenrod, actually a Lithuanian named Walter, who is impersonating a loyal Teutonic Knight, allows the Lithuanians to win against the Teutons by executing a long-planned misdirection. Aldona, a Lithuanian princess and his wife, who has entered a convent, searches for her love Walter, and finds him just before he is

sentenced to death for his deception. Rather than fall into the hands of the enemy, Walter drinks poison and dies in Aldona's arms.

575 [R440].
Costume Design for One of the Eight Young Girls in the Corps de Ballet, 1884.
Watercolor and ink.
Signed and dated lower right in Russian: "1884 Grigoriev."
10½ x 5½ in., 26.7 x 14 cm.
Other inscriptions: upper left: "8 Jeunes Filles"; upper right: "Aldona Opera" followed by the Russian word: "Ballet."
Provenance: Igor Dychenko, Kiev, 1970.
Reproduced in I40, No. 55.

GUDIASHVILI, Lado (Vladimir) Davidovich

Born 18 (30) March, 1896, Tiflis, Georgia; died 20 July, 1980, Tbilisi, Georgia.

1910-14 attended the School for the Encouragement of the Fine Arts in Tiflis; 1914 began to teach at a local high school; 1915 first one-man exhibition in Tiflis; from this time until the end of 1919 played a leading part in the activities of the Tiflis artistic and literary world, associating with the Neo-Symbolist group known as The Blue Horns; 1919 with David Kakabadze, Sergei Sudekin, and Kirill Zdanevich worked on mural designs for the cabaret called Khimerioni; October, 1919, left Tiflis for Turkey and Italy, arriving in Paris on 1 January, 1920; 1920-25 lived in Paris; attended the Académie Ranson; influenced by Léon Bakst and by the general trend toward Art Deco; 1925 worked for Nikita Baliev's Chauve-Souris, designing revues such as *Not Far From Tiflis;* 1926 returned to Tbilisi; one-man exhibition there; 1930s attempted to combine his Parisian experience with the subjects and styles of Medieval Georgian art; 1930s and 1940s painted portraits, illustrated books, designed many productions for the Paliashvili Theater of Opera and Ballet in Tbilisi; 1950s continued to design spectacles and to paint themes related to ancient Georgia.

Bibliography
M. Raynal: *Lado Goudiachvili*, Paris: Au Sans Pareil, 1925.
A. Mikhailov: *Lado Gudiashvili*, M: Sovetskii khudozhnik, 1968.
L. Zlatkevich: *Lado Gudiashvili*, Tbilisi: Ganatleba, 1971.
V. Narakidze: *Gudiashvili*, Tbilisi: Khelovneba, 1976.
John E. Bowlt: "Lado Gudiasvili" in B47, pp. 7-16.
M. Kagan: *Lado Gudiashvili*, L: Aurora, 1983.
L. Gagua, comp.: *Lado Gudiashvili. Kniga vospominanii. Stati. Iz perepiski. Sovremenniki o khudozhnike*, M: Sovetskii khudozhnik, 1987.
T. Kobaladze: *Lado Gudiashvili*, Tbilisi: Merani, 1988.

Lado Gudiasvili. Catalog of exhibition at the Complesso Monumentale di San Michele a Ripa, Rome, 1991.
Yu. Didenko et al.: *Lado Goudiachvili*. Catalog of exhibition at the TG and the RM, 2009.
Lidiia Iovleva: "'Nesravnennyi Lado!' / 'The Incomparable Lado'" in *Tretiakovskaia galereia / Tretiakov Gallery*, M, 2009, No. 4, pp. 102-09.

During his sojourn in Paris, especially in 1922-23, Gudiashvili made many drawings incorporating the motifs of Georgian maidens and animals, and a number of these are in private collections in Paris.[392] Although Gudiashvili worked for the Chauve-Souris in Paris, he did not treat stage design as a central discipline until after he returned to Tbilisi in 1926. In his drawings and paintings of the Paris period, Gudiashvili paid homage to several contemporary artists, and his evocations of feminine beauty bring to mind the ample odalisques of Léon Bakst, even if, as the critic Maurice Raynal remarked in 1925:

> Malgré leur souplesse, les personnages de Lado conservent une sorte de respect pour ces attitudes hiératiques qui, venues des origines byzantines, marquent quand même l'art géorgien.[393]

The meticulous head-dresses with Art Nouveau patterns worn by Gudiashvili's women also remind us of Aubrey Beardsley and, more immediately, of Erté. For all his further debt to André Derain and Amedeo Modigliani, Gudiashvili was praised in Paris for his exotic, oriental subjects and, in fact, he never really adapted to Western styles. As the historian Georgii Lukomsky wrote in 1921:

> Gudiashvili does not need Paris. He does not need Europe. Back, as soon as possible, to Georgia, to sing the praises of his native land.[394]

Indeed, Gudiashvili soon returned to Tbilisi, where he developed a fulsome, monumental style that might have earned him the title of the "Georgian Rubens" had the quality of his work not declined substantially.

Lado Gudiashvili, Tbilisi, 1970.

576

576 [R441].
Costume Designs for Two Georgian Dancers, 1922.
Pencil and watercolor.
Signed and dated lower right: "Lado Goudiachvili. Paris, 1922."
19⅝ x 12¾ in., 50 x 32.5 cm.
Provenance: Vladimir Hessen, New York, June, 1976.
Reproduced in J16, Lot 809.

577 [R442].
Two Dancing Girls with a Doe, 1923.
Pencil.
Signed and dated lower right: "Lado Goudiachvili. Paris, 1923."
19⅝ x 12¾ in., 50 x 32.5 cm.

Provenance: Alexander Raydon Gallery, New York, 1975.
Reproduced in I40, No. 56; I51, No. 117; M25; N23.

Non Loin de Tiflis: *a revue with music by Alexei Arkhangelsky. Produced by Nikita Baliev's Chauve-Souris at the Théâtre Femina, Paris, 1924, with designs by Lado Gudiashvili.*

578 [R443].
Design for the Backdrop with a Country Inn: Scene from the Caucasus Incorporating Local Georgian Life, ca. 1924.
Watercolor.
Signed lower right: "Lado Goudiachvili."
10⅜ x 13¾ in., 26.5 x 35 cm.
Other inscriptions: the sign above the entrance to the inn reads in Russian: "Tavern. Don't leave, my dear. Wine to drink here or to go."
Provenance: *Russian Pictures, Icons and Russian Works of Art,* London: Sotheby's, 15 February, 1984, Lot 81 (reproduced).
Reproduced in A34, p. 180; I. Dzutsova: "An Unknown Page in the Stage Design Activity of Lado Gudiashvili" (in Georgian) in *Sabchota khelovneba,* Tbilisi, 1985, No. 3, p. 68, where the author discusses the work and an analogous piece in the context of Gudiashvili's career in the 1920s. A similar work is reproduced in color in the Souvenir Program for *Théâtre de la Chauve-Souris,* Paris: Théâtre Femina, 1924, p. 13; it is also reproduced in other souvenir programs. The 1924-25 Paris season of the Chauve-Souris was one of Baliev's most successful (see Nos. 295 [R265], 297 [R266], 345-48 [R310-13], 949 [R963]).

392 Several drawings, similar to the works in question, are reproduced in Raynal, *Lado Gudiashvili* (cf. *La Voyante, Les Caresses, La Chasse,* etc.).
393 Ibid., p. 15.
394 Georgii Lukomsky in *Le Figaro,* Paris, 1921, 25 February. Quoted in Zlatkevich, *Lado Gudiachvili,* p. 29.

HOERSCHELMANN (Gershelman), Karl Karlovich

Born 26 February (10 March), 1899, Sevastopol, Ukraine; died 21 December, 1951, Eichstätt, Germany.

The son of the Baltic aristocrats Maria and Carl von Hoerschelmann, Karl Hoerschelmann spent his childhood in Odessa; 1906-16 a Cadet, enrolled in the Odessa, and then the St. Petersburg, Military Academy; 1918-20 served in Denikin's and Vrangel's armies; 1921 interned in Gallipoli; 1922 reached Riga via Rumania, Bulgaria, and Poland; 1922 settled in Reval (Tallinn); 1926 married Elizaveta Rozendorf (Elisabeth Rosendorf), who had worked as an artist for the State Porcelain Factory in Petrograd in 1919-20; 1920s onwards Hoerschelmann worked in many capacities, e.g., as a technical draftsman for the Ministries of Agriculture and Transport and for various factories, a studio painter, a stage and textile designer, and an illustrator; exhibited in many cities, including Tallinn, Helsinki, Kiel, and Königsberg; 1933 designed the cover and illustrations for Pavel Irtel's almanac *Virgin Soil;* 1933-38 member of the Tallinn Guild of Poets; 1940 after the Red Army's occupation of the Baltic states moved to Poland; 1945 moved to Eichstätt; continued to paint and write poetry until his death.

Bibliography
T. Pachmuss: *Russian Literature in the Baltic between the World Wars.* Columbus: Slavic, 1988, pp. 147-48.
Elisabeth von Hoerschelmann. Karl von Hoerschelmann. Catalog of exhibition at the Museum Ostdeutsche Galerie, Regensburg, 1989.
S. Suchkov: "Takoi smeshnoi, v shtanakh i pidzhake... " in *Russkaia mysl,* Paris, 2000, 27 January, p. 14.

577

S. Isakov, ed.: *K.K. Gershelman. "Ya pochemu-to dolzhen rasskazat o tom...."*, *Izbrannoe*, Tallin: Ingri, 2006.

Hoerschelmann was an amateur in the good sense of the word, experimenting with many disciplines and many methods, although his preferred style was a pleasing integration of Art Nouveau and Art Deco, manifest in the poster below. Influenced by the early work of Vasilii Kandinsky, especially the watercolors, Hoerschelmann also investigated the more emphatic delineations of Constructivism, an approach that functioned well in book illustrations and promotional material such as posters, i.e., media intended to catch the public eye. Hoerschelmann's clarity and simplicity of presentation earned him high praise from critics and poets such as Yurii Ivask in his adopted homeland.

579 [104; R861].
Poster Design for a Conjuror, 1923 (?).
Watercolor and India ink.
Signed middle right with the monogram in Russian: "K G."
20¾ x 10⅞ in., 52.6 x 27.8 cm.
Other inscription: the Russian word "Fokusnik" [Conjuror] appears at the top left of the work as part of the design.
Provenance: Anna Röder, daughter of Karl von Hoershelmann and Elisabeth Rosendorf, Andernach, Germany, February, 1993.
Reproduced in color in Isakov, *K.K. Gershelman. "Ya pochemu-to dolzhen rasskazat o tom...."*, *Izbrannoe*, p. 395; and in T21; T41; and *Elisabeth von Hoerschelmann. Karl von Hoerschelmann.* plate 39, p. 17.

579

HOUDIAKOFF, André
(Khudiakov/Chudiakoff/
Chudjakov, Andrei Timofeevich)

Born 30 November (12 December) 1894, Trubchevsk, Orel Region, Russia; died 1985, Newtown, Connecticut, USA.

1905-10 attended Trubchevsk City Institute; 1910 enrolled at MIPSA, taking lessons from Pavel Korin and Konstantin Korovin; 1911-18 member of the Circle of Art Lovers in Ivanovo-Voznesensk; 1917 joined the White Army; painted a portrait of Alexander Kerensky; 1920 emigrated to Berlin; 1921-24 designed numerous productions for Der Blaue Vogel; 1924 arrived in New York; 1920s worked for Nikita Baliev's Bat theater; 1920s-40s worked predominantly as a designer of stage designs, murals, and cartoons, especially for the Russian colony in New York; 1940s decorated part of the St. Regis Hotel, New York.

Bibliography
V. Zavalishin: "Pamiati Andreia Khudiakova" in *Novyi zhurnal*, New York, 1985, No. 161, pp. 286-92.
A53, Vol. 6, Book 3, p. 106.
H34, p. 594
Some information on Houdiakoff's association with the Blue Bird cabaret can be found in H31, passim.

Houdiakoff is one of the many artists of the Russian diaspora who, on emigrating to the West after the Revolution, seemed assured of a brilliant career, thanks to his exceptional talent, dashing personality, and auspicious entrée into flourishing companies such as the Blaue Vogel in Berlin and the Bat in New York. At the Blaue Vogel, whose logo he designed, Houdiakoff moved closely with Kseniia Boguslavskaia, Elena Lissner, Pavel Tchelitchew, and other young designers, most of whom were at the threshold of their careers. Here was a mercurial company of diverse styles that, on the one hand, could not maintain collegiate cohesion for long and, yet, on the other, created glitz and glamour, prompting impassioned audiences to speak of a "cabaret of colors."[395] Houdiakoff was largely responsible for this effervescence and in 1921-24 was virtually artist-in-residence at the Blaue Vogel, making the sets and costumes for Jascha Juschny's main such as *Bei den Zigeuner, Rjasaner Volkstanz, Bäuerinnen,* and *Träumerei.* Some of these colorful resolutions were seen in New York when the Blue Bird toured the USA in 1924 and 1931-32.

Much influenced by Korovin and Serge Sudeikin,[396] Houdiakoff described a Russia of lively Vankas playing accordions as mincing village maidens laughed and sang. Here was an innocuous distillation of Old Russia that, as Michaele Böhmig, has pointed out, still paid homage to the more grotesque art of David Burliuk, Mikhail Larionov, and other Neo-Primitivists of ca. 1910.[397] Houdiakoff's stylized interpretations of "colorful peasant women" and "stylish Katenkas"[398] delighted both the émigré and the German publics in Berlin, and Nikita Baliev, who thrived on such nostalgic merriness, made sure to hire Houdiakoff for the Bat when the artist moved to New York. Strangely enough, as designer and portraitist,[399] Houdiakoff almost vanished from the public arena after 1932 and Nicholas Martianoff even omitted him from his directory of Russian artists in America of that year (H11). Although Houdiakoff eked out a living by painting panneaux and portraits, he never justified the high hopes of the 1920s and to this day is neglected in studies of the emigration.[400]

Unidentified production for the Blaue Vogel Cabaret, Berlin, ca. 1920.

580 [NIRE].
Curtain Design, ca. 1920.
Gouache and gold paint on board.
15 x 20 in., 38 x 50.8 cm.

580

Provenance: *Dance. Theatre. Opera. Music Hall and Film,* New York: Sotheby's, 1984, 21 November, Lot 199 (reproduced), where it is described as a backdrop for several productions at the Blaue Vogel.

395 E.Tannenbaum: "Das Kabarett der Farben" in *Karussel,* Berlin, 1922-23, Book 1, pp. 9-10.
396 Conversation between André Houdiakoff and John E. Bowlt, Newtown, Connecticut, 15 October, 1981.
397 H31, p. 123.
398 S. Makovsky: "Siniaia ptitsa" in *Teatr,* Berlin, 1923, No. 12-13, p. 5.
399 For a reproduction of one of Houdiakoff's self-portraits see the second program for *Der Blaue Vogel,* Berlin, 1922, February, p. 10.
400 Houdiakoff's name is missing from the recent comprehensive surveys of Russian émigré culture in Berlin (e.g., H25, H28) and even the catalog of the panoramic exhibition "Moskau-Berlin" (K200).

IVANOFF, Serge (Ivanov, Sergei Petrovich)

Born 12 (24) December, 1893, Moscow, Russia; died 8 February, 1983, Paris, France.

1903-07 studied intermittently at MIPSA; 1918-22 enrolled in Pegoskhuma; studied under Vladimir Kozlinsky; 1920 studied under Dmitrii Kardovsky and Osip Braz; 1921 graduated from the Department of Painting; 1922 received the title of artist-painter; toured famine-stricken Volga regions, creating drawings which became the twenty-eight illustrations for his book on the famine in Bolshevik Russia, i.e. *La famine en Russie bolcheviste* (published by the Nouvelle Librairie Nationale in Paris in 1924); emigrated to Finland; 1923, arrived in Paris via England; 1925 illustrated J. Barbey d'Aurevilly's *Les Diaboliques*; 1920s onwards worked in commercial advertising and theater design; painted portraits, genre pictures, some blatantly erotic; 1928 exhibited in the "Salon des Tuileries," "Salon d'Automne," and "Société Nationale des Beaux-Arts" (of which he became a member in 1942); 1930-44 worked for the magazine *l'Illustration,* contributed drawings to the magazine *Plaisir de France* and to publications by and about leading fashion houses such as Moline, Paquin, and Elsa Schiaparelli; visited Brazil; made portraits of elders of the Catholic Church, including Pope Pius XI (1937), portraits of writers and artists, including Alexandre Benois, Viacheslav Ivanov, Natalia Goncharova, Serge Lifar, and Boris Zaitsev; 1942 exhibition at the Galeries de la Chaussée d'Antin (1942), 1950 moved to the USA; early 1960s returned to France; 1966 awarded gold medal by the Société Nationale des Beaux-Arts; 1988 Hotel Drouot held an auction of Ivanov's works, most of which were acquired by the Musée Carnavalet in Paris.

Bibliography
Atelier Serge Ivanoff. Catalog of auction at

581   582

Binoche et Godeau, Hôtel Drouot, Paris, 1988. 16 October.
H34, pp. 295, 296.
I. Shuvalova: "Zabytyi khudozhnik russkoi emigratsii (pamiati S.P. Ivanova)" in *Sranitsy istorii otechestvennogo iskusstva XII-XX vek,* SP, 2004, No. 4, pp. 100-07.
A. Avdeev et al.: *Serge Ivanoff. Ambassade de Russie à Paris.* Catalog of exhibition at the Embassy of the Russian Federation, Paris, May, 2006.
H51, passim.

Ivanoff is often associated with the artists of the St. Petersburgh World of Art such as Léon Bakst and Konstantin Somov, not least by virtue of his erotic subjects. As his grandson Alexandre Barberà-Ivanoff has observed :

> Ses recherches constantes lui permirent de développer sa fameuse 'belle matière', dans le genre de la nature morte et des scènes intimes.[401]

Ivanoff felt an especially close alliance with the St. Petersburg artist Dmitrii Kardovsky. His dancing couples, for example, are reminiscent of Kardovksky's illustrations for the ball scenes in Alexander Griboedov's play *Woe from Wit,*[402] although they also bring to mind Dobujinsky's dashing cossacks in *Platov's Cossacks in Paris* (see Nos. 430-31 [R463-64]). In any case, illustration was Ivanoff's forte and his drawings for French editions such as Charles Baudelaire's poetry[403] are fine examples of sensuous line and trenchant form. Indeed, Ivanoff implied that for him

583

the book was a physical object, a body which, almost like his female nudes depicted in tight embrace, could be felt, manipulated, and enjoyed.[404]

Note: Ivanoff produced the following items as illustrations to the article by Emile Vuillermoz, "Quelques Pas de Danse," which appeared in the December, 1937, issue of the Parisian journal *L'Illustration* (No. 4944).

Provenance: The watercolors were all acquired in January, 2008, after the auction of the same pieces at MacDougall's, London, on 29 November, 2007 (Lot 214, reproduced in color). The items had been sold previously as *Atelier Serge Ivanoff*, Paris: Binoche et Godau, Salle Drouot, Paris, on 16 October, 1988 (reproduced).

581 [NIRE].
Dancing Couples I (male partner from behind), Paris, ca. 1937.
Watercolor and pencil.
Signed lower right corner: "Serge Ivanoff."
9¼ x 6¼ in., 23.5 x 16 cm.

582 [NIRE].
Dancing Couples II (in profile), Paris, ca. 1937.
Watercolor and pencil.
Signed lower right corner: "Serge Ivanoff."
8¾ x 6 in., 22 x 15 cm.

583 [NIRE].
Two Dancing Couples: La Contredanse, Paris, ca. 1937.
Watercolor and pencil.
Signed lower right corner: "Serge Ivanoff."
8 x 4⅞ in., 20.5 x 12.5 cm.

401 A. Barberà-Ivanoff: untitled essay in Avdeev, *Serge Ivanoff. Ambassade de Russie à Paris*, p. 2.
402 For the cycle of Kardovsky's color illustrations see A. Griboedov: *Gore ot uma*, SP: Golike and Vilborg, 1913. For commentary see B. Zelinsky, ed.: *Slawische Buchillustration im 20. Jahrhundert. Russland, Polen, Tschechien, Slowakei*, Vienna: Böhlau, 1998, p. 42.
403 See Ivanoff's illustrations to the de luxe edition, of Baudelaire's *Petits Poèmes en prose*, Paris: Javal et Bourdeaux, 1933.
404 Conversation between Serge Ivanoff and John E. Bowlt, Paris, December, 1981.

Serge Ivanoff, 1976.

JACOVLEFF, Alexandre (Yakovlev, Alexander Evgenievich)

Born 13 (25) June, 1887, St. Petersburg, Russia; died 12 May, 1938, Paris, France.

1904-13 attended IAA, studying mainly under Dmitrii Kardovsky; established close contact with Isaak Brodsky, Boris Grigoriev, and Vasilii Shukhaev; 1909 onward contributed to many exhibitions at home and abroad, including the "World of Art" and the "Union of Russian Artists"; 1912 with Shukhaev designed Vsevolod Meierkhold's pantomime *The Lovers* at the Karabchevsky House, St. Petersburg; 1913 member of the World of Art society; 1914-15 with Vasilii Shukhaev resided in Italy and Spain on an Academy scholarship; 1916 with Grigoriev and Sergei Sudeikin worked on the interior of the Petrograd cabaret, The Comedians' Halt; with Shukhaev designed ceiling for the Firsanov mansion in Moscow; designed murals for the Orthodox Church of St. Nicholas in Bari, Italy, and for Kazan Station in Moscow; 1916-17 professor at the Institute of the History of Arts, Petrograd; 1917 with Kardovsky and Shukhaev established the Workshop of St. Luke in Petrograd; 1917-18 traveled in Mongolia, China, and Japan; 1919 settled in Paris; 1920 exhibited his Eastern scenes at the Galerie Barbazanges; 1922 one-man exhibition at the Art Institute, Chicago; published folio of drawings called *The Chinese Theater*; 1924-25 accompanied the Citroën Central Africa Expedition as official artist; 1926 one-man exhibition at the Galerie Charpentier, Paris; 1928 traveled to Ethiopia with Henry Rothschild; one-man exhibition at the Academy of Arts of the USSR, Leningrad; 1931 accompanied the Citroën Trans-Asiatic Expedition as official artist; 1934 appointed chairman of the Department of Painting at art school of the Boston Museum of Fine Arts; 1937 returned to Paris.

Bibliography
A. Iacovleff and S. Elisséeff: *Le théâtre japonais (kabuki)*, Paris: Brunhoff, 1933.
M. Birnbaum: *Jacovleff and Other Artists,* New York: Strick, 1946.
J. Kessel: *Alexandre Jacovleff 1887-1938.* Catalog of exhibition at the Galerie Vendôme, Paris, 1965.
Anon.: *Alexandre Iacovleff.* Catalog of exhibition at the Gropper Art Gallery, Cambridge, Mass., 1972. M2, Vol. 2, pp. 180-82.
N. Elizbarashvili, ed.: "Pisma V.I. Shukhaeva A.E. Yakovlevu iz Italii (1912-13) i Peterburga (1914-15)" in *Panorama iskusstv,* M, 1985, No. 8, pp. 173-90.
E. Yakovleva: "Eto bylo schastliveishee vremia…" in *Neva,* SP, 1987, No. 8, pp. 171-76.
V. Babiiak: "Aleksandr Evgenievich Yakovlev" in *Iskusstvo,* M, 1988, No. 8, pp. 62-68.
N. Uvarova, comp.: *A.E. Yakovlev, V.I. Shukhaev.* Catalog of exhibition at the State Russian Museum, L, and the State Museum of the Arts of the Georgian SSR, Tbilisi, 1988.
E. Yakovleva: "V. Shukhaev, A. Yakovlev. Kogda

kraska eshche svezha" in *Sovetskii muzei,* M, 1989, No. 2, pp. 42-53.
E. Yakovleva: "Shukhaev i Yakovlev. Novaia vstrecha" in *Sovetskii muzei,* M, 1990, No. 3, pp. 48-55.
G. Shcherbakova: "Khudozhnik-attashe" in *Khudozhnik,* M, 1990, No. 8, pp. 36-53.
E. Yakovleva, ed.: "Pisma V.I. Shukhaeva i A.E. Yakovleva D.N. Kardovskomu 1923-1934" in *Iskusstvo Leningrada,* L, 1991, No. 1, pp. 76-89; No. 2, 67-79.
L. Cerwinske: "An Emigrée's [sic] Life on Safari" in *Art and Antiques,* New York, 1993, May, pp. 62-67.
A. Aaron and M. Schaffer: *Alexandre Iacovleff.* Catalog of exhibition A La Vieille Russie, New York, 1993.
H34, pp. 657-60.
La Tradition Française. Tableaux modernes. Catalog of auction at the Hôtel des ventes, Fontainebleau, 2000, 16 April.
P. Rosenberg et al.: *Alexandre Iacovleff. Itinérances.* Catalog of exhibition at the Musée des Années 30, Boulogne-Bilancourt, 2004.
Works by Alexander Yakovlev and Nikolai Kalmakov from the Estate of a French Nobleman. Catalog of auction at Sotheby's, London, 10 June, 2008.
Art Moderne. Catalog of auction at Drouot-Richelieu, Paris, 21 November, 2008.
Jacovleff's own albums of sketches and paintings are also worthy of note: *Le Théâtre Chinois. Peintures, Sanguines et Croquis,* Paris: Brunoff, 1922; *Dessins et Peintures d'Afrique, Exécutés au Cours de l'Expedition Citroën Centre Asie.* Paris: Meynial, 1927.

Just before the 1917 Revolution, Jacovleff and his "double," Shukhaev, enjoyed acclaim as the representatives of a new classicism in Russian art. The "beautiful clarity"[405] of Jacovleff, Grigoriev, Kuzma Petrov-Vodkin, Shukhaev, and their colleagues within the second generation of World of Art artists brings to mind the concurrent poetry of Anna Akhmatova and Mikhail Kuzmin, leaders of the Acmeist movement. These graduates of the Academy of Arts and their literary colleagues moved in the same circles, frequenting St. Petersburg cabarets such as the Stray Dog and the Comedians' Halt and contributing to Sergei Makovsky's *Apollon* journal and salon.

Artistically and temperamentally Jacovleff was so close to Shukhaev that sometimes their portraits in red chalk are difficult to separate. "Sasha-Yasha," as Jacovleff was called, was a brilliant draftsman, and "lightness, clarity, healthiness, uncontrivedness"[406] were the hallmarks of his work. Just before the Revolution, Jacovleff was extremely popular as a teacher and he had many "apostles."[407] In Paris he moved closely with Russian and Ukrainian artists, e.g., Ivan Bilibin, Chana Orloff, and Konstantin Somov, and received a certain recognition for his interpretations of the Far East.[408] Although he had some experience of interior design (for the murals in the Comedians' Halt) and of book illustration (he worked for the journal *Satirikon*), Jacovleff was primarily a studio artist and his theatrical work was secondary.

584

585

584 [R1008].
Self-Portrait, 1935.
Oil on canvas.
11¾ x 8 in., 29.8 x 20.2 cm.
Signed and dated lower left: "A. Jacovleff
1935."
Provenance: *Icons, Russian Pictures and
Works of Art,* London: Sotheby's, 7 April,
1989, Lot 310 (reproduced). Now in a
private collection.
Reproduced in F107, p. 164; L37, Lot 310.

Sémiramis: *ballet-melodrama in three acts
and two interludes by Paul Valéry after the
tragedy by Voltaire (pseudonym of François-
Marie Arouet) with music by Arthur
Honegger. Produced by the Ida Rubinstein
Ballet at the Théâtre National de l'Opéra,
Paris, on 11 May, 1934, with choreography*

*by Michel Fokine, costumes by Alexandre
Benois, and sets by Alexandre Jacovleff.*

*Aided by Prince Assur, Sémiramis
(Semiramide), the Queen of Babylon, has
murdered her husband Nino. Enamored of
the youth Arsace, commander of her army,
Sémiramis is unaware that he is, in fact,
her son. At a gathering in the temple,
Nino's tomb opens and his ghost declares
that Arsace will be his successor and
summons Arsace to visit him. Enraged,
Assur anticipates the arrival of Arsace, who
is warned of the fact by Sémiramis. Arsace
then lunges at Assur, but Sémiramis
interposes herself and receives the mortal
blow. Arsace is then proclaimed King.*

585 [R1009].
Stage Design for Act I, 1934.
Gouache.
Signed and dated lower right: "A. Jacovleff,
1934."
27 x 32¼ in., 68.6 x 82 cm.
Provenance: Issar Gourvitch, Paris, 1967.
Reproduced in I14, No. 76; a version is
reproduced in I44, p. 50.

586 [R1010].
Stage Design for Act II, 1934.
Gouache and oil.
Signed and dated lower right: "A. Jacovleff
1934."
27 x 32¼ in., 68.6 x 82 cm.
Provenance: Iosif Lempert, Paris, October,
1976.
Reproduced in color in N188, p. 62; and in
black and white in A34, p. 463; I40, No.
148; I51, No. 118. A version in the
collection of The Fine Arts Museums of San
Francisco is reproduced in I44, No. 71.

586

587

588

587 [RI0I1].
Stage Design for Act III, **ca. 1934.**
Gouache.
Stamped with the monogram.
27 x 32¼ in., 68.6 x 82 cm.
Provenance: Iosif Lempert, Paris, October, 1976.
Reproduced in F107, p. 164; I40, No. 147.

588 [RI0I2].
Portrait of Sergei Sudeikin, **ca. 1935.**
Red chalk.
18⅛ x 13⅜ in., 46 x 34 cm.

Yurii Rakitin (formerly of the Moscow Art Theater) and the illustrator and designer Leonid Brailovsky; 1920-41 artist-in-residence at the People's Theater, Belgrade, where he designed 135 productions, including *The Inspector General, Coppelia, Macbeth* and, with Nicola Benois in 1938, *The Invisible City of Kitezh;* early 1930s organized the Little Berry Theater of Miniatures in Belgrade; 1941-50 lived in Zagreb; continued to design productions for various theaters; 1951-52 lived in Morocco, where he designed twelve productions for the Municipal Theater, Casablanca; 1952-74 lived in Paris; active as a stage designer until his death.

Bibliography
Žedrinski. Catalog of exhibition at the Museum of Visual Art, Belgrade, 1974.
F. Slivnik: "Vl. Žedrinski — scenograf in kostumograf v slovenskih gledališčih" in *Dokumenti Slovenskega gledališkega in filmskega muzeja,* Ljubljana, 1980, No. 34-35, pp. 63-94.
N. Lobanov: "Vladimir Jedrinsky" in B44, pp. 307-31.
O. Milanovič : *Vladimir Žedrinski.* Catalog of exhibition at the Muzej pozorišne umetnosti Srbije, Belgrade, 1987.

Provenance: Jeanne Palmer-Soudeikine, widow of Sergei Sudeikin, Norwalk, Connecticut, 1961.
Reproduced in F107, p. 154; I14, p. 63

Note: Presumably, Jacovleff made this portrait while he was living in Boston between 1934 and 1937 and while Sudeikin was living in New York.

405 This is the title of Mikhail Kuzmin's essay, i.e., "O prekrasnoi iasnosti" in *Apollon,* SP, 1909-10, No. 1, pp. 5-10.
406 N. Milioti: "Neskolko myslei po povodu vystavki A.E. Yakovleva" in *Chisla,* Paris, 1930-31, No. 4, pp. 195-96.
407 For a description of Jacovleff's studio and the "apostles" see O. Morozova: "Odna sudba" in *Novyi mir,* M, 1964, No. 9, p. 119.
408 See for example, his illustrations to *Tchou-Kia-Kien* in "Le Théâtre Chinois" in *Comoedia Illustré,* Paris, 1921, 6 June, pp. 456-60.

JEDRINSKY (Zhedrinsky), Vladimir Ivanovich

Born 30 May (11 June), 1899, Moscow, Russia; died 30 April, 1974, Paris, France.

1917 finished high school in Moscow; enrolled at IAA in order to study architecture, but then moved to Kiev; 1917-19 attended the Kiev Art Institute under Egor Narbut; met Pavel Tchelitchew; close to Georgii Lukomsky; worked for the Commission for the Preservation of Works of Art and Historical Monuments; 1920 emigrated to Yugoslavia; began to work on stage design for various productions in Belgrade; close contact with the producer

589

589 [R482].
Self-Portrait, **1924.**
Charcoal and white wash.
Signed with monogram and dated: "VJ 1924."
13⅜ x 10¼ in., 34 x 26 cm.
Provenance: Mariana Jedrinsky, Paris, July, 1981.

Note: Like Alexandre Jacovleff and Vasilii Shukhaev, Jedrinsky carried on the strong graphic traditions of the St. Petersburg and Kiev academies of art, and, in their sharp, prismatic quality, Jedrinsky's portraits of the

590

1920s have certain affinities with those of Nikolai Akimov. Of course, Jedrinsky did not limit himself to a single style. For example, in his design for an oriental ballet, he might use an ornamental style with striking color effects; on the other hand, architectural features might predominate in his design for a Shakespearean drama. Jedrinsky's designs are characterized primarily by his use of color, refinement in the layout, and mastery of composition.

Les Présages: *ballet in four acts based on music from Peter Tchaikovsky's Fifth Symphony. First produced by the Ballet Russe de Monte Carlo on 13 April, 1933, with choreography by Leonide Massine and designs by André Masson. Then produced at the People's Theater, Belgrade on 19 January, 1934, with choreography by Nina Kirsanova after Leonide Massine, and with designs by Vladimir Jedrinsky.*

This choreographic symphony has no developed plot, but treats the age-old theme of man's struggle with fate. Symbolic characters — Action, Passion, Fate, Frivolity and a Hero — celebrate, after countless dangers, their triumph over strife and evil.

590 [R483].
Stage Design for Act IV, 1932.
Watercolor, black ink, and pencil.
Initialed and dated in pencil lower right: "VJ 1932."
12¼ x 18⅛ in., 31 x 46 cm.
Provenance: Mariana Jedrinsky, Paris, July, 1981.
Reproduced in I51, No. 119.

591 [R484].
Costume Design for Passion, ca. 1934.
Watercolor.
Signed lower center in pencil: "V. Jédrinsky."
10¾ x 9 in., 27.3 x 23 cm.
Other inscriptions in French: lower center carries an identification: "La Passion,

solistes, Présage"; the reverse carries an identification in pencil by Mariana Jedrinsky.
Provenance: Mariana Jedrinsky, Paris, April, 1980.
Reproduced in I51, No. 120.

592 [R485].
Costume Design for the Hero, ca. 1934.
Watercolor.
10¾ x 9 in., 27.3 x 23 cm.
Inscriptions in right margin: "Présage. Le Héro (révolution), Matériel: Jersey"; lower margin: certification by Mariana Jedrinsky; reverse also carries an identification in Mariana Jedrinsky's hand and a Serbian stamp.
Provenance: Mariana Jedrinsky, Paris, April, 1980.
Reproduced in I51, No. 121.

593 [R486].
Costume Design for a Male Dancer in the Corps de Ballet in Scene 1, ca. 1934.
Watercolor and pencil.
10¾ x 9 in., 27.3 x 23 cm.
Inscriptions along lower right: "Corps de Ballet, I Partie. Matériel: Jersey et Velours"; certificate by Mariana Jedrinsky along lower margin in pencil; another certificate by her on the reverse together with an official Serbian stamp.
Provenance: Mariana Jedrinsky, Paris, April, 1980.
Reproduced in B44, p. 291. A version is reproduced in J37, Lot 81.

Note: The Monte Carlo production of *Les Présages* danced by Irina Baronova, Nina Verchinina, Tatiana Riabouchinska, David Lichine, and Leon Woizikowski, was one of Leonide Massine's most audacious choreographic experiments:

> I decided to avoid all symmetrical compositions and to render the flow of the music by fluctuating lines and forms both static and mobile. I deliberately chose to follow the movements of the symphony in a logical evolution of choreographic

591

592

593

phrases, successively amplifying and regrouping themselves into new shapes and patterns.[409]

Although critics praised this "transmutation of music into pure dancing,"[410] André Masson's surrealistic decorations were regarded as "not too happy."[411] No doubt, Jedrinsky's heroic, histrionic designs were most successful in the Belgrade production, since, as he always maintained, stage design, by its very nature, should harmonize with the plot of the ballet, the opera, or the play, for

> le décor doit être une pure fiction ornamentale, une illusion complète par des analogies de couleur et de ligne avec le drame.[412]

409 F28, p. 187.
410 D4, p. 9.
411 Ibid., p. 12.
412 V. Jedrinsky: untitled, undated manuscript on stage design, p. 8. Collection of the late Mariana Jedrinsky, Paris.

KALMAKOV, Nikolai Konstantinovich

Born 23 January (4 February), 1873, Nervi, Italy; died 1 February, 1955, Chelles, France.

Spent childhood in Italy, 1895 graduated from Law School, University of St. Petersburg; 1900 moved to Moscow; 1903 onward lived in St. Petersburg; influenced by Léon Bakst, Konstantin Somov, and other members of the World of Art group; 1908 designed Nikolai Evreinov's production of Oscar Wilde's Salomé at Vera Komissarzhevskaia's theater, St. Petersburg (withdrawn after the dress rehearsal); 1908 onwards active as a stage designer for various productions including Leonid Andreev's Black Masks and Anathema and Fedor Sologub's Nocturnal Dance; 1909 contributed to Nikolai Kulbin's exhibition "Impressionsists," St. Petersburg; 1911 worked for the Antique Theater, St. Petersburg; 1911-13 exhibited with the "World of Art" in Moscow and St. Petersburg; illustrated a number of books from the early 1910s onwards such as Nikolai Kronidov's Printsessa Lera [Princess Lera] (SP: Kronidov, 1911), Vladimir Elsner's translations of modern German poetry (Sovremennye nemetskie poety, M: Nekrasov, 1913), and Nikolai Gumiliev's Shater [Tent] (Reval: Bibliofil, 1921); 1915 with Yuliia Slonimskaia et al., organized the Theater of Marionettes in Petrograd, which opened in February, 1916; 1922 lived in Estonia; illustrated Gumiliev's Ditia Allakha [Child of Allah] (Berlin: Mysl); 1923 visited Helsinki; met Arthur Strindberg; emigrated to France via Latvia and Belgium; 1924 one-man show at the Galerie le Roy, Brussels; 1926 contributed to the "Exhibition of Russian Book Marks," Leningrad; 1928

one-man exhibition at the Galerie Charpentier, Paris.

Bibliography
R. Barotte: "L'aventure fantastique de Nicolai Kalmakoff" in *Paris-Presse-L'Intransigeant,* Paris, 1964, 2 February, p. 8E.
M2, Vol. 2, pp. 182-83.
M5.
P. Jullian: *Nicolas Kalmakoff 1873-1955.* Catalog of exhibition at Hartnoll and Eyre, London, 1970.
M9.
M.-C. Hugonot: "La descente aux enfers de Kalmakoff" in *Le Quotidien de Paris,* Paris, 1982, 26 August, No. 855.
G. Martin du Nord: *Kalmakoff.* Catalog of exhibition at the Musée-Galérie de la Seita, Paris, 1986.
M. Gibson: "'Angel of the Abyss' in Paris: Toils of a Russian Symbolist" in *International Herald Tribune,* Paris, 1986, 12-13 April, p. 6.
K. Sapgir: "Nikolai Kalmakov — vstrecha, polnaia neozhidannostei" in *Russkaia mysl,* Paris, 1986, 25 April, p. 11.
A14, Vol. 4, Book 2, pp. 94-95.
Yu. Balybina: "Nikolai Kalmakov. V poiskakh diavola" in *Novyi mir iskusstva,* M, 1999, No. 4, pp. 36-39.
E. Strutinskaia: "Legenda o Salomee" in *Russkoe iskusstvo,* M, 2004, No. 1, pp. 140-49.
Works by Alexander Yakovlev and Nikolai Kalmakov from the Estate of a French Nobleman. Catalog of auction at Sotheby's, London, 10 June, 2008.
D. Boult (J. Bowlt) and Yu. Balybina: *Nikolai Kalmakov i labirint dekadentstva,* M: Iskusstvo XXI vek, 2008.

A St. Petersburg Decadent, Kalmakov was fascinated by the erotic and the necrological, emphasizing these elements in his paintings, stage designs, and book illustrations and even signing his works with a monogram in the form of a stylized phallus. Kalmakov generated much commentary with his explicit images of sex and death, especially with his resolutions for the unrealized production of *Salomé* at Vera Komissarzhevskaia's Theater in 1908 (see Nos. 594-98 [R498-502]).[413] He was also strongly supported by Nikolai Evreinov, who, like him, emphasized the erotic element on stage and they collaborated on a number of productions such as Natalia Butkovskaia's production of Lope de Vega's *The Great Prince of Moscow* for the Antique Theater in St. Petersburg in 1911. This was one of Kalmakov's more auspicious endeavors, for he

> has proved to be a master of the stage, he has risen to the point where he has succeeded in making — from the costume itself — a strong and independent medium of scenic effect.[414]

According to one source, Kalmakov even worked for a production of Calderon de la Barca's *Life is a Dream* at the Chamber Theater, Moscow, but the published repertoire of the Chamber Theater does not mention this.[415] Like Evreinov, Kalmakov also tried to extend the theater into life by dressing outrageously, cultivating the part

of the dandy, and dabbling in the occult sciences, a pose that annoyed more moderate colleagues in the artistic world of St. Petersburg.[416]

Salomé: *drama in one act based on the Biblical story by Oscar Wilde. Dress-rehearsed at the Vera Komissarzhevskaia Theater, St. Petersburg on 27 October, 1908, with music by Christoph Willibald von Glück and designs by Nikolai Kalmakov.*

Salomé, daughter of Herodias, is corrupted by the depraved court of King Herod, her stepfather, and she seeks ever new pleasures. Although contrary to the law, the young captain Narraboth lets her see the captive John the Baptist. Fascinated, Salomé tries to seduce him, but in vain. Narraboth, who is enamored of Salomé, cannot endure the scene and kills himself. Salomé dances the Dance of the Seven Veils in front of Herod who desires her, and as her reward for the Dance she demands the head of John the Baptist. It is brought to Salomé, who kisses the dead lips. Horrified, Herod has her put to death by his guards.

594

594 [105; R498].
Costume Design for Salomé, 1908.
Watercolor.
Signed upper right with the Russian monogram in the form of a stylized phallus and dated 1908.
12¾ x 8¼ in., 32.5 x 21 cm.
Provenance: Anna Kashina-Evreinova, Paris, May, 1967.
Reproduced in color in F107, p. 283; I77, p. 67; Boult and Balybina, *Nikolai Kalmakov,* p. 97; and in black and white in B200, p. 39; I77, p. 125; P15; P36; P39.

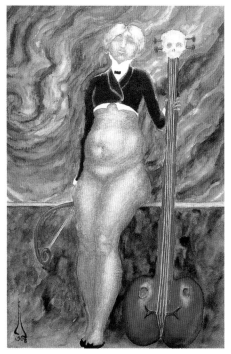

595

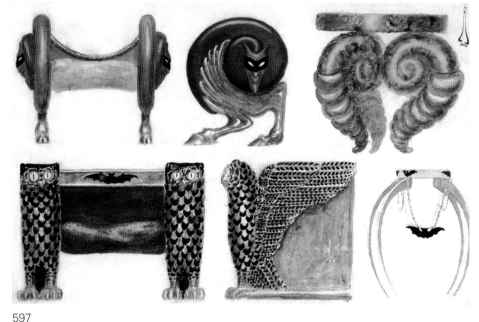

597

595 [106; R500].
Costume Design for a Cellist, 1908.
Watercolor.
Signed lower half with the Russian monogram in the form of a stylized phallus and dated 1908.
12¾ x 8¼ in., 32.5 x 21 cm.
Provenance: Anna Kashina-Evreinova, Paris, May, 1967.
Reproduced in color in F107, p. 144; Balybina: "Nikolai Kalmakov. V poiskakh diavola", p. 39; and Boult and Balybina, *Nikolai Kalmakov,* p. 93; in black and white in I77, pp. 103, 125.

596

596 [R499].
Costume Design for Narraboth, Captain of the Guard, Holding His Sword, 1908.
Watercolor and black wash.
Signed lower half with the Russian monogram in the form of a stylized phallus and dated 1908.
12¾ x 8¼ in., 32.5 x 21 cm.
Provenance: Mikhail Kolesnikov, Moscow, 1984.
Reproduced in color in Boult and Balybina, *Nikolai Kalmakov,* p. 93.

597 [R501].
Stage Details of Tables and Chairs, 1908.
Watercolor with silver paint and black ink.
Signed upper right with the Russian monogram in the form of a stylized phallus and dated 1908.
8⅝ x 13⅝ in., 22 x 34.5 cm.
Provenance: Mikhail Kolesnikov, Moscow, Moscow, 1984.
Reproduced in color in Boult and Balybina, *Nikolai Kalmakov,* p. 87.

598 [R502].
Stage Details of Fruit and Drinking Vessels, 1908.
Watercolor and pencil.
Signed upper right with the Russian monogram in the form of a stylized phallus and dated 1908.
8⅝ x 13⅝ in., 22 x 34.5 cm.
Provenance: Mikhail Kolesnikov, Moscow, 1984.
Reproduced in color in Boult and Balybina, *Nikolai Kalmakov,* p. 87.

Note: The details of this project for Vera Komissarzhevskaia's Theater in St. Petersburg are enveloped in myth and legend. According to one rumor (not confirmed), for example, Kalmakov designed the set for this one-act play in the form of the female private parts, and this, allegedly, caused the immediate prohibition of the play after the direct intervention of Nicholas II. Certainly, *Salomé* was banned, but the command was issued by the St. Petersburg police at the instigation of the Holy Synod on the grounds that the play itself was a sacrilegious treatment of a Biblical story (although Komissarzhevskaia had received formal permission to prepare and rehearse the play). The actor Andrei Zheliabuzhsky has left the following account of the episode:

> The joyful news arrived that permission to produce *Salomé* had been received. It stirred the whole theater, and everyone went around uplifted and animated. The hurriedly convoked art committee — and this time Vera Fedorovna [Komissarzhevskaia] took part — resolved to rush the production with every means available…
>
> The task seemed impossible. Indeed, Glück's pastorale *The Queen of May,* which had just been found and had never been performed, was added to *Salomé* — which was already complicated enough. This created difficulties for the dramatic theater since it contained intricate vocal parts (performed by Vera Fedorovna, A.N. Feona, and the singer A.I. Barynskaia specially invited for the role of the Queen of May…). The dress rehearsal took place on 27 October.
>
> Among the audience invited to the viewing were writers, journalists, and artists. Separate boxes were occupied by General Lysogorsky representing the City Governor and a group of rightist deputies from the State Duma. Vera Fedorovna together with Evreinov, and Fedor Fedorovich [Komissarzhevsky] were at the producer's desk.
>
> According to the many reactions of those who saw the rehearsal… it created a deep impression, and the play was recognized as a great theatrical achievement.

598

But the next day came a blow... *Salomé* had been banned. This was communicated to the theater at 10 a.m. The Black Hundreds had made a lot of noise regarding this business the day before. Arrant die-hards led by Markov, the famous Black Hundreds member and deputy of the State Duma, together with Evlogii and Antonin, members of the Holy Synod, had been trying to secure a ban on *Salomé* within the highest circles — and, no doubt, just as we were celebrating victory and the playbill was being approved at the City Governor's office, the ban had already been gotten.[417]

It would seem that the main element of the rehearsal that delighted the St. Petersburg bohemia and shocked the pillars of the establishment was not the acting or the story itself, but the sumptuous languor of Kalmakov's audacious costumes. Evreinov described the visual effect:

Surely, whoever attended the dress rehearsal of *The Princess* [Salomé] ... will quiver when they recall the harmonious mix of Kalmakov's grotesque style, the lapidary sphinx-like face of Herodias with her Medusa hair powdered blue, the bestial image of Herod, the golden hair of the totally pink Princess, the Prophet's greenish body as if fluorescing sanctity, the voluptuous convolution of the Syrian's gentle child-like body, the red square of Tigellinus's face beneath the pseudo-Classical plumage of his helmet with its unbearable brilliance, and, finally, the bright red hands and feet of the executioner Naaman as black as night.[418]

In spite of protests, the ban on *Salomé* was not lifted. But Kalmakov still indulged his "erotic and mystical phantasms"[419] in his other commissions for Komissarzhevskaia such as his designs for Leonid Andreev's *Black Masks* (1908) and in his illustrations for Kronidov's *Printsessa Lera* [Princess Lera] in 1911. Kalmakov and Evreinov revived the *Salomé* project in Paris in 1925, but once again it was not produced.

The Power of Love and Magic: *comic divertissement in three intermezzi for puppets based on a text by Tirso de Molina translated by Georgii Ivanov. Produced by Pavel Sazonov for Yuliia Slonimskaia's Marionette Theater, Petrograd, on 15 February, 1916, with music by Thomas von Hartmann and designs by Mstislav Dobujinsky, Nikolai Kalmakov, and Anna Somova-Mikhailova.*

The Fair of Saint-Germain in the late 18th century forms the backdrop for a variety of episodes: marquises dance a minuet, dwarfs run and tumble, Juno, surrounded by cupids, enters in a golden carriage drawn by peacocks, etc.

599 [R503].
Costume Design for a Devil, 1916.
Gouache.
Signed lower right with the Russian monogram in the form of a stylized phallus.
9½ x 13 in., 24 x 33 cm.
Provenance: Georges Martin du Nord, Paris, 1965.
Reproduced in color in B115, plate 77; F107, p. 145; and in black and white in I77, p. 150; I14, No. 77; and I51, No. 122, where it is described incorrectly as a design for *The Power of Magic and Death*. Nicola Benois included this piece in his 1981 portrait of Nikita D. Lobanov (see No. 360 [R324]).

Note: Yuliia Slonimskaia (Sazonova) and her husband Pavel Sazonov entertained the idea of establishing a puppet theater for grown-ups in 1915, and implemented their project in February, 1916. *The Power of*

Love and Magic (virtually, the only developed number in the repertoire) premiered at the Petrograd apartment of the artist Alexander Gaush as a benefit,[420] before being transferred to the People's House.[421] In spite of the inclement times (the First World War), Slonimskaia and Sazonov had high hopes for their venture and received the ready support of the Petrograd "bourgeois bohemia" associated with Sergei Makovsky's review *Apollon* [Apollo] such as Anna Akhmatova, Mikhail Kuzmin, and Olga Glebova-Sudeikina. Slonimskaia even published an article in *Apollon* in which she clarified her objectives:

The marionette provides a theatrical form without a carnal expression. Just as algebraic signs substitute certain desired quantities, so the conventional flesh of the marionette substitutes real human flesh... The infinite variety of the puppet repertoire had preserved one basic characteristic: indifference to the prose of everyday life.[422]

The same notion of an intensely stylized

599

theater had encouraged Nikolai Drizen and Evreinov to found their Antique Theater several years before,[423] and both were especially interested in Slonimskaia's ideas.

The Power of Love and Magic seems to have been the only spectacle played at the Marionette Theater, but, judging from contemporary reports, it was of an exceptionally high artistic caliber. After all, the costumes were designed by professional artists, the music was by a foremost composer of the time, the voices were provided by distinguished, professional singers such as Nikolai Andreev and Zoia Lodii, and *Apollon* gave wide coverage of the event.[424] Still, not everyone was enthusiastic. Konstantin Somov, whose sister Anna Somova-Mikhailova helped with the costumes, attended the dress rehearsal of the play on the evening of 14 February, 1916, and described his impressions:

> Infinitely long — from 8.30 through 12, intolerable. So the Theater is starting its activities in a very mediocre way. The movements are uniform, simple, the producer is not very bright. A lot of humdrum… Kalmakov did not distinguish himself. Some of the details are pleasant enough, for example, the dances of the shepherdess and the two shepherds, Gartman's music is okay, and the play itself is a good one for puppets. A lot of horrible, snobbish people. Ladies… Poets, writers and critics… Blok, Remizov, Akhmatova [illegible], Evreinov, etc., etc.[425]

1916 was an important year in the history of the Russian puppet theater, since the great puppeteer Nina Simonovich-Efimova made her debut at an evening of the Moscow Association of Artists. Simonovich-Efimova had started her career as a painter and then turned to the miniature theater as a medium of movement, for, as she affirmed, "[the puppets'] charm lies in movement, the meaning of their existence lies in play, the theater of Petrushka is the theater of action."[426] It was this "art of play" that attracted many modern Russian artists to puppetry, not least Alexandra Exter, Kalmakov, El Lissitzky, Liubov Popova, and Elizaveta Yakunina.

413 For commentary on the production of *Salomé* see N. Evreinov: "Khudozhniki v teatre V.F. Komissarzhevskoi" in *Alkonost*, SP, 1911, pp. 133-34; and M. Veikone: "Na generalnoi repetitsii, 'Salomei' v teatre V.F. Komissarzhevskoi," ibid., pp. 139-41; also see Bowlt and Balybina, *Nikolai Kalmakov*, Chapter IV.
414 "Khronika" in *Apollon*, SP, 1912, No. 4, February, p. 60.
415 Kalmakov's alleged participation in the Chamber Theater is mentioned in G10, Vol. 1, p. 147. For references to other productions in which Kalmakov was involved, including illustrations, see C25, p. 290; K153, pp. 182-83.
416 Konstantin Somov did not seem to find Kalmakov especially sympathetic. See Somov's diary entry for 26 February, 1915, in F51, p. 141.
417 Quoted in A. Altshuller, ed.: *Vera Fedorovna Komissarzhevskaia*, L-M: Iskusstvo, 1964, pp. 284-85.
418 Evreinov, op. cit.
419 Hugonot, "La descente."
420 According to unsigned and untitled text in *Liubov k trem apelsinam*, P, 1916, No. 1, p. 97.
421 Natalia Smirnova provides this information in her book on the puppet theater (E6, p. 58). However, according to a press report of March, 1916, the "organizers of the puppet theater in Petrograd, Yu.L. Slonimskaia and P.P. Sazonov, who hitherto have staged [their works] for a small circle of people, will be organizing six presentations — from 20 to 25 March — for a wider audience on the premises of the Lawyers' Art Circle (2 Baskov St.). The 17th century comic divertissement *The Power of Love and Magic* is being put on," ("Stolichnaia khronika" in *Teatr i kino*, Odessa, 1916, No. 13, p. 5). For a review of the production "in the apartment of A.F. Gaush" see *Liubov k trem apelsinam*, op. cit. One of Kalmakov's actual marionettes for *The Power of Love and Magic* and

relevant publicity materials are in the collection of the Demmeni Marionette Theater, St. Petersburg.
422 Yu. Slonimskaia: "Marionetka" in *Apollon*, P, 1916, No. 3, p. 30. For further information on Slonimskaia's and others' marionette theaters see E61.
423 See entries for Yurii Annenkov (No. 41 [R40]) and Evgenii Lanceray (Nos. 693-94 [R587-88]).
424 Smirnova has noted this in her pages devoted to the Marionette Theater (E6, pp. 56-59). Much of the March 1916 issue of *Apollon* was devoted to the Slonimskaia-Sazonov enterprise. Alexandre Benois also supported the project and published a positive article entitled "Marionetochnyi teatr" in *Rech*, P, 1916, 20 February.
425 Konstantin Somov. Diary entry for 15 February, 1916, in F51, p. 154. Somov is referring to the poet A.A. Akhmatova (1889-1966), and the playwright Evreinov. Yuliia Slonimskaia renewed her puppet theater in emigration at the Théâtre du Vieux Colombier, Paris, on 24 December, 1924. Natalia Goncharova, Mikhail Larionov, Nikolai Milioti and other Russian artists designed marionettes for her. See "Teatr marionetok" in *Teatr, iskusstvo, ekran*, Paris, 1925, January, pp. 12-13.
426 N. Simonovich-Efimova: *Zapiski petrushechnika*. M-L: State Publishing-House, 1925, pp. 25, 42. Also see E3.

KANDINSKY, Wassily (Vasilii Vasilevich)

Born 4 (16) March, 1866, Moscow, Russia; died 13 December, 1944, Neuilly-sur-Seine, near Paris, France.

Born in Moscow, Kandinsky spent his childhood in Odessa. 1886-92 studied law at Moscow University; 1892 offered a professorship in Roman Law at the University of Dorpat (Tartu, Estonia); 1889 joined ethnographical expedition to the Vologda Region; 1895 exhibition of French Impressionists, especially works by Monet, informed his artistic development; 1896 settled in Munich; studied under Anton Ažbè and then at the Akademie der bildenden Künste; 1901 organized Phalanx group; close to Gabriele Münter; early 1900s in touch with the World of Art group in St. Petersburg; began to contribute regularly to exhibitions; close to Alexej von Jawlensky, Alexander Sacharoff, Marianne Werefkin, Alexander Salzmann (Zaltsman), and other Russians in the Munich community; interested in the new theories of art, especially the ideas of Wilhelm Worringer; painted first abstract painting; represented at the "Jack of Diamonds" exhibition in Moscow; 1910s-20s painted abstract *Improvisations* and *Compositions*; 1911 co-founded the Blaue Reiter group; 1912 conributed to the Cubo-Futurist almanac, *A Slap in the Face of Public Taste*; published German version of theoretical essay *On the Spiritual in Art*; 1915 via Scandinavia returned to Moscow; 1917 married Nina Andreevskaia, his second wife; 1910s-30s published many theoretical and critical articles in German, Russian, and French journals; 1920 director of Inkhuk; professor at Moscow University; 1921 co-founder of RAKhN/GAKhN (Russian [later State] Academy of Artistic Sciences); emigrated to Germany; 1922-33 taught at

the Bauhaus; 1928 became a German citizen; 1929 first one-man exhibition in Paris; expelled from GAKhN; 1930 second one-man exhibition in Paris; 1933 moved to France, where he lived the rest of his life; 1939 became a French citizen.

Bibliography

Kandinsky is the subject of a very large number of monographs, catalogs, and articles. The titles below are a representative selection only.

M. Bill: *Wassily Kandinsky*, Paris: Maeght, 1951
W. Grohmann: *Wassily Kandinsky. Life and Work*, New York: Harry N Abrams, 1958
R.-C. Washton Long: *Kandinsky. The Development of an Abstract Style*, Oxford; Clarendon Press, 1980.
C. Poling: *Kandinsky — Unterricht am Bauhaus*, Weingarten: Kunstverlag Weingarten, 1982
H. Roethel and J. Benjamin: *Kandinsky. Catalogue Raisonné of the Oil paintings. Volume One, 1900-1915*, Ithaca; Cornell; 1982; *Volume Two, 1916-1944*, 1984.
P. Vergo and K. Frampton, eds.: *Wassily Kandinsky. Kandinsky, Complete Writings on Art*, Boston: Hall, 1982 (two volumes); reprinted New York: Da Capo Press, 1994.
J. Bowlt and R.-C. Washton Long: *The Life of Vasilii Kandinsky in Russian art: a Study of "On the Spiritual in Art" by Wassily Kandinsky*, Newtonville, Mass.: Oriental Research Partners, 1984.
V. Barnett: *Kandinsky Watercolours. Catalogue Raisonné. Volume One, 1900-1921*, Ithaca: Cornell, 1992; *Volume Two, 1922-1944*, 1994.
J. Hahl-Fontaine: *Kandinsky*, New York: Rizzoli, 1993.
N. Misler, ed. : *Wassili Kandinsky tra Oriente e Occidente. Capolavori dai musei russi*. Catalog of exhibition at the Palazzo Strozzi, 1993.
P. Weiss: *Kandinsky and Old Russia*, New Haven, CT: Yale University Press, 1995.
J. Boissel, ed.: *Kandinsky: Du Théâtre, Uber das Theater, O teatre*, Paris: Biro, 1998.
L. Romachkova: *Kandinsky et la Russie*. Catalog of exhibition at the Foundation Pierre Gianadda, Martigny, 2000.
V. Turchin: *Kandinsky v Rossii*, M: Society of the Friends of Kandinsky's Oeuvre, 2005.
I. Aronov, *Kandinsky's Quest: A Study in the Artist's Personal Symbolism, 1866-1907*, NewYork: Lang, 2006.
M. Tupitsyn: *Gegen Kandinsky / Against Kandinsky*. Catalog of exhibition at the Museum Villa Stuck, Munich, 2006.
I. Aronov: *Kandinsky. Istoki, 1866-1907*, M: Mosty kultury, 2010.
C. Short; *The Art Theory of Wassily Kandinsky, 1909-1928*, Oxford: Lang, 2010.

Although he spent many years abroad, Kandinsky maintained creative and personal connections with the Russian avant-garde, contributing, for example, to Mikhail Larionov's "Jack of Diamonds" exhibition in 1910 and to David Burliuk's anthology *Poshchechina obshchestvennomu vkusu* [A Slap in the Face of Public Taste] in 1912. In turn, Kandinsky ensured that Russian art was well represented in the Blaue Reiter almanac both in reproduction and in text. Even so, the connections were uneasy, for Kandinsky did not approve of the rude iconoclasm of his Moscow colleagues and saw much of their art to be disorderly, superficial, and lacking in the "spiritual" and prophetic value, which for him was the primary ingredient of the true work of art. Conversely, Kandinsky's Romantic interpretation of art won little sympathy with the later avant-garde, especially just after the October Revolution. When in 1917, the critic Nikolai Punin, champion of the Russian and Soviet avant-gardes, referred to Kandinsky as "confused and ephemeral,"[427] he was voicing the opinion of many radicals.

A salient characteristic of Kandinsky's discourses on art is the constant expression of disillusionment in the Positivist worldview of the later 19th century. Kandinsky's rejection of Materialism in favor of the spiritual constitutes the leit-motif of his many essays – from his complaint that critics read, but do not see, to his later explanations of abstract art. In aspiring from the material to the spiritual, Kandinsky shared with the Symbolists of the *fin de siècle* a common desire to replace the fragmentation of their age with a new wholeness — to synthesize the arts (identifying Wagner and the operatic drama as a paragon), to test new media, and to restore the purity of primitive cultures. Kandinsky's experimental work on *Pictures at an Exhibition* is strong witness to this aspiration.

If these priorities now constituted the common denominator, then documentary reproduction of the outer world was no longer a prerequisite for artistic creativity:

> Any object is, as it were, merely an allusion to the real, an allusion or aroma in the composition. So that's why there is no need for the object (the real object) to be reproduced with precision. On the contrary, its *impression* only intensifies the purely painterly composition.[428]

Kandinsky elaborated this argument in his principal essay, *On the Spiritual in Art,* and proceeded to explore it pictorially in the abstract imagery of the *Compositions* and *Improvisations.* Kandinsky never altered his commitment to this fundamental belief in the nobility of the creative act and in the esthetic experience which, for him, abstract art encapsulated and expressed.

***Bilder einer Ausstellung* [Pictures at an Exhibition]:** *dance production based on the music by Modest Mussorgsky. Staged by Vasilii Kandinsky in sixteen scenes for the Friedrich-Theater, Dessau, on 4 April, 1928, with his designs.*

A visitor to an exhibition responds in various ways to the pictures of people and places.

600 [NIRE].
Sound Harmonies (visual accompaniment), 1928.
Watercolor.
Signed with monogram and dated lower left: "K 28."
9¼ x 5¾ in., 23.5 x 14.5 cm.
Provenance: Baron Richard von Radack, Berlin.

600

Reproduced in color in F107, p. 163. For reproductions of other Kandinsky designs for *Pictures at an Exhibition* see Barnett, *Kandinsky Watercolours. Catalogue Raisonné Volume Two, 1922-1944,* pp. 176 88; and A. Seban, et al.: *Chagall et l'avant-garde russe.* Catalog of exhibition at the Centre Pompidou, Paris, 2011-12, pp. 201-04.

Note: Kandinsky's production of *Pictures at an Exhibition* is a clear example of his concept of the *Gesamtkunstwerk* which he and his Symbolist colleagues both in Russia and in Europe had been elaborating with such enthusiasm. Informed by Wagner's operatic dramas, by Alexander Skriabin's attempts to combine colors and sounds, and by the general interest in synesthesia which artists, composers, and writers of the time were expressing (Vladimir Baranoff-Rossiné, Mikalojus Čiurlionis, Nikolai Rimsky-Korsakov, Arthur Rimbaud), Kandinsky regarded the Mussorgsky project as a laboratory for testing pictorial, musical, and choreographic ideas. If Mussorgsky himself had tried to provide a musical evocation of the various scenes of Viktor Gartman's paintings and drawings which he saw at the retrospective exhibition organized by the St. Petersburg Society of Architects at the Imperial Academy of Arts in 1874,[429] Kandinsky now also followed the flow of the music with colorful forms, vivid light play, and kinetic accompaniment (dancers appeared in two scenes):

> At the first *espressivo* only three long, vertical strips appear in the background. They vanish. At the next *espressivo* the great red perspective is introduced from the right (double color). Then, from the left, the green perspective. The middle

figure emerges from the trap door. It is illumined with an intense colored light.[430]

Kandinsky's resolutions for the scenery and costumes in *Pictures at an Exhibition* such as the abstract and geometrical props, some of them in motion, suspended in front of a black backdrop so as to create the impression of an extended painting, also indicated a ready awareness of Oskar Schlemmer's parallel experiments on stage. To all accounts, the effect of the individual acts with the severe contrast between light and shadow, the movement of the white square over the stage, and the sequence of descent into the catacombs was magical. No doubt, in creating this total exercise in sound and color, Kandinsky was also remembering his own dramatic text, *The Yellow Sound,* of 1908.

427 N. Punin: "V zashchitu zhivopisi" in *Apollon,* P, 1917, No. 1, p. 62.
428 V. Kandinsky: "Kuda idet 'novoe' iskusstvo" in *Odesskie novosti,* Odessa, 1911, 9 February, p. 3.
429 See N. Misler: "Musorgskij e Hartmann," in F. Degrada and A. Morazzoni, eds.: *Musorgskij – l'opera, il pensiero, Convegno Internazionale – Teatro alla Scala,* Milano: Unicopli, 1985, pp.151-64; and A. Silbermann: *Wassily Kandinsky. Quadri di un'esposizione. Musica di Modesto Moussorgsky,* Macerata: Editore Università Europa, 1984.
430 Kandinsky writing in *Kunstblatt,* 1930. Quoted in Grohman, *Kandinsky,* p. 203.

KHODASEVICH, Valentina Mikhailovna

Born 13 (25) March, 1894, Moscow, Russia; died 25 May, 1970, Moscow, Russia.

Niece of the writer Vladislav Felitsianovich Khodasevich (1886-1939). Late 1900s attended CSIAI and the private studio of Fedor Rerberg; 1910-11 studied in Munich; 1911-12 studied with Kees Van Dongen and other artists in Paris; 1912 worked closely with Vladimir Tatlin, Alexander Vesnin, and other members of the Russian avant-garde in Moscow; 1913 married the artist Andrei Dideriks and moved to St. Petersburg; ca. 1914 close to the circle of artists and critics associated with the journal *Apollon* in St. Petersburg; 1917 helped with the interior design of the Café Pittoresque in Moscow; 1919 debut as a stage designer for a production of Nikolai Gumiliev's *Tree of Metamorphoses;* designed agit-prop decorations for streets and squares; 1919-22 worked for the Theater of People's Comedy in Petrograd, coming into close contact with Sergei Radlov; used various media in her designs — poster technique, montage, constructions; 1922 worked in and near Berlin; 1924-25 lived in England, France, and Italy, visiting Maxim Gorky in Sorrento; mid-1920s active as a stage designer in a number of theaters; 1932-36 head of the Art Section of the Kirov Academic Theater of Opera and Ballet in Leningrad; 1937 worked on the propaganda magazine *USSR in Construction;* 1953 onwards lived in Moscow.

Bibliography.
M. Kuzmin et al.: *Valentina Khodasevich*, L: Akademiia, 1927.
V. Lapshin: "'Kafe poetov' v Nastasinskom pereulke" in G31, Vol. 2, pp. 178-88. Italian version: "Il 'Caffè dei poeti' nel Vicolo Nastas'inskij" in *Rassegna sovietica,* Rome, 1985, No. 1, pp. 122-35.
Valentina Mikhailovna Khodasevich. Catalog of exhibition organized by the Union of Artists of the USSR, M, 1979.
R. Sylvester, ed.: *Valentina Khodasevich and Olga Margolina-Khodasevich. Unpublished Letters to Nina Berberova,* Berkeley: Berkeley Slavic Specialties, 1979.
N. Malaichuk: *Blagorodnaia simfoniia ritma: Teatralnye raboty V.M. Khodasevich.* Catalog of exhibition at Elizium, M, 2002.
K284, pp. 200-02.
Khodasevich's memoirs are also of interest. See: "Vstrechi" in *Novyi mir,* M, 1969, No. 7, pp. 180-215; "Gorod-teatr, narod-akter" in *Dekorativnoe iskusstvo,* M, 1979, No. 11, pp. 34-37; "Bylo," ibid., 1980, No. 3, pp. 40-42. The full text of her memoirs has been published as T. Ivanova, ed.: *Valentina Khodasevich. Portrety slovami. Ocherki,* M: Galart, 1995.

Before coming to the Theater of People's Comedy, Khodasevich had designed only one theater piece, i.e., Nikolai Gumiliev's *Tree of Metamorphoses* at the Theater Studio, Petrograd, in 1918. The Theater of People's Comedy made particular demands on Khodasevich since, within the space of two and a half years, she designed twelve productions there, including several elaborate interpretations of plays by Molière. As a matter of fact, the first part of the program for 1 November, 1921, was the comedy *Monsieur de Pourceaugnac* also with sets and costumes by Khodasevich. The actor Konstantin Miklashevsky (1886-1944) played principal roles in both pieces.

Khodasevich's work at the Theater of People's Comedy (which was sometimes compared to a London music-hall)[431] provided her with invaluable experience as a stage designer that witnessed a move from the early, painterly conception of the stage to a volumetrical and architectural one. Indebted to Tatlin and Alexander Vesnin, in particular, Khodasevich arrived at a simple, laconic, and highly effective resolution of costume and set design. The theater critic Alexander Movshenson wrote of her in 1927:

> Khodasevich presents the personality of the character by the cut of the costume, by its basic color, and by an extremely well-defined pattern. The color of the costume is always restrained within a certain scale, and it engraves itself upon the spectator's memory.[432]

Although committed to the Theater of People's Comedy in the 1920s, Khodasevich worked for other theaters in Leningrad such as the Free Theater and the Theater of the Classical Miniature. She continued to work on productions until the 1950s.

Harlequin-Skeleton, or Pierrot the Jealous: *pantomime by Jean-Gaspard Debureau. Produced by Sergei Radlov for the Theater of People's Comedy in the Iron Hall of the State People's House, Petersburg, 1 November, 1921, with designs by Valentina Khodasevich.*

A pantomime based on the traditional theme of Pantalone, Harlequin, Columbine, and Pierrot.

601

601 [R862].
Costume Design for Harlequin, 1921.
Watercolor and pencil.
Signed and dated lower right in Russian: "V. Khodasevich, 1921."
14 x 8¾ in., 35.6 x 22.2 cm.
Other inscription: upper right in Russian: "Harlequin, Miklashevsky."
Provenance: Mark Etkind, Leningrad, May, 1973.
Reproduced in color in B115, plate 122; and in black and white in I51, No. 123; I77, p. 151; N91, p. 138; and in I32, No. 43, where it is wrongly described as a design for a production of Molière's *Flying Doctor* (*Le Médecin volant*).

Monsieur de Pourceaugnac: *comedy-ballet by Jean-Baptiste Molière. Produced by Vladimir Soloviev for the Iron Hall of the Theater of People's Comedy, Petersburg, on 30 September, 1921, with designs by Valentina Khodasevich.*

The wealthy M. de Pourceaugnac arranges to marry Oronte's daughter, Julie, who is in love with Erast. But through various ruses, involving disguises, false accusations, and confused identities, Julie, Erast, and their devious servants have M. de Pourceaugnac put in jail on charges of bigamy. He escapes by bribing the police. Shocked by these unsavory events, Oronte begs Erast to marry Julie.

602

602 [R863].
Costume Design for Oronte Holding a Handkerchief, 1921.
Watercolor and pencil.
Signed and dated lower left in Russian: "V. Khodasevich, 1921."
16½ x 11⅝ in., 42 x 29.5 cm.
Other inscriptions in pencil in Russian: upper left: "Oronte Alekson"; upper right: "Monsieur de Pourceaugnac by Molière, Sheet No. 4a"; lower left: "Order No. 724." Provenance: Mark Etkind, Leningrad, May, 1973.

Volpone, or The Fox: *comedy in a prologue and five acts by Ben Johnson. Produced by Konstantin Khokhlov from a free interpretation by Stefan Zweig at the Comedy Theater, Leningrad, on 2 March, 1929, with music by Vladimir Deshevov and designs by Valentina Khodasevich.*[433]

The foxy Volpone and his servant Mosca amass a sizable fortune from gifts conned out of Volpone's friends, all eager to be named heir to his mythical fortune. Among the hopefuls duped are Corbaccio, who is persuaded to disinherit his son Bonaccio in hopes of Volpone's fortune, and Corvino, who agrees to give Volpone his wife Celia as a "cure." To hide the villainy of Corbaccio and Corbino, Celia and Bonaccio are falsely accused of trying to kill Volpone, but are spared when Volpone exposes the stupidity and guilt of the conspirators, who are duly punished by the court.

603 [R864].
Poster advertising the premiere of Volpone, 1929.
Colored lithograph.
20½ x 13½ in., 52 x 34.2 cm.
Inscriptions: the text provides the details of the production, including the names of the actors.
Printed in an edition of 4000 copies.

603

Provenance: Solomon Shuster, Leningrad, March, 1984.

Unidentified production, *ca. 1924.*

604 [R865].
Costume Design for a Female Dancer, ca. 1924.
Watercolor, collage of gold paper laid on green.
8⅝ x 5½ in., 22 x 14 cm.
Inscription: the reverse carries the following attribution by the Leningrad art historian

604

Evgenii Kovtun, in ink in Russian: "This design is by V. Khodasevich. Early 1920s. E. Kovtun. 17.04.1986."
Provenance: Mark Etkind, Leningrad, May, 1986.
Reproduced in I77, p. 144.

431 Yu. Annenkov: "Teatr chistogo metoda." Manuscript in RGALI, f. 2618, op.1, ed. khr. 14, l. 168.
432 A. Movshenson: "Dekorator V.M. Khodasevich i Teatr Narodnoi Komedii (1920-22)" in Kuzmin, *Valentina Khodasevich,* p. 64.
433 For reviews of this production see B. Mazing: "'Volpone' v Komedii" in *Rabochii i teatr*, L, 1929, No. 13, p. 5; S. M-sky: "Volpone" in *Zhizn iskusstva*, L, 1929, No. 13. p. 13.

KHVOSTENKO-KHVOSTOV
(Khvostov-Khvostenko),
Alexander Veniaminovich

Born 17 (29) April, 1895, Borisovka, Ukraine; died 16 December, 1968, Kiev, Ukraine.

1907-17 attended MIPSA, where he studied principally under Konstantin Korovin; 1914-17 worked as a scene painter in various theaters; 1915-16 contributed to the satirical magazine *Budilnik* [Alam-clock]; 1920-21 with Vasilii Ermilov worked for the UkrROSTA (the propaganda windows of the Ukrainian Telegraph Agency) in Kharkov; 1920 onwards active as a stage designer in Kiev, Kharkov, and Moscow, working on important productions such as Maiakovsky's *Mystery-Bouffe* (Kharkov, 1921), Reingold Glière's *Red Poppy* (1929), and Stanislav Moniushko's *Galka* (Kiev, 1949); in 1926-27 also worked on a projected version of Sergei Prokofiev's *Love for Three Oranges* in Kharkov, one of his most experimental endeavors; 1920s-60s contributed regularly to national and international exhibitions.

Bibliography
A. Drak: *Oleksandr Veniaminovich Khvostenko-Khvostov,* K: Mistetsvo, 1962.
G57, passim.
Oleksandr Veniaminovich Khvostov (Khvostenko) 1895-1968. Catalog of exhibition at the State Museum of Theatrical Art, K, 1986.
D. Gorbachev: *Oleksandr Khvostenko-Khvostov,* K: Mistetstvo, 1987.
D. Gorbačev: "O kazališnem scenografijama Oleksandra Hvostova" in K131, pp. 155-58.
A31, p. 612.
K265, pp. 240-53.
B356, passim.

While a student in Moscow in the 1910s, Khvostenko-Khvostov was confronted with the avant-garde experiments of Kazimir Malevich and Vladimir Tatlin, although it was the color geometries of Suprematism that left the deepest imprint on his development. Returning to the Ukraine after his Moscow schooling, Khvostenko-Khvostov also turned his attention to the decorative work of Alexandra Exter, and her immediate influence can be traced in the cubistic resolutions of his

early stage designs. As the Ukrainian historian Dmitrii Gorbachev asserts in his monograph, under Exter's influence Khvostenko-Khvostov moved to a "volumetrical, constructive design, something that transformed the scenic space." [434]

Along with Alexander Bogomazov, Vasilii Ermilov, and Alexander Petritsky, Khvostenko-Khvostov was a leader of the Ukrainian avant-garde in the 1920s and made a valuable contribution to both Ukrainian and Russian stage design. Sometimes his sets were remarkably abstract, e.g., for *Die Walküre* of 1929,[435] although many consider his most experimental costumes and sets to be those for the unrealized production of the *Love for Three Oranges* at the Berezil Theater in Kharkov in 1926-27.

605

605 [R858].
Dmitrii Moor: *Three Caricatures of Alexander Khvostenko-Khvostov,* 1922.
Pencil.
7¼ x 5 in., 18.5 x 12 cm.
Initialled in pencil and dated lower left corner in Russian: "D.M. 22."
Provenance: Igor Dychenko, Kiev, March, 1984.

Note: Dmitrii Moor (pseudonym of Dmitrii Stakhievich Orlov, 1883-1946) is now remembered for his forceful posters and political caricatures, especially at the time of the Civil War. During the 1910s and 1920s Moor and Khvostenko-Khvostov worked on satirical journals together in Moscow and, presumably, this drawing was done in one of the editorial offices where the artists were employed. While all three faces are Khvostenko-Khvostov's, it is not certain whether Moor drew them all or simply the one on the left that he has initialled.

Uncle Vanya. Scenes from Country Life: drama by Anton Chekhov in four acts performed in the Summer Theater, Meshchensk, in 1915 with designs by Alexander Khvostenko-Khvostov.

Uncle Vanya (Voinitsky) works hard on the estate of his niece Sonia, the daughter of his late sister and Professor Serebriakov. When the latter visits the estate, Uncle Vanya realizes that the man is shallow and egocentric and he makes a futile attempt to kill him. Sonia is in love with Dr. Astrov, who is in love with Elena, Serebriakov's second wife, but each love is unrequited. After the Serebriakovs leave, Uncle Vanya and Sonia continue their aimless life, hoping that one day their sufferings will be redeemed.

606 [R859].
Design for a Room, ca. 1915.
Watercolor.
Signed on reverse.
8⅝ x 11¼ in., 22 x 28.6 cm.
Provenance: Simon Lissim, Dobbs Ferry, New York, 1967.
Reproduced in I40, No. 57.

Love for Three Oranges: farcical opera in four acts by Sergei Prokofiev based on the comedy by Carlo Gozzi. Prepared, but not produced by the State Opera Company, Kharkov, for the 1926-27 season of the Berezil Theater with designs by Alexander Khvostenko-Khvostov.

See No. 32 [R31] for plot summary.

607

607 [R860].
Costume Design for the Black Servant of the Fata Morgana, Smeraldina, ca. 1926.
Watercolor over pencil and gold and silver paint with collage made of silver and gold paper.
Signed in pencil above right foot in Russian: "A. Khvostov."
21½ x 12¾ in., 39.5 x 32.5 cm.
Other inscriptions: in pencil in Russian: on reverse: "Love for Three Oranges. A.V. Khvostov"; upper right: "Love for Three

606

Oranges. A.V. Khvostov"; upper right: "Smeraldina. Chains made of cardboard covered in tin-plate."
Provenance: Igor Dychenko, Kiev, March, 1984.
Reproduced in color in B115, plate 162; I77, p. 162; and in black and white in A34, p. 198; I77, p. 144; M20; M112; T10; T27. Another version, in the collection of the State Museum of Art, Kiev, is reproduced in *Oleksandr Veniaminovich Khvostov,* p. 22.

Note: Les Kurbas's transference of his Berezil Theater from Kiev to Kharkov in 1926 was indicative of a remarkable upsurge of avant-garde activity there in the mid- and late 1920s. While Moscow and Leningrad were coming under increasing pressure to adapt their cultures to a more conservative taste, Kharkov still held out as a progressive center. It provided a forum for the Association of Contemporary Artists of the Ukraine, organized exhibitions of the new art, and published important journals such as *Nova generatsiia* (1927-30) and *Avangard* (1929). Khvostenko-Khvostov's dynamic costume for Smeraldina in the *Love for Three Oranges* communicates the dynamism of that highly charged epoch. As Ihor Ciszkewycz has noted:

> Kurbas felt the actor should create a memorable transformation on the stage in order that the audience be shocked and in the end, profoundly influenced by it. This transformation technique could be abstract, psychological, stylized, rhythmical, symbolic, metaphysical and numerous other types. These transformations even occurred in music, drama and stage décor.[436]

434 Gorbachov: *Oleksandr Khvostenko-Khvostov,* p. 9.
435 For a reproduction of a set for *Die Walkürie* see *The Berezil Theatre.* Catalog of exhibition organized by the Organization of Modern Ukrainian Artists, New York, 1980, unpaginated.
436 I. Ciszkewycz: "The Berezil Theatrical Association and Its Revolutionary Makeup," ibid., unpaginated.

KISELEV, Viktor Petrovich

Born 31 January (12 February), 1895 (some sources give 19 February [2 March], 1896), Moscow, Russia; died 24 May, 1984, Moscow, Russia.

1906-12 attended CSIAI; 1912-18 attended MIPSA / Svomas under Abram Arkhipov and Konstantin Korovin; 1918 onwards exhibited regularly; taught at Svomas in Riazan; 1920 onwards involved in the theater as a stage designer; 1921 codesigner of Vsevolod Meierkhold's production of *Mystery-Bouffe;* supported Constructivism; early 1920s especially interested in the formal experiments of Alexander Rodchenko and Vladimir Tatlin; ca. 1923 taught at Vkhutemas, Moscow; 1925-27 taught at the Mstera Art-Industrial Technicum; 1926 designed costumes for a production of Nikolai Gogol's *Inspector General;* 1926-29 member of OMKh; 1929 took part in the "First Stage Design Exhibition" and "Results of the Moscow Theater Season for 1928-29," both in Moscow; 1932 designed *The Last Victim* at the Ermolova Studio, Moscow; 1935 took part in the exhibition "Artists of the Soviet Theater over the Last 17 Years (1917-1934)" in Moscow and Leningrad; 1930s taught at the Moscow Textile Institute; worked for MKhAT and the Central Theater of the Red Army; continued to exhibit until the 1970s.

Bibliography
A7, Vol. 3, p. 43.
A14, Vol. 4, Book 2, pp. 492-93.
Viktor Petrovich Kiselev: Catalog of exhibition organized by the Union of Artists of the USSR, M, 1983.

As an artist of the stage, Kiselev is not widely known. But the fact that he produced such original resolutions for *Mystery-Bouffe* when he was only twenty-six and under contract to such a prestigious director as Meierkhold indicates the wealth and diversity that have yet to be discovered in the treasure-house of Russian stage design, especially of the 1920s. Many artists are worthy of note for their costumes and sets, yet they are still unfamiliar to the broader public and await rediscovery, among them Orest Allegri, Leonid Chupiatov, and Yurii Bondi.

True, Kiselev's encounter with the avant-garde and Constructivism was brief and he seems to have acquiesced to the more mundane demands of the academic theater in the late 1920s onwards. At the same time, the bizarre resolutions that Kiselev made for *Mystery-Bouffe* such as the costumes for the Lamplighter and Beelzebub, raise — once again — the vexed question as to how exactly such imaginary figures functioned in three dimensions on the material stage. The designs on paper are visually attractive, clever examples of Constructivist economy and understatement, but just how far this impression would have been reinforced by the actors moving in costumes of cloth with cuts and seams is hard to envision. The apparent discrepancy between the surface and volume, performance and reality in the projects of Kiselev and his colleagues caused one critic to observe of the 1921 premiere that

> The attempt to drag elements of the new way of life on to the stage fails. Afraid of descending into naturalism, the artists schematize — and go astray. The rejection of theatrical forms proves to be illusory.[437]

Mystery-Bouffe: *"A Heroic, Epic and Satirical Depiction of Our Epoch" in prologue and six acts by Vladimir Maiakovsky. Produced at the Theater of the RSFSR No. 1, Moscow, 1 May, 1921, by Vsevolod Meierkhold and Valerii Bebutov with music compiled by Alexander Orlov and with designs by Viktor Kiselev, Anton Lavinsky, and Vladimir Khrakovsky.*
See No. 520 [R395] for plot summary.

The following costume designs by Kiselev are ordered according to the sequence of characters specified at the beginning of Maiakovsky's play. Costumes for other characters are reproduced in C72, p. 266, and I26, pp. 80-81; also see G82, p. 150. Four costume designs, wrongly attributed to Vladimir Kozlinsky, are also reproduced in V. Komissarjevski: *Les Théâtres de Moscou*, M: Éditions en langues étrangères, 1959, p. 11. Provenance for Nos. 608-18 [R504-514]: Viktor Kholodkov, Moscow, September, 1989.

608 [R504].
Costume Design for the Lamplighter, ca. 1921.
Gouache and pencil.
9 x 7¼ in., 23 x 18.4 cm.
Inscriptions: lower right has identification by Kiselev in Russian: "Lamplighter. Mystery-Bouffe"; upper right carries the number "19," a reference to the sequence of dramatis personae; the reverse carries the name Ellis (a reference to the actor Ivan Vasilievich Ellis, 1893-1963, who played the

608

part) and body measurements for the costume maker.
Reproduced in I77, p. 139.

609 [R505].
Costume Design for the Lamplighter (Front), ca. 1921.
Gouache and pencil.
9⅛ x 7¼ in., 23.2 x 18.4 cm.
Inscribed upper right in pencil in Russian: "Costume, front view"; part of the Russian word for lamplighter is visible underneath this.
Reproduced in I77, p. 139.

610 [R506].
Costume Design for the Lamplighter (Back), ca. 1921.
Gouache and pencil.

609

610

9 x 6¾ in., 23 x 17 cm.
Inscribed upper right in pencil in Russian: "Costume, back view."
Reproduced in I77, p. 139.

611 [R507].
Costume Design for the Automobile Driver, ca. 1921.
Gouache and pencil.
9 x 7⅛ in., 23 x 18 cm.
Inscribed upper left with the number "18," a reference to the sequence of dramatis personae; lower right carries pencil annotations in Russian: "Driver. Mystery-Bouffe"; the reverse carries the name Levshin (a reference to the actor Alexander Ivanovich Levshin, 1899-1982, who played the part) and body measurements, including head size (55 cm.).
Reproduced in I77, p. 140.

611

612

614

615

612 [R508].
***Costume Design for the Coal Miner*, ca,
1921.**
Gouache and pencil.
9 x 7⅛ in., 23 x 18 cm.
Inscribed upper left with the number "20,"
a reference to the sequence of dramatis
personae; upper right carries the name
Nelli, Vl. In Russian (a reference to the actor
Vladimir Alexandrovich Nelli, 1895-1980,
who played the part); lower margin carries
pencil identification of the character; the
reverse carries body measurements,
including hat size (60 cm.).
Reproduced in I77, p. 140.

"Washerwoman. Mystery-Bouffe. Seamstress costume is the same, but with
sleeves"; the reverse carries the names
Subbotina (a reference to Sofia Innokentievna
Subbotina, 1889-1973, who played the part of
Washerwoman) and Zviagintseva (a reference
to Vera Klavdievna Zviagintseva, 1894-1972,
who played the part of the Seamstress), plus
respective costume sizes.
Reproduced in I77, p. 140.

614 [R510].
***Costume Design for the Engineer*, ca. 1921.**
Gouache and pencil.
9 x 7¼ in., 23 x 18.4 cm.
Inscribed upper left with the number "24,"
a reference to the sequence of dramatis
personae; lower margin carries pencil
annotations in Russian: "Engineer.
Mystery-Bouffe;" the reverse carries the
costume measurements.
Reproduced in I77, p. 140.

615 [107; R511].
***Costume Design for Beelzebub*, ca. 1921.**
Gouache and pencil.
14 x 8⅞ in., 35.5 x 22.4 cm.
Inscribed lower margin in pencil in Russian:
"Beelzebub. Mystery-Bouffe"; the reverse
carries details of costume measurements
plus the words in Russian: "Cover with red
copper."
Reproduced in color in B115, plate 124; and
in black and white in I77 p. 140.

616 [108; R512].
***Costume Design for the Devil Herald*, ca.
1921.**
Watercolor and pencil.
15 x 8⅞ in., 38 x 22.5 cm.
Inscribed on the Herald's chest with the
number "12" and the Russian word
"cleaned" (= "The twelfth man has been
cleansed"); his right hip carries the number
"711" (these elements are part of the basic
design); upper left carries the number "28,"
a reference to the sequence of dramatis

personae; lower right carries the pencil
annotation in Russian: "The Devil Herald.
Mystery-Bouffe"; the reverse carries
costume measurements.
Reproduced in color in B115, plate 123; and
in black and white in I77, p. 140. A similar
costume, identified as the Devil, is
reproduced in C89, p. 63.

613

613 [R509].
***Costume Design for the Washerwoman*, ca.
1921.**
Gouache and pencil.
9 x 7⅛ in., 23 x 18 cm.
Inscribed upper right in pencil in Russian:

616

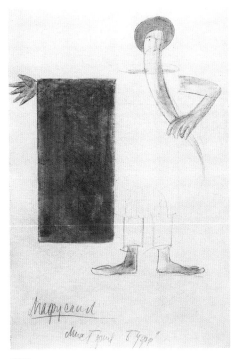

617

617 [R513].
Costume Design for Methuselah, ca. 1921.
Watercolor and pencil.
14 x 8⅞ in., 35.5 x 22.4 cm.
Inscriptions in pencil in Russian: lower margin: "Methuselah. Mystery-Bouffe"; the reverse: annotation "until clarification." Reproduced in I77, p. 140.

Kiselev as contributor:

618 [R514].
Designer unknown: Poster Advertising Mystery-Bouffe, 1921.
Lithograph in black and white.
18⅛ x 8⅝ in., 46 x 22 cm.
Inscriptions provide details on the production of *Mystery-Bouffe,* including the names of the actors.

Note: When Vladimir Maiakovsky finished his famous satire *Mystery-Bouffe* in September, 1918, he was hard put to interest any theater in its production, not least because many were disturbed by the blasphemous interpretation of the Biblical Flood, when God instructed Noah to take seven pairs of clean animals and one pair of each unclean on to his Ark. In the end, Maiakovsky appealed to friends and volunteers to help him and organized a special declamation of his text to attract potential actors. The result was the production of *Mystery-Bouffe* by Meierkhold, Vladimir Soloviev, and Maiakovsky himself at the Communal Theater of Musical Drama in Petrograd on 7 November, 1918 (after strong objections from the administration of that Theater). Meierkhold had first invited Georgii Yakulov to work on the designs for *Mystery-Bouffe,* but the artist's proposals did not satisfy either Meierkhold or Maiakovsky, so they then turned to Kazimir

Malevich. However, Malevich's costumes and sets (which have not survived), while radical in their resolution (e.g., all the "unclean" wore costumes of the same grey material), did not seem to function well on stage, and neither Meierkhold, nor Maiakovsky were happy with the result. As the critic Andrei Levinson wrote: "from the costumes it was impossible to tell a bricklayer from a chimney sweep."[438] After the third night (9 November, 1918), the play was taken off.

Undaunted by the mixed reception of *Mystery-Bouffe,* Meierkhold and Maiakovsky decided to make a "second edition" of the play in 1921. Maiakovsky then rewrote the section called "Land of Fragments", while Meierkhold tried to make the result crisper, more forthright, more politicized; and to introduce elements of the the *balagan* and the circus (the famous clown, Vitalii Lazarenko, played one of the devils). Maiakovsky also invited a trio of young experimental artists — Kiselev, Lavinsky, and Khrakovsky — to design the costumes and sets, and ensured that the level of acting was of the highest caliber (for example, Max Tereshkovich played the part of the Intellectual, Petr Repnin that of the Priest, Evgeniia Khovanskaia that of the Lady with Boxes, and Igor Ilinsky had his first major success with his interpretation of the Conciliator and the German).[439]

The designs were striking. Kiselev and his colleagues interpreted the Earth as a spatial construction of platforms and ladders (something that anticipated Liubov Popova's construction for *The Mag-nanimous Cuckold* the following year). Moreover, part of the design and of the dramatic activity "spilled over" into the auditorium, thereby bridging the gap between actor and audience. As the critic Emmanuil Beskin wrote:

> There is a monumental platform half moved out into the auditorium… It has broken away from all the machinery of the stage, has elbowed away the wings and gridirons, and has crowded up to the very roof of the building. It has torn down the suspended canvases of dead decorative art. It is all constructed, constructed lightly, sche-matically, farcically, made up of wooden benches, sawhorses, boards and painted partitions and shields. It does not copy life with its fluttering curtains and idyllic crickets. It is all composed of reliefs, counter-reliefs, and force lines.[440]

There is no question that this "spectacle of maximum theatrical excess"[441] encouraged the development towards Constructivism in the theater, emphasizing the tendencies that Vladimir Dmitriev had established for Meierkhold's production of *Les Aubes* in 1920. The radical critic, Nikolai Tarabukin, a champion of the Formal method in the early 1920s, even identified the 1921 production of *Mystery-Bouffe* as a "bridge towards Constructivism."[442]

618

The second edition of *Mystery-Bouffe* played more than forty times and, in spite of fears to the contrary, was received well by the proletarian audience who enjoyed its spontaneous, improvisational, carnival atmosphere. "Even the non-Party proletariat feels that this is 'their' play," wrote the critic Vladimir Blium.[443] Indeed, *Mystery-Bouffe* achieved lasting success, not only in Moscow (where, incidentally, Alexei Granovsky also produced a version with designs by Natan Altman at the Salomonsky Circus in 1921),[444] but in other centers, too, including Kiev in 1919, Omsk, Kharkov, Tambov and Saratov in 1921, Kazan in 1923, and then in Tbilisi in 1924 (see Nos. 520-24 [R395-99]). The many discussions that *Mystery-Bouffe* aroused among artists, intellectuals, and factory workers tended to be positive in the evaluation of the play, even though increasing criticism was addressed to the enormous sums of money that Meierkhold's theater consumed. In fact, *Mystery-Bouffe* was Meierkhold's last triumph at his Theater of the RSFSR No. 1 before it was closed down in September, 1921.[445]

619

The Inspector General: satire in five acts by Nikolai Gogol. Produced by Vsevolod Meierkhold at the Meierkhold Theater, Moscow, on 9 December, 1926, with décor by Meierkhold and costumes and stage details by Viktor Kiselev.
See No. 506 [R853] for plot summary.

Kiselev as contributor:

619 [R515].
Designer unknown: *Poster Advertising* **The Inspector General, 1926.**
Lithograph in black and red.
42½ x 28⅜ in., 108 x 72 cm.
Inscriptions (as part of the design) provide details on the production at the Meierkhold

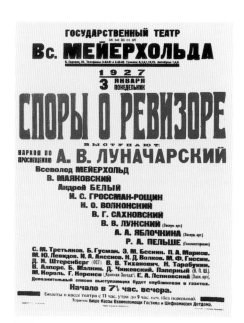

620

Theater on 9-12 and 14-19 December, 1926.
Provenance: Viktor Kholodkov, Moscow, September, 1989.

Kiselev as contributor:

620 [R516].
Designer unknown: *Poster advertising a Debate of* **The Inspector General, 1927.**
Lithograph in black and red.
35 x 28⅜ in., 89 x 72 cm.
Inscriptions (as part of the design) provide details on the debate that took place at the Meierkhold Theater, Moscow, on 3 January, 1927, in connection with Meierkhold's production of Gogol's play. Among the participants indicated are Andrei Bely, Anatolii Lunacharsky, Maiakovsky, Meierkhold, David Shterenberg, Tarabukin, and Sergei Tretiakov.
Provenance: Viktor Kholodkov, Moscow, September, 1989.

437 Anon.: "Teatr im. Meierkholda" (1928). Quoted in G82, p. 150.
438 A. Levinson: "'Misteriia-buff' Maiakovskogo" in *Zhizn iskusstva*, M, 1918, 11 November. Quoted in C72, p. 257. One of Malevich's designs for *Mystery-Bouffe* is reproduced in *Novyi zritel*, M, 1927, 7 November, p. 6.
439 See Ilinsky's memoirs in F66, pp. 195-98.
440 E. Beskin: "Revoliutsiia i teatr" in *Vestnik rabotnikov iskusstv*, M, 1921, No. 7-9, p. 31. Quoted in C72, p. 279.
441 S. Glagolin: "Vesna teatralnoi chrezmernosti" in *Vestnik rabotnikov iskusstv*, M, 1921, No. 11-11, p. 122. Quoted in C72, p. 278.
442 N. Tarabukin. Quoted in C72, p. 274.
443 V. Blium: "Teatr RSFSR Pervyi. 'Misteriia-Buff'" in *Vestnik teatra*, M, 1921, No. 91-92, p. 10. Quoted in C31, Vol. 1, p. 154.
444 For the reproduction of one of Altman's designs for this see M. Etkind: *Natan Altman*, M: Sovetskii khudozhnik, 1972, p. 125. The same design is attributed to Samokhvalov in C7, plate 278.
445 For further information on the 1921 production of *Mystery-Bouffe* see C31, Vol. 1, pp. 141-159; and C72, pp. 273-81.

KLIUN (Kliunkov), Ivan Vasilievich

Born 20 August (1 September), 1870, Bolshie Gorki, Vladimir Region (near Moscow), Russia; died 13 December, 1943 Moscow, Russia.

1880s studied at the Art Institute in Penza; 1889-90 studied at the school of the Society of the Encouragement of the Arts in Warsaw; 1900-05 studied in private studios, including that of Fedor Rerberg in Moscow, where he met Kazimir Malevich; 1907-14 studied at IAA; 1910-16 contributed to avant-garde exhibitions such as "Union of Youth," "Tramway V," "0.10," and "The Store"; 1913-14 befriended Alexei Kruchenykh, Mikhail Matiushin, and other members of the avant-garde; interested in French Cubism and Italian Futurism; 1916 together with Suprematist artists such as Alexandra Exter, Malevich, Liubov Popova, and Nadezhda Udaltsova worked at the Verbovka Village Folk Center, Ukraine; 1917-21 Head of the Central

Exhibition Bureau of the IZO NKP; 1918 took part in the November agit-decorations for Moscow; 1918 -21taught at Vkhutemas in Moscow; 1919 contributed to the "Tenth State Exhibition: Non-Objective Creation and Suprematism"; 1920 member of Inkhuk; 1922 contributed to "Erste Russische Kunstausstellung" in Berlin; 1920s-30s contributed to many exhibitions in the Soviet Union; 1923 illustrated Kruchenykh's *Faktura slova* [Texture of the Word]; 1925 member of the "Four Arts" group; turned to a more representational kind of painting much in the style of Ozenfant.

Bibliography
M. Kolpakchi, ed.: *Skulptura i risunki skulptorov kontsa XIX – nachala XX veka*, Moscow: Tretiakov Gallery, 1977, pp. 435-37.
B34, pp. 139-205.
J. Bowlt: *Ivan Vasilievich Kliun. Sketchbook 1916-1922.* Catalog of exhibition at the Matignon Gallery, New York, 1983.
B134, pp. 156-61.
B138, pp. 110-15.
K154, pp. 767-68.
S. Kliunkova-Soloveichik: *Ivan Vasilievich Kliun,* New York: TVK, 1994.
A. Sarabianov, comp.: *I.V. Kliun. Moi put v iskusstve,* Moscow: RA, 1999.
A. Sarabianov, ed.: *Ivan Vasilievich Kliun.* Catalog of exhibition at the Tretiakov Gallery, Moscow, 1999.
B284, passim.
K281, pp. 198-201.

Although Kliun studied many styles, including Symbolism, Cubism, and Futurism, his abstract compositions remain among his principal artistic accomplishments. A close friend and colleague of Kazimir Malevich, Kliun championed Suprematism and became a leading member of the Supremus group in 1916-18, sharing and reprocessing the concepts of geometric abstraction. As he announced in 1915, "before us has arisen the grand task of creating a form *out of nothing*."[446] Throughout the late 1910s and early 1920s Kliun continued to investigate Suprematism, although he expressed frustration with its geometric exclusivity, criticizing Malevich and, at one point, even referring to the Black Square as the "corpse of painterly art."[447]

Kliun was especially interested in the perception and variability of color and he elaborated a number of tabulations based on the results of his abstract painting in which he aspired to present a rational explanation of "color, form, light, and texture (the intensification of color via light and via contrasts, the influence of adjacent colors on the change of form."[448] Above all, Kliun was a studio painter and chose not to transfer his energies to design and the utilitarian arts, in spite of the pressure to place art in the service of politics after the October Revolution. He supported neither Vladimir Tatlin's extension of the abstract relief to practical ends, nor Malevich's endeavor to "suprematize" the world by applying geometric motifs to porcelain, textiles, and architecture. Apart from his occasional book illustrations, his projects for a memorial to Olga Rozanova, and his casual contribution to the agit-decorations for Moscow in 1918-19, Kliun remained committed to the esthetic of studio painting – and the costume design below is a highly unusual, if not, unique, example of his sally into the theater.

From the late 1920s onwards Kliun continued to experiment with various pictorial styles, although he gave increasing attention to the possibilities of a new figurative painting and sculpture — to a new "subjectness," as contemporary critics called it.[449] In his esthetic response, Kliun reasserted his earlier obligation to Cubism and manifested a particular interest in French Purism, paraphrasing and elaborating works by Jeanneret, Léger, and Ozenfant.

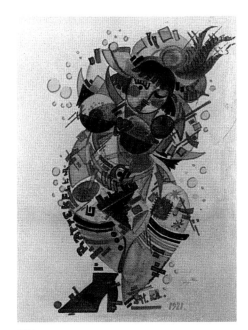

621

Unknown production, ca. 1921.

621 [NIRE].
Design for a Costume, 1921.
Watercolor.
Initialed and dated lower right in Russian: "I.Kl. 1921."
10⅝ x 7⅞ in., 27 x 20 cm.
Inscription on left contour of the figure: "Rattekeler" ["Ratskeller" is a colloquial German word for a restaurant or bar in a basement.]
Provenance: Hempel Kunstauktion, Munich, 4 September, 2007, Catalog II, Lot 184 (reproduced).

446 I. Kliun: "Primitivy XX veka" (1915). English translation in B12, p. 137.
447 I. Kliun: "Iskusstvo tsveta" (1919), English translation in B12, p. 143.
448 P. Pertsov: *Khudozhestvennye muzei Moskvy. Putevoditel,* M: Moskovskoe kommunalnoe khoziaistvo, 1925, p. 88.
449 A. Fedorov-Davydov: "Khudozhestvennaia zhizn Moskvy" in *Pechat i revoliutsiia,* M, 1927, Book 1, p. 98.

KLUTSIS Gustav Gustavovich (Klucis, Gustavs)

Born 4 (16) January, 1895, Rujena, Latvia; executed 26 February, 1938, Moscow, Russia.

1911-13 attended a teachers' seminary in Volmar (Valmiera, Latvia); 1914-15 studied at the Riga Art Institute under Vilhelms Purvitis (Purvit); 1915-18 studied at the Society for the Encouragement of the Arts in Petrograd; worked as a scene painter for the Okhta Workers' Theater there; 1918 moved to Moscow as a rifleman in the Ninth Latvian Infantry and worked in its art studio, painting scenes from army life; attended Ilia Mashkov's private studio; 1918-21 studied at Svomas/Vkhutemas under Konstantin Korovin and Anton Pevsner; contact with Kazimir Malevich; 1919-20 began to work on poster, typographical, and architectural designs; 1920 exhibited with Naum Gabo and Pevsner; with Sergei Senkin established his own studio within Vkhutemas; 1920-21 contributed to the Unovis exhibitions in Vitebsk and Moscow; 1920-22 influence of El Lissitzky; became especially interested in constructive projects and photomontage; 1921-23 member of Inkhuk; 1922 began to teach at the Painting Studio of the Sverdlov Club; contributed to the "Erste Russische Kunstausstellung" in Berlin; 1924-30 taught color theory at Vkhutemas/Vkhutein; 1925 contributed to the "Exposition Internationale des Arts Décoratifs et Industriels Modernes" in Paris; 1928 contributed to the "Pressa" exhibition in Cologne; cofounder of the October group; 1929 designed posters for the art department of the State Publishing-House; late 1920s taught at the Moscow Polygraphical Institute and the Communist Academy; 1920s-30s active as a poster and typographical designer; contributed to Soviet and international exhibitions; 1929-32 member of the Association of Revolutionary Poster Artists; 1937 collaborated on the design of the Soviet pavilion for the "Exposition Internationale" in Paris; 1938 arrested and transported to a labor camp.

Bibliography
L. Oginskaia: *Gustav Klutsis,* M: Sovetskii khudozhnik, 1981.
J. Bowlt: *Gustav Kluzis.* Catalog of exhibition at the Galerie Gmurzynska, Cologne, 1988.
Gustavs Klicis. Starp varu un mīlestību. Catalog of exhibition at the Valsts Mākslas Muzejs, Riga, 1988.
H. Gassner and R. Nachtigaller: *Gustav Klucis. Retrospektive.* Catalog of exhibition at the Museum Fridericianum, Kassel; and the Centro de Arte Reina Sofia, Madrid, 1991.
Anon.: *Gustav Klutsis; Soviet Propaganda Photomontage.* Catalog of exhibition at the Ubu Gallery, New York, 1997.
M. Tupitsyn: *Gustav Klutsis and Valentina Kulagina: Photography and Montage after Constructivism.* Catalog of exhibition at the International Center of Photography New York, 2004.
F. Hergott et al.: *Gustavs Klicis.* Catalog of exhibition at the Musée d'art moderne et contemporain, Strasbourg, 2005.
A. Snopkov and A. Morozov: *Gustav Klutsis, Valentina Kulagina, Plakat, Knizhnaia grafika, Zhurnalnaia grafika, Gazetnyi fotomontazh, 1922-1937,* M: Kontakt-Kultura, 2010.
S. Khan-Magomedov: *Gustav Klutsis,* M: Gordeev, 2011.

As in the case of Alexander Rodchenko, Klutsis embarked upon his artistic career as a studio painter, attending schools in Riga,

Petrograd, and Moscow, but he achieved recognition, above all, as a poster artist and photomontagist. From 1919 onwards Klutsis gave increasing attention to photomontage, using it documentarily, imaginatively, sometimes even capriciously — from the first experiment called *Dynamic City* (1919) to the *Pravda* layout of the mid-1930s. While often proposing utopian renderings of present and future, Klutsis's compositions are taut in their organization and direct in their message, and from the very beginning, the posters and, no doubt, the street decorations such as the one here, were oriented towards a mass consumer: in fact, *Dynamic City* is intended to be "viewed from all sides,"[450] and brings to mind Malevich's Suprematist compositions.

True, Klutsis's ideas and images are often analogous to those of Rodchenko and the two artists have sometimes been confused. Not surprisingly, Klutsis also contributed to the Constructivist magazine *Lef* [Left Front of the Arts], publishing his essay on photo-montage there in 1924. Klutsis also shared the group's interest in industrial art, programmatic art, and the unashamed application thereof to political ends, to which his designs for propaganda illumination bear strong witness. From the series of loudspeakers and radios of 1922 through his remarkable serial illustrations for the book *Lenin i deti* [Lenin and Children] (Moscow, 1925), the sports meets, and the reconstruction posters of the 1930s, Klutsis used his talent consciously and sincerely to disseminate the behests of Marx, Lenin, and Stalin. Tragically, Klutsis fell victim to the very ideological machine which he glorified so graphically.

622 [109; NIRE].
Design for Decoration of the Moscow Kremlin Celebrating the IV Congress of the Communist International and the Fifth Anniversary of the Revolution, 1922.
Watercolor over ink and pencil.
8⅞ x 12 in., 22.5 x 30.5 cm.
Provenance: Stockholms Auktionsverk, Stockholm, 4 October, 2007, Lot 125 (reproduced).
Reproduced in color in *ArtGorod,* SP, 2009, No. 11(21), p. 76. A similar design is illustrated in Gassner and Nachtigaller, *Gustav Klucis, Retrospektive,* at No. 81, where it is captioned: "The Bourgeoisie is trembling. Radio for the proletariat. Honor to the fallen in battle."

623 [NIRE].
Drawing on reverse of No. 622 [NIRE].
Charcoal.

Note: Klutsis devoted much time and energy to his celebratory designs for the IV Congress of the Communist International and many of his projects for loudspeakers, podiums, and movie screens of 1922 were connected to this important agit-project. Intended for Red Square or even inside the Kremlin (one of the Kremlin towers is visible

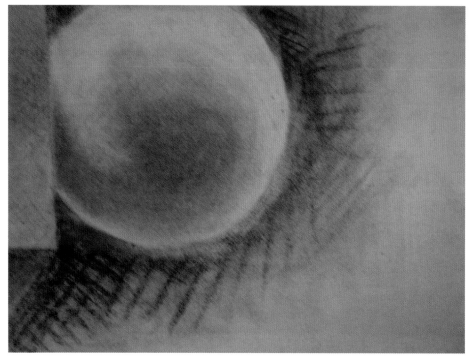

623

on the far left of the sketch), the ensemble was to have included both "hi-tech" paraphernalia such as wireless megaphones and simple slogans, incorporated into the design here, such as "Long Live the Anniversary," "Make the Bourgeois Tremble!", "Glory to the Fallen in Battle," and "Radio for the whole of [the proletariat]." With its simple, dynamic, geometric forms, the ensemble derived immediately from Klutsis's prior abstract experiments in painting and construction, encapsulated in his *Dynamic City* series of 1919.

450 Such is the inscription on one of the *Dynamic Cities* reproduced, for example, in B71, p. 6.

KOMARDENKOV, Vasilii Petrovich

Born 12 (24) April, 1897, Moscow, Russia; died 15 April, 1973, Moscow, Russia.

Ca. 1910 took private lessons with Dmitrii Shcherbinovsky; ca. 1912 attended CSIAI and then MIPSA, graduating in 1917; 1914-17 worked as a scene painter for Sergei Zimin's Opera Company, Moscow; influenced by Vladimir Egorov, Fedor Fedorovsky, Ivan Fedotov, and Ivan Maliutin; 1918 debut as a professional stage designer for the production of *Evgenii Onegin* at the Opera of the Moscow Soviet of Workers' Deputies; this was the first of more than seventy stage productions that he designed during his lifetime; close to Sergei Esenin, Georgii Yakulov, and the Imaginists; frequented the Café Pittoresque; worked in IZO NKP; helped Yurii Annenkov color his illustrations for the first hundred copies of the original edition of Alexander Blok's

poem *Dvenadtsat* [The Twelve]; 1918-19 attended Svomas in Moscow; 1919 co-founder of Obmokhu, contributing to its first and third exhibitions (1919 and 1921); influenced by Vladimir Tatlin; 1918-25 scene painter for Alexander Tairov's Chamber Theater, Moscow; 1920 frequented the House of Arts; 1922 contributed to the "Erste Russische Kunstausstellung" in Berlin; 1923 contributed to the "Moscow Stage Design Exhibition"; 1925 began to work on movie designs; contributed to the "Exposition Internationale des Arts Décoratifs," Paris; 1926-28 worked on productions for the Terevsat (Theater of Revolutionary Satire); 1927 designed *A Midsummer Night's Dream* for the Ivan Franko State Drama Theater in Kiev; 1929 contributed to the "First Stage Design Exhibition" in Moscow; 1937 represented at the "Exposition Internationale" in Paris; 1946 onwards taught at the Higher Art-Industrial Institute in Moscow; increasingly interested in studio painting.

Bibliography
I. Sats et al.: *Vasilii Petrovich Komardenkov.* Catalog of exhibition at the All-Union Theatrical Society, Moscow, 1986.
Anon.: "On govorit o dvukh vystavkakh" in *Sovetskaia kultura,* M, 1987, 3 February.
Vasilii Petrovich Komardenkov. Catalog of exhibition at the TG, 2008.
Komardenkov's memoirs are of particular interest, i.e., F38.

The "Class of '19" at the Moscow Svomas included a number of outstanding painters and designers who contributed much to the second wave of Russia's avant-garde. Besides Komardenkov, Nikolai Denisovsky, Sergei Kostin, Konstantin Medunetsky, and the Stenberg brothers — to mention but a few — received their Svomas diplomas that year. Not surprisingly, they held their mentors, especially Tatlin, in high regard, and tended to pursue similar cultural interests. On graduation, they founded Obmokhu which, with its four exhibitions (through 1924), contributed directly to the establishment and development of Constructivism; and many of these young artists, not least Komardenkov, quickly achieved recognition as stage designers.

Komardenkov was affected by many artistic influences and found inspiration in a wide variety of painters, from Fedor Fedorovsky to Aristarkh Lentulov, from Isaak Rabinovich to Sergei Sudeikin. But he was especially drawn to Yakulov's bohemian way of life and to Moscow's café culture during those revolutionary years. Komardenkov even helped decorate the interior of the premises of the All-Russian Union of Poets, where Futurists and Imaginists met and polemicized, recalling in his memoirs that "All kinds of fanciful forms were cut out of paper which were then stuck on the walls. The result was very variegated, but not all that beautiful."[451] In fact, it was at the All-Russian Union of Poets that Komardenkov came into close contact with the writers Sergei Esenin, Vasilii Kamensky, Anatolii Mariengof, and Vadim Shershenevich. Yakulov, a frequent visitor to the All-Russian Union, was already working at the Chamber Theater and, no doubt, through this connection Komardenkov was appointed scene painter there.

624 [R519].
Caricature of Charlie Chaplin, 1923.
Black ink.
Initialed lower right.
6¾ x 5¾ in., 17.2 x 14.5 cm.
Inscribed on the reverse in Russian: "Drawing reproduced in *Zrelishcha* [Spectacles] No. 40."
Provenance: Viktor Kholodkov, Moscow, September, 1989.

Note: The reference to *Zrelishcha* is to the leading performing arts journal of the 1920s. It was published in Moscow in

624

1922-24 and often carried portraits and caricatures of leading theater and movie personalities. Charlie Chaplin enjoyed a particular vogue in Soviet Russia in the 1920s and his autobiographical statement, "Chaplin o sebe," appeared in three numbers of *Zrelishcha* for 1923 (Nos. 33, 34, 38). However, in spite of the inscription on the reverse of this piece, issue No. 40 of *Zrelishcha* for 1923 does not carry a reproduction of Komardenkov's rendering of Charlie Chaplin.

A Midsummer Night's Dream: *comedy in five acts by William Shakespeare. Produced by Gnat Yura at the Ivan Franko State Drama Theater, Kiev, on 15 October, 1927, with designs by Vasilii Komardenkov. See No. 356 [R321] for plot summary.*

625

625 [R520].
Costume Design for Lysander, 1927.
Watercolor and pencil.
Signed lower left in pencil in Russian and dated: "V. Komar. '27."
13¾ x 10 in., 35 x 25.5 cm.
Other inscriptions in pencil in Russian: upper left: "Lysander"; cloth annotations throughout; the reverse carries the inscription: "Komardenkov. Midsummer Night's Dream. Franko Theater, Kiev, 1927," and also an unfinished drawing.
Provenance: Viktor Kholodkov, Moscow, September, 1989
Reproduced in color in I60, p. 4; and I68, p. 14; and in black and white in I77, p. 144. For a documentary photograph of the production containing this costume see G57, p. 125.

Signor Formica: *play by Vladimir Sokolov based on the story by E.T.A. Hoffmann. Produced by Vladimir Sokolov at the Chamber Theater, Moscow, on 13 June, 1922, with music by Anatolii Alexandrov*

and designs by Georgii Yakulov, assisted by Vasilii Komardenkov.

The artist Salvador Rosa befriends the surgeon and aspiring painter Antonia Scacciati. Rosa submits a painting by Scacciati to the Academy of St. Luke in Rome as a work by a dead Neapolitan painter, and Academicians accept it. Meanwhile, Scacciati, in love with the lovely Marianna, is at loggerheads with her father, Pasquale Capuzzi. In order to win the good graces of Capuzzi, Rosa asks his friend, Signor Formica, to sing some of Capuzzi's music in a local theater, which he does, albeit sardonically. Scacciati and Marianna elope to Florence and, after many misunderstandings, Capuzzi accepts their union.

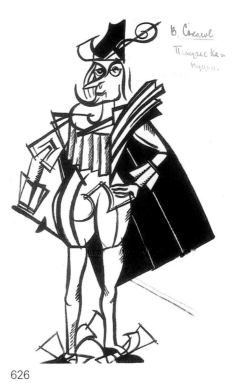

626

626 [R521].
Portrait of the Actor Vladimir Sokolov in the Role of Pasquale Capuzzi, 1922.
Ink.
Signed and dated on the reverse.
6¼ x 9½ in., 16 x 24 cm.
Other inscriptions in Russian: upper right in ink: "V. Sokolov. Pasquale Capuzzi"; on the reverse: "Chamber Theater. Sig. Formica. Designer: Yakulov in collaboration with Komardenkov. Sketch for Pasquale Capuzzi's costume by V. Komardenskov after the original by G. Yakulov. The journal *Ermitazh*, 1922, No. 7."
Provenance: Viktor Kholodkov, Moscow, September, 1989.
Reproduced in *Ermitazh*, M, 1922, No. 7, p. 11; *Modern Continental Paintings, Watercolours and Sculpture.* Catalog of auction at Phillips, Son and Neale, London, 1987, 24 February, Lot 118; and I77, p. 138. Also cf. Yakulov's design for *Signor Formica* at Nos. 1159-60 [R1014-15]. Vladimir Alexandrovich Sokolov (1889-1962) was a prominent actor with the Chamber Theater.

627

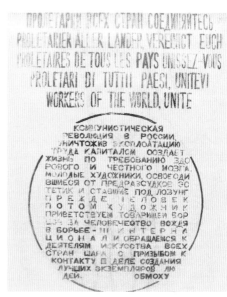

628

629

627 [R522].
Portrait of Igor Ilinsky in the Role of Salvador Rosa, 1922.
Pen and Ink.
Signed and dated on the reverse.
6¼ x 9½ in., 16 x 24 cm.
Other inscriptions: on the reverse in Russian: "Chamber Theater. 'Sig Formica'. Designer: Yakulov in collaboration with Komardenkov. Sketch for Salvador Rosa's costume by V. Komardenkov after the original by G. Yakulov. The journal *Ermitazh,* 1922, No. 7." The reference is to the celebrated actor, Igor Vladimirovich Ilinsky (1901-87; see F67).
Provenance: Viktor Kholodkov, Moscow, September, 1989.
Reproduced in *Ermitazh,* M, 1922, No. 7, p. 11; *Modern Continental Paintings, Drawings, Watercolours and Sculpture.* Catalog of auction at Phillips, Son and Neale, London, 1987, 24 February, Lot 117; and I77, p. 138. Also cf. Yakulov's designs for *Signor Formica* at Nos. 1159-60 [R1014-15].

Note: Unlike most modern Russian stage designers, Komardenkov had considerable experience as an actual scene painter, working at Zimin's Opera Company and then at the Chamber Theater (where, of course, he helped with the 1922 production of *Signor Formica*). Komardenkov knew, therefore, about the technical and material aspects of costume and set design and the direct relevance and appropriateness of a given project to its intended function on the three-dimensional stage. Consequently, he tended not to indulge in fantastic ornament, even though, for example, he appreciated Alexander Golovin's florid decorations. Komardenkov produced rational, but still attractive, designs that were both practicable and could be identified easily by the audience.

These qualities were evident in his resolutions for *A Midsummer Night's Dream* in Kiev — which he considered to be his most successful endeavor as a stage designer.[452]

Komardenkov as contributor:
628 [R523].
Designer unknown: Poster Advertising the "Third Exhibition of Obmokhu (Society of Young Artists)", Moscow, May-June, 1921.
Lithograph in black on pink paper.
15⅜ x 23⅝ in., 39 x 60 cm.
The text lists the participants, among whom are Nikolai Denisovsky, Vasilii Komardenkov, Sergei Kostin, Konstantin Medunetsky, Alexander Rodchenko, and the Stenberg brothers.
Provenance: Viktor Kholodkov, Moscow, September, 1989.
Reproduced in K154 (Russian edition), p. 163.

Note: Obmokhu (Society of Young Artists) was founded in 1919 by a group of graduates from the Moscow Svomas. Using a studio with metal-cutting machines and welding apparatus, they viewed art as an extra-esthetic, functional discipline. To this end, they designed and produced stencils for postcards and badges, worked on theater sets, constructed traveling libraries, and decorated streets and squares. Prominent members of Obmokhu were Komardenkov and the Stenberg brothers, who showed their works at the group's four exhibitions in Moscow between 1919 and 1923. Rodchenko joined the Society in 1921, a move that consolidated Obmokhu's position as a champion of applied art and Constructivism.

Komardenkov as contributor:
629 [R524].
Collective design by the artists of Obmokhu: Poster Carrying the Slogan "Workers of the World, Unite," 1921.
Stencil with black lettering.
Signed: Obmokhu.
20⅝ x 17½ in., 52.5 x 44.5 cm.

Other inscriptions (as part of the design): the top half of the poster carries the slogan "Workers of the World, Unite" in Russian, German, French, Italian, and English. The circle contains the following, somewhat recondite, information: "After destroying the exploitation of labor by capital, the Communist Revolution in Russia is now creating a life demanded by a healthy and honest brain. Having freed themselves from the prejudices of esthetics and standing under the banner 'First Man, Then Artist', young artists greet their comrade fighters for humanity and the leader in the struggle — the III International. We turn to the art workers of all countries of the world with an appeal to join us in an endeavor to create the finest exemplars of human beings." The reverse carries a pencil drawing of a nude male.
Provenance: Viktor Kholodkov, Moscow, September, 1989.

Note: Obmokhu issued this poster on the occasion of the III Congress of the Communist International that was convoked in Moscow in June and July, 1921. While an intensely political event, the Congress attracted a good deal of artistic and cultural attention — from Isaak Brodsky's sketches of Lenin there to Vladimir Tatlin's project for the monument to the Congress. Vsevolod Meierkhold even made a special Russo-German production of Vladimir Maiakovsky's *Mystery-Bouffe* (see Nos. 520 [R395] and 608 [R504]) for the Congress, so it is not surprising that the artists of Obmokhu were also interested in its proceedings.

451   F38, p. 66.
452   F38, p. 7.

KOROVIN, Alexei Konstantinovich

Born 23 June (5 July), 1897, Moscow, Russia; died (suicide) 17 December, 1950, Paris, France.

Through his father Konstantin Korovin, was introduced to stage design from an early age as well as to the artistic circles of Moscow and St. Petersburg; his mother, Anna Fidler, was a singer with Savva Mamontov's Private Opera Company; 1913 entered high school in Moscow; 1918 member of the World of Art Society, exhibiting in 1918 and 1921; 1920 contributed to the "XIX State Exhibition," Moscow; 1923 emigrated with his parents and settled in Paris; 1925 attempted suicide; during the 1920s worked for various cabarets as a designer and assisted his father with stage decorations; 1933 worked for the Teatro Colón, Buenos Aires; 1939 designed Bronislava Nijinska's production of *Sylphides* for the Ballet Russe de Monte Carlo; 1930s-40s copied many of his father's early paintings and designs.

Bibliography
Nothing substantial has been published on Alexei Korovin. For some information see the the general sources on Konstantin Korovin and the following.
V. Zeeler: "Aleksei Korovin" in *Russkaia mysl*, Paris, 1950, 28 December (No. 306).
H10.
F16.
M2, Vol. 2, p. 183.
F33.
H34, p. 343

A characteristic feature of modern Russian culture, including the theater, is the extent to which the creative momentum was maintained by the role of family connections, whether through blood relation or intermarriage, a phenomenon that allows us to speak of the "fathers and sons" of Russian stage design. Some of the "sons" achieved reputations almost as worthy as those of their mothers and fathers as in the case of Nicola and Alexandre Benois or Alexandre and Zinaida Serebriakov; but others such as Kirill Kustodiev (son of Boris)

630

and Alexei Korovin did not succeed in making independent professional careers.

The life of Alexei Korovin was hardly one of good fortune. Overshadowed by the international fame of his father, whom he often assisted and copied (some might say — plagiarized), Alexei Korovin seems not to have developed an original and enduring style. At best, along with Boris Bilinsky (Nos. 372-87 [R342-55]), Eugene Dunkel (No. 454 [R480]), Vladimir Jedrinsky (Nos. 589-93 [R482-86]), Simon Lissim (Nos. 745-50 [R626-30]), and Georges Pogedaieff (Nos. 824-27 [R703-06]), he can be regarded as a Russian advocate of Art Deco and the tinsel glamour of his set for *The Tale of the Invisible City of Kitezh and the Maid Fevronia* might have functioned equally well in a Hollywood movie.

631

The Tale of the Invisible City of Kitezh and the Maid Fevronia: *opera in four acts by Nikolai Rimsky-Korsakov with a libretto by Vladimir Belsky. Produced by Marie Kousnezoff's Opéra Privé de Paris at the Théâtre des Champs-Elysées, Paris, on 27 February, 1929, with designs by Alexei Korovin.*
See No. 369 [R339] for plot summary.

630 [110; R525].
Stage Design for Paradise (the City of Greater Kitezh), ca. 1929.
Watercolor, gold and silver paint, and ink.
Signed lower right: "Alexei Korovine."
18½ x 24⅜ in., 47 x 62 cm.
Other inscription: lower margin: "Légende de la ville invisible de Kitège. Acte IV tableau II."

632

633

634

Provenance: Mikhail Benois, Madrid, May, 1968.
Reproduced in I20, No. 55; I51, No. 124. A variant in the collection of The Fine Arts Museum of San Francisco is reproduced in I44, fig. 72.

631 [R526].
Stage Detail: the Wedding Chariot, ca. 1929.
Watercolor and black ink.
Signed lower left in ink: "A. Korovine."
10⅝ x 15⅜ in., 27 x 39 cm.
Other inscriptions: upper left: "Kitège"; lower left: "La Charette Nuptiale."
Provenance: Iosif Lempert, Paris, April, 1977.
Reproduced in B44, p. 294.

632 [R527].
Costume Design for Fevronia, ca. 1929.
Gouache, gold and silver paint, pencil and ink.
Signed lower left: "A. Korovine."
15⅛ x 10⅞ in., 38.5 x 27.5 cm.
Other inscriptions: upper left margin: "Kitège"; on right: "Fevronia."
Provenance: Mikhail Benois, Madrid, May, 1968.
Reproduced in I40, No. 62.[453]

633 [R528].
Costume Design for Prince Yurii Vsevolodovich, ca. 1929.
Gold paint, gouache, and ink.
Signed lower left: "A. Korovine."
15½ x 10⅞ in., 39.5. x 27.5 cm.
Other inscriptions: upper margin on left: "Kitège"; on right: "Prince Youri Vsevolodovitch."
Provenance: Mikhail Benois, Madrid, May, 1968.
Reproduced in A34, p. 213; I20, No. 56.

634 [R529].
Costume Design for Prince Vsevolod Yurievich, ca. 1929.
Gouache, silver and gold paint, and ink.
Signed lower left: "A. Korovine."
15⅛ x 10⅞ in., 38.5 x 27.5 cm.
Other inscriptions: instructions to the dress-maker in Russian; upper left margin: "Kitège"; on right: "Prince Vsevolod Yurievich."
Provenance: Mikhail Benois, Madrid, May, 1968.
Reproduced in A34, p. 213; I40, No. 59.

635 [R530].
Costume Design for Prince Vsevolod Yurievich Holding a Flower, ca. 1929.
Gouache, gold and silver paint.
Signed lower left: "A. Korovine"
15⅛ x 10⅞ in., 38.5 x 27.5 cm.
Other inscriptions: around the figure instructions in Russian to the dressmaker;

upper left margin: "Kitège"; on right: "Prince Vsevolod Yurievich."
Provenance: Mikhail Benois, Madrid, May, 1968.
Reproduced in I40, No. 60.

636 [I11; R531].
Costume Design for Bediai, a Tatar Chieftain, ca. 1929.
Gouache, silver paint, and black ink.
Signed lower left: "A. Korovine."
15⅛ x 10⅞ in., 38.5 x 27.5 cm.
Other inscriptions: instructions in Russian to the dressmaker; upper left margin: "Kitège"; on right: "Bediai"
Provenance: Mikhail Benois, Madrid, May, 1968.
Reproduced in I40, No. 63.

635

636

637

638

637 [112; R532].
Costume Design for Burundai, a Tatar Chieftain, ca. 1929.
Gouache, silver paint, and black ink.
Signed lower left: "A. Korovine"
15⅛ x 10⅞ in., 38.5 x 27.5 cm.
Other inscriptions: instructions to the dressmaker in Russian; upper left margin: "Kitège"; on right: "Bouroundai."
Provenance: Mikhail Benois, Madrid, May, 1968.
Reproduced in I40, No. 65.

638 [R533].
Costume Design for the Bard (Gusli Player), ca. 1929.
Gouache and gold.
Signed lower left: "A. Korovine."
15⅜ x 10⅞ in., 39 x 27.5 cm.

Other inscriptions: instructions in Russian to the dressmaker; upper left margin: "Kitège"; on right: "Le Barde."
Provenance: Mikhail Benois, Madrid, May, 1968. Now in a private collection.
Reproduced in I40, No. 61.

639 [R534].
Costume Design for the Bear Tamer, ca. 1929.
Gouache and ink.
Signed lower left: "A. Korovine."
15½ x 10 in., 39.5 x 25.5 cm.
Other inscriptions: upper left margin: "Kitège"; on right: "Dresseur d'ours."
Provenance: Mikhail Benois, Madrid, 1968. Now in a private collection.
Reproduced in I40, No. 64.

640 [R535].
Costume Design for a Tatar Holding a Shield and Dagger, ca. 1929.
Watercolor, silver paint, and ink.
Signed lower left: "A. Korovine."
15½ x 10⅞ in., 39.5 x 27.5 cm.
Other innscriptions: instructions for a dressmaker in Russian; upper left margin: "Kitège"; on right: "Tartares."
Provenance: Mikhail Benois, Madrid, 1969.
Reproduced in I40, No. 66.

641 [R536].
Costume Design for Tatar Warrior Holding a Dagger in Left Hand, ca. 1929.
Gouache, silver paint, and black ink.
Signed lower left: "A. Korovine."
15½ x 10⅞ in., 39.5 x 27.5 cm.
Other inscriptions: instructions to the dressmaker in Russian; upper left margin in French: "Kitège"; on right: "Tartares."
Provenance: Mikhail Benois, Madrid, 1969.
Reproduced in I20, No. 57.

Note: The designs for the 1929 Paris production of *The Tale of the Invisible City of Kitezh and the Maid Fevronia* remind us that Alexei Korovin was much indebted to his

father and, of course, they have much in common with Konstantin Korovin's resolution of the same opera (cf. No. 643 [R538]). At the same time, Alexei Korovin's extreme detail, his generous application of gold and silver, and his intense stylization in this stage design also bring to mind Ivan Bilibin's resolution of the same act (cf. No. 369 [R339]) and Boris Bilinsky's work for the 1930 production of *Ruslan and Liudmila* (cf. No. 377 [R344]). For details on the Opéra Privé de Paris, see notes to Nos. 367, 368 [R337, R338].

453 Nos. 632 [R527], 633 [R528], 635-38 [R530-33], 640 [R535], and 641 [R536] are also reproduced in the Souvenir Program for this production of *The Tale of the Invisible City of Kitezh,* i.e., *Opéra Privé de Paris. Première Saison,* Paris: Publicité Commerciale et Théâtrale, 1919, unpaginated.

639

640

641

KOROVIN, Konstantin Alexeevich

Born 23 November (5 December), 1861, Moscow, Russia; died 11 September, 1939, Paris, France.

1874 entered MIPSA, where he studied principally under Vasilii Polenov and Alexei Savrasov, who encouraged his work in landscape; 1885 made the acquaintance of the art patron and railroad magnate Savva Mamontov and became a primary member of the Abramtsevo colony; through Mamontov began to work as a stage designer, helping with Mamontov's production of *Sadko, Khovanshchina, Prince Igor,* etc., in the 1890s; close to Fedor Chaliapin and Valentin Serov; late 1880s and early 1890s traveled extensively in Europe; influenced by Impressionism; 1894 with Serov traveled in the Far North; 1896 worked on the interior design for Mamontov's Northern Pavilion at the "All-Russian Art and Industry Exhibition" in Nizhnii Novgorod; 1898 onward close to the World of Art group; 1900 appointed artist-in-residence at the Bolshoi Theater, Moscow, working on a number of productions there, e.g., Cesare Pugni's ballet *The Little Hump-Backed Horse* (1901); 1900s onward active in many opera and drama productions, including *Les Orientales* (1910) for Sergei Diaghilev in Paris; 1901-18 taught at MIPSA; 1923 emigrated and settled in Paris; during the 1920s worked for a number of émigré theater companies but had little success; 1929 one of the adjudicators for the Miss Europe Beauty Contest in Paris.

Bibliography
D. Kogan: *K. Korovin,* M: Iskusstvo, 1964. M2, Vol. 2, pp. 183-85.
R. Vlasova: *Konstantin Korovin,* L: Khudozhnik RSFSR, 1969. F33.
T. Kusubova: "A Note on Konstantin Korovin (1860-1939)" in *TriQuarterly,* Evanston, Ill., 1973, No. 28, pp. 558-69.
N. Moleva: *Zhizn moia – zhivopis,* M: Moskovskii rabochii, 1977.
A. Basyrov: *K.A. Korovin,* L: Khudozhnik RSFSR, 1985.
A. Gusarova: *Konstantin Korovin,* M: Sovetskii khudozhnik, 1990.
I. Khabarov, comp.: *Konstantin Korovin / Shaliapin. Vstrechi i sovmestnaia zhizn,* M: Moskovskii rabochii, 1993 (and reprintings).
V. Kruglov: *Korovin,* M: Izobrazitelnoe iskusstvo, 1997.
I. Nenarokomova: *Korovin,* M: Slovo, 1997.
K. Korovin: *Vospominaniia,* M: Sovremennyi literator, 1999 (editor not indicated).
V. Domiteeva: *Konstantin Korovin,* M: Terra, 2007.
E. Gromova: *Korovin: Albom,* M: OLMA Media, 2009.
T. Ermolaeva and T. Esina, eds.: *Konstantin Korovin: "To bylo davno… tam… v Rossii…,"* M: Russkii put, 2010 (two volumes).
Various authors: *Konstantin Korovin. Zhivopis. Teatr: K 150-letiiu so dnia rozhdeniia,* M: Skanrus, 2012.

Konstantin Korovin is one of Russia's most celebrated stage designers, although not necessarily one of the most audacious. Korovin belonged to the first generation of the new stylists of the late nineteenth and early twentieth centuries, a generation that also included Polenov, Viktor Vasnetsov (No. 1115 [NIRE]), and Mikhail Vrubel (1152-55 [R383-85]). Korovin made his debut as a theatrical painter in 1885, when he executed the sets and costumes for the production of *Snegurochka* at Mamontov's Private Opera Company (after Vasnetsov's designs) and, thereafter, emerged rapidly as an independent stage designer — decorating eighty operas, thirty-seven ballets, and seventeen dramas during his lifetime. Korovin brought to the Russian stage a vibrancy and richness that were lacking in the traditional Imperial theaters. Alexandre Benois, who saw performances by the Private Opera Company on tour in St. Petersburg in 1898, including *Sadko* with Korovin's designs, recalled his impression:

> [We] were able to see for ourselves how original and interesting Korovin's treatment of scenic painting was. I did not like everything — the planning was rather poor at times, and there was a certain roughness in the technique — but these shortcomings could have been explained by the very modest means the private company had at its disposal. On the whole, Korovine's décors amazed us by their daring approach to the problem and, above all, by their high *artistic* value.[454]

Vladimir Teliakovsky, Director of the Imperial Theaters, also responded favorably and in 1900 invited Korovin to become artist-in-residence at the Bolshoi Theater in Moscow. Korovin and his colleague Alexander Golovin, who also began work for the Imperial Theaters at this time, revolutionized the traditional concept of stage design as a banal confection or dull ethnographical exercise by emphasizing the color, the dynamism, and the artistic license afforded by the discipline of stage design.

Celebrated for the stylistic bravura and vivid palette with which he described both town and country, Korovin was recognized as Russia's premier Impressionist. In particular, his evocations of Paris by night and day and of the Black Sea Coast, where he often summered, engage and inspire with their play of light and radiant colors. Not surprisingly, with his ebullient character and raw artistic talent, Korovin still tended to regard stage design as an extension of two-dimensional painting, rather than as a constructive, volumetrical experience. Many of Korovin's sets are pointillist pictures, beautiful to behold in their Impressionist color harmonies, but not necessarily successful as scenic mechanisms. Perhaps for this reason, Sergei Diaghilev invited Korovin to design only one production for a Paris season, i.e., *Les Orientales* (No. 649 [R544]) in 1910 (assisted by Léon Bakst). In any case, Korovin felt more at ease when called upon to design operas and ballets treating of Russian history and legend, such as *Prince Igor, Sadko,* and *The Golden Cockerel,* and he designed sets and costumes for many such spectacles at home and abroad. The results were attractive artistically and accurate historically, even though they had none of Benois's wry humor or Bakst's eroticism. Korovin's years in emigration did not continue the artistic success of Moscow and St. Petersburg: his last major association was with Marie Kousnezoff's Opéra Privé de Paris in 1929-30, and he continued to design isolated productions in Paris, Barcelona, and other cities until his death. In competition with many other Russian designers and depressed by financial problems, by his psychotic son, and by the loss of his friendship with Chaliapin, Korovin "bowed his head and wept."[455]

Sadko: opera in seven scenes by Nikolai Rimsky-Korsakov with libretto by the composer and Vladimir Belsky. Produced at the Bolshoi Theater, Moscow on 27 October, 1906, with designs by Konstantin Korovin.

See No. 308 [R275] for plot summary.

642 [113; R537].
Stage Design for a Square in Novgorod, 1912.
Gouache.
Signed and dated lower left in Russian: "Korovin Konst. 1912."
15¾ x 24⅜ in., 40 x 62 cm.
Provenance: *Russian Works of Art*, New York: Sotheby Parke Bernet, 1968, 18 December, Lot 254 (reproduced).
Reproduced in I20, No. 58; I51, No. 125. This design is a 1912 repetition of the 1906 oil original in the BTM and has been reproduced in black and white many times, including F33, plate 62, where it is described as a set for *Prince Igor*. The BTM also contains a tempera sketch for the same scene. For a photograph of the actual production see Kogan, *K. Korovin,* p. 193.

Note: Korovin had already designed a production of *Sadko* in 1897, when he was working for Mamontov's Private Opera Company, but his 1906 resolution was at once more professional and more ambitious. His designs for this production (also shown at the Mariinsky Theater, St. Petersburg the same year) were a distinct success and critics agreed that the artist had captured the essence of Russian popular ornament to create stylizations that blended well with Rimsky-Korsakov's national music. But historical evocation aside, for many Korovin was also an artist of "fabulous, magical pictures beyond nationality and epoch." [456]

The Tale of the Invisible City of Kitezh and the Maid Fevronia: opera in four acts by Nikolai Rimsky-Korsakov with a libretto by Vladimir Belsky. Produced at the Mariinsky Theater, St. Petersburg, on 7 February, 1907, with designs by Konstantin Korovin and Apollinarii Vasnetsov assisted by Nikolai Klodt.
See No. 369 [R339] for plot summary.

643 [R538].
Costume Design for a Tatar, 1906.
Gouache.
Signed lower left in Russian: "Korovin."
13 x 8½ in., 33 x 21.5 cm.
Other inscriptions in Russian: upper right: "Kitezh, a Tatar"; upper margin carries the seal of the Imperial Theaters, St. Petersburg for 4 July 1906; lower margin carries the seal of the Bolshoi Theater Museum; the reverse carries two other seals; various instructions to the dressmaker surround the figure.
Provenance: Iosif Lempert, Paris, June, 1975.
Reproduced in I40, No. 69; I51, No. 126. Korovin made several versions of the costumes for this opera. A variant of this

643

costume for a Tatar is in the collection of the BTM and is reproduced in Kogan, p. 199; another is in the collection of the Wadsworth Atheneum and is reproduced in I11, fig. 106; yet another is reproduced in J22, Lot 55.

Note: When Korovin first heard Rimsky-Korsakov's music for *The Tale of the Invisible City of Kitezh* in March, 1906, he found it to be an "awful bore… tedious," [457] but he soon changed his mind. His designs for the 1907 production elicited various responses, some critics referring to the "most elevated aspects of human consciousness," [458] others to its "vulgar, realist colors." [459]

Prince Igor: opera in a prologue and four acts by Alexander Borodin with a libretto by the composer after a play by Vladimir Stasov; completed by Nikolai Rimsky-Korsakov and Alexander Glazunov. Produced on 14 December, 1909, at the Mariinsky Theater, St. Petersburg, with choreography by Michel Fokine and designs by Konstantin Korovin.
See No. 380 [R353] for plot summary.

644 [R539].
Costume Design for Khan Konchak Holding a Spear and Shield, ca. 1909.
Gouache, black ink, and gold paint.
Signed upper right in Russian: "Konst. Korovin."
11¾ x 12¼ in., 30 x 31 cm.
Other inscription in Russian: upper right: "Konchak. 4th Costume."
Provenance: Mikhail Benois, Madrid, May, 1968.
Reproduced in I20, No. 59.

644

645

645 [R540].
Costume Design for a Polovets, ca. 1909.
Watercolor, pencil, and gold paint.
13⅛ x 8⅝ in., 33.5 x 22 cm.
Inscriptions in Russian: "Prince Igor, a Polovets"; lower right carries the seals of the Imperial Theaters of St. Petersburg and the Bolshoi Theater Museum; reverse carries the seal of the Export Control Commission for Russian art; various instructions to the dressmaker surround the figure.
Provenance: M. Glinsky, Paris, January, 1969.
Reproduced in I51, No. 129.

646

646 [R541].
***Costume Design for Khan Konchak Holding
a Whip,* ca. 1909.**
Gouache, black ink, and gold paint.
Signed upper left in Russian: "Korovin
Konst."
11⅝ x 8⅛ in., 29.5 x 20.5 cm.
Provenance: Nina Stevens, New York,
December, 1968.
Reproduced in I20, No. 60.

647

647 [R542].
***Costume Design for a Persian Slave,* ca.
1909.**
Watercolor, pencil, and gold paint.
14⅛ x 10⅝ in., 36 x 27 cm.
Inscriptions: upper left in Russian: "Prince
Igor"; upper left carries the seal of the

Imperial Theaters, dated 24 October 1911;
lower left carries the seal of the Bolshoi
Theater Museum; the reverse carries the
seal of the Export Control Commission for
Russian Art.
Provenance: M. Glinsky, Paris, January,
1969.
Reproduced in I51, No. 128.

648

648 [R543].
***Costume Design for a Polovets with Hand
on Dagger,* ca. 1909.**
Watercolor, pencil, and ink.
13⅛ x 8⅝ in., 33.5 x 22 cm.
Inscriptions in Russian: upper left: "Prince
Igor"; upper right: "Ballet Polov[illegible]";
lower right carries the seal of the Bolshoi
Theater Museum; the reverse carries the
seal of the Imperial Theaters and the seal
of the Export Control Commission for

Russian Art; various instructions to the
dressmaker surround the figure.
Provenance: M. Glinsky, Paris, January,
1969.
Reproduced in black and white in I51, No.
127. Korovin repeated his costumes for
Prince Igor several times, and variants of
this costume are in the collection of the
Wadsworth Atheneum (reproduced in I11,
fig. 109) and the BTM (reproduced in G33,
fig. 46).

Les Orientales: *ballet with music by
Alexander Glazunov, Christian Sinding,
Antonii Arensky, Edvard Grieg, and
Alexander Borodin, with a theme by Sergei
Diaghilev interpreted by Michel Fokine.
Produced by Sergei Diaghilev for the
Ballets Russes on 25 June, 1910, at the
Théâtre National de l'Opéra, Paris, with
choreography by Michel Fokine and
designs by Léon Bakst and Konstantin
Korovin; principal parts danced by Tamara
Karsavina, Vaslav Nijinsky, and Catherine
Geltzer.*

This set of five choreographic sketches
has no developed plot and consists simply
of a series of exotic dances purporting to
represent the cultures of India, Persia,
China, and Arabia.

649 [R544].
***Stage Design for Sketch I,* 1910.**
Gouache.
Signed and dated lower right in Russian:
"Konst. Korovin 1910."
4¼ x 8½ in., 10.8 x 21.6 cm.
Provenance: Vladimir Hessen, New York,
May, 1974.
Reproduced in I40, No. 68; I51, No. 130.

Note: According to hearsay, the original
owner of this design, an associate of
Diaghilev and Korovin, described it as a set
for *Les Orientales,* an attribution which is
reasonable, even though there is no
specific indication on the work itself. The
design is typical of Korovin's Impressionist
style and brings to mind his celebrated
paintings such as *In the South of France*
(1908, TG) and *Paper Lanterns* (1895, TG).
Other contributions by Korovin to *Les*

649

Orientales have not been located, but visual comparisons with designs of the same period, as for the 1913 production of *The Tale of Tsar Saltan* (reproduced in color in G47, fig. 29), demonstrate that the piece follows Korovin's usual approach to scenic resolution. As he wrote:

> colors and forms in their combinations produce a harmony of beauty, an illumination. Colors can be a feast for the eye, just as music can be for the ear. The eyes communicate to your soul delight, enjoyment, paints, the chords of colors and forms. This is the task that I have set myself in designing for the theater, the ballet, and the opera.[460]

The Tale of Tsar Saltan: *opera in three acts by Nikolai Rimsky-Korsakov with a libretto by Vladimir Belsky after a poem by Alexander Pushkin. Produced at the Bolshoi Theater, Moscow, on 2 October, 1913, with designs by Konstantin Korovin. See No. 349 [R314] for plot summary.*

650

650 [114; R545].
Costume Design for Tsarevich Gvidon, 1912.
Gouache, ink, and silver and gold paint.
Signed upper left in black ink in Russian: "Konstantin Korovin."
14¼ x 10¼ in., 36.2 x 26 cm.
Other inscriptions n Russian: upper left: "Opera by Rimsky-Korsakov, Tsar Saltan, Imperial Theater, Petersburg 1912, Konstantin Korovin, Tsarevich Gvidon"; lower left in Russian: illegible phrase followed by signature of Korovin.
Provenance: Lidia Kamyshnikova, New York, 1964. Now in a private collection.
Reproduced as the cover to I12; and in A34, p. 221; F33, plate 61; G55, p. 279; I14, No. 78; and I51, No. 131.

Note: Korovin remarked that he "loved and breathed" *Tsar Saltan* before embarking on his decorations,[461] and as if recalling the passion and intensity with which he worked on the sets and costumes he wrote a little later:

> I feel that the theater cannot do without the artist... With his décors, the artist does what the singer does by inspiring the author's words with his sound. The ideal of the designer should be Chaliapin himself, the classical singer of our time who does, indeed, inspire the author's words with his sound. I cannot agree with the opinion that decorations hinder or efface the performers.[462]

Note: Inasmuch as Konstantin Korovin's son Alexei worked closely with his father on several productions in the 1920s some of the designs in the following sections (e.g. No. 668 [R563] may, in fact be the work of Alexei and not of Konstantin, in spite of traditional assumptions to the contrary and in spite of Konstantin Korovin's own signature. The issue of the correct attribution of the designs for the Kousnezoff productions of *Sneurochka* (1929) and *Prince Igor* (1929), therefore, remains a vexed one.

Snegurochka (The Snow Maiden): *opera in a prologue and four acts by Nikolai Rimsky-Korsakov after the play by Alexander Ostrovsky. Produced by Nikolai Evreinov for Marie Kousnezoff's Opéra Privé de Paris in 1929 with choreography by Boris Romanov and designs by Konstantin Korovin.*
See No. 33 [R32] for plot summary.

651

651 [R546].
Costume Design for Winter, 1928.
Watercolor and ink.
Signed and dated lower left: "Constantine Korovine Paris 1928."
18½ x 14 in., 47 x 35.5 cm.
Other inscriptions: upper left: "Snegourotchka"; upper right: "L'Hiver."
Provenance: Mikhail Benois, Madrid, May, 1968.
Reproduced in I40, No. 73, where it is attributed to Alexei Korovin; I51, No. 132.

652

652 [R547].
Costume Design for One of the Young Girls, 1928.
Gouache.
Signed and dated lower left: "Constant. Korovine, Paris, 1928."
10¼ x 14⅛ in., 26 x 36 cm.
Other inscriptions: upper left: "Korovine 'Snegourotchka"; in pencil in Russian: "cloud with thunder"; upper right: "jeunes filles, ballet"; cloth annotations throughout in Russian; lower right corner in blue pencil: "No. 75."
Provenance: Peter Tretiakov Gallery, New York, 1965. Now in a private collection.
Reproduced in I14, No. 79. A version is reproduced in F33, plate 58.

653

654

655

653 [R548].
Costume Design for the Tsar, 1928.
Watercolor, gold paint, and ink.
Signed and dated lower margin: "C. Korovine, Paris, 1928."
15⅜ x 10⅞ in., 39 x 27.5 cm.
Other inscriptions: upper left: "Snegourotchka en noir"; upper right: "Le Tzar."
Provenance: Mikhail Benois, Madrid, May, 1968. Now in a private collection.
Reproduced in the Souvenir Program for the *Opéra Privé de Paris. Première Saison,* Paris, 1929, unpaginated; F33, plate 59; I40, No. 70.

654 [R549].
Costume Design for the Snow Maiden, 1928.
Watercolor, ink, and silver paint.
Signed and dated lower left: "C. Korovine, 1928."
15⅜ x 10⅞ in., 39 x 27.5 cm.
Other inscriptions: upper left and right: "Snegourotchka."
Provenance: Mikhail Benois, Madrid, May, 1968. Now in a private collection.
Reproduced in I40, No. 71; a version is reproduced in F33, plate 55.

655 [R550].
Costume Design for Bobyl (Bakula), ca. 1928.
Watercolor.
Signed lower left: "C. Korovine, Paris."
15⅜ x 10⅞ in., 39 x 27.5 cm.
Other inscriptions: upper left: "Snegourotchka"; upper right: "Bobyl."
Provenance: Mikhail Benois, Madrid, May, 1968. Now in a private collection.
Reproduced in F33, plate 60; and in black and white in I40, No. 76.

656 [115; R551].
Costume Design for the Carnival, ca. 1928.
Watercolor, pencil, and ink.
Signed lower left: "Korovine."
15 x 10 in., 38 x 25.5 cm.
Other inscriptions: upper left: "Snegourotchka"; upper right: "Le Carnaval."
Provenance: Mikhail Benois, Madrid, May, 1968. Now in a private collection.
Reproduced in F33, plate 57; and in black and white in I40, No. 72.

657 [R552].
Costume Design for Bermiata, 1928.
Watercolor, gold paint, and ink.
Signed and dated lower left: "Constant. Korovine Paris 1928."
14⅛ x 10⅜ in., 36 x 26.5 cm.
Other inscriptions in French: upper left: "Snegourotchka"; upper right: "Bermiata."
Provenance: Mikhail Benois, Madrid, May, 1968.
Reproduced in the Souvenir Program for the *Opéra Privé de Paris. Première Saison,* Paris, 1929, unpaginated; and in black and white in I40, No. 75. Now in a private collection.

656

657

658

659

Snegurochka (Kapiton Zaporozhets, the great basso, sang the part of Winter and Korovin insisted that real Russian sleighs be used) had only a moderate success and did not recoup the substantial financial outlay that Marie Kousnezoff made for the production.

Prince Igor: *opera in a prologue and four acts by Alexander Borodin with a libretto by the composer after a play by Vladimir Stasov; completed by Nikolai Rimsky-Korsakov and Alexander Glazunov. Produced by Marie Kousnezoff for her Opéra Privé de Paris in January, 1929, with choreography by Michel Fokine and designs by Konstantin Korovin.*
    See No. 380 [R353] for plot summary.

658 [R553].
Costume Design for a Servant with a Bag, 1928.
Watercolor and ink.
Signed and dated lower left: "Constant. Korovine Paris 1928."
15⅜ x 10⅞ in., 39 x 27.5 cm.
Provenance. Mikhail Benois, Madrid, May, 1968. Now in a private collection.
Reproduced in I40, No. 75.

659 [R554].
Costume Design for the Second Herald, 1928.
Gouache, silver, and ink.
Signed and dated lower margin: "C.

Korovine Paris 1928."
15⅜ x 10⅞ in., 39 x 27.5 cm.
Other inscriptions: upper left: "Snegourotchka"; upper right: "2e Héraut."
Provenance: Mikhail Benois, Madrid, May, 1968. Now in a private collection.
Reproduced in F33, plate 56; I40. No. 77.

Note: Konstantin Korovin first designed a production of *Snegurochka* in 1911 at the Bolshoi Theater, Moscow, and thereafter he returned to the opera several times. His last interpretation was for the 1928-29 season of the Opéra Privé de Paris (see No. 368 [R338]), when he also designed a production of *Prince Igor.* Evreinov's staging of

660 [R555].
Stage Design for the Camp of the Polovtsy, 1930.
Gouache.
Signed and dated lower left: "C. Korovine, 1930."
20⅝ x 29¾ in., 52.5 x 75.5 cm.
Other inscription following the signature in Russian: "Polovtsian dances."
Provenance: Issar Gourvitch, Paris, March, 1967.
Reproduced in I14, No. 80.

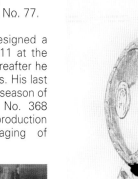

661

661 [116; R556].
Costume Design for Prince Igor with a Shield, 1928.
Gouache, and silver and gold paint.
Signed and dated lower left: "Korovine Paris 1928."
15 x 10¼ in., 38 x 26 cm.
Provenance: Mikhail Benois, Madrid, May, 1968.
Reproduced in the Souvenir Program *Opéra Privé de Paris. Première Saison,* Paris, 1929, unpaginated.

660

662

663

664

662 [R557].
Costume Design for Prince Igor Unarmed,
1928.
Watercolor, gold paint, and blue pencil.
Signed and dated lower left: "Korovine
Paris 1928."
15⅜ x 10⅜ in., 39 x 26.5 cm.
Other inscriptions: extensive dress
annotations in Russian upper left side.
Provenance: Mikhail Benois, Madrid, May,
1968.

663 [R558].
Costume Design for Prince Vladimir
Igorevich, 1928.
Gouache, silver paint, and blue pencil.
Signed and dated lower left: "Korovine
Paris 1928."
15⅜ x 10⅜ in., 39 x 27 cm.

Other inscriptions: upper left: "Le Prince
Igor"; upper right: "Vladimir."
Provenance: Mikhail Benois, Madrid, May,
1968.

664 [117; R559].
Costume Design for Khan Konchak, 1928.
Watercolor, gold paint, and ink.
Signed and dated lower left: "Korovine
Paris 1928."
15⅜ x 10¼ in., 39 x 26 cm.
Other inscriptions: upper left: "Le Prince
Igor"; upper right: "Le Khan Kontchak."
Provenance: Nina Stevens, New York,
December, 1968.
Reproduced in F33, plate 64.

665 [R560].
Costume Design for the Priest, ca. 1928.
Gouache and gold paint.

15⅜ x 10⅜ in., 39 x 27 cm.
Inscriptions: upper left: "Le Prince Igor";
upper right: "le Prêtre"; "Moiseenko."
Provenance: Mikhail Benois, Madrid,
September, 1968.

666 [R561].
Costume Design for a Polovtsian Warrior, ca.
1928.
Gouache and silver paint.
15⅜ x 10⅜ in., 39 x 27 cm.
Inscriptions: upper left: "Le Prince Igor";
upper right: "Ballet"; cloth and color
annotations in pencil throughout; performer's
name (Merkholenko?) almost erased.
Provenance: Mikhail Benois, Madrid, May,
1968.
Reproduced in B44, p. 297; F33, plate 63.
The identity of Merkholenko has not been
established.

665

666

667

668

669

670

667 [R562].
Costume Design for a Polovtsian Warrior Holding a Stringless Bow in Right hand, ca. 1928.
Gouache, and silver and gold paint.
15⅜ x 10⅝ in., 39 x 27 cm.
Inscriptions: upper left: "Le Prince Igor"; upper right: "Ballet"; cloth and color annotations in pencil throughout; performer's name (Baydaroff) almost erased.
Provenance: Mikhail Benois, Madrid, May, 1968.
A version is reproduced in black and white in C7, No. 79.
Vladimir Vasilevich Poliakov-Baidarov (Baydaroff, 1890-1952) was an opera singer working in in Paris, Nice, and Monte Carlo.

668 [R563].
Costume Design for a Polovtsian Warrior Holding a Lowered Bow in Left Hand, ca. 1928.
Gouache and silver paint.
15⅜ x 10⅝ in., 39 x 27 cm.
Inscriptions: upper left: "Le Prince Igor"; upper right: "Ballet"; performer's name (Bologovskoi) almost erased.
Provenance: Mikhail Benois, Madrid, May, 1968.
Vladimir Ignatievich Bologovskoi (1890-1971) was an actor and dancer.

669 [R564].
Costume Design for a Polovtsian Warrior Holding a Stringless Bow in Left Hand, ca. 1928.
Gouache, ink, and silver paint.
15⅜ x 10⅝ in., 39 x 27 cm.
Inscriptions: upper left: "Le Prince Igor"; upper right: "Ballet"; cloth and color annotations in pencil throughout; performer's name (Baratov) almost erased.
Provenance: Mikhail Benois, Madrid, May, 1968.
Leonid Vasilevich Baratov (1895-1964) was a singer, dancer, and producer.

670 [118; R565].
Costume Design for a Persian Slave Girl Holding Flowers, ca. 1928.
Gouache and ink.
15 x 10 in., 38 x 25.5 cm.
Inscriptions: upper left: "Le Prince Igor"; upper right: "Ballet"; cloth and color annotations in pencil throughout; performer's name (Lily Michel?) almost erased.
Provenance: Mikhail Benois, Madrid, May, 1968.
Reproduced in F33, plate 66.
The identity of Lily Michel has not been established.

671 [R566].
Costume Design for a Persian Slave Girl, ca. 1928.
Gouache and gold paint.
15 x 10 in., 38 x 25.5 cm.

671

Inscriptions: upper left: "Le Prince Igor"; upper right: "Ballet"; cloth and color annotations throughout; performer's name (Stark) almost erased.
Provenance: Mikhail Benois, Madrid, September, 1968.
Olga Nikolaevna Stark (1908-98) was a dancer.

672 [R567].
Costume Design for a Persian Slave Girl Inclining to Her Left, ca. 1928.
Gouache, ink, and silver and gold paint.
15⅜ x 10⅝ in., 39 x 27 cm.
Inscriptions: upper left: "Le Prince Igor"; upper right: "Ballet"; cloth and color annotations throughout plus performer's name (Dolina).
Provenance: Mikhail Benois, Madrid, May, 1968.
Reproduced in B44, p. 296.

672

673

674

675

673 [R568].
Costume Design for a Persian Slave Woman Playing the Saz, ca. 1928.
Gouache, ink, and gold paint.
Signed lower left: "Korovine."
15⅜ x 10⅝ in., 39 x 27 cm.
Other inscriptions: upper left: "Le Prince Igor"; upper right: "Ballet"; color and cloth annotations throughout almost erased.
Provenance: Mikhail Benois, Madrid, May, 1968.
Reproduced in B44, p. 296.

674 [R569].
Costume Design for a Polovtsian Girl with Rings on Her Fingers, ca. 1928.
Gouache, ink, and gold paint.
15⅜ x 10⅝ in., 39 x 27 cm.
Inscriptions: upper left: "Le Prince Igor"; upper right: "Ballet; cloth and color annotations throughout almost erased.
Provenance: Mikhail Benois, Madrid, May, 1968.
Reproduced in B44, p. 294.

675 [R570].
Costume Design for a Polovtsian Girl with a Feather in Her Hair, ca. 1928.
Gouache.
15⅜ x 10⅝ in., 39 x 27 cm.
Inscriptions: upper left: "Le Prince Igor"; upper right "Ballet"; cloth and color annotations throughout almost erased.
Provenance: Mikhail Benois, Madrid, May, 1968.
Reproduced in B44, p. 297.

676 [R571].
Stage Details: Two Barrels, Two Saz Musical Instruments, and Two Tables, ca. 1928.
Watercolor, black ink, and pencil.
10¼ x 15 in., 26 x 38 cm.
Inscriptions: annotations throughout in

Russian and French.
Provenance: Iosif Lempert, Paris, December, 1977.
Reproduced in B44, p. 295.

677 [R572].
Stage Details: Chair, Bench, Chair Cushion, Lace Frame, Stool, Table, and Rake, ca. 1928.
Watercolor, gold paint, and ink.
9⅞ x 14⅞ in., 25 x 37.8 cm.
Inscriptions: annotations throughout in Russian and French.
Provenance: Iosif Lempert, Paris, February, 1978.
Reproduced in B44, p. 295.

Boris Godunov: opera in a prologue and four acts by Modest Mussorgsky with libretto based on a play of the same name by

Alexander Pushkin and Nikolai Karamzin's History of the Russian State. *Production not known.*
    See No. 339 [R305] for plot summary.

678 [R573].
Costume Design for Fedor Chaliapin as Tsar Boris, 1932.
Gouache.
Signed and dated lower left: "Korovine Paris 5 février 1932."
15¼ x 10⅜ in., 38.8 x 26.5 cm.
Other inscription: upper left: "Boris."
Provenance: Michel Sokoloff, Paris, March, 1967.
Reproduced in I40, No. 67; M86.

Note: With his outgoing nature and good sense of humor, Fedor Ivanovich Chaliapin

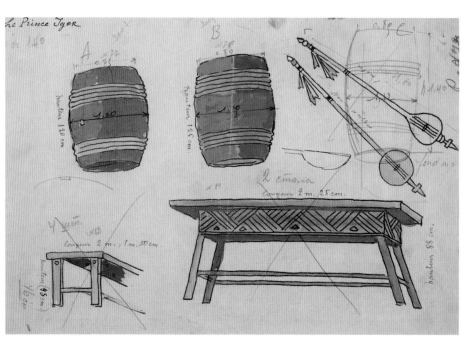

676

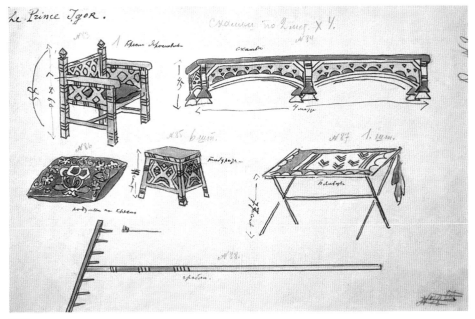

677

(Shaliapin, 1873-1938), was the friend of many artists and the subject of numerous portraits. Alexander Golovin, Boris Grigoriev, Nikolai Kharitonov, Boris Kustodiev, Ilia Repin, Valentin Serov (No. 912 [R780]), and Alexandre Jacovleff all portrayed him as did Nicola Benois (No. 354 [R319]) and Leonid Pasternak (No. 806 [R688]). Korovin, who designed many of the operas in which Chaliapin appeared in Moscow, St. Petersburg, and abroad, was a close friend of the great singer, admired his talent, and painted or drew several portraits of him, e.g., in 1905 (TG) and in 1911 (RM); Chaliapin also portrayed Korovin (see the 1906 sketch in C52, Vol. 2, opposite p. 241; and the 1932 sketch in F33, plate 35). In addition, Korovin wrote a book about Chaliapin in which he described his

678

meetings with the singer in Russia and France, conveying the essential assets of Chaliapin's artistic psychology:

> I was always struck by his [Chaliapin's] amazing comprehension of each character that he was creating. He never let on to his friends in advance how he would sing or perform this or that role. He never acted at rehearsal, just sang softly, and sometimes he even left out whole passages. It was only on stage that he astonished the audience with his new, brilliant incarnation and the mighty timbre of his unique voice.[463]

1932 marked the fiftieth anniversary of Korovin's artistic activity and he was given a lavish celebration in Paris (to which Chaliapin sent a rude telegram).[464] By then, Chaliapin was past his prime, and yet Korovin has depicted him here as the impressive Fedor Ivanovich of the early days.

454 F7, p. 197.
455 Conversation between André Houdiakoff and John E. Bowlt, Newtown, Connecticut, 15 October, 1981.
456 Review in *Russkie vedomosti*, M, 1906, 2 November. Quoted in Kogan, *K. Korovin*, p. 196.
457 From a memoir by Vasilii Shkafer. In F21, p. 353.
458 Review by Nikolai Kashkin in *Russkoe slovo*, M, 1908, 17 February. Quoted in Kogan, *K. Korovin*, p. 201.
459 This criticism was addressed more to the execution of certain designs by Nikolai Klodt than to Korovin's actual sets. See V. Shkafer: *Sorok let na stsene russkoi opery, Vospominaniia.* L: Kirov State Theater of Opera and Ballet, 1936, pp. 200-01.
460 Quoted in Moleva, *Zhizn moia – zhivopis*, p. 175. Original source not indicated.
461 Korovin on the Moscow theatrical season of 1913 in F21, p. 383. Original source not indicated.
462 K. Korovin: "Rol khudozhnika na stsene" in *Teatr*, SP, 1913, October. Quoted in Kogan, *K. Korovin*, p. 315.
463 K. Korovin: *Shaliapin*, Paris: La Renaissance, 1939, p. 195.
464 Ibid., p. 177.

KOSTIN, Sergei Nikolaevich

Born 26 October (7 November), 1896, Moscow, Russia; died 8 November, 1968, Moscow, Russia.

Nephew of Nikolai Sapunov; 1918-19 attended Svomas, studying under Boris Grigoriev and in the Studio without a Supervisor; close to Nikolai Denisovsky, Vasilii Komardenkov, Konstantin Medunetsky, Nikolai Prusakov, and the Stenberg brothers; contributed to the first exhibition of Obmokhu (1919); 1921 contributed to the third exhibition of Obmokhu; 1922-24 worked in Zagorsk at the Industrial Art Studio for Toys; 1924 started work at the State Publishing-House as a book and poster designer; helped establish OST, but did not take part in its exhibitions; 1925 with David Shterenberg designed the State Trade Section at the "Exposition Internationale des Arts Décoratifs" in Paris; 1927 visited Japan in connection with the exhibition of Soviet art in Tokyo; 1920s worked in a Constructivist idiom, both as a studio and as an applied artist; illustrated the satirical journal *Krokodil* [Crocodile], often collaborating with Nikolai Denisovsky; 1930s worked as a designer for the Bolshoi Theater, Moscow; 1938 contributed to the "Exhibition of Works by Theater Artists of the State Academic Bolshoi Theater" in Moscow; 1941-45 designed patriotic posters as a member of the Grekov Studio of Battle Painters in Moscow and contributed to poster exhibitions of the time such as "Exhibition of Agit-Visual Art" in Moscow (1943); 1946 onwards taught at the Surikov Institute of Visual Art, Moscow.

Bibliography
Nothing substantial has been published on Sergei Kostin. For some references see A34, p. 217; A49, p. 162.

Kostin belonged to the generation of the 1920s that favored the restoration of figurative painting after the abstractions of Kazimir Malevich and Vladimir Tatlin, and the utilitarian emphasis of Alexander Rodchenko and Varvara Stepanova. In many cases, the artists of this new school reached their conclusion after following the path of their mentors, and Kostin's close association with Obmokhu, for example, indicates that at first he also supported the move towards construction and industrial design. However, as a founding member of OST, Kostin — along with Denisovsky (No. 417 [R453]), Alexander Tyshler (Nos. 1102-07 [R841-45]), David Shterenberg, and Konstantin Vialov (Nos. 1143-51 [R386-93]) — came to argue for the "rejection of abstraction... of sketchiness as a phenomenon of latent dilettantism... [and] of pseudo-Cézannism as a disintegrating force."[465] Consequently, even if some of the *ostovtsy*, especially Tyshler, made substantial contributions to the discipline of stage design and influenced the development of Soviet theater, they still regarded figurative studio painting as a primary means of expression.

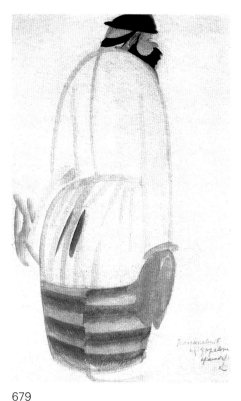

679

Unidentified production, *ca. 1923.*

679 [R574].
Costume Design for a Peasant (Back View),
ca. 1923.
Gouache.
Initialed in lower right in pencil in Russian:
"SK."
18⅞ x 12 in., 48 x 30.4 cm.
Inscribed above the initials in pencil in
Russian: "from the country."
Provenance: Evgenii Gunst, Moscow, 1974.

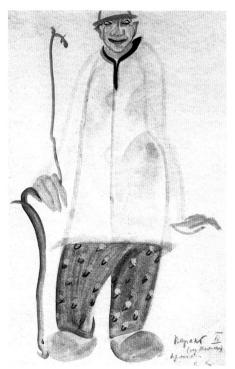

680

680 [R575].
Costume Design for a Man Holding a Long
***Stick,* ca. 1923.**
Gouache.
Initialed in lower right in pencil in Russian:
"SK."
18⅞ x 11⅞ in., 48 x 30.3 cm.
Inscribed in lower right in pencil in Russian:
"Lad II"
Provenance: Evgenii Gunst, Moscow, 1974.

465 Anon.: "Platforma OSTa" (1929). Quoted in B12,
p. 281.

KOZLINSKY, Vladimir
Ivanovich

Born 2 (14) April, 1891, Kronstadt (St.
Petersburg), Russia; died 17 July, 1967,
Snegiri (near Moscow), Russia.

1907 entered SSEA; studied at Elizaveta
Zvantseva's private art school where his
teachers were Léon Bakst and Mstislav
Dobujinsky; also took lessons from Dmitrii
Kardovsky; 1909-10 contributed to Nikolai
Kulbin's "Triangle" exhibition in St. Petersburg
and Vilna, Latvia; 1911-17 attended IAA;
close contact with Vladimir Lebedev and Nikolai
Punin; 1916 worked with Alexei Radakov on
productions for the Comedians' Halt cabaret
in Petrograd; 1918-21 designed agitprop
decorations for streets and squares in
Petrograd and Moscow; published album of
linocuts with Vladimir Maiakovsky, Pougny, et
al. called *Geroi i zhertvy revoliutsii* [Heroes
and Victims of the Revolution]; professor at
Svomas; 1919 with Lebedev worked on sets
for Velimir Khlebnikov's play *Death's Mistake*
(not produced); 1920 head of the Petrograd
ROSTA (propaganda windows of the Russian
Telegraph Agency) where he worked closely
with Lebedev; 1920s active as a book and
poster designer; 1924 helped with designs for
Sergei Radlov's production of *Lucrezia Borgia;*
1928 designed décor for Valentin Kataev's
Squaring the Circle; thereafter, designed
many productions for Leningrad and Moscow
theaters.

Bibliography
"Vladimir Ivanovich Kozlinsky" [Obituary] in
Moskovskii khudozhnik, M, 1967, 28 July.
L. Diakov: *Mastera sovetskoi karikatury. V.I.*
Kozlinsky, M: Sovetskii khudozhnik, 1978.
E. Kovtun: "Neizvestnyi albom V.I. Kozlinskogo"
in *Soobshcheniia Gosudarstvennogo Russkogo*
muzeia, M, 1975, No. 10, pp. 20-22.
L. Diakov: *Vladimir Kozlinsky,* M: Sovetskii
khudozhnik, 1978.
"V.I. Kozlinsky" in A. Sarabianov, comp.:
Khudozhestvennyi kalendar. Sto pamiatnykh dat,
1981, M: Sovetskii khudozhnik, 1980, pp. 96-99.
E. Kovtun: "V.I. Kozlinsky v gody revoliutsii" in
Sovetskaia grafika, M, 1986, No. 10, pp. 198-209.
E. Kovtun, intro.: *Sovremennyi Peterburg. Graviury*
V. Kozlinskogo, L: Khudozhnik RSFSR, 1987.

Along with Yurii Annenkov, Lebedev, Nicholas
Remisoff, and Yurii Yurkun, Kozlinksy estab-

lished a strong reputation on the basis of his
political and social satire, beginning his career
well before the Revolution as a caricaturist
and cartoonist for society journals such as
Lukomorie [Shore]. The new republic also
provided Kozlinsky with rich material for his
satirical eye — the new bourgeoisie, the
pitfalls of Soviet bureaucracy, the international
boycott — and his clear, incisive commentaries qualified him for instant inclusion in
the first generation of Soviet caricaturists led
by Deni (Viktor Denisov), Dmitrii Moor (No.
605 [R858]), and Radakov. Theirs was a
school of Soviet caricature that in its strength
of invective, caustic humor, and persuasive-
ness was unrivalled.

Of course, Kozlinsky and his colleagues
were drawing upon a strong pre-
Revolutionary tradition of social satire
manifest, for example, in the caricatures of
the underground press of 1905-06. But
these artists also owed much to the
esthetic elegance and graphic mastery of
the World of Art artists, such as Bakst,
Alexandre Benois, Dobujinsky, Elizaveta
Kruglikova, and Anna Ostroumova-
Lebedeva. In the World of Art tradition,
Kozlinsky found a clarity, understatement,
and stylization that he used to advantage in
his own linocuts and engravings, qualities
of simplicity and economy that he observed
even in his most tendentious cartoons and
stage designs — as he observed in his
article "The Object on Stage":

> The theater has one more law — scale.
> The objects that the actor uses must
> be made in correspondence with him;
> their dimensions do not depend upon
> the dimensions of the theatrical stage.
> This should be resolved... spatially,
> using a maquette in which the constant
> scale is the human figure.466

Responsible for designing more than thirty
major productions in Moscow and Leningrad,
Kozlinsky often approached the page of a
book or the social caricature as a miniature
stage. The album described below, *Sovre-*
mennyi Peterburg [Contemporary St.
Petersburg], can be interpreted as a theatralized description of Petrograd — just as the
other collection, *Geroi i zhertvy revoliutsii*
[Heroes and Victims of the Revolution], can
be identified as *dramatis personae* in the
tragic theater of war and revolution.

Two Designs with Theatrical Motifs from the
***album of twelve linocuts called* Sovremennyi**
Peterburg *[Contemporary St. Petersburg],*
1919. The album was not published, but was
issued in twenty copies. Provenance for
both: acquired from John E. Bowlt, New
York, December, 1975.

681 [R517].
***Street Scene* , ca. 1919.**
Black and white linocut.
Initialled in block.
15¾ x 11⅜ in., 40 x 29 cm.
Inscriptions in Russian (as part of the
design): the banner reads: "All Power to the
Soviets"; the posters on the fence read:

681

"Shal" (abbreviation for "Shaliapin [Chaliapin]"?) and "Theater."
Reproduced in I32, No. 45. A version is reproduced in Kovtun, "V.I. Kozlinsky," p. 205, and as sheet No. 7 in Kovtun, *Sovremennyi Peterburg,* where it is called *Night.*

682 [R518].
Man Drawing Curtain (Twelfth and Last Sheet from the Album), ca. 1919.
Black and white linocut.
10⅞ x 13¾ in., 27.5 x 35 cm.
Reproduced in I32, No. 44. A version is reproduced in Kovtun, "V.I. Kozlinsky," p. 208, and as the back cover to Kovtun, *Sovremennyi Peterburg.*

Note: These two linocuts are from an un-published cycle of images of Revolutionary Petrograd that Kozlinsky worked on in 1919. It followed the collective album of 1918, *Geroi i*

zhertvy revoliutsii [Heroes and Victims of the Revolution], that IZO NKP published with text by Vladimir Maiakovsky and illustrations by Kseniia Boguslavskaia, Kozlinsky, Sergei Makletsov, and Jean Pougny; and it preceded Nikolai Punin's famous *Russkii plakat 1917-1922* of 1922 (see No. 736 [R622]). All these albums contain examples of the revolutionary poster style — schematic, simple, vivid, topical — that we now associate with the ROSTA style, the propaganda windows of the Russian Telegraph Agency in Moscow, Petrograd, and other cities where Kozlinsky, Lebedev, Ivan Maliutin, Maiakovsky, et al. designed and painted cheap, colored "comic strips" with agitational, often satirical content. Actually, Kozlinsky produced his album *Contemporary Petersburg* in the same studio where Lebedev and he produced their ROSTA windows in 1920-21, and it would seem that these twelve sheets were intended to be hand-colored just as the cover was.

The images are instant stills from the Revolutionary reality, including *The Sailor, The Orator, The Meeting, The Couple,* and two pieces bearing the message "All Power to the Soviets." The one included here (No. 681 [R517]) seems to refer to a Chaliapin concert (during 1919 Chaliapin had many engagements at the Mariinsky and Mikhailovsky Theaters in Petrograd). As far as No. 682 [R518] is concerned, the late Evgenii Kovtun has written:

> From early youth Kozlinsky was not indifferent to the theater and theatricality, and it is not fortuitous, therefore, that *Contemporary Petersburg* ends with a sheet in which an obviously theatrical personage is represented — who is pulling the curtain with the word "Finish!" which hides a city landscape from the audience.[467]

466 V. Kozlinsky and E. Freze: "Veshch na stsene — detal obraza oformleniia" in G46, p. 113.
467 Kovtun, "Neizvestnyi albom," p. 22. Kovtun also reproduces other images from the album in his article. Also see B26, plates 14, 100, 101, 107.

KUDRIASHEV, Ivan Alexeevich

Born 1896, Kaluga, Russia; died 1972, Moscow, Russia.

1912-17 attended MIPSA; contact with Ivan Kliun and Kazimir Malevich; 1918 worked on propaganda designs for automobiles for the first anniversary of the Revolution; 1918-19 studied under Malevich at Svomas; his father, who worked as a constructor for the rocket engineer Konstantin Tsiolkovsky, introduced him to the ideas of space flight; 1919 went to Orenburg where he contributed to the "First State Exhibition" and worked on interior designs for the First Soviet Theater; 1920 worked for the Summer Red Army Theater in Orenburg and organized a branch of Unovis there; 1920s worked on the principles of luminosity and refractivity in painting, producing works similar to the "engineerist" paintings of Kliment Redko; 1922 contributed to the "Erste Russische Kunstausstellung" in Berlin; 1925 contributed to the "First State Traveling Exhibition of Paintings" in Moscow, Saratov, and other cities; joined OST; 1925-28 contributed to the first, second, and fourth OST exhibitions in Moscow; after 1928 stopped exhibiting.

Bibliography
Anon.: *Koudriachov.* Catalog of exhibition at the Galerie Jean Chauvelin, Paris, 1970.
V. Kostin: *OST,* L: Khudozhnik RSFSR, 1976, passim.
B34, pp. 223-32.
K215.
E. Petrova et al.: *V kruge Malevicha,* SP: Palace Editions, 2000, passim.
I. Vakar and T. Mikhienko, eds.: *Malevich o sebe. Sovremenniki o Maleviche,* M: RA, 2004 (two volumes), passim.
I. Smekalov: *UNOVIS v Orenburge. K istorii khudozhestvennoi zhizni v rossiiskoi provintsii,* Orenburg: Orenburgskoe knizhnoe izdatelstvo, 2011.

Kudriashev and his immediate colleagues, such as Solomon Nikritin and Redko, all graduates of Svomas/Vkhutemas in Moscow, were united in their belief that art should reflect and interpret technological progress not only in the form of particular mechanical constructions, but also in the form of abstract scientific categories. As Nikritin wrote in 1926:

> As for the themes in his work, the contemporary painter is hopelessly lagging behind events. The palette of our painter is more primitive, more lapidary, is poorer than that of the 18th century painter... Questions of color, light, perspective, questions of the spatial composition of objects and phenomena are being resolved in exactly the same way as they were during Leonardo's time. It's as if we were living in a century on which the researches of Lobachevsky, Gauss, and Einstein had no bearing at all.[468]

682

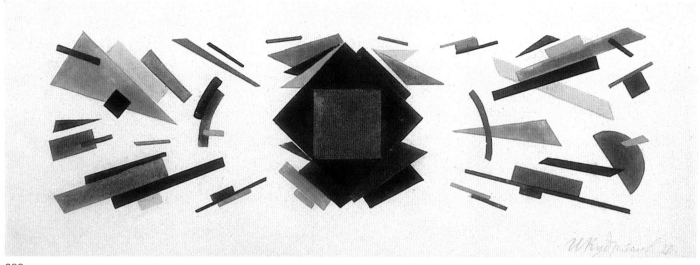

683

Kudriashev's Suprematist exercises of ca. 1920 (as in No. 683 [R576]) and then his illustrations of scientific phenomena, such as luminescence and fission, were intended to respond to the need, voiced by Nikritin, for art to be more actual and contemporary; one reason why the idea of Malevich to create a Suprematist universe was of profound importance to Kudriashev.

683 [R576].
Design for the Interior of the First Soviet Theater in Orenburg, 1920.
Gouache.
Signed and dated lower right in pencil in Russian: "I. Kudriashev, 1920."
7⅛ x 15½ in., 18 x 39.5 cm.
Provenance: Yakov Rubinshtein, Moscow, 1972.
Reproduced in F107, p. 285; I77, p. 128; I117, p. 555. There exist a number of similar designs by, or attributed to, Kudriashev for the Orenburg Theater, and this item may itself be a reprise. For reproductions of other Suprematist pieces see B34, pp. 224-26 (and inside front and back covers); K72, p. 16.

Note: Kudriashev, who was sent from Moscow to Orenburg in 1919 in order to establish a branch of Svomas there, made an elaborate Suprematist scheme for the interior of the First Soviet Theater, although it is not clear whether his designs were to cover the entire space (i.e., from the foyer through to the back of the stage) or just the auditorium. Although the designs seem not to have been realized,[469] Kudriashev's attempt to "suprematize" a theater was symptomatic of a tendency to introduce Malevich's abstract system to the stage — we remember Vera Ermolaeva's sketch for *Victory over the Sun* (No. 458 [R481]), El Lissitzky's marionette inventions for the same opera (see Nos. 752-64 [R632-43]), and Nina Kogan's Suprematist designs for a ballet in Vitebsk in 1920. This was a key moment in the history of the reconstruction of Soviet theaters, although no other theater building — metropolitan or provincial — was the recipient of such a radical abstract treatment as the First Soviet Theater in Orenburg.[470]

468 S. Nikritin. Quoted in Moskovskii Muzei zhivopisnoi kultury (=signatory as author): "O 'sovremennom' zhivopistse" in *Iskusstvo trudiashchimsia*, M, 1926, No. 3, pp. 8-11.
469 The authoritative surveys of the architecture and design of Soviet theaters, i.e., C12 and C85, make no reference to the Orenburg Theater in 1919-20.
470 For statistical tables of Soviet theater construction and reconstruction see C85, pp. 384-90.

KULBIN, Nikolai Ivanovich

Born 20 April (2 May), 1868, St. Petersburg, Russia; died 6 March, 1917, Petrograd, Russia.

Professor at the St. Petersburg Military Academy and doctor to the General Staff; taught himself to paint; 1908 organized the Impressionist group; organized the exhibition "Contemporary Trends" in St. Petersburg; 1909 group broke up; dissident members, including Elena Guro and Mikhail Matiushin, contributed to the founding of the Union of Youth, which opened in February, 1910; 1910 organized the "Triangle" exhibition in St. Petersburg; peripheral contact with the Union of Youth; close to the Burliuk brothers, Vladimir Markov (Matvejs), Olga Rozanova, et al.; 1911 contributed to the All-Russian Congress of Artists in St. Petersburg; 1912 designed several theater performances, including Vsevolod Meierkhhold's production of the pantomime *The Lovers* at the Association of Actors, Writers, Artists, and Musicians in Terioki (now Zelenogorsk), for whose theater he also designed the drop curtain; ca. 1913 illustrated Cubo-Futurist publications; 1914 host to Marinetti's visit to Russia.

Bibliography
S. Sudeikin, N. Evreinov, et al.: *Katalog-kniga "Kulbin,"* SP: Obshchestvo Intimnogo teatra, 1912.
A. Deich: "N.I. Kulbin" in *Muzy*, K, 1914, 15 January, No. 2, p. 6.
N. Evreinov: *Original o portretistakh*, M: GIZ, 1922.
E. Spandikov: "Anarkhist v iskusstve" in *Iskusstvo kommuny*, P, 1919, No. 18, pp. 2-3.
E. Kovtun: "Portretnaia grafika N.I. Kulbina" in *Pamiatniki kultury. Novye otkrytiia*, L: Nauka, 1986, pp. 358-64.
B144, passim.
B170.
B. Kalaushin et al.: *Nikolai Kulbin, Originator of the St. Petersburg Avant-Garde*, SP: Apollon, 1995, Vol. 1, Books 1 and 2.
J. Bowlt: "Vasilii Kandinsky and Nikolai Kul'bin" in *Experiment*, Los Angeles, 2003, No. 9, pp. 69-81.

Kulbin, the "doctor of Russian Futurism," was concerned with liberating art, literature, and music from conventional patterns and replacing these with what he called the "intuitive principle." In music he followed the atonal theories of Arnold Schoenberg and was much influenced by the current interest in sound-color connections elaborated by Vasilii Kandinsky, Alexander Skriabin, and the Theosophists. Similarly, Kulbin welcomed Alexei Kruchenykh's linguistic experiments; and in painting supported an entire range of eccentric principles, declaring at one point that "painting is the spontaneous projection of conventional signs from the artist's brain into the picture."[471] One of the conventional signs that Kulbin saw as recurrent in history was the triangle, and it assumed such importance for him that he organized an artist's group of that name and began to sign his writings with its graphic representation. It was at the "Triangle" and similar exhibitions that Kulbin presented experiments in automatic or intuitive painting: for example, a blind painter submitted canvases to "Contemporary Trends" and the peasant primitive Petr Kovalenko ("discovered" by David Burliuk) contributed five canvases to the "Wreath" subsection of the "Triangle." Kulbin himself was represented at the latter by a number of intuitive works with intriguing titles such as *Blue on White* and *White on Green*.

684 [R578].
Portrait of Alexei Kruchenykh, 1913.
Lithograph.
Signed with the Russian initials "NK" in a triangle lower left; hand-colored in watercolor probably by Olga Rozanova.

6¾ x 4½ in., 17 x 11.4 cm.
Provenance: Viktor Kholodkov, Moscow, March, 1988

Note: Kulbin's lithographic portrait of the poet and sometime painter Alexei Eliseevich Kruchenykh (1886-1969) appeared in three or more publications during 1913, i.e., in the first and second editions of Kruchenykh's Cubo-Futurist miscellany *Vzorval* [Explodity] (SP) and in Kulbin's own *Seriia litografii* [Series of Lithographs] (SP). The latter, published in an edition of only ca. 15 copies, also carried Kulbin's renderings of Marinetti and Nikolai Evreinov. Kulbin made another lithographic portrait of Kruchenykh in 1913 which he included in Kruchenykh's and Velimir Khlebnikov's *Bukh lesinnyi* [Forestly Rapid] (SP: EUY, 1913).

The distinctive feature of this particular lithograph, however, is that it is hand-colored, allegedly by Olga Rozanova, Kruchenykh's companion. The two editions of *Vzorval* differed in the illustrated contributions. The cover of the first edition, for example, was by Kulbin, but of the second by Rozanova, while Malevich contributed two lithographs to both editions; there also exist other "editions" or variants with discrepancies in cover designs and in numbers of pages and illustrations. This lithograph comes from a copy of the first edition (printed in 350 copies), which carries 11 rubber stamped pages, 15 lithographed pages of text, and seven lithographed illustrations (three by Rozanova, two by Malevich, one by Kulbin, and one by Natalia Goncharova).

Kruchenykh, with Khlebnikov, the inventor of *zaum,* or transrational language, felt at ease in all languages, adapting them to his own poetic expression, whether Russian, "Japanese," "Spanish," or "Hebrew." He announced: "On April 27, at 3 p.m., I mastered all languages in a momentary flash."[472] The year 1913 marked a high point in Kruchenykh's career since in December of that year, Khlebnikov, Malevich, and Mikhail Matiushin produced their transrational opera *Victory over the Sun* (see Nos. 770-84 [R648-62]).[473] Kulbin did much to disseminate the ideas of his radical colleagues in publications, conversations, and rambling lectures at public meetings. However, his own art was not particularly avant-garde — the "harmonious contemplation of a man whose soul is tranquil and forgiving."[474]

471 Quoted in L. Diakonitsyn: *Ideinye protivorechiia v estetike russkoi zhivopisi kontsa 19 – nachala 20 vv.,* Perm: Permskoe knizhnoe izdatelstvo, 1966, p. 151.
472 B17, No. 129.
473 For information on Kruchenykh see B21, passim; B66, especially pp. 69-121.
474 K. and O. Kovalskie: "Khudozhnik-idealist" in *Novaia Studiia,* SP, 1912, No. 6, 12 October, p. 10.

KUSTODIEV, Boris Mikhailovich

Born 23 February (7 March), 1878, Astrakhan, Russia; died 26 May, 1927, Detskoe Selo, near Leningrad, Russia.

1892-96 attended the Ecclesiastical Seminary in Astrakhan; 1893-96 took private lessons from a local artist; 1896 entered the Higher Art Institute of IAA; 1898 entered the studio of Ilia Repin there; 1900 contributed to the "Spring Exhibition" of IAA, the first of many exhibitions; 1902-03 helped Repin with the painting *The Session of the State Council* (RM); 1903 with Dmitrii Stelletsky visited Novgorod to study ancient Russian art; 1903-04 lived in Paris; studied under René Menard; joined the New Society of Artists, St. Petersburg; 1905 contributed cartoons to the satirical journal *Zhupel* [Bugbear]; 1907 member of the Union of Russian Artists; helped Alexander Golovin design sets at the Mariinsky Theater, St. Petersburg; visited Italy with Stelletsky; 1908 moved to Moscow; 1909 traveled in Austria, France, Italy, and Germany; 1910 onward contributed regularly to the World of Art exhibitions; 1911 visited Switzerland; thereafter traveled widely in Europe; 1914 worked on the production of Mikhail Saltykov-Shchedrin's *Death of Pazukhin* for the Moscow Art Theater, the first of several collaborations there; 1916 first symptoms of the creeping paralysis that later confined him to a wheelchair; 1918 took part in the anniversaries of the Revolution in Petrograd; 1920 one-man exhibition at the House of Arts, Petrograd; 1922 began to work with linocuts; 1923 member of the Association of Artists of Revolutionary Russia; 1925 designed Evgenii Zamiatin's *The Flea* for the Moscow Art Theater; contributed to the "Exposition Internationale des Arts Décoratifs," Paris.

Bibliography
V. Voinov: *Kustodiev,* L: Gosizdat, 1926.
M. Etkind: *B.M. Kustodiev,* L-M: Iskusstvo, 1960.
V. Lebedeva: *Boris Mikhailovich Kustodiev,* M: Nauka, 1966 (English version: M: Progress, 1981).

F26.
S. Kaplanova: *Boris Mikhailovich Kustodiev,* L: Aurora, 1971.
Boris Mikhailovich Kustodiev (1878-1927). Catalog of exhibition at the RM, 1978.
S. Kaplanova: *Novoe o Kustodieve,* M: Izobrazitelnoe iskusstvo, 1979.
Kustodiev v teatre. Catalog of exhibition at the BTM, 1979.
M. Etkind: *Boris Kustodiev,* M: Sovetskii khudozhnik, 1982.
M. Etkind: *Boris Kustodiev,* L: Aurora, 1982 (French and English versions: 1983).
M. Petrova: "Teatralnye raboty B.M. Kustodieva" in *Iskusstvo,* M, 1984, No. 12, pp. 37-41.
A. Turkov: *Kustodiev,* M: Iskusstvo, 1986.
V. Dokuchaeva: *B.M. Kustodiev,* M: Izobrazitelnoe iskusstvo, 1987.
N. Sautin: *Boris Mikhailovich Kustodiev (1878-1927),* L: Khudozhnik RSFSR, 1987.
V. Dokuchaeva: *Boris Kustodiev. Zhizn v tvorchestve,* M: Izobrazitelnoe iskusstvo, 1991.
V. Lebedeva: *Boris Kustodiev,* M: Trilistnik, 1997.
A. Turkov: *Kustodiev,* M: Terra, 1998.
V. Kruglov: *Boris Kustodiev.* Catalog of exhibition at the RM, 2003.
A. Alekseeva: *Tri muzy Borisa Kustodieva,* M: EKSMO, 2006.
A. Kudria: *Kustodiev,* M: Molodaia gvardiia, 2006.

Kustodiev is often remembered for his charming evocations of pre-Revolutionary Russian provincial life with its vigorous peasants and colorful merchants. Kustodiev's paintings evoke the sweet indolence of merchants' wives (the same Russian Venuses so beloved by Nicholas Remisoff and Sergei Sudeikin), the brilliance of the golden domes of village churches, and the intimacies of the tea-drinking ritual and the bathhouse. Much influenced by peasant art, especially by the art of the *lubok,* Kustodiev integrated the intense stylization of primitive ornament with an unusual mastery of academic convention. Such an artistic combination ensured him an immediate success in his stage designs for productions dealing with traditional Russian life, particularly the plays of Alexander Ostrovsky.

Georgii Vereisky: *Portrait of Boris Kustodiev,* **1921.** See No. 1119 [R371].

685

685 [R580].
Poster for "The Russian Art Exhibition," New York, 1924.
Chromolithograph.
28⅜ x 22 in., 72 x 56 cm.
Provenance: Viktor Kholodkov, Moscow, September, 1989.
Reproduced in color in F107, p. 153; Kaplanova, *Boris Mikhailovich Kustodiev*, No. 84; in black and white as the cover for B31, and elsewhere.

Note: "The Russian Art Exhibition," organized by the Soviet government through a committee headed by Igor Grabar, was seen at the Grand Central Palace in New York between 8 March and 21 April, 1924. It was primarily a commercial venture containing works by moderate artists — such as Alexandre Benois, Igor Grabar, Sergei Konenkov, Kustodiev, Konstantin Somov, and Serge Tchehonine — but it did not enjoy particular success either financially or artistically. Kustodiev designed the poster on the basis of his oil painting called *The Smart Coachman* (1923, private collection, M; reproduced in Etkind, *Boris Kustodiev*, p. 207). For detailed commentary on the exhibition see B31, pp. 70-88.

The Flea, or the Left-Handed Smith and the Steel Flea: *buffonade by Evgenii Zamiatin in four acts based on the tale by Nikolai Leskov. Produced by Alexei Dikii and directed by Vladimir Gotovtsev at the Moscow Art Theater 2, Moscow, on 11 February, 1925, with music by Viktor Oransky and designs by Boris Kustodiev.*

A steel flea of life size, made by an English smith, is presented to Alexander I. The Emperor then challenges the famous metalsmiths of Tula, including a left-handed one, to do better. They respond by shoeing each of the flea's feet in gold. As a reward, the left-handed smith is taken to England, although there he sees everything through Tulan eyes. On his return to Russia, the

Emperor presents him with a kaftan and money, and even though tipsy and at odds with the local policeman, he is happily united with his young lady Masha.

686 [119; R581].
Poster Advertising "The Flea", 1925.
Lithograph in red, black, and white.
Signed and dated lower right in the stone in Russian: "B. Kustodiev, 1925."
28⅜ x 42½ in., 72 x 108 cm.
Provenance: Viktor Kholodkov, Moscow, September, 1989.
The poster has been reproduced in color several times, e.g., in E38, plate 23; and in black and white, e.g., A34, p. 240. The original watercolor for this piece in the BTM is reproduced in *Kustodiev v teatre*, p. 38, where it is described as a design for the drop curtain.

687 [120; R582].
Stage Design for Act 2, Scene 1: Tula, 1925.
Pen and ink over watercolor, heightened with white.
Signed and inscribed lower right in Russian: "B. Kustodiev. Blokha. 1 kartina" [Flea. Scene 1].
14⅜ x 22 in., 36.5 x 56 cm.
Provenance: *Icons, Russian Pictures and Works of Art*, London: Sotheby's, 28 November, 1991, Lot 464 (reproduced).
Reproduced in color in B122, p. 260, and N188, p. 26; in black and white in N176. Other versions are reproduced in *Kustodiev v teatre*, pp. 38 and 39; and Etkind, *Boris Kustodiev* (Sovetskii khudozhnik), fig. 219.

Note: Kustodiev's sets and costumes for this production of *The Flea* by Studio 2 of

686

687

the Moscow Art Theater helped make this event the hit of the Moscow theater season for 1925. Alexei Dikii recalled:

> I have never experienced so complete, so inspired a harmony of ideas and opinions with a painter... Awakened and urged on by the painter and steered into the right channel by the stage manager, the actors' imaginations worked brilliantly and faultlessly.[475]

To a considerable extent, the production symbolized a sharp rebuttal of the concurrent avant-garde experiments in the Soviet theater that were being promoted by Vsevolod Meierkhold and Alexander Tairov. Anatolii Lunacharsky even went so far as to contend that this production had triumphed over Constructivism.[476] Apart from the sets and costumes, Kustodiev was also commissioned to make illustrations of the play for the journal *Ogonek* (not published). Kustodiev designed another poster for the Leningrad production of *The Flea* by the Bolshoi Dramatic Theater in 1926[477] as well as the illustrations for another tale by Nikolai Leskov, *Zver* [The Beast] (M-L: Novaia detskaia biblioteka, 1926).

There Was Not a Penny and Suddenly There Was a Pound (also-called From Rags to Riches): *comedy in five acts by Alexander Ostrovsky. Produced by Evtikhii Karpov for the Academic Theater of Drama, Leningrad, on 31 October, 1925, with designs by Boris Kustodiev.*

Set in a quiet merchants' district of old Moscow, the play treats the theme of match-making and money. Krutitsky, a retired civil servant, and his wife Anna have a niece Nastia, who complains of her bitter poverty, while Krutitsky, a wealthy man, suspects everyone of cheating him. Two love intrigues develop, one between Nastia and the eligible bachelor Baklushin, the other between Elesia, the stupid son of Migacheva, and Larisa, the daughter of the merchant Epishkin. After lots of tea-drinking and small talk, Nastia suddenly receives an inheritance from Krutitsky and is made happy.

688 [R583].
Stage Design for a Courtyard with Lamp-Post on the Right, Leningrad, 1925.
Watercolor.
Signed and dated lower left in Russian: "B. Kustodiev 1925."
12 x 19 in., 30.5 x 48.5 cm.
Provenance: Abram Hourvitch, New York, June, 1970.
Reproduced in color in G61; in black and white in I20, No. 61; I51, No. 134; N114; a version with the principal components inverted is reproduced in *Teatr,* M, 1979, No. 3, between pp. 96 and 97; and in *Iskusstvo*, M, 1984, No. 12, p. 38. The variant in No. 689 [R584] reverses some of the same scenic components.

689 [R584].
Stage Design for a Courtyard with Lamp-post on the Left, Leningrad, 1925.
Oil on board.

688

689

Signed and dated lower left in Russian: "B. Kustodiev, 1925."
19⅞ x 33¼ in., 50.5 x 84.5 cm.
Other inscription: the reverse carries a statement in Russian: "There Was Not a Penny and Suddenly There Was a Pound by Ostrovsky. Academic Theater of Drama, Leningrad. B.M. Kustodiev," followed by the line "Exhibition of the State Russian Museum No. 15" (1928).
Provenance: *Russian Pictures, Works of Art and Icons*, London: Sotheby's, 6 December, 1989, Lot 135 (reproduced).
Reproduced in color Etkind, *Boris Kustodiev* (Sovetskii khudozhnik), fig. 212. The variant in No. 688 [R583] reverses some of the scenic components. Other sets for the play are in the BTM (see *Kustodiev v teatre,* p. 48); Kustodiev's set for Act I of the 1920 production of *The Storm* is also very similar (see Voinov, *Kustodiev*, p. 128).

Note: Fedor Chaliapin, an admirer of Kustodiev's art, once asked, "Who else can better feel and depict Ostrovsky [than

Kustodiev]?"[478] Kustodiev treated the theme of mercantile Moscow and provincial towns with affection and a gentle irony, and his many stage designs for Ostrovsky's plays, especially for *The Storm,* were paralleled by his analogous paintings, such as *The Provinces* (1910, private collection, SP) and *Autumn* (1922, private collection, K). "Back to Ostrovsky!" exclaimed Lunacharsky in 1923.[479] Kustodiev sympathized with that sentiment.

Kustodiev first worked on designs for *There Was Not a Penny and Suddenly There Was a Pound* in 1917 for an unrealized production at the Moscow Art Theater,[480] and the play was staged at the Academic Theater of Drama, Petrograd, in 1921, but with designs by Petr Lambin. In spite of illness, 1925 was an auspicious year for Kustodiev because, in addition to his work for *There Was Not a Penny and Suddenly There Was a Pound*, he saw the implementation of perhaps his most successful stage undertaking — his sets and costumes for Dikii's production of Evgenii Zamiatin's *The*

Flea at the Moscow Art Theater.[481] For reproductions of other costume designs by Kustodiev see L120, Lots 65-83.

475   Quoted in Etkind: *Kustodiev* (Aurora, English version), p. 267.
476   Ibid.
477   Reproduced in Etkind, *Kustodiev* (Sovetskii khudozhnik), p. 373.
478   F. Shaliapin: "Chelovek vysokogo dukha." Quoted in F26, p. 379.
479   Quoted in C85, p. 21.
480   Costumes for the 1917 production are in the GMTMA and the RM.
481   Dikii was particularly close to Kustodiev in 1924-25 and his reminiscences and correspondence concerning the artist are of particular interest. See A. Dikii: *Povest o teatralnoi yunosti*, M: Iskusstvo, 1957, pp. 323-58; also see his *Stati. Perepiska. Vospominaniia*, M: VTO, 1967.

KUZNETSOV, Pavel Varfolomeevich

Born 5 November (17), 1878, Saratov, Russia; died 21 February, 1968, Moscow, Russia.

1897-1907 attended MIPSA, studying under Konstantin Korovin and Valentin Serov; met Kuzma Petrov-Vodkin and Martiros Sarian there; 1903 visited Norway; 1904 contributed to the "Crimson Rose" exhibition in Saratov; 1906 at Sergei Diaghilev's invitation visited Paris in connection with the Russian contribution to the "Salon d'Automne"; 1907 co-founder of the Blue Rose group of Symbolist painters; 1908 rejected Symbolist imagery in favor of more immediate interpretations of everyday life, epecially of the Kirghizian steppes; 1910 onwards member of the renewed World of Art movement; throughout the 1910s continued to exhibit regularly with various societies; designed *Sakuntala* for the Chamber Theater, Moscow; 1918 worked on agit-designs for the streets and squares of Moscow; 1924 member of the Four Arts group; 1924 visited Paris with his wife, the artist Elena Bebutova; 1929 one-man exhibition in Moscow; 1930s produced paintings on industrial and collective farm themes; 1940 one-man exhibition in Moscow; 1945 taught at the Moscow Central Industrial Design Institute; 1956 one-man exhibition in Moscow and then Leningrad (1957); 1964 one-man exhibition in Moscow.

Bibliography
A. Romm: *Pavel Varfolomeevich Kuznetsov*, M: Sovetskii khudozhnik, 1960.
M. Alpatov: *Pavel Varfolomeevich Kuznetsov*, M: Sovetskii khudozhnik, 1968 (second edition 1969).
L. Budkova and D. Sarabianov: *Pavel Kuznetsov*, M: Sovetskii khudozhnik, 1975.
A. Rusakova: *Pavel Kuznetsov*, L: Iskusstvo, 1977.
Pavel Kuznetsov. Catalog of exhibition organized by the Union of Artists of the USSR, M, 1979.
L. Mochalov: *Pavel Kuznetsov 1878-1968*, L: Khudozhnik RSFSR, 1979.
D. Sarabianov: *P. Kuznetsov*, M: Sovetskii khudozhnik, 1988.
P. Stupples: *Pavel Kuznetsov*, Cambridge: Cambridge University Press, 1989. B268.
O. Davydova: *Pavel Kuznetsov*, M: Art-Rodnik, 2010.
Pavel Kuznetsov. Puteshestvie v Aziiu. Catalog of exhibition at the Proun Gallery, M, 2010.

While not a radical artist in the way Kazimir Malevich and Vladimir Tatlin were, Kuznetsov was a leader of the Symbolist movement in Russia, even if the hushed tones and approximate forms of his pictures of the Blue Rose period seem to possess the same "spiritual" quality as the abstractions of Vasilii Kandinsky. Still, Kuznetsov, ultimately, remained a figurative artist, and adjusted readily to the new Realism of the 1930s. On the other hand, even in his renderings of the ordinary life, whether sheep-shearing or oil-wells, he maintained a strong sense of pictorial rhythm, an almost musical movement that became a distinguishing feature of his work. This strong plastic sense is evident in all media — studio painting, stage design, lithography.[482] As Mikhail Alpatov observed of Kuznetsov's pictures at the one-man exhibition of 1940:

> ...the flowers, the fruits, trees, grasses, distances, houses, people, and animals fused into a nocturnal chord. You could hear the ringing, the chimes of the colors as if they were effusing beyond the confines of the canvases.[483]

Sakuntala: Hindu mystery play by Kalidasa translated by Konstantin Balmont. Produced by Alexander Tairov at the Chamber Theater, Moscow, on 12 December, 1914, with music by Vladimir Pol and designs by Pavel Kuznetsov.

The powerful King Dusianta rides his chariot followed by his suite — his general, his buffoon, his poets, etc. In the forest he comes upon the beautiful Sakuntala, the adopted daughter of the hermit Kanva and his wife Gautami. To gratify a moment of lust, the King lures Sakuntala from her natural habitat. The gods do not tolerate such iniquity and, after much song and dance, order the King to marry Sakuntala so that she will become Queen.

690 [R577].
Costume Design for a Woman, ca. 1914.
Watercolor and pencil.
Initialed lower left in Russian: "P.K."
11⅞ x 6¾ in., 30 x 17 cm.
Other inscription: the reverse carries the dedication in pencil in Russian: "To my dear friends E.P. and E.A. Gunst in fond memory of Pavel Kuznetsov's theater work. E. Bebutova, 7.XI.1964." (The statement is by Elena Mikhailovna Bebutova, 1892-1970, Kuznetsov's wife, who presented this piece to the Moscow collector Evgenii Anatolievich Gunst, 1901-83, and his wife.)
Provenance: Evgenii Gunst, Moscow, 1972.
Reproduced in I77, p. 125.

Note: Tairov spent much of the summer of 1914 in English and French libraries and museums, including the British Museum, researching Ancient Hindu mythology and

690

ethnography in preparation for his production of *Sakuntala* He decided to inaugurate his Chamber Theater with a production of Kalidasa's play, because "its mystery attracted us, its beautiful majesty beckoned us." [484] This was also Kuznetsov's first major theatrical engagement and

> the decorations... were beautiful... They were simple and austere, almost awkward. But it was in this "almost" that their charm lay... The figures, their bodies painted plainly and wearing restrained tunics, moved about the free spaces of the stage.[485]

However, *Sakuntala* was not an unqualified success, even with Alisa Koonen in the title role. As several critics observed, the general conception, including Kuznetsov's design, was not especially innovative and belonged more to the Symbolist theater with its stylization and decorativism.[486] Tairov himself, while acknowledging the functionality of the costumes and the color harmonies of the sets, felt that his desire to emphasize motion and emotion had not been gratified. After commissioning Kuznetsov to design a second play, Mikhail Kuzmin's pantomime *The Day of the Spirits in Toledo,* in 1915 (which also had a cool reception), Tairov and the artist parted ways.

482   Kuznetsov's three albums of lithographs published in 1923 are of particular interest, i.e., *Turkestan. 1-ia seriia risunkov,* M-P: Gosizdat; *Turkestan. Avtolitografii 2-ia seriia,* M-P: Gosizdat; and *Avtolitografii v kraskakh. Ot Saratova do Bukhary. Gornaia Bukhara. Tsvetnye litografii.* M: Gosizdat.
483   Alpatov, *Pavel Varfolomeevich Kuznetsov*, p. 13.
484   C35, p. 97.
485   G17, p. xviii.
486   C11, p. 70.

LAMBIN, Petr Borisovich

Born 15 (27) May, 1862, St. Petersburg; died 11 January, 1923, Petrograd.

1884 graduated from the Higher Art Institute of IAA, where he studied under the celebrated stage designer Matvei Shishkov; 1885 onwards assisted Shishkov with many ballet and opera productions for the Imperial Theaters, supporting Shishkov's Romantic interpretation; 1893 became an independent designer; late 1890s became artist-in-residence for the Imperial Theaters, St. Petersburg (one of his disciples was Alexander Golovin); among Lambin's designs were those for Alexander Ostrovsky's *The Storm* (1907) and Lev Tolstoi's *The Fruits of Enlightenment* (1916); early 1900s taught at SCITD; 1912 designed the set for *Papillons* at the Mariinsky Theater, St. Petersburg (Léon Bakst did the costumes).

Bibliography
G2, pp. 94-95.
Ezhenedelnik petrogradskikh gosudarstvennykh akademicheskikh teatrov, P, 1923, No. 5, p. 12 (obituary).

Les Saisons (also called **Les Quatre Saisons**): *allegorical ballet in one act of four tableaux by Marius Petipa with music by Alexander Glazunov. Produced at the Hermitage Theater, St. Petersburg on 7 February, 1900, with choreography by Marius Petipa, costumes by Evgenii Ponomarev, and sets by Petr Lambin.*

The four tableaux constitute allegorical choreographies of Winter (Hoar-frost, Ice, Hail and Snow), Spring (Zephyr, fairies, and enchanted birds), Summer (Naiads, Satyrs, and Fauns), Autumn (dance of an Autumn Bacchanale), followed by the Apotheosis (iridescent constellations). The pastoral allegory incorporating the seasons of the year and their attendants — a girl, a boy, a faun, and a bacchante — provide the meteorological setting with a whiff of eroticism and decadence.

691 [R585]
Costume Design for Summer, 1900 (?).
Watercolor and pencil.
Signed lower left: "P. Lambin."
12¼ x 8⅝ in., 31 x 22 cm.
Other inscription: top right in Russian: "Ballet Four Seasons of the Year. Summer."
Provenance: Alexander Malitsky, Bay Shore, New York, May, 1974.
Reproduced in I40, No. 78.

Note: According to one documentary source,[487] Evgenii Ponomarev, not Lambin, created the costumes for this ballet production of *Les Saisons* in 1900, so it is possible that this particular rendering for Summer was either for an unrealized project or for the second presentation -- at the Mariinsky Theater, St. Petersburg, in 1907, again with Lambin's sets, but with costumes by Alexander Golovin. In any case, the 1900 production was especially

691

effective thanks to the character dancing by Alexander Gorsky, Matilda Kshesinskaia, Anna Pavlova, Mariia Petipa, and Olga Preobrazhenskaia. It is of interest to recall that part of the music for *Les Saisons* was used by Michel Fokine for *Cléopâtre* in 1909 (see No. 75 [R71]). Much later, Vasilii Shukhaev also tried his hand at *Les Quatre Saisons* (see No. 950 [NIRE]).

Lambin was one of the last "Victorian" designers for the Imperial stage in Russia and he extended the sumptuous traditions of Mikhail Bocharov and Shishkov. One of his pupils remembered Lambin in the following manner:

> Lambin used to exhibit splendid watercolors at the exhibitions and in his class used to teach [us], through direct visual example, how to paint big canvases in size paint [fixative]. He communicated his practical instructions on the principles of decorative composition and technical methods in direct visual form and confirmed them through example there and then.[488]

487 A20, p. 131.
488 P. Buchkin: *O tom, chto v pamiati*, L: Khudozhnik RSFSR, 1963, pp. 31-32.

LANCERAY (Lansere), Evgenii Evgenievich

Born 23 August (4 September), 1875, Pavlovsk, near St. Petersburg, Russia; died 13 September, 1946, Moscow, Russia.

Son of the sculptor Evgenii Alexandrovich Lanceray, nephew of Alexandre Benois, brother of the architect Nikolai Lanceray and Zinaida Serebriakova, and cousin of Nadia and Nicola Benois. 1892-95 attended SSEA; 1895 visited Paris, where he studied under Filippo Colarossi and Jean-Joseph Benjamin-Constant; 1898 returned to St. Petersburg, where he joined the World of Art society; established himself as a skilful graphic artist, and contributed subsequently to many publications, such as the journal *Zolotoe runo* [Golden Fleece] and the 1911 edition of Lev Tolstoi's *Hadji Murat;* 1905-06 worked for the satirical journals *Zritel* [Spectator] and *Zhupel* [Bugbear]; 1907 designed productions for the Antique Theater in St. Petersburg; 1913-26 made interior decorations for the Kazan Railroad Station in Moscow;1916 left Petrograd for Ust-Krestishche in Pskov Region; 1918 Golike and Vilborg, Petrograd, published Tolstoi's *Khadzhi-Murat* with Lanceray's illustrations; 1922-32 taught at the Academy of Arts, Tbilisi; 1924 published *Leto v Angore* [Summer in Angora]; continued to make paintings, drawings, and graphic designs until his death.

Bibliography
O. Podobedova: *Evgenii Evgenievich Lansere, 1875-1946,* M: Sovetskii khudozhnik, 1961.
O. Podobedova, comp.: *Evgenii Evgenievich Lansere, 1875-1946,* M: Sovetskii khudozhnik, 1964.
N. Mashkovtsev: *Lansere*. Catalog of exhibition at the Academy of Arts of the USSR, M, 1966.
A. Borovsky: *Evgenii Evgenievich Lansere*, L: Khudozhnik RSFSR, 1975.
N. Shantyko: *E. Lansere*. Catalog of exhibition at the RM, 1975.
V. Bialik, comp.: *Evgenii Lansere. Dnevniki*, M: Iskusstvo XXI vek, 2008 (three volumes).

Lanceray was born into a family of talented artists: his father, Evgenii Alexandrovich, was a famous sculptor; his sister was the painter Zinaida Serebriakova; his brother Nikolai was an architect and stage designer; and his uncle was Alexandre Benois, an ambiance that left a deep impression on his early career. While Lanceray did not possess the encyclopedic knowledge and artistic subtlety of his uncle, he shared many of the intellectual and philosophical pursuits of the World of Art group — a passion for 17th- and 18th-century Russia, a particular love of the theater and book design, and a strong orientation towards the graphic arts. As his Soviet biographer, Olga Podobedova, pointed out, Lanceray's graphic designs are distinguished by their "'constructivity', their clarity and precision of form... and their laconic artistic language."[489] Lanceray expressed his flair for the scenographic and the decorative in his work for the Antique Theater in St. Petersburg (see Nos. 693-94 [R587-88]), in his illustrations for journals (e.g., his cover and vignettes for *Zolotoe runo* [Golden Fleece]), and, curiously enough, in his murals for the Kazan Railroad Station in Moscow.

The Kazan Station (1913-26) extended an intellectual fascination with the Baroque, reflected, for example, in the writings of Lanceray's colleagues, such as Georgii Lukomsky, Pavel Muratov, and Alexander Trubnikov, and in the 1913 Russian publication of Heinrich Wölfflin's fundamental treatise on *Renaissance and the Baroque.* This realignment of historical pressures resulted in architectural *tours de force* in Neo-Baroque style that served to counteract the aggression of the avantgarde. Above all, one thinks of the vast "Baroque" interior of the Kazan Railroad Station in Moscow, Russia's latterday answer to the Sistine Chapel or the Palazzo Barberini. Supplementing the quaint façades and pilasters that the architect Alexei Shchusev had borrowed from the so-called Naryshkin Baroque of Moscow's18th century, the insets and panels, designed by Benois, Lanceray, and Serebriakova between 1914 and 1917 (and continued by Lanceray in the 1930s), duplicated the most audacious Baroque perspectives and elliptical configurations.

Even so, the visual impression leaves a lot to be desired — the images of the various nationalities (such as Benois's *Asia,* Lanceray's *Meeting of Europe and Asia,* and Serebriakova's *Siam*) squeezed into their cartouches lack the sensuous energy of Tiepolo and Caravaggio.

Generally speaking, Lanceray applied his measured style to national historical subjects as in his renderings of early St. Petersburg palaces and Moscow *osobniaki* [villas], and he tended to emphasize the Russian tradition rather than the cultures of Ancient Greece and Louis XIV, unlike Léon Bakst, Benois, and Konstantin Somov. In this concentration on the Russian patrimony, Lanceray was close to Mstislav Dobujinsky, although his *oeuvre* lacked the often sardonic and sometimes apocalyptic mood of Dobujinsky's urban cycles. Of the central World of Art members, Lanceray was the only one to resist emigration and, during the Soviet period, continued to enjoy acclaim, especially for illustrations to the Russian classics and for official commissions, such as his *plafond* for the main restaurant in the Hotel Moscow in the late 1930s — an anachronistic homage to Pietro da Cortona.

692 [R586].
Poster for the "Exhibition of Historic Russian Portraits," 1905.
Chromolithograph.
17⅞ x 25⅝ in., 45.5 x 65 cm.
Inscriptions (as part of the design) in Russian: "Beginning on the 6 March, 1905, the 'Historical-Artistic Exhibition of Russian Portraits' will be open at the Tauride Palace under the patronage of His Majesty the Emperor. It is being organized to benefit the

692

widows and orphans of soldiers who fell in battle." Lower left contains the words: "Approved by the censor, St. Petersburg, 14 March, 1905. Printed by R. Golike and A. Vilborg."
Reproduced in B24, p. 166.

Note: Throughout 1904 Sergei Diaghilev, the organizer of this exhibition, traveled extensively in Russia and Europe, searching for portraits in forgotten palaces and estates and borrowing from collections in Paris, Vienna, Berlin, Amsterdam, Weimar, and Geneva. The result was his spectacular "Exhibition of Historic Russian Portraits," which, with a generous subsidy from Nicholas II, opened at the Tauride Palace, St. Petersburg in March, 1905. With a complement of 4,000 canvases, including 35 portraits of Peter the Great, 44 of Catherine the Great, and 32 of Alexander I, with long forgotten works by Vladimir Borovikovsky, Dmitrii Levitsky, and Fedor Rokotov, and with a scholarly catalog in eight separate books compiled by Baron Nikolai Vrangel, the exhibition was itself a historic event. Between March and May, the month of its closure, the exhibition was visited by 45,000 people and its philanthropic mission — to benefit the widows and orphans of those who had fallen in the Russo-Japanese War — was profitable to the tune of 60,000 rubles.

The Tauride Palace exhibition was a grand visual record of Russia's Imperial history. Open during the tragic events of the first Russian revolution, the exhibition summarized a majestic and noble brilliance by then fast receding. Diaghilev himself was acutely aware of this conflict between past and present, as he indicated in a moving speech that he gave at a Moscow banquet held in honor of the exhibition:

Do you not feel that the long gallery of portraits of people great and small... is

but a grand and convincing reckoning of a dazzling but, alas, fossilized period of our history?[490]

In some respects, the "Exhibition of Historic Portraits" can be regarded as Diaghilev's first innovative "theatrical" production. True, he had long entertained chosen audiences with his pleasing baritone and he had supervised the abortive production of *Sylvia* at the Mariinsky Theater during his stormy tenure within the administration of the Imperial Theaters in 1901. Still, for its undoubted triumph, the Tauride exhibition, even if primarily an investigation into cultural and social history, drew upon Diaghilev's exceptional gifts of technical organization, esthetic arbitration, histrionic gesture and audience manipulation — a theatrical strategy that Diaghilev repeated with alacrity and aplomb when he established the Ballets Russes.

El Purgatorio de San Patricio: *drama in one act by Pedro Calderón de la Barca in a translation by Konstantin Balmont. Produced by Nikolai Drizen at the Antique Theater, St. Petersburg, on 9 December, 1911, with music by Ilia Sats and sets by Evgenii Lanceray and Vladimir Shchuko and costumes by Ivan Bilibin.*

Patrick, a Christian, brings the holy word to Egerius, King of Ireland, to the King's daughters, Lesbia and Polonia, and to other pagans. Lesbia warms to Patrick, but Polonia does not, preferring a rival and impure Christian, Luis. After invoking the appearance of a Good Angel, Patrick departs, while Luis perpetrates black deeds, including the killing of Polonia. Saddened by the woes of Ireland, Patrick resurrects Polonia, and also guides the King and the wicked Luis to a terrifying cave on a mountain — his Purgatory. However, the Purgatory purifies even the intransigent Luis and the play ends with the evocation of paradise.

693

694

Lanceray was a supporter of the Antique Theater from the very beginning and designed the production of Evreinov's *Fair of St. Denis* in 1908. The production of *El Purgatorio de San Patricio* which, apparently, was transposed to a 17th-century setting, marked a shift in the general trend of the Antique Theater away from the Medieval mystery to the Spanish Renaissance. Calderón enjoyed a distinct vogue in Moscow and St. Petersburg just before the Revolution, and his works were also staged by Vsevolod Meierkhold and Alexander Tairov. It is possible that these two designs were not for *El Purgatorio*, but for an unrealized production of Friedrich Schiller's *Kabale und Liebe* (1909-10), although the designs for this in the BTM are not similar to the ones under discussion. In any case, contemporary reviews of the Calderón production indicate that this attribution is a probable one. One critic made the following remarks:

> In the background, behind a tripartite portal, Evgenii Lanceray's decorative panels appeared as the action progressed. From a general standpoint, some of them are worthy of great praise…
>
> But from the standpoint of the Antique Theater, they really ought to be condemned: they have so little in common with Spanish painting, with the 17th century in general, or with the actual mood of Calderón's drama.[491]

489 Podobedova (1964), p. 48.
490 S. Diaghilev: "V chas itogov" in *Vesy*, M, 1905, No. 4, p. 45.
491 Review in *Apollon*, SP, 1912, No. 4, pp. 60-61. For other commentary see A. Rostislavov: "O postanovkakh Starinnogo teatra" in *Teatr i iskusstvo*, SP, 1911, No. 51, pp. 1002-03.

693 [R587].
Stage Detail, Table and Two Chairs, ca. 1911.
Watercolor and ink.
Signed lower right in Russian: "E. Lanceray."
3½ x 8¾ in., 9 x 22.2 cm.
Other inscription: lower right in Russian: "A detail XIV."
Provenance: John E. Bowlt, New York, August, 1974, who had purchased it in a bookstore in the Metropole Hotel building, Moscow, 1968.
Reproduced in I40, No. 82; I51, No. 135.

694 [R588].
Stage Design, ca. 1911.
Watercolor and pencil.
Signed lower left in Russian: "E. Lanceray."
10½ x 13⅞ in., 26.7 x 35.3 cm.
Provenance: John E. Bowlt, New York, August, 1974. who had purchased it in a bookstore in the Metropole Hotel building,

Moscow, 1968.
Reproduced in I40, No. 81; I51, No. 136.

Note: The Antique Theater opened in St. Petersburg in 1907 under the directorship of Nikolai Drizen and Nikolai Evreinov. Alexandre Benois was chief artistic and historical consultant, who, together with Ivan Bilibin, Dobujinsky, Lanceray, and Nicholas Roerich, contributed as designers. The Antique Theater opposed the Imperial Theaters and in its esthetic stance appealed largely to the World of Art artists. Until its closure in 1912, it served as an important outlet for their decorative talents. The essential aim of Drizen and Evreinov was to restore the theatrical forms and methods of the ancient European theater, especially that of the Middle Ages and the 15th and 16th centuries, and, consequently, to focus attention on the genres of the morality play, the miracle play, and the pastorale.

Konstantin Somov: Lithograph portrait of Evgenii Lanceray.

LAPIN, Lev Pavlovich

Born 14 (26) December, 1898, Moscow, Russia; died 24 February, 1962, Leningrad, Russia.

1917 graduated from high school in Moscow; after the Revolution the family moved to Petrograd; 1918 began work as a teacher in the orphanage in the former Buddhist Temple; 1920-30 worked as a research assistant at the Institute of Art History; attended lectures by Nikolai Radlov at the Academy of Arts; 1920s and early 1930s acquaintance with Kazimir Malevich, who exerted a strong influence on his artistic style; 1923 married Tatiana Krechetova, an art historian who worked for thirty years at the State Russian Museum, finishing her career there as head of the Department of Applied Arts; 1930-62 worked at the Molotov Steel Wire Factory on Vasilievsky Island; 1941 evacuated to the Urals during WWII.

Bibliography
I. Galeev: *Linograviury 30-kh godov.* Catalog of exhibition at Ildar Galeev Gallery, Moscow, 2006.
I. Galeev: *Lev Lapin,* M: Galeev, 2006.
For some references see A34, pp. 246-47.

Lapin's artistic legacy has yet to be recognized and systematized, although the recent retrospective exhibition at the Galeev Gallery in Moscow has done much to restore his name to the history of modern Russian art. Perhaps the main reason for this comparative obscurity is simply that, by profession, Lapin was a cable engineer and, however creative his aesthetic imagination, he preferred artistic media and genres that were modest and intimate, such as the linocut, the engraving, the pastel, and the watercolor, rather than the imposing oil painting or free-standing sculpture. Even so, Lapin was passionate in

695

696

his artistic searches, appreciating both the traditional masters and the abstract experiments of Vasilii Kandinsky and Kazimir Malevich and his followers, especially Nikolai Suetin. Evgenii Kovtun commented that:

> For many years Lev Pavlovich Lapin was connected with K.S. Malevich and studied under him. The paintings that have survived testify to his high artistic cultural level and to the fact that he was deeply aware of the peculiarities of Suprematist color and form.[492]

695 [NIRE].
Female Dancer, 1922.
Pencil with a touch of blue color.
Signed in Russian lower right: "LEV" and dated in lower left and right corners: "FEV RAL '22 g." [= February '22].
6¼ x 4½ in., 16 x 10.5 cm.
Provenance: the artist's daughter, Irina Zakharova, Leningrad, June, 1984.

Unidentified production, 1929.

696 [121; R589].
Costume Design for a Russian Peasant Woman Dancing, 1929.
Watercolor.
Dated in pencil lower left corner: "2/V/1929."
13¾ x 8⅝ in., 34.8 x 22 cm.
Other inscriptions: signed on the reverse and dated in pencil in Russian: "L. Lapin, 2 May, 1929."
Provenance: the artist's daughter, Irina Zakharova, Leningrad, June, 1984.
Reproduced in color in B115, plate 192; Galeev, *Lev Lapin,* p. 16; and in black and white in A34, p. 247; I77, p. 144.

492 Note by Evgenii Kovtun dated 24 October, 1988, accompanying L35, Lot 570.

LARIONOV, Mikhail Fedorovich

Born 22 May (3 June), 1881, Tiraspol, Kherson Region, Ukraine; died 10 May, 1964, Fontenay-aux-Roses, near Paris, France.

1898 entered MIPSA; 1900 met Natalia Goncharova, who became his life-long companion; 1902 expelled from MIPSA; 1906 traveled with Sergei Diaghilev to Paris in connection with the Russian Section at the "Salon d'Automne"; thereafter contributed to numerous exhibitions in Russia and abroad, including the three exhibitions organized by Nikolai Riabushinsky, editor of the journal *Zolotoe runo* [Golden Fleece]; 1910 with Goncharova et al. organized the "Jack of Diamonds" exhibition, and then the "Donkey's Tail" (1912), the "Target" (1913), and "No. 4" (1914); ca. 1910 worked in Primitivist, Cubist, and, in 1912-13, Futurist and Rayonist styles; 1914 (29 April) with Goncharova left for Paris to design Sergei Diaghilev's production of *Le Coq d'Or;* Galerie Paul Guillaume, Paris, and Galerie Der Sturm, Berlin, held an exhibition of both artists' work; 1915 back in Russia mobilized, wounded and hospitalized; 1916-17 after traveling with Diaghilev's company to Spain and Italy, settled in Paris with Goncharova; 1919 with Goncharova exhibited at the Galerie Barbazanges, Paris; 1920-21 with Goncharova contributed to the "Exposition internationale d'art moderne" in Geneva; 1920-22 designed *Chout* and *Le Renard* for Diaghilev's Ballets Russes; thereafter worked on several stage productions; 1922 with Goncharova exhibited at the Kingore Gallery, New York; 1923 exhibited at the Shiseido Gallery, Tokyo; after 1930, except for occasional commissions and contributions to exhibitions, Larionov and Goncharova lived largely unrecognized and impoverished; 1954 their names were resurrected at Richard Buckle's "The Diaghilev Exhibition" in Edinburgh and London; 1961 Art Council of Great Britain organized a major retrospective of Goncharova's and Larionov's works.

Bibliography
M. Chamot and C. Gray: *A Retrospective Exhibition of Paintings and Designs for the Theatre. Larionov and Goncharova.* Catalog of the exhibition at the City Art Gallery, Leeds; the City Art Gallery, Bristol; and the Arts Council Gallery, London, 1961.
W. George: *Larionov,* Paris: La Bibliothèque des Arts, 1966. Second edition, 1996.
T. Loguine: *Gontcharova et Larionov,* Paris: Klincksieck, 1971.
D. Sarabianov: "Primitivistskii period v tvorchestve Mikhaila Larionova" in D. Sarabianov: *Russkaia zhivopis kontsa 1900-kh – nachala 1910-kh godov.* M: Iskusstvo, 1971, pp. 99-116.
G. Ruzsa: *Larionov,* Budapest: Corvina, 1977.
M. Larionov: *Une Avant-Garde Explosive,* Lausanne: L'Age d'Homme, 1978.

T. Liberman: "M. Larionov i N. Goncharova v pismakh i risunkakh" in *Chast rechi*, New York, 1980, No. 1, pp. 243-51.

A. Parton: *Mikhail Larionov and the Russian Avant-Garde*, Princeton: Princeton University Press, 1993.
B170.

G. Kovalenko: *Natalia Goncharova. Mikhail Larionov. Vospominaniia sovremennikov*, M: Galart, 1995.

G. di Milia, intro.: *Mikhail Larionov. Manifestes*, Paris: Allia, 1995.

J. Boissel et al.: *Nathalie Gontcharova. Michel Larionov*. Catalog of exhibition at the Centre Georges Pompidou, Paris, 1995; and at the Fondazione A. Mazzotta, Milan, 1996.

Ye. Kovtun: *Mikhail Larionov*, Bournemouth, England: Parkstone, 1998.

E. Iliukhina: *M. Larionov. N. Goncharova. Parizhskoe nasledie v Tretiakovskoi galeree. Grafika, teatr, kniga, vospominaniia*. Catalog of exhibition at the TG, 1999.

A. Lukanova, comp.: *Larionov. Goncharova. Shedevry iz parizhskogo naslediia. Zhivopis*. Catalog of exhibition at the TG, 1999.

G. Kovalenko, ed.: *N. Goncharova, M. Larionov*, M: Nauka, 2001.

A. Kovalev, ed.: *Mikhail Larionov v Rossii*, M: Elizium, 2004.

G. Pospelov and E. Iliukhina: *Mikhail Larionov*, M: RA and Galart, 2006.

A. Inshakov: *Mikhail Larionov*, M: Gnozis, 2010.
D110.

Also see Bibliography for Natalia Goncharova.

Larionov brought to Russian art a vigor and vitality that contrasted sharply with the conventions of Realism and Symbolism still dominant in the mid-1900s. Inspired by indigenous primitive art forms, such as the *lubok*, the painted tin tray, the signboard, and the icon, Larionov and his colleagues, especially Goncharova, proceeded to "vulgarize" the high arts. As Larionov declared in 1913:

> We despise and brand as artistic lackeys all those who move against a background of old or new art and go about their trivial business. Simple, uncorrupted people are closer to us than this artistic husk that clings to modern art, like flies to honey.[493]

Larionov's new and radical approach to painting became immediately clear from his canvases of 1908 onward, such as *Sunset after the Rain* (1908, TG), in which the traditional narrative value of a painting was already superseded by a primary concern with the intrinsic properties of color, texture, and line. In order to propagate the new primitivism, Larionov established the Jack of Diamonds group in 1910, inviting a number of young, dynamic artists, including Goncharova, Aristarkh Lentulov, and Kazimir Malevich, to cultivate a "deliberate simplification and vulgarization of form."[494] The very title, Jack of Diamonds, was one of the several striking sobriquets of the time and its association with the uniforms of civil prisoners was in keeping with the social and cultural position of the new artist

as outcast.[495] In his naive paintings of the time such as his Venuses, farmyards, and barrack scenes, Larionov transmitted particular devices from the icon and the *lubok*, such as inverted perspective, bright, "rude" coloring, and flat rendering of figures, etc., thereby questioning the age-old traditions of Western academic painting. At the same time, Larionov, Goncharova, Malevich, and their friends began to give increased attention to the conditions of spontaneity and illogicality and to the notion of the game or play inherent in children's art. This attitude towards art found its most productive application in Larionov's work for the theater in the 1910s and 1920s.

Indeed, after the elegance of the World of Art artists — such as Alexandre Benois and Mstislav Dobujinsky — Larionov and Goncharova suddenly transformed the Russian stage into a buffoonery, imbuing it with an effervescence that it had possessed only with the old *skomorokhi* and *balagany*.[496] Larionov, in particular, restored the element of farce to the professional stage, achieving this not through a confirmation of historical or ethnographical fact, but rather through a contradiction of it: his projects for *Soleil de Nuit* (1915), *Histoires Naturelles* (1915), *Chout* (1921), and *Le Renard* (1922) rely for their effect precisely on this tension between narrative or choreographic sequence and unexpected visual displacement. The comic effect of Larionov's costume for the Merchant in *Chout* (No. 720 [R611]), for example, is generated by the fact that he is wearing his shirt both under and over his coat — and in an improbable array of colors and patterns. The emphatic arrangement of the ornamental fabrics, especially of the sash, reminiscent of Goncharova's *Costume Design for a Spanish Dancer* (ca. 1916, see No. 559 [R430]), helps to express what Goncharova and Larionov saw as the essential connection between "costume and movement, costume and the word":

> Le costume théâtral représente le signe particulier, le détail significatif contribuant à expliquer le personnage et ses possibilités; il aide à créer l'atmosphère voulue, avant même que l'interprète parle, danse ou chante. Il crée le grotesque par contraste, soutient par consonance, complique ou simplifie le geste ou le sens de la parole. C'est précisément là que se manifeste les rapports essentiels entre le costume et le mouvement, entre le costume et le verbe.[497]

697

Yurii Annenkov: *Portrait of Mikhail Larionov*, 1950. See No. 49 [R46].

697

697 [R590].
***Portrait of Natalia Goncharova*, ca. 1910.**
Pencil.
18⅞ x 14¾ in., 48 x 37.5 cm.
Provenance: Elisabeth Anderson-Ivantzova, New York, 1965.
Reproduced in D41, p. 275; F107, p.39; I14, p. 62.
The reverse carries the portrait of a soldier (No. 702 [R594]). Cf. No. 698 [R591].

Larionov as contributor:
700 [R593].
Designer unknown: Poster Advertising the "Donkey's Tail" Exhibition Moscow, 1912.
Black and white mechanical print on thin tan tissue paper.
11¾ x 39⅜ in., 30 x 100 cm.
Inscriptions (as part of the design) in Russian: "'Donkey's Tail.' Exhibition of paintings in the new exhibition building of the Institute of Painting, Sculpture and Architecture. Open 10 a.m. to 6 p.m. Entrance 50 kopecks, 25 kopecks for students. Participants: V.K. [= Yu.P.] Anisimov, V.S. Bart, S.P. Bobrov, V.D. Bubnova, N.S. Goncharova, A.S. Sdanevich [=K.S. Zdanevich], I.F. Larionov, M.F. Larionov, A.[=M.] V. Le-Dantiu, K.S. Malevich, V.I. Matvei, A.A. Morgunov, N.E. Rogovin, E.Ya. Sagaidachny, I.A. Skuie, V.E. Tatlin, A.V. Fon-Vizen, M. Chagall, A.V. Shevchenko, A.S. Yastrzhembsky and others. Printed by A.Z. Kiselev, Poliakov Building, corner of Tverskaia and Chernyshev Streets. Sent to press 6 March, 1912."
Provenance: Viktor Kholodkov, Moscow, 1989.
Reproduced in I60, p. 19; L22, Lot 638.

698

699

698 [R591].
Portrait of Natalia Goncharova, ca. 1930.
Pen and ink.
Initialed lower left: "M.L."
10¼ x 7⅞ in., 26 x 20 cm.
Provenance: Gregory Frumkin, London, August, 1971.
Reproduced in I20, p. 58; I51, No. 94. A similar drawing is reproduced under the title Head of a Young Girl and dated 1907 in W. George, Larionov (Paris: La Bibliothèque des arts, 1966, p. 42). This is one of many analogous pencil and pen portraits by Larionov of Goncharova done in the late 1920s and early 1930s, Cf. No. 697 [R590].

699 [R592].
Portrait of Vladimir Tatlin, ca. 1912.
Pen and ink.
5⅞ x 4¾ in., 15 x 12 cm.
Provenance: Nina Stevens, New York, July, 1979.
Reproduced in B60, p. 71; F107, p. 266; I20, p. 61; I51, No. 238; B104, p. 156; B183, p. 340. An almost identical version,

formerly in the collection of the late Nikolai Khardzhiev, Moscow, is reproduced in B217, Vol. 1, p. 283.

Note: Larionov and Tatlin were close friends ca. 1908-12. They both favored an artistic style dependent on primitive art forms and often contributed to the same exhibitions. Larionov made several portraits of Tatlin, including two oil paintings, i.e., the Portrait of Vladimir Tatlin in a Seaman's Blouse (1908, National Gallery of Australia, Canberra; reproduced in B60, p. 5) and the Rayonist Portrait of Vladimir Tatlin (1912 [?], Musée National d'Art Moderne, Paris; reproduced in B60, p. 39). Larionov drew No. 699 [R592] just when both artists (with Goncharova, Nikolai Rogovin, and Olga Rozanova) were contributing art works to the "Donkey's Tail" exhibition in Moscow in March-April, 1912 (see No. 700 [R593]), and illustrations to Alexei Kruchenykh's booklet Mirskontsa [World backwards] (Moscow) in December. The small pen and ink caricature portrait was a favorite discipline of the Russian Cubo-Futurists and there are striking parallels between this piece and contemporary portraits by the Burliuk brothers (Nos. 397-99 [R364-66]), Vladimir Maiakovsky, and Tatlin himself.

Note: Larionov founded his group, the Donkey's Tail, in December, 1911, after the incident at the "Salon des Indépendants" in Paris the year before, at which art students had shown a picture "painted" by a donkey under a fictional name. The critics had referred positively to the painting not knowing, of course, that it was the work of a donkey — whereupon the students revealed the identity of the "artist," much to the consternation of the critics. Larionov also liked to "shock the bourgeoisie" and, naturally, this incident appealed to him. In establishing his group, Larionov was reacting against what he felt was the academic tendency already manifested in his first group of 1910, i.e., the Jack of Diamonds. He explained:

> My task is not to affirm the new art because after that it would cease to be new, but as far as possible to try to move it forward… After organizing the "Jack of Diamonds" two years ago… I did not realize that under that name

would arise... such a popularization of works that have nothing in common either with the new art or with the old.[498]

The Donkey's Tail had one exhibition (11 March – 8 April, 1912) at MIPSA with nineteen participants (Bubnova, mentioned in the poster, did not contribute). The focus of attention was on Goncharova (56 works), Larionov (42), Kazimir Malevich (24), and Tatlin (44), and their experimental interpretations of Neo-Primitivism drew much comment — mostly negative — in the press.[499] Actually, as Varsonofii Parkin, the group's apologist, observed, "if it had not been for Larionov and Goncharova, the 'Donkey's Tail' would not have existed."[500] Certainly, they were the driving force and their exercises in "cinematography," "photography," and "immediate perception"[501] indicated that they were advancing further away from the static, measured forms of the Jack of Diamonds painters (e.g., of Robert Falk and Alexander Kuprin). It was shortly after the "Donkey's Tail" exhibition that Larionov promulgated his theory of Rayonism and painted his first Rayonist compositions — which he showed at his next group exhibition, the "Target," in March, 1913.

701

701 [NIRE].
Poster advertising the "Target" exhibition, Moscow, 24 March – 7 April, 1913.
Lithograph in dark brown on white paper.
27½ x 21¼ in., 70 x 54 cm.
Inscriptions (as part of the design) in Russian: "Open from 24 March to 7 April. "Target" exhibition of paintings; exhibition of Russian, Persian, and Japanese popular prints" followed by the list of participating artists: A.I. Abramov, Yu.P. Anisimov, S.P. Barov [=Bobrov], V.S. Bart, A.N. Beliaev, T.N. Bogomazov, Nataliia Goncharova, K.M.

[=K.S.] Zdanevich, I.F. Larionov, Mikhail Larionov, M.V. Le-Dantiu, V.V. Levkievsky, M. Mikhailov. K.S. Malevich, S.M. Romanovich, V.A. Obolensky, O.D. Olgina, E.Ya. Sagaidachny, I.A. Skuie, Niko Pirosmanashvili, T.E. Pavliuchenko, Morits Fabri, I.[=M] Chagall, A.V. Shevchenko, A.S. Yastrzhembsky, and others." Bottom line left: "Permitted for printing on 21 March, 1913," signed by Assistant Governor of Moscow Mr. Zakitin. Bottom right: Printers of the Moscow Imperial Theaters, by appointment to his Imperial Majesty, Skazov, and A.A. Levenson, Partners." Provenance: Viktor Kholodkov, Moscow, 1989.

Note: Larionov organized the "Target" exhibition at the Art Salon on Bolshaia Dmitrovka in downtown Moscow. On the eve of the opening, Larionov and his colleagues staged a public discussion at the Polytechnical Museum entitled "The East, National Identity, and the West" with lectures by Larionov on Rayonism, Ilia Zdanevich on Marinetti's Futurism, and Alexander Shevchenko on medieval Russian, Georgian, and Armenian painting.

The centerpiece of the "Target" exhibition was Larionov's contribution, which included major works such as *Seasons, Moldavian Venus, Jewish Venus, Provincial Girl,* as well as Rayonist paintings. Goncharova also sent a number of Rayonist works, including *Lilies* and *Cats.* The preface to the exhibition catalog, written by Larionov, announced thirteen key points:

1. Negative attitude to the praise of individualism.
2. Artworks must be taken into account without reference to author.
3. Granting a copy the status of an independent work of art.
4. Acknowledgement of all styles preceding us and of those which are being created right now such as Cubism, Futurism, and Orphism. We advocate every possible combination and mixing of styles. We have created our own style, "Rayonism," having to do with spatial forms and rendering the painting self-contained and subject to its own laws.
5. We gravitate towards the East and pay heed to traditional art.
6. We protest against enslavement to the West, which regurgitates to us our own Eastern forms in an arresting, if indiscriminate form.
7. We do not demand attention from society, but ask that we are not required to show it in return.
8. Above all, we value intensity of feeling and its lofty inspiration.
9. Above all, one must be good at what one does.
10. One must not reject anything.
11. Rejection must be for the sake of rejection, because this is closest to our cause.
12. We maintain that the whole world

— life, poetry, music, philosophy etc.
— is completely expressible through art forms.
13. We do not wish to form an artistic association, because in the past analogous institutions have led invariably to stagnation.[502]

In spite of such vociferousness, the number of visitors did not exceed 1500 and not a single work was sold.

702

702 [R594].
Portrait of a Soldier, ca. 1914.
Gouache with white paint in relief.
Initialed lower right: "M.L."
19¼ x 13¾ in., 49 x 35 cm.
The reverse carries a pencil portrait of Natalia Goncharova (No. 697 [R590]), painted probably in the late 1910s.
Provenance: Elisabeth Anderson-Ivantzova, New York, 1965.
Reproduced in F107, p. 284; M43 (c); M73, p. 92. A version is reproduced as the frontispiece to A. Blok: *The Twelve,* London: Chatto and Windus, 1920 (illustrations by Larionov).

Le Soleil de Nuit (Le Soleil de Minuit): ballet in one act based on a musical extract from Nikolai Rimsky-Korsakov's Snegurochka *with dances by Leonide Massine. Produced by Sergei Diaghilev for the Ballets Russes at the Grand Théâtre, Geneva, on 20 December, 1915, with choreography by Leonide Massine and designs by Mikhail Larionov.*

The ballet has no developed plot and consists of a sequence of Russian dances arranged after the scene of the returning Sun in Snegurochka *(see No. 33 [R32]). The characters — the Midnight Sun, the Snow Maiden, Bobyl, peasants, buffoons, etc. — are taken from Russian folklore.*

703

703 [122; R595].
Stage Design with Group of Dancers and Mask on Floor, 1915.
Watercolor and pencil.
Signed and dated lower right in red ink: "M. Larionow 915."
24⅞ x 30⅞ in., 63.3 x 78.6 cm.
Other inscriptions: lower right in pencil over red paint: "Soleil de Minuit"; lower left in pencil: "L. Massine dans le Ballet Soleil de Minuit donné pour la lère fois en 1915 à l'Opéra National de Paris au profit de la Croix Rouge Anglaise"; on reverse in red pencil "M. Larionov, No. 2, Ballet 'Soleil de Minuit'" together with Larionov's address, 16 rue Jacques Callot, Paris 6, and a French Customs stamp.
Provenance: John Carr-Doughty, Leicester, 3 November, 1981.
Reproduced in F107, p. 423; I51, No. 138; I77, pp. 126 and 143; I117, p. 357; M179; N112, p. 58; N128 (b); P17; program for 36. Berliner Festwochen 86. Magazin, W. Berlin, 1986, p. 31. Some of the variants of this piece have been reproduced, e.g., in D1, unpaginated; G51, p. 115; George, Larionov, pp. 97 and 127; K50 (b), unnumbered. Larionov made many individual sketches for the figures in the group, e.g., for the Sun, in the Wadsworth Atheneum (reproduced in color in G43, No. 43). For a color reproduction of Massine's magnificent costume see G58, p. 41; for documentary photographs see C7, Nos. 163, 168, 169; D51, p. 101.

704

704 [123; R596].
Costume Design for a Young Peasant Girl, 1915.
Watercolor over pencil.
Signed with the initials: "M.L."
12 x 9 in., 30.5 x 22.7 cm.
Other inscriptions: upper left: "Soleil de minuit Tina"; upper right: "Lausanne 1915."
Provenance: Ballet and Theatre Material, London: Sotheby's, 28 May, 1985, Lot 71 (reproduced).
Reproduced in color in I77, p. 68; and in

black and white in A34, p. 250; I77, p.126; I117, p. 357; M93; and Parton, Mikhail Larionov, p. 152.
The word "Tina" or "Cina" might be a reference to Nemtchinova who danced one of the peasant girls (see note below). However, according to the dancer Alexandra Danilova, Nemtchinova was not known by either of these nicknames. Danilova further recalls that, in performing this part, Nemtchinova wore a headdress different from the one in this design.[503]

Note: Le Soleil de Nuit marked an important milestone in the history of the Ballets Russes since it brought together for the first time three newcomers to Diaghilev's enterprise, i.e., Massine, Larionov, and the conductor Ernest Ansermet. Massine and Larionov enjoyed a particularly harmonious collaboration during their preparations for the ballet in Lausanne in 1915 — one result of this was Larionov's portrait of the choreographer (No. 706 [R598]). In turn, Le Soleil de Nuit also marked Diaghilev's move away from the well tried decorative principles of Léon Bakst and Alexandre Benois to more avant-garde methods represented by Goncharova, Larionov, and, later, Naum Gabo and Georgii Yakulov.[504] With Massine (holding the suns on the left in No. 703 [R595]) as the Sun, Nikolai Zverev (on the right) as Bobyl, and Nemtchinova (in the center) as one of the peasant girls, Le Soleil de Nuit scored a remarkable success at its premiere in Geneva and then at its French premiere at the Théâtre National de l'Opéra, Paris, on 29 December, 1915 — all the more surprising when we remember that this was Massine's first public choreography and Larionov's first independent ballet interpretation.

705 [R597].
Costume Design for a Dancer in Movement, 1915.
Gouache.
Signed and dated lower right in black ink: "M. Larionov / 915."
20 x 13 in., 51 x 33 cm.
Provenance: Ballet and Theatre Material, London: Sotheby's, 6 June, 1979, within Lot 160 (reproduced).
Reproduced in color in B115, plate 49; F107, p. 285; and in black and white in I51, No. 139; I61, p. 228; I77, p. 126; M76; R16; and as a gouache/silkscreen in N. Goncharova and M. Larionov: L'Art Décoratif Théâtral Moderne (Paris: La Cible, 1919; see Nos. 559, 562 [R430, R431]), where it is entitled Equilibre de Danse; reproduced in color in C7, plate 176, where it is entitled Movement. Also see the version in the Dance Collection of the New York Public Library at Lincoln Center, New York (reproduced in I15, no. 487), the one in the collection of the Museum of Modern Art, New York, which is dated 1916 and entitled Dance Balance (reproduced in M. Chamot, Goncharova [London: Oresko, 1979], p. 16), and the gouache entitled Study of Movement reproduced in color in

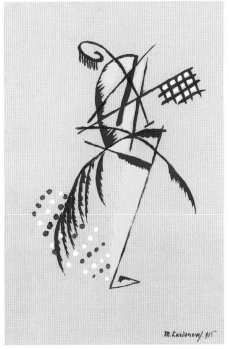

705

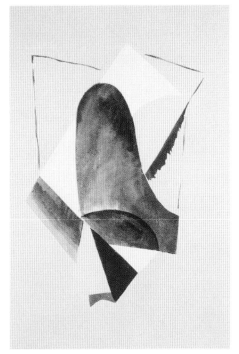

706

707

708

K160, p. 27. Two pieces analogous to the design here were auctioned at J30, Lot 266, and L2, Lot 41; also see J46, Lot 130; and a drawing called *Head* from the collection of the Museum of Modern Art, New York, is reproduced in *Novoe Russkoe Slovo,* New York, 1983, 29 November, p. 4.

Note: Larionov produced this design when he and Massine were working on the ballet *Soleil de Nuit* (see Nos 703, 704 [R595, R596]), and, when, through Larionov, Massine "first came to understand the true nature of these old ritual peasant dances."[505] Massine had already collaborated with Goncharova earlier that year on *Liturgie* and had posed for his portrait by her (published in the Goncharova / Larionov *Album de 14 Portraits Théâtraux* in 1916; see No. 561 [NIRE]); and the following year he and Larionov also collaborated on the production of the *Contes Russes*. Larionov at this time was still full of the Rayonist ideas that he had first formulated in Moscow in 1912, and both this portrait and the actual stage designs of the same period incorporate the "spatial forms that can arise from the intersection of the reflected rays of different objects."[506]

706 [124; R598].
Stage Mask: Portrait of Leonide Massine, 1916.
Gouache and black ink.
Signed and dated lower right in black ink: "M. Larionov / 916."
20 x 13 in., 51 x 33 cm.
Provenance: *Ballet and Theatre Material,* London: Sotheby's, 6 June, 1979, within Lot 160.
Reproduced in color in B115, plate 50; and in black and white in I51, No. 140; I61, p. 229; I77, p. 129; M36; and as a gouache/silkscreen in N. Goncharova and

Larionov, *L'Art Décoratif Théâtral Moderne* (Paris: La Cible, 1919; see Nos. 559, 562 [R430, R431]); reproduced in color in C7, plate 175; a version is also reproduced in black and white in C7, plate 173, where it is described as a light and shadow theatrical mask. A number of drawings for the *Stage Mask* are in the TG and there exist several versions of the design, some of which carry the name of Massine, being described as portraits of Massine. Also see J44, Lot 88. A gouache painting incorporating similar shapes is in a private collection and is reproduced in Chamot and Gray, *A Retrospective Exhibition of Painting and Designs for the Theatre. Larionov and Gontcharova,* No. 42.

Histoires Naturelles: *ballet by Jules Renard reworked by Mikhail Larionov and Michel Fokine with music by Maurice Ravel. Prepared by Larionov in Rome in 1917 with his designs, rehearsed, but not produced. Some of the designs entered the folio compiled by N. Goncharova and M. Larionov,* L'Art Décoratif Théâtral Moderne *(Paris: La Cible, 1919).*

707 [NIRE].
Costume Design for a Swan, ca. 1917.
Two-color engraving.
19¾ x 12¾ in., 50 x 33 cm.
Signed upper left in the plate: "M. Larionov".
Provenance: *Ballet and Theatre Material,* London: Sotheby's, 6 June, 1979, within Lot 160.
Reproduced in Goncharova and Larionov, *L'Art Décoratif Théâtral Moderne.* The original gouache for this so-called Mechanical Costume, formerly in the collection of the late Alexandra Tomilina, Paris, is reproduced in G49, p. 159.

708 [125; R599].
Costume Design for a Peacock, ca. 1917.
Gouache/silkscreen.
Signed lower right: "M. Larionow"; monogram stamp lower left.
20 x 13 in., 51 x 33 cm.
Provenance: Georges Yakoubovsky, Paris, 1968 (Yakoubovsky, Larionov's framer, lived at 18, rue Guenegaud, close to 16, rue Jacques Callot, the Paris home of Goncharova and Larionov).
Reproduced in Goncharova and Larionov, *L'Art Décoratif Théâtral Moderne.* The original gouache for this so-called Mechanical Costume, formerly in the collection of the late Alexandra Tomilina, Paris, and now in the TG, is reproduced in G49, p. 159.

709

Lot 267, and carried the additional data: "Rayonist Portrait of Catherine Devilliers" (cf. No. 559 [R430]).

Note: The original gouache carries indications to the effect that this is a mechanical costume set in motion principally by the voice and also through small springs. Pierre Bertin was to have taken the role of the peacock or what Larionov later called "The Modern Man."[507]

709 [R600].
Costume Design for a Cricket, ca. 1917.
Gouache/silkscreen.
19½ x 12⅝ in., 49.7 x 32.2 cm.
Provenance: Robert Brown, New York, December 1969.
Reproduced in Goncharova and Larionov, *L'Art Décoratif Théâtral Moderne.* The original gouache for this so-called Mechanical Costume, formerly in the collection of the late Alexandra Tomilina, Paris, is reproduced in G49, p. 159. A preliminary drawing for the *Cricket* is in the collection of the TG; the pencil and watercolor original for this gouache/silkscreen, in the collection of the Victoria and Albert Museum, London, is reproduced in B. Reade: *Ballet Designs and Illustrations 1881-1940,* London: Her Majesty's Stationery Office, 1967, plate 144.

Note: Larionov referred to this image as "The Social Cricket" — "a satirical drawing expressing the artist's reaction to what he terms the 'megalomania of modern society' and his conception of the bacteria of the brain."[508] Massine was to have taken the role of the cricket. Valentin Parnakh wrote in the context of these "natural history" designs:

> Des clowns maquillés, des jongleurs, des filles roses et bleues sur les trapèzes. Mouvements adroits. Les costumes sont mécaniques. On les met en mouvement par l'éléctricité. Les décors en relief sont faits de fer blanc, de ciment et peints au rispolin.[509]

Note: Larionov's design for a *Lady with Fans* is typical of his style of 1915-16 and relates closely to concurrent designs, especially to his costume for the Peacock in the same ballet.[510] Although Larionov's dynamic composition derives in part from his experiments with Rayonism in 1912-14, it also brings to mind the contemporary work of the Italian Futurists Fortunato Depero and Gino Severini. Depero did not establish a working relationship with the Ballets Russes until 1916, when Diaghilev commissioned him to design a "scena plastica e costumi meccanici" for a production of *Chant du Rossignol* (not realized). Giovanni Lista describes this project as follows:

> Utilisant cartons colorés, fil de fer et autres matériaux, Depero construit la plus grande partie de la scène et plusieurs costumes plastiques que Massine essaie avec enthousiasme. La scène apparaît comme une gigantesque flore tropicale cristallisée, avec éléments mécaniques et fluorescents, feuilles de six mètres, campanules diversement stylisées (d'où, semble-t-il, devait sortir la musique), formes suspendues, tiges rouges et jaunes qui se terminent par des couronnes d'épines de toutes couleurs, etc.[511]

Like Gino Severini, Depero was interested in the theme of the dance, drawing and painting works such as *Ballerina* (1915) and *Futurista – Movimento d'Uccelo* (1916).[512] The latter is especially close to Larionov's *Lady with Fans,* an apparent borrowing that Depero himself was quick to notice:

> After arranging them in his own manner, the painter Larionov published my designs in the album "Russian Theater. Gontcharova and Larionov," plagiarizing them completely.[513]

Although Larionov tended to cast aspersions on Italian Futurism, he was interested in its principles and admired its representatives. For example, a banquet was given in Larionov's honor by Filippo Marinetti when Larionov, Goncharova, and other Diaghilev associates were working in Rome in the late spring of 1917.

The lady in *Lady with Fans* is, no doubt, Catherine Devillier (Devilliers). Diaghilev had invited her to dance in the projected *Histoires Naturelles* and *España* (see No. 559 [R430]) and, presumably, Larionov portrayed her in the costume while she was rehearsing in Lausanne.

710

710 [126; R601].
Costume Design for a Lady with Fans, ca. 1916.
Watercolor and pencil.
Signed lower left: "M. Larionow" and initialed lower right "M-L."
13½ x 9⅞ in., 34.3 x 25 cm.
Provenance: Vladimir Hessen, New York, October, 1976.
Reproduced in color in B115, plate 48; F107, p. 266; I51, p. 12; I77, p. 80; I117, p. 153; N13, p. 121; and in black and white in I40, No. 79; I51, No. 141; I77, p. 134; I117, p. 358; N17; and Parton, *Mikhail Larionov,* p. 160; a drawing for this was auctioned at J16, Lot 728a (where it was misattributed as a design for *Contes Russes*); a pencil and gouache version was auctioned at J30,

711

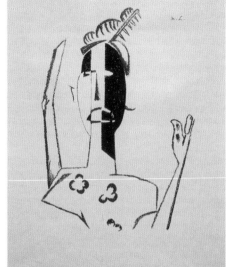

712

Contes Russes: *three choreographic miniatures with an epilogue and danced interludes by Leonide Massine. Music by Anatolii Liadov with a prelude and lament orchestrated by Arnold Bax. Produced by Sergei Diaghilev's Ballets Russes at the Théâtre du Châtelet, Paris, on 11 May, 1917, with choreography by Leonide Massine assisted by Mikhail Larionov and designs by Mikhail Larionov.*

A street vendor comes onto the stage carrying two puppets — the witch Kikimora and her cat. The first scene shows how the evil Kikimora kills her faithful cat. The second scene concerns Bova Korolevich, who rides the breadth of Russia to conquer evil; he beheads a dangerous beast, frees the Swan Princess, brings her back to life, and goes on his way. The third scene concerns the witch — the Baba-Yaga — who wants to eat a little girl lost in the forest, but the girl makes the sign of the cross and the evil forces disappear. The conclusion is a Russian feast and dance.

711 [127; R602].
Design for Backdrop for the Haunted Forest, the Home of the Witch Baba-Yaga, 1916.
Watercolor.
Signed upper left in blue paint: "M. Larionov" and signed and dated lower right in pencil: "M. Larionov, 1916."
10¼ x 16⅛ in., 26 x 41 cm.
Other inscriptions: on reverse in pencil: "Contes Russes, Rideau de Fond, 1916", plus French customs stamp.
Provenance: *Arts Anciens,* Geneva: Sotheby's, November 28, 1983, Lot 307 (reproduced).
Reproduced in color in B115, plate 47; G70; I117, p. 358; M23; and in black and white in L2, Lot 49; a similar design, entitled *Rayonnisme Rouge* and dated 1915, is reproduced in *Larionov.* Catalog of exhibition at the Acquavella Galleries, New York, April-May, 1969, No. 41.

712 [R603].
Make-up Design for Kikimora, ca. 1916.
Engraving in two colors.
Initialed upper right in the plate: "M.L.".
19⅝ x 12¾ in., 50 x 32.5 cm.
Provenance: *Ballet and Theatre Material,* London: Sotheby's, 6 June, 1979, within Lot 160.
Reproduced on many occasions, e.g., in M76. There exist several versions of this; see, for example, the reproductions in D1, unpaginated; G22, p. 81.

713 [R604].
Detail for the Magic Pool in Scene 3, ca. 1916.
Gouache/silkscreen.
Initialed lower right in the plate: "M.L.".
19⅝ x 13 in., 50 x 33 cm.
Provenance: *Ballet and Theatre Material,* London: Sotheby's, 6 June, 1979, within Lot 160.

Note: Both these images (Nos. 712, 713 [R603, R604]) were reproduced in *L'Art Décoratif Théâtral Moderne,* Paris: La Cible, 1919, under different titles.

Diaghilev gave a presentation of one of the miniatures from *Contes Russes,* i.e., *Kikimora,* at the Teatro Eugenia Victoria, San Sebastián in August, 1916, with Maria Shabelska in the title role (for some information see D26, p. 315). However, the entire set — this picture of "pagan Russian violence"[514] — was produced as an ensemble for the first time in May, 1917, in Paris. With Lydia Sokolova (Kikimora), Liubov Tchernicheva (the Swan Princess), Leon Woizikowsky (the Street Vendor), Stanislas Idzikowski (the Cat), and Nicholas Kremnev (the Baba-Yaga), the *Contes*

713

Russes was a "young" ballet, full of vitality and energy, and a long way from the staid elegance of Le Pavillon d'Armide or Giselle. Sokolova recalled:

> The work held the very essence of Russian folklore; I loved dancing the ferocious and hideous witch Kikimora, with her blue-striped face, who made her cat rock in her cradle and then in a fury chopped off its head with an axe.[515]

Massine experienced difficulties organizing his choreographical structure, but, helped by Larionov, he managed to "clear away much of the excess movement."[516] In any case, he was pleased with the sets and costumes, some of which had been commissioned by Diaghilev from Depero, but which Diaghilev had then rejected.[517] Massine praised the Larionov designs as

> among his most delightful creations, the elements of Russian folk-art being even more cleverly adapted than in Soleil de Nuit. Kikimora's cottage, with its canary-yellow walls and bulging green stove, had all the naive charm of a child's painting, and the cradle, decorated with huge sunflowers, added the right touch of grotesque fantasy to the composition.[518]

For his resolution of the costumes and sets, Larionov relied substantially on his latest stylistic discovery, Rayonism, which he had invented in Moscow in 1912-13 and according to which:

> if we wish to paint literally what we see, then we must paint the sum of rays reflected from the object. But in order to receive the total sum of rays from the desired object, we must select them deliberately — because together with the rays of the object being perceived, there also fall into our range of vision reflected reflex rays belonging to other objects... and then we will depict literally what we see.[519]

While Rayonism (as can be seen from No. 713 [R604]) had apparent cross-references with Franz Marc, Lyonel Feininger, and the Italian Futurists, the upsurge of interest in photography and cinematography in Russia at this time provided an undoubted stimulus to Larionov's concern with light rays and velocity. Whatever their stylistic derivation, Larionov's designs, colorful, angular, and abrasive, were a perfect match for the violent narrative of the ballet.

La Marche Funèbre sur La Mort de la Tante à Héritage: *musical composition by Lord Berners projected for a so-called Théâtre des Ombres Colorées, Paris, in 1919, with designs by Mikhail Larionov.*

One of a set of three satirical funeral marches ("pour un homme d'état, pour un canari, pour une tante à héritage") using colored shadows and dolls that poked fun at war and the military spirit.

714

714 [R605].
Design for a Personage, ca. 1919.
Gouache/silkscreen.
Signed upper left in the plate: "M. Larionov."
20 x 13 in., 51 x 33 cm.
Provenance: Sabine Zlatin, Paris, June, 1966.

715 [R606].
Design for the Kingfisher, ca. 1919.
Gouache/silkscreen.
Signed lower left in the plate: "M. Larionov."
19½ x 12¾ in., 49.7 x 32.2 cm.
Provenance: Robert Brown, New York, December, 1969.

715

Note: Both these images (Nos. 714, 715 [R605, R606]) were reproduced in *L'Art Décoratif Théâtral Moderne,* Paris: La Cible, 1919 and, according to Valentin Parnakh's explanation there, formed part of Larionov's invention, i.e., "le théâtre des ombres colorées, des poupées plates pour la musique de Lord Berners."[520] In subsequent literature, this "théâtre des ombres colorées" became capitalized as if it had been a real theater, but strong evidence suggests that Larionov's "invention" was simply a performance piece involving colors and shadows. In any case, the project coincided with the exhibition of works by Goncharova and Larionov at the Galerie Barbazanges, Paris, open in June and July of 1919. According to Anthony Parton:

> On the 18th, 20th and 24th June 1919 Pierre Bertin (for whom Larionov designed the mechanical *Peacock* costume in *L'Art Decoratif Theatral Moderne*) organized two concerts and a literary afternoon at the Galerie in conjunction with the exhibition. We know that Lord Berners' music was on the programmes for these events and so it has always seemed to me that Larionov might have mounted a shadow performance to accompany the playing of his compositions. However, there was also a soirée of music, dance and poetry at the Galerie Barbazanges on 12th July, 1919, for which Larionov designed the poster and this, too, might have proved a suitable venue for the production.[521]

Larionov and Lord Gerald Berners benefited from a strong creative alliance, Larionov even caricaturing him (see J4, Lot 199). Diaghilev introduced Goncharova and Larionov to Lord Berners in Rome in 1917.

Chout: *choreographic pantomime in six scenes with music by Sergei Prokofiev based on a legend interpreted by Mikhail Larionov. Produced by Sergei Diaghilev for the Ballets Russes at Théâtre de la Gaité-Lyrique, Paris, on 17 May, 1921, with choreography by Mikhail Larionov and Thadée Slavinsky, and designs by Mikhail Larionov.*

Chout, *subtitled "How One Young Buffoon Deceived Seven Old Buffoons and a Stupid Merchant," is a riotous farce about a village buffoon who plays tricks on his fellow buffoons. The village buffoon, the young hero, pretends to stab his wife and bring her back to life with a magic whip, whereupon the other buffoons buy the whip. But, after killing their wives and trying in vain to revive them by the whip, they try to avenge themselves on the charlatan. The situation is saved by the hero's wife, who disguises him as a nursemaid, and by the merchant who pays the damages.*

716

717

716 [128; R607].
Stage Design for Scene I, ca 1921.
Gouache.
Signed lower right in brown gouache: "M. Larionov."
19⅝ x 27⅛ in., 50 x 69 cm.
Provenance: Robert Kashey, New York, 1972. Reproduced in color in A34, p. 25; B88, p. 40; B115, plate 57; B122, p. 262; G99, p. 178; I61, p. 234; F107, p. 423; I127, p. 256; I117, p. 362; M23, p. 55, N156, p. 79; and on the Melodiia record sleeve of "The USSR Ministry of Culture Orchestra Conducted by Gennadii Rozhdestvensky, Playing Sergei Prokofiev's *Chout*," 1987; in

black and white in I67, p. 56; I77, p. 134; M87; N112, p. 56; N122; Q9.

Note: The design shows the interior of the house of the Young Buffoon (danced by Thadée Slavinsky) who has "revived" his wife (danced by Lydia Sokolova). The seven Old Buffoons (Errol Addison, Anatole Bourman, Jamoujinsky, Nicholas Kremnev, Lukin [Leighton Lucas], Nicolas Mikolaichik, and Okhimovsky) are begging him to sell them his "magic" whip with which he has "revived" his wife. For a documentary photograph closely related to this design see I42, p. 103.

717 [129; R608].
Stage Design for Scene V: The Bedroom, 1915.
Watercolor and gouache on board.
Signed and dated lower left: "M. Larionov 1915."
19⅛ x 25¼ in., 48.5 x 64 cm.
Provenance: *Dance, Theatre, Opera, Cabaret*, New York: Sotheby, Parke Bernet, 6 December, 1979, Lot 62 (reproduced). Reproduced in color in B88, p. 40; B115, plate 53; D41, p. 206; G49, plate 292; G99, pp. 168, 169; I67, p. 46; I68, p. 8; I117, p. 365; J22, Lot 62; and in black and white in I77, p. 135; M86; P12; R16; R19. A version is reproduced in color in I42, No. 285.

Note: The design shows the bedroom to which the Rich Merchant takes his newly chosen bride. She turns out to be the Young Buffoon disguised as a cook. In order to avoid being found out, the bride tells the merchant that she feels unwell and asks him to let her out via the window.

718 [R609].
Costume Design for an Old Buffoon, 1915.
Watercolor.
Signed and dated lower left: "M. Larionow / 915."
22 x 15 in., 56 x 38 cm.
Other inscription: upper right: "no. 2/7" (i.e., the second of the seven buffoons).
Provenance: private transaction.
Reproduced in color in B115, plate 56; D1, p. 207; G99, p. 179; and in black and white in G49, p. 161; I41, No. 77; I51, No. 142; I61, p. 232; I117, p. 363; and George, *Larionov*, p. 127. There are several versions of this costume — see D17, p. 157; G20, 136; sketches for three of the seven buffoons were auctioned in 1969 at J5, Lot 172, and then again in 1976 at J16, Lot 713. For a photograph of a dancer wearing this costume see C7, fig. 170.

718

719

719 [R610].
***Costume Design for One of the Two
Grooms, 1915.***
Watercolor, pencil, and collage.
Signed and dated upper left: "M. Larionov
1915."
21¼ x 15 in., 54 x 38.2 cm.
Provenance: *Dance, Theatre, Opera,
Music-Hall and Film. Décor and Costume
Designs, Books, Posters and Photographs,*
New York: Sotheby's, 15 December, 1981,
Lot 50 (reproduced).
Reproduced in color in B115, plate 55; and
in black and white in I77, p. 135; L2, Lot 50.

720 [130, R611].
Costume Design for the Merchant, 1921.
Gouache and pencil.
Signed and dated lower right: "M. Larionow
1921."
19⅝ x 14½ in., 50 x 37 cm.
Other inscriptions: upper left: "à mon cher ami
Micha S.W. 27"; lower left: "Michel Larionow,
maquette pour le ballet Chout 1921."
Provenance: private transaction.
Reproduced in color in B115, plate 54; and
in black and white in B88, p. 41; I40, No. 80;
I51, No. 143; I77, p. 135; I117, p. 363; a
similar costume is in the collection of the
Victoria and Albert Museum, London, and
is reproduced in color in George, *Larionov,*
p. 99, and in black and white in G36, p. 36;
another variant is reproduced in G19, p. 30.

Note: Larionov's designs for *Chout* carry
variously the dates 1915 or 1921. This
discrepancy can be explained by the fact that
his original projects for *Chout* date from 1915,
when Diaghilev commissioned Prokofiev to
compose the music and when Massine
began to give thought to the choreographic
sequence for the new ballet. Due to the
privations of the First World War, it was not
until 1921 that Diaghilev staged *Chout,*
although by then Massine had married Vera

Savina, had formed his own company, and
gone off to South America, causing Diaghilev
to dismiss him in January, 1921. Consequently, Diaghilev asked Larionov to be
choreographic consultant to Thadée Slavinsky,
whom Diaghilev appointed as principal
choreographer for *Chout.* On 15 March, 1921
Larionov was hired officially by Diaghilev and
started to work on the scheduled production.
As he wrote to Diaghilev on 24 March, 1921:

> I've studied *Chout* and learned it by
> heart. I've bought a big new notebook
> and am busy working out entrances
> and dance figures. The whole of Chout
> is in my head, ready to be staged. It's
> exhausting to keep it there![522]

Combining his interest in primitive art —
especially in the *lubok* — and his Rayonist
ideas, Larionov produced sets and costumes
that were at once vulgar and sophisticated,
"popular art in a renewed and vigorous
form."[523] However, from a practical standpoint, Larionov's costumes were unwieldy
and Diaghilev was forced to threaten the
dancers with penalties in order to make them
dance in clothes that interfered with the very
movements of their dancing. Even though
Diaghilev spoke of *Chout* in laudatory terms,
referring to its "new principle" and "highest
modernity,"[524] it had a cool reception in both
Paris and in London (where *Chout* was
performed on 9 June, 1921), causing the
critic of the *Times* to observe that "one
hardly finds in it a touch of that art which has
made the Diaghilev ballet famous throughout
Europe and beyond it."[525] Still, to a
considerable extent, *Chout* marked a new
departure in Diaghilev's ballet endeavor, for
thereafter his productions became increasingly experimental as he gave attention
to new composers, to Constructivism, to
untried choreographic systems, and to new
dancers (Slavinsky and his wife, Catherine

720

Devilliers, danced the main roles in *Chout).*
For Larionov, this period was a happy one, a
mood reflected in the "exclusive vitality and
saturation of color, in the distinctive
dynamism"[526] of his designs both for *Chout*
and for *Le Renard.*

Le Renard: *ballet burlesque with voices in
one act by Igor Stravinsky based on a
Russian folk tale adapted by Charles
Ferdinand Ramuz. Produced by Sergei
Diaghilev for the Ballets Russes at the
Théâtre National de l'Opéra, Paris, on 18
May, 1922, with choreography by Bronislava
Nijinska and designs by Mikhail Larionov.*

*A cock is fooled by a sly and greedy
fox. After some narrow escapes, the cock
is deplumed, but he outwits the fox and is
granted safe haven by a cat and a goat.*

721

721 [131; R612].
Stage Design, ca. 1922.
Gouache.
Initialed lower left in brown gouache: "M.L."
6¾ x 9½ in., 17 x 24 cm.
Provenance: private transaction.
Reproduced in color in I41, No. 79; N188, p. 28; and in black and white in I51, No. 144; I77, p. 135; and Parton, *Mikhail Larionov*, p. 190. There are several versions of this design, the more so since Larionov repeated sketches for the 1929 production and often failed to date them. One version is reproduced in the Souvenir Program for the *Ballets Russes à l'Opéra*, Paris, 1922, May-June, unpaginated; another version, in a private collection in Paris, is reproduced in I15, fig. 357; another, formerly in the collection of Boris Kochno, is reproduced in I18, fig. 105; another one is reproduced in George, *Larionov*, p. 127; another was auctioned in 1979 at J22, Lot 15; also see G49, p. 160; I63, p. 26; and J41, Lot 349. There are several drawings for this design: see, for example, J12, Lot 26; J15, Lot 62; an entire group of designs pertaining to *Le Renard* is reproduced together in D13, pp. 66-67. For photographs of the actual set on stage see G12, No. 14; D3, plate 44; D10, p. 90; I42, p.111.

722 [132; R613].
Costume Design for the Fox Disguised as a Beggar Woman, ca. 1922.
Gouache.
Initialed and dated lower right: "921 M.L."; signed upper left "M. Larionow."
20 x 14 in., 51 x 35.5 cm.
Other inscriptions: left upper margin: "Opera Nationale, Paris 1921, Role a La Nijinska, Paysanne"; top right: "Coton"; on reverse in Russian: "To V.N. Bashkirov from M. Larionov" (a reference to the businessman and collector, Vladimir

723

Nikolaevich Bashkirov [Bashkiroff], 1886-1969).
Provenance: Irina Bashkiroff, New York, April, 1970.
Reproduced in color in B115, plate 51; F107, p. 146; and in black and white in I51, No. 145; I77, p. 135; I117, p. 371; N91, p. 137. An identical design, lacking the description in the left margin, described as a costume for a peasant girl and ascribed to the collection of the Museum of Modern Art, New York, is reproduced in G21, plate 8; another version is in the collection of the Victoria and Albert Museum, London, and is reproduced in G36, fig. 147; another version is reproduced in D15, p. 87; yet another is reproduced in D17, p. 178.

723 [133; R614].
Costume Design for the Fox Disguised as a Nun, ca. 1922.
Gouache and pencil.
Signed upper right: "M. Larionow."
18¼ x 10 in., 46.5 x 25.5 cm.
Provenance: Mendes Synek, Paris, August, 1969.
Reproduced in color as the back cover to G24; F107, p. 146; I117, p. 371; and in black and white in I51, No. 146; I77, p. 135; and the Souvenir Program of the *Ballets Russes à l'Opéra*, Paris, 1922, May-June, unpaginated; I51, No. 146. A very similar piece is in the collection of the Museum of Modern Art, New York, and is reproduced in G21, plate 9; another version, in a private collection in Paris, is reproduced in I7, p. 62; yet another version, formerly in the

collection of Boris Kochno, is reproduced in D17, p. 177; yet another was auctioned in 1979 at J22, Lot 4; drawings for the designs were auctioned in 1978 at J20, Lots 43 and 49; a variant with the Fox facing the other way is in the Harvard College Library and is reproduced in I9, p. 25. Larionov also drew portraits of Bronislava Nijinska in the part of the Fox and Stanislas Idzikowski in the part of the Cock (see J12, Lot 27).

724 [134; R615].
Costume Design for the Rooster, ca. 1922.
Watercolor and black ink.
Initialed lower left and signed above this in pencil: "M. Larionov."
19¼ x 13 in., 49 x 33 cm.
Other inscriptions: upper right in pencil: instructions to the dressmaker; the reverse upper right: "Idzikowsky"; lower left carries two customs seals reading "Douane Centrale, Paris."
Provenance: *Ballet and Theatre Material*, London: Sotheby's, 6 June, 1979, Lot 23a (ex catalogue).
Reproduced in color in B115, plate 52; I77, p. 69; I117, p. 371; and in black and white in I51, No. 147; I77, p. 135; J12, Lot 24. Another costume for the Rooster is in the collection of Robert L. B. Tobin, San Antonio, and is reproduced in I43, fig. 53; a similar design is in the collection of The Fine Arts Museum of San Francisco, and is reproduced in I44, fig. 74; a drawing for this design was auctioned in 1979 at J22, Lot 18.

Note: Le Renard marked the last collaboration between Diaghilev and Larionov, except for the modified revival of the same ballet in 1929. Although Larionov helped Léopold Survage paint his designs for *Mavra* late in May, 1922, Larionov, with his Russian ingenuousness, seems to have appealed less and less to Diaghilev. Favoring more

722

724

SALLE BULLIER
31 avenue de l'Observatoire

Le Vendredi 23 Février 1923

GRAND BAL
TRA VESTI NSMENTAL

Organisé par l'Union des Artistes Russes
au profit de la caisse de secours des artistes

FOIRE DE NUIT

Chars, Encombrement des rues — Elections
de Reines, — Gigolos et Gigolettes — Femmes à
barbe — Manège de cochons, — Jeux de massacre
Fœtus à 4 têtes, — Sirènes et dadaïstes mytholo-
giques — originales en chair et en fil de fer, incassa-
bles, ininflammables, assurées contre les accidents du
travail, pouvant être mises entre les mains de tous
les enfants.

Défense de se pencher dehors et de toucher aux
objets exposés.

Gontcharova et sa boutique de masques, — Delaunay
et sa Compagnie Transatlantique de pickpockets,
Larionow et son Rayonnisme — Léger et son orches-
tre-décor. — Iliazde et ses accès de fièvre au 41e
degré, — Mme Widopff et sa poupée dansant sur une
corde. — André Lewinson et ses vedettes. — Marie
Wassilieff et ses poupons, — Serge Romoff ami des
pauvres. — Tristan Tzara et ses oiseaux gras, —
Nina Peyne et son Jazz-Band — Puscin et ses danses du ventre inédites. — Lizica Codréano dans la
chorégraphie de Larionow. Galerie des écrivains pré-
sentée par Iliade. Baraque des poètes où l'on vend
des poèmes au mètre.

725

5230

726

sophisticated artists such as Naum Gabo and Georgii Yakulov, Diaghilev remained a personal friend of Larionov and Goncharova until the very end, and it is perhaps fitting that one of the last spectacles under Diaghilev's jurisdiction was the second production of Le Renard with modified designs by Larionov and a new choreography by Serge Lifar at the Théâtre Sarah-Bernhardt, Paris on 21 May 1929. According to one source, Diaghilev originally gave the design commission for Le Renard to Sergei Sudeikin and the choreography to Larionov,[527] but Sudeikin would hardly have managed to produce such a vivid and original resolution as Larionov for the 1922 production and for the "Constructivist" interpretation of 1929.[528] Thanks to the innovative character of the entire presentation — Stravinsky's music, the four singers in the orchestra pit, the folkloristic designs, and the complex choreographic sequences danced by Bronislava Nijinska (the Fox) and Stanislas Idzikowski (the Cock) — Le Renard scored a remarkable success on both occasions. Even the demure Serge Grigoriev, who directed the first performance, was prompted to speak of the ballet's "charme et la naiveté [qui] me plurent beaucoup."[529]

Grand Bal des Artistes; *also known as* **Grand Bal Travesti Transmental:** *charity ball organized by Natalia Goncharova, Mikhail Larionov, et al. for the Union des Artistes Russes at the Salle Bullier, Paris, on 23 February, 1923, with publicity designs by Natalia Goncharova and Mikhail Larionov.*

725 [R616].
Double-sided Playbill Announcing The Grand Bal Travesti Transmental, 1923.
Lithograph in brown on green paper.
Signed in the plate under the design: "M.

Larionov."
19¾ x 5¼ in., 50.3 x 13.2 cm.
Other inscriptions (as part of the design): under the design in the lower half: "Salle Bullier, 31 Ave. de l'Observatoire, le vendredi 23 février 1923 Grand Bal Travesti Transmental organisé par l'Union des Artistes Russes au profit de la caisse de secours des artistes." There then follows a long description of the various attractions and performers at the Ball.
Provenance: Drouot-Richelieu, Aguttes Auction House, Paris, 2005, 19 December, Lot 185 (reproduced).
Reproduced in Loguine, *Gontcharova et Larionov,* p. 132.
The design on the upper half is similar to the ticket for the Grand Bal Travesti, see No. 726 [R617].

726 [R617].
Ticket for The Grand Bal Travesti Transmentale, 1923.
Colored lithograph in dark brown and ocher on white
8¾ x 11 in., 22.3 x 27.8 cm.
Signed lower center in the plate: "M. Larionov."
Other inscriptions (as part of the design): on the right half: "Grand Bal des Artistes Travesti Transmental, vendredi 23 février au profit de la caisse de secours mutuel de l'Union des Artistes Russes. Bullier, 31, Ave. de l'Observatoire Prix: 15 de 9 h. du soir a 5 h. du matin."
Provenance: *Ballet and Theatre Material,* London: Sotheby's, 22 October, 1987, 22 October, Lot 832 (reproduced).
The work has been reproduced many times, including V. Maiakovsky, *Solntse. Poema,* M-P: Krug, 1923; George, *Larionov,* p. 126; and J49, Lot 832.

727a-e

727a-e [NIRE].
Five Advertising Leaflets for **The Bal de la Grande Ourse, 8 May, 1925.**
Lithograph: black printing on brown, off-white, pink, green and orange papers.
12¼ x 5½ in., 31 x 14 cm.
Provenance: Drouot-Richelieu, Aguttes Auction House, Paris, 2005, 19 December, Lot 187 (reproduced), and Vintage Posters, London: Bloomsbury, 14 November 2012, Lot 167.

728

729

729a

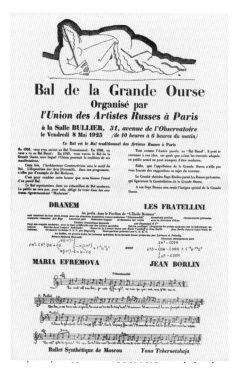

728 Reverse

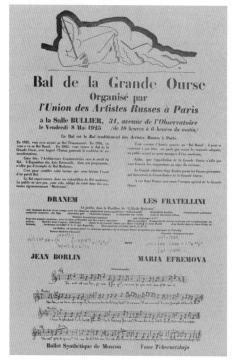

729 Reverse

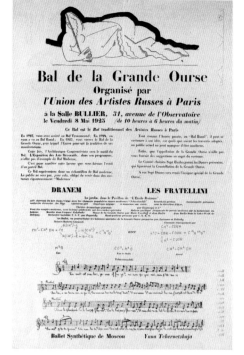

729a Reverse

Larionov as contributor:
728 [NIRE].
Henri Laurens (1885-1954): *Two-sided poster for The Bal de la Grande Ourse, 8 May, Paris, 1925.*
Lithograph in black on cream paper.
19⅝ x 12⅝ in., 50 x 32 cm.
Provenance: Drouot-Richelieu, Aguttes Auction House, Paris, 19 December, 2005, Lot 186 (reproduced).
Cf. No. 729 and 729A [NIRE].

729 and 729a [NIRE].
Henri Laurens (1885-1954): *Two-sided posters for The Bal de la Grande Ourse, 8 May, Paris, 1925.*
Lithograph: 729 black on grey and 729a brown on grey papers.
19⅝ x 12⅝ in., 50 x 32 cm.
Provenance: Vintage Posters, London: Bloomsbury, 14 November 2012, Lot 167 (reproduced).
Cf. No. 728 [NIRE].

Note: See commentary to Nos. 564-566b [R432-34], and 1116 [R370].

Group of Portraits by Mikhail Larionov

730 [NIRE].
Caricature of Georgii Yakulov, 1925.
Black ink on white paper.
Signed in lower margin in Russian: "M.
Larionov."
7⅔ x 8¼ in., 19.5 x 21 cm.
Inscribed by Larionov on lower margin in
Russian: "Yakulov on the street in Paris."
Provenance: Alexandra Tomilina, Paris,
1964.
Yakulov is urinating close to the Eiffel
Tower. On Yakulov see Nos. 1157-70
[R1013-25].

731 [R619].
*Sergei Diaghilev Watching Serge Lifar and
Other Dancers at Rehearsal, 1927.*
Pen and ink.
Initialed and dated lower left: "M.L. 927."
14 x 20⅞ in., 35.5 x 53 cm.
Other inscriptions: lower right: "Répétition -
Lifar et S.P.D." [=Sergei Pavlovich Diaghilev].
Provenance: Richard Buckle, London,

September, 1971.
Reproduced in D41, p. 31; F107, p. 246;
G70; I7, p. 40; I51, I117, p. 238; No. 149;
M157, p. 9; N13, p. 119; and George,
Larionov, p. 126; D13, p. 29; N114; and I.
Zilbershtein, *Parizhskie nakhodki,* M:
Izobrazitelnoe iskusstvo, 1993, p. 130,
where it is attributed to Jean Cocteau.
Larionov made several drawings on the
same subject with discrepant dates; see
G32, pp. 72-73, where a similar sketch is
dated 1924; also George, *Larionov,* p. 34,
where a similar sketch is dated 1921. For
another portrait see J32, Lot 71.

Note: If the date inscribed on this work is
correct, then the rehearsal depicted was
probably for the production of *La Chatte*
(performed in Monte Carlo on 30 April,
1927, and then in Paris on 27 May, 1927).
Serge Lifar (the Youth) was partnered in this
by Alice Nikitina (the Cat). See No. 512
[R394]. Lifar had arrived in France in
January, 1923, and had joined the Diaghilev
company that year.

730

731

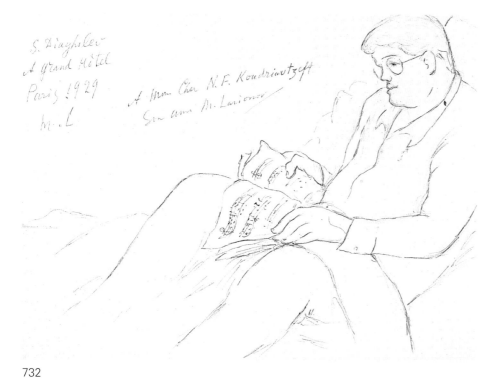

732

732 [R620].
Sergei Diaghilev in Bed at the Grand Hôtel, Paris, 1929.
Pencil, pen and ink.
Initialed and dated upper left: "S. Diaghilev A Grand Hôtel Paris 1929 M.L."
10⅞ x 16⅛ in., 27.5 x 41 cm.
Other inscription: in the center: "A Mon Cher N.F. Koudriavtzeff. Son Ami M. Larionov."
Provenance: Nicholas de Koudriavtzeff, Montreal, April, 1971.
Reproduced in F107, p. 487; I117, p. 236; M157, p. 7; a similar portrait is reproduced in D26, between pp. 392 and 393. Larionov made many versions of this image.
Nicholas Koudriavtzeff (1896-1980), impresario and balletomane, helped promote the Monte Carlo ballet in North America, moving from Paris to Montreal in 1934. He was, as Sol Hurok wrote:

> A man of fine culture, he is an idealistic business man of the theatre, and concert worlds; a gentle kind, able person, with an irresistible penchant for getting himself involved, for swimming in waters far beyond his depth, largely because of his idealism.[530]

733 [R621].
Portrait of Sergei Diaghilev, 1949.
Ink on personalized stationery.
Initialed lower right: "M.L."
10⅜ x 8½ in., 26.5 x 21.5 cm.
Other inscriptions in French: upper right dedication by Larionov to Yurii Annenkov: "A mon cher Ioury Annenkov, Ton Micha, chez Ira à Paris mai 1949."
Provenance: Yurii Annenkov, Paris, August, 1967.
Reproduced in F107, p. 496; I117, p. 235. Larionov made many versions of this portrait. For a very similar item see I31, p.

68; also J34, Lot 34; J36, Lot 171.
The stationery belonged to Irène François, daughter of Barbara Karinska (Varvara Andreevna Zhmudskaia Karinskaia, 1886-1983), the costume designer who worked for the Ballets Russes. She was especially close to Anton Dolin and Michel Fokine.[531]

Note: Larionov's portraits of Diaghilev from the 1920s onwards, casual and spontaneous, express the artist's sincere respect for his subject. A friend of Diaghilev from 1906, when they both traveled to Paris together in connection with the Russian Section at the "Salon d'Automne," Larionov "worshipped Diaghilev to the end of his days."[532] For numerous relevant drawings and photographs see D110.

733

734 [R618].
Portrait of Igor Stravinsky, ca. 1930.
Black and blue inks.
10¼ x 8¼ in., 26 x 21 cm.
Provenance: Iosif Lempert, Paris, 22 March, 1981.
Reproduced in I51, No. 148; N91, p. 137; M43 (c). A similar portrait, the head reversed, is reproduced in G32, p. 70; another version hangs in the Pit Lobby at Covent Garden, London.

734

Note: Larionov made several portraits of Stravinsky in the late 1910s and 1920s as a result of their collaboration. The artist and composer established an especially harmonious relationship in their work on *Le Renard,* which Stravinsky regarded as one of Larionov's "greatest successes."[533]

493 M. Larionov and N. Goncharova: "Rayonists and Futurists. A Manifesto" (1913). Translation in B12, p. 89.
494 Quoted in V. Lobanov: *Khudozhestvenny gruppirovki za 25 let,* M: AKhR, 1930, p. 62.
495 For a full explanation of the name, "Jack of Diamonds," see G. Pospelov: "O 'valetakh' bubnovykh i valetakh chervonnykh" in *Panorama iskusstv 77,* M, 1978, pp. 127-42; and B113, passim.
496 The *skomorokh* was an itinerant buffoon or mummer. His profession was an ancient one and constituted an important part of the Russian folk theater. The *balagan* was the fair-ground booth where the traditional counterpart to the Punch and Judy Show was presented. Benois drew on the *balagan* in his work for *Petrouchka* (Nos. 159-280 [R133-253]) as did Mikhail Bonch-Tomashevsky and Vladimir Tatlin for their *Emperor Maximilian and His Disobedient Son Adolf* (see No. 1014 [R837]).
497 G24, p. 37.
498 Statement by Larionov in V. Parkin et al.: *Oslinyi khvost i mishen,* M: Miunster, 1913, p. 54.
499 See, for example, M. Voloshin: "Oslinyi khvost" in *Russkaia khudozhestvennaia letopis,* SP, 1912, No. 7, p. 9 ; A. Benua: "Bazar khudozhestvennoi suety" in *Rech,* SP, 1912, 12 April; V. Parkin: "Oslinyi khvost i mishen" in *Oslinyi khvost i mishen,* op. cit., pp. 49-82.
500 Ibid., p. 50.
501 Goncharova contributed an *Autumn Study* subtitled "immediate perception"; Larionov contributed *Photographic Study of an Actual City Street, Photographic Study of Melting Snow in Spring,* and *Scene: Movie House.*

502 M. Larionov: "Predislovie" in *Mishen. Katalog vystavki kartin gruppy khudozhnikov Mishen,* M: 1913, pp. 6, 7 (publisher not indicated).

503 Letter from Alexandra Danilova to John E. Bowlt dated 25 September, 1985.

504 F28, p. 75.

505 Ibid., p. 75.

506 M. Larionov: *Rayonist Painting* (1913). Translation in B12, p. 93.

507 I. Narodny: "Art under the Soviet Rule" in *International Studio,* New York, 1923, March, p. 69.

508 Ibid., p. 68.

509 V. Parnach: *L'Art Décoratif Théâtral Moderne,* Paris: La Cible, 1919, p. 17. Both these silkscreens (Nos. 708-09 [R599-600]) were reproduced therein. Also see Nos. 712-13 [603-04]. In the catalog of the "Exposition des Oeuvres de Gontcharova et de Larionow" held at the Galerie Barbazanges, Paris, in June, 1919, Nos. 317-28 are listed as works for *Histoire Naturelle,* i.e., the title is in the singular.

510 The original watercolor for the Peacock is in the collection of the Musée des Beaux-Arts, Strasbourg, and is reproduced in I15, fig. 56. The image was used as a gouache/silkscreen by Goncharova and Larionov for their *L' Art Décoratif Théâtral Moderne* (Paris: La Cible, 1919).

511 I45, p. 55.

512 The painting *Futurista 1916 – Movimento d'Uccello,* formerly in Massine's collection, was auctioned in 1971 at J9, Lot 80. Also see G49, Nos. 190-91. For a number of analogous designs see K85, pp. 174-87. Giacomo Balla's designs for the 1917 production of Stravinsky's *Feu d'Artifice* are also reminiscent of the Larionov design; see I19, p. 22.

513 From a prospectus by Depero for the *Chant du Rossignol (Il Canto dell'Usignuolo)* on display in the Civico Museo Depero, Rovereto, Italy. Still, whether Larionov plagiarized here or not, it should be emphasized that he had been thinking about Futurist theater from the fall of 1913 onwards — a theater in which "the décors are in motion and follow the actor, the spectators lie in the middle of the auditorium" (unsigned article called "K proektu futuristicheskogo teatra v Moskve" in *Teatr v karikaturakh,* M, 1913, No. 1, p. 14).

514 F28, p. 101.

515 F17, p. 132.

516 F28, p. 101.

517 Ibid., p. 99.

518 Ibid., p. 100.

519 Larionov, "Rayonist Painting" (1913). Translation in B12, p. 98.

520 *L'Art Décoratif Théâtral Moderne,* p. 16. Lord Berners also invited Larionov to design the cover and four silkscreens for his *Trois Morceaux pour piano à quatre mains* in 1919; and in the same year he invited Goncharova to design his *Poisson d'or.* For reproductions see K80, p. 162.

521 Letter from Anthony Parton to John E. Bowlt dated 24 July, 2011.

522 Letter from Mikhail Larionov to Sergei Diaghilev dated 24 March 1921. Quoted in D17, p. 159.

523 D. Kobiakov: "Sovremennaia zhivopis. Larionov" in *Zemlia,* Paris, 1949, No. 2, p. 16.

524 Serge Grigoriev in Loguine, *Gontcharova et Larionov,* p. 112. For further information see I65, pp. 29-31.

525 F32, p. 102.

526 A. Maslovsky: "Balety S. Diaghileva i russkie khudozhniki" in *Teatr,* Berlin, 1922, April, No. 9, p. 6.

527 *Teatr i zhizn,* Berlin, 1921, December, No. 4, p. 13.

528 Larionov himself described the 1929 production as Constructivist, although his resolution had little in common with the principles supported by the Soviet Constructivists in the 1920s. For commentary see G24, p. 33.

529 Serge Grigoriev in Loguine, *Gontcharova et Larionov,* p. 112. For further information see I65, pp. 29-31.

530 F11, pp. 168-69.

531 See G80.

532 Larionov in conversation with Richard Buckle. Quoted in D26, p. 92.

533 F32, p. 102.

LATTRY (Latri), Mikhail Pelapedovich

Born 19 (31) October, 1875, Odessa, Ukraine; died 11 February, 1942, Paris, France.

Son of Ivan Aivazovsky's eldest daughter, Elena, and Pelopid Savvich Lattry, a doctor at the Odessa Hospital; introduced to painting from early age by his grandfather; 1885 after her husband's death, Elena married Anton Vladimirovich Rybitsky, Governor of Yalta, where Lattry spent his childhood, 1895 graduated from the Richelieu Gymnasium in Odessa; 1896 enrolled in Arkhip Kuindzhi's landscape painting course at IAA, St. Petersburg, 1897 traveled in Greece, Italy, Turkey, France; studied in Munich with Simon Hollósy and Ferenc "Ferry" Schmidt;1899 returned to IAA as an auditor; 1902 graduated from IAA; 1902 onwards participated in the IAA "Spring Exhibitions"; 1905 exhibited with the New Artists' Society; 1915; board member of the second World of Art society; 1905 left his country estate Boran-Eli near Feodosia in the Crimea, where he had been breeding prize cattle and also producing ceramics at a specially equipped workshop there; director of the Aivazovsky Art Gallery, which the maritime painter had bequeathed to the city of Feodosiia; 1909-10 contributed ceramics to Vladimir Izdebsky's "International Exhibition of Paintings, Sculpture, Engraving, and Drawings"; 1915 contributed to "Exhibition of 1915" in Moscow; 1920 emigrated to Greece; director of the Royal Ceramics Factory in Athens, participated in digs carried out by the French Archaelogical Institute; 1924 settled in Paris, where he founded an art and design studio as a charitable enterprise to aid Russian refugees; 1935 one-man exhibition in Rheims.

Bibliography

N. Barsamov, comp.: *Mikhail Latri.* Catalog of exhibition at the Art Museum, Simferopol, 1964. *Tri khudozhnika – vnuka I.K. Aivazovskogo: M.P. Latri, A.V. Ganzen, K.K. Artseulov.* Catalog of exhibition at the Aivazovsky Picture Gallery, Feodosiia, 1970.
S. Polun, comp.: *Mikhail Latri.* Catalog of centennial exhibition at the Art Museum, Simferopol, 1975.
Irina Porritt: Leaflet for Mikhail Lattry Exhibition at Pushkin House, London, November 9-20, 2007. K284, pp. 190, 191,195.

Lattry received some acclaim for his landscape paintings, especially of the Crimea and Ancient Greece, such as his Delos, Mykonos, and Piraeus cycles (as well as an extensive Venetian cycle). In Russia and the Ukraine, at least, the public knew him as a painter from his regular contributions to Moscow and St. Petersburg exhibitions and from reproductions in journals such as *Mir iskusstva* and *Ogonek.* However, from the early years, Lattry's preferred medium seems to have been pottery and in emigration he gained recognition in Europe and America primarily as a ceramicist with deft combinatons of Art Nouveau and Art Deco. He designed vases and dinner sets for Limoges and other manufacturers, and also panels and laquered screens for French furniture designers oriented towards the American market. His niece, the sculptress Ariadna Arendt, remembered:

> I was born in Simferopol, in 1906, in a family of many doctors. But I didn't go down that route. From earliest childhood I spent my summers in Baran-Eli (now Kashtanovka) near Staryy Krym, where my aunt Ariadne Nikolaevna Lattry lived. Her husband Mikhail Pelopidovich Lattry, the grandson of I.K. Aivazovsky, was himself an artist. In the summer Boran-Eli was the gathering place of creative intelligentsia — K.F. Bogaevskiy, M.A. Voloshin, V.P. Belkin and many others.

> Lattry had a ceramic workshop, where I continuously observed the miraculous appearance of pots and vases upon the pottery wheel. When I looked into the kiln I saw the ceramic reactions, searing, almost transparent, of extraordinary beauty. Yet when cooled and covered in their colored glazes, they became even more beautiful. For me this was like divine magic, just like a painting appearing on a blank canvas.[534]

735

735 [NIRE].
Dancing Couple, ca. 1920.
Watercolor and gouache.
Signed bottom right: "M. Lattry."
13 x 9⅞ in., 33 x 25 cm.
Provenance: Boisgirard auction house, Paris, 10 June, 2009, Lot 47 (reproduced). Reproduced in color in F107, p. 122; K288, p. 40. For color reproduction of a similar piece see L168, Lot 216.

534 A. Arendt: Preface to *Ariadna Arendt: Personalnaia vystavka. Skulptura, grafika.* Catalog of exhibition at the Moscow Union of Artists Moscow, 1991.

LEBEDEV, Vladimir Vasilievich

Born 14 (26) May, 1891, St. Petersburg, Russia; died 21 November, 1967, Leningrad, Russia.

1909 attended the studio of Alexander Titov, St. Petersburg; 1910-11 attended the studio of Frants Rubo, meeting Lev Bruni, Peter Lvov, and other young artists; 1912-14 attended the private studio of Mikhail Bernshtein; met Nikolai Lapshin, Viktor Shklovsky, and Vladimir Tatlin; 1912 saw the exhibition "100 Years of French Art" in St. Petersburg; 1912-16 attended IAA; contact with Boris Grigoriev, Vasilii Shukhaev, Alexandre Jacovleff; impressed by the sculpture and drawings of Rodin, by Cubism, and also by primitive art forms such as the store signboard; illustrated satirical magazines; 1918 professor at Svomas in Petrograd; with Vladimir Kozlinsky designed posters for the Okna ROSTA (propaganda windows for the Russian Telegraph Agency); 1922 contributed to the exhibition "Association of New Tendencies in Art," Petrograd, and the "Erste Russische Kunstausstellung," Berlin; 1923 designed Konstantin Khokhlov's production of Sem Benelli's *La Cena delle Beffe* at the Bolshoi Dramatic Theater, Petrograd; began to illustrate books, especially for children, by authors such as Rudyard Kipling and Samuil Marshak; 1925 contributed to the "Exposition Internationale des Arts Décoratifs" in Paris; 1930s-50s continued to paint, design, and exhibit.

Bibliography

N. Punin: *Vladimir Vasilievich Lebedev*, L: Komitet populiarizatsii khudozhestvennykh izdanii, 1928.
E. Levitin: *Vladimir Vasilievich Lebedev.* "*Natur-shchitsy.*" Catalog of exhibition at GMII, 1967.
V. Petrov: *V. Lebedev*, L: Khudozhnik RSFSR, 1972.
N. Popova: *Vladimir Vasilievich Lebedev.* Catalog of exhibition at the RM, 1973.
V. Pushkarev: *V.V. Lebedev. Risunki*, L: Aurora, 1974.
Yu. Gerchuk, ed.: *Khudozhnik V. Lebedev delaet knigu*, M: Sovetskii khudozhnik, 1982.
R. Messina: *V.V. Lebedev. Sette cicli favolistici.* Catalog of exhibition organized by the Comune di Rieti, Rieti, Italy, 1982.
B. Semenov: "Lebedev izdali i vblizi" in his *Vospominaniia. Vremia moikh druzei*, L: Lenizdat, 1982, pp. 245-57.
B88, pp. 60-75.
Yu. Gerchuk and I. Viskova: *Mastera sovetskoi karikatury. V. Lebedev*, M: Sovetskii khudozhnik, 1990.
N. Kozyreva et al: *Vladimir Lebedev.* Catalog of exhibition at the RM, 1994 (two volumes).
ROSTA: Bolshevik Placards 1919-1922. Catalog of exhibition at the Sander Gallery, New York, 1994.
M211.
M. Koval, N. Misler and C. Pérez y Françoise Lévèque: *Vladímir Lébedev.* Catalog of exhibition at the Museu Fundación Juan March, Palma; and the Museo de Arte Abstracto Espagñol, Cuenca, 2012.

As a graduate of the Academy of Arts in St. Petersburg, Lebedev possessed a fine talent for drawing and illustration, manifesting the same facility and acuity as did Yurii Annenkov and Boris Grigoriev. Lebedev's technique of the 1910s and 1920s is distinguished by a graphic ease, exemplified by his drawings for pre-Revolutionary journals such as *Novyi Satirikon* [New Satyricon] and his social caricatures of the NEP era epitomized in his saucy ballerinas and bustling sailors. Lebedev's illustrations for Nikolai Punin's 1922 booklet on Russian posters, *Russkii plakat 1917-1922* [The Russian Poster, 1917-1922], reveal the artist's ability to capture the salient characteristics of the new Russian street life by a simple and economic artistry. Yet Lebedev was also a fine studio painter and constructor, experimenting with Cubism and reliefs in the late 1910s and early 1920s. In his semi-abstract works, such as *Woman Ironing* (1920, RM), Lebedev followed a consistent and logical system of geometrical reduction. Furthermore, in his experimental works, Lebedev favored a strict compositional play of vertical and horizontal elements. This is manifest, for example, in his two paintings, both called *Cubism*, of 1922 (RM), which, in any case, are total reductions of his leitmotif of the woman ironing to a geometric configuration. The female figure in No. 736 [R622] can be accommodated within these exercises.

Lebedev soon returned to a figurative style at first reminiscent of a slightly ironical Impressionism as in his various female portraits of the 1930s (e.g., the series of *Girls with Bouquets* of 1933). This more academic style represented the artist's competent interpretation of the new Realism that, for better or for worse, replaced his energetic association with the avant-garde just after the Revolution. Unfortunately, the artistic heritage of Lebedev from the 1910s and 1920s is limited since, as Punin indicated in his 1928 appreciation, the artist worked on his Cubist works slowly and patiently, numbering each of them carefully and laboriously.[535] Moreover, as his friends, the artist Petr Neradovsky and the critic Vsevolod Petrov recalled, Lebedev had no qualms about destroying drawings and paintings that he felt to be "unsuccessful" and after a session his studio floor would often be covered with the remnants of rejected works.[536]

736 [R622].
Design for a Poster, ca. 1920.
Watercolor, brush and ink.
14 x 10⅜ in., 35.5 x 26.2 cm.
Provenance: *Russian Pictures, Icons and Russian Works of Art*, London: Sotheby's, 15 February, 1984, Lot 109 (i) (reproduced). Reproduced in I77, p. 161.

Note: This is a preliminary design for Lebedev's poster called "A work-woman. (Raising productivity through joining together small handworking and trade industries)." The finished poster, which was used in the ROSTA windows, was reproduced in color as Plate XVI in Nikolai Punin's booklet *Russkii plakat 1912-1922, Vypusk pervyi. V.V. Lebedev*, P: Strelets, 1922, where it is dated 1920 (cf. XXIII). This booklet was also

736

published in 1923 in English and French under the title *Russian Placards / Placard Russe 1917-1922* by the Izvestiia VTsIK, then printed by Strelets in an edition of 1700. Plate XVI represents the same woman as in No. 736 [R622], except that the facial features are missing and the left leg is hidden under a sewing machine. In the Russian edition of the Punin book, Plate XVI is described as a "Pattern Maker [Zagotovshchitsa] next to a Footwear Machine" and is dated December, 1920-February, 1921. Clearly, this kind of poster relates directly to Lebedev's famous series of *Washerwomen*. [537]

535 N. Punin: "Znachenie kubizma v tvorchestve V. Lebedeva" in *V. Lebedev.* Catalog of exhibition at the RM, 1928, pp. 25-47.
536 Petrov, *Vladimir Vasilievich Lebedev*, p. 261.
537 R. Messina: "I cartelloni di Lebedev nel primo libro sui manifesti della Rivoluzione russa" in R. Messina et al.: *Studi di Biblioteconomia e storia del libro in onore di Francesco Barberi*, Rome: Associazione Italiana Biblioteche, 1976. The poster in question is reproduced there as plate 32, figure 1.

Vladimir Lebedev.

LENTULOV, Aristarkh Vasilievich

Born 14 (26) March, 1882, Voronie, near Penza, Russia; died 15 April, 1943, Moscow, Russia.

1897-1903 attended the Penza School of Drawing; 1903-05 studied in Kiev; 1906 studied under Dmitrii Kardovsky in St. Petersburg; 1907-08 contributed to the "Wreath-Stephanos" exhibition in Moscow, the first of many involvements with avant-garde enterprises; 1910 moved to Moscow; with Robert Falk, Natalia Goncharova, Petr Konchalovsky, Mikhail Larionov, Ilia Mashkov, et al. formed the nucleus of the Jack of Diamonds group; 1911 visited Italy and France; studied under Henri Le Fauconnier in Paris; influenced by Albert Gleizes and Jean Metzinger; 1912 exhibited first Cubist works; 1913 developed a style of painting reminiscent of the parallel experiments of Robert and Sonia Delaunay; painted *St. Basil's Cathedral, Red Square,* one of his most important works; 1915 designed the production of the *Merry Wives of Windsor* for the Chamber Theater, Moscow; 1918 onward professor at Svomas in Moscow; member of IZO NKP; early 1920s designed a number of productions for Petrograd and Moscow theaters; 1925 coorganizer of the group called Moscow Painters which maintained the principles of Cézanne; 1926 joined AKhRR; 1930s onwards continued to paint, especially landscapes and portraits.

Bibliography
V. Kostin: *Aristarkh Lentulov.* Catalog of exhibition organized by the Union of Artists of the USSR, M, 1968.
M. Lentulova: *Khudozhnik Aristarkh Lentulov,* M: Sovetskii khudozhnik, 1969.
A. Korzukhin: "Sokhranennoe pamiatiu. A. Lentulov" in *Tvorchestvo,* M, 1979, No. 7, pp. 16-19.
A. Korzukhin: "Khudozhnik solntsa" in *Moskovskii khudozhnik,* M, 1982, 29 January, p. 2.
K75.
D. Sarabianov: *Aristarkh Lentulov.* Catalog of exhibition at the Central House of Artists, M, 1987.
E. Murina: *Aristarkh Lentulov,* Milan: Teti, 1988.
V. Manin: *A.V. Lentulov.* Catalog of exhibition at the Österreichische Galerie, Vienna, 1989.
E. Murina and S. Dzhafarova: *Aristarkh Lentulov,* M: Sovetskii khudozhnik, 1990.
V. Manin: *Aristarkh Lentulov,* M: Slovo, 1996.

Primarily a studio painter, Lentulov also contributed to a number of theatrical enterprises. His first experience of the theater was in 1914, when he designed décors for Vladimir Maiakovsky's tragedy *Vladimir Maiakovsky,* although the production did not take place. Lentulov's public debut as a stage designer came in 1915 with his work on Alexander Tairov's production of *The Merry Wives of Windsor* at the Chamber Theater, Moscow, and thereafter his repertoire extended to both classical and to modern spectacles. Just after the

Revolution, Lentulov participated in several intimate and innovative productions such as Anton Rubinstein's *Demon* at the so-called Experimental Theater within the Bolshoi Theater, Moscow and *The Unknown Lady* at the Café Pittoresque. In 1919-20 Lentulov also worked on designs for Igor Stravinsky's *Firebird,* but they were not used. From time to time Lentulov returned to the theater in the late 1920s and 1930s, although the portrait and the landscape were always more important to him as artistic disciplines.

737

Lentulov as contributor:
737 [NIRE].
Designer unknown: *Poster Advertising the "Exhibition of Paintings by the Jack of Diamonds,"* Moscow, 1914.
Lithograph in black on white.
36 x 25⅝ in., 91.5 x 65 cm.
Provenance: Viktor Kholodkov, Moscow, 1989.
Inscriptions (as part of the design) in Russian state that the exhibition will open in the Society of Art Lovers at the Levinson House on the Bolshaia Dmitrovka on 5 February [1914] with contributions by Georges Braque, Marie Vassilieff, Gendy (?), Albert Gleizes, André Derain, Robert Delaunay, Kirk [Conrad Kickert], Petr Konchalovsky, Alexander Kuprin, Aristarkh Lentulov, Fernand Léger, Henri Le Fauconnier, Ilia Mashkov, Kazimir Malevich, Jean Metzinger, Adolf Milman, Alexei Morgunov, Alexander Mogilevsky, Pablo Picasso, Liubov Popova, Valerian Pozharsky, Vasilii Rozhdestvensky, Viktor Savinkov, N. [=Antonina] Safronova, L.G. Turchenko, Nadezhda Udaltsova, Maurice de Vlaminck, Othon Friesz, Robert Falk, German Fedorov, Ivan Fedotov, Alexander Shevchenko, Lodewijk Schelfhout, Alexandra Exter, et al."

Note: Most of the names in the poster lack first names and, wherever possible, they have been supplied. "Gendy" has not been identified and is presumed to be a misprint. Initially,

"Jack of Diamonds" was the name of an exhibition organized by Mikhail Larionov, Natalia Goncharova, Robert Falk, Konchalovsky, Kuprin, Lentulov, Mashkov, Rozhdestvensky, and other students from MIPSA in December, 1910 – January, 1911. Towards the end of 1911 Larionov and his immediate colleagues rejected the title, replacing it with "Donkey's Tail" (see No. 700 [R593]) and then, in 1913, with "Target", (see No. 701 [NIRE]), and, finally, in 1914 with "No. 4." However, Falk, Konchalovsky, Kuprin, Lentulov, Mashkov, and Rozhdestvensky, disagreeing with Larionov, registered the Jack of Diamonds as a formal corporation in November, 1911, with Konchalovsky as chairman, Mashkov as secretary, and Kuprin as treasurer; the Realist painter, Vasilii Surikov (Konchalovsky's father-in-law), and the collector Sergei Shchukin were appointed honorary members. As a corporation, the Jack of Diamonds opened its first exhibition on 23 January, 1912, in Moscow. Subsequent exhibitions were held in February-March, 1913 (and later in April-May, 1913, in St. Petersburg), February, 1914, November-December, 1916, and November-December, 1917. During the early 1910s the Society advocated its views at various public discussions, the first on 12 February, 1912, at the Polytechnical Museum, where Nikolai Kulbin delivered his lecture on "The New Free Art as the Basis of Life", Kandinsky on "The Epoch of Great Spirituality" (read by Kulbin), and David Burliuk "On Cubism and Other Trends in Painting". Respondents included Goncharova, Larionov, and Maximilian Voloshin. At the debate on 1 February, 1913, Viktor Ardov, Burliuk, Georgii Chulkov, and Ilia Repin discussed the "attack" on Repin's painting *Ivan the Terrible and His Son* at the Tretiakov Gallery by the mental patient Balashev in January, 1913. In the same year the Society published an illustrated collection of essays on modern art by Ivan Aksenov, Guillaume Apollinaire, Henri Le Fauconnier, et al. Although this poster carries no year, it is presumed to be for the Moscow exhibition that opened on 5 February, 1914, the more so since the vast majority of the artists listed did participate in this session.

Aristarkh Lentulov.

The Unknown Lady: play in three acts by Alexander Blok. Produced by Samuil Vermel and Georgii Krol under the directorship of Vsevolod Meierkhold at the Café Pittoresque on 14 March, 1918.

The play opens with a scene in a St. Petersburg bar where a "man in blue," an astronomer, a poet, and the landlord argue among themselves. The scene then changes to the edge of town at the end of a bridge over a river from where a star is seen falling — only to turn into a woman of mystical appearance. The play ends in a fashionable salon where guests indulge in absurd conversations.

738 [135; R624].
Stage Design for Scene I, 1918.
Watercolor and pencil.
19¾ x 11½ in., 50.2 x 29.2 cm.
Provenance: Christophe Czwiklitzer, Paris, May 1975.
Reproduced in color in B115, plate 81; and in black and white in E27, p. 127; I32, No. 50; I51, No. 150; I77, p. 139; J4, Lot 4. A similar design for the entire stage, in the collection of the State Literary Museum, Moscow, is reproduced in color in M. Dolinsky, *Iskusstvo i Aleksandr Blok,* M: Sovetskii khudozhnik, 1985, pp. 220-21; costume designs in the BTM are reproduced in A. and M. Gordin, *Aleksandr Blok i russkie khudozhniki,* L: Khudozhnik RSFSR, 1986, pp. 274-75. Another design with similar elements, described as a project for a 1919 production of Anton Rubinstein's opera *The Demon,* is reproduced in K74, p. 66.

Note: The color scheme and pronounced curvatures of this design are typical of Lentulov's style in the 1910s, and the bold application of pink, yellow, gold, and green can

738

739

also be identified with Lentulov's major paintings, such as *St. Basil's Cathedral, Red Square* (1913, TG) and *Nizhnii Novgorod* (1915, TG). The arc, or rainbow, with gold stars, reminiscent of the color discs of the Delaunays and Georgii Yakulov, is also a recurrent motif: Lentulov used it, for example, in his set for *Vladimir Maiakovsky* (reproduced in Lentulova, *Khudozhnik Aristarkh Lentulov,* p. 29) and in his curtain design for the production of *Prometheus* at the Bolshoi Theater, Moscow, in 1918 (reproduced in I1, p. 3). Lentulov's organization of the scenery on the miniature stage in the Café Pittoresque was careful and controlled and entailed the use of sails, the transposition of which changed scene and setting. As Lentulov said of all his artistic endeavors, he worked here with "all the sensations of poetry."[538]

The Café Pittoresque opened in Moscow on 26 December, 1917,[539] and quickly became a center of literary and artistic activity. With interior designs by Alexander Rodchenko, Vladimir Tatlin, Yakulov, and other members of the avant-garde, the Café Pittoresque provided a forum for poetry readings, dramatic productions, lectures, etc. According to Yakulov, the Café Pittoresque was meant to "provide the basis of a new style not only in painting, but in all the branches of art, too."[540] A frequent visitor, Lentulov was an eager supporter of the "café culture" just before and after 1917, also contributing to the artistic life (and decoration) of the Poets' Café in Moscow, where he moved closely with David Burliuk, Velimir Khlebnikov, and Maiakovsky at the end of 1917 through the beginning of 1918.

Meierkhold, who had already produced *The Unknown Lady* at the Tenishev Hall, St. Petersburg, in 1914 (with designs by Yurii Bondi), staged the play at the Café Pittoresque with the help of Samuil Vermel and Georgii Krol. It was surprising to see a play by

Blok — a representative of the Symbolist generation already passé — in the repertoire of such a bohemian institution as the Café Pittoresque, as critics were quick to observe:

> Nobody thought that serious dramas like *The Unknown Lady* would be put on... This is not just an attempt to stage Blok in such an environment, but also an attempt to cultivate a new audience.[541]

L'Oiseau de Feu: ballet in two scenes with music by Igor Stravinsky based on the Russian fairy-tale. Prepared, but not produced, in Moscow in 1920.
See No. 370 [R340] for plot summary.

739 [NIRE].
Stage Design, 1919.
Watercolor and pencil.
Signed on reverse in Russian: "A.V. Lentulov Moscow 1919".
11⅛ x 8⅝ in., 28.2 x 22 cm.
Provenance: Christophe Czwiklitzer, Paris, May, 1975.
Reproduced in black and white in I40, p. 73. For a color reproduction of another set design for the same project, now in the Vereshchagin Art Museum in Nikolaev, see Sarabianov, *Aristarkh Lentulov,* p. 112.

538 From unpublished autobiographical notes by Aristarkh Lentulov written ca. 1941. Collection of the Institute of Modern Russian Culture at Blue Lagoon, Los Angeles.
539 According to B58, p. 234. However, according to a letter from Yakulov to Anatolii Lunacharsky dated 19 August, 1918, the café opened on 30 January, 1918. See GAU, f. 2306, op. 24, ed. khr. S4, 1.1.
540 Untitled typescript by Yakulov dated 20 September, 1918, in GAU, f. 2306, op. 24, ed. khr. S4, L. 3.
541 V. Ermans: "Neznakomka" in *Novosti sezona,* M, 1918, 18-19 March, No. 3480, p. 3. Quoted in V. Lapshin: "Iz tvorcheskogo naslediia G.B. Yakulova," in I. Kriukova et al., eds.: *Voprosy sovetskogo izobrazitelnogo iskusstva i arkhitektury,* M: Sovetskii khudozhnik, 1975, p. 289.

LEVIN, Moisei Zelikovich

Born 16 (28) or 18 February (1 March), 1896, Vilnius, Lithuania; died 19 July, 1946, Leningrad, Russia.

1911-14 attended the Vilnius Art Institute; 1915 mobilized; 1917 served in the Red Army; 1918 moved to Petrograd; 1919 enrolled at Svomas in Petrograd; studied under Natan Altman; 1922 after being demobilized, worked on many stage productions, especially for the Ligovsky Theater of the New Drama, Petrograd; also contributed designs to the Habima, Gaideburov, and Skarskaia theaters; 1923 began to design movies; 1924-25 worked as a puppet play designer; 1925-26 worked in the Comedy Theater, Leningrad; 1927 designed several spectacles to commemorate the 10th anniversary of the Revolution, including *Breaking, 10 October,* and *25th October;* 1927 onwards worked for the Bolshoi Dramatic Theater, Leningrad, designing many pieces such as Valentin Kataev's *Avant-Garde* (1930) and Yurii Olesha's *Three Fat Men* (1930); 1936 left the Bolshoi Dramatic Theater to concentrate on movie design; late 1930s lived and worked in Kazakhstan; chair of the Union of Artists of Kazakhstan; Merited Art Worker of Kazakhstan; 1944 returned to Leningrad.

Bibliography
K. Tverskoi: *M.Z. Levin,* L: Akademiia, 1927.
L. Oves, comp.: *M. Levin.* Catalog of exhibition at the Stanislavsky Palace of Arts, L, 1980.
L. Oves: "Moisei Levin: kultura 'idish' i ekspress-ionizm. Dve 'smerti' na stsene" in D284, pp. 518-30.
C182, pp. 425-32.

Moisei Levin, like Isaak Rabinovich and Nisson Shifrin, was one of the young Jewish stage designers who joined the ranks of the avant-garde after the Revolution. His real apprenticeship was with Natan Altman, through whom he studied the new movements such as Suprematism, although he never adapted their extreme conclusions to his stage work. In any case, Levin always regarded the theater designer as a codirector or coproducer. "Visual producership," he wrote in 1935, "is the art of the militant theater artist whose effect upon both the spectator and the theater [should be] an active one." [542] Along with Semeon Mandel, Levin is recognized as one of the leading designers of the Leningrad theater.

Dzhummi (Dzhuma) Mashid (Fire and Steel): *play by Georgii Venetsianov produced at the Bolshoi Dramatic Theater, Leningrad, on 3 March, 1928, by Alexei Gripich with music by Nikolai Strelnikov and designs by Moisei Levin.*

The plot, based on the author's personal experiences, deals with the British colonials in India and the new revolutionary movement there.

740

740 [R623].
Costume Design for Abdala Khan, One of the Three Moslems, ca. 1928.
Gouache and pencil.
10¾ x 7⅛ in., 27.3 x 18 cm.
Inscriptions in Russian: upper right: "Abdala Khan"; upper left: "scarf"; mid-left: "Three Moslems"; lower right margin: "Gafur Bugi"; on reverse in ink: "Gafur Bugi. Kamosov. Aivetus (?)" (Gafur is a Moslem first name. The Hindi word *urfu* denotes what in English is called a buggy. Since family names did not exist in India, Gafur Bugi can, therefore, be construed as the name of an individual, i.e., Mr. Gafur Bugi).
Provenance: Yakov Rubinshtein, Moscow, March, 1978
For reproductions of other costumes by Levin for *Dzhummi Mashid,* see I74, pp. 55, 56.

Note: The aim of Venetsianov and Gripich in their *Dzhummi Mashid* was to "construct a spectacle consonant to the authentic India, close to our worldview, active in organizing the psyche of the auditorium." [543] However, according to contemporary reviews, the production lacked "drama" and fell short of these expectations, not least because of Strelnikov's "tedious" music.[544] Even so, the actors played well and the sets and costumes elicited the "specific features of that 'wonderland' and its extraordinary class oppression." [545]

542 M. Levin: "Izobrazitelnaia rezhissura" in *Teatr i dramaturgiia,* M, 1935, No. 10. Reprinted with cuts in *M. Levin* (1980), pp. 5-9. This excerpt from p. 7.
543 Quoted in A. Verkhotursky: "'Dzhuma Mashid'" in *Zhizn iskusstva,* L, 1928, No. 12, 20 March, p. 11.
544 S. Mochulsky: "'Dzhuma Mashid'" in ibid., p. 12.
545 Verkhotursky, op. cit.

LIBAKOV, Mikhail (Moisei) Vadimovich

Born 11 (23) September, 1889, Vitebsk, Belorussia, died 25 March, 1953, Moscow, Russia.

1900s contact with Yurii Pen in Vitebsk; 1913-29 worked as a designer for the First Studio of the Moscow Art Theater and at what came to be called the Moscow Art Theater No. 2; during this time designed many plays by Russian and Western authors, including Charles Dickens, Gerhardt Hauptmann, Herman Heijermans, and Vladimir Volkenshtein, often collaborating with other designers, such as Ivan Gremislavsky, Boris Matrunin, and Alexei Radakov; among his important interpretations were *Hamlet* in 1924 and *Petersburg* (after the novel by Andrei Bely) in 1925; 1919 contributed to the "XI State Exhibition: Works of the Union of Applied Art and Industrial Design Workers" in Moscow; 1925 contributed to the "Exposition Internationale des Arts Décoratifs" in Paris; 1939 onwards member of the All-Russian Theatrical Society; 1930s designed plays at the Maly Theater, Moscow, and the Moscow Operetta Theater.

Bibliography
Nothing substantial has been published on Libakov. The reader will find some information on him in A7, Vol. 3, p. 522; and C172, pp. 433, 434.

Not a radical artist, Libakov did work for many years as actor and designer for the First and Second Studios of the Moscow Art Theater, contributing to a wide variety of productions, from *Hamlet* to *Uncle Tom's Cabin.* He was appreciated for his engaging, if restrained, designs for sets, costumes, and commercial promotions (including the poster for *The Cricket on the Hearth*) and Mikhail Chekhov, in particular, was his keen supporter. Libakov also collaborated readily with many writers and artists of the time, including Ivan Gremislavsky, Valentina Khodasevich, and Alexei Radakov, and also worked for other companies in Odessa, Kiev, Yalta and elsewhere.

The Cricket on the Hearth: *play by Boris Sushkevich based on the tale by Charles Dickens. Produced by Boris Sushkevich and Leopold Sulerzhitsky at the First Studio of the Moscow Art Theater on 24 November, 1914, with music by Nikolai Rakhmanov and designs by Mikhail Libakov and Pavel Uzunov.*

John Perrybingle, an elderly wagoner, comes home to his young wife Mary with a wedding cake intended for the marriage of sour old Gruff Tackleton to young May Fielding. An elderly stranger turns up in search of lodging, and secretly reveals himself to Mary as Edward, May's childhood sweetheart and the long lost son of Caleb Plummer, Gruff Tackleton's meek employee. At a pre-wedding supper, Perrybingle discovers his wife in the embrace of the elderly Stranger, who he realizes is a young man in disguise, and he suspects the worst. But the cricket that lives on his hearth as a

741

symbol of domestic bliss, paints for him a vision of Mary's innocence, and Perrybingle vows to stand by her. Edward soon enters with May after a secret marriage, and reveals himself to his father and blind sister Bertha. Tackleton is thus jilted of his bride, but accepts his fate with good grace and the company celebrates in a country dance.

741 [R625].
Costume Design for John the Coachman, 1914.
Watercolor and ink.
Signed and dated lower center in Russian: "Mikh. Libakov 1914."
11⅝ x 9 in., 29.5 x 23 cm.
Other inscription: upper right in Russian: "John."
Provenance: Boris Brodsky, Moscow, January, 1978.
Reproduced in *Teatr i muzyka*, M, 1923, No. 4, 28 January, p. 520; B44, p. 298.

Note: Konstantin Stanislavsky and Leopold Sulerzhitsky established their so-called First Studio of the Moscow Art Theater (MKhAT) in 1912 in order to elaborate and refine Stanislavsky's theatrical system. It opened to the public in January, 1913, with a production of Heijermans' *Op hoop van zegen* [The Destruction of Hope]. Primarily under Sulerzhitsky's direction, a number of important chamber productions were created there, including *The Cricket on the Hearth* (1913-15), *Twelfth Night* (1917), and August Strindberg's *Erik XIV* (produced by Sushkevich and Evgenii Vakhtangov in 1921). Stanislavsky regarded the interpretation of *The Cricket on the Hearth* as one of the most successful in the First Studio — "remarkably sincere and moving,"[546] and at its 500th presentation in December, 1922, the Moscow critics still enthused.[547]

546 F2 (2nd edition, 1936), pp. 509-10.
547 Skh [sic]: "Sverchok na pechi" in *Teatr i muzyka*, M, 1922, No. 11, 12 December, pp. 240-41.

LIBERTS, Ludolfs

Born 3 April 1895, Tirza, Latvia; died March 11, 1959, New York.

1900s attended J. Madernieks's studio in Riga; 1911-12 studied sculpture at CSIAI; 1914 onwards contributed regularly to national and international exhibitions; 1914-15 took lessons from Nikolai Feshin at the Kazan Art Institute; 1915 contributed to the "World of Art" exhibition" in Kazan; helped design productions at the Kazan Opera; 1915-18 artillerist in WWI; received combat medal; 1923 one-man exhibition (with Konrad Ubans) at the City Museum, Riga; 1923-32 professor at the Latvian Academy of Art in Riga; 1924-37 designed productions for opera and theater companies in Latvia, Bulgaria, Yugoslavia, Finland, and Sweden; 1924-39 member of the Riga group of artists called "Sadarbs"; 1929, 1930, 1931, and 1933 contributed to the "Salon d'Automne" in Paris; 1935-44 director of State Printing House and Mint in Riga; 1944 emigrated to Austria; 1950 emigrated to the USA; taught painting at New York City College.

Bibliography
J. Siliņš: *Ludolfs Liberts*, Riga: Apgāds, 1943.
G. Švītiņš and I. Kalniņa: *Ludolfs Liberts*. Catalog of exhibition sponsored by the Parekss Bank, Riga, 2000.

Along with Alexander Drevin and Gustav Klutsis, Liberts was one of several artists from the Baltic States who made a vital contribution to the development of "Russian" Modernism. Trained in Riga, Moscow, and Kazan, Liberts – like Mikhail Libakov and Viktor Simov – emphasized the technical craft of painting and design rather than the experimental or radical innovation and, if his stage designs tend to be pedestrian in their historical descriptions, they are also luminous and comprehensible. Liberts's sense of measure, good taste, and historical accuracy were qualities that made him an influential teacher both in Europe and America.

Boris Godunov: *opera in a prologue and four acts by Modest Mussorgsky with libretto based on a play of the same name by Alexander Pushkin and Nikolai Karamzin's* History of the Russian State. *Production not known, 1930s?*
     See No. 339 [R305] for plot summary.

742 [NIRE].
Stage Design for the Coronation Scene, 1930s?
Oil on board.
19⅞ x 24 in., 50.5 × 61 cm.
Provenance: *Russian Pictures, Works of Art and Icons*, London: Sotheby's, 29 November, 2005, Lot 100 (reproduced).

742

LIESSNER-BLOMBERG (Lisner; also Lissner), Elena Arturovna

Born 31 January (12 February), 1897, Moscow, Russia; died 1 January, 1978, Berlin, Germany.

Her mother, Natalia Lisner-Arnaumova, ran a corsetry store in Moscow frequented by celebrities such as Olga Knipper (wife of Anton Chekhov) and Ekaterina Peshkova (Volzhina, wife of Maxim Gorky); 1910s close to her uncle, Ernst Lissner, a student of Ilia Repin at IAA;[548] 1917 worked as a draughtswoman; 1919 secretary within IZO NKP; met Vladimir Maiakovsky, Georgii Yakulov, and other avant-gardists; conducted drawing lessons for children; 1920 studied at Vkhutemas under Anton Pevzner and Liubov Popova; studied the nationalized collections of Ivan Morozov and Sergei Shchukin; 1921 via Prague emigrated to Berlin; with Jean Pougny exhibited in the galleries of the Twardy bookshop; met Vasilii Kandinsky, Laszlo Moholy-Nagy, and other modern artists, writers, and theater people; created curtain design and logo for the Blaue Vogel cabaret; 1921-23 took part in exhibitions held by the Novembergruppe; contributed costume and set designs to the Blaue Vogel; 1923 married the architect Albrecht Blomberg; exhibition in the Galerie Garvens, Hanover; 1927 and 1929 visited her mother in Moscow; befriended Nikolai Kupreianov; 1932 contributed to the Berlin "Secession"; 1934 visited Bulgaria; 1936 and 1939 traveled extensively in Italy; 1948 exhibition in the Galerie Wimmer, Munich; 1950s-70s continued to paint, compose collages, and exhibit.

Bibliography
G. Wolf, ed.: *Elena Liessner-Blomberg oder Die Geschichte vom Blauen Vogel*, Berlin: Der Morgen, 1978.
A. Meyer zu Essen: *Elena Liessner-Blomberg*. Catalog of exhibition at the Kunsthalle Bremen, Bremen, 1983.
M. Schmidt-Wakel: *Elena Liessner-Blomberg, 1897-1978* (doctoral thesis), Hamburg: Universität Hamburg, 1984.
G. Busch: *Elena Liessner-Blomberg, 1897-1978: Collagen, Aquarelle, Zeichnungen*, Catalog of exhibition at Schwetzingen: K.F. Schimper-Verlag, 1989.
O. Westheider: *Elena Liessner: Ankunft in Berlin. Zeichnungen aus den frühen Zwanziger Jahren*, Catalog of exhibition at the Kunsthalle, Hamburg, 1996.
R. Weingart et al.: *Elena Liessner-Blomberg, 1897-1978. Eine Russin in Berlin*. Catalog of exhibition at the Staatliches Museum Schwerin, Schwerin, 2002.
R. Weingart, introd.: *Elena Liessner-Blomberg, 1897-1978. Eine russisch-deutsche Entdeckung / A German-Russian Discovery*. Catalog of exhibition at the Galerie Gmurzynska, Zug, 2004.

Liessner-Blomberg achieved her visible reputation as an artist not in Russia, but in Berlin from the 1920s onwards. Although she trained briefly at Vkhutemas and was among the ranks of the second avant-garde, the mature Liessner-Blomberg had more in common with Juan Gris and Henri Matisse than with Kazimir Malevich or Vladimir Tatlin. In any case, like Nina Aizenberg and Elizaveta Yakunina, Liessner seems to have been drawn more to the spontaneous sketch rather than to solid studio painting. Indeed, while avoiding the abstract systems of Kandinsky and Malevich, Liessner gave particular attention to "life" in the form of portraits and street scenes, eliciting character and mood in deft drawings and collages, sometimes informed by a mild Cubism.

***Unidentified production**, ca. 1921.*

743 [136; NIRE].
Costume Design for a Man with Stick and Hat, 1921.
Gouache.
Signed with initials and dated upper left in black ink in Russian: "EL, 1921, II [=February]."
11¾ x 8 in., 30 x 20.9 cm.
Other inscriptions: upper right: "Moscow"; on reverse: Russian stamp and sketches in pencil of a man's head and two women standing.
Provenance: Galerie Gmurzynska, Zurich, November, 2004.
Reproduced on cover of Weingart, *Elena Liessner-Blomberg, 1897-1978. Eine russisch-deutsche Entdeckung.*

Note: Liessner-Blomberg was one of the many talented artists who worked for the theaters "of small forms," such as the cabaret, the music-hall, and the puppet theater, during the 1920s, both in Soviet Russia and in emigration. For Jascha Juschny's Blaue Vogel, Liessner-Blomberg designed some of the main numbers, such as the *Grosse Internationale Revue* and even the drop curtain, collaborating there with

743

other young and still unknown Russian painters such as André Houdiakoff and Pavel Tchelitchew. Judging from the inscription, Liessner-Blomberg seems to have made this particular sketch just before she emigrated to Germany, perhaps for one of Moscow's new little theaters or for the projected production of Frank Wedekind's *Frühlingserwachen* for which Liessner-Blomberg made costume designs in 1921. In any event, the costume is engaging in its geometric simplicity and functionality, emphasizing what one critic has called the "crystal transparency" of her graphic work.[549]

548 Ernst Lissner is now remembered for his stylized illustrations to fairy-tales. See, for example, *Skazka o lisichke-sestrichke i volke* [A Tale About a Sister Fox and a Wolf], SP, 1900.
549 G. Busch "Elena Liessner-Blomberg" in Busch, *Elena Liessner-Blomberg, 1897-1978*, upaginated.

LISSIM, Simon (Lisim, Semeon Mikhailovich)

Born 11 (24) October 1900, Kiev, Ukraine; died 10 May 1981, Naples, Florida, USA.

1910s attended the Naumenko High School, Kiev, and also took violin lessons at the Kiev Conservatory of Music; 1917 studied art under Alexander Monko; worked at the Kiev Repertory Theater; met Alexandra Exter and Isaak Rabinovich; 1919 emigrated to Bulgaria, then to Yugoslavia, Austria, and Germany; 1921 arrived in Paris; worked closely with Léon Bakst; helped to edit the journal *Zhar-ptitsa* [Firebird]; 1923 began to work for the Théâtre de l'Oeuvre, Paris, one of many theatrical involvements from the 1920s onward; during this time also wrote a number of articles on contemporary Russian and Western art; worked for the Théâtre Royal de la Monnaie, Brussels, Colonel de Basil's Ballets Russes de Monte Carlo (1930s), and other companies; 1924 began to decorate porcelain; 1925 contributed to the "Exposition Internationale des Arts Décoratifs," Paris; 1928 one-man exhibition at the Galerie Charpentier, Paris; 1935 made his first trip to the US; 1936 one-man exhibition at the Wildenstein Gallery, New York; 1939-41 served in the French army; 1941 settled in the US; 1942 director of the Art Education Project of the New York Public Library, one of many administrative posts that he held during his American residence; 1944-71 taught at the City College of New York.

Bibliography
N. Misheev: "S. Lisim" in *Perezvony*, Riga, 1927, No. 33, pp. 1049-51.
A. Tessier: *Simon Lissim*, Paris: Trident, 1928.
R. Cogniat et al.: *Simon Lissim*, Paris: Aux Editions du Cygne, 1933.
G. Freedley: *Simon Lissim*, New York: Hendrickson, 1949.
R. Lister: *Simon Lissim*, Cambridge: Golden Head Press, 1962.
M2, Vol. 2, pp. 188-89.

T. Wood et al.: *Dreams in the Theater. Designs of Simon Lissim.* Catalog of exhibition at the New York Public Library at Lincoln Center, New York, 1975-76.
J. Bowlt: "Simon Lissim" in *Art News*, New York, 1975, November, pp. 123-25.
E. Dee: *The World of Simon Lissim. 90 Designs for the Theatre.* Catalog of exhibition circulated by the International Exhibitions Foundation, Washington, D.C., 1979.
H34, pp. 383, 384.

Although Lissim was born in Kiev and emigrated when he was only 19 years old, he remained one of the most "Russian" of the Paris émigrés. As one critic wrote of him in the 1920s, "il a porté sur soi la Russie."[550] Not surprisingly, Lissim was an enthusiastic supporter of the émigré art magazine *Zhar-ptitsa* [Firebird] (Paris/Berlin, 1921-26), which maintained the fine traditions of Russian art and architecture, and he did much to publicize the work of his elder colleagues by writing articles on Bakst, Alexandre Benois, Natalia Goncharova, and others for Berlin and Paris magazines.[551]

Like Boris Bilinsky and Alexei Korovin, Lissim maintained and expanded the decorative principles of the World of Art and the Diaghilev era, but he was also an artist of wide horizons, conversant with the Constructivism of Alexandra Exter and with the latest Western trends, especially with Art Deco. Lissim's artistic fantasy was, metaphorically, as fluent and as indefinable as water, one of his favorite motifs. Whether he evoked the mood of ancient Russia, as in *The Tale of Tsar Saltan*, concentrated on the convolutions of ceramic designs, or painted cloud formations above New York, Lissim remained faithful to this principle of fluency and mobility — perhaps deriving in part from his early training as a musician.

744 [R626].
Civis: *Portrait of Simon Lissim,* 1927.
Pen and ink.
Signed and dated lower left: "Civis 27."
13¾ x 9⅞ in., 35 x 25 cm.
Other inscriptions: upper right: "1¾ Civis."
Provenance: Simon Lissim, Dobbs Ferry, New York, March, 1967.
Reproduced in F107, p. 157; I20, No. 59; I51, No. 151.

Note: Civis, pseudonym of Sergei Antonovich Tsivinsky (1895-1941), a Russian émigré who lived in Latvia during the 1920s, was especially active as a caricaturist for the Russian newspaper *Segodnia* [Today]. In 1930, two collections of his caricatures were published in Riga, i.e., *Karikatury Tsivisa-Tsivinskogo* (Riga: Gramatu dragus, 1930; introduced by Petr Pilsky) and *Geroi nashego vremeni* (Riga: Rota, 1933). Simon Lissim wrote the following comment on this caricature:

> In 1927 I was in Riga, Latvia, where I designed the stage settings and costumes (and all furniture and props) for the National Theater of Latvia for *L'Aiglon* by Rostand. There were many articles about me in the Riga papers and the caricature was reproduced in the Russian daily *Segodnia,* and Civis (on the staff of the paper) specially made the caricature. He was a very gifted young artist.[552]

L'Oiseau Bleu: *play in four acts by Maurice Maeterlinck. Produced at the Théâtre de l'Oeuvre, Paris, projected, but not produced, in 1923, with designs by Simon Lissim.*
See No. 31 [R30] for plot summary.

745 [R627].
Costume Design for *Le Pain,* 1923.
Watercolor, gold paint, and pencil.
Signed and dated lower right: "S. Lissim 23."
13 x 9⅞ in., 33 x 25 cm.

745

Provenance: Simon Lissim, Dobbs Ferry, New York, May 1969.
Reproduced in G10, Vol. 2, fig. 293; I20, No. 68; I51, No. 152. A similar costume, reproduced in color in H5, No. 33 (1927), opp. p. 1056, is in the collection of the Ashmolean Museum, Oxford.

Note: Although Lissim signed and dated this design "1923," repertoire lists of the Théâtre de l'Oeuvre (La Maison de l'Oeuvre) do not carry a reference to a production of *L'Oiseau Bleu* in 1923.[553] True, an article in the London *Observer*, datelined Paris, does refer to a revival of Maeterlinck's *Blue Bird* with Cora Laparcerie, but does not name the theater,[554] and one critic of the time even described Lissim's designs for *L'Oiseau Bleu* as a "complete absence of half-tones. Silver and gold. And the total effect is a festival for the eye."[555] In any case, Lissim did work on

744

746

747

three other commissions for the Théâtre de l'Oeuvre, i.e. Henry Soumagne's *L'Autre Messie* (December, 1923), Henri Ghéon's *La Joyeuse Farce des "Encore"* (February, 1924), and Henri Soumagne's *Les Danseurs de gigue* (January, 1926).[556] Evidence suggests, therefore, that Lissim's design here was for a projected, not actual, production of *L'Oiseau Bleu*.

El Tsar Saltan: *opera in three acts by Nikolai Rimsky-Korsakov with a libretto by Vladimir Belsky after a poem by Alexander Pushkin. Produced at the Gran Teatro del Liceo, Barcelona, on 4 December, 1924, with designs by Simon Lissim.*
See No. 349 [R314] for plot summary.

746 [R628].
Stage Design for Act I, 1922.
Gouache.
Signed and dated lower right: "S. Lissim 22."
11 x 15¾ in., 28 x 40 cm.
Other inscriptions: lower margin: "Salon d'automne 1924" and identification.
Provenance: Issar Gourvitch, Paris, June, 1966.
Reproduced in H5, No. 33 (1927), p. 1050; G10, Vol. 2, fig. 233; I14, No. 83; I51, No. 153.

747 [R629].
Costume Design for the Tsar, 1967.
Gouache.
Signed and dated lower left: "Simon Lissim 1967."
16½ x 10½ in., 42 x 26.7 cm.
Provenance: Simon Lissim, Dobbs Ferry, New York, 1967.
Reproduced in I14, No. 84.
It is not known for which production of *The Tale of Tsar Saltan* this design was intended.

Note: Lissim's designs for *The Tale of Tsar Saltan,* while reminiscent of the stylizations of Viktor Vasnetsov and Léon Bakst, evoked the colorful primitivism of pre-Petrine Russia. As one critic maintained:

> Both the décors and the costumes communicate the atmosphere of the fairy-tale remarkably well... All is deliberate, 'not real,' but is intensely gratifying because it corresponds to your sensation and perception of the fairy-tale.[557]

Boris Godunov: *opera in a prologue and four acts by Modest Mussorgsky with libretto based on a play of the same name by Alexander Pushkin. Projected in Paris in 1926, but not produced.*
See No. 339 [R305] for plot summary.

748 [NIRE].
Decorative Panel with Costume Designs for the Boyars, 1926
Watercolor and black ink.
Signed and dated lower right: "Lissim 26."
7⅛ x 17⅛ in., 18 x 43.5 cm.
Provenance: Nicholas Wyrouboff, Paris.

Ballet based on Brahms's Fourth Symphony.
Projected, but not produced, by Colonel de Basil's Ballets Russes de Monte Carlo before 1933.

749 [R630].
Curtain.
Watercolor and gold.
Signed lower right in white paint: "Simon Lissim."
15 x 20⅞ in., 38 x 53 cm.
Provenance: Simon Lissim, Dobbs Ferry, New York, March, 1970.
Reproduced in Cogniat, *Lissim;* I20, No. 67.

748

749

550 Tessier: *Simon Lissim*, p. 42.
551 See, for example, the following articles by Lissim: "L.S. Bakst i teatralnyi kostium" in *Spolokhi*, Berlin, 1924, No. 12, p. 4; and "Alexandre Benois" in *La Revue de "l'Oeuvre*," Paris, 1926, No. 1, pp. 27-28.
552 Letter from Simon Lissim to John E. Bowlt dated 29 October 1980. For some information on Civis, including a partial list of his published caricatures, see A29, Vol. 4, pp. 290-93, and addendum (unpaginated).
553 See "Théâtres" in *Le Temps*, Paris, 1923, 25 September, p. 3, which lists the productions scheduled for the 1923-24 season. We are grateful to Lynn Garafola and Asya Speranskaia for much of the information regarding *L'Oiseau Bleu* and the Théâtre de l'Oeuvre.
554 P. Carr: "The Theatre in Paris. Two New Guitry Plays. Poignant Study by Jacques Copeau. A Satire on Doctors" in *The Observer*, London, 1924, 13 January, p. 7.
555 Misheev, "S. Lissim," p. 1050.
556 See Eliane Roussin: "Annexe II – Pièces créées à l'Oeuvre 1893-1929" in *Lugné-Poe et le Théâtre de l'Oeuvre*, (Ph.D. dissertation), Columbia University, New York, 1958, pp. 276-88.
557 Misheev, op. cit. For information on productions at the Liceo in Barcelona see Roger Alier: *El Gran Libre del Liceo*, Carroggio, 1999.

LISSITZKY, EL (Lisitsky, Lazar Markovich)

750

Born 10 (22) November, 1890, Pochinok, near Smolensk, Russia; died 30 December, 1941, Moscow, Russia.

1909-14 attended the Technische Hochschule in Darmstadt; also traveled in France and Italy; 1914 returned to Russia; worked in Moscow as an architectural draftsman; 1915-18 attended the Riga Polytechnical Institute in Moscow (evacuated from Riga during the War); 1916 designed the cover for Konstantin Bolshakov's book of poetry *Solntse na izlete* [Spent Sun]; 1917 exhibited with the World of Art in Petrograd and thereafter at many exhibitions in the Soviet Union and abroad; 1918 member of the IZO NKP; 1919 professor at the Vitebsk Popular Art Institute; close contact with Kazimir Malevich; began to work on his Prouns (Proun = Project for the Affirmation of the New); member of Unovis; close to Vera Ermolaeva, Lazar Khidekel, Ilia Chashnik, and Nikolai Suetin; 1920 member of Inkhuk, Moscow; 1920-21 professor at Vkhutemas, Moscow; 1922 with Ilya Ehrenburg edited the journal *Veshch / Gegenstand / Objet* in Berlin; worked increasingly on typographical and architectural design; published *Pro dva kvadrata* [About Two Squares]; created the Proun Room for the "Grosse Berliner Kunstausstellung" of 1923; 1923 published his six Proun lithographs in the *Kestnermappe* in Hanover and the album of figures for *Victory over the Sun;* designed the Berlin edition of Vladimir Maiakovsky's *Dlia golosa* [For the Voice]; 1925 returned to Moscow; taught interior design at Vkhutemas; thereafter active primarily as an exhibition and typographical designer, creating new concepts for the exhibition room as in his Abstrakte Kabinett at the Niedersächsische Landesgalerie in Hanover in 1927-28; 1928 joined the October group; 1930 published his treatise on modern architecture *Russland: Architektur für eine Weltrevolution;* 1930s worked for the propaganda magazine *USSR in Construction.*

Bibliography

Lissitzky is the subject of a very large number of monographs, catalogs, and articles. The titles below are a representative selection only.

H. Richter: *El Lissitzky*, Cologne: Czwiklitzer, 1958.
S. Lissitzky-Küppers: *El Lissitzky. Life, Letters, Texts*, London: Thames and Hudson, 1968; second edition, 1976.
S. Mansbach: *Visions of Totality*, Ann Arbor: UMI, 1980.
El Lissitzky. Catalog of exhibition at the Staatliche Galerie, Moritzburg, and the Galerie der Hochschule für Grafik und Buchkunst, Leipzig, 1982-83.
P. Nisbet et al.: *El Lissitzky 1890-1941*. Catalog of exhibition at the Busch-Reisinger Museum, Cambridge, Massachusetts, 1987.
P. Nisbet et al.: *El Lissitzky—1890-1941— Retrospektive*. Catalog of exhibition at the Sprengel Museum, Hanover, 1988.
M. Nemirovskaia: *L.M. Lisitsky 1890-1941*. Catalog of exhibition at the TG, 1990.
H. Puts et al.: *El Lissitzky. Architect, Painter, Photographer, Typographer*. Catalog of exhibition at the Municipal Van Abbemuseum, Eindhoven, and other cities, 1990.
V. Malsy: *El Lissitzky. Konstrukteur, Denker, Pfeifenraucher, Kommunist*. Catalog of exhibition at Mathildenhöhe, Darmstadt, 1990-91.
K. Simons: *El Lissitzky. Proun 23 N, oder Der Umstieg von der Malerei zur Gestaltung*, Frankfurt: Insel, 1993.
M. Tupitsyn et al.: *El Lissitzky. Jenseits der Abstraktion*, Munich: Schirmer-Mosel, 1999.
S. Morejko et al., eds.: *Sophie Lissitzky-Küppers. 36 Letters*, Jerusalem: Alphabet, 2001.
I. Prior: *Die geraubten Bilder: Der abenteuerliche Geschichte der Sophie Lissitzky-Küppers und ihre Kunstsammlung*, Cologne: Kiepenheuer und Witsch, 2002.
N. Perloff and B. Reed, eds.: *Situating El Lissitzky*, Los Angeles: Getty Research Institute, 2003.
E. Nemirovsky, comp.: *Konstruktor knigi El Lisitsky*, M: Fortuna El, 2006.
J. Milner: *Lissitzky – Overwinning op de Zon / Lissitzky – Victory over the Sun*. Catalog of exhibition at the Van Abbemuseum, Eindhoven, 2009-10.
I. Dukhan: *El Lisitsky*, M: Art-Rodnik, 2010.
S. Khan-Magomedov: *Lazar Lisitsky*, M: Gordeev, 2011.

Much indebted to the theory and practice of Malevich, Lissitzky developed certain aspects of Suprematism, but avoided the mystical dimension that Malevich tended to invoke. For Lissitzky and for Malevich, architecture and design in general presented themselves as obvious vehicles for the transference of basic Suprematist schemes into life itself. In this respect, Lissitzky's Prouns were of vital significance since they served as intermediate points between two and three dimensions or, as Lissitzky himself said, "as a station on the way to constructing a new form."[558]

The principles of the Proun — the rejection of the single axis, the convenience of entering the work at any junction, the idea of the "flotation device" — are operative in most aspects of Lissitzky's work during the 1920s, but especially in his graphic designs. The formative influence of his residence in

Vitebsk when he extended the Suprematist system into his formulation of the Proun can be seen, for example, in his book *Pro dva kvadrata* (conceived in Vitebsk in 1920; published in Berlin in 1922). This extraordinary "biblio-construction," which in many ways is similar to the album of figures for *Victory over the Sun* (also conceived in Vitebsk in 1920), has to be experienced as a "movie" rather than as a "book." The organization of this publication demonstrates how closely Lissitzky paid attention to the visual appearance of the object, convinced that design, especially the geometric esthetic, could serve as a visual Esperanto and replace some of the traditional functions of verbal language. Yet, in his earnest endeavor to "fuse art and life,"[559] Lissitzky never lost his sense of humor, and one of the appealing ingredients in his Constructivist compound is the gentle irony and whimsical jocularity evident in his collocation of forms and colors.

750 [NIRE].
Propaganda Poster "Beat the Whites with the Red Wedge," 1919.
Lithograph / printer's proof.
Initialed in Russian in the plate lower left: "LL."
19¾ x 28⅜ in., 50.2 x 72 cm.
Other inscriptions in Russian: as part of the design: "With the red wedge beat the Whites"; bottom margin left: "No. 19. Lithopublishers of the Political Authority of the Western Front"; and bottom margin right: "Unovis." (For information on Unovis see No. 458).
Provenance: Viktor Kholodkov, Moscow, September, 1986.

751 [137; R631].
Vladimir Tatlin at Work on the Monument to the III International, ca. 1922.
Silver print photograph heightened with two areas of India ink.
Signed in pencil upper margin with the initials "EL."
9 x 6⅝ in., 23 x 16.8 cm.
Other inscriptions: mathematical inscriptions at lower center form part of the design, while the reverse carries the name "El Lissitzky" in block capitals in pencil; beneath are the words: "'Der Konstruktor' für das Buch von Ehrenburg '6 Geschichten'."
Provenance: Viktor Kholodkov, Moscow, September, 1986.
Reproduced in M166. A larger version of this piece is reproduced in K12, No. 37; Lissitzky-Küppers, plate 73; and elsewhere.

Note: Called variously *Tatlin at Work, Tatlin and the Monument to the Third International, Tatlin Working on 3rd International Statue,* etc., this piece is the original photograph from which the illustration called *Tatlin at Work* was lithographed and reproduced for the story "Vitrion" in Ilya Ehrenburg's *Shest povestei o legkikh kontsakh* [Six Tales with Easy Endings] (M-Berlin: Gelikon, 1922; for a reproduction see B17, No. 61). Lissitzky photographed the image and heightened it with black so

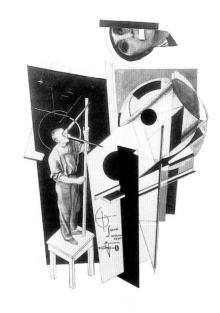

751

that it would carry the right tones for the illustration. The same book also included five other Lissitzky illustrations, among them the *Football Player, Black Ball,* and *[New] York – Hamburg* (for reproductions see Lissitzky-Küppers, plates 74, 71, 72), plus his cover design.

The photograph shows Tatlin at work on the model for his Monument, or Tower, for the III Communist International, which he started in 1919. He was assisted by his students Iosif Meerzon and Tevel Shapiro. The young artist Sofia Dymshits-Tolstaia, much influenced by Tatlin and a contributor to his exhibition called the "Store" in Moscow in 1916, was a keen observer of the undertaking. Until 1915 Dymshits-Tolstaia was the wife of the writer Alexei Tolstoi, the close colleague and friend of Ehrenburg, whom Lissitzky also knew in Petrograd and, in 1921-22, in Berlin. In one of the documentary photographs of Tatlin and his assistants constructing the model for the Monument in 1920 (reproduced, for example, on p. 54 of *Vladimir Tatlin* [1968]), Dymshits-Tolstaia is also present.

These connections explain the appearance of Dymshits-Tolstaia's face in a horizontal position at the top of the design. However, as in many of Lissitzky's works, there is an ironic comment in the image since Dymshits-Tolstaia, who was often regarded by artists and writers of the time as a mediocre artist and a chatterbox, has her mouth sealed with a collage. Lissitzky's irony does not end here, for there seems to be an implied suspicion of Tatlin's ability to really think and act as an engineer and as a mechanical theorist who understands higher mathematics. The figure of Tatlin holding the shaft of wood is taken directly from the 1920 photograph mentioned above, except that Tatlin's eye is replaced by a pair of compasses (inserted in the wrong place). This, together with Tatlin's now precarious position on the stool (not in the 1920 photograph) and the absence of the

Monument itself, indicate Lissitzky's doubts as to the feasibility of the project rather than praise and admiration for it. Even so, Lissitzky generally appreciated the artistic talents of Tatlin and gave him credit for the establishment of the Constructivist movement — which he emphasized in his book *Die Kunstismen* coauthored with Hans Arp in 1925 (Erlenbach-Zürich: Rentsch) by reproducing one of Tatlin's counter-reliefs as well as the detail of Tatlin holding the wooden shaft from the 1920 photograph.

The interplay of verticals and circles here is typical of Lissitzky's geometric work of this period and reminds one of his title page for the portfolio *Sieg über die Sonne* (see No. 754 [R634]). The insertion of the compasses in the composition is also a device common to Lissitzky's practice. They appear, for example, in the several versions of his photographic and photogramic self-portrait of 1924, where they are used, of course, not for ironic effect.

Victory over the Sun: opera in two actions with prologue by Velimir Khlebnikov, libretto by Alexei Kruchenykh, and music by Mikhail Matiushin. First produced at the Luna Park Theater, St. Petersburg, on 5 December, 1913, with designs by Kazimir Malevich. Produced by Unovis (Affirmers of the New Art) in Vitebsk on 6 February, 1920, with designs by Vera Ermolaeva and some costumes by Kazimir Malevich. Lissitzky's version, incorporating the set of puppets, was projected but not produced.
See No. 458 [R481] for plot summary.

752 [R632].
Wrapper for the portfolio "Figurinen, die Plastische Gestaltung der Elektro-Mechanischen Schau Sieg über die Sonne," 1923.
Red cardboard with black letter "F" superimposed.
21¼ x 18½ in., 54 x 47 cm.
Inscription: yellow tag with black letters on upper part of wrapper reads "El Lissitzky."
Provenance: Margo Schab, New York, 18 December, 1980.

752

753   754   755

The letter "F" is formed when the wrapper is closed.

Lissitzky also designed a cover for the proposed Russian edition of the portfolio incorporating the Cyrillic letter "Ф" [F] as a major component. The original gouache for this, in the TG, is reproduced in Lissitzky-Küppers, *El Lissitzky,* plate 54.

753 [R633].
Table of Contents for the Portfolio "Figurinen, die Plastische Gestaltung der Elektro-Mechanischen Schau Sieg über die Sonne," 1923.
Colored lithograph.
Signed in pencil and numbered in the plate; also numbered in red pencil by Lissitzky: "No. 26."
20½ x 17⅜ in., 52 x 44 cm.
Other inscriptions: lower right in ink: "Für die liebe Frau und Herrn Dr. Steinitz mit besten Grüssen. Hannover, Feb 1924"; signed in ink "El Lissitzky."

For the reproduction and description of copies of the folio see L162, p. 46; L211, Lot 16.
Provenance: Margo Schab, New York, July, 1979.

Note: Dr. Ernst Steinitz was Director of the Jewish Hospital in Hanover, where Lissitzky underwent medical tests for his tuberculosis in 1923. His wife, Käte Steinitz, was an artist and at one time was close to Kurt Schwitters. Dr. and Frau Steinitz were art patrons and collectors who played a leading role in Hanover cultural life.

754 [R634].
Title Page for the Portfolio "Figurinen, die Plastische Gestaltung der Elektro-Mechanischen Schau Sieg über die Sonne" (Figure 1), 1923.
Colored lithograph.
Signed in pencil and numbered in the plate.
20½ x 17⅜ in., 52 x 44 cm.
Provenance: Margo Schab, New York, July, 1979.

A pencil sketch for this design is reproduced in Lissitzky-Küppers, *El Lissitzky,* plate 56; also see G28, fig. 130A.

755 [138; R635].
Design for the Announcer (Ansager, Figure 2), 1923.
Colored lithograph.
Signed in pencil and numbered in the plate.
20½ x 17⅜ in., 52 x 44 cm.
Provenance: Margo Schab, New York, July, 1979.
Lissitzky used this design as an illustration to his interpretation of Maiakovsky's *Dlia golosa* [For the Voice], Berlin-Moscow: State Publishing-House, 1923.

756 [139; R636].
Design for the Sentinel (Posten, Figure 3), 1923.
Colored lithograph.
Signed in pencil and numbered in the plate.
20½ x 17⅜ in., 52 x 44 cm.
Provenance: Margo Schab, New York, July, 1979.

756   757   758

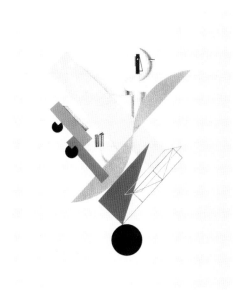

759

760

761

757 [140; R637].
Design for the Anxious One (Angstliche, Figure 4), 1923.
Colored lithograph.
Signed and numbered in the plate.
20½ x 17⅜ in., 52 x 44 cm.
Provenance: Louis Mestre, New York, 1974.

758 [NIRE].
Design for the Globetrotter in Time (Globetrotter in der Zeit, Figure 5), 1923.
Color print.
22 x 18 in., 56 x 45.7 cm.
Provenance: The Prints Shop, London, May, 1980.

759 [141; R638].
Design for the Globetrotter in Time (Globetrotter in der Zeit, Figure 5), 1923.
Colored lithograph.
Signed in pencil and numbered in the plate.
20½ x 17⅜ in., 52 x 44 cm.
Provenance: Margo Schab, New York, April 16, 1981.

760 [142; R639].
Design for the Sportsmen (Sportsmänner, Figure 6), 1923.
Colored lithograph.
Signed in pencil and numbered in the plate.
20½ x 17⅜ in., 52 x 44 cm.
Provenance: Margo Schab, New York, July, 1979.
A pencil sketch for this is reproduced in G28, fig. 130B.

761 [143; R640].
Design for the Troublemaker (Zankstifter, Figure 7), 1923.
Colored lithograph.
Signed in pencil and numbered in the plate.
21 x 18 in., 53.3 x 45.7 cm.
Provenance: the Fisher Gallery, London, 27 November, 1979.
A version of this is reproduced in *Zenit*, Belgrade, 1922, No. 17-18, p. 49.

762 [144; R641].
Design for the Old Man with Head Two Steps Back (Alter: Kopf 2 Schritt Hinten, Figure 8), 1923.

Colored lithograph.
Signed in pencil and numbered in the plate.
20½ x 17⅜ in., 52 x 44 cm.
Provenance: Louis Mestre, New York, 1975.
A pencil sketch for this is reproduced in Lissitzky-Küppers, *El Lissitzky*, plate 57; also see G28, fig. 130C.

763 [145; R642].
Design for the Gravediggers (Totengräber, Figure 9), 1923.
Colored lithograph.
Signed in pencil and numbered in the plate.
20⅞ x 18⅛ in., 53 x 46 cm.
Provenance: Galerie Gmurzynska, Cologne, October, 1978.

764 [146; R643].
Design for the New Man (Neuer, Figure 10), 1923.
Colored lithograph.
Signed in pencil and numbered in the plate.
20½ x 17⅜ in., 52 x 44 cm.
Provenance: Margo Schab, New York, July, 1979.

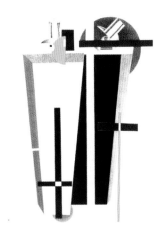

762

763

764

Note: Lissitzky's portfolio of ten figures based on the Cubo-Futurist opera *Victory over the Sun* was published by Leunis and Chapman, Hanover, in the summer of 1923 in an edition of seventy-five copies. Inspired by the production of the opera in Vitebsk in February, 1920 (see No. 458 [R481]), Lissitzky elaborated his idea of a number of figurines that would be used as a puppet interpretation of this "transrational" spectacle. Although the puppet version was not implemented, Lissitzky made designs for various personages in the opera, adding some of his own, and the result was the portfolio — which he hoped would appear as a Russian edition in 1920-21. One or two of the figures bear the same title as their predecessors of 1913 Luna Park production (e.g., *The New Man*), but most do not (e.g., there is neither a *Sentinel* nor an *Anxious One* in the 1913 libretto), and one can assume that these discrepancies were the result of Lissitzky's free interpretation rather than of an inaccurate German translation of the Russian titles; Kruchenykh, author of the 1913 libretto, seems to have liked Lissitzky's innovations.[560] Apparently, the Hanover publication did not include all the images that Lissitzky created for his project. A gouache and ink design for a so-called *Stage Machine,* in the collection of the Theatermuseum, Cologne, is reproduced in I62, p. 123. The drawing and lithograph for this are in the TG, and the former is reproduced in Lissitzky-Küppers, *El Lissitzky,* plate 63, and in the Leipzig, 1982-83, catalog, p. 84; all these items are missing from the portfolio. The Theatermuseum, Cologne, also possesses curious variants (reproduced in I62, p. 124), and a version of No. 763 [R642] is reproduced in I2, p. 51. Lissitzky had the following to say about his creation:

> The sun as the expression of the world's age-old energy is torn down from the sky by modern man; the power of his technological supremacy creates for itself a new source of energy. This idea is woven into the opera simultaneously with the action. The language is alogical. Individual singing parts are phonetic poems.
>
> The text of the opera compelled me to preserve something of the anatomy of the human body in my puppets. The colours of the individual sections of these pages are to be regarded in the same way as in my Proun works, as equivalent to materials; yellow or black parts of the puppets are not painted correspondingly, but rather they are made in corresponding material, for example in bright copper, dull iron and so on.[561]

It is important to remember that Lissitzky designed his figures primarily to teach children about the revolutionary events and the great future. Lissitzky's concern with the visual education of children (cf. his book *Pro dva kvadrata*) began with his colorful,

Chagall-like illustrations to the 1917 edition of *Khad Gadya* (a Passover book for children), but his attempts to transmit the idea of the new society and the new art through abstract images to a young audience bore fruit only in 1919-20. In 1919 Lissitzky illustrated a new edition of *Khad Gadya* with lithographed Proun designs and the following year he contributed abstract illustrations to children's stories by the Jewish writer Ben Zion Raskin to the "Jewish Art Exhibition" in Kiev. That Lissitzky wished to express clearly and concisely the political importance of his interpretation of *Victory over the Sun* is demonstrated by his concluding figure, the New Man. As one critic has written, this *deus ex machina*

> forcefully implies triumphant energy... Not only is the future man's dynamic heart communistic but so is his vision, for the left eye is formed by the Soviet red star.[562]

Lissitzky himself argued that the "Communist system of social life is creating a new man — from a tiny, insignificant wheel of a machine he has turned into its captain."[563] Lissitzky was not alone in his conception of the puppet as a vehicle for communicating new ideas. Both Liubov Popova and Alexandra Exter applied elements of their experimental artistic systems to the marionette, thereby enriching the traditions of the modern Russian puppet theater (see Note to No. 599 [R503]).

The portfolio is generally considered to be among the finest examples of Constructivist printmaking, but it is rarely found complete, especially with the wrapper intact, in part because under the Hitler régime many copies were destroyed in the late 1930s as examples of "degenerate art." (The entire set of the figures, except for the wrapper, is reproduced in Richter, *El Lissitzky,* unpaginated; part of the set is reproduced in color in Lissitzky-Küppers, *El Lissitzky,* plates 52-62).[564]

558   I. Erenburg: *A vse-taki ona vertitsia,* Berlin: Gelikon, 1922, p. 85.

559   See Lissitzky's article: "Kniga s tochki zreniia zritelnogo vospriiatiia — vizualnaia kniga" in *Iskusstvo knigi,* M, 1962, No. 3, pp. 164-68.

560   A photograph of Kruchenykh holding the Lissitzky portfolio is reproduced in M. Marzaduri, comp.: *Igor Terentiev. Sobranie sochinenii,* Bologna: S. Francesco, 1988, between pp. 416 and 417.

561   From Lissitzky's foreword to the portfolio *Figurinen, die Plastische Gestaltung der Elektro-Mechanischen Schau "Sieg über die Sonne,"* Hanover: Leunis and Chapman, 1923. Translation in Lissitzky-Küppers, *El Lissitzky,* p. 352.

562   Mansbach, *Visions of Totality,* p. 25.

563   L. Lisitsky: "Novaia kultura" in *Shkola i revoliutsiia,* Vitebsk, 1919, No. 23, p. 11. For an English translation see P. Nisbet: "El Lissitzky: The New Culture" in B183, pp. 257-84.

564   For detailed commentary on the folio see Milner, *Lissitzky – Overwinning op de Zon / Lissitzky-Victory over the Sun.*

MAK (pseudonym of Pavel Petrovich Ivanov; also known as Paul Mak)

Born 16 (28) June, 1891, Moscow, Russia; died 22 June, 1967, Brussels, Belgium.

Illegitimate son of Prince Alexander Vladimirovich Bariatinsky; half-brother of the theater critic and dancer Viktor Iving. Ca. 1910 attended Konstantin Yuon and Ivan Dudin's Art School in Moscow; 1911-13 cadet at the School of Cavalry Junkers and Ensigns of the Guard, St. Petersburg; ca. 1912 worked on the St. Petersburg satirical journal *Satirikon* [Satyricon] as a caricaturist, thereby establishing contact with other contributors to the journal such as Vladimir Lebedev and Nicholas Remisoff; 1910s worked in Kiev, St. Petersburg, and Moscow as a portrait painter, newspaper and magazine cartoonist (e.g., for *Zritel* [Spectator], *Golos Moskvy* [Voice of Moscow], and *Teatr v karikaturakh* [Theater in Caricatures]), and costume designer; ran a dance studio in Moscow, specializing in the tango; 1914 entered the Kiev Military Institute; 1914-18 served with the Death's Head Hussars; 1918 was jailed by the Bolsheviks for six months for refusing to discard his Imperial military uniform; 1920-21 worked at the Terevsat (Theater of Revolutionary Satire) in Moscow, establishing close contact with fellow designers there, such as Ivan Fedotov, Vasilii Komardenkov, and Ivan Maliutin; 1921 left Russia and, via Turkestan and Afghanistan, reached Iran in 1922; 1929 moved to France; 1934 one-man exhibition in London; 1930s lived in Iran, became interested in Persian miniatures; was appointed Court Painter to Reza Shah and was commissioned to paint the Coronation Picture of the Shah on the Peacock Throne; after brief sojourns in Athens and Cairo, moved to Belgium; 1958 received a Gold Medal at the "Exposition Universelle et Internationale," Brussels.[565]

Bibliography
P. Annenkov: "Pol Mak" in *Novoe russkoe slovo,* New York, 1967, 24 September.
P. Annenkov: "Khudozhnik-miniatiurist Pol Mak" in *Russkaia mysl,* Paris, 1967, 24 August (No. 2649).
C31, pp. 183, 188, 189.
E34, pp. 22-25.
H34, pp. 294, 295.
A. Shcherbatov and L. Krivoruchkina-Shcherbatova: *Pravo na proshloe,* M: Sretenskii Monastery, 2005, passim.
C190, especially chapters 9-12.

Mak began his artistic career as a professional caricaturist for the journal *Satirikon* (published in St. Petersburg between 1908 and 1913), a forum that brought him in contact with leading artists, writers, and actors. Apparently, Natalia Goncharova even painted his portrait in 1910.[566] "A man of sensitive nature," Mak was also a celebrated ballroom dancer and an actor, and he and his constant partner, Elsa Krüger (Elza Kriuger), were considered the "best pair of tango dancers in Moscow."[567] Like Mikhail Larionov, Mikhail Le-Dantiu, and other bohemians, Mak attracted public attention thanks to his civic and legal confrontations. For example, privy to inside information, Mak announced Marinetti's arrival in Russia in *Golos Moskvy* several days before the event and without the editor's permission — for which he was removed from his position. After asking the editor for an explanation, Mak slapped him in the face, an action that cost Mak a penalty of fifty rubles.[568]

765

766

767

765 [R644].
Self-Portrait as a Knight in a Fur Cape, 1953.
Gouache and pencil, heightened with gold. Signed and dated lower right in Russian: "Mak 1953."
13 x 9½ in., 33 x 24 cm.
Provenance: *Imperial and Post-Revolutionary Russian Art,* London: Christie's, 5 October, 1989, Lot 344 (reproduced). The work has been lost.

766 [R645].
Caricature of Konstantin Varlamov, 1911.
Watercolor and ink.
Signed and dated lower left in Russian: "Mak 1911."
8⅝ x 7⅝ in., 22 x 19.3 cm.
Provenance: John E. Bowlt, New York, August, 1974, who had purchased it in a bookstore in the Metropole Hotel building, Moscow, 1968.
Reproduced as the frontispiece in I40.

Note: Konstantin Alexandrovich Varlamov (1848-1915) was one of Russia's greatest actors, both comic and straight. Known as the "Tsar of Russian Laughter,"[569] Varlamov

spent practically his entire professional career at the Alexandrinsky Theater, St. Petersburg,[570] appearing in plays by Nikolai Gogol, Molière, Alexander Ostrovsky, Alexander Sukhovo-Kobylin, and many other authors. By the time Mak made this sketch, Varlamov was suffering from the advanced stages of elephantiasis, although the artist has softened the horror of the condition beneath the disguise of Henry VIII (cf. Alexander Golovin's portrait of Varlamov of 1914 in the National Gallery, Stockholm). For analogous designs see L164, Lots 199-203.

767 [R646].
Mak et al.: Poster Advertising the Journal Teatr v karikaturakh [The Theater in Caricatures], 1913.
Lithograph in black and white.
20⅝ x 15½ in., 52.5 x 39.3 cm.
Inscriptions: the text announces subscription policy and details for the year 1914 and provides details on the journal's orientation, frequency, prices, etc.; the name and address of the publishing house of the poster are also supplied: Russian Printing House, 14, Bolshaia Sadovaia, Moscow.

Provenance: Viktor Kholodkov, Moscow, 1989. The same composition is reproduced as a subscription reminder in *Teatr v karikaturakh,* M, 1913, 15 December, No. 15, p. 11.

The eight component images of No. 767 are as follows (anti-clockwise on the poster):

767a [R646a].
Ivik: Headpiece.
Reproduced in *Teatr v karikaturakh,* 1913, 6 October, No. 5, p. 5.
The design shows a satyr taking the photograph of a nude girl accompanied by a second satyr playing the pipes. The identity of the caricaturist Ivik has not been established, although it may be presumed that the reference is to Iving, Mak's half-brother, i.e. the theater and ballet critic, Viktor Petrovich Iving (Ivanov, 1888-1952), or perhaps to Mak himself. The work is reproduced in C190, p. 377, where it is captioned "In the Cinema" and attributed to "Paul."

767a

А. А. Бахрушинъ.

767c

Наташа Труханова на морскомъ пляжѣ.

767d

767b

767b [R646b].
Joe: *Stanislavsky and Nemirovich-Danchenko*.
Reproduced in *Teatr v karikaturakh,* 1913, 8 September, No. 1, p. 7.
Konstantin Sergeevich Stanislavsky (real name: Alexeev, 1863-1938) and Vladimir Ivanovich Nemirovich-Danchenko (1858-1943) were the founders of the Moscow Art Theater (opened in 1898). "Joe" ("Dzho") is the pseudonym of the caricaturist Vasilii Vasilievich Kniazev (1887-1937). The work is reproduced in C190, p. 460, where it is attributed to "Paul."

767c [R646v].
Ten: *A.A. Bakhrushin*.
Reproduced in *Teatr v karikaturakh,* 1913, 8 September, No. 1, p. 8.
Alexander Alexandrovich Bakhrushin (1865-1929) was a collector of theatrical art, founding his private museum in Moscow in

1894. In 1918 the museum was nationalized, although Bakhrushin was retained as director. Moscow's main museum of theatrical art bears his name and is still located in his villa. The wooden house on which Bakhrushin is seated in the caricature bears the words (in Russian) above the entrance: "My personal museum." "Ten" is the pseudonym of the caricaturist Konstantin Arsenievich Mikhailov (1868-1919).

767d [R646g].
Ten: *Natasha Trukhanova at the Beach*.
Reproduced in *Teatr v karikaturakh,* 1913, 8 September, No. 1, p. 5.
Natalia Vladimirovna Trukhanova (1885-1956) was a ballet dancer, now remembered for her involvement in the preparations for *La Péri* in 1912 (Nos. 89-90 [R84-85]). The work is reproduced in C190, p. 391, where it is captioned "Trukhanova in the Cinema" and attributed to "Tell."

767e [R646d].
Ten: *S.I. Zimin*.
Reproduced in *Teatr v karikaturakh,* 1913, 15 September, No. 2, p. 7.
Sergei Ivanovich Zimin (1875-1942) was the founder of the Zimin Opera Theater in Moscow (opened in 1904). Ivan Bilibin designed the *Golden Cockerel* there in 1909.

767f [R646e].
Mak: *V. Piontkovskaia in the Movies*.
Reproduced in *Teatr v karikaturakh,* 1913, 15 September, No. 2, p. 10.
Valentina Ivanovna Piontkovskaia (Piątkowska, 1877-1915) was an operetta singer.
The work is reproduced in C190, p. 394, where it is captioned "V. Piontkovskaia in the Embraces of the Cinema."

С. И. Зиминъ.

767e

В. Піонтковская въ кинематографѣ.

767f

К. А. Марджановъ.

767g

767g [R646zh].
Ten: K.A. Mardzhanov.
Reproduced in *Teatr v karikaturakh*, 1913, 13 October, No. 6, p. 14.
Kote Mardzhanishvili (Konstantin Alexandrovich Mardzhanov, 1872-1933), the Georgian theater director, was founder of the Free Theater in Moscow (see No. 953 [R783]). He supervised a number of experimental productions (see Nos. 520-24 [R395-99]).

767h

767h [R646z].
Mak: A.I. Yuzhin.
Alexander Ivanovich Yuzhin-Sumbatov (Sumbatashvili, 1857-1927) was a famous Moscow actor.

Note: The journal *Teatr v karikaturakh* was a Moscow weekly published between September, 1913, and November, 1914, under the editorship of Evgenii Ivanov. As the title would imply, the journal parodied and caricatured personalities and events connected with the stage (especially in Moscow). While it made frequent reference to the distinguished actors and impresarios of the day (e.g., Nikita Baliev, Boris Borisov, Nemirovich-Danchenko, Stanislavsky, Yuzhin, etc.), the journal also cultivated an interest, albeit an ironic one, in the exploits of the Moscow Futurists, particularly Goncharova and Mikhail Larionov, and ran a number of articles and interviews connected with their artistic and theatrical experiments. *Teatr v karikaturakh* was oriented towards the middle-class reader and gave wide coverage to programs in the Moscow cabarets, music-halls, private ballet evenings, dinner dances, etc. Mak was one of the team of caricaturists working for the journal, which also included Ten, Ivik, Tango, Chelli (Viacheslav Konstantinovich Vasiliev, 1888-1914), and also Dmitrii Moor (see No. 605 [R858]).[571]

565 Mak's son, Dimitri Doudrine-Mak of Brussels, and Ruben Markarian of London, a collector of Mak's work, have graciously provided much of the above information.
566 For a reproduction of the work see B137, p. 68.
567 N. Serpinskaia: "Memuary intelligentki dvukh epokh." Manuscript in RGALI, f. 1604, op. 1, ed. khr. 1248, p. 46, L. 90. For a photograph of Mak dancing see F36, between pp. 96 and 97. For some information on Mak and Kriuger as dance partners see Yu. Tsivian: "The Tango in Russia" in B183, No. 2, pp. 306-33; and G. Kovalenko: "Elza Kriuger," ibid., pp. 334-57.
568 According to the journal *Zhizn i iskusstvo*, K, 1914, No. 7, p. 9.
569 Such is the title of Eduard Stark's monograph on Varlamov, i.e., *Tsar russkogo smekha Konstantin Aleksandrovich Varlamov*, P: Evdokimov, 1916.
570 For photographs of Varlamov in various dramatic roles see the journal *Solntse Rossii*, P, 1915, No. 287, August, pp. 8-13.
571 For Mak's contributions see *Teatr v karikaturakh*, M, 1913, No.2, pp. 3, 10, 12. Also see his renderings in *Zritel*, K, 1913, No. 2, plate 8. For reproductions of late works see, for example, L104, Lots 225-27.

MALEVICH, Kazimir Severinovich

Born 11 (23) February, 1879, near Kiev, Ukraine; died 15 May, 1935, Leningrad, Russia.

1904 audited courses at MIPSA; 1905-10 studied under Fedor Rerberg in Moscow; ca. 1910 influenced by Neo-Primitivism; 1910-17 contributed to many exhibitions including the "Jack of Diamonds," "Union of Youth," "Donkey's Tail," "Target," "Tramway V," "0.10" (first public showing of Suprematist works), and "Store"; 1913 met with Alexei Kruchenykh and Nikolai Matiushin for a weekend at the latter's dacha, which meeting was declared the First All-Russian Congress of Futurists; designed the sets and costumes for the transrational opera *Victory over the Sun* in St. Petersburg; illustrated avant-garde booklets by Velimir Khlebnikov, Kruchenykh, and other poets; 1914 met Filippo Marinetti on the latter's arrival in Russia; 1915 publicized his invention of Suprematism; 1918 active on various levels within IZO NKP; 1919-22 taught at the Vitebsk Popular Art Institute / Vitebsk Art-Practical Institute; coorganized Unovis; attracted many young artists including Ilia Chashnik, Vera Ermolaeva, El Lissitzky, and Nikolai Suetin; 1922 moved to Petrograd where he began to work for Ginkhuk; 1920s active on various levels; wrote many essays on art; gave attention to the architectural possibilities of Suprematism, inventing his so-called *arkhitektony, planity*, and *zemlianity;* 1927 visited Warsaw and Berlin with a one-man exhibition; established contact with the Bauhaus; late 1920s returned to a figurative kind of painting, even working on social themes such as *Working Woman* and *The Smith*.

Bibliography
Malevich is the subject of a very large number of monographs, catalogs, and articles. The titles below are a representative selection only.

T. Andersen, ed.: *K.S. Malevich. Essays on Art,* Copenhagen: Borgen, 1968-78 (four volumes).
T. Andersen. *Malevich,* Amsterdam: Stedelijk Museum, 1970.
A.B. Nakov, ed.: *Malévitch. Ecrits,* Paris: Champ Libre, 1975.
J. Bowlt and C. Douglas, eds.: *Kazimir Malevich 1878-1935-1978.* Special issue of *Soviet Union* (Tempe, Arizona), Vol. 5, Part 2 (1978).
A. Gmurzynska et al.: *Malewitsch.* Catalog of exhibition at the Galerie Gmurzynska, Cologne, 1978.
J.-C. Marcadé, ed.: *Malévitch. Actes du Colloque international tenu au Centre Pompidou, Musée national d'art moderne, Paris,* Lausanne: L'Age d'Homme, 1979.
C. Douglas: *Swans of Other Worlds: Kazimir Malevich and the Origins of Abstraction in Russia,* Ann Arbor: UMI, 1980.
J. Bowlt: *Journey into Non-Objectivity. The Graphic Work of Kazimir Malevich and Other Members of the Russian Avant-Garde.* Catalog of exhibition at the Dallas Museum of Fine Arts, Dallas, Texas, 1980.
J.H. Martin et al.: *Malévitch: Oeuvres de Casimir Severinovitch Malévitch (1878-1935),* Paris: Centre Georges Pompidou, 1980.
W.S. Simmons: *Kasimir Malevich's Black Square and the Genesis of Suprematism 1907-1915,* Ann Arbor: UMI, 1981.
L. Zhadova: *Malevich. Suprematism and Revolution in Russian Art 1910-1930,* London: Thames and Hudson, 1982 (this is a translation of B23).
E. Petrova et al.: *Kazimir Malevich. Artist and Theoretician,* Paris: Flammarion, 1990.
J. D'Andrea et al.: *Kazimir Malevich.* Catalog of exhibition at the National Gallery of Art, Washington, D.C., the Armand Hammer Museum of Art and Cultural Center, Los Angeles, and the Metropolitan Museum of Art, New York, 1990-91.
R. Crone and D. Moos: *Kazimir Malevich. The Climax of Disclosure,* Chicago: University of Chicago, 1991.
V. Zavalishin and J. Bowlt: *Kazimir Malevich,* New York: Effect, 1992.
S. Fauchereau: *Malévitch,* Paris: Cercle d'Art, 1992. Translated to English as: *Malevich,* London: Academy, 1993.
A. Shatskikh and D. Sarabianov: *Malevich,* Moscow: Iskusstvo, 1993.
A. Shatskikh, comp.: *K.S. Malevich. Sobranie sochinenii v 5 tt.,* M: Gileia, 1995-2004 (five volumes).
E. Weiss: *Kasimir Malewitsch.* Catalog of exhibition, Cologne: Museum Ludwig, 1995-96.
J. Milner: *Kazimir Malevich and the Art of Geometry,* New Haven: Yale University Press, 1996.
A. Shatskikh: *Kazimir Malevich,* M: Slovo, 1996.
T. Kotovich, ed.: *Malevich. Klassicheskii avangard, Vitebsk,* Vitebsk: Pankov, 1997 onwards (twelve issues until 2010).
V. Gusev et al.: *Kazimir Malevich,* SP: Palace Editions, 2000.
E. Petrova et al.: *V kruge Malevicha,* SP: Palace Editions, 2000.
A. Shatskikh: *Malevich. Chernyi kvadrat,* SP: Azbuka, 2001.
M. Drutt: *Suprematism.* Catalog of exhibition at the Solomon R. Guggenheim Museum, New York, 2002.
A.B. Nakov: *Malewicz,* Paris: Biro, 2002.

C. Beltramo et al.: *Kasimir Malevič: Oltre la figurazione, oltre l'astrazione.* Catalog of exhibition at the Museo del Corso, Rome, 2005.
A.B. Nakov: *Kazimir Malewicz. Le peintre absolu,* Paris: Thalia, 2006-07 (four volumes).
C. Douglas and C. Lodder, eds.: *Rethinking Malevich,* London: Pindar, 2007.
T. Goriacheva and I. Karasik: *Prikliucheniia chernogo kvadrata / The Adventures of the Black Square,* SP: Palace Editions, 2007.
A. Shatskikh: *Vitebsk. The Life of Art,* New Haven: Yale university Press, 2007.
F. Malsch et al.: *Malewitsch und sein Einfluss.* Catalog of exhibition at the Kunst Museum Liechtenstein, Vaduz, 2008.
A. Shatskikh: *Kazimir Malevich i obshchestvo Supremus,* M: Tri kvadrata, 2009.
S. Khan-Magomedov: *Kazimir Malevich,* M: Gordeev, 2010.
R. Bartlett and S. Dadswell, eds.: *Victory over the Sun,* University of Exeter Press, 2012.
T. Goriacheva; intr.: *Nas budet troe. Kazimir Malevich. Ilia Chashnik.* Nikolai Suetin. Catalog of exhibition at TG, 2012.
A. Shatskikh: *The Black Square and the Origin of Suprematism,* New Haven: Yale University, 2012.

Malevich recalled how, from a very early age, he was drawn to the element of paint and how, as a young boy in Kiev, he found a sensual delight in using a house painter's paints: "I was so gratified by the paint itself. I experienced a very pleasant sensation from the very paint on the brush." [572] In other words, Malevich was drawn to the physical, tactile property of art, an attraction that he expressed in the thick strata of his Neo-Primitivist canvases of 1909-11 and in the fibrous textures of his Suprematist lithographs. There was, indeed, something vigorous and vital about Malevich, a natural, spontaneous character that brought him close to the Russian peasants whose way of life he depicted and whom he emulated.

During the period 1912-18 Malevich was at the height of his inventive powers. He produced original paintings, contributed to public debates and manifestos, participated in radical exhibitions such as "0.10", and published three versions of his important artistic credo *Ot kubizma i futurizma k suprematizmu. Novyi zhivopisnyi realizm* [From Cubism and Futurism to Suprematism. The New Painterly Realism]. Malevich welcomed the Revolution, regarding it as an overture to the complete transvaluation of esthetic values, which he saw as the task of Suprematism, his particular system of abstract art. The leftist dictatorship of the first years of the Bolshevik régime granted him, together with many colleagues (such as Ivan Kliun, Liubov Popova, and Alexander Rodchenko), an unprecedented artistic and pedagogical freedom. Malevich exploited these new opportunities as widely as he could during his brief tenure at the Vitebsk Popular Art Institute / Vitebsk Art-Practical Institute, where he exerted a profound and permanent influence on his talented students, especially Ilia Chashnik, Ivan Chervinka, Vera Ermolaeva, Lissitzky, and Nikolai Suetin. No doubt, for the messianic Malevich this was the most satisfying period of his life.

768

769

768 [R647].
Artist unknown: Portrait of Kazimir Malevich, ca. 1927.
Pencil.
10⅜ x 5⅞ in., 26.5 x 15 cm.
Reproduced in L4, Lot 12.
The reverse carries another drawing (No. 769 [R647a]).
Previously attributed to Malevich.

769 [R647a].
Artist unknown: Study for an Arkhitekton, ca. 1927.
Pencil.
10⅜ x 5⅞ in., 26.5 x 15 cm.
Reproduced in L4, Lot 12.
The reverse carries another drawing (No. 768 [R647]).
Previously attributed to Malevich.

Note: It is difficult to identify the artist of these two drawings, but, presumably, they would have been by one of Malevich's numerous students, such as Lazar Khidekel or Nikolai Suetin. Judging from documentary photographs, Malevich adopted this more sinuous hairstyle in ca. 1927. This was also the moment when Malevich was giving particular attention to the three-dimensional extension of his Suprematist system in the form of architectural designs for his so-called *planity, zemlianity,* and *arkhitektony* (models of visionary buildings for the future).

Victory over the Sun: *opera in two actions with prologue by Velimir Khlebnikov, libretto by Alexei Kruchenykh and music by Mikhail Matiushin. Produced at the Luna Park Theater, St. Petersburg, on 3 and 5 December, 1913, with designs by Kazimir Malevich.*
See No. 458 [R481] for plot summary.

The following designs for *Victory over the Sun* are all silkscreens, and their measurements are uniform, i.e., 16½ x 11½ in., 42 x 29.2 cm.

770

770 [147; R648].
Design for the Backcloth for Action I, Scene 2, 1913 (1973).
Inscriptions in Russian: right margin in Russian: "green before the funeral"; lower margin in Russian: "Scene 2. Green and black. Action I. No. 162, IV, 6/173."

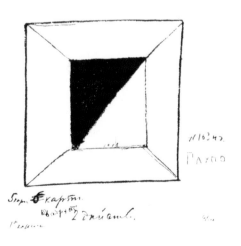

771

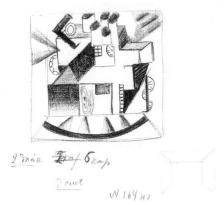

772

773

774

771 [148; R649].
Design for the Backcloth, Action II, Scene 5, 1913 (1973).
Inscriptions in Russian right margin: "No. 163 [illegible] Stupid"; lower left in Russian: "Scene 5. Scene ("6" crossed out). Square. Acti[on] II"; lower margin in Russian: "Scene 1 2nd act[ion]."

Note: Some scholars regard this design as "abstract" and as the point of departure for Malevich's Suprematist painting of 1915 onward; others, however, identify the composition as a figurative one:

> Although at first glance the inner square seems to be divided by a diagonal into a black and white triangle, this in fact is not the case. The dividing line between black and white is actually curved downward slightly so that it intersects the small square on its lower edge, about a tenth of the way along the total width of the square. Thus the inner square may well be meant to show a small section of an enormous sun.[573]

772 [R650].
Design for a House, Action II, Scene 6, 1913 (1973).
Inscriptions: lower margin in Russian: "2nd Action. 2nd Scene, Scene 6. House. No. 164."

773 [149; R651].
Costume Design for a Futurist Strongman, 1913 (1973).
Initialed lower right in Russian.
Other inscription: lower margin in Russian: "1st Futurist strongman. 4-2 pieces."

774 [150; R652].
Costume Design for Nero, 1913 (1973).
Inscribed right margin in Russian: "Nero."

775 [151; R653].
Costume Design for a Mugger, 1913 (1973).
Inscribed lower right in Russian: "Mugger."

776 [152; R654].
Costume Design for a Coward, 1913 (1973).
Inscribed lower margin in Russian: "Costume design for the cowards."

777 [R655].
Costume Design for the Old Timer, 1913 (1973).
Inscribed lower right in Russian: "Old timer."

775

776

777

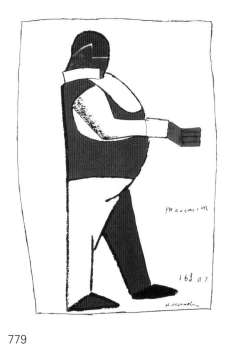

778

779

780

778 [R656].
Costume Design for Many and One, 1913 (1973).
Inscribed lower margin in Russian: "Costume for many and one [Sun] bearers, [the latter] same but green."

779 [153; R657].
Costume Design for a Fat Man, 1913 (1973).
Signed lower right margin in Russian: "KMalev."
Other inscription: right margin in Russian: "A fat man 165 II 7."

780 [R658].
Costume Design for a Guy with Bad Intentions, 1913 (1973).
Initialed lower right in Russian.

Other inscription: right margin in Russian: "a certain guy with bad intentions" and "12 IIX 166."

781 [R659].
Costume Design for a Singer in the Chorus, 1913 (1973).
Inscribed lower margin in Russian: "a singer in the chorus, the same, one light blue, one indigo."

782 [154; R660].
Costume Design for a New Man, 1913 (1973).
Inscribed lower margin in Russian: "8 IV x costume for the new men."

783 [R661].
Costume Design for an Attentive Worker, 1913 (1973).
Inscribed lower margin in Russian: "An attentive worker"; right margin: "167 i g."

784 [155; R662].
Costume Design for the Enemy, 1913 (1973).
Signed and dated lower left in Russian: "K. Malevich 1913."
Other inscription: lower right in Russian: "The enemy."

Note: These designs for *Victory over the Sun* are from the set of fifteen silkscreens produced as a portfolio in an edition of 150 copies by the Galerie Gmurzynska,

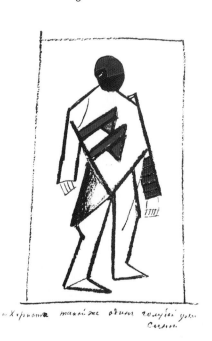

781

782

783

7.

784

572 K.   Malevich: "Autobiography"   (1923)   in
     Malewitsch, pp. 16-17.
573 C. Douglas, "Victory over the Sun" in G55, p. 82.
     For further commentary on the 1913 production of
     Victory over the Sun see G. Erslöh: "*Pobeda nad
     solntsem.*" Ein futuristisches Drama von A.
     Kručenych, Munich: Sagner, 1976. Also see V. and
     J.-C. Marcadé, eds.: *La Victoire sur le Soleil,*
     Lausanne: L'Age d'Homme, 1976; and G87, pp.
     27-64. Kruchenykh described the production and
     the preparations for it in his memoirs, *Nash
     vykhod / Our Arrival.* See B184, pp. 59-69.
574 In 1980 a recreation in English translation was
     undertaken by the California Institute of Arts (see
     footnote 254 in Ermolaeva section). According to
     various sources, including Douglas, *Swans of
     Other Worlds,* p. 85, Malevich produced more
     costumes for *Victory over the Sun* in the late
     1920s.
575 Anon.: "Peterburg" in *Muzy,* K, 1913, No. 1, 25
     December, p. 20.
576 For additional information on the decorations for
     Victory over the Sun, see M. Etkind: "'Soiuz
     molodezhi'   i   ego   stsenograficheskie
     eksperimenty" in G50, 1981, pp. 258-59.
577 Letter from Kazimir Malevich to Alexei Kruchenykh
     dated 27 May, 1915. Quoted in B15, p. 95.
578 For a reproduction of one of the Malevich
     costumes for the 1920 production see B23, p.
     308. Note that all the original designs for the 1913
     production are reproduced in color, for example, in
     G49, p. 91, and I61, pp. 298-301.

Cologne, in 1973, one of which was presented to Nina and Nikita Lobanov-Rostovsky in New York in 1973 by Antonina Gmurzynska, then owner of the Galerie Gmurzynska. The silkscreens are enlarged copies of the original designs in the GMTMA (reproduced in color in G49, p. 91; and in black and white in B2, pp. 162-63; B23, pp. 26-35; also see K50 (a), pp. 383, 396; K50 (b), unnumbered), and were published under the title *Kasimir Malewitsch "Sieg über die Sonne" 1913-1973.*

The Cubo-Futurist or "transrational" opera, *Victory over the Sun,* performed on 3 and 5 December 1913 in St. Petersburg,[574] not only integrated a number of different artistic and musical ideas of the time, but also served as an important iconographic source for concurrent and subsequent paintings and graphics by Malevich. *Victory over the Sun* was an experiment in literary, musical, and pictorial alogicality. The language, often neologistic and recondite, told the story of a band of Futurist strongmen who endeavored to disrupt all norms by challenging and conquering the Sun. The music depended on intense chromatics, bold consecutive fifths, and melismata produced by an out-of-tune piano and a student choir that sang flat. For his sets and costumes Malevich relied on a highly geometrized conception that, if still illustrating a certain scene or figure, reduced it to schematic components.

Naturally, the opera caused a scandal and evoked a good deal of audience participation. The following eyewitness report provides the description of a number of details that have often been overlooked in the general literature on *Victory over the Sun*:

> The second spectacle was dedicated to the opera *Victory over the Sun,* which was preceded by V. Khlebnikov's prologue under the title "Unskilled Newslets."

> A. Kruchenykh also read a "prologue" against the background of a curtain made out of a regular old bed sheet with "portraits" of Kruchenykh, Malevich, and Matiushin daubed on it. As for the kind of "prologue" it was, well one can tell from the fact that it was dominated by the following kind of inhuman expressions:
>
> "Bytavy, ukravy, mytavy."
>
> Actually, the public did understand something — realizing that it would soon be the recipient of sounds from some kind of "pipe dream."
>
> Since the Futurists did not wish to be like "everyone else," instead of pulling up the curtain, they tore it in halves.
>
> That was when the "opera," if I may call it that, began...
>
> It became tedious at the end, so the public itself chipped in to help the exhausted Futurists. After almost every cue, you could hear some witty remark from the public, so that, very shortly, instead of one spectacle in the theater, we had two: one on stage, the other in the audience. The occasional "music" was replaced by cat-calls which, incidentally, harmonized very well with the crazy décors and with the gibberish that resounded from the stage... [575]

Central images from the opera such as bayonets, fish, a saw, and piano keys recur in Malevich's paintings of the time, e.g., *Portrait of the Composer Mikhail Matiushin* (1913, TG) and *Englishman in Moscow* (1914, Stedelijk Museum, Amsterdam). In addition, the strutted wheels of the ill-fated airplane that crashes to the stage during the course of the action became a regular motif for Malevich and may explain the curious "droplets" in the *Portrait of Matiushin. Victory over the Sun* played a major role in Malevich's creative life and its symbols firmly implanted themselves in his artistic imagination.

As far as the "abstract" design for Action II, Scene 5, is concerned (No. 771 [R649]), later on Malevich regarded its geometry as an important junction in his own artistic development. Whether the image was, indeed, a rendering of the sun or not,[576] in preparing a second collection of designs for a new edition of the booklet *Pobeda nad solntsem* [Victory over the Sun] in May, 1915 (not published), Malevich actually drew a black square. As he wrote to Kruchenykh at that time: "This sketch is going to have great significance in painting; what had been done unconsciously is now yielding remarkable fruits."[577] Malevich returned to *Victory over the Sun* in 1920 in Vitebsk, when, with Vera Ermolaeva and the Unovis group, he contributed designs to a new production. What his new response to the square within a square was for this production is not known.[578] (Cf. Nos. 458 [R481], 752-64 [R632-43].)

MALIAVIN, Filipp Andreevich (Maliavine, Philippe)

Born 10 (22) October, 1869, Kazanka, Samara Region, Russia; died 23 December, 1940, Nice, France.

1885-91 studied icon painting in the studios of the St. Panteleimon Monastery, Agion Oros, Greece; 1891 on the recommendation of the sculptor Vladimir Beklemishev decided to pursue the career of professional painter; 1892-99 attended IAA, studying under Pavel Chistiakov and then Ilia Repin; 1895 began to paint scenes from peasant life and also portraits of contemporaries; 1899 his picture *Laughter* created a furor at the IAA exhibition; in close contact with Sergei Diaghilev and the World of Art society; 1900 visited France; contributed to the "Exposition Universelle" in Paris, where *Laughter* earned him a Gold Medal; from this time onwards contributed to many exhibitions at home and abroad; married Natalia Novak-Savich and retired to an estate near Riazan; 1903 onwards member of the Union of Russian artists; 1910s worked mainly on his estate; contacted by Konstantin Mardzhanov to design a production of Nikolai Gogol's *Fair at Sorochintsy* for the Free Theater, Moscow; 1920 moved to Moscow; 1921 made several portraits of Lenin and other political dignitaries at the III Congress of the Communist International in Moscow; 1922 contributed to the "Association of Artists of Revolutionary Russia"; emigrated to France; 1920s-30s lived mainly in Paris and Nice; 1930s several one-man exhibitions, including Belgrade and Prague (1933), Nice (1934, 1937), London and Stockholm (1935).

Bibliography
V. Pica: *Philippe Maliavine,* Milan: Galleria Bardi, 1929.
Philippe Maliavine. Catalog of exhibition at the Camerata degli Artisti, Rome, 1932.
N. Aleksandrova: *Filipp Maliavin,* M: Sovetskii khudozhnik, 1966.
O. Zhivova: *Filipp Andreevich Maliavin,* M: Iskusstvo, 1967.
N. Murashova: *Filipp Andreevich Maliavin.* Catalog of exhibition at the Scientific-Research Museum of the Academy of Arts of the USSR, L, 1969.
J50.
A. Korobtsova: *Philip Maliavin,* L: Aurora, 1988.
Philip Andreyevich Maliavin. Works from the Artist's Studio. Catalog of auction at Sotheby's, London, 1998, 19 February.

Maliavin is remembered above all for his colorful renderings of Russian peasant women (in Russian: *baby*) whose "immobile, iconic visages"[579] emerge from the seething floridity of red, orange, and yellow dresses. The riot of color in Maliavin's picture *Laughter,* for example, bewildered visitors to the 1899 Academy of Arts exhibition in St. Petersburg. However, it so captivated the French critics when it was shown at the "Exposition Universelle" in Paris in 1900 that the artist was awarded a Gold Medal and the following year the picture was acquired by the Ca' Pesaro in Venice — prestigious moments that boded well for Maliavin's future career. Indeed, living at his estate near Riazan, Maliavin continued to paint his *baby* and *muzhiki,* dynamic canvases that impressed by their "magic" and "iridescence."[580] In canvases such as *Whirlwind* (1906, TG) and *Verka* (1913, RM) Maliavin emphasized the massive strength of the peasants vaunting the bold patterns of their dresses and headscarves, but he manifested little interest in the social connotations of the toiling masses or in the sentimental philosophy that afforded a special messianic status to the Russian peasantry — such as we might sense in the rural descriptions of Abram Arkhipov, Andrei Riabushkin, and Zinaida Serebriakova.

A primary student of Repin, Maliavin was a master of the spontaneous portrait, rendering likeness and mood in quick, concentrated strokes of the pencil or brush. Maliavin's portraits of contemporaries, such as Léon Bakst, Igor Grabar, Anna Ostroumova-Lebedeva, and Konstantin Somov, demonstrate strong powers of observation and technical bravura that remind us of the concurrent work of Leonid Pasternak, Valentin Serov, and Mikhail Vrubel. His early oil portraits, e.g., of Kontantin Somov (1895) and Elizaveta Martynova (1897) (both in the RM), are especially successful in their rendering of the sudden gesture and the casual pose, evoking a veracity and vivacity that appealed to his advocates, such as Alexandre Benois and Diaghilev. However, these qualities weakened as time passed, and his portraits of the late 1910s and 1920s, especially the more official commissions, are less adventurous.

785

785 [R663].
Self-Portrait, ca. 1925.
Black ink and red crayon.
Signed lower right: "Ph. Maliavine."
11 x 7½ in., 28 x 19 cm.
Provenance: *Russian Paintings, Drawings, Watercolors and Sculpture,* London: Sotheby's, 14 May, 1980, Lot 115 (reproduced). Now in a private collection.

786 [R664].
Portrait of Anatolii Lunacharsky, Lenin, and Lev Trotsky, 1921.
Pencil, heightened with white chalk.
Signed lower right in pencil in Russian: "F. Maliavin"
11¾ x 17⅜ in., 30 x 44 cm.
Other inscription: on reverse in ink a certificate by Maliavin's daughter, Zoya, in Russian: "I certify that this design was made from life by my late father, Academician Filipp Maliavin in 1921 in Moscow."
Provenance: *Nineteenth and Twentieth Century European Paintings, Drawings, Watercolours and Sculpture and Russian Paintings, Drawings and Watercolors,* London: Sotheby's, 28 February, 1983, Lot 210 (reproduced).
Reproduced in F107, p. 39. Another version is in a private collection in Nice.

Note: Vladimir Ilich Lenin (pseudonym of Vladimir Ilich Ulianov, 1870-1924) is pictured here with Anatolii Vasilievich Lunacharsky (1875-1933) on the left and Lev Davidovich Trotsky (pseudonym of Lev Davidovich Bronshtein, 1879-1940) on the right. At this time Lunacharsky was head of NKP, holding responsibility for all the arts; while Trotsky was then Commissar for War. It is not known exactly when Maliavin made this triple portrait, but if the date is June-July of 1921, then the time and place are probably one of the meetings of the III Congress of the Communist International in the Kremlin. Maliavin had also been commissioned to paint an oil portrait of Lenin and, to that end, made many preparatory sketches, although none of them conveys the energy and acuity manifest, for example, in Natan Altman's and Isaak Brodsky's renderings of the same period.[581]

Shortly after these sessions, in January, 1922, Maliavin wrote to Lenin asking permission to take his one-man exhibition through Europe and Russia and to organize the publication of a series of reproduction albums of his paintings and drawings "which [would] demonstrate typical proletarian art."[582] Lenin, who liked the idea, showed the request to Lunacharsky, who while voicing reservations about Maliavin's

786

ultimate esthetic worth, felt his art to be "democratic." Lunacharsky wrote:

> He's certainly not a run-of-the-mill painter, he's distinctive, profound, democratic, spontaneous, a great guy... [But] he has a terrifyingly high opinion of himself and the slightest doubt in his being Russian — or even European artist No. 1, well, he regards that as a personal insult.[583]

579　Murashova in Filipp Andreevich Maliavin, p. 8.
580　Mikhail Nesterov spoke of Maliavin's "iridescent color" and "magic." Quoted in Korobtsova, *Philip Maliavin*, p. 5.
581　Other sketches of Lenin by Maliavin are or were in the collection of the Central Lenin Museum, Moscow. For reproductions see I. Zilbershtein: *Lenin v zarisovkakh i v vospominaniiakh khudozhnikov*, M-L: State Publishing-House, 1928, pp. 5, 9 (both dated 1920); G. Zlobin, comp.: *Vashim, tovarishch, serdtsem i imenem*, M: Progress, 1976, Vol. 2, plate 35 (dated early 1920s); O. Krivoshein: *V.I. Lenin. Zhivopis, skulptura, grafika iz sobraniia Tsentralnogo muzeia V.I. Lenina*, M: Izobrazitelnoe iskusstvo, 1986, plates 110, 111 (both dated 1921); also see A. Shefov: *Leniniana v sovetskom izobrazitelnom iskusstve*, L: Iskusstvo, 1986, pp. 56-61.
582　Letter from Filipp Maliavin to Lenin dated no later than 14 January, 1922. In V. Shleev, comp.: *V.I. Lenin i izobrazitelnoe iskusstvo*, M: Izobrazitelnoe iskusstvo, 1977, p. 483.
583　Letter from Anatolii Lunacharsky to Lenin dated 16 January, 1922. Ibid., p. 484.

MANDEL, Semeon Solomonovich

Born 27 October (9 November), 1907, Vinnitsa, Ukraine; died 19 September, 1974, Leningrad, Russia.

1920s student at the Vinnitsa Electrotechnical School; 1925 designed production of the ballet *Little Hunchback Horse* for a local theater; 1925-31 student at the Kiev Art Institute, attending courses in sculpture, painting, and film design (the latter supervised by Vladimir Tatlin); 1931 worked in the Kiev Film Studios; 1931 onwards worked as a designer for the theater, circus, musicals, and film; 1933 moved to Leningrad; 1941-43 designed anti-German posters and caricatures during the Leningrad blockade; 1942 designed propaganda plays for the House of the Red Army, Leningrad; 1948 awarded the Stalin Prize for his work on the film *The Russian Question*; 1940s-70s collaborated with celebrated producers and actors, such as Georgii Tovstonogov and Arkadii Raikin; worked at the Leningrad Theater of Miniatures; 1952 artist-in-residence for the Lenin Komsomol Theater in Leningrad; 1953 designer for the film *Masters of the Russian Ballet*; 1969 Merited Art Worker of the RSFSR.

Bibliography
V. Bazanov: "Semeon Solomonovich Mandel" in E. Davydova, comp.: *Leningradskie khudozhniki teatra*, L: Khudozhnik RSFSR, 1971, pp. 65-94.
K. Shulzhenko: *Kogda Vy sprosite menia*, M: Molodaia gvardiia, 1981, pp. 83-109, 125.
E. Grushvitskaia and G. Tovstonogov: *Semion Mandel. Teatr, kino, estrada.* Catalog of exhibition at the GMTMA, 1988.
E. Uvarova: "Mandel, Semion Semionovich" in A54, pp. 339, 340.

An outstanding artist of the theater and cinema, Mandel exerted an appreciable influence on the development of stage design in Leningrad, especially after WWII. He designed decorations for numerous theaters and also directed many public festivities in stadiums and parks. Mandel believed that the set should not be a mere background to action, but a principal component of the entire spectacle, capable of connecting organically with plot, performers, music, and audience. He built his own sets, believing that, in creating the mise-en-scène, he could provide — immediately — direction, instruction, and orientation to the actor. Indeed, Mandel thought theatrically: able to imagine the two-dimensional design in its three-dimensional or moving application. In addition to dramatic theater, Mandel directed no less than forty films, including *The Russian Question*, *A Musical Story*, and *The Wedding*.

Unknown production, Leningrad, ca. 1929

787 [R379].
Costume Design for a Narrator, ca. 1929.
Previously attributed to Alexander Vesnin.
Watercolor and pencil.
14⅜ x 10⅝ in., 36.4 x 27 cm.
Inscribed upper left in Russian in pencil: "Narrator."
Reproduced in color in B115, plate 27; I77, p. 89; and in black and white in I77, p. 138; and P55, where attributed to Alexander Vesnin.

787

Note: Elena Grushvitskaia, art historian and curator at the GMTMA, writes:

> In the mid-1980s, I was helping to organize [Mandel's] retrospective exhibition. He had already passed away and we were selecting the works together with his widow, an actress with the Leningrad Komsomol Theater... There were a set of four pieces. Mandel's widow explained that they dated from his sojourn at the Kiev [Art] Institute, where his teacher had been Tatlin. He enrolled there in ca. 1926, so this piece must be from ca. 1929, maybe it's even his graduation assignment? His widow and I were unable to establish the literary source for any relevant design. She presented three of them to the [St. Petersburg Theater] Museum and we still have them.[584]

584　Letter from Elena Grushvitskaia to John E. Bowlt, 31 August, 2010.

MATRUNIN, Boris Alexandrovich

Born 16 (28) June, 1895, Moscow, Russia; died 13 October, 1959, Moscow, Russia.

1916 graduated from the Higher Institute of Construction and Architecture in Moscow; 1917 attended MIPSA, taking courses with Konstantin Korovin; joined the Chaliapin Studio at MKhAT-2; 1922 with Fedor Fedorovsky designed production of *Eugene Onegin* for the Opera Studio of the Bolshoi Theater; thereafter responsible for designing many ballets, operas, and plays at various national theaters, e.g. Andrei Bely's *Petersburg* and Nadezhda Bromlei's *King of the Square Republic* (with Mikhail Libakov) (1925), Viktor Oransky's ballet *Three Fat Men* (1935), *Prince Igor* (1944), *Carmen* (1945), etc.; 1920s-50s contributed to many exhibitions, including the "All-Belarus Art Exhibition" (Moscow, 1927); "Moscow Theaters of the October Decade" (Moscow, 1928); "Exhibition of the Association of Workers of the Visual Arts" (Moscow, 1932); and "Gorky and the Theater" (Moscow, 1937); 1937 onwards artist-in-residence for Igor Moiseev's State Ensemble of Folk Dances; 1944 artist-in-residence for the Theater of Opera and Ballet in Perm; 1947 arrested; 1955 rehabilitated; 1959 Merited Art Worker of the RSFSR.

Bibliography

Nothing substantial has been published on Matrunin. The reader will find occasional references to him in the general publications on modern Russian art and design such as A7, Vol. 3, p. 743.

Trained as an architect, Matrunin approached the theatrical space in a rational

788

and calculated manner, facilitating the actor's movements and the visual recognizability of a particular scene. This is clear, for example, from the sets for the 1922 *Eugene Onegin* and the 1935 *Three Fat Men*,[585] which, in their economy of means and stylistic integration, elicit the "spirit of the time, the atmosphere of the epoch".[586] Like Libakov (No. 741 [R625]), Viktor Simov (No. 951 [NIRE]), and other artists working in the MKhAT tradition, Matrunin avoided the excesses of the avant-garde, exercising good judgement and common sense in his evocation of a given historical era or individual character, whether in a dramatic play, opera, or ballet, and this quality earned him high praise in a variety of productions — from Shakespeare's *Taming of the Shrew* (MKhAT, 1918) to *The Tale of Ivan the Fool and His Brothers* that Mikhail Chekhov adapted from Lev Tolstoi's prose (MKhAT, 1921).

Even so, Matrunin is now remembered more for his numerous scenic contributions to Moiseev's State Ensemble of Folk Dance in the late 1930s, for which he designed sets, costumes, and props for all manner of Russian, Georgian, Kazakh, Ukrainian, and Belorussian popular spectacles. In this capacity, and mindful of the directives of Socialist Realism, Matrunin diversified and diluted his talents, losing something of his artistic physiognomy amid the often chintzy interpretations of folk culture. This might explain why, in spite of more than thirty years on stage, Matrunin does not command wide critical recognition — the six volume history of the Soviet dramatic theater, for example, carries only one casual reference to his work.[587]

Unknown production, *ca. 1922.*

788 [NIRE].
Design for a Costume, 1922.
Watercolor and pencil on board.
Signed and dated lower right in Russian: "B Matrunin 1922."
9 x 5½ in., 23 x 14 cm.
Provenance: Valerii Dudakov, Moscow, January, 2000.

585   For reproductions see G29, Nos. 20, 102.
586   G53, p. 153.
587   C29, Vol. 4, p. 249.

MEDUNETSKY, Konstantin (Kazimir) Konstantinovich

Born 1899, Moscow, Russia; died 1934, Moscow, Russia.

Son of a civil engineer; 1914 attended CSIAI, specializing in stage design; met Vasilii Komardenkov, Nikolai Prusakov, and Mikhail Sapegin there; 1919 with Prusakov, the Stenberg brothers, and others coorganized Obmokhu; contributed to its first exhibition; worked on abstract, free-standing constructions; 1920 member of Inkhuk; contributed to the second Obmokhu exhibition; 1921 with the Stenbergs organized the exhibition "The Constructivists" in Moscow; contributed to the third Obmokhu exhibition; 1922 with the Stenbergs designed Joseph Henry Benrimo and George C. Hazelton's *The Yellow Jacket* for the Studio-School of the Chamber Theater, Moscow; contributed to the "Erste Russische Kunstausstellung," Berlin; 1923 with the Stenbergs visited Paris; 1924 took part in the "First Discussional Exhibition of Associations of Active Revolutionary Art" in Moscow; designed movie posters at this time; with the Stenbergs made designs for Alexander Tairov's production of Alexander Ostrovsky's *The Storm* at the Chamber Theater; 1925 contributed to the "Exposition Internationale des Arts Décoratifs" in Paris; late 1920s and early 1930s continued to contribute to exhibitions at home and abroad.

Bibliography
Nothing substantial has been published on Medunetsky. The reader will find references to him in the general publications on modern Russian art and design such as B59, K55, and K154, p. 758. Also see the biographies of Georgii and Vladimir Stenberg and B312, passim.

The life and work of Medunetsky have still to be documented and evaluated. If the achievements of his immediate colleagues in Obmokhu, such as Georgii and Vladimir Stenberg and Alexander Rodchenko, have received wide acclaim via publications and exhibitions, Medunetsky's have not. In part, this lacuna is due to the scarcity of his works, because, apart from a handful of abstract

constructions at the Yale Art Gallery in New Haven, the TG, and the Museum of Fine Arts in Rostov, there exists very little testimony to his artistic development. Even so, judging from these pieces alone and from the designs that he made for *Phèdre* in 1922, Medunetsky was an artist of singular vision, like Tatlin, eager to incorporate the tactile and the physical into the work of art, and a strong champion of construction over composition. As Maria Gough explains:

> In order to distinguish construction from composition, therefore, [Vladimir] Stenberg and Medunetskii both deploy conventionally opposed drawing materials (drafting ink versus crayons and soft pencils) as well as an equally conventional dichotomy of rendering (sharp contour versus predominance of modeling). Each artist thus relies on a very old dichotomy of contour and chiaroscuro in order to delimit construction and composition...[588]

Phèdre: tragedy in five acts by Jean Racine, translated into Russian by Valerii Briusov. Produced by Alexander Tairov for the Chamber Theater, Moscow on 8 February, 1922, and presented on tour in Berlin (Deutsches Theater) and Paris (Théâtre des Champs-Elysées) in February and March, 1923, with designs by Alexander Vesnin and renderings for program publicity by Konstantin Medunetsky and Georgii and Vladimir Stenberg.
See No. 57 [R53] for plot summary.

789 [R665].
Headgear Design for Thérämène, 1923.
Pencil.
Signed and dated lower right in Russian: "K. Medunetsky 1923."
13¾ x 9⅞ in., 35 x 25 cm.
Other inscriptions: lower left typewritten label appended: "Arcadine rôle de Thérämène Etude de Masque pour Phèdre."
Provenance: H. Le Maire via André B. Nakov, Paris, November, 1976.

789

Reproduced in *Paris-Journal,* Paris, 1923, 6 March, p. 3; I40, No. 84; I51, No. 173; I77, p. 138; N91, p. 139. A version is reproduced in Catalog No. 7 of the Ex Libris bookstore, New York, 1977, No. 319; a curious version is reproduced in I100, No. 17.

Note: Phèdre was one of Alexander Tairov's favorite plays and he had considerable experience of it before taking the Chamber Theater on tour to Berlin, Paris, and other cities in February and March, 1923.[589] Tairov started working on the Russian version of *Phèdre* in Valerii Briusov's translation in October, 1921, and he staged its premiere at the Chamber Theater, Moscow on 8 February, 1922, with Alisa Koonen in the principal role and with designs by Alexander Vesnin (Nos. 1137-42 [R377-82]). As Anatolii Lunacharsky wrote: "Tairov's victory was *indisputable...* The spectacle left the impression of a beautiful shock. This is a monumental spectacle... "[590]

On 21 February, 1923, the company of the Chamber Theater left Moscow for the European tour, where the production (in Russian) of *Phèdre* in Berlin and Paris also scored an unqualified success. With Koonen again in the lead role, Nikolai Tsereteli as Hippolyte, Konstantin Eggert as Thésée, and Ivan Arkadin as Théramène, the spectacle left no one indifferent.[591] Even though the Russian émigrés in Paris felt that it was "essential to withstand the influence of the Bolshevik theater," the French critics felt that thenceforth it would be impossible to remain satisfied with the conventional French interpretations of Racine's tragedy.[592] The European tour of the Chamber Theater was accompanied by a number of publicity materials in the form of prospectuses, handouts, and special issues of newspapers. Medunetsky and the Stenberg brothers contributed drawings to these publications of Arkadin, Koonen, Tsereteli, and Eggert in their respective roles, wearing the headgears designed by Alexander Vesnin.[593]

Medunetsky as contributor:

790 [R666].
Designer unknown: *Poster Advertising the "First Discussional Exhibition of Associations of Active Revolutionary Art,"* 1924.
Lithograph in red, black, and white.
22⅞ x 16⅞ in., 58 x 43 cm.
Inscriptions describe the composition of the exhibition.

Note: The "First Discussional Exhibition of Associations of Active Revolutionary Art" opened on the premises of Vkhutemas at 54, Tverskaia, Moscow), on 11 May, 1924. It consisted of eight sections, of which four advanced independent declarations. Those without declarations were the *Byt* [Everyday Life] group, consisting of the artists Ivan Papkov and Konstantin Parkhomenko (this group is not mentioned in the poster); the Association of Three (Alexander Deineka, Andrei Goncharov, and Yurii Pimenov, also omitted here); a faction of the Constructivists, including Konstantin Medunetsky and Georgii and Vladimir

790

Stenberg (Nos. 969-73 [R795-99]); and small one-man exhibitions of the sculptor Iosif Chaikov and the graphic artist Nikolai Prusakov. The groups that did advance declarations were the Concretists, the Projectionist Group (see No. 1107 [R845]), the First Working Group of Constructivists, and the First Working Organization of Artists.[594]

What the poster does not explain is that the Constructivists actually represented two factions or groups, one consisting of Medunetsky and the Stenberg brothers, the other led by Gan and consisting of Olga and Galina Chichagova, Grigorii Miller, Alexandra Miroliubova, Liudmila Sanina and Nikolai Smirnov. This second group issued its own manifesto, compiled probably by Gan, which announced:

> In rationalizing artistic labor, the constructivists put into practice — not in verbal, but in concrete terms — the real qualifications of the *object:* they are raising its quality, establishing its social role, and organizing its forms in an organic relationship with its utilitarian meaning and objective.[595]

So as to prove their point, Gan's group, calling itself the First Working Group of Constructivists, contributed typographical designs, specimens of industrial clothing, illustrations to children's books, and other "utilitarian" items to the exhibition.

Essentially, the "First Discussional Exhibition" served as a platform that brought together two main directions in contemporary Soviet art — studio painting and industrial design. The title of the exhibition also implied the quandary in which many artists were finding themselves by the mid-1920s, since the word "discussional" [*diskussionyi*] has the connotation not only of "concerned with discussion or debate," but also of "open to debate, questionable."

588 B312, p. 42.
589 See entry for Stenbergs. For information on Tairov's European tour see C183.
590 A. Lunacharsky: "Fedr" in *Izvestiia* , M, 1922, 11 February. Quoted in C35, p. 513.
591 From a Paris review of *Phèdre,* 1923. Quoted in F43, p. 285, where the original source is not given.
592 Jacques-Emile Blanche in his review of *Phèdre,* 1923. Quoted in F43, p. 285. Many theater personalities were enthusiastic about Tairov's Paris production, including Jean Cocteau and Eugene O'Neill. Fernand Léger even wrote several letters of praise to Tairov after seeing *Phèdre,* referring to the Chamber Theater as the "first theater born of the Revolution" ("Pismo Lezhe" in *Teatr i muzyka,* M., 1923, No. 35, 9 October, p. 116. Much of this issue, incidentally is devoted to the French reception of *Phèdre.* For other statements by Léger and Cocteau see C35, p. 543).
593 All four headgears by Alexander Vesnin, rendered by Medunetsky and the Stenberg brothers, were reproduced in *Paris-Journal,* Paris, 1923, 6 March, pp. 2 and 3. Two of the Stenberg pieces (Nos. 969 [R795] and 971 [R797]) were reproduced in the brochure *Gastspiel im Deutschen Theater/Berlin. Moskauer Kamerny Theater,* Berlin, 1923, pp. 10 and 9.
594 For details, including translations of the manifestos, see B12, pp. 237-43.
595 Ibid., p. 241.

MELLER, Vadim Georgievich

Born 26 April (8 May), 1884, St. Petersburg, Russia; died 4 May, 1962, Kiev, Ukraine.

1892-1903 attended various schools in Erevan, Tiflis, and Kiev; 1903-08 attended Law School at Kiev University; 1905-08 audited at the Kiev Art Institute; 1907 published caricatures in the newspaper *Kievskaia mysl* [Kiev Thought]; 1908-12 attended the Akademie der bildenen Künste, Munich; 1912-14 studied and exhibited in Paris; returned to Kiev; 1917 moved to Moscow; 1918-19 after a short residence in Odessa moved back to Kiev, working in Alexandra Exter's studio; contributed designs to the anniversary celebrations of the Revolution; collaborated with Bronislava Nijinska, producing costume designs for her ballets such as *Mephisto Valse* and *Fear;* 1921-23 worked at the Shevchenko Theater, Kiev; 1922 onwards designer for the Berezil Theater in Kiev; designed many productions there, including *Jimmy Higgins* (1922) and *Destruction of the Squadron* (1933); 1924-25 designed movies; 1925 contributed to the "Exposition Internationale des Arts Décoratifs," Paris; 1926 moved to Kharkov with the Berezil Theater; mid-1920s active as a book illustrator; 1948 artist-in-residence for the Kiev Theater of Musical Comedy; 1953-59 head of the Art Section of the Ivan Franko State Drama Theater, Kiev.

Bibliography
M. Bazhan et al., eds.: *Slovnik khudozhnikiv Ukraini,* K: URE, 1973, pp. 148-49.
Z. Kucherenko: *Vadim Meller,* K: Mistetstvo, 1975.
D. Gorbachev: "Rezhisser i khudozhnik v ukrainskom opernom teatre 20-kh godov" in G50 for 1978, M, 1980, pp. 255-64.
G57, passim.
Z. Kucherenko: *Zasluzhennyi deiatel iskusstv USSR, Vadim Meller (1884-1962). Teatralno-dekoratyvne mistetstvo. Zhivopis. Grafika.*

791

Catalog of exhibition organized by the Union of Artists of the Ukraine, K, 1984.
I. Dichenko: "Toi nizhnii vikhor barv" in *Ukraina,* K, 1984, No. 13, p. 16.
B77, passim.
I65, passim.
A31, p. 396.
K265, pp. 214-21.

Meller, a primary representative of the Ukrainian avant-garde, came to stage design in the late 1910s while experimenting with abstract painting and reliefs, clearly under the influence of Exter, Kazimir Malevich, and Vladimir Tatlin. Along with other young students, such as Ivan Kudriashev and Anatolii Petritsky, Meller developed his conception of the new art according to the rigors of formal analysis, devoid of the often messianic and transcendental dimensions that accompanied the researches of older colleagues, such as Vasilii Kandinsky and Malevich. Meller received acclaim as a designer for Bronislava Nijinska's ballets in Kiev in 1919, especially for her solo concerts *Mephisto Waltz* and *Fear,* among the most exciting undertakings of her studio. Subordinating color to the "melody of lines," Meller used his designs as an instrument for emphasizing the "expression of the turns of the head, the rhythm of the folds and scarves... the dynamic of the dance".[596]

Mephisto Waltz: *plotless ballet with abstract choreography by Bronislava Nijinska based on the music of Franz Liszt for* Mephisto Valse *arranged by Karl Müller-Berghaus. Produced by Bronislava Nijinska, assisted by her students, for her Choreographic Studio (École de Mouvement) at the State Opera Theater, Kiev, 1919; and then under the title* Mephisto *in 1920, with designs by Alexandra Exter and Vadim Meller.*

791 [NIRE].
Costume Design for a Female Dancer, 1919.
Watercolor, gouache, pencil, and black ink.
Signed lower right in Russian: "Vadim Meller"; and dated lower left: "1919".
20½ x 13⅜ in., 52 x 34 cm.
Other inscriptions: top right in Russian: "Mask."
Provenance: *The Russian Sale,* London: Sotheby's, 31 May, 2006, Lot 141 (reproduced).
The attribution to Meller has been questioned.

792 [156; NIRE].
Costume Design for Bronislava Nijinska, 1919.
Watercolor, gouache, pencil, and India ink.
23⅝ x 17⅜ in., 60 x 44 cm
Provenance: Gleb Ivakin, Kiev, in 1999, who had acquired it from the artist's daughter, Brigitta Vetrova, Kiev, in 1971.
Reproduced in color in N188, p. 32. A version formerly in the Nijinska Archives, now in the Music Division of the Library of Congress, Washington, D.C., is reproduced in color in I65, p. 24; another version in the BTM is also reproduced in color in *Vitchizna,* K, 1973, No. 3, p. 140; and in G. Kovalenko: *Aleksandra Ekster,* M: Galart, 1993, p. 212, where it is described as a costume for a ballet called *City* and dated 1921.

Note: The production was a revised version of the 1919 solo performance, *Mephisto Valse.* Because of disruption caused by the Civil War, the costume designs by Meller and Exter were not executed and tunics made by Bronislava Nijinska herself were used for the performances.
   One of the most innovative centers of the Ukrainian avant-garde was Nijinska's Choreographic Studio, which sponsored experiments in both Classical and modern dance. Attracting young designers, especially Meller, Nijinska proceeded to incorporate the methods of the *danse plastique,* eurhythmics, and even gym-

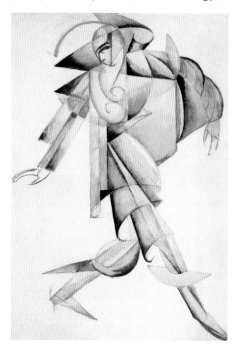

792

nastics into her choregraphical interpretations. It would seem, in fact, that some of the numbers — such as *Mephisto Valse* — were offered simply as creative platforms for experimental movement and design rather than as narratives to be illustrated. According to Dmitrii Gorbachev, "*Mephisto Valse* was a solo performance by B. Nijinska or her dancers... Meller's designs were not implemented and [simply] served as a visual analogy of Nijinska's ballet style."[597] This brief, but fruitful episode in Kiev prepared Nijinska for her more celebrated choreographic interpretations in the early 1920s, especially for Sergei Diaghilev in Paris, such as *Le Renard, Mavra,* and *Les Noces* (see Nos. 721-24 [R612-15], 1012 [R835], 1013 [R836], 568 [R436]).

793

793 [R667].
Cover Design for the Magazine Teatr [Theater], 1920.
Ink.
Signed and dated lower right in Russian: "V. Meller 1920 Kiev."
13¾ x 10½ in., 35 x 26.7 cm.
Provenance: Igor Dychenko, Kiev, 1975.
Reproduced in Kucherenko, *Meller,* p. 11; I32, No. 67; I77, p. 165.

Note: Teatr was the weekly stage magazine published by the Theater Section of the Subdepartment of Arts of the People's Education Secretariat, Kiev. Although the project here is dated 1920, the magazine appeared only in 1921 (running through 1923).

Mazeppa: *drama in five acts by Juliusz Słowacki. Directed by Konstantin Berezhnoi for the Shevchenko First State Ukrainian Dramatic Theater, Kiev, 1921, with designs by Vadim Meller.*[598]
   The Ukrainian hetman Mazeppa, fickle supporter of Peter the Great, has reaped rich rewards for his attack — together with Prince Golitsyn — on the Crimea. The clergy and plutocracy are content. Through his

mercenary Cossack army and régime of fear and oppression, Mazeppa brings order to his unruly state, ignoring the sorrow of his populus and and punishing civil disobedience. However, displeased with Mazeppa's passion for his daughter, the military judge Kochubei informs Peter the Great of the hetman's iniquities. Peter comes to the Ukraine to solicit Mazeppa's support against the Swedes only to discover that Mazeppa is currying favor with the Swedish court.

794

794 [NIRE].
Costume Design for a Monk, 1920-21.
Gouache and India ink.
19⅞ x 12¾ in., 50.5 x 32.5 cm.
Provenance: Gleb Ivakin, Kiev, in 1999, who had acquired it from the artist's daughter, Brigitta Vetrova, Kiev, in 1971.
Reproduced in B212, fig. 194; K154 (Russian edition), fig. 515, *Vitchizna*, No. 3, 1973, p. 140 (black and white); K31; B212, fig. 194.

Carnival: *play based on Romain Rolland's play* Liluli. *Produced by Mikola Tereshchenko for the Art of Action Group at the Hnat Mykhaily-chenko Theater, Kiev, on 8 September, 1923, with designs by Vadim Meller.*
        This allegory of human greed and frailty takes place beyond space and time inasmuch as representatives from many historical eras participate. Symbolic characters such as Liluli, or Illusion, Chirridi, or Truth, the Goddess Llop'ih, or Opinion, mingle with real person-ages such as Janot, the donkey-driver, or the Grand Khan. During the various confron-tations, the themes of war, revolution, imperialism, and religion are examined and interpreted, the orientation being toward Socialism and Communism. In spite of the role of the workmen and the simple people, Liluli triumphs at the end, as everything crashes down onto the stage.

795

795 [R668].
Costume Design for a Female with Right Leg Raised, ca. 1923.
Gouache and black ink.
17⅛ x 9 in., 43.5 x 23 cm.
Inscribed upper left in Russian: "Carnival."
Provenance: Igor Dychenko, Moscow, 1981.
Reproduced in color in B115, plate 164; and in black and white in I51, No. 174; I77, p. 144. A very similar design in another private collection is reproduced in color in I74, No. 65.

Note: For a review of this production see the newspaper *Bil'shovyk*, K, 1923, 7 Sep-tember; for general information on *Carnival*, see C23, pp. 133-36. For information on the artistic environment of this production and on the Berezil Theater, see M. Kachaniak: "Beresil" in *The International Theater*, New York: International Union of the Revolutionary Theatre, 1933, pp. 36-40; *The Berezil Theatre Exhibition.* Catalog of exhibition compiled by Ihor Ciczkewycz for the Organization of Modern Ukrainian Artists, New York, 1980; N. Kornienko, "Les Kurbas i khudozhniki" in G50, M, 1983, No. 5, pp. 332-54.

The Mikado: *operetta in two acts by Arthur Sullivan with libretto by William Schwenk Gilbert with a text modernized by Maik Yogansen, Mikola Khvylev and Ostap Vyshnia. Produced by Valerii Inkizhinov at the Berezil Theater, Kharkov, on 13 April, 1927, with designs by Vadim Meller.*
        Nanki-Poo has fled the court of his father, the Mikado, to the town of Titipu, because of the misguided advances of the elderly Katisha. Disguised as a wandering

796

minstrel, he harbors true love for Yum-Yum, who is betrothed to her guardian Ko-Ko, the Lord High Executioner of Titipu. Pooh-Bah, the Lord High Executioner of Everything Else, proceeds to arrange the wedding festivities, even though Yum-Yum does not love Ko-Ko. The Mikado is distressed by the lack of executions in Titipu, and so, in order to please his imperial majesty, Ko-Ko invites the disguised Nanki-Poo to be beheaded. Nanki-Poo agrees on condition that he can marry Yum-Yum, except that it transpires that, by custom, Yum-Yum must be buried alive with her new husband. Ko-Ko then fakes the execution to spare her life. The ruse is discovered; the Mikado is overjoyed to see his son again, Ko-Ko is persuaded to marry Katisha, and Yum-Yum and Nanki-Poo live happily united.

796 [R669].
Costume Design for Ko-Ko, ca. 1927.
Colored pencil and watercolor.
Faded signature upper right-hand corner in pencil in Russian.
16½ x 12⅝ in., 42 x 32 cm.
A similar design is reproduced in *Vadim Meller (1884-1962)*, p. 46. For a documentary photograph from the 1927 Kharkov production see the catalog of the exhibition "The Berezil Theatre Exhibition," op. cit., unpaginated.[599]

596 Kucherenko: *Vadim Meller*, p. 39.
597 Letter from Dmitrii Gorbachev to John E. Bowlt dated 2 August, 1999.
598 There is a discrepancy in the dating of this production of *Mazeppa*. Both Kucherenko (*Meller*, p. 34) and Verikivska (G57, p. 91) date the production as 1921, although the exhibition catalog for "The Great Utopia" (K154, Russian edition, p. 785) gives 1920 and Verikivska also dates Meller's maquette as 1920 (G57, p. 90). The main source of information on Kurbas (C85) omits any reference to such a production.
599 For further information on the production of *Mikado* and the Berezil Theater see R. Cherkashyn and Yu. Fomina: *My—Bereziltsi*, Kharkiv: Akta, 2008; and B356, especially Parts 3-5.

MILIOTI (Millioti, Miliotti, Miliuti), Nikolai Dmitrievich

Born 16 (28), January, 1874, Moscow, Russia; died 26 December, 1962, Paris, France.

1894-1900 studied at MIPSA under Abram Arkhipov, Leonid Pasternak, and Valentin Serov; visited Konstantin Korovin private studio in Moscow; 1898 enrolled in the Department of History and Philology at Moscow University; early 1900s studied at the Sorbonne, Paris; 1906 contributed to the "World of Art" exhibition in Moscow and the "Salon d'Automne" in Paris; 1907 member of the Society of Free Esthetics; first one-man exhibition there; founding member of the Blue Rose group of Symbolist artists in Moscow; contributing to its exhibition; thereafter contributed regularly to international exhibitions in Brussels, Rome, Berlin, and Paris; 1908 contributed to "Wreath" exhibition in St. Petersburg; 1909 contributed to Sergei Makovsky's "Salon" in St. Petersburg; 1909 onwards member of the editorial board of the journal *Apollon*; 1906-08 and in 1910 exhibited with the Union of Russian Artists; 1910 onwards member of the World of Art society; 1914-17 mobilized, seeing action in the Carpathians; 1918 member of the Commission for the Protection of Artistic Treasures in Yalta; 1920 emigrated. first to Sofia, then, in 1921-22, to Berlin; co-founder of the House of the Arts there; 1923 settled in Paris; 1924, with Natalia Goncharova, worked for Yuliia Sazanova-Slonimskaia's puppet theater at the Théâtre Le Vieux-Colombier; 1924 designed production of *La Princesse de Carizme* by Le Sage; 1925 visited USA; 1929 onwards taught at the Académie Russe in Paris; 1940-42 lived in Biarritz.

Bibliography
"Pamiati N.N. Sapunova. Beseda s N.D. Milioti" in *Golos Moskvy*, M, 1912, 17 June.
V. Zeeler: "Vystavka N.D. Millioti" in *Illiustrirovannaia Rossiia*, Paris, 1938, 4 June, pp. 14, 15.
K209, passim.
H34, pp. 425, 226.
H51, passim.
K. Tribble and R. Davis, intro: "Pisma N.D. Milioti k V.N. Buninoi (1927–1958). Materialy k letopisi zhizni i tvorchestva N.D. Milioti" in O. Korosteleva and R. Davis: *I.A. Bunin. Novye materialy*, M: Russkii put, 2011, No. 2, pp. 400-64.
L209, pp. 128-36.

Nikolai Milioti and his brother, Vasilii, the "pale, black-bearded Greeks,"[600] were among Moscow's "gilded youth" in the 1900s and were strong supporters of the Symbolist enterprises such as the journal *Zolotoe runo* [Golden Fleece], the Society of Free Esthetics (directed by the poet Valerii Briusov), and the important Symbolist exhibition, the "Blue Rose" of 1907. Indeed, much influenced by Mikhail

Vrubel, the early Nikolai Milioti received critical acclaim for his decorative panels, such as *Angel of Sadness*; Igor Grabar, for example, speaking of the painter's "sonorous fanfares"[601] and Sergei Makovsky of his "resounding interfusions of colors,"[602] although for Pavel Muratov this vivid gamut was merely illustrating a "coarse fantasy."[603]

Certainly, in momentum of brushtroke and density of color, Milioti differed from his immediate colleagues in Moscow such as Pavel Kuznetsov and Petr Utkin, who preferred a paler and more muted palette, and he does not seem to have shared the eschatological sensibility of the *fin de siècle* generation. Indeed, a bon vivant, Milioti remained content with the beauty of the material world and, in emigration, at least, gained a lasting reputation for his solid portraits and landscapes.

Princesse de Carizme: *comic opera in three acts with music by Alain René Lesage and Joseph de la Font (Lafont) projected, but not produced, by Yuliia Sazonova for her Théâtre de l'Atelier in Paris in 1925.*

Based on a story from One Thousand and One Nights, *and placed in a romantic, but satirical, setting, a Persian prince, and his companion and confidant Arlequin experience many adventures, including tumultuous love affairs.*

797

Reproduced in L1, Lot 57, where it is called "Odalisque – Princess Bounteous".

Note: Keith Tribble, a specialist in the work of Nikolai Milioti writes:

> After the May 1925 season of Sazonova's puppet theater at the Théâtre de l'Atelier she continued rehearsing her puppets and attempting to find new repertory for them. It is probably for this purpose that Milioti designed the costumes for *La Princesse de Carizme*. Maybe some of the play was rehearsed and performed in her studio on the rue Tonnerre during the summer of 1925. However in August she fell ill with appendicitis and was hospitalized for a long time. Marionette activity was not resumed until the company toured Holland in 1926 without *La Princesse de Carizme*. Milioti made many sketches of costumes, curtain and set designs for the proposed production some of which were exhibited in London ("Exhibition of Russian Art", 4-13 July, 1935, p. 133-34, 142); one costume design is in the collection of Cyrille Makhrov in Paris, another in the collection of Alex Rabinovich in New York. The catalogue for the London 1935 exhibition states that the work was staged in 1925, but this evidently refers to the planned production by Sazonova's theater, which, as I said, was not publicly performed. Incidentally, Milioti consistently misspells the title of the play (he writes *La Princesse de Carisme* instead of *La Princesse de Carizme*). For the correct title see: "La Princesse de Carizme. Pièce en trois actes par Monsieur de S**" in *Le Théâtre de la Foire, ou l'Opéra-Comique. Contenant les meilleures Pièces qui ont été representées aux Foires de S. Germain et de S. Laurent. Recueillies, revues, et corrigées.* Par Mrs. <Alain-René> Le Sage et <Jacques-Philippe> d'Orneval, Tome III, Paris: Pierre Gandouin, 1737, pp. 92-199. [604]

600 A. Bely: *Mezhdu dvukh revoliutsii*, L: Izdatelstvo pisatelei v Leningrade, 1934, p. 237.
601 I. Grabar: "Golubaia roza" in *Vesy*, 1907, No. 5, p. 95.
602 S. Makovsky: "Golubaia roza" in *Zolotoe runo*, 1907, No. 5, p. 27.
603 P. Muratov: "Vystavka kartin 'Golubaia roza'" in *Russkoe slovo*, M, 1907, 1 April, No. 75, p. 3.
604 Letter from Keith Tribble to John E. Bowlt, 6 February, 2011.

797 [NIRE]
Costume Design for an Odalisque, 1925.
Gouache and pencil on board.
Signed lower right: "Milioti."
14 x 9 in., 35.5 × 22.9 cm.
Provenance: *Important Russian Pictures*, London: Christie's, 30 November, 2004, Lot 330 (reproduced).

MILLER, Grigorii Lvovich

Born 5 (17) January, 1899; Moscow, Russia; died 6 June, 1963, Moscow, Russia.

1915 attended the Odessa Art Institute; 1916 transferred to the Kharkov Art Institute; 1920-24 studied at Svomas / Vkhutemas, Moscow; worked in Alexander Rodchenko's studio; 1920 onward with Alexei Gan, Nikolai Smirnov, et al. founded the First Working Group of Constructivists; 1921 designed the cover for Riurik Rok's book of Nothingist poetry *Ot Riurika Roka Chteniia* [Readings from Riurik Rok] (M: Khobo), and for Georgii Shtorm's *Karma Ioga. Poema* [Karma Yoga. a Poem] (M); 1923 designed costumes for a production of Molière's *Le Médicin Volant*; 1924 contributed to the "First Discussional Exhibition of Associations of Active Revolutionary Art," Moscow; 1924-27 taught at the Central House for Communist Education in Moscow; 1927 designed the production of Anatolii Glebov's play *Growth* at the Theater of Revolution; 1928 contributed to the "Third Exhibition of Graphics" at the Press House, Moscow; assisted El Lissitzky on the latter's design for the Soviet pavilion at the "Pressa" exhibition in Leipzig; 1920s onward designed and illustrated books and posters; used photomontage extensively; 1942 contributed to the exhibition "The Komsomol in the Fatherland War," Моэcow.

Bibliography
Nothing substantial has been published on Miller. The reader will find references to him in B10, B55, K77, and K154, p. 759.

Salomé: *drama based on Oscar Wilde's poem of the same name. Projected by Vsevolod Meierkhold (?) in Moscow, 1920 (?) with designs by Grigorii Miller.*
         See No. 594 [R498] for plot summary.

798a [157; R670].
Costume Design for King Herod, ca. 1920.
Watercolor, gold paint, and black ink.
7¾ x 3⅝ in., 19.7 x 9.2 cm.
Role identification on the reverse in Russian.
Provenance: Varvara Rodchenko, Moscow, 1971.
Reproduced in I32, No. 68; I51, No. 175; I77, p. 139.

Note: The theme of *Salomé*, whether as drama, opera, or ballet, enjoyed great popularity in Russia just before and after 1917. Indicative of this decadent interest was Ida Rubinstein's production of *La Tragédie de Salomé* in Paris in 1912, Nikolai Evreinov and Vera Komissarzhevskaia's preparation of the play in 1908 (Nos. 594-98 [R498-502]), and Alexander Tairov's production of the drama at the Chamber Theater, Moscow, in 1917, with designs by Alexandra Exter.[605] This was complemented by several other productions of the play at the Troitsky Theater, Petrograd, in 1917

798a

(with designs by Iosif Shkolnik), at the Maly Theater, Moscow, in 1918, and at the Hermitage Theater, Petrograd, in 1919. According to one source,[606] Vsevolod Meierkhold contemplated a production of the play at the Theater of the RSFSR No. 1, Moscow, in 1920, and Miller's costume may have been for this project. Clearly, Miller's design derives in part from the contemporary work of Exter and Alexander Vesnin, and, as a student in Moscow at this time, he would have been aware of both artists' contributions to the Chamber Theater.

605 See remarks on Mikhail Mordkin under Anatolii Petritsky.
606 C31, Vol. 1, p. 144.

MUKHINA, Vera Ignatievna

Born 19 June (1 July), 1889, Riga, Latvia; died 6 October, 1953, Moscow, Russia.

1898-1904 attended high school in Feodosiia, Crimea, where she took lessons in drawing and landscape painting; 1904-06 lived in Kursk; 1908-11 attended Konstantin Yuon and Ivan Dudin's Art School in Moscow; also attended courses in sculpture at Nina Sinitsyna's studio in Moscow; 1911-12 worked in Ilia Mashkov's studio in Moscow; 1912 visited Paris, where she enrolled in the Académie de la Grande Chaumière, taking lessons from Antoine Bourdelle; made the acquaintance of Jacques Lipchitz and Ossip Zadkine; close friends with Liubov Popova; 1914 traveled with Iza Burmeister and Popova to Italy; returned to Russia at the outbreak of World War I; 1915-16 as Alexandra Exter's assistant at the Chamber Theater, Moscow, designed costumes for various plays (not produced); 1918 married Alexei Zamkov, a physician; 1918-20s worked on posters, magazine designs, and monuments such as *Flame of the Revolution* (1919); early 1920s gave increasing attention to monumental sculpture; designed posters, candy wrappers, commercial labels; 1923 worked with Exter et al. at the Atelier of Fashions, Moscow, on dress designs; helped Exter with designs for the movie *Aelita*; 1925 contributed to the "Exposition Internationale des Arts Décoratifs" in Paris; with Nadezhda Lamanova published the album *Iskusstvo v bytu* [Art in Everyday Life]; 1926-27 taught at Vkhutemas; 1926-30 taught at Vkhutein; 1930-32 exiled to Voronezh; 1930s-40s designed porcelain and glassware, monuments and interiors; 1937 designed the *Worker and Collective Farm Girl* placed on the roof of the Soviet pavilion at the "Exposition Internationale" in Paris; 1941 awarded State Prize of the USSR for *Worker and Collective Farm Girl* (which became the Mosfilm logo); 1941-42 evacuated to the Urals; 1947 member of the Academy of Arts of the USSR; 1940s-50s continued to produce monumental sculptures, portraits, glassware, and stage designs.

Bibliography
V. Mukhina: *A Sculptor's Thoughts,* M: Foreign Languages Publishing-House, n.d. (after 1953).
R. Klimov, ed.: *Mukhina,* M: Iskusstvo, 1960 (3 vols.).
O. Voronova: *V.I. Mukhina,* M: Iskusstvo, 1976.
P. Suzdalev: *Vera Ignatievna Mukhina,* M: Iskusstvo, 1981.
Vera Ignatievna Mukhina. Catalog of exhibition at the TG and the RM, 1989.
N. Voronov: *Vera Mukhina,* M: Izobrazitelnoe iskusstvo, 1989.
M. Kolesnikov: "Aleksandra Ekster i Vera Mukhina" in *Panorama iskusstv,* M, 1989, No. 12, pp. 89-110.
I. Lipovich: *V.I. Mukhina,* L: RM, 1989.
N. Voronov: "Rabochii i kolkhoznitsa," M: Moskovskii rabochii, 1990.
E. Vasilievskaia et al.: *Vera Mukhina.* Catalog of exhibition at the RM, 2009.
G. Kovalenko: *Teatr Very Mukhinoi.* Catalog of exhibition at the Moscow Museum of Contemporary Art, M, 2012.

Along with Anna Golubkina, Vera Isaeva, and Beatrisa Sandomirskaia, Mukhina was one of Russia's greatest sculptresses and her influence on the course of Soviet sculpture was profound and permanent. While not avant-garde in the way Kazimir Malevich and Vladimir Tatlin were, Mukhina demonstrated a strong confidence in the classical tradition and an artistic vitality that became especially appropriate to her interpretations of Socialist Realism. True, Mukhina's admiration of Rodin and Bourdelle and her exposure to French Cubism left an imprint on her early figures, such as *Pietà* (1916), and on her dynamic projects (not produced) for several plays that Alexander Tairov prepared for his Chamber Theater in the mid-1910s, such as *La Cena delle Beffe* and *The Rose and The Cross*. An assistant to Exter there, Mukhina took particular note of Exter's subtle conception of volume and construction, mentioning later on that "Exter exerted a deep influence on my entire life."[607] Mukhina combined the need for historical accuracy with an impetuous fantasy, prompting the critic Boris Ternovets, Mukhina's long-time friend, to speak of her "vividness and expressivity of decorative invention."[608] Although later on Mukhina adjusted her artistic vision to the conventions of the Stalin style, her love of the histrionic was no less evident in her monumental statues, such as the famous *Worker and Collective Farm Girl* created for the Soviet pavilion at the Paris World's Fair in 1937.

Mukhina is now remembered for her documentary and often tendentious sculpture, reflecting her commitment to the Revolution and to the fundamental tenets of Socialist Realism. The grandeur of Mukhina's artistic vision appealed to both the Party and the masses alike, ensuring her prestigious political commissions in the 1930s-50s, such as her figures for the Hotel Moscow and the buxom harvesters for the New Moscow River Bridge (late 1930s), the group *We Demand Peace* (1951), and her many statues to cultural heroes, from Tchaikovsky (1953) to Maxim Gorky (1952). However, Mukhina could also produce more intimate and pensive sculpture such as her renderings of relatives and friends, including several heads of her son. Moreover, Mukhina's interest in unexpected media, such as glass and her numerous pencil and charcoal drawings, show an esthetic diversity and flexibility that are not always apparent from her more familiar public sculpture.

La Cena delle Beffe: *play in four acts by Sem Benelli translated into Russian by Valerii Briusov. Produced by Alexander Tairov at the Chamber Theater, Moscow, on 9 December, 1916, with choreography after Marius Petipa and preliminary designs by Vera Mukhina replaced by definitive designs by Nikolai Foregger.*

This drama of treachery and black deeds takes place in Florence during the time of the Medici. The wicked Nera antagonizes the youth Giannetto while Ginevra, the languorous femme fatale, provides the target of various amorous advances as the action moves from the house of Tornaquinci to her chambers, to the subterranean rooms of the Medici Palace and back to her luxurious villa.

798b

798b [R671].
Costume Design for a Swordsman, 1916.
Gouache and gold paint.
Signed and dated lower right in pencil in Russian: "Vera Mukhina 1916."
24¾ x 17⅞ in., 63 x 45.5 cm.
Provenance: *Costume and Décor Designs for Ballet, Theatre and Opera,* London: Sotheby's, 30 May, 1974, Lot 25 (reproduced).
Reproduced in color in B115, plate 80; F107, p. 420; N188, p. 34; and in black and white in I32, No. 69; I51, No. 175; I77, p. 136; M131.

A number of similar designs are reproduced in Klimov, *Mukhina,* Vol. 3, plates 26-35; and *Vera Ignatievna Mukhina,* p. 51; and D. Molok: "Rabochie risunki skulptora" in *Skulptura,* M, 1985, No. 5, p. 256.

799 [158; R672].
Costume Design for a Runner, 1916.
Gouache, gold paint, pencil, and black ink.
Initialed on reverse lower left in Russian: "V.M."
19½ x 26⅞ in., 49.7 x 68 cm.
Provenance: the artist's son, Vsevolod Zamkov, Leningrad.
Reproduced in color in G79, p. 32; and in black and white in A34, p. 304; I77, pp. 105 and 136; P5; P7; P11; P48; and in Klimov, Vol. 3, plate 27. Analogous designs are in *Vera Ignatievna Mukhina,* p. 51.

The Rose and the Cross: *play in four acts by Alexander Blok. Projected, but not produced, by the Chamber Theater, Moscow, in 1916 with designs by Vera Mukhina.*

The elderly Count Archambaut, lord of a castle in Languedoc, is beset by military and conjugal rivalries. His young wife, Isaure (Izora), bored, but languorous, is courted by Aliscan the page and Bertrand the hapless knight, while her servant Alisa is pursued by the portly chaplain. Defying his own sentiments, the devoted Bertrand, bearer of the Rose, ushers Aliscan into the tower whither the Count had banished Isaure. Fatally wounded in an attack by the armies of Toulouse, Bertrand remains at his post, symbolizing the triumph of noble duty over religious bigotry and petty liaisons.

799

800

800 [159; R673].
Costume Design for Bertrand, the Knight of Misfortune, ca. 1916.
Gouache, silver, and black ink.
27½ x 19⅛ in., 70 x 48.5 cm.
Provenance: the artist's son, Vsevolod Zamkov, Leningrad.
Reproduced in color in B115, plate 79; G79, p. 132; and in black and white in I77, p. 137; S57; S61; and Klimov, Vol. 3, p. 44, and *Vera Ignatievna Mukhina*, p. 51, which also list other versions, each of different dimensions. For a color reproduction of other designs for *The Rose and the Cross* see M. Dolinsky, *Iskusstvo i Aleksandr Blok*, M: Sovetskii khudozhnik, 1985, p. 230; and A. and M. Gordin: *Aleksandr Blok i russkie khudozhniki*, L: Khudozhnik RSFSR, 1986, pp. 229-30.

Note: In 1915-16 Mukhina worked on several projects for the Chamber Theater, Moscow, but none of them was produced with her designs. They included the ballet *Nal and Damayanti* and Arthur Schnitzler's *Der Schleier der Pierrette,* as well as *La Cena delle Beffe* and Alexander Blok's *Rose and the Cross*. As Exter's assistant at the Chamber Theater, Mukhina made a close study of the former's designs for the famous production of *Thamira Khytharedes* of 1916 (Nos. 460-62 [R973-74]), and there are distinct parallels between these and Mukhina's costumes for *La Cena delle Beffe.*

607   Quoted in Voronova, *V.I. Mukhina,* p. 42.
608   B. Ternovets: *V.I. Mukhina,* M-L: Ogiz, 1937, p. 24.

NIVINSKY, Ignatii Ignatievich

Born 30 December, 1881 (11 January, 1882), Moscow, Russia; died 27 October, 1933, Moscow, Russia.

1893-98 attended CSIAI; 1899-1906 taught there; 1900 studied under the architect Ivan Zholtovsky; 1904 onwards traveled frequently to Italy; 1906-12 supervised the interior decorations for the Alexander III Museum, later known as Pushkin State Museum of Fine Arts (GMII); 1908-10 attended the Moscow Archaeological Institute; 1909 took lessons from Stanislav Zhukovsky; began to contribute regularly to exhibitions; 1911 onwards worked mainly with etchings, especially of Italian landscapes; 1913 contributed to exhibitions of the World of Art and the Moscow Association of Artists; 1916 contributed to the "Moscow Association of Artists"; 1916-17 produced a cycle of etchings devoted to the Crimean landscape; 1917-18 taught at MIPSA/Svomas; 1918 headed the Section of People's Festivities in Moscow; 1919 chairman of the Union of Engravers; 1920 began to work with Evgenii Vakhtangov, culminating in his designs for the production of *Princess Turandot* at the Vakhtangov Theater, Moscow, in 1922; 1920-21 visited and sketched in various provincial cities such as Zvenigorod; 1921-30 taught at Vkhutemas-Vkhutein in Moscow; 1923-26 worked on etchings devoted to the Caucasus; 1924 member of the Four Arts group; worked at the Moscow Art Theater; made designs for Boris Vershilov's production of *Golem* at the Habima Theater, Moscow; 1925 received a Gold Medal for his contribution to the "Exposition Internationale des Arts Décoratifs," Paris; 1927 onwards traveled widely in Georgia and Armenia; 1928 with the Vakhtangov Theater visited Paris, where he had a one-man show; 1933 Konstantin Stanislavsky invited him to design a production of the *Barber of Seville* for his Opera Theater in Moscow.

Bibliography
P. Ettinger and N. Romanov: *Oforty Ign. Nivinskogo*. Catalog of exhibition at the State Museum of Fine Arts, M, 1925.
V. Polonsky: *Mastera sovremennoi graviury i grafiki,* M: Gosizdat, 1928, pp. 257-72.
N. Petoshina: *I.I. Nivinsky.* Catalog of exhibition at the RM, 1960.
V. Dokuchaeva: *I.I. Nivinsky,* M: Iskusstvo, 1969.
K. Bezmenova: *Ignatii Ignatievich Nivinsky 1880-1933.* Catalog of exhibition organized by the Union of Artists, M, 1980.
K. Bezmenova: "O vystavke I.I. Nivinskogo" in *Sovetskaia grafika,* M, 1983, No. 8, pp. 300-03.
I122, pp. 96-105.

Nivinsky found a primary inspiration in Italy and Italian culture. As one of his biographers wrote, Nivinsky embarked upon the "trail along which the old Venetian artists had advanced."[609] Well into the 20th century, Italy continued to be an obligatory halting place on the grand European tour for Russian artists (even for avant-gardists such as Pavel Filonov and Liubov Popova), an itinerary that repeated

the pilgrimage of Russia's 19th century *pensionnaires*. Along with Andrea Beloborodoff, Eugène Berman, Konstantin Bogaevsky, and Alexandre Jacovleff, in particular, Nivinsky paid homage to the Italian legacy, not, however, to Futurism, but rather to Roman antiquity, the Renaissance, and Neo-Classicism. These artists refracted their Italian passion in various ways, some paraphrasing the methods of the great masters, as Bogaevsky did with the landscapes of Mantegna, others by clothing their models in period costume as Jacovleff was wont to do, and yet others by simply rendering motifs from Italian sculpture and monuments. Strongly influenced by his mentor Ivan Zholtovsky, Nivinsky paid particular attention to Palladian architecture, rendering the façades and columns of countless palazzi in his pencil sketches and etchings. Drawn especially to the art of Leonardo da Vinci and Piranesi, Nivinsky expressed his Classical nostalgia in friezes, panneaux, and decorations for Moscow villas, something that harmonized well with the new Neo-Classicism that in the 1910s undermined the current fashion for Art Nouveau.

La Dama Duende **[The Phantom Lady]:** *comedy in three acts by Pedro Calderón de la Barca. Produced by Mikhail Chekhov at the Second Studio of the Moscow Art Theater on 9 April, 1924, with designs by Ignatii Nivinsky.*
See No. 470 [R979] for plot summary.

801

801 [R682].
Costume Design for a Man from the Crowd with Hand on Hip, 1923.
Gouache and pencil.
Signed and dated lower right in Russian: "Ign Nivinsky 1923."
22⅛ x 16⅛ in, 56.2 x 41 cm.
Other inscriptions in Russian: upper left in pencil: "Phantom Lady. Man from the

crowd"; lower left: "3 costumes"; lower right: "No. 2."

Provenance: Igor Dychenko, Kiev, February, 1984.

Reproduced in A34, p. 315. A similar costume is reproduced in color in Dokuchaeva, p. 200.

Note: Nivinsky was working on several experimental productions for the Second and Third Studios of the Moscow Art Theater at this time, all of which "captivated by their elegance, grace, and vivid sense of theater."[610] His major design undertaking at the Third Studio, i.e. for Evgenii Vakhtangov's production of Carlo Gozzi's *Princess Turandot* in 1922, an interpretation of "China via Italy,"[611] revealed the "lightness, elegance, and grace peculiar to the actors of the Italian Comedy"[612] which identified Nivinsky's art in general. Also see Nos. 470-73 [R979-81].

802

802 [R684].
Portrait of Alexandra Exter, 1928.
Pen and ink wash.
Signed and dated lower right: "Ign. Nivinsky 1928."
20⅝ x 15¾ in., 52.5 x 40 cm.
Other inscriptions: upper left in Russian: "To my dear Georgii from Ignatii."[613]
Provenance: Simon Lissim, Dobbs Ferry, New York, September, 1969.
Reproduced in F107, p. 157; I20, No. 58; and I51, No. 78, where the work is wrongly attributed to Ignatii Fenbaum; and G. Kovalenko, *Alexandra Exter,* M: Galart, 1993, p. 219.

Note: Nivinsky was not an advocate of extreme tendencies, but he did receive acclaim for his experimental designs for *Princess Turandot* in 1922 and, no doubt, Exter would have approved of them. Collaborating with her on the decorations for the *Izvestiia* Pavilion at the "All-Russian

Agricultural Exhibition" in Moscow in 1923[614] and perhaps for a production of *La Dama Duende* in 1924 (see notes to Nos. 470-73 [R979-81] and 801 [R682]), Nivinsky established a close relationship with Exter, one that continued even after she emigrated to France. The exact circumstances in which Nivinsky made this portrait are not known, although it is probable that he executed it during his trip to Paris in 1928.[615]

609   Dokuchaeva, *I.I. Nivinsky,* p. 40.
610   Vera Dokuchaeva writing on *La Dama Duende* in Dokuchaeva, p. 206.
611   From a conversation between Nivinsky and Vakhtangov. Quoted in Dokuchaeva, p. 94.
612   Ibid., p. 194.
613   Presumably, the dedication is to Exter's second husband, Georgii Nekrasov.
614   The architecture for the exhibition was supervised by Ivan Fomin, Alexei Shchusev, Vladimir Shchuko, and Nivinsky's mentor Zholtovsky. Apart from Exter and Nivinsky, the contingent of decorative artists also included Fedor Fedorovsky, Kuzma Petrov-Vodkin, Evgeniia Pribylskaia, and Isaak Rabinovich.
615   See M. Kolesnikov: "Aleksandra Ekster i Vera Mukhina" in *Panorama iskusstv,* M, 1989, No. 12, p. 104.

OSTROUKHOV, Ilia Semenovich

Born 20 July (1 August), 1858, Moscow, Russia; died 8 July, 1929, Moscow, Russia.

1871-76 attended the Moscow Practical Academy of Commercial Sciences; 1876 met Anatolii Mamontov and through him his family, including Savva Mamontov; 1880s-90s played a primary role at the latter's Abramtsevo artists' colony; close to Konstantin Korovin, Isaak Levitan, Vasilii Polenov, Ilia Repin, Valentin Serov, and the Vasnetsov brothers; influenced by Polenov; painted landscapes; 1882-84 attended IAA, studying under Pavel Chistiakov; 1887 contributed to the "XIV Exhibition of the Wanderers"; thereafter continued to participate regularly in their exhibitions; Pavel Tretiakov acquired his painting *Golden Fall* for his gallery; traveled in Italy; 1889 visited Berlin; married Nadezhda Botkina; 1890s gravitated increasingly towards collecting works of art, especially icons and modern paintings; 1898-1903 served on the Advisory Committee for the Tretiakov Gallery, Moscow, playing an active part in the campaign to clean and restore works of art; 1901-09 wrote the text for promotional guide to the Tretiakov Gallery, i.e., *Moskovskaia gorodskaia khudozhestvennaia galereia Pavla i Sergeia Tretiakovykh* [The Moscow City Art Gallery of Pavel and Sergei Tretiakov]; 1903 member of the Union of Russian Artists, contributing to its exhibitions; 1905-13 trustee of the Tretiakov Gallery; 1918 his own collection was nationalized and he was allowed to remain its curator until his death.

Bibliography
Yu. Rusakov: *Ilia Semenovich Ostroukhov,* M: Iskusstvo, 1954.

Yu. Rusakov: *I.S. Ostroukhov. Albom,* M-L: Iskusstvo, 1962.
S. Kudriavtseva: *Ilia Ostroukhov,* L: Khudozhnik RSFSR, 1982.
O. Ptitsyna: *Moskovskii kollektsioner I.S. Ostroukhov,* M: Surgutneftegaz, 2001.
Russkoe iskusstvo, M, 2009, No. 3 (whole issue devoted to Ostroukhov).

A passionate collector of Russian icons, Ostroukhov is remembered above all for his services to the wider appreciation of Medieval Russian painting, for he did much to preserve and restore an artistic heritage that had long suffered from neglect and ignorance.[616] Ostroukhov was also a competent landscape painter, especially of the Moscow countryside and Abramtsevo, where he spent much time with Savva and Elizaveta Mamontov. As one historian has commented, "perhaps no artist owed as much to Abramtsevo as Ostroukhov did."[617] Ostroukhov took an active role in the amateur theatricals at Abramtsevo and also worked for Mamontov's Private Opera Company, designing, for example, the production of *Carmen* in 1886.

Unidentified production, ca. 1890.

803

803 [R685].
Set Design, ca. 1890.
Oil on cardboard.
Signed lower left in black paint in Russian: "I. Ostroukhov."
15¾ x 10 in., 35 x 25.5 cm.
Other inscriptions in Russian: under the signature in black paint: "Design for a production." The reverse carries in blue pencil: "From the collection of Vargunina (?), Tverskoi Boulevard."
Provenance: Yakov Rubinshtein, Moscow, February, 1985.

616   On Ostroukhov's collection see N. Vrangel: "Sobranie I.S. Ostroukhova" in *Apollon,* SP, 1911, No. 10, pp. 5-14.
617   N. Pakhomov: *Abramtsevo,* M: Moskovskii rabochii, 1969, p. 198.

PASTERNAK, Leonid Osipovich

Born 22 March (3 April), 1861, Odessa, Ukraine; died 31 May, 1945, Oxford, England.

1879 attended the Odessa Institute of Drawing; 1881 studied medicine at Moscow University; 1882 attended the studio of Evgraf Sorokin in Moscow; 1882-85 attended Law School at Novorossiisk University in Odessa; attended the Akademie der bildenen Künste in Munich; 1885-86 served in the army; 1888 showed his *Letter from Home* at the "Exhibition of the Society of Wanderers," which was then bought by Pavel Tretiakov; 1889 moved back to Moscow; saw examples of French Impressionism in Paris; 1889-94 directed a private sketching school in Moscow; late 1880s onwards contributed as an illustrator to books and magazines, including the commemorative edition of Mikhail Lermontov's collected works in 1899-91; 1892 illustrated Lev Tolstoi's *War and Peace,* making the author's acquaintance the following year; 1894-1921 professor at MIPSA/Svomas; 1898 contributed to Sergei Diaghilev's "Exhibition of Russian and Finnish Artists" in St. Petersburg; 1900 represented at the "Exposition Universelle" in Paris; founding member of the group known as the 36; 1903 onwards member of the Union of Russian Artists; 1910s traveled widely in Europe; 1921 moved to Berlin, 1939 moved to Oxford, England.

Bibliography
H. Struck: *Prof. L. Pasternak. Portrait-Album,* Berlin: Jibneh-Verlag of Jerusalem, 1923.
C. Bialik and M. Osborn: *L. Pasternak. His Life and Work,* Berlin: Sztybel of Warsaw, 1924 (in Yiddish).
D. Buckman: *Leonid Pasternak. A Russian Impressionist, 1862-1945,* London: Maltzahn Gallery, 1974.
F44.
L.O. Pasternak. Catalog of exhibition at the TG, 1979.
J. Pasternak: *Leonid Pasternak, 1862-1945.* Catalog of exhibition at the Museum of Modern Art, Oxford, 1982-83.
A. Hilton: *A Russian Impressionist. Paintings and Drawings by Leonid Pasternak.* Catalog of exhibition circulated by the Smithsonian Institution Traveling Exhibition Service, Washington, D.C., 1987.
R. Salys: "Boris Pasternak and His Father's Art" in *Oxford Slavonic Papers,* Oxford, 1992, Vol. 25, pp. 120-36.
R. Salys: "A Tale of Two Artists. Valentin Serov and Leonid Pasternak" in *Oxford Slavonic Papers,* Oxford, 1993, Vol. 26, pp. 75-86.
W. Salmond: "Leonid Pasternak: Autobiographical Fragments" in B183, pp. 35-44.
R. Salys: *Leonid Pasternak. The Russian Years, 1875-1921. A Critical Study and Catalogue,* Oxford: Oxford University Press, 1999 (two volumes).

Not an artist of radical convictions, Pasternak attained a pleasing integration of Realism and Impressionism, prompting observers to mention his work in the context of Louis Corinth, Max Liebermann, and Adolf von Menzel, a comparison that is not surprising given his schooling at the Akademie der Künste in Munich in the early 1880s.

Pasternak was much sought after for his portraits of contemporaries such as Fedor Chaliapin and Serge Rachmaninoff and he was a popular teacher at MIPSA. However, Pasternak was the servant of a double allegiance, "neither Russian, nor Jewish," as the St. Petersburg lawyer Oskar Gruzenberg commented in his memoirs.[618] Here was a Moscow intellectual and a leading sponsor of the Union of Russian Artists, who was "raised in a Russian environment, received a Russian education, and grew up in the Russian 1880s, a decade when Jews were assimilated and expected to serve the Russian people."[619] On the other hand, the predicament of the Jewish artist in Tsarist Russia and the issue of Jewish art and literature were common motifs in Pasternak's art and essays, indicated by his portraits of Jewish writers such as Chaim-Nachman Bialik and David Ben Saul Frishman.

Like his fellow Jews Mark Antokolsky, Naum Aronson, and Ilia Gintsburg, Pasternak also praised the cultural achievements of his territorial homeland and had every admiration for Russian artists and writers, particularly the august Tolstoi, who, for him, symbolized the highest ethical and artistic aspirations of mankind. A frequent visitor to Tolstoi and illustrator of his books, including *Resurrection,* Pasternak commented that

> even before I came to know him personally, I was drawn to him not only as a great artist, but also as a man in whom I discerned the presence of spiritual qualities, which condition the basic expression of morality: sympathy, compassion—the principle of love for one's neighbor.[620]

A colleague of Konstantin Korovin and Valentin Serov at MIPSA, Pasternak welcomed some of the new trends, although, certainly, he had little sympathy for the avant-garde. Pasternak was not granted a full professorship (presumably because of his Jewish ethnicity), but he considered the Moscow Institute to be a center of liberal and enlightened views in just conflict with the Ministry of the Court and, philosophically and esthetically, more progressive than the St. Petersburg Academy, which as late as 1916 was still limiting the Jewish student quota to "six."[621] Pasternak's transfer to Germany in 1921 and the publication of two monographs on him, reinforced his reputation — but as a Jewish, rather than a Russian, artist.

804 [R686].
Self-Portrait, ca. 1922.
Etching.
Monogram in the plate lower right in Russian.
11 x 8⅞ in., 28 x 22.5 cm.
Other inscriptions: in English by Pasternak's daughter, Lydia Pasternak-Slater, in pencil lower left: "Self portrait"; lower right:

804

"Etching by Leonid Pasternak"; lower margin in Russian: "To dear Nikita and his wife with heartfelt greetings and best wishes from the Pasternak sisters. Oxford, 1962."
Provenance: the artist's daughters Josephine and Lydia Pasternak, Oxford; 1962. Now in a private collection.
Pasternak made many self-portraits, but this etching is especially close to the pastel self-portrait reproduced in Struck, *Pasternak,* unpaginated. The portrait was Nina and Nikita Lobanov-Rostovsky's wedding present.

805

805 [R687].
Portrait of Count Lev Tolstoi, 1901.
Charcoal and pastel on prepared paper (washed with watercolor).
Signed and dated lower right in Russian: "Pasternak. 10.VI.01."
12¼ x 11⅜ in., 31 x 29 cm.
Provenance: *Icons, Russian Pictures and*

Works of Art, Christie's, London, 6 March, 1986, Lot 153 (reproduced). Now in a private collection.

Reproduced in F44 (1982) between pp. 112 and 113, where other renderings of Lev Tolstoi are also reproduced; and F107, p. 421. This charcoal and pastel sketch is similar to another portrait in the TG (for a reproduction see L207, p. 66) and, presumably, is a preparatory design for Pasternak's oil portrait of Tolstoi (reproduced in L207, Lot 164).

Note: Lev Nikolaevich Tolstoi (1828-1910) was one of Pasternak's favorite authors. Pasternak not only drew and painted Tolstoi numerous times after his first visit to the latter's estate in Yasnaia Poliana in 1893, but he also illustrated the novels *War and Peace* and *Resurrection.*

806

806 [R688].
Portrait of Fedor Chaliapin Rehearsing, 1924.
Autolithograph in black and white.
Signed and dated in the stone in Russian: "L. Pasternak, 24."
20⅞ x 15 in., 53 x 38 cm.
Other inscriptions: under the signature in pencil: "Hotel Bristol"; lower margin a dedication to his daughter Josephine and his son-in-law Friedrich: "Meinen lieben Kindern Friedrich und Josephine von Vater, L. Pasternak. Berlin 24.IX.1924."
Provenance: the artist's daughter, Josephine Pasternak, Oxford, 1962.
Reproduced in *Zeitbilder. Beilage zur Dossischen Zeitung,* Berlin, 1925, No. 37, 13 September, p. 2; N114; O31.

Note: Pasternak made portraits of many artists, actors, musicians, and writers, such as Gordon Craig, Joseph Hoffmann, Sergei Rachmaninoff, Alexander Skriabin, and the famous group portrait, often reproduced, of Alexander Benois, Diaghilev, Nikolai Milioti, et al. listening to a concert by Wanda Landowska at the Literary-Artistic Circle in Moscow.[622]

Pasternak seems to have made the acquaintance of the singer Fedor Chaliapin (see No. 678 [R573]) in the 1890s when he was in touch with the patron Savva Mamontov and hence with Mamontov's Private Opera Company, where Chaliapin was singing. In the early 1900s Pasternak became especially close to Chaliapin, thanks in part to the latter's rapport with members of the Union of Russian Artists in Moscow such as Konstantin Korovin, Serov, and Pasternak himself; Pasternak even described the great basso as his "best friend."[623] Pasternak also made a number of group portraits that included Chaliapin, such as the evocative *Evening Party at Korovin's* of 1912(?),[624] but the 1924 lithograph *Chaliapin Rehearsing* or, more literally, *At the Rehearsal,* seems to have been the last interpretation. Pasternak remembered the scene:

> I saw Chaliapin for the last time in 1924 in the Hotel Bristol in Berlin when I did a sketch of him in his room for the subsequent autolithograph *At the Rehearsal.* Chaliapin was sitting in his flowery dressing-gown at the piano. Suddenly he leapt up, took a match, dipped it in ink and with two or three strokes he drew on hotel note paper a caricature of himself singing. On one side he wrote with the match: "To my very dear friend, Leonid Osipovich Pasternak. F. Chaliapin, 1924." I have kept this little sketch as a dear memento of him.[625]

According to the artist's daughter Josephine, Pasternak made only a small number of prints (no more than ten) of the Chaliapin piece and never returned to it, even though he intended to make modifications. Chaliapin never forgot Pasternak; as he made clear when he happened to see Josephine Pasternak in Salzburg (date not provided):

> "Pasternak!...," he kept repeating, with a touch of nostalgia in his voice: "Those times... How fond I was... how fond I am of your father... Oh, give him my love when you see him next, and tell him that he is always with me... here...," and with a true Chaliapin gesture he pointed to his heart.[626]

618 Oskar Gruzenberg entitled one section of his memoirs, "Moe dvoeverie: Ne to evrei, ne to russkii. V evreiskom mestechke." See his *Vchera. Vospominaniia,* Paris: Dom knigi, 1938, pp. 21-24.
619 Salmond, "Leonid Pasternak: Autobiographical Fragments," op cit., p. 40.
620 F44 (1982), p. 126.
621 As reported in Anon.: "Khudozhestvennye vesti" in *Evreiskaia nedelia* M, 1916, 17 January, No. 3, p. 42.
622 The pastel *An Evening with Wanda Landowska at the Artistic Circle* (1908) is reproduced, for example, in D26, opposite p. 136; and I42, p. 11.
623 F44 (English translation), p. 86.
624 In F44 (Russian text) the work is dated 1916; in C52, Vol. 1, opposite p. 304, it is dated 1912. A probable sketch for this, in the Pasternak-Ramsay collection, is reproduced in *Yale Literary Magazine,* New Haven, 1981, Vol. 148, No. 4, p. 63.
625 F44 (English translation) p. 86.
626 Letter from Josephine Pasternak to Nikita D. Lobanov dated 10 October, 1984.

PESTEL, Vera Efremovna

Born 13 (25) May, 1883, Moscow, Russia; died 18 November, 1952, Moscow, Russia.

1905 attended CSIAI; 1906-07 attended Konstantin Yuon and Ivan Dudin's Art School in Moscow; 1907 first trip to Italy and Germany; 1909-11 attended Károly Kiss's studio in Moscow; 1912-13 lived in France, where she attended La Palette, studying under Le Fauconnier and Metzinger; close to Sofia Karetnikova and Nadezhda Udaltsova; 1915 began to contribute to exhibitions, including "0.10"; close to Liubov Popova, Vladimir Tatlin, and Lev Zhegin; 1916 contributed to the "Store" and the "Jack of Diamonds" exhibitions in Moscow; interested in Kazimir Malevich's Suprematism; 1917 contributed to the "World of Art" exhibition in Petrograd; 1918 contributed to the "Fifth State Exhibition. From Impressionism to Non-objective Art" in Moscow; 1918-19 worked on agit-designs for Moscow; 1921 contributed to the "World of Art" exhibition in Moscow; 1922 contributed to the "Erste Russische Kunstausstellung" in Berlin; leading member of the Makovets group (through 1927); 1926 with Zhegin coorganized the Path of Painting group; 1927 showed at "l'Araignée" exhibition in Paris; 1920s onwards continued to paint and exhibit; became especially interested in art education for children.

Bibliography
B. Berman: "Zhivopis i grafika V.E. Pestel v muzeinykh sobraniiakh" in *Muzei,* M, 1981, No. 2, pp. 76-81.
B67, passim.
B291, passim.

Pestel belonged to the avant-garde generation that was distinguished by its strong female presence, to the "Amazons of Russian art."[627] A colleague of Alexandra Exter, Vera Mukhina, Popova, and Udaltsova, Pestel studied in Paris at La Palette, assimilating the principles of Cubism. Later, as a frequent visitor to Tatlin's collective studio, the Tower, in Moscow, explored the concept of the abstract relief: one of Pestel's most successful works of the mid-1910s is her portrait of Tatlin playing his bandura. Pestel was also drawn to Malevich's Suprematism, painting compositions in 1915-16 that, like Udaltsova's of the same period, integrated the figurative contours of Cubism (e.g. of a guitar) and the colored planes of Suprematism. However, the four such works that she contributed to "0.10" encountered only misunderstanding and indignation, one critic describing this section of the exhibition as reaching the "limits of human morality beyond which begin robberies, murders, and piracy."[628]

Pestel chose not to pursue the abstract idiom and by the early 1920s had moved from her Cubist interpretations to a lyrical, intimate style of painting reminiscent of the Moscow Symbolists. A member of the moderate group called Makovets, Pestel avoided the demands for political compliance and didactic Realism, using her self-portraits and interiors to express a hushed and private vision of the world. In this volte-face she was close to Alexander Drevin, Artur Fonvizin, Udaltsova, and Lev Zhegin, who also resisted the temptations of abstraction to reaffirm the force of painting as an instrument of both concrete description and emotional evocation.

807

807 [R690].
Self-Portrait, ca. 1930.
Pencil.
12 x 8⅞ in., 30.5 x 22.5 cm.
Provenance: Valery Dudakov, Moscow, March, 1984.
The reverse (808 [NIRE]) carries the portrait of a young girl and a baby.

808

808 [NIRE].
Young Girl with a Baby, ca. 1930.
Pencil.
12 x 8⅞ in., 30.5 x 22.5 cm.
Reverse of No. 807 [R690].

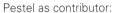

809

Pestel as contributor:
809 [R691].
Designer unknown: *Poster Advertising the Living Almanacs Revue at The Musical Snuffbox Cabaret, 1918.*
Lithograph in black on pink paper.
24⅜ x 19¼ in., 62 x 49 cm.
Inscriptions (as part of the design) identify the participants in these events (Vasilii Chekrygin, Lev Nikulin, Alexander Osmerkin, Vera Pestel, Sergei Spassky, Alexei Toporkov, et al.), the location (the Café Kade, Moscow), and the dates of the performances (June). Pestel's act is described (under the subtitle "Suprematists in the 'Snuffbox'") as an illustration of the theme "Down with Kings" through the demonstration of a deck of cards.
Another poster advertising events at The Musical Snuffbox and Living Almanacs is reproduced in A. Nikich, ed.: *Osmerkin,* M: Sovetskii khudozhnik, 1981, p. 39.

Note: Living Almanacs (also known as Living Almanac) was part of a revue organized at the shortlived cabaret called Musical Snuffbox within the Café Kade (on the corner of the Petrovka and Kuznetskii Most, Moscow). In 1918, when the Musical Snuffbox was functioning, Pestel was an active member of the avant-garde, especially close to Popova and Udaltsova. Vladimir Maiakovsky and the artist Chekrygin used to visit the Musical Snuffbox, even though Malevich referred to it as "old-fashioned."[629]

Unidentified production, ca. 1922.

810 [R692].
Costume Design for a Female Dancer, ca. 1922.
Watercolor, pencil, and silver paint.
10 x 8 in., 25.5 x 20.2 cm.
Inscriptions in Russian: color annotations on both sides in pencil: lower left (abbreviated): "Red"; center right: "[illegible] white silver"; on reverse: "3r"

(i.e., 3 rubles).
Provenance: Igor Dychenko, Kiev, February, 1984.
Reproduced in A34, p. 324; I77, p. 144; M26.

Unidentified production, ca. 1922.

810

811

811 [R693].
Costume Design for a Chinaman Holding a Fan, ca. 1922.
Watercolor, pencil, and gouache.
Signed on the reverse upper right in pencil: "Pestel."
12⅜ x 8⅝ in., 31.5 x 21.8 cm.
Provenance: Yakov Rubinshtein, Moscow, 1974.
The reverse also carries a pencil design for another costume for a Chinaman.

Note: Pestel was at her most creative and innovative in the 1920s, especially as a member of the Makovets group. In its wistful expression and loose style, Pestel's self-portrait is close to the concurrent drawings of her colleagues within that group such as Nikolai Chernyshev, Konstantin Zefirov, and Zhegin. Her encounter with the theater in the early 1920s was brief, although she worked for private ballet studios, including the one established by Antonina Shalomytova in Moscow in 1921.[630] The following year Pestel designed two productions there, i.e., Lope de Vega's comedy *Fuente Ovejuna* (The Sheep Well) and a piece called *Scenes from Chinese Life,* and it is possible that these costumes were for one of these enterprises.[631]

627 Anon.: "0,10" in *Golos Rusi,* P, 1916, 21 January. Reproduced in H. Berninger and J.A. Cartier: *Pougny. Catalog de l'oeuvre. Russie – Berlin, 1910-1923,* Tübingen: Wasmuth, Vol, 1, 1972.
628 Ibid.
629 See K. Malevich: "Reply" (1918) in T. Andersen, ed.: *K.S. Malevich. Essays on Art,* Copenhagen: Borgen, 1968, Vol. 1, p. 52.
630 For commentary on Shalomytova see A. F: "Tantsuiushchaia degeneratsiia" in *Teatr i muzyka,* M, 1922. For her own ideas on ballet see A. Shalomytova: "Voprosy baleta" in *Zrelishcha,* M, 1922, No. 17, 19-25 December, p. 16. For a color reproduction of a ballet set design by Pestel see K108, No. 74.
631 I74, No. 78 reproduces a costume dated 1920 allegedly for *Princess Turandot.*

PETRITSKY, Anatolii Galaktionovich

Born 31 January (12 February), 1895, Kiev, Ukraine; died 6 March, 1964, Kiev, Ukraine.

1910-18 attended the Kiev Art Institute; influenced by Impressionism and Post-Impressionism; close to Fedor Krichevsky; 1914 onward contributed regularly to Ukrainian, Russian, and international exhibitions; 1917 onward became increasingly involved in stage design; influenced by Alexandra Exter; 1920 designed posters and agit-prop decorations; 1922 worked with Kasian Goleizovsky on Eccentric Dances for the Moscow Chamber Ballet; 1922-24 attended Vkhutemas in Moscow; exponent of Constructivism; 1924 made designs for an unrealized production of a ballet based on the theme of Richard Wagner's *Tristan und Isolde;* 1925 contributed to the "Exposition Internationale des Arts Décoratifs" in Paris; moved to Kharkov; 1920s with Alexander Bogomazov, Vasilii Ermilov, Les Kurbas, Mikhailo Semenko, and other artists, producers, and writers, leading member of the Ukrainian avant-garde; active as a caricaturist and painter of proletarian scenes as well as a stage and book designer; 1928-32 painted portraits of Ukrainian literary and theatrical celebrities; 1930s-50s continued to work on theatrical design, mainly for Kiev productions, although he also worked for the Bolshoi Theater, Moscow, in the 1940s; 1944 was made People's Artist of the U.S.S.R.

Bibliography
V. Khmuryi: *Anatol Petritskii. Teatralnii stroi,* Kharkov: State Publishing-House, 1929 (in Ukrainian).
I. Vrona: *Anatol Petritskii,* K: Mistetstvo, 1968.
D. Gorbachev: *Anatolii Galaktionovich Petritskii,* M: Sovetskii khudozhnik, 1971.
M20.
I. Dychenko: "Bezoshibochnym glazom (Novoe ob Anatole Petritskom)" in *Vitchizna,* K, No. 12 (1974).
D. Horbachov: "Soviet Ukrainian Art: A Retro of Achievement" in *Ukraina,* K, 1980, November, pp. 14-17.
D. Gorbachev: "Rezhisser i khudozhnik v ukrainskom opernom teatre 20-kh godov" in G50 for 1978. M, 1980, pp. 255-64.
G57, *passim.*
D. Horbachov et al.: *Anatolii Petritskii. Spogadi pro khudozhnika,* K: Mistetstvo, 1981 (in Ukrainian).
N. Kornienko: "Les Kurbas i khudozhniki" in G50, No. 5, pp. 332-54.
M. Mudrak: "Modern Expression and Folk Tradition in the Theatrical Art of Anatol' Petryts'kyi" in *Cross Currents,* New York, 1984, No. 3, pp. 385-95.
I. Dychenko: "Shchedrii na barvi" in *Ukraina,* K, 1985, No. 8 (in Ukrainian).
B77, *passim.*
V. Ruban: *Anatol Petritskii. Portreti suchasnikiv,* K: Mistetstvo, 1991.
A31, p. 453-54.
K265, pp. 240-53.
D. Horbachov: "Gra-drazhnilka iuviliara" in *Fine Art,* K, 2010, No. 2, pp. 23-27.
D. Horbachov et al.: *Anatol Petritskii. Teatralnii stroi ta dekoratsii zi zbirki Muzeiu teatralnogo, muzichnogo ta kinomistetstva,* Kiev-Lvov: Maister-knig, 2012 (in Ukrainian).

Petritsky was a pioneer in the artistic and theatrical renaissance that occurred in the Ukraine in the late 1910s and 1920s and was a leading exponent of the Ukrainian interpretation of Constructivism in stage design.[632] Beginning in 1918, Petritsky decorated ballets, operas, and dramas for numerous theaters in the Ukraine and Russia and was quickly recognized as an original practitioner and theorist of stage design. As he wrote in the avant-garde journal *Nova generatsiia* [New Generation] in 1930:

> The artist builds the theatrical costume like a functional object which embodies this or that idea of the general stage design. The artist balances this object within the general composition and creates an organic link between the object of the design, the actor and the costume by means of the mechanics of the action. The costume should also be built from the inside out.[633]

Of particular importance to Petritsky's early development as a stage designer was his collaboration with the ballet dancer Mikhail Mordkin in Kiev in 1918 on *Spanish Dance.*

Mordkin was an exponent of the "new ballet" and, along with Nikolai Foregger, Goleizovsky, Lavrentii Novikov, and Vladimir Riabtsev, he did much to change the conventions of classical ballet in Moscow, Kiev, and after 1923, the year of his emigration, in New York. Mordkin also worked for the Chamber Theater, Moscow, even instructing Alisa Koonen for her Dance of the Seven Veils in Alexander Tairov's 1917 production of *Salomé* — thereby establishing close contact with the designer Exter. Mordkin also collaborated with Georgii Yakulov on projects for the Chamber Theater and, as an associate of the Bolshoi Theater in Moscow, traveled a great deal during the Civil War period, spending 1919 in Kiev and then 1921-22 in Tiflis. Thanks to Mordkin, Petritsky gained valuable knowledge and experience of the ballet and theater worlds, and it was logical that Petritsky accepted Mordkin's invitation to design the New York production of *Nur and Anitra* in 1923. After Mordkin's emigration, Petritsky continued to collaborate with experimental choreographers, contributing designs to Mikhail Moiseev's productions of *Le Corsaire* in 1926 and *Taras Bulba* in 1928 in Kharkov. As one critic has written recently of Petritsky the stage designer:

> The main thing is movement, speed. And Petritsky expressed this "speed" thesis in his designs where — not without irony — he elucidated the energic scheme of the dance. But he was not satisfied with schemes. The artist was skeptical of those who, by the term "contemporary," understand a break with the culture of the past... Using new visual media and elements of bygone styles in many of his productions, the artist restored the living physiognomy of the past to the stage.[634]

Nur and Anitra: *ballet in one act by Alexander Gorsky to music by Alexander Ilinsky. Projected, but not produced, by Morris Gest for the Greenwich Village Follies, New York, in the fall of 1923, with choreography by Mikhail Mordkin and designs by Anatolii Petritsky.*

The Indian knight Nur comes to the castle of a beautiful enchantress, Queen Anitra. With the help of a talisman from a magician, Nur attempts to conquer the Queen, whose charms had destroyed many before him. The dances of the Queen's maidens do not affect the bearer of the talisman, so the Queen then lures him away to a magic grotto and, with her song, induces him to sleep. However, the magician saves Nur from this induction. Much angered, the Queen and her servants express their injured pride in a frenzied dance.

812

813

News from Ukraine, K, 1985, No. 9. A design close in composition is reproduced in Mudrak, "Modern Expression," p. 384.

Note: From the style and theme, it would appear that this design was for one of the numbers produced at the variety theater called Crooked Jimmy and organized in Kiev in 1919 on the basis of the Petrograd cabaret Bi-Ba-Bo. Directed by Konstantin Mardzhanov, Crooked Jimmy maintained the traditions of its St. Petersburg and Moscow precedents, i.e., The Crooked Mirror and The Bat, and, in fact, it owed much to Nikolai Evreinov's notion of the miniature theater (see Note to No. 41 [R40]). In 1922, Crooked Jimmy moved to Moscow and, directed by Alexei Alexeev, opened in the former cellar of The Bat; in 1924, it became the Moscow Theater of Satire. This piece may have been for the revue called Jimmy, the Rascal, produced at the Crooked Jimmy, Moscow, in 1923.

814

812 [160; R694].
Costume Design for Nur, 1923.
Watercolor and collage.
Signed and dated upper right in Russian: "Act II, Warriors, Men Sc. 4."
21¾ x 15½ in., 55.3 x 39.5 cm.
Provenance: Igor Dychenko, Kiev, June, 1974.
Reproduced in color in B115, plate 161; and in black and white in I32, No. 71; I51, No. 177; I77, p. 159. A version of this design, without the elaborate collage, is reproduced in Khmuryi, Anatol Petritskii, unnumbered. Another version, with the collage, is in the BTM, and a set of the costumes, including a version of this design, is reproduced on the cover of Zrelishcha, M, 1924, No. 71 (see also ibid., p. 13), and this is reproduced again in G57, p. 87.

813 [161; R695].
Costume Design for the Musician, 1923.
Watercolor, collage, and pencil.
Signed and dated upper center in Russian: "An. Petritsky 23."
21⅞ x 15½ in., 55.5 x 39.5 cm.
Other inscriptions: upper center in Russian: "Musician Buffoon 2 XX."
Provenance: Igor Dychenko, Kiev, 1973.
Reproduced in color in B115, plate 160; G79, p. 133; and as the cover to I32; and in black and white in I32, No. 70; I51, No. 178; I61, p. 320; I77, p. 159; a version of this design, without the elaborate collage, is reproduced in Khmuryi, Anatol Petritskii, unnumbered; another version, with the collage is in the BTM, and a set of the costumes, including a version of this design, is reproduced on the cover of Zrelishcha, 1924, No. 71, and this is reproduced again in G57, p. 87. Part of the collage in this design is made from the

application of pieces of a colored reproduction of Natalia Goncharova's designs for the project Foire Espagnole (1916), which was printed in the journal Zharptitsa, Paris-Berlin, 1922, No. 7, pp. 2-4.

Note: Nur and Anitra, which had premiered in Moscow on 2 December, 1907, marked the high point in Mordkin's and Petritsky's artistic collaboration, even though this 1923 production was not implemented. In any case, Petritsky had already finished his maquette and costume designs in August, 1923,[635] but Mordkin arrived in the USA only at the end of November, 1924.[636] According to some observers, Petritsky managed to evoke the spirit of India, even though the costumes were "far from any sense of everyday life... two or three characteristic details (for example, Anitra's headdress) waive any possibility of making a mistake: this is India."[637] Seven designs by Petritsky for Nur and Anitra are known to exist: three are in the BTM, two in a private collection in Kiev,[638] and two in the Lobanov-Rostovsky collection.

Unidentified production, ca. 1923.

814 [R696].
Costume Designs for a Figure Emerging from a Suitcase, a Gentleman, and a Lady.
Black ink and grey wash.
11 x 8½ in., 28 x 21.7 cm.
The reverse carries the pencil design of a man and a reclining figure.
Provenance: Dmitrii Gorbachev, Kiev, February, 1984.
Reproduced in I68, p. 16; I77, pp. 117, 147; M20, p. 5; O14; P35; R2; T6; T8; T32; D. Horbachov: "'I Feel Life Passionately'" in

Le Corsaire: ballet in three acts and five (or seven) scenes by Joseph Mazilier and Jules-Henri Vernoy de Saint-Georges with music by Adolphe Charles Adam, based loosely on Lord Byron's poem The Corsair. Produced by Mikhail Moiseev at the Kharkov Opera Theater early in 1926 with choreography by Marius Petipa and designs by Anatolii Petritsky.

The Greek slave Medora is abducted by Conrad the Corsair, but through treachery and cunning, her master Isaac Lankedem regains possession of her and sells her to the Pasha Seid who lives in a palace on the Bosphorus. In love with Medora, Conrad enters the palace, frees her, and the couple flee on his boat. Tossed by the waves, the boat is shipwrecked, but Medora and Conrad reach the shore, are saved, and live happily ever after.

815

816

817

815 [162; R697].
Costume Design for Medora, 1925.
Collage, colored crayon, silver and gold paint, tinsel paper (added later), pencil, and black ink.
19⅞ x 14¼ in., 50.5 x 36.2 cm.
The reverse carries a rough sketch of a female dancer (see No. 816 [R697a]) under which (lower margin) is inscribed in pencil in Ukrainian: "'Ballet 'Corsaire'. Medora, wife of the Sheikh. State Opera, Kharkov, 1925."
Provenance: Igor Dychenko, Kiev, June, 1974.
Reproduced in color in A34, p. 331; B115, plate 159; I68, p. 15; M78; M140; N120; N156, p. 80; N187, p. 36; P16; T10; Khmuryi, *Anatol Petritskii,* unpaginated; and in black and white in I77, p. 144.

816 [R697a].
Sketch of a Female Dancer, ca. 1925.
Watercolor and pencil.
19⅞ x 14¼ in., 50.5 x 36.2 cm.
This is the reverse of No. 815 [R697].

817 [R698].
Costume Design for a Native, ca. 1926.
Collage, silver paper (added later), black crayon, and pencil.
19½ x 14 in., 49.5 x 35.5 cm.
Provenance: Igor Dychenko, Kiev, June, 1974.
Reproduced in I77, p. 144.

Note: After opening in the fall of 1925, the Kharkov Opera Theater soon became a prestigious center for artistic experiment, thanks to the presence there of Foregger, Goleizovsky, Moiseev, and Petritsky. Coming to the Kharkov Opera after working for Goleizovsky at the Moscow Chamber Ballet and then designing the production of Nikolai Gogol's *Vii* at the Ivan Franko Ukrainian Dramatic Theater (also in Kharkov), Petritsky consolidated his position as a leader of the Ukrainian avant-garde. Although a Con-

structivist by inclination, Petritsky adjusted easily to the needs of a given spectacle and was willing to use ornament and "illusion" if the production so dictated. Consequently, he had no difficulty in evoking the historical ambiance for operas such as *Prince Igor* (Odessa, 1926), *Taras Bulba* (Kiev, 1927; Kharkov, 1928) and, of course, *Le Corsaire;* and he did this while still emphasizing the formal qualities of the piece. He wrote in 1930:

> You must... construct the costume from inside, and be guided not just by nice appearances, but also by your

relationship to it as a form that is supplementary to the image created by the actor — as one of the components interconnected to the logical mechanics of the whole.[639]

Petritsky had very definite ideas about the way in which his costumes were to function, especially for *Le Corsaire.* The dancer Valentina Dulenko, for example, who danced the part of Medora in Kharkov had a hard time convincing Petritsky that elementary adjustments had to be made — otherwise the costumes would have impeded the movements.[640] Petritsky also

818

created a complex set, suspending planes of different colors and forms from the gridiron, which changed their shape and depiction as the ballet progressed.[641]

The Flea or The Left-Handed Smith and the Steel Flea: buffoonery by Evgenii Zamiatin in four acts based on a tale by Nikolai Leskov. Projected for the Ivan Franko Ukrainian Dramatic Theater, Kharkov, in May, 1927, with designs by Anatolii Petritsky (?).
See No. 686 [R581] for plot summary.

818 [R699].
Stage Design for Act III with a Boat in Front of a City, 1927.
Gouache.
4½ x 17¾ in., 36.7 x 45 cm.
Inscriptions in silver paint as part of the design: lower left: "4.V.1927"; lower right in Ukrainian: "The Flea (by Zamiatin). III Act."
Provenance: Igor Dychenko, Kiev, June, 1974.
Reproduced in I77, pp. 107 and 145.
The attribution to Petritsky has been questioned.

Note: Since there is no documented record of a production of Zamiatin's *The Flea* with designs by Petritsky in 1927, it is assumed that this design, attributed to Petritsky, was for a project that was not implemented. The Leskov/Zamiatin social satire became immediately popular after its premiere at the Moscow Art Theater in February, 1925, when Alexei Dikii produced it with designs by Boris Kustodiev (see No. 686 [R581]). Clearly, Petritsky's interpretation, with its shooting star, electric lights, and electricity wires, would have been more "contemporary" than Kustodiev's, but it is difficult to imagine how it would have functioned vis-à-vis the dramatic text.

632 For information on the Ukrainian avant-garde, see B77; B356; K131; K150; K161. Also see the entries for Bogomazov and Meller in this catalog.
633 A. Petritsky: "Oformleniia stseni suchasnogo teatru" in *Nova generatsiia*, Kharkov, 1930, No. 1, pp. 41, 42.
634 D. Gorbachev: *Problema traditsii i novatorstva v tvorchestve A. G. Petritskogo*, K: Academy of Sciences of the Ukrainian SSR, 1970, p. 10. This is the typewritten summary of Gorbachev's *kandidat* dissertation for the Rylsky Institute of Art History, Folklore, and Ethnography, Kiev.
635 See "Khronika" in *Zrelishcha*, M, 1923, No. 50-52, p. 11.
636 A notice in *Teatr i muzyka*, M, 1923, No. 35, p. 1119, indicates that Mordkin was leaving for the USA at the end of October, 1923, but, in fact, he delayed his trip for one year. For further information see D67, p. 146.
637 E. Kuzmin on Petritsky's designs for *Nur and Anitra*. Quoted in Gorbachev, *Anatolii Galaktionovich Petritsky*, p. 38.
638 For the reproduction of one of the designs in the private collection in Kiev (a Warrior) see *Mistetska tribuna*, K, 1974, December, p. 164. For commentary see M20.
639 Petritsky: "Oformleniia stseni suchasnogo teatru", op. cit., p. 42.
640 V. Dulenko: "Maister baletnogo kostiuma" in Horbachov et al., op. cit., pp. 44-45. Dulenko recalls that Petritsky designed five costumes for Medora. This piece would seem to be for Scene 2.
641 This according to Gorbachev, *Anatolii Galaktionovich Petritsky*, p. 66.

PETROV-VODKIN, Kuzma Sergeevich

Born 24 October (5 November), 1878, Khvalynsk, Saratov Region, Russia; died 15 February, 1939, Leningrad, Russia.

1895-97 attended SCITD; 1897-1904 attended MIPSA, studying under Konstantin Korovin, Valentin Serov, et al.; 1901 visited Munich, where he took lessons from Anton Ažbé; 1904 visited London; 1905-09 traveled extensively in Germany, France, Italy, Turkey, and Africa; influenced by Viktor Borisov-Musatov and Mikhail Vrubel; 1906 married a Serb, Maria Jovanovič 1906-08 lived in France; 1910 painted *The Dream*; began to exhibit with the World of Art and to teach; 1912 painted *The Bathing of the Red Horse;* 1918 onwards taught at Pegoskhuma and the Petrograd Svomas, where he occupied a variety of pedagogical and administrative posts; 1910s developed his spatial theory based on spherical perspective; 1921 under the auspices of the Academy of Material Culture took part in an expedition to Central Asia, including Samarkand; 1920s painted and drew portraits, for example, of the writers Anna Akhmatova and Andrei Bely; 1924-26 lived in France; late 1920s concentrated on his autobiographical writings; 1932 elected president of the Leningrad Union of Artists; 1930s while still active as an studio painter, also worked on stage design; 1936-37 one-man exhibition in Leningrad and Moscow.

Bibliography
V. Kostin: *Kuzma Sergeevich Petrov-Vodkin,* M: Sovetskii khudozhnik, 1966.
Yu. Rusakov: *Risunki K.S. Petrova-Vodkina,* M: Iskusstvo, 1978.
S. Kaplanova: *Ot zamysla i natury k zakonchennomu proizvedeniiu,* M: Iskusstvo, 1981, pp. 140-203.
Petrov-Vodkin's memoirs and commentaries on art are of particular interest. See Yu. Rusakov, ed.: *K. Petrov-Vodkin. "Khlynovsk. Prostranstvo Evklida. Samarkandiia,"* L: Iskusstvo, 1970 (second edition, 1982).
Yu. Rusakov: *K.S. Petrov-Vodkin,* L: Aurora, 1986.
E. Selizarova, ed.: *K.S. Petrov-Vodkin. Pisma. Stati. Vystupleniia. Dokumenty,* M: Sovetskii khudozhnik, 1991.
V. Leniashin: *Kuzma Sergeevich Petrov-Vodkin,* SP: Palace Editions, 2001.
V. Chaikovskaia: *Tri lika russkogo iskusstva XX veka. Robert Falk, Kuzma Petrov-Vodkin, Aleksandr Samokhvalov,* M: Iskusstvo XXI veka, 2006.
T. Grodskova, ed.: *K.S. Petrov-Vodkin i XXI vek,* Saratov: Radishchev State Art Museum, 2008.
M. Petrova-Vodkina: *Moi velikii russkii muzh,* Saratov: SGKHM imeni A.N. Radishcheva, 2008.
E. Gribonosova-Grebneva: *Tvorchestvo K.S. Petrova-Vodkina i zapadnoevropeiskie "realizmy" 1920-1930-kh,* M: Galart, 2010.
V. Uspensky: *Kuzma Sergeevich Petrov-Vodkin. Materinstvo,* SP: Arka, 2010.
S. Daniel: *Kuzma Petrov-Vodkin,* SP: Aurora, 2011.

The artistic career of Petrov-Vodkin has been overshadowed by the more exuberant achievements of the Russian avant-garde, although he also "endeavored to liberate painterly trends from the fortuitousness of polyglot confusion."[642] Petrov-Vodkin matured during the Symbolist age of Viktor Borisov-Musatov and the Blue Rose group, and his painting, early and late, often elicits an intimate mood and mystical dimension. Petrov-Vodkin was important not only as a painter, but also as a theorist of pictorial space — of a "spherical perspective" in which "form conditions color" and in which "symptoms of growth are visible in object-phenomena."[643] Interested in non-Euclidian geometry, Petrov-Vodkin often based the composition of his paintings on a spherical, planetary perspective. Both form and color were of equal import to Petrov-Vodkin and his early works, e.g., *The Bathing of the Red Horse,* owed much to his analyses of the techniques and compositions of old Russian icons.

Petrov Vodkin's forays into the discipline of design were rare and he is remembered primarily as a studio painter. Except for his contribution to the production of *The Marriage of Figaro* at the Leningrad Bolshoi Theater of Drama in 1935, practically all his stage designs remained as projects, including those for *Boris Godunov* (1923) and for *The Brothers Karamazov* (1927).[644]

The Brothers Karamazov: drama based on the novel by Fedor Dostoevsky. Projected, but not produced by Gennadii Ge at the Leningrad Academic Theater of Drama in 1927 with designs by Kuzma Petrov-Vodkin.

Fedor's three sons — the sensual Dmitrii, the atheist Ivan, and the novice Alexei — meet in their home town. Fedor, a profligate businessman, scoffs at the church elder Father Zosima in their presence. Dmitrii confesses to Alexei how he had caroused with Grushenka, a lady of easy virtue, using the money of his betrothed, Ekaterina. He then asks Alexei to secure him money from their father. Meanwhile, Zosima dies, causing much anxiety among some disciples, inasmuch as his holy body starts to decompose. Alexei sees Grushenka. Through a series of confusions, Dmitrii is accused of killing his father, but Smerdiakov, Fedor's epileptic servant, confesses to the murder before hanging himself. In spite of counter-evidence by Ivan, Dmitrii is still convicted — thanks in part to compromising evidence given by the jealous Ekaterina. Alexei, wishing to sacrifice his own life for truth, prepares to go with Dmitrii to Siberia.

819

819 [R700].
Stage Design, ca. 1927.
Watercolor.
Signed lower right margin in ink in Russian:
"K. Petrov-Vodkin."
15 x 20¼ in., 38 x 51.5 cm.
Provenance: Solomon Shuster, Leningrad,
February, 1984.

Reproduced in I77, p. 145; M25, p. 19. A
version is in the TG. Another set design,
now in the Museum of Private Collections,
Moscow, is reproduced in B159, p. 187. Yet
another design is in the collection of the
RM.
It is unclear why this particular production
was cancelled.

The Commander of the Second Army:
tragedy by Ilia Selvinsky. Produced by
Vsevolod Meierkhold at the Meierkhold
Theater, Moscow, on 4 May, 1929, with
music by Vissarion Shebalin and designs by
Meierkhold, Sergei Vakhtangov, Vasilii
Pochitalov, and Kuzma Petrov-Vodkin.

Commander Chub, a worker from the
peasantry who has endured the Tsarist labor
camps, encounters the writer and intel-
lectual Okonny. Both are Reds, but their
attitudes towards the revolutionary cause
are very different. Okonny develops a plot
against Chub, whom he regards as
incapable of making major military deci-
sions. Nevertheless, Chub is a doer and
thinks only of the great victory, while
Okonny is impractical and merely
daydreams.

Petrov-Vodkin as contributor:
820 [R701].
Designer unknown: *Poster Advertising the*
Premiere of **The Commander of the**
Second Army, 1929.
Lithograph in black and white.
28¾ x 35⅜ in., 73 x 90 cm.
Inscriptions (as part of the design) provide
details on the presentation dates of *The*
Commander of the Second Army (4, 5, 6,
and 7 May). Among the actors was Zinaida
Raikh.

Petrov-Vodkin as contributor:

821 [R702].

Designer unknown: *Poster Advertising* **The Bed Bug** *and* **The Commander of the Second Army, 1929.**

Lithograph in black on yellow paper.

22 x 28⅜ in., 56 x 72 cm.

Inscriptions (as part of the design) provide details on the presentation dates of *The Bed Bug* (25, 26, 27 November) and *The Commander of the Second Army* (29, 29, 30 November), and also on the Slovo Printing-House at 25 October Prospect, Moscow. For information on *The Bed Bug* see Nos. 867-72 [R750-54a]).

Note: The primary sources on Meierkhold give the premiere of *The Commander of the Second Army* as 24 July, 1929, in Kharkov (see C32, Vol. 2, p. 606; C46, p. 290; C72, p. 470),[645] although the first poster here advertises 4 May, 1929. In fact, the Moscow premiere was on 30 September, 1929.[646] Petrov-Vodkin was only one of the many collaborators on this production, but the theme of the Red Army appealed to him, as evidenced by his painting *Death of a Commissar* (1928, TG), which, undoubtedly, Meierkhold had seen. In a letter to his wife dated 17 November, 1929, Petrov-Vodkin wrote: "Yesterday we went to the Meierkhold Theater to see *Commander of the Second Army,* for which I was consultant."[647]

642 I. Levkova-Lamm: "'Narodnye massivy' Petrova-Vodkina" in *Novoe russkoe slovo,* New York, 1983, 19 August, p. 4.
643 Rusakov, *K. Petrov-Vodkin* (second edition), pp. 487, 554.
644 For reproduction of Petrov-Vodkin's theater designs, including a set for *The Brothers Karamazov,* see Rusakov, *K.S. Petrov-Vodkin,* plates 218-31.
645 See C31, Vol. 3, Part 1, p. 269, 301 (Note 2).
646 Ibid.
647 Selizarova, op. cit., p. 262.

PEVSNER, Antoine (Pevzner, Nota / Natan / Anton Berkovich / Abramovich / Borisovich) [648]

Born 18 (30) January, 1886, Klimovichi (Klimavichy), Mogilev Region, Belorussia (some sources give Orel, Russia); died 12 April, 1962, Paris, France.

1902-09 attended the Kiev Art Institute, impressed by Isaak Levitan and Mikhail Vrubel; 1909-10 attended IAA; 1910 contact with the Jack of Diamonds group in Moscow; visited the Shchukin and Morozov collections of modern French painting in Moscow; 1911-14 worked in Paris with brief trips to Russia; influenced by Cubism; contact with Archipenko and Modigliani; 1915-17 stayed with his brother Naum Gabo in Norway; 1917 returned to Russia; 1918 contributed to the "First Exhibition of Paintings by the Professional Union of Artists in Moscow"; 1918-19 contributed to the "V State Exhibition of Paintings" in Moscow; 1918-21 professor at Svomas / Vkhutemas; 1920 with Gabo issued the *Realistic Manifesto;* 1922 contributed to the "Erste Russische Kunstausstellung" in Berlin; 1923 emigrated to Berlin and then to Paris; began to work on constructions of zinc, copper, brass, and celluloid; 1926-27 worked with Gabo on sets and costumes for Diaghilev's production of *La Chatte;* 1930 became a French citizen; 1932 founder-member of the Abstraction-Création group in Paris; 1940s supporter of the Réalités Nouvelles group; 1948 with Naum Gabo, retrospective exhibition at the Museum of Modern Art, New York; 1940s onwards produced monumenral public sculptures, for example, for the City of Caracas and the General Motors Technical Center in Warren, Michigan.

Bibliography

K. Dreier et al.: *Antoine Pevsner,* Paris: Drouin, 1947.
Gabo – Pevsner. Catalog of exhibition at the Museum of Modern Art, New York, 1948.
R. Massat: *Antoine Pevsner et le Constructivisme,* Paris: Caractères, 1956.
P. Peissi and C. Giedion-Welcker: *Antoine Pevsner,* Neuchâtel: Griffon, 1961.
A. Pevsner: *Naum Gabo and Antoine Pevsner. A Biographical Sketch of My Brothers,* Amsterdam: Augustin and Schoonman, 1964.
J. Cassou: *Pevsner au Musée National d'Art Moderne. Les Ecrits de Pevsner,* Paris: Ministère d'Etat, 1964.
B. Dorival: *Antoine Pevsner,* Paris: Prisme, 1965.
B. Dorival: *I maestri della scultura. Pevsner,* Milan: Fabbri, 1966.
J.-C. Marcadé, ed.: *Pevsner,* Paris: Art Edition, 1995.
J.-J. Aillagon et al.: *Antoine Pevsner.* Catalog of exhibition at the Centre Georges Pompidou, Paris, 2001.
E. Lebon and P. Brullé, comps.: *Antoine Pevsner. Catalogue raisonné de l'oeuvre sculpté,* Paris: Les Amis d'Antoine Pevsner / Galerie-Editions Pierre Brullé, 2002.

The study of anatomical construction played a major part in the curricula of the Art Institute in Kiev and the Academy of Arts in St. Petersburg; while most of Pevsner's student drawings have not survived, it can be assumed that his interest in skeletal form was no less profound than Gabo's. Some of Pevsner's later constructions even recall anatomical and musculatory specimens or, more precisely, seem to be schematic paraphrases of them. Pevsner's purpose, however, is contrary to that of the traditional academy. As with the geometric elements of Malevich's Suprematism, Pevsner took the didactic tables of cones and cylinders and conceived them not as a guide to the attainment of Classical beauty, but rather as a new artistic alphabet that could provide an infinite number of new lexical arrangements. Like Gabo and Rodchenko, Pevsner offered a complex of inner connections as the finished work of art, whereas the traditional academy viewed it as a means to an end and as the basic framework upon which to construct the outward material illusion — the very façade that Pevsner and his colleagues wished to demolish.

The son of an engineer, Pevsner must have been fascinated to discover mechanical parallels between zoological bone structures and the industrial skeletons of the new iron frame buildings towering above Moscow and St. Petersburg. As he viewed these somatic compositions, he may well have recalled his arrival at the Briansk (now Kiev) Railroad Station in Moscow en route for St. Petersburg: Vladimir Shukhov's cantilevered metal construction with its exposed sockets, articulations, and joints must have appeared to Pevsner (and also perhaps to his brother Gabo, to Alexander Rodchenko, the Stenberg brothers, and Vladimir Tatlin) as some gigantic technological counterpart to the human and animal skeletons that he was copying in the St.

822

823

Petersburg Academy and the Zoological Museum. Still, Pevsner did not necessarily equate structural engineering with artistic invention in the way that the Moscow Constructivists did in the early 1920s. For Pevsner there was an essential difference between science and art, as he explained in the second issue of *Abstraction-Création, art non figuratif* in 1933:

> If there still exists an exterior likeness between a technical creation and an artistic construction, the first aids in calculating the perturbations of planetary mechanics, while the other gives us the possibility of bringing to light the hidden forces in nature. [649]

Unidentified production, *ca. 1918.*

822 [NIRE].
Costume Design for the Head of a Bird, 1918 (?).
Black ink and mauve wash.
Signed and dated: "A. Pevsner, 18-5."
11⅜ x 8¼ in., 29 x 21 cm.
Provenance: Annely Juda Gallery, London, October, 1975.
Reproduced in I32, p. 51, No. 72.

La Chatte: *ballet in one act by Sobeka (a composite pseudonym where S=Sauguet, B=Balanchine, K=Kochno) based on a fable by Aesop reworked by Boris Kochno with music by Henri Sauguet. Produced by Sergei Diaghilev's Ballets Russes at Monte Carlo on 30 April, 1927, with choreography by George Balanchine and designs by Naum Gabo and Antoine Pevsner. The production was then given in Paris on 27 May, 1927, at the Théâtre Sarah-Bernhardt.*
See No. 512 [R394] for plot summary.

823 [R689].
Stage Detail, 1927 (?).
Pencil.
Signed lower right: "Pevsner."
5⅞ x 5⅛ in., 14.8 x 13 cm.
Other inscription: the number "23" lower right.
Provenance: Annely Juda Fine Art, London, October, 1975.

Reproduced in I40, No. 85; K13, No. 51a; and in Dorival, *Antoine Pevsner,* p. 54, where it is dated 1924 and described as a drawing for a bas-relief.

Note: There is some question as to whether this design was intended for *La Chatte,* even though it was acquired from the Pevsner family precisely as a component for the ballet. The work is clearly a preparatory drawing for the metal relief called *Bust* of 1924 (reproduced in Dorival, p. 55), although it is possible that Pevsner also applied the design towards his statue of Venus on center stage. See entry for Gabo at No. 512 [R394].

648 Pevsner's full name appears in several Russian variations, although according to his birth certificate, he was registered as "Nota Berkovich Pevsner." However, during 1902-10 two other variants appear, i.e., Nota Abramovich and Natan Abramovich; and in emigration Pevsner was addressed as Anton Borisovich. We would like to thank Jean-Claude Marcadé for this information.

649 A. Pevsner: [Reply to questions posed by the Committee of the Abstract-Création Association] in *Abstraction-Création,* Paris, 1933, No. 2, p. 35. English translation in *Gabo – Pevsner* (1948), op. cit., p. 57.

Antoine Pevsner.

POGEDAIEFF, Georges (Pozhedaev/Pozhidaev, Grigorii Anatolievich)

Born 13 (25) January, 1894, Pozhedaevka, Kursk Region, Russia; died 3 August, 1971, Ménerbes, Vaucluse, France.

1908 took drawing lessons with Yan Tsionglingsky (Jan Ciągliński) in St. Petersburg; 1911-14 trained with the Nicholas Cadet Corps in St. Petersburg; joined the Hussars Regiment; 1915 enrolled in MIPSA; 1916 enrolled in IAA; 1917-18 started to work as a stage designer in Petrograd; moved to Moscow; 1918-19 designed Kasian Goleizovsky's interpretation of Nikolai Cherepnin's ballet *Red Masks* for the Bolshoi Theater, Moscow (not produced); also worked with Goleizovsky on a ballet scenario called *Gamelin, or the Revolution Will Conquer* (not produced); 1920 emigrated to Romania; 1921 executed designs for a production of *Hamlet* in Vienna; 1921-24 lived in Berlin; 1922 one-man exhibition at Der Sturm in Berlin; worked for Jascha Juschny's Blaue Vogel cabaret, designing numbers such as *Die traurige Prinzessin, Die zwei Feine,* and *Pique Dame;* 1924 one-man exhibition in Vienna; 1925 moved to Paris; mid-1920s worked for the Chauve-Souris, Paris, designing numbers such as *Le Crocodile et Cléopâtre* and *Le Grand Guignol;* from the late 1920s onward designed stage productions, illustrated books (Chekhov, Dostoevsky, Gogol, Lermontov), and wrote poetry; 1946 and 1955 one-man exhibitions in Paris; 1953 awarded the Order of the Legion of Honor for cultural services rendered.

Bibliography
J.R. Thomé: "G. de Pogédaieff ou la comédie humaine à travers les classiques russes" in *Le Courier graphique,* Paris, 1949, No. 35, pp. 11-18.
L. Réau: *Georges A. Pojedaieff.* Catalog of exhibition at the Galerie R. Creuse, Paris, 1958.
M2, Vol. 2, pp. 189-90.
G36, pp. 43-44.
M73, Vol. 26, pp. 80-81.
H34, 465, 466.
H51, passim.
K252, pp. 270-73.
N. Dolgopolov: "Parizh s russkim aktsentom" in *Rossiiskaia gazeta,* M, 2010, 11 November.
Recent exhibitions of stage designs have featured Georges Pogedaieff's work. See, for example, I116, p. 56.
Some of Pogedaieff's poetry was published in *Vozrozhdenie,* Paris, 1954, No. 34, pp. 7-22.

Designer and dancer (and poet), Pogedaieff commenced his alliance with the performing arts in the mid-1910s when he designed the cover for the score of *Prelude,* a song by Kasian Golzeiovsky and Vasilii Nebolsin.[650] He collaborated further with Goleizovsky by designing experimental ballets, especially the *Gamelin, or the Revolution Will Conquer* in 1918-19 which was to have consisted of a "suite of national French dances" with a finale celebrating the Revolution.[651] Unfortunately, these projects were not produced — partly because of Pogedaieff's emigration in late 1919 (?) and partly because of protests from the more conservative dancers and producers.[652] According to Nikolai Dolgopolov, the artist's nephew, Pogedaieff even helped design costumes for Sergei Diaghilev's ballet productions and in the early emigration made ends meet by drawing portraits in Montmartre.[653] Reminiscent of the scintillating designs of Boris Bilinsky and Simon Lissim, Pogedaieff's art is distinguished by richness of color and bold flourish of line, a combination that was especially suited to his exotic commissions in the late 1920s and 1930s such as *Princess Turandot* and *Khovanshchina*.

824

824 [R703].
Self-Portrait, 1930s?
Pencil.
Monogram lower left in pencil in French.
5¾ x 4⅛ in., 14.5 x 10.5 cm.
Other inscription: dated lower right: "1968."
Provenance: the artist, Ménerbes, Vaucluse, France. 1968.
Reproduced in F107, p. 147; I51, No. 179; M157, p. 71.

Turandot: *opera in three acts by Giacomo Puccini (completed by Franco Alfano) based on a drama by Carlo Gozzi. Projected, but not produced, in Paris in 1929 with designs by Georges Pogedaieff.*
    See No. 39 [R38] for plot summary.

825 [R704].
Costume Design for Ping, Grand Chancellor of China, 1929.
Watercolor.
Signed and dated lower left: "Georges A. de Pogedaieff, Paris 1929."
21⅞ x 14½ in., 55.5 x 37 cm.
Provenance: Michel Flax, Paris, March, 1966.
Reproduced in color in M157, p. 71; and in black and white in I14, No. 85; I51, No. 180; M88.

825

826

Unidentified production, *ca. 1930.*

826 [R705].
Costumes for a Persian and His Servant, 1930.
Watercolor, black ink, and gold paint; cut-outs glued on gray paper.
Signed and dated lower left in watercolor: "Georges A. de Pogedaieff, Paris, 1930."
18⅛ x 15⅝ in., 46 x 39.7 cm.
Provenance: The Ballet Shop, New York, February, 1979.
Reproduced in color in F107, p. 147; M157, p. 71; and in black and white in B44, p. 298; M73, p. 93.

827 [163; R706].
Costume Design for a Male Dancer, ca. 1930.
Watercolor and gold paint.
Signed lower left in ink: "Georges A. de Pogedaieff, Paris."
17½ x 11 in., 44.5 x 28 cm.
Other inscription lower right in Russian:

827

"Dear Boris Alexeevich, We will try to finish our ballets just as successfully as we started them, joyfully. Sincerely captivated by your talent, the author."
Provenance: The Ballet Shop, New York, February, 1979.
Reproduced in I51, No. 181; I77, p. 130.
The dedication to the choreographer, Boris Alexeevich Kniaseff (Kniazev) (1900-75), indicates that the design was for a projected ballet.

650 For a reproduction of the cover see B94, p. 78.
651 D28, p. 162.
652 For some information on the conflict see ibid., p. 164.
653 Dolgopolov, "Parizh s russkim aktsentom."

Georges Pogedaieff: *Poster for Dolinoff's Troupe Tour, 1928.*

POLIAKOFF, Serge (Poliakov, Sergei Georgievich; or another identity)

Born 8 (21) January, 1906, Moscow, Russia; died 12 October, 1969, Paris, France.

1919 fleeing the consequences of the Revolution, an aunt took him to Constantinople; 1922 he or another Sergei Poliakov designed and illustrated Viktor Yablonsky's book of poetry called *V sumerkakh* [In the Twilight] (M: Author's publication; 1923 via Belgrade and Berlin arrived in Paris; 1924 settled in Paris, where he made his living as a musician; 1930 onwards studied at the Trochot and Grande Chaumière academies; contributed to the "Salon des Indépendants"; made the acquaintance of Robert and Sonia Delaunay, Vasilii Kandinsky, and other avant-garde artists; 1935-37 studied at the Slade School in London; 1937 back in Paris; 1945 first one-man show in Paris; 1953 one-man show in Brussels; 1962 became a French citizen.

Bibliography:
M. Ragon: *Poliakoff*, Paris: Fall, 1956.
Serge Poliakoff. Catalog of exhibition at the Kunstverein, Hamburg, 1958.
D. Vallier: *Serge Poliakoff,* Paris: Cahiers d'Art, 1959.
Serge Poliakoff. Catalog of exhibition at the Musée national d'art moderne, Paris, 1970.
Serge Poliakoff. Catalog of exhibition at the Fondation Dina Vierny and the Musée Maillol, Paris, 1995.

A. Poliakoff and G. Durozoi: *Serge Poliakoff. Monograph and Catalogue Raisonné,* Paris: Acatos, 2005 (n two volumes).
C. Lange and N. Ohlsen: *Serge Poliakoff. Retrospektive*. Catalog of exhibition at the Kunsthalle der Hypo-Kulturstiftung, Munich, 2007.
M.-V. Poliakoff, *Serge Poliakoff, Mon Grand-Père*, éd. du Chêne, 2011.

828

The Judges. A Tragedy by Stanisław Wyspiański. First produced in Lvov on 11 November, 1908.

Natan, son of the Jewish inn-keeper Samuil, leads Evdokha, the servant-girl astray and impels her to kill their baby. Natan is convinced that he should marry a Jewish girl, so he and his father decide to

829

830

831

832

833

834

do away with Evdokha. One day when Otpushnik, Evdokha's brother, visits the tavern, Natan picks a quarrel with him and, by design, a shot from Otpushnik's revolver kills the remorseful Evdokha, whereupon Natan accuses him of killing her. But Samuil's younger son, Ioas, understands the criminal plot between his father and Natan, and so, during the judicial investigation, he points to Samuil as the real murderer. Ioas, however, then dies of a heart attack, and this loss of his favorite son brings the father to his senses and he confesses his complicity.

The designs below bear the Russian signature "S. Poliakov," which does not prove, of course, that the artist is Sergei Poliakoff, the famous Russo-French abstract painter. Circumstantial evidence is not especially persuasive, the more so since Serge Poliakoff would have been only seventeen years old if he had projected these sophisticated costumes and, in any case, he received his professional training in art only in Paris in the 1930s. According to the standard exhibition lists, other S. Poliakovs in Russia in the mid-1920s were active as painters, but not as stage designers, although information on them

has not been forthcoming. For example, one "S.B. Poliakov" is listed in the catalog of the "Exhibition of Contemporary Russian Painting" that Nadezhda Dobychina organized at her Art Bureau in Petrograd in 1915 and the internet also yields a certain S. Yablonsky-Poliakoff. In spite of these hesitations and in the absence of more concrete information, the provisional attribution is to Serge Poliakoff. The provenance of all the works, executed in black ink and white wash on paper and signed lower right in ink in Russian "S. Poliakov, 1923," is Viktor Kholodkov, Moscow, May, 1989. The entire set is reproduced in I77, p.155.

828 [R708].
Set Design for the Court Room, 1923.
8¹/₁₆ x 11¼ in., 20.5 x 28.5 cm.
Other inscription: on the reverse in pencil in Russian: "Draw[ing], black ink."

829 [R709].
Costume Design for the Judge, 1923.
10¼ x 5½ in., 26 x 14 cm.
Other inscriptions: lower right in pencil in Russian: "The Judge"; on the reverse in pencil in Russian: "Draw[ing] in India ink."

830 [R710].
Costume Design for the Jury Foreman, 1923.
10¹/₁₆ x 4¾ in., 25.6 x 12 cm.
Other inscription: lower right in pencil in Russian: "Jury foreman."

831 [R711].
Costume Design for the Apothecary, 1923.
10 x 4¾ in., 25.5 x 12 cm.
Other inscription: lower right in pencil in Russian: "Apothecary."

832 [R712].
Costume Design for Natan, 1923.
10¼ x 5¼ in., 26 x 13.4 cm.
Other inscription: lower margin in pencil in Russian: "Natan."

833 [R713].
Costume Design for Samuil, 1923.
10 x 5 in., 25.3 x 12.8 cm.
Other inscription: lower center in pencil in Russian: "Samuil."

834 [R714].
Costume Design for Evdokha, 1923.
10¼ x 5¼ in., 26 x 13.4 cm.
Other inscriptions: lower right in pencil in Russian: "Evdokha"; on the reverse in pencil in Russian: "Draw[ing] in India ink."

654 For more information on Wyspiański see Alicja Okońska: *Stanisław Wyspiański*, Warsaw: Wiedza Powszechna, 1971; Russian translation: *Vyspianskii*, M: Iskusstvo, 1977. On *The Judges* see especially pp. 109-15 of the Russian edition.

835

836

837

835 [R715].
Costume Design for the Old Man Ukli, 1923.
10 x 5¼ in., 25.3 x 13.2 cm.
Other inscription: lower right in pencil in Russian: "Ukli."

836 [R716].
Costume Design for Ioas, 1923.
10 x 5 in., 25.5 x 12.7 cm.
Other inscription: lower right corner in pencil in Russian: "Ioas."

837 [R717].
Costume Design for a Beggar, 1923.
10¼ x 5¼ in., 26 x 13.4 cm.
Other inscription: lower right in pencil in Russian: "Beggar."

Note: Stanisław Wyspiański, the *fin de siècle* Polish playwright and artist, was known for his plays of violence and despair, and *The Judges* is typical of his output.[654] He wrote the tragedy in 1899, although it was not published until 1906, the year before his death. It is not known for which production Poliakov designed these pieces, although Wyspiański's plays were popular in Russia and Eastern Europe during the 1910s and 1920s, and, if the Poliakov here is, indeed, Serge Poliakoff, the production would have been in Constantinople, Belgrade, or Berlin. One of the most famous productions of *The Judges* was given by the Reduta Theater in Vilnius in 1927.

POPOVA, Liubov Sergeevna

Born 24 April (6 May), 1889, on the family's estate "Krasnovidovo," Ivanovskoe Village, Moscow Region, Russia; died 25 May, 1924, Moscow, Russia.

1889-1901 received art lessons at home; 1906 graduated from the Arseniev Gymnasium; 1907 attended the private studio of Stanislav Zhukovsky; 1908-09 attended Konstantin Yuon and Ivan Dudin's Art School; met Alexander Vesnin; 1910 visited Italy, where she was especially impressed by Giotto; that summer traveled to Pskov and Novgorod to study icons; 1911 made several trips to Medieval Russian cities; 1912 worked in the Moscow studio known as The Tower with Ivan Aksenov, Viktor Bart, Alexei Grishchenko, Vladimir Tatlin, and Kirill Zdanevich; visited the Shchukin collection of modern French art; 1912-13 with Nadehda Udlastova went to Paris, enrolling in La Palette and studying under Henri Le Fauconnier, Jean Metzinger, and André Dunoyer de Segonzac; 1913 met Alexander Archipenko and Ossip Zadkine; after spending May in Brittany with Vera Mukhina and Boris Ternovets returned to Russia; again worked closely with Tatlin, Udaltsova, and Alexander Vesnin; 1914 visited France and Italy again, accompanied by Mukhina; 1914-15 her Moscow home became a regular meeting place for the new artists and writers; 1914-16 contributed to the "Jack of Diamonds" (Moscow, 1914 and 1916), "Tramway V," "0.10," the "Store," and other exhibitions; 1916 visited Samarkand; 1916-17 member of the Supremus group; 1916-18 painted architectonic compositions; 1917 made embroidery designs for Natalia Davydova's enterprise in Verbovka; joined the Professional Union of Artists and Painters; 1918 married Boris von Eding; worked on agit-designs; in November gave birth to a son; 1919 contributed to the "X State Exhibition: Non-Objective Art and Suprematism"; husband died from typhoid fever; 1919-21 painted so-called painterly constructions; 1920 made stage designs for *Romeo and Juliet* projected by Alexander Tairov; designed marionettes for a children's theater; taught at Svomas-Vkhutemas, compiling a program on "color discipline"; joined Inkhuk; 1921 contributed to "5 x 5 = 25," Moscow; thereafter became active as an applied Constructivist, designing book covers, porcelain, stage sets, textiles; taught at the State Higher Theater Studios; 1921-24 designed book and sheet music covers; 1922 created the sets and costumes for Vsevolod Meierkhold's production of *Magnanimous Cuckold*; contributed to the "Erste

Russische Kunstausstellung" in Berlin; 1923 designed Meierkhold's production of *Earth on End;* 1923-24 worked on textile and dress designs for the First State Textile Factory; 1924 posthumous exhibition opened in Moscow (21 December).

Bibliography
O.Brik: *Posmertnaia vystavka proizvedenii konstruktora L.S. Popovoi.* Catalog of post-humous exhibition at the Museum of Artistic Culture, M, 1924.
J. Bowlt: "From Surface to Space: The Art of Liubov Popova" in *The Structurist,* Saskatoon, 1976, No. 15-16, pp. 80-88.
V. Vorobiev: "Kak Liubovi Popovoi povezlo" in *Russkaia mysl,* Paris, 1979, 4 October, p. 10. K52, pp. 174-214.
A. Law: "'Le Cocu Magnifique' de Crommelynck" in *Les Voies de la création théâtrale,* Paris, 1980, No. 7, pp. 14-43.
J. Bowlt: "Liubov Popova, Painter" in B44, pp. 227-51.
N. Adaskina: "Formirovanie dizainerskoi kontseptsii L.S. Popovoi, GVYTM-VKHUTEMAS 1921-1923 goda" in *Trudy VNIITE. Tekhnicheskaia estetika,* M, 1983, No. 41, pp. 43-60.
N. Adaskina: "Rabota L. Popovoi po sozdaniiu 'tsvetovoi distsipliny' Vkhutemasa" in I. Gofman, ed.: *Gosudarstvennaia Tretiakovskaia galleria. Materialy i issledovaniia,* L: Khudozhnik RSFSR, 1983, pp. 172-87.
C. Douglas: *Liubov Popova: Spatial Force Constructions 1921-22.* Catalog of exhibition at Rachel Adler Gallery, New York, 1985.
Gouaches and Drawings by Liubov Popova and Kazimir Malevich. Catalog of exhibition at the Leonard Hutton Galleries, New York, 1986.
N. Adaskina and D. Sarabianov: *Liubov Popova,* New York: Abrams, 1990 (French edition: *Lioubov Popova.* Paris: Sers, 1989).
D. Sarabianov and N. Adaskina: *L.S. Popova 1889-1924.* Catalog of exhibition at the TG and the RM, 1990.
B109, pp. 99-116.
M. Dabrowski: *Liubov Popova.* Catalog of exhibition at the Museum of Modern Art, New York, and other institutions, 1991-92.
D. Sarabianov: *Liubov Popova,* M: Galart, 1994.
L. Monakhova et al.: *Priamaia i obratnaia perspektiva russkogo minimalizma / Gerade und umgekehrte Perspektive des russischen Minimalismus. Ljubov Popova. Aleksandr Konstantinov.* Catalog of exhibition at the Tsaritsyno Museum, M; and the Palais Liechtenstein, Feldkirch, 1994.
K224, passim.
K236.
M. Tupitsyn: *Rodchenko and Popova.* Catalog of exhibition at Tate Modern, London, State Museum of Contemporary Art, Thessaloniki, and the Museo Nacional Centro de Arte Reina Sofia, Madrid, 2009-10.
N. Adaskina: *Liubov Popova,* M: Gordeev, 2011.

838 [R718].
Self-Portrait, ca. 1920.
Pencil.
7 x 3⅞ in., 18 x 10 cm.
Provenance: Vasilii Rakitin, Moscow.
Reproduced in Adaskina and Sarabianov, *Liubov Popova,* p. 342; and B107, p. 51. A similar drawing in the Costakis collection,

838

designated provisionally as a self-portrait, is reproduced in B34, No. 738.

Like Alexandra Exter, El Lissitzky, and Alexander Rodchenko, Popova possessed the rare gift of thinking in terms of both two dimensions and three. Her desire to introduce space as a creative agent into her art, encouraged by her friendship with Mukhina and Tatlin, was already evident in 1915 in her series of still-lifes and paintings, which she subtitled "plastic painting," and in her occasional reliefs of the same period. Popova's interest in sequential spatial relationships was also manifest in her graphics and linocuts of 1920-21, in which she often imposed a grid of conflicting lines above a complex of color planes — a concept that she used with great success in her textile designs of 1923-24.

A logical outcome of Popova's interest in pictorial space was her work on stage design in the early 1920s, which, she felt, would enable her to avoid the "frontal, visual character [of art]."[655] It was in the theater that Popova showed herself to be one of the few authentic Constructivists of the Russian theater: in her economy of means, austerity of organization, and subtle combination of real form and real space, Popova expanded the elementary concepts of Rodchenko's wooden and metal constructions of 1918-21 into her inventions for *The Magnanimous Cuckold,* which premiered in April, 1922 (see Nos. 974-75 [R800-01]). The artist Louis Lozowick recalled his impression of the production:

> The stage was bare — no curtain, no proscenium arch, wings, backdrop, flood lights. On the background of the bare wall of the building with its open brickwork, one saw a simple, skeleton-like construction, a scaffolding designed

by Popova consisting of one large black wheel and two small ones, red and white, several platforms at various levels, revolving doors, stairs, ladders, chutes, square, triangular, and rectangular shapes.[656]

Inevitably, Popova's construction provoked criticism not only from the traditionalists who compared her interpretation to a piece of vaudeville, but also from the Constructivists themselves, some of whom regarded it as mere ornament and descriptive scenery.[657] Whatever the responses, Popova's work for *The Magnanimous Cuckold* marked the culmination to her relentless effort to resolve the dichotomy between surface and space and to move from pictorial space to open, real space.

The Tale of the Country Priest and His Dunderhead Servant: *story by Alexander Pushkin. Produced at the First State Children's Theater of NKP, Moscow, 1920, with designs by Liubov Popova.*

A crafty country priest hires a servant as cheaply as he can. The servant, who does not seem to be very bright, says he will accept as remuneration groats as his rations and the privilege of flicking the priest's forehead with his fingers three times a year. The priest proceeds to give the servant, a robust personage, various chores, including the removal of the Devil from a nearby pond. The servant tries to do this with a rope and, after various adventures, triumphs over the Devil's wiles. When the servant claims his remuneration, his first flicking of the priest's forehead causes the priest to jump to the ceiling, the second to strike him dumb, and the third to drive him crazy.

839 [NIRE]. *Costume Design for the Priest's Daughter, En Face,* ca. 1920.
Color print.
21½ x 13½ in., 54.6 x 34.3 cm.
Provenance: internet purchase, 2 February 2012. Now in a private collection.

839

840

841

842

840 [164; R719].
Costume Design for the Dunderhead Servant with Hat, ca. 1920.
Watercolor.
21½ x 13½ in., 54.6 x 34.3 cm.
Provenance: Dmitrii Sarabianov, Moscow, May, 1971.
Reproduced in color in B115, plate 154; and in black and white in I32, No. 16; I51, No. 183; I77, p. 151; M14; N140.

841 [165; R720].
A Second Costume Design for the Dunderhead Servant without Hat, ca. 1920.
Watercolor and gouache.
19⅞ x 14 in., 50.5 x 35.6 cm.
Provenance: Leonard Hutton Galleries, New York, September, 1974.
Reproduced in color in B115, plate 152; B122, p. 267; and in black and white in I32, No. 79; I51, No. 184; I77, p. 151; M14; N140. Another version is reproduced in Adaskina and Sarabianov, *Liubov Popova*, p. 236.

842 [166; R721].
Costume Design for the Priest's Daughter, in Profile, ca. 1920.
Watercolor.
21½ x 13½ in., 54.6 x 34.3 cm.
Provenance: Dmitrii Sarabianov, Moscow, May, 1971.
Reproduced in color in B115, plate 153; B122, p. 267; I77, p. 91; and in black and white in I32, No. 77; I51, No. 185; I77, p. 151; M86; P16; P26; R1; R16; R17. Another version is reproduced in *L.S. Popova 1889-1924*, No. 241; and Adaskina and Sarabianov, *Popova*, p. 239.
Compare with No. 839 [NIRE].

843 [167; R722].
Costume Design for the Devil, ca. 1920.
Watercolor and gouache.
19⅞ x 14 in., 50.5 x 35.7 cm.
Provenance: Leonard Hutton Galleries, New York, September, 1974.
Reproduced in I32, No. 78; I51, No. 186; I77, p. 151. Another version is reproduced in Adaskina and Sarabianov, *Liubov Popova*, p. 236.

Note: At the end of October, 1918, the Theater of Marionettes, Petrouchkas, and Shadows opened in Moscow in what had been the Theater of Miniatures or the Lukomorie [Sea-shore]. Situated on Mamonovskii Lane, the theater was known more familiarly as the Children's Theater (of the

843

Moscow Soviet) and was run by Natalia Sats with the close collaboration of the sculptor Ivan Efimov and his wife Nina Simonovich-Efimova, the noted puppeteer (who had produced puppet shows in Moscow and elsewhere during 1917). An important precedent to the Children's Theater in Moscow was Yuliia Sazonova's Theater of Marionettes in Petrograd in 1915 (see No. 599 [R503]), although this had been oriented more towards the intellectual elite than towards children.

Until it suspended its activities in June, 1919, a number of important literati and artists were associated with the Children's Theater in Moscow, writing scenarios, collaborating as producers, and creating designs, including Vladimir Favorsky, Pavel Florensky, and Konstantin Istomin. Alexandra Exter and Popova were also involved in the Children's Theater as designers for the often satirical fables acted out by the puppets. In 1920, the Children's Theater was revived as the First State Theater for Children of NKP, producing several plays such as *Mowgli* in 1920 and *Adalmina's Pearl* (designed by Alexander Vesnin) in July, 1921, in which, however, real actors, played instead of puppets.

It is presumed that Popova designed *The Tale* for one of the productions at the First State Theater for Children in 1920, probably within the framework of a Pushkin celebration (she made at least seventeen designs for the occasion).[658] After this, Popova gave little attention to puppetry, although, along with Efimov and Exter, she contemplated the organization of a puppet laboratory in Moscow at the beginning of 1921. Exter went on to produce her extraordinary set of marionettes for a movie in 1926, and El Lissitzky, of course, created his marionette interpretations of *Victory over the Sun* in 1923 (see Nos. 752-64 [R632-43]).[659]

844

845

844 [168; R723].
Costume Design for a Lady in a Blue Cape, ca. 1920.
Watercolor and pencil.
Signed upper right in Russian: "L.S. Popova."
13 x 8¾ in., 33 x 22.2 cm.
Provenance: Dmitrii Sarabianov, Moscow, May, 1971.
Reproduced in B115, plate 156; I32, No. 74; I51, No. 187, where the piece is described as a costume for *The Locksmith and the Chancellor.* For similar costumes see *Liubov Popova 1889-1924,* No. 228; and Adaskina and Sarabianov, pp. 230-33. A similar design was auctioned at *Art Russe,* Paris: Tajan, 10 December, 2004, Lot 210 (reproduced).

845 [169; R724].
Costume Design for a Man in Green, with Feather in Cap, ca. 1920.
Watercolor and pencil.
14 x 10¼ in., 35.6 x 26 cm.
Provenance: Dmitrii Sarabianov, Moscow, May, 1971
Reproduced in B115, plate 157; I32, No. 75; I51, No. 188, where the piece is described as a costume for *The Locksmith and the Chancellor.* For similar costumes see *Liubov Popova 1889-1924,* No. 228; and Adaskina and Sarabianov, *Liubov Popova,* pp. 230-33. A similar design was auctioned at *Art Russe,* Paris: Tajan, 10 December, 2004, Paris, Lot 218 (reproduced).

Romeo and Juliet: *Tragedy in five acts by William Shakespeare. Projected, but not produced, by the Chamber Theater, Moscow, in 1920, with designs by Liubov Popova.*

During a ball at the House of the Capulets in Verona, Romeo, of the rival Montague family, professes his love for Juliet, a Capulet. Defying the family feud, Romeo proposes marriage, Juliet consents, and they are betrothed by a friar. The two families clash: Tybalt of the Capulets *stabs Mercutio of the Montagues. Enraged, Romeo kills Tybalt and is forced to flee. The Capulets demand that their daughter marry Paris, but Juliet, fearing the arrangement, swallows a secret potion and swoons. Believing her to be dead, the Capulets lay her in the family vault, where Tybalt also lies. On seeing this, Romeo concludes in horror that Juliet has died and drinks a vial of poison. At that moment Juliet awakens, is embraced by the dying Romeo, and kills herself with his dagger.*

846

847

846 [170; NIRE].
Costume Design for a Woman, 1920.
Gouache and ink.
13⅞ x 10½ in., 35.2 × 26.8 cm
Provenance: Vladimir Asriev, London, June, 2005.
Reproduced in color in Adaskina, *Liubov Popova* (2011), p. 93; and in black and white in Adaskina and Sarabianov, *Liubov Popova,* p. 232.

Note: Romeo and Juliet was Popova's first major professional theatrical commission and she worked on the sets and costumes with enthusiasm and inventiveness. With Exter, Aristarkh Lentulov, Mukhina, and Alexander Vesnin among the designers, the Chamber Theater at this time was a veritable scenographic laboratory, and Popova must have been drawn to the theater precisely for this

reason. However, perhaps because of her relative inexperience as a stage artist or because of the excessive geometry of her designs, Alexander Tairov rejected Popova in favor of Exter, producing *Romeo and Juliet* the following year with Exter's designs.

The Chancellor and the Locksmith: *play in ten scenes by Anatolii Lunacharsky. Produced by Andrei Petrovsky at the Comedy Theater (formerly the Korsh Theater), Moscow, in May, 1921, with designs by Liubov Popova.*[660]

Based on recent political events in Germany, this play was an allegory of two opposing worlds — the vulgar pseudo-democratic world of the bourgeoisie and the world of the underprivileged workers. The

actual geographical and political names, such as Norlandia, Tifliandia, etc., are conventional. The Chancellor, von Turau, is the class enemy; the Locksmith, Stark, is the protagonist, while Frei is the compromising Socialist. Although not unequivocal, the play ends with the condemnation of the Chancellor and the extolment of the Locksmith.

847 [171; R725].
Set Design for the Chancellor's Study, ca. 1921.
Gouache.
10⅜ x 14 in., 26.5 x 35.5 cm.
Provenance: *Russian Avant-Garde. Pictures from the Collection formed by George Costakis,* Sotheby's: London, 4 April, 1990, Lot 511 (reproduced).
Reproduced in color in B34, p. 398; F107, p. 100; G79, p. 130; I77, p. 86; N188, p. 38; and in black and white in I77, p. 145; P56. A version dated 1920 is reproduced in color in *L.S. Popova 1889-1924,* No. 247; Adaskina: *Liubov Popova* (2011), p. 94; and Sarabianov, *Liubov Popova,* p. 244; and I81, p. 77. Yet another version, in the collection of the late Abram Chudnovsky, is reproduced in K168, p. 88.

Note: The Chancellor and the Locksmith, Lunacharsky's "purely Communist play,"[661] saw several productions in the early 1920s, when Lunacharsky, perhaps more competent as Commissar of Enlightenment than as a playwright, was still aspiring to make his name as a creative writer. Although Von Turau embodied "all the former might of the bourgeoisie,"[662] the character of Stark was regarded as too weak to communicate the correct ideological message.

Earth on End: *play in eight episodes by Sergei Tretiakov based on the novel La Nuit by Marcel Martinet. Produced by Vsevolod Meierkhold at the Meierkhold Theater, Moscow, on 4 March, 1923, with designs by Liubov Popova.*

848

A tale of military revolution, the play was meant to reveal the emptiness of bourgeois militarism. At the same time, it emphasized that the order and discipline of the Red Army was the result of a rational organization of the human collective. The play communicated its propaganda message through eight episodes, i.e., "Down with War!", "At Ease!", "The Truth about the Trenches," "The Black International," "All Power to the Soviets!", "A Knife in the Back of the Revolution," "Shearing the Sheep," and "Night."

Popova as contributor:
848 [R726].
Designer unknown: Poster Advertising the Premiere of Earth on End, 1923.
Lithograph in red and black.
28 x 42 in., 71 x 106.5 cm.
Inscriptions (as part of the design) provide details on the date and place of the premiere, stating that Meierkhold is director of action while Sergei Tretiakov is director of diction.

Note: Earth on End marked the culmination of Popova's involvement in the theater. Drawing on her design experience of the previous year (The Magnanimous Cuckold), Popova used a mobile construction as a centerpiece and orientation point for the actors, while introducing real telephones, motorbikes, and automobiles on stage in order to emphasize the authenticity and contemporary relevance of the play.

Tarquinius, the High Priest: *play by S. Polivanov (pseudonym of Naum Sheinfeld). Projected, but not produced, by the Atheist Theater, Moscow, in 1923, with designs by Liubov Popova.*

On his death-bed, the high priest Avraam summons his successor, Tarquinius, and tells him that henceforth he must live with a bitter truth: God does not exist. According to ritual, the high priest's widow must also be buried with her husband, but Tarquinius secretly loves Avraam's wife Maria. As he sees her being led away, Tarquinius commands her to be freed — and announces to the people that God is dead. The other priests declare that Tarquinius has been sent to test the faith and, at their bidding, the people stone Tarquinius and Maria to death.

849 [172; R727].
Costume Design for a Soldier with Billowing Scarf, ca. 1923.
Watercolor.
22¾ x 16 in., 57.8 x 40.7 cm.
Inscription on the reverse in Russian: "Tarquinius the High Priest."
Provenance: Dmitrii Sarabianov, Moscow, May, 1971.
Reproduced in color in B115, plate 158; I77, p. 90; and in black and white in A34, p. 336; I20, No. 70; I32, No. 73; I51, No. 189; I77, p. 142; S57; S58; S63. A similar costume for a Soldier (dated 1922, in a private collection) is reproduced in color in *L.S. Popova 1889-1924*, No. 269; and in Adaskina and Sarabianov, *Popova*, p. 243. A curious version is reproduced in color in I100, No. 727.

849

Note: Polivanov's play *Tarquinius, the High Priest* was published by the Moscow publishing-house Atheist in 1922 and, according to various reports, the same house was about to organize a theater of the same name in the fall of 1923 with Polivanov's play in the repertoire.[663] Apparently, however, the idea was not implemented, although Polivanov's play did enjoy a certain vogue as anti-religious propaganda. In May, 1922, Meierkhold was approached by Nadezhda Krupskaia (Lenin's wife) to produce the play because of its didactic value, but he decided against the idea. The play was staged at the Belorussian State Theater in Minsk by Evstignei Mirovich with designs by Oskar Mariks, and in 1924 was given at the Goznak Theater in Leningrad.

655 From Popova's lecture on her set for *The Magnanimous Cuckold*, which she delivered at Inkhuk on 27 April 1922. Quoted in E. Rakitina: "Liubov Popova. Iskusstvo i manifesty," in G44, Vol. 1, p. 154.
656 F90, p. 246.
657 Popova was the subject of the most varied evaluations in the early 1920s. On the one hand, she was nicknamed (benevolently) the "mother of scenic Constructivism" (Anon.: "Samoe predstavlenie 'Velikogo rogonostsa'" in *Zrelishcha*, M, 1923, No. 67, p. 8); on the other, people wondered whether her designs were "charlatanism or stupidity" (P. Krasikov: "Sharlatanstvo ili glupost" in *Rabochaia Moskva*, M, 1922, No. 16).
658 We are grateful to Natalia Adaskina for her assistance in establishing the exact chronological sequence of productions at the Children's Theater and for commenting on Popova's involvement. For further information on the Theater see F55, pp. 118-25; see also N. Sats: *Deti prikhodiat v teatr. Stranitsy vospominanii*, M,1961, p. 70. Also see C89, pp. 67-69.
659 For information on the history of the early Soviet marionette theater see E6.
660 For reproductions of other costume designs by Popova for this play see T. Strizenova: *Moda e rivoluzione*, Milan: Electa, pp. 60-61.
661 A. Lunacharsky: "O zadachakh teatra v sviazi s reformoi Narkomprosa" in C31, Vol. 2, p. 42.
662 C20, p. 178.
663 See *Teatr i muzyka*, M, 1923, No. 36, 6 November, p. 1160.

POUGNY, Jean (Puni, Ivan Albertovich)

Born 22 February (6 March), 1890, Kuokkala, Finland (now Repino near St. Petersburg, Russia); died 26 November, 1956, Paris, France.[664]

Grandson of Cesare Pugny, the Italian composer who conducted at the Paris Opéra before emigrating to St. Petersburg. Received early education in St. Petersburg; 1910 attended the Académie Julian in Paris; 1912 back in St. Petersburg; contact with David and Vladimir Burliuk, Kazimir Malevich, and other members of the Russian avant-garde; associated with the Union of Youth; 1912-14 contributed to the two "Union of Youth" exhibitions, 1913 married the painter Xana (Ksana, i.e., a diminutive of Kseniia) Boguslavskaia; 1914 contributed to the avant-garde book *Rykaiushchii Parnas* [Roaring Parnassus] subsidized by Boguslavskaia; 1915-16 coorganized and financed "Tramway V" and "0.10" exhibitions, issuing with Boguslakvskaia a Suprematist Manifesto at the latter; 1917 contributed to the "Jack of Diamonds"; 1918 professor at the Petrograd Svomas; 1918-29 exhibited at many Soviet exhibitions such as "Russian Landscape" in Petrograd (1919) and the "Exhibition of New Trends" in Leningrad (1927); 1918-19 took part in agit-decoration for the streets and squares of Petersburg; 1919 taught at the Vitebsk Art School under Marc Chagall; 1920 emigrated to Berlin; illustrated children's literature and other books such as Sergei Rafalovich's *Marc Antoine, Tragédie* (Berlin, 1923); 1922 rejected Suprematism, voicing a preference for Vasilii Kandinsky over Malevich; contributed to the "Erste Russische Kunstausstellung" in Berlin; 1924 settled in Paris; in emigration supported a figurative kind of painting, reminiscent of Pierre Bonnard and Edouard Vuillard; 1946 granted French citizenship; 1947 awarded the Legion of Honor.

Bibliography
V. Viale et al.: *Jean Pougny*. Catalog of exhibition at the Galleria Civica d'Arte Moderna, Turin, 1962-63. M2, Vol. 2, pp. 190-91.
H. Berninger and J.A. Cartier: *Pougny. Catalog de l'oeuvre. Russie-Berlin, 1910-1923*, Tübingen: Wasmuth, Vol, 1, 1972.
H. Berninger and J.A. Cartier: *Pougny. Catalog de l'oeuvre. Paris – Côte d'Azur 1924-1956*, Tübingen: Wasmuth, Vol, 2, 1992.
P. Lufft: "Der Gestaltwandel im Werk von Jean Pougny" in E. Hüttinger and A. Lüthy, eds.: *Gotthard Jedlicka. Eine Gedenkschrift*, Zürich: Füssli, 1974, pp. 181-98.
Iwan Puni (Jean Pougny) 1892-1956. Catalog of exhibition at the Haus am Waldsee, Berlin, and other institutions, 1975.
A. Bakrakh: "Puni" in *Novoe russkoe slovo*, New York, 1979, 11 November, p. 5.
Pougny Peintre / Bogratchew Sculpteur. Catalog of exhibition at the Musée Bourdelle, Paris, 1989.
E. Roters and H. Gassner: *Iwan Puni. Synthetischer Musiker*, Berlin: Berlinische Galerie, 1992.

S. Pagé et al.: *Jean Pougny.* Catalog of exhibition at the Musée d'Art Moderne de la Ville de Paris, Paris, and the Berlinische Galerie, Berlin, 1993.
V. Viale et al.: *Iwan Puni (1892-1956). Werke und Dokumente (1915-1919) aus dem Puni-Archiv, Zürich.* Brochure for exhibition at the Kunsthaus, Zurich, 1999.
M73, Vol. 26, pp. 81-82.
G. Magnaguagno et al.: *0.10: Ivan Puni.* Catalog of exhibition at the Museum Jean Tinguely, Basel, 2003.
M. Daniel and M Lista: *Jean Pougny (1892-1956).* Catalog of exhibition at the Galerie Zlotowski and the Galerie Le Minotaure, Paris, 2003.
D. Sarabianov: *Ivan Puni,* M: Iskusstvo XXI vek, 2007.

Pougny worked with many media, but he was a studio painter above all. Even his reliefs of ca. 1915 were a radical extension of the two-dimensional surface rather than spatial constructions. It was the constant tension between the emotional, expressionistic forces of Pougny's temperament, manifested especially during the Union of Youth days, and his "vernünftiger Logik"[665] which prompted him to swing rapidly from the synthetic style of the early Fauvist paintings shown at the Union of Youth shows in 1912-13 and 1913-14 to an analytical conception, mirrored in his Suprematist pieces of 1915-16 — and then back to his synthetic, highly colored still-lifes of 1917-19. Only with the commencement of his Berlin period did this oscillation decrease when Pougny suddenly dismissed his Suprematist achievements as transitory and superficial — and voiced his support for Kandinsky on the one hand, and Picasso on the other.[666]

Even so, Pougny's criticism of his own abstract works does not belittle their significance and, indeed, the Suprematist Manifesto issued by Pougny and Boguslavskaia at "0.10" in 1915-16 was of vital importance to the development of non-objective art. The assertion that a "picture is a new conception of abstracted real elements, deprived of meaning,"[667] was, together with Malevich's concurrent statements, among the first unequivocal promotions of a purely self-sufficient art form.

Street Procession, *February, 1921.*

850 [173; R728].
Costume Design for a Lady with the Figure 8, *ca. 1921.*
Watercolor and pencil.
Signature stamped lower right: "Pougny".
9½ x 6½ in., 24 x 16.5 cm.
Provenance: the artist's widow, Ksenia Bogouslavskaia, Paris, 1967.
Reproduced in color in B115, plate 82; F107, p. 148; I68, back cover; M157, p. 63; and in black and white in A34, p. 345; E27, p. 125; I20, No. 71; I32, No. 80; I51, No. 190; I61, p. 341; I77, p. 129; M73, p. 93 (where it is dated "1916"); M91; M111.

Note: Pougny designed this costume for a "Cubist" street procession in Berlin in February, 1921, organized to advertise the vernissage of his exhibition at the Galerie Der

850

851

Sturm, Berlin. This design may also have been used for the so-called Letter Ballet at the Sturm-Bal on 8 March, 1921. A number of similar costumes were displayed at the Pougny exhibition as *Theaterkostüme* and were listed in the catalog as such.[668]

While costume and set design was not Pougny's artistic forte, he did work for the theater in its broadest sense during his sojourn in Berlin in 1920-24 and his first years in Paris. He and his wife, Boguslavskaia, worked for Jascha Juschny's Blaue Vogel cabaret in Berlin, for the Renaissance Theater there, for the Grand Opera in Prague, and for the Folies-Bergères in Paris. In their temporary orientation towards the world of design (stage design and book illustration), Pougny and Boguslavskaia paid homage to a current emphasis on the applied arts both in Germany and in the Soviet Union. Pougny, in fact, had even discussed the "principle of utilitarianism" in his article in the avant-garde journal *Iskusstvo kommuny* in 1919.[669]

Unidentified production, *ca. 1923.*

851 [R729].
Costume Design for a Lady with a Fan, *1923.*
Watercolor and gouache.
Signed and dated lower right in pencil: "Pougny Paris, 1923."
16½ x 10⅞ in., 42 x 27.5 cm.
Provenance: the artist's widow, Ksenia Bogouslavskaia, Paris, 1966. Now in a private collection.
Reproduced in I14, No. 86; I51, No. 191; I61, p. 341.

Note: It is not known whether this design was for an actual production. The reference to Paris, 1923, indicates that Pougny made the design on one of his brief visits to Paris from Berlin before settling there per-

manently in 1924. For reproductions of other theatrical costumes by Pougny see, for example, *Jean Pougny* (1993), pp. 191-97.

Unidentified production, *ca. 1923.*

852 [R730].
Costume Design for a Persian Man with a Sword, *ca. 1923.*
Gouache and collage.
Signature stamped lower right: "Pougny".
18⅛ x 12 in., 46 x 30.5 cm.
Provenance: the artist's widow, Ksenia Bogouslavskaia, Paris, 1967. Now in a private collection.
Reproduced in I20, No. 72; I51, No. 192.

852

Комитетъ 1-ой футуристической выставки

Трамвай В

покорнѣйше проситъ Васъ пожаловать

на верниссажъ 3-яго Марта, отъ 1 ч. до 5 ч.

Малый залъ Имп. Общ. Поощ. Худ.

Морская 38

853

Note: It has not proved possible to establish whether this design was for an actual production. It follows the traditional interpretation of Shah Shahriar or Hassan in *Schéhérazade*, but there is no record of such a production with designs by Pougny.

Pougny as contributor:
853 [R759].
Designer unknown: *Invitation Card for the "Tramway V" Exhibition*, 1915.
Black on white.
3¾ x 5⅞ in., 9.5 x 15 cm.
The full text on the card reads: "The Committee of the First Futurist Exhibition Tramway V respectfully invites you to attend the vernissage on 3rd March between 1 and 5 p.m., Minor Hall of the Imperial Society for the Encouragement of the Arts, 38, Morskaia St."

Note: The reference is to the exhibition "Tramway V" that Pougny coorganized in Petrograd in March-April, 1915. This was one of the most famous exhibitions of the Russian avant-garde and participants included Alexandra Exter, Ivan Kliun, Malevich, Liubov Popova, Jean Pougny, Olga Rozanova, Vladimir Tatlin, and Nadezhda Udaltsova. The most radical part of the exhibition was Tatlin's contribution of seven reliefs.

664   There are discrepancies regarding the birth date of Pougny (A42, p. 525, for example, gives 20 November 1894; other sources give 20 February and 6 May, 1894). 22 February, 1890 is taken from Pougny's birth certificate reproduced in Berninger and Cartier, *Pougny*, op. cit., p. 245.
665   I. Puni, untitled essay in P. Westheim, ed.: *Künstlerbekenntnisse*, Berlin: Propyläen, 1925, p. 346.
666   Pougny expounded his ideas in a lecture that he gave at the Haus der Künste in Berlin in conjunction with the "Erste Russische Kunstausstellung," Berlin, in November, 1922. He then published his lecture as a book, i.e., *Sovremennaia zhivopis*, Berlin: Frenkel, 1923; French translation: *L'Art Contemporain*, Berlin: Frenkel, 1923.
667   I. Puni et al.: "Suprematist Manifesto" (1915). Translation in B12, p. 112.
668   *Iwan Puni*. Catalog of exhibition at the Galerie Der Sturm, Berlin, 1921, p. 10.
669   I. Puni: "Tvorchestvo zhizni" in *Iskusstvo kommuny*, P, 1919, 5 January, No. 5, p. 1.

RABINOVICH (Rogaler), Isaak Moiseevich

Born 27 February (11 May), 1894, Kiev, Ukraine; died 4 October, 1961, Moscow, Russia.

1906-12 attended the Kiev Art Institute, studying under Alexander Prakhov, Grigorii Diadchenko, and Alexander Murashko; 1911 onwards worked regularly as a stage designer; 1914 contributed to the "Ring" exhibition, Kiev; 1917 worked closely with Nikolai Evreinov at the Petrograd cabaret Bi-Ba-Bo; 1918 worked closely with Alexandra Exter in Kiev; close to other students there such as Boris Aronson, Liubov Kozintseva, Nisson Shifrin, Alexander Tyshler, and Sofia Vishnivetskaia; 1919 worked on May Day agit-designs for Kiev; member of Kultur-Lige; designed a production of Lope de Vega's drama *Fuente Ovejuna* directed by Konstantin Mardzhanov in Kiev (assisted by Tyshler); 1920 lived briefly in Kharkov before moving to Moscow permanently; made Moscow debut as a stage designer for a production of Anton Chekhov's *The Wedding* at the Moscow Art Theater Studio Three (MKhAT 3); 1923 designed *Lysistrata* for the MKhAT Musical Studio; 1924 designed the sets for Yakov Protazanov's movie *Aelita* (Exter designed the costumes); 1926-30 taught at Vkhutein in Moscow; designed many productions for various theaters, including the State Jewish Chamber Theater, the Bolshoi Theater, and the Maly Theater; 1936 designed a lavish production of *Sleeping Beauty* for the Bolshoi Theater; 1939-48 artist-in-chief for the projected Palace of Soviets in Moscow.

Bibliography
A. Efros: "Khudozhniki teatra Granovskogo" in *Iskusstvo,* M, 1928, Book 1-2, pp. 53-74.
A7, Vol. 4, pp. 504-07.
F. Syrkina: *I. Rabinovich,* M: Sovetskii khudozhnik, 1972.
G38, pp. 211-29.
A. Shifrina: *Isaak Moiseevich Rabinovich 1894-1961*. Catalog of exhibition, M, BTM, 1984.
A31, p. 483.
K281, pp. 268-71.
C169, passim.
G. Kazovsky: *Khudozhniki Kultur-Ligi / The Artists of the Kultur-Lige,* Jerusalem: Gesharim; M: Mosty kultury, 2003, passim.
E. van Voolen et al.: *Russisch-Joodse Kunstenaars, 1910-1940. Moderne meesterwerken uit Moskou / Russian Jewish Artists, 1910-1940 / Modern Masterpieces from Moscow*. Catalog of exhibition at the Joods Historisch Museum, Amsterdam, 2007, passim.
G. Kazovsky et al.: *Kultur-Liga: Khudozhnii avangard 1910-1920-kh rokiv / Artistic Avant-Garde of the 1910s-1920s*. Catalog of exhibition at the National Art Museum, Kiev, and other venues, 2007, passim.

854 [R731].
***Self-Portrait*, 1911.**
Pencil.
Signed and dated on the left of center in Russian: "Isaak Rabinovich, 6 Jan., 1911."

854

8⅝ x 12⅝ in., 22 x 32 cm.
Provenance: Igor Dychenko, Kiev, February, 1984.
Reproduced in M20.

Note: Rabinovich was one of the more gifted students of Alexandra Exter in Kiev, so it is not by chance that she chose him to assist her with the decorations for the "All-Russian Agricultural Exhibition" in Moscow in 1923 and to design the sets for *Aelita* the following year (see Nos. 465-69 [R976-78]). Rabinovich kept in close contact with other young artists who attended Exter's studio in 1918-19, especially Shifrin and Tyshler, and often referred to her influence on his artistic development. As Rabinovich wrote to Shifrin in 1918 (?), Exter was "practically and theoretically the herald of the French."[670] Rabinovich's assimilation of French Cubism via Exter is especially noticeable in his early stage designs as for *Salomé* at the Solovtsov Theater, Kiev, in 1919.

The Love for Three Oranges: *a farcical opera in four acts by Sergei Prokofiev based on the comedy by Carlo Gozzi. Produced at the Bolshoi Theater, Moscow, by Alexei Dikii on 17 May, 1927, with designs by Isaak Rabinovich.*
     See No. 32 [R31] for plot summary.

855

855 [174; R732].
Costume Design for the Glutton, 1927.
Gouache on paper on board.
Signed and dated lower right in blue pencil in Russian: "Isaak Rabinovitch 1927."
24¾ x 18⅞ in., 63 x 48 cm.
Other inscription: the reverse carries a signature by Sergei Lifar.
Provenance: *Ballet Material and Manuscripts from the Serge Lifar Collection,* London: Sotheby's, 9 May, 1984, Lot 65. (reproduced).
Reproduced in color in B115, plate 163; I77, p. 95; and in black and white in A34, p. 347;

G14, plate 107; I77, p. 145; M25, p. 18; P26; P38. Two similar designs, in the BTM, are reproduced in Syrkina, *Rabinovich,* p. 124. For other relevant reproductions see G14, plates 104-06.

Note: Rabinovich brought a rich theatrical experience to his scenographic resolution for *The Love for Three Oranges,* even though, by 1927, he was more accustomed to the intimate stage, e.g., of the State Jewish Chamber Theater, than to the large space of the Bolshoi. Still, Rabinovich's artistic psychology was a dynamic and expansive one and he was able to move with ease from tragedy to comedy, from cabaret to high drama. In this sense, he maintained the artistic flexibility of Exter, one of his principal mentors.
     Although Rabinovich elicited criticism for his experimental sets and was obliged to mollify his enthusiasm for Constructivism, he did avoid the political obviousness of the new didactic Realism. His sets for *Lysistrata* of 1923, for example, emphasized the restrained harmony of Constructivist forms and the hieratic simplicity of Classical columns, while his sets and costumes for *The Love for Three Oranges* seemed to recapture more of the cabaret atmosphere of Bi-Ba-Bo and Crooked Jimmy (see No. 814 [R696]) than of a professional opera. He described his work on the production:

> In this work all the elements of the vivid stage action reach their flowering. Suffice it to refer to the scenes in which about fifty masks participated, from minute ones to very big ones... It was here that, for the first time, I made use of light not only as a source of illumination, but also as a source of design: I use the lighting apparatus to create an even greater visual effect. [671]

Although Prokofiev was still living in Paris in 1927 and, therefore, did not supervise the Soviet premiere of his opera (conducted by Nikolai Golovanov), the production enjoyed a distinct musical success, especially since Antonina Nezhdanova, Nadezhda Obukhova, Alexander Pirogov, and other distinguished singers took part; the production was even broadcast and recorded, so that Prokofiev was actually able to hear the rendering (in 1928). As for the scenic resolution, Rabinovich interpreted the opera as a *bouffonnerie* with sharp contrasts in color and form, volumetrical decors that were light and transparent, and exaggerated, caricatural costumes. Flora Syrkina, Rabinovich's biographer, emphasizes just how eccentric and unexpected the designs were:

> By intensifying and underlining the expressivity of the constructed architecture, he created an architecture of light, achieving a fantastic, fairy-tale spectacle.[672]

Not everyone was pleased, the Bolshoi management noting that the general

sequence of designs was full of "external appurtenances... creating a sharp breach with the musical content."[673] In fact, in February, 1928, a special committee was established to "rework *The Three Oranges* from the scenographic standpoint"[674] — a sign for Rabinovich of more difficult times ahead. Nevertheless, Rabinovich's satirical costumes and masks for the Glutton, the Drunkards, etc. found a further, strictly political application: according to the historian Samuil Margolin, they formed the basis for a series of effigies representing the Pope, International Capitalism, Fascism, etc., that Rabinovich and his students built for a political carnival in the Park of Culture and Recreation in Moscow.[675]

670 Undated Letter from Rabinovich to Shifrin in RGALI, Call number f2422, op. 1, ed. khr. 314, l. 5.
671 G8, p. 220.
672 Syrkina: *Rabinovich,* p. 30.
673 C31, Vol. 2, p. 134.
674 Ibid.
675 G16, p. 111.

REMISOFF, Nicholas (Remizov, Nikolai Vladimirovich; real surname: Vasiliev; also known as Re-Mi)

Born 6 (18) May, 1887, St. Petersburg, Russia; died 4 August, 1975, Palm Springs, California, USA.

1896-1904 studied at the Boginsky High School in St. Petersburg; 1905 onwards contributed caricatures to journals such as *Strely* [Arrows] and *Vesna* [Spring] in St. Petersburg; thereafter active especially as a social and political caricaturist, working for *Satirikon* [Satyricon] and *Novyi Satirikon* [New Satyricon] just before and during World War I; 1908-16 attended IAA, studying under Dmitrii Kardovsky; established close contact with Alexandre Jacovleff; 1913 contributed to the "World of Art" exhibition in St. Petersburg and Kiev; published his own collections of caricatures such as *Prekrasnye Sabinianki* [The Beautiful Sabines]; in collaboration with the writers Arkadii Averchenko and Arkadii Bukhov, et al., illustrated various miscellanies of satire and caricature such as *Vestnik znaniia Novogo Satirikona. Entsiklopedicheskii slovar. Khrestomatiia dlia detochek* [The "Novyi Satirikon" Herald of Knowledge. An Encyclopedic Dictionary. A Collection for Little Children] (1917); early 1910s worked for the Crooked Mirror theater in St. Petersburg; 1916 designed productions for the Comedians' Halt, Petrograd; 1918 member of Alexandre Jacovleff and Vasilii Shukhaev's Workshop of St. Luke; left Petrograd for Kherson; 1920 arrived in Paris; worked for Nikita Baliev's Chauve-Souris there; 1922 with Nikita Baliev and the Chauve-Souris emigrated to the USA; one-man exhibition at the Wildenstein Gallery, New York; designed the interior for the New York home of the Chauve-Souris, i.e., the attic of the house over The

Century Theater; 1920s onward worked on many ballet and film productions for US companies; designed interiors for movie stars in Hollywood; among the most famous movies that he designed were *Of Mice and Men* (1939), *My Life with Caroline* (1941), and *Ocean's Eleven* (1960).

Bibliography
I. Yasinsky: "Vystavka risunkov Re-Mi i dr." in *Birzhevye vedomosti,* SP, 1913, 14 December.
G. Saber: "Through the Eyes of Remizov" in *Arts and Decoration,* New York, 1922, June, pp. 124, 155, 156.
M2, Vol. 2, pp. 191-93, listing his theatrical productions.
J. Bowlt: "Art and Violence: the Russian Caricature in the Early Nineteenth and Early Twentieth Centuries" in *20th Century Studies,* Canterbury, 1975. No. 13/14, pp. 56-76.
B16, Vol. 1, p. 112.
V. Zavalishin: "Yubilei zamechatelnogo khudozhnika" in *Novoe Russkoe Slovo,* New York, 1977, 4 August, p. 6.
B. Efimov: *N. Re-mi, B. Malakhovsky, V. Deni,* M: Sovetskii khudozhnik, 1985.
M73, Vol. 26, pp. 82-83.
H34, pp. 485-86.
L213, pp. 94-97.

Remisoff was a master of caricature, book illustration, stage and movie design, and portraiture, although, like Boris Bilinsky in France, he preferred the medium of film, especially the entertainment movie in which he could indulge his vivid imagination. Remisoff also used satire and parody as outlets for his fantasy, a dramatic model for which he found in the ancient traditions of the Punch and Judy show.[676] As Viacheslav Zavalishin has noted: "In painting and graphics [Remisoff] has done for Russian satire approximately what Arkadii Averchenko and Mikhail Bulgakov did for satire in literature."[677] The Chauve-Souris, with its revues, comedies, and music-hall numbers, also served as an important context for Remisoff's light-hearted comments on social mores and society personalities.

856 [R733].
Self-Portrait, ca. 1962.
Gouache.
Initialed lower left.
18⅛ x 12 in., 46 x 30.5 cm.
Provenance: the artist, Palm Springs, California, November, 1967.
Reproduced in I14, p. 63; I51, No. 193.

857 [R734].
Poster Advertising The Bat Cabaret, 1914.
Lithograph in black and white.
19⅝ x 9⅞ in., 50 x 25 cm.
Provenance: N. Skarovsky, Moscow, 1984.

Note: Remisoff designed the logo for Nikita Baliev's cabaret theater known as The Bat (in emigration: Chauve-Souris). This poster advertises a gala performance of fourteen numbers by The Bat at the Passage Theater in St. Petersburg on 7, 8, 9, and 10 April, 1914. For information on The Bat see C51, pp. 162-70; E1; E21; E35; E52, pp. 19-36, 340-77.

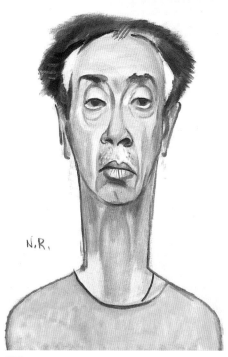

856

Zaria-Zarianitsa (lit. *Dawn-Lightning,* **known as The Miracle of the Holy Virgin):** *play by Fedor Sologub with music by Nikolai Suvorovsky. Produced by Nikita Baliev for the Théâtre de la Chauve-Souris, Paris, March, 1921, with designs by Nicholas Remisoff.*

A group of young novices assembles at the door of a chapel to listen to an old pilgrim chant a sacred legend. This legend describes how the Holy Virgin, dressed as a simple peasant woman, is refused alms as she wanders through a certain village on her way to the holy places. St. Elijah, the Prophet, mounts his fiery chariot to chastise the villagers for their callousness. However, the Holy Virgin intervenes, telling St. Elijah that she has forgiven the villagers for the sake of their children.

857

858 [175; R735].
Stage Design, ca. 1921.
Watercolor.
Signed upper right: "N. Remisoff."
10½ x 13¾ in., 26.5 x 35 cm.
Provenance: the artist, Palm Springs, California, November, 1967.
Reproduced in color in the Souvenir

858

859

860

861

program for the *Théâtre de la Chauve-Souris*, Paris, March, 1921, unpaginated, and in several subsequent programs; I20, No. 73; I51, No. 194; M86.

Note: Zaria-Zarianitsa was part of the repertoire of the Chauve-Souris as early as 1918 in Moscow.[678]

A Quartet of Merry Artists: *revue produced by Nikita Baliev for the Chauve-Souris Theater, New York, 31 January, 1922, with designs by Nicholas Remisoff.*

859 [R736].
Caricature of a Quartet of Artists and Nikita Baliev, 1922.
Black ink.
Signed and dated lower left: "N. Remisoff 22."
18⅛ x 13 in., 46 x 33 cm.
Provenance: the artist, Palm Springs, California, November, 1967.
Reproduced in I20, No. 74; I51, No. 195; N91, p. 139; M73, p. 93. A painted version of this caricature is reproduced in the Souvenir Program of *Balieff's Théâtre de la Chauve-Souris*, New York, 1922, unpaginated.

Note: From left to right the figures are Mikhail Vavitch (Mikhail Ivanovich Vavich, 1881-1930, operetta singer and then manager of The Bat), Georgii (George) Birse, Arcady (Arkadii) Stoianovsky, and Zotoff, who were the actors in *A Quartet of Merry Artists;* the fifth person is Nikita Baliev himself, compère of the Chauve-Souris. This particular revue (a more appropriate translation of the Russian title, *Kvartet veselykh artistov,* would have been *A Quartet of Merry Artistes,* or *Actors*) was a popular one, and Remisoff designed both the New York and the Paris productions in 1922. Remisoff and Baliev collaborated on a number of projects in the early 1920s and Remisoff did many caricatures of the colorful impresario. (Cf. Nos. 51 [R47], 948 [R962]).

862

Moscow Fiancées: *play produced by Nikita Balieff's Théâtre de la Chauve-Souris at the Théâtre Femina, Paris, 1923.*
A riotous comedy of rivalries, betrothals, and happy unions.

860 [NIRE].
Stage design, 1923.
Watercolor and pencil laid on cardboard.
Signed bottom right: "N. Remisoff."
7⅞ x 18⅜ in., 20 x 46.6 cm.
Provenance: the artist's wife, Sophia Remisoff, Palm Springs, November, 1967.
Reproduced in I40, p. 75.

861 [NIRE].
Stage design, 1923.
Gouache and silver foil.
10⅝ x 20½ in., 27 x 52 cm.
Provenance: the artist's wife, Sophia Remisoff, Palm Springs, November, 1967.
Reproduced in I40, p. 75.

862 [NIRE].
Backdrop for "A Scene in the Snow", 1923.
Gouache.
Signed bottom left: N. Remisoff."
7⅝ x 16⅞ in., 19.4 x 42.8 cm.
Other inscriptions: top left: "d'après lubok

863

864

russe. N. Remisoff, 1923."
Provenance: the artist's wife, Sophia
Remisoff, Palm Springs, November, 1967.
Reproduced in I40, p. 75.

Arlecchinata: *ballet based on the
Commedia dell'Arte with Pantalone,
Harlequin, Columbine, and Pierrot. Music
by Jean-Joseph Cassanéa de Mondonville
and choreography by Adolph Bolm.
Produced by the Bolm Ballet Company at
the Chamber of Music, Washington, D.C.
on 27 April, 1928, with designs by Nicholas
Remisoff.*

863 [R737].
**Stage Design with Three Characters of the
Commedia dell'Arte, ca. 1928.**
Gouache.
Signed upper left: "N. Remisoff."

13 x 26 in., 33 x 66 cm.
Provenance: the artist, Palm Springs,
California, November, 1967.
Reproduced in I14, No. 88.
The center figure is alleged to be the dancer
Adolph (Emilii) Rudolfovich Bolm (1884-
1951).

The Fair at Sorochinsk: *ballet based on the
story by Nikolai Gogol and taken from the
unfinished opera of the same name by
Modest Mussorgsky with choreography by
David Lichine. Produced by the Ballet
Theater at the Metropolitan Opera, New
York, on 14 October, 1943, with designs by
Nicholas Remisoff.*

*Cherevik has brought his daughter
Parasia to the fair where, legend tells, the
devil likes to appear in the form of a pig
seeking the sleeve of a garment pawned*

many years before. Gritsko, the son of a
friend, asks Parasia's hand in marriage, but
Khivria, Parasia's stepmother, as well as the
mistress of the priest's son, does not
consent. Cherevik's carousal is interrupted
by the appearance of a pig at the window.
He then consents to his daughter's marriage,
and the two sweethearts celebrate in spite
of Khivria's dissatisfaction.

864 [R738].
Stage Design for Act II, ca. 1943.
Gouache.
Signed lower right: "N. Remisoff."
14 x 16⅞ in., 35.5 x 43 cm.
Provenance: the artist, Palm Springs,
California, November, 1967.
Reproduced in I14, No. 87.

676 Remisoff even wrote an article on the subject. See
      "The Punch and Judy Theatre" in *Western
      Architect,* Minneapolis, 1930, Vol. 39, pp. 182-83.
677 Zavalishin, "Yubilei zamechatelnogo khudozhnika."
678 A documentary photograph of the production is
      reproduced in E1, p. 17.

RIABUSHKIN, Andrei Petrovich

Born 17 (29) October, 1861, Stanichnaya
Sloboda Village near Borisoglebsk in
Tambov Region, Russia; died 27 April (10
May), 1904, at Didvino estate on the River
Trigoda, near St. Petersburg, Russia.

Born into a peasant family in which the
father and elder brother were icon painters;
1875-82 attended MIPSA, where he
studied under Vasilii Perov; his colleagues
included Abram Arkhipov, Konstantin
Korovin, Isaak Levitan, and Mikhail
Nesterov; attended lectures by Vasilii
Kliuchevsky on Russian history; 1880
showed his *Peasant Wedding* at the
Moscow Institute students' exhibition,
which Pavel Tretiakov then acquired; 1882-
90 attended IAA; 1880s onwards illustrated
magazines such as *Niva* [Field] and
Vsemirnaia illiustratsiia [Global Illustration];
1890 visited old Russian towns such as
Moscow, Rostov, Kiev, Pskov, and
Novgorod; 1891 first contributed to an
exhibition of the *peredvizhniki* [Society of
Wandering Exhibitions] with his painting
*Waiting for the Newlyweds Coming from
the Church, Novgorod Province;* 1890s
produced paintings based on traditional,
pre-Petrine Russian society; 1895 contributed to the first exhibition of the Society of
Artists of Historical Painting; 1900 contributed to the "Exposition Universelle,"
Paris; close to the World of Art group; 1903
ill with tuberculosis, traveled to Switzerland
and Germany; returned to his home in the
St. Petersburg countryside.

Bibliography
A. Voskresensky: *Andrei Petrovich Riabushkin,*
SP: Butkovskaia, 1912.
A. Rostislavov: *Andrei Petrovich Riabushkin,* M:
Knebel, [1913].

865

A. Savinov: Andrei Petrovich Riabushkin, L: Aurora, 1973.

E. Odinokova: Andrei Petrovich Riabushkin, M: Iskusstvo, 1977.

N. Masalina: Andrei Riabushkin, M: Aurora, 1986.

V. Mekhanikova: A.P. Riabushkin, L: Khudozhnik RSFSR, 1989.

E. Shilova: Andrei Riabushkin. Catalog of exhibition at the RM, 2009.

Like Sergei Maliutin, Mikhail Nesterov, Ilia Ostroukhov (No.803 [R685]), Elena Polenova, and the Vasnetsov brothers, Apollinarii and Viktor (No. 1115 [NIRE]), Riabushkin contributed much to the national revival in Russian art towards the end of the 19th century, and he is now remembered as an illustrator of court and village life of seventeenth-century Moscow and Novgorod. Unlike some of his colleagues, however, Riabushkin did not idealize Medieval Russia, implying that, in spite of the colorful folklore, it could also be a harsh and rigid society (cf. the blind beggar in the painting A Moscow Street on a Holiday, 1895, RM). As Alexandre Benois wrote in 1912: "[Riabushkin] never descended into icky and sentimental artificiality."[679] On the other hand, Riabushkin was not a Realist in the way that Ilia Repin or his mentor Perov were and he gave little attention to the "accursed questions." Rather, Riabushkin was attracted to the costumes, celebrations, and rituals of Old Russia — as Alexander Rostislavov wrote in 1913:

> This love of Riabushkin [for Old Russia] was spontaneous and quite without ideological tendentiousness, for this was a love of the forms of Russian beauty, of the Russian festival, of a beauty that lived in olden times and is still alive in the life of the real people.[680]

During his short career, Riabushkin received limited attention (he died when he was only 43). Retiring by nature, he exhibited infrequently, and, being of peasant background, preferred to live in the country. It was only towards the end of his life when, incidentally, his style began to assimilate the influence of Art Nouveau and Symbolism (cf. Winter Morning, 1903, Museum of the Academy of Arts, SP) that he prompted increasing comment, especially among the members of the World of Art group: Benois, Sergei

Diaghilev, and Igor Grabar were fond of his work, and Diaghilev made sure that Riabushkin was represented in the group's magazine and exhibitions.

865 [R761].
At the Wedding, ca. 1901.
Watercolor, wash, and pencil.
Signed lower right in pencil in Russian: "Drawn by Riabushkin."
8⅞ x 24⅝ in., 22.5 x 62.5 cm.
Other inscriptions: lower left in brown ink: "No. 38"; on the reverse in pencil in Russian: "A. Riabushkin. At the Wedding."
Provenance: Yakov Rubinshtein, Moscow, October, 1974.

Note: Riabushkin often depicted the rituals and festivities of Medieval Russia, and there are a number of paintings and drawings that concern weddings, e.g., A Wedding Train in Moscow (17th Century) (1901, TG). For other sketches relating to this subject see Rostislavov, Andrei Petrovich Riabushkin, p. 38; and Savinov, Riabushkin, No. 16.

679   "Khudozhestvennye pisma. Dve vystavki" in Rech, SP, 1912, 12 October. Quoted in Odinokova: Riabushkin, p. 8. Benois was reviewing Riabushkin's posthumous exhibition at IAA in 1912.

680   Rostislavov: Riabushkin, p. 80.

RODCHENKO, Alexander Mikhailovich

Born 23 November (5 December), 1891, St. Petersburg, Russia; died 3 December, 1956, Moscow, Russia.

1910-14 attended the Kazan Art School under Nikolai Feshin (Fechin); then moved to CSIAI; influenced by Art Nouveau; 1913 met Varvara Stepanova, who became his life-long companion; 1916 contributed to the "Store"; 1917 with Vladimir Tatlin, Georgii Yakulov, et al. designed the interior of the Café Pittoresque, Moscow; 1918 onward worked at various levels in IZO NKP; contributed to many national and international exhibitions; 1918-21 worked on spatial constructions; 1918-26 taught at the Moscow Proletkult [Proletarian Culture] School; 1920 member of Inkhuk; created costumes for Alexei Gan's

unrealized spectacle We; 1920-30 professor at Vkhutemas/Vkhutein; 1921 contributed to the third exhibition of Obmokhu [Society of Young Artists] and to "5 x 5 = 25" in Moscow, at which he showed three monochrome paintings; 1922-28 associated with the journals Lef [Left Front of the Arts] and Novyi lef [New Left Front of the Arts], which published some of his articles and photographs; 1925 designed a workers' club, contributed to the "Exposition Internationale des Arts Décoratifs" in Paris; late 1920s onward concentrated on photography, including press photographs of sports meets and the White Sea Canal; contributed to the propaganda journal USSR in Construction; 1930 joined October, a group of designers that also included Alexei Gan, Gustav Klutsis, and El Lissitzky; early 1940s produced paintings in an Abstract Expressionist style.

Bibliography
Rodchenko is the subject of a very large number of monographs, catalogs, and articles. The titles below are a representative selection only.

G. Karginov: Rodcsenko, Budapest: Corvina, 1975 (and subsequent translations into French and English).

V. Rodchenko, comp.: A.M. Rodchenko. Stati. Vospominaniia. Avtobiograficheskie zapiski. Pisma, M: Sovetskii khudozhnik, 1982.

Alexander Rodtschenko und Warwara Stepanowa. Catalog of exhibition at the Wilhelm-Lehmbruck Museum Duisburg, 1982.

W. Rodtschenko and A. Lawrentjew: Alexander Rodtschenko, Dresden: VEB Kunst, 1983.

S. Khan-Mogomedov: Rodchenko: The Complete Work, Cambridge: MIT, 1987.

A. Lavrentiev, comp.: Alexandre Rodtchenko. Ecrits complets sur l'art, l'architecture et la révolution, Paris: Sers, 1988 (French translation and annotation of V. Rodchenko, A.M. Rodchenko).

A. Lavrentiev: A.M.Rodchenko, V.F. Stepanova, Moscow: Kniga, 1989.

D. Elliott and A. Lavrentiev: Alexander Rodchenko. Works on Paper, 1914-1920, London: Sotheby's, 1991.

J. Bowlt and A. Lavrentiev: Alexander Rodchenko. Museum Series Portfolio, M: Rodchenko/Stepanova Archives, and Los Angeles / New York: Schickler Lafaille, 1994.

M. Dabrowski: Aleksandr Rodchenko. Catalog of exhibition at the Museum of Modern Art, New York, 1998.

V. Rodchenko: Vospominaniia, dnevniki, pisma, M: Grant, 1998.

A. Rennert: *Rodčenko. Metapmorphosen,* Munich: Deutsche Kunstverlag, 2008.

M. Tupitsyn: *Rodchenko and Popova.* Catalog of exhibition at Tate Modern, London, State Museum of Contemporary Art, Thessaloniki, and the Museo Nacional Centro de Arte Reina Sofia, Madrid, 2009-10.

A. Lavrentiev: *Aleksandr Rodchenko,* M: Ruskii avangard, 2011.

Rodchenko's artistic evolution was a broad and rapid one, encompassing the early Symbolist pieces of ca. 1913, the graphics done with compass and ruler of 1915, the non-figurative paintings and three mono-chrome canvases exhibited at "5 x 5 = 25," the free-standing and suspended con-structions of 1918-21, and the photographic work of the 1920s and 1930s. While Rodchenko's studio painting was innovative, it derived its stimulus from various sources: including the Suprematism of Kazimir Malevich (Rodchenko's *Black on Black* of 1918 was an obvious gesture to Malevich's original black on white square of 1915) and Liubov Popova's architectonic painting. However, Rodchenko's experiments in three dimensions were, indeed, pioneering, and his suspended constructions acted as the brilliant culmination to the tradition of the relief initiated by Tatlin in 1914.

In transferring his energies to typo-graphy and photography in the 1920s, Rodchenko ostensibly moved from the esthetic exercise of the abstract painting to a utilitarian medium — to stage and book design, interior design, clothing, and even playing cards. At the same time, Rodchenko did not cease to experiment with the purely formal aspects of his new disciplines, and "Rodchenko perspective" and "Rodchenko foreshortening" became current terms in the 1920s. Furthermore, it seems probably that Rodchenko's innovative use of light and shadow exerted an appreciable influence on Sergei Eisenstein, Lev Kuleshov, and Dziga Vertov. In true Constructivist fashion, Rodchenko attempted to expose the mechanism of the camera and to exploit the photographic method to its maximum, just as he had disclosed the essence of space and form in his constructions. For this, Rodchenko came under strong attack during the hegemony of Socialist Realism in the 1930s and 1940s.

866 [176; R749].
Costume Design for the Black Mask Champion (Holland), 1918.
Gouache, watercolor, and colored ink.
Signed in Russian lower left: "Rodchenko".
14¼ x 10¾ in., 36.2 x 27.2 cm.
Other inscriptions: lower right in Russian: "Champion 'black mask' (Holland)"; the reverse carries the name and date "A.M. Rodchenko 1918" with stamps from the Rodchenko/Stepanova collection and archive; the word "Varst" (pseudonym of Varvara Stepanova) and the number "164" have been crossed out.
Provenance: Leonard Hutton Galleries, New York, 1974.
Reproduced in color in I68, p. 14; I77, p. 75;

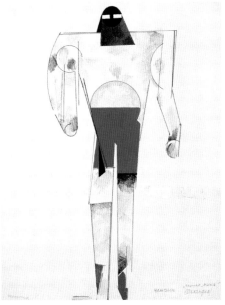

866

and in black and white in A34, p. 355; B200, p. 45; I77, p. 162; N173; P18.

Note: While Rodchenko is often remem-bered for his abstract paintings, it would be misleading to assume that he ignored the human element during the late 1910s and early 1920s. Indeed, perhaps one reason why he investigated the medium of the collage from 1915 onwards (especially 1918-21), using photographic fragments, pieces of newspaper and advertisements, etc. (all with direct references to concrete life), is that it helped to reintroduce a "readable" content to the work of art and, in this sense, to oppose the self-sufficient studio paintings of the same period. Certainly, it would be an exaggeration to claim that, while producing non-figurative art, Rodchenko felt nostalgia for the figurative content, but one cannot help noticing the anthropomorphic forms in some of the so-called abstract paintings, constructions, and architectural designs of 1918-21. Conversely, if some of Rodchenko's abstractions can be perceived as schematic figures, so some of his costume designs for the theater can be read as abstract paintings. This is true, for example, of his set of costumes for Alexei Gan's play *We,* which Gan asked him to produce in November, 1920 (but which Gan actually never completed).

Black Mask Champion (Holland) is a clear specimen of Rodchenko's constant concern with human depiction at this time and extends one of his life-long interests — the circus, the sports rally, and martial arts. He painted and photographed these subjects many times especially in the 1920s and 1930s. This piece is one of the series called *The Wrestlers,* which Rodchenko produced in 1918-19, but it bears an uncanny resemblance to Kazimir Malevich's 1913 costume for the Mugger in *Victory over the Sun* (see No. 775 [R653]). Lissitzky's design for Three

Sportsmen in the same opera (1920-23) also comes to mind (see No. 760 [R639]). Another costume design from Rodchenko's *Wrestlers,* called *Red Mask Champion from Germany,* dated 1919, is reproduced in color in K59, p. 253; others — called *Champions of England and France* and *Champion of Canada* — are reproduced in Khan-Magomedov, *Rodchenko,* pp. 33, 89. For commentary on Black Mask wrestlers in Russia see A. Mazur: *Sem Ivanov,* M: Stolitsa, 1995, pp. 128-29.

The Bed Bug: *comedy in nine scenes by Vladimir Maiakovsky. Produced by Vsevolod Meierkhold at the Meierkhold Theater, Moscow, on 13 February, 1929, with music by Dmitrii Shostakovich and designs by Meierkhold, the Kukryniksy,[681] and Alexander Rodchenko.*

A crafty operator by the name of Prisypkin, who is a product of the new Soviet bourgeoisie, tries to ingratiate himself with the Party. The result, however, is disaster: he is immersed in ice and unfrozen by scientists in 1979 in what was meant to be the ideal Communist world. Prisypkin is quarantined together with his only possessions: a guitar and a bed bug. Having found the bed bug on himself, he keeps it as his one and only friend.

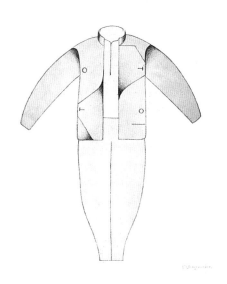

867

867 [R750].
Costume Design for the Director of the Zoo, ca. 1929.
Watercolor and pencil.
Signed lower right in Russian: "Rodchenko."
12¾ x 14⅛ in., 32.4 x 36 cm.
Provenance: the artist's daughter, Varvara Rodchenko, Moscow, 1970.
Reproduced in I32, No. 83; I51, No. 196; I77, p. 142. A similar design is reproduced in Khan-Magomedov, *Rodchenko,* p. 209.

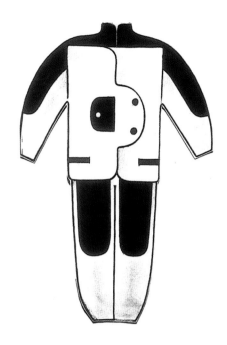

868

869

870

868 [R751].
Costume Design for the Master of Ceremonies, ca. 1929.
Collage, India ink, and pencil.
Stamped signature on reverse in Russian.
Provenance: the artist's daughter, Varvara Rodchenko, Moscow, 1970.
14⅛ x 10⅝ in., 36 x 27 cm.
Reproduced in I32, No. 84; I51, No. 197; I77, p. 142. A similar design, the front reversed, in the collection of the Rodchenko family in Moscow, is reproduced in Karginov, *Rodcsenko,* plate 164; and in Khan-Magomedov, *Rodchenko,* p. 209. For other costumes similar to this and to No. 867 [R750], see G29, plates 21, 22; I26, p. 90; C46, p. 93; K59, p. 90; also see *Rodčenko / Stepanova,* p. 74; *Realtà Sovietica,* Rome, 1984, May-June, pp. 35, 39. A curious version is reproduced in L15, Lot 203 bis.

Note: The Bed Bug was a satire on the life of the new Soviet bourgeoisie and bureaucracy that appeared in the wake of NEP (New Economic Policy, 1921-29), which had allowed a partial return to the free enterprise system. *The Bed Bug* was, as Maiakovsky said, intended to

> expose the philistines of today… this is a great heap of philistine facts which came into my hands and head from all over the place during my newspaper and publishing work.[682]

This was one of Meierkhold's major productions, even though, theatrically, it was not an unqualified success, mainly as a result of the bizarre sets and costumes. According to one commentator:

> Nearly all the costumes and properties were bought over the counter in Moscow shops in order to demonstrate

the pretentious ugliness of current fashions… Part Two, set in 1979, was designed by the Constructivist artist, Alexander Rodchenko; but his vision of a disciplined, scientific Communist future was so lifeless and hygenic that the spectator was hard put to decide where the parody really stopped.[683]

Other reviews were more favorable. Isaak Turkeltaub praised Rodchenko for his "splendid, material design," [684] while Pavel Novitsky liked the "simple and clear forms created by an industrial and scientific-laboratorial technology." [685]

Rodchenko as contributor:
869 [R752].
Designer unknown: *Poster Advertising the Premiere of* **The Bed Bug, 1929.**
Lithograph in blue and white.

42½ x 28½ in., 108 x 72.5 cm.
Inscriptions as part of the design provide details on the date of the premiere (12 February, 1929), the list of actors, and other information on the production.
Provenance: Viktor Kholodkov, Moscow, 1989.
Reproduced in C30, p. 371.

870 [R753].
Designer unknown: *Poster Advertising* **The Bed Bug on Tour, 1929.**
Lithograph in black and white.
12¼ x 6⅛ in., 31 x 15.7 cm.

871

872

873

Inscribed in Russian at bottom: "Printed by Nizhpoligraf. Edition of 850."
Provenance: Viktor Kholodkov, Moscow, 1989.
Reproduced in A. Favorsky, comp.: *Maiakovsky. Piesy,* M: Detskaia literatura, 1976, p. 160.

871 [R754].
Layout by Alexander Rodchenko and text by Vladimir Maiakovsky: *Poster Advertising* **The Bed Bug, 1929.**
Lithograph in black and white.
7⅛ x 10¼ in., 18 x 26 cm.
The Russian script reads: "People are laughing and knitting their brows in the Meierkhold Theater at the Comedy *Bed Bug.*"

Provenance: Viktor Kholodkov, Moscow, 1989.
For verso of this poster see No. 872 [R754a].

872 [R754a].
Layout by Alexander Rodchenko and text by Vladimir Maiakovsky: *Poster Advertising* **The Bed Bug (verso), 1929.**
Lithograph in black and white.
7⅛ x 10¼ in., 18 x 26 cm.
The large Russian script reads "Citizen, hurry to the showing of *The Bed Bug.* There's a line at the box office, there's a crowd in the theater, just don't be angry at the insect's jokes. This is not about you, but about someone you know." The small Russian script in lower margin reads: "Moscow.

Glavlit [=Censor] A.30.383 Edition of 15,000. Published by the Meierkhold Theater, Moscow. Printed by Mospolitgraf, 16th Printing House, 9 Trekhprudnyi, Moscow."
Provenance: Viktor Kholodkov, Moscow, 1989.
Reproduced in Khan-Magomedov, *Rodchenko,* p. 201; also see *Maiakovsky. Piesy,* op. cit., after p. 169.
This is the verso of No. 871 [R754].

Rodchenko as contributor:
873 [NIRE].
Designer unknown: *Poster Advertising Seven Lectures and Readings Dedicated to Vsevolod Meierkhold's 35th Anniversary as Actor and Director at the Club of Masters of Art, Moscow,* **1934.**
Lithograph in black and red.
Photomontage with a portrait of Meierkhold.
27¾ x 34⅝ in., 70.5 x 88 cm.
Inscriptions (as part of the design) provide the names of the lecturers (speaking of Meierkhold and the revolutionary theater, music, St. Petersburg, Maiakovsky, and drama) and actors of the Meierkhold company scheduled to read passages from plays performed at the Meierkhold Theater, and also the dates of these events during March and April, 1934. Among the presentations is a lecture by Osip Brik on Meierkhold's productions of Vladimir Maiakovsky's *Bathhouse* and the *Bed Bug.* Printed by Moskoprompechat, Moscow, in an edition of 6,000

874

Rodchenko as contributor:
874 [R755].
Designer unknown: *Poster for the "Exhibition of Works by Alexander Mikhailovich Rodchenko" at the State Literary Museum, Moscow,* **1962.**
Lithograph in black and red.
19½ x 27½ in., 49.5 x 70 cm.
The photograph above the exhibition

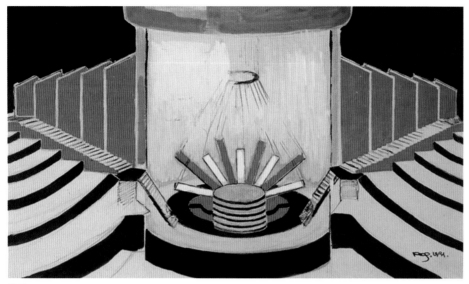

875

announcement is of Dmitrii Shostakovich, Vladimir Maiakovsky, Vsevolod Meierkhold, and Rodchenko working on the production of *The Bed Bug* in 1929. Under the announcement: "Collaboration with Maiakovsky and Meierkhold on the play *Bed Bug.* Collaboration with Maiakovsky on books, magazines, and advertisements, photomontages, photo studies, photo portraits of writers. State Literary Museum, 38, Dmitrovka, Moscow. Printed by Krasnaia Zvezda printing house, 73, Verkhniaia Maslovka, Moscow." The smaller Russian script lower left reads: "The Museum is open: Monday, 10.00-16.00; Wednesday and Friday 14.00-21.00; Thursday, Saturday, and Sunday 11.00-18.00; closed Tuesdays. Public transport: Oktiabrskaia Metro Station, streetcar No. 4, bus No. 5 to Literary Museum. Entrance fee: 10 kopecks. Information by phone: B1-00-60." The script in the box lower right reads: "On Wednesday, Thursday and Friday, during the exhibition, from 17.00 to 18.00, you can hear recordings of Maiakovsky's poetry read by Vl. Yakhontov and Edgar Valdman."
Provenance: Viktor Kholodkov, Moscow, 1999.

Note: Rodchenko's costumes for *The Bed Bug* are of particular interest since they extend the principles of *prozodezhda*, which Varvara Stepanova elaborated in 1922-23 (see Nos. 977-80 [R803-06]) and which Rodchenko applied to his idea for a worker's suit (the photographs of Rodchenko wearing this suit, taken by Stepanova, have been reproduced many times; see, for example, the frontispiece to Karginov, *Rodcsenko*).[686] To Rodchenko, who in his work for the second part of *The Bed Bug* was attempting to predict clothes of the future, the simple, undecorated costume with its associations with mechanical precision and industrial efficiency (qualities that the Constructivists advocated), seemed to be a reasonable solution.

Although Rodchenko had already contributed designs to a number of stage and movie undertakings, including Gan's *We* (1920, not produced) and Dziga Vertov's *Kino-Truth* (1922 onward), and although he had worked on clothes and textile design in 1923-24, *The Bed Bug* marked Rodchenko's real entry into the theater and his first collaboration with Meierkhold. Rodchenko worked on *The Bed Bug* on Maiakovsky's initiative from 14 January through 13 February, 1929, and produced about sixty costumes and décors. Stepanova recalled that "Meierkhold passed the designs without making any corrections, which astonished everyone in the theater."[687] Immediately after *The Bed Bug*, Rodchenko went on to design Anatolii Glebov's play *Inga* staged by Nikolai Gorchakov at the Theater of the Revolution also in 1929. Gorchakov then employed Rodchenko for the ambitious production of *One Sixth of the World* in 1931 and the same year Rodchenko designed *The Army of the World* for Zavadsky's Studio in Moscow — Rodchenko's last major theatrical endeavor.

One Sixth of the World: *revue in three acts by Alexander Yarkov and Nikolai Ravich. Produced by Nikolai Gorchakov at the Music-Hall, Moscow, on 22 February, 1931, with choreography by Kasian Goleizovsky and designs by Alexander Rodchenko.*

An expatriate American millionaire comes to the Soviet Union to try and persuade his brother to emigrate. The brother refuses, making a long speech in which he denounces American Imperialism. The political theme is supplemented by singing, ballet numbers, and declamations, and the cast is some two hundred strong.

875 [R756].
Stage Design for Act I, 1931.
Gouache, silver paint, black ink, and pencil. Signed and dated lower right in Russian: "Rod. 1931."
8½ x 14 in., 21.6 x 35.6 cm.
Other inscription on reverse: "To esteemed Nikolai Mikhailovich Gorchakov, the first author of *One Sixth of the World,* from the

second. A. Rodchenko, 1931."
Provenance: André B. Nakov, Paris, 1976. Reproduced in I40, No. 89; I51, No. 198; I77, pp. 110, 153; P45. A very similar design, in the collection of the Rodchenko family, Moscow, is reproduced in K59, p. 279; a photograph of the maquette is reproduced in *Alexander Rodtschenko und Warwara Stepanowa,* p. 64. Also see Khan-Magomedov, *Rodchenko,* pp. 166, 204, 205.
The theater producer and critic Nikolai Mikhailovich Gorchakov (1898-1958) was a close friend of Rodchenko and Stepanova.

Note: According to Varvara Rodchenko, who is in possession of her father's explanatory drawings for this project, the central component of this design in the shape of a tumbler was mobile and the extended platforms were to move up and down. The tiers on either side of the "tumbler" were part of a permanent stage installation that the Stenberg brothers had constructed just before the production of *One Sixth of the World* and were not part of Rodchenko's design.[688]

876

876 [R757].
Costume Design for the Intourist Guide, 1931.
India ink and colored crayon.
13¾ x 10¼ in., 35 x 26 cm.
Inscriptions in Russian: top right in pencil: "Music-Hall"; lower right: "Intourist guide" in ink and "Zlotnik" in pencil. The reverse carries the stamp of the Rodchenko studio and the inscription "1/6 of the world" and the costume dimensions.
Provenance: the artist's daughter Varvara Rodchenko, Moscow, 1986.

877

878

877 [NIRE].
Costume Design for the General, Second Version, 1931.
Pencil, colored crayon, and ink.
13 x 8⅞ in., 33 x 22.5 cm.
Inscribed lower right in orange pencil in Russian: "General, second version"; the reverse carries the Russian atelier stamp: "Rodchenko."
Provenance: the artist's daughter, Varvara Rodchenko, Moscow, 1986.

878 [NIRE].
Costume Design for an Uzbek Wearing a Turban, 1931.
Gouache and pencil on paper laid on cardboard.
Signed, inscribed, and dated lower right in Russian: "Uzbek, Rod. 1931."
12⅝ x 9⅞ in., 32 x 25 cm.
Other inscriptions: upper left in pencil: "No. 1"; upper right in black ink the names of eight actors who were to wear Uzbek

costumes: "Drozdov, Manuilov, Viktorov, Poluektov, Skvortsov, Zhizhin, Antonov, Ermolov"; instructions to the dressmaker throughout in pencil.
Provenance: the artist's daughter, Varvara Rodchenko, Moscow, 1986.
A costume design for an Uzbek woman is reproduced in Khan-Magomedov, *Rodchenko. The Complete Work*, p. 205.

879 [NIRE].
Three Preparatory Costume Designs, 1931.
Pencil.
Stamped lower right in Russian: "Rodchenko."
9½ x 12⅝ in., 24 x 32 cm.
Provenance: the artist's daughter, Varvara Rodchenko, Moscow, 1986.

Note: Rodchenko had given thought to the theme of *One Sixth of the World* as early as 1926 when he designed a brochure by Izmail Uvarov advertising Dziga Vertov's movie also-called *One Sixth of the World*.[689] This 1931 production was Rodchenko's only design contribution to vaudeville, although contemporary critics felt that the simplicity and efficiency of his set was just what the music-hall needed:

> No painted glad rags, no perfumery — the entire construction was expedient, simple, and clever, and provides the opportunity for any kind of trans-formation for a rapid scene change.[690]

681 The Kukryniksy is the composite abbreviation of three names — Mikhail Vasilievich Kupriianov (1903-91), Porfirii Nikitich Krylov (1902-91), and Nikolai Aleksandrovich Sokolov (1903-2001). This three-man team, best known for its political caricatures and cartoons, designed the first four scenes of *The Bed Bug*, while Rodchenko designed the last five scenes — the so-called utopian part.
682 Maiakovsky on *The Bed Bug*. Quoted in Ch. Zalilova, ed.: *V.V. Maiakovsky. Sochineniia v trekh tomakh*, M: Khudozhestvennaia literatura, 1970, Vol. 3, p. 571. Also see B160 and J. Stepanian-Apkarian: "Alexander Rodchenko: 'Vladimir Maiakovsky'" in B183, pp. 271-80.
683 C34, p. 236.
684 Quoted in C33, p. 404.
685 Ibid.
686 For information on the principles of *prozodezhda* as formulated by Liubov Popova and Varvara Stepanova, see B59, passim; G34; K75.
687 V. Stepanova: "Occasional Notes" in K59, p. 139.
688 Letter from Varvara Rodchenko to John E. Bowlt dated 17 October, 1981.
689 I. Uvarov: *Shestaia chast mira*, M: Kinopechat, 1926.
690 From a review in *Sovetskoe iskusstvo*, M, 1931, 12 March. Quoted in Karginov, *Rodscenko*, p. 193. For photographs of the actual performance of *One Sixth of the World*, see E15, Vol. 2, pp. 38, 39; Khan-Magomedov: *Rodchenko*, p. 205.

879

ROERICH, Nicholas (Rerikh, Nikolai Konstantinovich)

Born 27 September (9 October), 1874, St. Petersburg, Russia; died 13 December, 1947, Kulu, North India.

1893 entered simultaneously the Law School at St. Petersburg University and the Higher Art Institute of IAA; during the 1890s displayed a keen interest in archeology and took part in a number of expeditions and digs; researched the art and religious rites of the ancient Slavs and began to use them as subjects for his paintings;1895 onwards pupil of Arkhip Kuindzhi; 1897 graduated from IAA; his diploma painting *The Messenger* was acquired by Pavel Tretiakov; 1900-01 traveled in France; early 1900s close contact with the World of Art group; 1903 took part in ethnographical and archeological expedition through the ancient cities of Russia, which became the subjects of his paintings; 1903-10 member of the Union of Russian Artists; 1906-18 director of the school at the Society for the Encouragement of the Arts in St. Petersburg; 1907 debut as a stage designer; 1908-14 collaborated with Princess Mariia Tenisheva on the interior decoration of her church at Talashkino; accepted one of several decorative commissions for private chapels and monasteries; 1909 designed Sergei Diaghilev's production of *The Polovtsian Dances* in Paris; elected member of the IAA; 1910 appointed chairman of the renewed World of Art society; 1913 responsible for the sets and costumes of Igor Stravinsky's *Sacre du Printemps* staged by Diaghilev in Paris; 1916 lived in Karelia, which in 1918 became Finnish territory; 1918-19 one-man shows in Stockholm, Copenhagen, and Helsinki; 1920 arrived in the USA; one-man exhibition in Chicago, where he established the Cor Ardens artists' association; 1920s studied Indian philosophy such as the works of Swami Vivekananda and Rabindranath Tagore; founded the Master Institute of United Arts (1921), the International Cultural Center "Corona Mundi" (1922), and in 1923 the Nicholas Roerich Museum in New York; 1929 established the Roerich Pact for the identifiication and protecton of artistic monuments worldwide; 1935 departed for extensive trips through India and Central Asia, not returning to the USA; 1942 at his house in Kulu in the Himalayas, received Jawaharlal Nehru and his daughter Indira Gandhi.

Bibliography

Over the last two decades a formidable amount of literature has appeared on Nicholas Roerich and only part is included in the list below. A full bibliography for Roerich is listed in V. Shishkova et al.: *Nikolai Konstantinovich Rerikh: Bibliograficheskii ukazatel,* M: International Roerich Center, 1999.

Yu. Baltrushaitis: *Rerich,* P: Svobodnoe iskusstvo, 1916

S. Ernst: *N. K. Rerikh,* P: Obshchina Sv. Evgenii, 1918.

M2, Vol. 2, pp. 193-94, listing his theatrical productions.

E. Poliakova: *Rerikh,* M: Iskusstvo, 1973 (second edition 1985).

P. Ekstrom: *Nicholas Roerich.* Catalog of exhibition at Cordier and Ekstrom Gallery, New York, 1974.

M. Kuzmina et al., eds.: *N.K. Rerikh. Zhizn i tvorchestvo. Sbornik statei,* M: Izobrazitelnoe iskusstvo, 1978.

E. Kiseleva: *Katalog eskizov dekoratsii i kostiumov N.K. Rerikha k muzykalnym postanovkam (1906-1944 gg.),* Alma-Ata: TUDSM, 1984.

J. Decter: *Nicholas Roerich,* Rochester, Vermont: Park Street, 1989.

E. Bazzarelli et al.: *Scritti italiani su N. Roerich,* Rubbettino: Soveria Mannelli.1993.

E. Dementieva et al., eds.: *Nikolai Rerikh. Listy dnevnika,* M: Bisan-Oazis, 1995-2002 (four volumes).

P. Belikov and V. Kniazeva: *Nikolai Konstantinovich Rerikh,* Samara: Agni, 1996.

A. Korotkina: *Nikolai Konstantinovich Rerikh,* SP: Khudozhnik Rossii, 1996.

E. Yakovleva: *Teatralno-dekoratsionnoe iskusstvo N.K. Rerikha,* Samara: Agni, 1996.

V. Melnikov, ed.: *Peterburgskii Rerikhovskii sbornik,* SP: Academic Gymnasium of St. Petersburg University, 1998-2008 (eight volumes).

K. Archer: *Roerich: East and West,* Bournemouth, England: Parkstone, 1999.

T. Rottert and I. Lipskaia, comps.: *Yubileinaia vystavka proizvedenii Rerikhov iz chastnykh sobranii.* Catalog of exhibition at the International Roerich Center, M, 1999.

N. Spirina and V. Larichev, eds.: *Rerikhovskie chteniia,* Novosibirsk: Siberian Roerich Society, 2000.

V. Melnikov, ed.: *Rerikhovskoe nasledie. Trudy konferentsii I,* SP: St. Petersburg State University, 2002.

N. Sergeeva: *Rerikh i Vrubel,* M: International Roerich Center, 2002.

A. Sobolev, ed.: *Nikolai Rerikh v russkoi periodike,* SP: Firma Kosta, 2004-08 (five volumes).

R. Drayer: *Nicholas and Helena Roerich,* Wheaton, Ill.: Quest, 2005.

E. Matochkin: *Nikolai Rerikh: Mozaiki, ikony, rospisi, proekty tserkvei,* Samara: Agni, 2005.

A. Sobolev, ed.: *N.K. Rerikh, 1917-1919. Materialy k biografii,* SP: Firma Kosta, 2008.

A. Shaposhnikova, ed.: *Mech muzhestva,* M: International Roerich Center, 2008.

T. Knizhnik and N. Mikhailova, comps.: *Rossiia i nasledie Rerikhov,* M: International Roerich Center, 2010 (Vol. 1).

Before the Revolution, Roerich played many important roles in Russian artistic and social life. For example, he was president of SSEA and was chairman of the revived World of Art society from 1910 onwards ("despite our coldness toward him," as Anna Ostroumova-Lebedeva later recalled).[691] Roerich also possessed genuine creative powers and he applied his extensive knowledge of primitive cultures to many enterprises — from his early cycle of paintings called *Ancient Russia* which he first showed at the 1902 "World of Art" exhibition in Moscow to his impressive sets and costumes for *The Polovtsian Dances* and *Le Sacre du Printemps*. True, Roerich's designs may be more sober than Bakst's and less reasoned than Benois's, but they still appeal as models of historical and ethnographical reconstruction, as with the designs for *The Polovtsian Dances*. The costumes for *The Tale of Tsar Saltan* are also extensions of national tradition, carrying more than casual allusions to Russian icons. Roerich's deep interest in cultures of the remote past and the primeval forces of nature parallels the work of contemporaries such as Mikhail Vrubel (the critic Sergei Makovsky once referred to them both as "otherworldly"[692]) and Viktor Vasnetsov.

Although indisputably an accomplished painter, stage designer, anthropologist, and poet, Roerich still occupies an uneasy position in the history of twentieth-century Russian culture. His artistic achievements are overshadowed by the less auspicious traits of his personality — self-glorification, financial machinations, and exaggerated interest in Eastern religion, which some observers saw as little more than charlatanism:

> By instinct he was the mystical messiah of a curious religious cult that flourished in New York in the 1920s and 1930s and involved a number of subsequently embarrassed converts.[693]

Ultimately, Roerich was perhaps too cautious to break fully with academic stricture and to develop a consistently original style: in this sense, Roerich's art may be regarded more as a symptom of the fashionable interests of his age — the occult, the national revival, the cult of the decorative arts — rather than as a deviant from them.

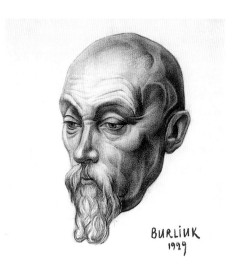

David Burliuk: *Portrait of Nicholas Roerich,* 1929. See No. 400 [R367].

880

881

The Polovtsian Dances: *ballet in one act extracted from* Prince Igor, *the unfinished opera in a prologue and four acts by Alexander Borodin with a libretto by the composer after a play by Vladimir Stasov; completed by Nikolai Rimsky-Korsakov and Alexander Glazunov. Produced on 19 May, 1909, at the Théâtre du Châtelet, Paris, with choreography by Michel Fokine and designs by Nicholas Roerich.*

See 380 [R353] for plot summary.

880 [177; NIRE].
Costume Design for Ovlur, 1909.
Gouache, watercolor, and silver on paper on board.
9⅝ x 7⅛ in., 24.5 x 18 cm.
Provenance: Gleb Ivakin, November, 1999. In a letter of 23 November, 1999, from Kiev, Gleb Ivakin writes: "This Roerich made its way into the collection before 1963 from the Kiev collector David Sigalov."
Reproduced in color in I117, p. 263; I127, p. 119 (full page); N188, p. 40; and in black and white in *Vitchizna*, 1973, No. 3, p. 140; and as item No. 34 in Yakovleva, *Teatralno-dekoratsionnoe iskusstvo N.K. Rerikha*, p. 117.[694]

Note: Sharing the spirit of Neo-Nationalism that Borodin echoed in his music, Roerich was the obvious choice for the decoration of the Paris and London productions of *Polovtsian Dances*. With dancers (in the Paris version) who included Adolph Bolm, Sofiia Fedorova, and Elena Smirnova, alongside the singing of Fedor Chaliapin, and Roerich's brilliant evocations of Ancient Russia, the production created a furor:

At the end, when Sofiia Fedorova, like one possessed before her colleagues, led the dance, the conductor seemed about ready to leap over the footlights, and the dancers, surging right up to the edge of the stage, stopped face to face with the audience now stamping and screaming.[695]

The Polovtsian Dances saw many interpretations by Russian designers and 1909 even saw a second elaborate production back home — with designs by Konstantin Korovin (644-48 [R539-43] for the Mariinsky Theater, St. Petersburg.

The Maid of Pskov (Pskovitianka): *opera in three acts and six scenes by Nikolai Rimsky-Korsakov. The libretto was written by the composer and is based on the drama of the same name by Lev Mei. The opera was staged on 19 May, 1909, at the Théâtre du Châtelet, Paris, by Sergei Diaghilev under the title* Ivan the Terrible *because of the dominance of his role, with designs by Nicholas Roerich.*

Princess Olga, daughter of Prince Tokmakov, hears of Ivan the Terrible's repression of Pskov and Novgorod. Her beloved, Mikhail Tucha, is leader of the uprising in Pskov, although she is betrothed to the boyar Nikita Matuta. Tokmakov tells Matuta that Olga is not his own daughter, but the child of his sister-in-law Vera Sheloga. In Pskov, Tucha and his associates plan to rebel. The Tsar asks to be attended by Princess Olga and is shaken to learn that Vera Sheloga is Olga's mother. He says that she will be taken to Moscow and that he will choose her groom. Tucha and his

forces attack the Tsar's camp. As they are repelled, Olga is fatally shot and over her body, Ivan reveals that he is her father.

881 [R739].
Set Design for the Monastery in Pskov, 1920.
Oil on canvas.
Signed with the Russian monogram and dated lower left: "NR 1920."
35¼ x 53⅛ in., 89.5 x 135 cm.
Provenance: *Diaghilev and Reinhardt Ballet Material*, London: Sotheby's, 9-10 July, 1969, Lot 120 (estate of Mary Garden, London; reproduced). Now in a private collection.
Reproduced in color in *Perezvony*, Riga, 1926, No. 13, opposite p. 376; and in Yakovleva,*Teatralno-dekoratsionnoe iskusstvo N.K. Rerikha*, p. 229; in black and white in No. 77; I51, No. 200; I61, p. 205. Also see *Stolitsa i usadba*, P, 1916, No. 57, p. 9; and G31, No. 157. A very similar design, dated 1908, from which this piece may have been copied, is in the GMTMA.

Le Sacre du Printemps: *Ballet in two acts with music by Igor Stravinsky and libretto by Nicholas Roerich and Igor Stravinsky. Produced by Sergei Diaghilev at the Théâtre des Champs-Elysées, Paris, on 29 May, 1913, with choreography by Vaslav Nijinsky and designs by Nicholas Roerich.*

At the foot of a sacred hill, youths and maidens await the wise man's signal to dance. They enter into convulsive, tempestuous dances to mark their adoration of the earth. In the second act, young people rejoice as the Chosen Virgin dances herself to death, sacrificing herself to Yarilo, the god of spring.

882

882 [R740].
Five Costume Designs, 1913 or 1920.
Gouache.

13¾ x 19⅝ in., 35 x 50 cm.

Provenance: Cordier-Ekstrom Gallery, New York, June, 1975. Now in a private collection. Reproduced in Yakovleva, *Teatralno-dekoratsionnoe iskusstvo N.K. Rerikha*, p. 228, where it is dated "1920";[696] and in *Nicholas Roerich*. (Catalog of exhibition at Cordier and Ekstrom Gallery, No. 3); F58, plate 101; I40, No. 90; I51, No. 201; I61, p. 204. A similar group is reproduced in J21, Lot 33. Similar costumes are in the BTM, the GMTMA, and the Radishchev Museum, Saratov. Documentary photographs from the 1913 performance, showing some of the costumes, are reproduced in I24, unpaginated. For color illustrations of some of the actual costumes used see J53, pp. 26-31.

Note: To a considerable extent, *Le Sacre du Printemps* was the creative result of Roerich's particular interests in ancient Russian history. Of direct relevance to his research for *Le Sacre* were his visits to Talashkino and his friendship with Princess Tenisheva, whose large collection of peasant artifacts provided Roerich with important ethnographical materials. At Talashkino, Roerich saw the workshops for wood-carving, embroidery, balalaika making, etc., which the Princess had founded with the explicit intention that they apply indigenous motifs and methods. Roerich also designed the interior of the church at Talashkino, his exotic fresco above the altar depicting Our Lady and the "perilous river of life"[697] reminding some observers of Tibetan and Thai religious paintings.[698] Perhaps Roerich

thought of Talashkino when he designed his sets and costumes for *Le Sacre* with their "broad, 'cosmic' upsurge."[699]

Stravinsky recognized Roerich's artistic and archaeological prowess and regarded him as the perfect visual interpreter of his "lapidary rhythms."[700] Nijinsky also felt a particular sympathy with Roerich and, according to Bronislava Nijinska, "the only time Vaslav appeared relaxed during rehearsals was when he was with Roerich."[701] *Le Sacre du Printemps* was perhaps the most audacious and provocative production of the pre-World War I Diaghilev seasons and it shocked more than it delighted its Paris audience. Jacques-Emile Blanche referred to its "realism of trembling, huddled fear,"[702] while Jacques Rivière likened it to a "physical image of the tortures of the soul."[703]

The Tale of Tsar Saltan: *opera in three acts by Nikolai Rimsky-Korsakov with a libretto by Vladimir Belsky after a poem by Alexander Pushkin. Projected production for the Royal Opera House, Covent Garden, London in 1919 with designs by Nicholas Roerich.*

See No. 349 [R314] for plot summary.

883 [178; R741].
Costume Design for a Warrior, ca. 1919.
Gouache.

Signed and initialed lower left with the Russian monogram "NR" and in Latin script lower right: "N. Roerich."

12 x 9½ in., 30.5 x 24 cm.

Provenance: Alexander Yaremenko, New York, September, 1967.

Reproduced in A34, p. 359; I40, No. 92; I51, No. 202; I61, p. 204; and Yakovleva, *Teatralno-dekoratsionnoe iskusstvo N.K. Rerikha*, p. 221.

884 [179; R742].
Costume Design for a Standard Bearer, ca. 1919.
Gouache.

Signed and initialed lower right with the

883

884

885

Russian monogram "NR" and in Latin script lower left: "N. Roerich."
11 x 9½ in., 28 x 24 cm.
Provenance: Alexander Yaremenko, New York, 1965.
Reproduced in color in G61; M45; and Yakovleva, *Teatralno-dekoratsionnoe iskusstvo N.K. Rerikha*, p. 223.

885 [180; R743].
Costume Design for a Boyar's Wife, ca. 1919.
Gouache, ink, and pencil.
Signed lower right with the Russian monogram: "NR."
12 x 9½ in., 30.5 x 24 cm.
Inscribed upper right in Russian: "Scene IX."
Provenance: Alexander Yaremenko, New York, December, 1968.
Reproduced in color in G61; in black and white in Kiseleva, p. 56; N114; Yakovleva, *Teatralno-dekoratsionnoe iskusstvo N.K. Rerikha,* p. 222.

886 [R744].
Costume Design for a Gusli Player, ca. 1919.
Gouache and ink.
Signed lower right with the Russian monogram: "NR."
12 x 9½ in., 30.5 x 24 cm.
Provenance: Alexander Yaremenko, New York, December, 1968. Now in a private collection.
Reproduced in I40, No. 95; Yakovleva, *Teatralno-dekoratsionnoe iskusstvo N.K. Rerikha,* p. 222.

Snegurochka (The Snow Maiden): *opera in a prologue and four acts by Nikolai Rimsky-Korsakov after the play by Alexander Ostrovsky. Produced by the Civic Opera Company, Chicago, on 16 November, 1922, with incidental dances by the Bolm Ballet and designs by Nicholas Roerich.*
See No. 33 [R32] for plot summary.

886

888

887 [181; R745].
Costume Design for a Village Maiden, 1920.
Pencil, colored crayon, and India ink.
Signed with the Russian monogram and dated lower left: "NR 1920."
14 x 10 in., 35.5 x 25.5. cm.
Provenance: Alexander Yaremenko, New York, December, 1968.
Reproduced in I40, No. 91; J5, Lot 72; and Yakovleva, *Teatralno-dekoratsionnoe iskusstvo N.K. Rerikha,* p. 235.

888 [182; R746].
Costume Design for a Maiden, 1921.
Tempera.
Signed with the Russian monogram and dated lower left: "NR 1921."
19¼ x 8¼ in., 49 x 21 cm.
Provenance: Alexander Yaremenko, New York, 1965. Now in a private collection.
Reproduced in *Mysl,* Riga, 1939, No. 1, p. 66, where it is described as *Kupava;* I4, No. 90; Yakovleva, *Teatralno-dekoratsionnoe iskusstvo N.K. Rerikha,* p. 232.

889

887

889 [183; R747].
Costume Designs for Snegurochka and Tsar Berendei, 1921.
Gouache and gold paint.
Signed with the Russian monogram and dated lower left: "NR 1921."
12 x 9½ in., 30.5 x 24 cm.
Provenance: Alexander Yaremenko, New York, December, 1968.
Reproduced in I20, No. 75; I51, No. 203; Kiseleva, p. 58; I61, p. 204; Yakovleva, *Teatralno-dekoratsionnoe iskusstvo N.K. Rerikha,* p. 235.

890 [R748].
Costume Design for Snegurochka, ca. 1921.
Gouache, pencil, and ink.
13¾ x 10 in., 35 x 25.5 cm.
Provenance: Alexander Yaremenko, New York, September, 1967. Now in a private collection.
Reproduced in I20, No. 76; Yakovleva,

890

Teatralno-dekoratsionnoe iskusstvo N.K. Rerikha, p. 235.

Note: Completed in 1880, *Snegurochka* premiered in St. Petersburg in 1882. Rimsky-Korsakov's opera became especially popular at the turn of the century, coinciding with the revival of interest in Russia's indigenous culture supported by the artistic communities of Abramtsevo, Talashkino, and the World of Art. As Rimsky-Korsakov himself wrote: "My mild interest in the ancient Russian customs and heathen pantheism flamed up." [704] One of the most successful productions of *Snegurochka* was by Savva Mamontov's Private Opera Company in 1885 in Moscow with sets and costumes by Viktor Vasnetsov, and Roerich, no doubt, was familiar with these designs.

Roerich contributed to several productions of *Sneguruchka*. For example, in 1908 he designed sets for a performance at the Opéra Comique in Paris, and in 1912 designed the production of Alexander Ostrovsky's play of the same name at the Reineke Dramatic Theater in St. Petersburg.[705] Roerich also created several designs for a production of the opera scheduled for 1921 in Chicago, but because of the unavailability of the complete musical score, it was postponed until November, 1922 (ten months after the American premiere of the opera was held at the Metropolitan Opera in New York with designs by Boris Anisfeld). With Roerich's dynamic sets and costumes and with Anna Ludmila and Adolph Bolm in the lead dance roles, the Chicago interpretation "became the striking success of the season, artistically and financially." [706]

691 F5, Vol. 2, p. 129.
692 S. Makovsky: *Siluety russkikh khudozhnikov*, Prague: Nasha rech, 1922, p. 111.
693 B29, p. 111.
694 We would like to thank Elena Yakovleva for her commentary on this and other Roerich pieces in the collection.
695 Boris Kochno. Quoted in I15, p. 47.
696 Reconfirmed in letter from Elena Yakovleva to John E. Bowlt dated 15 April, 1997.
697 N. Rerikh: "Tsaritsa Nebesnaia (Stenopis Khrama Sv. Dukha v Talashkine)" in N. Rerikh: *Sobranie sochinenii*, M: Sytin, 1914, Book 1, p. 310.
698 S. Shcherbatov: "Russkie khudozhniki" in *Vozrozhdenie*, Paris, 1951, No. 18, p. 117.
699 S. Ernst: *N.K. Rerikh*, P: Obshchina Sv. Evgenii, 1918, pp. 80-81.
700 F37, p. 470.
701 F58, p. 461.
702 Quoted in I9, p. 42. Original source not given.
703 Ibid. For more information on Roerich and *Le Sacre du Printemps* see E. Yakovleva: "N.K. Rerikh i balet I.F Stravinskogo 'Vesna sviashchennaia'. K istorii pervoi postanovki" in G. Vagner et al., eds.: *Pamiatniki kultury. Novye otkrytiia 1992*, M: Nauka, 1993, pp. 275-85; also see P.C. van den Toorn: *Stravinsky and "The Rite of Spring,"* Berkeley: University of California Press, 1987.
704 From Rimsky-Korsakov's notes of 1880. Quoted in M. Calvocoressi and G. Abraham: *Masters of Russian Music*, New York: Tudor, 1944, p. 376.
705 See Nemo: "Stsenicheskie illiustratsii N. Rerikha k skazke A. Ostrovskogo" in *Novaia studiia*, SP, 1912, No. 2, pp. 9-10.
706 E. More: *Forty Years of Opera in Chicago*, New York: Liveright, 1930, p. 256.

ROZANOVA, Olga Vladimirovna

Born 21 June (3 July), 1886, Melenki, Vladimir Region, Russia; died 7 November, 1918, Moscow, Russia.

1896-1904 attended the Women's Gymnasium in Vladimir; 1904-09 attended Konstantin Yuon and Ivan Dudin's Art School in Moscow; 1907 audited the Bolshakov Painting and Sculpture Institute, Moscow; 1907-10 audited courses at CSIAI; 1911 moved to St. Petersburg; attended the Zvantseva Art School; in close contact with the Union of Youth, contributing to its journal; 1911-18 contributed to the "Union of Youth," "Tramway V," "0.10," "Jack of Diamonds," and other avant-garde exhibitions; 1912 made the acquaintance of Alexei Kruchenykh; 1912 onwards illustrated Cubo-Futurist books such as *Te li le* (SP, 1914) and *Zaumnaia gniga* [Transrational Gook] (M, 1915); 1914 met Marinetti in St. Petersburg; contributed to the "Prima Esposizione Libera Futurista Internationale" in Rome; 1915 executed fashion and textile designs, some of which she contributed to "Women Artists for the Victims of War" in Moscow; worked with Kruchenykh on the album *Voina* [War] (Petrograd, 1916); moved to Moscow; 1916-17 with Kazimir Malevich, Mikhail Matiushin, Liubov Popova, Nikolai Roslavets, et al. member of the Supremus group and secretary of its journal (not published); contributed to the last "Jack of Diamonds" exhibition; contributed poems to Kruchenykh's *Balos* (Tiflis, 1917); 1918 helped to decorate the Moscow streets and squares for May Day; member of IZO NKP; with Alexander Rodchenko in charge of its Art-Industry Sub-Section; helped to organize Svomas in several provincial towns; published in the newspaper *Anarkhiia* [Anarchy]; secretary of the Leftist Federation of the Professional Union of Artists and Painters and contributed to its first exhibition; contributed to Kruchenykh's "Exhibition of Moscow Futurists" in Tiflis; died of diptheria; December: posthumous exhibition opened as the "I State Exhibition" in Moscow with more than 250 of Rozanova's paintings and drawings.

Bibliography
I. Kliun: *Pervaia Gosudarstvennaia vystavka. Katalog posmertnoi vystavki kartin, etiudov, eskizov i risunkov O.V. Rozanovoi*. Catalog of posthumous exhibition within the "I State Exhibition" at the Art Salon, M: 1919.
A. Efros: "O.V. Rozanova" in *Profili*. M: Federatsiia, 1930, pp. 228-29. This article first appeared as an obituary to Rozanova under the title "Vo sled ukhodiashchim" in *Moskva. Zhurnal literatury i iskusstva*, M, 1919, No. 3, pp. 4-6.
K52, pp. 215-56.
N. Gurianova: "Na puti k novomu iskusstvu. Olga Rozanova" in *Iskusstvo*, M, 1989, No. 1, pp. 24-30.
V. Terekhina: "Nachalo zhizni tsvetochno aloi..." in *Panorama iskusstv*, M, 1989, No. 12, pp 38-62.
N. Gurianova: "Voennye graficheskie tsikly N. Goncharovoi i O. Rozanovoi" in *Panorama iskusstv*, M, 1989, No. 12, pp 63-88.
B109, pp. 81-98.
V. Terekhina: *Olga Rozanova 1886-1918*. Catalog of exhibition at the Helsingin Kaupungin Taidemuseo, Helsinki, 1992.
V. Terekhina: "Zhenshchina russkogo avangarda" in *Chelovek*, M, 1993, No. 6, pp. 128-31.
N. Gurianova: "Olga Rozanova: Colore Libero" in *Art e Dossier*, Florence, 1993, December, No. 85, pp. 37-43.
N. Gurianova: *Rozanova, Filonov, Tatlin, Goncharova, Larionov, Malevich, Kulbin*, M: Avant-Garde; and Paris: La Hune, 1994.
N. Gurianova: *Exploring Colour: Olga Rozanova and the Culture of the Russian Avant-garde, 1910-1918*, London: G+B Arts International, 1999.
K222, passim.
K234.
N. Gurianova: *Olga Rozanova i rannii russkii avangard*, M: Gileia, 2002.
A. Sarabianov and V. Terekhina: *Olga Rozanova. "Lefanta chiol...."*, M: RA / Palace Editions, 2002.
R. Mason: *Guerres: trois suites insignes sur un thème: Natalija Gontcharova, Ol'ga Rozanova, Aleksej Kruchenykh*. Catalog of exhibition at the Musée d'Art et d'histoire, Paris, 2003.
T. Goriacheva and V. Terekhina: *Olga Rozanova... Uvidet mir preobrazhennym*, M: Pinakoteka, 2007.

Olga Rozanova was one of the few members of the Russian avant-garde to translate and paraphrase the principles of Italian Futurism without imbuing them with extraneous ideas. She did not, for example, use the jocular non sequiturs that Mikhail Larionov liked to apply to his paintings such as *Boulevard Venus* (1912, private collection) or the Neo-Primitivist additions that Natalia Goncharova favored as in her *Bicyclist* (1912, RM). In her careful identification and application of the Italians' concepts of mechanical speed, explosivity, and mobility, Rozanova was joined — to some extent — by Malevich (cf. his *Knife-Grinder*, 1912, Yale University Art Gallery, New Haven) and by Ivan Kliun (cf. his *Ozonator*, 1912-14, RM). Still, by and large, she operated with this esthetic somewhat in isolation.

Rozanova derived the visual subject of her poster (No. 891 [R758]) from the force lines and collisions of an urban environment, emphasizing the articulations of dynamic space, just as she did in analogous paintings such as *Factory and Bridge* (1913, MOMA, New York). On this level, Rozanova brings to mind the parallel experiments of Alexandra Exter (cf. her *City at Night* of 1915 in the RM), a process that led to her remarkable Suprematist pieces of 1916 onwards. In fact, Rozanova was among the first of the Russian avant-garde to advocate a non-figurative art form and she had little patience with those who remained behind:

> Only the absence of honesty and of true love of art provides some artists with the effrontery to live on stale cans of artistic provisions stocked up for years, and, year in year out, until they are fifty, to mutter about what they had first started to talk about when they were twenty.[707]

891

Foreign to the the philosophical under-pinnings of Vasilii Kandinsky, Malevich and Mikhail Matiushin, Rozanova's visual deductions are calculated and formal, based upon sharp juxtapositions of colors without allusion to the traditional narrative or perspectival role of color and form, especially in her abstract color painting of 1917-18. Occasionally, Rozanova applied the term "Suprematist" to figurative works (cf. *Metronome* and *Oil-Stove* of 1915-16 in the TG), but she was consistent and rational in her methodology whether in paintings, drawings, or book designs. Her premature death in 1918 was "one less world in the universe,"[708] for, as Kliun wrote in his obituary,

> Her ever searching soul, her exception-ally developed sense of intuition could never compromise with the old forms and always protested against all repetition whether in everyday life or in art.[709]

891 [R758].
Poster for The First World Productions by the Futurists of the Theater, 1913.
Color lithograph.
Signed lower left in the plate in Russian: "O. Rozanova."
35⅞ x 25¾ in., 91 x 65.5 cm.
Inscriptions (as part of the design) in Russian read: "Union of Youth Society of Artists. The First World Productions by the Futurists of the Theater. 2, 3, 4, 5 December, 1913. Luna Park Theater. 3, Officers' Street." The words "Futur teatr" [Future Theater] can be distinguished within the central image.
Provenance: Viktor Kholodkov, Moscow, 1989.
Reproduced in color in B115, plate 58; and in black and white in A34, pp. 366; I26, p. 50; I60, p. 20.

Note: The poster is for the Union of Youth's presentation of the two Cubo-Futurist spectacles at the Luna Park Theater, St. Petersburg: Vladimir Maiakovsky's *Vladimir Maiakovsky. A Tragedy* on 2 and 4 December (designed by Pavel Filonov and Iosif Shkolnik) and the Kruchenykh / Matiushin / Malevich opera *Victory over the Sun* on 3 and 5 December. For commentary see the entries for Ermolaeva, Filonov, and Malevich.[710]

Rozanova as contributor:
892 [R760].
Designer unknown: *Poster Advertising the "First Six State Exhibitions Organized by IZO NKP", Moscow, 1918.*
Black on white lithograph.
32¼ x 21⅝ in., 82 x 55 cm.
Inscriptions provide details of six exhibitions organized by the Visual Arts Department of the People's Commissariat of Enlightenment at various locations in downtown Moscow.

Note: IZO NKP organized twenty-one exhibitions of paintings, drawings and sculptures in 1918-21 — all in Moscow. They covered a wide range of styles, both moderate and radical, although the first in the series, the "1st Posthumous Exhibition of Paintings by Comrade O.V. Rozanova" (as it is described here), which opened in December, 1918, was one of the most important. It showed 250 works of all periods and was accompanied by a catalog introduced by Kliun. Among the other exhibitions listed on this poster, the 5th (with contributions by Vladimir Bekhteev, Vasilii Kandinsky, Kliun, Aristarkh Lentulov, Antoine Pevsner, Rodchenko, Varvara Stepanova, et al.) and the 6th (engravings by Elizaveta Kruglikova, Ignatii Nivinsky, Leonid Pasternak, Vladimir Favorsky, et al.)

892

are also worthy of attention. The most remarkable of the entire twenty-one was the "X State Exhibition: Non-Objective Creativity and Suprematism" (1919) at which the latest experiments in painting and graphics by the leaders of the avant-garde — Kliun, Malevich, Popova, Rodchenko, the late Rozanova, Stepanova et al. — were shown along with the accompanying manifestos.[711]

707 O. Rozanova: "Osnovy novogo tvorchestva i prichiny ego neponimaniia" in *Soiuz molodezhi*, SP, 1913, March, p. 20. Translation in B12, p. 109.
708 Yu. Annenkov: "Teatr chistogo metoda." Manuscript in RGALI, f. 2618, op. 1, ed. khr. 14, L. 173.
709 Kliun, *Pervaia Gosudarstvennaia vystavka*, p. III.
710 For reproductions of Rozanova's graphic work from the same period see, for example, B21, passim; B73, pp. 125-27; K85, pp. 404, 405.
711 For translation of the statements see B12, pp. 138-51.

SAPUNOV, Nikolai Nikolaevich

Born 17 (29) December, 1880, Moscow, Russia; died 14 June, 1912, Terrioki, Finland (now Zelenogorsk, near St. Petersburg, Russia).

Uncle of Sergei Kostin. 1893-1901 attended the MIPSA, studying under Nikolai Kasatkin, Konstantin Korovin, Isaak Levitan, Leonid Pasternak, and Valentin Serov; late 1890s close to Pavel Kuznetsov; 1900-01 acquainted with Savva Mamontov; 1901-02 worked as a set painter under Viktor Simov at the Bolshoi Theater, Moscow; 1902 contributed to the "World of Art" exhi-bition; visited Italy, Austria, Germany, and Poland; 1902-03 designed productions for Mamontov's Opera Company; 1904 contri-buted to the "Crimson Rose" exhibition in Saratov; 1904-11 attended IAA; 1905 designed production of *Evgenii Onegin* at the Girsh Theater, Moscow; started to collaborate with Vsevolod Meierkhold; designed the December issue of the journal *Vesy* [Scales]; 1907 contributed to the "Blue Rose" exhibition in Moscow; member of the Society of Free Esthetics; 1908 member of the Union of Russian Artists; 1909 onward active as a designer in St. Petersburg theaters; 1910 with Mikhail Kuzmin, Meierkhold, and Sergei Sudeikin founded the House of Interludes; resigned from the Union of Russian Artists and joined the new World of Art society; 1912 drowned in a boating accident; 1912-13 posthumous exhibition organized by the World of Art in Moscow and St. Petersburg.

Bibliography
V. Briusov et al.: *N. Sapunov*, M: Karyshev, 1916.
M. Voloshin et al.: *Pamiati N.N. Sapunova*, P: Apollon, 1916.
M. Alpatov and E. Gunst: *N. Sapunov*, M: Iskusstvo, 1965.
E. Gunst: *N.N. Sapunov*, M: Izobrazitelnoe iskusstvo, 1974.

J. Bowlt: "The Blue Rose: Russian Symbolism in Art" in *The Burlington Magazine*, London, 1976, August, pp. 566-74.
M. Kiselev: "Iskusstvo Sapunova" in *Iskusstvo*, M, 1981, No. 3, pp. 60-67.
K. Rudnitsky: "Nikolai Sapunov" in G50, 1981, pp. 230-44.
D. Kogan: *Nikolai Sapunov*, M: Iskusstvo, 1998.
I. Gofman: *Nikolai Sapunov*, M, 2003.
I. Gofman: *Nikolai Sapunov 1880-1912*. Catalog of exhibition at the TG, 2003.

Although Sapunov started his career as a studio painter, playing a leading role in the Blue Rose group of Symbolist artists in Moscow, he quickly turned his attention to the theater. Together with Sergei Sudeikin, Sapunov joined Vera Komissarzhevskaia's Theater in St. Petersburg at the beginning of 1906, where he collaborated with Vsevolod Meierkhold on a number of projects — culminating in the historic production of Alexander Blok's play *Balaganchik* [Fairground Booth] in December, 1906.[712] This event marked a high point in the development of the Symbolist theater in Russia and also pointed forward to Meierkhold's concept of theatricality that he continued to elaborate throughout the 1910s and 1920s.

In the winter of 1910 and the spring of 1911, Sapunov affirmed his decisive move from studio painting to stage design by contributing sets and costumes to five separate productions in St. Petersburg. Vivid color contrasts, a sardonic wit, and a love of the exotic characterized these spectacles, which included Fedor Komissarzhevsky's interpretation of *Le Bourgeois Gentilhomme* for the Nezlobin Theater in 1911. In all these productions Sapunov was successful as a decorator, because he was able to apply his artistic conception to the ethos of a given play and to regard the stage as a dynamic, three-dimensional art form. It is a matter of conjecture as to how Sapunov's decorative art would have evolved had he lived, the more so since Diaghilev wanted him to design a production for the Saisons Russes. In his obituary, Alexandre Benois wrote:

> Death has snatched away our wonderful painter N.N. Sapunov, a genuine colorist among Russian artists, a magician who compelled colors to sound and to sing in their charming musicality.[713]

Uncle Vanya. Scenes from Country Life: drama by Anton Chekhov in four acts projected, but not produced, in 1908, with designs by Nikolai Sapunov.
See No. 606 [R859] for plot summary.

893 [184; R762].
Set Design for Act II, The Dining-Room in the Serebriakov House, 1908.
Oil on canvas.
Signed lower right in black paint in Russian: "N. Sapunov."
19⅝ x 26¾ in., 50 x 68 cm.
Other inscription lower right prior to the signature in black paint in Russian: "Uncle

893

Vania. Act 2. 1908."
Provenance: Evgenii Gunst, Moscow, 1981.
Reproduced in A34, p. 370; I77, p. 145. A close version is in the BTM.
The attribution to Sapunov has been questioned.

Note: The connection of this design with Sapunov and *Uncle Vania* is tentative. If the attribution and date are correct, then Sapunov was already an experienced stage designer, having worked on Humperdinck's *Hansel and Gretel* (1904), Wedekind's *Dance of Death* (1907), and, above all, Kommisarzhevskaia's productions of Henrik Ibsen's *Hedda Gabler* and Alexander Blok's *Fairground Booth* in 1906. In this interior, assumed to be for the dining-room, Sapunov is, to some extent, paraphrasing his main set for the *Fairground Booth* with its ornate wallpaper, central doorway, table, and window on the right. Describing this design or one like it, the late Evgenii Gunst observed that the "little green flowers protrude importunately from the fancy wallpaper, capable of driving any living person out of the interior."[714]

Le Bourgeois Gentilhomme: comedy-ballet by Jean-Baptiste Molière. Produced by Fedor Komissarzhevsky at the Nezlobin Theater, Moscow, on 1 September, 1911, with designs by Nikolai Sapunov.
See No. 288 [NIRE] for plot summary.

894 [R763].
Costume Design for the Turk, ca. 1911.
Watercolor and pencil.
11¾ x 9¼ in., 29.9 x 23.5 cm.
Inscriptions in pencil in Russian: upper right:

894

"12 Turks (in fours)"; top margin to the left: a transposed column of twelve names (actors?); "12" to the left of the figure and elsewhere instructions to the dressmaker.
Provenance: Yakov Rubinshtein, Moscow, March, 1972.
Reproduced in I40, No. 96; I51, No. 204.

Princess Turandot: drama by Carlo Gozzi in three acts produced by Fedor Komissarzhevsky at the Nezlobin Theater, Moscow, on 23 October, 1912, with designs by Nikolai Sapunov (completed by Anatolii Arapov).
See No. 39 [R38] for plot summary.

895

895 [R764].
Costume Design for an Attendant to
Princess Turandot Carrying a Fan, ca. 1912.
Watercolor and black ink.
13¾ x 10 in., 35 x 25.5 cm.
Other inscriptions: the reverse of the work
carries the label of the "World of Art"
exhibition for January, 1913 (St.
Petersburg): "No. 394. Author: N. Sapunov.
Title: costume for 'Princess Turandot'.
Owner: Address: January, 1913."
Provenance: Evgenii Gunst, Moscow, 1981.
Reproduced in I51, No. 205. Other
costumes for *Princess Turandot* in the RM,
the GMTMA, the TG, and Russian private
collections have been reproduced, for
example, in *Stolitsa i usadba*, P, 1916, No.
57, p. 18; B1, Vol. 10, Book 2, p. 213; G31,
No. 190; A13, Vol. 4, p. 208.

Note: From all reports, Sapunov's designs
for *Princess Turandot* were vivid and
dynamic and constituted a contrasting
precedent to the more famous production
of *Princess Turandot* by Evgenii Vakhtangov
staged at the Third Studio of the Moscow
Art Theater in 1922 with designs by Ignatii
Nivinsky.   Sapunov died before the
Komissarzhevsky production of *Princess
Turandot* premiered, so his designs were
modified and realized by his friend and
fellow painter Anatolii Arapov.

712 For a color reproduction of Sapunov's painting based
     on his set for Blok's play see Gunst and Alpatov,
     Sapunov, plate 8. For an analysis of Sapunov's
     designs for the production see I. Gutt: "Uslovnyi teatr
     i formirovanie zhivopisnoi sistemy N.N. Sapunova" in
     T. Kovalenskaia, ed.: *Voprosy russkogo i sovetskogo
     iskusstva*, M: the TG, 1973, No. 2, pp. 119-37.
713 A. Benois: "Khudozhestvennye itogi" in *Rech*
     (1913). Quoted in Gunst, *N.N. Sapunov,*
     unpaginated.
714 Gunst and Alpatov, *Sapunov*, p. 11.

SARIAN, Martiros Sergeevich

Born 16 (28) November, 1880, Nor-
Nakhichevan (Rostov-on-Don), Russia; died
5 May, 1972, Erevan, Armenia.

1897-1903 attended MIPSA; 1903-04
attended the studios of Konstantin Korovin
and Valentin Serov; 1904 contributed to the
"Crimson Rose" exhibition in Saratov; in
contact with Symbolist artists such as
Viktor Borisov-Musatov, Pavel Kuznetsov,
and Kuzma Petrov-Vodkin; 1907 contributed
to the "Blue Rose" exhibition; 1908-14
exhibited regularly, e.g., at the shows
organized by the *Golden Fleece* journal and,
after 1910, with the World of Art group;
favored an "orientalist" or Primitivist style;
1910-11 traveled in Turkey and Egypt; 1912
contributed to the "Second Post-
Impressionist Exhibition" in London; 1913
visited Persia; 1916 lived briefly in Tiflis,
where he married Lusik Agaian, daughter of
a celebrated Armenian writer; 1917
returned to Nor-Nakhichevan; 1919
organized a museum of Armenian art in
Rostov-on-Don; 1921 director of the
National Armenian Museum in Erevan;
1926-28 lived in Paris; late 1920s onwards
continued to contribute to exhibitions at
home and abroad; began to work as a stage
designer; 1937 made a mural for the
"Exposition Internationale" in Paris; 1940s-
60s continued to paint and exhibit.

Bibliography
M. Sarian: *Iz moei zhizni*, M: Izobrazitelnoe
iskusstvo, 1970 and later editions. French
translation: *Fragments de ma vie,* M: Progress,
1976.
A. Kamensky: *Etiudy o khudozhnikakh Armenii,*
Erevan: Sovetakan Grokh, 1979, pp. 5-77.
Sh. Khachatrian: *Martiros Sarian,* Erevan:
Sovetakhan Grokh, 1979; second edition 1980.
P. Hulten: *Sarian.* Catalog of exhibition at the
Centre Georges Pompidou, Paris, 1980.
Sh. Khachatrian: *Martros Sarian. Izbrannye
proizvedeniia,* M: Sovetskii khudozhnik, 1983.
A. Kamensky: *Martiros Saryan,* L: Aurora, 1985.
L. Mirzoian and Sh. Khachatrian: *Tsvety,* M:
Sovetskii khudozhnik, 1987.
S. Khachatrian and L. Mirzoian: *Sarian,* L: Aurora,
1987.
A. Agasian: *Martiros Sarian. Rannee tvorchestvo,*
Erevan: Akademiia nauk Armenii, 1992.
I. Gofman: *Martiros Sarian. Skazki i sny 1903-
1908.* Catalog of exhibition at the TG and the RM,
1995.
V. Rasdolskaja: *Martiros Sarjan,* Bournemouth,
England: Parkstone, 1998.
J.-L. Andral et al.: *Sarian: Au pays du soleil volant.*
Catalog of exhibition at the Musée Picasso,
Antibes, 2003.
R. Sarian: *Sarian i Rossiia,* Erevan: Tigran Mets,
2006.

While playing a substantial role in Moscow
artistic life, especially before the
Revolution, Sarian stands somewhat apart
from the mainstream of Russian art
inasmuch as his national identity is

Armenian and his artistic temperament
"Oriental." Primarily a studio painter, Sarian
rarely turned to stage design and, in fact,
his first major scenic undertaking came as
late as 1927 with the production of the
fairy-tale ballet *Ziuleika* in Paris; and in the
1930s he designed a number of pieces
(only some realized) such as Alexander
Spendiarov's opera *Almast* in Odessa in
1930 and Aro Stepanian's *The Bold Nazar*
in Erevan in 1934. Occasionally, Sarian was
also active as a book illustrator and
designer: of particular note are his images
for the miscellany *Armianskie skazki*
[Armenian Fairy-tales] (several editions) and
the covers for Avetik Isaakian's collection of
poems (1929) and Ovanes Tumanian's
Skazki [Fairy-tales] (1930).

The hallmark of Sarian's art is the
particularly vivid and emphatic combination
of colors that he used to accentuate the
outwards surfaces and forms of concrete
reality, whether the arid slopes of
mountains, the sultry alleys of an Armenian
village, or the brilliant blueness of the
southern sky. Sarian reaffirmed the vitality
of everyday existence, although, in the late
1930s and '40s he was often criticized for
his exuberant and "loose" style, which had
more to do with Gauguin and Matisse than
with Socialist Realism. Sarian did much for
the art of Armenia and, as a mark of respect
to his patriotism, a Sarian Muscum was
opened in Erevan in 1967.

**Natan Altman: *Caricature of Martiros
Sarian. ca. 1913.*** See No. 15 [R14].

The Golden Cockerel: *opera-ballet in three
acts with music by Nikolai Rimsky-
Korsakov and libretto by Vladimir Belsky
based on a fairy-tale by Alexander Pushkin.
Produced at the Moscow Stanislavsky
Opera Theater on 4 May, 1932, with
costume designs and one set (Act II) by
Martiros Sarian (sets for Acts I and III by
Sergei Ivanov).*
See No. 299 [R268] for plot summary.

896

896 [R765].
Costume Design for the Cyclops, 1931.
Watercolor and pencil.
Signed and dated lower right in Russian:
"M. Sarian, 1931."
13 x 10 in., 33 x 25.5 cm.
Inscribed lower right in pencil in Russian:
"'Golden Cockerel'. From the mythology
for the 'Golden cockerel'."
Provenance: Garabed Basmadjian, Paris,
March 12, 1983.
The BTM possesses other costumes for
this production.

Note: Stanislavsky had begun to think of a
production of *The Golden Cockerel* at his
Opera Theater as early as 1929, but was
unable to find an appropriate artist. At first he
thought of inviting one of the Palekh artists,
discussed the project with Alexander
Golovin, and then invited Sarian after seeing
one of his landscapes in the Moscow
apartment of the actor Nikolai Podgornyi in
1931. Even though Sarian's maquette for the
set in Act II looked like a "painted cake"[715]
and contrasted sharply with Ivanov's more
prosaic renderings for the other acts,
Stanislavsky enthused about and liked both
the set and the costumes. Unfortunately, the
disagreements between Sarian and Ivanov
and the fact that his ambitious set required a
complicated scene change and technical
apparatus impeded the production and it was
taken off after only a short run.[716]

715 According to Sh. Khachatrian: *Teatralno-dekorativnoe iskusstvo Sovetskoi Armenii*, M, 1979, p. 39.
716 For more information see ibid., pp. 38-44. Also see P. Rumiantsev: *Stanislavsky i opera*, M, 1969, pp. 450-51.

SEREBRIAKOFF, Alexandre
(Serebriakov, Alexander
Borisovich)

Born 7 (20) September, 1907 at
"Neskuchnoe," the family estate, Kursk
Region, near Kharkov, Ukraine; died 10
January, 1995, Paris, France.

Son of Zinaida Serebriakova and nephew of
Nicola Benois. After her husband's death in
1919, Serebriakova moved to France in
1924 and was joined there by her son in
1925. 1925 onwards often assisted Nicola
Benois with stage designs, e.g., for
productions by Ida Rubinstein's company in
Paris; 1926 painted geographical maps as
decorative components for temporary
exhibitions at the Musée des Arts
Décoratifs in Paris; contributed to the
"Exposition d'Art Russe," Paris; 1931 after
the "Exposition Coloniale" in Paris painted
decorative panels for the Musée des
Colonies in Paris; 1930s traveled widely in
France and Belgium painting landscapes;
illustrated books, especially for children,
such as *Notre France (Album pour enfants)*
(1934); *Venok* [A Wreath] (poetry by Lolli
Lvov, 1938) and *The Twilight of the Gods*
(1938); also worked as a designer for
French movies; 1941 onwards designed
architectural projects for, and painted
interiors of, the Château de Groussay;
thereafter, depicted many interiors of
châteaux and other residences in France,
England, and Austria; 1947 made
maquettes for the ballet *La Sylphide* for the
Ballets Roland Petit in Paris; 1951 painted
scenes from the Bal Costumé organized by
Charles de Beistegui at the Palazzo Labia in
Venice; 1969 painted scenes from the Bal
Oriental given by the Baron de Redé at
l'Hôtel Lambert on the Ile St. Louis in Paris;
1985 with his sister Catherine Serebriakoff,
retrospective exhibition in Paris; 1987
retrospective exhibition at the Didier Aaron
Gallery, New York.

Bibliography
A. de Gaigneron: "Les Sérébriakoff" in
Connaissance des Arts, Paris, 1985, May, No. 399.
H. Dorsey: "The Fête Goes on in Paris" in
International Herald Tribune, Paris, 1985, 28 May.
T. Serebriakova: "Kartiny minuvshego" in
Sovetskii balet, M, 1988, No. 3, pp. 33-37.
P. Mauries: *Alexandre Sérébriakoff. Portraitiste
d'intérieurs*, Milan: Galleria Franco Maria Ricci,
1990.
V. Shleev: "Nasledie semii Serebriakovykh" in
Otchizna, M, 1991, No. 3, pp. 20-25.
G. de Brissac: *Alexandre Sérébriakoff.
Portraitiste d'intérieurs*. Catalog of exhibition at
the Musée national des Châteaux de Malmaison
et Bois-Préau, Paris, 1994.
M73, Vol. 26, pp. 83-84.
M83.
M85.
V. Shleev: "Mnogogrannyi talant. Pamiati
Aleksandra Serebriakova" in *Golos Rodiny*, M,
1995, No. 3, p. 8.
H34, pp. 519, 520.
H41, passim.

Alexandre Serebriakoff, his sister
Catherine, and Dimitri Bouchène
represented the last generation of the
World of Art artists with their disciplined
combinations of graceful decoration and
historical accuracy. Like his great-uncle,
Alexandre Benois, Serebriakoff was also
drawn to the Baroque and Neo-Classical
styles, especially as reflected in estate
architecture and interiors, subjects that he
often approached in a theatrical manner,
stressing integration of outer ornament and
inner structure. At the same time,
Serebriakoff also worked with more
intimate formats such as book design, and
his illustrations and covers for French and
Russian editions from the 1930s onwards
are simple and enchanting, e.g., the green,
white, and black cover for Boris
Panteleimonov's *Zelenyi shum* (Paris:
Podorozhnik,1947). Like the original World
of Art artists, especially Alexandre Benois,

Zinaida Serebriakova: *Portrait of
Alexandre Serebriakoff, the Artist's Son,
1935.* See No. 906 [R774].

Zinaida Serebriakova: *Portrait of Alexandre
Serebriakoff, 1950.* See No. 906a [NIRE].

Serebriakoff was an expert in the ways of watercolor, preferring its malleability and lightness to the heavier quality of oil. In fact, in using the medium of the watercolor — translucent and unstable — Serebriakoff seemed to be evoking the very fragility of the bygone eras of elegant luxury that so enchanted and inspired him.

The Ball at the Palazzo Labia: *a fête and masked ball organized by Carlos (Charlie) de Beistegui at the Palazzo Labia, Venice, on 3 September, 1951, with costumes by Cecil Beaton, Christian Dior, Jacques Fath, Oliver Messel, et al.*

897

897 [185; R766].
The Ballroom Frescoed by G.B. Tiepolo: the Arrival of the Giants, 1951.
Watercolor, varnished.
Signed and dated lower left: "A. Serebriakoff 1951."
23⅝ x 17¾ in., 60 x 45 cm.
Other inscription: "Bal du Palazzo Labia, Venise, le 3 septembre, 1951. L'Entrée des Géants."
Reproduced in color in B115, plate 198; and in black and white in *Connaissance des Arts,* Paris, 1964, January, No. 143, p. 65; and in M71.
Provenance: the artist, Paris, October, 1981. Now in a private collection.
Reproductions of analogous scenes of another sumptuous ball by Serebriakoff are in *L'Oeil,* Paris, 1971, December, No. 204.

Note: Serebriakoff commented as follows:

> The giants — a group of fantastic black and white figures — representing the ghosts of Venice — were made up of Salvador Dalí, Christian Dior and his suite. The smallest figure was Dior.
>   Watching them we have Lady Diana Cooper & the Baron de Cabrol, costumed as Antony & Cleopatra, for a

group tableau based on Tiepolo's mural in the Palazzo Labia;
      Carlos de Beistegui to the left, in red, dressed as a Procurator of the Venetian Republic and towering over his guests thanks to eight inch platform shoes hidden by his robes. He is leaning on a cane so as not to fall over;
      Johnny de Beistegui stands next to him, receiving guests;
      AS [Alexandre Serebriakoff] in the foreground holding his sketching pad, and dressed in a traditional Venetian carnival mask & costume;
      Princess Paley as a canteen-keeper in a blue & red outfit;
      Cecil Beaton as an abbot in black robes;
      Orson Welles, standing behind C. Beaton with plumed headgear.[717]

The ghosts or giants "of Venice" that Serebriakoff rendered so skillfully in his picture would seem to be arriving from Barcelona rather than from Venice, for they belong to an ancient Spanish tradition. This is evident from Sacheverell Sitwell's description of the procession preceding a bullfight that he once attended in "ancient Tarragona":

> [The procession] consisted of gigantes and cabezudos (giants and big-heads), with several bands playing feverishly, many ecclesiastics, and long lines of children holding candles. The giants looked almost terrifying, tottering down the long dark street from the cathedral. The two tallest, a king and a queen, must be eighteen to twenty feet high...
>   So popular did the Gigantes used to be that the old houses of Barcelona were built with especially high doorways so that the giants could enter and dance in the courtyards. There are these Gigantes all over Spain.[718]

898 [186; R767].
The Arrival of the Couturier Jacques Fath (Dressed as the Sun King), His Wife Geneviève, and Other Guests at the Palazzo Labia, 1951.
Watercolor, varnished.
Signed lower right in black ink: "A. Serebriakoff." Also signed and dated lower left: "A. Serebriakoff, 1951."
23⅝ x 17¾ in., 60 x 45 cm.
Provenance: the artist, Paris, October, 1981. Now in a private collection.
Reproduced in color in B115, plate 197; M157, p. 97; and in black and white in H32, p. 410; M83.

Serebriakoff commented as follows:

> Part of this watercolor represents the arrival of the couturier Jacques Fath (dressed as the Sun King) and his wife Geneviève in a white and gold dress.
>   Princess Radziwill in a white dress standing next to an "Inca."

898

> Countess de Mun in a blue costume (Tiepolo);
>   Jean Tierney, as a canteen-keeper in red, white and blue;
>   Mme. Edouard Bourdet, in a red dress, to the right;
>   In the door, three princesses — 2 were Italians and the 3rd the Vicomtesse de Ribes;
>   Emilio Terry in the window to the left, dressed as J.-J. Rousseau in a lounge robe with leopard skin lapels and a matching night cap;
>   Johnny de Beistegui (nephew and heir to C. de Beistegui) on the balcony dressed as Puncinello with a long, high, white hat;
>   to the left and the right on the embankment, the Italian police guarding the great, carved & gilded ceremonial gondolas lent by the City of Venice.[719]

According to another source:

> Après avoir magnifiquement restauré le palais Labia, acquis en 1948, Charles de Beistegui — don Carlos — y convia le Gotha international en 1951 pour un bal *in costume del settecento, maschere e domino* dont la Sérénissime gardera à jamais le souvenir. L'art photographique n'aurait pas rendu la même nostalgie les épisodes de la fête la plus anachronique du siècle. Abandonnant ses "natures mortes" et renouant avec les artifices du théâtre qui l'avaient fait connaître, Alexandre Sérébriakoff illustra principaux événements de cette folle nuit. Arrivés en gondole et accueillis par un maître de maison en Procurateur de la République, les masques envahirent le dix-huit salons de l'étage noble.[720]

899

900

899 [187; R768].
The Entrance of Arturo Lopez as the Emperor of China together with His Suite, 1951.
Watercolor, varnished.
Signed lower right in black ink: "A. Serebriakoff."
18¼ x 24⅜ in., 46.5 x 62 cm.
Other inscription: detailed and dated lower left: "Bal du Palazzo Labia, 3 sept., 1951."
Provenance: the artist. Paris, October, 1981. Now in a private collection.
Reproduced in M83.

Serebriakoff commented as follows:

Arturo Lopez's entrance was spectacular. The suite and its costumes were the creation of Georges Geffroy.
        A. Lopez carried in a palanquin, preceded by Baron A. de Rede dressed as the Chinese Ambassador;
        Mme. Lopez in a small open carriage surrounded by three princesses, one of them Princess Ghislaine de Polignac;
        Preceding the suite, dressed in a blue costume we have Enrico Lopez, cousin of Arturo Lopez;
        Georges Geffroy, closing the suite and holding The Bird of Paradise;
        To the right, towering above his guests, dressed in a red robe we have C. de Beistegui, next to him, in black, Mrs. Winston Churchill.[721]

Note: The eighteenth-century Palazzo Labia (now the headquarters of RAI, the Italian broadcasting network) on the Fondamenta di Cannaregio in Venice, was famous for its extravagant balls and parties. Its last private owner, the Mexican-Spanish millionaire Carlos (Charles) de Beistegui, decided to continue

this tradition by organizing a spectacular masked ball there on 3 September, 1951, "the last great ball."[722] The costumes were intended to evoke the 1740s and the highlight of the evening was the reenactment by Lady Diana Cooper and Baron de Cabrol of the Anthony and Cleopatra tableau after G.B. Tiepolo's frescoes in the Palazzo's ballroom. According to one source:

A une heure du matin furent ouvertes les portes de la salle des fêtes. Accueillies par Antoine et Cléopatre — lady Diana Cooper et le baron de Cabrol — descendus des fresques de Tiepolo couvrant les immenses parois, les "entrées" se succédèrent, réglées par Boris Kochno et la princesse Nathalie Paley. Si la plus exotique fut celle de l'empereur et de l'impératrice de Chine, la plus nombreuse celle de l'ambassade du Grand Turc — quatre-vingts personnes! — l'entrée la plus onirique fut celle des "fantômes de Venise," masques blafards démesurés rêvés par Salvador Dali et Christian Dior (c'est Dior lui-même qui se cache sous le petit fantôme).[723]

900 [R769].
Design for a Private Theater at the Château de Groussay, 1945.
Watercolor and black ink.
Signed lower margin in black ink in French and dated: "A. Serebriakoff, mai, 1945."
15¾ x 13⅜ in., 40 x 34 cm.
Other inscription: lower margin in black ink: "Projet de Théâtre. pour le Pavillon de Pyramide à Groussay par E. Terry."
Provenance: the artist, Paris, October, 1981. Now in a private collection.
Reproduced in the magazine *La France Vie*, Paris: Librarie Plon, 1946.

Note: Charles de Beistegui, bought the Château de Groussay near Versailles in the late 1930s and "for the next three decades used it as a vehicle for his own genius for color and fantasy."[724] De Beistegui organized many social events at the Château to gratify his passion for the decorative arts and in the 1940s commissioned Serebriakoff and the Cuban-born architect Emilio Terry to design ornaments for the Château and follies in the park. One of their many projects was this one for a theater in a pyramid pavilion in the park, but to Terry's chagrin, the project was not implemented, even though a pyramid pavilion was built. In the 1950s, however, Terry did design and build a theater in one of the wing pavilions added to either side of the Château.

Giselle: *ballet pantomime in two acts by Vernoy de Saint-Georges, Théophile Gautier, and Jean Coralli, with music by Adolphe Adam. Projected, but not produced, in 1950 with designs by Alexandre Serebriakoff.*
See No. 152 [R126] for plot summary.

901 [R770].
Set Design for Act I, 1950.
Watercolor and pencil.
Signed lower left in ink in French and dated: "A. Serebriakoff, 1950."
17½ x 23¼ in., 44.3 x 59 cm.
Provenance: the artist, Paris, October, 1981.
Reproduced in color in M157, p. 97; and in black and white in M73, p. 94.

901

902

902 [R771].
Oriental Ball: The Staircase Leading to the
Grande Galerie d'Hercule, 1969.
Watercolor, black ink, and pencil.
Signed and dated in ink: "A. Serebriakoff 69."
17⅛ x 12⅜ in., 43.4 x 31.5 cm.
Provenance: the artist. Paris, October,
1981. Now in a private collection.
Reproduced in F107, p. 149. A variant is
reproduced in L'Oeil, Paris, 1971, No. 204,
December, p. 40.

Note: The Baron Alexis de Rédé (Rosenberg) organized the Oriental Ball at his
home, the Hôtel Lambert (former home of
the Czartoryski family on the Eastern tip of

the St. Louis Island, the smaller of the two
islands on the Seine in the center of Paris),
in December, 1969, and Serebriakoff
painted several pictures of the event. In this
particular scene the artist draws attention
to the procession up the stairs and past the
two tapestries based on cartoons by
Andrea Pozzo (1642-1709).

717 Letter from Alexandre Serebriakoff to John E.
     Bowlt dated 18 May 1987.
718 S. Sitwell: *Truffle Hunt with Sacheverell Sitwell,*
     London: Hale, 1953, pp. 171, 291.
719 Comments made by Alexandre Serebriakoff to
     Nina Lobanov-Rostovsky on 30 July, 1987, Paris.
720 Mauries: *Alexandre Sérébriakoff. Portraitiste*
     d'intérieurs, planche 22.
721 Ibid.
722 M. Blume: "When Paris Put on its Best Dress" in
     International Herald Tribune, Paris, 1987, 3
     August, p. 14.
723 Mauries: *Alexandre Sérébriakoff. Portraitiste*
     d'intérieurs, planche 23.
724 C. Aslet: "Château de Groussay — The House of
     Juan de Beistegui" in *Country Life,* London, 1987,
     18 June, p. 156. Juan (Johnny) was the nephew
     and heir of Charles de Beistegui.

SEREBRIAKOVA, Zinaida Evgenievna

Born 28 November (10 December), 1884,
at "Neskuchnoe," the family estate, Kursk
Region, near Kharkov, Ukraine; died 19
November, 1967, Paris.

Daughter of the sculptor Evgenii
Alexandrovich Lanceray, niece of Alexandre
Benois, sister of Evgenii Evgenievich
Lanceray and Nikolai Lanceray, an architect,
and cousin of Nadia and Nicola Benois. 1866
after the death of the father, the family moved
to St. Petersburg; 1901 Zinaida graduated
from the Kolomenskii Women's Gymnasium,

St. Petersburg, and entered Princess Mariia
Tenisheva's Art School; 1902-03 visited Italy;
1903-05 studied under Osip Braz; 1905
married Boris Serebriakov; 1905-06 studied at
the Académie de la Grande Chaumière, Paris;
1906-17 lived in St. Petersburg;1910
contributed to the "Union of Russian Artists"
exhibition and the "Exhibition of Contemporary Female Portraits"; 1911 began to
exhibit regularly with the World of Art group;
1914 visited Switzerland and Italy; 1916 with
Evgenii Lanceray, Alexandre Benois, et al.
worked on interior designs for the Kazan
Railroad Station, Moscow; 1918-20 lived in
Kharkov; 1919 husband died; 1920 returned
to Petrograd; 1921-24 painted and drew
pictures concerned with the ballet, especially
portraits of ballerinas at the Mariinsky Theater,
Petrograd; 1924 emigrated to Paris; took part
in the "Exhibition of Russian Painting," New
York; 1920s-60s continued to paint and
exhibit.

Bibliography
S. Ernst: *Z.E. Serebriakova,* P: Akvilon, 1922.
A. Savinov: *Serebriakova.* Catalog of exhibition
organized by the Union of Artists of the USSR,
M, 1965.
V. Lapshin: *Serebriakova,* M: Sovetskii
khudozhnik, 1969.
A. Savinov: *Zinaida Evgenievna Serebriakova,* L:
Khudozhnik RSFSR, 1973.
V. Kniazeva: *Zinaida Evgenievna Serebriakova,* M:
Izobrazitelnoe iskusstvo, 1979.
N. Senkovskaia, comp.: *Z. Serebriakova.* Catalog
of exhibition at the TG, 1986.
N. Aleksandrova: *Risunki Zinaidy Evgenievny*
Serebriakovoi. Catalog of exhibition at the GMII,
1987.
V. Kniazeva, comp.: *Zinaida Serebriakova. Pisma.*
Sovremenniki o khudozhnike, M: Izobrazitelnoe
iskusstvo, 1987.
C. Mons et al.: *Z. Sérébriakova.* Catalog of
exhibition organized by the Alliance Russe, Paris,
1995.
N. Aleksandrova: *Zinaida Serebriakova,* M: Belyi
gorod, 2001.
V. Drozdova: *Serebriakova,* M: Terra – Knizhnyi
klub, 2001.
A. Benois et al.: *Zinaida Serebriakova.* Catalog of
exhibition at the Nashchokin House Gallery, M,
2003.
V. Kruglov: *Zinaida Evgenievna Serebriakova,* SP:
Zolotoi vek, 2004.
E. Efremova: *Zinaida Serebriakova,* M: Art-rodnik,
2006.
A. Rusakova: *Zinaida Serebriakova,* M: Iskusstvo
XXI vek, 2006.
A. Rusakova: *Zinaida Serebriakova,* M: Molodaia
gvardiia, 2008; second edition, 2011.
A. Benois et al.: *Zinaida Serebriakova: Zhivopis,*
grafika. Catalog of exhibition at the Nashchokin
House Gallery, M, 2010-11.

A leading member of the revived World of
Art group, Serebriakova was a champion of
the restrained, esthetic identifiable with the
best works of Alexandre Benois, Mstislav
Dobujinsky, and Konstantin Somov.
Serebriakova applied her talents with
particular success to the female nude and
the portrait, especially of ballerinas,
patronesses, and fellow artists during the

1920s; in their spontaneity and intimacy some of her renderings of the Mariinsky dancers, such as Ekaterina Geidenreikh and Lidia Ivanova, bring to mind the ballet compositions of Edgar Degas. Serebriakova often imbued her portraits with a melancholic, contemplative mood, something especially noticeable in her several self-portraits. However, as one observer has remarked of Serebriakova in the early 1920s:

> In spite of her great grief and insuperable difficulties in everyday life she looked much younger than her years and one was struck by the freshness and color of her face. The deep inner life which she led created an outward charm that was impossible to resist.[725]

904

Georgii Vereisky: *Portrait of Zinaida Serebriakova,* **1922.** See No. 1126 [NIRE].

903 [NIRE].
Self-Portrait, **1925.**
Black and white lithograph.
18½ x 14¾ in., 47 x 37.5 cm.
Provenance: the artist's son, Alexandre Serebriakoff, Paris, October, 1981.

903

904 [R772].
Self-Portrait with Palette, **1925.**
Oil.
Signed and dated upper right corner: "Z. Serebriakova 1925."
28¾ x 23⅝ in., 73 x 60 cm.
Provenance: the artist's son, Alexandre Serebriakoff, Paris, October 20, 1981.
Reproduced in F107, p. 150; I51, No. 206; M175; M212. A similar self-portrait, dated 1956, in the collection of the Tula Regional Art Museum, is illustrated in S. Nechaeva, comp., *Tulskii oblastnoi khudozhestvennyi muzei,* L: Khudozhnik RSFSR, 1983, unpaginated. Several other Serebriakova self-portraits of the 1910s-20s have been reproduced, for example, in Ernst, *Z.E. Serebriakova,* passim; Kniazeva, *Zinaida Evgenievna Serebriakova,* p. 145; also see R. Drampian, *Gosudarstvennaia kartinnaia galereia Armenii,* M: Iskusstvo, 1982, p. 169.

905

905 [R775].
***Portrait of Alexandra Danilova as one of the Seven Demoiselles d'Honneur from "Le Mariage d'Aurore" in* La Belle au Bois Dormant, 1925.**
Pastel.
Signed and dated lower left in pencil: "Z. Serebriakova, Paris 1925."
23⅝ x 18⅛ in., 60 x 46 cm.
Other inscription: lower left: "Alexandra Danilova."
Provenance: the artist's son, Alexandre Serebriakoff, Paris, January, 1981.
Reproduced in color in F107, p. 151; N188, p. 42; and in black and white in I51, No. 207; M43 (c).

Note: Alexandra Dionisievna Danilova (1904-97) had recently arrived from Leningrad to join Sergei Diaghilev's company in Paris when Serebriakova painted this portrait. In 1925 Danilova danced as one of the Demoiselles d'Honneur in the last act of *La Belle au Bois Dormant* produced by Diaghilev in Paris with designs by Alexandre Benois, and this marked the beginning of her highly successful career as a dancer and teacher in Western Europe and the US. In this portrait, however, Serebriakova seems to have idealized Danilova, because after the production George Balanchine told Danilova: "Well, you are much too fat and you danced abominably."[726] Diaghilev told her the same thing — which quickly resolved her to lose weight and assume the svelte proportions that Serebriakova had already bestowed upon her.
    Serebriakova painted several portraits of Danilova both in Russia and in the West, one of the most charming of which is of Danilova in a costume for the ballet *The*

906

Serf Dancer (1922; reproduced in G33, plate 86). Danilova was also the subject of portraits by other Russian artists, including Alexandre Jacovleff.[727]

906 [R774].
Portrait of the Artist's Son, Alexandre Serebriakoff, 1935.
Oil on canvas.
Signed and dated lower left: "Paris 1935, Z. Serebriakova."
25¾ x 21¼ in., 65.5 x 54 cm.
Provenance: the artist's son, Alexander Serebriakoff, Paris, 20 October, 1981. Now in a private collection.
Reproduced in color in F107, p. 149; M157, p. 97 (see entries for Alexandre Serebriakoff).

906a

906a [NIRE].
Portrait of Alexandre Serebriakoff, 1950.
Pencil on white paper.
Initialed and dated lower right: "Z.S. 25 Nov. 1950."
12¼ x 10¼ in., 31 x 26 cm.
Provenance: the artist's son, Alexandre Serebriakoff, Paris, 20 October, 1981.

907 [R776].
Portrait of Georges Tcherkessoff, 1939.
Pastel.
Signed lower right in Russian: "Z. Serebriakova."
23⅝ x 18⅛ in., 60 x 46 cm.
Other inscription: lower left in Russian: "Yura Cherkesov October, 1939, Paris."
Provenance: the artist's son, Alexandre Serebriakoff, Paris, 20 October, 1981.
Reproduced in F107, p. 137; M212.
See entries for Georges Tcherkessoff.

908 [R773].
Portrait of Alexandre Benois, 1955.
Pastel.
22 x 18 in., 56 x 45.5 cm.
Inscribed upper left by Zinaida Serebriakova's daughter Ekaterina: "Alexandre Benois par Z. Serebriakova, Paris, 1955."
Provenance: the artist's son, Alexandre Serebriakoff, Paris, May, 1981. Now in a private collection.
Reproduced in color in F107, p. 120; I51, No. 33; M212.

Note: Benois was Serebriakova's uncle and the two artists moved in the same intellectual and social circles in St. Petersburg and Paris. This portrait of Benois (he was already 85) is one of the last artistic renderings of the great artist and critic by a fellow World of Art artist.

907

908

725 Letter from Galina Teslenko to Alexander Savinov dated 16 April, 1967. Quoted in Kniazeva, *Zinaida Evgenievna Serebriakova,* p. 150.
726 A. Twysden: *Alexandra Danilova,* London: Beaumont, 1945, p. 57.
727 A portrait by Jacovleff of Danilova in *Le Beau Danube* is reproduced as the frontispiece in ibid.

SEROV, Valentin Alexandrovich

Born 7 (19) January, 1865, St. Petersburg, Russia; died 22 November, 1911, Moscow, Russia.

Son of the composer Alexander Nikolaevich Serov and musician Valentina Bergman; 1872 following the death of his father lived in Munich with his mother; 1874 with his mother moved to Paris; took lessons from Ilia Repin there; 1875 spent the summer at Abramtsevo; 1875-76 attended Mai's Gymnasium in St. Petersburg; 1876 moved to Kiev; 1878 moved to Moscow; resumed art lessons from Repin; 1880-85 attended IAA, studying under Pavel Chistiakov; 1885 returned to Munich; visited Holland; late 1880s onward created many portraits of artists, actors, society ladies, etc.; 1894 painted portrait of Alexander III and his family; 1895 onward made illustrations for a special edition of Ivan Krylov's fables; 1897 painted the portrait of Grand Duke Pavel Alexandrovich; until 1909 taught at MIPSA; 1898 onward member of the Society of Wandering Exhibitions; 1899 painted post-humous portrait of Alexander III; moved closely with the World of Art group; ca. 1900 changed his artistic direction from Realism to a style more reliant on the *style moderne;* began to give particular attention to historical themes such as *Peter the Great at Monplaisir;* 1903 joined the Union of Russian Artists; 1904 visited Italy; 1907 with Léon Bakst visited Greece; began to elaborate themes such as the *Rape of Europa* and *Odysseus and Nausica;* 1910 painted portrait of Ida Rubinstein; 1910 onward member of the revived World of Art society; 1911 began to paint murals for the Nosov mansion in Moscow; created a drop curtain on the theme of *Schéhérazade* for Sergei Diaghilev's Ballets Russes in Paris; began to work on designs for a production of *Daphnis et Chloë.*

Bibliography
I. Grabar: *Valentin Aleksandrovich Serov. Zhizn i tvorchestvo,* M: Knebel, 1914.
S. Ernst: *V. A. Serov,* P: Committee for the Popularization of Art Editions at the Russian Academy for the History of Material Culture, 1921.
M. Kopshitser: *Serov,* M: Iskusstvo, 1967.
D. Sarabianov: *Serov,* M: Iskusstvo, 1974.
D. Sarabianov: *Valentin Serov,* L: Aurora (English and French Editions), 1982.
V. Leniashin et al.: *Valentin Serov.* Catalog of exhibition at the TG and the RM, 1991.
R. Salys: "A Tale of Two Artists. Valentin Serov and Leonid Pasternak" in *Oxford Slavonic Papers,* Oxford, 1993, Vol. 26, pp. 75-86.
V. Lapshin: *Valentin Serov. Poslednii god zhizni,* M: Galart, 1995.
E. Allenova: *Valentin Serov,* M: Slovo, 1996.
A. Kudria: *Sluzhenie krasote, ili zhizn khudozhnika Serova,* M: Raduga, 2001.
E. Valkenier: *Valentin Serov: Portraits of Russia's Silver Age,* Evanston: Northwestern University Press, 2002.
V. Leniashin and V. Kruglov: *Valentin Aleksandrovich Serov,* SP: Palace Editions, 2003.
A. Kudria: *Valentin Serov,* M: Molodaia gvardiia, 2008.
I. Zolotinkina and Yu. Solonovich: *Valentin Serov. Grafika iz sobraniia Russkogo muzeia.* Catalog of exhibition at the Ekaterinburg Museum of Visual Arts, Ekaterinburg, 2011.

Serov is remembered above all as a portraitist, and his pictorial interpretations of his contemporaries such as *Girl with Peaches* (Savva Mamontov's daughter, Vera, 1887), *Genrietta Girshman* (1907) (both in the TG), and *Princess Olga Orlova* (1911, RM) are important social documents of the Silver Age. Serov produced an entire gallery of artistic and theatrical personalities — from *Sergei Diaghilev* (1904, RM) to *Fedor Chaliapin* (e.g., of 1905), from *Konstantin Korovin* (1891) to *Mariia Ermolova* (1905) (last three in the TG). Serov was also involved in a number of important stage productions, an interest nurtured by his mother and father and then developed by his close association with Savva Mamontov and the Abramtsevo circle. While still a teenager, Serov helped Vasilii Polenov design the various charades and amateur theatricals that the Abramtsevo colony put on in the spring and summer evenings.

Serov's first important engagement was for a production of his father's opera *Judith* for Mamontov's Private Opera Company in 1898 in Moscow with Chaliapin in the role of Holophernes (cf. No. 911 [R779]). Serov returned to this three times in 1900, 1908, and 1909. In 1898 Serov also designed the production of *King Saul* composed by Savva and Sergei Mamontov at the latter's Moscow house in 1899. In 1900-01 Serov, along with Bakst, Benois, Korovin, and Evgenii Lanceray, was invited by the Imperial Theaters to contribute to a production of Léo Delibes's *Sylvia,* but the spectacle was canceled. Although Serov's contribution to the Diaghilev enterprise was limited to his famous Pavlova poster for the first Paris season, his *Schéhérazade* curtain, and his sets for *Judith,* he hoped to involve himself more fully for, as he wrote to Walter Nouvel in July, 1911, "the only thing that I acknowledge is the ballet; everything else is fiddlesticks."[728] Serov also created many pertinent portraits, e.g. of Tamara Karsavina (1909, TG), Michel Fokine (1909, present whereabouts unknown), and Vaslav Nijinsky (1910, GMTMA). Serov worked on a variety of opera and ballet productions during the 1900s and his untimely death cut short a promising career in stage design.

909 [R777].
Poster Advertising the Inauguration of the First "Russian Season" at the Théâtre du Châtelet, Paris, in May-June, 1909.
Lithograph in black and white on a blue background.
Initialed in the plate lower right and dated 1909.
90⅞ x 70 in., 231 x 177.7 cm.
Other inscriptions: at the top: "Théâtre du Châtelet Saison Russe Mai-Juin 1909 Opéra et Ballet"; lower left: "Administration G.

909

Astruc & Cie Villon de Hanovre. 32 Rue Louis-le-Grand"; lower right along margin: "Eugène Verneau, 108 Rue Folie Mericourt, Paris."
Provenance: *Poster Auctions International,* New York, 3 May, 1987, Lot 278 (reproduced). Reproduced in color in D17, p. 23; G99, p. 165; I117, p. 256; M157, p. 7; in black and white in D13, fig. 47; M148; and elsewhere. The poster also exists in a reduced format, i.e., 70⅝ x 63½ in.; 187 x 158 cm. (For a color reproduction see G72, unpaginated.) The original design for the poster, formerly in the collection of Mikhail and Sergei Botkin and now in the RM, was litho-graphed by Andrea Beloborodoff in 1921 (see No. 118 [R97]).

Note: Sergei Diaghilev opened his first season of the Ballets Russes in Paris on 1 May, 1909, with *Le Pavillon d'Armide,* the *Polovtsian Dances,* and *Le Festin.* This was followed by his presentation of *Les Sylphides* and *Cléopatre* on 2 June. In his interpretation here Serov has captured the ethereal Anna Pavlova dancing the part of the First Sylphide in *Les Sylphides* (see No. 118 [R97]). A friend and admirer of Serov, the writer Vasilii Rozanov responded to the poster in the following manner: "A head, air, blueness and nothing... Nothing has been made and yet the idea of dance has been expressed so perfectly."[729]

Judith: opera in five acts by Alexander Serov with a libretto by Ivan Giustiniani. Produced by Sergei Diaghilev at the Théâtre du Châtelet, Paris, on 6 June, 1909, with designs by Léon Bakst and Valentin Serov.

The Jewish city of Bethulia is besieged by the army of Holophernes, the general of Nebuchadnezzar. Judith, a Jewish widow, manages to enter the enemy's camp and seduces Holophernes. While he is slumbering, rather the worse for drink, Judith cuts off his head and, in triumph, returns to Bethulia. Encouraged by this, the Jews make a sortie and put the enemy to flight.

910

910 [188; R778].
Stage Design for the Orgy in Holophernes's Camp, 1908.
Watercolor and pencil.
8¼ x 13⅛ in., 21 x 33.5 cm.
Inscribed lower left in Russian: "Stage design by V.A. Serov for the opera *Judith*. Witnessed by Konstantin Korovin, 1908."
Provenance: Alexandre Djanchieff, Paris, February, 1978, who in turn had acquired it from Semeon Belitz.
Reproduced in A34, p. 380; I42, No. 89; I51, No. 208.

911 [R779].
Costume Design for Chaliapin as Holophernes, ca. 1909.
Gouache and charcoal.
Signed lower left in Russian: "V. Serov."
21¾ x 14⅛ in., 55.2 x 36 cm.
Provenance: Alexandre Djanchieff, Paris, September, 1978.
Reproduced in color in B115, plate 15; F107, p. 276; I42, No. 88; in black and white in I51, No. 209. Variants of the costume for the 1909 and other productions are reproduced in G31, plate 56; C26, p. 60; J7, Lot 153. A photograph of Chaliapin as Holophernes in the 1898 production is reproduced in C24, between pp. 64 and 65; and a 1907 version is reproduced in Sarabianov, *Valentin Serov,* p. 351. Bakst designed a similar costume for Holophernes (dated 1922) and this is reproduced in C. Spencer, *Bakst,* London: Academy Editions, 1973, plate 43.

Note: Judith, first performed at the Mariinsky Theater, St. Petersburg in 1863, was perhaps

Alexander Serov's most successful work and it saw many subsequent revivals in Russia. Valentin Serov (the son of the composer) and Chaliapin worked on the opera four times — in 1898 for Savva Mamontov's Private Opera Company in Moscow, in 1900 for the Bolshoi Theater, Moscow, in 1908 for the Mariinsky Theater, St. Petersburg, and in 1909 in Paris.[730] Chaliapin recalled this collaboration:

> We often conducted conversations about our imminent work. Serov talked to me about the spirit of ancient Assyria with enthusiasm. But I was troubled by the question of how to present Holophernes on stage… I wanted to provide an image of the ancient Assyrian satrap that was both alive and characteristic… When I was in Serov's studio one day… I came upon an album in which I saw photographs of bas-reliefs, stone depictions of tsars and military leaders… I was struck by the profile movement of the hands and feet of these people — always going in the same direction… A great serenity, a regal unhurriedness and at the same time a powerful dynamism could be felt in these lapidary poses. "It wouldn't be a bad idea," I thought, "to depict Holophernes like this with these typical movements, lapidary, terrifying…" I asked Serov what he thought of my strange fancy. Serov gave a joyful start, thought for a moment and said, "Well, that would be great. Really great!"[731]

As for Serov's conception of Chaliapin's costume for Holophernes in No. 911 [R779], it

would seem to rely substantially on Chaliapin's impressions noted above.[732] In any case, evidently, it blended well with the other designs for the opera. Alexander Golovin, for example, who portrayed Chaliapin in Serov's costume (1909, TG), observed that "of his [Serov's] theatrical designs, those for

911

912

913

913 [R780a].
Study for the Painting Odysseus and Nausica, ca. 1910.
Pencil and watercolor.
This is the reverse of No. 912 [R780]
Reproduced in I20, No. 78, where it is described wrongly as a design for the opera *Judith;* I51, No. 211. Serov's classical theme *Odysseus and Nausica,* which he seems to have first contemplated even before his trip through Greece and Crete with Bakst in 1907, exists in several versions, although none of them is definitive.[735] Perhaps the most impressive version is the tempera painting in the TG (reproduced in Ernst, *V.A. Serov,* between pp. 64 and 65); another tempera study is also in the TG (reproduced in B33, plate 46), as is a sketch (reproduced in Kopshitser, *Serov,* plate 47). For reproductions of a series of versions see Sarabianov, *Valentin Serov,* plates 198-201.

914 [189; R781].
The Rape of Europa, 1910.
Pencil and watercolor.
Signed and dated lower right in Russian: "Serov 910."
11⅜ x 18⅛ in., 29 x 46 cm.
Provenance: *Russian Paintings, Drawings, Watercolours and Sculpture,* London: Sotheby's, 14 May, 1980, Lot 133 (reproduced). Now in a private collection, Moscow. Reproduced in color in A34, p. 378; B115, plate 114; F107, p. 134; and in black and white in M78; M183; M212; N13, p. 118; O3; O12.

Note: Serov painted several versions of this theme: a tempera and gouache version and a pencil study are in the RM (reproduced in N. Novouspensky, *The Russian Museum, Leningrad. Painting,* L: Aurora, 1979, plate 88; and in K139, p. 184); a large tempera is in the TG and has been reproduced many times, e.g., in K43, p. 98, and K50 (a), p. 74; a watercolor version, formerly in the collection of Ilia Ostroukhov, is reproduced in Ernst, *V.A. Serov,* between pp. 80 and 81; another version, formerly in the collection of the Malmo Museum, is reproduced in D. Arkin and I. Chvojnik, *Samtida Konst i Ryssland,* Malmo: Ljustrycksanstalt, 1930, p. 67. Also see I. Barsheva, *Muzei-kvartira I.I. Brodskogo,* M: Izobrazitelnoe iskusstvo, 1985, plate 71; and Sarabianov, *Serov* (1982), plates 202-07. Nicola Benois included this piece in his 1981 portrait of Nikita D. Lobanov (No. 360 [R324]).

Rumor has it that the model for Europa in Serov's *Rape of Europa* was Ida Lvovna Rubinshtein (Ida Rubinstein, 1885-1960), the dancer, actress, and patroness, whose nude portrait Serov painted in the summer of 1910 in Paris, which Ilia Repin described indignantly as a "galvanized corpse."[736] Although Serov created at least six versions of *The Rape of Europa* and made a plaster sculpture on the same theme in 1910 (translated into porcelain and bronze posthumously in 1915), he did not exhibit them during his lifetime. The public first saw *The Rape of Europa* (and *Odysseus and Nausica*) at Serov's posthumous exhibition in Moscow in 1913-14. Opinions regarding *The Rape of Europa* varied. Igor

Judith were the best."[733] Chaliapin's dramatic appearance, his majestic voice (matched by that of the soprano Felia Litvin, who performed Judith) as well as the impressive sets by Bakst and Serov brought forth loud applause at the Paris premiere. It is difficult to determine exactly for which production Nos. 910 [R778] and 911 [R779] were created. The date of 1908 on No. 910 [R778] may indicate that it was made for the production of *Judith* at the Mariinsky Theater, St. Petersburg, in November of that year; on the other hand, it may have been an advance design for the 1909 Paris production.

912 [R780].
Fedor Chaliapin and His Two Wives Depicted as Centaurs, ca. 1910.
Pencil.
10 x 18⅛ in., 25.5 x 46 cm.
Provenance: Irina Bashkiroff, Valira Farm, New Preston, Connecticut, March, 1971. Now in a private collection.
Reproduced in F107, p. 262; I20, No. 79; I51, No. 210; N188, p. 44. On the reverse of this piece is a sketch for the painting *Odysseus and Nausica* (see No. 913 [R780a]).

Note: Chaliapin's first wife, with whom he lived until 1906, was Iola Tornaghi, the prima ballerina with Savva Mamontov's Private Opera Company (where Chaliapin met her). In 1906 Chaliapin married his second wife, Mariia Elukhen, with whom he lived in St. Petersburg. The late Ivan Boiarsky, a Moscow expert on twentieth-century Russian opera, has written:

> Of course, malicious tongues gossiped that he [Chaliapin] had one wife in St. Petersburg and another one in Moscow. Chaliapin had two houses, one in Moscow, where Tornaghi lived with her children (and, of course, Chaliapin lived there when he sang at the Bolshoi Theater, etc.), the other in St. Petersburg, where he lived with his second wife. But he was not a bigamist. Even Chaliapin was not allowed that.[734]

Serov made several portraits of Chaliapin, e.g., in 1897 (private collection, M; reproduced in I. Grabar, *Serov-risovalshchik,* M: Academy of Arts, 1962, unnumbered) and 1905 (TG; reproduced in B33, plate 48). Serov was also fond of animals, especially horses, drawing an entire album of them for Krylov's fables. In 1910 Chaliapin transposed the theme of the centaur to his own caricature of Diaghilev (see J30, Lot 58).

914

Grabar, Serov's early biographer, felt that the work contained "a too obvious compromise — an aspiration to combine a certain decorative style with observations of everyday life."[737] Sergei Ernst offered a more constructive commentary:

> The strict and measured compositional distribution of masses that controls the scheme, the colors, and mood, and finally, the 'otherworldly,' pure colors in bold contrast — such are the visual and emotional impressions of the viewer in front of The Rape of Europa.[738]

728 Letter from Valentin Serov to Walter Nouvel dated 29 Juy, 1911. Quoted in F69, Vol. 2, p. 305.
729 Quoted in F34, Vol. 2, p. 469. Also see ibid., p. 473, for some details on the general reception of Serov's poster.
730 In his memoirs, *Stranitsy moei zhizni*, Chaliapin mentions that he made his debut as Holophernes in the Solodovnikov Theater, Moscow, in 1897, although Serov did not contribute to that production. See the extracts from Chaliapin's memoirs reprinted in F34, Vol. 2, pp. 279-80. For commentary on Chaliapin's involvement with Mamontov's Private Opera see C184.
731 Ibid.
732 However, according to one source, Chaliapin also gave particular attention to a Vrubel pen and ink drawing variously called *My Soul is Gloomy* and *Saul and David*. See *Studiia*, M, 1911, 1 October, No. 1, pp. 8 (opposite) and 31.
733 F16, p. 34.
734 Letter from Ivan Boiarsky to John E. Bowlt dated 24 October, 1981.
735 In his *V.A. Serov*, p. 67, Sergei Ernst mentions that there was a total of five versions of *Odysseus and Nausica* and that two of these were done before Serov went to Greece. Ernst dates the tempera painting as before 1907, but contemporary Russian scholars always date it as 1910. For further commentary see O. Morozova: "Drevniaia Gretsiia v zhivopisnykh panno Serova i Golovina" in *Russkoe iskusstvo*, M, 2005, No. 1; reprinted in No. 11 for 2012, pp. 86-96.
736 Quoted in ibid., p. 72. Nicola Benois, in a conversation with John E Bowlt and Nikita D. Lobanov-Rostovsky in 1981, maintained that Ida Rubinstein was the model for *The Rape of Europa*. See F107, p. 134.
737 Grabar, *Valentin Aleksandrovich Serov*, p. 228.
738 Ernst, *V.A. Serov*, p. 68.

SHCHEKATIKHINA-POTOTSKAIA, Alexandra Vasilievna

Born 8 (20) May, 1892, Alexandrovsk (now Zaporozhie), Ukraine; died 23 October, 1967, Leningrad, Russia.

Born into a family of Old Believer merchants. 1908-15 studied under Ivan Bilibin and Nicholas Roerich at SSEA; during her school years visited Talashkino, where she assisted Roerich with the designs for the church; 1910 with her classmate Mariia Lebedeva toured Northern Russia; 1912 onward began to work as a stage designer; 1913 visited Greece, Italy, and France; studied at the Académie Ranson in Paris under Maurice Denis, François Vallotton, and Paul Sérusier; upon her return to Talashkino assisted Nicholas Roerich with his designs for Sergei Diaghilev's production of *Sacre du Printemps*; 1915 married the lawyer Fedor Pototsky; 1915 onwards participated in the World of Art exhibitions; 1916 designed a production of *Rogneda* for Sergei Zimin's Moscow Private Opera; 1918-23 worked at the State Porcelain Factory in Petrograd; 1920 death of her husband; 1923 with her son Mstislav, went to Berlin to study porcelain manufacture, and then joined Ivan Bilibin in Egypt on his invitation, who soon became her husband; 1924-25 with Bilibin traveled in Egypt, Syria, and Palestine; 1925-36 lived with Mstislav and Bilibin in Paris; painted on Sèvres and Limoges porcelain; 1926 one-woman exhibition at the Galerie Druet; 1920s-30s contributed to many European exhibitions; 1936 with Bilibin and Mstislav returned to Leningrad, resuming work at the State Porcelain Factory under the direction of Nikolai Suetin; 1937 with Bilibin designed sets and costumes for *The Tale of Tsar Saltan* at the Kirov Theater; 1955 one-woman exhibition in Leningrad.

Bibliography
N. Yaglova: *Aleksandra Vasilievna Shchekatikhina-Pototskaia*. Catalog of 1955 [sic] exhibition organized by the Union of Artists of the USSR, Leningrad, 1958.
V. Noskovich: *Aleksandra Vasilievna Shchekatikhina-Pototskaia*, L: Khudozhnik RSFSR, 1959.
G. Golynets and S. Golynets: *I.Ya. Bilibin; A.V. Shchekatikhina-Pototskaia*. Catalog of exhibition organized by the Union of Artists of the RSFSR, Leningrad, 1977.
A42, pp. 725-26.
H34, pp. 636-38.
E. Petrova, ed.: *Aleksandra Shchekatikhina-Pototskaia*, SP: Palace Editions, 2009.

Although Shchekatikhina-Pototskaia[739] is now remembered primarily as a ceramic artist, she was an artist of many parts, working also as a studio painter, book illustrator, and stage designer. In 1913 and 1914 she assisted Roerich in his designs for *The Rite of Spring* and *Prince Igor*, before turning to Anton Rubinstein's opera *Demon* for the Zimin Opera, Moscow, in 1919, Rimsky-Korsakov's *Sadko* for the People's House, Petrograd, in 1920, and a ballet based on Mussorgsky's *Night on a Bald Mountain* (not produced). Consequently, the following designs for *Sadko* and *The Tale of Tsar Saltan* depend on her considerable experience as a professional designer, reflecting both the taste and style of her chief mentors, Bilibin and Roerich.

915 [R964].
Self-Portrait, 1913.
Colored pencil.
11 x 8⅞ in., 28 x 22.5 cm.
Inscribed on the reverse in pencil in Russian: "This is me with Iv. Yak. [Bilibin], 1913." The inscription would indicate that this is part of a larger double portrait.
Another self-portrait, dated 1931, is reproduced in Golynets and Golynets, *I.Ya. Bilibin, A.V. Shchekatikhina-Pototskaia*, unpaginated.
Provenance: the artist's son, Mstislav Pototsky, St. Petersburg. Now in a private collection.

915

916

917

Sadko: *opera in four acts and seven scenes by Nikolai Rimsky-Korsakov with libretto by the composer and Vladimir Belsky. Produced at the People's House Theater, Petrograd, on 20 November, 1920, with designs by Alexandra Shchekatikhina-Pototskaia.*

See No. 308 [R275] for plot summary.

916 [R965].
Set Design for the Port of Novgorod in Scene IV, 1920.
Watercolor and gold and silver paint.
Signed upper left in pencil in Russian: "A. Shchekotikhina P."
9½ x 12¾ in., 24 x 32.5 cm.
Other inscriptions: upper left by the artist in pencil in Russian: "Op[era] 'Sadko', People's House; upper right in ink "Scene IV."
Provenance: the artist's son, Mstislav Pototsky, St. Petersburg. Now in a private collection.

Unidentified production, *ca. 1923.*

917 [NIRE].
Costume Design for a Russian Maiden, 1923.
Gouache.
Signed with the initials and dated lower right in Russian: "A Shch P 1923."
14¾ x 11 in., 37.5 x 28 cm.
Provenance: *Russian Pictures, Works of Art and Icons*, London: Sotheby's, 30 November, 2006, Lot 108 (reproduced).

918 [R970].
Motherhood, 1924.
Watercolor, gold, and pencil.
Signed and dated lower right in brown paint in Russian: "A. Shchekotikhina, 1924."
25 x 18¾ in., 63.5 x 47.5 cm.
Other inscriptions: signed on the reverse in red pencil in French: "A. Shchekotikhina"; followed by the name and address of a

previous owner: "M. Pierre Haas, 260 Bd. St. Germain [Paris]." The reverse also carries a warehouse label: "Tailleur fils, Garde meuble," and a framer's label: "A. Buccelati, Artistic Materials, Photo Store, Maidan El Azhare, Cairo."
Provenance: auction, London: Bonhams, 19 September, 1991, Lot 109 (reproduced). Reproduced in color in F107, p. 147.

Note: Shchekatikhina also used the central motif in this design in her plate called *Motherhood* of 1920. For a color reproduction of the plate see N. Lobanov-Rostovsky: *Revolutionary Ceramics,* London: Studio, 1990, fig. 135; also see L. Andreeva: *Sovetskii farfor 1920-1930,* M: Sovetskii khudozhnik, 1975, p. 165.

The Tale of Tsar Saltan: *opera in three acts by Nikolai Rimsky-Korsakov with a libretto by Vladimir Belsky after a poem by Alexander Pushkin. Produced by Nikolai Evreinov for Marie Kousnezoff's Opéra Privé de Paris at the Théâtre des Champs-Elysées, Paris, in February, 1929, with designs by Ivan Bilibin and some costumes by Alexandra Shchekatikhina-Pototskaia, executed by Alexandre Shervashidze.*

See No. 349 [R314] for plot summary.

919 [R966].
Costume Design for the Deacon, 1929.
Watercolor, gold and silver paint, black ink, and pencil.
Signed lower right in pencil in Russian: "TchekoPotocka."
18¾ x 12⅜ in., 47.5 x 31.5 cm.

918

919

920

921

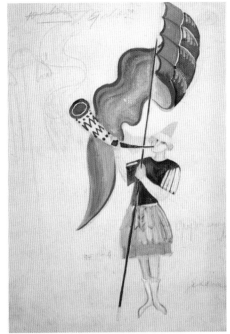

922

Other inscriptions: upper right in ink: "No. 6"; and in pencil in Russian: "Deacon, silvery white beard, caftan cassock."
Provenance: the artist's son, Mstislav Pototsky, St. Petersburg.
Reproduced in I77, p.158.

920 [R967].
Costume Design for the Six Elders, 1929.
Watercolor and pencil.
Signed lower right in black ink in Russian: "Shchekotikhina."
20⅛ x 13¾ x 51 x 35 cm.
Other inscriptions in Russian: lower left in black ink: "Tsar Saltan"; upper left in pencil: "Long white beards, cloaks light brown (siena-like) and ocher yellow reminiscent of saintly old men."
Provenance: the artist's son, Mstislav Pototsky, St. Petersburg
Reproduced in I77, p. 158.

921 [R968].
Costume Design for a Maiden, 1929.
Watercolor, silver and gold paint, pencil, and black ink.
Signed lower right in blue pencil in Russian: "A. Shchekotikhina-P."
18¼ x 13¾ in., 46.5 x 35 cm.
Other inscriptions in Russian: lower right in pencil: "Golden hats, almost flat, with silver straps. Round coat with no angles. Petticoats sticking out, made of tulle."
The reverse carries another design (see No. 922 [R968a]).
Provenance: the artist's son, Mstislav Pototsky, St. Petersburg

922 [R968a].
Costume Design for a Standard Bearer Blowing a Horn, ca. 1929.
Inscriptions in Russian (illegible).
This is the reverse of No. 921 [R968].

923 [R969].
Costume Design for the Swan Princess, 1929.
Gouache and silver paint.
Initialed lower left in black ink in Russian: "AShch-P."
10⅝ x 13¾ in., 60 x 35 cm.
Other inscriptions: upper right in ink: "No. 14"; lower margin, in pencil, in Russian: "Swan Princess's kokoshnik is with feathers sewn with sequins. Necklace is with fake stars." The upper part of the reverse carries Russian instructions in pencil to the seamstress from Nikolai Evreinov: "Received 25 Dec., in the evening. Budikova. Alter the headgear in this costume (flat bird's skull with one egret plume in the silver crown) and the wings which have to contain

the hands. N. Evreinov. 27.XII.1928." The lower half bears a costume identification in pencil in Russian: "A. Shchekotikhina-Pototskaia, Swan Bird, Tsar Saltan."
Marie Budíková-Jeremiášová (1904-84) was a Czech soprano.
Provenance: the artist's son, Mstislav Pototsky, St. Petersburg. Now in a private collection.
For three other costume designs for The Swan Princess see the commemorative program, unpaginated.

739 Until the end of 1930 Shchekatikhina-Pototskaia wrote the second syllable of her name with an "o" and thereafter with an "a". The second part of her name, Pototskaia, appeared as a result of her first marriage in 1915. She signed her work in numerous ways: Tcheka-Potocka, A. Sh-P, Shch-P, ASHEP, ASHCHEP, A. Shchekatikhina-P, Shchekatikhina, A.Sh.; A. Shchek.-P., Shchek, etc.

923

Alexandra Shchekatikhina-Pototskaia.

SHERVASHIDZE (CHACHBA), Alexandre Konstantinovich

Born 12 (24) December, 1867, Feodosiia, Crimea, Ukraine; died 17 August, 1968, Monte Carlo, Monaco.

1889 graduated from the Kiev Secondary School; took art lessons from Ivan Seleznev; 1891 audited classes at MIPSA; 1894, on the advice of Vasilii Polenov, went to Paris, where he took art lessons in various studios; established contact with Alexandre Benois, Viktor Borisov-Musatov, Valentin Serov, Maximilian Voloshin, and other artists and writers, often painting their portraits; 1899 returned to Russia; 1904-06 lived in Paris again; 1907 appointed artist-in-residence at the Imperial Theaters, St. Petersburg; 1907-18 contributed to more than forty productions such as *Hamlet, Khovanshchina, Lakmé,* Gounod's *Faust;* 1910 onward exhibited regularly with the World of Art group; wrote a number of texts on modern European and Russian artists; 1911 onward designed several productions for The Antique Theater, St. Petersburg; 1917 appointed artist-in-residence of the Petrograd State Theaters; accepted the Revolution inasmuch as it seemed to promise independence to his ancestral country Abkhazia; 1918-19 traveled to Sukhumi, capital of Abkhazia, to organize an art school and the Sukhumi Theatrical Society; staged several plays by Nikolai Evreinov there; joined by other St. Petersburg and Moscow friends such as Natalia Butkovskaia and Vasilii Kamensky; 1919 traveled to the Crimea; 1920 at the invitation of Sergei Diaghilev emigrated to Paris; 1922 onward designed many plays and ballets in Paris and elsewhere; 1926 designed Sacheverell Sitwell's *Le Triomphe de Neptune* for Diaghilev's Ballets Russes in London; 1940 settled in Monte Carlo; continued to paint and design until his death.

Bibliography
N. Evreinov: *Original o portretistakh,* M: Svetozar, 1922, pp. 61-65.
M2, Vol. 2, pp. 194-95, listing his theatrical productions.
B. Adzhindzhal: "Khudozhnik A.K. Chachba (Shervashidze)" in *Materialy po arkheologii i iskusstvu Abkhazii,* Sukhumi: Academy of Sciences of the Georgian SSR, 1974.
A.K. Chachba (Shervashidze). Catalog of exhibition at the Abkhazia State Museum, Sukhumi, 1978.
R. Shervashidze: "Razum i serdtse rodine" in *Literaturnaia Gruziia,* 1984, Tbilisi, No. 4, pp. 202-13.
R. Shervashidze: "Apsny, tvoi drevnii klich zvuchit kak zvuk dalekii" in *Ertsakhu,* Sukhumi: Alashara, 1984, pp. 206-23.
B. Atsyntsial (Adzhindzhal): *Apstazaara du adakiakua,* Akua: Alashara, 1985.
Aleksandr Shervashidze (Chachba) 1867-1968. Catalog of exhibition organized by the Union of Artists of the USSR, Moscow and Sukhumi, 1986-87.
N. Kornienko and L. Taniuk: "A. Chachba-Shervazshidze i Vs. Meierkhold" in A. Vasiliev et

Alexandre Benois: *Portrait of Prince Alexandre Shervashidze, 1906.* See No. 120 [R99].

al., eds.: *Khudozhnik i zritel,* M: Sovetskii khudozhnik, 1990, pp. 328-44.
B. Adzhindzhal, intro.: *Kniaz Aleksandr Chachba (Shervashidze). Statii ob iskusstve. Otryvki iz pisem i zapisnykh knizhek,* SP: Razumova, 1998.
R. Sadykhova: *A.K. Shervashidze, S.B. Virsaladze, R.I. Gabriadze, G.V. Aleksi-Meskhishvili.* Catalog of exhibition at the GMTMA, 2008.

The "embodiment of an Eastern, knightly nobility,"[740] Shervashidze is not widely known either as a stage designer or as a portraitist, even though he was a productive artist and was chief designer for the Imperial Theaters in St. Petersburg from 1907 until 1918, contributing to over forty productions. Until his emigration in 1920, Shervashidze worked almost exclusively in Russia, scoring some success with his historical reincarnations. Of particular importance were his sets and costumes for Vsevolod Meierkhold's production of *Tristan und Isolde* at the Mariinsky Theater, Petrograd in 1918, of which the critic Sergei Auslender noted that "it was difficult to wish for a better combination of colors."[741]

A Merry Death: a harlequinade in one act by Nikolai Evreinov. Produced by the Sukhumi Theatrical Society at the Aloizi Theater, Sukhumi on 30 March, 1919. with music by Nikolai Evreinov, choreography by Natalia Butkovskaia, and designs by Alexandre Shervashidze.
Knowing that the aged Harlequin must die at midnight, Pierrot puts the clock back two hours so as to prolong Harlequin's life. However, when Pierrot's suspicion that Harlequin is deceiving him with Columbine is confirmed certainty (for Harlequin, wishing to dine for his last time, requests

three places at table together with Death and Columbine who is singing a love song), Pierrot corrects the time. Satisfied with his vendetta, Pierrot feigns indifference as he watches the love scene between Harlequin and Columbine, until Death arrives.

924 [R941].
Costume Design for a Harlequin, 1919.
Watercolor and ink.
Signed and dated lower right in Russian: "Shervashidze 1919."
9½ x 8⅝ in., 24 x 22 cm.
Other inscriptions: upper left in Russian: "'A Merry Death' by N. Evreinov"; upper right in Russian: "Harlequin" followed by "Mr. Roger Allard" in French.
Provenance: Anna Kashina-Evreinova, Paris, February, 1969.
Reproduced in I20, No. 80; I51, No. 214.

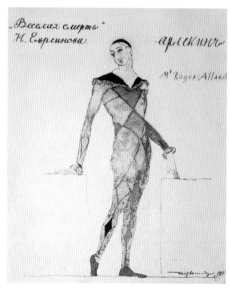

924

925

927

925 [R942].
Costume Design for Columbine, ca. 1919.
Watercolor, pencil, and ink.
8½ x 7⅛ in., 21.5 x 18 cm.
Inscriptions in Russian: upper left: "'A Merry Death' by N. Evreinov"; upper right: "Columbine."
Provenance: Anna Kashina-Evreinova, Paris, February, 1969.
Reproduced in I20, No. 81; I51, No. 215. A similar piece in the collection of the Sukhumi Picture Gallery is reproduced in *A.K. Chachba (Shervashidze),* plate 48; and in *Aleksandr Shervashidze,* unnumbered.

926 [NIRE].
Costume Design for Death, ca. 1919.
Watercolor, pencil, and ink.
9½ x 8⅝ in., 24 x 22 cm.
Provenance: Anna Kashina-Evreinova, Paris, February, 1969. Now in a private collection.

926

Note: Evreinov published his play *A Merry Death* in 1909 in St. Petersburg and it was first performed at Fedor Komissarzhevsky's Merry Theater for Elderly Children, St. Petersburg, with designs by Mstislav Dobujinsky and Nikolai Kalmakov. The play was revived in Petrograd for the Comedians' Halt in 1917, in Kiev in 1918, and then in Sukhumi in 1919, and then again in March, 1922, at the Théâtre du Vieux Colombier, Paris, under the direction of Jacques Copeau. As far as the Sukhumi production was concerned, it scored an immediate success thanks to Shervashidze's "original, stylish, fine costumes, very interesting décors, and general restraint of tone." [742]

Les Sylphides: *ballet in one act based on music by Frederic Chopin with choreography by Michel Fokine. Produced by the Original Ballet Russe at the Hollywood Theater, New York, in late fall of 1940 with designs by Alexandre Shervashidze.*
See No. 118 [R97] for a summary.

927 [R943].
Design for Act I, 1939.
Watercolor.
Signed and dated lower left in Russian: "Shervashidze, 1939."
12½ x 19¾ in., 34.5 x 50 cm.
Provenance: Issar Gourvitch, Paris, November, 1966, who had acquired it from the artist.
Reproduced in A34, p. 388; I14, No. 91.

Note: Les Sylphides, in Fokine's choreographic interpretation, was a basic part of the repertoire of the so-called Original Ballet Russe, and it was played in many cities in Europe, Australia, and the USA. The 1940-41 American tour does not seem to have been a financial success, at least according to Sol Hurok, who contracted the company.[743] As far as this particular design is concerned, it evokes associations with Benois's romantic interpretations for *Giselle*

(see Nos. 152-58 [R126-32]), and perhaps Shervashidze had the earlier Diaghilev traditions in mind when he was working on this production.

740 Evreinov, *Original o portretistakh,* p. 81.
741 Quoted in *A.K. Chachba (Shervashidze),* p. 6.
742 Kin: "Spektakl N.N. Evreinova" in *Nashe slovo,* Sukhumi, 1919. Quotation supplied by Rusudama Shervashidze, Sukhumi.
743 See F11, p. 131 et seq. Also see D29 and D31, passim.

SHKOLNIK, Iosif (Osip) Solomonovich

Born 30 November (12 December), 1883, Balta, Ukraine; died 26 August, 1928, Leningrad, Russia.

Early 1900s attended the Odessa Art Institute; 1905-07 attended IAA; 1906 contributed caricatures to the journal *Kosa* [Scythe]; 1908 contributed to the "Contemporary Trends" exhibition in St. Petersburg; 1909 contributed to the "Impressionists" in St. Petersburg; close to Nikolai Kulbin; influenced by Henri Matisse and the Fauves; 1910 joined the Union of Youth society, contributing to its exhibitions and becoming its secretary; 1911 traveled extensively in Northern Europe; 1912-13 studied antiquities in the Ukraine; 1913 with Pavel Filonov worked on the designs for the production of Vladimir Maiakovsky's *Vladimir Maiakovsky. A Tragedy;* 1914-17 artist-in-residence at the Troitskii Theater, St. Petersburg; 1910s worked on a number of theatrical presentations such as *Cain, Fée des poupées, The Swan, Salomé, A Merry Day of Princess Elizabeth,* and *The Guslar Player;* 1917 worked on agit-designs for the Revolutionary celebrations; 1918-19 worked as designer for the Maly Theater in Petrograd; 1918-26 directed the Institute of Decorative Art in

Petrograd; 1920s continued to contribute to exhibitions such as the "Exhibition of Paintings and Sculpture by Jewish Artists" (Moscow, 1918), the "I State Free Exhibition of Works of Art" (Petrograd, 1919), the "Erste Russische Kunstausstellung" (Berlin, 1922), and the "Exhibition of the Latest Trends in Art" (Leningrad, 1927).

Bibliography
Nothing substantial has been published on Shkolnik, although most studies of the avant-garde carry passing references to him as a stage designer and member of the Union of Youth (for example, B138, pp. 305-07).
Recent exhibitions of stage designs have featured Iosif Shkolnik's work, e.g. see I116, p. 14.

As a member of the St. Petersburg Union of Youth, Shkolnik was close to many radical artists including Pavel Filonov and Olga Rozanova. Although he did not share their extreme ideas and did not investigate abstract painting, he was especially interested in the relationship of indigenous, primitive traditions to modern art, studying the art of the old store signboard and painted trays, for example, and incorporating their images into his own compositions. Indeed, one of Shkolnik's favorite motifs was the main square in the provincial town where vestiges of Old Russia — such as signboards — could still be encountered. In its bright colors and choice of subject, his painting is reminiscent of the Neo-Primitivism of the milder members of the Jack of Diamonds, such as Alexander Kuprin and Ilia Mashkov, even though his cityscapes and still-lifes seem to be more contemplative, more melancholy, and more "Jewish" than their more boisterous canvases. In any case, Shkolnik was able to integrate these various influences into the pleasing, if not always radical, "stylistics of Fauvism."[744]

Unidentified production, *ca. 1913.*

928 [R944].
Village Square, **ca. 1913**
Gouache on paper laid on cardboard.
19½ x 21¾ ins., 49.7 x 55.4 cm.
Provenance: Yakov Rubinshtein, Moscow, 1974.
Reproduced in color in A34, p. 382; B151, p. IX; M78; and in black and white in I77, pp. 106, 145.

Note: It is possible that this design of a village square was for the second of the Union of Youth's two Cubo-Futurist productions at the Luna Park Theater, St. Petersburg, i.e., Maiakovsky's *Vladimir Maiakovsky. A Tragedy,* shown on 2 and 4 December, 1913 (designed by Filonov and Shkolnik and directed by Vladimir Maiakovsky). The other production was of *Victory over the Sun* on 3 and 5 December. For commentary see the entries for Malevich. For reproductions of Shkolnik's set designs for *Vladimir Maiakovsky* see I73, p. 123; I81, p. 102. It is also possible that this item is a studio painting, not intended for the theater.

928

929 [NIRE].
Poster for the "Exhibition of Monuments of the Russian Theater from the Collection of L.I. Zheverzheev", 1915.
Chromolithograph.
Signed in the plate in Russian: "I. Shkolnik."
41¾ x 30½ in., 106 x 77.5 cm.
Inscriptions (as part of the design) state that the exhibition is opening on 3 December [1915, Petrograd] and that the poster is printed by B. Avidon, Petrograd, 1915.
Provenance: *Important Silver, Russian Works of Art and Paintings,* London: Christie's, 25 November, 2003, Lot 205 (reproduced).

Note: Levkii Ivanovich Zheverzheev (1881-1942), the foremost St. Petersburg collector of stage designs, was passionate about the theater. A businessman who made his money from the sale of church supplies in the Neo-Russian style, Zheverzheev also financed the activities of the St. Petersburg Union of Youth group, including the avant-garde opera *Victory over the Sun* (see Nos. 770-84 [R648-62]) and in December, 1915, organized a major exhibition of his collection at the Dobychina Art Bureau in Petrograd, issuing not only this handsome poster, but also a solid catalog, which, to this day, is a primary sourcebook for information on Russian stage designs.[745]
After the October Revolution, Zheverezheev chose not to emigrate, remaining as curator of his nationalized collection at the Leningrad Theater Museum (today the Glinka Museum of Theatrical and Musical Art, St. Petersburg). His daughter Tamara Zheverzheeva went

929

on to become a famous ballerina, dancing with the Diaghilev company and the Ballet Russe de Monte Carlo under the pseudonym of Tamara Geva, and even marrying George Balanchine.

744 B138, p. 305.
745 L. Zheverzheev and N. Evreinov: *Opis vystavlennykh v polzu lazareta shkoly narodnogo iskusstva ee Velichestva Gosudaryni Imperatritsy Aleksandry Fedorovny pamiatnikov russkogo teatra iz sobraniia L.I. Zheverzheeva.* P: Shmidt, 1915 (G2).

SHLEPIANOV, Ilia Yulievich

Born 27 October (9 November), 1900, Chernigov, Ukraine; died 21 December, 1951, Moscow, Russia.

1904 family moved to Kiev; 1919 graduated from the First Commercial Institute in Kiev; took painting lessons from A. Menko, a local painter, and worked in Alexei Smirnov's theater studio; 1919-20 served in the Red Army; 1922-25 attended the State Higher Theater Studios in Moscow under Vsevolod Meierkhold; 1923-26 designed three productions for Meierkhold's theater, i.e., *Come on, Europe,* or *The D.E. Trust* (1924), *Bubus the Teacher* (1925), and *The Mandate* (1925); 1925 contributed to the "Exposition Internationale des Arts Décoratifs" in Paris; 1926 contributed to the "First Exhibition of Graphics" in Moscow; 1926-28 artist-in-residence at the Baku Workers' Theater; 1928-37 artist-in-residence and director at the Moscow Theater of Revolution; 1929 contributed to the exhibition "Results of the 1928-29 Theater Season" in Moscow; 1920s worked closely with many theatrical and musical celebrities of the time, including Dmitrii Kabalevsky, Meierkhold, and Sergei Prokofiev; 1938 worked as artist and/or director at various theaters, including the Bolshoi Theater of Opera and Ballet in Minsk, the Moscow Theater of Satire, and the Kirov Academic (Mariinsky) Theater of Opera and Ballet in Leningrad; 1944-51 artistic director of the Kirov; 1946 and 1951 awarded Stalin Prizes.

Bibliography
B. Graeva, ed.: *Ilia Shlepianov,* M: Iskusstvo, 1969.
C89, passim.
G62, passim.
Sourcebooks on Meierkhold carry copious references to Shlepianov, e.g. C30, C32, C33, C50, C99, C130, C132, C137.

Shlepianov began his independent career as a theater director and designer when he broke with Meierkhold in 1926 and went to Baku with several other students. The group, which also included Vasilii Fedorov, who had made his name with his designs for Sergei Tretiakov's *Roar, China!* at Meierkhold's theater in 1926, implemented a number of important productions in Baku, including *Sunset* by Isaak Babel. Shlepianov was much indebted to the Constructivist principles of Meierkhold, Liubov Popova, Alexander Rodchenko, and Varvara Stepanova, sharing the premise that:

> The theater not only reflects life, but it also remakes it... Our theater is not a theater of the dramaturgist, the producer, the artist, the musician, or the actor, but it is a theater of the collective interrelationship of all the components of the theatrical-creative organism.[746]

930

931

930 [R945].
Self-Portrait, 1926.
Black ink.
Initialed in ink and dated lower right in Russian: "I.Sh. 1926."
10 x 6½ in., 25.3 x 16.5 cm.
Provenance: the artist's son, Alexander Shlepianov, Moscow, 1980s.

Sunset: play in eight scenes by Isaak Babel produced by Vasilii Fedorov at the Workers' Theater, Baku, on 23 October, 1927, with designs by Ilia Shlepianov.

Local Jewish merchants from Odessa are wining and dining at the house of the carter Mendel Krik and his wife Nekhama. The guests are telling stories, cracking jokes and gossiping when the old man Mendel, cruel and domineering, arrives. This and the ensuing scenes in a tavern and a synagogue demonstrate that there is no love lost between the old man and his children Benia, Levka, and Dvoira, and the result is a bloody fight between Mendel, and Levka and Benia. Although, finally, there is reconciliation, it is clear that the sun has set on Mendel's family and business empire.

931 [R946].
Costume Design for Mendel Krik (?), ca. 1927.
Black ink.
Initialed and dated lower right in Russian: "I. Sh. 1927."
18 x 12¾ in., 45.6 x 32.5 cm.
Provenance: the artist's son, Alexander Shlepianov, Moscow, 1980s.
Reproduced in I78, p. 155.

Note: Written in 1924, *Sunset* describes the twilight life of Odessa Jews, who were hounded by the Tsarist régime and yet who

were often themselves crass materialists, bigoted and insensitive. Mendel and his sons are such types, contributing to a community that Babel, born and raised in Odessa, knew well and described so ably in his many short stories. Shlepianov, too, knew this reality in Chernigov and responded to the play by trying to evoke the colorful but staid traditions of merchant life in pre-Revolutionary Russia (the action takes place in 1913) — as, for example, in the costumes:

> A black and grey scale dominated the costumes, but this was offset by costumes of other tones — emerald green, light blue, violet and claret. The designs communicated the atmosphere of the play wonderfully and really helped to disclose its content.[747]

The designers of Nos. 932-46 [R947-60] are unknown, with Shlepianov as contributor. Provenance for all is the artist's son, Alexandre Shlepianov, Moscow, 1980.

The D.E. Trust (Come on, Europe!): *play in three parts and seventeen episodes adapted by Mikhail Podgaetsky from stories by Ilya Ehrenburg and Bernard Kellermann. Produced by Vsevolod Meierkhold for the Meierkhold Theater in the Greater Hall of the Leningrad Conservatoire on 15 July, 1924, with choreography by Kasian Goleizovsky, jazz music by Valentin Parnakh, and designs by Ilia Shlepianov.*

An American corporation tries to destroy Europe and settle it with colonists from Africa and workers from the USSR. As the representatives of the bourgeois past dance their last moments in night clubs, Soviet sailors, hailing the future, do gymnastics.

932

933

934

935

932 [R948].
Poster Advertising the Premiere of **The D.E. Trust, 1924.**
Lithograph in red and black.
57½ x 26¾ in., 146 x 68 cm.
Inscriptions (as part of the design) provide details on the dates of the premiere (15 and 16 July, 1924), its location, and information on the production, including Meierkhold's system of bio-mechanics.

933 [R949].
Poster Advertising the Premiere of The D.E. Trust *and* The Forest, 1924.
Lithograph in red and black.
26 x 41½ in., 66 x 105.5 cm.
Inscriptions (as part of the design) supply the dates: "14, 16, and 18" and "15, 17, and 19 [October 1924]." Inscriptions also indicate that on the 16th there was a special performance for the Union of Printers and that the poster was published in an edition of 600 copies by Gublit, Moscow.
Reproduced in L69, Lot 110.

Bubus the Teacher: *musical comedy in three acts by Alexei Faiko. Produced by Vsevolod Meierkhold at the Meierkhold Theater, Moscow, on 29 January, 1925, with music by Frédéric Chopin and Franz Liszt, and designs by Ilia Shlepianov.*
The cowardly teacher Bubus hides in the garden of the ruler Van Kamperdaf after taking part in a workers' demonstration that has been broken up by the police. By a twist of fate he finds himself nominated to a government position, but he proves to be superfluous even to the ruling class. Conciliatory and rhetorical, he then fails to join with the forces of the Revolution and the historic moment passes him by.

934 [R950].
Poster Advertising Performances of **Bubus the Teacher, 1925.**
Lithograph in red, black, and white.
42½ x 28 in., 108 x 71 cm.
Inscriptions (as part of the design) provide details on the dates of the performance (29-31, January, and 1 February, 1925), on the production, and the actors' names.
Reproduced in M53; M86; another copy is reproduced in color in G82, p. 184.

935 [R951].
Poster Advertising a Debate on **Bubus the Teacher, 1925.**
Lithograph in blue, black, and white.
35 x 28 in., 89 x 71 cm.
Inscriptions (as part of the design) provide details on the date and location of the debate (23 March, 1925, at the Meierkhold Theater, Moscow), on the main lecture by Alexei Gvozdev on "Creative Theater," and on the other participants, including Meierkhold and Anatolii Lunacharsky (master of ceremonies). Among the speakers "for" is Georgii Yakulov; among those "against" is Pavel Markov.
Provenance: the artist's son, Alexander Shlepianov, Moscow, 1980s.

936

937

938

939

939 [R947].
Poster Advertising a Public Debate on the Theme "Lef or Bluff," 1927.
Lithograph in black and white.
36⅝ x 26¾ in., 93 x 68 cm.
Inscriptions (as part of the design) provide details on the date of the debate (23 March [1927]), chaired by Vladimir Friche, the issues to be debated, and a list of participants (Nikolai Aseev, Osip Brik, Vladimir Maiakovsky, Alexander Rodchenko, Viktor Shklovsky, Varvara Stepanova et al.).

Note: The individuals in the poster are from the group of writers and artists connected to the journal *Lef* [Left Front of the Arts] established in Moscow in 1923. The champions of *Lef* rejected the art of the bourgeois past and were enthusiastic supporters of Formalism and Constructivism. However, some regarded this position as too radical and *Lef* had many antagonists — among them Osip Beskin, Vasilii Ermilov, and Viacheslav Polonsky, as this poster indicates. The subjects for discussion listed

936 [R952].
Poster Announcing the Forthcoming Performance of Bubus the Teacher at the Meierkhold Theater, 1925.
Lithograph in red and white.
14⅛ x 42½ in., 36 x 108 cm.

937 [R958].
Poster Advertising the Forthcoming Performance of The Mandate at the Meierkhold Theater, 1925.

Lithograph in blue and white.
14⅛ x 42½ in., 36 x 108 cm.

938 [R953].
Poster Advertising Bubus the Teacher at the Meierkhold Theater, 1925.
Lithograph in green, black, and white.
28⅜ x 42⅛ in., 72 x 107 cm.
The photographs are of fifteen actors involved in the production, among them Nikolai Okhlopkov, Zinaida Raikh, and Boris Zakhava.

940

941

in the poster, e.g., "What is Lef?" "Where is the theory of Lef?" "Whom are you with?" are similar to the polemical issues raised in the first two numbers of the *Lef* journal. The title of the debate, *Lef ili blef* [=Lef or Bluff], is a play on words.

940 [NIRE].
Poster Advertising a Tour by the State Meierkhold Theater in the Cities of Baku, Tiflis, Rostov-on-Don, Krasnodar, Kharkov, and Leningrad, ca. 1928.
Lithograph in black and white.
Photomontage with twenty-three photographs of performances and fourteen portraits of performers.
42 x 27½ in., 106.5 x 70 cm.
Inscriptions (as part of the design) provide the names of the actors and administrators of the Meierkhold company together with the repertoire of six plays, i.e. *Forest, Come On, Europe!, Bubus the Teacher, Mandate, Roar, China!,* and *Inspector General.* Printed by the Gosizdat First Model Printing-House, Moscow, in an edition of 2000.

The Mandate: *comedy in three acts by Nikolai Erdman. Produced by Vsevolod Meierkhold at the Meierkhold Theater, Moscow, on 20 April, 1925, with designs by Ilia Shlepianov.*

Satirizing Moscow life under NEP (New Economic Policy), the action exposes the opportunism and fraudulence of the Soviet bourgeoisie. The retiring Guliachkin declares himself to be a Communist and marries off his sister, an old maid, so that he can profit from her husband. Nastia, a cook, is taken for the Grand Duchess Anastasia Nikolaevna, a mistaken identity that leads to a grand comedy of errors.

942

943

944

946

945

(22, 23, 25 August, 1925, at the Greater Hall of the Leningrad Conservatory).

945 [R959].
Poster Advertising the End of the Season Performance of **The Mandate** *at the Meierkhold Theater,* 1925.
Lithograph in black and white.
21 x 14⅛ in., 53.5 x 36 cm.
Inscriptions (as part of the design) provide details on the names of the performers, listing Shlepianov as the designer of the production.

946 [R960].
Poster Advertising the Performance of the Meierkhold Theater in the Leningrad Conservatoire, 1925.
Photomontage lithograph in black and white.
14 x 21¼ in., 35.5 x 54 cm.
Inscriptions (as part of the design) indicate the commencement and location of the performances (on 22 August, 1925, at the Bolshoi Hall of the Leningrad Conservatoire with a repertoire of *The Mandate, Bubus the Teacher, The D.E. Trust,* and *The Forest*).
Provenance: the artist's son, Alexander Shlepianov, Moscow, 1980s.

746 I. Shlepianov: "Nash revoliutsionnyi tvorcheskii put (1922-1932)" in Graeva, *Ilia Shlepianov,* p. 18.
747 S. Maiorov: "Pervye shagi" in Graeva, *Ilia Shlepianov,* p. 67.

941 [R954].
Poster Advertising the First Performances of **The Mandate** *at the Meierkhold Theater, Moscow,* 1925.
Lithograph in red, green, black, and white.
28⅜ x 42½ in., 72 x 108 cm.
Inscriptions (as part of the design) provide details on the date and location of the performances (20-22 April, 1925) and the names of the actors.

942 [R955].
Poster Advertising Performances of **The Mandate** *at the Meierkhold Theater, Moscow,* 1925.
Lithograph in green, black, and white.
28⅜ x 42½ in., 72 x 108 cm.
Inscriptions provide details on the dates and location of the performances (5-10 May, 1925).

943 [R956].
Poster Advertising Performances of **The Mandate** *at the Meierkhold Theater, Moscow,* 1925.
Lithograph in yellow, black, and white.
28⅜ x 42½ in., 72 x 108 cm.
Inscriptions (as part of the design) provide details on the dates and location of the performances (12-17 May, 1925), announcing that these are the last of the 1924-25 winter season.

944 [R957].
Poster Advertising Performances of **The Mandate** *by the Meierkhold Theater, Leningrad,* 1925.
Lithograph in blue, green, and white.
28⅜ x 42½ in., 72 x 108 cm.
Inscriptions (as part of the design) indicate the date and location of the performances

SHUKHAEV, Vasilii Ivanovich

Born 12 (24) January, 1887, Moscow, Russia; died 14 April, 1973, Tbilisi, Georgia.

1897-1905 attended CSIAI; 1906-12 attended the Higher Art Institute of IAA, where he studied under Dmitrii Kardovsky and Vasilii Savinsky; established close contact with Alexandre Jacovleff; 1912 with Jacovleff designed Vsevolod Meierkhold's pantomime *The Lovers* at the Karabchevsky House, St. Petersburg; 1912-14 lived in Rome as an IAA *pensionnaire;* 1915 contributed to the "New Society of Artists" exhibition in Petrograd; 1917 onward member of the World of Art Society; 1918 taught at Pegoskhuma; 1920 lived in Finland; 1921 went to France; 1922 with Jacovleff exhibited at the Galerie Barbazanges, Paris; 1922 onward lived in Western Europe, mainly in Paris; 1924 contributed to the "Russian Art Exhibition," New York; 1924-25 designed several spectacles for Nikita Baliev's Chauve-Souris cabaret, such as *A Country Festival, The Arrival at Bethlehem, A Country Picnic in a Distant Province of Russia;* during the 1920s was active as a portraitist, stage designer, book illustrator, and muralist (e.g., designed the interior of La Maisonnette Russe, a cabaret and restaurant in Paris, in 1928); 1930 visited Morocco; 1935 returned to the Soviet Union, settling in Leningrad; 1937-47 exiled to Magadan in Eastern Siberia, where he designed for the Magadan Music and Drama Theater; 1947 moved to Tbilisi, where he became professor of drawing at the Academy of Arts.

Bibliography
F. Fishkova, ed.: *V.I. Shukhaev.* Catalog of exhibition organized by the Union of Artists of the USSR and the Union of Artists of the Georgian SSR, M, 1958.
M2, Vol. 2, pp. 195-96, listing his theatrical productions.
I. Miamlin: *Vasilii Ivanovich Shukhaev,* L: Khudozhnik RSFSR, 1972.
S. Erlashova: *Vasilii Ivanovich Shukhaev.* Catalog of exhibition at the State Museum of Art of the Peoples of the East, M, 1977.
N. Elizbarashvili, ed.: "Pisma V.I. Shukhaeva A.E. Yakovlevu iz Italii (1912-13) i Peterburga (1914-15)" in *Panorama iskusstv,* M, 1985, No. 8, pp. 173-90.
N. Uvarova et al., comp.: *A.E. Yakovlev (1887-1938) V.I. Shukhaev (1887-1973).* Catalog of exhibition at the RM and the State Museum of Arts of the Georgian SSR, Tbilisi, 1988.
A42, pp. 722-24.
E. Yakovleva: "Zhivopis Shukhaeva v Russkom muzee" in *Khudozhnik,* M, 1989, No. 9, pp. 17-24.
E. Yakovleva, ed.: *Vasilii Shukhaev. Zhizn i tvorchestvo,* M: Galart, 2010.

Like his close friend Alexandre Jacovleff (Nos. 584-88 [R1008-12]), Shukhaev is known primarily as a superb draftsman, especially in the medium of sanguine. Although he explored many subjects and genres, Shukhaev gave particular attention to portraits of artistic, literary, and theatrical celebrities both in Europe and the Soviet Union. For example, during his sojourn in France, Shukhaev made a number of memorable portraits of Fedor Chaliapin, Serge Prokofiev, Igor Stravinsky, etc., as well as those of Nikita Baliev and Anna Pavlova included here. In some cases, such portraits resulted from his collaborations in opera, ballet, and drama productions. His Soviet biographer Igor Miamlin wrote:

> [Shukhaev] 'squeezes' his model into the frame and so arranges the figure or face of the person being portrayed that at times the sensation is one of tightness. Presumably, he did this to achieve the maximum concentration of attention on what was important, so that neither the details, nor the space inhabited by the person would deflect the viewer.[748]

Shukhaev played an active role in the early Russian emigration in Paris, allying himself with artists such as Alexandre Benois, Ivan Bilibin, Dimitri Bouchène, Boris Grigoriev, Georgii Lukomsky, and Konstantin Somov in their endeavor to maintain the elegance and measured taste of the World of Art. Shukhaev reinforced these traditions in his book designs, as is clear from his pochoir illustrations to the deluxe editions of Alexander Pushkin's *Boris Godunov* and *Queen of Spades,*[749] and in his oil paintings of French landscapes, some of which were reproduced in the journal *Zhar-ptitsa.* Like many others of his generation, such as Viktor Bart and Bilibin, Shukhaev did not find artistic success in Western Europe and, beckoned by illusory promises of material welfare and artistic opportunity, returned to Soviet Russia — and to the tragic consequences that such a move entailed.

Alexandre Benois: *Portrait of Vasilii Shukhaev, 1926.* See No. 298 [R267].

947

947 [R961].
Portrait of Anna Pavlova, **1922.**
Sanguine and charcoal.
Signed and dated lower right: "B. Schoukhaeff, Paris 1922."
35⅜ x 25⅝ in., 90 x 65 cm.
Reproduced in A34, p. 398; I51, No. 217.
Provenance: Boris Melikoff, Paris, March, 1981.

Note: This sanguine sketch recalls Shukhaev's 1921 oil portrait of the famous ballerina, which was shown at the exhibition "Le Monde d'Art," Paris, in 1921 (reproduced in the journal *Zhar-ptitsa,* Berlin, 1921, No. 2, p. 3) and also at the exhibition "Art Russe," Brussels in 1930 (reproduced in K8, plate 47; and also in Yakovleva, *Vasilii Shukhaev. Zhizn i tvorchestvo,* ill. 20). Pavlova (see No. 118 [R97]) is presented here in a pose reminiscent of movements in *Chopiniana* (cf. the photograph of her in *Chopiniana* in A. Oliveroff: *The Flight of the Swan. A Memory of Pavlova,* New York: Dutton, 1932, opposite p. 72). Of course, Pavlova was the subject of many portraits by Russian artists, including Léon Bakst (reproduced in G51, p. 107), Jacovleff (reproduced in V. Svetloff: *Anna Pavlova,* Paris: Brunoff, 1922, p. 127), and Savelii Sorin (reproduced, for example, in Oliveroff, opposite p. 114; and also in L112, Lot 144). For photographs of Pavlova posing for the Shukhaev portraits see Elizbarashvili, pp. 184-85.

948 [R962].
Portrait of Nikita Baliev, **1924.**
Sanguine and black chalk.
Signed and dated lower left: "B. Schoukhaeff, Paris 24/6 24."
22¼ x 20 in., 56.6 x 50.8 cm.
Other inscription: lower left carries a dedication in Russian from Shukhaev to Baliev: "To Nikita Fedorovich in memory of V. Shukhaev. Paris. 1.10.1924."
Provenance: *Dance, Theatre, Opera, Music-Hall and Film. Décor and Costume*

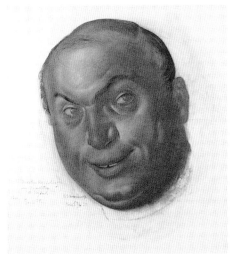

948

Designs, Books, Posters and Photographs, New York: Sotheby, Parke Bernet, 1981, 15 December, Lot 37 (reproduced).
Reproduced in color as the cover for the program Balieff's "Chauve-Souris," London season, 1924; also reproduced in subsequent programs; reproduced in black and white in I51, No. 218; O26. A very similar portrait in the GMTMA is reproduced in Yakovleva, Vasilii Shukhaev. Zhizn i tvorchestvo, ill. 38. (Cf. Nos. 51 [R47], 859 [R736].)

Note: In 1924-25 Shukhaev was especially close to Nikita Baliev, the founder and director of the cabaret the Bat/Chauve-Souris, and contributed a number of designs to his productions, and not surprisingly, he portrayed the impresario "in the shape of a round, smiling full moon."[750] To some extent, therefore, Shukhaev was responsible for the phenomenal success of the cabaret in Paris, London, and New York precisely during this period (see No. 949 [R963]) — when reviewers offered nothing but praise for Baliev's entreprise which transformed

> poupées en hommes et les hommes en poupées; elle présente des opéras qui durent trois minutes, anime les tableaux et fige la foule vivante en

949

> tableaux. Elle souligne le sens dans le non-sens, elle pénètre dans "l'âme des objets" et cherche surtout et partout "l'inattendu."[751]

Partie Champêtre dans une Lointaine Province Russe: revue by Nikita Baliev with music by Alexei Arkhangelsky. Produced by Nikita Baliev's Chauve-Souris at the Théâtre Femina, Paris, 1924, with designs by Vasilii Shukhaev.
A group of Hussars and their ladies in crinolines flirt as they picnic in the Caucasus Mountains.

949 [R963].
Costume Design for the Georgian Maid, ca. 1924.
Watercolor.
14 x 9⅞ in., 35.5 x 25 cm.
Annotations throughout in Russian with precise instructions to the dressmaker.
Provenance: Salomé Halpern, London, 1966.

Note: Partie Champêtre dans une Lointaine Province Russe (known as A Country Picnic

in a Distant Province of Russia when it was presented to English-speaking audiences) was produced during one of Baliev's most successful seasons. Somov, a colleague of Shukhaev in Paris, attended one of the performances and was much impressed by Shukhaev's contribution:

> Quite unexpected for me is Shukhaev — he's a very, very good décor and costume designer. His old-fashioned Russian picnic somewhere in Lermontov's Caucasus with its hussars and ladies in crinolines is charming. The selection of colors for the costumes is excellent.[752]

Les Quatre Saisons: allegorical ballet in one act of four tableaux by Marius Petipa with music by Alexander Glazunov. Projected, but not produced, in Paris in 1931, with designs by Vasilii Shukhaev.
See No. 691 [R585] for plot summary.

950 [NIRE].
Set Design for Summer, 1931.
Watercolor and gouache
Signed and dated lower right: "B. Schoukhaeff 1931."
8⅝ x 20 in., 22 x 51.5 cm.
Reproduced in I20, No. 82.
Provenance: Issar Gourvitch, Paris, 1964.
Now in a private collection.
Reproduced in I20, No. 82.

Note: Les Quatre Saisons (also known as Les Saisons) was first performed by the Imperial Ballet at the Hermitage Theater in St. Petersburg on 7 February, 1900, with designs by Petr Lambin and Evgenii Ponomarev (see No. 691 [R585]). Later on Les Quatre Saisons became a staple number for various companies, assuming a primary place in the repertoire of Anna Pavlova.

748 Miamlin: Vasilii Ivanovich Shukhaev, p. 86.
749 A. Pouchkine: La Dame de Pique, Paris: La Pléiade, 1923; A. Pouchkine: Boris Godunov, Paris: La Pléiade, 1925.
750 D. Aminado: Poezd na tretiem puti, New York: Chekhov, 1954, p. 169.
751 (unsigned): "Le Théâtre de la Chauve-Souris" in program for the 1924-25 season at the Théâtre Femina, Paris; 1924, p. 16.
752 Letter from Konstantin Somov to his sister, Anna Somova-Mikhailova, dated 7 March, 1925. Quoted in F51, p. 269.

SIMOV, Viktor Andreevich

Born 2 (14) April, 1858, Moscow, Russia; died 21 August, 1935, Moscow, Russia.

1875-82 studied at MIPSA under Vasilii Perov, Illarion Prianishnikov, Alexei Savrasov, and other Realists; 1883-93 contributed to several sessions of the Society of Wandering Exhibitions; 1885-86 invited by Savva Mamontov to work for the Krotkov Opera Company; 1887 designed Gerhard Hauptmann's *Drowned Bell* for the Society of Art and Literature, Moscow; 1896 made acquaintance of Konstantin Stanislavsky; 1898 joined MKhAT, where he worked as artist-in-residence until 1912, designing, for example, Chekhov's *Seagull* (1898), *Uncle Vania* (1899), *Three Sisters* (1901), and *Ivanov* (1904); 1910s worked for various Moscow theaters, including the Free Theater, the Chamber Theater, the Maly Theater, and the Sukhodolsky Dramatic Theater; 1920 contributed to the "First State Exhibition of Art and Science," Kazan; 1923 contributed to "Theatrical and Decorative Art of Moscow," Moscow; 1924 helped design sets for the movie *Aelita*; 1925-35 in charge of the Experimental-Decoration Studio at MKhAT; 1927 designed Vsevolod Ivanov's *Armored Train 14-69* for MKhAT; contributed to "10 Years of Work at the Little Theater," Moscow; 1928 member of the Association of Realist Artists; contributed to "Moscow Theaters of the October Decade," Moscow.

Bibliography
O. Nekrasova: *Simov,* M: Iskusstvo, 1952.
I. Gremislavsky: *Kompozitsiia stsenicheskogo prostranstva v tvorchestve V.A. SImova,* M: Iskusstvo, 1953.
A7, Vol. 4, pp. 934-35.
C42, passim.
F53, passim.
Yu. Nekhoroshev: *Khudozhnik V.A. Simov,* M: Sovetskii khudozhnik, 1984.
G67, pp. 186-96.
Sourcebooks on the Moscow Art Theater carry copious references to Simov, e.g. C15, C134, C158, C174.

The success of the Moscow Art Theater (MKhAT) is closely linked to the decorative contributions that Simov made, epecially in the first years of its evolution. Together with Stanislavsky and Nemirovich-Danchenko, Simov reformed the Russian theater by emphasizing a new "psychological" Realism after the illusionistic overindulgence of the preceding decades. To this end, Simov always tried to elicit both the actuality of the time and place of a given play and the emotional color, studying, for example, Vologda folklore in preparation for *Snegurochka* (1900), Moscow flophouses for *The Lower Depths* (1902), and Roman ruins for *Julius Caesar* (1903). In many respects, Simov, therefore, was the ideal artist for Chekhov — economical and sparse, but also, according to critics, capable of "destroying the even surface of the floor and combining landings, staircases, and passages"[753] so as to make the production alive and convincing. At all times, Simov was solicitous of the welfare of the actor,

maintaining that "in putting together the maquette, mentally I took the place of the actors."[754] No wonder, then, that Simov was charged with designing the premieres of *Seagull, Uncle Vania, Three Sisters, Cherry Orchard,* and *Ivanov* — from any standpoint a prestigious repertoire.

Although also a studio painter and caricaturist, Simov was at home in the theater. He was a skilled artisan, knew how to turn a two-dimensional drawing into a three-dimensional object, and, in creating his sets and costumes, was able to assume the changing perspectives of audience, actor, and director. Simov declared:

> The decorations should accompany [the performance] like a simple, cordial melody. If it is possible to read between the lines, then let the viewer read between the pictures of the scenic design[755]

True, his esthetic was basically a Realist one (his resolutions were very different from those of his Symbolist rival at MKhAT, Vladimir Egorov) and he had little patience with avant-garde experiment. How satisfied he must have been when Stanislavsky called upon him to "save" the 1927 production of *Armored Train 14-69* from the highly inventive, but totally impracticable, designs of Leonid Chupiatov. For some, this episode was a "death sentence" to free experimentation in the Soviet theater, for others it marked the beginning of a new and healthy Realism.[756]

The Storm: *play in five acts by Alexander Ostrovsky. Projected, but not produced, for the Sukhodolsky Dramatic Theater, Moscow, in November, 1915, with designs by Viktor Simov.*

Katia Kabanova lives a tedious life in a small town on the River Volga with her jealous husband Tikhon and her spiteful mother-in-law Marfa. One day she discovers true love with Boris, a local

gentleman, but torn by divided obligations and fallen victim to moral unrest, she throws herself into the river.

951 [NIRE].
Set Design, 1915.
Oil on board.
Signed lower right in Russian: V. Simov."
19¼ x 28 in., 49 x 71 cm.
Inscribed on the reverse in Russian: "To dear Isaak Ezrovich in memory of a radiant time working together at the Dramatic Theater. From Simov, November, 1915." The reference is to Ivan (Isaak) Ezrovich Duvan-Tortsov (1873-1939), actor and director of the Sukhodolsky Dramatic Theater, Moscow, and with Jascha Juschny's Blaue Vogel cabaret in Berlin.
Provenance: *Russian Paintings and Works of Art,* London: Christie's, 7 July, 2000, Lot 208 (reproduced and described as a stage design for *Khovanshchina*).

Note. The reference to the [Sukhodolsky] Dramatic Theater and to the date 1915 in the inscription suggests that the piece is a design for the presentation of *The Storm* for which Simov had been engaged, but which was not produced.[757] Moreover, the houses and dress of the two women suggest the 19th-century Russian provinces (the ambience of *The Storm*) and certainly not the fabulous Moscow of boyars and princes of *Khovanshchina*. During its brief life, the Sukhodolsky Dramatic Theater produced plays by a wide variety of authors, including Dmitrii Merezhkovsky, Alexei K. Tolstoi — and also Ostrovsky.

753 A7, Vol. 4, p. 934.
754 Statement by Simov. Quoted in Nekhoroshev, *Khudozhnik V.A. Simov,* p. 239, where neither source, nor date is given.
755 Statement by Simov. Quoted in Gremislavsky, *Kompozitsiia...,* p. 28, where neither source, nor date is given.
756 See C19, p. 236.
757 Nekhoroshev, *Khudozhnik V.A. Simov,* p. 271.

SOMOV, Konstantin Andreevich

Born 18 (30) November, 1869, St. Petersburg, Russia; died 6 May, 1939, Paris, France.

Son of Andrei Ivanovich Somov, Senior Curator at the Hermitage, St. Petersburg. 1879-88 studied at Karl Mai's Gymnasium, St. Petersburg; 1884 attended evening classes at SSEA; 1888-97 attended IAA, studying under Pavel Chistiakov, Ilia Repin, Vasilii Vereshchagin, et al.; 1890 traveled in Europe, the first of many trips abroad; 1897-99 lived in Paris, studying at the Académie Colarossi; attended Whistler's studio; interested in the work of Chardin, Ingres, Watteau, and Poussin; 1899 after a short visit to England, returned to St. Petersburg; primary member of the World of Art Society, contributing to all its exhibitions; 1901 visited Berlin and Dresden; especially interested in the art of the Simplicissimus group in Munich; 1903 one-man exhibition at the Contemporary Art enterprise, St. Petersburg; widely recognized as an accomplished portraitist, landscapist, and book illustrator; 1910 co-founder of the second World of Art Society; popular as a fashionable portrait painter; 1913 received the title of Academician from IAA; 1914 worked on murals for Evfimiia Nosova's house in Moscow; 1915 involved in the organization of Yuliia Sazonova's puppet theater in Petrograd; 1915-18 taught at Elizaveta Zvantseva's school in Petrograd; 1919 one-man exhibition at the TG; 1923 traveled to New York with the "Russian Art Exhibition"; 1925 settled in Paris; 1928 acquired a farm in Normandy; 1920s-30s continued to paint portraits and landscapes and to illustrate books.

Léon Bakst: *Portrait of Konstantin Somov Seated in a Chair,* 1899. See 56 [R52].

Georgii Vereisky: *Portrait of Konstantin Somov,* 1922. See 1127 [NIRE].

Georgii Vereisky: *Portrait of Konstantin Somov,* 1922. See 1129 [NIRE].

Fedor Zakharov: *Portrait of Konstantin Somov,* 1923. See 1182 [R782].

Bibliography
S. Ernst: *K.A. Somov,* P: Obshchina Sv. Evgenii, 1918.
I. Pruzhan: *Konstantin Andreevich Somov.* Catalog of exhibition at the RM, 1971.
I. Pruzhan: *Konstantin Somov,* M: Izobrazitelnoe iskusstvo, 1972.
A. Gusarova: *Konstantin Andreevich Somov,* M: Iskusstvo, 1973.
F51.
E. Zhuravleva: *K.A. Somov,* M: Iskusstvo, 1980.
H34, pp. 534-36.
L. Korotkina: *Konstantin Andreevich Somov,* SP: Zolotoi vek, 2004.
H51, passim.
P. Golubev: "'Nichego osobennogo, no kakaia zhizn.' Konstantin Somov v 1926 godu" in *Mitin zhurnal,* Tver, 2011, No. 65, pp. 204-64.

An inveterate theater-goer, Somov rarely designed for the stage, even if many of his images, such as those of Harlequin and Columbine, were inspired by prevalent theatrical tastes of the early twentieth century. For example, in his several *Harlequinades* of the 1910s, the figures seem to be taking part in some intimate *ballet mécanique* in which every movement and gesture is controlled and predetermined. In these theatralized paintings Somov concentrates all actions within the tight confines of the stage, refusing to connect them with the concrete world outside. The exquisite balance of forms and colors, the rhythmic lines of figures and foliage, the uniform montage of night sky, the calculated choreography of the participants — these elements often guide the eye toward the center of the composition. In the case of the *Harlequinades*, this may be a fountain or a rainbow, symbols perhaps of the unattainable and the vainglorious.

The concept of the miniature theater, which can be associated readily with many of Somov's studio paintings, might be applied also to his book illustrations — perhaps Somov's most successful discipline. Beginning in 1898, Somov executed numerous head- and tail-pieces, letterheads, and other vignettes for magazines and books and he produced full-scale illustrations for several deluxe editions, such as the celebrated erotic miscellany *Kniga markizy* (*Le Livre de la Marquise*, 1908 and subsequent editions); he also designed advertisements, posters, menus, visiting-cards, ex-libris plates, and theater bills. In their effusion of silken ribbons, carnations, lace, and daisy chains, Somov's designs prompt comparison with the gentle delights of Boucher and Fragonard, although the total effect of Somov's decorations tends to be a disturbing and lugubrious one. In the swoon of love beneath fireworks that celebrate no great event, in the aimless walks beneath rainbows that herald no better day, in the intricate ornaments worn by his phantoms from Versailles, Somov was surely depicting the diversions of his own society in the face of imminent destruction. From the endless panorama of marquises and cavaliers, Columbines and Harlequins, devils and cupids, there exudes a great weariness and

952

953

behind the gay colors and erotic play of Somov's *dramatis personae*, there looms the shadow of death. These things reflect the very ethos of the Russian *fin de siècle* — what Alexandre Benois described as an "effeminate, spiritually tormented and hysterical time."[758]

Unidentified production, *ca. 1910.*

952 [R785].
Set Design, ca. 1910.
Pencil.
8½ x 4⅜ in., 21.5 x 11 cm.
Inscriptions carry instructions in Russian for the stage hands, painters, and dressmakers; the reverse also carries a similar scene and inscriptions in French: "demoiselle malgardée," "l'imitation."
Provenance: the artist's nephew, Evgenii Mikhailov, Leningrad, September, 1970.

Note: It is not known for which production, if any, this design was made. It may be a preparatory sketch for a book illustration or simply one of Somov's numerous doodles, perhaps on the theme of Red Riding-Hood. The words "gouache le Toison d'Or" on the far right of the drawing may refer to a potential illustration for the Moscow Symbolist journal *Zolotoe runo / Toison d'or,* which published many of Somov's pictures and vignettes.

953 [R783].
Design for the Drop Curtain at the Free Theater, Moscow, ca. 1913.
Gouache.
25⅝ x 38 in., 65 x 96.5 cm.
Provenance: the artist's nephew, Evgenii Mikhailov, Leningrad, September, 1970.
Reproduced in color in I73, p. 115; and in black and white in I20, No. 83; I51, No. 220. The actual curtain (7.6 x 11.46 meters; now in the collection of the State Museum of the Arts of Georgia, Tbilisi) has been reproduced several times, e.g., in *Baian,* M, 1914, No. 1, opposite p. 66; *Stolitsa i usadba,* P, 1916,

No. 57, p. 15; *Dekorativnoe iskusstvo,* M, 1981, No. 4, p. 44. A watercolor design for the curtain dated 1913, now in the BTM (formerly in the collection of Vladimir Girshman, Mocow), is reproduced in M. Kuzmin: *K.A. Somov,* P: Kamena, 1916, plate 27; Pruzhan, *Konstantin Somov,* plate 60; G66, plate 19. The dating of the work to ca. 1913 has been questioned.

Note: Somov's drop curtain for the Free Theater in Moscow incorporated many of his favorite motifs and images and elaborated a vocabulary that he had been using in his evocations of the Italian Comedy and in the *Livre de la Marquise.* As a matter of fact, it was the actress and director Vera Kommissarzhevskaia who first invited Somov to make a drop curtain for her own theater in St. Petersburg, but he refused the commission. She then asked Léon Bakst to fulfill the commission — which he did by basing his curtain composition on his painting called *Elysium* (1906; now in the TG). Bakst's curtain (now in the RM), unfortunately, was damaged by water.[759] Somov's curtain was commissioned in 1913 by Konstantin Mardzhanishvili (Mardzhanov; see No. 767g [R646zh]), founder of the Free Theater and himself caught up in the "whirlwind of Columbines and Harlequins."[760] In establishing his Free Theater, Mardzhanov wished to "overcome the division between ballet-dancer, acrobat, actor, singer,"[761] although his undertaking did not last long. By the late spring of 1913 Somov had already painted one design surrounded by a frieze (the one now in the BTM) and, with Mardzhanov's approval, he, his sister (Anna Somova-Mikhailova), and fifty embroideresses set to work on the final product — embroidered in silk, velvet, brocade, and other fabrics.[762] The curtain was ready by October, 1913 and was installed shortly thereafter. Somov himself preferred the designs to the curtain and observers tended to agree: "The world of his [Somov's] mannered dolls should remain small, doll-like, almost a joke. Vast dimensions require vast images... Nevertheless, the impression of the curtain is a vivid and unusual one."[763]

Sinfonia: *suite of dances based on Bach's* Christmas Oratorio *performed by Tamara Karsavina at Carnegie Hall, New York, on 1 November, 1924.*

954 [R784].
Costume Design for Tamara Karsavina, 1924.
Watercolor.
Signed and dated lower right in ink: "C. Somoff, Paris 1924."
13⅛ x 9¾ in., 33.3 x 24.7 cm.
Provenance: John Carr-Doughty, Leicester, 3 November, 1981.
Reproduced in A34, p. 406; F107, p.152; and in N118 (a), where it is described as a costume for the Countess in Mozart's *Marriage of Figaro.*

Note: This is one of Somov's rare costume designs for the stage, a discipline that he

954

tended to avoid,[764] and it is reasonable to assume that he produced this work as a favor to his friend Karsavina rather than as the result of any deep commitment to theatrical design. Karsavina wore this costume of an angel during the dance recital. Somov, who was in New York at this time, designed two costumes for the presentation and, unexpectedly, he was rather pleased with the result:

> They turned out to be very successful, charming in color and material... At first Tamara was cold, but she then began to be herself and to dance better and better.[765]

The second costume that Somov designed for this production — for Karsavina as a marquise — is in the collection of the Ashmolean Museum, Oxford (reproduced in *Dancing Times*, London, 1967, July, p. 532; also see G30, No. 94). In addition, Somov designed a costume for Karsavina's opposite in the Carnegie Hall production, i.e., Pierre Vladimirov (also reproduced in the same issue of *Dancing Times*, p. 533). Somov designed occasional costumes for other ballerinas as well, such as Anna Pavlova (see reproduction in F51, No. 39) and Vera Nemtchinova (see reproduction in J34, Lot 39).

758 A. Benois: *Istoriia russkoi zhivopisi v XIX veke*, SP: Evdokimov, 1901, pp. 271-72.
759 See *Teatr, muzyka i sport*, SP, 1913, No. 2, p. 12.
760 A. Mgebrov: *Zhizn v teatre*, M-L: Akademiia, 1932, p. 2.
761 C25, p. 215.
762 The design for the curtain (now in the BTM) and the curtain itself were made in 1913. The date of the version in the Lobanov-Rostovsky collection has not been established and it is assumed that this is a later repetition.
763 V. Zv.: "Zanaves Svobodnogo Teatra" in *Baian*, M, 1914, No. 1, p. 67.
764 For commentary, see N. Lobanov: "K.A. Somov and the Stage" in M2, Vol. 6, pp. 89-93; N118 (a).
765 Letter from Konstantin Somov to his sister, Anna Somova-Mikhailova, dated 2 November, 1924. Quoted in F51, p. 255. Also see the brief commentary by Karsavina herself in her article "Touring in America" in *Dancing Times*, op. cit., p. 533.

STELLETSKY, Dmitrii Semeonovich

Born 1 (13) January, 1875, Brest-Litovsk, Belorussia; died 21 February, 1947, Sainte Geneviève-des-Bois, near Paris, France.

1896-1903 attended the Higher Art Institute of IAA; at first studied architecture and then switched to sculpture; 1903 with Boris Kustodiev visited Novgorod to research Medieval Russian art, his lifelong interest; lived in Paris; attended the Académie Julian; 1903-13 lived in St. Petersburg; worked in various disciplines, including painting, sculpture, stage design, and book illustration; contributed to the exhibitions of the New Society of Artists, the Union of Artists, the World of Art, and other societies; with Ivan Bilibin, Mstislav Dobujinsky, and others, visited Talashkino; 1905-06 contributed illustrations to satirical magazines, including *Adskaia pochta* [Hellish Post]; 1906 created an album of illustrations to *The Lay of the Host of Igor;* 1907 with Kustodiev visited Italy; 1907-13 made many trips to Medieval Russian towns; visited Western Europe several times; 1908-09 designed productions of Alexei K. Tolstoi's *Tsar Fedor Ioannovich* and Nikolai Rimsky-Korsakov's *Snegourochka;* 1909 designed costumes for Sergei Diaghilev's production of *The Maid of Pskov* in Paris; 1912 joined the revived World of Art group; contributed to the "Exhibition of Paintings by Russian Artists and Sculpture by Boris Fredman-Kliuzel" at the Lemercier Gallery, Moscow; 1914 onward lived in France, where he worked as a sculptor, muralist, and stage designer; 1920 built a house and studio near Cannes; painted murals for villas in the south of France; 1925 cofounded the Icône society; 1925-27 supervised murals for the church of Saint Serge in Paris; 1930s painted murals for other Orthodox churches.

Bibliography
A. Benois: "Iskusstvo Stelletskogo" in *Apollon*, SP, 1911, No. 4, pp. 5-16. Reprinted as "D. Stelletsky" in *Novyi mir iskusstva*, SP, 1998, No. 1, pp. 8-9.
G. Lukomskij: "Dimitri Semenowitsch Stelezkij" in *Kunst*, Berlin, 1930, No. 61, pp. 228-32.
S. Makovsky: "D.S. Stelletsky" in *Grani*, Frankfurt, 1956, No. 31, pp. 153-64.
B19, pp. 567-73.
F18, pp. 313-30.
K48 (b), p. 39.
M2, Vol. 2, p. 199, listing his theatrical productions.
H34, pp. 544-46.
H51, passim.
Relevant correspondence, memoirs, and documents concerning Stelletsky will be found in G. Vzdornov, Z. Zalesskaia, and O. Lelekova: *Obshchestvo "Ikona" v Parizhe*, M-Paris: Progress-Traditsiia, 2002, pp. 140-80.
For color reproductions of some of Stelletsky's early works see S. Nechaeva, comp.: *Tulskii oblastnoi khudozhestvennyi muzei*, L: Khudozhnik RSFSR, 1983, unpaginated.

Painter and sculptor, Stelletsky was associated with the World of Art group, contributed to their exhibitions, and shared their retrospective mood, especially the evocations of Medieval Russia (cf. Ivan Bilibin). Stelletsky was particularly interested in icons and church frescoes, interpreting this legacy in both image and method, to which end he mixed his own paints according to Medieval recipes, avoiding chemical compounds. His activity as a scenic designer was intermittent, although Diaghilev thought highly enough of his work to invite him to design *Liturgie* in 1915 (see Note to Nos. 542-58 [R414-29]). In France and along with Dimitri Bouchène, Alexandre Serebriakov, and Boris Zvorykin, Stelletsly maintained the high graphic and decorative standards of the World of Art, accepting both serious and more ephemeral commissions such as designs for concert programs and menus for the émigré community. Writing of the effect of Byzantine and Medieval Russian painting on Bilibin, Roerich, and Stelletsky, Sergei Golynets concludes that

> colors become more resonant and saturated, preserving their locality and planarity... Under artificial light the paints appear to be luminous. Sometimes the representation is reminiscent of baffled enamel.[766]

Boris Godunov: *opera in four acts by Modest Mussorgsky. Produced by Sergei Diaghilev for the first Saison Russe at the Théâtre National de l'Opéra, Paris, on 19 May, 1908, with set designs by Alexandre Benois, sets and costumes by Alexander Golovin, and costumes by Ivan Bilibin and Dmitrii Stelletsky. See No. 339 [R305] for plot summary.*

955

955 [R786].
Costume Design for the Holy Fool (Yurodivyi), ca. 1908.
Gouache and pencil.
Initialed lower right in pencil in Russian: "D.S."

959

Note: The exact date of the production of
this poster is difficult to establish, although
it cannot be later than 1917, since Rodin,
described here as Honorary President, died
on 17 November, 1917.

Rite Matrimonial Russe: *theatrical number
based on Mikhail Glinka's* Ruslan and
Liudmila *arranged by Alexei Arkhangelsky.
Produced by Nikita Baliev's Chauve-Souris
at the Théâtre de la Madeleine, Paris, 1926
with designs by Dmitrii Stelletsky.*
        See No. 377 [R344] for plot summary.

959 [190; R790].
Stage Design, 1926.
Gouache.
Signed and dated lower right in Russian:
"D. Stelletsky, Paris 1926."
39⅜ x 47¼ in., 100 x 120 cm.
Provenance: Nicholas Wyrouboff, Paris,
May, 1968.
Reproduced in color in G79, p. 131; N188,
p. 46; and as the cover for B179; and in
black and white in I20, No. 86; I51, No. 225;
I77, p. 153; and Q8.

766   F30, p. 13.

STENBERG BROTHERS

Stenberg, Georgii Avgustovich

Born 20 March (2 April), 1900, Moscow, Russia;
died 15 October, 1933, Moscow, Russia.

Stenberg, Vladimir Avgustovich

Born 23 March (4 April), 1899, Moscow,
Russia; died 1 May, 1982, Moscow, Russia.

1912-17 attended CSIAI; 1917-19 attended
Svomas, Moscow, where they were enrolled
in the so-called Studio without a Supervisor;
with Nikolai Denisovsky, Vasilii Komardenkov,
Sergei Kostin, Konstantin Medunetsky,
Nikolai Prusakov, and Sergei Svetlov, they
were among the first Svomas graduates;
1918 contributed to May Day agit-decorations in Moscow, working on designs for
the Napoleon Movie House and the Railroad
Workers' Club; 1919-21 members of
Obmokhu; 1920 members of Inkhuk; 1921
with Alexei Gan, Alexander Rodchenko,
Varvara Stepanova, and others opposed
"pure art" and championed industrial
Constructivism; 1922 with Medunetsky
worked on a production of *The Yellow Jacket*
for the School of the Chamber Theater,
Moscow, the first of several collaborations
with Medunetsky; 1923 began to work on
movie posters; 1923-25 closely associated
with the journal *Lef*; 1924-31 worked on sets
and costumes for productions at Alexander
Tairov's Chamber Theater in Moscow; 1925
contributed to the "Exposition Internationale
des Arts Décoratifs" in Paris; 1929-32 taught
at the Architecture-Construction Institute,
Moscow; 1933 onwards, after Georgii's

death, Vladimir continued to work on poster
design.

Bibliography
D. Aranovich: "2 Stenberg 2" in *Krasnaia niva*,
M, 1929, No. 40, pp. 20-21.
K31.
M. Constantine and A. Fern: *Revolutionary
Soviet Film Posters*, Baltimore: Johns Hopkins
University Press, 1974.
K32.
I. Dychenko: "Kist i palitra — ulitsam i
ploshchadiam" in *Trudovaia zhizn*, K, 1976, May.
V. Stenberg: "O moei rabote s A. Ya. Tairovym i
V.E. Meierkholdom" in G50, 1981, pp. 210-22.
D. Ades: *Posters*, New York: Abbeville, 1984,
passim.
*Stenbergi. Teatr. Monumentalnoe iskusstvo.
Plakat. Dizain.* Catalog of exhibition organized by
the Union of Artists of the USSR, M, 1984.
Sowjetische Stummfilmplakate. Catalog of
exhibition at the Kunsthalle, Düsseldorf; and the
Kulturzentrum Alte Hauptfeuerwache,
Mannheim, 1985.
2 Stenberg 2. Catalog of exhibition at the Central
House of Writers, M, 1989.
*Stenberg Brothers: Constructing a Revolution in
Soviet Design.* Catalog of exhibition at the
Museum of Modern Art, New York, 1997; and
the Armand Hammer Museum and Cultural
Center, Los Angeles, 1999.
M. Tillberg: "2 Stenberg 2: Constructivists and
Designers for the Revolutionary Mass Stagings
at the Red Square" in *Konsthistorisk Tidskrift*,
Stockholm, 1998, Vol. 67, No. 3, pp. 175-88.
B312, passim.
S. Khan-Magomedov: *Vladimir i Georgii
Stenbergi*, M: RA, 2008.

The Stenberg brothers were typical of the
young generation of artists sympathetic to the
cause of the Revolution, moving rapidly from
the traditional conception of art as a purely
"esthetic" experience (the free-standing
constructions of 1919-20) to that of art as a
utilitarian, social activity (the stage designs
and movie posters). True, even the "esthetic"
constructions of the Stenberg brothers, like
those of Rodchenko and Medunetsky, were
outside the conventional process of
"deformation" that the Cubists and Futurists
had pursued so swiftly and drastically. The
new constructors now reaffirmed form, i.e.,
the interaction of material and space; they
rebuilt it consciously and logically, and
produced an art that, to paraphrase
Rodchenko, was one of analysis, not of
synthesis.[767] The possibility of experimenting
with an entire range of new formal combinations imbued the Stenberg constructions
with a great vitality and potency and, just as
"you can't isolate part of luminous space,"[768]
so the upward thrust of the Stenberg
structures seems to contain an unfinished
movement, a line of direction that will carry
on into external space.
        The Stenbergs applied their formal exper-
iments to their functional art, specifically to
the stage designs and movie posters (which
often carry the joint signature "2 Sten" or "2
Stenberg 2"). The stage sets and costumes,
especially for Tairov's major productions such
as *The Storm* and *Saint Joan* (both 1924),

960

961

962

maintained the principles of dynamic interaction between solid and space identifiable also with the "esthetic" constructions. Moreover, like Liubov Popova and Varvara Stepanova, the Stenbergs regarded the actor and not the text as the central attribute of theater and ensured a maximum of movement by using multilevel constructions, ladders, inclines, etc. The actors, therefore, now operated in a variety of positions, relating to each other and to the audience vertically, horizontally, and diagonally.

As for the more decorative movie posters of the mid- and late 1920s, such as *October* (1927) and *Man with a Movie Camera* (1929), the Stenbergs continued to emphasize dramatic contrasts in form and movement. The thrust of diagonals, rendered often by a figure's outstretched arms, as in the poster for *Man with a Movie Camera,* the skillful photomontage, and hence the inclusion of several strata of action often produce the impression of a three-dimensional construction rather than of a two-dimensional surface. The peculiarly mobile *trompe l'oeil* effect of these posters forms a striking parallel to the illusion of perpetual movement in space, which the constructions create by means of their forceful lines of direction.

960 [NIRE].
Georgii Stenberg: *Illustration for the Poem "October" by Konstantin Medunetsky, 1919.*
Black ink and red watercolor.
Signed.
10⅞ x 7⅜ in., 27.5 x 18.7 cm.
Provenance: Vladimir Stenberg, Moscow, 1972.
Reproduced in I32, p. 58.

961 [NIRE].
Georgii Stenberg: *Costume Design for a Dancer, 1919.*
Watercolor.
Signed and dated lower right in Russian: "Georgii Stenberg, 1919."
11⅜ x 9½ in., 29 x 24 cm.
Provenance: Vladimir Stenberg, Moscow, 1972.
Reproduced in I32, p. 59.

962 [NIRE].
Georgii Stenberg: *Portrait of Alexander Tairov behind Bars, 1922.*
Pencil and black ink.
9½ x 7⅛ in., 24 x 18 cm.
Provenance: *Russian Twentieth Century and Avant-Garde Art,* London: Sotheby's, 6 April,1989, Lot 722 (reproduced).
Reproduced in F107, p. 277.

Unidentified production: *at Inna Chernetskaia's Studio of Synthetic Dance (also called the Studio of Dramatic and Plastic Dance), Moscow, 1922, with designs by Georgii and Vladimir Stenberg.*

963 [R791].
Costume Design for a Man with Hands in Pockets, 1922.
Watercolor and pencil.
Signed and dated on the reverse in Russian: "2 Stenberg 2 1922."
10½ x 6¼ in., 26.7 x 16 cm.
Provenance: Vladimir Stenberg via André B. Nakov, Paris, August, 1976.
Reproduced in I32, No. 89. Another male costume for the Chernetskaia Studio is reproduced in I60, p. 35.

963

964

965

966

967

968

964 [NIRE].
Costume Design for a Young Man with Right Hand behind His back, 1922.
Signed and dated on the reverse in Russian: "2 Stenberg 2 1922."
10½ x 5½ in., 26.5 x 14 cm.
Provenance: Vladimir Stenberg, Moscow, 1972.
Reproduced in I32, No. 90.

965 [NIRE].
Costume Design for a Man with a Beard, 1922.
Signed and dated on the reverse in Russian: "2 Stenberg 2 1922."
10½ x 5½ in., 26.5 x 14 cm.
Provenance: Vladimir Stenberg, Moscow, 1972.
Reproduced in I32, No. 91.

966 [R792].
Costume Design for a Figure in a Cape, ca. 1922.
Watercolor and pencil.
11 x 6¾ in., 28 x 17 cm.
Provenance: Vladimir Stenberg via André B. Nakov, Paris, August, 1976.
Reproduced in I32, No. 93; I77, p. 146.

Note: The Studio of Synthetic Dance directed by of Inna Samoilovna Chernetskaia (1894-1963), located at 10, Bolshaia Sadovaia in Moscow, was an intimate dance center that specialized in "rhythmic and Swedish gymnastics, plastic and individual dancing, free form and style dancing, mime

dance, etc."[769] In 1920 Chernetskaia re-organized her school into the Studio of Dramatic and Plastic Dance. It is not known

for which particular spectacle these costumes were made, although the Studio was known for its balletic presentations of fairy-tales, games, and poetry.[770]

The Lawyer from Babylon: *satire by Anatolii Mariengof. Produced by Vladimir Sokolov for the Chamber Theater, Moscow, on 15 April, 1924, with music by Alexander Metner and designs by Georgii and Vladimir Stenberg.*

The plot is based on the Biblical story of Daniel the Prophet who is loved by Zera, the slave of Susanna. Characters include Jehoiakim, the husband of Susanna; Jacob; the Lioness of Babylon; Ashpenaz, the King's Eunuch, etc.

967 [R793].
Costume Design for a Man in Striped Socks, 1924.
Pencil, black ink, and watercolor.
8¼ x 6¾ in., 21 x 17.2 cm.
Inscribed on the reverse in Russian: "The Lawyer from Babylon. Drawing of a man in profile. Chamber Theater. By Vladimir Sokolov. Moscow, 1924, April."
Provenance: Vladimir Stenberg via André B. Nakov, Paris, August, 1976.
Reproduced in I51, No. 226; I77, p. 146; and I32 No. 92, where it is wrongly described as a design for a production at Inna Chernetskaia's ballet Studio, Moscow. Also see I2, p. 73; and *Stenbergi*, p. 7.

968 [R794].
Costume Design for a Woman with a Raised Leg, 1923.
Pencil and watercolor.
Signed and dated lower right in Russian: "2 Stenberg 2 1923."
10 x 4¾ in., 25.4 x 12.1 cm.

969

970

971

Other inscription: on reverse in Russian: "The Lawyer from Babylon" plus a drawing of a man in profile.
Provenance: Vladimir Stenberg via André B. Nakov, Paris, August, 1976.
Reproduced in color in I77, p. 77; and in black and white in I51, No. 227; I77, p. 146; and I32, No. 88, where it is wrongly described as a design for a production at Inna Chernetskaia's Ballet Studio, Moscow. Also see I2, p. 73; and *Stenbergi*, p. 7. The BTM also possesses nine costumes for *The Lawyer from Babylon,* some of which are similar to Nos. 967 [R793] and 968 [R794]. Three other costumes in a private collection are illustrated in I74, nos. 121-23.

Note: Anatolii Borisovich Mariengof (1897-1962), member of the Imaginist group of writers and artists in the early 1920s, which included Sergei Esenin and Georgii Yakulov, was known for his histrionic behavior and eccentric novels such as *Roman bez vrania* [A Novel without Fibs] of 1927. His wife, Anna Borisovna Nikritina, who played Zera in *The Lawyer from Babylon,* recalled that the play was written in honor of their newborn son in 1923, but that the text was never published.[771] In his book *Zapiski rezhissera* [Notes of a Director], Tairov referred to *The Lawyer from Babylon,* along with two other works produced for the 1924-25 season, i.e., Alexander Ostrovsky's *The Storm* and *Kukirol* (by Pavel Antokolsky et al.), but his comments were non-committal:

> We were searching for dramatic material that would respond to our conception of reality. And, of course, we were obliged first and foremost to look for such dramatic material among those playwrights who had created their images on the basis of a reality which was an incubator for us as well.[772]

Alisa Koonen, the leading star of the Chamber Theater, who seems not to have played in *The Lawyer from Babylon,* referred to the play as a contemporary satire that "left no noticeable trace in the repertoire."[773]

Phèdre: tragedy in five acts by Jean Racine, translated into Russian by Valerii Briusov. Produced by Alexander Tairov for the Chamber Theater, Moscow, on 8 February 1922, and presented on tour in Berlin (Deutsches Theater) and Paris (Théâtre des Champs-Elysées) in February and March, 1923, with designs by Alexander Vesnin and renderings for program publicity by Konstantin Medunetsky and Georgii and Vladimir Stenberg.[774]
See No. 57 [R53] for plot summary.

969 [191; R795].
Georgii Stenberg: *Design for Phèdre's Headgear,* 1923.
Pencil.
Signed and dated lower right in Russian: "G. Stenberg 1923."
18½ x 12½ in., 47 x 32 cm.
Other inscription: the reverse carries the following in Russian: "For Paris. Moscow Chamber Theater. *Phèdre* by Racine. Alisa Koonen in the role of Phèdre"; this is followed by the same in French: "Le Kamerny Théâtre de Moscou. *Phèdre* de Racine. Alice Koonen dans *Phèdre.* " The reverse is also stamped with the seal of the Chamber Theater, Moscow.
Provenance: H. Le Maire via André B. Nakov, Paris, November, 1976.
Reproduced in *Paris-Journal,* Paris, 1923, 6 March, p. 2; *Gastspiel im deutschen Theater / Berlin. Moskauer Kamerny Theater,* Berlin, 1923, p. 10; I40, No. 97; I77, p. 115; K50 (a), p. 395, (b), unnumbered; P58; T28; also see C35, p. 439. A variant is also in C35 (1923 edition), p. 29; and in Catalog No. 7

of the bookstore Ex Libris, New York, 1977, No. 319; also see A34, p. 410; a curious version is reproduced in I100, No. 26.

970 [R796].
Georgii Stenberg: *Design for Hippolytus's Headgear,* 1923.
Pencil.
Signed and dated lower right in Russian: "G. Stenberg 1923."
18½ x 12⅝ in., 47 x 32 cm.
Other inscription: the reverse carries the following inscription in Russian: "Moscow Chamber Theater. *Phèdre.* Nikolai Tsereteli in the role of Hippolytus." This is followed by the same inscription in French: "Le Kamerny Theatre de Moscou. *Phèdre.* Nicolas Tsereteli dans Hippolyte."
Provenance: H. Le Maire via André B. Nakov, Paris, November, 1976.
Reproduced in *Paris-Journal,* Paris, 1923, 6 March, p. 3; A34, p. 411; I32, No. 87; I40, No. 98; I51, No. 229; I77, pp. 114, 138; a variant is reproduced in K32, p. 51; also see C35 (1923 edition), p. 29; and the Catalog No. 7 of the bookstore Ex Libris, New York, 1977, No. 319.

971 [R797].
Vladimir Stenberg: *Design for Thésée's Headgear,* ca. 1923.
Pencil.
Signed lower right in Russian: "V. Stenberg."
18¾ x 12½ in., 47.5 x 31.7 cm.
Provenance: H. Le Maire via André B. Nakov, Paris, November, 1976.
Reproduced in *Paris-Journal,* 6 March 1923, p. 3; *Gastspiel im deutschen Theater / Berlin. Moskauer Kamerny Theater,* Berlin, 1923, p. 9; I40, No. 100; I51, No. 230; I77, p. 138; K50 (a), p. 395, (b), unnumbered; another version reproduced in C35 (1923

972

973

767 A. Rodchenko: "Sistema Rodchenko," in catalog
     X Gosudarstvennaia vystavka "Bespredmetnoe
     tvorchestvo i suprematizm," M, 1919, p. 26.
768 P. Florensky: "Nebesnye znameniia" in Makovets,
     M, 1922, No. 2, p. 15.
769 Adverisement in Teatralnaia nedelia, M, 1914,
     No. 7, p. 4.
770 For information on Chernetskaia see N. Misler:
     "Designing Gestures in the Laboratory of Dance"
     in I81, pp. 157-73; and D116, passim.
771 Letter from Gordon McVay to John E. Bowlt dated
     9 March, 1987.
772 C35, p. 209.
773 F43, p. 306.
774 See entry for Medunetsky. For information on
     Tairov's European tour see C183.
775 A. Lunacharsky: "K desiatiletiiu Kamernogo
     teatra" in Iskusstvo trudiashchimsia, M, 1924, No.
     4-5, p. 5.
776 P. Markov: "Liubov pod viazami" in Pravda, M,
     1926, 19 November. Quoted in C35, p. 517.
777 See, for example, their article "Kakim dolzhno byt
     nashe teaoformlenie" in Brigada khudozhnikov, M,
     1931, No. 7, p. 14.

a theory of stage design,[777] ended with Georgii's premature death in a motorcycle accident in 1933.

edition), p. 30; K32, p. 51; and the Catalog No. 7 of the bookstore Ex Libris, New York, 1977, No. 319.

972 [R798].
Vladimir Stenberg: Poster Advertising Performances by the Moscow Chamber Theater at the Théâtre des Champs-Elysées, Paris, 6-23 March, 1923.
Lithograph.
The right side carries a long dedication in Russian to a friend, signed "V. Stenberg" and dated 1967.
27 x 17½ in., 68.5 x 44.5 cm.
Provenance: H. Le Maire via André B. Nakov, Paris, November, 1976.
Reproduced in I51, No. 231; K50 (a), p. 395; (b) unnumbered.

Note: This was one of the first Constructivist posters designed by Vladimir Stenberg who, with his brother, produced many such posters throughout the 1920s. The basic composition here — the circular axis — recurs in later Stenberg posters such as *The Poet and the Tsar* (1927), *The Eleventh* (1928), and *Man with a Movie Camera* (1929). For reproduction of such posters, see Constantine and Fern, *Revolutionary Soviet Film Posters;* and Ades, *Posters.*

Desire under the Elms: *play in three parts by Eugene O'Neill. Produced by Alexander Tairov at the Chamber Theater, Moscow, on 13 November, 1926, with choreography by Natalia Glan and designs by Georgii and Vladimir Stenberg.*

Eben, the son of the elderly farmer Cabot, is jealous of his father's young wife Abbie, fearing that her offspring will deprive him of his inheritance. To put Eben's mind at rest, Abbie seduces Eben, has his child, and falls in love with him. Eben then tells Cabot

that the child is his, but Cabot interprets Abbie's behavior simply as a ruse to gain the inheritance. To prove her love for Eben, Abbie murders the child and is arrested, but Eben also declares his complicity, and both are imprisoned.

973 [R799].
Poster Advertising Desire under the Elms, 1926.
Lithograph in red, white, and black.
Signed in the poster.
24⅜ x 28 in., 107.5 x 71 cm.
Other inscriptions: "Published by the Chamber Theater, Moscow; printed at the New Village Printing-House, Moscow."
Provenance: Viktor Kholodkov, Moscow, 1984.

Note: Alexander Tairov's production of *Phèdre* with designs by Alexander Vesnin (see Nos. 1137-1142 [R377-82]) and incidental drawings by Konstantin Medunetsky (see No. 789 [R665]) and the Stenbergs marked the beginning of an intense collaboration between the Stenbergs and the Chamber Theater. Their Moscow debut came with their designs for the productions of *The Lawyer from Babylon, The Storm,* and *Kukirol,* and, thereafter, they were involved in the designs for eight major productions, including Bernard Shaw's *Saint Joan* (1924) and Berthold Brecht's *The Beggars' Opera* (1930). The Stenbergs' experimental sets and costumes of the 1920s elicited a variety of responses. Anatolii Lunacharsky referred to their "rather artificial constructive decoration" for *The Storm;*[775] while Pavel Markov praised their "starkness of exterior design" in Eugene O'Neill's *Love under the Elms* (1926).[776] The Stenbergs' fruitful cooperation with Tairov, which prompted them to elaborate

STEPANOVA, Varvara Fedorovna (pseudonym: Varst)

Born 23 October (4 November), 1894, Kovno (Kaunas), Lithuania; died 20 May, 1958, Moscow, Russia.

1910-13 attended the Kazan Art Institute; 1913 moved to Moscow; studied under Mikhail Leblan, Ilia Mashkov, and Konstantin Yuon; met Alexander Rodchenko, who became her life-long companion; 1913-14 attended CSIAI; gave private lessons; 1914 exhibited with the "Moscow Salon"; 1915-17 worked as an accountant and secretary in a factory; 1917 onward composed experimental visual poetry, producing graphic poems such as "Rtny khomle" and "Zigra ar"; 1918 contributed to the "First Exhibition of Paintings of the Young Leftist Federation of the Professional Union of Artists and Painters"; closely involved with IZO NKP; 1919 contributed to the "V State Exhibition" and the "X State Exhibition: Non-Objective Creativity and Suprematism"; illustrated Alexei Kruchenykh's book *Gly-Gly;* 1920-23 member of Inkhuk, where in 1920-21 she was research secretary; 1920-25 taught at the Krupskaia Academy of Social (Communist) Education; 1921 contributed to the exhibition "5 x 5 = 25"; 1922 made collages for the journal *Kino-fot;* designed sets and costumes for Vsevolod Meierkhold's production of *The Death of Tarelkin;* made linocuts on the subject of Charlie Chaplin; 1923-28 closely associated with the journals *Lef* and *Novyi Lef;* 1924-25 worked for the First State Textile Factory as a designer; taught in the Textile Department of Vkhutemas; 1925 contributed to the "Exposition internationale des arts décoratifs" in Paris; 1926-32 worked predominantly as a book and journal designer, fulfilling major government commissions; 1928 designed sets and costumes for Yurii Tarich's movie *Svoi i chuzhie* [Friends and Enemies]; late 1930s resumed painting; 1941-42 lived in Perm; 1940s-50s continued to paint, design, and exhibit.

Bibliography
E. Kovtun: "Das Antibuch der Warwara Stepanova / Varvara Stepanova's Anti-book" in K31, pp. 57-64, 142-51.
A. Lavrentiev: "V.F. Stepanova o rannem konstruktivizme" in *Trudy VNIITE*, M, 1979, No. 21, pp. 111-17.
K52, pp. 270-84.
A. Lavrentiev: "Poeziia graficheskogo dizaina v tvorchestve Varvary Stepanovoi" in *Tekhnicheskaia estetika*, M, 1980, No. 5, pp. 22-26.
A. Law: "'The Death of Tarelkin.' A Constructivist Vision of Tsarist Russia," in J. Bowlt, ed.: *Russian History*, Tempe, 1982, Vol. 8, Parts 1-2, pp. 145-98.
V. Stepanova: "Aufzeichnungen / Occasional Notes (1919-1940)" in K59, pp. 122-44.
A. Lavrentiev: "The Graphics of Visual Poetry in the Work of Varvara Stepanova" in *Grafik*, Budapest, 1982, No. 1, pp. 46-51.
V. Quilici: *Ročenko / Stepanova*. Catalog of exhibition at the Palazzo dei Priori, Perugia, and elsewhere, 1984.
K75, pp. 292-339.
A. Lavrentiev and N. Misler: *Stepanova*, Milan: Idea Books, 1988.
A. Lavrentiev and J. Bowlt: *Stepanova*, Cambridge, Mass.: MIT, 1988.
B109, pp. 141-56.
A. Garcia: *Rodchenko / Stepanova*. Catalog of exhibition at the Fundación Banco Centrale Hispanoamericano, 1992.
V. Rodchenko and A. Lavrentiev, eds.: *Varvara Stepanova: Chelovek ne mozhet zhit bez chuda*, M: Sfera, 1994.
K224, passim.
K236.
B275.
A. Lavrentiev: *Geometricheskie tsvety na konstruktivistskom pole*, M: Grant, 2002.
A. Lavrentiev: *Varvara Stepanova*, M: Russkii avangard, 2009.
N. Avtonomova et al.: *Aleksandr Rodchenko and Varvara Stepanova: Visions of Constructivism*. Catalog of exhibition at the Metropolitan Teien Art Museum, Tokyo, and other venues, 2010.

Until ca. 1921 Stepanova was concerned primarily with studio painting and graphics, investigating abstract art and transrational poetry,[778] as she demonstrated in her statement for the "X State Exhibition" in 1919:

> Non-objective creativity is still only the beginning of a great new epoch, of an unprecedented Great Creativity, which is destined to open the doors to mysteries more profound than science and technology.[779]

Of the leading members of the Russian avant-garde who concerned themselves with industrial and functional design in the 1920s, only Stepanova had received training in the applied arts (at CSIAI) and

974

she drew particular benefit from this while working on her textile designs at the First State Textile Factory. It was there that Stepanova, like Liubov Popova, strove

> to eradicate the ingrown view of the ideal artistic drawing as the imitation and copying of nature. To grapple with the organic design, orienting it towards the geometrization of forms. To propagate the productional tasks of Constructivism.[780]

Perhaps the most remarkable consequence of Stepanova's theory was her designs for *prozodezhda*, especially her sports tunic, in which she combined an economy of material with emphatic contrasts in color (for

the purposes of team identification), while removing ornamental or "esthetic" elements as superfluous. Stepanova followed a similar conception in her work for the theater, as evidenced by her sets and costumes for *The Death of Tarelkin* and her projects for evenings of propaganda entertainment at the Academy of Communist Education in Moscow in the early 1920s.

The Magnanimous Cuckold: *farce in three acts by Fernand Crommelynck, was produced by Vsevolod Meierkhold for the Meierkhold Theater, Moscow on 25 May, 1922, with designs by Liubov Popova (see commentary on Popova at No. 839 [R718] above).*[781]

A miller suspects his wife of being unfaithful, and the action unfolds as he follows his farcical searches through the village in pursuit of his wife's lovers.

The Death of Tarelkin: *play in three acts by Alexander Sukhovo-Kobylin. Produced by Vsevolod Meierkhold for the Meierkhold Theater, Moscow on 24 November, 1922, with designs by Varvara Stepanova.*

Tarelkin, the hero of this anti-tsarist satire, fakes his death in order to avoid his creditors. Taking the identity of a recently deceased neighbor, Korylov, he intends to disappear for a time and then to return by using stolen documents, but his plan is foiled when his toupee and false teeth are found in his apartment. He is arrested and interrogated, but set free — doomed to spending the rest of his life under his assumed identity of Korylov.

Stepanova as contributor:
974 [R800].
Designer unknown: *Poster for* **The Magnanimous Cuckold** *and the Premiere of* **The Death of Tarelkin** *from the Workshop of* **Vsevolod Meierkhold at GITIS, 1922.**
Lithograph in black, red, and white.
42 x 27¾ in., 106.7 x 70.5 cm.

975

Provenance: the artist's daughter, Varvara Rodchenko, Moscow, October, 1971.
Reproduced in I51, No. 232. For other posters of this kind see C65, between pp. 160-61.

Stepanova as contributor:
975 [R801].
Designer unknown: *Poster for* The Death of Tarelkin *and* The Magnanimous Cuckold, 1922.
Lithograph in black, red, and white.
42 x 27¾ in., 106.7 x 70.5 cm.
Inscriptions (as part of the design) provide details on the two productions, the *The Death of Tarelkin* being in the upper half.
Provenance: the artist's daughter, Varvara Rodchenko, Moscow, October, 1971.
Reproduced on the cover of G55; I51, No. 233.

Stepanova as contributor:
976 [R802].
Alexander Liubimov: *Poster for* The Death of Tarelkin *from the Workshop of Vsevolod Meierkhold at GITIS, 1922.*
Lithograph in black, red, and white.
27¾ x 42⅛ in., 70.5 x 107 cm.
Provenance: the artist's daughter, Varvara Rodchenko, Moscow, October, 1971.
Reproduced in G55, p. 160; and *Rodcenko / Stepanova*, p. 80.
The box at the bottom center states in Russian: "This design is dedicated to V. Meierkhold"; and underneath it: "the designer of this work A. Liubimov" – presumably, Alexander Mikhailovich Liubimov (1879-1955). Also listed as directors – lab technicians Sergei Eisenstein and Valerii Ivanovich Inkizhinov (Inkijinoff, 1895 – 1973)

977 [192; R803].
Costume Design for Tarelkin, ca. 1922.
Watercolor.
Signed lower right in pencil with the Russian acronym: "Varst."

976

11⅜ x 8¼ in., 29 x 21 cm.
Other inscription: along lower margin in blue watercolor in block capitals in Russian: "Tarelkin."
Provenance: Artcurial Gallery, Paris, June 24, 1983.
Reproduced in color in B115, plate 126; K65, p. 52; M23; and in black and white in I77, p. 141; N175; S33. Two similar designs are reproduced in *Rodčenko / Stepanova,* p. 81.

978 [R804].
Costume Design for Tarelkin (Coverall), 1922.
Watercolor and blue pencil.
10⅝ x 8¾ in., 27 x 22.3 cm.
Inscriptions: The reverse carries the stamp of Stepanova's studio and pencil inscriptions by Varvara Rodchenko*: "Death of Tarelkin.* Tarelkin's coverall, 1922."
Provenance: the artist's daughter, Varvara

Rodchenko, Moscow, September, 1971.
Reproduced in color in A34, p. 383; F107, p. 278.

979 [R805].
Costume Design for Raspliuev, Chief of Police, ca. 1922.
Black ink and color pencil.
Signature stamped on reverse.
13¼ x 8¾ in., 33.6 x 22.3 cm.
Inscriptions: lower margin in Russian: "Military uniform (Raspliuev. *The Death of Tarelkin*). Constructor Stepanova."
Provenance: the artist's daughter, Varvara Rodchenko, Moscow, October, 1971.
Reproduced in G55, p. 186; I32, No. 95; I51, No. 234; I61, p. 336; I77, p. 141; N107, p. 80. For a set of similar designs see G55, pp. 186-87; *Rodcenko / Stepanova,* p. 81.

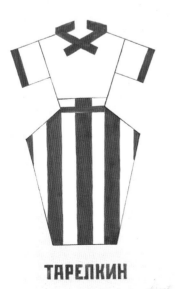

ТАРЕЛКИН

977

978

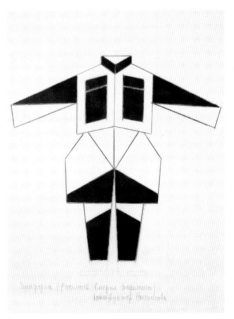

979

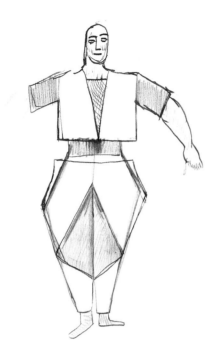

980

980 [R806].
Costume Design for Man with Right Arm Missing, ca. 1922.
Ink, watercolor, and pencil.
Signature stamped on reverse with identification by Varvara Rodchenko.
14 x 9 in., 35.6 x 22.9 cm.
Provenance: the artist's daughter, Varvara Rodchenko, September, 1971.
Reproduced in I32, No. 94; I51, No. 235; I61, p. 336; I77, p. 141; N107, p. 80. This costume is probably a preliminary sketch for the costume of one of the seven clerks (cf. G55, p. 186-87).

Note: Stepanova's sets and costumes for *The Death of Tarelkin* owed an appreciable debt to Liubov Popova's Constructivist conception for *The Magnanimous Cuckold* produced earlier in 1922 as well as to Rodchenko's ideas for *prozodezhda* (see Nos. 867 [R750], 868 [R751]). Meierkhold even so far as to speak of Stepanova's jealous wish to "outdo" Popova.[782] Still, the rivalry between Popova and Stepanova and the strained relations between Meierkhold and Stepanova notwithstanding, it is clear that Stepanova was genuinely concerned with the Constructivist notion of maximum effect through economy of means. In this sense and like Popova and Rodchenko, Stepanova stood in complete antithesis to the World of Art designers, who, as one observer mentioned, "wrapped up the actor like candy in a pretty piece of paper."[783]
Stepanova and her colleagues unwrapped him. This return of the body as a highly visible but controlled mechanical force to costume design was paralleled by Meierkhold's rejection of makeup and, in broader terms, by the general concern in the 1920s with mass gymnastics and athletics inside and outside the Soviet theater, an

appropriation that Stepanova also welcomed. Inevitably, some critics rejected Stepanova's costumes in *The Death of Tarelkin* for the "obvious estheticism of all these stripes, tabs, and little pockets"[784] and in any case argued that the actors were too straight for Meierkhold's balagan interpretation.[785] Stepanova herself countered such remarks by arguing that she had not been given enough time to coordinate the actors and the costumes. On the other hand, she felt that she had succeeded in

> showing spatial objects in their utilitarian content wherein I wished to present genuine objects — a chair, a table, armchairs, screens, etc.[786]

The play *The Death of Tarelkin* enjoyed popularity with the Russian avant-garde: Meierkhold first produced it at the Alexandrinsky Theater, Petrograd, in October, 1917, and Alexandra Exter also designed a production scheduled for the First Studio of the Moscow Art Theater in 1921 (not realized). Looking back, critics now emphasize that the 1922 production, dedicated to the memory of Evgenii Vakhtangov, who had intended to stage the play with designs by Isaak Rabinovich, marked a milestone in the history of the Russian theater:

> Today we can appreciate this extraordinary production as a landmark of "Eccentrism" in the theatre and as one of the most fascinating pages in the history of theatrical Constructivism. At the time, however, this *Tarelkin* pleased almost no one.[787]

778 Stepanova wrote and illustrated transrational (*zaum*) poetry. Some examples were displayed at the "X State Exhibition," M, 1919. See K31, pp. 143-51; K59, p. 164 et seq.
779 V. Stepanova: "Bespredmetnoe tvorchestvo" in catalog of *X Gosudarstvennaia vystavka "Bespredmetnoe tvorchestvo i suprematizm,"* M, 1919, p. 9.
780 Statement by V. Stepanova. Quoted in G34, p. 97.
781 For a detailed discussion of Meierkhold's production of *The Magnanimous cuckold,* see A. Law: "*Le Cocu magnifique* de Crommelynck" in C69, 1980, Vol. 7, pp. 14-43.
782 C32, Vol. 2, p. 79.
783 A. Ivanov: "Teatralnyi kostium" in G7, p. 157.
784 V. Bezard: "Meierkhold i russkii teatr" in *Zrelishcha,* M, 1922, No. 15, 5-11 December, p. 9.
785 See S. Margolin: "Balagannoe predstavlenie" in *Teatr i muzyka,* M, 1922, No. 11, 12 December, p. 231. The poet and critic Sergei Bobrov was especially negative in his appraisal of Stepanova's designs, referring to the "murder of Tarelkin." See S. Bobrov: "V poriadke ideologicheskoi' borby... Istoriia ubiistva Tarelkina" in *Zrelishcha,* 1922-23, No. 18, 26-31 December / 1-2 January, p. 10.
786 [A. Gan]: "Beseda s V.F. Stepanovoi" in ibid., No. 16, 12-18 December, pp. 11-12.
787 A. Law: "The Death of Tarelkin" in G55, p. 145.

SUDEIKIN, Sergei Yurievich (Soudeikine, Serge)

Born 7 (19) March, 1882, St. Petersburg, Russia; died 12 August, 1946, Nyack, New York, USA.

1897-1909 attended MIPSA, where he studied principally under Konstantin Korovin and Valentin Serov; established close contact with Savva Mamontov and the Abramtsevo group, and then with the World of Art group; 1904 took part in the "Crimson Rose" exhibition, Saratov; 1905 worked at Konstantin Stanislavsky's and Vsevolod Meierkhold's Theater-Studio in Moscow; thereafter designed productions for Vera Komissarzhevskaia, Alexander Tairov, Nikolai Evreinov, and other directors; 1906 on the invitation of Sergei Diaghilev went to Paris in connection with the Russian Section of the "Salon d'Automne"; 1907 contributed to the "Blue Rose" exhibition; 1908 moved away from Symbolism to a more Primitivist style; 1909 settled in St. Petersburg, where he attended IAA until 1910; 1911-12 designed panneaux for the Stray Dog cabaret; 1913 designed sets and costumes for Diaghilev's production of *La Tragédie de Salomé,* one of many stage presentations that Sudeikin designed in Russia, Europe, and the US; 1916 designed one of the rooms for the Comedians Halt cabaret in Petrograd; 1917-20 worked in the Crimea and then Georgia and Azerbaijan; 1920 emigrated to Paris; 1922 settled in New York; during the 1920s worked for Nikita Baliev's Chauve-Souris cabaret; designed several productions for the Metropolitan Opera; painted portraits; 1920s-30s several one-man exhibitions, including "Paintings of the American Scene" at the Stendahl Galleries, Los Angeles; 1930 continued to design operas, including Rouben Mamoulian's production of George Gershwin's *Porgy and Bess;* designed Samuel Goldwyn's movie *We Live Again* (1934; after Lev Tolstoi's *Resurrection*); 1943 designed sets and costumes for the revived Chauve-Souris in New York.

Bibliography
O. Sayler: "Sergei Sudeykin, Court Painter" in *Morris Gest Presents Nikita Balieff,* New York: Chauve-Souris Theater, 1928-29 Season Program, pp. 29-31.
M2, Vol. 2, pp. 196-99 (includes list of Sudeikin's theatrical productions).
D. Kogan: *Sergei Sudeikin,* M: Iskusstvo, 1974.
M. Babenchikov: "Teatr Sudeikina" in *Dekorativnoe iskusstvo,* M, 1975, No. 12, p. 39-40.
Yu. Zorin: "Neznakomyi Sudeikin" in *Novoe Russkoe Slovo,* New York, 1975, 21 December, p. 5; 28 December, pp. 5-8; 1976, 4 January, p. 5.
Yu. Zorin: "Vnov obretaemyi profil" in *Novoe Russkoe Slovo,* 1976, 15 August, pp. 7-8.
M. Kiselev: "Zhivopis S.Yu. Sudeikina. K 100-letiiu so dnia rozhdeniia khudozhnika" in *Iskusstvo,* M, 1982, No. 2, pp. 49-55.
I. Dzutsova: "Gruzinskie Temy v Russkoi Teatralnoi Zhivopisi," *Vechernii Tbilisi,* 1983, 2 July.

M53, Vol. 26, pp. 84-85.

F85, passim.

J. Bowlt: "Of Miracles and Simple Nonsense: The Petrograd Diaries of Vera Sudeikina" in *Europa Orientalis*, Rome, 1997, No. 2, pp. 249-74.

Vera Sudeikina's diaries are of interest. See I. Menshova, ed.: *Vera Sudeikina. Dnevnik. Petrograd, Krym, Tiflis*, M: Russkii put, 2006; and the journal *Experiment*, Los Angeles, 2007, No. 13 (special issue devoted to Vera Sudeikina).

Like Nikolai Sapunov, in many ways his rival, Sudeikin started his career as a studio artist, but achieved his real reputation, at least in the West, as a stage designer. As early as 1905, Sudeikin worked under Vsevolod Meierkhold and Konstantin Stanislavsky in the latter's experimental Theater Studio in Moscow. The following year Sudeikin entered into a fruitful association with the Vera Komissarzhevskaia Theater in St. Petersburg, where, for example, he designed a successful production of Maurice Maeterlinck's *Soeur Béatrice*. By 1908 Sudeikin moved away from his early Symbolist preoccupations toward a more stylized conception of painting and design that relied substantially on amusing evocations of nineteenth-century mercantile Russia — a choice of theme that won him many supporters among the St. Petersburg and Moscow *nouveaux riches*. During the early 1910s Sudeikin received wide recognition as a fashionable artist and man-about-town and was given many design commissions.

Perhaps the highlight of Sudeikin's career as a stage designer came with his participation in Alexander Tairov's production of the *Marriage of Figaro* at the Chamber Theater, Moscow, in 1915. In spite of an enthusiastic reception, Tairov was not altogether satisfied with Sudeikin's "stylized, contrived screens, bouquets, and curtains" [788] and observers even argued that the bright golds and reds of the sets, the extreme decorativism, and loud dissonances detracted from, rather than enhanced, the action and dialogue. On the other hand, however, this kind of criticism simply emphasized the deeply theatrical nature of Sudeikin's art, for, as the critic Nadezhda Giliarovskaia remarked in 1924,

> Sudeikin is a theater unto himself, he has assimilated the Italian Commedia dell'Arte, the most theatrical of all theatrical acts... More than anybody else he can be considered the father of the theater's theatricality. [789]

981

982

981 [R807].
Self-Portrait, 1918.
Pencil.
Signed and dated lower right in Russian: "Sudeikin 1918."
14 x 11¼ in., 35.5 x 28.5 cm.
Provenance: the artist's widow, Jeanne Palmer-Soudeikine, New York, April, 1969. Now in a private collection.
Reproduced in B162, between pp. 160 and 161; D41, p. 282; F107, p. 154; I20, p. 61; I51, No. 222; M157, p. 85; N98; O26.

Note: This is one of several self-portraits that Sudeikin painted and drew in the 1910s and 1920s. The meaning of the image of the Queen of Hearts in this context remains unclear.

Alexandre Jacovleff: *Portrait of Sergei Sudeikin, ca. 1935.* See No. 588 [R1012].

982 [R808].
Portrait of Vera Sudeikina, 1921.
Watercolor and pencil.
Signed and dated lower right: "Serge Soudeikine Paris 1921."
14 x 11¼ in., 35.5 x 28.5 cm.
Provenance: the artist's widow, Jeanne Palmer-Soudeikine, New York, April, 1969. Now in a private collection.
Reproduced in F70, p. 12; I20, p. 61. Another portrait of Vera Sudeikina, in a Russian private collection, is reproduced in Kogan, *Sudeikin*, p. 128; another is reproduced on the dust jacket of F70; yet others are reproduced in color in F85, including one of 1917 on the dust jacket.

Note: Vera Sudeikina (Soudeikine; née Vera Arturovna Bosset, 1888-1983) was Sudeikin's second wife. He and other artists

> often portrayed her in this fashion, that is, wearing a kerchief. Vera had a collection of 'Moscow kerchiefs' and several times in her Diaries she mentions posing for Sudeikin wearing a kerchief. [790]

Their marriage weakened in 1921 after Vera met Igor Stravinsky in Paris — a primary reason for Sudeikin's departure for the USA in August, 1922. See her memoirs in F70, F85, and *Experiment*, 2007, No. 13.

983

984

La Tragédie de Salomé: *ballet in one act by Florent Schmitt after a poem by Robert d'Humières. Produced by Sergei Diaghilev at the Théâtre des Champs-Elysées, Paris on 12 June, 1913, with choreography by Boris Romanov and designs by Sergei Sudeikin.*

See No. 594 [R498] for plot summary.

983 [193; R809].
Costume Design for Salomé Danced by Tamara Karsavina, 1913.
Watercolor.
Initialed lower center in Russian: "SS."
18½ x 11¾ in., 47 x 29.8 cm.
Other inscription: by Sudeikin in Russian lower right: "Salomé."
Provenance: Konstantin Stramentov, London, May, 1977.
Reproduced in color in I20, No. 90; and in black and white in *Stolitsa i usadba*, P, 1916, No. 57, p. 4; A34, p. 415; I51, No. 223. A close variant is reproduced in color in *Comoedia Illustré*, Paris, 1913, No. 17, unpaginated; D23, plate 7; and in color in D1, unpaginated. For a documentary photograph of Karsavina wearing the costume see D23, p. 80. Also see G63, p. 143.

Note: Florent Schmitt composed his *La Tragédie de Salomé* in 1907 when the subject was enjoying a particular vogue in Europe and Russia (see Nos. 594-98 [R498-502] and 798a [R670]). Igor Stravinsky was enthusiastic about Schmitt's music and Diaghilev decided to include the ballet in the 1912-13 season, sensing that a spectacle with "l'idée de maléfice ajoutée à celle de séduction"[791] would go down well with a Paris audience. According to the ballet critic Valerian Svetlov, Sudeikin did, indeed, evoke this spirit of malevolence and mysticism in his designs, especially in his costume for Salomé. From the Vrubelian colors of dark blue and gold to the single rose that Sudeikin painted on Salomé's knee at each performance, the ensemble captivated by its exoticism and boldness.[792]

Le Carnaval de la Vie: *play by Saint-Georges de Bouhélier (?) produced at the Chamber Theater, Moscow, on 7 November, 1915, with designs by Sergei Sudeikin.*

984 [R810].
Stage Design, 1915.
Oil on cardboard.
14½ x 27¼ in., 37 x 69.2 cm.
Provenance: Semeon Bolan, New York, 1960.
Reproduced in G17, p. 16; I77, p. 136; and M43 (c).

Note: Details on the production of this play at the Chamber Theater have not been forthcoming, the more so since a play by the name of *Le Carnaval de la Vie* does not figure within the oeuvre of Saint-Georges de Bouhélier (unless the reference here is to his three-act play, *Le Carnaval des enfants*). The primary chronology for the Theater (C35) does not include the play or its author, although one source does ascribe the

984a

production designed by Sudeikin to Tairov's repertoire (C31, Vol. 1, p. 178). Sudeikin was especially interested in the theme of the carnival, especially Schumann's *Carnaval: Scènes mignonnes* and he contributed a large painting with the title *Carnaval* (together with many studies on the same theme) to the "Art in the Crimea" exhibition in Yalta in October, 1918, and to the "Little Circle" exhibition in Tiflis in May, 1919. Sudeikin's picture was actually "12 colored drawings" that were called *Figures of the Carnaval* (No. 212 in the Yalta exhibition catalog; one of these pieces is now in the State Museum of the Arts of Georgia, Tbilisi), described by the poet Sergei Gorodetsky as a "colorful illustration to Schumann's compositions."[793] Sudeikin also contributed a painting called *Russian Winter Carnival* to the "Exhibition of Russian Painting and Sculpture" at the Brooklyn Museum, New York, in 1923 (present whereabouts unknown; reproduced in the catalog, unpaginated).

The Tales of Hoffmann: *opera by Jacques Offenbach projected, but not produced, for Sergei Zimin's Opera Company, Moscow, in 1915, with designs by Sergei Sudeikin.*

The plot is based on stories by E.T.A. Hoffmann, including Coppélia *(see No. 449 [R476]).*

984a [R811].
Costume Design for a Jester, 1915.
Gouache.
6¾ x 4 in., 17 x 10 cm.
Initialed lower center in Russian: "S.S."
The reverse carries an ink drawing.
Provenance: Evgenii Gunst, Moscow, 1985.

Unidentified production, perhaps for Nikita Baliev's Chauve-Souris, Moscow, *ca. 1916.*

985 [R812].
Costume designs for Four Military Gentlemen, ca. 1916.
Watercolor.
Signed lower left in Russian: "Drawn by Boyar Serezha Sudeikin, son of Yurii."
9¼ x 12⅝ in., 23.5 x 32 cm.
Other inscriptions: left to right under the four figures in Russian: "Count Vasilii

985

986

Vasilievich Orlov-Denisov; Adjutant General Prince Mikhail Dmitrievich Gorchakov; General of Artillery Alexei Petrovich Ermolov; His Imperial Highness Grand Duke Nikolai Konstantinovich."
Provenance: Semeon Bolan, New York, 1960.
Reproduced in F107, p. 154; N106.

Note: According to Jeanne Palmer-Soudeikine (Sudeikin's widow), this piece was for a number produced at Baliev's Chauve-Souris cabaret in Moscow in 1916. However, the Chauve-Souris repertoire for 1916 does not carry a reference to a spectacle that might

have incorporated such a design. The personages represented here in sardonic fashion were prominent military men active at the time of the Decembrist revolt (see No. 1034 [R908]), i.e., V.V. Orlov-Denisov (1759-1844), M.D. Gorchakov (1793-1861), A.P. Ermolov (1777-1861), and N.K. [=N.P.] Romanov (1796-1855). Sudeikin has made a mistake (deliberate or not) in calling the latter Nikolai Konstantinovich; the reference is to Nikolai Pavlovich, Tsar Nicholas I after 1825.

Romances: *musical medley by Mikhail Glinka, Peter Tchaikovsky, and others,*

Produced by Nikita Baliev's at the Théâtre de la Chauve-Souris, Paris, 23 December, 1920, with designs by Serge Sudeikin
    This loose revue contains romances by Glinka, gypsy and folk songs, and a pas de deux from Tchaikovsky's Nutcracker.

986 [NIRE].
Costumes for Glinka's Romances, ca. 1921.
Gouache.
8⅝ x 10⅝ in., 22 x 27 cm.
Signed lower left in Russian: "Sudeikin."
Inscribed in pencil along the lower margin in Russian: "Romances of Glinka."
Provenance: the artist's widow, Jeanne Palmer-Soudeikine, New York, 1962.
Reproduced in I14, p. 53, No. 95.

Note: Although the date of the premiere was on 23 December, 1920, Baliev gave an informal preview of the *Romances* on 19 December.

Petrouchka: *ballet in four acts by Alexandre Benois and Igor Stravinsky. Produced at the Metropolitan Opera, New York, on 13 March, 1925, with choreography by Adolph Bolm and designs by Sergei Sudeikin.*
    See No. 159 [R133] for plot summary.

The following costume designs for *Petrouchka* are all signed "Soudeikine" in the lower right except for No. 988 [R814], which is signed lower middle; their measurements are also identical, i.e., 14 x 9 in., 35.5 x 23 cm.

987 [R813].
Costume Design for Petrouchka, ca. 1925.
Watercolor and ink.
Provenance: Semeon Bolan, New York, Vasiliy Wyrouboff, Buenos-Aires, May, 1969.
Reproduced in color in Kogan, *Sudeikin,* p. 153; N188, p. 48; and in black and white in G10, No. 237; I40, No. 104.

987

988

990

992

988 [R814].
Costume Design for the Ballerina, ca. 1925.
Watercolor and ink.
Provenance: Semeon Bolan, New York,
Vasiliy Wyrouboff, Buenos-Aires, May, 1969.
Reproduced in color in Kogan, *Sudeikin,* p.
152; I40, No. 105; in black and white in
G10, No. 237.

989 [R815].
*Costume Design for the Bulgarian Monkey
Trainer, ca. 1925.*
Watercolor and black ink.
Provenance: Semeon Bolan, New York,
Vasiliy Wyrouboff, Buenos-Aires, May, 1969.
Reproduced in I40, No. 106.

990 [R816].
*Costume Design for the Flute-Playing Bear
Keeper, ca. 1925.*
Watercolor.
Provenance: the artist's widow, Jeanne
Palmer-Soudeikine, New York, June, 1968.
Reproduced in I40, No. 107.

991 [R817].
Costume Design for the Bear, ca. 1925.
Watercolor.
Provenance: the artist's widow, Jeanne
Palmer-Soudeikine, New York, June, 1968.
Reproduced in I40, No. 108.

992 [194; R818].
*Costume Design for the Bear Tamer, ca.
1925.*
Watercolor and ink.
Provenance: Semeon Bolan, New York,
Vasiliy Wyrouboff, Buenos-Aires, May, 1969.
Reproduced in I40, No. 109.

993 [R819].
Costume Design for a Priest, ca. 1925.
Watercolor.
Provenance: Semeon Bolan, New York,
Vasiliy Wyrouboff, Buenos-Aires, May, 1969.
Reproduced in I40, No. 110.

989

991

993

994

996

998

994 [R820].
Costume Design for the Wet Nurse, ca. 1925.
Watercolor.
Provenance: Semeon Bolan, New York, Vasiliy Wyrouboff, Buenos-Aires, May, 1969. Reproduced in color B115, plate 174; in Kogan, *Sudeikin,* p. 152; in black and white in I40, No. 111.
This is a variation of No. 995 [NIRE].

995 [195; NIRE].
Costume Design for the Wet Nurse, ca. 1925.
Gouache on cardboard.
Other inscriptions on upper left in pencil in French: "Nourrice (1) et 12." Upper right: "1 solo Ballet." Lower left margin: consecutive number "39".

Provenance: Semeon Bolan, New York, Vasiliy Wyrouboff, Buenos-Aires, May, 1969. This is a variation of No. 994 [R820].

996 [R821].
Costume Design for an Old Man Dancing, ca. 1925.
Watercolor.
Provenance: Semeon Bolan, New York, Vasiliy Wyrouboff, Buenos-Aires, May, 1969. Reproduced in color in B115, plate 172; and in black and white in I40, No. 112.

997 [196; R822].
Costume Design for the Rooster, ca. 1925.
Watercolor.
Provenance: Semeon Bolan, New York, 1960. Reproduced in color in B115, plate 173; and in black and white in I14, No. 98.

998 [197; R823].
Costume Design for a Gypsy Man, ca. 1925.
Watercolor.
Provenance: Peter Tretiakov Gallery, New York, 1965.
Reproduced in I14, No. 96.

999 [198; R824].
Costume Design for a Gypsy Woman, ca. 1925.
Watercolor.
Provenance: Peter Tretiakov Gallery, New York, 1965.
Reproduced in I14, No 97.

995

997

999

1000

1002

1004

1001

1003

1000 [199; R825].
Costume Design for The Moor, ca. 1925.
Watercolor and ink.
Provenance: Semeon Bolan, New York;
Vasiliy Wyrouboff, Buenos-Aires, May, 1969.
Reproduced in color in B115, plate 175; and
in black and white in G10, No. 237; I20, No.
84.

1001 [R826].
Costume Design for the Drummer, ca. 1925.
Watercolor.
Provenance: Jeanne Palmer-Soudeikine,
New York, 1964.

Reproduced in color in B115, plate 176; F107,
p. 98; and in black and white in I14, No. 99.

1002 [200; R827].
*Costume Design for the Tea Vendor, ca.
1925.*
Watercolor.
Provenance: Alexis Gregory, New York,
1964.
Reproduced in color in Kogan, *Sudeikin,* p.
153; in black and white in I14, No. 100.

1003 [201; R828].
*Costume Design for the Chimney Sweep, ca.
1925.*
Watercolor.
Provenance: Semeon Bolan, New York,

Vasiliy Wyrouboff, Buenos-Aires, May, 1969.
Reproduced in I20, No. 85.

1004 [NIRE].
Costume Design for a Nobleman, ca. 1925.
Watercolor.
Provenance: Semeon Bolan, New York,
Vasiliy Wyrouboff, Buenos-Aires, May, 1969.

Le Rossignol: opera in three acts with
incidental dances by Igor Stravinsky and
Stepan Mitusov based on a tale by Hans
Christian Andersen. Produced at the
Metropolitan Opera, New York, on 7
March, 1926, with choreography by Boris
Romanov and designs by Sergei Sudeikin.
  See No. 281 [R254] for plot summary.

1005 [202; R829].
Costume Design for Death, ca. 1926.
Gouache.
Signed lower center in pencil: "Soudeikine."
11 x 9¼ in., 28 x 23.5 cm.
Other inscription: upper right corner in ink:
"1 La Mort."
Provenance: Semeon Bolan, New York,
1965.
Reproduced in color in B115, plate 177; and
in black and white in I40, No. 101; I51, No.
224.

1006 [R830].
*Costume Design for a Priest in a Wide Hat,
ca. 1926.*
Gouache.
Signed lower center in pencil: "Soudeikine."
11 x 9 in., 28 x 23 cm.
Inscribed upper right in ink: "9."
Provenance: Semeon Bolan, New York,
1965.
Reproduced in I40, No. 103.

1005

1006

1007

1007 [R831].
Costume Design for a Priest, ca. 1926.
Gouache.
Signed lower center in pencil: "Soudeikine."
11 x 9 in., 28 x 23 cm.
Inscribed upper right in ink: "10. Prêtre."
Provenance: Semeon Bolan, New York, 1965.
Reproduced in I40, No. 102.

Note: Ever since Diaghilev's production of *Le Rossignol* in Paris in 1914 with choreography by Boris Romanov and designs by Alexandre Benois (Nos. 281-84 [R254-56]), *Le Rossignol* had occupied an important place in the repertoire of Russian "balletic operas." The last time that Diaghilev staged *Le Rossignol* was in 1925 at the Théâtre de la Gaité-Lyrique with designs by Henri Matisse and choreography by George Balanchine. The following year the Metropolitan Opera also presented *Le Rossignol,* but with Romanov's original choreography and with new sets and costumes by Sudeikin. According to Anna Kashina-Evreinova (widow of Nikolai Evreinov), who saw the 1926 production, Sudeikin's designs were so vivid that they deafened the music.[794] Irving Kolodin, the opera historian, also remarked that "Soudeikine's settings... were among the best he has ever done for the Metropolitan."[795] Sudeikin was an enthusiastic interpreter of Stravinsky's music on stage — for example, in 1925 he designed Michel Fokine's revival of *Petrouchka* also at the Metropolitan Opera. For reproductions of analogous designs for the 1929-30 production of *Sadko* at the Metropolitan Opera see L209, Lot 508.

The Chief Thing: *play in four acts by Nikolai Evreinov produced at the Theatre Guild, New York, on 22 March, 1926, with designs by Sergei Sudeikin.*
The loose plot concerns love (or the illusion of love) — "the chief thing" or nothing in particular. Through many references to the conventions and characters

of the Italian Commedia dell'Arte, the play depends upon an amusing dialogue on life and love between fortune tellers, a civil servant, a barefoot dancer, a typist, a student, a landlady, Nero, Petronius, etc. The play ends with a discourse between Harlequin, the director, and the producer, whose closing remarks begin with: "The chief thing is to end the play effectively."

1008 [R832].
Poster for The Chief Thing, 1926.
Lithograph in red, grey, black, and white.
26⅛ x 14 in., 66.5 x 35.7 cm.
For photographs of the actual sets used in the production see E. Proffer: *Evreinov. A Pictorial Biography,* Ann Arbor: Ardis, 1981, pp. 33-38.
Provenance: the artist's widow, Jeanne Palmer-Soudeikine, New York, June, 1968.
Reproduced in color in F107, p. 155; M157,

1008

p. 85; and in black and white in M73, p. 94; M138; Q17; R11.

Note: Evreinov wrote *The Chief Thing* while he was living in Tiflis in 1919 and it proved to be his most successful and famous play. One reason for this is that it commented upon — and ridiculed — the recent Symbolist dramaturgy wherein characters had philosophized long and agonizingly over the meaning of life. *The Chief Thing* also poked fun at the "sex question" that had been a favorite topic for discussion among "liberated" Russian playwrights just before the Revolution. Evreinov deflated these conventions and relied for appeal on a rapid fire of asides, non-sequiturs, ironic remarks — all of which constituted an "illusion or a surrogate that the author and his representative, Dr. Fregoli, consider to be 'the chief thing.'"[796]
The Chief Thing was first produced by Evreinov at the Free Comedy Theater, Petrograd, on 20 February, 1921, with designs by Yurii Annenkov (see Nos. 47 [R44], 48 [R45]), and thereafter it saw many interpretations in Russian, German, French, Italian, and English. Although it enjoyed a particular success in Paris in the 1920s under the title *La Comédie du bonheur,* the New York presentation elicited a mixed reaction, one reviewer noting that

> *The Chief Thing* ... is remarkable as a farce which tries to say something instead of just sitting still and being farcical. Admittedly, it doesn't say anything of any momentous value. Of all M. Evreinov's talk of life and happiness and the theatre, what is true does not seem to be particularly new, and what is new seems to me to be singularly untrue.[797]

Evreinov and Sudeikin had been in close contact in Russia. Both, for example, had been active supporters of the Stray Dog and Comedians' Halt cabarets in St. Petersburg/Petrograd.

1010

The Patriot: *play by Alfred Neuman. Produced by Gilbert Miller at the Majestic Theater, New York on 19 January, 1928, with designs by Sergei Sudeikin.*

The subject is the brief, but adventurous reign of Paul I in Russia (Tsar from 1796 to 1801). Thanks to his psychotic militarism, Paul makes many enemies: he defines the peasants' corvée and quarrels with Alexander Suvorov, Russia's greatest general. Paul sends Suvorov to Italy to drive out the French from the Apennines. Paul then tries to woo Napoléon and to implement a joint invasion of India, but he is murdered before his schemes can bear fruit.

1009

1009 [R833].
Poster for The Patriot, ca. 1928.
Chromolithograph.
Signed lower right in the plate: "Soudaykin."
21⅞ x 14 in., 55.5 x 35.5 cm.
Provenance: the artist's widow, Jeanne Palmer-Soudeikine, New York, 1968.

Les Noces: *choral ballet in four scenes by Igor Stravinsky. Produced by the League of Composers at the Metropolitan Opera, New York, on 25 April, 1929, with choreography by Elisabeth Anderson-Ivantzova and designs by Sergei Sudeikin.*

See No. 568 [R436] for plot summary.

1010 [R834].
Stage Design for Act II, ca. 1929.
Pencil.
16⅛ x 20⅛ in., 41 x 51 cm.
Provenance: Elisabeth Anderson-Ivantzova, New York, 1965.
Reproduced in the souvenir program for *Les Noces,* New York, 1919, p. 6; I14, No. 94; Kogan, *Sudeikin,* p. 164.

788 C35. p.104.
789 I1, p. 11.
790 F85, p. 18.
791 Letter from Robert d'Humières to Florent Schmitt dated 1913. Quoted in I42, p. 59.
792 See Kogan, *Sergei Sudeikin,* p. 74. Sudeikin also designed a drop curtain for *Salomé* relying on these "Vrubelian" colors. For a color reproduction see C7, plate 58.
793 S. Gorodetsky: "Rabotniki iskusstva na yuge [interviu, vziatoe redaktsiei u S.M. Gorodetskogo]" in *Zhizn iskusstva,* M, 1920. Quoted in Kogan: *Sergei Sudeikin,* p. 137.
794 Kogan,*Sergei Sudeikin,* p. 151.
795 I. Kolodin: *The Metropolitan Opera 1883-1935.* New York: Oxford University Press. 1936, p. 336.
796 Atelstan: "Samoe glavnoe" in *Teatr, Literatura, muzyka, balet, grafika, zhivopis, kino,* Kharkov, 1922, No. 1, p. 10.
797 Review by R.S. in *The Grants,* New York, 1927, 2 December. Quoted in *Nicolas Evreinoff 1873-1953.* Catalog of exhibition at the Bibliothèque Nationale, Paris, 1981, p. 37.

SUETIN, Nikolai Mikhailovich

Born 25 October (6 November), 1897, Matlevskaia, near Kaluga; Russia; died 25 January, 1954, Leningrad, Russia.

1915-17 served part of his mobilization in Vitebsk during the First World War and the October Revolution; 1918-22 studied at the Popular Art Institute / Art-Practical Institute, Vitebsk; 1919 made the acquaintance of Jean Pougny and then Kazimir Malevich; 1920 founding member of Posnovis (later Unovis); supporter of Suprematism; 1922 after Malevich's departure for Petrograd, Suetin followed, along with other members of the group, including Ilia Chashnik, Lev Yudin, and Vera Ermolaeva; 1923 joined the staff of the Lomonosov State Porcelain Factory, where he produced Suprematist designs for plates, cups, saucers, etc.; 1923-24 with Chashnik helped Malevich to construct the architectural models known as *arkhitektony, planity,* and *zemlianity;* 1923-26 member of Ginkhuk; 1925 contributed to the "Exposition Internationale des Arts Décoratifs" in Paris, and in 1926 to the the "Exhibition of Soviet Porcelain"; 1927 especially interested in architectural and furniture design; 1928 with Chashnik designed residential quarters for the Bolshevik Confectionery Factory in Leningrad; 1927-30 worked at the Institute of Art History; 1932 onwards artist-in-residence at the Art Laboratory of the Leningrad Lomonosov Porcelain Plant; 1937 chief interior designer of the Soviet pavilion at the "Exposition Internationale des Arts et Techniques dans la Vie Moderne" in Paris; 1938 interior designer of the Soviet pavilion at the "World's Fair" in New York; 1940s continued to work as designer.

Bibliography
A. L[eporskaia]: "Nikolai Suetin" in K42, pp.167-68.
K54, passim.

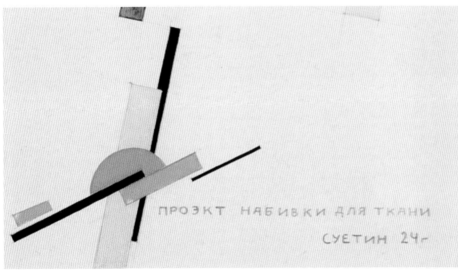

1011

in Vitebsk and then Leningrad, developing the Suprematist formulae and applying them to porcelain, furniture, and architectonic projects. Indeed, of all of Malevich's disciples perhaps Suetin achieved the highest success as a designer, playing a primary role, for example, in the interior resolutions for the Paris and New York World's Fairs in 1937 and 1939, respectively — in which, in spite of the weight of Socialist Realism, Suetin still followed the Suprematist line, emphasizing economy, efficiency, and simple geometric composition. In this way, Suetin was also expressing Malevich's — and El Lissitzky's — fundamental desire that Suprematism advance from two to three dimensions, from surface to space and thereby help reconstruct the material world. As Szymon Bojko writes, Suetin's idea was to "apply the principles of Suprematism to commodities of mass producton: the square becomes a cube; the circle becomes a cylinder."[798] Similarly, Suetin's textile designs are also — ultimately — oriented towards volume, i.e. towards the kinetic mass of the human body.

1011 [NIRE].
Textile Design with Suprematist Motif, 1924.
Watercolor and ink.
Signed and dated lower right in pencil in Russian block capitals: "Suetin 24."
12⅝ x 16½ in., 32 x 42 cm.
Other inscriptions lower right above signature in Russian block capitals, in pencil: "Design for cloth print."
For similar decorative compositions, see K154, figs. 166 and 167; and also Rakitin, *Nikolai Mikhailovich Suetin*, pp. 188-91.
Provenance: private collector, Moscow.

798 S. Bojko: "Practical Application of Suprematism" in I42, p. 168.

SURVAGE, Léopold (Shtiurtsvage, Leopold Lvovich sometimes given as Leopoldovich)

Born 31 July (12 August), 1879, Lappeenranta, Finland; died 31 October, 1968, Paris, France.

1899 enrolled in MIPSA, where he studied under Konstantin Korovin and Leonid Pasternak; 1907-08 contributed to the "Wreath-Stephanos" exhibition in Moscow; 1908 traveled through Russia and Europe; 1909 settled in Paris; impressed by the piano recitals of Wanda Landowska; 1910 contributed to the "Jack of Diamonds" exhibition, Moscow; 1911 created first abstract compositions called *Rythmes colorés*, 1912 in close contact with the Delaunays, Picasso, Gino Severini, and other contemporary artists; 1913 contributed to the "Salon d'Automne" and the "Salle des Cubistes" within the "Salon des Indépendents"; 1914 published his explanation of *Rythmes colorés* in the

V. Rakitin: "Plus X. Nikolai Suetin – der Schuler wird zum Meister" in K105, pp. 168-70.
V. Rakitin, comp.: *Suprematismus. Werke von Kasimir S. Malewitsch, Nikolai M. Suetin, Ilja G. Tschaschnik aus dem Archiv Lev Nussberg.* Catalog of exhibition at the Galerie Schlegl, Berlin, 1989.
V. Rakitin: *Suprematisti russi degli anni 20. Suetin, Čašnik, Leporskaja.* Catalog of exhibition at the Galleria Marconi, 1991.
V. Rakitin: *Malewitsch. Suetin. Tschaschnik.* Catalog of exhibition at the Galerie Gmurzynska, Cologne, 1992.
K154, pp. 808-09.
B154, pp. 278-81.
V. Rakitin: *Nikolai Mikhailovich Suetin,* M: RA and SP: Palace Editions, 1998.
E. Basner, ed.: *Malevich's Circle,* SP: Palace Editions, 2000, passim.
B283 (English version), passim.
P. Yuzhik et al., eds.: *Vitebsk. Klassika i avangard,* Vitebsk: Vitebskaia oblastnaia tipografiia, 2004, passim.
A. Shatskikh et al.: *Malevich, Suetin, Chashnik, Ermilov.* Catalog of exhibition at the Gary Tatintsian Gallery, M, 2006.
A. Shatskikh: *Vitebsk, The Life of Art,* New Haven: Yale University Press, 2007, passim.
V. Rakitin: *Nikolai Suetin,* SP: Palace Editions, 2008.
T. Goriacheva: *Nikolai Suetin,* M: Gordeev, 2010.
T. Goriacheva: *Nas budet troe. Kazimir Malevich. Il'ia Chashnik. Nikolai Suetin.* Catalog of exhibition at TG, 2012.
T. Goriacheva: *Nikolai Mikhailovich Suetin,* Sepherot Foundation, Vaduz, 2012.

Suetin was one of Malevich's most earnest and devoted students and a cardinal influence on his painting and design was, of course, the Suprematist system. In the 1920s Suetin worked closely with Malevich

newspaper *Les Soirées de Paris;* 1917 with Irène Lagut exhibited at the Galerie Bougard (curated by Apollinaire); 1919 contributed to the "Exhibition of Modern French Painting" in London; 1919 developed the idea of *tons sourds;* 1922 designed the sets and costumes for *Mavra;* 1928 decorated the interior of the Union Catholique du Théâtre, Paris; 1920s many one-man exhibitions in Europe and the USA; 1933 designs textiles for Chanel; 1937 interior designs for pavilions at the "Exposition Internationale' in Paris; 1954 painted sets and costumes for Antonio Veretti's opera *La Petite marchande d'allumettes* for the Théâtre da Cagliari, Paris; 1950s-60s continued to paint and exhibit;1963 awarded Légion d'Honneur.

Bibliography
S. Putman: *The Glistening Bridge: Léopold Survage and the Spatial Problem in Painting,* New York: Covici-Friede, 1929.
P. Fierens: *Survage,* Paris: Quatre Chemins, 1931.
M. Gauthier: *Survage,* Paris: Les Gémeaux, 1953.
Survage, Exposition Rétrospective. Catalog of exhibition at the Musée Galliera, Paris, 1966.
J. Warnod: *Léopold Survage,* Paris: André de Rache, 1983.
H. Seyrès: *Survage. Ecrits sur la peinture,* Paris: l'Archipel, 1992.
H34, pp. 559-61.
H51, passim.
F. Luchert: *Léopold Survage.* Catalog of exhibition at the Galerie Zlotowski, Paris, 2008.
K274, pp. 198, 203.

Like Vladimir Baranoff-Rossiné (see No. 108 [NIRE]), Survage found an artistic and ethnic license in Paris that enabled him to develop his peculiar theory of "colored rhythms" which along with Vasilii Kandinsky's *Improvisations* and Sonia Delaunay's Simultanism, were among the first exercises in non-objective painting. Although the forces of Cubism, Futurism, and Orphism can be recognized in Survage's abstract compositions of 1912-13, he seems to have also been aware of Theosophical thought forms and of the Symbolists' ideas about synesthesia. However, Survage's sally into abstraction was short-lived, for most of his ensuing art was representational (landscapes, portraits, stage designs), tinged concurrently with a mild Surrealism and a Neue Sachlichkeit. Even so, a just and esthetically pleasing pictorial organization remained fundamental to Survage's artistic worldview:

> La synthèse plastique c'est le seul moyen qui nous permette, non pas de représenter les objets tels que nous les voyons, mais de nous servir d'eux pour former et créer un monde poétique, constitué et exprimé par des moyens exclusivement plastiques dont la base est le rythme.[799]

Mavra: comic opera in one act by Igor Stravinsky with libretto by Boris Kochno based on Alexander Pushkin's poem The Little House in Kolomna. *Produced by Sergei Diaghilev at the Hôtel Continental, Paris on 29 May, 1922, and then at the Théâtre de l'Opéra, Paris, on 3 June, 1922, with choreography by Bronislava Nijinska and designs by Léopold Survage.*

The young girl Parasha has her lover Vasilii disguise himself as the servant Mavra that her mother has asked her to employ. After some amusing incidents, the couple is united.

1012

1012 [R835].
Costume Design for Parasha, 1922.
Brush and ink.
Signed, stamped with the atelier stamp, and dated lower right: "Survage 22."
17 x 10 in., 43.3 x 25.4 cm.
Provenance: the artist's wife, Hélène Moniuschko, Paris, September, 1967.
Reproduced in I20, No. 87; I51, No. 236. A close variant, now in the collection of the Wadsworth Atheneum, Hartford, Connecticut, is reproduced in the souvenir program for the *Ballets Russes à l'Opéra,* Paris; 1922, May-June, unpaginated; also in I9, p. 26; K50 (b), unnumbered; also see G59, p. 117.

1013 [R836].
Costume Design for Vasilii the Hussar, 1922.
Pencil and watercolor.
Signed, stamped with the atelier stamp and dated lower right: "Survage 22."
17 x 10 in., 43.3 x 25.4 cm.
Other inscription: lower right: "Grigori."
Provenance: the artist's wife, Hélène Moniuschko, Paris, September, 1967.
Reproduced in A34, p. 418; I20, No. 88; I51, No. 237; *Peintres et Sculpteurs Russes de France* (Catalog of exhibition at the Office

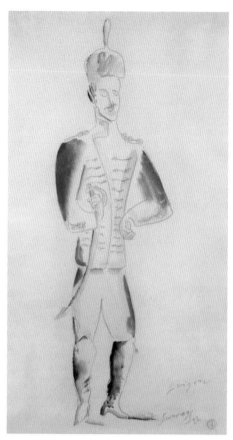

1013

Culturel de Bry, Bry-sur-Marne, 1983, p. 72). A close variant, now in the collection of the Wadsworth Atheneum, Hartford, Connecticut, is reproduced in the souvenir program for the *Ballets Russes à l'Opéra,* Paris; 1922, May-June, unpaginated; also in I11, No. 169; K50 (b), unnumbered; also see G59, p. 117.

Note: Diaghilev first commissioned Léon Bakst to design *Mavra,* but he was dissatisfied with the result and, on Mikhail Larionov's recommendation, transferred the commission to Survage. Survage recalled:

> "Come along," [Larionov] said, "Diaghilev wants to see you." We set out for the Hotel [Le] Meurice [probably the Continental], and found Diaghilev on the sixth floor in a servant's bedroom furnished only with a bed, a table and a chair. Diaghilev sat on the bed, I on the chair, and Larionov remained standing. Diaghilev explained that he wanted me to make designs for Stravinsky's opera *Mavra;* but he wanted them by the next morning. I thanked Larionov and made two sketches during the night, of which Diaghilev chose one.[800]

Bakst then initiated a court proceeding against Diaghilev for reimbursement. The entire incident forced a breach between Diaghilev and Bakst with the sad result that the two men ended their long artistic relationship once and for all.

799 L. Survage: «Notes pour les entretiens d'atelier» in Seyrès, *Survage. Ecrits sur la peinture,* p. 106.
800 Quoted from D26, p. 402.

TATLIN, Vladimir Evgrafovich

Born 16 (28) December, 1885, Moscow, Russia; died 31 May, 1953, Moscow, Russia.

Ca. 1900 ran away from home; joined the merchant navy; 1902-03 attended MIPSA; 1904-09 attended the Penza Art Institute, where he studied under Ilia Goriushkin-Sorokopudov and Alexei Afanasiev; 1904 – ca. 08 as a seaman visited many ports in the Mediterranean; 1909-10 reenrolled at MIPSA; 1909-11 close to Burliuk, Mikhail Larionov, and other members of the avant-garde; 1910-11 contributed to Vladimir Izdebsky's "Salon 2"; 1912 onwards contributed to many exhibitions, including the "Donkey's Tail" and the "Target"; 1914 visited Berlin and Paris, where he met Picasso; on his return to Moscow began to work on reliefs; worked closely with Liubov Popova, Nadezhda Udaltsova, Alexander Vesnin, and other avant-garde artists; 1915 contributed reliefs to "Tramway V"; 1915-16 contributed to "0.10"; organized the "Store" exhibition; 1917 helped with the interior decoration for the Café Pittoresque, Moscow; 1918 appointed head of IZO NKP in Moscow; 1918-20 professor at Svomas; 1919-24 professor at Pegoskhuma; 1919 began to work on his model for the Monument to the III International; 1922-26 head of the Department of Material Culture at the Museum of Artistic Culture / Ginkhuk, Petrograd / Leningrad; 1923 organized a production of Velimir Khlebnikov's dramatic poem *Zangezi* in Petrograd; 1925-27 professor at the Kiev Art Institute; 1927-30 professor at Vkhutein; 1929-32 developed project for a glider called Letatlin; 1931-33 headed the Scientific Research Laboratory for the Plastic Arts, Moscow; 1930s-40s worked on stage design; returned to figurative painting.

Bibliography
N. Punin: *Tatlin (Protiv kubizma)*, P: IZO NKP, 1921. Reprinted as *O Tatline*, M: RA, 1994.
T. Andersen: *Vladimir Tatlin*. Catalog of exhibition at the Moderna Museet, Stockholm, 1968; and the Van Abbemuseum, Eindhoven, 1969.
A. Strigalev: "O proekte 'Pamiatnika III Internatsionala' khudozhnika V. Tatlina," in I. Kriukova et al., eds.: *Voprosy sovetskogo izobrazitelnogo iskusstva*, M: Sovetskii khudozhnik, 1973, pp. 409-52.
L. Zhadova: *V.E. Tatlin*. Catalog of exhibition organized by the Union of Writers of the USSR, the Union of Artists of the USSR, and other agencies, M, 1977.
J. Bowlt: "Un voyage dans l'espace: l'oeuvre de Vladimir Tatlin" in *Cahiers du Musée National d'Art Moderne*, Paris, 1979, No. 2, pp. 216-27.
L. Zhadova: "Tatlin – proektirovshchik materialnoi kultury," in *Sovetskoe dekorativnoe iskusstvo '77/78*, M: Sovetskii khudozhnik, 1980, pp. 204-34.
S. Khan-Magomedov: "Dizainerskaia kontseptsiia V.E. Tatlina v sisteme khudozhestvennykh distsiplin dermetfaka VKHUTEINa (1927-30)" in *Trudy VNIITE*, M, 1981, No. 28, pp. 42-59.
B60.
L. Zsadova et al.: *Tatlin*, Budapest: Corvina, 1984. English translation: L. Zhadova et al.: *Tatlin*, London: Thames and Hudson, 1987.
A. Strigalev: "Vladimir Tatlin" in *Arkhitektura SSSR*, M, 1985, No. 6, pp. 86-92.
B85, pp. 22-26.
Tatlin, Vladimir Evgrafovich (1885-1953). Catalog of exhibition at the Savitsky Art Institute, Penza, 1987.
A. Parnis: "Kievskie epizody teatralnoi biografii Tatlina" in *Russkaia mysl*, Paris, 1990, 16 February.
A. Kovalev: "'Letatlin'. Poisk novogo mira" in *Iskusstvo*, M, 1990. No. 6, pp. 28-34.
M. Ray: "Tatlin e la cultura del Vchutemas, 1920-1930, Rome: Officina, 1992.
Yu. Nagibin: *Tatlin / Vermeer*, Milan: Spirali, 1993.
J. Harten, ed.: *Tatlin: Leben, Werk, Wirkung; ein internationales Symposium*, Cologne: DuMont, 1993.
A. Strigalev and J. Harten: *Tatlin*. Catalog of exhibition at the Kunsthalle, Düsseldorf, and other cities, 1993-94.
B170.
N. Lynton: *Tatlin's Tower. Monument to Revolution*, New Haven: Yale University Press, 2009.
A. Strigalev: *Bashnia 3-go Internatsionala*, M: Gordeev, 2011.
A. Strigalev: *Tatlin*, M: Gordeev, 2011.
S. Baier et al.: *New Art for a New World*. Catalog of exhibition at the Museum Tinguely, Basel, 2012.

Tatlin's artistic activities — his reliefs, his Monument to the III International, his functional designs, his glider — represent a consistent extension of the endeavor to replace the particular by the universal, to "reach out," and to change the concept of art as a vehicle of individual, private expression into an object of social need and public consumption. Both before and after the Revolution, Tatlin worked as the leader or member of a collective and his Moscow studio witnessed the fruitful collaboration between many artists. Even though Alexander Vesnin felt that it was "impossible to work with Tatlin,"[801] the studio was reminiscent of a Medieval guild in which common ideas and materials were shared and explored and in which topical issues such as Byzantine art, the Russian icon, and Cubism were discussed and interpreted.

Tatlin summarized his attitude to the work of art as an "anonymous" endeavor when he declared that in the art of the past

> every connection between painting, sculpture and architecture has been lost; the result was individualism, i.e., the expression of purely personal habits and tastes.[802]

Symptomatic of this spirit of collectivity is the fact that the drawings and designs for the Monument to the III International were exhibited in Petrograd as the "collective work of the central group of the Association of New Trends of Art."[803]

Tatlin's attempt to move from the surface of the traditional painting out into public space was evident on many levels — in his concern with the method of display in the Tretiakov Gallery in Moscow,[804] in his active participation in professional societies such as the Professional Union of Artists-

Mikhail Larionov: *Portrait of Vladimir Tatlin*, *ca. 1912. See No. 699 [R592].*

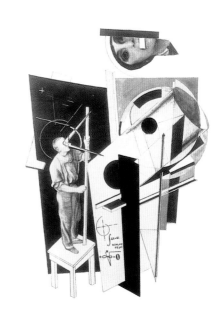

El Lissitzky: *Vladimir Tatlin at Work on the Monument to the III International*, *ca. 1922. See No. 751 [R631].*

Painters in Moscow in 1917, in his efforts to establish (with Nikolai Punin) the journal *Internatsional iskusstv* [International of the Arts] in 1918, and even in his demand for a motorcycle in 1922 so that he could visit "at least fifteen factories."[805] Tatlin's "impersonality" was also demonstrated by his unchanging mode of dress and hairstyle — the old jacket and sagging roll-neck sweater visible in photographs of 1916 or 1950. Viewed against this simple physical and psychological background, Tatlin's creation of the reliefs, the stage designs, the Monument, and the glider can be regarded as attempts to resolve what he called "the problem of the correlation between man and the object,"[806] so as to produce an art that would be material, concrete, and universally accessible.

The Emperor Maximilian and His Disobedient Son Adolf. *tragedy in two acts based on an 18th-century folk drama. Produced by Mikhail Bonch-Tomashevsky at the Literary-Artistic Circle, Moscow on 6 November, 1911, with music by Mikhail Rechkunov and designs by Vladimir Tatlin.*

The Emperor demands obedience from his son Adolf to the gods of trade, but Adolf refuses, is imprisoned and executed. The narrative is accompanied by fights and dances, and is enhanced by the traditional folk characters such as a priest, a doctor, a gravedigger, a tailor, etc.

1014

1014 [203; R837].
Costume Design for a Pipe Player, ca. 1911.
Watercolor and ink.
Initialed lower right in Russian: "V.T."
12⅝ x 7⅝ in., 32 x 19.5 cm.
Other inscription: upper left in Russian: "A pipe player."
Provenance: Nina Stevens, New York, May, 1969.
Reproduced in color in B115, plate 74; N188, p. 50; and in black and white in B60, p. 30; I20, No. 89; I32, No. 96; I51, No. 239; I77, p. 146; M75. The design seems to be based on the 18th-century *lubok* (hand-colored print) called *Farnos the Clown Riding a Pig* (reproduced in Yu. Ovsiannikov: *Lubok,* M: Sovetskii khudozhnik, 1968, No. 37). For reproductions of similar costumes for *The Emperor Maximilian,* see B60, pp. 30-31; G39, No. 50; I61, pp. 303-04; *Studiia,* Moscow, 1911, No. 4, pp. 7-8; *Dekorativnoe iskusstvo,* M, 1975, No. 12, p. 23; Zsadova, *Tatlin,* Nos. 39-41.

Note: According to G2, *The Emperor Maximilian and His Disobedient Son Adolf* was staged in St. Petersburg by the Union of Youth society on 27 January, 1911, with designs by Avgust Ballier, Alexander Gaush, Mikhail Le-Dantiu, Savelii Shleifer, Eduard Spandikov et al., supervised by Evgenii Sagaidachnyi.[807] According to the late Mark Etkind, however, this production took place at the end of 1910 and Alexander Shevchenko and Tatlin were among the decorators, but this information is not corroborated by other evidence.[808] In any case, Bonch-Tomashevsky staged his own version in Moscow in November, 1911, for which Tatlin assumed responsibility for all the designs, and then took the production to the Troitsky Theater, St. Petersburg, in January, 1912. In his endeavor to revitalize the modern theater by incorporating the "low" elements of folk theater, Bonch-Tomashevsky even took part in a real *balagan* theater so as to "sense the popular psychology more intimately." [809] Still, as one critic wrote of the Moscow production,

> the outer thoroughness of the production, all the vivid details, could not conceal the squalor and decrepitude of the action itself.[810]

A Life for the Tsar (also called Ivan Susanin): *opera in four acts and an epilogue by Mikhail Glinka based on a text by Egor Rozen. Production projected, but not realized, in Moscow, 1913, with designs by Vladimir Tatlin.*

Ivan Susanin, a peasant, reports that the Polish army is advancing on Moscow. Sobinin, a Russian soldier, allays the people's fears and expresses his hope that he will soon marry Antonida, Susanin's daughter. Meanwhile the first Romanov Tsar is elected and the Poles plan to capture him. The Polish troops enter and order Susanin to take them to the Tsar. He leads them astray deliberately, admits his action, and is killed for this.

1015 [204; R838].
Costume Design for a Peasant Girl, 1913.
Watercolor.
Initialed lower right and dated: "V.T. 1913."
18⅛ x 11⅜ in., 46 x 29 cm.
Provenance: Nina Stevens, New York, January, 1968.
Reproduced in color in A34, p. 427; B60, p. 42; B115, plate 73; K108, No. 127; and in black and white in I20, No. 90; I32, No. 97; I51, No. 240; I77, p. 146; N112, p. 57. The Lobanov-Rostovsky collection also contains a second version of this item (see No. 1016 [R839]). Two other costumes for peasant girls from *A Life for the Tsar,* in the GMTMA, are reproduced in Zhadova, *V.E. Tatlin,* pp. 52-53; also see B60, pp. 54-56; many costumes are reproduced in Zsadova, *Tatlin,* Nos. 141-53, including a version of this one (No. 144). For reproductions of sets for the drama see B60, p. 29; Zsadova, Nos. 137-40; also see G49, p. 97; I61, p. 303; K67, No. 19.

1015

1016 [R839].
Costume Design for a Peasant Girl, ca. 1913.
Watercolor.
Signed upper left in pencil in Russian "V. Tatlin."
18⅛ x 11⅜ in., 46 x 29 cm.
Other inscription: upper right in pencil in Russian: "Cher[nyi]" [Black]; upper part crossed out, presumably, by Tatlin. Note that the signature and annotation were erased during restoration and that this reproduction is from a photograph taken before cleaning.
Provenance: Nina Stevens, New York, January, 1968.
Reproduced in I77, p. 146.

1016

Note: In the late 1900s Tatlin's colleagues, especially Goncharova and Larionov, were giving particular attention to the icon, the *lubok,* and other traditional arts, an interest that Tatlin supported with particular enthusiasm. Not surprisingly, certain formal parallels between Tatlin's work of ca. 1912 and that of Goncharova and Larionov can be distinguished. For example, Tatlin's design for the stage set of the Grove of Kostroma Forest in *A Life for the Tsar* is close to Goncharova's painting called *The Grove* of 1913; both artists resort to the geometric, stylized forms of the icon and the *lubok,* and, similarly, Tatlin's folkloristic, florid backgrounds and costumes for *The Emperor Maximilian and His Disobedient Son Adolph* are reminiscent of Goncharova's Neo-Primitivist designs — for example, her sets and costumes for the Diaghilev production of *Le Coq d'Or* in 1914 (Nos. 534-40 [R407-12]).

1017 [NIRE].
Designer unknown: *Poster for the Futurist Exhibition "The Store," Petrograd, 30 March,* 1916.
Lithograph in black and white.
20½ x 10⅜ in., 52 x 26.5 cm.
Inscriptions (as part of the design) provide the details of the exhibition, i.e. top right: "1916", followed by:

> PETROVKA, HOUSE NO. 17
> FUTURIST EXHIBITION "THE STORE"
> OPENS
> From 20 March until 20 April [1916]
> With the participation of painters from Moscow, St. Petersburg, and Paris
> Vernissage on 19 March, from 1 until 7 pm. Entrance fee 1 ruble.
> OPENING OF THE EXHIBITION 20 MARCH, from 10 am till 7 pm. Ticket price 59 kopecks, students 35 kopecks.
> Organizer V.E. Tatlin.

Followed by:

> In line with the highest approval by the Council of Ministers of 22 November, 1915, in addition to the supreme decision approved on 6 May, 1892, on the recommendation of the State Council, a special tax is levied on all tickets, payable with stamps issued by the Office of Empress Mariia, without which tickets are invalid.

Lower margin, in small print:

> Permitted for printing on 17 March, 1916. Signed for the City of Moscow Governor by his acting deputy Durov. Printer of the Moscow Imperial Theaters. By appointment to the Imperial Court, Serov Partnership, A.A. Levenson. Moscow Tverskaia, 206 Mamonovskii Lane, Room 3.

Note: The Futurist exhibition "Store," organized by a group of Moscow avant-garde artists headed by Vladimir Tatlin and

1017

Alexander Rodchenko, opened on 20 March, 1916, on the premises of a disused store at 17 Petrovka in downtown Moscow. Contributors included Lev Bruni, Alexandra Exter, Ivan Kliun, Alexei Morgunov, Vera Pestel, Liubov Popova, Rodchenko, Tatlin, Sofia Tolstaia, Nadezhda Udaltsova, Marie Vassilieff, and Valentin Yustitsky. One of the initiators, Kazimir Malevich, removed his works on the eve of the opening owing to disagreements with other participants. Among the works on show were Cubist paintings (Pestel. Popova, and Udaltsova), abstract painting, sculptures, and constructions (Bruni and Rodchenko), and Tatlin's counter-reliefs. Early in 1917 the participants in the "Store" and their colleagues established the Store Association, subtitled Society for the Perfection of Sight and Sound. A protocol submitted to a meeting of the Union of Professional Artists on 14 April, 1917, listed Bruni, Sergei Isakov (secretary), Petr Lvov, Vladimir Milashevsky, Petr Miturich, Pestel, Rodchenko, Tatlin (chairman), Tolstaia, Vassilieff, Nokolai Yasinovsky, and Boris Zenkevich, as well as composer Arthur Lourié and art critic Nikolai Punin as members.

1018 [NIRE].
Designer unknown: *Poster for the "Exhibition of the Model for the Design of the Monument to the Third International" and a Meeting, Petrograd,* 1920.
Lithograph in black and white.
12¾ x 9⅞ in., 32.5 x 25 cm.

1018

Note: This temporary exhibition of Tatlin's wooden maquette of his celebrated and ambitious project — monument to the III Communist International — took place in Tatlin's studio "of volume, material, and construction" in Svomas (formerly the Imperial Academy of Fine Arts) in Petrograd, from 8 November until 1 December, 1920. The poster not only advertises the exhibition, but also invites the public to a discussion of the monument in Tatlin's studio (formerly the Mosaic Studio) on 8 November. For relevant documentary photographs see Zsadova, *Tatlin,* figs. 179-206.

801 From a letter from Alexander Vesnin to his brother Leonid dated January, 1915. Quoted in A. Chiniakov: *Bratia Vesniny,* M: Stroiizdat, 1970, p. 38.

802 V. Tatlin, T. Shapiro, I. Meerzon, P. Vinogradov: "Nasha predstoiashchaia rabota" (1920). From the translation in *Vladimir Tatlin* (1968), p. 51.

803 Zhadova, *V.E. Tatlin,* p. 8.

804 Appointed director of the Tretiakov Gallery in 1912, Igor Grabar embarked on an ambitious program of reforms, something that incurred the wrath of many conservatives. One result of this was a heated debate and exchange of letters on the aims and intentions of Grabar. Many young artists encouraged Grabar, and, on 4 February, 1916, they published a joint declaration under the title "Zaiavlenie khudozhnikov i deiatelei iskusstva" in the Moscow newspaper *Russkie vedomosti* in order to demonstrate support. Among the cosignatories was Tatlin.

805 Tatlin in his lecture "Doloi tatlinizm" in Petrograd, 1922. Quoted in K. Miklashevsky: *Gipertrofiia iskusstva,* P: Akademiia, 1924, p. 60.

806 This is the title of one of Tatlin's articles, i.e., "Problema sootnosheniia cheloveka i veshchi" in *Rabis,* M, 1930, No. 15, p. 9.

807 See A. Zhurin: "Poeziia balagana" in *Studiia,* M, 1911, 16 October, No. 3, pp. 8-10.

808 M. Etkind: "'Soiuz molodezhi' i ego stsenograficheskie eksperimenty" in G50, 1981, pp. 249-50.

809 "Khronika" in *Studiia,* M, 1911, No. 4, p. 27. For commentary on the relationship of *Emperor Maximilian* and the *balagan* see Zhurin, op. cit.

810 Max-li: "Tragicheskii balagan" in *Studiia,* 1912, 5 November, No. 6, p. 7.

TCHEHONINE, Serge (Chekhonin, Sergei Vasilievich)

Born 21 September (3 October) (some sources give 14 [26] February), 1878, Lykoshino, near Novgorod, Russia; died 23 February, 1936, Lörrach, Germany.

1896-97 attended SSEA; 1897-1900 took lessons in painting from Ilia Repin at Princess Mariia Tenisheva's Art School in St. Petersburg (in 1900 renamed the Free Studio); 1902-07 worked with sculpture and ceramics under Petr Vaulin at the Abramtsevo Ceramic Studio in Moscow; helped with the decorations for the Metropole Hotel in Moscow; 1903-04 contributed to the designs of the Contemporary Art enterprise in St. Petersburg; 1905-07 contributed caricatures and cartoons to revolutionary journals; 1906-07 worked in Paris; 1906 onwards designed and made illustrations for books and magazines, which became his major occupation in the ensuing years; 1907-15 continued to work under Vaulin at the Kikerino workshop near St. Petersburg; 1908 returned to St. Petersburg; worked on interior designs for various residences; contributed to the "Wreath" exhibition in St. Petersburg; thereafter contributed to many national and international exhibitions; 1910 joined the revived World of Art society and contributed regularly to its exhibitions until 1924; 1913-18 head of the Art Section of the Craft Industries at the Ministry of Agriculture; 1917-20s taught at SCITD; 1918-23 and from 1925 onward Artistic Director of the State Porcelain Factory, Petrograd-Leningrad; 1923-25 lived in Novogord Region;1925 contributed to the "Exposition Internationale des Arts Décoratifs," Paris; 1928 emigrated to Paris; in emigration worked as a designer for Nikita Baliev's Chauve-Souris cabaret and for the Ballets Russes de Vera Nemtchinova in Paris; 1929 worked for *Vogue* magazine; designed porcelain and jewelry; 1933 took out a patent for a

1019

machine for multicolor fabric printing; 1934 visited New York; 1935 prototype machine was constructed for a textile dye and printing plant at Weil am Rhein in Germany near Basel.

Bibliography
A. Efros and N. Punin: *S. Chekhonin*, M-P: State Publishing House, 1923 (editions in Russian, English and French).
M2, Vol. 2, pp. 199-200, listing his theatrical productions.
N. Lianda: "Novye materialy o dorevoliutsionnom periode tvorchestva S.V. Chekhonina" in *Problemy razvitiia russkogo iskusstva*, L, 1974, No. 6, pp. 71-77.
L. Andreeva: "O poslednikh godakh tvorchestva S. Chekhonina" in K. Rozhdestvensky et al., eds.: *Sovetskoe dekorativnoe iskusstvo '76*, M: Sovetskii khudozhnik, 1978, pp. 230-48.
N. Lianda: "Sergei Chekhonin and the New Soviet Porcelain" in B31, pp. 157-69.
Yu. Gerchuk: "Iskusstvo Sergeia Chekhonina" in *Tvorchestvo*, M, 1978, No. 2, pp. 20-23.
R. Gerra (Guerra): "S. Chekhonin — master russkoi grafiki" in *Russkii almanakh*, Paris, 1981, pp. 184-87.
I. Lipovich: "Albom S.V. Chekhonina iz sobraniia Gosudarstvennogo Russkogo muzeia" in *Muzei*, M, 1988, No. 9, pp. 152-58.
M20.
I. Lipovich: "Satiricheskie simvoly Chekhonina" in *Tvorchestvo*, M, 1990, No. 1, pp. 30-32.
E. Ivanova and I. Lipovich: *Sergei Vasilievich Chekhonin 1878-1936*. Catalog of exhibition at the RM, 1994.
M73, Vol. 26, pp. 87-88.
E. Kuznetsov: "Prevrashcheniia Sergeia Chekhonina: Zigzagi russkogo estetizma" in *Novyi mir iskusstva*, SP, 1998, No. 2, pp. 20-23.
H34, pp. 606-09.
H51, passim.
K284, passim.

During the 1910s Tchehonine made his reputation as a book designer and illustrator, often of publications concerned with the theater. For example, designs similar to No. 1019 [R893] can be found on the frontispiece of Alexander Izmailov's *Krivoe zerkalo* [Crooked Mirror] (SP: Shipovnik, 1912) and Nikolai Efros's *Teatr Letuchaia mysh* [The Bat Theater] (M: Svetozar, 1918). Tchehonine's decorative talent and his

Serge Tchehonine, Paris, 1930.

1020

proximity to theater celebrities, such as Nikolai Evreinov and Vladimir Nemirovich-Danchenko, encouraged him to explore the discipline of stage design. According to the dates on some of Tchehonine's designs, he started to project sets and costumes in 1918, but received his first official stage commission only in 1925, when he designed the production of Natalia Venkstern's play *In 1825* at the experimental Moscow Art Theater-2. However, Tchehonine seems to have made his real public debut as a stage designer only in 1928-29 in Paris when he joined forces with Vera Nemtchinova and Nikita Baliev to assist with their ballets and variety shows.[811] As a friend observed of Tchehonine's costumes and sets for these enterprises, they testified to "your change of location, to your museum visits, and simply to the aroma of Paris which has invested your creativity... with much that is new and diverse."[812]

Provenance for Tchehonine in Lobanov-Rostovsky collection: unless stated otherwise, Nos. 1019-65 [R893-938] were acquired from the artist's adopted stepson, Pierre Ino, Paris, September, 1968.

1019 [R893].
Design for Three Theatrical Masks, 1911.
Black ink.
Initialed and dated lower margin in Russian: "S.Ch. 1911."
3¾ x 4½ in., 9.2 x 11.5 cm.
Reproduced in F107, p. 6; H3, 1921, No. 1, p. 19; I40, No. 126; I51, No. 241.

Unidentified production: Nine miniature stage designs, *1918-20.*

1020 [R894].
Design with Curtain on Left Carrying a Suprematist Motif, ca. 1918.
Pencil and watercolor.
1½ x 2½ in., 3.9 x 6.4 cm.
Reproduced in color in M157, p. 109; and in black and white in I32, No. 102, I51, No. 242 (i); I77, p. 153.

1021 [R895].
Design Marked with Figure "4", ca. 1918.
Watercolor.
1½ x 2¾ in., 3.9 x 7 cm.
Reproduced in color in B151, p. 61; and in black and white in I32, No. 103; I51, No. 242 (ii); I77, p. 153.

1022 [R896].
Design with Suprematist Curtain, ca. 1918.
Pencil and watercolor.
1⅛ x 2¼ in., 3 x 5.6 cm.
Reproduced in color in I77, p. 87; M157, p. 109; and in black and white in I32, No. 104; I51, No. 242 (iii); I77, p. 153.

1023 [R897].
Design Marked with Figure "2", ca. 1918.
Watercolor.
1⅜ x 2⅜ in., 3.5 x 6 cm.
Reproduced in I32, No. 105; I51, No. 242 (iv); I77, p. 153.

1021

1022

1023

1024

1025

1026

1024 [R898].
Design with a Cone, **ca. 1918.**
Watercolor and pencil.
2¾ x 4⅜ in., 7 x 11 cm.
Reproduced in color in I77, p. 87; N160, p.
81; and in black and white in I32, No. 106;
I51, No. 242 (v); I77, p. 153.

1025 [R899].
Design Carrying Two Spherical Motifs in
Each Half, **ca. 1918.**
Watercolor and pencil.
1½ x 2½ in., 3.9 x 6.4 cm.
Reproduced in I32, No. 107; I51, No. 242
(vi); I77, p. 153.

1026 [R900].
Design with Tree, **1918.**
Watercolor and pencil.
Signed and dated lower right in Russian:
"S. Chekhonin 1918."
2⅜ x 3⅞ in., 5.9 x 9.8 cm.
Reproduced in I32, No. 108; I51, No. 242
(vii); I77, p. 153.

Serge Tchehonine: Poster for Christmas
Tree at an Antiquarian Book Shop. 12th
Exhibition of Antique Trinkets at the Popoff
Store, Paris, 1939.

1027

1029

1028

1030

1027 [R901].
Stage Design with White Rectangle, 1920.
Watercolor.
Initialed and dated in pencil lower margin in
Russian: "S.Ch. 1920."
5 x 6¾ in., 12.7 x 17.2 cm.
Reproduced in I32, No. 109; I51, No. 243;
I77, p. 153.

1028 [R902].
**Stage Design with a Human Figure, ca.
1920.**
Watercolor and pencil.
4¾ x 7 in., 12.1 x 17.8 cm.
Reproduced in I32, No. 110; I51, No. 244;
I77, p. 153.

Unidentified production, *1922.*

1029 [205; R903].
**Costume with Celestial Motifs for a Clown,
1922.**
Watercolor and ink.
Initialed and dated lower margin in Russian:
"S.Ch. 1922."
6⅞ x 4 in., 17.5 x 10 cm.
Reproduced in color in B115, plate 180;
F107, p. 196; and in black and white in I20,
No. 95; I77, p. 149.

1030 [R904].
Cover for the Book Teatr dlia detei **[The
Theater for Children], 1922.**
Black ink.
Signed and dated lower right hand column
in Russian: "Chekhonin 1922."
10¾ x 7¾ in., 27.3 x 19.7 cm.
Reproduced in F107, p. 156; I40, No. 127.

1031

1032

1033

1031 [R905].
***Illustration for the Book* Teatr dlia detei [The Theater for Children], ca. 1922.**
Black ink.
Signed at the base in Russian: "Sergei Chekhonin."
10¾ x 7¾ in., 27.3 x 19.7 cm.
Reproduced in I40, No. 125.

Note: The book *Teatr dlia detei,* written by Elizaveta Ivanovna Vasilieva (known more commonly by her pseudonym Cherubina de Gabriak, 1887-1928) and Samuil Yakovlevich Marshak (1887-1964), was published in 1922 by Raduga in Petrograd and Moscow. The collection of essays was based on the experiences of Marshak, Vasilieva, and others in the Theater of the Young Spectator in Petrograd in 1921-22. For some information see C31, Vol. 1, p. 289.

1032 [R906].
***Cover for the Book* Moskovskii Khudozhestvennyi teatr [Moscow Art Theater], 1924.**
Black ink and gouache.
Signed at the base in Russian: "Sergei Chekhonin."
13 x 10 in., 33 x 25.4 cm.
Reproduced in I40, No. 123.

Note: The book *Moskovskii Khudozhestvennyi teatr,* written by Nikolai Efimovich Efros (1867-1923), was published by the State Publishing-House, Moscow and Petrograd in 1924 to commemorate the 25th anniversary of the Moscow Art Theater (founded in 1898) — hence the silhouettes of its founders on the front cover: Konstantin Stanislavsky (pseudonym of Konstantin Sergeevich Alexeev, 1863-1938) on the left, and Vladimir Ivanovich Nemirovich-Danchenko (1858-1943) on the right. It is of interest to note that Tchehonine designed a number of books connected with the Moscow Art Theater, e.g., Nikolai Efros's *K.S. Stanislavsky* (P: State Printing House, 1918), and *"Tri sestry"; piesa A.P. Chekhova v postanovke Moskovskogo*

Khudozhestvennogo teatra (P: Svetozar, 1919).

1033 [R907].
***Cover for the Book* Moskovskii Malyi teatr [The Moscow Maly Theater], ca. 1924.**
Black ink.
Signed at the base in Russian: "Sergei Chekhonin."
13⅝ x 10⅝ in., 34.5 x 27 cm.
Reproduced in F107, p. 156; I20, p. 64.

Note: The book *Moskovskii Maly teatr* edited by Alexander Ivanovich Sumbatov (known under the pseudonym of Yuzhin, 1857-1927) was published by the State Publishing-House, Moscow in 1924 to commemorate the 100th anniversary of the Maly Theater.

In 1825: *play by Natalia Venkstern. Produced at MKhAT-2 (the Second Studio of the Moscow Art Theater) on 16 September, 1925, with designs by Serge Tchehonine.*
The plot concerns the insurrection perpetrated by the Decembrists, i.e., the group of noblemen led by Mikhail Bestuzhev-Riumin, Petr Kakhovsky, Sergei Muraviev-Apostol, Pavel Pestel, and Kondratii Ryleev, who in December, 1825 (hence the name Decembrists), forcibly interrupted the Imperial army's swearing of allegiance to the new tsar, Nicholas I. Nicholas would have none of the Decembrists' utopian demands for civil liberties and ordered his troops to take reprisals. The leaders and others were hanged or sent to Siberia.

1034 [R908].
Costume Design for a Lady, 1925.
Watercolor.
Signed and dated lower right in Russian: "S. Chekhonin 1925."
12⅝ x 7¼ in., 32 x 18.5 cm.
The reverse carries the inscription in Russian: "Koreneva – V.E. Kuindzhi, The Decembrists, Art Theater."
Reproduced in I40, No. 118.

Note: This production of *In 1825* was one of many experimental interpretations staged at the MKhAT Studios Nos. 1 and 2 (see Note to No. 741 [R625]). Although little is known about this production, it can be assumed from the annotations on No. 1034 [R908] that Lidiia Mikhailovna Koreneva (1885-1982) and/or Valentina Efimovna Kuindzhi (1899-1971) played the role of this lady (presumably, one of the Decembrists' wives). The BTM possesses a costume design for the same production (for the Decembrist poet Kondratii Ryleev), while the RM possesses many set and costume designs (see *Sergei Vasilievich Chekhonin,* pp. 48-50, 76, 77).

1034

1035

Unidentified production, *1925.*

1035 [R909].
Stage Design, with Man Standing, ca. 1925.
Pastel.
Signed lower right in Russian: "S. Chekhonin."
7¼ x 8½ in., 18.4 x 21.6 cm.
Reproduced in I32, No. 98.
Cf. No. 1036 [R910].

1036

1037

1036 [R910].
Costume Design for Male Figure, 1925.
Charcoal and red pencil.
Signed and dated lower center in Russian: "S. Chekhonin 1925."
12¼ x 7¾ in., 31.1 x 19.7 cm.
Reproduced in I32, No. 100.
The figure would seem to be a preliminary element for No. 1035 [R909].

1037 [R911].
Costume Design for a Man Wearing a Dark Cloak, 1925.
Charcoal.
Signed and dated lower right in Russian: "S. Chekhonin 1925."
13¼ x 9⅞ in., 33.5 x 25.1 cm.
Reproduced in I32, No. 99.

Note: It is not known for which production, if any, 1035-37 [R909-11] were designed. The set and costumes may have been for a production of William Shakespeare's *Hamlet,* but there is no record of a *Hamlet* presented in Leningrad or Moscow in 1925 with designs by Tchehonine.

Unidentified productions, *1925-29:* Nos. 1038-46 [R912-18].

1038

1038 [206; R912].
Costume Design for a Clown with Protruding Belly, 1926.
Watercolor and pencil.
Signed and dated lower right in Russian: "S. Chekhonin, 1926."
13⅛ x 11 in., 33.3 x 28 cm.
Reproduced in color in B115, plate 182; I68, front cover; I77, p. 93; M78; and in black and white in I20, No. 99; I32, No. 111; I51, No. 245; I77, p. 149; S29; S47; S60; S61; T1; T6; T11; T13; T20; T25; T28; T30; T33; T34; T37; T45; T46.

1039

1040

1041

1039 [NIRE].
Costume Design for a Female Dancer with a Guitar, Moscow, 1926.
Watercolor.
Signed lower right in Russian: "S. Chekhonin."
11⅜ x 8⅝ in., 29 x 22 cm.
Reproduced in I20, p. 51, No. 97.

1040 [NIRE].
Costume Design for a Female Dancer with Castanets, 1926.
Watercolor and pencil.
Signed lower left in Russian: "S. Chekhonin."
11¾ x 9½ in., 30 x 24 cm.
Reproduced in I20, p. 52, No. 98.

1041 [207; R913].
Costume Design for a Clown Wearing a High-Heeled Shoe, 1927.
Watercolor and ink.
Signed and dated lower left in Russian: "S. Chekhonin, 1927."
7⅛ x 3⅛ in., 18 x 8 cm.
Reproduced in I32, No. 93; I77, p. 149.

1042 [R914].
Costume in Cubist Style for a Female Dancer, 1928.
Watercolor and pencil.
Signed and dated lower left, along the skirt: "S. Tchehonine 1928."
6½ x 4⅜ in., 16.5 x 11 cm.
Reproduced in I20, p. 51, No. 96.

1043 [208; R915].
Costume Design for a Guitar Player, 1928.
Watercolor.
Signed along the leg on the right: "S. Tchehonine" and dated "1928" along the leg on the left.
6¾ x 4⅛ in., 17 x 10.5 cm.
Reproduced in color in B115, plate 181; I77, p. 154; and in black and white in I20, No. 101; I32, No. 112; I51, No. 246; Andreeva, "O polednikh godakh," p. 234.

1042

1043

1044

1045

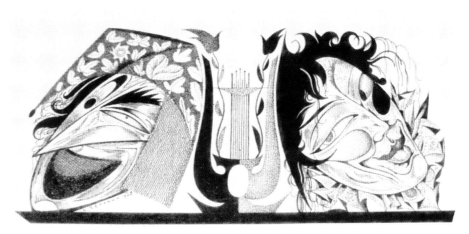

1046a

1047

1046

1044 [R916].
***Costume Design for a Dancer with a Big
Head, ca. 1928.***
Watercolor and pencil.
Initialed lower right in pencil in Russian: "S.Ch."
10¼ x 9 in., 26 x 23 cm.
Reproduced in I77, p. 154; M9.

1045 [R917].
Costume Design for a Devil (?), ca. 1928.
Pencil and wash.
Initialed lower right in pencil in Russian:
"S.Ch."
12⅝ x 6⅝ in., 32 x 16.8 cm.
Reproduced in I32, No. 101; I77, p. 154.

1046 [R918].
Costume Design for a Russian Doll, 1929.
Watercolor.
Signed and dated lower right: "Serge
Tchekhonine, Paris 1929."
15 x 9¼ in., 38 x 23.5 cm.
Reproduced in I20, No. 94; I77, p. 151.

1046a [R919].
***Graphic Illustration: Two Theatrical Masks,
1928.***
Black ink.
Signed and dated lower left in Russian: "S.

Chekhonin 1928."
5 x 7⅞ in., 12.8 x 20 cm.
Reproduced in I40, p. 6; M58; N11; N12, p.
114.

The Blind Street Musician: *theatrical
number with music by Nikita Baliev at the
Chauve-Souris Theater, New York, 1928-29
season, with designs by Serge Tchehonine.*

*A blind musician and his group of
fellow musicians entertain the passersby
on a Moscow street.*

1047 [R920].
Set Design with Four Musicians, 1929.
Gouache.
Signed and dated lower left: "Serge
Tchekhonine Paris 1929."
17¾ x 21½ in., 45 x 54.5 cm.
Reproduced in color in B115, plate 183; and
in black and white in I20, No. 92, where it is

1048

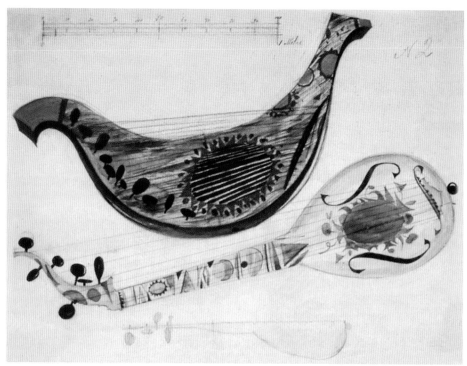

1049

1050

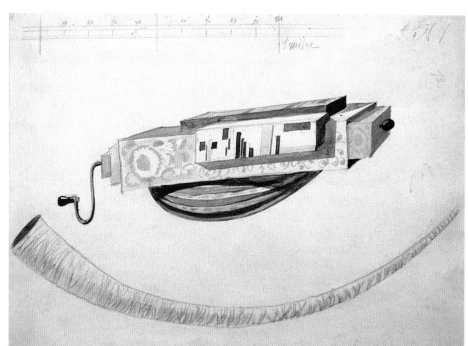

1051

described wrongly as a design for *Ruslan and Liudmila;* I51, No. 247; I77, p. 154; N84, p. 60. A photograph of the actual performance incorporating this backdrop is reproduced in *Morris Gest Presents Nikita Balieff. Théâtre de la Chauve-Souris,* New York, 1928, p. 10.

1048 [209; R921].
Costume Design for an Old Gusli Player, ca. 1929.
Watercolor and pencil.
Signed lower right: "S. Tchekhonine."
12⅝ x 9½ in., 32 x 24 cm.
Now in a private collection.

Reproduced in I40, No. 114.

1049 [R922].
Stage Detail for Gusli and Mandolin, ca. 1929.
Watercolor and pencil.
9⅞ x 12¾ in., 25 x 32.5 cm.
Now in a private collection.
Reproduced in I40, No. 116.

1050 [210; R923].
Costume Design for a Blind Barrel Organ Player, ca. 1929.
Watercolor.
Signed lower right: "S. Tchekhonine."
12¼ x 9½ in., 31 x 24 cm.
Reproduced in I14, No. 102; I77, p. 154.

1051 [R924].
Stage Detail for a Trumpet and a Barrel Organ, ca. 1929.
Watercolor.
9⅞ x 12¾ in., 25 x 32.5 cm.
Now in a private collection.
Reproduced in I40, No. 117.

1052

1053

1052 [R925].
Costume Design for a Trumpet Player, ca.
1929.
Watercolor and pencil.
Signed lower right "S. Tchekhonine."
12⅝ x 9½ in., 32 x 24 cm.
Now in a private collection.
Reproduced in I40, No. 115.

Ruslan and Liudmila: opera in five acts by
Mikhail Glinka after a poem by Alexander
Pushkin. Excerpts produced by Nikita
Baliev for the Théâtre de la Chauve-Souris,
Paris, 1929, with designs by Serge
Tchehonine.
    See No. 377 [R344] for plot summary.

1053 [R926].
Backdrop, ca. 1929.
Gouache.
Signed lower right: "S. Tchekhonine."
3¼ x 5⅝ in., 8.3 x 14.3 cm.
Now in a private collection.
Reproduced in *Krasnaia panorama,* L, 1929,
17 May, p. 12; I14, No. 113.

1054 [211; R927].
Costume Design for Ruslan, ca. 1929.
Watercolor.
Signed lower right: "S. Tchekhonine."
12¼ x 9 in., 31 x 23 cm.
Other inscription: on reverse on supporting
cardboard: "Ruslan, la Chauve-Souris, Serge
Tchekhonine, 31, Rue Greuze, Paris 16."
Provenance: Issar Gourvitch, Paris, June,
1966. Now in a private collection.
Reproduced in I14, No. 103.

1055 [212; R928].
Costume Design for a Male Dancer Wearing
a Turban, ca. 1929.
Watercolor and pencil.
Signed lower right in ink: "Serge
Tchekhonine, Paris."
13 x 10 in., 33 x 25.5 cm.
Reproduced in R44 p. 299; I77, p. 154; T6.

1056 [R929].
Costumes for Two Female Dancers, ca. 1929.
Watercolor and pencil.
Signed lower right: "Serge Tchekhonine,
Paris."
15⅜ x 11 in., 39 x 28 cm.
Reproduced in I40, No. 121.

1054

1055

1056

1057

1058

1059

Publicity Designs for Vera Nemtchinova's Ballets Russes at the Théâtre des Champs-Elysées, Paris, 1930.

1057 [R930].
Design for a Program Cover, ca. 1930.
Watercolor.
Signed lower left: "Serge Tchekhonine."
12⅝ x 9⅝ in., 32 x 24.5 cm.
Reproduced in color on the cover of the Souvenir Program of the ballet *Islamey* produced by Vera Nemtchinova's Ballets Russes, Paris, 1930; A34, p. 115; B115, plate 185; and in black and white in B34, p. 299; I51, No. 248; I77, pp. 104, 167; N91, p. 139; N128 (a); R1; T17. Tchehonine designed several versions of this program cover. For illustrations see J4, Lot 90; J8, Lot 29; J16, Lot 812.

1058 [R931].
Design for a Poster, ca. 1930.
Watercolor.
Signed lower right: "Serge Tchekhonine."
24½ x 16 in., 62 x 41 cm.
Reproduced in color in B115, plate 186; and in black and white in I40, No. 119; I77, p. 167.

1059 [R932].
Design for a Poster, ca. 1930.
Watercolor.
Signed lower right: "Serge Tchekhonine."
13¾ x 12⅝ in., 35 x 32 cm.
Reproduced in color in B115, plate 184; and in black and white in I77, p. 167.

Note: While reminiscent of Valentin Serov's famous poster depicting Anna Pavlova used during the first season of Sergei Diaghilev's Ballets Russes in 1909 (No. 118 [R97], 909 [R777]) and also of Konstantin Korovin's poster of Pavlova (see J23, Lot 44), Tchehonine's program and posters here contain artistic references — to Cubism, Suprematism, Art Deco — that distinguish them immediately from such prototypes. The inspiration for these pieces was the dancer Vera Nemtchinova (see No. 433 [R467]), some of whose productions

Tchehonine designed in 1930 (Nos. 1060-64 [R933-37]), including the ballet *Islamey* (No. 28 [R27]), after Milii Balakirev's music choreographed by Nicolas Zverev (see No. 432 [R466]) that premiered on 21 January, 1930, at the Théâtre des Champs-Elysées. Nemtchinova also commissioned Tchehonine to design evening gowns for her.

Snegurochka (The Snow Maiden): *ballet in one act by Alexander Glazunov after the play by Alexander Ostrovsky. Prepared for production, but not realized, by the Ballets Russes de Vera Nemtchinova in Paris, 1930, with choreography by Bronislava Nijinska and designs by Serge Tchehonine. See No. 33 [R32] for plot summary.*

1060 [R933].
Backcloth for Tsar Berendei's City, ca. 1930.
Watercolor.
Signed lower right: "Serge Tchekhonine."
10⅝ x 14⅝ in., 27 x 37 cm.
Reproduced in color in N188, p. 56; and in black and white in I20, No. 91; I51, No. 249.

1061 [R934].
Costume Design for the Snow Maiden, 1931.
Gouache.
Signed and dated lower right: "Serge Tchekhonine Paris 1931."
12¼ x 10 in., 31 x 25.5 cm.
Now in a private collection.

1060

1061

1062

1063

1062 [R935].
Costume Design for One of the Snow Maiden's Friends, ca. 1930.
Watercolor.
Signed lower left: "Paris, Serge Tchekhonine."
13 x 10 in., 33 x 25.5 cm.
Now in a private collection.
A version is reproduced in I44, p. 60.

Unidentified production, *1930.*

1063 [213; R936].
Costume Designs for a Male and Female Dancer, 1930.
Watercolor and pencil.
Signed and dated lower right: "Serge Tchekhonine Paris 1930."
12⅝ x 10¼ in., 32 x 26 cm.
Other inscription: on reverse "Ballets Nemtchinova."
Reproduced in color in B115, plate 187; and in black and white in I20, No. 100; I68, p. 16; I77, p. 154; M63.

Unidentified production, *ca. 1930.*

1064 [R937].
Group of Four Dancers, ca. 1930.
Pencil and sanguine.
Signed lower left: "Serge Tchekhonine Paris."
15 x 11⅝ in., 38 x 29.5 cm.
Reproduced in I40, No. 120, where it is described as a design for three Polovtsian dancers carrying a female slave dancer.

1065 [R938].
Poster Advertising the "Tenth Exhibition at the Store of Alexandre Popoff", Paris, 1937.
Engraving in black on white.
Signed in the stone lower left: "Serge Tchekhonine."
20 x 25⅝ in., 51 x 65 cm.
Other inscriptions: as part of the general design, the text in Tchehonine's hand, reads: "10-me exposition des petits cadeaux anciens pour Noël et le Nouvel An

1064

chez Alexandre Popoff, 48, Rue Cambon, Paris, 1937."
Reproduced in M73, p. 95.

Note: Alexandre Alexandrovich Popoff (1880-1964) owned an antique store in Paris in the 1920s and 1930s that specialized in Russian porcelain and furniture. For some information see L193 and L194.

811   C31, Vol.2, p. 393.
812   Letter from A. Brodsky to Tchehonine dated 10 April, 1929. Quoted in Andreeva, "O poslednikh godakh tvorchestva S. Chekhonina," p. 238.

1065

TCHELITCHEW
(Chelishchev, Tchelicheff, Tchelitcheff, Tschelitchew), Pavel Fedorovich

Born 21 September (3 October), 1898, Kaluga, Russia; died 31 July, 1957, Frascatti, near Rome, Italy.

1916-18 attended art courses at Moscow University; 1918-20 attended the Kiev Art Institute; also took lessons from Alexandra Exter and Adolf Milman in Kiev, establishing contact with other young artists there such as Nisson Shifrin and Alexander Tyshler; influenced by Cubism and Constructivism; 1919 designed agit-decorations for Kiev; designed an unrealized production of Sidney Jones and Ivan Caryll's *The Geisha* at Konstantin Mardzhanishvili's (Mardzhanov's) Theater in Kiev; joined the Volunteer Army; 1920 left Sevastopol for Istanbul; 1920-21 designed several ballet productions for Boris Kniaseff and six ballet productions for Viktor Zimin's Ballet Company in Istanbul; 1921 left for Sofia, where he designed the book *Iskhod k Vostoku. Predchuvstviia i sversheniia. Utverzhdenie evraziitsev* [Exodus to the East: Forebodings and Events: an Affirmation by the Eurasians]; arrived in Berlin in the fall; 1921-23 worked in Berlin, designing plays and variety shows for the Blaue Vogel Theater (such as *Der König rief seinen Tambour* and *Die drei Trommler*), the Russisches Romantisches Theater and the Königgrätzerstrasse Theater (such as *Savonarola*); 1923 onward settled in Paris; cultivated a deep interest in astrology and the occult; read widely, especially Dante; began to paint in a Surrealist manner; worked as a designer for Sergei Diaghilev (e.g., for *Ode* in 1928) and then George Balanchine (e.g., *Orfeo* in 1936); close to Gertrude Stein, Dame Edith Sitwell, and other celebrities; 1936-38 painted *Phenomena;* 1940-42 painted *Hide and Seek;* 1940s-50s continued to paint his anatomical Surrealism and to illustrate books such as Parker Tyler's poem, *Yesterday's Children* (1944); 1952 became US citizen, but later moved to Italy.

Bibliography
J. Soby: *Tchelitchew. Paintings. Drawings.* Catalog of exhibition at the Museum of Modern Art, New York, 1942.
P. Tyler: *The Divine Comedy of Pavel Tchelitchew,* London: Weidenfeld and Nicolson, 1967.
M2, Vol. 2, pp. 200-201, listing his theatrical productions.
M7.
R. Nathanson: *Pavel Tchelitchew. A Selection of Gouaches, Drawings and Paintings.* Catalog of exhibition organized by Richard Nathanson at The Alpine Club, London, 1974.
R. Nathanson: *Pavel Tchelitchew (1898-1957). A Collection of Fifty-Four Theatre Designs c. 1919-1923.* Catalog of exhibition organized by Richard Nathanson at The Alpine Club, London, 1976.
P. Cummings et al.: *Pavel Tchelitchew. Nature Transformed.* Catalog of exhibition at the Michael Rosenfeld Gallery, New York, 1993.
M. Rosenfeld at al.: *Perceivable Realities. Louis Michel Eilshemius, Morris Graves, Henry Ossawa Tanner, Pavel Tchelitchew.* Catalog of exhibition at the Michael Rosenfeld Gallery, New York, 1994.
L. Kirstein: *Tchelitchev,* Santa Fe: Twelvetree Press, 1994.
M. Duncan and B. Bloemink: *Pavel Tchelitchew. The Landscape of the Body.* Catalog of exhibition at the Katonah Museum of Art, Katonah, NY, 1998.
M73, Vol. 26, pp. 85-87.
V. Kaskin-Youritzin: *Tchelitchew.* Catalog of exhibition at the Fred James Jr. Museum of Art, University of Oklahoma, Norman, 2002.
A. Shumov: *Le Paradis de Pavel Tchelitchew,* M: Elinin, 2005.
Yu. Girba: *Pavel Tchelitchew, 1898-1957* at Our Artists Gallery, Moscow, 2006-07.
Yu. Girba: *Tchelitchew.* Catalogue of exhibition at Our Artists Gallery, Moscow, 2011.
E. Sadykova: "Rannee tvorchestvo Pavla Chelishcheva" in *Russkoe iskusstvo,* M, 2012, No. 1, pp. 74-79.
A. Kuznetsov: *Pavel Tchelitchew Metamorphoses,* Stuttgart: Arnoldsche Art Publishers, 2012.

The intimate Russian theater enjoyed one of its most exciting moments in the early 1920s in Berlin, as one after the other émigré cabarets began to open up — Carousel, Vanka-Vstanka, Jascha Juschny's Blaue Vogel, and Boris Romanov's Romantisches Theater.[813] The Blaue Vogel, in particular, situated on Goltzstrasse in the center of the Russian colony, was a popular rendezvous:

> Müde von Politik und Alltag suchte der Russe beim Besuch seines Cabarets eine vollkommene Loslösung von der Wirklichkeit des Lebens, suchte ein heiteres Suchvergessen in Musik, Farbe und Spiel.[814]

Between 1920 and the 1930s, the Blaue Vogel presented numerous sketches and reviews, often designed by talented young artists, including Tchelitchew. True, within the Berlin Russian emigration of the early 1920s, Tchelitchew's experimental conception was the exception rather than the rule, but whatever their artistic standard, the Berlin cabarets did serve as a cultural and social meeting-place for thousands of homeless and homesick Russians. The cabarets also attracted Germans, but as one Russian reviewer wrote, "they merely guffaw at those moments when we feel like crying."[815]

In the six productions that he designed for the Blaue Vogel, Tchelitchew regarded the sets and costumes as practical extensions of the lessons he had learned from Exter in Kiev. Often constructed according to a spiralic or circular scheme and depending on emphatic, exotic color contrasts, his designs generate an extraordinary sense of movement. Tchelitchew removed the simple horizontal, the plane, and the right angle from his compositions and compelled his immobile forms to become mobile, to interact with the real space of the stage so that "every object has the spherical dimension of life."[816] At the same time Tchelitchew adapted the geometric severity of Constructivism efficiently and elegantly — as he demonstrated in his cover and ornaments for the Eurasian miscellany *Iskhod k vostoku. Predchuvstviia i sversheniia. Utverzhdenie evraziitsev* (Sofia, 1921) and his cover for the literary almanac *Na putiakh* [On the Roads] (Berlin,1922).

During the 1920s and 1930s Tcheltchew gained a strong reputation for his bold and original theater designs, often incorporating innovative materials and dramatic lighting. Among his masterpieces are designs for *Ode* (see below), *Wanderer* (music by Franz Schubert, Théâtre des Champs-Elysées, Paris, 1933), *Noblissima Visione* (music by Paul Hindemith, directed by Leonide Massine, London, 1938), and the play *Ondine* (by Jean Giraudoux, Paris, 1939).

1066

1066 [R866].
Self-Portrait, ca. 1923.
Pencil.
15¾ x 12¼ in., 40 x 31 cm.
Provenance: Solomon Shuster, Leningrad, November, 1984.
Reproduced in color in F107, p. 155; M157, p. 118.

The Geisha: *operetta by Sidney Jones adapted by Ivan Caryll. Projected, but not produced by Konstantin Mardzhanov in Kiev in 1919 with designs by Pavel Tchelitchew.*

An English naval officer falls in love with a geisha — O Mimosa San — at a teahouse. The lovers are parted after their brief encounter, although not tragically. The Englishman weds a comely English girl and O Mimosa San marries an Oriental.

1067

1069

1067 [214; R867].
Costume Design for the Geisha, ca. 1919.
Watercolor and ink.
Signed on the reverse in Russian: "P.
Chelishchev."
12¾ x 8½ in., 32.5 x 21.5 cm.
Provenance: the artist's sister, Alexandra
Zaoussailoff, Paris, June, 1972.
Reproduced in color in B115, plate 183; and
in black and white in I32, No. 113; I77, p.
146.

Note: Sidney Jones's operetta enjoyed a
certain popularity in Russia and the Ukraine
just after the Revolution. For example,
Nikolai Popov directed a production at the
Moscow Theater of Comic Opera in 1920
and there was a production at the Nikitsky

Theater, Moscow, the following year. No
doubt, Tchelitchew's resolution would have
been the most audacious rendering, i.e.,
scenografically, were it to have been
implemented. According to Donald
Windham, these *Geisha* designs were
simple, involving no complexities of light
and color, but illustrated the idea he had
then temporarily embraced, that in a
spherical world all things are essentially
spherical and no straight line exists.[817]

Unidentified productions *for Viktor Zimin's
Ballet Company at the Strelna Theater,
Istanbul, in 1920-21 with choreography by
Boris Kniaseff and designs by Pavel
Tchelitchew.*

1068 [NIRE].
*Costume Designs for Two Russian Peasant
Women, ca. 1920.*
Watercolor
9¼ x 25⅜ in., 23.5 x 64.5 cm.
Provenance: Niki Yakovlev (via Boris Kniaseff),
Athens, 1966. Now in a private collection.
Reproduced in I20, No. 102.

1069 [R868].
Design for an Oriental City Street, ca. 1920.
Watercolor.
The reverse carries the atelier stamp: "P.
Tchelicheff."
10⅜ x 13⅛ in., 26.5 x 33.3 cm.
Provenance: Richard Nathanson, London,
December, 1976.
Reproduced in color in *Pavel Tchelitchew
(1898-1957)*, p. 13; I40, No. 139; I51, No. 256;
I77, p. 159; N188, p. 54. Cf. No. 1070 [R869].

1068

1070

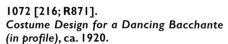

1071

1070 [R869].
Design for an Oriental City Street, ca. 1920.
Charcoal and pencil.
8¼ x 13¼ in., 21 x 33.5 cm.
Atelier stamp on reverse: "P. Tchelicheff."
Provenance: Richard Nathanson, London, December, 1976.
Reproduced in *Pavel Tchelitchew (1898-1957)*, p. 12; I40, No. 140.
This is a preliminary design for No. 1069 [R868].

1071 [215; R870].
Costume Design for a Male Dancer in the Ballet Sketch "Caprice", 1920.
Watercolor and collage.
Signed lower left in Russian: "P. Chelishchev"; and in lower right corner "P.Ch."
12⅝ x 8½ in., 32 x 21.5 cm.

Other inscriptions: lower left in Russian: "Ballet Caprice by Viktor Zimin"; on reverse in French: "Dessin de Pavel Tchelischev, Konstantinopol 1920. Zimin, Danseur Russe."
Provenance: Niki Yakovlev (via Boris Kniaseff), Athens, July, 1966.
Reproduced in color in B115, plate 85; and in black and white in I14, No. 105; I32, No. 115; I77, p. 159.

1072 [216; R871].
Costume Design for a Dancing Bacchante (in profile), ca. 1920.
Watercolor and pencil.
Signed lower right in Russian: "P. Chelishchev."
12⅝ x 8⅝ in., 32 x 22 cm.
The reverse carries a sketch of the frontal

view for the same costume (see No. 1073 [R871a]).
Provenance: Niki Yakovlev (via Boris Kniaseff), Athens, July, 1966.
Reproduced in color in B115, plate 86; I77, p. 88; and in black and white in I14, No. 108; I32, No. 118; I54, No. 255; I77, p. 159; N112, p. 55. A curious version is reproduced in I100, No. 33.

1073 [R871a].
Costume Design for a Dancing Bacchante (front view), ca. 1920.
Watercolor and pencil.
12⅝ x 8⅝ in., 32 x 22 cm.
Inscriptions: stamped lower right: "Corsi superiori [di danza classica] Boris Kniazeff"

1072

1073

1074

1075

1076

1077

and the words in pencil in Russian: "Property of V.P. Zimin. Bacchanalia"; also instructions in Russian to the dressmaker: "red 3 meters, orange 2 meters, half meter black."
This is the verso of No. 1072 [R871].

1074 [R872].
Costume Design for a Male Dancer with a Scarf in Left Hand, 1920.
Watercolor.
13½ x 9½ in., 34.4 x 24 cm.
Inscriptions on reverse: "Etude d'un costume de mes ballets par P. Tchelicheff, 1920, Konstantinopol, Boris Kniazeff," plus a stamp: "Boris Kniazeff, Corsi Superiori di Danza Classica."
Provenance: Niki Yakovlev (via Boris Kniaseff), Athens, July, 1966.
Reproduced in color in B115, plate 84 (where it is described as a costume for a warrior); and in black and white in I14, No. 104, I32, No. 114; I51, No. 252; I61, p. 414; I77, p. 159.

1075 [217; R873].
Costume Design for a Male Dancer with Leopard Motif on Trousers, ca. 1920.
Gouache.
10⅝ x 8⅛ in., 27 x 20.5 cm.
Stamped on reverse: "Boris Kniazeff, Corsi Superiori di Danza Classica."
Provenance: Niki Yakovlev (via Boris Kniaseff), Athens, July, 1966.
Reproduced in color in B115, plate 91; F107, p. 426; as the cover to I14; I68, p. 10; I77, p. 88; N140; B329, Vol. 3; and in black and white in I32, No. 120; I77, p. 159; N128 (b); O14.

1076 [218; R874].
Costume Design for a Male Turkish Dancer Wearing a Turban, 1920.
Watercolor.
Signed on the reverse in Russian: "P. Chelishchev."
13 x 9 in., 33 x 23 cm.
Other inscriptions: on reverse: "Etude d'un costume de mes ballets par Tchelischev, 1920, Konstantinopol, Boris Kniazeff"; also instructions to the dressmaker.
Provenance: Niki Yakovlev (via Boris Kniaseff), Athens, July, 1966.
Reproduced in color in B155, ill. 67; I68, p. 10; and in black and white in I14, No. 106; I32; No. 116; I51, No. 250; I77, p. 159; M74; N122; N128 (b); S33; U1. A variant of this costume, dated 1919, and entitled *Turkish Dancer*, is reproduced in J5, Lot 168.

1078

1077 [219; R875].
Costume Design for a Female Dancer Wearing a Bead Necklace, 1920.
Watercolor.
Signed lower right in Russian "P. Chelishchev."
12⅝ x 8⅛ in., 32 x 20.5 cm.
Other inscriptions: on reverse: "Etude d'un costume de mes ballets par P. Tchelischev, 1920, Konstantinopol, Boris Kniazeff"; and stamped "Corsi Superiori di Danza Classica."
Provenance: Niki Yakovlev (via Boris Kniaseff), Athens, July, 1966.
Reproduced in color in B115, plate 88; F107, p. 156; G70; on the back cover of I51; I68, p. 11; M78; N156, p. 78; N13, p. 125; and in black and white in I14 No. 107; I32, No. 117; I51, No. 251; I61, p. 415; I77, p. 159; M111; N17; P16; P49; P53; P54; and program for *36. Berliner Festwochen 86. Magazin*, W. Berlin, 1986, p. 37.

1078 [R876].
Costume Design for a Man with a Whip, ca. 1920.
Watercolor.
Signed with the atelier stamp on the reverse: "P. Tchelitcheff."
10 x 7⅜ in., 25.5 x 18.8 cm.
Provenance: Richard Nathanson, London, December, 1976.
Reproduced in color in B115, plate 90; and in black and white in I40, No. 138; I51, No. 257; I77, p. 159; and *Pavel Tchelitchew (1898-1957)*, p. 10.

1079

1081

1083

1079 [220; R877].
Costume Design for a Female Dancer with a Tambourine, ca. 1920.
Watercolor.
Signed with the atelier stamp on the reverse: "P. Tchelicheff."
11 x 9½ in., 28 x 24 cm.
Provenance: Richard Nathanson, London, December, 1976.
Reproduced in color in B115, plate 94; and in black and white in I40, No. 136; I51, No. 258; I77, p. 159; and *Pavel Tchelitchew (1898-1957)*, p. 8.

1080 [221; R878].
Costume Design for a Female Dancer with Chains, ca. 1920.
Watercolor.
10 x 7⅜ in., 25.5 x 18.8 cm.
Signed with the atelier stamp on the reverse: "P. Tchelicheff."
Provenance: Richard Nathanson, London, December, 1976.

Reproduced in color in B115, plate 89; I77, p. 88; and in black and white in I40, No. 137; I77, p. 160; and *Pavel Tchelitchew (1898-1957)*, p. 10.

1081 [222; R879].
Costume Design for a Fishmonger, ca. 1920.
Watercolor.
Signed with the atelier stamp on the reverse: "P. Tchelicheff."
11¾ x 8¾ in., 30 x 22.3 cm.
Provenance: Richard Nathanson, London, December, 1976.
Reproduced in color in B115, plate 92; I77, p. 88; and G. Kovalenko, *Alexandra Exter*, M: Galart, 1993, p. 219; and in black and white in A34, p. 428; I40, No. 135; I77, p. 160; *Pavel Tchelitchew (1898-1957)*, p. 9.

1082 [R880].
Costume Design for a Rabbi, ca. 1920.
Watercolor.
Signed on the reverse in ink: "P. Tchelicheff."
11¾ x 9 in., 30 x 23 cm.
Provenance: the artist's sister, Alexandra Zaoussailoff, Paris, June, 1972.
Reproduced in color in B115, plate 93; and in black and white in H32, p. 414; I32, No. 119; I61, p. 414; I77, p. 160.

1083 [R881].
Costume Design for a Fat Turk, ca. 1920.
Watercolor.
Signed on the reverse: "P. Tchelicheff."
12¾ x 8½ in., 32.5 x 21.5 cm.
Provenance: the artist's sister, Alexandra Zaoussailoff, Paris, June, 1972.
Reproduced in color in B115, plate 95; and in black and white in I32, No. 121; I61, p. 414; I77, p. 160; R15.

Note: Nos. 1068-83 [R868-81] are designs that Tchelitchew executed for Viktor Zimin's Ballet Company in Istanbul during 1920-21. Viktor Petrovich Zimin (18??-1964) had been a pupil of Mikhail Mordkin in Kiev, who, after a brief interlude in Istanbul, settled in Paris. Zimin's chief choreographer at this time was Boris Kniaseff (Boris Alexeevich Kniazev 1905-75), who had been a pupil of the experimental balletmaster Kasian Goleizovsky in Moscow. With Tchelitchew, Kniaseff departed for Sofia in 1921 and then to Paris in 1924, where he quickly made his name as a ballet teacher.

1080

1082

1084

1085

Danse Espagnole: *concert number produced by Jascha Juschny at the Blaue Vogel cabaret, Berlin, in December, 1921, with designs by Pavel Tchelitchew.*

1084 [223; NIRE].
Costume Design for a Spanish Dancer, 1921.
Watercolor.
Signed on reverse in Russian: "P. Chelishchev."
15 x 8⅝ in., 38 x 22 cm.
Provenance: auction, Berlin: Bassenge Auction House, 1 December, 2007, Lot 7169 (Catalog No. 90; reproduced).
Reproduced in color in the program for *Théâtre Russe, L'Oiseau Bleu,* Berlin, 1921;

p. 30; in the program for *Der Blaue Vogel,* (Berlin: Season 1921-22); in *Das Theater Kunstblatt,* Berlin, 1921, p. 10; and in F107, p. 280.

1085 [224; NIRE].
Costume Design for a Spanish Guitar Player, 1921.
Watercolor.
15 x 8⅝ in., 38 x 22 cm.
Inscriptions on reverse: stamp: "Blaue Vogel Berlin" and label in Russian: "No. 44/58 (in red ink), name: Spaniard with a guitar, Artist: Chelishchev, Series: sketch."
Provenance: auction, Berlin: Bassenge Auction House, 1 December, 2007, Lot 7170 (Catalog No. 90; reproduced).
Reproduced in black and white in the program for *Théâtre Russe, L'Oiseau Bleu,* Berlin, 1921, p. 43; in the program for *Der Blaue Vogel* (Berlin: Season 1921-22), p. 9; in *Das Theater Kunstblatt,* Berlin, 1921, p. 10; and in F107, p. 280.

Die Pagode: *film produced by Olga Tschechowa for Olga Tschechowa-Film GmbH, Berlin, with designs by Pavel Tchelitchew. Released in 22 May, 1922.*

Information on the plot of Die Pagode *has not been forthcoming, although it is known that the actors included Olga Tschechowa (Knipper), Ernst Deutsch, Wilhelm Dieterle, and Paul Bildt.*

1086 [R882].
Costume Design for an Oriental Warrior, 1921.
Gouache and collage.
Signed and dated lower right: "Pavel Tchelitcheff 1921 Berlin."
18⅞ x 12 in., 48 x 30.5 cm.
Other inscription: lower right: "Film Die Pagode."
Provenance: *Ballet, Opéra, Théâtre, Music-Hall. Projets de Costumes et de Décors,* Monte Carlo: Sotheby, Parke Bernet, 26 June, 1976, Lot 778 (reproduced).
Reproduced in I40, No. 129; I77, p. 148; M112. A documentary photograph reproduced in Tyler, *Divine Comedy,* between pp. 90 and 91, includes an actor wearing a costume similar to this one.

Savonarola: *tragedy in ten scenes after Joseph-Arthur de Gobineau's play* La Renaissance *adapted by Petr Suvchinsky. Produced at the Königgrätzers Strasse Theater, Berlin in December, 1922, by Carl Meinhard and Rudolf Bernauer with music by Vladimir Biutsov and designs by Pavel Tchelitchew.*

The play concerns the life of the Italian reformer and martyr Girolamo Savonarola (1452-98), who devoted his life to a fanatical struggle against the corruption and duplicity of the Italian church. Commanding popular respect and espousing provocative ideas about the need to turn the City of Florence into a City of God, he elicited the jealousy and displeasure of Pope Alexander VI. Ultimately, Savonarola was put on trial for his opposition to the church and was burned at the stake as a common criminal.

1087 [225; NIRE].
Costume Design for Girlolamo Savonarola, Berlin, 1921.
Mixed media on cardboard.
Signed and dated lower right: "P. Tschelitcheff. 1921."
16 x 14⅛ in., 40.7 x 36.2 cm.
Other inscriptions: "'Savonarola' Berlin" (under signature), illegible (upper left), numbered "24" upper center.
Provenance: *Russian Art,* New York: Sotheby's, 28 April, 2006, Lot 522 (reproduced).
Reproduced in F107, p. 469.

1086

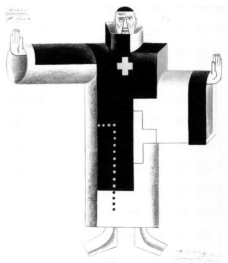

1087

1088

1088 [R883].
Costume Design for the Milanese Messenger, 1921.
Gouache and gold paint.
Signed and dated lower right: "Paul Tschelitcheff 1921, Berlin."
20⅛ x 13¾ in, 51 x 35 cm.
Other inscription: lower right "Savonarola"; "Milano" as part of the design on the front of the costume.
Provenance: *Ballet, Opéra, Théâtre, Music-Hall. Projets de Costumes et de Décors*, Monte Carlo: Sotheby, Parke Bernet, 26 June, 1976, Lot 791 (ii) (reproduced).
Reproduced in I40, No. 131; I51, No. 259; I77, p. 160.

1089

1089 [226; R884].
Costume Design for a Gentleman at Court and His Moorish Boy Servant, ca. 1921.
Gouache and collage.
Signed lower right: "Berlin. P. Tschelitcheff."
14 x 17⅜ in., 35.5 x 44 cm.
Other inscriptions: lower right "Savonarola"; upper right "Begleiter"; top left "Mohrenkind."
Provenance: *Ballet, Opéra, Théâtre, Music-Hall. Projets de Costumes et de Décors*, Monte Carlo: Sotheby, Parke Bernet, 26 June, 1976, Lot 780 (reproduced).

Reproduced in color in B115, plate 98; I61, p. 413; in black and white in I40, No. 132; I51, No. 260; I77, p. 160.

1090 [R885].
Costume Design for Bourdillon, a Knight in Armor, 1921.
Gouache and collage on cardboard.
Signed and dated lower right: "*Savonarola* P. Tschelicheff 1922 Berlin."
19⅞ x 14⅜ in., 50.5 x 36.5 cm.
Other inscription: "Bourdillon Alten."
Provenance: *Ballet, Opéra, Théâtre, Music-Hall. Projets de Costumes et de Décors*, Monte Carlo: Sotheby, Parke Bernet, 26 June, 1976, Lot 784 (reproduced).
Reproduced in color in B115, plate 96 (where it is described as a costume for Cornazano); and in black and white in I40, No. 134; I77, p. 160.

1091 [227; R886].
Costume Design for Cornazano, a Knight, 1921.
Gouache and collage.
Signed and dated upper left and lower right: "*Savonarola* Pavel Tchelicheff Berlin 1921."
20⅛ x 14⅜ in., 51 x 36.5 cm.
Provenance: *Ballet, Opéra, Théâtre, Music-Hall. Projets de Costumes et de Décors*, Monte Carlo: Sotheby, Parke Bernet, 26 June, 1976, Lot 783 (reproduced).
Reproduced in color in B115, plate 97 (where it is described as a costume for Bourdillon); I40, No. 130; I77, p. 160.

1090

1091

1092

1092 [R887].
***Costume Design for a Lady*, ca. 1921.**
Gouache.
Signed lower right: "Savonarola P. Tschelitcheff Berlin."
20⅛ x 14⅜ in., 51 x 36. 5 cm.
Provenance: *Ballet, Opéra, Théâtre, Music-Hall. Projets de Costumes et de Décors,* Monte Carlo: Sotheby, Parke Bernet, 26 June, 1976, Lot 791 (i) (reproduced).
Reproduced in I40, No. 133; I77, p. 160.

Note: According to Donald Windham, Tchelitchew's resolution for this production of *Savonarola* stipulated that

> the sets be constructed on a revolving stage with some of the actors built into the décor and unable to move of their own accord. He endeavored to create a maximum of character in a maximum of geometry... The costumes, however heavy they appeared, were constructed of the lightest materials mounted on frames of horsehair and whalebone, but still their very size hampered the movements of the actors, who gesticulated only with difficulty.[818]

Tchelitchew's costumes did not function very well, however impressive they might have been as extensions of the Cubist ideas that he had assimilated from Exter. One reviewer even spoke of

> a tendency toward an excessive exaggeration of dimensions, a capricious fancy of detail... What has all this to do with de Gobineau's play and the Italian Renaissance?[819]

Le Coq d'Or: *opera-ballet in three acts with music by Nikolai Rimsky-Korsakov and libretto by Vladimir Belsky, based on a fairy-tale by Alexander Pushkin and adapted by Alexandre Benois. Produced at the Staatsoper, Berlin on 18 June, 1923, with designs by Pavel Tchelitchew.*
See No. 299 [R268] for plot summary.

1093

1093 [228; R888].
***Costume Design for Three Turks*, ca. 1923.**
Watercolor, gold and silver paint, and pencil.
Signed on reverse: "P. Tchelitcheff."
12¾ x 9⅞ in., 32.5 x 25 cm.
Provenance: the artist's sister, Alexandra Zaoussailoff, Paris, June, 1972.
Reproduced in I40, No. 127.

1094 [NIRE].
***Costume Design for General Polkan*, ca. 1923.**
Watercolor and pencil.
12¾ x 9⅞ in., 32.5 x 25 cm.
Provenance: the artist's sister, Alexandra Zaoussailoff, Paris, June, 1972. Now in a private collection.

1094

Ode: *ballet in two acts with a choir, two solo voices and a symphony orchestra with music by Nicolas Nabokov and a libretto based on a poem by Mikhail Lomonosov. Produced by Sergei Diaghilev at the Théâtre Sarah-Bernhardt, Paris on 6 June, 1928, with choreography by Leonide Massine and designs by Pavel Tchelitchew.*
Nature descends from her pedestal and answers questions of her pupil. She shows him the diverse phenomena of heaven and earth, but the pupil is not satisfied and asks Nature to show him the Aurora Borealis. Nature complies, but the pupil is so captured by its beauty that he rushes forth into the Aurora, thus destroying the vision. Nature then becomes a statue again.

1095

1095 [R890].
***Portrait of Serge Lifar*, ca. 1928.**
Ink.
Stamped on the reverse with the atelier signature: "P. Tchelitchew."
21⅝ x 17⅜ in., 55 x 44 cm.
Provenance: the artist's sister, Alexandra Zaoussailoff, Paris, June, 1972. Now in a private collection.
Reproduced in F107, p. 245; M43 (c).
The work is probably a study for the watercolor portrait of Lifar in the collection of the Wadsworth Atheneum, reproduced, for example, in I11, p. 2. For another similar portrait in a private collection see K284, p. 176.

1096

1097

1098

1096 [229; NIRE].
Portrait of Serge Lifar, ca. 1928.
Watercolor.
11¾ x 8¼ in., 30 x 21 cm.
Inscribed lower left in Russian: "To Sergei, as a keepsake from Pavel."
Provenance: A. Gorbat (Gorbatov), New York.
Reproduced in F107, p. 156, and in *Serge Diaghilev: The Centenary Exhibition of Les Ballets Russes 1909-2009.* Catalog of exhibition of Julian Barran at the Daniel Katz Gallery, London, 209, p.16.
Serge Lifar (Sergei Mikhailovoich Lifar; 1905-86) is depicted in the costume for his role as Mikhail Lomonosov in *Ode*.

1097 [R889].
Design for a Group of Figures, ca. 1928.
India ink and wash.
16¾ x 14 in., 42.5 x 35.5 cm.
Provenance: *Dance, Theatre, Opera, Music Hall and Film,* New York: Sotheby, Parke Bernet, 21 November, 1984, Lot 101 (reproduced).
Reproduced in B88, p. 44; I77, pp. 113, 135; B88, p. 44.
The reverse carries three studies of a girl's head.

Note: It is assumed that this drawing is a preliminary item for one of the designs for *Ode* since Tchelitchew's cover design for the souvenir program (reproduced in Tyler, *The Divine Comedy,* between pp. 282-83) also incorporates a double figure holding a hoop. The Wadsworth Atheneum owns a fuller design for the project (reproduced in I11, p. 82) which, unexpectedly, is reminiscent of No. 1097 [R889].

The hoop motif has several derivations, not least from occult and alchemical sources such as the Hermetic Cosmos and the Hermetic Scheme of the Universe (for illustrations see Tyler, op. cit., between pp. 186-87), and such elements must have seemed rather surprising to the "unmystical"

Diaghilev. In any case, Tchelitchew's request for movie cameras, neon lights representing a "galaxy of celestial manifestations,"[820] and a spotlight beamed at the audience was rejected by Diaghilev, although he seems not to have been too perturbed by the "unadorned white all-over tights" that the dancers wore. Boris Kochno reported the dress rehearsal as "indescribable chaos"[821] and Nicolas Nabokov remembers that Tchelitchew managed to keep up the spirits of the stage technicians only by wine and flattery.[822] The premiere was, however, a success, thanks in no small degree to the tolerance and comprehension of the principal dancers: Alexandra Danilova, Felia Dubrovska, Lifar, Alicia Markova, Massine, and Alicia Nikitina. Danilova has left the following description of *Ode*:

> It was an odd ballet. It opened with a movie — nobody dancing, just a movie of a flower. There was a rope draped across the back of the stage — I think that was meant to be the Milky Way with all the stars. One end of the rope was loose, and Lifar danced a variation holding on to it, never letting go. For the set Tchelitchev continued the perspective to its vanishing point: there was a line of corps girls moving up the stage, and then a row of dolls that got smaller and smaller, so it looked as if the stage were very deep and full of people, much like they did it at the Mariinsky, when we children were positioned at the back of the stage to look like adults from afar. Tchelitchev's costumes were white leotards and tights — it was the first time we didn't wear anything on top of our leotards. Doubrovska and I had white caps that covered all our hair.[823]

Orpheus and Eurydice: *opera in three acts with music by Christoph Willibald Gluck. Produced at the Metropolitan Opera House, New York, on 22 May, 1936, with choreography by George Balanchine and designs by Pavel Tchelitchew.*

Orpheus mourns the loss of Eurydice,

who was fatally bitten by a snake, but he vows to rescue her from Hades. Advising Orpheus that love can overcome all obstacles, Amore, the god of love, issues a single condition for Eurydice's deliverance: Orpheus is not to touch or look at her until they have ascended. Orpheus accepts the challenge. Descending, he encounters the Furies, goddesses of vengeance, and Scarlet Demons, but his singing inspires them to let him pass. When Orpheus arrives at the Elysium, Eurydice is presented to him, blindfolded, by the gods. Without looking at her and in silence, Orpheus leads Eurydice from Hades, but she takes his detachment to be rejection, so Orpheus turns to answer Eurydice — and she dies once more. Distraught, Orpheus attempts suicide, but Amore intervenes, reviving Eurydice and reuniting the lovers.

1098 [230; NIRE].
Costume Design for a Scarlet Demon, 1936.
Watercolor.
Signed lower margin under the image in pencil: "P. Tchelitchew."
11¾ x 8⅝ in., 30 x 22 cm
Label on reverse: reads: "Pavel Tchelitchew, 1928? White Guard Homosexual. Dr. A. Gorbat, 103 East 78 St., New York City, 1942/05."
Provenance: a Ukrainian relative of A. Gorbat (alias Gorbatov, Tchelitchew's physician) in 2007.
Reproduced in color in the journal *ArtGorod,* SP, 2009, No. 11 (21), p. 78; F107, p. 122. A very similar design, incorporating a second figure, is reproduced in Shumov, *Le Paradis de Pavel Tchelitchew,* p. 11.

Note: Tchelitchew designed Hades as a concentration camp, the Elysian Fields as "ether dream", and paradise as "eternity we know from a planetarium."[824] Part of the cost of the ambitious production was borne by Edward Warburg.

813 For information on the Blaue Vogel see the brochure
     Der Blaue Vogel, Berlin, 1922, Vol. 1 (no further
     volumes issued), and the album of photographs of
     productions at the Blaue Vogel entitled *Der Blaue
     Vogel / L'Oiseau Bleu*, date and publisher not
     indicated. On the Russisches Romantisches Theater,
     see the brochure *Russisches Romantisches Theater*,
     Berlin: Europa-Verlag, 1923 [?]. For background
     information on the Russian theaters and cabarets in
     Berlin see E19 and H31.
814 *Der Blaue Vogel*, op. cit., p. 11.
815 Baian: "Russkoe iskusstvo za granitsei" in *Teatr i
     zhizn*, Berlin, 1922, No. 10, p. 14.
816 D. Windham: "The Stage and Ballet Designs of
     Pavel Tchelitchew" in *Dance Index*, New York, Vol.
     III, Nos. 1-2, January-February, p. 4.
817 Ibid.
818 Ibid., pp. 5, 6.
819 A.V.: "'Savonarola'" in *Teatr*, Berlin, 1923, No. 1,
     p. 14.
820 Tyler, *The Divine Comedy*, p. 331.
821 D17, p. 260.
822 N. Nabokov: *Old Friends and New Music*, Boston:
     Little, Brown, 1951, p. 98.
823 F71, p. 93.
824 See Tyler, p. 282.

TCHERKESSOFF, Georges (Cherkesov, Yurii Yurievich)

Born 16 (29) December, 1900, St. Petersburg, Russia; died 31 July, 1943 (suicide), Paris, France.

1917-25 attended IAA / Pegoskhuma-Svomas, taking courses predominantly with Kuzma Petrov-Vodkin; interested in the work of Mstislav Dobujinsky, Boris Kustodiev, and other members of the World of Art group; also aware of the avant-garde experiments and, for example, with Vladimir Kozlinsky, Liubov Popova, Jean Pougny, et al. contributed to the "Exhibition of Contemporary Painting and Drawing" in Petrograd in 1918; 1919 married Alexandre Benois's daughter, Anna, thereby establishing direct contact with the World of Art group; 1922 contributed to their exhibition in Petrograd; 1924 contributed to the "Russian Art Exhibition," New York; in the early 1920s began to illustrate children's books such as *Prazdnik igrushek* [Festival of

Zinaida Serebriakova: *Portrait of Georges Tcherkessoff*, 1939. See No. 907 [R776].

1099

Toys] (P, 1922) and *La Fête Foraine* (Paris: Larousse, N.D.); 1925 emigrated to Paris; thereafter worked for fashion houses and publishers; interested in landscape painting; contributed to many French exhibitions; 1937 received a Gold Medal at the "Exposition Internationale" in Paris for his woodcut illustrations to *Hamlet*; 1941-43 as a Soviet citizen, interned in Royallieu-Compiègne, a French concentration camp; 1943 one-man exhibition; 1944 retrospective at the "Salon des Indépendants," Paris; 1963 retrospective at the Meudon Museum (suburb of Paris).

Bibliography
Nothing substantial has been published on Tcherkessoff. For some references see A37, pp. 496-97.

1099 [R891].
Self-Portrait, 1933.
Pencil.
14 x 11⅞ in., 35.5 x 30.3 cm.
Inscribed on reverse by the artist's son

Alexandre: "Georges Tcherkessof, 1933, Autoportrait."
Provenance: the artist's son, Alexandre Tcherkessoff, Paris, January, 1984.
Reproduced in F107, p. 137.

1100 [R892].
Design for a Decorative Panel at the Cricket on the Hearth Cabaret, 1925.
Watercolor and pencil.
Signed and dated lower right in ink: "G. Tcherkessoff '25."
13⅜ x 17¾ in., 34 x 45 cm.
Other inscription on reverse in Russian: "Project for a decorative panel for the cabaret 'Cricket on the Hearth.'"
Provenance: the artist's son, Alexandre Tcherkessoff, Paris, November 1983.
Reproduced in color in N156, p. 76; and in black and white in A34, p. 111.

Note: The Cricket on the Hearth was one of the ephemeral "little theaters" that opened in St. Petersburg/Petrograd/Leningrad during the 1910s and early 1920s. Created along the lines of Parisian cabarets, the Cricket on the Hearth opened on 12 January, 1922, at 30, Nevsky Prospect, Petrograd. The basic fare was dramatizations and separate numbers, such as Georgian Kinto singing and dancing, Old French songs, and American dances.[825] Like other little cabarets of its kind, such as The Little Berry (founded in October, 1922), the Cricket on the Hearth grew up in direct response to the taste and demands of the new bourgeoisie that appeared thanks to Lenin's New Economic Policy (NEP) with its partial return to the free enterprise system. Many artists became involved in these cabarets, not least Yurii Annenkov, Nicola Benois, Kirill Kustodiev (Boris Kustodiev's son), and Georges Tcherkessoff.

825 See *Vestnik teatra i iskusstva*, P, 1922, No. 7, 24-26 January, p. 4.

1100

TELINGATER, Solomon Benediktovich

Born 29 April (12 May), 1903, Tiflis, Georgia; died 1 October, 1969, Moscow, Russia.

Grew up in an artistic family; attended gymnasium in Baku and graduated from the Baku Art Institute. 1920-21 studied at Vkhutemas in Moscow under Vladimir Favorsky; 1921-24 contributed designs to various newspapers in Baku such as *Rabota* [Work]; 1922 illustrated an edition of Alexander Blok's *Dvenadtsat* [The Twelve] in Baku; 1923 designed a poster for the Baku Soviet elections, his first major typographical exercise; 1925 back in Moscow, started work for various publishing-houses as a designer of books and journals; influenced by the Constructivist concepts of the Lef group of artists such as Alexei Gan, Gustav Klutsis, and Alexander Rodchenko; 1927 contributed to the exhibition "The Moscow Ex-Libris for the Year 1926" in Moscow; received a diploma in industrial design; 1927-32 much influenced by Lissitzky, produced Constructivist covers for journals; 1928 with Lissitsky et al. helped design the layout for the Soviet pavilion at the "Pressa" exhibition in Cologne; 1928 member of the October group, cosigning its manifesto and designing its booklet (1931); 1932 worked for the Down with Illiteracy Publishing-House; 1936 with Sergei Tretiakov produced the first monograph on John Heartfield; 1943 became a member of the Communist Party of the Soviet Union; 1946 winner of the Stalin Prize followed by other accolades; 1963 received the Gutenberg Award in Leipzig for his lifetime achievements in typography.

Bibliography
Telingater's own writings on typographical design and layout are of particular interest, e.g., (with L. Kaplan): *Iskusstvo aktsidentnogo nabora,* Moscow: Kniga, 1965. The following sources provide information on his life and work:
Yu. Gerchuk: "S.B. Telingater" in *Iskusstvo knigi 1963-1964,* M, 1968, No. 5, pp. 134-45.
Yu. Molok: *Solomon Benediktovich Telingater.* Catalog of exhibition organized by the Union of Artists of the USSR, M, 1975.
M. Zhukov: "Aktsidentsii Telingatera" in *Dekorativnoe iskusstvo,* M, 1978, No. 12, pp. 34-38.
S. Telingater: *Telingater: Typograf 1922-1933* (facsimile album of eleven designs by Telingater), Hamburg: Hochschule für bildende Kunst, 1979.
V. Telingater: "Monia-komsomolets" in *Iskusstvo kino,* M, 2004, No. 8, pp. 111-27.
V. Telingater: *Solomon Telingater. Konstruktor graficheskikh ansamblei,* M: Galart, 2008.

Although Telingater is now remembered for his typographical designs and his concern with the "architectonic totality of the book,"[826] his interests were wide-ranging and he did much to propagate the "new" arts of the 1920s such as radio, photography, statistical diagrams, etc. He believed that art could serve the cause of ideology without compromising its esthetic effect, as he emphasized in his many articles of the late 1920s onwards:

> We are profoundly convinced that the spatial arts ... can escape their current crisis only when they are subordinated to the task of serving the concrete needs of the proletariat, as a hegemon showing the way to the peasantry and backwards peoples.[827]

To this end, Telingater produced many political posters such as his anti-League of Nations collage of 1925 and photomontages that illustrated the topical issues of the time.[828]

Telingater was not a professional stage designer, but he was fascinated by the possibilities of the theater as a mass medium and produced a number of related works such as book covers for the Moscow Theatrical Publishing-House. In 1926 he even designed costumes for Shakespeare's *Twelfth Night* (not produced) and in 1931 he made a foldout program for the revue *They're Getting Ready* at the Central Club of the Red Army in Moscow. In 1933 he also designed a poster for the Red Army Theater.

1101 [231; R840].
Design for a Propaganda Truck for the Red Army, 1932.
Collage, watercolor, and ink.
Signed upper left in pencil in Russian: "S. Telingater," and dated "22.IV.32."
9⅞ x 24⅜ in., 25 x 62 cm.
Other inscriptions in pencil in Russian: upper left: "Solomon. Prepared for..."; lower right carries censor's authorization.
Provenance: Viktor Kholodkov, Moscow, 1984.
Reproduced in A34, p. 429; F107, p. 282; I60, p. 31 where it is incorrectly dated as 1922; I77, p. 146. Similar designs are reproduced in I74, No. 127; K56, cover; and K59, p. 82. A larger version is in the collection of Merill Berman, Scarsdale, New York.

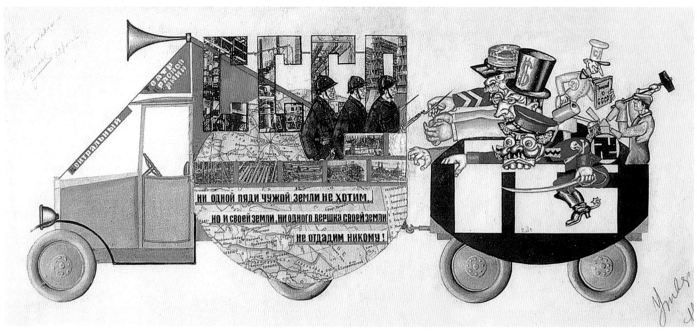

1101

Solomon Telingater: *Font Composition,*
Lithograph, 1960.

Note: Like his colleagues in the October
group, Telingater was drawn to the concept
of the mass festival, arguing that, along with
architecture, the design of objects for mass
consumption, and art education, it was a new
and vital area of concentration.[829] For the
October artists such as Klutsis, Lissitzky, and
Sergei Senkin, the mass festival was important because it could both transmit a direct
political and social message and involve the
public more actively in the artistic process. As
at a fairground, the Communist carnival and
procession (like the mass actions of ca. 1920)
enabled the viewer to "join in."

This design for a propaganda or agit-
truck is for one such carnival organized by
the Maly Theater of the Red Army (later the
Central State Academic Theater of the Red
Army) in Moscow on 22 December, 1932,
and, in fact, the caption strung diagonally
above the front of the truck reads: "Central
Theater of the Red Army." The idea of agit-
transport (propaganda floats) had been
developed with particular enthusiasm just
after the Revolution, especially in the form
of trains and steamboats, although agit-
buses and agit-trucks were also used.
These vehicles participated in the parades
and manifestations that became an integral
part of Soviet public life, especially for May
Day and the October anniversary.

This particular piece shows the USSR
riding in the front part of the truck (with the
letters "CCCP" on top, Red Army soldiers,
photographs of industrial scenes, a map of
part of Soviet Russia, and the lines from a
popular song "We do not want a single foot of
foreign land, but we will not give up an inch of
our land to anyone!"), which is still attached
to the "chariot of world imperialism"
containing representatives of the foreign
powers, i.e. Marshal Foch (?) of France, Henry
Hoover (?) of the USA, and Paul von
Hindenburg (?) of Germany. The "Mad

Hatter" with the long (Jewish) nose and a
watering can is Lev Trotsky, who had adopted
an especially hostile position towards Stalin in
1923 and who had been expelled from the
Soviet Union in 1929: he is wearing a hat with
the letters SD (a reference to his conciliatory
attitude towards the Social Democrats in
Europe — something that had caused Lenin
to distrust him) and carrying his book *Trotsky
o SSSR* [Trotsky on the USSR].[830] This
particular group of enemies was a popular
subject for agit-processions in 1931-32 and
appeared in other propaganda trucks, statues,
and "avenues of enemies" in public spaces
in Moscow and Leningrad.[831]

826 Untitled statement by Telingater. Quoted in
     Gerchuk, "S.B. Telingater," pp. 144-45, where
     neither source, nor date are given.
827 S. Telingater et al.: "Oktiabr. Obiedinenie novykh
     vidov khudozhestvennogo truda. Deklaratsiia"
     (1928). Translation in B12, p. 274-75.
828 For a list of relevant designs see Molok, *Solomon
     Benediktovich Telingater,* unpaginated.
829 See Telingater et al.: "Oktiabr," op. cit., p 277.
830 Trotsky's book was not, of course, published in the
     Soviet Union, but an English translation, introduced by
     Max Eastman, appeared in New York (Harcourt, Brace
     and Co.) in 1928 as *The Real Situation in Russia.*
831 For the reproduction of another agit-truck called
     Trotsky in the Chariot of World Imperialism see
     B72, Vol. 2, No. 299.

TYSHLER, Alexander Grigorievich

Born 14 (26) July, 1898 Melitopol, Ukraine;
died 23 June, 1980, Moscow, Russia.

1912-17 attended the Kiev Art Institute;
1917-18 attended the Kiev studio of
Alexandra Exter, establishing contact with
Boris Aronson, Isaak Rabinovich, Nisson
Shifrin, et al.; 1919-21 during the Civil War
served with the Red Army; contributed to
the Okna ROSTA (propaganda windows of
the Russian Telegraph Agency) in Melitopol;
1921 moved to Moscow; enrolled in
Vkhutemas, studying under Vladimir
Favorsky; collaborated with TsIT (Central
Institute of Labor); painted abstract
paintings; 1922 founding member of the
Projectionist group; met Eduard Bagritsky,
Sergei Esenin, Vera Inber, Velimir
Khlebnikov, Vladimir Maiakovsky, Petr
Miturich, and other progressive writers and
artists; early and mid-1920s worked in a
somewhat Expressionist or Surrealist
manner in various media; 1925 principal
member of OST, supporting the group's
general return to a figurative esthetic; late
1920s began to work as a stage designer;
1930s through early 1960s established
himself as one of the most original Soviet
stage designers, especially for Shakespeare's plays, such as *Richard III*
(Leningrad, 1935) and *King Lear* (Moscow,
1935); 1940s onward continued to work
predominantly for the theater; 1950 onward
worked with wood sculpture, but also
continued to paint and design.

Bibliography
F. Syrkina: *Aleksandr Tyshler,* M: Sovetskii
khudozhnik, 1967.
F. Syrkina: *Aleksandr Tyshler.* Catalog of
exhibition organized by the Union of Artists of the
USSR, M, 1969.
Yu. Molok: "Aleksandr Tyshler" in *Iskusstvo knigi
'65/66,* M, 1970, No. 6, pp. 54-65.
F. Syrkina: *Aleksandr Tyshler.* Catalog of
exhibition organized by the Union of Artists of the
USSR, M, 1978.
G. Levitin: *A.G. Tyshler. Teatr. Zhivopis. Grafika. Iz
leningradskikh sobranii.* Catalog of exhibition at
the GMTMA, 1981.
F. Syrkina and D. Sarabianov: *Aleksandr Tyshler
1898-1980.* Catalog of exhibition organized by
the Union of Artists of the USSR, M, 1983.
F. Syrkina: *Alexander G. Tischler. Drawings,* M:
Sovetsky khudozhnik, 1987.
F. Syrkina: *Aleksandr Tyshler,* M: Galart, 1998.
G. Kazovsky: *Khudozhniki Kultur-Ligi / The Artists
of the Kultur-Lige,* Jerusalem: Gesharim; and M:
Mosty kultury, 2003, passim.
E. van Voolen et al.: *Russisch-Joodse Kunstenaars,
1910-1940. Moderne meesterwerken uit Moskau /
Russian Jewish Artists, 1910-1940. Modern
Masterpieces from Moscow.* Catalog of exhibition
at the Joods Historisch Museum, Amsterdam,
2007, passim.
H. Kazovsky et al.: *Kultur-Liga: Khudozhnii
avangard 1910-1920-kh rokiv / Artistic Avant-
Garde of the 1910s-1920s.* Catalog of exhibition
at the National Art Museum, Kiev, and other
venues, 2007, passim.
K. Svetliarov: *Aleksandr Tyshler,* M: Art-Rodnik,
2007.
B. Dergachev: "Zagadka Tyshlera. Zametki resta-
vratora" in *Sobranie,* M, 2008, No. 4, pp. 20-25.
V. Chaikovskaia: *Tyshler. Neposlushnyi vzroslyi,*
M: Molodaia gvardiia, 2010.

Like Boris Aronson, Anatolii Petritsky, and
Isaak Rabinovich, Tyshler worked in
Alexandra Exter's studio in Kiev, although
later on he maintained that he had not been
deeply affected by her artistic principles.[832]
Still, contact with Exter helped him learn
about Cubism, Futurism, and Suprematism
and reinforced his interest in both studio
painting and design. In the 1920s Tyshler,
along with Alexander Deineka and
Konstantin Vialov, was one of the more
active members of OST, advocating the
return and restoration of the figurative studio
painting after the experiments in abstract
painting and Constructivism. To this end, he
developed a style that, on the one hand,
dealt with contemporary reality and yet, on
the other, often incorporated metaphysical
references as in *Woman and an Airplane* of
1927 (private collection, M). In the late 1920s
and 1930s, Tyshler's lyrical visions encountered an increasingly negative reception
among critics, one remarking that Tyshler's
choice of themes revealed "[his] indubitable
petit-bourgeois sympathies and limited
outlook."[833] However, Tyshler found a more
secure haven for his rich imagination in the
theater, where he worked creatively and pro-
vocatively for many years.

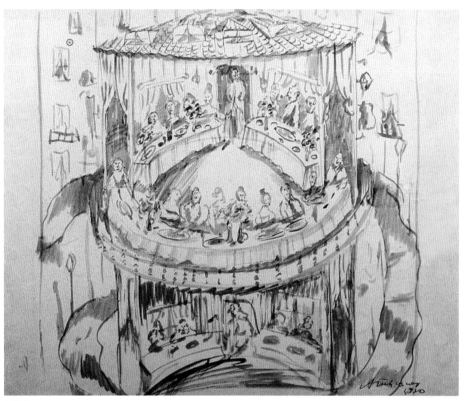

1102

1103

Other inscriptions in Russian: lower margin in pencil character identifications: under man in bowler hat: "Valodor Shylia"; under figure in fur hat: "Pavich"; under woman: "Nadina." Provenance: Igor Dychenko, Kiev, February, 1984.
Reproduced in I77, p. 156.

Note: It is possible that these costumes were part of Tyshler's design contribution to Mikhail Rafalsky's production of the play *Tops and Bottoms* based on David Bergelson's *Deaf Man.* This was staged at the Belorussian State Jewish Theater in Minsk in 1929.

Twelfth Night: *play by William Shakespeare. Produced by Leonid Vivien at the State Pushkin Academic Theater of Drama, Leningrad, on 28 May, 1951, with music by A.S. Zhivotov and designs by Alexander Tyshler.*

The twins Viola and Sebastian are separated after a shipwreck, each believing the other to have drowned. Viola is cast up on the shore of Illyria, where, dressed as a page called Cesario, she enters the service of the Duke of Orsino. Orsino sends him (her) to woo the Countess Olivia on his

Unidentified production, *1930.*

1102 [R841].
Stage Design on Two Tiers, 1930.
Watercolor.
Signed and dated lower right in Russian: "A. Tyshler, 1930."
13¾ x 16½ in., 35 x 42 cm.
The reverse carries another stage design perhaps not by Tyshler. See No. 1103 [NIRE].
Provenance: Igor Dychenko, February, 1984.
Reproduced in I77, p. 156.

1103 [NIRE].
Stage Design, 1930.
Watercolor.
This is the verso of No. 1102 [R841].
The attribution to Tyshler is tentative.

Note: It has been suggested that No. 1102 [R841] is a variant of Tyshler's set for Samuil Margolin's production of Lipe Reznik's *Die Letzte* at the Kharkov State Jewish Theater in 1928.[834] However, it may also be connected to one of the productions on which Tyshler worked for the Belorussian State Jewish Theater in Minsk in the late 1920s and early 1930s.

Unidentified production, *1930.*

1104 [R842].
Two Costumes for a Woman and a Man, 1930.
Watercolor and pencil.
Signed twice lower margin in pencil in Russian: "A. Tyshler" and below this in ink with the date: "A. Tyshler, 1930."
18½ x 15¾ in., 47 x 40 cm.

Other inscriptions in Russian: under the woman's costume in pencil the word "Peiza" (?); under the male figure in pencil in Russian the word "Oke" (?).
Provenance: Igor Dychenko, Kiev, February, 1984.
Reproduced in A34, p. 436; I77, pp. 118, 156.

1105 [R843].
Three Costumes, for Two Men and a Woman, 1930.
Watercolor and pencil.
Signed and dated lower center in pencil in Russian: "A. Tyshler, 1929"; also signed and dated underneath in ink in Russian: "A. Tyshler, 1930."
18⅛ x 20⅛ in., 46 x 51 cm.

1104

1105

behalf, but the Countess, who resides with her servant Maria and the carousing Sir Toby Belch and Sir Andrew Aguecheek, falls in love with Cesario, who loves only the Duke. Meanwhile, Sebastian has also been rescued and, by chance, comes to the court of the Duke Orsino, where his rescuer the Captain Antonio is arrested. After a series of mistaken identities is corrected, Viola marries Orsino and Sir Toby — Maria.

1106

1106 [R844].
Costume Design for Olivia, ca. 1951.
Gouache and pencil.
Signed lower center in Russian: "A. Tyshler."
15¾ x 12¼ in., 40 x 31.1 cm.
Other inscriptions: lower left corner: "Olivia"; left of the skirt: cloth annotations.
Provenance: Nina Stevens, New York, December, 1968.
Reproduced in I40, No. 141. A version very similar item held in the GMTMA is reproduced in *A.G. Tyshler,* p. 9.

Note: Tyshler achieved his positive reputation as a stage designer and, specifically, as an interpreter of Shakespeare, thanks mainly to his unfailing imagination. Even though his *oeuvre* is marked by a cyclical application of themes (e.g., women in veils and/or supporting elaborate headgear), Tyshler was careful to consider the demands of each spectacle. He summarized his artistic philosophy when, in an imaginary interview with a theater director, he stated:

> I do not become the slave of the stage. I have my own floor, ceiling, my own walls, my own, so to say, malleable household. I like my design to completely accommodate itself in the pupil of the eye — like a silhouette, like an architectural image; I like it to accommodate itself in the consciousness...
>
> An ironic nuance is characteristic of my work — a plastic paradox, something

grotesque. I always want to strike the viewer, to amaze him. Maybe that's not a very solid quality for an artist, but what can you do? That's me.[835]

Tyshler as contributor:
1107 [R845].
Designer unknown: Poster for the Studio of the Projectionist Theater, 1923.
Lithograph in black and white.
32⅝ x 24¾ in., 83 x 63 cm.
Reproduced in I60, p. 38.
The full text of the poster reads as follows:

> 1923-16-V. Hall of Columns in the House of Unions [Moscow]. Studio of the Projectionist Theater Performs. Object 1: Workers: Amkhanitskaia, Bogatyrev, Viliams Grei (Reskin), Luchishkin, Svobodin. Work instruments: Nikolai Triaskin's system. Costume: Worker's uniform. Stage trampoline. Anatolii Mariengof's tragedy Conspiracy of Fools. Rhythmo-dynamic montage of the text and movement phonation: Nikritin's systems. Starts at 8:30 p.m. Supervisor: A.Ya. Reznikov. Tickets on sale at: Box office, House of Unions, 1 Bolshaia Dmitrovka (Entrance No. 5) and at 5 Petrovka. Special cheap tickets for workers, Komsomol members, and students.

Anna Amkhanitskaia and Alexander Bogatyrev were actors, Luchishkin, Solomon Nikritin, Nikolai Triaskin, and Petr Viliams artists, Anatolii Mariengof a writer, and A. Svobodin a member of the Proletkult Theater. Grei (Reskin) and Reznikov and have not been identified, although the former may have been a pseudonym of Petr Viliams.

Note: The Projectionist Group was founded in Moscow in 1923 by Tyshler, Sergei Luchishkin, Solomon Nikritin, Mikhail Plaksin, Kliment Redko, Nikolai Triaskin, et al., and their initial activities in both studio and applied work brought them into close

alliance with the Constructivists. The artists were all young, graduates or graduating from Vkhutemas, and at the beginning of 1925 some of them became founding members of OST (see No. 1148-51 [R390-93]). The Projectionist Group issued a manifesto in conjunction with their contribution to the "First Discussional Exhibition of Associations of Active Revolutionary Art" in the spring of 1924 at the Moscow Vkhutemas (see No. 790 [R666]), in which they asserted that:

> 1. Industrial production regulates social attitudes...
>
> 4. Painting and volumetrical constructions are the most convincing means of expressing *(projecting)* the method of organizing materials...
>
> 5. The artist is not the producer of consumer objects (cupboard, picture), but (of projections) of the method of organizing materials...
>
> 6. Art is the science of an objective system of organizing materials.[836]

In order to sustain their affirmation, they submitted blueprints, maquettes, models, scale drawings, "tectonic researches," and analytical paintings to the exhibition — carefully avoiding the words "beauty" and "esthetic."

As far as the Projectionist Theater was concerned, the prime mover was Nikritin, who in 1923 produced a number of experimental plays, including Mariengof's historical tragedy *Conspiracy of Fools* and his so-called *A, O, U Tragedy.* Anatolii Mariengof was a leading supporter of Imaginism, a close friend of the poet Sergei Esenin and the artist Georgii Yakulov (see Nos. 1157-70 [R1013-25]), and a "poet-clown, a verbal juggler, a representative of the bohemia."[837] In their application of "workers' uniforms" and "work instruments," Nikritin and his colleagues were borrowing freely from the Constructivist, bio-mechanical vocabulary of Vsevolod Meierkhold and Liubov Popova and perhaps also of Nikolai Foregger and Kasian Goleizovsky. Moreover, their reference to the production here as an "object" (Russian: *veshch*) also invokes a primary concept of the Constructivists (cf. El Lissitzky's and Ilya Ehrenburg's Berlin journal called *Veshch/Gegenstand/Objet* of 1922) — to the effect that the artifact or theatrical presentation is of the same category as the factory made object. The Projectionist Group and Theater were disbanded in late 1924 and many of the artists involved (Tyshler being an exception) returned exclusively to studio painting.

1923 — 16 — V
Колонный Зал ДОМА СОЮЗОВ
МАСТЕРСКАЯ
ПРОЭКЦИОННОГО
ТЕАТРА
ВЫСТУПАЕТ.
ВЕЩЬ 1:

РАБОТАЮТ: АМХАНИЦКАЯ, БОГАТЫРЕВ, ВИЛЬЯМС ГРЕИ (РЕСКИН), ЛУЧИШКИН, СВОБОДИН. ■ ОРУДИЯ РАБОТЫ: СИСТЕМЫ—НИКОЛАЯ ТРЯСКИНА. ■ КОСТЮМ: РАБОЧАЯ ФОРМА. СЦЕНИЧЕСКИЙ ТРАМПЛИН: ТРАГЕДИЯ АНАТОЛИЯ МАРИЕНГОФА: „ЗАГОВОР ДУРАКОВ". РИТМОДИНАМИЧЕСКИЙ МОНТАЖ ТЕКСТА, ЗВУЧАНИЯ ДВИЖЕНИЯ: СИСТЕМЫ НИКРИТИНА.

Начало в 8½ в. Для этого издает А. Я. Резников.
Билеты: Касса Дома Союзов. Б. Дмитровка. № 1 под кат. 5 и Петровка. 5. Рабочим, комсомольцам и учащимся СПЕЦ. ДЕШ. БИЛЕТЫ.

1107

832 According to the Flora Syrkina in conversation with John E. Bowlt, Moscow, 16 June, 1986.
833 L. Zivelchinskaia: *Expressionizm,* M-L: Ogiz-Izogiz, 1933, p. 83.
834 According to Syrkina in conversation with Bowlt, Moscow, 16 June 1986.
835 G38, p. 255.
836 Untitled statement by the Projectionist Group. Translation in B12, p. 240.
837 A8, Vol. 4, p. 613.

UDALTSOVA, Nadezhda Andreevna

Born December 29, 1885 (10 January, 1886), Orel, Russia; died 25 January, 1961, Moscow, Russia.

1905 enrolled in Konstantin Yuon and Ivan Dudin's Art School, making the acquaintance of Vera Mukhina, Liubov Popova, and Alexander Vesnin; 1908 visited Sergei Shchukin's collection; visited Berlin and Dresden; 1912-13 with Popova studied under Henri Le Fauconnier, Jean Metzinger, and André Dunoyer de Segonzac at La Palette in Paris; 1913 with Alexei Grishchenko, Popova, Vesnin, et al. worked in Tatlin's studio known as the Tower; 1914 onwards contributed to exhibitions such as "Jack of Diamonds," "Tramway V," "0.10," and "The Store"; 1916 commissioned by Natalia Davydova to design textiles; 1916-17 helped prepare the journal *Supremus* (not published); 1917 Yakulov invited her to take part in the decoration of the Café Pittoresque; 1918 collaborated with Alexei Gan, Alexei Morgunov, Malevich, and Alexander Rodchenko on the newspaper *Anarkhiia* [Anarchy]; 1918-30 taught at Svomas/Vkhutemas/Vkhutein; 1920 married Alexander Drevin; 1920-21 member of Inkhuk; 1922 contributed to the "Erste Russische Kunstausstellung" at the Galerie Van Diemen in Berlin; 1923 contributed to "Exhibition of Paintings" at Vkhutemas; 1924 contributed to the Venice Biennale; 1928 joint exhibition, with Drevin, at the State Russian Museum in Leningrad; 1934 joint exhibition, with Drevin, in Erevan; 1938 Drevin arrested; 1945 painted portraits of actors from the Romen Gypsy Theater, Moscow; one-woman exhibition at the Moscow Union of Soviet Artists.

Bibliography
M. Miasina, comp.: *Stareishie sovetskie khudozhniki o Srednei Azii i Kavkaze,* M: Sovetskii khudozhnik, 1973, pp. 220-25.
K52, pp. 286-312.
K75, pp. 291-339.
B109, pp. 157-72.
E. Drevina: *Aleksandr Drevin. Nadezhda Udaltsova.* Catalog of exhibition organized by the Union of Artists of the USSR, M, 1991.
B180.
E. Drevina: *Nadezhda Udaltsova,* M: Trilistnik, 1997.
K224, passim.
K236, pp. 271-95.
S. Aleksandrov: *Aleksandr Drevin i Nadezhda Udaltsova.* Catalog of exhibition at the Nashchokin House Gallery, M, 2008.

One of the "Amazons" of the Russian avant-garde, Udaltsova made a substantial contribution to the development of Russian Cubism and then Suprematism. With Popova, she studied the principles of Cubism under Le Fauconnier and Metzinger in Paris before the First World War and then, in 1915-16, changed her allegiance to Malevich and his Suprematist doctrine, wherein

forms change in perspective, according to light or the influence of the atmosphere and surrounding forms, and only the individual desire of the artist will show them on the canvas in this or that aspect.[838]

However, Udaltsova's interest in Suprematism was not exclusive, for she also attended the lessons of Tatlin before turning back to Cubism and then, in the 1920s, to a Realist style with which she interpreted Russian and Central Asian landscapes. Udaltsova was primarily a studio painter and, although she applied Suprematist motifs to textile design in the late 1910s and worked on the interior design of the bohemian Café Pittoresque in Moscow, her contributions to scenography are rare and the circumstances of her collaboration with Nikita's Baliev's Bat (Chauve-Souris) in 1916 have not been clarified.

1108 [NIRE].
Efrosinia Fedoseevna Ermilova-Platova (1895-1974): *Portrait of Nadezhda Udaltsova, 1940.*
Pencil
Signed and dated under the portrait in pencil in Russian: "1940 E. Erm.-Pl."
7½ x 6⅞ in., 19 x 17.5 cm.
Provenance: Ekaterina Drevina, grand-daughter of Nadezhda Udaltsova, Moscow, May, 1984.

Unidentified production, 1916.

1109 [R846].
Stage Design, 1916.
Gouache and black ink
10⅞ x 14 in., 27.5 x 35.5 cm.

1108

Inscribed on the reverse in pencil in Russian by the artist's grand-daughter, Ekaterina Drevina: "Udaltsova, N.A. Study for a decoration. 1916 P[aper], gouache, India ink, 27.5 x 35.5."
Provenance: the artist's grand-daughter, Ekaterina Drevina, Moscow, May, 1984.
Reproduced in K110, p. 64, where it is described as a "*Decorative Sketch,* 1910s, watercolor and ink on paper." A similar piece in the collection of the Galerie Gmurzynska, Cologne, is reproduced in Drevina, *Nadezhda Udaltsova,* p. 9.

1109

1110

Unidentified production, *1945.*

1110 [R847].
Costume Designs for Female and Male Gypsy Dancers, 1945.
Watercolor, gouache, and pencil
7¼ x 9 in., 18.5 x 23 cm.
Inscribed on the reverse in pencil in Russian by Ekaterina Drevina, the artist's grand-daughter: "Udaltsova, N.A. Gypsies. 1945. P[aper], watercolor, gouache, bronze, 18.5 x 23."
Provenance: the artist's grand-daughter, Ekaterina Drevina, Moscow, May, 1984.

838 N. Udaltsova: untitled text for the unpublished journal *Supremus*, 1917. Quoted in K226, p. 347.

ULIANOV, Nikolai Pavlovich

Born 2 (14) May, 1875, Elets, Lipetsk Region, Russia; died 5 May, 1949, Moscow, Russia.

1887 family moved to Moscow; 1887-88 apprentice in an icon studio; 1888-89 took art lessons from Vasilii Meshkov; 1889-1900 attended MIPSA under Nikolai Ge, Nikolai Nevrev, Illarion Prianishnikov, and then Valentin Serov, becoming the latter's teaching assistant in 1900-03; 1900-07 taught at the Zvantseva Art School in St. Petersburg; 1904 made the acquaintance of Anton Chekhov and Sergei Diaghilev; 1905 debut as a stage designer for Konstantin Stanislavsky and Vsevolod Meierkold's production of Hauptman's *Schluck und Jau,* 1906 designed part of the Stanislavsky-Meierkhold production of Hamsun's *Drama of Life*; 1906-09 close to the artists and writers of the journal *Zolotoe runo* [Golden Fleece], contributing to its exhibitions; also contributed regularly to exhibitions in Moscow, St. Petersburg, and other cities; 1907 toured Italy, visiting Venice, Padua, Ferrara, Ravenna, Florence, Rome, and Bologna; 1909-12 traveled in France and Germany; concentrated on Classical and mythological scenes; 1914 mobilized; 1915-18 taught at CSIAI; 1916 initiated a cycle of portraits and renderings based on Pushkin's life and work, called *My Pushkin*, which he continued through the 1930s; 1917 onwards created designs for the Revolutionary festivities; 1919 contributed to the "IV State Exhibition" in Moscow; 1919-21 taught at Svomas-Vkhutemas; 1924 founding-member of the Four Arts Society; 1920 contributed to the "I State Exhibition of Art and Science" in Kazan; 1920s-30s designed several productions for Stanislavsky, including Mikhail Bulgakov's *Days of the Turbins*; 1930s-40s concentrated on scenes, often politically charged, such as *Barricades on the Sadovaia* (1948); 1942-45 taught at the State Art Institute, Moscow; 1946 illustrated Alexander Griboedov's *Woe from Wit*.

Bibliography
P. Muratov and B. Griftsov: *Nikolai Pavlovich Ulianov*, M-L: Gosizdat, 1925.
Yu. Lobanova: *Nikolai Pavlovich Ulianov*. Catalog of exhibition at the Academy of Arts, M, 1951.
O. Roitenberg: *Nikolai Pavlovich Ulianov*, M: Sovetskii khudozhnik, 1953.
O. Lavrova: *Nikolai Pavlovich Ulianov*, M: Iskusstvo, 1953.
M. Sokolnikov, ed.: *N.P. Ulianov: Moi vstrechi,* M: Akademiia khudozhestv SSSR, 1959.
V. Leniashin: *Nikolai Pavlovich Ulianov*, L: Khudozhnik RSFSR, 1976.
K. Kravchenko: *A.V. Kuprin, S.D. Lebedeva, N.P. Ulianov.* Catalog of exhibition at the Scientific Research Museum of the Academy of Arts, L, 1977.
A34, p. 440.
L. Pravoverova, comp.: *Nikolai Ulianov. Liudi epokhi sumerek,* M: Agraf, 2004.

Ulianov wrote in his memoirs that "If Serov... was my guide in painting, then Stanislavsky... was my teacher of the stage."[839] Much influenced by the portraiture of Valentin Serov, Ulianov assimilated many styles and motifs — from Classical antiquity to contemporary Decadence — and some works of the 1910s such as *Café* (1917-18, TG) and *At the Barber's, Self-Portrait* (1919, TG) even betray a fleeting interest in Cubism and perhaps Rayonism. Ulianov also found inspiration in the new poetry and philosophy, discussing Symbolist ideas with Andrei Bely and Viacheslav Ivanov, a connection that inspired his portraits of contemporaries such as Konstantin Balmont (1909, TG) and Viacheslav Ivanov (1920, RM). The Blue Rose artists such as Pavel Kuznetsov and Sergei Sudeikin were frequent visitors to Ulianov's Moscow studio, although formally he was not a member of the group.

Through his acquaintance with the Chekhov family and Stanislavsky, in particular, Ulianov portrayed many representatives of the performing arts, including Fedor Chaliapin, Anton Chekhov, Mariia Ermolova, Olga Knipper, Vladimir Nemirovich-Danchenko, Alexander Skriabin, and Stanislavsky. Although his whimsical costumes for *Schluck und Jau* in 1905 demonstrated an indubitable talent for stage design (and Stanislavsky praised them highly[840]), the theater did not play the primary role in Ulianov's artistic career. As he wrote: "the theater doesn't give as much as it takes"[841] and for many years after his initial collaboration with Meierkhold and Stanislavsky, he concentrated on other media, returning to the theater only after the Revolution, when he renewed his collaboration with major companies. Of particular importance were his designs for Stanislavsky's interpretations at the Moscow Art Theater of Mikhail Bulgakov's *The Days of the Turbins* (1926) and his *Molière* (1933, not produced) and then for an adaptation of Georges Bizet's *Carmen* at the Stanislavsky Opera Theater in 1935.

Examining Ulianov's student works, his mentor Nikolai Ge once exclaimed "You will be a fantastic artist."[842] Ulianov may not have been "fantastic," but he was a competent and often original portraitist, book illustrator, and stage designer; and in all his endeavors, whether as Classicist, Symbolist, or Cubist, Ulianov "sought to combine the beautiful and the eternal."[843]

1111

Les Fourberies de Scapin: comedy in three acts by Jean-Baptiste Molière, produced by Sergei Aidarov at the Maly Theater, Moscow, on 19 December, 1918, with designs by Nikolai Ulianov.

The arrogant, but clever, Scapin uses deceit and falsehood to advance in life, but he also uses his skills to keep young lovers together. In their fathers' absence, Octave has married Hyacinthe and Léandre has fallen in love with Zerbinette, but the fathers return, each with his own plan for an arranged marriage. Heeding the lovers' pleas for help, Scapin ensures that they stay betrothed, helps organize the marriage feast, and is even received as the guest of honor.

1111 [NIRE].
Costume Designs for the Turkish Captain with Two Blackamoors Carrying His Train, 1918.
Watercolor and pencil.
11¾ x 14¼ in., 30 x 36 cm.
Provenance: Natalia Alexandrova, Moscow, 1980s.

1112 [NIRE].
Costumes for Three Egyptian Slaves Appearing in Act III, Scene 1, 1918.
Gouache and pencil.
13¼ x 14½ in., 34 x 37 cm.
Provenance: Natalia Alexandrova, Moscow, 1980s.

Note: Les Fourberies de Scapin enjoyed a marked success at the Maly Theater, running as a regular component of the repertoire until 1924. According to one source, however, the selection of Les

Fourberies de Scapin (see Nos. 1111-12 [NIRE]), Le Médecin volant, and Monsieur de Pourceaugnac (see No. 602 [R863]), and the general emphasis on the farces and "comedy ballets" of Molière, rather than on

the "politically saturated" Tartuffe or Misanthrope, indicated a conscious — and pernicious — aspiration to provide the masses with easy recreation and spectacle rather than with healthy ideological fare.[844] In 1920 Ulianov suddenly returned to the theater, working on several projects, including a version of Molière's L'Avare, also for the Maly Theater, Vladimir Nemirovich-Danchenko's interpretation of Offenbach's Orpheus for the Music Studio of the Moscow Art Theater (not produced), and Stanislavsky's plans for productions of A Nest of Gentlefolk (by Vladimir Rebikov after Ivan Turgenev) and Uncle Tom's Cabin. These tentative efforts prepared Ulianov for his Soviet triumphs: the sets and costumes for the productions of The Days of the Turbins in 1926 and Carmen in 1935, both of which expressed Ulianov's conviction that "historical truth is not always artistic truth."[845]

Woe to Wit: play by Vsevolod Meierkhold and Mikhail Korenev based on Alexander Griboedov's four-act comedy Woe from Wit. Produced by Meierkhold at the Meierkhold Theater, Moscow, on 12 March, 1928, with designs by Viktor Shestakov and Nikolai Ulianov.

The conservative Famusov, director of an important government department, is a pillar of the establishment. His colleagues such as Molchalin, the cunning secretary, and Repetilov, the coffee-room lawyer, all pretend to be upright and decent. The exceptions are Sophia, Famusov's daughter, and the idealist Chatsky, who,

1112

1113

1114

with his eloquence and fantasy, condemns and revolts against the narrow world of philistines and pharisees.

Ulianov as contributor:
1113 [R678].
Designer unknown: *Poster Advertising a Debate on Woe to Wit*, 1928.
Lithograph in black and white.
41⅜ x 28 in., 105 x 71 cm.
Inscriptions (as part of the design) provide details on the date and location of the debate (2 April, 1928, Meierkhold Theater, Moscow) and a list of contributors, including Leopold Averbakh, Henry Dana, Mikhail Gnesin, Pavel Markov, Vsevolod Meierkhold, Diego Rivera, and Vladimir Sarabianov.
Provenance: Viktor Kholodkov, Moscow, May, 1984.

Note: Henry Wadsworth Longfellow Dana (1881-1950) was an American theatrical historian, collector of theatrical memorabilia, and curator of the Longfellow House in Cambridge, Mass.

Ulianov as contributor:
1114 [NIRE].
Designer unknown: *Poster Advertising Performances by the State Meierkhold Theater at the Lunacharsky Theater in Sverdlovsk*, 1928.
Lithograph in black and white.
Photomontage with photographs of performances and a portrait of Vsevolod Meierkhold.
40¾ x 27⅜ in., 103.5 x 69.5 cm.
Inscriptions (as part of the design) provide the names of the actors and administrators of the Meierkhold company together with the repertoire of the seven plays scheduled for performance during May and June, 1928, i.e. *Inspector General, Come On, Europe!, Mandate, Roar, China!, Magnanimous*

Cuckold, Forest, and *Woe to Wit*. Printed by the Mospoligraf 16th Printing-House, Moscow, in an edition of 1500.

839 Sokolnikov, *N.P. Ulianov. Moi vstrechi*, p. 150.
840 Stanislavsky also felt that Ulianov would have made a talented director. See Lavrova, *Nikolai Pavlovich Ulianov*, p. 36.
841 Ibid., p. 41.
842 Quoted in Leniashin, *N.P. Ulianov*, p. 15.
843 Ibid., p. 26.
844 C10, p. 138. According to the two-volume history of the Maly Theater (C58, Vol. 1, p. 576), *Les Fourberies de Scapin* premiered there in October, 1847, but the same source (Vol. 2) makes no reference to a 1918 Soviet production.
845 Sokolonikov, *N.P. Ulianov. Moi vstrechi*, p.149.

VASNETSOV, Viktor Mikhailovich

Born 3 (15) May, 1848, Lopial Village, Viatka Region, Russia; died 23 July, 1926, Moscow, Russia.

1858-67 attended the Viatka Ecclesiastical School and then Viatka Seminary; 1867 moved to St. Petersburg; 1868-75 attended IAA, taking classes with Petr Basin, Pavel Chistiakov, Vasilii P. Vereshchagin, et al.; 1873 onwards contributed regularly to the exhibitions of the Wanderers Society; 1876-77 lived in France; 1878 moved to Moscow; 1881 painted *Alenushka* and started *Bogatyrs*, soon achieving acclaim for his Russian historical pictures; 1882 designed Alexander Ostrovsky's *Snegurochka* for Savva Mamontov; 1882-85 worked on his *Stone Age* frieze for the Historical Museum, Moscow; 1885 designed Nikolai Rimsky-Korsakov's *Snegurochka* for Mamontov's Private Opera Company in Moscow; travelled in Europe; 1892

appointed professor of painting by IAA; 1893-94 designed and built his own house in the Russian style in Moscow; 1896 contributed to the "All-Russian Art and Industry Exhibition" in Nizhnii Novgorod; 1899 one-man exhibition at IAA; 1900 contributed to the "Exposition Universelle" in Paris; 1903 began to contribute to the exhibitions of the Union of Russian Artists; 1905 one-man exhibition of religious paintings at IAA; 1914-15 helped the war effort by designing posters and contributing to philanthropic enterprises, such as the exhibition "Artists to Comrade Warriors"; 1922 contributed to the "Erste Russische Kunstausstellung," Berlin; 1924 contributed to the "Russian Art Exhibition," New York.

Bibliography
N.-N.: *V.M. Vasnetsov*, M: Maevsky, 1913.
M. Vasnetsov: *Russkii khudozhnik Viktor Mikhailovich Vasnetsov*, Prague: Khutor, 1948.
M. Kholodovskaia: *Viktor Vasnetsov*, M: GMII, 1949.
V. Lobanov: *Viktor Vasnetsov v Moskve*, M: Moskovskii rabochii, 1961.
V. Bakhrevsky: *Viktor Vasnetsov*, M: Molodaia gvardiia 1989.
L. Iovleva, G. Sternin, et al.: *Viktor Vasnetsov*. Catalog of exhibition at the TG, 1990.
L. Kudriavtseva: *Khudozhniki Viktor i Apollinarii Vasnetsovy*, M: Detskaia literatura, 1991.
L. Iovleva, ed.: *Viktor Mikhailovich Vasnetsov 1848-1926*, M: TG, 1994.
E. Paston: *Viktor Vasnetsov*, M: Slovo, 1996.
N Yaroslavtseva: *Moskva Viktora Vasnetsova*, M: Novosti, 1998.
L. Korotkina, comp.: *Viktor Vasnetsov. Pisma. Novye materially*, M: ARS, 2004.
E. Shilova: *Viktor Vasnetsov*, M: Art-Rodnik, 2004.
G. Pikulina: *Mir Vasnetsova 1848-1926*, M: Terra, 2008.
L. Efremova: *Vasnetsov: Albom*, M: Olma Media Grupp, 2010.

Along with other Neo-Nationalist artists and patrons at Abramtsevo and Talashkino, Viktor Vasnetsov breathed the "oxygen of art" that helped revive and refurbish the Russian arts and crafts at the end of the 19th century.[846] For Vasnetsov, this "seer of the eternal in the ephemeral,"[847] stage and book design were not the mere hand-maidens to painting, but were equal parts in the esthetic synthesis to which the Neo-Nationalists and then the Symbolists aspired so eagerly.

True, Vasnetsov's early works, such as *Fairground on the Outskirts of Paris* (1876, TG), show a clear debt to French and German genre painting and his religious nostalgia often brings to mind the English Pre-Raphaelites. Still, Vasnetsov is remembered, above all, for his reconstructions of "Old Russia" through fable, myth, and religious parable. Although to some observers Vasnetsov's mythological and historical evocations, such as *Magic Carpet* (late 1870s, TG), *Alenushka* (1880s), and *Bogatyrs* (1898, TG), may seem sentimental, if not melodramatic, they express and confirm the artist's genuine passion for the

1115

artistic achievements of pre-Petrine Russia.

On this level, Vasnetsov had much in common with Sergei Maliutin, Elena Polenova, and Andrei Riabushkin (see No. 865 [R761]), and, naturally, was a champion of the Neo-Nationalist movement at the Abramtsevo colony. Like the Mamontovs, the Prakhovs, and Vladimir Stasov, too, Vasnetsov focused attention on the organic traditions of Medieval Russian culture as mirrored especially in church architecture, icons, woodcarving, and illuminated manuscripts. Vasnetsov examined and interpreted these sources in his studio paintings and designs in an earnest attempt to "understand the Russian people."[848] Identifying Russia's finest hour with the triumph of Orthodoxy, Vasnetsov sought to reclaim the virtues of humility, spirituality, wisdom, and resoluteness in the face of evil, for which many of his pictures serve as metaphors, such as *The Battle of Dobrynia Nikitich and the Seven-Headed Serpent Gorynych* (1913-18, Vasnetsov House-Museum, Moscow).

Even so, when, in his survey of the new developments in Russian art, the critic Sergei Makovsky remarked that the "conflagration had begun with Vasnetsov,"[849] he seemed to have in mind not the artist's evocation of the brave deeds of legendary heroes and the sterness of the Orthodox saints, but his flamboyant attention to the richness and diversity of Russian ornament and design. Vasnetsov was fascinated by the traditional arts and crafts, studying embroideries, costumes, parchments, icons, and prints in Moscow's Historical Museum, while he

reminisced, no doubt, about the glorious country fairs and bazaars of his childhood. Asked whence he had borrowed his vivid colors for the *Snegurochka* designs, Vasnetsov responded:

> from the interfusing play of pearls, beads and colored stones on the headdresses, jackets, coats, and other female attire that I saw at home [in Viatka] and Moscow.[850]

Vasnetsov elaborated the colors and motifs that he found in national art, transferring them to his designs for the productions in Abramtsevo and Moscow, such as *Black Turban, Crimson Rose*, and, above all, *Snegurochka*. After the pompous sets of the Imperial designers, such as Mikhail Bocharov and Matvei Shishkov, Vasnetsov's lively renderings of boyars and buffoons seemed both historically tenable and artistically inventive. Here was a theatrical combination of ethnography and imagination that Vasnetsov himself may not have intended,[851] but which formed a strong precedent to the later folkloric explorations of Ivan Bilibin, Alexander Golovin, and Natalia Goncharova for ballet, fashion, and book design.

Unidentified production, 1880s.
1115 [232; NIRE].
Maiden in Medieval Dress, 1880s.
Watercolor, pencil, and gouache.
Signed lower left in Russian: "V. Vasnetsov."
10⅝ x 6¼ in., 27 x 16 cm.
Provenance: *Icons, Russian Pictures and Works of Art*, London: Sotheby's, 8 October, 1998, Lot 1113 (reproduced).
Reproduced in F107, p. 469.

Note: It is possible that this is a design for a female costume in one of the two *Snegurochka* productions, i.e., the Ostrovsky play at the Mamontovs' Moscow home in 1881 or the Rimsky-Korsakov opera at Mamontov's Private Opera Company, Moscow, in 1885.

846 Lobanov, *Viktor Vasnetsov v Moskve*, p. 79.
847 V. Vasnetsov, statement quoted in *Viktor Vasnetsov*. Catalog of exhibition at the the TG, p. 30.
848 F22, p. 515.
849 S. Makovsky: *Siluety russkikh khudozhnikov*, Prague: Nasha rech, 1922, p. 28.
850 Lobanov, *Viktor Vasnetsov v Moskve*, p. 124.
851 See V. Vasnetsov: "Vospminaniia o Savve Ivanoviche Mamontove" in V. Mamontov: *Vospominaniia o russkikh khudozhnikakh*, M: Akademiia khudozhestv SSSR, 1950, p. 101.

VASSILIEFF, Marie (Vasilieva, Mariia Ivanovna)

Born 22 February (5 March), 1884, Smolensk, Russia; died 14 May, 1957, Nogent-sur-Marne, France.

1902 studied medicine and the fine arts in St. Petersburg; received a stipend to study in Paris; 1905 made an extended visit to Paris; 1907 moved to Paris permanently, where she became a correspondent for Russian news-papers; especially interested in the work of Henri Matisse; in close contact with Max Jacob; 1908 sent an essay by Matisse to the Moscow art journal *Zolotoe runo* [Golden Fleece] (published as "Zametki khudozhnika" [An Artist's Notes], 1909, No. 6); 1909 established the Académie Libre (also known as the Académie Russe) in Paris; met Paul Poiret, André Salmon, and many other artistic and literary celebrities; began to exhibit regularly with professional societies, including the Salon d'Automne and the Salon des Indépendants; 1909-14 traveled extensively in Western Europe, Scandinavia, Romania, Poland, and Russia; 1910s contributed to a number of avant-garde exhibitions in Russia; 1911 withdrew from the board of the Académie; 1912 founded the Académie Vassilieff; 1913-14 invited Fernand Léger to deliver two lectures at her Académie; 1914 joined the French Red Cross as an ambulance attendant; 1915 contributed to exhibitions in New York and Harbin, China; 1915-16 visited Russia; contributed to "0.10"; 1915-17 turned her Paris studio into a canteen to help friends during wartime, welcoming many artists, writers, musicians, and dancers, such as Braque, Friesz, Léger, Modigliani, Picabia, Valadon, Cendrars, Gide, Jacob, Poulenc, and Satie; 1916 contributed to Vladimir Tatlin's exhibition the "Store"; 1917 being a Russian citizen, was placed in confined residence in Fontainebleau as a result of the Brest-Litovsk Treaty; 1920s often exhibited in London and Paris; 1924-37 created costumes and sets for various companies, including the Ballets Suédois; 1925 contributed to the "Exposition Internationale des Arts Décoratifs" in Paris; gave particular attention to furniture design; 1928-30 one-woman exhibitions in London and Rome; 1937 contributed to the "Exposition Internationale" in Paris; 1938 settled in the south of France; 1945 returned to Paris.

Bibliography
A. Salmon and W. George: *Un peintre cubiste méconnue Marie Vassilieff 1884-1957*. Catalog of exhibition at the Galerie Hupel, Paris, 1969.
Collection Didier-Cottoni. Marie Vassilieff. Catalog of auction at the Palais des Congrès, Versailles, 1970, 8 March.
Y. Moch: *Oeuvres postérieures au cubisme de Marie Vassilieff. Toiles des années 1920 et 1930*. Catalog of exhibition at the Galérie Hupel, 1971.
A. Shatskikh: "Russkaia akademiia v Parizhe" in *Sovetskoe iskusstvoznanie*, Moscow, 1986, No. 21, pp. 352-65.
M. Beckers: *Marie Vassilieff 1884-1957. Eine russische Künstlerin in Paris*. Catalog of exhibition at the Das Verborgene Museum, Berlin, 1995.

H34, pp. 192-94.
H51, passim.
K252, pp.334-39.
K284, passim.
P. Restany: *Les artistes russes hors frontière.*
Catalog of exhibition at the Musée du Montparnasse, Paris. 2010, passim.

Marie Vassilieff was one of the many Russian and Ukrainian ex-patriates living permanently in Paris before the Revolution. Others included Alexander Archipenko, Chana Orloff, and Léopold Survage, whose artistic careers were fashioned more by their Parisian encounters with Cubism than by their Slavic roots and who achieved their real recognition as members of the international, rather than the Russian, avant-garde. Their lives and work were tempered by a Gallic elegance and restraint foreign to the Russian Cubo-Futurists and Suprematists, and Vassilieff conforms to this context, for she owed little to the radical cultural innovations in Moscow and St. Petersburg in the 1910s.

Still, Vassilieff was not entirely isolated from developments in Russia and the many artists who visited her Académie Libre and Académie Vassilieff informed her of the new movements and individuals back home. In particular, during the First World War she organized a canteen, where, as Ilya Ehrenburg recalled "artists would congregate... to declaim their poetry, to prognosticate events or just to shout out."[852] In any case, from time to time Vassilieff made brief visits to Russia — in 1914 and, in spite of the War, in 1915.[853] This would explain her contribution of six Cubist works to the "0.10" exhibition in Petrograd in December, 1915 – January, 1916, and of eleven Cubist works to the "Store" in Moscow in March, 1916, a fact that would indicate her acquaintance with both Kazimir Malevich and Tatlin, the driving forces behind these exhibitions. The occasion for her participation in such radical enterprises is not clear, although her acquaintance with Liubov Popova and Nadezhda Udaltsova in Paris in 1912-13 must have facilitated the alliance, the more so since both Popova's and Udaltsova's contributions to the two exhibitions were also Cubist rather than Suprematist. One critic even mentioned that Vassilieff's *Spanish Landscape* at "0.10" had set the record in creative novelty — "a white wooden board... lying on the window sill."[854]

The exact chronology of Vassilieff's evolution is difficult to establish, although evidence, including observations by André Salmon, suggests that by 1909 she was already the adept of a "violent and lyrical Cubism."[855] By then, the year she founded her Académie, she counted Braque and Picasso among her personal friends and had mastered the principles of Cubism — division of the object into particular elements, reduction to intersecting planes, difraction of light — as is demonstrated by the "voluptuous science"[856] of her portaits and landscapes. Waldemar George once observed of Vassilieff that "j'ai rarement vu quelqu'un présenter un tel contraste entre ses attitudes et sa réalité intérieure,"[857] and it

was this more subjective quirk of character that in the 1920s and 1930s expressed itself in a style informed by Surrealism and the metaphysical school. An accomplished artist of many media and styles, Vassilieff is also remembered for her humanitarian aid to indigent artists in Paris during the First World War and the early 1920s.[858]

1116 [R370].
Poster for the **Deuxième Bal des Artistes,** *Paris, 23 May,* 1924.
Chromolithograph.
Signed in the plate lower right: "Marie Vassilieff" and monogrammed in lower left. 48½ x 33 in., 123 x 84 cm.
Other inscriptions (as part of the design): "2me Bal de L'A.A.A.A., Attractions de Cortèges Travesti"; on the personage: "Peintres, Sculpteurs, Graveurs, Décorateurs"; in lower half, as part of the design: "Aide Amicale Aux Artistes; Bullier, 23 mai 1924"; lower margin contains details as to where tickets can be purchased for the Ball; lower left margin, perpendicularly: "Risacher et Cie, 161 Rue Montmartre, Paris" [= the name of the printer].
Provenance: *Posters*, New York: Swann Galleries auction, 6 August, 1992, Lot 282 (reproduced)
Reproduced in color in A34, p. 449; F107, p. 139; and in black and white in M93; R15; *Marie Vassilieff 1884-1957. Eine russische Künstlerin in Paris,* p. 64.

Note: The *Deuxième Bal des Artistes,* also known as the *Bal de Cortèges Travesti,* was organized for the benefit of artists at the Salle Bullier, Paris, on 23 May, 1924. It was one of several such philanthropic balls held in Paris in the early 1920s, involving a number of important Russian artists such as Natalia Goncharova and Mikhail Larionov

1116

(see Nos. 564-66b [R432-34], 725-26 [R616-17]). The writer Nina Berberova has left the following memoir regarding these boisterous events:

Opposite the Closerie des Lilas in the early 1920s, near the Luxembourg Gardens, the huge Bal Bullier stood, a wooden barracks in which Paris artists held their charity balls. Some of the Russian artists had been granted a long life — for example, Mikhail Larionov, who had lived in Paris long before World War I, together with his wife, Natalia Goncharova (he died in 1964). Soutine and Bakst died comparatively young. On the day of the ball in Bullier — in the summer — half-naked artists, made up as savages, Indians, or African Negroes, walked around Montparnasse, from La Rotonde to La Coupole, faces daubed in all colours of the rainbow, with their models, young and pretty, painted, hardly covered by bits of material. Here you could see everyone: the calm patrician Derain and Zadkine and Pevsner and Braque. All would end in a noisy and orgiastic fête at someone's studio; and once it was a nocturnal gathering at Kostya Tereshkovich's, then still a bachelor, to which he invited [the émigré writers] Bunin, Zaitsev, and Aldanov. Aldanov was what is called "shocked" by everything he saw, and left quite early. Bunin was at first overwhelmed by the spectacle, but then not without relish joined the bacchanalia; Zaitsev sat and drank and looked around a little, and finally zealously joined: all this was very familair to him from his youth.

At dawn, everyone had a faded look, dishevelled and somewhat obscene. All went home along empty streets, where cesspool cleaners' barrels rumbled and farmers on high carts took cabbages and carrots to the central market.[859]

852 Ilya Ehrenburg. Quoted in H30, p. 191.
853 The "Eléments Biographiques" included in the exhibition catalog *Oeuvres postérieures au cubisme de Marie Vassilieff. Toiles des années 1920 et 1930* held at the Galerie Hupel, Paris, in 1971 (unpaginated) mentions that Vassilieff traveled in Scandinavia, Rumania, Poland, and Russia between 1909 and 1914. The biographical entry for Vassilieff in K65, p. 30, however, mentions that she was in Russia in 1915.
854 Anon.: "Po vystavkam" in *Petrogradskie vedomosti,* P, 1915, 22 December. Reproduced in H. Berninger and J.-A. Cartier: *Pougny,* Tübingen: Wasmuth, 1972, p. 57.
855 Ph. Hupel: "Marie Vassilieff vue par André Salmon" in *Un peintre cubiste méconnu,* unpaginated.
856 Statement by Guillaume Apollinaire in 1910. Quoted in K65, p. 30.
857 Hupel, op. cit.
858 For example, Vassilieff opened a cafeteria-cum-bar at her Académie in 1915 for the artists of Montparnasse, which today is the Musée Montparnasse. See E.R.: "Cantine. Kabachok" in *Frantsuzskie novosti,* Paris, 1998, July-August, No. 10-11.
859 N. Berberova: *The Italics Are Mine,* London: Chatto and Windus, 1991, pp. 290-91. Larionov did not settle in Paris before the First World War. Vassilieff's frescoes for the interior of La Coupole are still extant.

VEREISKY, Georgii Semeonovich

Born 18 (30) July, 1886, Proskurov (now Khmelnitskii), Ukraine; died 19 December, 1962, Leningrad, Russia.

1895 and 1900-04 took lessons from Egor Shreider in Kharkov; 1904-12 intermittently attended Law School at St. Petersburg University; 1904 onwards contributed regularly to exhibitions; 1905 arrested for participating in the revolutionary movement; 1905-07 lived in Germany and Italy; 1912-15 studied under Evgenii Lanceray in St. Petersburg; 1912-17 worked as an illustrator for various magazines, including *Teatr i iskusstvo* [Theater and Art] and *Golos zhizni* [Voice of Life]; began to gain recognition as a sketcher and lithographer, especially of portraits; 1916-18 mobilized; 1918 taught at SCITD; 1918-30 Chief Curator of engravings at the Hermitage; 1920 drew portraits of Lenin at the Third Communist International; 1921-23 taught at Vkhutemas in Petrograd; 1922 produced his folio of lithograph portraits of contemporary artists; 1924 one-man exhibition in Kazan; 1920s-30s made portraits of literary figures, including Samuil Marshak and Boris Pilniak, culminating in a second folio of lithographs (1928); early 1940s produced anti-Fascist posters; thereafter continued to draw and design.

1117

Bibliography
G. Chernova: *G.S. Vereisky*, M: Iskusstvo, 1965.
D. Shmarinov and L. Bogino: *G.S. Vereisky. Akvareli i risunki,* M: Sovetskii khudozhnik, 1973. A14, Vol. 2, pp. 236-37.
L. Voronikhina: *Georgii Semeonovich Vereisky,* L: Khudozhnik RSFSR, 1987.
N. Ilina, introd.: *Orest Vereisky, Vstrechi v puti,* M: Iskusstvo, 1988.
S. Ros, ed.: *Boris Suris,* SP: Iskusstvo Rossii, 2003, pp. 43-112.

1118   *A. Ostroumova - Lebedeva.*

1119   *B. Kustodiev*

Vereisky is remembered above all for his sketches and lithographic portraits of contemporaries, of which his two deluxe albums (see below) are superb examples. Neither radical, nor ultra-conservative, Vereisky used the pencil and pen with a high degree of technical proficiency — indeed, with a virtuosity which also allowed him a freedom and flexibility in his endeavor to record not only the outward likeness of the sitter, but also the psychological landscape. Vereisky was one of many distinguished artists in St. Petersburg who maintained the strong traditions of *blanc et noir* and who continued to use the drawing and the engraving as vehicles of documentary registration. That is why he enjoyed a special affinity with the *miriskusniki* [World of Art artists] who also did much to raise the standards of the Russian graphic arts after their decline in the later 19th century. Benois, Lanceray, Somov, and Yaremich, in particular, all responded favorably to Vereisky's portraits.

The following black and white lithographs, **Nos. 1117-29 [NIRE]**, are from Vereisky's album of ten portraits plus list of contents entitled *Portrety russkikh khudozhnikov. Avtolitografii Vereiskogo. 10 portretov* [Portraits of Russian Artists. Autolithographs by Vereisky. 10 Portraits] published by the Committee for the Popularization of Art Editions, St. Petersburg [sic], in 1922. Each is initialed and dated in the plate and measures 18 x 14 in., 45.5 x 35.5 cm. Their provenance is Berta Popoff, Paris, October, 1981.

1117 [NIRE].
Portrait of Petr Neradovsky, 1921.
Inscription: sitter's signature under portrait in the plate.
Petr Nikolaevich Neradovsky (1875-1955) was an artist, critic, and museum worker.

1118 [NIRE].
Portrait of Anna Ostroumova-Lebedeva, 1921.
Inscription: sitter's signature under portrait in the plate.
Anna Petrovna Ostroumova-Lebedeva (1871-1955) was an artist, noted especially for her engravings.

1119 [R371].
Portrait of Boris Kustodiev, 1921.
Inscription: sitter's signature under portrait in the plate.

1120 [NIRE].
Studio of Georgii Vereisky, 1922.

1121 [NIRE].
Portrait of Alexandre Benois, 1922.
Inscription: in the plate in Russian: "Contents."

1122 [NIRE].
Portrait of Alexandre Benois, 1922.
Inscription: sitter's signature under portrait in the plate.

1123 [NIRE].
Portrait of Osip Braz, 1922.
Inscription: sitter's signature under portrait in the plate.
Osip Emmanuelovich Braz (1873-1936) was an artist, noted especially for his portraits.

1124 [NIRE].
Portrait of Mstislav Dobujinsky, 1922.
Inscription: sitter's signature under portrait in the plate.

1125 [NIRE].
Portrait of Dmitrii Mitrokhin, 1922.
Inscription: sitter's signature under portrait in the plate.
Dmitrii Isidorovich Mitrokhin (1883-1973) was an artist, noted especially for his drawings and lithographs.

1120

1124　　　　　*M Добужинский*

1121

1125　　　　　*Д. Митрохин*

1122　　　　*Александр Бенуа*

1123　　　　*I. Браз*

1126

1128

1130

1126 [NIRE].
Portrait of Zinaida Serebriakova, 1922.
Inscription: sitter's signature under portrait in the plate.

1127 [NIRE].
Portrait of Konstantin Somov, 1922.
Inscription: sitter's signature under portrait in the plate.

1128 [NIRE].
Portrait of Stepan Yaremich, 1922.
Inscription: sitter's signature under portrait in the plate.
Stepan Petrovich Yaremich (1969-1939) was an artist and critic.

1129 [NIRE].
Portrait of Konstantin Somov, 1922.

1130 [R372].
Portrait of Alexander Golovin, 1925.
Lithograph in black on white.
Signed and dated lower left in the plate in Russian: "G. Vereisky 1925."
24⅝ x 16⅞ in., 62.5 x 43 cm.
Other inscription: lower right in black ink in Golovin's hand in Russian: "To dear and much loved Ripsime Karpovna Tamantseva with best wishes from A. Golovin, 23 January, 1928." At this time Ripsime Karpovna Tamantseva (Tamantsova, 1889-1958) was Konstantin Stanislavsky's personal secretary and director's aide at the Moscow Art Theater.

Provenance: Berta Popoff, Paris, October, 1981.
Reproduced in A34, p. 446.

1131 [R373].
Portrait of Alexandre Benois, 1926.
Lithograph in black and white.
Signed and dated lower left in the plate in Russian: "G. Vereisky 1926."
17⅞ x 14 in., 45.5 x 35.5 cm.
Other inscription: sitter's signature under portrait in the plate.
Provenance: Anna Tcherkessoff, Paris, May, 1979. Now in a private collection.

1127

1129

1131

1132

1132 [R374]
Portrait of Sergei Prokofiev Playing the Piano, **1927.**
Lithograph in black and white.
Initialed and dated center right in the stone in Russian: "GV 1927", and signed lower right in Russian: "G. Vereisky."
18¾ x 12¼ in., 47.5 x 31 cm.
Other inscriptions: signed and dated lower margin by Prokofiev after a musical extract (i.e. the beginning of his First Violin Concerto): "S. Prokofiev 1927."
Provenance: Berta Popoff, Paris, October, 1981. Now in a private collection.
The original sketch, in the RM, is reproduced in Voronikhina, *Vereisky,* plate 10; and in K91, p. 290. It is also the frontispiece to B. Asafiev et al.: *Liubov k trem apelsinam,* L: Gosudarstvennyi akademicheskii teatr opery i baleta, 1934. For another reproduction and contextual commentary see M. Nestieva: *S.S. Prokofiev,* M: Muzyka, 1981, p. 80.

Note: Vereisky was especially active as a drawer of portraits, making many renderings of contemporary artists and literati. In 1928 the Committee for the Popularization of Art Editions, the Soviet continuation of the Society of St. Eugenia (see No. 74 [R68]), issued Vereisky's second deluxe folio of portraits, i.e. *Chetrynadtsat portretov. Avtolitografii G.S. Vereiskogo* [Fourteen Portraits. Autolithographs by G.S. Vereisky], in an edition of one hundred numbered copies. No. 1132 [R374] is one of the portraits therein.

VESNIN, Alexander Alexandrovich

Born 16 (28) May, 1883, Yurievets, near Nizhnii Novgorod, Volga Region, Russia; died 7 November, 1959, Moscow, Russia.

The youngest of the three Vesnin brothers (the others being Leonid and Viktor), who worked closely on many architectural and design projects during the 1910s, 1920s, and early 1930s. 1901-12 after graduating from the Moscow Practical Academy, Alexander Vesnin entered the Institute of Civil Engineers, St. Petersburg; 1912-14 worked in Vladimir Tatlin's Tower studio in Moscow, establishing contact with Liubov Popova, Nadezhda Udaltsova, et al.; 1918 worked on agit-decorations for the streets and squares of Petrograd and Moscow; 1920 designed sets and costumes for Paul Claudel's *L'Annonce faite à Marie* produced by Alexander Tairov at the Chamber Theater, Moscow; thereafter active in a number of stage productions, including his most experimental, G.K. Chesterton's *The Man Who Was Thursday,* produced by Tairov in 1923; joined Inkhuk; 1921 contributed to the exhibition "5 x 5 -25"; 1923-25 close to *Lef*; keen supporter of Constructivism; 1923-33 worked with his brothers on various industrial designs and architectural projects, such as the Lenin Library, Moscow, the Palace of Soviets, Moscow, communal housing for Stalingrad, etc.; co-founded OSA (Association of Contemporary Architects); late 1930s-40s with the death of Leonid in 1933 and the censure of Constructivism, Alexander Vesnin reduced his architectural and artistic activities considerably.

Bibliography
A. Chiniakov: *Bratia Vesniny,* M: Stroiizdat, 1970.
K. Usacheva: "Teatralnye raboty A.A. Vesnina" in I. Kriukova et al., eds.: *Voprosy sovetskogo izobrazitelnogo iskusstva i arkhitektury.* M: Sovetskii khudozhnik, 1975, pp. 304-31.
A. Lupandina: "Khudozhniki Kamernogo teatra" in *Tvorchestvo,* M, 1980, No. 19, pp. 14-18.
E. Vasiutinskaia et al., comps.: *Katalog-putevoditel po fondam muzeia. Vesniny,* M: TsNTI, 1981 (catalog of the Vesnin holdings at the Shchusev Museum, Moscow).
S. Khan-Magomedov: *Aleksandr Vesnin,* M: Znanie, 1983.
S. Khan-Magomedov: "A. Vesnin — khudozhnik teatra" in *Dekorativnoe iskusstvo,* M, 1983, No. 6, pp. 37-40.
A. Manina: *Arkhitektory bratia Vesniny.* Catalog of exhibition at the Shchusev Museum, M, 1983.
S. Chan-Magomedov: *Alexandre Vesnine.* Catalog of exhibition at the Institut Français d'Architecture, Paris, December, 1984.
K. Rudnitsky: "Khudozhniki teatra Tairova" in

Dekorativnoe iskusstvo, M, 1985, No. 10, pp. 30-35.
S. Khan-Magomedov: *Alexander Vesnin,* New York: Rizzoli, 1986.
M. Petrova: "Teatralnyi khudozhnik Aleksandr Vesnin" in *Muzei,* M, 1987, No. 7, pp. 101-11.
S. Khan-Magomedov: *Aleksandr Vesnin i konstruktivizm,* M: Arkhitektura "S", 2010.

Alexander Vesnin is remembered as a Constructivist architect rather than as a stage designer. However, he made a vital contribution to the development of Soviet stage design, especially through his sets and costumes for five major spectacles for the Chamber Theater, Moscow — *L'Annonce faite à Marie, Adalmina's Pearl, Romeo and Juliet* (not realized), *The Man Who Was Thursday,* and *Phèdre,* the latter being the most famous. Vesnin was a prolific theater artist: the Shchusev Museum in Moscow, for example, contains over five hundred of his costumes and décors.
    Vesnin made his debut as a stage designer in 1919-20 when he collaborated on several productions for the Maly Theater, Moscow, including *The Marriage of Figaro,* Nikolai Gogol's *The Inspector General* and Anatolii Lunacharsky's *Olivor Cromwell.* In 1920 Vesnin also worked with Popova and Vsevolod Meierkhold on a "mass action" installation to celebrate the Second Congress of the III Communist International (not realized) and in 1921 with the composer Ilia Sats on *Adalmina's Pearl* at the Children's Theater, Moscow, run by Sats's daughter Natalia. However, the most important period of Vesnin's theatrical career began when Alexander Tairov commissioned him to design the productions of *L'Annonce faite à Marie* (usually translated as *The Tidings Brought to Mary*) in 1920 and *Romeo and Juliet* in 1921. True, Vesnin's costume designs for these pieces were informed by the ideas of Alexandra Exter and Popova, indeed his set for *Phèdre* is very reminiscent of Exter's for Tairov's production of *Salomé* in 1917. In turn, and again like Exter, Vesnin also derived inspiration from the simple but emotive forms for his scenic constructions, levels, and inclines from Adolphe Appia's earlier formulations of scenic space:

> Stairs by their straight lines and breaks maintain the necessary contrast between the curves of the body and the sinuous lines of its evolution, their practical use offering at the same time distinct facilities of expression.[860]

Romeo and Juliet: *tragedy in five acts by William Shakespeare. Commissioned by Alexander Tairov from Alexander Vesnin in 1921, but not produced. For reasons unknown, Vesnin's designs were scrapped at the last moment and Alexandra Exter was commissioned to redesign the entire production.*

See No. 844 [R723] for plot summary.

1133 [234; NIRE].
Costume Design for Romeo, 1922.
Gouache.
Signed and dated lower right in Russian in ink: "A. Vesnin 22."
14⅛ x 9¼ in., 36 x 23.5 cm.
Provenance: *The Russian Sale,* London: Sotheby's, 31 May, 2006, Lot 139 (reproduced).
A variant is reproduced in color in Khan-Magomedov, *Alexander Vesnin,* p. 59, and Khan-Magomedov, *Aleksandr Vesnin i konstruktivizm,* p. 120, where the design is dated 1921.

L'Annonce Faite à Marie: *play by Paul Claudel with music by Henri Forter. Produced by Alexander Tairov at the Chamber Theater, Moscow, on 16 November, 1920, with designs by Alexander Vesnin.*

The mason Pierre de Craon, who is helping to build the Cathedral of St. Justitia at Rheims, is attracted to the beautiful but unwilling Violaine. One year later he is struck down with leprosy, which he interprets as divine punishment. Violaine, betrothed to Jacques, kisses Pierre adieu, contracts leprosy, and is banished to the forest. Her jealous sister Mara, who witnessed Violaine's gesture, marries Jacques, but their child is still-born, whereupon she implores the saintly Violaine, now blind, to revive the infant. Violaine dies and Pierre scatters violets upon her virginal body. As they lament her passing, Mara and Pierre ponder upon their moral imperfections.

1134 [R375].
Costume Design for Mara, 1923.
Gouache.
Signed on the reverse in ink in Russian: "A. Vesnin."
26¾ x 17½ in., 68 x 44.5 cm.
Provenance: Alexander Shlepianov, Moscow, 1990, who in turn had acquired it from Natalia Vesnina.
Reproduced in color in I77, p. 89; and in black and white in I77, p. 137. The original design is reproduced in color in F66, fig. 80; and in black and white in Khan-Magomedov, *Aleksandr Vesnin,* fig. 2; and in Khan-Magomedov, *Aleksandr Vesnin i konstruktivizm,* p. 120; also see I73, p. 162.

1135 [R376].
Costume Design for Violaine, 1923.
Gouache.
Signed on the reverse in ink in Russian "A. Vesnin."
26 x 18¼ in., 66 x 46.5 cm.
Provenance: Alexander Shlepianov, Moscow, 1990, who in turn had acquired it from Natalia Vesnina.

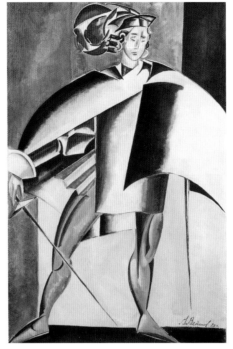

1133

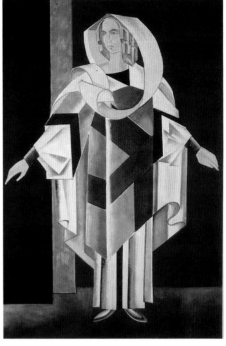

1134

Reproduced in color in I77, p. 89; and in black and white in I77, p. 137. The original design is reproduced in color in Khan-Magomedov, *Aleksandr Vesnin i konstruktivizm,* p. 111. A photograph of an actress wearing a similar costume is reproduced in Khan-Magomedov, *Alexander Vesnin* (1986), p. 57.

1136 [235; R376a].
Costume Design for Jacques, 1921.
Gouache.
Signed and dated lower right corner in black ink in Russian: "A. Vesnin 21."
15⅜ x 9⅝ in., 39 x 24.5 cm.

1135

Provenance: Alexander Shlepianov, Moscow, 1990, who, in turn, had acquired it from Natalia Vesnina.
Reproduced in color in M78. For reproductions of variants see Khan-Magomedov, *Aleksandr Vesnin i konstruktivizm,* p. 108. A photograph of the actor wearing the costume is reproduced in Khan-Magomedov, *Alexander Vesnin* (1986), p. 57.

Note: Nos. 1134-35 [R375-76] are allegedly copies made by Natalia Vesnina. See Note to No. 1141 [R381].

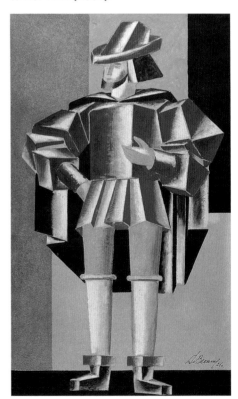

1136

1137

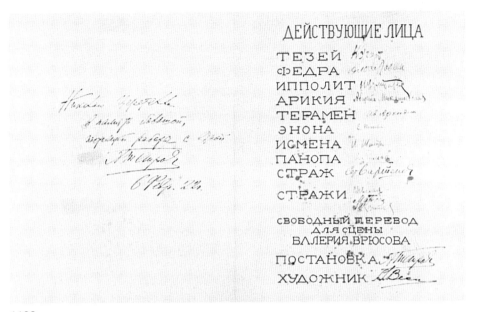

1138

Phèdre: tragedy in five acts by Jean Racine, translated into Russian by Valerii Briusov. Produced by Alexander Tairov for the Chamber Theater, Moscow, on 8 February, 1922, and presented on tour in Berlin (Deutsches Theater) and Paris (Théâtre des Champs-Élysées) in February and March, 1923, with designs by Alexander Vesnin and renderings for program publicity by Konstantin Medunetsky and Georgii and Vladimir Stenberg.

See No. 57 [R53] for plot summary.

1137 [R377].
Program Cover Showing Designs for Phèdre and Thésée, 1922.
Gouache, gold and silver paint, black ink, and pencil.
Signed on the second page in ink in Russian: "A. Vesnin."
18¾ x 12½ in., 47.5 x 31.8 cm.
The program consists of a sheet folded in half, thus providing four open sides (see No. 1138 [R377a] for a description of the reverse).
Provenance: Mikhail Grobman, London, November 21, 1981.
Reproduced in color in B115, plate 128; I77, p. 78; I81, p. 84; N188, p. 10; and in black and white in the almanac *Leviafan,* Jerusalem, 1979, April, p. 8; I51, No. 261; I77, p. 137; N183, p. 49. The BTM has a very similar design (reproduced in color in D72, plate 26), and a version of the cover adjusted by Vesnin to a design for a curtain is in Usacheva, "Teatralnye raboty," p. 327. A reproduction of Phèdre in the same pose as here appears in *Le Figaro,* Paris, 1984, 20 December, p. 35.

1138 [R377a].
Reverse of Program Cover, 1922.
See No. 1137 [R377].
The left-hand side of the sheet carries a dedication in blue ink in Russian from Alexander Tairov reading: "To Nikolai Tsereteli in memory of a great and genuine project. With faith, A.

Tairov, 6 February, 1922." The right-hand side of the sheet carries a list of the parts in the production compiled by Vesnin with signatures of the performers. It reads as follows:

DRAMATIS PERSONAE
THESEE, K.V. Eggert
PHEDRE, Alisa G. Koonen
HIPPOLYTEN, Tsereteli
ARICIE, Avgusta Miklashevskaia
THERAMENE, Arkadin
OENONE, Pozoeva
ISMENE, Shtein
PANOPE, Geiman
GUARD, Matissen
GUARDS, Voronkov, Matissen (?), and [illegible]
FREE TRANSLATION FOR THE STAGE BY VALERII BRIUSOV

PRODUCTION, A. Tairov
DESIGNER, A. Vesnin

Another program page like this, carrying the signatures of all the principal participants in the *Phèdre* production is reproduced in C35, p. 442.

1139 [R378].
Stage Design, ca. 1922.
Gouache.
6¾ x 8½ in., 17 x 21.5 cm.
Provenance: Simon Lissim, Dobbs Ferry, New York, September, 1969.
Reproduced in I20, No. 103; I32, No. 122; I51, No. 262; I77, p. 137. A variant is reproduced in color in Lupandina, "Khudozhniki Kamernogo teatra," p. 16; another variant is reproduced in color in G17, No. 73; also see G33, No. 79;

1139

1140

1141

a three-dimensional maquette based on the design and dated 1921 is reproduced in I5, unpaginated; as well as in I1, p. 14; a similar maquette is reproduced in C7, No. 202; in C55, p. 109; and in I61, p. 333; also see Usacheva, "Teatralnye raboty," p. 327. For photographs of the actual staging see C35, between pp. 448 and 449; and G14, Nos. 83, 84.

1140 [R380].
Costume Design for Thesée, 1923.
Gouache.
Signed on the reverse in ink in Russian: "A. Vesnin."
26⅝ x 17⅛ in., 67.5 x 43.5 cm.
Provenance: Alexander Shlepianov, Moscow, 1990, who in turn had acquired it from Natalia Vesnina.
Reproduced in I77, p. 138. A similar design with different color schemes is reproduced in color in Khan-Magomedov (1987), p. 51.

1141 [R381].
Costume Design for Théramène, 1923.
Gouache.
Signed on the reverse in ink in Russian: "A. Vesnin."
27⅛ x 16⅞ in., 69 x 43 cm.
Provenance: Alexander Shlepianov, Moscow, 1990, who in turn had acquired it from Natalia Vesnina.
Reproduced in color in I77, p. 89; and in black and white in A34, p. 451; I77, p. 138. A

similar design with color and structural variations is reproduced in color in Khan-Magomedov, *Alexander Vesnin* (1986), p. 51.

Note: In February, 1923, the Chamber Theater went on its tour, transporting the original costumes and decorations for its international repertoire (see I51, p. 218). This occurred just as the exhibition "Moscow Stage Design 1918-23" was opening in Moscow. Allegedly, Victor Vesnin's first wife, Natalia Vesnina, made copies from her brother-in-law's sketches for the exhibition. This was done with Vesnin's permission — hence his signature on the reverse of Nos. 1134-35 [R375-76] and 1140-41 [R380-81].

A. Vesnin as contributor:
1142 [R382].
Designer unknown: Poster Advertising a Public Debate on the Chamber Theater's Production of Phèdre Together with Other Events, 1922.
Lithograph in black and white.
24¾ x 11 in., 63 x 28 cm.
Inscriptions (as part of the design) provide details on the *Phèdre* debate scheduled for 8 February, 1922, at the Press House, Moscow; introduction by Petr Kogan, main lecture by Valerii Briusov, and contributions by Ivan Aksenov, Boris Ferdinandov, Nikolai Foregger, Anatolii Lunacharsky, Vsevolod Meierkhold, Tairov, et al. The poster also lists other upcoming productions at the

Press House by Foregger, Sergei Gorodetsky, and Vladimir Maiakovsky.
Provenance: Viktor Kholodkov, Moscow, 1984.

Note: Alexander Tairov began to prepare his production of *Phèdre* in October, 1921, and, already familiar with Vesnin's experimental designs for other projects, invited him to collaborate. Vesnin made at least three maquettes for the set of *Phèdre*, which, as Tairov asserted, not only served

> as an apparatus for the acting, but in turn demonstrates a tendency… to become a figure of objective reality, to become an environment in constant interconnection with the figures of the actors."[861]

Tairov liked Vesnin's central set because it was like a boat deck "at the moment of imminent shipwreck, of catastrophe."[862] Vesnin applied similar formal ideas to his elaborate construction for Tairov's production of *The Man Who Was Thursday* (1923), although this was little more than a paraphrase of Liubov Popova's set for *The Magnanimous Cuckold* of 1922.

The restrained hieratic form of Racine's tragedy with its reliance on the equal functioning of all artistic components, appealed to Tairov and Vesnin and they used their production as a vehicle for integrating an elegant Classicism with a calculated

1142

Constructivism. Alisa Koonen, who took the part of Phèdre, remembered that

> visually, Phèdre gave the impression of severe beauty and majesty. The arrangement of the stage was remarkably successful. It afforded the director much scope and was very convenient for the actors. The costumes looked great. They were simple, severe."[863]

Although critics were not unanimous in their appreciation of Tairov's production of *Phèdre,* most felt that Vesnin's costumes, rather than his sets, were the more original feature of the decoration. As Abram Efros remarked:

> Certain basic characteristics of the Hellenic dress were expressed by the plasticity of new forms: helmet, armor, cloak, shield, spear, sword, tunic, women's headgear. They were all reduced to two or three planes, volumes, curves, colors... New expression had been given to the laws of the Classics.[864]

860 Adolphe Appia. Quoted in G42, p. 185, where original source is not given.
861 C35, p. 207.
862 C33, p. 441.
863 F43, p. 273.
864 G17, p. XXXIV.

VIALOV, Konstantin Alexandrovich

Born 6 (19) April, 1900, Moscow, Russia; died 12 July, 1976, Moscow, Russia.

1914-17 attended CSIAI; specialized in textile design; 1917-23 attended Svomas-Vkhutemas, studying under Aristarkh Lentulov and Alexei Morgunov; 1922-25 directed the Visual Arts Studio of the Teenagers' Club attached to the NKP Test Station; developed his theory of "montage of meaning," using an often stenographic, poster-like style; 1924 designed a production of *Stenka Razin;* co-founded OST, contributing to its exhibitions until 1928; 1925 contributed to the "Exposition Internationale des Arts Décoratifs" in Paris; during the 1920s designed many books and posters; 1932 joined the Moscow Union of Soviet Artists; 1932-41 took part in numerous naval and other expeditions to Kronstadt, Leningrad, Arkhangelsk, Sebastopol, and other places; 1930s painted industrial scenes; 1937-40 worked on designs for the "All-Union Agricultural Exhibition" in Moscow; 1941-42 designed anti-Fascist posters; thereafter continued to paint and design; 1940s onwards continued to paint and exhibit, giving increasing attention to landscape.

Bibliography
V. Lobanov: *Konstantin Vialov,* M: Sovetskii khudozhnik, 1968.
V. Kostin: *OST,* L: Khudozhnik RSFSR, 1976, passim.
V. Leshin: *Konstantin Vialov.* Catalog of exhibition organized by the Union of Artists of the USSR, M, 1981.
J. Bowlt: "The Society of Easel Artists (OST)" in *Russian History,* Tempe, 1982, Vol. 9, Parts 2-3 pp. 203-26.
T. Durfee: *A Glimpse of Tomorrow.* Catalog of exhibition at the Institute of Modern Russian Culture, Los Angeles, 1992.
K281, pp. 118-25.

Many artists of the second generation of the Russian avant-garde who matured just after the Revolution derived their creative strength from either Kazimir Malevich or Vladimir Tatlin. For those who followed Tatlin, the relief — the three-dimensional assemblage of modern materials — formed an exciting departure-point for further constructive experiments. Lev Bruni, Vladimir Lebedev, Konstantin Medunetsky, Georgii and Vladimir Stenberg, and Vialov were among those disciples who, albeit briefly, investigated the possibilities of the relief and the three-dimensional construction, although some, including Lebedev and Vialov, soon returned to figurative painting and sculpture. Interested in the new set and costume resolutions elaborated by Liubov Popova and Alexander Vesnin, in particular, Vialov also explored space and volume as esthetic agents through his scenic designs as, for example, in the 1924 *Stenka Razin.* Even so, Vialov's involvement in the theater was sporadic and his real vocation was studio painting, for he and his colleagues in OST

defended visual art and saw in it the intrinsically valuable elements of the painterly craft. They insisted that the painting as such would not die and would, in fact, continue to develop.[865]

The Camorra of Seville: *play projected by Evgenii Prosvetov at the Theater of the Revolutionary Military Soviet, Moscow, in 1923, with designs by Konstantin Vialov.*
The play is set in Medieval Seville, seat of the criminal society that would become the Camorra.

1143 [236; R386].
Costume Design for an Abbot Wearing Glasses, ca. 1923.
Watercolor and black ink over pencil.
10⅜ x 5¾ in, 26.4 x 14.5 cm.
The design carries the identification "Abbot" in Russian letters on the dress and between the feet.
Provenance: Boris Kerdimun, Rego Park, New York, January, 1984.
Reproduced in color in I77, p. 72; and in black and white in I77, p. 128; M26; P62. A version of this design is in the BTM.

Note: In his book on OST Vladimir Kostin referred to a presentation of *The Camorra of Seville* in a "studio from which would later grow the Central Theater of the Red Army,"[866] but the standard reference books on the history of Soviet theater make no mention of this production or of a play of this name, from which it may be assumed that the work was projected, but not produced.[867] This particular design is close in style to Vialov's costumes for *Stenka Razin* of 1924.[868]

1143

Stenka Razin: play by Vasilii Kamensky with music by Nikolai Popov. Produced by Valerii Bebutov at the Theater of Revolution, Moscow, on 6 February, 1924, with designs by Konstantin Vialov.

Stenka Razin, leader of a pirate host, routs government troops in Central Russia. Attracting increasing popular support, he equips a fleet and sails the Caspian Sea as far as Persia. He then sails up the River Volga as far as Astrakhan, pirating and plundering, killing nobles, and looting churches and stores. After these bloody encounters he is caught by the Ataman of the Don Cossacks and is sent to Moscow, where he is executed.

1144

1144 [R387].
Stage Design for Razin's Boat, ca. 1924.
Black ink and watercolor.
Signed lower right in Russian: "K. Vialov."
7⅛ x 6⅛ in., 18 x 15.5 cm.
The reverse carries an unfinished watercolor.
Provenance: Boris Kerdimun, Rego Park, New York, January, 1984.
Reproduced in A34, p. 460. A preliminary sketch for this design is reproduced in B34, No. 1136. A similar maquette (undated) is reproduced in C7, No. 305. Another version, in the BTM, carries the words in Russian "Theatrical presentation, Cinema, 1922"; yet another version, carrying the words "'Theatrical motif," is reproduced in K281, p. 121.

1145 [237; R388].
Stage Design for Razin's Boat with Mast in the Center, ca. 1924.
Watercolor, black ink, and pencil.
Signed lower right in Russian: "Art[ist] K. Vialov."
16⅜ x 13 in., 41.5 x 33 cm.
The diagonal caption means: "Up to the prow, gang" or "Scum, to the bow!"(see No. 1147 [R389]). The reverse carries a sketch by Elena Melnikova (see No. 1146 [NIRE]).

1145

Provenance: Boris Kerdimun, Rego Park, New York, January, 1984.
Reproduced in color in B115, plate 168; F107, p. 286; I77, p. 128; M78; and in black and white in I60, p. 37; M26; M76; R16; S61. A similar design is reproduced in B34, No. 1137, and I73, p. 197.

1146 [NIRE].
Elena Melnikova: untitled drawing, ca. 1924.
Pencil.
Signed in Russian: "E.K. Melnikova."
16⅜ x 13 in., 41.5 x 33 cm.
This is the verso of No. 1145 [R388].
Elena Konstantinovna Melnikova (1902-80), the wife of Konstantin Vialov, was also a member of OST.

1147 [238; R389].
Stage Design for the Upper Deck of Razin's Boat, ca. 1924.
Watercolor, black ink, and wash.
Signed lower right in Russian: "Art[ist] K. Vialov."
16⅜ x 13 in., 41.5 x 33 cm.
The Russian caption at top right reads: "Scum, to the bow!"[869]
Provenance: Boris Kerdimun, Rego Park, New York, January, 1984.
Reproduced in color in B115, plate 169; M23, p. 55; and in black and white in I60, p. 36; I77, p. 128; P55. A similar maquette is reproduced in B34, No. 1135; and I62, p. 78; yet another version, in the collection of the Theater-museum, Cologne, is reproduced in I62, p. 77.

1147

1146

Note: The theme of Stenka Razin was a popular one just after the Revolution, when this legendary insurgent was widely identified as a positive manifestation of the class struggle and revolutionary process in Tsarist Russia. Consequently, Razin was celebrated in art, literature, and the theater because "each of us is Stenka Razin." [870] Yet Kamensky's text left a lot to be desired and Yurii Annenkov even wondered how this gifted Cubo-Futurist poet could have written something so devoid of talent. [871] As far as the Bebutov production of Kamensky's play is concerned, Vialov tried consciously to apply the lessons he had learnt from his observations of the Projectionist Theater (see No. 1107 [R845]). He conceived the play as a "buffoonery," using "Cubist constructions, bright light effects, music, and dynamic elements," [872] and the surviving set and costume designs certainly demonstrate this. As Bebutov remarked, the company wished to avoid all references to the "*style russe*" and "cabaret falsification." [873]

1149

Vialov as contributor:
1149 [R391].
Designer unknown: *Poster Advertising "OST 2nd Exhibition of Paintings, Drawings and Sculpture"*, 1926.
Lithograph in black and white.
42⅞ x 28¼ in., 109 x 72 cm.

Inscriptions provide details of the exhibition that opened at the State Historical Museum, Moscow, on 3 May, 1926, with contributions by Alexander Deineka, Nikolai Denisovsky, Andrei Goncharov, Ivan Kudriashev, Alexander Labas, Sergei Luchishkin, Yurii Pimenov, Alexander Tyshler, Nisson Shifrin, David Shterenberg, Vialov, Petr Viliams, et al.
Provenance: Viktor Kholodkov, Moscow, 1984.
Reproduced in Kostin, *OST,* p. 47; and L69, Lot 134.

Vialov as contributor:
1150 [R392].
Designer unknown: *Poster Advertising "OST 3rd Exhibition of Paintings, Drawing and Sculpture"*, 1927.
Lithograph in red, black, and white.
28 x 42⅛ in., 71 x 107 cm.

Inscriptions provide details of the exhibition that opened in the Museum of Painterly Culture, Moscow, on 3 April, 1927, with contributions by Barshch, Nikolai Denisovsky, Andrei Goncharov, Alexander Labas, Sergei Luchishkin, Yurii Pimenov, Alexander Tyshler, Nisson Shifrin, David Shterenberg, Vialov, Petr Viliams, et al. It is possible that the designer of this poster was Alexander Osipovoch (Evseevich) Barshch (1897-1971).
Provenance: Viktor Kholodkov, Moscow, 1984.
Reproduced in M183, p. 7.

1148

Vialov as contributor:
1148 [R390].
Designer unknown: *Poster Advertising the "First Exhibition of OST (Society of Studio Artists)"*, 1925.
Lithograph in black and white.
37 x 24⅜ in., 94 x 62 cm.

Inscriptions (as part of the design) provide details of the exhibition that opened at the Museum of Painterly Culture, Moscow, on 26 April, 1925, with contributions by Barshch, Alexander Deineka, Andrei Goncharov, Ivan Kliun, Ivan Kudriashev, Sergei Luchishkin, Yurii Pimenov, Nisson Shifrin, David Shterenberg, Vialov, et al. It is possible that the designer of this poster was Alexander Osipovich (Evseevich) Barshch (1897-1971).
Provenance: Viktor Kholodkov, Moscow, 1984.
Reproduced in Kostin, *OST,* p. 35.

1150

1151

Vialov as contributor:

1151 [R393].

Designer unknown: *Poster Advertising the "4th Exhibition of Paintings, Drawings and Sculpture by OST,"* 1928.

Lithograph in red, black, and white.
28¾ x 42⅞ in., 73 x 109 cm.
Inscriptions (as part of the design) provide details of the exhibition that opened at the Museum of Painterly Culture, Moscow, on 22 April, 1928, with contributions by Yurii Annenkov, Nikolai Denisovsky, Andrei Goncharov, Ivan Kudriashev, Alexander Labas, Sergei Luchishkin, Yurii Pimenov, David Shterenberg, Nisson Shifrin, Vialov, Petr Viliams, et al. Provenance: Viktor Kholodkov, Moscow, 1984.

Note: OST (the Society of Studio Artists) arose as an untitled group after the "First Discussional Exhibition of Associations of Active Revolutionary Art" in late 1924 (see Nos. 790 [R666] and 1107 [R845]) and was established formally at the beginning of 1925. Founding members included Annenkov, Deineka, Pimenov, Shterenberg (chairman), Vialov, and Viliams, and its membership encompassed leading figures of the new Soviet art. OST had four exhibitions, all in Moscow (Deineka contributed only to the first two, leaving the group in 1927). Although OST supported studio painting and searched consciously for a figurative style that would be experimental while still drawing on contemporary themes, it did not reject the achievements of the old avant-garde; Kliun,

for instance, was invited to contribute to the first exhibition. Even so, OST questioned the validity of Constructivism and industrial design as the new "legitimate" proletarian art, and argued that "revolutionary contemporaneity and clarity of subject matter" were essential components of Socialist culture.[874]

865 T. Durfee: "Konstantin Aleksandrovich Vialov 1900-1976" in *A Glimpse of Tomorrow*, p. 4.
866 Kostin, *OST*, p. 73.
867 See, for example, C31, Vol. 2.
868 Some are reproduced in color in the exhibition catalog Leshik, *Konstantin Vialov*, unpaginated; also in I61, pp. 342-45.
869 The words, "Saryn na kichku" (lit. "scum to the bow") are a Volga criminal argot. According to tradition, the command "Saryn na kichku!" was issued by pirates on the River Volga to the boatmen of the boat that they were about to capture. The words became something of a catchphrase after the Revolution, thanks, in no small measure, to Kamensky's use of the idiom in his *Stenka Razin*. For a discussion of the context see S. Gints: *Vasilii Kamensky*, Perm: Permskoe knizhnoe izdatelstvo, 1974, pp. 126-45.
870 Quoted in I62, p. 78, in which the source is not given.
871 Yu. Annenkov: Untitled, undated note on Vasilii Kamensky in RGALI, f. 2618, op. 1, ed. khr. 14, l. 2.
872 Kostin, *OST*, p. 73.
873 From a conversation between Valerii Bebutov and a correspondent for the journal *Zrelishcha* (January, 1924). Quoted in C31, Vol. 2, p. 235. For information on the popularity of the Razin theme see I62, pp 78-79. For information on the first production of Kamensky's *Stenka Razin* in Perm in 1920 (with designs by Alexander Kuprin) and this 1924 production, see Gints, *Vasilii Kamensky*, pp. 142-44.
874 From the OST declaration called "Platform" (1929). Translation in B12, p. 281.

VRUBEL, Mikhail Alexandrovich

Born 5 (17) March, 1856, Omsk, Russia; died 1 April, 1910, St. Petersburg, Russia.

1864-69 attended courses at SSEA; 1874-80 attended Law School at St. Petersburg University; 1880-84 attended IAA, studying there under Pavel Chistiakov; 1884-85 restored frescoes in the Church of St. Cyril, Kiev; visited Venice, one of many trips to Western Europe; 1887 designed murals for the Cathedral of St. Vladimir, Kiev; 1889 moved to Moscow; kept in close contact with Savva Mamontov and the Abramtsevo group; interest in the applied arts, especially in stage design and ceramics; 1890-91 illustrated Mikhail Lermontov's poem *The Demon* for the jubilee edition of Lermontov's works; image and concept of the Demon became central to Vrubel's painting, culminating in several remarkable canvases, such as *The Demon Downcast* (1902); 1890s in contact with Princess Mariia Tenisheva and the Talashkino colony; married Nadezhda Zabela, a singer with Mamontov's Private Opera Company; 1890s-1900s influenced by Art Nouveau and Symbolism; deeply interested in Slavic mythology; 1898 onwards in close contact with the World of Art group; 1899-1903 his decorative panel *Princess Reverie* installed on the front of the new Metropole Hotel, Moscow; 1902 onward increasing symptoms of insanity; 1906 went blind; 1910 died in a lunatic asylum in St. Petersburg.

Bibliography
S. Yaremich: *Mikhail Aleksandrovich Vrubel*, M: Knebel, 1911.
E. Gomberg-Verzhbinskaia, comp.: *Vrubel. Perepiska. Vospominaniia o khudozhnike*, L: Iskusstvo, 1963; second edition 1976.
M2, Vol. 2, pp. 201-02, lists Vrubel's theatrical productions.
N. Tarabukin: *M.A. Vrubel*, M: Iskusstvo, 1974.
D. Kogan: *Vrubel*, M: Iskusstvo, 1980; second edition: M: Terra-Knizhnyi klub, 1999.
D. Sarabianov: *Vrubel*, M: Izobrazitelnoe iskusstvo, 1981.
A. Isdebsky-Pritchard: *The Art of Mikhail Vrubel (1856-1910)*, Ann Arbor: UMI, 1982.
P. Suzdalev: *Vrubel, muzyka, teatr*, M: Izobrazitelnoe iskusstvo, 1983.
N. Dmitrieva: *Vrubel*, L: Khudozhnik RSFSR, 1984.
P. Suzdalev: *Vrubel. Lichnost, mirovozzrenie, metod*, M: Izobrazitelnoe iskusstvo, 1984.
P. Suzdalev: *Vrubel,* M: Sovetskii khudozhnik, 1991.
M. Allenov: *Mikhail Vrubel*, M: Slovo, 1996.
M. Allenov et al.: *Michail Wrubel. Der russische Symbolist*. Catalog of exhibition at the Kunsthalle, Düsseldorf, and the Haus der Kunst, Munich, 1997.
A. Gusarova: *Mikhail Vrubel*, M: Trilistnik, 1997 (second edition: 2000).
I. Gutt, ed.: *Mikhail Vrubel v Tretiakovskoi galeree, muzeiakh i chastnykh sobraniiakh Moskvy*. Catalog of exhibition at the TG, 1997.
M. Alpatov and G. Anisimov: *Zhivopisnoe*

masterstvo Vrubelia, M: Lira, 2000.

N. Shumsky: *Vrubel. Zhizn i bolezn,* SP: Akademicheskii proekt, 2001.

N. Sergeeva: *Rerikh i Vrubel,* M: Mezhdunarodnyi tsentr Rerikhov, 2002.

V. Leniashin and V. Kruglov: *Mikhail Vrubel iz sobraniia Russkogo muzeia,* SP: Palace Editions, 2006.

K. Zacharias: *Vom Symbol zum «Diabol»: über das Prinzip der Entzweinung in der Kunst der russischen Symbolisten Michail Wrubel,* Kassel: Kassel University Press, 2006.

G. Polikarpova et al.: *Mikhail Vrubel: Iz sobraniia Russkogo muzeia,* SP: Palace Editions, 2007.

L. Efremova: *Vrubel,* M: Olima, 2009.

G. Sternin: *Ot Repina do Vrubelia,* M: Galart, 2009.

N. Ermilchenko, *M. Vrubel,* M: Belyi gorod, 2010.

M. German: *Mikhal Vrubel,* SP: Aurora, 2010.

O. Pirumova and E. Tabanokhina, eds.: *Mikhail Vrubel,* SP: Aurora, 2010.

E. Skorobogacheva: *Mikhail Vrubel,* M: Art-Rodnik, 2010.

1152

Vrubel's philosophy of art, his approach to technique, form, and content were both similar to, and different from, the principles supported by his World of Art colleagues. Whereas Alexandre Benois, Ivan Bilibin, and Konstantin Somov reached esthetic conclusions early in their careers, and tended to remain at the same point, entertaining few subsequent modifications, Vrubel's search was constant and his late paintings, such as *Demon Downcast* (1902, TG) and the *Portrait of Briusov* (1906, TG), demonstrate that he never found an adequate response to the fateful questions that tormented him. Whether the Versailles scenes of Benois and Somov and the fairy-tale illustrations of Bilibin are to be accepted as mere bibelots with a certain nostalgic charm or as implicit commentaries on what some observers would see as a degenerate and enfeebled society, they retain a balance, symmetry, and harmony lacking in the restless, nervous visions of Vrubel with their "monstrous and dazzling inferno."[875]

On one level, Vrubel's stage designs, frescoes, and book illustratons can be regarded as an extension of the fashionable interest in the applied arts in Russia in the late 19th century and, certainly, Mamontov and the Abramtsevo circle encouraged his orientation towards decoration and ornament. Some might even criticize his studio painting for an excess of ornament, as in the *Fortune-Teller* (1895, TG), or for presenting a subject as if it were part of a stage set, as in *Venice: The Bridge of Sighs* (1890s, TG). On the other hand, Vrubel was fascinated by the construction of the artifact and both his paintings and his stage designs are distinguished by their careful architectural arrangement. For example, the two versions for the drop curtain entitled *Neapolitan Night* for Mamontov rely for their effect on the subtle interchange of horizontal plane and diagonal thrust. Vrubel developed this method in his magnificent set for the City of Ledenets in *The Tale of Tsar Saltan* (produced by Mamontov's company in 1900). He used the long sweep

of an arched gateway not only to reveal a receding cityscape below, but also to join one spatial division with the next and to integrate background with foreground. Vrubel's aspiration to treat stage design as architecture — to join inside and outside, while exposing the function — testified to his strong potential as a stage designer. It is to be regretted that, with the disbandment of Mamontov's opera company in 1901, Vrubel turned away from the theater, although his studio paintings of 1901-06 were often inspired by his experience of the stage.

1152 [R383a].
Leaves, ca. 1904.
Watercolor and pencil.
13 x 8½ in., 33 x 21.6 cm.
Inscriptions in pencil in Russian concern the further execution of these sketches.
This is the verso of No. 1153 [R383].

1153 [R383].
Costume Design for a Lady Wearing Cothurni, ca. 1904.
Pencil.
13 x 8½ in., 33 x 21.6 cm.
Provenance: Leonard Hutton Galleries, New York, 1976.
Reproduced in *Apollon,* St. Petersburg, 1913, May, between pp. 16-17; Kogan, *Vrubel,* plate 92, in which it is dated 1904; D23, p. 17, in which the provenance is given as the TG; I40, No. 146; I51, No. 263; I77, p. 125; I117, p. 328; K17, unpaginated; and N188, p. 12. An undated drawing in the RM, called *Seraph,* repeats a number of the elements.
The reverse (No. 1152 [R383a]) carries sketches of leaves.

Note: There is evidence to assume that this piece is a costume design for Vrubel's wife, Nadezhda Zabela-Vrubel, in the role of Aida in the opera of the same name. According to the late Dora Kogan,[876] Vrubel saw a production of Verdi's *Aida* in 1904, although Zabela-Vrubel herself does not seem to

have taken the role in any public performance of *Aida* and, certainly, the knight in armor on his horse in the background does not tally with the story of *Aida.*[877] While there is no absolute proof that this design was, in fact, inspired by *Aida,* the date of 1904 would seem to be correct, for the convoluted, intricate conglomeration of strokes is typical of Vrubel's artistic style in 1904-05 and brings to mind more familiar works of the period, such as *Campanulas* (RM) and *The Pearl* (TG). Furthermore, both iconographically and technically, this image finds close parallels with the several versions of *The Six-Winged Seraph* (1904-05, the GMII; the RM; and elsewhere).

Vrubel collaborated on a number of productions for Mamontov's Private Opera

1153

Company. In 1890, for example, just after his move to Moscow, he designed the sets for the Biblical drama *King Saul* written by Savva and Sergei Mamontov. During the 1890s and early 1900s Vrubel emerged as a professional stage designer, contributing, among others, to the 1899 production of Nikolai Rimsky-Korsakov's *The Tsar's Bride*, and, more importantly, to the 1900 production of Rimsky-Korsakov's *The Tale of Tsar Saltan*. As one observer recalled, the designs were a "revelation, the entire audience applauded the artist, so captivating was this picture."[878] Vrubel's work for *The Tale of Tsar Saltan* was indicative of his keen interest in the culture of the East or at least of a romanticized Orient as described in *One Thousand and One Nights*. Vrubel expressed his fascination with the exotic worlds of Persia and Egypt in many works, not least the painting *A Tale of the East* (1886, Museum of Russian Art, Kiev), the illustrations to Lermontov's works, and the majolica head *An Egyptian Girl* (1899-1900, TG). Consequently, No. 1153 [R383], whether or not it is a theatrical piece, can be accommodated easily within this context of Vrubel's art.

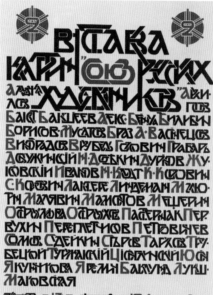

1154

1154 [R384].
***Portrait of a Violinist*, ca. 1904.**
Pencil and ink.
7½ x 5 in., 19 x 12.7 cm.
The reverse bears an inscription in Russian by Alexander Arnshtam: "This drawing by the painter Vrubel was purchased in Moscow. I am selling it to Mr. N.D. Lobanov." Then follows Arnshtam's signature and a note in French: "Dessin (crayon et plume) de M.A. Vrubel (1856-1910)."

Provenance: Alexander Arnshtam, Paris, March, 1966.
Reproduced in I14, No. 110, in which it is described as a portrait of Eugène Ysaye.

Note: It has been suggested that this portrait is of one of the concert violinists who performed in Moscow and St. Petersburg, such as Leopold Auer (1845-1930) or Eugène Ysaye (1858-1931). However, when compared to documentary photographs and other portraits of the period (e.g. Valentin Serov's pencil sketch of Ysaye, now in the Museum of Private Collections, Moscow, reproduced in D. Sarabianov, *Valentin Serov*, L: Aurora, 1982, p. 335; B159, p. 217; and K141, p. 27), Vrubel's rendering does not resemble either of these celebrities.

1155

1155 [R385].
***Poster Advertising the "Exhibition of Paintings by the Union of Russian Artists,"* 1904.**
Lithograph in red, black, and white.
26⅝ x 18½ in., 67.5 x 47 cm.
Inscriptions (as part of the design): after the exhibition announcement follows a list of the participants: "Aladzhalov, Arkhipov, Bakst, Baksheev, Alex. Benois, Bilibin, Borisov-Musatov, Braz, A. Vasnetsov, Vinogradov, Vrubel, Golovin, Grabar, Dobujinsky, N. Dosekin, Durnov, Zhukovsky, S. Ivanov, M. Klodt, K. Korovin, S. Korovin, Lanceray, Lindeman, Maliutin, Maliavin, Mamontov, Meshchersky, Ostroumova, Ostroukhov, Pasternak, Pervukhin, Perepletchikov, Petrovichev, Somov, Sudeikin, Serov, Tarkhov, Trubetskoi, Tsionglinsky (Jan Ciągliński), Yuon, Yakunchikova, Yaremich, Baklund, Luksh-Makovskaia." The list is followed by the details: "Open from 13 February, 1905, for one month in the Building of the Anchor Insurance Company on the corner of the Petrovka and Stoleshnikov Lane." The small print in the lower left margin reads: "Printing permission granted on 11 February, 1905, by the Moscow Chief of Police, Major General Volkov"; lower right:

"Published by the A.A. Levenson Press, Moscow."
Vrubel's initial application of the design — to the poster for the first and second exhibitions of the Society of the 36 in Moscow in 1901-03 — is reproduced in V. Lapshin, *Soiuz russkikh khudozhnikov*, L: Khudozhnik RSFSR, 1974, p. 33; and K183, p. 24.

Note: The Union of Russian Artists was founded in Moscow in 1903 as an outgrowth of the exhibition society called the 36. The 36, founded in 1901 by Moscow artists such as Konstantin Korovin, Andrei Riabushkin, and Vrubel, opposed the monopoly of the World of Art and supported different exhibition procedures, although, as a matter of fact, many of the World of Art artists participated in the exhibitions of the 36 and the Union of Artists (and vice versa). The question of organizing a new exhibition group arose at the closure of the February, 1903, "World of Art" exhibition in St. Petersburg, which, to a considerable degree, also heralded the end of the World of Art society as a whole. Igor Grabar recalled the scene:

> I was silent and began to realize that an open fight between Moscow and St. Petersburg was on... But what was most unexpected was that some of the Petersburgers... took the side of Moscow. Still more unexpected was Benois's speech — he declared himself in favor of the organization of a new society.[879]

The outcome of this meeting was the establishment of a new exhibition society, the Union of Russian Artists, in November, 1903. Despite ill health, Vrubel was one of the most active agitators for the new society and it was he who suggested the title. Moreover, he adapted his original poster design for the second exhibition of the 36 of 1902 to the first exhibitions of the Union, retaining the basic format and simply changing the list of participants' names. Léon Bakst, Alexandre Benois, Ivan Bilibin, Mstislav Dobujinsky, Evgenii Lancéray, Anna Ostroumova, Konstantin Somov, and other World of Art members joined the Union and contributed regularly to its exhibitions at least until 1910, when a new World of Art society was created. The Union itself continued to hold exhibitions in Moscow and St. Petersburg/Petrograd until 1923.

This poster is for the second exhibition of the Union of Artists, which was first open in St. Petersburg from 31 December, 1904 through 30 January, 1905, before going to Moscow (with a slightly different list of participants). It was open there from 13 February through 27 March, 1905, with a contingent of 39 artists and 332 works of art plus a posthumous showing of works by Mariia F. Yakunchikova. The list of names on this poster differs from that published in the exhibition catalog: Manuil Aladzhalov and Elena Luksh-Makovskaia, for example, are missing from the catalog.

875 The poet Alexander Blok argued that Vrubel went insane because "art is a monstrous and dazzling inferno." See A. Blok: "O sovremennom sostoianii russkogo simvolizma" (1910) in V. Orlov, ed.: *Aleksandr Blok. Sochineniia v odnom tome*, M-L: Khudozhestvennaia literatura, 1946, p. 407. Sergei Sudeikin also noted the "restlessness" of Vrubel's painting. See his article "Dve vstrechi s Vrubelem" in *Novoe russkoe slovo*, New York, 1981, 18 September, p. 6; 19 September, p. 6.

876 See Kogan, *Vrubel*, pp. 341, 342.

877 See L. Barsova: *N.I. Zabela-Vrubel glazami sovremennikov*, L: Muzyka, 1982. Vrubel's sketch of Zabela-Vrubel on the stage of the Noblemen's Assembly (undated), reproduced there between pp. 64 and 65, is reminiscent, at least in pose, of 1153 [R383].

878 V. Shkafer: *40 let na stsene russkoi opery. Vospominaniia*, L, 1936. Quoted in W. Salmond: "Mikhail Vrubel' and Stage Design: The Production of *Tsar Saltan*" in G55, p. 11.

879 I. Grabar: *Moia zhizn*, M-L: Iskusstvo, 1937, p 188.

YAKIMCHENKO, Alexander Georgievich

Born 1878, Nezhin, Chernigov Region, Ukraine; died 20 February, 1929, Moscow, Russia.

1900 graduated from CSIAI; visited Paris; early 1900s much influenced by Sergei Maliutin, Elena Polenova, and Mikhail Vrubel; contributed to the exhibitions of the World of Art and the Union of Russian Artists; 1905 onwards made decorations for the Moscow journal *Vesy* [Scales]; 1906 contributed to the "Exhibition of Young Artists" organized by the Leonardo da Vinci Society; 1910s worked as a book designer and illustrator for the Knebel Publishing-House in Moscow; member of the Moscow Association of Artists; 1911 contributed to the "Salon des Indépendants" in Paris; and the "Exhibition of Paintings by Russian Artists and of Sculpture by Boris Fredman-Kliuzel" at the Lemercier Gallery, Moscow; 1912-13 worked in Belgium and France; 1913 contributed decorations to the St. Petersburg journal *Apollon* [Apollo]; 1918 contributed to the first and second "Exhibition of Paintings by the Professional Union of Artist-Painters" in Moscow; 1919 contributed to the "IV State Exhibition of Paintings" in

Moscow; 1920 helped decorate agit-trains; 1921 completed an album of linocuts called *Gorod* [City]; 1920s contributed to many exhibitions, including the "Erste Russische Kunstausstellung" in Berlin (1922), the first and sixth exhibitions of the Association of Artists of Revolutionary Russia in Moscow (1922, 1924), the Venice Biennale for 1924, the "Exposition des Arts Décoratifs" in Paris (1925), both the "All-Union Polygraphic Exhibition" and the "Engraving in the USSR over the Last 10 Years" in Moscow (1927), and "Works on Revolutionary and Soviet Themes" in Moscow (1929); 1929 posthumous exhibition in Moscow.

Bibliography

I. Vrochevsky et al.: *Vystavka graviur V.D. Falileeva, I.A. Sokolova, S.M. Kolesnikova, A.G. Yakimchenko, M.A. Dobrova*. Catalog of exhibition at the Art Gallery of the Perm State Regional Museum, Perm, 1927.

A. Sidorov: *Posmertnaia vystavka graviur i risunkov A.G. Yakimchenko*. Catalog of posthumous exhibition at the All-Union Theater Society, Moscow, 1929.

B100, p. 31.

A. Sidorov: *Aleksandr Georgievich Yakimchenko*. Catalog of exhibition at the All-Union Theater Society, Moscow, 1986.

M. Kiselev: "Vozvrashchenie khudozhnika" in *Iskusstvo*, M, 1990, No. 4, pp 22-27.

A34, p. 462.

Of the same generation as Vasilii Denisov, Vadim Falileev, Vladimir Favorsky, Vasilii Masiutin, Dmitrii Mitrokhin, Georgii Narbut, and Viktor Zamirailo, Yakimchenko contributed much to the renaissance of the Russian graphic arts at the beginning of the century. Like them, he integrated the most diverse motifs and methods from the work of Aubrey Beardsley, the Simplicissimus group, and Japanese engravings into his own artistic vision, which in the 1900s drew heavily upon the conventions of the *style russe*. Yakimchenko also cultivated an eager interest in contemporary French artists and writers, many of whom he met through Elizaveta Kruglikova and Maximilian Voloshin in Paris in the 1900s.[880] Yakimchenko even exhibited alongside Alexander Archipenko, Marc

Chagall, Vasilii Kandinsky, Osip Zadkine, and other expatriates at the "Salon des Indépendants" in 1911, constituting a faction that "in artistic quality is in no way inferior to the others."[881] As his elaborate vignettes and filigrees for Symbolist publications such as *Vesy* demonstrate, Yakimchenko sympathized with the ideas of the Symbolist poets and philosophers, supporting their general move "away from the world of realities into the fantastic, as if afraid of actuality."[882]

Much influenced by the engravings of Ivan Pavlov, Yakimchenko attracted critical attention for his linocuts of city scenes and architectural monuments. In an appreciation of the Russian graphic arts of the Revolutionary period, Alexei Sidorov described Yakimchenko as a "very mature and independent artist,"[883] while Yakov Tugendkhold also mentioned him favorably in his survey of the period 1917-1927.[884]

The Firebird: *traditional Russian fairy-tale on which Igor Stravinsky based the ballet of the same name* (L'Oiseau de Feu).
        See No. 370 [R340] for plot summary.

1156 [R707].
Design for a Panneau for the Dining Room in Vera Firsanova's House, Moscow, 1909.
Watercolor.
8⅛ x 24¾ in., 20.5 x 63 cm.
Inscription: the right side carries the numbers 1 through 10 in ink.
Provenance: Issar Gourvitch, Paris, 1964, when the attribution was to Elena Polenova. Reproduced in color in B88, p.134; and B122, p. 160; and in black and white in I51, No. 182; I77, p. 129; B179, p. 213, in which it is misattributed to Polenova; and I14, No. 42, in which it is misattributed to Ivan Bilibin. A photograph of the interior of the Firsanova house, showing the panneau identified as the work of Yakimchenko, is reproduced in *Ezhegodnik Obshchestva arkhitektorov-khudozhnikov*, M, 1909, p. 149; two photographs of the interior are also reproduced in B122, p. 181.

Note: Although not a stage design, this draft for a panneau showing Ivan Tsarevich confronting the Firebird in the forest glade

at night, relates directly to the current concern with Russian national culture and, of course, parallels Igor Stravinsky's *L'Oiseau de Feu* (see No. 370 [R340]). The piece betrays Yakimchenko's proximity to Maliutin, Polenova, and Viktor Vasnetsov (No. 1115 [NIRE]); their Neo-Nationalist style can easily be recognized in the surviving photographs of the furniture, fixtures, and interior decorations for the house of the wealthy philanthropist, Vera Ivanovna Firsanova (1863-1932), on Novinskii Boulevard (now Tchaikovsky St.) in Moscow (designed by the architect Alexander Tamanov). The exuberant wings of the bird and swirling shape of the panneau also reflect an interest in European Art Nouveau, the mosaic-like surface reminiscent of the art of Jan Toorop, which Yakimchenko may have seen during his travels in France. The parallels with the various panneaux that Mikhail Vrubel made for Moscow houses (for example, Alexei Morozov's) are very striking.

Although the details of this commission are unknown, it is tempting to assume that Yakimchenko (or Firsanova) was paying homage to the vogue for splendid birds (in some sense the motif of the Russian firebird recurrent in the *style russe* is of the same species as the peacock in European Art Nouveau). Certainly, Yakimchenko was drawing upon Russian precedents, not least, Polenova's illustrations to the fairy-tale reproduced in the *World of Art* magazine and the panneau that she embroidered for the "All-Russian Art and Industry Exhibition" in Nizhnii Novgorod in 1896. Her description of this project could apply equally well to Yakimchenko's resolution:

I have chosen as my subject the fabulous Firebird who guards the golden apples. I am depicting a dark night, clouds above, and you can see the moon and stars between them. In the middle is a tree with golden fruit, and a fiery bird is perched somnolently upon it. Around the tree twine and intertwine fabulous flowers and grasses. Down below, hares have taken shelter among the roots of the tree, and even lower there are bog grasses, reeds and water weeds. Everything is very stylized.[885]

880 See E. Kruglikova: "Iz vospominanii o Makse Voloshine" in R. Popova: comp.: *Maksimilian Voloshin, khudozhnik*, M: Sovetskii khudozhnik, 1976, p. 99.
881 Alexander Archipenko (1911). Quoted in V. Lapshin: *Valentin Serov. Poslednii god zhizni*, M: Galart, 1995, pp. 187-88.
882 D. Mitrokhin: "Vystavka molodykh khudozhnikov" in *Utro*, Kharkov, 1907, 2 January. Quoted in L. Chaga, comp.: *Kniga o Mitrokhine*, L: Khudozhnik RSFSR, 1986, p. 433.
883 A. Sidorov: Russkaia grafika za gody revoliutsii, 1917-1922, M: Dom pechati, 1923, p. 67.
884 Ya. Tugendkhold: "O nashei grafike" (1928). Reprinted as "Graviura i grafika" in T. Kazhdan, comp.: *Ya.A. Tugendkhold*, M: Sovetskii khudozhnik, 1987, p. 252.
885 Letter from Elena Polenova to Vladimir Stasov dated 29 January, 1896. Quoted in F22, pp. 545-44. First published in V. Stasov: "E.D. Polenova" in *Mir iskusstva*, SP, 1899, No. 13, p. 45.

YAKULOV, Georgii (Georges) Bogdanovich

Born 2 (14) January, 1882, Tiflis, Georgia; died 28 December, 1928, Erevan, Armenia.

Born into an Armenian family. 1893-99 attended the Lazarev Institute of Oriental Languages in Moscow; 1901-03 attended MIPSA; 1903 served in the army; 1904 mobilized for the Russo-Japanese front; spent time in Manchuria; 1905 began to develop his theory of light; 1907 contributed to the "Moscow Association of Artists"; thereafter contributed to many exhibitions in Russia and abroad; 1910-11 often involved as a decorator in private balls, amateur theatricals, etc.; 1913 visited Paris, where he met the Delaunays and found that his ideas on light related to their theory of Simultanism; 1914-17 military service (with interruptions); 1917 assisted by Alexander Rodchenko, Vladimir Tatlin, Nadezhda Udaltsova, et al., designed the interior of the Café Pittoresque in Moscow; 1918 onward active as a stage designer, particularly for Alexander Tairov's Chamber Theater; 1919 close to the writers Sergei Esenin and Anatolii Mariengof; cosigned the Imaginist manifesto; professor at Svomas; painted murals for the Stable of Pegasus Café; early 1920s active principally as a stage designer, but also involved in fashion design; 1923 designed monument to the 26 Baku Commissars (not realized); 1925 visited Paris; contributed to the "Exposition Internationale des Arts Décoratifs"; worked on the décor for Sergei Diaghilev's production of *Le Pas d'Acier* (realized in 1927); returned to Moscow later that year.

Bibliography
M. Sarkisian: *Georgii Yakulov*. Catalog of exhibition at the State Picture Gallery of Armenia, Erevan, 1967.
M2, Vol. 2, pp. 202-03.
Notes et Documents Edités par la Société des Amis de Georges Yakoulov, Nos. 1-4, Paris, 1967-75.
S. Aladzhalov: *Georgii Yakulov*, Erevan: Armenian Theatrical Society, 1971.
M. Sarkisian et al.: *Georgii Yakulov*. Catalog of exhibition at the State Picture Gallery of Armenia, Erevan, and the State Museum of Art of the Peoples of the East, M, 1975.
V. Lapshin: "Iz tvorcheskogo naslediia G.B. Yakulova" in I. Kriukova et al., eds.: *Voprosy sovetskogo izobrazitelnogo iskusstva i arkhitektury*, M: Sovetskii khudozhnik, 1975, pp. 275-303.
E. Kostina: *Georgii Yakulov 1884-1928*, M: Sovetskii khudozhnik, 1979.
C. Amiard-Chevrel: "*Princess Brambilla* d'après E.T.A. Hoffmann. Mise en Scène de Tairov" in *Les Voies de la Création Théâtrale*, Paris, 1980, Vol. 7, pp. 127-53.
R. Casari and S. Burini: *L'Altra Mosca: Arte e Letteratura nella cultura russa tra ottocento e novecento*, Bergamo: Moretti & Vitali, 2000, pp. 158-86.
V. Badalian: *Georgii Yakulov 1884-1928, Khudozhnik, teoretik iskusstva*, Erevan: National Gallery of Armenia, 2010.

Mikhail Larionov: *Caricature of Georgii Yakoulov*, 1925. See 730 [NIRE].

The art of Georgii Yakulov cannot be contained within one stylistic category. He gave his artistic allegiance neither to Cubism nor to Futurism nor to Constructivism, and yet he derived his strength from all these movements. As one critic noted, Yakulov, like Vsevolod Meierkhold, carried the theater within him, "his own evolution was a theater unto itself."[886] It was in two productions in particular — *Princess Brambilla* (1920, in which Yakulov himself performed) and *Giroflé-Girofla* (1922), both of which played at the Chamber Theater, Moscow — that Yakulov demonstrated his acute sense of the theater. As a matter of fact, Yakulov's set and costume designs for these two spectacles seemed destined more for the circus or "happenings" than for the conventional stage: Yakulov used chance, coincidence, and intuition resulting either in brilliant success (as in *Giroflé-Girofla*) or in lukewarm audience response (as was the case with *Signor Formica* of 1922). The element of guesswork imbued Yakulov's art with a spontaneity and immediacy that appealed to a broad public, for, as he liked to say, "Art exists for the ignoramus. The greatness of art lies in its right to be illiterate."[887]

Consequently, Yakulov tended to regard the theater precisely as a mass circus experience and, in turn, emphasized its simplest and most basic ingredient — "the principle of perpetual motion, the kaleidoscope of forms and colors."[888] In order to express this movement in *Giroflé-Girofla*, Yakulov resorted to an intricate system of kinetic "machines" that "moved forward some parts, removed others, rolled out platforms, let down ladders, opened up traps, constructed passageways."[889] This crazy, chaotic spectacle, which Yakulov repeated in modified form in his conception of *Le Pas d'Acier* (in 1927), could not fail to evoke mirth and it was the most popular entertainment in Moscow in 1922. As

Anatolii Lunacharsky said, the common man had the right to relax after the hard days of the Revolution, and Yakulov gave him the chance to do so.[890]

1157

1158

1157 [NIRE].
Self-Portrait, 1925.
Gouache and black ink.
3 x 3½ in., 7.5 x 9 cm.
Inscribed and dated lower right in Russian: "Me 1925."
Provenance: Viktor Kholodkov, Moscow, 1974.

1158 [239; R1013].
Design for the Interior of the Stable of Pegasus Café, 1919.
Gouache and black ink.
Signed lower margin in Russian: "Georgii Yakulov."
5⅞ x 9⅝ in., 15 x 24.5 cm.
Provenance: Alexander Shlepianov, Moscow, 1989.
Reproduced in color in A34, p. 467; B115, plate 131; F107, p. 285; M78; and in black and white in I77, p. 127; Badalian, p. 139. An analogous piece with the composition reversed is reproduced in color in Kostina, p. 122; also see ibid., p. 123; and Aladzhalov, p. 127.

Note: The café, cabaret, and night-spot Stable of Pegasus opened on Tverskaia Street in Moscow in November, 1919, under the directorship of Ivan Startsev. Nicknamed the Association of Free Thinkers, the Stable of Pegasus was a popular center for the Moscow bohemia, especially for the Imaginists Esenin, Mariengof (see Note to Nos. 967-68 [R793-94]), and Vadim Shershenevich. It was at the Stable of Pegasus, for example, that the group devised and elaborated the contents of their magazine called *Gostinitsa dlia puteshestvuiushchikh v prekrasnom* [Hotel for Those Traveling the Beautiful]. Applying his decorative experience from the Café Pittoresque (see No. 738 [R624]), Yakulov designed part of the exterior and the interior of the Stable, creating an ambiance of:

> Light doubled in mirrors, tables piled up virtually on top of each other because

of the narrow space. A Rumanian orchestra. Stage. Murals by the artist Yakulov and poetical slogans by the Imaginists on the walls.[891]

Signor Formica: *Play by Vladimir Sokolov based on the story by E.T.A. Hoffmann. Produced by Alexander Tairov at the Chamber Theater, Moscow on 13 June, 1922, with music by Anatolii Aleaxandrov and designs by Georgii Yakulov, assisted by Vasilii Komardenkov.*
See No. 626 [R521] for plot summary.

1159 [R1014].
Costumes for Four Academicians, ca. 1922.
Gouache and pencil.
12⅜ x 18⅝ in., 31.5 x 47.4 cm.
Inscribed lower right in Russian: "4 Academicians."
Provenance: Gregory Frumkin, London, July, 1974.

Reproduced in color in B115, plate 129; and in black and white in A34, p. 465; J4, Lot 80; I32, No. 126; I51, No. 264; I77, p. 138. A similar design for six Academicians in the BTM is reproduced in Aladzhalov, *Georgii Yakulov*, p. 237, and in Kostina, *Georgii Yakulov*, p. 162, in which it is described wrongly as a design for *Princess Brambilla*. A sketch for one Academician is reproduced in C7, No. 221. Yakulov used similar costumes for the proposed production of Tirso de Molina's *El Burlador de Sevilla y Convidado de Pieda* in 1918, and one is reproduced in Kostina, p. 188.

Note: In the spirit of E.T.A. Hoffmann, a favorite author among Russian artists and writers of the Silver Age,[892] Yakulov interpreted *Signor Formica* as a carnival of personages parodying human foibles. True to his instinctive understanding of the theater, Yakulov conceived the actors and

1159

their locale as moving volumes rather than as mere decorations. In his own words, Yakulov combined "not only colors, but also architectural constructions."[893] By and large, the critical reception of *Signor Formica* was fairly positive and Yakulov was commended for avoiding superfluous detail[894] — although some observers did feel the result to be "very boring."[895] Vasilii Komardenkov, Yakulov's friend and fellow artist, was much impressed by the production and made several portraits of the actors playing their roles (see Nos. 626-27 [R521-22]).

Rienzi: *opera in five acts by Richard Wagner based on the novel by Edward Bulwer-Lytton. Projected by Valerii Bebutov and Vadim Shershenevich for the RSFSR Theater No. 1, Moscow, in 1921 with pantomime scenes directed by Vsevolod Meierkhold and designs by Georgii Yakulov. A smaller version was produced at the Great Hall of the Moscow Conservatoire on 8 July, 1921, and Yakulov also contributed the same and supplementary designs to Nikolai Prostorov's production of the opera at the Free Theater, Moscow, on 3 April, 1923.*

Set in Rome, the opera tells the life of Cola di Rienzi, a Medieval populist, who outwits and defeats the nobles and their followers and raises the power of the people. In turn, he crushes the nobles' rebellion against the people's power, but popular opinion changes and even the Church, which had urged him to action, turns against him. In the end, the populace burns the Capitol, in which Rienzi and a few adherents have made a last stand.

1160

1160 [R1015].
Three Costumes for the Peace Delegates, 1921.
White paint on black paper.
Inscribed and dated lower left in white paint in Russian: "Peace delegates, 27.V.1921."
5¼ x 8⅝ in., 13.3 x 22 cm.
Other inscription: lower center: "42."
Provenance: Christophe Czwiklitzer, Paris, October, 1975.
Reproduced in Aladzhalov, *Georgii Yakulov,* p. 153. For other costume designs for *Rienzi* see Kostina, *Georgii Yakulov,* p. 166, 167; and Badalian, *Georgii Yakulov,* p. 162.

King Lear: *tragedy in five acts by William Shakespeare. Prepared for production, but not realized, by the National Armenian Theater, Erevan in 1925, with designs by Georgii Yakulov.*

The senile King Lear decides to divide his kingdom among his three daughters, Goneril, Regan, and Cordelia. Displeased with Cordelia's definition of her filial love, Lear tells her that her dowry will be truth. Cordelia then marries the King of France, who prepares to invade England. The scene shifts to the Earl of Gloucester and the evil designs perpetrated against him by his sons, Edgar and Edmund. Gloucester has his eyes gouged out. Allied with the Dukes of Cornwall and Albany (Regan's and

Goneril's husbands), Edmund commands the British forces and, after Lear regains his clarity of mind and recognizes Cordelia, he takes both Lear and Cordelia prisoner. Cordelia is put to death, Goneril poisons Regan and kills herself. Lear dies of anguish.

1161

1161 [R1016].
Costume Design for King Lear, ca. 1925.
Pencil, India ink, and watercolor with traces of gold and silver paint.
10½ x 7 in., 26.8 x 17.8 cm.
Inscribed upper right in Russian: "Lear."
Provenance: *Dance, Theatre, Opera, Music Hall,* New York: Sotheby, Parke Bernet, 18 December, 1980, Lot 122B (reproduced).
Reproduced in I77, p. 147; J4, Lot 79.

1162

1162 [R1017].
Costume Design for Cordelia, Daughter of King Lear, ca. 1925.
Pencil, watercolor, and silver paint.
10½ x 7 in., 26.7 x 17.8 cm.
Provenance: *Dance, Theatre, Opera, Music Hall,* New York: Sotheby, Parke Bernet, 18 December, 1980, Lot 122A (reproduced)
Reproduced in J4, Lot 78; I77, p. 147.

1163

1164

Le Pas d'Acier: *ballet in two scenes by Sergei Prokofiev and scenario by Prokofiev and Georgii Yakulov. Produced by Sergei Diaghilev at the Théâtre Sarah-Bernhardt, Paris on 7 June, 1927, with choreography by Leonide Massine and designs by Georgii Yakulov.*

The ballet describes the new Socialist Russia. The first scene presents a picture of the old régime changing in the face of the revolutionary epoch. The second scene, concentrating on a double-tiered Constructivist setting with mobile elements, glorifies the new reality of the factory and the machine.

1165 [R1020].
Stage Set, ca. 1927.
White gouache on black paper.
9 x 12 in., 23 x 30.5 cm.
Inscriptions in Russian: left margin with instructions to the dressmaker; the right margin with instructions regarding the planning of the stage and lighting, including references to cables, screens, color projectors, etc.
Provenance: Christophe Czwiklitzer, Paris, October, 1975.
Reproduced in I77, pp. 112, 136; L2, Lot 105; I32, No. 125. A similar sketch is reproduced in D17, p. 263. A maquette, described as belonging variously to Serge Lifar and Alexandra Larionova (Tomilina), incorporating some of the details in this design, is reproduced in I15, plate 106, and in J24, Lot 75.

1163 [240; R1018].
Costume Design for the Earl of Gloucester (?), ca. 1925.
Watercolor, gold and silver paint, and pencil.
10⅝ x 6⅞ in., 27 x 17.5 cm.
Provenance: Jean Chauvelin, Paris, July, 1969.
Reproduced in I20, No. 106; I51, No. 265; I77, p. 147; N183, p. 49. Two other designs for this proposed production described wrongly as projects for a 1920 production at the Habima Jewish Theater, Moscow, are reproduced in J4, Lots 78, 79.

1164 [R1019].
Costume Design for Regan, 1925.
Watercolor and pencil.
10⅝ x 7⅛ in., 27 x 18 cm.
Provenance: Jean Chauvelin, Paris, July, 1969.
Reproduced in I20, No. 105; I51, No. 266; I77, p. 147.

Note: A distinctive aspect of Yakulov's theatrical activity was his ability to approach both old and new repertoires in a fresh and experimental manner. His sets and costumes for *Measure for Measure* (1919) and *Oedipus* (1921), both at the Moscow State Model Theater, for *Rienzi* (1921-23), and for the projected production of *Hamlet* at the RSFSR Theater No. 1 in 1920 demonstrate a clear understanding of the principles of classical drama, while providing a new "urban" interpretation. Until recently, it was not known that Yakulov had also worked on designs for *King Lear* since neither he, nor his contemporaries, nor relevant directories mention the project.[896] However, when his one-time friend and fellow Imaginist, the poet and artist Alexander Kusikov, died in Paris in 1966, a

number of Yakulov sketches, including the ones in question, were discovered in the estate, some of which were established as designs for *King Lear.*

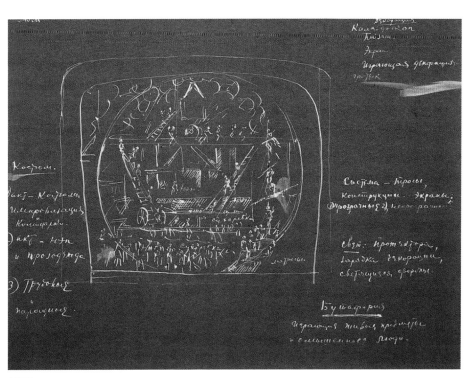

1165

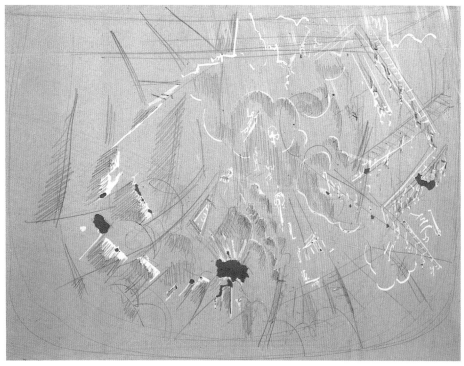

1166

1166 [R1021].
Stage Design, ca. 1927.
Pencil, gouache, and black ink.
9 x 12 in., 23 x 30.5 cm.
Provenance: Christophe Czwiklitzer, Paris, October, 1975.
Reproduced in color in B115, plate 130; and in black and white in I77, p. 136; L2, Lot 106; I51, No. 268. A similar design is reproduced in I32, No. 124.

1167 [R1022].
Costumes for the Three Dancers of the Clockwork Snuffboxes, ca. 1927.
Pencil and watercolor.
8¾ x 13¼ in., 22.2 x 31 cm.
Inscribed lower left in Russian: "The Clockwork Snuffboxes"; the reverse carries a design for a lady in a large hat.
Provenance: *Designs for Costumes and Décors: Ballet, Opera, Theatre*, New York: Sotheby Parke Bernet, 6 May, 1970, Lot 154 (reproduced).
Reproduced in color in N188, p. 64; and in

black and white in I19, No. 104; I32, No. 123; I51, No. 269; I77, p. 136.

Note: Le Pas d'Acier was the last of Sergei Diaghilev's "industrial" ballets. Produced in the same season as *La Chatte* (Monte Carlo, 30 April; Paris, 27 May, 1927), *Le Pas d'Acier* symbolized Diaghilev's wish to relate ballet, still regarded by many as a "classical art," to twentieth-century concerns. For this he was accused of destroying hallowed values and of encouraging musicians to make noise, not music.[897] Yakulov's mechanical props, including real hammers, for *Le Pas d'Acier* contributed a great deal to this development. By introducing such "unartistic" elements into the ballet, Yakulov endeavored to represent not only a choreography of factory workers, but a choreography of machines as well.[898] The connections between Yakulov and Picasso in this context of "modernization" are especially close.[899]

1168

Yakulov as co-signatory:
1168 [R1023].
Designer unknown: Manifesto: "We and the West", 1914.
Lithograph in black and white.
16⅛ x 10¼ in., 41 x 26 cm.
Provenance: Viktor Kholodkov, Moscow, 1984.
See translation at No. 1169 [R1024], the French version of the poster.

1169 [R1024].
Designer unknown: Manifesto: "We and the West" (French Version), 1914.
Lithograph in black and white.
16⅛ x 10¼ in., 41 x 26 cm.
Provenance: Viktor Kholodkov, Moscow, 1984.
French version of No. 1168 [R1023].

1167

Nous et l'Occident

(Placard № 1)

L'Europe a été atteinte dans ses aspirations créatrices (restées sans réalisation!) d'une crise, qui s'est manifestée dans l'orientation vers l'Orient. Cependant **la compréhension de l'Orient est hors du pouvoir de l'Occident**, car ce dernier a perdu la notion des limites de l'art (sont confondus les problèmes philosophiques et esthétiques avec les méthodes d'incarnation dans l'art). **L'art de l'Europe est archaïque et il n'y a et il ne peut y avoir d'autre art**, vu que ce dernier se base sur les éléments **cosmiques** tandis que tout l'art de l'Europe est **territorial**. **La Russie** est l'unique pays qui jusqu'à présent n'a pas d'art territorial. Tout le travail de l'Occident a été de défendre les résultats acquis par le vieil art (l'esthétique précédente). Tous les autres essais de l'Occident à construire une nouvelle esthétique, étant aprioriques et non pas aposterioriques, sont **fatalement catastrophiques**: l'esthétique nouvelle suit l'art nouveau, et non pas inversement. Tout en reconnaissant la divergence dans l'évolution des arts—occidental et oriental—(l'art de l'Occident est l'incarnation de la conception mondiale géométrique, conception se dirigeant de l'objet au sujet; l'art de l'Orient—est l'incarnation de la conception mondiale algébrique, se dirigeant du sujet à l'objet)—nous admettons comme principes directeurs, **communs** pour la peinture, la poésie et la musique:

1) le spectre spontané,
2) la profondeur spontanée,
3) l'autosuffisance des temps, comme méthodes d'incarnation, et des rythmes comme absolus;

et comme principes **speciaux**:

A la peinture:	A la poésie:	A la musique:
1) la negation de la construction d'après le conus, comme représentant la perspective trigonometrique; 2) les dissonances.	1) la continuité de la massé simple; 2) la differenciation des masses de rarefications diverses: lithoïdes, fluides et phosphénoides; 3) l'élimination de la conception accidentaliste.	1) l'élimination de la linéarité (de l'architectonique) au moyen de la perspective interne (la synthèse-primitive); 2) substantivité des éléments.
Georges Jacouloff.	Benoît Livschitz.	Arthur-Vincent Lourié.

St.-Pétersbourg, 1-er Janvier, 1914.

Éd. „TAVR".

1169

The poster reads:

WE AND THE WEST[900]
(POSTER NO. 1)

In her creative aspirations (and she attained nothing!) Europe has been overtaken by crisis, which finds its outward expression in her appeal to the East. *But the West does not have the East's power of comprehension* because the former has lost the concept of the limitations of art (questions of philosophy and esthetics have been confounded with the methods of artistic incarnation). European art is archaic. Europe has no new art and cannot have it for this is founded on *cosmic* elements. All the art of the West is *territorial*. The only country that, hitherto, has had no territorial art is *Russia*. All the endeavors of the West rely on the *formal basis* of the achievements of the old art (the old esthetics). All attempts of the West to erect a new esthetics, *a priori* and not *a posteriori*, have been *fatally catastrophic:* a new esthetics follows a new art and not vice versa. Recognizing the difference in the artistic processes of West and East (the art of the West is the embodiment of a geometric worldview proceeding from subject to object), we affirm — as the *general* bases for painting, poetry and music —

1) arbitrary spectrum;
2) arbitrary depth;
3) the self-sufficiency of tempi as methods of artistic embodiment, and of rhythms which are immutable; and as *particular* bases:

For Painting:
1) rejection of construction according to the cone — a trigonometric perspective;
2) dissonances.

Georgii Yakulov

For Poetry:
1) continuity of the single verbal mass;
2) differentiation of masses at varying degrees of rarefication lithoidal, fluid and phosphenoidal;
3) overcoming the accidentalist approach.

Benedikt Livshits

For Music:
1) overcoming linearity (architectonic) by means of inner perspective (primitive synthesis);
2) substantiality of elements.

Arthur-Vincent Lourié
St. Petersburg, 1st January, 1914

Note: The three cosignatories of this manifesto (written on 1 January, 1914), Yakulov, Benedikt Konstantinovich Livshits (1886-1939), and Arthur-Vincent Lourié (1892-1966), were representatives of the new Russian art (painting, poetry, music), convinced that the Russian avant-garde was superior to the "geometric worldview" of the West. In his memoirs, Livshits recalled the atmosphere in which the text was drafted:

As soon as we sat at the table to compose the declaration (this took place at Lourié's flat) our damn susceptibility to "isms" and to science-like abracadabra immediately made itself felt. Moreover, in our excitement we forgot that negative formulae did not constitute a programme. This was especially obvious in the case of Yakulov.[901]

Livshits also mentions that the manifesto was published in Russian, French, and Italian "since we considered Italy and France as the

1170

only nations practising avant-garde art."[902] As a matter of fact, Guillaume Apollinaire published the French text in *Mercure de France,* adding with tongue in cheek, that "Il est vrai que *la négation de la construction d'après le connu* est tout un programme."[903]

Yakulov as contributor:
1170 [R1025].
Designer unknown: *Poster Advertising the Opening of the "First Obmokhu Exhibition,"* 1919.
Lithograph in black and white.
14¾ x 9⅞ in., 37.4 x 25 cm.
The poster announces the opening of the exhibition of Obmokhu (Society of Young Artists) on Sunday, 2 May, 1919, at Svomas in Moscow. Among the participants in the exhibition are Nikolai Denisovsky, Sergei Kostin, Konstantin Medunetsky, and the Stenberg brothers. The speakers include Anatolii Lunacharsky [then head of NKP] (introductory remarks) followed by Lev Kamenev, Olga Kameneva, David Shterenberg, Osip Brik, and Georgii Yakulov. Among other details the poster communicates that the exhibition will be open from 2 through 16 May [1919].
Provenance: Viktor Kholodkov, Moscow, 1984.
Reproduced in K154 (Russian edition), p. 164.

886 I1, p. 15.
887 Quoted in I1, p. 46.
888 Ibid., p. 45.
889 G17, p. XXXVI.
890 A. Lunacharsky: "Zhirofle-Zhirofla" in C12, p. 36.
891 I Startsev: "Moi vstrechi s Eseninym" (1965). Quoted in Aladzhalov, p. 59.
892 For information on the position of E.T.A. Hoffmann in modern Russian culture, see N. Ingham: *E.T.A. Hoffmann's Reception in Russia,* Würzburg: Jal Verlag, 1974.
893 G. Yakulov: "Znachenie khudozhnika v sovremennom teatre" (1921). Quoted in Kostina, *Georgii Yakulov,* p. 86. For Yakulov's own conception of his tasks in *Signor Formica* see G. Yakulov: "Moia kontrataka" in *Ermitazh,* M, 1922, No. 7, pp. 10-11.
894 V. Bitt: "Posledniaia postanovka Moskovskogo kamernogo teatra" in *Teatr, literatura, muzyka, balet, grafika, zhivopis, kino,* Kharkov, 1922, No. 6, 14 October, p. 14.
895 A. Vinokurova: "A.Ya. Zakushniak." Manuscript in RGALI, f. 2378, op. 1, ed. khr. 182, l.132.
896 See, for example, M. Babaian, comp.: *Armianskii dramaticheskii teatr. Annotirovannyi ukazatel bibliograficheskikh i spravochnykh materialov 1920-1980,* M: Ministerstvo kultury SSSR, 1983.
897 From *The Lady,* London, 1927, 14 July. Quoted in D24, p. 350. For a detailed discussion of *Le Pas d'Acier,* see L.-A. Sayers: "Sergei Diaghilev's 'Soviet' Ballet: *Le Pas d'Acier* and Its Relationship to Russian Constructivism" in B183, No. 2, pp. 100-25.
898 G. Yakulov: "'Stalnoi skok' Sergeia Prokofieva" (1928). Quoted in Kostina, p. 88.
899 See K. Passuth: "Jakulov et Picasso" in *Cahiers du Musée national d'art moderne,* Paris, 1980, No. 3, pp. 86-97.
900 This is the title of Chapter 7 in Benedikt Livshits's memoirs *Polutoraglazyi strelets,* L: Izdatelstvo pisatelei, 1933. See translation by John E. Bowlt: *Benedikt Livshits. "The One and a Half-Eyed Archer,"* Newtonville: ORP, 1977, pp. 181-213.
901 Bowlt, *Benedikt Livshits,* p. 177.
902 Ibid. The manifesto was first published as a handout and then reprinted in the miscellany *Gramoty i deklaratsii russkikh futuristov,* SP: Svirelga, 1914.
903 G. Apollinaire: "Spectre spontané" in *Mercure de France,* Paris, 1914, 16 April, pp. 882-83.

YAKUNINA, Elizaveta Petrovna

Born 1 (13) September, 1892, St. Petersburg, Russia; died 16 January, 1964 Leningrad, Russia.

1916 graduated from SCITD; 1918-20 attended the Kurmastsep (Courses in the Art of Stage Productions) supervised by Vsevolod Meierkhold; came into contact with Konstantin Derzhavin, Vladimir Dmitriev, Valentina Khodasevich, Kuzma Petrov-Vodkin, and other young artists and critics associated with Kurmastsep; 1920 onwards worked at the People's Comedy Theater, Petrograd; close to Sergei Radlov; designed *Smeraldina's Pranks* there; 1922 contributed to the "Exhibition of Designs for Theatrical Decorations and Works from the Studios of the Decorative Institute for 1918-1922" in Petrograd; 1927 contributed to the "Exhibition of Stage Design 1917-X-1927," Leningrad; 1930 worked for the Moscow Theater of Satire, e.g., on the operetta *Ah, My Lady!;* 1931-33 worked at the Leningrad Theater of Musical Comedy; 1930s worked for children's theaters; close to Evgenii Shvarts; 1935 became artist-in-residence at the New Theater for Children, Leningrad; contributed to the exhibition "Artists of the Soviet Theater over the Last 17 Years" in Moscow and Leningrad; 1940s-50s continued to exhibit and to work on Leningrad productions, e.g., for Alexander Ostrovsky's *The Storm* at the Navy Dramatic Theater, Leningrad, 1950.

Bibliography
L. Oves: *E.B. Slovtsova. B.M. Erbshtein. E.P. Yakunina.* Catalog of exhibition at the State Museum of Theatrical and Musical Art, L, 1987. Recent exhibitions of stage designs have featured Elizaveta Yakunina's work. See, for example, I116, p. 32.

1171

Along with Moisei Levin and Semeon Mandel, Yakunina was one of the younger stars in the artistic firmament of Leningrad in the 1920s onwards, achieving a sound reputation as a designer for lighter genres, such as the circus and the puppet theater, rather than for the ballet or dramatic stage. Yakunina viewed the arena as a playful, jocular, and spontaneous medium, where bright colors, sharp movements, and even moments of vulgarity, contortion, and audience baiting were part and parcel of the spectacle. When not involved in the circus, Yakunina also designed sets and costumes for comedies, skits, and musicals, often imbuing her works with the elements of caricature, parody, and hyperbole.

The Circus (also called The Circus of Archibald Fox): *comedy review by Konstantin Gibshman reworked by Samuil Marshak. Produced at the Petrograd Theater of Marionettes (part of the Theater of the Young Spectator) by Liubov Shaporina-Yakovleva in the fall of 1923 with designs by Elizaveta Yakunina.*

A parade of circus people, such as clowns, acrobats and jugglers.

1171 [R1026].
Costume Design for a Fat Clown, ca. 1923.
Watercolor, pencil, and black ink.
Signed lower right in Russian: "E. Yakunina 19."
12 x 9¼ in., 30.5 x 23.5 cm.
Other inscription: the reverse carries the exhibition label No. 17 (or 77).
Provenance: Yakov Rubinshtein, Moscow, 1972.
Reproduced in color in B115, plate 121; and in black and white in A34, p. 468; I60, p. 38; I77, p. 150. For reproductions of other comparable costume designs by Yakunina see I74, pp. 47-52.

Note: Yakunina designed this costume for a marionette for the Petrograd Marionette Theater, which until 1924 was an important part of the Theater of the Young Spectator (TYuZ). At one time, Yulii Klever (fils), Nikolai Kochergin, and Moisei Levin (No. 740 [R623]) were also among the designers employed there under the able supervision of Alexander Briantsev. The actor Nikolai Petrov recalled his impressions of the Petrograd Marionette Theater:

> This was not a "naturalistic" theater that copied the human theater and the puppets themselves were not a "copy" of a man… the artists came to realize that puppets — and not just hand puppets but specifically marionettes — have the right to their own independent and interesting existence.[904]

Yakunina was involved in a number of productions at the Marionette Theater. However, she is best known for her designs for *The Circus,* which implemented the principles she had assimilated from the Courses in the Art of Stage Productions

under Vsevolod Meierkhold where the focus of attention was precisely on the theoretical elaboration and implementation of the maquette and the costume.[905]

904   N. Petrov: *Vospominania* . Quoted in E6, p. 173.
905   For some information on the Courses in the Art of Stage Productions see C51, p. 63.

YUON, Konstantin Fedorovich

Born 12 (24) October, 1875, Moscow, Russia; died 11 April, 1958, Moscow, Russia.

1894-98 attended MIPSA, studying under Abram Arkhipov, Leonid Pasternak, Nikolai Kasatkin, and Konstantin Savitsky; 1898-1900 studied there under Valentin Serov; 1899 contributed to the 28th exhibition of the Society of Wandering Exhibitions, Moscow; visited Austria, Switzerland, and Italy; 1900-17 director of Konstantin Yuon and Ivan Dudin's Art School in Moscow; 1900 took part in the 7th exhibition of the Moscow Association of Artists; thereafter contributed to many exhibitions in Russia and abroad; 1900 onward visited Medieval Russian towns such as Pskov, Novgorod, and Uglich; 1904-23 member of the Union of Russian Artists; 1905 visited Germany and France; 1908 visited Paris for Sergei Diaghilev's first Paris season; first major professional stage designs for the Moscow Art Theater production of Nikolai Gogol's *Inspector General;* 1910 designed Petr Yartsev's play *Sweet Miracle* at the Nezlobin Theater, Moscow; 1913 designed costumes for Diaghilev's production of *Boris Godunov* in Paris; 1921 member of RAKhN; 1925 member of AKhRR; 1931 member of the Moscow Union of Soviet Artists; 1939-40 professor at the Academy of Arts, Leningrad; active as a painter and teacher until his death.

Bibliography
A. Koiransky: *K.F. Yuon,* M: Kogan, 1918.
Ya. Apushkin: *Yuon,* M: Vsekokhudozhnik, 1936.
K. Yuon: *O zhivopisi,* L: Izogiz, 1937.
N. Tretiakov: *Konstantin Fedorovich Yuon,* M: Iskusstvo, 1957.
A. Galushkina, ed.: *K.F. Yuon ob iskusstve,* M: Sovetskii khudozhnik, 1959 (two vols.).
V. Sidorenko: *Konstantin Fedorovich Yuon.* Catalog of exhibition at the TG, 1962.
I. Rostovtseva: *Konstantin Fedorovich Yuon,* L: Khudozhnik RSFSR, 1964.
N. Sobolevsky: *Konstantin Fedorovich Yuon,* M: Sovetskii khudozhnik, 1968.
T. Nordshtein: *Yuon,* L: Aurora, 1972.
T. Vendelshtein et al.: *Konstantin Fedorovich Yuon.* Catalog of exhibition at the RM and the TG, 1976.
Yu. Osmolovsky: *Konstantin Yuon,* M: Sovetskii khudozhnik, 1982.
N. Mamonova: *Konstantin Yuon,* M: Belyi gorod, 2001.

Yuon is known as a painter of the Russian

countryside, of the Russian seasons, and of old Russian churches and monasteries. His contributions to stage design are of less import than his studio paintings, and even though he designed thirteen productions between 1910 and 1925, he possessed neither the artistic imagination, nor the universal knowledge of contemporaries, such as Léon Bakst and Alexandre Benois. However, Yuon was an unquestionable expert in the culture of Medieval Russia and for this reason Diaghilev invited him to create some of the costumes and sets for *Boris Godunov* in Paris in 1913. True to his conception of stage design as an auxiliary and illustrative mode, Yuon insisted that the

> painted decorations should be esthetically valuable and beautiful. Beauty of stage design means a well thought-out harmony of colors and paint spots and the artistic resonance of the entire colored ensemble as well as the precise expression of the style and character [of the production].[906]

Boris Godunov: *opera in four acts by Modest Mussorgsky. Produced by Sergei Diaghilev and directed by Alexander Sanin at the Théâtre des Champs-Elysées, Paris, on 22 May, 1913, with designs by Léon Bakst, Ivan Bilibin, and Konstantin Yuon.*
See No. 339 [R305] for plot summary.

1172

1172 [R1005].
Costume Design for a Boyar in a Pointed Hat, ca. 1913.
Watercolor.
Initialed lower right in Russian: "K.Yu."
8¾ x 6⅜ in., 22.3 x 16.3 cm.
Other inscription: upper right in Russian: "A boyar, VI."
Provenance: the artist's grandson, Oleg Yuon, Moscow, May, 1973
Reproduced in I40, No. 143; I51, No. 270.

1173

1173 [R1006].
Costume Design for a Boyar in a Fur Hat, ca. 1913.
Watercolor.
8¾ x 6⅜ in., 22.3 x 16.3 cm.
Inscribed: upper right in Russian: "A boyar VI"; upper left "68."
Provenance: the artist's grandson, Oleg Yuon, Moscow, May, 1973.
Reproduced in I40, No. 144.

1174 [R1007].
Costume Design for a Boyarynia, ca. 1913.
Watercolor.
Initialed lower right in Russian: "K.Yu."
8¾ x 6⅜ in., 22.3 x 16.3 cm.
Other inscriptions: upper right in Russian: "A boyarynia or a woman in peasant clothes;" upper left: "15."
Provenance: the artist's grandson, Oleg Yuon, Moscow, May, 1973.

1174

Reproduced in I40, No. 145; I51, No. 271.

Note: Yuon had already had experience of *Boris Godunov* before the 1913 production since he had helped to paint Alexander Golovin's costume designs for Diaghilev's Paris production in 1908 (along with Boris Anisfeld, Evgenii Lanceray, and Stepan Yaremich). In the same year Yuon also illustrated the brochure that accompanied the *Boris Godunov* production, i.e., *Boris Godunov de Modeste Moussorgsky. Théâtre National de l'Opéra.* According to Anatolii Lunacharsky who saw the 1913 production, it was

> unprecedented in its beauty...The distinctive beauty of the Russian version of the religious splendor of Byzantium shone with its iridescent fire, with its brocade during the extraordinarily picturesque scene of the coronation.[907]

1175

Unknown production, ca. 1930.

1175 [NIRE].
Costume design for a Russian Female Dancer, ca. 1930.
Watercolor and pencil
Initialed lower right in Russian: "K.Yu."
10¼ x 7 in., 26 x 17.8 cm.
Provenance: Nina Stevens, New York, 1968.
Reproduced in I14, p. 93, Fig. 142.

906 K. Yuon: "Zhivopis v teatre" (1938). Quoted in Galushkina, ed.: *K.F. Yuon ob iskusstve,* Vol. 2, p. 161.
907 Review by A. Lunacharsky. Quoted in Apushkin, *Yuon,* p. 110.

ZACK, Léon (Zak, Lev Vasilievich)

Born 12 (24) July, 1892, Nizhnii Novgorod, Russia; died 30 March, 1980, Paris, France.

Cousin of the philosopher Semeon Frank. 1905 onwards studied art and exhibited in Moscow and elsewhere; 1907 contributed a portrait of Alexander Skriabin to the program for the "Cinq Concerts Historiques Russes" in Paris; 1913 studied literary history at Moscow University; early 1910s enrolled in the private studios of Fedor Rerberg and Ilia Mashkov; began to write poetry under the names of Khrisanf and Rossiiansky; member of the Ego-Futurist movement and Mezzanine of Poetry; especially close to the poet Vadim Shershenevich; co-published miscellanies of new poetry, such as *Vernissazh* [Vernissage]; 1916 and 1917 contributed to the "Moscow Association of Artists"; 1920 emigrated, lived in Florence; 1922 moved to Berlin, where he worked for Russian theaters, including the Russisches Romantisches Theater; 1923 arrived in Paris; deeply interested in philosophy; 1930 contributed designs to the production of *Giselle* by the Ballets Russes Vera Nemtchinova in Paris, one of several productions that he designed in Paris; 1943 designed the productions of *Stenka Razin* and *Prince Igor* for the Nouveaux Ballets de Monte Carlo; 1945 broke with figurative painting to develop his own abstract style; 1940s onwards continued to paint, especially in an abstract idiom, and to exhibit.

Bibliography
E. Znosko-Borovsky: "A propos de quatre artistes: Larionov, L. Zak, Modzalevsky, Bilinsky" in *La Revue de "l'Oeuvre,"* Paris, 1927, November, p. 25.
Pierre Courthion et al.: *Léon Zack*, Paris: Le Musée de Poche, 1961; second edition 1976.
M2, Vol. 2, p. 204, listing his theatrical productions.
Rossiiansky: *Utro vnutri*, Munich: Fink Verlag, 1970 (a collection of Zack's poetry edited by Vladimir Markov).
J.C. Marcadé: "Poeticheskaia filosofiia zhivopisi L.V. Zaka" in *Russkaia mysl*, Paris, 1979, 17 May, p. 11.
A14, Vol. 4, p. 196.
A. Rannit: "Pismennaia beseda s poetom Rossiianskim Leonom Zakom" in Z. Shakhovskaia et al.: *Russkii almanakh*, Paris: P.I.U.F., 1981, pp. 250-52.
J.-M. Dunoyer: *Léon Zack*, Paris: Editions de la Différence, 1989.
J.-M. Maulpoix: *Léon Zack ou l'instinct de ciel*, Paris, Editions de la Différence, 1990.
A. Pizerra: *Léon Zack*, Paris: Editions de la Différence, 1991.
P. Cabanne et al.: *Léon Zack. Catalogue raisonné de l'oeuvre peint*, Paris: Editions de l'Amateur, 1993.
H34, pp. 280-83.
H51, passim.

Zack first attracted public attention as a writer when, as an active supporter of the Ego-Futurist group in Moscow, he published several books of poetry. As Vladimir Markov has pointed out, Zack the poet was a distinctive and original representative of the Russian avant-garde, exerted an appreciable effect on Vladimir Maiakovsky and, in his experimentation with verbal textures, shared some of Velimir Khlebnikov's ideas,[908] even if much of his writing still remains in manuscript form. Zack seems to have started painting in the late 1910s, shortly before he left Moscow, but he reached his own "Zackian" style of lyrical abstraction only in the late 1940s — what J.-C. Marcadé calls the "poetical philosophy of Zack's painting."[909] Beginning in 1922, Zack collaborated as a stage designer with Boris Romanov, Vera Nemtchinova, Bronislava Nijinska, and other choreographers, and his contributions to Romanov's productions at the Russisches Romantisches Theater in Berlin in 1922-23 are especially worthy of note.

1177

1176

1176 [R487].
Self-Portrait, 1969.
Pencil.
Signed and dated lower right: "Léon Zack 69."
4⅛ x 3 in., 10.5 x 7.5 cm.
The reverse also carries two other self-portraits (see No. 1177 [R487a]).
Provenance: the artist, New York, April, 1969.
Reproduced in I20, p. 61.

1177 [R487a].
Two Studies of Heads (Self-Portraits), ca. 1969.
Pencil.
4⅛ x 3 in., 10.5 x 7.5 cm.
Reproduced in I51, No. 272.
Inscriptions: top right with the numbers "676 80."
Reproduced in I51, No. 272.
The reverse carries a self-portrait (see No. 1176 [R487]).

Les Miliions d'Arlequin: opera-ballet in two acts by Ivan Vsevolozhsky with music by Riccardo Drigo. Produced at the Russisches Romantisches Theater, Berlin, on 14 October, 1922, with choreography by Boris Romanov and designs by Vladimir Boberman, Fedor Goziason (Philipp Hosiasson), and Léon Zack.
See No. 17 [R16] for plot summary.

1178 [R488].
Stage Design, ca. 1922.
Watercolor.
Signed lower right: "Léon Zack."
15½ x 22⅝ in., 39.5 x 57.5 cm.
Other inscription: stamped upper right: "B. Romanoff."
Provenance: Elena Smirnova, wife of Boris Romanov, New York, December, 1969.
Reproduced in I20, No. 109; I51, No. 273, in which it is described as a stage design for Darius Milhaud's *Champions*.

1179 [R489].
Costume Design for an African Woman with a Hookah, ca. 1922.
Watercolor.
Signed lower right: "Léon Zack."
18⅞ x 12⅜ in., 48 x 31.5 cm.
Other inscription: left margin: illegible annotation; lower right: stamp "B. Romanoff"; the reverse carries a pencil sketch of a Chinese dancer.

1178

1179

Provenance: Elena Smirnova, wife of Boris Romanov, New York, December, 1969.

Note: It is assumed that Nos. 1178 [R488] and 1179 [R489] are designs for the 1922 production of *Les Millions d'Arlequin* in Berlin. Previous sources have described No. 1178 [R488] as a stage design for a production of Darius Milhaud's *Champions* that, according to M2, p. 204, Anna Pavlova staged in the 1920s. However, this design is very similar to other early pieces that Zack designed for The Blue Bird cabaret in Berlin (see album of photographs entitled *Die Blaue Vogel / L'Oiseau Bleu,* Berlin, n.d., no author, unpaginated, but ca. 1922). For commentary on *Les Millions d'Arlequin* see Nos. 17-18 [R16-17].

Giselle: *ballet in two acts with scenario by Théophile Gautier, Vernoy de Saint-Georges, and Jean Coralli and music by Adolphe Adam. Produced by the Ballets Russes Vera Nemtchinova at the Théâtre des Champs-Elysées, Paris, in 1930 with choreography by Boris Romanov and designs by Léon Zack.*

See No. 152 [R126] for plot summary.

1180 [R490].
Costume Design for a Hunter, 1927.
Watercolor.
Signed lower right and dated: "Léon Zack 1927."
19½ x 13 in., 49.5 x 33 cm.
Provenance: Elena Smirnova, wife of Boris Romanov, New York, December, 1969.
Reproduced in I20, No. 107; I51, No. 274.

1180

1181 [R491].
Costume Design for a Young Nobleman, ca. 1927.
Watercolor.
Signed lower right: "Léon Zack."
18⅞ x 12¼ in., 48 x 31 cm.
Provenance: Elena Smirnova, wife of Boris Romanov, New York, December, 1969.
Reproduced in I20, No. 108.

1181

Note: Before the production for Vera Nemtchinova in 1930, Zack and Romanov had already collaborated on *Giselle* at the Russisches Romantisches Theater, Berlin, in 1922.

908 See V. Markov: *Russian Futurism*, Berkeley: University of California Press, 1968, especially pp. 113-16.
909 This is the translation of the title of J.-C. Marcadé's Russian article on Zack.

Léon Zack, Paris, 1960.

ZAKHAROV, Fedor Ivanovich

Born 1882, Astrakhan, Russia; died 28 August, 1968, New York, USA.

1910-16 attended MIPSA; 1911 onwards participated in numerous exhibitions, such as the "Moscow Association of Artists," the "World of Art," and the "Union of Russian Artists"; 1915 the Rumiantsev Museum in Moscow acquired some of his engravings; 1918-20 taught at Svomas; 1922 made illustrations for Berlin edition of Alexander Pushkin's *Count Nulin*; 1923 as a member of the advisory committee for the "Russian Art Exhibition," traveled to New York via Riga, Berlin, and London; designed a poster for the same; 1920s onwards worked in the US primarily as a portrait painter and ex-libris designer; patronized by the American businessman and philanthropist Charles Richard Crane; had several one-man exhibitions in Philadelphia, Paris, New York, and other cities; 1965 put on a large one-man exhibition at the North Carolina Museum of Art in Raleigh, North Carolina.

Bibliography
P. Ettinger: "Fedor Zakharoff as a Portrait Painter" in *The Studio,* London, 1924, Vol. 88, pp. 22-27.
P. Galtsev: "Pamiati F.I. Zakharova" in *Russkaia mysl,* Paris, 1968, 26 September, No. 2705.
A53, Vol. 2, p. 591.
H34, pp. 287.

Zakharov achieved some reknown as a portrait painter, both in Russia and in emigration, although his primary artistic merit lies in his ex-libris designs, silhouettes, and book vignettes. Not surprisingly, he was regarded highly by the Russian bibliophiles Pavel Ettinger and Alexei Sidorov, the former praising his miniature portraits for their "unexpected degree of excellence."[910]

1182 [R782].
Portrait of Konstantin Somov, 1923.
Ink and pencil.
Signed and dated upper right in Russian: "Zakharov, Riga, 18 December 1923."
12 x 9½ in., 30.5 x 24 cm.
Provenance: Elena Somova, New York, April, 1969. Now in a private collection.
Reproduced in I51, No. 219.

Note: Although Zakharov received his training at MIPSA, he was in close touch with St. Petersburg artists and, from 1911 onward was a regular contributor to the "World of Art" exhibitions. Zakharov made this portrait of Somov when both men were in Riga traveling from Petrograd as committee members for the "Russian Art Exhibition," which opened in New York in March, 1924 (see No. 685 [R580]). In a letter to his sister, Anna Somova-Mikhailova, dated 11 December, 1923, and posted in Riga, Somov wrote: "Of my companions the most pleasant is Zakharov. He looks a bit simple, has the appearance

1182

of a monkey, but I think he's a sincere, pleasant man and, moreover, has a sharp sense of humor."[911]

910   Ettinger, "Fedor Zakharoff as a Portrait Painter," p. 22.
911   F51, p. 221.

ZDANEVICH, Ilia Mikhailovich (pseudonyms: Eli Eganbiuri; Iliazd)

Born 9 (21) April, 1894, Tiflis, Georgia; died 25 December, 1975, Paris, France.

Younger brother of Kirill Zdanevich, the avant-garde painter (see next artist entry). 1911 after attending the Tiflis Gymnasium went to Batum and then to St. Petersburg, where he entered Law School at St. Petersburg University; met Viktor Bart and Mikhail Le-Dantiu; 1912 with his brother Kirill and Le-Dantiu "discovered" the primitive artist Niko Pirosmanashvili; moved to Moscow; 1913 published a monograph on Natalia Goncharova and Mikhail Larionov under the pseudonym Eli Eganbiuri; advocated the new movement of *vsechestvo* [Everythingness]; with Goncharova and Larionov co-signed the manifesto "Why We Paint Ourselves"; involved in many Futurist happenings; 1914 met Marinetti in Moscow; joined the Centrifuge group, which also included Boris Pasternak; 1915-17 Caucasus correspondent for the Petrograd newspaper *Rech* [Discourse] and for the *Manchester Guardian;* 1917 received diploma in law; left Petrograd for Tiflis; visited Turkey; back in Tiflis established the 41° group with the avant-garde writers Alexei Kruchenykh and Igor Terentiev; cosigned several 41° manifestos; 1921 arrived in Paris, becoming a prominent member of the international artistic community there; 1930 published a novel, *Voskhishchenie* [Rapture]; until his death active as an avant-garde writer and illustrator.

Bibliography
P. Hulten et al.: *Iliazd.* Catalog of exhibition at the Centre Georges Pompidou, Paris, 1978.
F. Le Gris-Bergmann: *Iliazd, Maître d'oeuvre du livre moderne.* Catalog of exhibition at the Galerie d'art de l'Université du Québec, Montreal, 1984.
A. Isselbacher and F. Le Gris-Bergmann: *Iliazd and the Illustrated Book.* Catalog of exhibition at the Museum of Modern Art, New York, 1987.
H. Iliazd: *Iliazd,* Paris: Union, 1987.
T. Sanikidze: *Kirill Zdanevich. Ilia Zdanevich.* Catalog of exhibition at the State Museum of Arts of the Georgian SSR, Tbilisi, 1989.
A. Calcagni Abrami: *I libri di Iliazd.* Catalog of exhibition at the Biblioteca Nazionale Centrale, Florence, and other institutions, 1991.
M. Muller and F. Le Gris-Bergmann: *41°. Ilya and Kirill Zdanevich.* Catalog of exhibition at Modernism Gallery, San Francisco, 1991.
R. Flak et al.: *Iliazd. Ses Peintres. Ses Livres.* Catalog of exhibition at Galerie Flak, Paris, 1991.
R. Gayraud and T. Nikolskaia, ed.: *Iliazd. 1. Parizhachi,* M: Gileia; Düsseldorf: Goluboi vsadnik, 1994.
R. Gayraud and T. Nikolskaia, ed.: *Iliazd. 2. Voskhishchenie,* M: Gileia; Düsseldorf: Goluboi vsadnik, 1995.
R. Gayraud (postface): *Iliazd. Ledentu le phare,* Paris: Allia, 1995.
R. Gayraud, tr.: *Nathalie Gontcharova Michel Larionov par Elie Eganbury,* Paris: Clémence Hiver, 1996.
R. Gayraud, ed.: *Iliazd et ses peintres,* Paris: Les Carnets de l'Iliazd Club, 1997.
R. Geiro and S. Kudriavtsev, eds.: *Ilia Zdanevich (Iliazd). Filosofiia futurista. Romany i zaumnye dramy,* M: Gileia, 2008.
I. Arsenishvili: *Zdanevich.* Catalog of exhibition at the National Museum of Georgia, Tbilisi, 2009.
For general descriptions of the avant-garde in Georgia see M. Marzaduri et al., eds.: *L'avanguardia a Tiflis,* Venice: Università degli Studi di Venezia, 1982; M. Marzaduri: *Dada Russo,* Bologna: Il cavaliere azzurro, 1984; M. Marzaduri et al., eds.: *Russkii literaturnyi avangard. Materialy i issledovaniia,* Trento: Università di Trento, 1990; and L. Magarotto et al., eds.: *Zaumnyi futurizm i dadaizm v russkoi kulture,* Berlin: Lang, 1991; the two issues of *Terentievskii sbornik,* M: Gileia, 1997 and 1998; F85, passim; B273; and B290.

Ilia Zdanevich (Iliazd) played an important role in the Russian-Georgian-French avant-garde, especially as an apologist and disseminator of pictorial and calligraphic ideas.[912] He contributed to many debates, publications, and exhibitions, and, with Goncharova and Larionov, was a practitioner of "face painting" in 1912-13.[913] He designed Cubo-Futurist booklets and posters, often using asymmetrical typographical shifts to draw attention to a certain word or concept.[914] Iliazd has every right to be considered a Russian (or Georgian) Dadaist.

1183

1183 [R492].
Sigizmund Valishevsky (?): *Portrait of Ilia Zdanevich*, ca. 1919.
Oil on canvas.
21⅛ x 9⅛ in., 53.5 x 48.5
Provenance: *Imperial and Post-Revolutionary Russian Art*, London: Christie's, 5 October, 1989, Lot 414 (reproduced).
According to some specialists, the artist of this portrait is Sigizmund (Ziga) Vladimirovich Valishevsky (Zygmunt Waliszewski, 1897-1936), a close friend of Ilia Zdanevich in Tiflis; according to others, it is by Mikhail Vasilievich Le-Dantiu (1891-1917), although this would predate the work. It may also be a self-portrait.

Zdanevich as contributor:
1184 [R494].
Designer unknown: *Poster Advertising Four Lectures by Ilia Zdanevich on Italian Futurism at the Futurist University, Tiflis*, 1918.
Lithograph in black and white.
7 x 10⅞ in., 17.7 x 27.5 cm.

The text of the poster provides details on the topics, place, and date of the presentations:

> 1-2 F.T. Marinetti's Doctrine
> 3 Italians and the Word
> 4 Painterly Doctrine
> in the auditorium of the Fantastic Tavern, 12, Golovinskii, in the courtyard, on Mondays 12, 19, and 26 of February, and 5 March, 1918. Lectures begin at 8 p.m. Fee for 4 lectures is 5 rubles. Registration is through the Women's Militia Patrol, in the Office, or at the entrance.

In B179, p. 144, it is reproduced on the wrong page, i.e., it should head the description of R494 rather than of R493. Provenance: Viktor Kholodkov, Moscow, 1984.

Note: The diaspora that followed in the wake of the Revolution led Russian artists and writers to converge in the most unlikely places as they sought refuge from the Bolsheviks dominant in Petrograd and Moscow. One such bohemian center was the "fantastic city"[915] of Tiflis (renamed Tbilisi in 1936), capital of Georgia that in May, 1918, became the new Menshevik Republic of Georgia. It was here, rather than in Berlin or Paris, that the Russian avant-garde continued to develop their iconoclastic ideas. Even though "only the main streets are cleaned,"[916] Tiflis boasted an active and vociferous intellectual community *au courant* with the latest trends in European and Russian Modernism. As is clear from No. 401 [R493], Tiflis had long attracted the Russian avant-garde: David Burliuk, Vasilii Kamensky, Nikolai Kulbin, and Vladimir Maiakovsky had all lectured in Tiflis before World War I, Ilia Zdanevich, a native of Tiflis, published his manifesto "What Is Futurism" there in 1914, and he and his brother Kirill propagated Neo-Primitivism, Cubo-Futurism, and Everythingism, organized Kirill's one-man exhibition in 1917, and entertained Kruchenykh in their home for much of 1919.

By the beginning of 1917, in spite of war and civil discontent, Tiflis had become an important laboratory for avant-garde activity: Kruchenykh arrived there in 1916 and Kirill Zdanevich returned from the front to publish, with Kruchenykh and Kamensky, the collection *1918*, in which the latter reproduced his Futurist map of Tiflis. New little magazines sprang up and exhibitions opened, ranging from children's drawings to "Paintings and Drawings by Moscow Futurists," while Kruchenykh, Igor Terentiev, and Ilia Zdanevich even ran the so-called "Futur vseuchbishche" announced in No. 1184 [R494] (a neologism that might be translated as "Futurist University"). Radical poetry and painting flourished thanks especially to the talent of Kruchenykh, who in January 1918 organized the First Evening of Transrational Poetry and who served as a primary stimulus to the group called 41° and the single issue of its magazine (July, 1919).

Perhaps the most important cultural event in Tiflis, however, was the opening in November, 1917, of the bohemian cabaret called the Fantastic Tavern, which witnessed many Dada events during its brief existence of less than two years. Tempered by the "ironic wisdom" of the poet Yurii Degen,[917] the Fantastic Tavern became a meeting-place for poets, painters, composers, actors, and critics who aspired to maintain the momentum of the St. Petersburg and Moscow Silver Age. Consisting of one room decorated by Degen, Lado Gudiashvili, Ziga Valishevsky, and Ilia Zdanevich, the Fantastic Tavern was dominated by the "three fools" (Kruchenykh, Terentiev, and I. Zdanevich) and their 41° group that endeavored to "incarnate a new poetical school by renewing the current poetical language so as to lead it toward the total abstraction of *zaum*."[918]

The poetry declamations, loud polemics, scandalous lectures, such as Kruchenykh's and Terentiev's on anal eroticism, and the general mix of creative improvisation and intellectual régime has led some critics to compare the Fantastic Tavern to the Café Voltaire in Zürich.[919] Certainly, the Tavern, like 41°, wished to "use all the great discoveries of its collaborators and place the world on a new axis."[920] Among the habitués of the Fantastic Tavern were the Georgian poets Semeon Chikovani, Paolo Yashvili, and Titsian Tabidze, "who always used to walk around with a muzzled bear"[921] and who in 1924, together with the artists Iraklii Gamrekeli and Beno Gordesiani, founded the group known as H₂SO₄ (the chemical formula for sulfuric acid) and published the two issues of its journal. Although the language used here was Georgian, not Russian, the group owed much to Kruchenykh's elaboration of *zaum* and to

футур всеучбище
ТИФЛИС
в аудиторип ФАНТАСТИЧЕСКАГО КАБАЧКА головинский 12 во дворе
по понедельникам 12 19 26 февраля 5 марта 18 года
4 лекции
ИЛЬИ ЗДАНЕВИЧА
о италианском футуризме
1—2 УЧЕНИЕ Ф Т МАРИНЕТТИ   3 СЛОВО У ИТАЛИАНЦЕВ
4 ЖИВОПИСНАЯ ДОКТРИНА
начало лекций в 8 час неч   плата за 4 лекции 5 рублей
запись в женской дружине · канцелярия · и при входе

Moscow Cubo-Futurism in general, and, as in the case of Goncharova, Larionov, and Maiakovsky, scandal and violence were part and parcel of their esthetic consciousness. This was acutely manifest, for example, in Konstantin Mardzhanov's proposed production of Maiakovsky's play *Mystery-Bouffe* with designs by Gamrekeli in Tiflis in 1924 (see Nos. 520-24 [R395-99]).

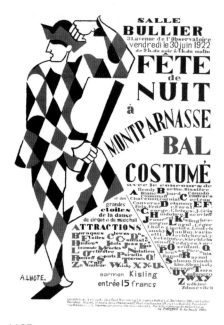

1185

1185 [R495].
(with André Lhote: *Poster Advertising the Montparnasse Costume Ball "Fête de Nuit,"* 1922.
Llithograph in brown and white.
53¾ x 38¼ in., 136.5 x 97 cm.
Provenance: Robert Brown, New York, 1973.
Inscriptions (as part of the design) provide details on the date and location of the Ball: the Salle Bullier, 31, Ave. de l'Observatoire, Paris, for the night of 30 June, 1922, from 9.00 p.m. through 4.00 a.m. The list of participants includes Viktor Bart, Sonia Delaunay, Fernand Léger, Sergei Sudeikin, and I. Zdanevich (cf. Goncharova's version at No. 564 [R432]).
Reproduced in color in J. and S. Müller-Brockmann, *Geschichte des Plakates,* Zürich: ABC, 1971, p. 82; N188, pp. 22 and 24.

Note: Ilia Zdanevich is first mentioned as the co-designer of this poster (with André Lhote, 1885-1962) in *Iliazd and the Illustrated Book,* p. 85, but the exact circumstances of the alleged alliance are not known. It should be pointed out that the poster carries only Lhote's signature, for the name Zdanevich included in the lower right corner is simply the last entry in the alphabetical list of participants.

912 For example, under the pseudonym Eli Eganbiuri, he authored the first monograph on Goncharova and Larionov, i.e., *Mikhail Larionov i Natalia Goncharova,* M: Miunster, 1913.

913 See the manifesto, "Pochemu my raskrashivaemsia" [Why We Paint Ourselves] signed by Goncharova, Larionov, and Zdanevich in *Argus,* M, 1913, December, pp. 114-18. For translation see B12, pp. 79-83.
914 The sources mentioned in the Bibliography for this section contain other examples of Zdanevich's typographical experiments.
915 G. Robakidze in *1928,* No. 4, p. 71. Quoted in *Iliazd, Maître d'oeuvre du livre moderne,* op. cit., p. 11.
916 G. Moskvin: *Prakticheskii putevoditel po Kavkazu,* Odessa: Levinson, 1899, pp. 303-05, 333.
917 Marzaduri, *Dada Russo,* p. 29.
918 From the credo of the 41° group on the first page of their journal. Quoted in *Iliazd, Maître d'oeuvre du livre moderne,* op. cit., p. 13.
919 Ibid., p. 31.
920 From the credo of 41°. Quoted in Ibid, p. 13.
921 G. Sciltian: *Mia avventura,* Milan: Rizzoli, 1963, pp. 131-32.

ZDANEVICH, Kirill Mikhailovich

Born 9 (21) July, 1892, Tiflis, Georgia; died 1 September, 1969, Tbilisi, Georgia.

Older brother of Ilia (Iliazd), the avant-garde poet and artist (see previous artist entry). 1902 attended a local art school in Tiflis; ca. 1910 studied in Moscow; 1912 met the Georgian primitive painter Niko Pirosmanashvili; close to Natalia Goncharova and Mikhail Larionov; contributed to their "Donkey's Tail"; 1913 signed the manifesto "Rayonists and Futurists" and contributed to the "Target" (together with Goncharova, Larionov, Kazimir Malevich, and other members of the avant-garde); collected paintings by Niko Pirosmanashvili; studied in Paris, where he soon gained a reputation as an accomplished Cubist painter; made the acquaintance of Alexander Archipenko and Serge Charchoune there; 1914 mobilized;

1917-19 with Ilia Zdanevich, Alexei Kruchenykh, and Igor Terentiev organized the Futurist group known as 41° in Tiflis; 1920 visited Paris; returned to Tiflis; 1920s onward continued to paint, design theater productions, and publish books and articles, particularly on Pirosmanashvili.

Bibliography
I. Dzutsova: "Gruzinskie temy v russkoi teatralnoi zhivopisi," *Vechernii Tbilisi,* 1983, 2 July.
B. Kerdimun: *Kirill Zdanevich and Cubo-Futurism.* Catalog of exhibition at Rachel Adler Gallery, New York, 1987.
A14, Vol. 4, pp. 274-75.
T. Sanikidze: *Kirill Zdanevich. Ilia Zdanevich.* Catalog of exhibition at the State Museum of Arts of the Georgian SSR, Tbilisi, 1989.
I. Arsenishvili: *Zdanevich.* Catalog of exhibition at the National Museum of Georgia, Tbilisi, 2009.
Also see Bibliography for Ilia Zdanevich.

Unidentified production, *ca. 1919.*

1186 [R496].
Stage Design, ca. 1919.
Watercolor, collage, pencil, pen and ink.
8⅛ x 10⅝ in., 20.5 x 27 cm.
Various inscriptions in Russian are on the reverse.
Provenance: *Impressionist and Modern Paintings, Drawings, Watercolors and Sculptures,* London: Sotheby's, 27 February, 1980, Lot 100 (reproduced).
Reproduced in color in B115, plate 102; and in black and white in A34, p. 477; I51, No. 275; I77, p. 147; N98; O26. A similar design, incorporating Suprematist elements, in the collection of Valerii Dudakov and Marina Kashuro, Moscow, is reproduced in color in K147, p. 129. For the reproduction of another stage design see L128, Lot 38.

1186

1187

1189

Note: With his brother, Ilia (Iliazd), Lado Gudiashvili (Nos. 576-78 [R441-43]), David Kakabadze, Sergei Sudeikin, Iraklii Gamrekeli (Nos. 520-24 [R395-99]), and others, Kirill Zdanevich played an active role in the Tiflis bohemia during 1919-20.[922] With his colleagues, he contributed designs to a number of avant-garde productions at the 41° Theater and the Fantastic Tavern. According to the Georgian scholar Irina Dzutsova,[923] No. 1186 [R496] is probably a design for the interior of the Tiflis café called The Boat of the Argonauts — an "americanized bar"[924] where local artists and writers used to meet. Unfortunately, it is not known for which spectacle Zdanevich designed No. 1186 [R496].

Schéhérazade: *a choreographic poem in one act with music by Nikolai Rimsky-Korsakov and designs by Kirill Zdanevich. Date and place of production unknown.*
    See No. 81 [R77] for plot summary.

1187 [R497].
Stage Design, ca. 1919.
Watercolor.
26 x 30⅜ in., 66 x 100 cm.
Provenance: Hélène Zdanevich, wife of Ilia Zdanevich, Paris, 1967. Now in a private collection.
Reproduced in color in B115, plate 101; and G70.

Note: Although there are no written indications on this design, two similar works in the collection of Petr Navashin in Moscow (a smaller version of No. 1187 [R497] and a preliminary sketch for a poster) are clearly for a production of *Schéhérazade.* Unfortunately, information on such a production, intended or implemented, has not been forthcoming.

922 For information on artistic life in Tiflis in 1919-20 see I. Dzutsova and N. Elizbarashvili: "S. Yu. Sudeikin v Gruzii" in *Muzei,* M, 1980, No. 1, pp. 23-26; B47, passim.
923 N98.
924 Letter from Irina Dzutsova to Nikita D. Lobanov-Rostovsky dated 30 January, 1984.

MISCELLANEOUS ITEMS

The following items do not relate to any particular artist or production in the Catalogue Raisonné. Except for Nos. 1195 and 1196 [both NIRE], the designers are unknown. The provenance for Nos. 1188-94 [R674-77] is Viktor Kholodkov, Moscow, May, 1984.

1188

1188 [R674].
Poster Advertising Productions at the Imperial Theaters, St. Petersburg, 1867.
Lithograph in black on pale blue paper.
22¾ x 16⅞ in., 58 x 43 cm.
Inscriptions (as part of the design) provide details (mostly in French and German) on various productions at the Alexandrinsky, Bolshoi, Mikhailovsky, and Mariinsky Theaters.

1189 [R675].
Poster Advertising Productions at Two Imperial Theaters, Moscow, 1896.
Lithograph in black on pink paper.
18¾ x 15 in., 47.5 x 38 cm.
Inscriptions (as part of the design) provide details on the performances of Ruggiero Leoncavallo's *Pagliacci,* Georgii Konius and José Mendes's *Daita,* Denis Fonvizin's *The Minor,* and Nikolai Gogol's *Wedding* at the Bolshoi and Maly Theaters.

1190

1190 [NIRE].
Poster Advertising a Soirée of the Enchanted Wanderer in the Concert Hall of the Petrovsky School, St. Petersburg, on 11 December, 1915.
Lithograph in black on light green paper.
15 x 9⅞ in., 38 x 25 cm.

Inscriptions announce the appearance of Viktor Khovin with his lyrical-critical pages "Airheads, Madcaps, Dreamers" and the participation of the Futurists Natan Vengrov, Ada Vladimirova, Riurik Ivnev, Tatiana Klado, Mikhail Kozyrev, Alexander Tolmachev and Ekaterina Guro reading the unpublished poems of her late sister Elena (1877-1913). *Ocharovannyi strannik* [Enchanted Wanderer] is a reference to Mikhail Matiushin's publishing-house in Petrograd, which, inter alia, published the almanac *Ocharovannyi strannik,* which Khovin edited and to which Nikolai Evreinov, Ivnev, Velimir Khlebnikov, Khovin, and other Futurists contributed. *Ocharovannyi strannik* was also the title of one of Nikolai Leskov's popular stories (1873).

1192

training, movement coordination, and an interest in the psychotechnics of the theater), and on the academic calendar (entrance examinations on 21-23 September [1922] with the semester beginning on 25 September [1922]).

1193

1193 [R677].
Poster Advertising the Theater School and Laboratory of the Theater of Expressionism, ca. 1922.
Lithograph in black on pink paper.
15 x 11 in., 38 x 28 cm.
Inscriptions provide details on the academic courses offered at the Theater School by Alexei Chicherin (Speech), and Nikolai Lvov (Rhythmodynamics of Movement), Valentin Parnakh (Eccentric Dance), Ippolit Sokolov (Gymnastics, Reflexology, etc.), and Vitalii Zhemchuzhnyi (Destruction of the Magical Forms of the Theater).

Note: The Moscow group of Expressionist writers, artists and dramatists was founded in 1920. Led by Ippolit Vasilievich Sokolov (1902-74), the group had little in common with the Expressionist movement in the West represented by artists such as Ernst Ludwig Kirchner and Max Pechstein. The Moscow group advocated bodily expression as an art form — the use of gymnastics, reflexology, Taylorism, etc. — which Sokolov discussed in his several pamphlets on the subject, e.g. *Sistema trudovoi gimnastiki* (M: publishing-house not indicated, 1922). These Moscow Expressionists opened their Laboratory Theater in September, 1922, but it functioned for only a very short time.

1194

1194 [NIRE].
Poster Advertising the Exhibition of Paintings by the Wing Group of Painters, 1927.
Lithograph in black and white.
30⅛ x 22¼ in., 76.5 x 56.5 cm.
Inscriptions (as part of the design) announce that the exhibition is taking place from 17 February through 13 March, 1927, in the Historical Museum on Red Square, Moscow, and provide the names of the sixteen participants: Boris Borisov, Vasilii Grigoriev, Nikolai Grigoriev, E.N. Ivanov, Mikhail Karneev, Sergei Kirov, Vasilii Novozhilov, Alexander Osmerkin, Georgii Rublev, Viktor Sadkov, Moisei Feigin, Anton Chirkov, Boris Shabl-Tabulevich, Vasilii Sherishev, Fedor Shmelev, and Tatiana Konchalovskaia. Printed by Mosgublit at the Politrafprom Printing House, Moscow, in an edition of 1000.

Note: Led by Osmerkin, the Wing group emphasized what they regarded as the essential prerogatives of the craft of painting (color, brushstroke, texture, density), while relegating the didactic purpose of subject matter to a secondary position. For some information on Wing see A32, p. 98.

1191

1191 [NIRE].
Poster Announcing the Moscow Region Theater of the Proletarian Lads, Moscow, 1921.
Lithograph in orange on light green paper.
12¾ x 8⅝ in., 32.5 x 21.8 cm.
Inscriptions (as part of the design) announce three productions in a former church on the Bolshaia Ordynka in Moscow of *The Chapaev Men* by Vasilii Liubimov, *The Administration of Village North* by Nikolai Shestakov, and *Fugitives* by Vasilii Liubimov et al. Mass games, singing and dancing are to precede the spectacles.

1192 [R676].
Poster Advertising the Laboratory of the Theater of Expressionism, ca. 1922.
Lithograph in black on pink paper.
18⅞ x 13¾ in., 48 x 35 cm.
Inscriptions (as part of the design) provide details on the location of the Theater (on the premises of Labor School No. 21 at 18, Znamenka Street, Moscow), on entrance requirements (good health, gymnastic

1195

1195 [NIRE].
Liudmil Chekhlarov (Bulgarian): Poster advertising *Mystery-Bouffe* **for the production at the State Satire Theater, Sofia, Bulgaria, 1967.**
Lithograph.
Signed in the plate.
52⅜ x 37⅜ in., 133 x 95 cm.
Other inscription (as part of the design): upper left: "Misteriia Buf."
A version is reproduced in A. Fevralsky (compiler): *Maiakovsky. Piesy,* M: Detskaia literatura, 1976, opposite p. 65.
Provenance: Liudmil Chekhlarov, Sofia, October, 1972.

Note: Liudmil Chekhlarov (b. 26 November, 1938, in Dobrich, Bulgaria) specializes in poster and book design and has contributed to numerous exhibitions in Bulgaria and abroad. For the plot summary of *Mystery-Bouffe* see 520 [R395].

1196 [NIRE].
Caran D'ache: *Poster for "Exposition Russe Hippique et Etnographique,"* **Paris, 1895.**
Color lithograph poster.
Signed in the plate, as part of design: "Caran D'ache."
33½ x 13⅞ in., 85.2 x 35.2 cm.
Other inscriptions: in the right margin: "Imp. Hérold, — 131 Bould. St. Michel, Paris."
Provenance: Pai-Lix: Rare Posters, New York: Poster Auctions International, 18 November 2012, Lot 112 (reproduced). Now in a private collection.

Note: Caran D'ache (a Gallicized version of the Russian word *karandash* = pencil) was the pseudonym of Emmanuel Poiré (born November 6, 1858, Moscow, died February 26, 1909, Paris). His grandfather was an Officer-Grenadier in Napoleon's Grande Armée who had been wounded during the Battle of Borodino and had stayed behind in

1196

Russia. Known as one of the fathers of the comic strip, Caran D'Ache was a master at creating visual stories in sequence. In 1877, Caran d'Ache emigrated to France, took French citizenship and joined the army for five years, during which he designed uniforms for the War Ministry and also contributed to their journal *La Vie militaire.* Subsequently, he worked for several Paris papers, his most renowned cartoon being *The Dreyfus Affair* for *Figaro* in 1898. The same year, with Jean-Louis Forain, he cofounded the weekly *Psst...!* magazine (85 issues in all) that was composed entirely of cartoons, caricaturing society and its scandals, showing violent anti-Semitism, as well as defending the honour of the French army. Expositions Russes were held by the Franco-Russian Alliance to surround the Russian monarch's visits to France with cultural events.

Note on Transliteration

Many of the Russian artists, dancers, producers, and critics mentioned in this book spent their lives traveling from country to country. Often their names received diverse, often unconventional, transliterations from the original Russian into the language of their adopted home. Because of these discrepancies and because of the frequent variants in the spelling of Russian names in Western languages, the following transliteration system has been followed:

For those artists, dancers, producers, etc. who emigrated from Russia, took up permanent residence in the West, and established a consistent spelling of their names, this has been retained in the main text. In many cases, the spelling may contradict standard American or British transliteration systems, but this approach has been followed in deference to the individuals themselves. Examples are: Alexandre Benois (not Aleksandr Benua), Dimitri Bouchène (not Dmitrii Bushen), André Houdiakoff (not Andrei Khudiakov), Vladimir Jedrinsky (not Vladimir Zhedrinsky), Jean Pougny (not Ivan Puni), and Nicholas Roerich (not Nikolai Rerikh). In the main text, "Aleksandr", "Aleksandra", and "Aleksei" have been rendered as "Alexander", "Alexandra", and "Alexei" respectively.

For most of those artists and their colleagues who did not emigrate or who emigrated temporarily and returned to the Soviet Union, such as Ivan Bilibin and Vasilii Shukhaev, the names are transliterated in accordance with a modified system of the Library of Congress, although the Russian soft and hard signs have either been omitted or rendered by an "i" (e.g., Grigoriev). This system is also used throughout the footnotes and the bibliographical data where references involve Russian language sources.

Note on Iconographic References

The Lobanov-Rostovsky Collection has been represented at exhibitions worldwide and many works have been reproduced in printed and electronic media. Such sources are usually indicated by a bibliographical code within the curatorial data for each item (e.g. B115, plate 1), together with comparative material. Exceptions are lithographs, silkscreens (pochoirs), and other works reproduced in multiple editions, unless a given item is exceptionally rare (e.g. No. 1116), and also Alexandre Benois's enormous cycle of variants and versions for his several interpretations of *Petrouchka*, which would warrant a separate compilation and analysis. A few of the items are double-sided (e.g. No. 1152) and wherever the verso is of particular importance, this has been given a sequential number (e.g. No. 1153). The iconographic references are not exhaustive and are intended only as a guide to the visual accessibility of the collection within the public domain.

List of Abbreviations

The following abbreviations have been used in both volumes (see Glossary for further explanation of terms):

AKhRR	Association of Artists of Revolutionary Russia
BTM	Bakhrushin State Central Theater Museum, Moscow
CSIAI	Central Stroganov Industrial Art Institute, Moscow
Comintern	Communist International
ed. khr.	*edinitsa khraneniia* (unit of preservation). This refers to the item number within a particular file in Russian archives
f.	*fond* (fund). This refers to the file number in Russian archives
GAKhN	See RAKhN
GAU	Chief Archive Administration, Soviet of Ministers of the USSR, Moscow
Ginkhuk	State Institute of Artistic Culture
GITIS	State Institute of Theater Art (now the Russian Academy of Theater Arts), Moscow
GMTMA	Glinka Museum of Theatrical and Musical Art, St. Petersburg
IAA	Imperial Academy of Arts, St. Petersburg
Inkhuk	Institute of Artistic Culture, Moscow
IZO	Subsection of NKP (Commissariat of Enlightenment) responsible for the visual arts
K	Kiev
l.	*list* (sheet). This refers to the sheet number in Russian archives
L	Leningrad
LEF	Left Front of the Arts
M	Moscow
MIPSA	Moscow Institute of Painting, Sculpture, and Architecture (Russian acronym MUZhV7)
NIRF	Not In Russian Edition (i.e., not listed in B179)
NKP	People's Commissariat for Enlightenment
Obmokhu	Society of Young Artists
OMKh	Society of Moscow Artists
op.	(opus). This is the general heading used for a particular section within a Russian archive *fond*.
OST	Society of Studio Artists
P	Petrograd
Pegoskhum	Petrograd State Free Art Studios
RAKhN	Russian Academy of Artistic Sciences
RGA	Russian State Archive, Moscow
RGALI	Russian State Archive of Literature and Art, Moscow
RM	State Russian Museum, St. Petersburg
RSFSR	Russian Soviet Federative Socialist Republic
SCITD	Stieglitz Central Institute of Technical Drawing, St. Petersburg
SP	St. Petersburg
SSEA	School of the Society for the Encouragement of the Arts, St. Petersburg
Svomas	Free Studios
TG	State Tretiakov Gallery, Moscow
Unovis	Affirmers of New Art
Vkhutein	Higher State Art-Technical Institute
Vkhutemas	Higher State Art-Technical Studios
VNIITE	All-Union Scientific Research Institute of Technical Esthetics
Vsekokhudozhnik	All-Russian Cooperative Association "Artist"
Zhivskulptarkh	Collective for "Painting-Sculpture-Architecture" Synthesis

INDEX

"0.10" exhibition: 15, 297, 314, 331, 332, 430, 431

"1905 Russie – 1917 – URSS 1935" festival, Toulouse: 160

"1917-X-1927" (Stage Design in the USSR 1917-X-1927) exhibition: 14, 452

"10 Years of Work at the Little Theater" exhibition, Moscow: 374

14 Portraits de Théâtre 1915-1916, album: 207, 208, 269

20th Century Studies, Canterbury, journal: 335

"20 Years of Work" exhibition: see "Exhibition of Works by Vladimir Maiakovsky"

"30th Anniversary of the Moscow Artists Union" exhibition: 179

"100 Years of French Art" exhibition, St. Petersburg: 282

"5 x 5 = 25" exhibition: 161, 326, 338, 339, 383, 435

"IV State Exhibition of Paintings", Moscow: 427, 445

"V State Exhibition of Paintings", Moscow: 321, 383

"X State Exhibition: Non-Objective Art and Suprematism": 236, 326, 349, 383, 384, 386

"XI State Exhibition: Works of the Union of Applied Art and Industrial Design Workers": 285

"XIV Exhibition of the Wanderers": 312

"XIX State Exhibition", Moscow: 241

"No. 4" exhibition: 200, 264, 283

A.B.A. Gallery, New York: 135

Aaron, Didier: 221

Abbot, James: 34

Abkhazia State Museum, Sukhumi: 364

Abraham, Gerald: 348

Abramov, A.I.: 267

Abramtsevo art colony: 197, 244, 312, 348, 358, 386, 400, 429, 430, 443

Abramtsevo Ceramic Studio: 400

Abstraction-Création group: 189, 321, 322

Academia Publishing-house: 31, 53, 183, 185

Academic Theater of Drama / Pushkin Academic Theater of Drama, Leningrad: 14, 15, 98, 259, 319, 378, 424

Academic Theater of Opera and Ballet, Leningrad: see Mariinsky (Kirov) Theater

Académie Cormon, Paris: 134

Académie de la Grande Chaumière, Paris: 31, 215, 309, 324, 355

Académie de la Palette, Paris: 31, 139, 314, 326, 426

Académie Julian, Paris: 182, 331, 377

Académie Ranson, Paris: 118, 131, 217, 361

Académie Russe / Académie Libre, Paris: 15, 308, 430, 431

Académie Vassilieff: see Vassilieff, Marie

Academy of Applied Arts, New York: 215

Academy of Art, Tbilisi: 261, 372

Academy of Artistic Sciences, State / Russian (GAKhN/RAKhN): 52, 53, 228, 452

Academy of Arts, St. Petersburg / Petrograd / Leningrad: 52, 119, 184, 221, 229, 264, 282, 302, 313, 321, 322, 399, 452

Academy of Arts of the USSR, Moscow: 197, 221, 261, 309

Academy of Commercial Sciences, Practical, Moscow: 312, 435

Academy of Fine Art, Santiago, Chile: 215

Academy of Fine Arts, Imperial, St. Petersburg: see Academy of Arts, St. Petersburg / Petrograd / Leningrad

Academy of Material Culture, Petrograd / Leningrad: 319

Academy of Music, Brooklyn, New York: 160

Academy of Sciences, Novosibirsk: 137, 183

Academy of Social (Communist) Education: see Krupskaia Academy

Accademia di San Luca (Academy of St. Luke), Rome: 239

Acquavella Galleries, New York: 271

Adalmina's Pearl, play: 328, 435

Adam, Adolphe: 68, 317, 354, 455

Adam, Adolphe Charles: 317

Adam de la Halle: 146

Adaskina, Nataliia: 327, 328, 330, 331

Addison, Errol: 273

Adelphi Gallery, London: 111

Ades, Dawn: 196, 379

Adskaia pochta, St. Petersburg, journal: 20, 377

Adzhindzhal, B.: 364

Aelita, film: 161, 162, 165-166, 178, 190, 309, 333, 334, 374

Aeschylus: 178

Aesop: 190, 322

Afanasiev, Alexei: 397

Agaian, Lusik: 351

Agasian, Ararat: 351

Aida, opera: 141, 142, 443

Aiglon, L', play: 288

Aillagon, Jean-Jacques: 231

Aivazovsky Art Gallery, Feodosia: 281

Aivazovskaia (Lattry, Rybitskaia), Elena: 281

Aivazovsky, Ivan: 184, 281

Aizenberg, Nina: 11-13, 287

Akademie der bildenden Künste, Munich: 228, 305, 313

Akhmatova, Anna: 29, 221, 227, 228, 319

Akhmeteli, Sandro: 194

AKhRR: see Association of Artists of Revolutionary Russia

Akimov, Nikolai: 14-15, 133, 144, 216, 224

Aksenov, Ivan: 157, 283, 326, 438

Alabama-Halle, Munich: 160

Aladin, ou la Lampe Merveilleuse, variety show: 36, 161

Aladzhalov, Manuil: 444

Aladzhalov, Semeon: 446, 447, 448, 451

Albatros: see Société des Films Albatros

Albeniz, Isaak: 208

Albert Hall, Royal, London: 118

Albright-Knox Art Gallery, Buffalo: 139

Aldanov, Mark: 431

Aldona (I Lituani), drama: 217

Aleko, opera: 137, 138

Aleksandrov, P.: 189

Aleksandrov, Sergei: 426

Aleksandrova, Natalia: 57, 302, 355, 428

Alekseev-Yakovlev, Alexei: 143

Alekseeva, Adel: 257

Alexander Nevsky, film: 156, 157

Alexander Raydon Gallery, New York: 218, 378

Alexander I, Emperor of All the Russias: 258, 262

Alexander III, Emperor of All the Russias: 358

Alexander III Museum: see Pushkin State Museum of Fine Arts (GMII)

Alexander VI, Pope: 417

Alexander, Sidney: 137, 138

Alexandrinsky Theater, St. Petersburg / Petrograd: 35, 40, 53, 145, 197, 198, 295, 378, 386; see also Pushkin Academic Theater of Drama, Petrograd / Leningrad

Alexandrov, Anatolii: 447

Alexeev, Alexei: 317

Alexeev, Konstantin: see Stanislavsky, Konstantin

Alexeev, Valerii: 193

Alfano, Franco: 26, 323

Alfieri, Marco: 158

Algaroff-Metzl, Youli (Algarov, Yulii): 214

Alhambra Theater, London: 49, 50, 154

Alier, Roger: 290

Almast, opera: 351

Alpatov, Mikhail: 260, 349, 351, 442

"All-Belarus Art Exhibition", Moscow: 303

"All-Russian Agricultural Exhibition" / "All-Union Agricultural Exhibition", Moscow: 161, 312, 334, 439

All-Russian Air Club, Imperial: 136

"All-Russian Art and Industry Exhibition", Nizhnii Novgorod: 244, 429, 446

All-Russian Congress of Artists, St. Petersburg: 256

All-Russian Congress of Futurists, First: 297

All-Russian Theatrical Society: 285

All-Russian Union of Poets: 239

All-Ukrainian Visual Arts Committee: 129

All-Union Children's Film Studios: see Soiuzdetfilm

"All-Union Polygraphic Exhibition", Moscow: 445

All-Union Scientific Research Institute of Technical Esthetics (VNIITE), Moscow: 327, 384, 397

All-Union Theater / Theatrical Society: 144, 181, 197, 238, 445

Allard, Roger: 364

Allegri, Orest: 99, 110, 111, 233

Allegri, R. 111, 117, 155

Allenov, Mikhail: 442

Allenova, Ekaterina: 358

Alliance Russe, Paris: 355

Almedingen, Boris: 137

Aloizi Theater, Sukhumi: 364

Alpine Club, The, London: 412

Altman, Natan: 15-16, 29, 30, 32, 52, 179, 235, 236, 285, 351

Altshuller, Anatolii: 228

Amadeo, pseudonym: see Dobuzhinsky, Mstislav

American Ballet Theater / Ballet Theatre: 138, 151, 156, 337

American Federation of Arts: 20

Amiard-Chevrel, Claudine: 10, 31, 446

Amiranashvili, Shalva: 194

Amkhanitskaia, Anna: 425

Amour autour de la maison, L', film: 31

Amour et Hiérarchie / *Love in the Ranks*, revue: 111, 112

Anarkhiia, Petrograd, newspaper: 348, 426

Anathema, play: 225

Andersen, Hans Christian: 96, 392

Andersen, Troels: 297, 316, 397

Anderson Galleries, New York: 32

Anderson-Ivantzova, Elisabeth: 265, 267, 394

Andral, Jean-Louis: 351

Andrea Chénier, opera: 65

Andreenko (Andrienko-Nechitailo), Mikhail: 16-19, 162

Andreev, G.: 26

Andreev, Leonid: 19, 225, 227

Andreev, Nikolai: 227

Andreev, Viacheslav: 32

Andreeva, Lidiia: 362, 400, 406, 411

Andreeva, Mariia: 30

Andronikova, Salomeya: see Halpern, Salomé

Andronnikov, Iraklii: 52

Angeles, Victoria de los: 160

Angermuseum, Erfrut: 200

Anikieva, Vera: 183

Anisfeld, Boris: 19 26, 348, 453

Anisimov, Grigorii: 442

Anisimov, Yurii: 266

Anna Karenina, play: 144

Anna Ludmila: 348

Annely Juda Fine Art / Annely Juda Gallery, London: 190, 322

Annenkov, Boris: 30

Annenkov, Pavel: 294

Annenkov, Yurii: 27-31, 32, 92, 102, 159, 228, 231, 238, 254, 265, 280, 282, 349, 393, 421, 441, 442

Annenkova (Galpern), Elena: 28

Annensky, Innokentii: 162, 178

Annonce faite à Marie, L' / *The Tidings Brought to Mary*, play: 435, 436

Ansermet, Ernest: 43, 268

Antikvar, Moscow, journal: 160

Antipova, Rimma: 215

Antique Theater [Starinnyi teatr], St. Petersburg: 58, 146, 225, 227, 261, 262, 263, 364

Antokolsky, Mark: 313

Antokolsky, Pavel: 382

Antonov, V.: 214

Apollinaire, Guillaume: 137, 139, 182, 283, 431, 451

Apollo, London, journal: 57, 111

Apollon, St. Petersburg, journal: 33, 52, 146, 178, 214, 221, 223, 227, 228, 229, 263, 308, 312, 377, 378, 443, 445

Appia, Adolphe: 163, 178, 435, 439

Après-midi d'un Faune, L', ballet: 45, 160

Apushkin, Yakov: 452, 453

"Araignée'l" exhibition, Paris: 314

Aranovich, David: 379

Arapov, Anatolii: 164, 350, 351

Archaeological Institute, French: 281

Archaeological Institute, Moscow: 311

Archaeological Institute, Petrograd: 159

Archer, Kenneth: 344

Archipenko, Alexander: 52, 321, 326, 431, 445, 446, 458

Architecture-Construction Institute, Moscow: 379

Archives d'Architecture Moderne, Brussels: 165

Archivio del '900, Rovereto: 162

Ardov, Viktor: 283

Arendt, Ariadna: 281

Arensky, Antonii: 21, 22, 41, 140, 246

Argutinsky-Dolgorukov, Vladimir: 51-52, 102

Arkadin (Arcadine), Ivan: 304, 305, 437

Arkhangelsky, Alexei: 112, 113, 148, 218, 373, 379

Arkhipov, Abram: 179, 232, 308, 337, 444, 452

Arkhitektura SSSR, Moscow, journal: 397

Arkin, David: 360

Arlecchinata, ballet: 337

Armand Hammer Museum of Art, Los Angeles: 297, 379

Armored Train 14-69, play: 14, 15, 374

ARMU: see Association of Revolutionary Art of the Ukraine

Army of the World, The, play: 342

Arnberg, George: 118

Arnshtam (Arnstam), Alexander: 27, 31-32, 444

Arnstam, Cyril (Kirill): 31

Aronov, Igor: 228

Aronson, Boris: 15, 32-33, 333, 423

Aronson, Lisa: 33

Aronson, Naum: 313

Arp, Hans: 52, 291

Arrival at Bethlehem, The: 372

Arseniev Gymnasium, Moscow: 326

Arsenishvili, I.: 456, 458

Art, L', Paris, journal: 214

Art of Action Group, Kiev: 307

Art and Antiques, New York, journal: 221

Art and Decoration, New York, journal: 26

Art Bulletin, New York, journal: 136

Art Bureau, Petrograd: see Dobychina, Nadezhda

"Art Décoratif Théâtral Moderne" exhibition, Paris: 200, 201, 207, 208, 214, 268, 269, 270, 271, 272, 281

Art-Divage / Art-Divazh gallery, Moscow: 53, 183

Art e Dossier, Florence, journal: 348

Art Education Project, New York: 287

Art Education Union of Workers'
    Organizations, Moscow: 181
Art-Industry Sub-Section: 348
Art Institute, Chicago: 221
Art Museum, Simferopol: 281
Art Salon on Bolshaia Dmitrovka,
    Moscow: 267, 283
Art School for Sailors, Petrograd: 144
Art Curial: 182
Art et les artistes, Paris, journal: 125
Art et Industrie, Paris, journal: 160
Art Gallery of Ontario: 20
"Art in the Crimea" exhibition, Yalta:
    132, 388
Art Institute, Kiev: see Kiev Art Institute
Art Institute, Odessa: see Odessa Art
    Institute
Art Institute, Penza: see Savitsky Art
    Institute, Penza
Art Journal, New York, journal: 200
Art News, New York, journal: 162, 288
Art-Practical Institute, Vitebsk: see
    Vitebsk Popular Art Institute
Art Russe, auction, Paris: 329
"Art Russe" exhibition, Bruxelles: 55,
    372
"Art Russe, L'", Paris: 132
Art Salon, Moscow: 267, 348
Art School, Konstantin Yuon's and Ivan
    Dudin's, Moscow: 31, 129, 156,
    179, 294, 309, 314, 326, 348, 383,
    426, 452
Artcurial Gallery, Paris: 385
Artémis Troublée, ballet: 50
Artforum, New York, journal: 162
ArtGorod, St. Petersburg, journal: 420
"Artists of the RSFSR over the Last 15
    Years" exhibition, Leningrad: 15, 183
"Artists of the Soviet Theater over the
    Last 17 years (1917-1935)"
    exhibition, Leningrad / Moscow: 15,
    181, 232, 452
"Artists to Comrade Warriors"
    exhibition: 429
Arts Anciens, Geneva: 271
Arts and Decoration, New York, journal:
    335
Arts Council Gallery, London: 200, 264
Artseulov, Konstantin: 181
Arvatov, Boris: 15, 143, 196
Asafiev, Boris: 435
Ascher, Celia: 140
Aseev, Nikolai: 10, 159, 369
Ashmolean Museum, Oxford: 52, 96,
    288, 377
Ashton, Frederick: 118
Ashton, Geoffrey: 70, 76
Aslet, Clive: 355
Asriev, Vladimir: 330
Association of Actors, Writers, Artists,
    and Musicians, Terioki: 256

Association of Artists of Revolutionary
    Russia (AKhRR): 257, 301, 445, 452
Association of Contemporary Architects
    (OSA): 196, 435
Association of Contemporary Artists of
    the Ukraine: 232
Association of Free Thinkers: 447
Association of Independents: 156
"Association of New Tendencies in Art"
    exhibition, Petrograd: 282
Association of New Trends of Art: 397
Association of Realist Artists: 374
Association of Revolutionary Art of the
    Ukraine (ARMU): 129
Association of Revolutionary Poster
    Artists: 237
Association of Russian-American
    Scholars in USA: 146
Association of Stage Designers,
    Moscow: 10
Association of Three: 305
Association of Workers of the Visual
    Arts: 303
Astrakhan Ecclesiastical Seminary: 257
Astruc, Gabriel: 358
At the Gate of the Kingdom / *Ved
    Rigets Port*, drama: 198
Atelier de Création Populaire: 160
Atelier of Fashions, Moscow: 30, 161,
    309
Atheist, Publishing-House, Moscow:
    331
Atheist Theater, Moscow: 331
Aubert, Louis: 51
Aubes, Les, play: 144, 145, 235
Auction at Hôtel Drouot / Auction at
    Nouveau Drouot, Paris: 57, 131,
    132, 163, 165, 166, 167, 210, 220,
    221
Auction at Phillips, Son and Neale,
    London: 239, 240
Auer, Leopold: 444
Aurora's Wedding, ballet: 110
Auslender, Sergei: 364
Autre Messie, L', revue: 289
Avangard, Moscow, journal: 232
"*Avant-Garde in Russia 1910-1930:
    New Perspectives, The*", exhibition:
    160
Avare, L', play: 428
Avdeev, Alexandre: 220, 221
Averbakh, Leopold: 429
Averchenko, Arkadii: 334, 335
Avidon, B. (V.?): 366
Avtonomova, Nataliia: 384
Axjonow, Iwan: see Aksenov, Ivan
Axman, Gladys: 22
Azadovsky, Konstantin: 57
Ažbè, Anton: 134, 146, 228, 319
Aziade, ballet: 21, 22, 25

Babaian, Mariiam: 451
Babel, Isaak: 367
Babenchikov, Mikhail: 26, 29, 386
Babiiak, Viacheslav: 221
Bach, Johann Sebastian: 376
Badalian, Viktoriia: 446, 447, 448
Bagritsky, Eduard: 423
Baian, Moscow, journal: 376, 377
Baian, pseudonym: 421
Baier, Simon: 397
Baiguzina, Elena: 34
Bakhrevsky, Vladislav: 429
Bakhrushin State Central Theater
    Museum (BTM), Moscow: 29, 40,
    41, 60, 144, 162, 164, 199, 203,
    245, 246, 257, 258, 263, 284, 296,
    306, 317, 333, 334, 346, 350, 352,
    376, 377, 382, 404, 437, 439, 440,
    447
Bakhrushin, Alexander: 296
Baklund, Elsa: 444
Bakos, Katalin: 200
Bakrakh, Alexander: 331
Baksheev, Vasilii: 444
Bakst (Rozenberg), Léon (Lev): 7, 20,
    33-52, 56, 57, 58, 71, 102, 123, 125,
    127, 131, 137, 141, 142, 145, 147,
    162, 163, 181, 191, 198, 199, 215,
    217, 220, 225, 244, 246, 254, 261,
    262, 268, 287, 288, 289, 290, 302,
    358, 359, 360, 372, 375, 376, 396,
    431, 444, 453
Bakst, Liubov: see Gritsenko, Liubov
Baku Art Institute: 422
Baku Workers' Theater: 367
Bal Banal, The, Paris: 209, 210, 211,
    212
Bal de Cortèges Travesti / Deuxième Bal
    des Artistes, The, Paris: 431
Bal Costumé, Venice: 352
Bal "Fête de Nuit", Montparnasse
    Costume, Paris: 457
Bal de la Grande Ourse, Paris: see
    Grande Ourse Bal
Bal Olympique, Paris: 210, 212
Bal Oriental, Paris: 352, 355
Balaganchik, play: 17, 350
Balaganchik [Fairground Booth] theater,
    Petrograd: 14, 15, 30, 31
Balagin, Alexander: 193
Balakirev, Milii: 19, 21, 410
Balan, Semeon: 81, 90
Balanchine, George / Balanchine
    Company: 110, 144, 190-191, 322,
    357, 366, 393, 412, 420; see also
    Young Ballet
Balashev, Abram: 283
Balashova, Alexandra: 123
Balet, Moscow, journal: 138
Baliev (Balieff, Balian), Nikita: 14, 32,
    101, 112, 113, 148, 219, 297, 334,

335, 336, 372-373, 389, 401, 407, 409
Ball at the Palazzo Labia, The: 353
Balla, Giacomo: 281
Ballet Rambert: see Rambert, Marie / Rambert Dance Company
Ballet Review, New York, journal: 52
Ballet Russe de Monte Carlo: 33, 118, 125, 149, 154, 156, 201, 224, 241, 366
Ballet Shop, The, New York: 323
Ballet Theatre: see American Ballet Theater
Ballet Troupe of the Royal Siamese Court: 47
Ballets Roland Petit, Paris: 352
Ballets Romantiques Russes: 161
Ballets Russes: 8, 33, 34, 41, 43, 45, 46, 52, 56, 58, 59, 65, 70, 96, 118, 125, 128, 147, 149, 160, 180, 181, 190, 199, 201, 203, 207, 208, 212, 213, 214, 246, 262, 264, 267, 268, 270, 271, 272, 274, 275, 280, 287, 289, 322, 358, 364, 396, 400, 410, 420, 454, 455
Ballets Suédois: 48, 430
Ballier, Avgust: 398
Balmont, Konstantin: 260, 262, 427
Baltrushaitis, Jurgis: 344
Balybina, Yulia: 225, 226, 228
Baranoff-Rossiné (Baranov), Vladimir (Wladimir): 52-53, 125, 229, 396
Baranovskaia, Vera: 98
Baratov, Leonid: 251
Barber of Seville / Barbiere di Siviglia, opera: 181, 182, 311
Barberà-Ivanoff, Alexandre: 220, 221
Barbey d'Aurevilly, J.: 220
Barbier, Jules: 99
Baritainsky, Alexander: 294
Barkov, Semeon: 132
Barmer Ruhmeshalle: 53
Barna, Yon: 156
Barnett, Vivian: 228, 229
Baron, Stanley: 139
Baronova, Irina: 224
Barotte, R.: 225
Barov, S.: see Bobrov, Sergei
Barran, Julian: 200, 420
Barry, André: 41
Barsacq, Mila: 35
Barsamov, Nikolai: 281
Barshch, Alexander: 441
Barsheva, Irina: 21, 360
Barsova, Liudmila: 445
Bart, Viktor: 211, 266, 267, 326, 372, 456, 458
Bartet: 378
Barthes, Roland: 160
Bartlett, Rosamund: 298
Bartoli, Federico: 125

Bartoshevich, Andrei: 14, 15
Barynskaia, A.: 226
Baschet, Marcel: 182
Bashkiroff, Irina: 201, 213, 275, 360
Bashkiroff (Bashkirov), Vladimir: 275
Basil, Wassily de (Vasilii Voskresensky): 109, 123, 160, 201, 212, 213
Basin, Petr: 429
Baskakov, Nikolai: 186
Basmadjian, Garabed: 16, 352
Basmajan, Gallery, Paris / Garik Basmajan, Gallery 134
Basner, Elena: 138, 200, 395
Bassekhes, Alfred: 197, 198
Bassenge Auction House, Berlin: 417
Basyrov, Anatolii: 244
Bat cabaret / Chauve-Souris / Letuchaia mysh: 10, 14, 31, 32, 100, 101, 111, 112, 113, 148, 200, 217, 218, 219, 317, 322, 335, 336, 372, 373, 379, 386, 388, 389, 400, 407, 409, 426
Bathhouse, play: 341
Battleship Potemkin, The, film: 156, 157
Baudelaire, Charles: 43, 220, 221
Bax, Arnold: 271
Baydaroff: see Poliakov-Baidarov, Vladimir
Bayer, Josef: 37
Bazanov, Vadim: 303
Bazetoux, Denise: 200
Bazhan, Mikola: 305
Beardsley, Aubrey: 161, 217, 445
Beaton, Cecil: 353
Beaumont, Cyril: 20, 21, 47, 141
Beauvais manufactory: 182
Bebutov, Valerii: 181, 182, 233, 440, 441, 442, 448
Bebutova, Elena: 260
Beckers, Marion: 430
Bed Bug, The, play: 320, 321, 339-342, 343
Bedel Storage House, Paris: 43
Begichev, Vladimir: 150, 198
Beggars' Opera, The, opera: 383
Beistegui, Carlos (Charles) de: 352, 353, 354, 355
Beistegui, Johnny de: 353, 355
Bekhteev, Vladimir: 53-55, 158, 359
Bekkerman, Sonya: 20
Beklemishev, Vladimir: 301
Beliaev, clown: 55
Beliaev, A.N.: 267
Beliaev, Yurii: 35, 52
Beliakov, Vladimir: 120
Belikov, Pavel: 344
Belikov, Vladimir: 146
Belitz, Semeon: 359
Belkin, Veniamin: 281
Belle Eccentrique, La: 48
Beloborodoff (Beloborodov), Andrei: 55-

56, 311, 358
Belodubrovsky, Mark: 189
Belorussian State Jewish Theater, Minsk: 424
Belorussian State Theater, Minsk: 331
Belsky, Vladimir: 103, 113, 114, 122, 124, 201, 241, 244, 245, 247, 289, 346, 351, 362, 419
Beltramo, Claudia: 298
Bely, Andrei (pseudonym of Boris Bugaev): 35, 52, 236, 285, 308, 319, 427
Benelli, Sem: 282, 310
Benjamin, Jean: 228
Benjamin-Constant, Jean-Joseph: 261
Benois (Benua), Alexandre: 5, 6, 17, 19, 33, 34, 37, 41, 42, 43, 50, 52, 56-111, 112, 120, 121, 122, 123, 124, 131, 133, 136, 146, 147, 180, 201, 212, 215, 220, 222, 228, 241, 244, 254, 258, 261, 262, 263, 265, 268, 280, 288, 290, 302, 314, 338, 350, 351, 352, 355, 357, 358, 364, 372, 376, 377, 389, 393, 419, 432, 434, 443, 444, 453
Benois, Anna (Atichka): see Tcherkessoff, Anna
Benois (Kavos) Kamilla: 56
Benois, Leontii: 111
Benois, Mikhail: 122, 124, 242, 243, 245, 247, 248, 249, 250, 251, 252
Benois, Nadia (Benua, Nadezhda): 56, 111, 355
Benois, Nicola (Benua, Nikolai): 14, 73, 74, 75, 78, 79, 80, 81, 82, 83, 84, 85, 86, 87, 88, 89, 90, 91, 92, 93, 94, 95, 97, 111-117, 118, 147, 151, 155, 223, 227, 241, 253, 261, 352, 355, 360, 361, 421
Benois, Nikolai Leontievich: 56
Benois family: 55, 57, 58, 70, 76, 79, 95, 96, 97, 101, 111
Benrimo, Joseph Henry: 304
Berberova, Nina: 146, 155, 230, 431
Berès, A. / Galerie Berès: 182, 183
Berezhnoi, Konstantin: 306
Berezil Theater, Kharkov: 231, 232, 305, 307
Berezil Theater, Kiev: 305
"Berezil Theatre Exhibition", New York: 307
Berezkin, Viktor: 144, 145, 178
Berg, Alban: 153
Bergelson, David: 424
Berlin, Irving: 160
Berlinische Galerie, Berlin: 189, 331, 332
Berman, Boris: 26, 314
Berman, Eugène (Evgenii): 118-119, 311
Berman, Leonid: 118

Berman, Merrill: 162, 422

Bernardt, Grigorii: 57, 97

Bernauer, Rudolf: 417

Berners, Gerald: 272, 281

Berninger, H.: 315, 331, 333, 431

Bernshtein, Mikhail: 159, 282

Bertin, Pierre: 270, 272

Beskin, Emmanuil: 235

Beskin, Osip: 369

Besovskoe deistvo [A Devilish Act], play: 146

Bespalova, Elena: 34, 125

Bestuzhev-Riumin, Mikhail: 146

Bezard, V.: 386

Bezhin Meadow, film: 157

Bezmenova, Kseniia: 311

Bi-Ba-Bo cabaret, Kiev: 317, 334

Bi-Ba-Bo cabaret, Petrograd: 333

Bialik, Chaim-Nachman: 313

Bialik, Valentina: 261

Biblioteca Nazionale Centrale, Florence: 456

Bibliothèque Nationale, Paris: 29, 97, 139, 394

Bich, Petrograd, journal: 142

Biches, Les, ballet: 149

Bilibin, Alexander: 118-119

Bilibin, Ivan (Bilibine, J.): 16, 101, 118, 119-125, 132, 221, 262, 263, 296, 361, 362, 372, 377, 378, 430, 443, 444, 445, 453

Bilinsky, Boris: 31, 33, 52, 125-129, 241, 288, 323, 335, 454

Bilinsky-Clémenti, René: 129

Bilinsky-Clémenti, Valeria: 125, 126, 127, 128, 129

Bill, Max: 228

Bilshovyk, Kiev, newspaper: 307

Binevich, Evgenii: 133, 134

Birkos, Alexander: 157-158

Birnbaum, M.: 221

Birot, Pierre-Albert: 182

Birse, Georgii (George): 336

Birzhevye vedomosti, St. Petersburg, newspaper: 335

Bitt, V.: 451

Biutsov, Vladimir: 417

Bizet, Georges: 180, 198, 427

Black and White, operetta: 27

Black Masks, play: 225, 227

Blanche Neige, ballet-opera: 131

Blanche, Jacques-Emile: 305, 346

Blanter, Matvei: 191

Blaue Reiter group and exhibition: 53, 135, 228

Blaue Vogel, Der: see Blue Bird cabaret

Blind Street Musician, The, theatrical number: 407

Blium, Vladimir: 235, 236

Blockade of Russia, mass action: 31

Bloemink, Barbara: 412

Blok, Alexander: 27, 43, 228, 267, 284, 310, 311, 445

Blomberg, Albrecht: 287

Blue Bird cabaret / Der Blaue Vogel [Siniaia ptitsa]: 32, 125, 214, 219, 220, 287, 322, 332, 374, 412, 417, 421, 455

Blue Bird, The / *L'Oiseau Bleu*, play: 19, 21, 22, 26, 48, 150, 288-289, 290

Blue Blouse / Siniaia bluza theater: 10-14, 158, 191

Blue God, The / *Le Dieu Bleu*, ballet: 7, 25, 36, 46, 47

Blue Horns, The [Golubye rogi] group, Tiflis: 217

"Blue Rose" [Golubaia roza] exhibition and group: 260, 308, 319, 349, 350, 351, 386, 427

Blum, Stella: 160

Blume, Mary: 355

Blumenfeld, Felix: 122

Boberman, Vladimir: 17, 454

Bobrov, Sergei: 266, 267, 386

Bobyshev, Mikhail: 154

Boccioni, Umberto: 130

Bocharov, Mikhail: 48, 216, 261, 430

Bode, Andreas: 119

Bogaevsky, Konstantin: 281, 311

Bogatyrev, Alexander: 425

Bogino, Liudmila: 432

Boginskii High School, St. Petersburg: 334

Bogomazov, Alexander: 129-131, 231, 316, 319

Bogomazov, Timofei: 267

Bogorodsky, Fedor: 53

Boguslavskaia (Bogouslavskaia), Kseniia (Xana, Ksana): 219, 255, 331, 332

Bohème, La, opera: 181, 182

Bohm Duchen, M.: 137

Böhmig, Michaela: 219

Boiarsky, Ivan: 360, 361

Boissel, Jessica: 200, 203, 228, 265

Boito, Arrigo: 116

Bojko, Szymon: 10, 395

Bolan, Semeon: 388, 389, 390, 391, 392, 393

Bold Nazar, The, opera: 351

Bolero, orchestral work: 97

Boll, André: 170

Bolm, Adolph (Emilii) / Bolm Ballet Company: 20, 21, 46, 147, 180, 337, 345, 347, 348, 389

Bologovskoi, Vladimir: 251

Bolshakov Painting and Sculpture Institute, Moscow: 348

Bolshakov, Konstantin: 290

Bolshevik Confectionery Factory, Leningrad: 394

Bolshoi Dramatic Theater, Petrograd / Leningrad: 146, 259, 282, 285

Bolshoi Theater, Moscow: 25, 52, 53, 78, 116, 132, 144, 145, 180, 181, 197, 198, 215, 244, 245, 247, 249, 253, 283, 284, 303, 316, 322, 333, 334, 349, 359, 360

Bolshoi Theater Museum, Moscow: 245, 246

Bolshoi Theater of Drama, Leningrad: 319

Bolshoi Theater of Opera and Ballet, Minsk: 367

Bolt, ballet: 11, 133, 134

Bonch-Bruevich, Vladimir: 196

Bonch-Tomashevsky, Mikhail: 280, 398

Bondi, Yurii: 233

Bonham's auctions: 139, 161, 208

Bonnard, Pierre: 331

Bordwell, David: 157

Boris Godunov, opera: 17, 58, 109, 112, 114, 115, 119, 120, 121, 122, 125, 180, 197, 198, 217, 252-253, 286, 289, 319, 372, 373, 377-378, 452, 453

Boris Godunov, Tsar: 17

Borisov, Boris: 297, 460

Borisov-Musatov, Viktor: 319, 351, 364, 444

Borisovskaia, Nataliia: 34, 44, 49

Borodin, Alexander: 128, 245, 246, 249, 345

Borodina, Alexandra: 178

Borovikovsky, Vladimir: 147, 262

Borovsky, Alexander: 191, 261

Bosch, Hieronymus: 184

Bosshard, Emil: 184

Bost, Pierre: 26

Boston Museum of Fine Arts: 221

Boston Public Library: 57

Botkin, Mikhail: 358

Botkin, Sergei: 358

Botkina, Nadezhda: see Ostroukhova, Nadezhda

Botticelli, Sandro: 21, 53

Bouchène, Dimitri (Bushen, Dmitrii): 118, 131-132, 352, 372, 377

Boucher, François: 375

Bouguereau, William: 182

Bouhélier, Saint-Georges de: 388

Boulgakov, Alexei: see Bulgakov, Alexei

Bour, Armand: 50, 99

Bourdelle, Antoine: 309, 310

Bourdet, Edouard: 353

Bourgeois Gentilhomme, Le, play: 10, 98, 350

Bourman, Anatole: 273

Bowlt, John: 6, 14, 15, 19, 31, 33, 34, 50, 56, 57, 117, 118, 129, 134, 135, 146, 155, 156, 162, 183, 184, 185, 188, 191, 192, 193, 195, 200, 214, 217, 220, 221, 225, 228, 236, 237, 253, 254, 256, 263, 281, 288, 290,

295, 297, 303, 307, 308, 327, 335,
    338, 343, 348, 350, 355, 361, 383,
    384, 387, 397, 425, 439, 451
Bozherianov, Ivan: 151
Brahms, Iohannes / Brahms's *Fourth
    Symphony*, ballet: 289
Brailovskaia, Rimma: 132
Brailovsky, Leonid: 132
Braque, Georges: 52, 161, 182, 183,
    283, 430, 431
Braz, Osip: 132, 220, 355, 432, 444
Brecht, Berthold: 383
Bret, Gustav: 123, 125
Briantsev, Alexander: 452
Brigada khudozhnikov, Moscow,
    journal: 383
Brik, Lilia: 143
Brik, Osip: 10, 11, 14, 143, 196, 327,
    341, 369, 451
Brinton, Christian: 19, 20, 26, 215
Brissac, Gilles de: 352
British Museum, London: 260
Britten, Benjamin: 116
Briullov, Karl: 133
Briusov, Valerii: 163, 304, 308, 310, 349,
    382, 437, 438, 443
Brodsky, Alexander: 411
Brodsky, Boris: 286
Brodsky, Isaak: 21, 221, 302, 360
Bromlei, Nadezhda: 303
Bronx production: 33
Bronze Horseman, The, ballet: 57, 154
Brooklyn Academy of Music, New York:
    160
Brooklyn Museum, New York: 19, 20,
    156, 215, 388
Brosse-Ferrand, Violaine de la: 182
Brothers Karamazov, play: 319, 321
Brown, Robert: 207, 208, 270, 272, 458
Brueghel (Bruegel), Pieter: 184
Brullé, Pierre: 231
Brunelleschi, Umberto: 127
Bruni, Fedor: 133
Bruni, Georgii: 132
Bruni, Lev: 16, 133, 282, 399, 439
Bruni, Tatiana: 11, 133-134, 216
BTM: see Bakhrushin State Central
    Theater Museum, Moscow
Bubnova, Varvara: 266, 267
Bubus the Teacher, play: 367-369, 370,
    371
Buchinskaia, Nadezhda: see Teffi
Buchkin, Petr: 52, 261
Buck, Robert: 139
Buckle, Richard: 57, 63, 70, 264, 279,
    281
Buckman, David: 313
Budennyi, Semeon: 143, 188
Budíková-Jeremiášová, Marie: 363
Budilnik, Moscow satirical magazine:
    231

Budkova, L.: 260
Bukhov, Arkadii: 334
Bulgakov (Boulgakov), Alexei 66, 68
Bulgakov, Mikhail: 335, 427
Bulgakova, Oksana: 157
Bullier Balls: 212
Bulwer-Lytton, Edward: 448
Bunin, Ivan: 48, 207, 214, 308, 431
Bunina, Vera: 308
Burini, Silvia: 446
*Burlador de Sevilla y Convidado de
    Pieda, El*, play: 447
Burlington Magazine, The, London,
    journal: 350
Burliuk, David: 130, 134-137, 179, 189,
    219, 256, 283, 284, 331, 344, 457
Burliuk, Liudmila: 134
Burliuk (Elenevskaia), Maria (Marusia):
    135, 137
Burliuk, Nadia (Nadezhda): 134
Burliuk, Nikolai: 134, 135, 136
Burliuk, Vladimir: 134, 135, 331
Burliuks: 130, 135, 256, 266, 397
Burtsev, Alexander: 215
Busch, Günter: 287
Busch-Reisinger Museum, Cambridge,
    Mass.: 201, 290
Butkovskaia, Nataliia: 225, 337, 364
Buzoter, Leningrad / Moscow, journal:
    142
By the Lake, film: 191
Byckling, Lisa: 146
Byron, George: 14
Byt [Everyday Life] group: 305

Cabanne, Pierre: 454
Cabin in the Sky: 32
Café Kade, Moscow: 315
Café Pittoresque, Moscow: 136, 229,
    238, 283, 284, 338, 397, 426, 446,
    447
Café Voltaire, Zürich: 457
Cahiers du monde russe et soviétique,
    Paris, journal: 142
Cain, play: 365
Calcagni Abrami, A.: 456
Calderon de la Barca, Pedro: 166, 225,
    262-263, 311
California Institute of the Arts, Los
    Angeles: 160, 301
Caligula: 159
Calvaresi, Ornella: 157
Calvocoressi, Michel: 348
Cambridge Arts Theatre, Cambridge,
    England: 153
Camerata degli Artisti, Rome: 302
Camorra of Seville, The, play: 439
Campanini, Cleofonte: 23
Canadian-American Slavic Studies,
    journal: 135
Canaletto: 147

Capannina di Porfiri, Rome: 125
Caprice, ballet: 414
Caran D'ache: see Poiré, Emmanuel
Caravaggio: 262
Carmeli, Haviva: 34
Carmen, opera: 180, 198-199, 303, 312,
    427, 428
Carmen, opera-parody: 13
Carmichael, Joel: 119
Carnaval: Scènes, piano work: 388
Carnaval de la Vie, Le, play: 388
Carnegie Hall, New York: 376, 377
Carnival, ballet: 25
Carnival, play: 307
Carousel cabaret, Berlin: 412
Carousel cabaret, Petrograd: 14, 15
Carr, P.: 290
Carr-Doughty, John: 47, 212, 268, 376
Carré, Michel: 99
Carter, Huntly: 168
Cartier, Jean-Albert: 315, 331, 333, 431
Caryathis: see Jouhandeau, Elise
Caryll, Ivan: 412
Casa d'Arte Bragaglia, Rome: 125
Casadesus: 378
Casanova, revue: 161
Casanova, film: 125, 127
Casari, Rosanna: 446
Casse-Noisette, ballet: 65
Cassou, Jean: 321
Catherine the Great, Empress of all the
    Russias: 262
Cena delle Beffe, La, play: 164, 282,
    310, 311
Cendrars, Blaise: 48, 137, 139, 142, 430
Center for the Performing Arts, New
    York: 153
Central Club of Red Army: 422
Central Cooperative Alliance: 138
Central Exhibition Bureau of the IZO
    NKP: 236
Central House for Communist
    Education, Moscow: 309
Central House of Artists, Moscow: 283
Central House of Writers, Moscow:
    199, 379
Central Institute of Labor (TsIT),
    Moscow: 188, 423
Central Lenin Museum, Moscow: 303
Central School of Arts, London: 118
Central Stroganov Industrial Art Institute
    (CSIAI), Moscow: 132, 142, 180,
    181, 182, 191, 215, 229, 232, 238,
    286, 304, 311, 314, 338, 348, 372,
    379, 383, 384, 427, 439, 445
Central Theater of the Soviet Army /
    Central Theater of the Red Army,
    Moscow: 181, 232, 422
Centre Georges Pompidou, Paris: 47,
    137, 138, 139, 183, 200, 203, 229,
    265, 297, 321, 351, 456

Centro de Arte Reina Sofia, Madrid: see
     Museo Nacional Centro de Arte
     Reina Sofia, Madrid
Century Theater, The, New York: 335
Cervantes, Miguel: 164
Cerwinske, Laura: 221
Cézanne, Paul: 179, 180, 283
Chachba, Alexandre: see Shervashidze,
     Alexandre
Chachoin, Henri: 45, 47, 48
Chaga, Lidiia: 446
Chagall (Rosenberg, Rozenberg), Bella:
     137, 138
Chagall (Meyer), Ida: 137
Chagall, Marc (Shagal, Mark): 32, 33,
     52, 137-138, 151, 159, 160, 229,
     266, 267, 294, 331, 445
Chagall Museum, Marc, Vitebsk: 146
Chaikov, Iosif: 32, 305
Chaikovskaia, Vera: 179, 319, 423
Chaliapin (Shaliapin), Fedor: 115, 120,
     122, 125, 181, 244, 247, 252-253,
     255, 259, 303, 313, 314, 345, 358,
     359, 360, 361, 372, 427
Chaliapin (Tornagi), Iola: 360
Chaliapin (Elukhen), Mariia: 360
Chamber Ballet, Goleizovsky's: see
     Goleizovsky, Kasian
Chamber Theater [Kamernyi tetar],
     Moscow: 16, 17, 18, 19, 33, 145,
     158, 161, 162, 163, 164, 170, 171,
     178, 191, 200, 225, 228, 238, 239,
     240, 260, 283, 304, 305, 309, 310,
     311, 316, 329, 330, 374, 379, 381,
     382, 383, 387, 388, 435, 436, 437,
     438, 446, 447; see also Studio-
     School of the Chamber Theater
Chamber Theater, Jewish, Moscow:
     see Jewish Chamber Theater,
     Moscow
Chamber Theater, Miklashevsky's,
     Odessa: 16, 19
Chambers (Chembers)-Bilibina, Mary: 118
Chamot, Mary: 111, 200, 205, 206, 208,
     213, 214, 264, 268, 269
Champions, ballet: 454, 455
Chancellor and the Locksmith, The,
     play: 330
Chanel, Coco: 396
Chanin, Abraham: 189, 191
Chan-Magomedov, Selim: see Khan-
     Magomedov, Selim
Chant du Rossignol, Le (Il Canto
     dell'Usignuolo), symphonic poem:
     197, 270, 281
Chaplin, Charlie: 239, 383
Charchoune, Serge: 458
Chardin, Jean-Baptiste: 375
Charonoff, Basile (Sharonov, Vasilii): 97
Chashnik, Ilia: 138, 159, 290, 297, 298,
     394, 395

Chast rechi, New York, almanac: 265
Chat Noir, La, cabaret, Paris: 216
Chat Noir Theater, Moscow: 12
Château-Musée de Cagnes-surmer: 215
Chatfield-Taylor, Charles: 20
Chatfield-Taylor, Mara: 20, 21, 22, 23,
     24, 26
Chatte, La, ballet: 162, 189, 190-191,
     279, 321, 322, 450
Chauve-Souris, Le: see Bat, The
Chauvelin, Jean: 52, 162, 163, 164, 165,
     166, 169, 255, 449
Chavasse, Jules: 46
Chekhlarov, Liudmil: 461
Chekhonin, Sergei: see Tchehonine,
     Serge
Chekhov, Anton: 32, 132, 232, 287,
     322, 333, 350, 374, 404, 427
Chekhov, Mikhail: 146, 166, 167, 188,
     285, 304, 311
Chekhov family: 427
Chekhova, Olga: see Tschechowa, Olga
Chekrygin, Vasilii: 315
Chelishchev, Pavel: see Tchelitchew,
     Pavel
Chelovek, Moscow, journal: 348
Chelsea Art Club: 118
Chepalov, Alexander: 188
Cherepnin (Tcherepnine), Alexander:
     213
Cherepnin (Tcherepnine), Nikolai: 41,
     44, 59, 60, 140, 322
Cherez group: 140
Cherkashyn, Roman: 307
Cherkesov, Yurii: see Tcherkessoff,
     Georges
Chernetskaia, Inna / Chernetskaia's
     Studio of Synthetic Dance, Moscow:
     380, 381, 382, 383
Cherniak, Yakov: 137
Chernian, Lord: 191
Chernov, Alexander: 135
Chernova, Bella: 192
Chernova, Galina: 432
Chernyshev, Nikolai: 315
Cherry Orchard, play: 374
Cherubina de Gabriak: see Vasilieva,
     Elizaveta
Chervashidze, Alexander: see
     Shervashidze, Alexander
Chervinka (Chervinko), Ivan: 138-139,
     159, 298
Chesterton, Gilbert Keith: 435
Chevalier, Maurice: 151
Chicago Opera Company: 19
Chichagova, Galina: 305
Chichagova, Olga: 305
Chicherin, Alexei: 460
Chief Archive Administration (GAU): 284
Chief Committee of NKP (Glavprofobr):
     142

Chief Thing, The, play: 27, 30, 32, 393
Chikovani, Semeon: 457
Children of the Sun, play: 181
Children's Theater, Kharkov: see
     Kharkov Children's Theater
Children's Theater, Moscow: see
     Moscow Children's Theater
Chilova, Alla: 200
Chinese Theater, Tsarskoe Selo: 198
Chiniakov, Alexei: 435
Chirkov, Anton: 460
Chisla, Paris, journal: 223
Chistiakov, Pavel: 301, 312, 358, 375,
     429, 442
Chopin, Frédéric: 51, 56, 365, 368
Chopiniana, ballet: 56, 372
Choreographic Studio Bronislava
     Nijinska's, Kiev: 162, 306
Chota Roustaveli, ballet: 213-214
Chout, ballet: 264, 265, 272-274
Chout, St. Petersburg, journal: see Shut
Christie's Auctions: 42, 63, 148, 295,
     308, 314, 366, 374, 457
Christmas Carol, A, play: 27
Chudiakoff (Chudiakov), Andrei: see
     Houdiakoff, André
Chudnovskaia, Evgeniia: 216
Chudnovsky, Abram: 330
Chuguev, Vladimir: 119
Chugunov, Gennadii: 146
Chulkov, Georgii: 283
Chupiatov, Leonid: 216, 233, 374
Chushkin, Nikolai: 144
Chuzhak, Nikolai: 143
Chvojnik, Ignatii: 360
Ciagliński, Jan: see Tsionglinsky, Yan
Ciczkewycz, Ihor: 307
Cinderella, film: 14
Ciné-Eye [Kino-glaz], documentary film:
     192
Cinémaction, Paris, journal: 125
Cinematography Polytechnic, State,
     Moscow: 191
Ciofi degli Atti, Fabio: 162
Circle of Art Lovers, Ivanovo-
     Voznesensk: 219
Circle, film: 192
Circus, ballet: 172-173
Circus, The / The Circus of Archibald
     Fox, comedy review: 452
Circus, Leningrad: 134
Circus, State / First State Circus,
     Moscow: 14, 53, 54, 158, 159
Cirque et le Music-Hall, Le: 26
Ciszkewycz, Ihor: 232
Citroën Central Africa Expedition: 221
Citroën Trans-Asiatic Expedition: 221
City Art Gallery, Bristol: 200, 264
City Art Gallery, Leeds: 200, 264
City College of New York: 287
City Museum, Petrograd: 159

City Museum, Riga: 286
City Theater, Brno: 124
Ciurlionis (Čiurlionis), Mikalojus: 229
Civic Opera Company, Chicago: 23, 347
Civico Museo Depero, Roverto, Italy: 281
Civis (Tsivis, Sergei Tsivinsky): 288, 290
Claudel, Paul: 435, 436
Clement, Rémi: 70, 76, 79, 95, 96, 97
Clémenti-Bilinsky, V.: see Bilinsky-Clémenti, V.
Cleopatra: 21, 41, 42
Cléopâtre / Cleopatra, choreographic drama: 22-33, 41, 42, 43, 46, 70, 139, 140, 141, 142, 261, 358
Cliazde: see Zdanevich, Ilia
Club of Masters of Art, Moscow: 341
Clustine, Ivan: 46, 48
Coates, Albert: 109
Cobb, J.: 132
Cocteau, Jean: 42, 47, 182, 183, 279, 305
Coeur à Gaz, Le, play: 140
Coeur de la Marquise, Le, play: 33
Cogniat, Raymond: 191, 287, 289
Cohen, Arthur: 139, 142
Cohen, Ronny: 162
Colarossi, Filippo / Académie Colarossi: 261, 375
Coliseum, St.: Petersburg: 22
Coliseum Theatre, London: 131, 140
Collective of Masters of Analytical Art (School of Filonov): 183, 184-185, 187, 188
Collin-Delavaud, Marie: 162
Colombe, La, opera: 100
Color and Rhyme, New York, journal: 135
Come on, Europe! or The D.E. Trust, play: 367-368, 370, 371, 429
Comedians' Halt [Prival komediantov] cabaret, Petrograd: 146, 215, 216, 221, 254, 334, 365, 393
Comins-Richmond, Allison: 33
Comintern: see Communist International
Commander of the Second Army, play: 320-321
Commission for the Preservation of Works of Art and Historical Monuments: 223
Commission for the Protection of Artistic Treasures, Yalta: 308
Committee for the Popularization of Art Editions: 432, 435
Communal Theater of Musical Drama, Petrograd: 235
Communist Academy, Moscow: 119, 237
Communist International (Comintern) / Congress of the Communist

International: 238, 240-241, 291, 301, 302, 397, 399, 432, 435; see also Third International
Communist University of Workers of the East, Club, Moscow: 12
Community of St. Eugenia: see Society of St. Eugenia
Comoedia Illustré, Paris, journal: 44, 180, 181, 223, 388
Company, musical: 33
Complesso Monumentale di San Michele a Ripa, Rome: 217
Compton, Susan: 137
Comune di Rieti, Rieti, Italy: 282
Connaissance des Arts, Paris, journal: 352, 353
Conservatoire, St. Petersburg / Leningrad: 42, 367, 371
Conspiracy of Feelings, play: 14
Conspiracy of Fools, play: 425
Constantine, Mildred: 379, 383
Constantinowicz, Marie: 37, 44
"Construction and Art of the National Republics", Moscow: 194
Constructive Gopak, ballet: 188
"Constructivists, The" exhibition, Moscow: 304
Conte du Tsar Saltan, Le: see The Tale of Tsar Saltan
"Contemporary Painting" exhibition, Petrograd: 16
"Contemporary Trends" exhibition, St. Petersburg: 256, 365
Contenson, Bernadette: 139
Contes Russes, Les, choreographic miniatures: 269, 270, 271
Cooper, Diana: 353, 354
Cooper, Emil: 152
Copeau, Jacques: 290, 365
Copenhagen Opera House, 74
Coppelia, ballet-pantomime: 153, 154, 223, 388
Coq d'Or, Le / The Golden Cockerel / Zolotoi petushok, opera: 101-102, 119, 120, 124, 121, 200, 201-203, 214, 244, 264, 296, 351-352, 399, 419
Cor Ardens artists' association: 344
Coralli, Jean: 68, 354, 455
Cordier and Ekstrom Gallery, New York: 344, 346
Corinth, Louis: 313
Corona Mundi, International Cultural Center: 344
Corot, Jean: 156
Corriere d'Italia, Rome, newspaper: 117
Corsaire, Le, ballet: 316-318
Cortona, Pietro da: 262
Cosmopolitan, New York, journal: 161
Costakis, George: 327, 330
Country Festival, A, revue: 372

Country Picnic in a Distant Province of Russia, A / Partie Champêtre dans une Lointaine Province Russe, revue: 372-373
Courier graphique, Paris, journal: 322
Courses in the Art of Stage Productions / Meierkhold's Kurmastsep: 144, 452
Courthion, Pierre: 26, 454
Covent Garden, London: 75, 78, 111, 156, 213, 280, 346
Craig, Edward Gordon: 163, 314
Cranach, Lucas: 184
Crane, Charles Richard: 456
Creative Committee of Unovis: see Unovis
Crespelle, Jean: 48
Crespi Morbio, Vittorio: 125
Cricket on the Hearth cabaret, Petrograd / Leningrad: 421
Cricket on the Hearth, A, play: 285-286
"Crimson Rose" [Alaia roza] exhibition: 260, 349, 351, 386, 430
Cristallo, Bolzano, journal: 195
Crocodile et Cléopâtre, Le, revue: 322
Crommelynck, Fernand: 195, 327, 384
Crone, Rainer: 297
Crooked Jimmy cabaret, Kiev: 317, 334
Crooked Jimmy cabaret, Moscow: 191, 317
Crooked Mirror [Krivoe zerkalo] theater, St. Petersburg: 14, 26, 27, 31, 317, 334
Cross Currents, New York, newsletter: 316
CSIAI: see Central Stroganov Industrial Art Institute, Moscow
Cueva de Salamanca, La, play: 164
Cuevas, George, Marquis de: 160
Culture-League, Kiev: 32
Cummings, Paul: 412
Cupid's Revenge, opera: 57, 65, 110
Czartoryski family: 355
Czech Folk Theater, Prague: 18
Czwiklitzer, Christophe: 284, 448, 449, 450

D.E. Trust, The: see Come on, Europe
D'Ache, Caran: 6
D'Andrea, Jeanne: 297
D'Annunzio, Gabriele: 43, 45, 47, 50, 52
D'Humières, Robert: 388
D'Oettingen, Hélène: 182
Dabrowski, Magdalena: 327, 338
Dadswell, Sarah: 298
Daily Telegraph, The, London: 132
Daita, play: 459
Dalí, Salvador: 118, 353, 354
Dallas Museum of Fine Arts: 189, 297
Dalmatoff, Mikhail: 112
Dama Duende, La, play: 166, 167, 311-312

Damase, Jacques: 139
Dame aux Camelias, La, play: 99
Dames de Bonne Humeur, ballet: 50
Dana, Henry: 429
Dance of the Budennyi Cavalry, ballet: 188
Dances of the Machines, dance number: 188
Danse Espagnole, concert number: 417
Daniel, Macha: 332
Daniel, Sergei: 319
Danilova, Alexandra: 33, 118, 191, 268, 281, 357, 420
Dance of Death, play: 350
Danseurs de gigue, Les, dramatized novel: 289
Dante Alighieri: 412
Daphnis et Chloë, ballet: 358
Dark Elegies, ballet: 111
Daughter of the Sun, film: 166
Davis, Richard: 308
Davydova, E.: 133, 303
Davydova, Nataliia: 326, 426
Davydova, Olga: 260
Day of the Spirits in Toledo, play: 260
Days of the Turbins, The, play: 427, 428
De Santi, Pier-Marco: 157
Deaf Man, story: 424
Death of the Commune, mass action: 31
Death of Pazukhin, play: 257
Death of Tarelkin, The, play: 54, 162, 190, 195, 383, 384-386
Death Ray, film: 192
Death's Mistake, play: 144, 254
Debureau, Jean-Gaspard: 230
Debussy, Claude: 45
Decter, Jacqueline: 344
Dee, Elaine Evans: 288
Degas, Edgar: 356
Degen, Yurii: 457
Degrada, Francesco: 229
Deich, Alexander: 256
Deineka, Alexander: 142, 305, 423, 441, 442
Dekorativnoe iskusstvo, Moscow, journal: 165, 178, 216, 230, 376, 386, 398, 422, 435
Delaunay, J.-L.: 139
Delaunay, Robert: 52, 139, 140, 141, 283, 324
Delaunay (Terk), Sonia: 52, 139-142, 211, 283, 324, 396, 458
Delaunays: 137, 284, 395, 446
Delibes, Léo: 58, 153, 358
Delteil, Joseph: 142
Demenni Marionette Theater, St. Petersburg: 228
Dementieva, Elena: 344
Demidenko, Yuliia: 34
Demon, opera: 361

Den, St. Petersburg, newspaper: 26
Denham, Serge: 33
Deni: see Denisov, Viktor
Denikin, Anton: 218
Denis, Maurice: 26, 118, 361
Denisov, Sergei: 135
Denisov, Vasilii: 445
Denisov, Viktor (Deni): 254, 335
Denisovsky, Fedor: 142
Denisovsky, Nikolai: 142-143, 238, 240, 253, 379, 441, 442, 451
Deotto, Patrizia: 111
Department for the Preservation of Monuments and Antiquities, Moscow: 53
Depero, Fortunato: 54, 270, 272, 281
Derain, André: 217, 283, 431
Dergachev, Boris: 423
Derzhavin, Konstantin: 28, 163, 452
Descent of Hans into Hell, The, revue: 30
Deshevov, Vladimir: 230
Desire under the Elms, play: 383
Destinée, revue: 30
Destruction of Hope, The / Op hoop van zegen, play: 286
Destruction of the Squadron, play: 305
Detective Story, The, play: 33
Deutsch, Ernst: 417
Deutsche-Russische Zeitung, Berlin: 58
Deutsches Theater, Berlin: 304, 382, 437
Deuxième Bal des Artistes, Le: see Bal de Cortèges Travesti
Devil's Holiday, The / Le Diable s'Amuse, ballet: 118
Devillier (Devilliers), Catherine (Ekaterina): 208, 214, 270, 274
Devils, dramatized novel: 146
Diable Blanc, Le, film: 125
"Diaghilev Exhibition, The", Edinburgh / London: 60, 70, 200, 264
Diaghilev Festival, Groeningen: 46
Diaghilev, Sergei: 19, 20, 21, 22, 31, 33, 34, 41, 42, 43, 44, 45, 46, 47, 49, 50, 52, 56, 57, 58, 59, 60, 62, 63, 65, 68, 70, 71, 76, 96, 97, 99, 100, 110, 118, 119, 120, 121, 122, 124, 131, 134, 139, 140, 141, 147, 149, 162, 180, 181, 189, 190, 191, 197, 198, 199, 200, 201, 202, 203, 207, 208, 212, 213, 214, 244, 246, 260, 262, 263, 264, 267, 268, 270, 271, 272, 274, 275, 276, 279, 280, 281, 288, 301, 302, 306, 313, 314, 321, 322, 323, 338, 344, 345, 346, 350, 357, 358, 360, 361, 364, 365, 366, 377, 386, 388, 393, 396, 399, 410, 412, 419, 420, 427, 446, 449, 450, 451, 452, 453
Diakonitsyn, Lev: 257

Diakov, Lev: 254
Dichenko, Igor: see Dychenko, Igor
Dickens, Charles: 27, 285
Didenko, Yulia: 179, 217
Dideriks, Andrei: 229
Didier Aaron Gallery: 352
Didier-Cottoni Collection: 430
Dieterle, Wilhelm: 417
Dieu Bleu, Le: see *The Blue God*
Dikii, Alexei: 258, 259, 319, 334
Dimshits, Eduard: 130
Dior, Christian: 353, 354
Disney, Walt: 52, 125
Dix, Otto: 215
Djanchieff, Alexandre: 76, 123, 154, 359
Dmitriev, Pavel: 8, 143-144
Dmitriev, Vladimir: 144-145, 164, 178, 182, 235, 452
Dmitriev, Vsevolod: 215, 216
Dmitriev-Kavkazsky, Lev: 146, 183
Dmitrieva, Nina: 442
Dobin, Efim: 197
Dobrushin, Ekhezkel: 179
Dobujinsky (Doboujinsky / Dobuzhinsky), Mstislav: 14, 26, 41, 55, 56, 58, 101, 131, 137, 146-155, 159, 180, 198, 199, 220, 227, 254, 262, 263, 265, 355, 365, 377, 421, 432, 444
Dobujinsky, Vsevolod: 149, 150, 151, 152, 153, 154, 155
Dobychina, Nadezhda / Dobychyna Art Bureau, Petrograd: 16, 325, 366
Dokuchaeva, Vera: 257, 311, 312
Dolgopolov, Nikolai: 322, 323
Dolin, Anton: 40, 149, 280
Dolinoff's Troupe (Anatolii Dolinov): 323
Dolinsky, Mikhail: 284, 311
Doll Bazaar, Philanthropic, St. Petersburg: 41
Domiteeva, Vera: 244
Don-Aminado (Aminodav Shpoliansky): 373
Don Carlos, opera: 178
Don Juan, play: 14, 98, 132, 166, 168, 169, 170, 171, 174, 177, 178
Don Juan and Death, play: 174
Don Juan in Hell, ballet: 177
Don Juan ou Le Festin de Pierre, ballet: 169, 170
Don Quixote, ballet: 133
Donetsk Miners, film: 191
Dongen, Kees Van: 229
"Donkey's Tail" [Oslynyi khvost] exhibition and group: 137, 200, 207, 264, 266, 267, 280, 283, 297, 397, 458
Dorfles, Gillo: 57
Dorival, Bernard: 321, 322
Dornand, Guy: 16
Dorpat (Derpt, Tartu) University: 228

Dorsey, Hebe: 352
Dosekin, Nikolai: 444
Dostoevsky, Fedor: 146, 319, 322; also
    see *The Brothers Karamazov*
Doubrovska (Dubrovska), Felia: 212, 420
Doudrine-Mak, Dimitrii: 297
Douglas, Charlotte: 160, 297, 298, 301,
    327
Drak, A.: 231
Drama of Life, play: 427
Drama Review, New York, journal: 188
Dranishnikov, Vladimir: 145
Drayer, Ruth: 344
Drei Trommler, Die, revue: 412
Dreier, Katherine: 315, 321
Drevin, Alexander: 286, 315, 426
Drevina, Ekaterina: 426, 427
Drigo, Riccardo: 17, 37, 454
Drizen, Nikolai: 227, 262, 263
Drouot Hôtel: see Auction at Hôtel
    Drouot
Drowned Bell, play: 374
Drozd, Tatiana: 133, 134
Drozdov: 343
Drozdova, V.: 355
Drutskaia, Vera: 158
Drutskoi (Drutsky), Boris: see Erdman,
    Boris
Drutt, Mathew: 297
Dudakov, Valerii (Valerian): 215, 304,
    315, 458
Dudin, Ivan: see Art School, Konstantin
    Yuon's and Ivan Dudin's, Moscow
Dukas, Paul: 45, 46
Dukhan, Igor: 290
Dulenko, Valentina: 318, 319
Dumas, Alexandre: 99, 216
Duncan, Isadora: 21, 45
Duncan, Michael: 412
Dunkel, Andrei: 156
Dunkel, Elizabeth: 156
Dunkel, Eugene (Evgenii): 156, 241
Dunkel, George: 156
Dunoyer, Jean-Marie: 454
Dunoyer de Segonzac, André: 139, 326,
    426
Dürer, Albrecht: 184
Durfee, Thea: 200, 439, 442
Durnov, Modest: 444
Durov, Anatolii: 53, 189, 399
Durozoi, Gerard: 324
Duvan-Tortsov, Ivan (Isaak): 374
Dychenko, Igor: 27, 129, 130, 131, 217,
    231, 232, 306, 307, 312, 315, 316,
    317, 318, 319, 334, 379, 424
Dymshits-Tolstaia, Sofia: 291, 399
Dzhafarova, Svetlana: 283
*Dzhummi (Dzhuma) Mashid / Fire and
    Steel*, play: 285
Dzutseva, Irina: 218, 459

Earth on End, play: 327, 330-331
Eastman, Max: 422
Eberling, Alfred: 132, 133
Eccentric Group: see FEKs
Eding (Edding), Boris von: 326
Efimov, Boris: 335
Efimov, Ivan: 328
Efremova, Elena: 355
Efremova, Liudmila: 429, 443
Efros, Abram: 29, 137, 138, 164, 333,
    348, 400, 439
Efros, Nikolai: 178, 400, 404
Eganbiuri, Eli (Zdanevich, Ilia): 200
Eggert, Konstantin: 305, 437
Egoroff, Wladimir (Egorov, Vladimir): 26,
    198, 238, 374
Egyptian Ballet, An, ballet: 22
Egyptian Night, An (aka *Egyptian
    Nights*), ballet: 21-22, 41, 140
Ehrenburg (Erenburg), Ilya: 158, 290,
    291, 367, 425, 431
Einstein, Albert: 255
Eisenstein (Eizenshtein), Sergei: 156-
    158, 188, 189, 191, 195, 339, 385
Ekho, Moscow, journal: 191
Ekstrom, Parmenia: 344
Electra, play: 131
Elena Borisovna: see Annenkova, Elena
Elisséeff, Serge: 221
Elizabeth II, Queen of England: 189
Elizarova, I.: 133, 134, 319
Elizbarashvili, Nonna: 221, 372, 459
Elizium Gallery, Moscow: 57, 111, 179,
    230, 265
Elkin, Boris: 216
Elliott, David: 157, 338
Ellis, Ivan: 233
Elsner, Vladimir: 225
Embassy of the Russian Federation,
    Paris: 220
Emdin, Anatolii: 179
*Emperor Maximilian and his
    Disobedient Son Adolf, The*, play:
    144, 280, 398, 399
Enchanted Kingdom, The, film: 156
Enchanted Tailor, play: 179
End of Krivorylsk, The, play: 14-15
Enei, Evgenii: 193
"Engraving in the USSR over the Last
    10 Years" exhibition, Moscow: 445
Ensigns of the Guard, St. Petersburg:
    294
Epstein, Jean: 126
Erbslöh, Gisela: 301
Erdman (Drutskoi, Drutsky), Boris: 10,
    11, 13, 53, 158-159
Erdman, Nikolai: 158, 370
Erenburg, I.: see Ehrenburg, Ilya
Erik XIV, play: 286
Erlashova, Sofia: 372
Ermans, Viktor: 284

Ermilchenko, Natalia: 443
Ermilov, Vasilii: 231, 298, 316, 369, 395
Ermilova-Platova, Efrosinia: 426
Ermitazh, Moscow, journal: 158, 189,
    191, 239, 240, 451
Ermitazh, museum: see Hermitage
Ermolaeva, Tatiana: 244
Ermolaeva, Vera: 138, 159-160, 256,
    290, 291, 297, 298, 301, 349, 394
Ermolov, Alexei: 389
Ermolov, Mikhail: 112, 113, 343
Ermolova, Mariia: 358, 427
Ermolova Studio, Moscow: 232
Ernst, Sergei: 131, 348, 355, 356, 358,
    360, 361, 375
Ershov, Gleb: 183
Ershov, Ivan: 145
"Erste Russische Kunstausstellung"
    exhibition, Berlin: 26, 137, 142, 159,
    189, 236, 237, 238, 255, 282, 304,
    314, 321, 331, 333, 366, 426, 429,
    445
Erté (Romain de Tirtoff, Roman Tyrtov):
    33, 126, 127, 160-161, 217
Esenin, Sergei: 97, 230, 239, 382, 423,
    425, 446, 447, 451
Esina, Tamara: 57, 244
Eskevich, Irina: 157
Esman Gallery, Rosa, New York: 133
España, ballet: 207-208, 214, 270
Essem, pseudonym: see Makovsky,
    Sergei
Estorick, Eric: 160, 161
Estorick, Salome: 160
Etkind, Mark: 15, 57, 65, 71, 97, 98,
    104, 110, 184, 188, 230, 231, 236,
    257, 258, 259, 260, 301, 398, 399
Ettinger, Pavel: 34, 52, 311, 456
Eugene Onegin, opera: 133, 145, 238,
    303, 304, 349
Euripides: 35
Europa Orientalis, Salerno, journal: 56,
    146, 387
European Herald, London, newspaper:
    119
Evdaev, Nobert: 135
Evenings of New Dance, Moscow: 158
Evergreen Museum, Baltimore: 34
Evgrafov, Nikolai: 186, 187
Evreinov, Nikolai (Evreinoff, Nicolas): 14,
    17, 26, 27, 28, 29, 30, 31, 32, 33,
    54, 122, 123, 125, 127, 146, 225,
    226, 227, 228, 247, 249, 256, 257,
    263, 309, 317, 333, 362, 363, 364,
    365, 366, 386, 393, 394, 401, 460
Evropeiskii vestnik, London, journal: 31,
    125
Ex Libris bookstore, New York: 305,
    382, 383
Exhibition at Complesso del Vittoriano,
    Rome: 137

Exhibition at Mairie du 7-e
    Arrondissement, Paris: 125
"Exhibition of 1915", Moscow: 281
"Exhibition of Agit-Visual Art",
    Moscow: 253
"Exhibition of Association of Workers of
    the Visual Arts", Moscow: 303
"Exhibition of Contemporary Female
    Portraits", St. Petersburg: 355
"Exhibition of Contemporary Painting
    and Drawing", Petrograd: 15, 421
"Exhibition of Contemporary Russian
    Painting", Petrograd: 325
"Exhibition of Designs for Theatrical
    Décors of Works from the Studios
    of the Decorative Institute",
    Petrograd: 15, 452
"Exhibition of Graphics", Moscow: 309
"Exhibition of Historic Russian
    Portraits": see "Historical-Artistic
    Exhibition of Russian Portraits"
"Exhibition of Icon-painting and Artistic
    Antiquities", St. Petersburg: 120
"Exhibition of Latest Trends in Art",
    Leningrad: 366
"Exhibition of Masters of Analytical
    Art", Leningrad: 187, 188
"Exhibition of Modern French Painting",
    London: 396
"Exhibition of Moscow Futurists", Tiflis:
    348
"Exhibition of New Trends", Leningrad:
    331
"Exhibition of Paintings" (1923): 426
"Exhibition of Paintings by Russian
    Artists and Sculpture by Fredman-
    Kliuzel", Moscow: 377, 445
"Exhibition of Paintings by David
    Davidovich Burliuk", New York: 136
"Exhibition of Paintings and Sculpture
    by Jewish Artists", Moscow: 366
"Exhibition of Paintings by Petrograd
    Artists of All Directions": 138, 144,
    183
"Exhibition of Paintings by the
    Professional Union of Artist-
    Painters", Moscow: 445
"Exhibition of Paintings by the Union of
    Russian Artists": 444
"Exhibition of Russian Art", London:
    308
"Exhibition of Russian Book Marks",
    Leningrad: 225
"Exhibition of Russian Painting and
    Sculpture", New York: 215, 355, 388
"Exhibition of Russian Theater from
    Collection of L.I. Zheverzheev": 366
"Exhibition of Society of Georgian
    Artists", Tiflis: 194
Exhibition of Soviet Art, Tokyo: 253
"Exhibition of Soviet Illustrations to

Creative Literature over the Last 5
    Years (1931-1936)", Moscow: 15
"Exhibition of Soviet Porcelain": 394
"Exhibition of Stage Design Art",
    Moscow: 10, 452
"Exhibition of Works by Theater Artists
    of the State Academic Bolshoi
    Theater", Moscow: 253
"Exhibition of Works by Vladimir
    Maiakovsky" / "20 Years of Work",
    Moscow / "Vladimir Maiakovsky,
    1893-1930": 196-197
"Exhibition Russian and Finnish
    Artists", St. Petersburg: 203, 313
Experiment, Los Angeles, journal: 132,
    162, 183, 188, 200, 256, 387
Experimental / Experimental-Heroic
    Theater, Moscow: 158, 283
Experimental-Decoration Studio at
    MKhAT: 374
Export Control Commission for the
    Russian Art: 245, 246
"Exposition Coloniale", Paris: 352
"Exposition d'Arte Russe", Paris: 352
"Exposition Internationale" /
    "Exposition Internationale des Arts
    et Techniques dans la Vie Moderne"
    / World's Fair (1937), Paris: 139,
    237, 238, 309, 310, 351, 394, 395,
    396, 421, 430
"Exposition Internationale d'art
    moderne", Geneva: 200, 264
"Exposition Internationale des Arts
    Décoratifs et Industriels" (1925),
    Paris: 53, 125, 126, 139, 142, 158,
    161, 180, 237, 238, 253, 257, 282,
    285, 304, 305, 309, 311, 316, 338,
    367, 379, 383, 394, 400, 430, 439,
    446
"Exposition Russe Hippique et
    Etnographique:, Paris: 461
"Exposition Universelle" (1900), Paris:
    182, 197, 301, 302, 313, 337, 429
"Exposition Universelle et
    Internationale", Brussels: 294
Exter (Grigorovich), Alexandra: 16, 19,
    28, 30, 32, 33, 129, 130, 142, 145,
    158, 161-178, 190, 228, 231, 236,
    283, 287, 288, 294, 305, 306, 309,
    310, 311, 312, 314, 316, 327, 328,
    330, 333, 334, 348, 386, 399, 412,
    416, 419, 423, 435, 436
Exter (Ekster), Nikolai: 161
*Extraordinary Adventures of Mr. West
    in the Land of the Soviets*, film: 191
Ezh, Leningrad, children journal: 159
*Ezhenedelnik petrogradskikh
    gosudarstvennykh akademicheskikh
    teatrov*, Petrograd, journal: 261

Fabri, Morits: 267

Faccioli, Erica: 188
Faiko, Alexei: 15, 158, 165, 191, 368
Fair at Sorochintsy, The, ballet: 301, 337
Fait, Andrei: 192
Falconet, Etienne: 154
Falileev, Vadim: 445
Falk, Robert: 159, 179-180, 267, 283,
    319
Famine en Russie bolcheviste, La: 220
Famous Players Company / Famous
    Players-Lasky Corporation, New
    York: 156
"Fan and Folly" exhibition, New York:
    156
Fantasy, ballet: 191
Farrère, Claude: 215
Fashion houses: 30, 131, 161, 220, 421
Fath, Geneviève: 353
Fath, Jacques: 353
Faucher, Paul: 162, 165, 166, 168, 170,
    174, 175
Fauchereau, Serge: 297
Faust, opera: 364
Favorsky, A.: 194, 341
Favorsky, Vladimir: 191, 328, 349, 422,
    423, 445
Fear, ballet: 305
Feast during the Plague, play: 98
Fedor Ioannovich, Tsar: 17
Fedorov, Andrei: 178
Fedorov, German: 283
Fedorov, Mikhail: 191
Fedorov, Vasilii: 367
Fedorov-Davydov, Alexei: 237
Fedorova, Alexandra: 65, 67, 68
Fedorova, Sofiia: 345
Fedorovsky, Fedor: 180-181, 238, 239,
    303, 312
Fedoruk, Oleksandr: 16
Fedotov, Ivan: 164, 181-182, 238, 283,
    294
Fée des Poupées, La / Die Puppenfee,
    ballet: 33, 37-39, 40-41, 365
Feigin, Moisei: 460
Feininger, Lyonel: 272
FEKs (Factory of the Eccentric Actor)
    group: 28, 156, 157
Feminist Art Journal, New York, journal:
    200
Fenbaum, Ignatii: 312
Férat, Edouard: see Férat, Serge
Férat, Serge (Serge Jastrebzoff, Sergei
    Yastrebtsov, Sergei Rudnev): 182-
    183
Ferdinandov, Boris: 158, 438
Fern, Alan: 379, 383
Feshin (Fechin), Nikolai: 136, 286, 338
Festin, Le, ballet: 48, 199, 358
Festin de Pierre, Le, ballet: 169, 170
Fête de Nuit: see Bal "Fête de Nuit"
Feu d'Artifice, orchestral suite: 281

Fevralsky, Alexander: 54, 55, 461
Fiddler on the Roof, musical: 33
Fidelio, opera: 182
Fidler, Anna: see Korovina (Fidler), Anna
Fierens, Paul: 396
"Fifth State Exhibition. From Impressionism to Non-objective Art", Moscow: 314
Figaro, Le, opera: 110, 218, 437
Figner, Medea: 40
Fille mal gardée, La, ballet: 133
Filonov, Pavel: 130, 159, 183-188, 311, 348, 349, 365, 366
Finale Balance, play: 33
Fine Arts Museum of San Francisco, The: 65, 128, 222, 242, 275
Firebird, Berlin / Paris, journal: see *Zhar-ptitsa*
Firebird, The / *L'Oiseau de Feu* [Zhar-ptitsa], ballet: 48, 71, 124, 131, 197, 198, 199, 201, 212-213, 283, 284, 445, 446
Fireground Booth: see *Balaganchik*, play
Firsanova, Vera: 445, 446
"First Discussional Exhibition of Associations of Active Revolutionary Art", Moscow: 196, 304, 305, 309, 425, 442
First Distiller, The, play: 28
"First Exhibition of Graphics", Moscow: 191, 196, 367
"First Exhibition of the Group of Young Artists", Tiflis: 194
"First Exhibition of Paintings and Sculpture by the Association of United Artists", Yalta: 132
"First Exhibition of Paintings by the Professional Union of Artists in Moscow": 321
"First Exhibition of the Young Leftist Federation of the Professional Union of Artists and Painters": 383
"First Jewish Art Exhibition", Kiev: 32
First Stage Design Exhibition, Moscow: 10
First State Exhibition, Moscow: 348
"First State Exhibition of Art and Science", Kazan: 374, 427
First State Free Art Exhibition / First State Free Exhibition of Works of Art, Petrograd: 15, 52, 183, 366
First State Movie Factory: 156
First State Painting and Decorative Studio, Kiev: 129
First State School of Theatrical Art, Moscow: 188
First State Textile Factory: 327, 383, 384
First State Theater for Children / First State Children Theater, Moscow:

188, 327
"First State Traveling Exhibition of Paintings": 255
First Studio of the Moscow Art Theater: 162, 285, 286, 386
First Working Group of Constructivists: 196, 305, 309
First Working Organization of Artists: 305
First Working Theater, Moscow: 156, 188
Firtich, Nicholas: 160
Fisher Gallery, London: 293
Fishkova, F.: 372
Five Dollars, revue: 30
Flak, Roland / Galerie Flak, Paris: 456
Flax, Michel: 323
Flea or the Left-Handed Smith and the Steel Flea, The, play: 257, 258-259, 319
Flint, Janet: 19
Florensky, Pavel: 328, 383
Flying Doctor / *Le Médicin Volant*, play: 230, 309
Fogel, Vladimir: 158, 192
Fokina, Vera: 44
Fokine, Michel (Fokin, Mikhail) / Fokine Ballet Company: 19, 20, 21, 22, 25, 26, 40, 41, 42, 43, 44, 45, 46, 47, 56, 58, 59, 60, 68, 70, 71, 90, 101, 118, 131, 132, 141, 147, 198, 100, 201, 203, 212, 222, 245, 246, 249, 261, 269, 280, 345, 358, 365, 393
Folies Bergère, Paris: 160, 161, 332
Follie viennesi, opera: 125
Followers of the New Art: see Posnovis
Fomin, Ivan: 312
Fomina, Yulia: 307
Fondation Ryback, Paris: 41
Fondazione A. Mazzotta, Milan: 200, 265
Fonteyn, Margot: 111
Fonvizin (Fon-Vizen), A.: 266
Fonvizin, Denis: 18, 459
Footballers, ballet: 188
Forain, Jean-Louis: 461
Foregger (von Greifenturn), Nikolai / Foregger's Mastfor [workshop]: 13, 53, 54, 156, 157, 158, 188-189, 191, 310, 316, 318, 425, 438
Forest, The, play: 195, 368, 370, 371, 429
Forestier, Sylvie: 137
Forter, Henri: 162, 436
Foundation Dina Vierny: 234
Four Arts Society: 236, 260, 311, 427
Four Lady-Killers, farce: 16
Fourberies de Scapin, Les, play: 428, 429
Fragonard, Jean-Honoré: 375
Frampton, Kenneth: 228

France, Anatole: 42
François, Irène: 280
Frank: see Liutse-Fedorov, V.
Frank, Semeon: 454
Franko State Drama Theater / Ivan Franko Ukrainian Dramatic Theater, Kharkov: 238, 239, 305, 318, 319
Fred James Jr. Museum of Art, University of Oklahoma, Norman: 412
Fredman-Kliuzel, Boris: 377, 445
Free Comedy Theater, Petrograd: 14, 30, 393
Free Studio, St. Petersburg: 400
Free State Art Studios (Svomas): 10, 15, 52, 111, 132, 142, 143, 144, 146, 179, 180, 191, 216, 232, 237, 238, 240, 253, 254, 255, 256, 282, 283, 285, 309, 311, 313, 319, 321, 326, 331, 348, 379, 397, 399, 421, 426, 427, 439, 446, 451, 456
Free Theater, Moscow: 297, 301, 374, 376, 448
Free Theater, Petrograd / Leningrad: 27, 230
Freedley, George: 287
Frette, Guido: 117
Freze, Ervin: 255
Friche, Vladimir: 369
Friedrich-Theater, Dessau: 229
Friesz, Othon: 283, 430
Frishman, David Ben Saul: 313
Frolov, Viktor: 57
From Rags to Riches: see *There Was Not a Penny and Suddenly There Was a Pound*
Froman, Margarita: 147
Fruits of Enlightenment, play: 261
Frumkin, Gregory: 120, 266, 447
Fuente Ovejuna [The Sheep Well], play: 194, 316, 333
Fundación Banco Centrale Hispanoamericano: 384
Futurist University, Tiflis: 457

Gabo (Pevzner), Naum: 162, 189-191, 237, 268, 276, 321, 322
Gabrilovitch, Anna: 203
Gabrilovitch, Elena: 203
Gad, Peter: 166
Gagua, Lamara: 217
Gaideburov and Skarskaia Theater: 285
Gaigneron, Axelle de: 352
GAKhN/RAKhN: see Academy of Artistic Sciences, State / Russian
Galadzhev, Petr: 158, 191-193
Galadzheva, Nataliia: 191, 192
Galeev, Ildar / Ildar Galeev Gallery, Moscow: 53, 98, 159, 183, 264
Galeeva, Tamara: 215, 216
Galeffi, Carlo: 115

Galerie J. Allard, Paris: 156

Galerie Alex Lachmann, Cologne: 191

Galerie Barbazanges / Barbazanges-Hodebert, Paris: 137, 200, 221, 264, 272, 281, 372

Galerie de Beaune, Paris: 182

Galerie Bonjean, Paris: 182

Galerie Bougard, Paris: 395

Galerie Brusberg, Berlin: 52

Galerie Charpentier, Paris: 26, 44, 55, 139, 221, 225, 287

Galerie R. Creuse, Paris: 322

Galerie d'art de l'Université du Québec, Montreal: 456

Galerie der Hochschule für Grafik und Buchkunst, Leipzig: 290

Galerie Der Sturm, Berlin: 53, 137, 139, 161, 162, 200, 264, 322, 332, 333

Galérie Druet, Paris: 118, 361

Galerie Garvens, Hanover: 287

Galerie Gmurzynska, Cologne / Zurich: 139, 183, 190, 237, 287, 293, 297, 300, 395, 426

Galerie Hupel, Paris: 430, 431

Galerie Jean Chauvelin, Paris: 52, 255

Galerie Katia Granoff, Paris: 137

Galerie Le Minotaure, Paris: 332

Galerie Natan Fedorowskij, Berlin: 191

Galerie Orlando, Zurich: 192

Galerie Paul Guillaume: see Guillaume, Paul

Galerie Percier, Paris: 189

Galerie Piltzer, Paris: 183

Galerie Povolozky, Paris: 215

Galerie le Roy, Brussels: 225

Galerie Sauvage, Paris: 200, 208

Galerie Schlegl, Berlin: 395

Galerie Van Diemen, Berlin: 426

Galerie Vendôme, Paris: 221

Galerie Werner Kunze, Berlin: 139, 162

Galerie Wimmer, Munich: 287

Galerie Wolfgang Ketterer, Munich: 200

Galerie Zlotowski, Paris: 332, 396

Galerie-Editions Pierre Brullé: 231

Galeries de la Chaussée d'Antin: 220

Galka, opera: 231

Galleria Civica d'Arte Moderna, Turin: 331

Galleria del Levante, Milan: 41

Galleria Franco Maria Ricci, Milan: 352

Galleria Marconi, Milan: 395

Galleria Martini and Ronchetti: 200

Galleria di piazza San Marco, Milan: 139

Galleries of the Twardy Bookshop, Berlin: 287

Gallet, Louis: 42

Galli, Rosina: 25

Galpern, Elena: see Annenkova, Elena

Galtsev, P.: 456

Galushkina, Anna: 452

Game of Life, The, play: 198

Gamelin, or the Revolution Will Conquer, ballet scenario: 322

Gamrekeli, Iraklii: 194-195, 457, 458, 459

Gan, Alexei: 29, 31, 189, 196-197, 305, 309, 338, 339, 342, 379, 386, 422, 426

Gandhi, Indira: 344

Ganzen, Alexei: 281

Garafola, Lynn: 52, 290

Garcia, Aurora: 384

Garden, Mary: 160

Gartman, Foma: see Hartmann, Thomas von: 227, 228

Gartman (Hartmann), Viktor: 229

Gary Tatintsian Gallery, Moscow: 298, 395

Gas, play: 26

Gasco, Alberto: 115, 117

Gascoigne, Bamber: 28

Gassner, Hubertus: 237, 238, 331

Gastev, Alexei: 188

GAU: see Chief Archive Administration

Gauguin, Paul: 139, 351

Gaulois, Le, Paris, newspaper: 26

Gaush, Alexander: 227, 228, 398

Gauss, Carl Friedrich: 255

Gauthier, Maximilian: 396

Gautier, Théophile: 21, 59, 68, 354, 455

Gavazzeni, Gianandrea: 116, 117

Gavronsky, Alexander: 192

Gayraud, Régis: 200, 456

Ge, Gennadii: 319

Ge, Nikolai: 427

Geffroy, Georges: 354

Geidenreikh, Ekaterina: 356

Geiro, Rezhis (Gayraud, Régis): 456

Geisha, The, operetta: 412-413

Gelikon Publishing-house: 31, 291, 294

Geltser, Vasilii: 150, 198

Geltzer, Catherine: 246

Gendy (?): 283

General Line, The, film: 156

Gente, Milan, journal: 110, 117, 155

Gentle People, The, play: 32

George, Waldemar: 32, 33, 214, 264, 266, 268, 273, 274, 275, 276, 279, 430, 431

Georges-Michel, Michel: 214

Georgii Saakadze, play: 194

Gerasimov, Sergei: 193

Gerchuk, Yurii: 282, 400, 422, 423

Gerdt, Pavel: 66, 68

Geriusy Studio: 131

German, Mikhail: 443

Germanova, Mariia: 98

Geroi i zhertvy revoliutsii [Heroes and Victims of the Revolution], album: 254

Gerra, René: see Guera, René

Gershelman, Karl: see Hoerschelmann, Karl

Gershwin, George: 386

Gessen, Iosif: 98

Gessen, Vladimir: see Hessen (Gessen), Vladimir

Gest, Morris: 316, 386, 408

Geva, Tamara: see Zheverzheeva, Tamara

Ghéon, Henri: 52, 289

Ghislanzoni, Antonio: 217

Gibshman, Konstantin: 452

Gibson, Michael: 225

Giedion-Welcker, Carola: 321

Gilbert, William Schwenk: 307

Giliarovskaia, Nadezhda: 180, 181, 387

Gills, Gabrielle: 378

Gilman Galleries, Chicago: 20

Gimpel Gallery, New York: 142

Ginkhuk (State Institute of Artistic Culture), Petrograd / Leningrad: 159, 183, 297, 394, 397; also see Inkhuk

Gints, Savvatii: 442

Gintsburg, Ilia: 313

Giotto di Bondone: 326

Giraudoux, Jean: 102, 131, 412

Girba, Yuliia: 146, 412

Giroflé-Girofla, play: 54, 446, 451

Girsh Theater, Moscow: 349

Girshman, Genrietta: 358

Girshman, Vladimir: 376

Giselle, ballet-pantomime: 58, 59, 68-70, 133, 272, 354, 365, 454, 455

GITIS (State Institute of Theater Art), Moscow: 158, 384, 385

Giuliano (Dzuliano), G.: 56, 146

Giustiniani, Ivan: 358

Giutel, Joseph: 25

Glagolin, Sergei: 236

Glan, Natalia: 158, 383

Glazunov, Alexander: 33, 41, 56, 111, 140, 149, 245, 246, 249, 261, 345, 373, 410

Glebov, Anatolii: 309, 342

Glebova, Tatiana: 185, 187, 188

Glebova-Sudeikina, Olga: 227

Gleizes, Albert: 211, 283

Glière, Reingold: 154, 194, 231

Glinka State Museum of Theatrical and Musical Art, St. Petersburg (GMTMA): 20, 21, 27, 44, 69, 97, 133, 199, 260, 301, 303, 345, 346, 351, 358, 364, 366, 373, 378, 398, 423, 425

Glinka, Mikhail: 41, 127, 140, 379, 389, 398, 409

Glinsky, M.: 149, 245, 246

Gluck, Christoph Willibald: 170, 225, 420

Glyndebourne: 160

GMII: see Pushkin State Museum of Fine Arts (GMII)

GMTMA: see Glinka State Museum of

Theatrical and Musical Art, St. Petersburg

Gmurzynska, Antonina: 297, 301; see also Galerie Gmurzynska, Cologne / Zurich

Gnesin, Mikhail: 429

Gobineau, Joseph-Arthur de: 417, 419

Gofman, Ida: 197, 198, 199, 327, 350, 351

Gogol, Nikolai: 32, 146, 160, 183, 185, 186, 187, 232, 236, 295, 301, 318, 322, 337, 435, 452, 459

Gogolitsyn, Yurii: 43, 201

Golden Age, The, ballet: 134

Golden Cockerel, The: see *Le Coq d'Or*

Golden Fleece / Toison d'or, journal: see *Zolotoe runo*

Goldoni, Carlo: 98, 200

Goldwyn, Samuel: 386

Goleizovsky, Kasian: 15, 158, 189, 191, 316, 318, 322, 342, 367, 416, 425

Golem, play: 311

Golike, Roman: 217, 221, 261, 262

Gollerbakh, Erik: 146, 155, 197, 199

Golos Moskvy, Moscow, newspaper: 294, 295, 308

Golos Rodiny, Moscow, journal: 352

Golos Rusi, Petrograd, newspaper: 315

Golos zhizni, Petrograd, newspaper: 432

Golovanov, Nikolai: 334

Golovin, Alexander: 19, 53, 111, 120, 121, 125, 145, 146, 197-199, 213, 240, 244, 253, 257, 261, 295, 352, 359, 361, 377, 430, 434, 444, 453

Goltsshmidt, Anna: 137

Goltsshmidt, Vladimir: 137

Golubev, P.: 375

Golubkina, Anna: 309

Golynets, Galina: 119, 124, 125, 361

Golynets, Sergei: 34, 37, 42, 46, 119, 124, 125, 361, 377

Gomberg-Verzhbinskaia, Eleonora: 442

Goncharov, Andrei: 305, 441, 442

Goncharova (Gontcharova), Natalia: 21, 50, 135, 184, 200-214, 220, 228, 257, 264, 265, 266, 267, 268, 269, 270, 272, 276, 281, 283, 294, 297, 308, 317, 348, 399, 430, 431, 456, 458

Good Treatment of Horses, dramatized poem: 157, 188

Goodman, Susan: 137

Gorbachov (Gorbachev, Gorba ev, Horbachov), Dmitrii: 130, 131, 162, 231, 232, 305, 306, 307, 316, 317, 319

Gorbat (Gorbatov), A.: 420

Gorchakov, Mikhail: 146, 389

Gorchakov, Nikolai: 342

Gorchakova (Kharitonenko) Natalia: 146

Gorchakovs: 147

Gordesiani, Beno: 457

Gordin, Mikhail: 284, 311

Gordon, Mel: 188

Goriacheva, Tatiana: 298, 348, 395

Goriushkin-Sorokopudov, Ilia: 397

"Gorky and the Theater" exhibition: 303

Gorky Film Studios, Moscow: 191

Gorky, Maxim: 30, 111, 181, 229, 287, 303, 310

Gorodetsky, Sergei: 388, 394, 438

Gorsky, Alexander: 54, 261, 316

Goskino (State Cinema): 192

Gosvoenkino (State Military Cinema): 192

Gostiny Dvor / Une Bouffonerie de l'Ancien Petersbourg, revue: 113

Gotovtsev, Vladimir: 258

Götterdämmerung, Die, opera: 58, 68

Gottschalk, Louis: 37

Gough, Maria: 304

Gounod, Charles: 99, 100, 364

Gourvitch, Issar: 35, 48, 49, 71, 122, 189, 198, 199, 222, 249, 289, 365, 373, 378, 409, 445

Goziason, Fedor (Hosiasson, Philipp): 17, 454

Goznak Theater, Leningrad: 331

Gozzi, Carlo: 23, 26, 145, 152, 216, 232, 312, 323, 334, 350

Grabar, Igor: 258, 302, 308, 338, 358, 360, 361, 399, 444, 445

Graeva, B.: 367, 371

Grafik, Budapest, journal: 384

Gran Kursal, San-Sebastian, Spain: 109

Gran Teatro del Liceo, Barcelona: 289

Grand Bal des Artistes / Grand Bal Travesti Transmental / Grand Bal de Nuit, Paris: 209-211, 276

Grand Guignol, Le, revue: 322

Grand Opéra, Paris: 101, 147, 190

Grand Opera, Prague: 322

Grand Ourse Bal, Paris: 211, 277-278

Grand Théâtre, Geneva: 267

Grande Galerie d'Hercule: 355

Grani, Frankfurt, journal: 377

Granovsky, Alexei: 137, 180, 235, 333

"Graphic Art" exhibition, St. Petersburg: 31

Grassi, Marco: 184

Gray, Camilla: 200, 264, 269

Gray, Frank: 119

Gray, Thomas: 178

Great American Goof, The, musical: 32

Great Prince of Moscow, The, play: 225

"*Great Utopia*" exhibition: 307

Grebenshchikov, Georgi: 215, 216

Grechaninov, Alexander: 17

Gregor, Joseph: 31

Gregory, Alexis: 392

Greifenturn, Nikolai von: see Foregger, Nikolai

Grekov Studio of Battle Painters, Moscow: 253

Gremislavsky, Ivan: 285, 374

Griboedov Russian Dramatic Theater, Tbilisi: 194

Griboedov, Alexander: 220, 221, 427, 428

Gribonosova-Grebneva, Elena: 319

Grieg, Edvard: 52, 246

Griftsov, Boris: 427

Grigorieff, Cyrille: 215, 216

Grigoriev (Grigorieff), Boris: 20, 27, 29, 101, 136, 215-216, 221, 253, 282, 372

Grigoriev, Mikhail: 216

Grigoriev, Nikolai: 460

Grigoriev, Pavel: 217

Grigoriev, Serge: 45, 62, 100, 147, 213, 276, 281

Grigoriev, Vasilii: 460

Grigoriev family: 215

Grin, Milica: 214

Gripich, Alexei: 285

Gris, Juan: 183, 211, 287

Grishchenko, Alexei: 326, 426

Gritsenko (Tretiakov), Liubov: 41, 52

Gritsenko, Nikolai: 41

Grobman, Mikhail: 437

Grodskova, Tamara: 319

Grohman, Will: 220, 229

Gromov, Andrei: 193

Gromova, Ekaterina: 244

Gromova, Natalia: 200

Gropius, Walter: 189

Gropper Art Gallery, Cambridge, Mass.: 221

Gross, Vitalii: 188

"Grosse Berliner Kunstausstellung": 290

Grosse Internationale Revue, revue: 287

Grosvenor Galleries, London and New York: 160, 212

Grosz, George: 215

Growth, play: 309

Grünewald, Matthias: 184

Grushvitskaia, Elena: 303

Gruzenberg, Oscar (Oskar): 313, 314

Gruzenberg, Sergei: 118

Gubarev, Alexander: 72

Gudiashvili, Lado (Vladimir): 14, 101, 112, 156, 194, 195, 217-218, 457, 459

Gudiashvili, Nino: 194

Guerra, Nicola: 50

Guerra, René: 16, 100, 400

Guggenheim Museum, New York: 137, 297

Guillaume, Paul / Galerie Paul Guillaume: 48, 200, 264

Guitry, Sacha: 378

Gulbenkian Ballet Festival, Lisbon: 131, 132
Gumiliev, Nikolai: 225, 229, 230
Gunst, Elena: 260
Gunst, Evgenii: 41, 199, 254, 260, 349, 350, 351, 388
Gunzburg, Dmitrii: 52
Gurianova, Nina: 200, 348
Guro, Ekaterina: 460
Guro, Elena: 256, 460
Gurvich, Boris: 185
Gusarov, V.: 57
Gusarova, Alla: 57, 146, 244, 375, 442
Gusev, Vladimir: 31, 297
Gusliar Player, The, play: 365
Gutt, Irina: 351, 442
Gvozdev, Alexei: 145, 188, 368
GVYTM: see State Higher Theater Studios

H2SO4 group: 194, 195, 457
Habima Jewish Theater, Moscow: 32, 285, 311, 449
Hahl-Fontaine, Jelena: 228
Hahn, Reynaldo: 47
Halévy, Ludovic: 198
Hall, F.: 132
Halpern, Salomé (Andronikova, Salomeya): 373
Hamlet, play: 14, 194, 285, 322, 364, 405, 421, 449
Hamlet, Right on [Daesh Gamleta], play: 14
Hammer, Armand: see Armand Hammer Museum of Art
Hammer, Martin: 191
Hamsun, Knut: 198, 427
Hanka, Erika: 76
Hansel and Gretel, opera: 350
Hanson, L.: 157
Hari, Mata: 160
Harlequin-Skeleton, or Pierrot the Jealous, pantomime: 230
Harlequinade: see *Millions d'Arlequin, Les*
Harper's Bazaar, New York, journal: 160, 161
Harrison, Michael: 190
Harsányi, Tibor: 213
Harshav, Benjamin: 137
Harten, Jürgen: 183, 397
Hartford Music Festival, Connecticut: 118
Hartmann, Thomas von (Gartman, Foma): 227
Hartmann, Viktor: see Gartman, Viktor
Hartnoll and Eyre Gallery, London: 225
Harvard College Library: 275
Harvard Theatre Collections, Cambridge, Mass.: 33
Haskell, Arnold: 131, 132

Hauptmann, Gerhard: 285, 374, 427
Haus am Waldsee, Berlin: 331
Haus der Kunst, Munich: 442
Havemeyer, Mary: 41
Hazelton, Georges: 304
Hearst, William / Hearst's Cosmopolitan Corporation: 160
Heartbreak House, play: 195
Heartfield, John: 422
Hebrew University, Jerusalem: 10
Hedda Gabler, play: 350
Heijermans, Herman: 285, 286
Heim, Jacques: 139
Heimkehr, film: 31
Hekking, André: 378
Helpmann, Robert: 111
Helsingin Kaupungin Taidemuseo, Helsinki: 348
Hempel Kunstauktion, Munich: 237
Henderson, Marina: 142, 216
"Herbstsalon", Berlin: 139
Hergott, Fabrice: 237
Hermitage, journal: see *Ermitazh*, journal
Hermitage Museum, St. Petersburg / Petrograd / Leningrad: 22, 28, 57, 58, 131, 133, 158, 375, 432
Hermitage Theater, St. Petersburg / Petrograd: 22, 28, 37, 65, 261, 309, 373
Hessen (Gessen), Vladimir: 73, 75, 99, 110, 136, 218, 246, 270
Hicks, A.: 161
Higher Art-Industrial Institute, Moscow: 238
Higher Art Institute of IAA, St. Petersburg: 119, 215, 257, 261, 344, 372, 377
Higher Courses for Workers: 14
Higher Institute of Construction and Architecture, Moscow: 303
Higher State Art-Technical Institute: see Vkhutein
Higher State Art-Technical Studios: see Vkhtemas
Hilton, Alison: 313
Hindemith, Paul: 19, 412
Hines, Jerome: 152
Hippodrome Theater, New York: 48
Hippolytus, tragedy: 33, 35, 382
Hirshhorn Museum and Sculpture Garden, Washington, D.C.: 160, 162
Histoires Naturelles, ballet: 265, 269-270
Historical Museum, Moscow: 429, 430, 460
"Historical-Artistic Exhibition of Russian Portraits": 262
Hochzeit der Sobeide, play: 19
Hoerschelmann, Carl von: 218
Hoerschelmann, Elizabeth (Rozendorf,

Elizaveta): 218
Hoerschelmann (Gershelman), Karl: 53, 218-219
Hoerschelmann, Maria von: 218
Hoffman, Ernst Theodor Amadeus: 146, 239, 388, 446, 447, 451
Hoffman, Joseph: 314
Hofmannsthal, Hugo von: 19
Hollósy, Simon: 146, 281
Hollywood Theater, New York: 365
Holy Synod: 226, 227
Homann, Joachim: 201
Homo Sapiens, play: 26
Honegger, Athur: 51, 213, 222
Hopkinson, Cecil: 43
Hosiasson, Philipp (Hossiason, Fedor): see Goziason, Fedor
Houdiakoff, André (Khudiakov, Chudiakoff, Chudiakov, Andrei): 8, 14, 219-220, 253, 287
Hourvitch, Abram: 259
House of Arts, Berlin: 308
House of Arts, Petrograd: 146, 238, 257
House of Interludes, St. Petersburg: 349
House of Photography, Moscow: 191
House of the Red Army, Leningrad: 303
Houston-Brown Galérie, Paris: 16
Hudson Theater, New York: 33
Hugonot, M.-C.: 225, 228
Hulten, Pontus: 351, 456
Humperdinck, Engelbert: 350
Hupel, Philippe: 431
Hurok, Sol: 118, 280, 365
Hüttinger, Eduard: 331
Hutton, Leonard / Leonard Hutton Galleries, New York: 125, 162, 327, 328, 339, 443
Hymn to Liberated Labor, The, mass drama: 26

IAA: see Imperial Academy of Arts, St. Petersburg
I Miss My Swiss, revue: 111, 112
Ibsen, Henrik: 144, 350
Icare, ballet: 118
"Icons and Broadsheets" exhibition, Moscow: 201
Idzikowski, Stanislas: 271, 275, 276
Ignatieva, M.: 20
Ignatiuk, Mikhail: see Lenin, Mikhail
"Ikona" society, Paris: 377
Il Ventaglio, play: 200
Iliazd: see Zdanevich, Ilia
Ilina, Nataliia: 432
Ilinsky, Alexander: 316
Ilinsky, Igor: 235, 236, 240
Iliukhina, Evgeniia: 200, 204, 205, 206, 265
Illiustrirovannaia Rossiia, Paris, journal: 128, 308

Illustration, L', Paris, journal: 43, 220, 221

Imhoff, Hans-Christoph von: 184

Imperial Academy of Arts, St. Petersburg (IAA): 19, 33, 52, 55, 56, 111, 119, 132, 143, 156, 183, 215, 217, 221, 223, 229, 236, 254, 257, 261, 281, 282, 287, 301, 312, 321, 322, 334, 337, 338, 344, 349, 358, 365, 372, 375, 377, 386, 399, 421, 429, 442; also see Academy of Arts; Higher Art Institute of IAA, St. Petersburg

Imperial Naval School, St. Petersburg: 160

Imperial Theaters, Moscow / St. Petersburg: 19, 58, 184, 197, 198, 244, 245, 246, 261, 262, 263, 267, 358, 364, 399, 459

"Impressionists" exhibition, St. Petersburg: 215, 365

In 1825, play: 401

Inber, Vera: 423

Industrial Art Studio for Toys, Zagorsk: 253

Ingham, Norman: 451

Ingles, Elisabeth: 34

Ingres, Jean Auguste: 375

Inkhuk (Institute of Artistic Culture), Moscow: 15, 52, 196, 228, 236, 237, 290, 304, 326, 331, 338, 379, 383, 426, 435

Inkizhinov (Inkijinoff), Valerii: 307, 385

Ino, Pierre: 401

Inshakov, Alexander: 265

Inspector General, The, play: 183, 185-187, 188, 223, 232, 236, 370, 429, 435, 452

Institut Français d'Architecture, Paris: 435

Institut Valencià d'Art Modern (IVAM), Valencia: 189

Institute of Civil Engineering, St. Petersburg / Petrograd: 156, 435

Institute of Decorative Art, Petrograd: 365-366

Institute of the History of Arts / Institute of Art History, Petrograd: 221, 264, 394

Institute of IAA, St. Petersburg: 119, 215, 257, 261, 344, 372, 377

Institute of Labor, Central (TsIT), Moscow: see Central Institute of Labor (TsIT), Moscow

Institute of Modern Russian Culture (IMRC), Los Angeles: 284, 439; see also *Experiment*

Institute of Rhythm: 132

International Center of Photography, New York: 237

"International Exhibition of Paintings,

Sculpture, Engraving, and Drawings" / "Salon" Izdebsky's, Odessa: 132, 135, 281

International Exhibitions Foundation, Washington, DC: 288

International Herald Tribune, Paris, newspaper: 225, 352, 355

"International Theater Exhibition", New York: 32

"Internationale Ausstellung für Buchgewerbe und Graphik" exhibition, Leipzig: 16

Internatsional iskusstva, journal: 397

Intimate Theater: see Nevolin, Boris / Nevolin's Intimate Theater

Intransigeant, L', Paris, newspaper: 183

Ioffe, Ya.: 378

Iovleva, Lidiia: 34, 184, 217, 429

Irtel, Pavel: 218

Isaakian, Avetik: 351

Isaeva, K.: 191, 193

Isaeva, Vera: 309

Isakov, Sergei: 183, 217, 219, 399

Iskusstvo, Moscow, journal: 26, 111, 114, 130, 138, 180, 257, 259, 333, 348, 350, 386, 397, 445

Iskusstvo kino, Moscow, journal: 422

Iskusstvo Leningrada, Leningrad, journal: 221

Iskusstvo kommuny, Petrograd, journal: 159, 256, 332, 333

Iskusstvo trudiashchimsia, Moscow, journal: 255

Islamey, ballet: 19, 20, 21, 410

Israel Museum, Jerusalem: 34, 48

Isselbacher, Audrey: 456

Istomin, Konstantin: 328

Ivakin, Gleb: 28, 306, 307, 345

IVAM: see Institut Valencià d'Art Modern, Valencia

Ivan Susanin: see *Life for the Tsar, A*

Ivan the Terrible, film: 156, 157, 158

Ivan the Terrible / Tsar Ivan the Terrible, opera: 217, 345

Ivan the Terrible, Tsar of All Russia: 17, 156, 345

Ivanoff, Serge (Ivanov, Sergei): 220-221

Ivanov, play: 374

Ivanov, Alexander: 386

Ivanov, Dmitrii: 56

Ivanov, Evgenii: 297, 460

Ivanov, Georgii: 29, 227

Ivanov, Pavel: see Mak

Ivanov, Sergei: 351, 352, 444

Ivanov, Viacheslav Iv.: 56, 163, 220, 374, 427

Ivanov, Viacheslav Vs.: 157

Ivanov, Victor: see Iving

Ivanov, Vsevolod: 14, 15, 374

Ivanova, Elena: 400

Ivanova, Lidiia: 356

Ivanova, Tamara: 230

Ivask, Yurii: 218

Ivensky, Semeon: 131

Iving (Ivanov), Victor: 256, 294, 295

Ivnev, Riurik: 460

Izdebsky, Galina: 169, 171

Izdebsky, Vladimir: 132, 135, 171, 172, 175, 281, 397

Izdebsky-Pritchard (Isdebsky-Pritchard), Alina: 168, 442

Izmailov, Alexander: 400

IZO NKP (Visual Arts Section of the People's Commissariat of Enlightenment): 15, 159, 179, 236, 238, 255, 283, 287, 290, 297, 338, 348, 349, 383, 397

Izvestiia, Moscow, newspaper: 305

Izvestiia khudprosotdela Moskovskogo Soveta, Moscow, newspaper: 182

Jack of Diamonds [Bubnovyi valet] exhibitions and group: 15, 53, 134, 137, 161, 179, 181, 200, 207, 228, 264, 265, 266, 267, 280, 283, 297, 314, 321, 326, 331, 348, 366, 395, 426

Jackson, Ernest: 118

Jacob, Max: 430

Jacovleff, Alexandre (Yakovlev, Alexander): 14, 29, 101, 111, 215, 216, 221-223, 253, 282, 311, 334, 357, 372, 387

Jamoujinsky: 273

Janacopulos, Vera: 378

Jangfeldt, Bengt: 143

Jastrebzoff, Serge: see Férat, Serge

Jawlensky, Alexej: 53, 228

Jeanneret, Pierre: 237

Jedrinsky, Marianna: 132, 224

Jedrinsky (Zhedrinsky), Vladimir: 223-224, 241

Jesus Christ: 203, 206, 207

Jesus Christ, Superstar, musical: 28

Jeu de Robin et Marion, play: 146

Jeux, ballet: 190, 191

"Jewish Art Exhibition", Kiev: 32, 294

Jewish (Yiddish) Chamber Theater, Moscow: 32, 33, 137, 333, 334

Jewish National Museum: 179

Jewish Society for the Encouragement of the Arts: 179

Jewish Society for the Promotion of the Arts, Moscow: 52

Jewish Theater, Belorussian State, Minsk: 424

Jewish Theater, State, Moscow (GOSET): 179, 180

Jimmy Higgins, play: 305

Johnson, Ben: 230

Johnson, Edward: 152

Jones, Sidney: 412, 413

Joods Historisch Museum, Amsterdam: 333

Jooss, Kurt: 131

Joseph-Charles: 209

Jouhandeau, Elise: 41, 47, 48

Jouhandeau, Marcel: 48

Joyeuse Farce des "Encore", La, farce: 289

"Jubilee Exhibition of the Art of the Peoples of the USSR", Leningrad / Moscow: 15, 194

Judges. A Tragedy, The, play: 324-326

Judith, opera: 358-360

Julien Levy Gallery, New York: see Levy, Julien

Julius Caesar, play: 111, 374

Jullian, Philippe: 52, 225

Juschny, Jascha: 219, 287, 322, 332, 374, 412, 417

Kabale und Liebe, play: 263

Kabalevsky, Dmitrii: 367

Kachalov, Vasilii: 98

Kachaniak, M.: 307

Kadina, Iraida: 111

Kaiser, George: 26

Kaiser Wilhelm Universität, Berlin: 31

Kakabadze, David: 188, 217, 459

Kakhovsky, Petr: 404

Kalaushin, Boris: 135, 256

Kalidasa: 260

Kalmakov, Nikolai: 20, 117, 221, 225-228, 365

Kameneff, Vladimir: 191

Kamenev, Lev: 451

Kameneva, Olga: 451

Kamensky, Alexander: 15, 137, 215, 351

Kamensky, Vasilii: 53, 135, 136, 137, 144, 158, 189, 239, 364, 440, 441, 442, 457

Kamyshnikova, Lidiia: 247

Kandinsky (Andreevskaia), Nina: 228

Kandinsky, Wassily (Vasilii): 52, 53, 130, 135, 137, 189, 190, 219, 228-229, 256, 260, 264, 283, 287, 306, 324, 331, 332, 349, 396, 445

Kantadze, D.: 195

Kapitonenko, Alexander: 135

Kaplan, L.: 422

Kaplanova, Sofia: 257, 258, 319

Karabchevsky house, St. Petersburg: 221, 372

Karalli, Vera: 68

Karamzin, Nikolai: 114, 252, 286

Karasik, Irina: 298

Kardovsky, Dmitrii: 19, 111, 156, 215, 216, 220, 221, 254, 283, 334, 372

Karelia Museum of Visual Arts, Petrozavodsk: 40

Karetnikova, Anna: 125

Karetnikova, Sofia: 314

Karginov, German: 338, 340, 342, 343

Karinska, Barbara (Karinskaia, Varvara): 280

Karneev, Mikhail: 460

Karpov, Dmitrii: 135

Karpov, Evtikhii: 259

Karsavina, Tamara: 21, 40, 44, 47, 56, 65, 66, 67, 68, 69, 70, 147, 181, 198, 199, 208, 246, 358, 376, 377, 388

Karussel, Berlin, journal: 220

Kasatkin, Nikolai: 349, 452

Kashchei the Immortal, film: 191

Kashey, Elizabeth: 20

Kashey, Robert: 20, 273

Kashina-Evreinova, Anna: 15, 225, 226, 364, 365, 393

Kashkin, Nikolai: 253

Kashnitsky, Vladimir: 185

Kashuro, Marina: 458

Kaskin-Youritzin, V.: 412

Kataev, Valentin: 10, 254, 285

Katia, film: 31, 125

Katkow, Cyril: 125

Katonah Gallery, Katonah, New York: 33

Katonah Museum of Art, Katonah, New York: 412

Katz, Daniel: 420

Kaufman, Mikhail: 192

Kaunas State Art School: 146

Kaunas State Theater: 149

Kautsky, Robert: 76

Kazan Art Institute: 134, 286, 383

Kazan Art School: 338

Kazan Opera: 286

Kazan, Elza: 33

Kazhdan, Tatiana: 446

Kazovsky, Hillel (Gillel): 333, 423

Kellermann, Bernard: 367

Kelly, Catriona: 166

Kemfert, Beate: 200

Kerdimun, Boris: 439, 440, 458

Kerensky, Alexander: 219

Kessel, Joseph: 221

Khabarov, Igor: 57, 244

Khachatrian, Shaen: 351, 352

Khan-Magomedov (Chan-Magomedov), Selim: 237, 290, 298, 339, 340, 341, 342, 343, 379, 397, 435, 436, 438

Khardzhiev, Nikolai: 190, 191, 266

Kharitonov, Nikolai: 253

Kharkov Art Institute: 309

Kharkov Children Theater: 14

Kharkov State Jewish Theater: 424

Kharkov Theater of Opera and Ballet / Kharkov Opera Theater: 188, 317, 318

Kharms, Daniil: 159, 188

Kherson Agricultural Institute: 129

Khidekel, Lazar: 138, 159, 290, 298

Khimerioni cabaret, Tiflis: 217

Khlebnikov, Velimir: 135, 136, 144, 159, 184, 254, 257, 284, 291, 297, 298, 301, 397, 423, 454, 460

Khmuryi, Vasyl: 316, 317, 318

Khodasevich, Olga: Margolina-Khodasevich, Olga

Khodasevich, Valentina: 27, 133, 144, 158, 229-231, 285, 452

Khodasevich, Vladislav: 229

Khokhlov, Konstantin: 193, 230, 282

Khokhlova (Botkina), Alexandra: 192

Kholmskaia, Zinaida: 27

Kholodkov, Viktor: 11, 135, 136, 143, 145, 194, 195, 233, 236, 239, 240, 257, 258, 266, 267, 283, 291, 295, 325, 340, 341, 342, 349, 383, 422, 429, 438, 441, 442, 447, 450, 451, 457, 459

Kholodovskaia, Mariia: 429

Khostov-Khostenko, Alexander: see Khvostenko-Khvostov, Alexsander

Khovanshchina, opera: 152, 180, 181, 244, 323, 364, 374

Khovanskaia, Evgeniia: 235

Khovin, Viktor: 460

Khrakovsky, Vladimir: 233, 235

Khrzhanovsky, Yurii: 188

Khudiakov, Andrei: see Houdiakoff, André

Khudozhestvennyi zhurnal, Moscow, journal: 31

Khudozhnik, Moscow, journal: 33, 221, 372

Khvostenko-Khvostov (Khostov-Khostenko), Alexander (Oleksandr): 145, 231-232

Khvylev, Mikola: 307

Kiaksht, Georgii: 40

Kiaksht, Lidiia: 68

Kibrik, Evgenii: 185

Kiev Art Institute: 32, 129, 161, 223, 303, 305, 316, 321, 333, 397, 412, 423

Kiev Conservatory of Music: 287

Kiev First Commercial Institute: 367

Kiev Film Studios: 303

Kiev Military Institute: 294

Kiev Secondary School: 364

Kiev Theater of Musical Comedy: 305

Kiev University: 305

Kievskaia mysl, Kiev, newspaper: 305

King Gaikin I / Activist Gaikin, agit-play: 183, 187, 188

King Lear, play: 168, 178, 423, 448-449

King of the Square Republic, play: 303

King Saul, play: 358, 444

Kingore Gallery, New York: 200, 264

Kino-fot, journal: 198, 383

Kino-glaz, Moscow, journal: 191

Kino-Truth, film: 342

Kipling, Tudyard: 282; see also *Mowgli*
Kirchner, Ernst Ludwig: 460
Kirillova, A.: 188
Kirk (Conrad Kickert): 283
Kirov Academic Theater of Opera and
    Ballet (Kirov Theater), Leningrad:
    see Mariinsky (Kirov) Theater
Kirov Academy of Ballet, Washington,
    D.C.: 67
Kirov, Sergei: 460
Kirsanov, Semeon: 11, 13, 14
Kirsanova, Nina: 224
Kiselev, A.Z.: 266
Kiselev, Alexander: 215
Kiselev, Mikhail: 350, 386, 445
Kiselev, Valentin: 15
Kiselev, Viktor: 195, 232-236
Kiseleva, Ekaterina: 347
Kiss, Károly: 314
Klado, Tatiana: 460
Kleberg, Lars: 157
Klee, Paul: 189
Kleiman, Naum: 157
Klejman, M.: 157
Klever, Yulii: 452
Klimoff (Klimov), Evgenii: 57, 120
Klimov, Alexander: 137
Klimov, Grigorii: 120
Klimov, R.: 178, 309, 310, 311
Kliuchevsky, Vasilii: 337
Kliun (Kliunkov), Ivan: 130, 236-237,
    255, 298, 333, 348, 349, 399, 441,
    442
Kliunkova-Soloveichik, Svetlana: 236
Klodt, Mikhail: 444
Klodt, Nikolai: 245, 252
Klop: see Ustinov, Johann
Klutsis (Klucis, Gustavs / Gustav): 10,
    189, 237-238, 286, 338, 422, 423
Knebel Publishing-House: 445
Kniazeff (Kniazev, Kniaseff), Boris: 209,
    323, 412, 413, 414, 415, 416
Kniazev, Vasilii (Joe): 296
Kniazeva, Valentina: 344, 355, 356, 357
Knight of Malta, play: 27
Knipper (Knipper-Chekhova), Olga L.:
    18, 287, 427
Knipper (Chekhova), Olga: see
    Tschechowa, Olga
Knirr's Studio, Heinrich, Munich: 53
Knizhnik, T.: 344
Knot, film: 193
Kobaladze, T.: 217
Kobiakov, Dmitrii: 281
Kochergin, Nikolai: 452
Kochno, Boris: 76, 190, 212, 275, 322,
    348, 354, 396, 420
Kogan, Dora: 53, 55, 158, 245, 253,
    350, 386, 387, 389, 390, 391, 392,
    394, 442, 443, 445
Kogan, Nina: 159, 256

Kogan, Petr: 438
Koiransky, Alexander: 19, 452
Kolesnikov, Mikhail: 162, 226, 309, 312
Kolesnikova, Larisa: 143
Kolodin, Irving: 393, 394
Kolpakchi, Mariia: 236
Kolupaev, Dmitrii: 193
Komardenkov, Vasilii: 158, 181, 182,
    192, 238-241, 253, 294, 304, 379,
    447, 448
Komfut [Communist Futurism] group:
    15
Komissarjevski (Komissarzhevsky),
    Viktor: 233
Komissarzhevskaia Dramatic Theater,
    Leningrad: 216
Komissarzhevskaia, Vera /
    Komissarzhevskaia Theater, St.
    Petersburg: 19, 27, 181, 182, 199,
    225, 226, 227, 228, 309, 350, 386,
    387
Komissarzhevsky, Fedor
    (Komissarjevsky, Theodore): 19,
    181, 182, 226, 350, 351, 365
"Komsomol in the Fatherland War",
    exhibition: 309
Konchalovskaia, Tatiana: 460
Konchalovsky, Petr: 179, 283
Kondratiev, Pavel: 185, 187
Konenkov, Serei: 31, 158, 258
König rief soinon Tambour, Der, play:
    412
Königgrätzerstrasse Theater, Berlin:
    412, 417
Konius, Georgii: 459
Konstantin Yuon's and Ivan Dudin's Art
    School: see Art School, Konstantin
    Yuon's and Ivan Dudin's, Moscow
Konsthistorisk Tidskrift, Stockholm: 379
Koonen, Alisa: 260, 305, 316, 382, 437,
    439
Kop ivová, Anastasie: 148
Kopshitser, Mark: 358, 360
Korbut, Evgeniia: 14
Korenev, Mikhail: 428
Koreneva, Lidiia: 404
Korin, Pavel: 219
Kornienko, Nelli: 307, 316, 364
Korobtsova, A.: 302, 303
Korolev, Yurii: 155
Korostelev, Oleg: 308
Korotkina, A.: 344
Korotkina, Liudmila: 375, 429
Korovin, Alexei: 124, 127, 241-243, 247,
    288
Korovin, Konstantin (Korovine,
    Constantine): 24, 35, 48, 58, 123,
    125, 133, 179, 180, 197, 198, 219,
    231, 232, 237, 241, 244-253, 260,
    303, 308, 312, 313, 314, 319, 337,
    345, 349, 351, 358, 359, 386, 395,

    410, 444
Korovin, Sergei: 444
Korovina (Fidler), Anna: 241
Korovine, C.: see Korovin, Konstantin
Korsakaite, I.: 155
Korsh Theater, The: 330
Korshikov, Georgii: 133, 134
Korshikova, Valentina: 134
Korzukhin, Alexei: 283
Kosa, St. Petersburg, journal: 365
Kosmatov, Leonid: 192
Kostandi, Yurii: 133
Kostin, Sergei: 238, 240, 253-254, 349,
    379, 451
Kostin, Vladimir: 143, 283, 319, 439,
    441, 442
Kostina, Elena: 144, 180, 446, 447, 448,
    451
Kostrichkin, Andrei: 193
Kostrovitskaia, Vera: 133
Kotovich, Tatiana: 297
Koudriavtzeff, Nicholas: 280
Kousnezoff, Marie (Kuznetsova, Mariia)
    / Marie Kuznezoff's Opéra Privé de
    Paris / Marie Kuznezoff's Opéra
    Russe: 34, 42, 43, 52, 103, 122,
    123, 124, 125, 199, 241, 243, 244,
    247, 249, 362; see also Opéra
    Russe à Paris
Kousnezoff-Massenet, Marie: see
    Kousnezoff, Marie
Koussevitsky, Serge: 202
Koval, A.: 162
Koval, Masha: 282
Kovalenko, Georgii: 162, 164, 168, 170,
    173, 175, 177, 200, 265, 297, 306,
    309, 312, 416
Kovalenko, Petr: 256
Kovalenskaia, Tatiana: 351
Kovalev, Alexander: 265, 397
Kovalskie, K and O.: 257
Kovtun, Evgenii (Yevgenii): 159, 183,
    188, 231, 254, 255, 256, 264, 265,
    384
Kozintsev, Grigorii: 15, 28, 157, 193
Kozintseva, Liubov: 333
Kozlinsky, Vladimir: 134, 220, 233, 254-
    255, 282, 421
Kozlovsky, Sergei: 165, 190
Kozyrev, Mikhail: 460
Kozyreva, Natalia: 282
Kramova (Fridland-Kramova), Nadezhda:
    31
Krasikov, P.: 331
Krasnaia gazeta, Leningrad: 15, 188,
    216
Krasnaia niva, Moscow, journal: 165,
    379
Krasnaia panorama, Leningrad, journal:
    409
Krasnaia Presnia Komsomol House: 197

Krasnyi militsioner, Moscow, journal: 31, 379
Krasovskaia, Vera: 44
Kravchenko, Kseniia: 427
Krebbs, Stanley: 26
Krechetova, Tatiana: 264
Kremnev, Nicholas: 271, 273
Kressel, N.: 157
Krichevsky, Fedor: 316
Kriuger Elza: see Kruger, Elza
Kriukova, Irina: 284, 397, 435, 446
Krivoruchkina-Shcherbatova, Larisa: 294
Krivosheina, Olga: 303
Kříž, Jan: 183
Krol, Georgii: 284
Krotkov Private Opera: 374
Krasnopevtsev, Dmitrii: 179
Krokodil, Moscow, journal: 142, 143, 253
Kronidov, Nikolai: 225
Kruchenykh, Alexei: 135, 159, 201, 236, 256-257, 266, 291, 294, 297, 298, 301, 348, 349, 383, 456, 457, 458
Kruger (Kriuger, Krüger), Elza: 170, 172, 173, 178, 295, 297
Kruglikova, Elizaveta: 254, 349, 445, 446
Kruglov, Vladimir: 52, 53, 57, 215, 216, 244, 257, 355, 358, 443
Krupensky, Alexander: 60
Krupskaia Academy of Social (Communist) Education: 383
Krupskaia, Nadezhda: 331
Krylov, Ivan: 159, 358, 360
Krylov, Porfirii: 343
Kryzhitsky, Grigorii: 28, 157
Kshessinskaia, Matilda: 261
Ktorov, Anatolii: 192
Kubanova, Galina: 160
Kucherenko, Zoia: 305, 306, 307
Kudashev lithographic workshop: 40
Kudria, Arkadii: 257, 358
Kudriashev (Koudriachov), Ivan: 255-256, 306, 441, 442
Kudriavtsev, Sergei: 188, 456
Kudriavtseva, Lidiia: 429
Kudriavtseva, Sofia: 312
Kugel, Alexander: 27, 28
Kuhlmann, Charles: 152
Kuibyshev Theater of Opera and Ballet: 188
Kuindzhi, Arkhip: 281, 344
Kuindzhi, Valentina: 193, 404
Kukryniksy group: 339, 343
Kulagina, Valentina: 237
Kulbin, Nikolai: 26, 29, 225, 254, 256-257, 283, 348, 365, 457
Kuleshov, Lev: 191, 192, 339
Kultkino-Goskino: 192
Kultur-Lige: 179, 333
Kulturzentrum Alte Hauptfeuerwache,

Mannheim: 379
Kunst, Berlin, journal: 377
Kunst Museum Liechtenstein, Vaduz: 298
Kunsthalle, Bremen: 287
Kunsthalle, Düsseldorf: 183, 379, 397, 442
Kunsthalle, Hamburg: 287
Kunsthalle St. Annen, Lübeck: 200
Kunsthalle der Hypo-Kulturstiftung, Munich: 324
Kunsthaus, Zurich: 332
Kunstmuseum, Bern: 53
Kunstverein, Hamburg: 324
Kupferstichkabinett, Berlin: 184
Kupreianov, Nikolai: 287
Kupriianov, Mikhail: 343
Kuprin, Alexander: 53, 179, 267, 283, 366, 427, 442
Kurbas, Les: 232, 307, 316
Kurikol, play: 382, 383
Kurmastsep: see Courses in the Art of Stage Productions, Meierkhold's
Kurtz, Efrem: 151
Kusikov, Alexander: 137, 449
Kustodiev, Boris: 111, 241, 253, 257-260, 319, 377, 421, 432
Kustodiev, Kirill: 111, 241, 421
Kusubova, Tatiana: 244
Kutuzov, Nikolai: 193
Kuzmin, Evgenii: 319
Kuzmin, Mikhail: 29, 31, 135, 136, 221, 223, 227, 230, 231, 260, 349, 376
Kuzmina, M.: 344
Kuzminsky, Konstantin: 135
Kuznetsov, Alexander: 412
Kuznetsov, Erast: 15, 400
Kuznetsov, Evgenii: 143
Kuznetsov, Pavel: 158, 164, 260, 308, 349, 351, 427
Kuznetsova, Mariia: see Kousnezoff, Marie
Kuznezoff's Opéra Privé de Paris, Marie / Marie Kuznezoff's Opéra Russe, Paris: see Kousnezoff, Marie

Labas, Alexander: 166, 441, 442
Lacerba, Florence, journal: 183
Ladies' Home Journal, New York, journal: 161
Ladurner, Helga: 135
Lady Macbeth of Mtsensk, opera: 134
Ladyzhnikov publishing-house: 31
Lafont (La Font), Joseph de: 308
La Fontaine, Jean de: 137
Lagut, Irène: 182, 396
Lahowska, Ada: 142
Lake Liul, play: 191
Lakmé, opera: 364
Laks, Anna: 183, 184
Lamanova, Nadezhda: 309
Lamartine, Alphonse: 21

Lambin, Petr: 156, 259, 261, 373
Lanceray, Evgenii A.: 261, 355
Lanceray (Lansere), Evgenii: 33, 56, 58, 111, 228, 261-263, 355, 358, 432, 444, 453
Lanceray, Nikolai: 261, 355
Landowska, Wanda: 314, 395
Lange, Christiane: 324
Laparcerie, Cora: 288
Lapin Aglie cabaret: 182
Lapin, Lev: 264
Lapina, I.: 378
Lapo, Olga: 146
Lapshin, Nikolai: 282
Lapshin, Vladimir: 137, 230, 284, 355, 358, 444, 446
Larichev, Vitalii: 344
Larionov, Ivan: 266, 267
Larionov, Mikhail (Michel): 9, 30, 31, 53, 101, 125, 135, 184, 201, 202, 203, 204, 205, 206, 208, 209, 211, 214, 219, 228, 264-281, 283, 295, 297, 348, 396, 397, 399, 431, 446, 454, 456, 458
Larionova, Alexandra: see Tomilina, Alexandra
La Scala, Milan: 57, 65, 72, 73, 110, 111, 114, 116, 117, 125, 229
Lassaigne, Jacques: 139, 142
Last Victim, The, play: 232
Lattry, Ariadne: 281
Lattry, Elena: see Aivazovskaia, Elena
Lattry (Latri), Mikhail: 281-282
Lattry, Pelopid: 281
Latvian Academy of Art, Riga: 286
Latvian Infantry, Ninth: 237
Laurens, Henri: 278
Lauri-Volpi, Giacomo: 25
Lavinsky, Anton: 233, 235
Lavrentiev, Alexander: 196, 338, 339, 384
Lavrova, Olga: 427, 429
Lavrovsky, Leonid: 144
Law, Alma: 327, 384, 386
Lawyer from Babylon, The, play: 381-382, 383
Lawyers' Art Circle: 228
Lazarenko, Vitalii: 158, 189, 235
Lazarev Institute of Oriental Languages, Moscow: 446
Leal, Brigitte: 139
Lebedev, Vladimir: 16, 134, 159, 254, 255, 257, 282, 294, 439
Lebedeva, Mariia: 361
Lebedeva, Sarra: 427
Lebedeva, Viktoriia: 257
Leblan, Mikhail: 383
Lebon, Elisabeth: 321
Lecocq, Charles: 151
Le-Dantiu, Mikhail: 266, 267, 295, 398, 456

Lee, Marshal: 160

Lef (Left Front of the Arts) journal and group: 143, 156, 238, 338, 369-370, 383, 435

Le Fauconnier, Henri: 283, 314, 326, 426

Leftist Federation of the Professional Union of Artists and Painters: 348, 383

Legat, Nikolai: 33, 37, 40

Legat, Sergei: 33, 37, 40

Légende de Joseph, La, ballet: 50

Léger, Fernand: 52, 137, 211, 237, 283, 305, 430, 458

Léger's Académie Moderne: 161

Le Gris-Bergmann, Françoise: 456

Leikind, Oleg: 8

Lelekova, Olga: 377

Lelong, Lucien: 44

Le Maire, Henri: 304, 382, 383

Lemercier Gallery, Moscow: 377, 445

Lempert, Iosif: 143, 144, 222, 223, 242, 245, 252, 280

Leniashin, Vladimir: 319, 358, 427, 429, 443

Lenin Komsomol Theater, Leningrad: 303

Lenin Library / Lenin Public Library, Moscow: 197, 435

Lenin Museum, Central, Moscow: 303

Lenin Railroad Club, Alatyr: 13

Lenin (Ignatiuk), Mikhail: 29

Lenin (Ulianov), Vladimir: 138, 142, 157, 238, 241, 301, 302, 303, 331, 423, 432

Leningrad Bolshoi Theater of Drama: see Bolshoi Dramatic Theater, Petrograd / Leningrad

Leningrad Conservatoire: see Conservatoire, St. Petersburg / Leningrad

Leningrad Ensemble of Stage Workers: 133

Leningrad Theater of Miniatures: 303

Leningrad Union of Artists: 319

Lenka's Canary, play: 187

Lentulov, Aristarkh: 283-284, 330, 349, 439

Lentulova, Marianna: 283, 284

Leonard Hutton Galleries, New York: see Hutton, Leonard

Leonard, Robert: 126

Leonardo da Vinci: 311

Leonardo da Vinci Society, Moscow: 445

Leoncavallo, Ruggiero: 459

Leporskaia, Anna: 394, 395

Le Rider, Georges: 139

Lerman, Zoia: 57

Lermontov, Mikhail: 21, 53, 197, 198, 313, 322, 373, 442, 444

Leroux, Xavier: 19

Le Sage (Lesage, Alain-René): 308

Leshin, V.: 439

Leskov, Nikolai: 258, 259, 319, 460

Let There Be Joy, play: 146

Levenson, Alexander: 267, 283, 399, 444

Lévèque, Françoise: 282

Levin, Moisei: 133, 144, 285, 452

Levina, Tatiana: 179

Levinson, Andrei (André): 31, 43, 44, 49, 50, 52, 68, 110, 191, 235, 236

Levitan, Isaak: 312, 321, 337, 349

Levitin, Evgenii: 282

Levitin, Grigorii: 14, 15, 133, 134, 423

Leviton, Rebekka: 186

Levitsky, Dmitrii: 262

Levitsky, Vladimir: 31, 125

Levkievsky, Viacheslav: 267

Levkova-Lamm, Inessa: 321

Levshin, Alexander: 233

Levy, Julien / Julien Levy Gallery, New York: 118

LewAllen Modern, Santa Fe: 135

Leyda, Jay: 157, 158

Leymarie, Jean: 52

Lhote, André: 142, 458

Liadov, Anatolii: 37, 56, 271

Liakhov, Volia: 185

Lianda, Nataliia: 400

Liandsberg, Artur: 186, 187

Liapunov, Sergei: 21

Libakov, Mikhail (Moisei): 285-286, 303, 304

Liberman, Alexander: 200

Liberman (Yakovleva), Tatiana: 265

Liberts, Ludolfs: 286

Library of Congress, Washington, DC: 306

Lichine, David: 224, 337

Liebermann, Max: 313

Liessner-Blomberg (Lisner, Lissner), Elena: 219, 287

Lieven, Petr: 65

Lifar, Serge (Sergei): 46, 102, 118, 125, 131, 151, 190-191, 213, 214, 220, 276, 279, 334, 378, 419, 420, 449

Life for the Tsar, A (Ivan Susanin), opera: 398-399

Life is a Dream, play: 225

Ligeia, Paris: 162

Ligovsky Theater of the New Drama, Leningrad: 285

Liluli, play: 307

Limpid Stream, The, ballet: 134

Lincoln Center, New York: 33, 61, 146, 153, 162, 268, 288

Lindeman, Agnessa: 444

Lingenauber, Eckard: 20, 21, 22, 23, 24, 25, 26

"Link" [Zveno] exhibition, Kiev: 52, 129, 130, 134, 161

Lion des Mogols, Le, film: 125, 126

Lipkovskaia, Lidiia: 109

Lipovich, Innesa: 309, 400

Lipshitz (Lipchitz), Jacques: 52, 309

Lipskaia, Irena: 344

Lisenko (Lissenko), Natalia: 126

Lisner (Lissner), Elena: see Liessner-Blomberg, Elena

Lisner-Arnaumova, Natalia: 287

Lissim, Simon (Lisim, Semeon): 33, 50, 112, 118, 125, 162, 163, 165, 166, 167, 168, 171, 178, 232, 241, 287-290, 312, 323, 437

Lissitzky, El (Lissitsky, Lazar): 32, 159, 179, 190, 196, 228, 237, 256, 290-294, 297, 298, 309, 327, 328, 338, 339, 395, 397, 422, 423, 425

Lissitzky-Küppers, Sophie: 290, 292, 293, 294

Lissner, Ernst: 287

Lista, Giovanni: 270

Lista, Marcella: 332

Lister, Raymond: 287

Liszt, Franz: 21, 306, 368

Literary Museum, Moscow: see State Literary Museum, State, Moscow

Literary-Artistic Circle, Moscow: 314, 398

Literaturnaia gazeta, Moscow: 143

Literaturnaia Gruziia, Tbilisi, journal: 364

Lithuanian National Opera and Ballet, Kaunas: 149, 154

Little Berry cabaret, Petrograd: 111, 223, 421

Little Berry Theater of Miniatures, Belgrad: 223

"Little Circle" exhibition, Tiflis: 388

Little House in Batavia, The, revue: 30

Little Hump-Backed Horse, The, ballet: 244

Little Hunchback Horse, ballet: 303

Little Review Gallery, New York: 189

Liturgie, ballet: 203-207, 208, 214, 269, 377

Litvin, Felia: 360, 378

Liubimov, Alexander: 385

Liubimov, Vasilii: 460

Liubimova, Alisa: 130

Liubov k trem apelsinam, journal: see Love for Three Oranges, journal

Liushin, Vladimir: 166

Liutse-Fedorov, Vladimir (Frank): 189

Living Almanacs revue: 315

Livshits, Benedikt: 130, 135, 136, 451

Lobachevsky, Nikolai: 255

Lobanov, Viktor: 143, 280, 429, 430, 439

Lobanov-Rostovsky, Nikita: 6, 28, 48, 98, 117, 131, 209, 223, 227, 301, 313, 314, 360, 361, 362, 377, 444, 459

Lobanov-Rostovsky, Nina: 6, 46, 52, 155, 301, 313, 355

Lobanova, Yuliia: 427

Locandiera, La, play: 98

Lochakoff, Alexandre: 126

Locksmith and the Chancellor, The, play: 329

Lodder, Christina: 191, 298

Lodii, Zoia: 227

Loguine (Loginoff-Muravjeff), Tatjana: 200, 209, 214, 264, 276, 281

Lois, Michel: 156

Lomonosov State Porcelain Factory: see State Porcelain Factory

Lomonosov, Mikhail: 419, 420

Lomtatidze, Lili: 194

London Coliseum: 132

London Group and Artistes Silencieux, Brussels exhibition: 118

London, Jack: 156

Lope de Vega, Félix Arturo: 194, 225, 316, 333

Lopez, Arturo: 354

Lopez, Enrico: 354

Lo Presti, Salvatore: 128

Lopukhov, Fedor: 133, 144

Los Angeles County Museum: 160

Lossky, Boris: 131

Louis XIV, King of France: 49, 161, 262

Louis XVI, King of France: 188

Lourié, Arthur: 399, 451

Love for Three Oranges [Liubov k trem apelsinam], Petrograd, journal: 23, 228

Love for Three Oranges, The [Liubov k trem apelsinam], opera: 19, 23, 145, 152, 178, 231, 232, 334, 435

Love in the Ranks: see *Amour et Hiérarchie*

Lovers, The, pantomime: 221, 256, 372, 412

Lövgren, Håkan: 157

Lower Depths, The, play: 374

Lozowick, Louis: 327

Lucas, Leighton (Lukin): 273

Lucie-Smith, Edward: 135

Luchert, F.: 396

Luchishkin, Sergei: 425, 441

Lucrezia Borgia, play: 254

Lufft, Peter: 331

Lukanova, Alla: 200, 265

Lukin: see Lucas, Leighton

Lukin, Lev / Lev Lukin's Moscow Free Ballet / Ballet Studio: 54, 158, 189, 191

Lukomorie, St. Petersburg, journal: 254

Likomorie, Theater of Miniatures, Moscow: 328

Lukomsky (Lukomskij), Georgii: 217, 218, 223, 262, 372, 377

Luksh-Makovskaia, Elena: 444

Luna-park Theater, Petrograd: 144, 159, 184, 291, 294, 298, 349, 366

Lunacharsky Theater, Sverdlovsk: 429

Lunacharsky, Anatolii: 27, 45, 52, 97, 110, 158, 159, 181, 196, 236, 259, 284, 302, 303, 305, 330, 331, 368, 383, 429, 435, 438, 447, 451, 453

Lupandina, A.: 435, 437

Lurie, Doron: 34

Lustigen Weiber von Windsor, Die / Vindzorskie prokaznitsy, play: 181, 182

Lüthy, Hans: 331

Lutskaia, Elena: 10, 158

Lvov, Lolli: 131, 352

Lvov, Nikolai: 460

Lvov, Peter: 282, 399

Lyceum Theater, London: 127, 212

Lynes, Russell: 118

Lynn, Nicholas: 209

Lynton, Norbert: 397

Lyon Corporation: 139

Lysistrata, play: 333, 334

Lysogorsky, Vladimir: 184, 226

Macdonald, Nesta: 199

MacDougall's, auction: 20, 212, 221

Machida City Museum of Graphic Arts, Japan: 135

Madernieks studio / Julijs Madernieks, Riga: 286

Madsen, Axel: 139

Maeterlinck, Maurice: 19, 22, 23, 26, 32, 157, 288, 387

Magadan Music and Drama Theater: 372

Magarill, Sofia: 193

Magarotto, Luigi: 188, 456

Maggio Musicale Fiorentino, Florence: 56

Magidovich, Marina: 32

Magnanimous Cuckold, The / Le Cocu magnifique, play: 54, 190, 195, 326, 327, 331, 384, 385, 386, 429, 438

Maiakovsky Museum, State, Moscow: 135, 143

Maiakovsky, Vladimir: 10, 11, 15, 27, 53, 134, 135, 136, 137, 143, 159, 183, 184, 188, 189, 194, 195, 196, 197, 231, 233, 235, 236, 241, 254, 255, 266, 276, 283, 284, 287, 290, 292, 315, 339, 340, 341, 343, 343, 349, 365, 366, 369, 423, 438, 454, 457, 458, 461

Maid of Pskov, The [Pskovitianka], opera: 19, 197, 345, 377

Maiorov, Sergei: 371

Maison de la Culture de Bourges: 200

Maison Worth: 47

Maisonnette Russe, La, cabaret and restaurant, Paris: 272

Majestic Theater, New York: 394

Mak (Pavel Ivanov / Paul Mak): 181, 294-297

Makarenko, Mikhail: 183

Makarenko, Nikolai: 130

Makhrov, Kirill (Cyrille): 8, 308

Makovets group and journal: 314, 316, 383

Makovskaia, Elena: see: Luksh-Makovskaia, Elena

Makovsky, Konstantin: 72

Makovsky, Sergei (pseudonym Essem): 14, 132, 216, 220, 221, 227, 308, 344, 348, 430

Makovsky, Vladimir: 197

Maksakova, Mariia: 145

Malade, La, opera: 98

Malaichuk, Natalia: 230

Malevich, Kazimir: 16, 27, 53, 130, 133, 135, 137, 138, 139, 159, 161, 166, 179, 184, 231, 235, 236, 237, 238, 253, 255, 256, 257, 260, 264, 265, 266, 267, 283, 287, 290, 291, 297-301, 306, 309, 314, 315, 316, 321, 327, 331, 332, 333, 339, 348, 349, 366, 394, 395, 399, 426, 431, 439, 458

Maliavin, Filipp (Maliavine, Philippe): 301-303, 444

Maliavina (Novak-Savich), Natalia: 301

Maliavina, Zoia: 302

Malikoff, Nikolai: 125

Malitsky, Alexander: 212, 261

Maliutin, Ivan: 181, 182, 238, 255, 294,

Maliutin, Sergei: 338, 430, 444, 445, 446

Malmo Museum, Sweden: 360

Malmstad, John: 139

Malochet, Annette: 139, 140

Malsch, Friedemann: 298

Maltzahn Gallery, London: 313

Maly Opera Theater, Leningrad: 133

Maly Theater, Moscow: 10, 132, 285, 309, 333, 374, 404, 428, 429, 435, 459

Maly Theater, Petrograd: 365

Maly Theater of the Red Army, Moscow: 423

Mamelles de Tirésias, Les, play: 182

Mamonova, Natalia: 452

Mamontov, Anatolii: 312

Mamontov, Savva: 244, 312, 314, 349, 358, 374, 386, 429, 430, 442, 443, 444; see also Private Opera Company, Mamontov's

Mamontov, Sergei: 358, 444

Mamontov, Vsevolod: 430

Mamontova, Elizaveta: 312

Mamontova, Vera: 358

Mamontov family: 430

Mamoulian, Rouben: 386

Mam'zelle Angot, ballet: 151, 152
Man Who Was Thursday, The, play: 435, 438
Man with a Movie Camera, film: 380
Mandate, play: 367, 369, 370-371, 429
Mandel, Semeon: 285, 303, 452
Manhattan Opera House, New York: 19
Manifesto "We and the West": 450-451
Manin, Vitalii: 283
Manina, Antonina: 435
Manna d'Oro, La, Spoleto: 198
Mansbach, Steven: 290, 294
Manson, J.: 111
Mantegna, Andrea: 147, 311
Marc, Franz: 272
Marcadé, Jean-Claude: 16, 19, 52, 53, 138, 139, 142, 297, 301, 321, 322, 454, 455
Marcadé, Valentina: 16, 19, 52, 301
Marche Funèbre sur La Mort de la Tante à Héritage, La, musical composition: 272
Mardzhanov, Konstantin (Mardzhanishvili, Kote): 194, 195, 297, 301, 317, 333, 376, 412, 458
Margolin, Samuil: 334, 386, 424
Margolina-Khodasevich, Olga: 230
Mariage d'Aurore, or Mariage de la Belle au Bois Dormant, La, ballet: 50, 150, 212, 357
Mariengof, Anatolii: 239, 381-382, 425, 446, 447
Mariinsky (Kirov) Theater, St. Petersburg / Petrograd / Leningrad: 17, 21, 22, 33, 37, 40, 43, 48, 58, 59, 60, 65, 123, 133, 144, 145, 154, 156, 197, 198, 199, 229, 245, 255, 257, 261, 262, 345, 355, 356, 359, 360, 361, 364, 367, 420, 459
Mariks, Oskar: 331
Marinetti, Filippo: 207, 256, 257, 267, 270, 295, 297, 348, 457, 458
Marion Koogler McNay Art Museum, San Antonio, Texas: 200
Marionette Theater, Petrograd: see Theater of Marionettes, Petrograd
Maris Contents, play: 19
Markarian, Ruben: 297
Markin, Yurii: 183
Markov, Pavel: 158, 178, 189, 368, 383, 429
Markov, Vladimir (Matvejs, Voldem rs): 256, 266
Markov, Vladimir: 454, 455
Markova, Alicia: 138, 420
Marriage of Figaro, The, opera: 181, 319, 376, 387, 435
Marshak, Samuil: 282, 404, 432, 452
Martianoff, Nicholas: 219
Martin, Jean-Huber: 183, 297
Martin, John: 138

Martin, Leslie: 189, 191
Martin du Nord, Georges: 225, 227
Martinet, Marcel: 330
Martynova, Elizaveta: 302
Martyre de Saint Sébastien, Le, ballet: 35, 36, 45, 47, 52
Marx, Karl: 138, 238
Mary, Queen of England: 111
Marzaduri, Marzio: 188, 294, 456, 458
Masalina, Natalia: 338
Mashkov, Ilia / Mashkov's Private Studio: 10, 32, 158, 178, 179, 237, 283, 309, 366, 383, 454
Mashkovtsev, Nikolai: 261
Masiutin, Vasilii: 445
Mask of the Red Death, ballet: 118; see also *Red Masks*, ballet
Maslovsky, Alexander: 97, 110, 281
Mason, Rainer: 348
Masquerade, play: 53, 197, 198
Mass, Vladimir: 189
Massat, René: 321
Massenet, Jules: 25, 42
Massine, Leonide (Leonid): 138, 140, 141, 149, 151, 190, 203, 207, 208, 224, 267, 268, 269, 270, 271, 272, 274, 281, 412, 419, 420, 449
Masson, André: 224, 225
Master Institute of United Arts, New York: 344
Masters of the Russian Ballet, film: 303
Mastfor: see Foregger, Nikolai
Matelots, Les, ballet: 149
Matignon Gallery, New York: 236
Matisse, Henri: 97, 179, 287, 351, 365, 393, 430
Matiushin, Mikhail: 26, 111, 130, 159, 236, 256, 257, 291, 297, 298, 301, 348, 349, 460
Matochkin, Evgenii: 344
Matoum en Matoumoisie, puppet play: 182
Matrunin, Boris: 285, 303-304
Mattioli Collection, Milan: 131
Matvejs (Matvei), Voldem rs: see Markov, Vladimir
Maulpoix, Jean-Michel: 454
Mauries, Patrick: 352, 355
Maver Lo Gatto, Anjuta: 52
Mavra, opera: 275, 306, 396
Max, Eduoard: 47
May Night, opera: 180
Mayer, Charles: 34
Mayer, Louis: 160
Mayo, Eileen: 190
Mazeppa, drama: 306-307
Mazeppa, Ivan, hetman: 306-307
Mazeppa, opera: 56
Mazilier, Joseph: 317
Mazur, Alexander: 338
McClintic, Miranda: 1 62

McEvoy, Ambrose: 118
McNay Art Museum, San Antonio, Texas /Marion Koogler McNay: 118, 200
McVay, Gordon: 383
Measure for Measure, play: 449
Mechlin, Leila: 20, 26
Médecin malgré lui, Le, play: 99-100, 132
Medunetsky, Konstantin (Kazimir): 35, 238, 240, 253, 304-305, 379, 380, 382, 383, 437, 439, 451
Medvedkova, Olga: 125
Meerzon, Iosif: 291, 399
Mefistofele, opera: 116
Mei, Lev: 345
Meierkhold, Vsevolod: 8, 10, 14, 23, 26, 28, 42, 47, 52, 53, 54, 144, 145, 146, 156, 158, 159, 181, 182, 188, 189, 190, 191, 195, 197, 198, 221, 232, 233, 235, 236, 241, 259, 263, 284, 309, 320, 321, 326, 327, 330, 331, 339, 340, 341, 342, 349, 350, 364, 367, 368, 369, 370, 371, 372, 378, 379, 383, 384, 385, 386, 387, 425, 427, 428, 429, 435, 438, 446, 448, 452
Meilhac, Henri: 198
Meinhard, Carl: 417
Mekhanikova, Valentina: 338
Mekk (Meck), Vladimir fon: 33
Melbourne Slavonic Studies, Melbourne, journal: 31
Melikoff, Boris: 372
Meller, Vadim: 305-307, 319
Melnikov, Vladimir: 344
Melnikova, Elena: 440
Menaechmi, play: 16
Menard, René: 257
Mendés, Catulle: 19
Mendes, José: 459
Menko, A.: see Monko, Alexander
Menzel, Adolf van: 313
Mephisto Waltz / Mephisto Valse, ballet: 305, 306
Merchant of Venice, The, play: 132, 177
Merezhkovsky, Dmitrii: 18, 35, 146, 163, 374
Merimée, Prosper: 198
Merkert, John: 189, 190
Merry Day of Princess Elizabeth, A, play: 365
Merry Death, play: 17, 364-365
Merry Theater for Elderly Children, St. Petersburg: 365
Merry Wives of Windsor, play: 164, 182, 283
Merzliakov, I.: 158
Meshchersky, Arsenii: 444
Meshkov, Vasilii: 427
Mesley, Roger: 20

Messel, Oliver: 353
Messina, Roberto: 282
Mestre, Louis: 293
Metelitsa, Natalia: 20
Metner, Alexander: 381
Metropole Hotel, Moscow: 197, 263, 295, 400, 442
Metropolis, film: 125
Metropolitan Museum of Art, New York: 45, 46, 47, 203, 297
Metropolitan Opera, New York: 19, 22, 23, 25, 26, 33, 43, 70, 118, 138, 151, 152, 156, 337, 348, 386, 389, 392, 393, 394, 420
Metropolitan Teilen Art Museum, Tokyo: 384
Metzinger, Jean: 211, 283, 314, 326, 426
Meudon Museum: 421
Mexican, The, film: 156, 157
Meyer zu Essen, Annette: 287
Meyer, Franz: 137, 138, 160
Meyer, Meret: 137
Mgebrov, Alexander: 184, 188, 377
Miamlin, Igor: 372, 373
Miasina, Marianna: 426
Midas, comic ballet: 146, 147
Midnight Sun: see *Le Soleil de Nuit*
Midsummer Night's Dream, A, play: 116, 238, 239, 240
Mies van der Rohe, Ludwig: 189
Mikado, operetta: 307
Mikhail Fedorovich (Romanov), Tsar: see 398
Mikhailov, Alexei: 217
Mikhailov, Evgenii: 376
Mikhailov, Konstantin (Ten): 296, 297
Mikhailov, M.: 267
Mikhailova, Alla: 8
Mikhailova, N.: 344
Mikhailovsky Theater, St. Petersburg: 42, 459
Mikhienko, Tatiana: 138, 255
Miklashevskaia, Avgusta: 437
Miklashevsky, Konstantin: 16, 230, 399
Mikolaichik, Nicolas: 273
Milanovi, Olga: 223
Milashevsky, Vladimir: 399
Milhaud, Darius: 454, 455
Milia, Gabriella di: 265
Milioti (Millioti, Miliotti, Miliuti), Nikolai: 101, 223, 228, 308, 314
Milioti, Vasilii: 308
Military Academy, Odessa: 63, 125
Military Academy, St. Petersburg: 110, 129, 218, 256
Military Institute, Kiev: 294
Miller, Gilbert: 394
Miller, Grigorii: 305, 309
Millions d'Arlequin, Les, opera-ballet: 17, 454-455

Milloss, Aurelio: 125
Milman, Adolf: 283, 412
Milner, John: 290, 294, 297
Milstein, Nathan: 152
Ministries of Agriculture and Transport: 218
Minor, The, play: 18, 459
MIPSA: see Moscow Institute of Painting, Sculpture, and Architecture (MUZhVZ)
Mir i iskusstvo, Paris, journal: 131
Mir iskusstva, St. Petersburg, journal: 125, 281, 446; see also: *World of Art*
Miracle of the Holy Virgin, The [Zaria-Zarianitsa], play: 335-336
Miroliubova, Alexandra: 305
Mirovich, Evstignei: 331
Mirsky, Dmitrii: 19
Mirzoian, Lusik: 351
Misanthrope, play: 428
Misheev, Nikolai: 119, 287, 290
"Mishen": see "Target"
Misler, Nikoletta: 183, 184, 185, 188, 200, 228, 229, 282, 383, 384
Miss: see Remizova, Alexandra
Mistetska tribuna, Kiev, journal: 319
Mitin zhurnal, Tver, journal: 375
Mitrokhin, Dmitrii: 432, 445, 446
Miturich, Petr: 399, 423
Mitusov, Stepan: 96, 97, 392
MKhAT: see Moscow Art Theater
Moch, Yvette: 430
Mochalov, Lev: 260
Mocher Seforim, Mendele: 179
Mochulsky, S.: 285
Moderna Museet, Stocholm, 397
Modernism Gallery, San Francisco: 456
Modigliani, Amedeo: 52, 217, 321, 430
Mogilevsky, Alexander: 283
Mohaupt, Richard: 151
Moholy-Nagy, Laszio: 287
Moi zhurnal dlia nemnogikh, St. Petersburg, journal: 215, 216
Moiseev's State Ensemble of Folk Dances / Igor Moiseev: 303, 304
Moiseev, Mikhail: 316, 317, 318
Moleva, Nina: 244, 253
Molière, play: 427
Molière (Jean-Baptiste Poquelin): 14, 98, 99, 100, 132, 216, 230, 295, 309, 350, 427, 428
Moline, fashion house: 220
Moloda gvardiia, Kiev, newspaper: 129, 130
Molok, Dmitrii: 310
Molok, Yurii: 15, 422, 423
Moments Fugitives / Visions Fugitives, piano composition: 132
Monakhova, Liudmila: 327
Monastyrskaia, Vanda: 130

Monde Artiste, Le: 101
"Monde d'Art, Le" exhibition, Paris: 372
Mondonville, Jean-Joseph de: 337
Monet, Claude: 228
Moniushko, Hélène: 296
Moniushko, Stanislav: 231
Monko (Menko), Alexander: 287, 367
Mons, Christian: 355
Monsieur de Pourceaugnac, play: 230, 428
Monte Cristo, film: 125
Month in the Country, A, play: 146, 155
Moody, Christopher: 31
Moor (Orlov), Dmitrii: 231, 254, 297
Moos, David: 297
Morazzoni, Anna: 229
Mordkin, Mikhail / Mordkin Russian Ballet Company: 25, 66, 68, 70, 118, 120, 156, 309, 316, 317, 319, 416
Mordvinova, Alevtina: 188
More, Edward: 348
Morejko, S.: 290
Morgunov, Alexei: 266, 283, 399, 426, 439
Morozov, Alexei: 237, 446
Morozov, Ivan: 287, 321
Morozova Olga: 361
Morozova, Olga G.: 223
Moscow Art Theater (MKhAT): 14, 18, 23, 26, 57, 58, 98, 100, 144, 146, 158, 162, 164, 166, 167, 197, 223, 257, 258, 259, 285, 286, 296, 311, 312, 319, 333, 351, 374, 386, 401, 404, 427, 428, 434, 452
Moscow Art Theater (MKhAT) Studios: 162, 166, 167, 258, 285, 286, 303, 311, 312, 333, 351, 374, 386, 404, 444
Moscow Association of Artists: 132, 180, 228, 311, 445, 446, 452, 454, 456
Moscow Central Industrial Design Institute: 260
Moscow Children Theater: 181, 328, 331, 435; see also First State Children Theater
Moscow Conservatory: 448
"Moscow Ex-libris for the Year 1926, The" exhibition: 422
Moscow Fiancées, revue: 336-337
Moscow Institute of Painting, Sculpture, and Architecture (MIPSA / MUZhVZ): 132, 135, 156, 179, 197, 200, 219, 220, 231, 232, 238, 244, 255, 260, 264, 266, 267, 283, 297, 303, 308, 311, 313, 319, 322, 337, 349, 351, 358, 364, 374, 386, 395, 397, 427, 446, 452, 456
Moscow Kino Center: 191
Moscow Music-Hall: 342

Moscow News Weekly, Moscow, newspaper: 215
Moscow Operetta Theater: 285
Moscow Painters group: 179, 283
Moscow Polygraphical Institute: 237
Moscow Practical Academy of Commercial Sciences: 312, 435
Moscow Private Opera: see Zimin's Moscow Private Opera
Moscow Railroad Workers' Club: 379
Moscow Region Theater of the Proletarian Lads, Moscow: 460
"Moscow Salon" exhibition: 383
Moscow Society of Independent Artists: 128
"Moscow Stage Design" exhibition: 238, 438
Moscow State Art Institute: see Surikov Institute of Visual Art, Moscow
Moscow State Model Theater: 449
Moscow Textile Institute: 232
Moscow Theater of Comic Opera: 413
"Moscow Theaters of the October Decade" exhibition: 10, 303, 374
Moscow Union of Soviet Artists: 426, 439, 452
Moscow University: 31, 228, 308, 313, 412, 454
Moscow Writers' Club: 196, 197
Mosenthal, Herman von: 182
"Moskau-Berlin" exhibition: 220
Moskovskii khudozhnik, Moscow, newspaper: 254, 283
Moskva, Moscow, journal: 348
Moskvich, Grigorii: 168
Moskvin, Andrei: 193
Moskvin, Ivan: 18, 32
Mouchoir de Nuages, play: 19
Mouveau, Georges: 99
Movshenzon (Movsheson), Alexander: 15, 230, 231
Mowgli, play: 328
Mozart and Salieri, opera: 98
Mozart, Wolfgang Amadeus: 132, 376
Mozzhukhin (Mosjoukine), Ivan: 126
Mr. Brown's Riding Lesson, circus number: 159
Mrazovsky, Vladimir: 11
Mrs. Denny's Riding Lesson, circus number: 159
Mstera Art-Industrial Technicum: 232
Mudrak, Myroslava: 316, 317
Mukhina, Vera: 30, 162, 164, 165, 178, 190, 309-311, 312, 314, 326, 327, 330, 426
Muller, Martin: 456
Müller-Berghaus, Karl: 306
Müller-Brockmann, Josef and Shizuko: 457
Müller-Groholski (Mme Muller), Nita (Anna): 211

Mun, Countess de: 353
Munich University: 189
Municipal Van Abbemuseum, Eindhoven: 290, 397
Municipal Theater, Casablanca: 223
Münter, Gabriele: 228
Murashko, Alexander: 32, 333
Murashova, Nonna: 302, 303
Muratov, Pavel: 262, 308, 427
Muraviev-Apostol, Sergei: 404
Murina, Elena: 283
Murray, Alden: 110
Murray, William: 26
Musatov, Nikolai: 158
Musée Bourdelle, Paris: 331
Musée Carnavalet, Paris: 220
Musée Château de Tours, Château de Tours: 162
Musée d'Art et d'histoire, Paris: 348
Musée d'Art Moderne, Toulouse: 130
Musée d'Art Moderne de la Ville de Paris: 137, 139, 332
Musée d'Art Moderne et Contemporain, Strasbourg: 237
Musée de l'Opéra, Paris: 76
Musée des Années 30, Boulogne-Bilancourt: 221
Musée des Arts Décoratifs, Paris: 44, 352
Musée des Arts et Métiers, Paris: 161, 162
Musée des Beaux-Arts, Lyon: 156
Musée des Beaux-Arts, Strasbourg: 281
Musée des Colonies, Paris: 352
Musée du Montparnasse, Paris: 431
Musée Galliera, Paris: 396
Musée Maillol, Paris: 324
Musée National d'Art Moderne, Paris: 52, 188, 266, 297, 321, 324, 397, 451
Musée National des Châteaux de Malmaison et Bois-Préau, Paris: 352
Musée National Message Biblique Marc Chagall, Nice: 137
Musée-Galérie de la Seita, Paris: 225
Museo de Arte Abstracto Español, Cuenca: 282
Museo de Bellas Artes, Santiago, Chile: 215
Museo del Corso, Rome: 298
Museo Nacional Centro de Arte Reina Sofia, Madrid: 237, 327, 339
Museo Teatrale alla Scala, Milan: 111
Museu Fundación Juan March, Palma: 282
Museum Fridericianum, Kassel: 238
Museum für Kunsthandwerk, Frankfurt: 34, 57
Museum of Academy of Arts (IAA), St. Petersburg: 338
Museum of Artistic Culture, Moscow: 327, 397

Museum of City of New York: 156
Museum of Contemporary Art, Moscow: 162, 309
Museum of Contemporary Art, Thessaloniki: 327, 339
Museum of Fine Arts, Rostov: 304
Museum of Modern Art (MOMA), New York: 33, 118, 137, 138, 157, 189, 203, 268, 269, 275, 321, 327, 338, 348, 379, 412, 456
Museum of Modern Art, Oxford: 313
Museum of Painterly Culture, Moscow: 441, 442
Museum of Private Collections, Moscow: 48, 98, 320, 444
Museum of Society for the Encouragement of the Arts, Petrograd: 131
Museum of Visual Art, Belgrade: 223
Museum of Visual Art, Grozny (Chechen Republic): 65
Museum of Visual Arts, Ekaterinburg: 184
Museum Ostdeutsche Galerie, Regensburg: 218
Museum Tinguely, Basel: 397
Music Box Revue, revue: 160
Musical America, New York, journal: 152
Musical Snuffbox cabaret: 315
Musical Story, A, film: 303
Mussorgsky, Modest: 109, 112, 114, 119, 121, 152, 180, 181, 229, 252, 286, 289, 337, 361, 377, 453
Mutiny of the Machines, play: 26
Muzei, Moscow, journal: 314, 400, 435, 459
Muzej pozorišne umetnosti Srbije, Belgrade: 223
MUZhVZ: see Moscow Institute of Painting, Sculpture, and Architecture
Muzy, Kiev, journal: 188, 256, 301
My Grandmother, film: 194
My Life with Caroline, film: 335
Mykhailychenko, Hnat / Hnat Mykhailychenko Theater, Kiev: 307
Mysterium of Liberated Labor, mass action: 31
Mystery-Bouffe, play: 15, 159, 194-195, 231, 232-235, 236, 241, 458, 461

Nabokov, Nicolas: 419, 420, 421
Nachtigaller, Roland: 237, 238
Nagibin, Yurii: 397
Nakov, André B.: 130, 131, 160, 162, 297, 298, 304, 342, 381, 382, 383
Nal and Damayanti, ballet: 311
Napoleon Bonaparte: 394
Napoleon Movie House, Moscow: 379
Narakidze (Norakidze), V.: 217
Narbut, Egor (Georgii): 223, 445

Narcisse, ballet: 44, 45, 48
Narodny, Ivan: 281
Nash, Steven: 189, 190
Nashchokin House Gallery, Moscow: 355, 426
Nashe nasledie, Moscow journal: 34, 215
Nashe slovo, Odessa, newspaper: 19
Nashe slovo, Sukhumi, newspaper: 365
Naslund (Näslund), Erik: 34, 57
Nathanson, Richard: 412, 414, 415, 416
National Armenian Museum, Erevan: 351
National Armenian Theater, Erevan: 448, 451
National Art Gallery, Wellington, New Zealand: 200
National Art Museum, Kiev: 135, 333, 423
National Gallery, Stockholm: 295
National Gallery of Armenia, Erevan: see State Pictury Gallery of Armenia, Erevan
National Gallery of Art, Washington, D.C.: 297
National Gallery of Australia, Canberra: 266
National Museum of Georgia, Tbilisi: 456, 458
National Theater of Latvia, Riga: 288
Nationalbibliothek, Vienna: 19, 99, 208
Naumov, Pavel: 118
Naumova, Lidiia: 157
Navashin, Petr: 459
Navy Dramatic Theater, Leningrad: 452
Nebolsin, Vasilii: 322
Nechaeva, Sofia: 356, 377
Nehru, Jawaharal: 344
Nekhoroshev, Yurii: 374
Nekrasov, Georgii: 161, 312
Nekrasova, Olga: 374
Nekrylova, Anna: 143
Nelidova, Lidiia: 47
Nelli, Vladimir: 234
Nemirovich-Danchenko, Vladimir: 98, 146, 296, 297, 374, 401, 404, 427, 428
Nemirovskaia, Mirra: 290
Nemirovsky, Evgenii: 290
Nemo, pseudonym: 348
Nemtchinova, Vera: 149, 268, 377, 400, 401, 410, 411, 454, 455
Nenarokomova, Irina: 244
Neradovsky, Petr: 282, 432
Nero: 159
Nest of Gentlefolk, A, dramatized novel: 428
Nesterov State Art Museum, Ufa: 135
Nesterov, Mikhail: 303, 337, 338
Neue Künstlervereinigung, Munich: 53
Neuman, Alfred: 394

Neuvecelle, Jean: 56
Neva, St. Petersburg, journal: 221
Nevolin, Boris / Nevolin's Intimate Theater: 158, 191
Nevrev, Nikolai: 427
New Art Studio, Petrograd: 14, 111
New Lef [Novyi lef], Moscow, journal: 338, 383; also see *Lef*
"New Society of Artists" exhibition cycle, St. Petersburg / Petrograd: 53, 257, 372, 377
New Theater for Children, Leningrad: 452
New York City College: 286
New York City Opera / New York City Center Opera: 152, 153
New York Evening World, New York, newspaper: 52
New York Public Library: 61, 146, 153, 162, 268, 287, 288
New York Times, New York, newspaper: 26, 118, 138, 156
Nezhdanova, Antonina: 334
Nezlobin Theater: 31, 350, 452
Nicholas Cadet Corps, St. Petersburg: 322
Nicholas Cavalry Academy, St. Petersburg: 27
Nicholas I, Emperor of All the Russias: 389, 404
Nicholas II, Emperor of All the Russias: 226, 262
Nicolai, Otto: 181, 182
Niedersächsische Landesgalerie, Hanover: 290
Night Dancers, play: 27
Night in the Old Market, The, play: 179
Night on a Bald Mountain, orchestral composition: 361
Nightingale, The, opera: see *Rossignol, Le*
Nijinska, Bronislava / Nijinska's Choreographic Studio / Nijinska's Théâtre Choréographique: 33, 44, 49, 99, 103, 109, 113, 123, 125, 127, 128, 161, 162, 190, 212, 214, 241, 274, 275, 276, 305, 306, 346, 396, 410, 454
Nijinsky, Kira: 40
Nijinsky, Vaslav: 19, 22, 44, 46, 47, 56, 61, 65, 67, 68, 70, 181, 191, 199, 206, 246, 345, 346, 358
Nikich, Anatolii: 315
Nikisch, Artur: 21
Nikitin, Anderi: 157
Nikitin, Nikolai: 32
Nikitina, Alicia: 190, 191, 279, 420
Nikitsky Theater, Moscow: 413
Nikolai Konstantinovich, Grand Duke: 389
Nikolskaia, Tatiana: 188, 456
Nikritin, Solomon: 255, 256, 425

Nikritina, Anna: 382
Nikulin, Lev: 30, 315
Nisbet, Peter: 290, 294
Niscemi, Maria: 78
Niva, St. Petersburg, journal: 337
Nivinsky, Ignatii: 162, 166, 167, 311-312, 349, 351
Noblissima Visione, ballet: 412
Noces, Les / *Les Noces Villageoises* [Svadebka], ballet: 212, 214, 306, 394
Noi vivi, film: 56
Non Loin de Tiflis, revue: 218
Nora, play: 144
Nordshtein, Tatiana: 452
North Carolina Museum of Art, Raleigh
Noskovich, Viktor: 361
Nosov, Viktor: 358
Nosova, Evfimiia: 375
Not Born for Money, film: 135
Not Far From Tiflis, revue: 217
Nouveaux Ballets de Monte Carlo: 454
Nouvel, Walter: 52, 358, 361
Nouvelle Librairie Nationale, Paris: 220
Nova generatsiia, Kharkov, journal: 232, 316, 319
Novaia studiia, Moscow, journal: 19, 257, 348
Novembergruppe: 189, 287
Novikov, Lavrentii / Novikoff, Laurent: 21, 56, 152, 316
Novitsky, Alexander: 132
Novitsky, Pavel: 340
Novoe russkoe slovo, New York, newspaper: 19, 26, 31, 214, 269, 294, 321, 331, 335, 386, 445
Novoe vremia, St.-Petersburg, newspaper: 52
Novorossiisk University, Odessa: 125, 313
Novosti sezona, Moscow, newspaper: 284
Novouspensky, Nikolai: 360
Novozhilov, Vasilii: 460
Novyi Mir, Moscow, journal: 223, 230
Novyi Mir iskusstva, St. Petersburg, journal: 31, 32, 225, 377, 400
Novyi Satirikon, St. Petersburg, journal: 215, 282, 334
Novyi Zhurnal, New York, journal: 117, 215, 219
Novyi Zritel, Moscow, journal: 11, 14, 236
Nue, revue: 30
Nuit Ensorcelée, La, ballet: 51
Nuitter, Charles: 153
Nur and Anitra, ballet: 316-317, 319
Nusch-Nuschi, opera: 19
Nussberg, Lev: 395
Nutcracker, The, ballet: 33, 111, 389

Oberiu group: 159
Obmokhu (Society of Young Artists):
    142, 238, 239, 240-241, 253, 304,
    338, 379, 451
Obolenskaia Gymnasium, St.
    Petersburg: 159
Obolensky, Vladimir: 267
Obozrenie teatrov, St. Petersburg,
    journal: 199
Observer, London, newspaper: 288,
    290
Obukhova, Nadezhda: 334
Obukhova-Zelinskaia, I.: 27
Ocean, play: 19
Ocean's Eleven, film: 335
October, film: 156, 380
October group of artists: 10, 196, 237,
    290, 338, 422, 423
Ode, ballet: 412, 419-420
Odessa Art Institute: 15, 52, 134, 309,
    365
Odessa Drawing School: 19
Odessa Institute of Drawing: 313
Odessa University: see Novorossiisk
    University, Odessa
Odesskie novosti, Odessa, newspaper:
    229
Odinokova, Elizaveta: 338
Oedipus, play: 449
Oedipus at Colona, play: 35, 45
Oeil, L', Paris, journal: 353, 355
Oenslager, Donald: 166, 167
Of Mice and Men, film: 335
Offenbach, Jacques: 428
Office Culturel de Bray, Bry-sur-Marne:
    396
Oginskaia, Larisa: 237
Ogonek, Moscow, journal: 98, 216, 259
Ogonek, St. Petersburg, journal: 281
O'Henry (pseudonym of William Sydney
    Porter): 216
Ohio State University: 20
Ohlsen, Nils: 324
Oiseau Bleu, L': see *Blue Bird*
Oiseau de Feu, L' / *Firebird* [Zhar-ptitsa],
    ballet: 71, 124, 131, 197, 198, 199,
    201, 212, 213, 284, 445, 446
Okhimovsky, Jean: 273
Okhlopkov, Nikolai: 369
Okhta Workers' Theater, Petrograd: 237
Okna ROSTA: see ROSTA Windows
Okna TASS (Windows of the Soviet
    Telegraph Agency): 143
Oko ska, Alisja: 326
Olesha, Yurii: 14, 158, 285
Olgina, O.: 267
Oliver Cromwell, play: 435
Olivéroff, André: 372
Olson, Ruth: 189, 191
OMKh: see Society of Moscow Artists
Omphale, dramatized novel: 59

O'Neill, Eugene: 305, 383
Ondine, play: 412
One-Sixth of the World, film: 194, 342-
    343
Onufrieva, Svetlana: 197, 199
Opelvillen, Rüsselsheim: 200
Opera House, Cologne: 170, 178
Opera House, Sofia: 209
Opera National at the Royal Opera
    House, Bucharest: 17
Opera of Soviet of Workers' Deputies,
    Moscow: 238
Opéra Privé de Paris: see Kouznezoff,
    Marie / Kuznezoff's Opéra Privé de
    Paris / Marie Kuznezoff's Opéra
    Russe, Paris
Opéra Russe à Paris / Opéra Russe de
    Paris: 108, 109, 122, 123, 125, 127,
    128
Opera Studio of the Bolshoi Theater,
    Moscow: 303
Operetta, operetta: 173, 174
Oransky, Viktor: 258, 303
Orenburg First Soviet Theater: 256
Orenburg Summer Red Army Theater:
    255
Orenstein, Gloria: 200
Orfeo, ballet: 412
Organization of Modern Ukrainian
    Artists, New York: 232, 307
Oriental Ball: see Bal Oriental
Orientales, Les, ballet: 46, 244, 246-247
Original Ballet Russe: 365
Orloff, Chana: 221, 431
Orlov, Alexander: 233
Orlov, Dmitrii: see Moor, Dmitrii
Orlov, Vladimir: 445
Orlova, Olga: 358
Orlov-Denisov, Vasilii: 389
Orphée aux Enfers, opera-buffa: 428
Orpheus, ballet: 197
Orpheus and Eurydice, opera: 420
OSA: see Association of Contemporary
    Architects
Osborn, Max: 16, 312
"Oslynyi khvost": see "Donkey's Tail"
Osmerkin, Alexander: 10, 189, 315, 460
Osmolovsky, Yurii: 452
OST: see Society of Studio Artists
Ostroukhov, Ilia: 312, 338, 360, 444
Ostroukhova (Botkina), Nadezhda: 312
Ostroumova-Lebedeva, Anna: 34, 52,
    56, 254, 302, 432, 444
Ostrovsky, Alexander: 23, 195, 216,
    247, 257, 259, 261, 295, 304, 347,
    348, 374, 382, 410, 429, 430, 452
Othello, play: 169, 171, 178, 194, 197
Otsep, Fedor: 165
Our Artists Gallery, Moscow: 146, 412
Oves, Liubov: 285, 452
Ovid: 44, 147

Ovsiannikov, Yurii: 125, 398
Oxford Slavonic Papers, Oxford, journal:
    313, 358
Ozarovsky, Yurii: 35
Ozenfant, Amédée: 139, 236, 237, 260

Pachmuss, Temira: 218
Pacific Overtures, musical: 33
Pagani Cesa, Giovanna: 188
Pagé, Suzanne: 137, 332
Pagliacci, opera: 459
Pagode, Die, film: 417
Painting Studio of the Sverdlov Club,
    Moscow: 237
"Paintings of the American Scene"
    exhibition: 386
"Paintings, Sculpture and Drawings by
    American and European Artists",
    Brooklyn: 156
Pakhomov, Nikolai: 312
Palacio de Bellas Artes, Mexico City: 138
Palazzo Strozzi, Florence: 228
Paleologue, Maurice: 55
Palette, La, Paris: see Académie de la
    Palette, Paris
Paley, Nathalie: 353, 354
Paliashvili Theater of Opera and Ballet,
    Tbilisi: 194, 217
Palmer-Soudeikine, Jeanne: 223, 387,
    389, 390, 392, 393, 394
Panorama iskusstv, Moscow, journal:
    162, 188, 200, 221, 280, 309, 312,
    348, 372
Panov, Alexander: 135
Pantomime of the Great Revolution,
    mass action: 31
Papillons, ballet: 146, 261
Papkov, Ivan: 305
Paquet (Rossini-Paquet), Françoise: 137
Paquin, fashion house: 220
Paramount Picture Corporation: 156
Paramount Theater: 156
Paray, Paul: 50
Parco della Musica, Rome: 157
Parekss Bank, Riga: 286
Paris, film: 160
Paris Opéra / Opera National de Paris: 137
Paris-Journal, Paris, journal: 305, 382
Paris-Presse-L'Intransigeant, Paris,
    newspaper: 225
Parisi, Valentina: 34
Parizhskii Vestnik, Paris, journal: 31
Parkhomenko, Konstantin: 305
Parkin, Varsonofii: 267, 280
Parnakh (Parnach, Parnac), Valentin:
    158, 208, 270, 272, 280, 367, 460
Parnis, Alexander: 183, 397
*Partie Champêtre dans une Lointaine
    Province Russe*, revue: see *A
    Country Picnic in a Distant Province
    of Russia*

Parton, Anthony: 200, 201, 203, 204, 208, 209, 212, 213, 214, 265, 268, 270, 272, 275, 281

Pas d'Acier, Le [Stalnoi skok], ballet: 134, 190, 446, 449-450, 451

Pashkova, Lidiia: 149

Passage Theater, St. Petersburg: 335

Passuth, Krisztina: 451

Pasternak, Boris: 313, 456

Pasternak, Josephine: 313, 314

Pasternak, Leonid: 179, 253, 302, 308, 313-314, 349, 358, 395, 444, 452,

Pasternak-Slater, Lydia: 313

Paston, Eleonora: 429

Path of Painting group: 314

Patriot, The, play: 394

Paul I, play: 18

Paul I, Emperor of All the Russias: 394

Pavel Alexandrovich, Grand Duke: 358

Pavillon d'Armide, Le, ballet: 57, 59-68, 70, 71, 102, 110, 272, 358

Pavillon de Paris theater, Petrograd: 30

Pavliuchenko, T.: 267

Pavlov, Ivan: 445

Pavlova, Anna: 19, 21, 22, 40, 48, 52, 55, 56, 68, 70, 120, 261, 358, 372, 373, 377, 410, 455

Pazzi, Ellen de': 135

Pechat i revoliutsiia, Moscow, journal: 26, 237

Pechstein, Max: 460

Pegoskhuma (Petrograd State Free Art Studios): 111, 132, 133, 144, 146, 220, 319, 372, 397, 421

Peissi, Pierre: 321

Pelléas et Mélisande, play: 125

Pen, Yurii: 285

Penza Art Institute: see Savitsky Art Institute, Penza

Penza School of Drawing: 283

People's House / People's House Theater, Petrograd: 21, 230, 361, 362

People's Theater, Belgrade: 223, 224

Perepletchikov, Vasilii: 444

Pérez, C.: 282

Perezvony, Riga, journal: 287, 345

Péri, La, ballet: 45-46, 52, 296

Perloff, Nancy: 290

Perm State Regional Museum: 445

Perm Theater of Opera and Ballet: 303

Perov, Vasilii: 337, 338, 374

Perrault, Charles: 48, 110, 111, 149

Perrot, Jules: 68

Perts, Vadim: 216

Pertsov, Petr: 237

Pervukhin, Konstantin: 444

Peshkova (Volzhina), Ekaterina: 287

Pestel, Pavel: 404

Pestel, Vera: 314-316, 399

Peter the Great (Peter I), Emperor of All

the Russias: 144, 154, 262, 306, 307, 358

Peterburgskaia gazeta, St. Petersburg, newspaper: 26, 52

Peterburgskaia zhizn, St. Petersburg, newspaper: 33

Peterburgskii listok, St. Petersburg, newspaper: 26

Petersburg, dramatized novel: 285, 303

Petersburg University, St. Petersburg: 16, 26, 56, 119, 146, 344, 432, 442, 456

Petipa, Marius: 40, 48, 49, 110, 111, 149, 212, 217, 261, 310, 317, 373

Petit Casino, Madrid: 139

Petite marchande d'allumettes, La, opera: 396

Petoshina, N.: 311

Petritsky, Alexander: 231

Petritsky, Anatolii: 306, 309, 316-319, 423

Petrograd State Free Art Studios: see Pegoskhuma

Petrogradskie vedomosti, Petrograd, newspaper: 431

Petrouchka cabaret: 328

Petrouchka [Petrushka], ballet: 5, 6, 17, 19, 57, 58, 59, 60, 70-96, 144, 280, 389, 393

Petrov, Nikolai (Kolia Peter): 14-15, 27, 28, 30, 378, 452

Petrov, Vsevolod: 282

Petrov-Vodkin, Kuzma: 144, 179, 216, 221, 260, 312, 319-321, 351, 421, 452

Petrov-Vodkina (Jovanovi), Maria: 319

Petrova, Ekaterina: 133

Petrova, Evgeniia: 159, 183, 255, 297, 361

Petrova, Liudmila: 146

Petrova, M.: 257, 435

Petrovichev, Petr: 444

Petrovsky, Andrei: 330

Peverelli, Maria de: 184

Pevsner, Antoine (Pevzner, Nota / Natan / Anton): 162, 189, 190, 191, 237, 321-322, 349, 431

Phalanx group: 228

Phèdre (*Phaedra*), tragedy: 35, 163, 304-305, 382-383, 435, 437-439

Philadelphia Museum of Art: 137

Philémon et Baucis, opera: 100

Pica, Vittorio: 302

Picabia, Francis: 430

Picasso, Pablo: 151, 161, 179, 182, 183, 211, 283, 332, 395, 397, 431, 450, 451

Picture Gallery of the Siberian Section of the USSR Academy of Sciences, Novosibirsk: 183

Pictures at an Exhibition / Bilder einer

Ausstellung [Kartinki s vystavki], orchestral composition: 32-33, 229

Pikuleva, Galina: 429

Pilniak, Boris: 432

Pilsky, Petr: 288

Pimenov, Yurii: 305, 441, 442

Pincus-Witten, Robert: 161

Piontkovskaia (Piątkowska), Valentina: 296

Piotrovsky, Adrian: 15, 188

Piranesi, Giovanni: 311

Piriutko, Yurii: 216

Pirogov, Alexander: 334

Pirosmanashvili, Niko: 267, 456, 458

Pisanella, La, ou la Mort Parfumée, play: 47

Pittoresque Café, Moscow: see Café Pittoresque

Pius XI, Pope: 220

Pizerra, Alain: 454

Pizzetti, Ildebrando: 47, 50, 51

Pizzini, Luca: 195

Plaisir de France, Paris, journal: 220

Plaksin, Mikhail: 425

Plastic Arts: 397

Plastici, Valori: 182, 183

Platov, Matvei: 148

Platov's Cossacks in Paris, revue: 148, 220

Platonov, Yurii: 180, 181

Plautus, Titus Maccius: 16

Pleshcheev, Alexander: 34, 52, 56

Plus Ça Change, Paris: music-hall revue, 160

Pochitalov, Vasilii: 320

Podgaetsky, Mikhail: 367

Podgornyi, Nikolai: 352

Podkopaeva, Yuliia: 57

Podobedova, Olga: 261, 263

Poe, Edgar Allan: 118

Poets' Café, Moscow: 136, 137, 284

Pogedaieff, Georges (Pozhedaev / Pozhidaev, Grigorii): 241, 322-323

Poiré, Emmanuel (Caran D'ache): 461

Poiret, Paul: 160, 430

Pokrovskaia, S.: 180

Pokrovsky, Oleg: 188

Pol, Vladimir: 260

Polenov, Vasilii: 197, 244, 312, 358, 364

Polenova, Elena: 197, 338, 430, 445, 446

Poliakoff, Alexis: 324

Poliakoff, Marie-Victoire: 324

Poliakoff, Serge (Poliakov, Sergei): 324-326

Poliakov, Mark: 136

Poliakov-Baidarov (Baydaroff), Vladimir: 251

Poliakov-Litovtsev, Solomon: 169

Poliakova, E. 344

Poliakova, Olga: 103

Polignac, Ghislaine: 354
Polikarpova, Galina: 443
Poling, Clark: 228
Political Authority of the Western Front:
    291
Polivanov, S. (Naum Sheinfeld): 331
Polonsky, Viacheslav: 311, 369
Polun, Sergei: 281
Polytechnic Engineering School,
    Munich: 189
Polytechnic Museum, Moscow: 267,
    283
Polytechnical Institute, Riga: 290
Polovtsian Dances: 126, 128, 188, 249,
    344, 345, 358, 411
Ponchielli, Amilcare: 216
Ponomarev, Evgenii: 261, 373
Popoff, Alexandre / Popoff Store, Paris:
    402, 411
Popoff, Berta: 432, 434, 435
Popov, Andrei: 72
Popov, Nikolai: 413, 440
Popova, Liubov: 139, 182, 195, 196,
    228, 235, 236, 283, 287, 294, 298,
    309, 311, 314, 315, 326-331, 333,
    339, 343, 348, 349, 367, 380, 384,
    386, 397, 399, 421, 425, 426, 431,
    435, 438, 439
Popova, N.: 282
Popova, Raisa: 446
Popova, Vera: 125, 192
Popovich, Vlodimir: 16, 19
Popular Art Institute: see Vitebsk
    Popular Art Institute / Art-Practical
    Institute
Poret, Alisa: 185, 187, 188
Porgy and Bess, opera: 386
Porritt, Irina: 281
Posnovis [Followers of the New Art]:
    159, 394
Pospelov, Gleb: 215, 265, 280
Poster Auctions International, New
    York: 45, 47, 358, 461
Posters Advertising: 11, 12, 13, 14, 30,
    40, 45, 47, 56, 136, 176, 185, 192,
    193, 196-197, 209-211, 219, 230-
    231, 235, 236, 240, 258, 262, 266,
    267, 278, 282, 283, 291, 295, 305,
    315, 320-321, 323, 331, 335, 340-
    341, 349, 358, 366, 368-371, 378,
    383, 384-385, 393, 394, 399, 402,
    410-411, 425, 429, 431, 438, 440-
    442, 444, 451, 457, 458-459, 460-
    461
Potemkin, Petr: 112, 148, 169
Pototsky, Fedor: 361
Pototsky, Mstislav: 361, 362, 363
Pouchkine, A.: see Pushkin, Alexander
Pougny, Jean (Puni, Ivan / Iwan): 26,
    159, 254, 255, 287, 316, 331-333,
    394, 421, 431

Poulenc, Francis: 430
Poussin, Nicolas: 375
Power of Love and Magic, The, puppet
    play: 227, 228
Pozharskaia, Militsa: 144, 146, 198
Pozharsky, Valerian: 283
Pozhedaev (Pozhidaev), Grigorii: see
    Pogedaieff, Georges
Pozoeva, Elena: 437
Pozzo, Andrea: 355
Prague National Theater: 119
Prakhov, Alexander: 333
Prakhov family: 430
Prampolini, Enrico: 54
Pravda, Moscow, newspaper: 134, 238,
    383
Pravoverova, Liudmila: 184, 427
Préludes, Les, ballet: 19, 21
Preparation of State Papers, St.
    Petersburg: 121
Présages, Les, ballet: 224
Press House, Leningrad: 159, 183, 185,
    187, 188
Press House, Moscow: 191, 438
"Pressa" exhibition, Cologne: 237, 422
"Pressa" exhibition, Leipzig: 309
Prianishnikov, Illarion: 374, 427
Prianishnikov, Ivan: 197
Pribylskaia, Evgeniia: 312
Prikker, Thorn: 53
"Prima Esposizione Libera Futurista
    Internationale", Rome: 348
Prince Igor, opera: 128, 180, 244, 245,
    246-247, 249-252, 303, 318, 345,
    361, 454
Princess Brambilla, play: 446, 447
Princess Turandot, play: 26, 311, 312,
    316, 323, 350-351; see also
    Turandot
Princesse Cygne, La, ballet: 128, 129
Princesse de Carizme, La, comic opera:
    308
Prior, Ingeborg: 290
Private Angelo, film: 111
Private Opera, Mamontov's, Moscow:
    181, 241, 244, 245, 314, 348, 349,
    358, 359, 360, 361, 429, 430, 442,
    443; see also Krotkov Private Opera
Professional Union of Artists-Painters,
    Moscow: 321, 326, 348, 383, 397
Proffer, Ellendea: 393
Project for the Affirmation of the New:
    see Proun
Projectionist Group: 305, 423, 425
Prokofiev, Sergei: 19, 23, 97, 132, 134,
    145, 152, 231, 232, 272, 273, 274,
    334, 367, 372, 435, 449, 451
Proletkult [Proletarian Culture]: 14, 156,
    188, 425
Proletkult [Proletarian Culture] School,
    Moscow: 338

Prometheus, symphonic work: 284
Pronina, Irina: 184
Propert, Walter: 199, 207
Proposing to the USSR, revue: 10
Prostorov, Nikolai: 446
Prosvetov, Evgenii: 439
Protazanov, Yakov: 165, 333
Proun (Project for the Affirmation of the
    New): 260, 290, 291, 294
Proun Gallery, Moscow: 260
Prusakov, Nikolai: 253, 304, 305, 379
Pruzhan, Irina: 34, 35, 40, 41, 42, 43,
    44, 46, 52, 199, 375, 376
Pskov State Combined Historical,
    Architectural, and Art Museum: 215
Pskovitianka: see The Maid of Pskov
Psst...!, Paris, journal, 461
Ptitsyna, Olga: 312
Publishing-Houses: 53, 71, 216, 237,
    253, 331, 404, 422, 445
Puccini, Giacomo: 19, 26, 181, 323
Pudovkin, Vsevolod: 158, 192
Pugni, Cesare (Pougny, César / Puni,
    Tsezar): 244
Pulcinella, ballet: 144
Pulver, Lev: 179
Puni, Ivan (Iwan): see Pougny, Jean
Punin, Nikolai: 215, 216, 229, 254, 255,
    282, 397, 399, 400
Puppet Theater, Yuliia Sazonova-
    Slonimskaia's, Paris: see Sazonova-
    Slonimskaia, Yuliia
Purgatorio de San Patricio, El, play: 262-
    263
Purvitis (Purvit), Vilhelms: 237
Pushkarev, Vasilii: 282
Pushkin Academic Theater of Drama,
    Petrograd / Leningrad: 14, 378, 424,
    see also Alexandrinsky Theater, St.
    Petersburg / Petrograd
Pushkin House, London: 281
Pushkin State Museum of Fine Arts
    (GMII), Moscow: 52, 179, 208, 282,
    311, 355, 429, 443
Pushkin, Alexander: 57, 98, 101, 109,
    113, 114, 120, 122, 127, 137, 138,
    146, 154, 201, 247, 252, 286, 289,
    327, 328, 346, 351, 362, 372, 396,
    409, 419, 427, 456
Putnam, Samuel: 396
Puts, Henk: 290

Quaderni del Vittoriale, Milan, journal:
    52
Quartet of Artists, A / Quartet of Merry
    Artistes, revue: 336
Quatre Chemins, Les, Paris: bookstore,
    161, 162, 171, 203, 396
Quatre Saisons, Les, ballet: see Les
    Saisons
Que Viva Mexico!, film: 156, 157

Queen of May / May Queen, operetta: 226

Queen of Spades, opera: 58, 112, 144, 372

Queen's Mistake, The, play: 10

Quilici, Vieri: 384

Quotidien de Paris, Le, Paris, newspaper: 225

Rabinovich, Alexander (Alex): 182, 308

Rabinovich (Rogaler), Isaak: 23, 145, 158, 161, 165, 178, 190, 239, 285, 287, 312, 333-334, 386, 423

Rabinovich, Saul: 188

Rabochaia Moskva, Moscow, newspaper: 331

Rabochii i teatr, Leningrad, journal: 15, 145

Rachel Adler Gallery, New York: 327, 458

Rachmaninoff, Serge (Sergei): 52, 313, 314

Racine, Jean: 35, 304, 305, 382, 437, 438

Radack, Richard von: 229

Radakov, Alexei: 254, 285

Radio CBS: 156

Radio October, play: 10

Radishchev Museum, Saratov: 345

Radlov, Nikolai: 14, 132, 215, 264

Radlov, Sergei: 145, 229, 230, 254, 452

Radziwill, Princess: 353

Rafalovich, Sergei: 331

Rafalsky, Mikhail: 424

Ragon, Michel: 324

Raikh, Zinaida: 320, 369

Raikin, Arkadii: 15, 303

Railing, Patricia: 162

Raizman, Yurii: 192

Rakhmanov, Nikolai: 285

Rakitin, Vasilii: 137, 165, 178, 327, 395

Rakitin, Yurii: 223

Rakitina, Elena: 331

Rambert, Marie / Rambert Dance Company / Ballet Rambert: 111, 153, 154

Ramuz, Charles: 274

Rannit, Alexis: 452

Rapée, Erno: 138

Rasdolskaja, Vera: 351

Rasimi, B. (Madame): 160

Raskin, Ben Zion: 294

Rasputin, der Dämon der Frauen, film: 31

Rassegna Sovietica, Rome, journal: 111, 137, 158, 230

Räuber, Die, play: 146, 194

Ravel, Maurice: 97, 103, 180, 207, 208, 269

Ravich, Nikolai: 342

Ray, Man: 397

Raymonda, ballet: 149

Raynal, Maurice: 217, 218

Razin, Stepan (Stenka): 440; see also *Stenka Razin*, play

Read, Herbert: 111, 189, 191

Reade, Brian: 270

Realtà Sovietica, Rome, journal: 340

Réau, Louis: 215, 322

Rebikov, Vladimir: 428

Rech, St. Petersburg / Petrograd, newspaper: 178, 199, 228, 280, 338, 351, 456

Red Army: 11, 53, 136, 142, 156, 218, 285, 321, 331, 367, 422, 423

Red Army Central Club, Moscow: 422

Red Army House, Leningrad: 303

Red Cross, The: see Society of St. Eugenia

Red Masks, ballet: 322; see also *Mask of the Red Death*, ballet

Redé, Alexis Baron de (Rosenberg): 352

Reed, Brian: 290

Redko, Kliment: 255, 425

Reduta Theater, Vilnius: 326

REF (Revolutionary Front of the Arts): 196

Regnier, Henri de: 14, 56, 131

Reifenscheid, Beate: 137, 138

Reine Fiammette, La, opera: 19

Reine, Bella: 151

Reineke Dramatic Theater, St. Petersburg: 348

Reinhardt, Max: 125

Reisinger, Vaclav: 150, 198

Re-mi: see Remisoff, Nicholas

Remisoff, Nicholas (Remizov, Nikolai; Vasiliev; Re-mi): 14, 31, 101, 112, 254, 257, 294, 334-337

Remisoff, Sophia: 336, 337

Remizov, Alexei: 146, 228

Remizova, Alexandra (Miss): 31

Renaissance Theater, Berlin: 332

Renard, Le, ballet: 144, 264, 265, 274-276, 280, 306

Renard, Jules: 269

Renée Maubel Conservatoire, Paris: 182

Rennert, Anne: 339

Repin, Ilia: 19, 41, 119, 215, 253, 257, 283, 287, 301, 302, 312, 338, 358, 360, 375, 400, 443

Repnin, Petr: 235

Rerberg, Fedor: 129, 229, 236, 297, 454

Rerikh, Nikolai: see Roerich, Nicholas

Restless Sex, film: 126, 160

Restany, Pierre: 431

"Results of the 1928-29 Theater Season" exhibition, Moscow: 367

Resurrection, play: 144, 313, 314, 386

Revalles (Revales), Flore: 43

Revolutionary Front of the Art: see REF

Revue: 175, 178

Revue de "l'Oeuvre", La, Paris, journal: 99, 125, 290 454

Revue of the Fairground Booth, revue: 30

Reza Shah: 294

Reznik, Lipe: 424

Reznikov, A.: 425

RGALI: see Russian / Central State Archive of Literature and Art, Moscow

Rhythm Institute, Moscow: 132

Riab, St. Petersburg / Petrograd, journal: 15

Riabouchinska, Tatiana: 224

Riabtsev, Vladimir: 316

Riabushinsky, Nikolai: 200, 264

Riabushkin, Andrei: 144, 302, 337-338, 430, 444

Rich, Frank: 33

Richard III, play: 423

Richter, Hans: 290, 394

Ricqlès, François de: 163, 165, 166

Rienzi, opera: 448, 449

Rienzi, Cola di: 448

Riga Art Institute: 237

Rilke, Rainer Maria: 57

Rimbaud, Arthur: 229

Rimsky-Korsakov, Andrei: 214

Rimsky-Korsakov, Nikolai: 19, 20, 23, 29, 41, 43, 101, 103, 113, 114, 119, 120, 122, 124, 128, 140, 152, 180, 201, 203, 229, 241, 244, 245, 247, 249, 267, 289, 345, 346, 347, 348, 351, 361, 362, 377, 419, 429, 430, 444, 459

"Ring" exhibition, Kiev: 128, 131, 161, 333

Rite Matrimonial Russe, revue: see *Ruslan and Liudmila*

Rite of Spring, The: see *Le Sacre du Printemps*

Riumin, Alexander: 146

Rivera, Diego: 429

Rivière, Jacques: 346

RM: see Russian Museum, State

Roar, China!, play: 370, 429

Robakidze, Grigol: 458

Rocher-Jauneau, Madeleine: 156

Rodchenko, Alexander: 10, 16, 182, 190, 194, 196, 232, 237, 238, 240, 253, 284, 298, 304, 309, 321, 327, 338-343, 348, 349, 367, 369, 379, 383, 384, 386, 399, 422, 426, 446

Rodchenko, Varvara: 309, 338, 385, 386

Rodchenko family: 340, 342

Röder, Anna: 219

Rodin, Auguste: 282, 310, 378, 379

Roerich Museum, New York: 136, 344

Roerich, Helena: 344

Roerich, Nicholas (Rerikh, Nikolai): 16,

19, 24, 41, 133, 136, 197, 263, 344-348, 361, 377, 443

Roethel, Hans: 228

Rogaler, Isaak: see Rabinovich, Isaak

Rogneda, opera: 361

Rogovin, Nikolai: 266

Roi de Lahore, Le, opera: 22, 25

Roi Fait Battre les Tambours, revue: 101

Roitenberg, Olga: 427

Rok (Hering), Riurik: 309

Rokotov, Fedor: 147, 262

Rolland, Romain: 307

Romachkova, Lidiia: 228

Romance of a Mummy, The, ballet: 22

Romances, musical medley: 389

Romanoff, Alexander: 78

Romanov (Romanoff), Boris / Romanov's Romantisches Theater: 17, 62, 96, 109, 123, 125, 127, 200, 247, 388, 392, 393, 412, 454, 455

Romanov, first, Tsar: see Mikhail Fedorovich, Tsar

Romanov, Nikolai: 311

Romanov, N.P. [N.K.]: see Nicholas I

Romanova, Anastasiia: 157

Romanovich, Sergei: 267

Romantic Adventure of an Italian Ballerina and a Marquis, A, ballet: 200

Romashov, Boris: 14, 15

Romen Gypsy Theater, Moscow: 426

Romeo and Juliet, play: 162, 163, 170, 326, 329-330, 435, 436

Romm, Abram: 200

Romoff, Serge: 140, 211

Room, Abram: 158, 191

Rose and the Cross, The, play: 146, 310-311

Rosenberg (Rozenberg), Bella: see Chagall, Bella

Rosenberg, Pierre: 221

Rosenfeld, Michael / Michael Rosenfeld Gallery, New York: 412

Rosenkavalier, Der, comic opera: 160

Rosing, Vladimir: 152

Roslavets, Nikolai: 348

Rossignol, Le [The Nightingale / Solovei], opera: 96, 97, 100, 110, 392-393

Rossiiansky, M.: see Zack, Léon

Rossiiskaia gazeta, Moscow, newspaper: 322

Rossini, Gioacchino: 181

ROSTA Windows [Windows for the Russian Telegraph Agency / Okna ROSTA]: 134, 197, 254, 255, 282, 423

Rostand, Edmond: 288

Rostislavov, Alexander: 263, 337, 338

Rostovtseva, Irina: 452

Roters, Eberhard: 331

Rothschild, Henry: 221

Rothschild, James: 34, 43, 48

Rottert, T.: 344

Rousseau, Henri (le Douanier): 182

Rousseau, Jean-Jacques: 353

Rousselière, Charles: 378

Roussin, Eliane: 290

Royal Academy of Art, London: 118, 137, 138, 238

Royal Ceramics Factory, Athens: 281

Royal Opera House, London: 156, 346

Royal Opera Theater, Bucharest: 17

Royal Society of Watercolour Artists: 118

Royal Theater, Stockholm: 21

Rozai, Georgii: 62, 63

Rozanov, Vasilii: 358

Rozanova, Olga: 130, 200, 237, 256, 257, 266, 333, 348-349, 366

Rozen, Egor: 398

Rozenberg (Rosenberg), Bella: see Chagall, Bella

Rozendorf, Elizaveta (Rosendorv, Elisabeth): see Hoerschelmann, Elizabeth

Rozhdestvensky, Gennadii: 103, 273

Rozhdestvensky, Konstantin: 400

Rozhdestvensky, Vasilii: 179, 283

Ruban, Valentina: 316

Rubinshtein, Ida: see Rubinstein, Ida

Rubinshtein, Yakov: 15, 34, 164, 256, 285, 312, 315, 338, 350, 366, 452

Rubinstein, Anton: 37, 283, 284, 361

Rubinstein Ballet Company: 103, 111, 222, 352

Rubinstein (Rubinshtein), Ida: 33, 35, 41, 42, 43, 45, 47, 50, 51, 52, 97, 99, 128, 197, 309, 358, 360, 361; see also Rubinstein Ballet Company

Rublev, Georgii: 460

Rubo, Frants: 282

Ruche, La, artist's colony: 52

Rudnev, Sergei: see Férat, Serge

Rudnitsky, Konstantin: 350, 435

Rudzitsky, Artur: 160

Rumiantsev Museum, Moscow: 456

Rumiantsev, Pavel: 352

Rumnev, Alexander: 158

Rusakov, Yurii: 312, 319, 321

Rusakova, Alla: 260, 355

Ruslan and Liudmila, opera: 127, 243, 379, 408, 409

Russian Art Exhibition, New York: 258, 372, 375, 421, 429, 456

Russian Ballet Company, Philadelphia: 25

Russian Chamber Theater / Ruské komorni divadlo, Prague: 17, 18

Russian Cultural Center, Washington, D.C.: 133

"Russian Landscape" exhibition, Petrograd: 331

Russian Museum, State (RM, Gosudarstvennyi Russkii muzei), Leningrad / St. Petersburg: 26, 31, 52, 56, 65, 72, 96, 110, 124, 125, 135, 160, 183, 184, 186, 188, 207, 217, 221, 253, 254, 257, 259, 260, 261, 264, 282, 302, 309, 311, 320, 327, 338, 348, 351, 358, 360, 372, 375, 376, 400, 404, 426, 427, 435, 443, 452

Russian Musical Publishing-House: 71

Russian Question, film: 303

Russian / Central State Archive of Literature and Art, Moscow (RGALI / TsGALI): 52, 231, 297, 334, 349, 442, 451

Russian Sale, The, London: 53, 161, 206, 208, 306, 436

Russisches Romantisches Theater, Berlin: 17, 412, 421, 454, 455

Russkaia khudozhestvennaia letopis, journal, St. Petersburg: 216, 280

Russkaia mysl, Paris, newspaper: 16, 125, 131, 215, 218, 225, 241, 294, 327, 397, 454, 456

Russkie novosti, Paris, newspaper: 214

Russkie vedomosti, Moscow, newspaper: 253, 399

Russkii plakat 1917-1922 [Russian Poster / Russian Placards]: 255, 282

Russkoe iskusstvo, Moscow, journal: 34, 125, 225, 312, 361, 412

Russkoe slovo, Moscow, newspaper: 253, 308

Rustaveli, Chota (Shota): 313

Rutland Gallery, London: 52

Ruzsa, Gyorgy: 264

Ryback, Sonia: 170

Rybitskaia, Elena: see Aivazovskaia, Elena

Rybitsky, Anton: 281

Ryleev, Kondratii: 404

Rylov, Arkadii: 16

SA [Sovremennaia arkhitektura], journal: 196

"*S.W.D.*" [Soiuz velikogo dela / Union of the Great Cause], film: 193

Sabar, Shalom: 10

Saber, G.: 335

Sacharoff, Alexander: 228

Sacre du Printemps, Le / *The Rite of Spring* / *Vesna sviashchennaia*, ballet: 160, 344, 345-346, 348, 361

"Sadarbs" group of artists: 286

Sadko, opera-ballet: 19, 20, 21, 103-109, 119, 120, 121, 244, 245, 361, 362, 393

Sadkov, Viktor: 460

Sadler's Wells Theatre, Islington, London: 111
Sadykhova, Roza: 364
Sadykova, Elena: 412
Safonov Theater, Moscow: 158
Safronova, Nina (Antonina): 283
Sagaidachnyi, Evgenii: 266, 267, 398
Saint Joan, play: 379, 383
Saint-Léon, Arthur: 153
Saint-Rat, André de: 26, 214
Saisons, Les / Les Quatre Saisons, ballet: 261, 373
Sakhalin Regional Art Museum, Yuzhno-Sakhalinsk: 179
Sakuntala, play: 164, 260
Sala Ex Cavallerizza, Brescia: 111
"Salle des Cubistes", Paris: 395
Salmina-Haskell, Larissa: 50
Salmon, André: 430, 431
Salmond, Wendy: 125, 313, 314, 445
Salomé: 225, 365; see also *La Tragédie de Salomé*
Salomé, play: 41, 42, 161, 162, 163, 164, 178, 194, 225, 226, 227, 228, 309, 316, 334, 365, 435
Salomonsky Circus, Moscow: 235
"Salon" Makovsky's, St. Petersburg: 308
"Salon" Izdebsky's, Odessa: see "International Exhibition of Paintings, Sculpture, Engraving, and Drawings"
"Salon 2" Izdebsky's, Odessa: 132, 135, 397
"Salon d'Automne", Paris: 19, 132, 137, 200, 220, 260, 264, 280, 286, 289, 308, 386, 395, 430
"Salon des Indépendants", Paris: 52, 137, 139, 182, 183, 266, 324, 421, 430, 445
"Salon des Tuileries": 220
Saltykov-Shchedrin, Mikhail: 257
Salykhova, R.: 20
Salys, Rimgaila: 313, 358
Salzmann (Zaltsman), Alexander: 228
Samokhvalov, Aleksandr: 179, 236, 319
Samuel, Claude: 97
Sander Gallery, New York: 282
Sandomirskaia, Beatrissa: 309
Sandoz, Maurice: 56
Sanikidze, Tamaz: 456, 458
Sanin, Alexandre: 109, 113, 114, 453
Sanina, Liudmila: 305
Sapegin, Mikhail: 304
Sapgir, Kira: 225
Sapunov, Nikolai: 199, 253, 308, 349-351, 387
Sarabianov, Andrei: 52, 53, 56, 183, 236, 254, 348
Sarabianov, Dmitrii: 179, 260, 264, 283, 284, 297, 327, 328, 329, 330, 331,

332, 358, 359, 360, 423, 442, 444
Sarabianov, Vladimir: 429
Sarian, Martiros: 16, 179, 260, 351-352
Sarian, Ruzan: 351
Sarkisian, M.: 446
Sasha-Yasha: see Jacovleff, Alexandre
Sashin, Andrei: 185, 186, 187, 188
Satie, Erik: 48, 99, 430
Satirikon, St. Petersburg, journal: 26, 215, 294, 334; see also *Novyi Satirikon*
Sats, Igor: 238
Sats, Ilia: 262, 435
Sats, Natalia: 328, 331, 435
Sauguet, Henri: 190, 322
Sautin, Nikolai: 257
Savina, Vera: 274
Savinkov, Viktor: 283
Savinov, Alexander: 202, 338, 355, 357
Savinsky, Vasilii: 372
Savitsky Art Institute, Penza: 236, 397
Savitsky, Konstantin: 452
Savonarola, play: 412, 417-419, 421
Savonarola, Girolama: 417
Savrasov, Alexei: 244, 374
Sayers, Lesley-Anne: 451
Sayler, Oliver: 386
Sazonov, Pavel: 227, 228
Sazonova-Slonimskaia (Slonimskaia, Sazonova), Yuliia / Theater of Marionettes, Sazonova's (Slonimskaia's) / Puppet Theater, Sazonova's / Théâtre de l'Atelier: 200, 225, 227, 228, 308, 328, 375
Scenes from Chinese Life, play: 315
Scenic Mimes, dance number: 151
Schab, Margo: 291, 292, 293
Schaffer, Alexander: 155
Schaffer, Mark: 221
Schaffer, Ray: 155
Schéhérazade, ballet: 25, 41, 43-44, 46, 48, 52, 70, 125, 126, 127, 150, 333, 358, 459
Schéhérazade cabaret, Paris: 127
Schelfhout, Lodewijk: 283
Schiaparelli, Elsa, fashion house: 220
Schiller, Friedrich: 146, 194, 216, 263
Schirn Kunsthalle, Frankfurt: 137
Schleier der Pierrette, Der, play: 311
Schlemmer, Oskar: 229
Schluck und Jau, play: 427
Schmidt, Ferenc (Ferry): 281
Schmidt-Wakel, Monica: 287
Schmitt, Florent: 388, 394
Schneider-Maunoury, Monique: 139
Schnitzler, Arthur: 311
Schoenberg, Arnold: 256
School for the Encouragement of the Fine Arts, Tiflis: 217
School of the Art Institute of Chicago, The: 19

School of Cavalry Junkers, St. Petersburg: 294
Schouvaloff, Alexander: 34, 45
Schubert, Franz: 412
Schumann, Robert: 388
Schünemann, Emil: 165
Schwarz, Boris: 134
Schwitters, Kurt: 292
Scientific-Research Laboratory, Moscow: 397
Scientific-Research Museum of the Academy of Arts of the USSR: 302, 427
Sciltian, Gregorio: 458
Seagull, play: 374
Seasons, The, oratorio: 111
Seban, Alain: 137, 229
"Secession", Berlin: 287
"Secession", Munich: 56, 215
"Secession", Viennese: 40
"Second Post-Impressionist Exhibition", London: 351
Second Studio of the Moscow Art Theater: see Moscow Art Theater Studios
"Section d'Or" group: 182
Section of People's Festivities, Moscow: 311
Segodnia, Riga, newspaper: 56, 288
Seibu Museum, Tokyo: 160
Seleznev, Ivan: 32, 364
Seleznev, Leonid: 135
Selezneva, Ekaterina: 137
Selizarova, Elena: 319, 321
Selvinsky, Ilia: 320
Semenko, Mikhailo: 316
Semenoff, Simon: 118
Semenov, Boris: 282
Semenov, Nikolai: 212
Semenov, Oleg: 119
Sementchenkoff, Alexandre: 148
Sémiramis [Semiramide], opera: 222
Senkin, Sergei: 10, 237, 423
Senkovskaia, Nadezhda: 355
Serebriakoff, Alexandre (Serebriakov, Alexander): 241, 352-355, 356, 357
Serebriakoff, Catherine: 352
Serebriakov, Boris: 355
Serebriakova, Tatiana: 352
Serebriakova, Zinaida: 56, 57, 101, 110, 261, 111, 241, 261, 262, 302, 352, 355-357, 421, 434
Sergeeva, Natalia: 344, 443
Serger, Helen: 139
Sergeyev, Nicholas: 49
Sergeyeva, K.: 118
Serov, Alexander: 358, 359
Serov, Valentin: 33, 34, 54, 56, 58, 117, 179, 244, 253, 260, 302, 308, 313, 314, 319, 349, 351, 358-361, 364, 386, 399, 410, 427, 444, 446, 452

Serova (Bergman), Valentina: 358
Serpinskaia, Nina: 297
Sesti, Mario: 157
Seven against Thebes, play: 178
*Seven Daughters of the Mountain King,
    The*, ballet: 21
Severini, Gino: 130, 131, 270, 395
Severiukhin, Dmitrii: 8
Seyrès, Hélène: 396
Shabelska, Maria: 25, 271
Shabl-Tabulevich, Boris: 460
Shaikevich, Anatolii: 216
Shakespeare, William: 116, 169, 182,
    197, 224, 239, 304, 329, 405, 422,
    423, 424, 425, 436, 448
Shalom Aleichem: 137
Shalomytova, Antonina: 315, 316
Shantyko, Nina: 261
Shapiro, Tevel: 291, 399
Shaporin, Yurii: 378
Shaporina-Yakovleva, Liubov: 452
Shaposhnikova, A.: 344
Sharp, Jane: 200
Shatskikh, Alexandra: 15, 52, 138, 139,
    159, 297, 298, 395, 430
Shaw, Bernard: 195, 383
Shchekatikhina-Pototskaia, Alexandra:
    101, 122, 123, 361-363
Shchekin-Krotova, Angelina: 179, 180
Shcherbakova, G.: 221
Shcherbatov, Alexei: 294
Shcherbatov, Sergei: 33, 125, 129, 348
Shcherbinovsky, Dmitrii: 191, 215, 238
Shcherbov, Pavel: 202, 203
Shchukin, Sergei: 283, 287, 321, 326, 426
Shchuko, Vladimir: 26, 111, 262, 312
Shchusev Museum, Moscow: 435
Shchusev, Alexei: 262, 312
Shebalin, Vissarion: 320
Shefov, Alexander: 303
Sheldon, Richard: 117
Shepherd and Derom Gallery, New
    York: 20
Sheremetievskaia, Natalia: 188
Sherishev, Vasilii: 460
Sherpets: 158
Shershenevich, Vadim: 158, 192, 239,
    447, 448, 454
Shervashidze family: 58
Shervashidze (Chervashirze; Chachba),
    Alexandre: 58, 110, 122, 213, 214,
    362, 364-365
Shervashidze, Rusudana: 364
Shestakov, Nikolai: 460
Shestakov, Viktor: 15, 191, 428
Shevchenko First State Ukrainian
    Theater / Taras Shevchenko Theater,
    Kiev: 188, 305, 306
Shevchenko, Alexander: 266, 267, 283,
    398
Shidlovsky, Boris (Vidi): 26

Shifrin, Nisson: 32, 285, 333, 334, 412,
    423, 441, 442
Shifrina, Anna: 181, 333
Shilova, Ekaterina: 338, 429
Shiseido Gallery, Tokyo: 200, 264
Shishkin, Andrei: 56
Shishkov, Matvei: 48, 65, 216, 261, 430
Shishkova, V.: 344
Shkafer, Vasilii: 198, 253, 445
Shkandrij, Myroslav: 135
Shklovsky, Viktor: 29, 31, 112, 117, 156,
    158, 282, 369
Shkolnik, Iosif (Osip): 183, 184, 309,
    349, 365-366
Shleev, Vladimir: 303, 352
Shleifer, Savelii: 398
Shlepianov, Alexander: 367, 368, 436,
    438, 447
Shlepianov, Ilia: 158, 367-371
Shmarinov, Dmitrii: 432
Shmelev, Fedor: 460
Shmidtgof, Vladimir: 27
Shock Group: 11, 12
Shoplo, Vera: 188
Short, Christopher: 228
Shostakovich, Dmitrii: 15, 133, 134,
    339, 342
Shota Rustaveli, ballet: see *Chota
    Roustaveli*, ballet
Shota Rustaveli Dramatic Theater, Tiflis /
    Tbilisi: 194
Shpinel, Iosif: 157
Shreider, Egor: 432
Shterenberg, Abram: 197
Shterenberg, David: 236, 253, 441, 442,
    451
Shtiurtsvage, Leopold: see Survage,
    Léopold
Shtorm, Georgii: 309
Shuisky brothers: 17
Shukhaev, Vasilii: 14, 29, 32, 101, 111,
    112, 215, 216, 221, 223, 261, 282,
    334, 372-373
Shukhov, Vladimir: 321
Shulzhenko, Klavdiia: 303
Shumov, Alexander: 412, 420
Shumsky, Nikolai: 443
Shuster, Solomon: 30, 40, 231, 320, 412
Shut, St. Petersburg, journal: 9, 143,
    217, 265
Shuvalova, Irina: 220
Shwarts, Evegenii: 452
Sichinsky, Vladimir: 19
Sicilia, La, Catania, journal: 128
Sickert, Walter: 118
Sidlina, Natalia: 190
Sidorenko, Vladimir: 452
Sidorov, Alexei: 158, 178, 445, 446, 456
Sieg über die Sonne: see *Victory over
    the Sun*
Sigalov, David: 216, 345

Signor Formica, play: 54, 239-240, 446,
    447-448, 451
Silberman, A.: 229

Siliņš, Jānis: 286
Simmons, William Sherwin: 297
Simon Boccanegra, opera: 132
Simonov, Konstantin: 197
Simonov, Nikolai: 15
Simonovich-Efimova, Nina: 228, 328
Simons, Katrin: 290
Simov, Viktor: 165, 190, 286, 304, 349, 374
Simplicissimus cabaret, Munich: 375
Simplicissimus group: 375, 445
Sims, Charles: 118
Sinding, Christian: 246
Sinfonia, suite of dances: 376
Sinitsyna, Nina: 309
Sirena, Voronezh, journal: 158
Sitwell, Edith: 412
Sitwell, Sacheverell: 355, 364
Skarovsky, N.: 335
Skazov: 267
Skibine, George: 138
Skorobogacheva, Ekaterina: 443
Skriabin, Alexander: 52, 125, 229, 256,
    314, 427, 454
Skuie, Illarion: 266, 267
Skulptura, Moscow, journal: 310
Slade School of Art, London: 324
Slavic and East European Performance,
    New York, journal: 10
*Slavic and Eastern European
    Information Resources*, Abingdon,
    journal: 34
Slavica Hierusalymitana, Jerusalem,
    journal: 155
Slavinsky, Thadée: 272, 273, 274
Sleeping Beauty, ballet: 34, 36, 48-50,
    52, 58, 65, 110, 111, 133, 149, 150,
    212, 333
Sleeping Princess, The, ballet: 34, 48,
    49, 50, 111
Sleeping Soldier, The, agit-play: 181
Slivnik, Frančiška: 223
Slonimskaia, Yuliia: see Sazonova-
    Slonimskaia, Yuliia
Slovo Printing-House: 321
Słowacki, Juliusz: 306
Smekalov, Igor: 255
Smena, Leningrad, newspaper: 188
Smeraldina's Pranks, play: 452
Smirnov, Alexander: 139, 142
Smirnov, Alexei: 367
Smirnov, Nikolai: 305, 309
Smirnov, Viktor: 133
Smirnova, Elena: 345, 454, 455
Smirnova, Nataliia: 228
Smithsonian Institution Traveling
    Exhibition Service, Washington,
    D.C.: 313

Smolich, Nikolai: 378

Snegurochka / Snegourochka / Snow Maiden, opera: 19, 23, 32, 33, 119, 121, 180, 215, 244, 247-249, 267, 347-348, 374, 410-411, 429, 430

Snopkov, Alexander: 237

Snow Maiden: see *Snegurochka / Snegourochka*

Sobeka, pseudonym of Sauguet, Balanchine, Kochno: 190, 322

Sobolev, A.: 344

Sobolevsky, Nikolai: 452

Sobolevsky, Petr: 193

Sobranie, Moscow, journal: 423

Soby, James: 412

Société des Films Albatros: 126

"Société Nationale des Beaux-Arts": 220

Society for the Encouragement of the Arts, St. Petersburg / Petrograd: 16, 131, 237, 333, 344

Society of Architects, St. Petersburg: 229

Society of Art and Literature, Moscow: 374

Society of Art Lovers: 283

Society of Artists of Historical Painting: 337

Society of Encouragement of the Arts, Warsaw: 236

Society of Free Esthetics, Moscow: 200, 308, 349

Society of Lovers of the Fine Arts, Kherson: 16

Society of Moscow Artists (OMKh): 232

Society of St. Eugenia (The Red Cross) / St. Eugenia Charitable Society / Obshchina Sv. Evgenii, St. Petersburg: 37, 41, 121, 122, 147, 344, 348, 435

Society of Studio Artists (OST): 441-442

Society of Water-colorists: 132

Society of Young Artists: see Obmokhu

Soeur Béatrice, play: 387

Soffici, Ardengo: 161

Soirée du Coeur à Barbe, revue: 140

Soirées de Paris, Les, Paris, newspaper: 182, 396

Soiuz molodezhi: see Union of Youth

Soiuzdetfilm (All-Union Children's Film Studios): 191

Sokolnikov, Mikhail: 427, 429

Sokolov, Evgenii: 185

Sokolov, Ippolit: 460

Sokolov, Ivan: 445

Sokolov, Mikhail: 184

Sokolov, Nikolai: 56, 343

Sokolov, Vladimir: 239, 381, 447

Sokolova, Lydia: 141, 271, 272, 273

Solara: 191

Soleil de Nuit / Soleil de Minuit, Le /

Midnight Sun, ballet: 265, 267-269, 272

Solianikov, Nikolai: 66

Sollertinsky, Ivan: 15, 134

Solntse Rossii, St. Petersburg / Petrograd, journal: 31, 52, 156, 297

Solntseva, Yuliia: 166

Solodovnikov Theater, Moscow: 361

Sologub, Fedor: 27, 29, 225, 335

Solonovich, Yuliia: 57

Soloviev Vladimir: 230, 235

Solovtsov Theater, Kiev: 334

Somov, Andrei: 375

Somov, Konstantin: 17, 34, 52, 55, 56, 131, 136, 215, 220, 221, 225, 228, 258, 262, 263, 302, 355, 372, 373, 375-377, 432, 434, 443, 444, 456

Somova, Elena: 456

Somova-Mikhailova, Anna: 227, 228, 373, 376, 377, 456

Sophocles: 35, 163

Sorbonne, Paris: 308

Sorcerer, The, play: 178

Sorin, Savelii: 372

Sorokin, Evgraf: 313

Sosnovskaia, Alla: 10

Sotheby's auctions: 11, 20, 29, 34, 40, 43, 46, 52, 57, 62, 63, 65, 103, 106, 124, 133, 142, 164, 179, 183, 190, 206, 208, 216, 218, 220, 221, 222, 225, 258, 259, 268, 269, 271, 274, 275, 276, 282, 286, 302, 306, 310, 330, 334, 338, 345, 360, 362, 378, 380, 417, 430, 436, 458

Soudeikine, Serge: see Sudeikin, Sergei

Soudeikine, Jeanne: see Palmer-Soudeikine, Jeanne

Souhami, Diana: 34

Soumagne, Henry: 289

Soupault, Philippe: 142

Soupault, Philippe: 142

Society of Studio Artists (OST)

Sovetskaia kultura, Moscow, newspaper: 34, 238

Sovetskii balet, Moscow, journal: 133, 162, 352

Sovetskii ekran, Moscow, journal: 192

Sovetskii muzei, Moscow, journal: 221

Sovkino [Soviet Cinema]: 193

Sovremennik, St. Petersburg, journal: 110

Sovremennyi Peterburg [Contemporary Petersburg], album: 254-255

Spandikov, Eduard: 256, 398

Spanish Pantomime, revue: 168, 176, 178

Spassky, Sergei: 137, 315

Spencer, Charles: 34, 37, 41, 42, 43, 46, 47, 50, 52, 160, 359

Spendiarov, Alexander: 351

Speranskaia, Asia: 290

Spessivtseva (Spessiva), Olga: 190, 191

Spirina, Natalia: 344

Spolokhi, Berlin, journal: 290

Sprengel Museum, Hanover: 290

"Spring Exhibition", St. Petersburg: 257, 281

Squaring the Circle, play: 254

St. Eugenia Charitable Society: see Society of St. Eugenia (The Red Cross)

Staatliche Galerie, Moritzburg: 290

Staatliches Museum Schwerin, Schwerin: 287

Staats, Leo: 51

Staatsoper, Berlin: 419

Staatsoper, Vienna: 73, 75, 76, 78

Staatsopera, Munich: 109

Stable of Pegasus café [Stoilo Pegasa], Moscow: 446, 447

Stael, A. de: 214

"Stage Design of the Last 5 Years" exhibition, Kazan: 181

Stakhovich, Alexei: 98

Stalin (Dzhugashvili), Iosif: 143, 157, 158, 238, 423

Stanislavsky Dramatic Theater, Moscow: 158

Stanislavsky Opera Theater, Moscow: 351, 427

Stanislavsky Palace of Arts, Leningrad: 285

Stanislavsky (Alekseev), Konstantin: 58, 98, 146, 164, 285, 286, 296, 297, 311, 352, 374, 386, 387, 404, 427, 428, 429, 434

Star Wars, opera: 166

Stark, Eduard (pseudonym Ziegfrid): 199, 297

Stark, Olga: 251

Startsev, Ivan: 447, 451

Starye gody, St. Petersburg, journal: 57

Starye gody Gallery, Moscow: 180

Stasov, Vladimir: 152, 180, 245, 249, 345, 430, 446

State Cinema: see Goskino

State exhibitions: 349

State Higher Theater Studios (GVYTM), Moscow: 326, 327, 367

State Institute of Theater Art, Moscow: see GITIS

State Literary Museum, Moscow: 52, 196, 197, 284, 341, 342

State Military Cinema: see Gosvoenkino

State Museum of Art, Kiev: 232

State Museum of Art of the Peoples of the East, Moscow: 372, 446

State Museum of Arts of the Georgian SSR / Georgia, Tbilisi: 221, 372, 376, 388, 456, 458

State Museum of Theatrical Art, Kiev: 231

State Opera Company, Kharkov: 232

State Opera Theater, Kiev: 306

State Pictury Gallery of Armenia / National Gallery of Armenia, Erevan: 179, 356, 446

State Porcelain Factory / Lomonosov State Porcelain Factory, Petrograd / Leningrad: 218, 361, 394, 400

State Printing House and Mint, Riga: 286

State Publishing-House, Moscow / Petrograd: 237, 253, 404

State Satire Theater, Sofia, Bulgaria: 461

Stedelijk Museum, Amsterdam: 297, 301

Stein, Gertrude: 412

Steinberg, Maximilian: 147

Steinitz, Ernst: 292

Steinitz, Käte: 292

Steladovsky: 91

Stelletsky, Dmitrii: 101, 121, 197, 207, 257, 377-379

Stenberg, Georgii: 305, 379-382, 439

Stenberg, Vladimir: 304, 305, 379-383, 437, 439

Stenberg brothers: 11, 13, 35, 145, 163, 238, 240, 253, 304, 305, 321, 342, 379-383, 451

Stendhal Galleries, Los Angeles: 386

Stenka Razin, play: 144, 439-441, 442, 454

Stepanian, Aro: 351

Stepanian-Apkarian, J.: 343

Stepanov, Zakharii: 134

Stepanova, Angelina: 158

Stepanova, Varvara (Varst): 139, 195, 196, 253, 338, 339, 340, 342, 343, 349, 367, 369, 379, 380, 383-386

Sterligov, Vladimir: 188

Sternin, Grigorii: 57, 429, 443

Stevens, Nina: 246, 250, 266, 398, 425, 453

Stevens, Rise: 152

Stijl, De group: 189

Stockholms Auktionsverk: 238

Stoianovsky, Arkady (Arkadii): 336

Stokowski, Leopold: 52, 125

Stolitsa i usadba, St. Petersburg, journal: 31, 110, 345, 351, 376, 388

Stoll, Oswald: 50

Stommels, Serge-Aljosja: 215

Stone Guest, The, play: 98, 158

"Store" [Magazin] exhibition, Moscow: 161, 236, 291, 297, 314, 326, 338, 397, 399, 426, 430, 431

Storm, The [Groza], play: 259, 261, 304, 374, 379, 382, 383, 452

Storming of the Winter Palace, The, mass spectacle: 26, 28, 29, 31

Stoska, Polyna: 152

Stramentov, Konstantin: 202, 388

Strathcona Publishing Co.: 31

Strauss, Richard: 21

Stravinsky, Igor: 40, 49, 56, 70, 71, 96, 97, 110, 131, 180, 199, 207, 212, 214, 274, 276, 280, 281, 283, 284, 344, 345, 346, 348, 372, 387, 388, 389, 392, 393, 394, 396, 445, 446

Straw Hat, The, play: 164

Stray Dog [Brodiachaia sobaka] cabaret, St. Petersburg: 30, 221, 386, 393

Strelets publishing house: 282

Strelna Theater, Istanbul: 413

Strelnikov, Nikolai: 285

Strely, St. Petersburg, journal: 334

Strigalev, Anatolii: 155, 397

Strike, film: 157

Strindberg, Arthur: 225, 286

Strizenova, Tatiana: 331

Stroganov Central Industrial Art Institute, Moscow: see Central Stroganov Industrial Art Institute, Moscow

Stroitel, St. Petersburg, journal: 132

Strong Feeling, A, revue: 30

Struck, Hermann: 313

Structurist, Saskatoon, journal: 327

Struggle for a Horse, The, circus number: 159

Strutinskaia, Elena: 225

Struzhinskaia, A.: 26

Studies in the Decorative Arts, New York, journal: 34

Studiia, Moscow, journal: 199, 361, 398, 399

Studio of Central Directorate for State Circuses, Leningrad: 14

Studio of Synthetic Dance / Studio of Dramatic and Plastic Dance, Moscow: see Chernetskaia, Inna

Studio-School of Chamber Theater, Moscow: 304, 379

Stupples, Peter: 260

Sturm, Der, gallery, Berlin: 53, 137, 139, 161, 162, 200, 264, 322, 332, 333

Sturm-Ball: 332

Subbotina, Sofia: 234

Suchasnist, Munich, journal: 19

Suchkov, Sergei: 218

Sudeikin, Sergei (Soudeikine, Serge): 14, 20, 32, 112, 132, 133, 145, 215, 216, 219, 221, 223, 239, 256, 257, 276, 349, 350, 386-394, 427, 444, 445, 458, 459

Sudeikina (Soudeikine), Vera (Bosset): 132, 387

Suetin, Nikolai: 138, 264, 290, 297, 298, 361, 394-395

Sugrobova-Roth, Olga: 20, 21, 22, 23, 24, 25, 26

Sukhodolsky Dramatic Theater: 374

Sukhovo-Kobylin, Alexander: 295, 384

Sukhumi Picture Gallery: 365

Sukhumi Theatrical Society: 364

Sulerzhitsky, Leopold: 285, 286

Sulimo-Samuillo, Vsevolod: 188

Sullivan, Arthur: 307

Sumbatov-Yuzhin, Alexander: see Yuzhin (-Sumbatov), Alexander

Summer Theaters: 12, 232

Sunset, play: 367

Sunset Glow, play: 198

Supremus group: 138, 236, 298, 326, 348, 426, 427

Surikov Institute of Visual Art, Moscow: 253, 427

Surikov, Vasilii: 283

Surits, Elizaveta: 138, 191

Survage, Léopold (Shtiurtsvage, Leopold): 211, 275, 395-396, 431

Susanin, Ivan: 398

Sushkevich, Boris: 285, 286

Suvchinsky, Petr: 417

Suvorin's Theater, St. Petersburg: 16

Suvorov, Alexander: 394

Suvorov, Innokentii: 188

Suvorovsky, Nikolai: 335

Suzdalev, Petr: 309, 442

Sverchkov, Nikolai: 211

Sverdlov Club, Moscow: 237

Svetliarov, Kirill: 423

Svetlov, Sergei: 379

Svetlov (Svetloff), Valerian: 22, 26, 372, 388

Švītiņš, Guntis: 286

Svobodin, Alexander: 158, 425

Svoi i chuzhie [Friends and Enemies], film: 384

Svomas: see Free State Art Studios

Swan, The, play: 365

Swan Lake, ballet: 133, 150, 198

Swann Galleries, New York: 431

Sweet Miracle, play: 452

Sylphide, La, ballet: 352

Sylphides, Les, ballet: 19, 56, 58, 156, 241, 358, 365

Sylvester, Richard: 230

Sylvia, ballet: 33, 58, 262, 358

Symphonie Fantastique, symphonic composition: 125

Synek, Mendes: 275

Syrkin, Maxim: 179, 180

Syrkina, Flora: 181, 182, 333, 334, 423, 425

Szmuszkowicz, Nechama: 161

Sznajderman, Eva: 34, 48

Tabaniukhina, Elena: 443

Tabidze, Titsian: 457

Tager, Elena: 53

Tagor, Rabindranath: 344

Tairov, Alexander: 35, 158, 161, 162, 163, 164, 171, 178, 188, 191, 200, 238, 259, 260, 263, 283, 304, 305, 309, 310, 316, 326, 330, 379, 380,

382, 383, 386, 387, 388, 435, 436, 437, 438, 439, 446, 447

Talalai, Mikhail: 111

Talashkino art colony: 344, 346, 348, 361, 377, 429, 442

Tale of the Country Priest and His Dunderhead Servant, The, puppet play: 327-328

Tale of the Invisible City of Kitezh and the Maid Fevronia, The, opera: 120, 124, 127, 156, 241-243, 245

Tale of Ivan the Fool and His Brothers, The, play: 304

Tale of Tsar Saltan, The / Le Conte du Tsar Saltan / El Tsar Saltan / Zar Saltan, opera: 113-114, 122-123, 128, 201, 247, 288, 289, 344, 346-347, 361, 362-363, 443, 444, 445

Tales of Hoffmann, The, opera: 388

Tallinn Guild of Poets: 218

Tamanov, Alexander: 445

Tamantseva (Tamantsova), Ripsime: 434

Taming of the Shrew, play: 304

Taneev, Alexander: 65, 110

Taneev, Sergei: 41, 56, 140

Taniuk, Leonid: 364

Tannenbaum, E.: 220

Tarabukin, Nikolai: 194, 235, 236, 442

Taras Bulba, opera: 316, 318

"Target" [Mishen] exhibition and group: 137, 264, 267, 280, 281, 283, 397, 458

Tarich, Yurii: 384

Tarkhov, Nikolai: 444

Tarkhovskaia, Zinaida: 191

Tarquinius, the High Priest, play: 331

Tartuffe, play: 14, 428

Taskin, Alexei: 40

Tate Gallery / Tate Modern, London: 111, 189, 327, 339

Tatlin, Vladimir: 16, 111, 133, 161, 166, 190, 229, 230, 231, 232, 236, 238, 239, 241, 253, 260, 266, 280, 282, 284, 287, 291, 303, 304, 306, 309, 314, 321, 326, 327, 333, 338, 339, 397-399, 426, 430, 431, 435, 439, 446

Tavel, Hans Christoph von: 53

Taylor, Frederick / Taylorism: 460

Taylor, J.: 20

Tchaikovsky, Petr (Peter): 37, 48, 49, 56, 65, 110, 111, 112, 138, 144, 149, 150, 198, 216, 224, 310, 389

Tchehonine, Serge (Chekhonin, Sergei): 8, 258, 400-411

Tchelitchew (Chelishchev, Tchelicheff, Tchelitcheff, Tschelitchew), Pavel: 118, 161, 223, 287, 412-421

Tcherepnine, Nikolai: see Cherepnin, Nikolai

Tcherkessoff, Alexandre: 61

Tcherkessoff (Benois), Anna: 56, 58, 60, 61, 62, 63, 65, 66, 67, 68, 69, 70, 71, 72, 73, 76, 77, 79, 81, 83, 86, 88, 89, 90, 91, 92, 96, 97, 98, 99, 100, 101, 102, 103, 104, 105, 106, 107, 110, 146, 147, 155, 434

Tcherkessoff, Georges (Cherkesov, Yurii): 61, 66, 357, 421

Tchernicheva, Lubov: 21, 68, 141, 181, 271

Teatr, Berlin, journal: 110, 125, 214, 220, 281, 421

Teatr, Kiev, journal: 306

Teatr, Moscow, journal: 132, 158, 162, 181, 188, 259, 306, 421

Teatr, St. Petersburg, journal: 253

Teatr-iskusstvo-ekran, Paris, journal: 16, 19, 52, 165, 168, 228

Teatr, literatura, myzyka, balet, grafika, zhivopis, kino, Kharkov, journal: 394, 451

Teatr, muzyka i sport, St. Petersburg, journal: 377

Teatr i dramaturgiia, Moscow, journal: 285

Teatr i iskusstvo, St. Petersburg, journal: 26, 52, 125, 263, 432

Teatr i kino, Odessa, journal: 228

Teatr i musyka, Moscow, journal: 286, 305, 316, 319, 331, 386

Teatr i zhizn, Berlin, journal: 52, 281, 421

Teatr v karikaturakh, Moscow, journal: 214, 281, 294-297

Teatralnaia gazeta, Moscow, newspaper: 137

Teatralnaia nedelia, Moscow, journal: 383

Teatralnaia zhizn, Moscow, journal: 162

Teatro alla Scala, Milan: see La Scala, Milan

Teatro Colón, Buenos-Aires: 111, 113, 124, 241

Teatro Eugenia Victoria, San Sebastián: 271

Teatro Liceo, Barcelona: 141

Teatro Lirico, Milan: 51

Teatro Reale dell'Opera, Rome: 109, 111, 115, 117

Technische Hochschule, Darmstadt: 290

Teffi (Nadezhda Buchinskaia): 32

Tekhnicheskaia estetika, Moscow, journal: 384

Tel-Aviv Museum of Art: 34, 200

Teliakovsky, Vladimir: 35, 52, 244

Telingater, Solomon: 422-423

Telingater, Vladimir: 422

Temps, Le, Paris, newspaper: 290

Ten: see Mikhailov, Konstantin

Tenishev Hall, St. Petersburg: 284

Tenisheva's Art School, St. Petersburg: 119, 355, 400

Tenisheva, Mariia: 56, 119, 202, 344, 346, 442

TEO NKP: see Theater Section of the People's Commissariat for Enlightenment

Terekhina, Vera: 215, 348

Terentiev, Igor: 183, 185, 187, 188, 294, 456, 457, 458

Terenzio, Stephanie: 19

Tereshchenko, Mikola: 307

Tereshkovich, Konstantin: 431

Tereshkovich, Max: 235

Terevsat, Moscow: see Theater of Revolutionary Satire, Moscow

Terkel, Elena: 34

Ternovets, Boris: 310, 311, 326

Terry, Emilio: 353, 354

Teslenko, Galina: 357

Tessa, play: 131

Tessier, André: 287, 290

TG: see Tretiakov Gallery, Moscow

Thaïs, opera: 42-43

Thamar, ballet: 46

Thamira Khytharedes [Famira Kifared], play: 161, 162-164, 178, 311

Theater Guild, New York: 155

Theater Institute, Ostrovsky State, Leningrad / St. Petersburg: 133

Theater Museum, Leningrad / St. Petersburg: see Glinka Museum of Theatrical and Musical Art

Theater School Laboratory of the Theater of Expressionism, Moscow: 460

Theater Section of the People's Commissariat for Enlightenment (TEO NKP): 158, 196

Theater of Baltic Fleet, Petrograd: 144

Theater of Classical Miniature, Petrograd: 230

Theater of Comedy / Theater of Satire / Theater of Satire and Comedy, Leningrad: 14, 178, 216, 230, 497

Theater of Drama and Comedy, Leningrad: 133

Theater of Four Masks, Moscow: 188

Theater of Free Comedy, Petrograd: 27

Theater of Marionettes (part of Theater of Young Spectator), Petrograd: 452

Theater of Marionettes, Yulia Sazonova's (Slonimskaia's), Petrograd: see Sazonova-Slonimskaia, Yuliia

Theater of Miniatures: see Likomorie, Moscow

Theater of Musical Comedy, Leningrad: 14, 452

Theater of Musical Drama, Petrograd: 156, 235

Theater of Opera and Ballet, Kharkov:
see Kharkov Theater of Opera and
Ballet
Theater of Opera and Ballet, Kirov,
Leningrad: see Mariinsky Theater
Theater of Opera and Ballet, Kuibyshev:
see Kuibyshev Theater of Opera and
Ballet
Theater of Opera and Ballet, Perm: see
Perm Theater of Opera and Ballet
Theater of People's Comedy [Teatr
narodnoi komedii], Petrograd: 229,
230
Theater of People's House, Moscow:
161
Theater of People's House, Odessa: 16
Theater of Press House, Leningrad:
185, 187
Theater of Proletarian Actor, Petrograd:
132
Theater of Red Army, Central State
Academic / Maly Theater of the Red
Army, Moscow: 232, 422, 423, 439
Theater of Revolution, Moscow: 15, 52,
53, 158, 191, 309, 342, 367, 439,
440
Theater of Revolutionary Military Soviet,
Moscow: 439
Theater of Revolutionary Satire
(Terevsat), Moscow: 181, 182, 238,
294
Theater of RSFSR 1, Meierkhold's,
Moscow: 144, 181, 233, 235, 309
Theater of Satire, Moscow: 317, 367,
452
Theater of Soviet of Workers' Deputies,
Moscow: 181, 182
Theater of Young Spectator (TYuZ),
Petrograd: 216, 404, 452
Theater-Studio, Petrograd: 230
Theater-Studio of MKhAT, Moscow: see
Moscow Art Theater (MKhAT)
Studios
Theatermuseum, Cologne: 168, 294
Théâtre Choréographique, Bronislava
Nijinska's: 161, 162
Théâtre Costanza, Rome: 71
Théâtre da Cagliari, Paris: 396
Théâtre de l'Arc-en-Ciel: 19
Théâtre de l'Atelier, Paris: see
Sazonova-Slonimskaia, Yulia
Théâtre de l'Oeuvre / La Maison de
l'Oeuvre, Paris: 287, 288, 289, 290
Théâtre de la Cigale: 19
Théâtre de la Danse, Paris: 128
Théâtre de Sarah Bernhardt: 99, 190,
276, 322, 419, 449
Théâtre de Monte Carlo: 99, 103, 213
Théâtre de la Gaîté-Lyrique, Paris: 212,
272, 393
Théâtre de la Madeleine, Paris: 148, 379

Théâtre des Champs-Elysées, Paris: 48,
99, 103, 104, 108, 109, 122, 180,
181, 241, 304, 345, 362, 382, 383,
388, 410, 412, 437, 453, 455
Théâtre des Ombres Colorées: 272
Théâtre du Châtelet, Paris: 20, 41, 44,
45, 47, 56, 59, 70, 140, 271, 345,
358
Théâtre du Vieux-Colombier, Paris: 228,
308, 365
Théâtre Edouard VII, Paris: 99
Théâtre Femina, Paris: 112, 113, 218,
336, 373
Theatre Guild, New York: 393
Théâtre National de l'Opéra, Paris: 41,
43, 50, 96, 121, 131, 199, 201, 212,
222, 246, 268, 274, 377, 453
Théâtre National de l'Opéra Comique,
Paris: 128, 308, 348
Théâtre Royal de la Monnaie, Brussels:
150, 287
"Theatrical and Decorative Art of
Moscow" exhibition, Moscow: 374
Theatrical Publishing-House: 422
There Was Not a Penny and Suddenly
There Was a Pound / From Rags to
Riches, play: 259
They're Getting Ready, revue: 422
Third International: 31, 240, 291, 397,
399
Thomé, J.R.: 322
Three Fat Men, play: 158, 285, 303, 304
Three Sisters [Tri sestry], play: 374, 404
Thyssen-Bornemisza Foundation: 34, 57
Thyssen-Bornemisza, Museo, Madrid:
188
Tibbett, Lawrence: 152
Tidings Brought to Mary, The: see
Annonce faite à Marie, L'
Tiepolo, Giovanni: 262, 353, 354
Tierney, Jean: 353
Tiflis School of Painting and Sculpture:
194
Tiflis State Theater: 136
Tillberg, Margareta: 379
Times, The, London, newspaper: 160,
161, 274
Timoshenko, Semeon: 27
Tintori, Giampier: 111
Tirso de Molina: 227, 447
Tirtoff, R. de: see Erté
Titanus Films: 125
Titov, Alexander: 282
Tivoli Theater, Lisbon: 131
Tkachenko, Leonid: 183
Tobin, Robert / Tobin Collection: 118,
208, 275
Tod über Shanghai, film: 31
Today Workshop of Artists: 159
Tolmachev, Alexander: 460
Tolstaia, Sofia: see Dymshits-Tolstaia,

Sofia
Tolstoi, Alexei K.: 17, 18, 374, 377, 378
Tolstoi, Alexei N.: 26, 27, 165, 166, 215,
216, 291
Tolstoi, Lev: 28, 31, 144, 261, 304, 313-
314, 386
Tombeau de Columbine, ballet: 191
Tomilina (Larionova), Alexandra: 201,
202, 203, 204, 205, 206, 208, 209,
269, 270, 279, 449
Tomilovskaia, E.: 162
Toorn, Pieter van der: 348
Toorop, Jan: 53, 446
Tooth, Athur: 111
Toporkov, Alexei: 315
Tops and Bottoms, play: 424
Tourjansky, Victor: 125
Tourneur, Maurice: 31, 125
Tovstonogov, Georgii: 303
Tower, The, Moscow, studio: 314, 326,
426, 435
Towards the World Commune, mass
action: 31
Tragédie de Salomé, La, ballet: 386,
388, 394
Train Bleu, Le, ballet: 190
Traline, Boris: 213
TRAM (Theaters of Working Youth): 134
"Tramway V" exhibition: 161, 236, 297,
326, 331, 333, 348, 397, 426
Transactions of the Association of
Russian-American Scholars in USA,
New York, journal: 146
Trauberg, Leonid: 28, 31, 157, 188, 193
Travels of Benjamin III, The, play: 179,
180
Tree of Metamorphoses, play: 229, 230
Tretiakov Gallery [Tretiakovskaia galerea]
(TG), Moscow: 34, 41, 44, 57, 60,
66, 72, 98, 135, 137, 146, 200, 203,
205, 206, 208, 217, 236, 238, 246,
247, 253, 265, 269, 270, 283, 284,
292, 294, 301, 302, 304, 309, 312,
313, 314, 320, 321, 327, 338, 349,
350, 351, 355, 358, 359, 360, 375,
376, 391, 397, 399, 427, 429, 430,
442, 443, 444, 452
Tretiakov Gallery, New York / Peter
Tretiakov Gallery: 98, 247, 391
Tretiakov, Nikolai: 144, 145, 452
Tretiakov, Pavel: 41, 312, 313, 337, 344
Tretiakov, Sergei: 312, 331
Tretiakov, Sergei, poet: 10, 13, 236,
330, 331, 367, 422
"Triangle" exhibition, St. Petersburg:
161, 215, 254, 256
Triaskin, Nikolai: 425
Tribble, Keith: 308
Tribuna, La, Rome, newspaper: 115,
117
Triomphe de Neptune, Le, ballet: 364

TriQuarterly, Evanston, journal: 16, 244
Tristan und Isolde, opera: 316, 364
Trochot Academie, Paris: 324
Troitsky Theater, St. Petersburg /
    Petrograd: 27, 156, 309, 365, 398
Trotsky (Bronshtein), Lev: 302, 423
Trubchevsk City Institute: 219
Trubetskoi, Pavel: 444
Trubnikov, Alexander: 262
Trukhanova, Natalia (Trouhanova,
    Nathalie): 46, 52, 296
Trutnev, Ivan: 156
Tsar Fedor Ioannovich, play: 17-18, 377,
    378
Tsar's Bride, The, opera: 444
Tsaritsyno Museum, Moscow: 327
Tschechowa (Knipper, Chekhova), Olga /
    Olga Tschechowa-Film, Berlin: 417
Tsereteli (Zereteli), Alexei: 109, 123,
    127, 128
Tsereteli, Nikolai: 163, 305, 382, 437
Tsibasov, Mikhail: 185
Tsiolkovsky, Konstantin: 255
Tsionglinsky, Yan (Ciągliński, Jan): 26,
    53, 322, 444
Tsipkevitch (Tsipkevich), Bertha: 43, 44,
    45, 46, 47, 48, 49, 50, 51
Tsirk i estrada, Moscow, journal: 159
TsIT: see Central Institute of Labor,
    Moscow
Tsitsishvili, Eteri: 195
Tsivian, Yurii: 297
Tsivinsky, Sergei: see Civis
Tsvetaeva, Marina: 200
Tugendkhold, Yakov: 52, 162, 163, 178,
    445, 446
Tula Regional Art Museum: 356, 377
Tumanian, Ovanes: 351
Tupitsyn, Maragrita: 228, 237, 327, 339
Turandot, opera: 19, 22, 25, 26, 323
Turchenko, L.: 283
Turchin, Valerii: 228
Turgenev, Ivan: 32, 146, 155, 428
Turkeltaub, Isaak: 340
Turkov, Andrei: 257
Tverskoi (Kuzmin-Karavaev), Konstantin:
    15, 285
Tvorchestvo, Moscow, journal: 159,
    183, 283, 400, 435
Tvorchestvo, Vladivostok, journal: 137
Twain, Mark: 216
Twardy bookstore, Berlin: 287
Twelfth Night, play: 286, 422, 424-425
Twysden, Aileen: 357
Tyler, Parker: 412, 417, 420
Tyrtov, Nicholas: 160
Tyrtov, R. de: see Erté
Tyshler, Alexander: 32, 161, 162, 253,
    333, 334, 412, 423-425, 441
Tzara, Tristan: 19, 140, 142

Ubans, Konrad: 286
Ubu Gallery, New York: 237
Udaltsova, Nadezhda: 236, 283, 314,
    315, 326, 333, 397, 399, 426-427,
    431, 435, 446
UFA-Film (Universum Film
    Aktiengesellschaft): 126
Ukraina, Kiev, journal: 130, 306, 316
Ukrainske mistetstvoznavstvo, Kiev,
    journal: 130
Ukrainskii teatr, Kiev, journal: 162
UkrROSTA (Windows of the Ukrainian
    Telegraph Agency): 231
Ulianov, Nikolai: 427-429
Ulukhanov, Alexander: 122
Uncle Tom's Cabin, play: 285, 428
Uncle Vanya. Scenes from Country Life,
    play: 232, 350, 374
Une Nuit d'Egypte, ballet: 19, 20
"Union of Art Workers" exhibition: 16
Union Artists of Georgian SSR: 372
Union Artists of Ukraine: 306
Union Catholique du Théâtre, Paris: 396
Union des Artistes Russes, l': 209, 210,
    276-278
Union of Artists of Kazakhstan: 285
Union of Artists of USSR: 14, 15, 143,
    179, 191, 230, 232, 260, 283, 355,
    361, 364, 379, 397, 422, 423, 426,
    439, 452
Union of Circus Artists, International,
    Moscow: 188
Union of Engravers: 311
Union of Metalworkers in Golutvin and
    Kolomna: 12
Union of Russian Art Workers,
    Belgrade: 132
"Union of Russian Artists" (Soiuz
    russkikh khudozhnikov) exhibition
    cycle: 19, 129, 211, 221, 257, 301,
    308, 312, 313, 314, 344, 349, 355,
    358, 429, 444, 445, 452, 456
Union of Writers of the USSR: 196, 197,
    397
Union of Youth group, journal, and
    exhibition cycle: 15, 26, 159, 161,
    183, 184, 236, 256, 297, 331, 332,
    348, 349, 365, 366, 398, 399
University of Brighton Gallery: 119
Unknown Lady, The, play: 283, 284
Unovis (Affirmers of New Art): 138,
    159, 160, 237, 255, 290, 291, 297,
    301, 394
Urban, Joseph: 26
Uriel Akosta, play: 179
Usachev, Alexander: 98
Usacheva, K.: 435, 437, 438
Uspensky, Vasilii: 319
Uspensky, Vladimir: 191
USSR in Construction, Moscow, journal:
    230, 290, 338

Ustinov family: 111
Ustinov, Johann (Jona, Klop): 111
Ustinov, Peter: 111
Utkin, Petr: 308
Uvarov, Izmail: 343
Uvarova, Elizaveta: 14, 31, 303
Uvarova, N.: 221, 372
Uzunov, Pavel: 285

Vagner, Georgii: 162, 348
Vakar, Irina: 138, 255
Vakhtangov Theater, Moscow: 14, 311,
    312
Vakhtangov, Evgenii: 286, 311, 312,
    351, 386
Vakhtangov, Sergei: 320
Valadon, Suzanne: 430
Valdman, Edgar: 342
Valéry, Paul: 222
Valkenier, Elizabeth: 358
Valishevsky, Sigizmund (Waliszewski,
    Zygmunt; Ziga): 457
Vallier, Dora: 324
Valloton, Félix: 26
Vallotton, François: 361
Valse, La, ballet: 103
Valsts Mākslas Muzejs, Riga: 237
Valter (Walter), Viktor: 60
Van Abbemuseum, Eindhoven: see
    Municipal Van Abbemuseum,
    Eindhoven
Van Gogh, Vincent: 139
Van Norman Baer, N.: 214
Vanderbilt, Jr., William, Mrs.: 22
Vanka-Vstanka cabaret, Berlin: 412
Vargunin: 312
Varlamov, Konstantin: 295, 297
Varlikh, Guido: 28
Varsher, Tatiana: 56
Varst: see Stepanova, Varvara
Vasilenko, Sergei: 158
Vasiliev, Alexander A.: 131
Vasiliev, Alexander P.: 131, 364
Vasiliev, Nikolai: see Remisoff, Nicholas
Vasiliev, Viacheslav (Chelli): 297
Vasilieva, Elizaveta (Cherubina de
    Gabriak): 404
Vasilieva, Mariia: see Vassilieff, Marie
Vasilievskaia, Elena: 309
Vasilievsky Island Metalworkers Club,
    Leningrad: 183, 187
Vasilii Kikvadze, play: 194
Vasilisa the Beautiful, play: 120-121
Vasiutinskaia, Elena: 435
Vasnetsov-House Museum, Moscow:
    430
Vasnetsov, Apollinarii: 179, 245, 312,
    338, 429, 444
Vasnetsov, Viktor: 24, 144, 197, 244,
    289, 312, 338, 344, 348, 429-430,
    446

Vassilieff, Marie (Vasilieva, Maria) / Marie Vassilieff's Académie Russe / Académie Vasilieff: 15, 212, 283, 399, 430-431
Vaudoyer, Jean Louis: 199
Vaughan, David: 52
Vaulin, Petr: 400
Vavitch (Vavich), Mikhail: 336
Vechten, Carl van: 70
Vedekhov, L.: 181
Veidle, Vladimir: 131
Veikone, Mikhail: 228
Veil of Pierette, pantomime play: 164
Veisberg, Vladimir: 179
Vendelshtein, Tatiana: 452
Venetsianov, Georgii: 285
Vengrov, Natan: 460
Venice Biennale: 161, 426, 445
Venkstern, Natalia: 401, 404
Verborgene Museum, Das, Berlin: 430
Verbovka Village Folk Center: 236
Verchinina, Nina: 224
Verdi, Giuseppe: 132, 141, 443
Vereisky, Georgii: 57, 146, 198, 257, 356, 375, 432-434
Vereisky, Orest: 432
Vereshchagin Art Museum, Nikolaev: 284
Vereshchagin, Vasilii: 184, 375, 429
Veretti, Antonio: 396
Vergo, Peter: 228
Vergun, Tatiana: 57, 111
Verhaeren, Émile: 144
Verikivska, Irina: 307
Verizhnikova, Tatiana: 120
Verkhotursky, A.: 285
Vermel, Samuil: 32, 284
Verneau, Eugene: 45, 358
Vernoy de Saint-Georges, Jules-Henri: 68, 317, 354, 455
Vershilov, Boris: 311
Vershiny, Petrograd, journal: 31
Vertov, Dziga: 192, 339, 342, 343
Veshch / Gegenstand / Objet, Berlin, journal: 290, 425
Vesna, St. Petersburg, journal: 334
Vesnin, Alexander: 35, 145, 163, 229, 230, 303, 304, 305, 309, 326, 328, 330, 382, 383, 397, 399, 426, 435-439
Vesnin, Leonid: 399, 435
Vesnin, Viktor: 435, 438
Vesnina, Natalia: 436, 438
Vesnins (Alexander, Leonid, Viktor), brothers (Vesniny, bratia): 399, 435
Vestnik rabotnikov iskusstv, Moscow, journal: 236
Vestnik teatra, Moscow, journal: 159, 236
Vestnik teatra i iskusstva, Petrograd, journal: 421

Vesy, Moscow, journal: 263, 308, 349, 445
Vetrova (Meller), Brigitta: 306, 307
Viale, Vittorio: 331, 332
Vialov, Konstantin: 142, 253, 423, 439-442
Viatka Seminary: 429
Vice Versa, film: 111
Vichet, J. de: 57
Victoria and Albert Museum, London: 61, 111, 160, 205, 206, 212, 213, 270, 274, 275
Victory over the Sun [Pobeda nad solntsem], play: 133, 159, 160, 184, 256, 257, 290, 291, 292-294, 297, 298-301, 328, 339, 349, 366
Vidal, Paul: 68
Vidi: see Shidlovsky, Boris
Vie militaire, La, Paris, journal: 461
Vieille Russie, A la, New York: 155, 221
View from the Bridge, play: 33
Vii, play: 318
Vilborg, Artur: 217, 221, 261, 262
Viliams, Petr: 425, 441, 442
Vilnius Art Institute: 285
Vilnius Sketching Scholl: 156
Vincent Astor Gallery, New York: 33
Vincent, S.: 111
Viñes, Ricardo: 378
Vinnitsa Electrotechical School: 303
Vinogradov, Pavel: 399
Vinogradov, Sergei: 444
Vinogradova, N.: 197
Vinokurova, Antonina: 451
Virginia Museum of Fine Arts, Richmond: 205
Vishnivetskaia, Sofia: 333
Viskova, Irina: 282
Visual Arts Studio, Moscow: 439
Vitali, Christoph: 137
Vitchizna, Kiev, journal: 306, 307, 316, 345
Vitebsk Popular Art Institute / Art-Practical Institute: 137, 138, 146, 159, 290, 297, 298
Vivekananda, Swami: 344
Vivien, Leonid: 424
Vkhutein (Higher State Art-Technical Institute): 179, 237, 309, 311, 333, 338, 397, 426
Vkhutemas (Higher State Art-Technical Studios): 10, 14, 32, 52, 161, 179, 180, 191, 232, 236, 237, 255, 287, 290, 305, 309, 316, 321, 326, 327, 338, 383, 422, 423, 425, 426, 427, 432, 439
Vladimir Maiakovsky, A Tragedy, play: 183, 184, 185, 365, 366
Vladimirov, Pierre: 377
Vladimirova, Ada: 460
Vlaminck, Maurice de: 283

Vlasova, Raisa: 244
VNIITE: see All-Union Scientific Research Institute of Technical Esthetics
Vogue, New York, journal: 26, 118, 161, 400
Voies de la Création Théâtrale, Paris, journal: 31, 327, 446
Voinov, Vsevolod: 19, 215, 216, 257, 259
Voiskounski (Voiskunskaia), Natella: 135
Volkenshtein, Vladimir: 285
Volkoff, Alexandre: 125, 126, 127
Volkonsky, Sergei: 58, 163, 203, 214
Volkov, Moscow Chief of Police: 125
Volkov, Solomon: 134
Voloshin, Maximilian (Maks): 280, 283, 349, 364, 445, 446
Volpin, Mikhail: 10
Volpone, or The Fox, play: 230-231
Voltaire (François-Marie Arouet): 101, 222
Voolen, Edward van: 333, 423
Voprosy teatra, Moscow, journal: 26
Vorobiev, Vladimir: 327
Voronikhina, Liudmila: 432, 435
Voronov, Nikita: 309
Voronova, Olga: 178, 309, 311
Voroshilov, Kliment: 142
Voskresensky, Apollinarii: 337
Voskresensky, Vasilii: see Basil, Wassily de
Vostretsova, Liudmila: 184
Voynow, Zina: 157, 158
Vozrozhdenie, Paris, journal: 16, 56, 322, 348
Vrai Bal Sportif, Paris: 211
Vrangel, Mariia: 215
Vrangel, Nikolai: 262, 312
Vrangel, Petr / Vrangel's armies: 218
Vrochevsky, I.: 445
Vrona, Ivan: 316
Vrubel, Mikhail: 21, 26, 120, 180, 184, 190, 197, 203, 244, 302, 308, 319, 321, 344, 361, 388, 394, 442-445, 446
Vsekokhudozhnik (All-Russian Cooperative Association "Artist"): 452
Vsemirnaia illiustratsiia, St. Petersburg, journal: 337
Vsevolozhsky, Ivan: 17, 19, 48, 49, 110, 111, 454
Vuillard, Edouard: 118, 331
Vuillermoz, Emile: 51, 220
Vulf, Vitalii: 158
Vulfson, Yurii: 37
Vvedensky, Alexander: 159
Vydrin, Ivan: 57
Vyshnia, Ostap: 307
Vzdornov, Gerold: 377

Wadsworth Atheneum, Hartford, CT: 24, 65, 66, 190, 212, 245, 246, 268, 296, 419, 420
Wagner, Richard: 52, 229, 316, 448
Wakhevitch, Georges: 131
Walküre, Die, opera: 231, 232
Wallmann, Margarita: 116
Walter, Thomas: 160
Walter, V.: see Valter, Viktor
Wanderer, piano composition: 412
Wanderers [Peredvizhniki] Society and exhibition cycle: 312, 313, 337, 358, 374, 429, 452
War and Peace, Mayakovsky's: 159
War and Peace [Voina i mir], Lev Tolstoi's: 313, 314
Warburg, Edward: 420
Warnod, Jeanine: 182, 396
Washton Long, Rose-Carol: 228
Watteau, Antoine: 375
We Live Again, film: 386
Weber, Andreas: 52
Weber, Nicholas: 20
Wedding, The: 303 (film), 333 (Chekhov), 459 (Gogol)
Wedekind, Frank: 287, 350
Weingart, Ralf: 287
Weiss, Evelyn: 297
Weiss, Peg: 228
Weldman, Charles: 152
Weldon, Jill: 152
Welles, Orson: 353
Wells, Herbert: 214
Werefkin, Marianne: 228
Werner, Wolfang / Kunsthandel Wolfang Werner, Bremen: 139, 162
Western Architect, Minneapolis, journal: 337
Westheider, Ortrud: 287
Westheim, Paul: 333
Wiener Slawistischer Almanach, Vienna, journal: 135
When the Trees Were Tall, film: 191
Whistler, James / Whistler's studio: 375
White Army: 219
Wilde, Oscar: 194, 225, 309
Wildenstein Gallery, New York: 287, 334
Wilhelm, Emperor: 22
Wilhelm-Lehmbruck Museum, Duisburg: 338
Wilson, Mme: 76
Wilson, V.: 52
Windham, Donald: 413, 419, 421
Winestein, Anna: 57
Wing Group of Painters: 460
Winnipeg Art Gallery, Winnipeg: 135
Winokan, Viola: 191
Woe from Wit [Gore ot uma], play: 220, 427, 428
Woe to Wit, play: 428-429
Woizikowski, Leon: 224, 271

Wolf, Gerhard: 287
Wolff, Albert: 22
Wölfflin, Heinrich: 189, 190, 262
"Women Artists for the Victims of War", Moscow: 348
Wood, Thor: 33, 146, 288
Workshop of St. Luke, Petrograd: 221, 334
Workshops: 40, 125, 131, 157, 158, 159, 188, 221, 281, 334, 346, 384, 385, 400
Workers Art Education Union: 191
"Works on Revolutionary and Soviet Themes" exhibition, Moscow: 445
World's Fair, Paris: see "Exposition Internationale" (1937)
World's Fair, New York: 394, 395
World of Art (Mir iskusstva) group, journal, and exhibition cycle: 19, 26, 31, 32, 33, 34, 37, 52, 55, 56, 57, 101, 118, 119, 120, 125, 131, 136, 146, 147, 180, 197, 198, 215, 220, 221, 225, 228, 241, 244, 254, 257, 260, 261, 262, 263, 265, 281, 286, 288, 290, 301, 308, 311, 314, 319, 334, 337, 338, 344, 348, 349, 351, 352, 355, 357, 358, 361, 364, 372, 375, 377, 386, 400, 421, 432, 442, 443, 444, 445, 446, 456
Worringer, Wilhelm: 228
Worth: see Maison Worth
Wozzeck, opera: 153
"Wreath" exhibition, St. Petersburg: 256, 308, 400
"Wreath-Stephanos" exhibition, Moscow: 52, 134, 283, 395
Wymetal, Wilhelm von: 25
Wyrouboff (Wyruboff), Nicolas: 127, 289, 379
Wyrouboff, Vasilii: 389, 390, 391, 392
Wyspiański, Stanisław: 324, 326

Yablonsky, Viktor: 324
Yablonsky-Poliakoff, S.: 325
Yaglova, Nina: 361
Yakhontov, Vladimir: 342
Yakimchenko, Alexander: 445-446
Yakobson, Leonid: 133
Yakobson, Miron: 132
Yakoubovsky, Georges: 269
Yakovlev, Alexander: see Jacovleff, Alexandre
Yakovlev, Kondrat: 98
Yakovleva, Elena: 221, 345, 346, 347, 348, 372, 373
Yakovleva, Liubov: see Shaporina-Yakovleva, Liubov
Yakulov, Georgii (Yakoulov, Georges): 53, 54, 139, 142, 158, 188, 235, 239, 240, 268, 276, 279, 284, 287, 316, 338, 368, 382, 425, 426, 446-451

Yakunchikova, Mariia: 197, 444
Yakunina, Elizaveta: 133, 144, 228, 287, 452
Yale Literary Magazine, New Haven, journal: 314
Yale University Art Gallery, New Haven: 190, 304, 348
Yamshchikov, Savelii: 34
Yanchevsky, Nikolai: 103
Yaremenko, Alexander: 346, 347
Yaremich, Stepan: 432, 434, 442, 444, 453
Yarkov, Alexander: 342
Yaroslavtseva, Nina: 429
Yartsev, Petr: 452
Yashvili, Paolo: 457
Yasinovsky, Nikolai: 399
Yasinsky, Ieronim: 335
Yastrebtsov, Sergei: see Férat, Serge
Yastrzhembsky, Anton: 266, 267
Yellow Jacket, The, play: 304, 379
Yermolinsky, Sergei: 192
Yifat, Dori: 200
Yogansen, Mark: 307
Young Ballet, George Balanchine's: 132, 144
Ysaye, Eugène: 444
Yudin, Lev: 159, 394
Yunger, Alexander: 14
Yunovich, Sofia: 216
Yuon, Konstantin: 444, 452-453; see also Art School, Konstantin Yuon's and Ivan Dudin's, Moscow
Yuon, Oleg: 453
Yura, Gnat: 239
Yurenev, Leonid: 193
Yurenev, Rostislav: 157
Yureneva, Vera: 30
Yurkun, Yurii: 254
Yustitsky, Valentin: 399
Yusupov, Felix: 55
Yutkevich, Sergei: 13, 156, 157, 158, 189
Yuzhanin, Boris: 10
Yuzhik, Petr: 395
Yuzhin (Sumbatov-Yuzhin, Sumbatashvili), Alexander: 297, 404
Yuzhnaia Rus, Odessa, newspaper: 19
Yvain, Maurice: 231

Zabela (Zabela-Vrubel), Nadezhda: 26, 442, 443, 445
Zabrodin, Vladimir: 157
Zabolotsky, Nikolai: 159
Zacharias, Kyllikki: 443
Zack, Léon (Zak, Lev): 17, 118, 125, 161, 454-455
Zadkine, Ossip (Osip): 309, 326, 431, 445
Zagorsky, Nikolai: 188
Zainchkovskaia, Antonina: 159

Zaitsev, Boris: 220, 431

Zakharov, Fedor: 375, 456

Zakharov, Rostislav: 154

Zakharova, Irina: 264

Zakhava, Boris: 369

Zakitin (Zakkitin): 267

Zakushniak, Alexander: 451

Zalesskaia, Zinaida: 377

Zalilova, Chulpan: 343

Zamiatin, Evgenii: 29, 31, 32, 257, 258, 259, 319

Zamirailo, Viktor: 445

Zamkov, Alexei: 309

Zamkov, Vsevolod: 310, 311

Zaoussailoff, Alexandra: 412, 416, 419

Zapiski russkoi akademicheskoi gruppy v SShA, New York, journal: 160

Zaporozhets, Kapiton: 109, 249

Zaria, New York, journal: 138

Zaria-Zarianitsa: see *The Miracle of the Holy Virgin*

Zavadsky's Studio, Moscow: 342

Zavadsky, Yurii: 166, 191; see also Zavadsky's Studio, Moscow

Zavalishin, Viacheslav: 19, 219, 297, 335, 337

Zborovsky, Nikolai: 52

Zdanevich, Hélène: 459

Zdanevich, Ilia (Eli Eganbiuri, Iliazd): 140, 182, 200, 211 (Cliazde), 214, 267, 456-458, 459

Zdanevich (Sdanevich), Kirill: 53, 136, 217, 266, 267, 326, 456, 457, 458-459

Zeeler, Vladimir: 241, 308

Zefirov, Konstantin: 315

Zeidenberg, Savelii / Zeidenberg private art school, St. Petersburg: 14, 26, 137

Zelenaia, Rina (Ekaterina): 30

Zelinsky, Bodo: 221

Zelinsky, Faddei: 163

Zemlia, Paris, journal: 281

Zenit, Belgrade, journal: 293

Zenkevich, Boris: 399

Zereteli, Alexei: see Tsereteli, Alexei

Zevi, Claudia: 137

Zhadova (Zsadova), Larisa: 297, 397, 398, 399

Zhar-ptitsa, Berlin / Paris, journal: 43, 146, 287, 288, 317, 372

Zhedrinsky, Vladimir: see Jedrinsky, Vladimir

Zhegin, Lev: 314, 315, 316

Zheliabuzhsky, Andrei: 226

Zheliabuzhsky, Yurii: 165

Zhemchuzhnyi, Vitalii: 460

Zheverzheev, Levkii: 133, 366

Zhivotov, Alexei: 424

Zhivotovskaia-Dega, Irina: 30

Zhivova, Olimpiada: 302

Zhizn iskusstva, Petrograd / Leningrad, journal: 31, 145, 164, 183, 188, 231, 236, 285, 394

Zhmudskaia, Varvara: see Karinska, Barbara

Zholtovsky, Ivan: 311, 312

Zhukov, Maksim: 422

Zhukovsky, Stanislav: 311, 326, 444

Zhupel, St. Petersburg, journal: 20

Zhuravleva, Elizaveta: 375

Zhurin, A.: 399

Ziegfeld Follies, film: 160

Ziegfrid, pseudonym: see Stark, Eduard

Zilbershtein, Ilia: 48, 98, 199, 279, 303

Zimin, Sergei: 182, 296; see also: Zimin's Moscow Private Opera

Zimin, Viktor: 415, 416; see also: Zimin's Ballet Company

Zimin's Ballet Company, Viktor, Istanbul: 412, 413, 414, 416

Zimin's Moscow Private Opera: 119, 120, 180, 181, 191, 238, 240, 361, 388

Ziuleika, ballet: 351

Zivelchinskaia, Lia: 425

Zlatin, Sabine: 272

Zlatkevich, Lidiia: 217, 218

Zlobin, Georgii: 303

Zlodeichik, ballet: 209

Znosko-Borovsky, Evgenii: 125, 454

Zolotoe runo, Moscow, journal: 31, 33, 58, 110, 200, 261, 262, 264, 308, 351, 376, 427, 430

Zolotukhina, Irina: 179

Zoological Museum, St. Petersburg: 322

Zorin, Yurii: 386

Zotoff: 336

Zrelishcha, Moscow, journal: 55, 158, 159, 189, 191, 239, 316, 317, 319, 331, 386, 442

Zritel, St. Petersburg, journal: 261, 294, 297

Zukor, Adolph: 156

Zv., V.: 377

Zvantseva, Elizaveta / Zvantseva's Art School, St. Petersburg / Petrograd: 137, 144, 254, 348, 375, 427

Zverev, Nicholas (Nikolai): 149, 150, 268, 410

Zviagintseva, Vera: 234

Zvorykin, Boris: 377

Zweig, Stefan: 230